POPE GREGORY VII

POPE GREGORY VII

1073–1085

H. E. J. COWDREY

CLARENDON PRESS · OXFORD
1998

Oxford University Press, Great Clarendon Street, Oxford OX2 6DP

Oxford New York

Athens Auckland Bangkok Bogotá Buenos Aires Calcutta
Cape Town Chennai Dar es Salaam Delhi Florence Hong Kong Istanbul
Karachi Kuala Lumpur Madrid Melbourne Mexico City Mumbai
Nairobi Paris São Paolo Singapore Taipei Tokyo Toronto Warsaw
and associated companies in
Berlin Ibadan

Oxford is a trade mark of Oxford University Press

Published in the United States
by Oxford University Press Inc., New York

British Library Cataloguing in Publication Data
Data available

Library of Congress Cataloging in Publication Data
Cowdrey, H. E. J. (Herbert Edward John)
Pope Gregory VII / H. E. J. Cowdrey.
p. cm. Includes bibliographical references and index.
1. Gregory VII, Pope, ca. 1015–1085. 2. Popes—Biography. I. Title.
BX1187.C68 1998 282'.092—dc21 97–47467
ISBN 0–19–820646–1

Typeset by Alliance Phototypesetters, Pondicherry
Printed in Great Britain
on acid-free paper by
Bookcraft Ltd., Midsomer-Norton
Nr. Bath, Somerset

Miserationes tuae Domine super omnia opera tua

(From Ps. 144: 9; cited in the Rota of Gregory VII's charters)

Ministerium evangelizandi accepimus, ve nobis, si non evangelizaverimus

(*Reg.* 1.53, p. 80/19–20)

Nemo repente fit summus et alta aedificia paulatim aedificantur

(*Reg.* 2.43, p. 180/14–15)

Omnipotens Deus mentem tuam illuminet sicque te faciat per bona transire temporalia, ut merearis addipisci aeterna

(*Reg.* 2.71, p. 232/3–4)

Summopere procuravi ut sancta aecclesia, sponsa Dei, domina et mater nostra, ad proprium rediens decus libera, casta, et catholica permaneret

(*Epp. vag.* no. 54, p. 132/30–2)

PREFACE

Despite his standing as one of the very greatest of the popes, it is more than fifty years since Gregory VII has been the subject of a comprehensive study in any language. But during these years there have been a daunting weight and variety of books and articles which bear upon his pontificate. Moreover, in both religious and political respects, the standpoints from which modern scholars regard it have profoundly changed. An attempt to write about Gregory must, therefore, begin afresh from the sources and especially from Gregory's own correspondence; for the fortunate survival of his original Register as well as of other letters provides an approach to his personality, actions, and thoughts which is not comparably available for any other pope of his age. The study that follows seeks to take advantage of this circumstance. It does not aspire either to present Gregory comprehensively against the background of his times or to establish his place in the longer development of the medieval church or of Latin Christendom. Light may be shed in passing on both these things. But its purpose is the more modest one, which must be pursued before these wider matters can usefully be addressed, of considering Gregory himself: what were his characteristics as a man, as a Christian of his time, and as pope; and what were the inner springs of his actions and ways of thinking with regard both to the church and to Christian society?

Some other limitations of this study must be acknowledged. I have attempted little appraisal of the sources, since they are well and comprehensively discussed in such works of reference as Wattenbach–Holtzmann and Potthast. More seriously, perhaps, I have been sparing in my footnotes of citations of modern authorities as distinct from primary sources. This has been done in order to keep the footnotes within reasonable bounds, since I have aimed at providing full source references. An inevitable consequence is that I may seem to have failed duly to acknowledge my debts to other scholars. Such debts are, in fact, legion; I must ask that notice in the Bibliography at the end of this book may be accepted as some token of due recognition. It may be added that the Bibliography makes no pretence to completeness. It is intended to indicate sources and authorities to which I am specifically indebted in my study of Gregory; it also serves as a guide to abbreviations in the footnotes. It has not been possible to take account of work that has been published, or that has become available to me, since the autumn of 1996.

In biblical references, titles of books follow prevailing English usage, but chapters and verses are cited according to the Vulgate. Since translation implies interpretation, all translations in this book are my own.

Certain other obligations that I have incurred call for acknowledgement. My colleagues in Oxford, the principal and fellows of St Edmund Hall, allowed me to spend my final years of active service to the college as a senior research fellow; this set me free to make progress with the earlier stages of writing this book. After my retirement, the Leverhulme Trustees awarded me an emeritus fellowship which facilitated its completion. I am grateful to the following for allowing me to reproduce, or to draw substantially upon, material already published elsewhere: Editrice LAS, Rome, for some paragraphs on England and Scandinavia from *Studi Gregoriani* 13; Herzog August Bibliothek Wolfenbüttel, for part of my discussion of Berengar of Tours in the collection *Auctoritas und Ratio*; James Hogg, for excerpts from my consideration of Gregory's spirituality in *Analecta Cartusiana* 130; and Judith Loades, for some ideas canvassed in *Medieval History* 1. To my publisher, the Oxford University Press, my accumulated debt is very great. I especially mention Tony Morris, whose invincible confidence over many years that I would one day complete this study, together with his wise counsel and friendly encouragement, has unfailingly sustained me; also my copy-editor, Tom Chandler for expert advice and assistance during the process of seeing the book through the press. I am extremely grateful to Toni Tattersall for her indefatigable patience, co-operation, and skill in single-handedly word-processing the whole of this book from my far from readily legible drafts.

CONTENTS

ABBREVIATIONS

AA. SS. Boll.	*Acta sanctorum quotquot toto orbe coluntur*, ed. J. Bolland and G. Henschen (Antwerp, 1643–)
Abh. Bay.	*Abhandlungen der bayerischen Akademie der Wissenschaften, philosophisch-historische Abteilung*
Abh. Berlin	*Abhandlungen der Akademie der Wissenschaften zu Berlin*
Abh. Gött.	*Abhandlungen der Gesellschaft der Wissenschaften zu Göttingen, philologisch-historische Klasse*
Abh. Heidelberg	*Abhandlungen der Heidelberger Akademie der Wissenschaften, philosophisch-historische Klasse*
AC	*Analecta Cartusiana*
AD	*Archiv für Diplomatik*
AHC	*Annuarium historiae conciliorum*
AHP	*Archivum historiae pontificiae*
AHR	*American Historical Review*
AK	*Archiv für Kirchengeschichte*
Annales OSB	J. Mabillon, *Annales ordinis sancti Benedicti*, 6 vols. (Paris, 1703–39)
ANS	*Anglo-Norman Studies*
Archiv	*Archiv der Gesellschaft für ältere deutsche Geschichtskunde*
ASI	*Archivio storico italiano*
ASP	*Archivio della deputazione romana di storia patria*
AU	*Archiv für Urkundenforschung*
Aus. Quell.	*Ausgewählte Quellen zur deutschen Geschichte des Mittelalters*
BÉC	*Bibliothèque de l'École des chartes*
Ben.	*Benedictina*
BH	*Bulletin hispanique*
BISI	*Bollettino dell'Istituto storico italiano per il medio evo e Archivio muratoriano*
BMCL	*Bulletin of Medieval Canon Law*
BPH	*Bulletin philologique et historique du comité des travaux historiques et scientifiques*
BRAH	*Boletín de la real academia de la historia*
BS	*Biblioteca sanctorum*, 13 vols. (Rome, 1961–70)
CCL	*Corpus Christianorum, series Latina*
CCM	*Corpus Christianorum, continuatio mediaevalis*
CHMPT	*The Cambridge History of Medieval Political Thought*, ed. J. H. Burns (Cambridge, 1988)
CHR	*The Catholic Historical Review*
CSEL	*Corpus scriptorum ecclesiasticorum Latinorum*
DA	*Deutsches Archiv für Erforschung des Mittelalters*
DBI	*Dizionario bibliografico degli Italiani*
Dölger, *Regesten*	Dölger, F., *Regesten der Kaiserurkunden der oströmschen Reiches*, 2: 1025–1204 (Munich, 1925)

DSP Modena	*Deputazione di storia patria per le antiche provincie Modenesi. Biblioteca*
EHR	*English Historical Review*
Epp. HIV	*Die Briefe Heinrichs IV.*, ed. C. Erdmann and F.-J. Schmale, in *Quellen HIV*, 5–20, 51–141, 469–83
ES	*España Sagrada*, ed. H. Florez
FBAM	*Forschungen und Berichte der Archäologie des Mittelalters in Baden-Württemberg*
FDA	*Freiburger Diözesan-Archiv*
FDG	*Forschungen zur Deutschen Geschichte*
Fonti	*Fonti per la storia d'Italia*
FS	*Frühmittelalterliche Studien*
GGA	*Göttingische Gelehrte Anzeigen*
GP	*Germania Pontificia*
H	*Die Hannoversche Briefsammlung*, ed. C. Erdmann, in *Briefsammlungen der Zeit Heinrichs IV.*, pp. 1–187
Hefele–Leclercq	C. J. von Hefele, *Histoire des conciles*, trans. H. Leclercq, 8 pts. in 16 vols. (Paris, 1907–21)
HJ	*Historisches Jahrbuch*
HS	*Historische Studien*
HSJ	*The Haskins Society Journal*
HSac.	*Helvetia sacra*
HZ	*Historische Zeitschrift*
IP	*Italia pontificia*
Jaffé, *Bibl.*	*Bibliotheca rerum Germanicarum*, ed. P. Jaffé, 6 vols. (Berlin, 1864–73)
JEH	*The Journal of Ecclesiastical History*
JGF	*Jahrbuch für Geschichte des Feudalismus*
JL	*Regesta pontificum Romanorum*, ed. P. Jaffé, 2 vols. (2nd edn. by W. Wattenbach, S. Loewenfeld, F. Kaltenbrunner, and P. Ewald, Leipzig, 1885–8)
JTS	*The Journal of Theological Studies*
La Mendola	*Atti dei Settimani internazionali di studio, La Mendola*
M	*Weitere Briefe Meinhards von Bamberg*, ed. C. Erdmann, in *Briefsammlungen der Zeit Heinrichs IV.*, pp. 189–248
MGH	*Monumenta Germaniae Historica*
AA	*Auctores antiquissimi*
Briefe	*Die Briefe der deutschen Kaiserzeit*
Capit.	*Capitularia regum Francorum*
Conc.	*Concilia*
Const.	*Constitutiones et acta publica imperatorum et regum*
DD	*Diplomata regum et imperatorum Germaniae*
OIII	Otto III
HII	Henry II
Arduin	Arduin
HIII	Henry III
HIV	Henry IV

Epp. sel.	*Epistolae selectae*
Font. iur. Ger. ant.	*Fontes iuris Germanici antiqui*
L. de L.	*Libelli de lite imperatorum et pontificum saeculis XI et XII con-* *scripti*
Lib. mem.	*Libri memoriales et Necrologia*
Necr.	*Necrologia Germaniae*
Quell. Geistesgesch.	*Quellen zur Geistesgeschichte des Mittelalters*
Schriften	*Schriften der MGH*
SRG	*Scriptores rerum Germanicarum*
SS	*Scriptores*
S. und T.	*Studien und Texte*
MH	*Medieval History*
MHP	*Miscellanea historiae pontificiae*
MIÖG	*Mitteilungen des Institute für österreichische Geschichtsforschung*
Misc. cassin.	*Miscellanea cassinese*
NA	*Neues Archiv der Gesellschaft für ältere deutsche Geschichte*
Nach. Gött.	*Nachrichten der Gesellschaft der Wissenschaften in Göttingen,* *philologisch-historische Klasse*
NJL	*Niedersächsisches Jahrbuch für Landesgeschichte*
OLD	*Oxford Latin Dictionary*, ed. P. G. W. Glare (Oxford, 1982)
PBA	*Proceedings of the British Academy*
PL	*Patrologiae cursus completus, series Latina*, ed. J. P. Migne
Potthast	*Repertorium fontium historiae medii aevi primum ab Augusto* *Potthast digestum, nunc cura collegii historicorum e pluribus* *nationibus emendatum et auctum* (Rome, 1962–)
P–W	*Paulys Real-Encyclopädie der classischen Alterthumswissenschaft* (new edn. begun by G. Wissowa, Stuttgart, 1894–1963)
QFIAB	*Quellen und Forschungen aus italienischen Archiven und* *Bibliotheken*
QSG	*Quellen zur schweizer Geschichte*
RAM	*Revue d'ascétique et de mystique*
RB	*Revue Bénédictine*
RDFE	*Revue de droit français et étranger*
Reg. Pap. XIIIe s.	*Bibliothèque des Écoles françaises d'Athènes et de Rome, Registres et* *lettres des papes du XIIIe siècle*
RH	*Revue historique*
RHE	*Revue d'histoire ecclésiastique*
RHGF	*Recueil des historiens des Gaules et de la France*, ed. M. Bouquet and others, 24 vols. (Paris, 1738–1904)
RIS^2	*Rerum italicarum scriptores*, new series
RM	*Revue Mabillon*
RQ	*Römische Quartalschrift*
RS	*Rolls Series—Rerum Britannicarum medii aevi scriptores*
RSCI	*Rivista di storia della chiesa in Italia*
RTAM	*Recherches de théologie ancienne et médiévale*
RWAWG	*Rheinisch-Westfälische Akademie der Wissenschaften,* *Geisteswissenschaften*

SA	*Studia Anselmiana*
SB Ak. DDR	*Sitzungsberichte der Akademie der Wissenschaften der Deutschen Demokratischen Republik, Gesellschaftswissenschaften*
SB Berlin	*Sitzungsberichten der deutschen Akademie der Wissenschaften zu Berlin, philosophisch-historische Klasse*
SB München	*Sitzungsberichte der bayerischen Akademie der Wissenschaften in München, philosophisch-philologisch und historische Klasse*
SB Wien	*Sitzungsberichte der österreichischen Akademie der Wissenschaften in Wien, philosophisch-historische Klasse*
SC	*Sources chrétiennes*
SCH	*Studies in Church History*
SE	*Sacris erudiri*
SG	*Studi Gregoriani*
SM	*Studi medievali*
SMGBO	*Studien und Mitteilungen zur Geschichte des Benediktiner-Ordens*
Spoleto	*Atti dei Congressi internazionali di studi sull'alto medioevo, Spoleto*
ST	*Studi e testi*
Stud. Grat.	*Studi Gratiani*
Todi	*Convegni del Centro di studi sulla spiritualità medievale, Todi*
TRHS	*Transactions of the Royal Historical Society*
VSD	*Vitae sanctorum Danorum*, ed. M. C. Gertz (Copenhagen, 1908–12)
Wattenbach–Holtzmann	W. Wattenbach and R. Holtzmann, *Deutschlands Geschichtsquellen im Mittelalter. Die Zeit der Sachsen und Salier*, new edn. by F.-J. Schmale, 3 vols. (Darmstadt, 1967–71)
WF	*Wege der Forschung*
WG	*Die Welt als Geschichte*
ZBLG	*Zeitschrift für bayerische Landesgeschichte*
ZDG	*Zeitschrift für deutsche Geistesgeschichte*
ZGO	*Zeitschrift für die Geschichte des Oberrheins*
ZKG	*Zeitschrift für Kirchengeschichte*
ZRG germ. Abt.	*Zeitschrift der Savigny-Stiftung für Rechtsgeschichte, germanische Abteilung*
ZRG kan. Abt.	*Zeitschrift der Savigny-Stiftung für Rechtsgeschichte, kanonistische Abteilung*

I

Background

Pope Gregory VII (1073–85) entered the historical scene under the name of Hildebrand during the crisis that overtook the church at Rome in 1044–9, in the course of which the German emperor Henry III (1039–56) instituted its thorough reform. Few popes have ever been so fully identified with the church and city of Rome as was Gregory VII or so conscious of a lifelong commitment to the service of St Peter and St Paul, its apostolic patrons. It is, therefore, with the Rome of Gregory's young manhood that a study of him may begin.

1.1 The City of Rome

The picture of the city as Gregory knew it is a sombre one.[1] Early in the twelfth century, Hildebert of Lavardin's elegy told how the memory of Rome's imperial past was preserved in a vista of devastated monuments and wasted lands:

> Rome, you know no peer, though you are almost completely in ruins;
>> How great you were in your prime, your very rubble proclaims.
> Long centuries have humbled your pride; levelled in the mire,
>> Caesar's citadels and the temples of the gods lie prostrate.[2]

Before and, still more, after its sacking of 1084 by Gregory VII's Norman allies, Rome was, indeed, in physical terms the mere shadow of its ancient self. In the fourth Christian century, its population was perhaps as much as half a million; the city in which Gregory grew up is unlikely have had more than 25–30,000 residents. The area of effective occupation was much smaller than that defined by the city walls—the massive Aurelian walls built between AD 272 and 279 which encompassed not only a huge area to the east of the River Tiber but also Trastevere to its west, together with the Leonine walls surrounding St Peter's basilica on the Vatican which Pope Leo IV had constructed between 847 and 853. The inhabited and the uninhabited parts of the city—the *abitato* and the *disabitato*—were fairly well demarcated. The Leonine city surrounding St Peter's was a region apart; otherwise, the centres of population were mostly situated, not on the hills of Rome, but in the low-lying lands to the west near the Tiber. Such lands were liable to flood, and a source of the fevers that terrified would-be visitors and pilgrims. But if the waters of the Tiber were dangerous, the river was essential for the city's internal and external communications and for its

---

[1] The best introduction to the medieval city is Krautheimer, *Rome*, which is particularly valuable for its illustrations from old drawings and photographs; Gregorovius, *Geschichte der Stadt Rom* remains fundamental.

[2] Hildebert of Le Mans, *Carmina minora*, no. 36, lines 1–4, pp. 22–3.

food supplies: apart from providing access for imported commodities, it was a source of fish; it supplied power for the floating mills that ground the city's corn. The centres of densest population were to the north-west of the Capitol and around the Pantheon; in Gregory VII's lifetime, a slowly expanding population was causing these centres to coalesce and to expand towards the Tiber and towards the *disabitato*. In Trastevere, which was becoming something of a business centre, the population was still concentrated near the river. The few bridges connecting the east bank with the Leonine city and with Trastevere were of the utmost importance, especially the Ponte S. Angelo which crossed to the Leonine city and to the adjacent Castel S. Angelo (originally the Mausoleum of Hadrian but in the eleventh century also known as the House of Theoderic and the Tower of Crescentius), the two bridges that crossed to the Tiber Island—the Cestian and the Fabrician (known in the Middle Ages as the Pons Quattuor Capi), and the Ponte S. Maria, near the church of S. Maria in Cosmedin (formerly the Aemilian Bridge and nowadays the Ponte Rotto). To the north, the limits of the *abitato* ran approximately from the Tiber near the Ponte S. Angelo along the line of the ancient Via Recta—the modern Via del Coronari, and thence eastward to the Piazza Colonna. Here they turned southward down the Via Lata (the modern Via del Corso) to the north of the Capitoline Hill, where they turned westward to the river at the Ponte S. Maria. There were also small, outlying areas of *abitato* round the church of S. Maria Maggiore, the Lateran palace, and in the area of the Colosseum and the church of S. Maria Nuova. Very much of the *abitato* was in the proprietorship of Roman churches and monasteries. Beyond it lay the *disabitato*—a region of fields, vineyards, and pasture, with isolated farmsteads from which pigs were driven through inhabited parts of the city;[3] there were few churches, and for the most part they were in disrepair.

Neither in respect of its agriculture nor of its commerce was Rome a prosperous city. Such wealth as it had came largely from the pilgrims, penitents, and suppliants who came from all over Latin Christendom and beyond to honour the princes of the apostles, St Peter and St Paul, to see the Christian marvels of the city in their ancient setting, to seek the remission of their sins, and to seek justice or other benefits from the pope and his agents. They needed to be housed and fed, and they could be exploited and imposed upon. They took part in the yearly round of religious observance that, it should never be forgotten, was the business of the church and city, shaping the lives of residents and visitors alike. In those who came to it for whatever reason, Rome elicited a spectrum of reactions which ranged from profound and life-changing conversion to the faith of the apostles to revulsion and cynicism in face of the cupidity and exploitation which were endemic in a centre of pilgrimage and of ecclesiastical business.

1.2 The Lands of St Peter

If the city of Rome was thus decayed and underpopulated, the lands of the Roman church were also largely without administrative order or unity. The history of these

3 Peter Damiani, *Briefe*, no. 70, 2. 319/12–17.

lands was long and complex; it bequeathed to the eleventh-century papacy a variety of precedents and hazards, but a dearth of clear guidelines or reliable support.[4]

From the peace of the church in the time of the Emperor Constantine (died 337), the Roman church received large endowments in Italy. But these endowments suffered severely from the Gothic and Lombard invasions. It is, therefore, in Carolingian times, with the donations that the collection of papal biographies, the *Liber pontificalis*, associated with the Frankish rulers Pippin (757) and Charlemagne (774), that the continuous history of the papal patrimony in Central Italy begins.[5] The donations of these rulers appear from the *Liber pontificalis*, which is the only record, to have been on a generous scale; they covered the parts of Central Italy that had fallen to the Lombards and followed a boundary running from Luna through Parma, Reggio, and Mantua to the Adriatic coast just north of the River Adige; they included the former exarchate of Ravenna as well as Venetia and Istria, and also the island of Corsica. A further landmark was the *pactum* which, in 817, the Emperor Louis the Pious made with Pope Paschal I, a text of which survives.[6] Although much interpolated, it envisaged a more southerly limit to the papal lands, running approximately from Populonia to Orvieto and Perugia, and thence northwards to include Bologna and Ferrara; it finally followed the River Adige to the sea. Of the duchy of Spoleto, only Sabina remained to the papacy, but lands near Naples and Salerno were added, as, almost certainly, were the islands of Sardinia and Sicily.

The lands which were thus donated did not form or grow into a consolidated territory such as the papal state was to become in the thirteenth century; they were essentially an assemblage of properties, rights, and claims. Nevertheless, in so far as they comprised a number of ecclesiastical dioceses in which areas of episcopal jurisdiction were established, the territorial boundaries of the papal lands were often sufficiently clear. So far as public authority is concerned, the Emperor Lothar's *Constitutio Romana* of 824 was of significance as establishing an element of papal and imperial condominium over Rome and its neighbouring lands, so that two *missi*, a papal and an imperial, shared judicial functions.[7] However limited the practical effects of such measures may have been, a basis was laid for future imperial claims at Rome in Ottonian, Salian, and Hohenstaufen times. After the Carolingian period, the Emperor Otto I's privilege of 962 for Pope John XII envisaged boundaries of the papal lands that were more like those that had been set in 774; with some modifications, the Emperor Henry II's *pactum* of 1020 with Pope Benedict VIII confirmed Otto's dispositions.[8]

This succession of acts by which lands were granted or restored to the papacy was the basis of its claims to lordship in Italy. In practice, during the latter half of the

---

[4] For the history of the lands of St Peter, see esp. Jordan, 'Das Eindringen', pp. 2–32; Partner, *The Lands of St Peter*, pp. 1–109; Toubert, *Les Structures*, 2. 935–1039.

[5] *LP* 1.447–9, 498.

[6] Haller, *Die Quellen*, pp. 238–41; for the history and development of this text between 817 and 962, see Stengel, 'Die Entwicklung des Kaiserprivilegs'.

[7] *MGH Capit.* 1.322–4, no. 161.   [8] *MGH Const.* 1.23–7, 65–70, nos. 12, 33.

eleventh century, the heartland of the *terra sancti Petri* extended along the coast of the Tyrrhenian Sea in Roman Tuscany as far north as Acquapendente and Orvieto, in Sabina, in the county of Tivoli, in the Roman Campagna, and in Maritima as far south as Terracina; the evocative name *respublica* was sometimes given to papal lands in this region.[9] From Rome, a narrow strip of land which followed the River Tiber by way of Perugia led northwards to lands along the Adriatic in Romagna and the Pentapolis from the River Adige to just beyond Ancona. Against this background, the term *terra sancti Petri* was variously applied in the later eleventh century, and each instance of its use must be understood in its context. Thus, the term was especially applied to the heartland which has just been described; but it was also on occasion used of much wider areas of South Italy or of adjacent islands which had found mention in imperial grants.[10] The term had a fluidity that must not be overlooked, especially in papal dealings with the Normans.

1.3 The Roman Families

Important though the provisions made by successive emperors undoubtedly were, their practical involvement in the affairs of Rome and its vicinity before the Emperor Henry III's intervention in 1046 was not great;[11] the sole exception is the Emperor Otto III (983–1002) with his juvenile vision of a Rome-centred empire and with his plan to establish an imperial palace upon the symbolically eloquent site of the Palatine hill, but he left no lasting mark upon the city.[12] Following the precedent set by Charlemagne in 800, emperors were bound to come to Rome for imperial coronation at the hands of the pope. The prestige and the power of the emperors made it inevitable that particular factions at Rome should from time to time look for their support. Yet, from 962 to 1046, emperors who came to Rome for their coronation normally stayed but briefly; even while they were present in the kingdom of Italy, they paid little heed to Rome and its local affairs, and they showed little inclination to become involved.

The popes themselves were placed in a weak position on account of the electoral basis of their office. With the intention of protecting them from local pressures of an improper kind, legislation in Carolingian times had proclaimed the independence of the Roman clergy in the making of a pope. The Lateran synod of 769 provided that a cardinal-priest or deacon of the Roman church should be elected; the laity should merely salute 'as lord of all' ('sicut omnium dominum') whomever the clergy chose. In 817, Louis the Pious's *pactum* confirmed that election was to be in the hands of the

---

[9] e.g. *Reg.* 1.25, to Erlembald of Milan, 27 Sept. 1073, p. 42/10–11; 8.5, to the bishops of South Italy, 21 July 1080, p. 522/13–15.

[10] Deér, *Papsttum und Normannen*, pp. 70–2.

[11] Toubert's discussion remains fundamental; for the Roman families themselves, this section is also greatly indebted to Whitton, 'Papal Policy'. See also Hüls, *Kardinäle*, pp. 255–72. There are useful genealogical tables in Toubert, *Les Structures*, 2. 1083–7, as well as in Whitton's thesis.

[12] For Otto's measures with regard to Rome and the lands of the Roman church, see esp. *MGH DDOIII*, nos. 389, 418.

Romans and that no one from outside ('ex regno nostro') might intervene against their will. In 824, Lothar I's *Constitutio Romana* reiterated that no one from outside Rome should impede the Romans in the exercise of their ancient right of electing the pope.[13] But there was little guidance as to how the electoral process should proceed, and in practice it was open to the pressures of interested parties at Rome and in its vicinity. For better or worse, Roman families came to exercise control of the succession to the papacy and over papal administration. After the coronation in 962 of the Emperor Otto I, the rulers of Germany were able to increase their influence according to their circumstances and wishes, and sometimes to have a decisive say in papal elections.

To begin with after the Carolingian endowments, some direct economic exploitation of papal lands near Rome was possible. Popes Zacharias (741–52) and Hadrian I (772–95) were able to establish in the *terra sancti Petri* a number of rural estates ('domuscultae') like Hadrian's at Capracorum, near Veii. But during the long Carolingian decline, papal lands came under the control of local families. They came to enjoy the economic benefit of exploiting the land, won control of judicial, administrative, and military institutions, and used their power and wealth to control the principal offices in the papal *palatium* at Rome. The first half of the tenth century saw a particularly intensive period of lay rule. From 904 to 924, Theophylact, the head of a local family whose earlier history is obscure, was *vestararius* and *magister militum* of the apostolic see; he thus combined financial with military functions. His power passed through his daughter Marozia (924–32) to his grandson Alberic, prince of Rome (932–54). Alberic's son Octavian was pope from 955 until his deposition in 963, under the name of John XII;[14] it was he who performed the imperial coronation of Otto I. The period of rule by the house of Theophylact gave rise to many scandalous stories; however, it should not be unduly denigrated, for it provided Rome and its surrounding lands with stable government, defence against the Saracens, and a measure of internal order. In any case, with the spread in the tenth century of *incastellamento*—the concentration of rural populations in fortified villages which underpinned the development of local family power, the growth of aristocratic control was inevitable; the house of Theophylact provided the papacy with the best protection that was available in the circumstances to which *incastellamento* gave rise.

During the eighty years between 960s and the 1040s, much of the history of Rome and the papacy must be written in terms of two families or clans which modern historians have conveniently called the Crescentians and the Tusculans; they have divided the Crescentians into the two branches of the Stephanians and the Octavians. Both families were descended from the house of Theophylact. Broadly speaking, the Crescentians continued to exercise control much as Theophylact and Alberic had done: they saw to the succession of popes who were closely linked with their family, a predominant lay member of which controlled public affairs. From *c.*975, the Crescentians revived the title of *patricius* in order to express their function as

---

[13] *MGH Conc.* 1.86–7, no. 14, *MGH Capit.* 1.322–4, 352–5, nos. 161, 172.
[14] John was the first pope to adopt a new name upon taking office.

advocates or protectors of the apostolic see. But, unlike Theophylact and Alberic, they could never be unmindful of the empire which Otto I had renewed, however sporadic imperial concern with Rome might in practice be. Moreover, whereas Theophylact and Alberic had been effectively masters at Rome, the Crescentians tended to share authority with the popes in a kind of balance of power. It was a characteristic of the tenth century that, however weak or unworthy popes might individually be, the prestige of Rome as the apostolic see, that is, as the see of the princes of the apostles St Peter and St Paul, tended to increase.

In 1012, the Crescentian predominance at Rome came to an end with the election to the papacy of Theophylact, son of Count Gregory of Tusculum; Theophylact reigned as Pope Benedict VIII (1012–24) and was succeeded by his brother, Pope John XIX (1024–32). Both were reputable and competent men whose pontificates in many ways prepared for and foreshadowed those of the reform popes after 1046. The Tusculan family did not claim the title of *patricius*. It used its resources to help with the keeping of public order and with the husbanding of the resources of the Roman church. If Benedict and John benefited from the local support of their family, they also enjoyed the goodwill and, in many respects, the co-operation of the Emperors Henry II and Conrad II. But the fragile beneficence of the Tusculan papacy was eclipsed under a pope of the next generation, Benedict IX, whose twelve-year pontificate came to an end in the crisis period for the papacy of 1044 to 1049. In those years, the Crescentians and the Tusculans lost most of their capacity to control papal affairs; although it should not be overlooked that the papacy thereby lost the considerable local support in administrative and economic terms that had for long been forthcoming. The relationship between the papacy and these two families had not been without benefits for both sides.

At Rome as Gregory VII knew it as archdeacon and as pope, the severance of the relationship left both families weakened. After the death in 1055 of the sometime Pope Benedict IX, the Tusculans, in particular, slipped to the margin of political events. Nevertheless, both the Tusculans and the Crescentians retained a significant place in the pattern of landholding. Evidence for the distribution of the Tusculans' property comes to a large extent from sources connected with Montecassino; it may have been distorted by the editorial hand of the Cassinese monk Peter the Deacon who probably himself belonged to the family.[15] But the heartland of Tusculan possessions undoubtedly lay around Tusculum itself; the family wielded extensive, but not exclusive, influence in the vicinity of Alban Hills. In the later eleventh century, it no longer had possessions to the north of Rome and in Sabina; in the city, it had once held property near the Via Lata and perhaps in Trastevere, but here, too, evidence for its residence gradually fails. The family was weakened by fragmentation as well as by the loss of its power over the papacy; it fairly quickly ceased to be a serious opponent of the reform papacy, and there is little sign that any of its members gave significant support after 1080 to Henry IV or to the anti-pope. The fortunes of the Crescentians

---

[15] On Peter and the Cassinese evidence, see Hoffmann, 'Petrus Diaconus'.

were similar. Their history is complex, but the Stephanians lost most of their property in the days of the Tusculan pope, Benedict VIII; after the late 1050s, they disappear. The main regions of Crescentian power had been to the north and east of Rome—in Sabina and around Tivoli and Palestrina, especially in the vicinity of the imperial abbey of Farfa. They had never had a significant holding of property in the city itself. The Octavians, however, remained active into the twelfth century; their members were often rectors of Sabina. After 1084, they gave some support to Henry IV and to the anti-pope Clement III; but during Gregory VII's years as archdeacon and pope, they were never a major political force.

In Rome, the decline of the Tusculans and Crescentians was to a limited extent balanced by the emergence of newer families which were to provide valuable support for Gregory VII and the popes who followed him. One was the Frangipani. First mentioned in 1014 and present in the city from *c.*1039, they had connections outside Rome, but their principal strength came to lie in the nerve-centre of Roman city life round the Colosseum and on the slopes of the Palatine. They acquired numerous towers and mansions, and they protected such places as Montecassino's principal Roman dependency, the church of S. Maria in Pallara, and the nearby *turris cartularia* with its scriptorium and repository for papal archives. The family was in a position to protect communications between the Vatican in the north-west of the city and the Lateran in the south-east. In Gregory VII's day, there was an element of opportunism in the loyalty of some of its members, but by and large they were his supporters. Of great reliability were the Pierleoni, a family that emerged a little later than the Frangipani. They were probably of Jewish origin, but by the middle of the eleventh century, their leading members had converted to Christianity. The earliest-known member of the family is Benedictus Christianus, who died in 1051; in the days of Pope Alexander II, it was headed by Leo, son of Benedict. The name Pierleoni was a later development. The original location of the family's property is not known, but by 1072 its members were well settled on and around the Tiber Island; like the Frangipani, they were critically important for their control of communications in the city. As a mercantile and banking family, they gave financial support to the reform papacy which did something to compensate the papacy's loss of access to the resources of the Crescentians and Tusculans. Trastevere also provided support from such figures as the John Tiniosus whom Pope Nicholas II (1059–61) made city prefect, and as his probable kinsman Gregory Brachiuti. John Tiniosus's son Cencius was city prefect under Alexander II (1061–73) and Gregory VII, until his assassination in 1077.

Pro-papal writers, in particular, made much of certain figures who opposed the reform popes, and who were on or beyond the fringe of the more prominent families and connections. One such was Count Gerard of Galeria. He was a son of Count Rainer of Tuscany who, under the Tusculan popes, had established himself at Galeria, the site of one of Pope Hadrian I's sometime *domuscultae* situated some thirty kilometres to the north-west of Rome. Cardinal Peter Damiani, who stigmatized him as 'non Romanus sed suburbanus', wrote of his sponsorship of the anti-pope Honorius

II against Pope Alexander II. Until his death in the mid-1060s, he was a thorn in the side of the popes.[16] Another lay figure of whom sources favouring the papacy made much was another Cencius, known as *de prefecto Stephano*, who belonged to the Ottavianeschi, a group decended from the Octavians. Under Alexander II, Cencius was the unsuccessful rival of his namesake the son of John Tiniosus for the city prefectship. He had a considerable foothold in the city, especially by reason of a house in the region known as Parrione which lay between the Pantheon and the Tiber. His resistance to Gregory VII and capture of him at Christmas 1075 will be noticed later; his brother murdered Gregory's ardent supporter the prefect Cencius, son of John.[17] Yet such figures were exceptional among the lay families of Rome and its neighbourhood. During Gregory's lifetime, the prevailing atmosphere amongst such families was one of quiet rather than of partisanship or of turbulence.

1.4 The Government of Rome

The administration and policing of the city of Rome were critical for papal peace and security. In the time of Gregory VII, arrangements for the ordering of the city which took clear shape in the twelfth century were still unformed, and details of them are scarce and incomplete. In particular, the division of the city into regions (*rioni*), twelve to the east of the River Tiber and two to the west, which is well attested from the twelfth century, had its origins as long ago as the 950s. But eleventh-century sources yield few references to it, even as a means of locating buildings or lands, although the description of the house of Cencius *de prefecto Stephano* as being 'in Parrione' is an example.[18] As Cencius's designation illustrates, the most prominent city official was the prefect ('prefectus urbis Romae'), whose office had been revived by the Crescentians; from 965, a fairly complete list of prefects has been drawn up. The prefect was chief of police in Rome and its environs. He also functioned as a judge, especially in criminal matters; as a layman, he could impose sentences of blood. He held office by papal authority.[19]

At the centre of Roman administration was the so-called Lateran palace ('palatium sacrum Lateranense') which adjoined the Lateran basilica. Even during Gregory VII's time as pope, the word *curia* was not used to describe it; the word appears only from the time of Pope Urban II (1088–99). The *palatium* had its staff of officials. Of especial prominence were the papal chancellor and librarian who were concerned with affairs both in the city and more widely; under Benedict IX, these offices were combined in the hands of a single person. Lower in the official scale were the seven *iudices palatini* whose designations were ancient and whose offices had a

---

[16] Peter Damiani, *Briefe*, no. 89, 2.561, 569, 571.

[17] Bonizo of Sutri, *Lib. ad amic.* 6, p. 595, 7, pp. 603–6, 8, pp. 610–11; Paul of Bernried, caps. 45–57, pp. 498–505. For Cencius, see Borino, 'Cencio del prefetto Stefano'.

[18] Hüls, *Kardinäle*, pp. 22–38, with map at p. 39.

[19] Halphen, *Études*, pp. 16–27, 147–56; cf. *Chron. s. Huber. Andeg.* cap. 25, p. 853; Georgi and Balzano, *Il Regesto di Farfa*, 5.16–17, no. 1017; Peter Damiani's letters to Cencius, son of John Tiniosus: *Briefe*, nos. 135, 145, 155, 3.456–62, 527–31, 4.71–3.

long history both before and after Gregory VII's time. The *primicerius* and the *secundicerius* were senior among them; there followed the *arcarius*, *primus defensor*, *nomenculator*, *sacellarius*, and *protoscriniarius*. They were in minor orders and had ceremonial functions, but they were also concerned with civil pleas. They could act alone, but they were sometimes assisted by *iudices dativi* who might be laymen but who could act only in concert with them.[20] Other officials functioned more restrictedly within the papal household, such as the *vestararius* who had charge of the papal treasure and vestments, and the *vicedominus* who had oversight of the papal palace. By the middle of the eleventh century, the duties of these officials devolved upon the archdeacon of the Roman church, thus preparing the way for the prominence of the office when it was held by Hildebrand.

Especially in its higher echelons, the papal *palatium* was by no means a static and unchanging institution; one of its strengths was its capacity to assimilate fresh ways and means, and thus to meet new needs. Especially after the Emperor Otto I's intervention at Rome in 962, it drew upon such sources as the so-called *Constitutum Constantini* (the 'Donation of Constantine'), Byzantine imperial administration, and the arrangements of the *palatium* of the Italian kingdom at Pavia.[21] The way was thus prepared for it to meet the wider responsibilities that it was required to assume with the coming of the reform papacy in the mid-eleventh century. There was a marked if gradual advance in its use of means of communication. Thus, as a writing material, papyrus largely gave way to the more durable and transmissible parchment. In place of the older curial script, documents were increasingly written in a minuscule that was more generally readable elsewhere in Latin Christendom. Especially in the early years of the reform papacy, significant changes took place in the form of papal charters which expressed the gathering prestige and effectiveness of the papal office. Under Pope Leo IX (1049–54), in particular, papal charters gained a new and eloquent solemnity. At the end, the ancient monogram which embodied the pope's *Bene valete* was now accompanied by a *comma* of uncertain significance and by a *rota*. The *rota* had the form of two concentric circles set close together; they were divided into four segments by a cross, each segment containing a letter of the pope's name (LEO . P). The symbolism was that of the round world which was entirely subject to the cross as the sign of the Christian religion and therefore to the sovereign pontiff. Each of the four ends of the cross, which were somewhat enlarged, pointed to a phrase of a motto from the Psalms which was written between the circles of the *rota*, Leo's motto being 'Misericordia | DOMINI | plena est | terra' (Pss. 32: 5, 118: 64). The changes in the eschatocol of the charters were simplified by later popes, but the symbolism of the *rota* persisted.[22] Leo IX's innovation aptly illustrated how, very gradually, the ways and means of a still rudimentary papal administration were

---

[20] Halphen, *Études*, pp. 37–52, 89–146.

[21] Elze, 'Sacrum palatium Lateranense'; for the *Constitutum Constantini*, see the edn. by Fuhrmann, *Das Constitutum Constantini*.

[22] For the *rota*, see Dahlhaus, 'Aufkommen und Bedeutung der Rota'. Its forms under Gregory VII may be studied in the plates at the end of *QF*.

adapted to meet the needs, not only of Rome and of its environment, but also of a papacy that came to see its function as being one of world-wide vigilance and activity.

1.5 The Roman Church

By contrast with its life in economic, social, and political respects, Rome's ecclesiastical institutions were complex and well structured. The Roman church had behind it a thousand years of history, and it had for long been of universal fame as a place of pilgrimage. It carried an authority that belonged to it as the church of St Peter and St Paul, the princes of the apostles who had been martyred in the city. Its life was expressed in a liturgical round which was the business of the pope no less than of his subordinate clergy and of the Roman laity. The liturgical life of the Roman church must be kept in view if the mind and work of an eleventh-century pope are to be understood.[23]

The Roman church centred upon the two great basilicas that stood at opposite sides of the city: in the south-east St John Lateran with the adjacent palace that was the pope's residence and the centre of his administration, and in the north-west, across the Tiber, St Peter's which was the basilica of the prince of the apostles whose vicar the pope was. Although at some distance from the more populated regions, the Lateran basilica was the cathedral church of Rome which was assigned to the pope as bishop of the city.[24] It proclaimed itself to the world as the head, mother, and mistress of all other churches, since it brought them solace and guidance by providing for their welfare and by watching over them. In 1057 Peter Damiani called it the church of churches and the holy of holies. One of its names was the church of the Saviour; as Christ was head of the elect, so the Lateran was the head and apex of all churches, to which it should provide an example of right living through an exemplary clergy. For the citizens of Rome itself, it was the temple of mercy whose doors stood open for sanctuary by day and by night.

Yet St Peter's stood nearer than did the Lateran to the *abitato*. Surrounded by its *borgo* and with the protection on its side of the Tiber of the Castel S. Angelo, it was a stronghold as well as a shrine. As a shrine, it was built over the *confessio* or supposed tomb of St Peter. Therefore it was equipped to be a stronger magnet of popular piety than the Lateran; when visitors from afar came 'ad limina apostolorum'—to the

---

[23] The 11th cent. left no comprehensive description of the churches and liturgical life of Rome, but much light is shed by 11th- and 12th-cent. sources of which the most useful are: *Desc. eccles. Lat.* of which there were three redactions between the late 11th and early 12th cent.: see C. Vogel, 'La *Descriptio ecclesiae Lateranensis*'; Benedictus, a canon of St Peter's whose *Liber politicus* was written *c.*1140/3; Albinus, who wrote his *Eglogarum digesta pauperis scholaris Albini* just before becoming cardinal-bishop of Albano in 1189; and Peter Malleus (Pet. Mall.), whose *Descriptio basilicae Vaticanae* has two recensions of late 12th- and early 13th-cent. date. On such treatises, see Schimmelpfennig, *Die Zeremonienbücher*, esp. pp. 6–16, and 'Die Bedeutung', pp. 48–51. Bernold's *Micrologus*, written after 1086, offers a conspectus of the Roman liturgical year after Gregory VII had made significant reforms. Jounel, *Le Culte des saints*, has material on the Roman calendar of saints. The articles of Salmon which are listed below in the Bibliography illustrate the value of surviving liturgical books.

[24] Peter Damiani, *Briefe*, no. 48, 2. 55/8–11, 56/12–14, 57/9–12; *Descr. eccles. Lat.* pp. 542, 547.

threshold of the apostles—it was to St Peter's that they first directed their steps. For the Romans, Pope Gregory the Great (who, like the seventh of his name, was a thoroughly Roman pope) was but the most renowned of St Peter's vicars who were buried near his relics; it was a matter of pride for the clergy of St Peter's basilica that Gregory I had loved and endowed it. They claimed for it a pre-eminence over the Lateran, for it was the basilica of the apostle to whom Christ had addressed his promise 'You are Peter' and his charge 'Feed my sheep'. It was from the altar of St Peter's that the pope gave the *pallium*—the lamb's-wool scarf that signified participation in the apostolic office—to the archbishops of distant churches. In 1027, Pope John XIX had initiated a major reform of the basilica, and had given the bishop of Silva Candida special responsibilities for it and for the Leonine city.[25]

St John Lateran and St Peter's were two of the five so-called patriarchal basilicas of Rome. The others were St Mary Major which was within the city walls but to the east of the *abitato* and the third major focus of worship on greater feasts, St Lawrence's-without-the-Walls eastwards in the cemetery of S. Ciriaco, and St Paul's-without-the-Walls well to the south along the Via Ostia. Together with the other great pilgrimage centres of St Sebastian along the Via Appia and St Agnes on the Via Nomentana, the patriarchal basilicas commanded the Roman network of roads. Communications were important, not least because there was throughout the city a proliferation of churches. The most important of them were the so-called title-churches whose principal clergy had an obligation to perform liturgical service in the patriarchal basilicas; but they had their own places in the liturgical arrangements of the city.

If the organization of the Roman churches was complex, so was that of its clergy. The upper levels of clerical organization may be seen in the ranks of the Roman cardinals. In the eleventh century, the later college of cardinals was moving tentatively towards a form which it definitively assumed only in the next century; Gregory VII's pontificate belongs to its prehistory rather than to its history.[26] Nevertheless its prehistory was a long one. Ever since the seventh century there had existed a group of seven cardinal-bishops. They were the bishops of a sometimes changing list of sees in the vicinity of Rome which are often known as the suburbicarian sees. In the middle of the eleventh century the list was Ostia, Porto, Albano, Palestrina, Silva Candida, Labiacum, and Velletri. Between 1060 and 1073 Labiacum was transferred to Tusculum and Velletri was united with Ostia; the vacancy so created was filled by Sabina. Under Gregory VII, Silva Candida was left vacant; from 1079 it was replaced by Segni. Because the cardinal-bishops held sees of their own they were in an ambivalent position with regard to the Roman clergy. There was a persistent usage, which for most of the eleventh century was not integrated with the threefold scheme

---

[25] Pet. Mall. caps. 4–6, 37–41, pp. 385–7, 402–7. For papal measures concerning St Peter's, see John XIX (1026) and Benedict IX (1037), Zimmermann, *Papsturkunden*, nos. 569, 608, 2. 1081/42–4, 1147/16–17.

[26] For the development of the college of cardinals, see also Cowdrey, *The Age of Abbot Desiderius*, pp. 51–5, and the sources and literature there cited.

that included bishops, whereby only clergy based within the walls of the city were described as *cardinales*. This term sometimes excluded bishops but embraced, besides cardinal-priests and -deacons, other palatine clergy including subdeacons and others in minor orders;[27] accordingly, the young Hildebrand appears in charters as 'cardinalis subdiaconus sanctae Romane ecclesiae'. Nevertheless, the suburbicarian bishops had liturgical duties by weekly rota at the principal altar of the Lateran basilica; apart from the pope himself, they alone had access to it for the celebration of mass.[28] For centuries, the bishops of Ostia, Porto, and Albano had enjoyed the right of consecrating a new pope. From the time of Pope Leo IX, the increasing importance of the cardinal-bishops and the widening of their concerns from liturgical to governmental functions were apparent from the priority of their names in attendance lists at papal synods held in the Lateran. For the moment at least, they could be described as a senate of the Roman church.[29]

The self-conscious core and centre of the Roman clergy were, however, not the bishops but the cardinal-priests. Their responsibilities as such lay entirely within the city of Rome, where they were the senior clergy and pastors of the title-churches. Twenty-eight in number, seven of them were assigned to each of the patriarchal basilicas apart from the Lateran. Like the bishops at the Lateran, they performed liturgical duties at the principal altars of their basilicas throughout the year. On greater festivals they also assisted the pope in services at the Lateran itself.[30]

The latest part of the college of cardinals to take shape was the cardinal-deacons, whose manifold duties were liturgical, administrative, and caritative. Their definitive emergence as a group took place only after Gregory VII's death. But for a long time past, the archdeacon and six palatine deacons had been particularly associated with the service of the Lateran where their duties included the liturgical reading of the gospel at mass. In other churches twelve regional deacons performed a similar service.[31] Below the deacons were the subdeacons, an important group of whom was the seven palatine subdeacons who read lections and the epistle at papal masses in the Lateran basilica, and performed a like service at the papal dinner table in the Lateran palace. A *schola cantorum* chanted the liturgy whenever the pope celebrated mass in the Lateran or elsewhere. There was a complement of clerks in the various grades of minor orders.

The second half of the eleventh century witnessed two developments in the recruitment of the Roman cardinals which served to enhance their role in papal counsels and policies. First, whereas almost all had hitherto been of local Roman background, a significant number of them now came to be drawn from reforming circles further afield. Pope Leo IX made it a matter of policy to replace simoniacal local clergy by men from distant provinces of the church.[32] In the third quarter of

---

[27] For this usage, see e.g. Zimmermann, *Papsturkunden*, no. 522, 2. 994.
[28] Peter Damiani, *Briefe*, no. 48, 2. 55/32–4; *Descr. eccles. Lat.* pp. 548–9.
[29] Peter Damiani, *Briefe*, no. 97, 3.80.   [30] *Descr. eccles. Lat.* pp. 548–9, 553–4.
[31] *Descr. eccles. Lat.*, ed. Georgi, pp. 549, 554.
[32] Bonizo of Sutri. *Lib. ad amic.* 5.588/18–25.

the eleventh century, such appointments were especially made to the cardinal-bishoprics: for example, to Albano were appointed the Apulian Boniface and the Vallombrosan monk Peter Igneus, to Ostia the hermit-monk Peter Damiani from Fonteavellana and Gerald who was grand prior of Cluny, and to Silva Candida Humbert, monk of Moyenmoutier and Mainard, abbot of Pomposa. Among cardinal-priests, notable examples of outside appointments were the abbots of Montecassino Frederick of Lorraine to S. Grisogono and Desiderius to S. Cecilia, as well as Hugh Candidus from Remiremont, who later apostatized from Gregory VII, to S. Clemente. The abbots of Montecassino as well as Mainard of Silva Candida illustrate a second development, that of the appointment of 'external' cardinals who retained their preferments away from Rome while also holding Roman cardinalates.[33] Such appointments of non-Roman and actively reforming clergy did much to open the ranks of the cardinals and to increase their serviceability in the general purposes of the popes. Nevertheless, it should not be forgotten that, like the rest of the cardinals, they had local functions; when in Rome they were involved in the liturgical round of the Roman church.

The ordered liturgical observance of the Roman church was based upon the ancient and meticulously regulated sequence through the year of 'stations' within the city at which the principal service of the day was held. In the later eleventh century, they were some eighty-five in number; a large proportion of them were assigned to days between Advent and Pentecost. On stational days, the pope, or if he were absent from Rome or otherwise not available his deputy, celebrated mass in a patriarchal basilica or other major church with appropriate solemnity. He was assembled by suburbicarian bishops, by many of the Roman clergy, and by laity from all regions of the city. Each grade of the clergy and laity occupied its due place in a manner that did much to define their loyalties and social awareness.[34] Lay participation in the liturgy was a strong feature, and Eastertide was marked by a general renewal of baptismal vows.[35]

On many stational days, the pope met the Roman clergy and people at a special place of assembly, or *collecta*, at which prayers were said before processing to the stational church. On major festivals, the pope solemnly processed from his residence at the Lateran through the principal streets of the city, where its classical monuments and Christian churches added to the dignity of the occasion.[36] With the greater festivals were also associated papal coronations which occurred eighteen times a year;[37] at the principal mass and during the processions, papal *laudes* were chanted

---

[33] For individual cardinals, see Hüls, *Kardinäle*, and for the external cardinals Ganzer, *Die Entwicklung des auswärtigen Kardinalats*.

[34] Pet. Mall. cap. 9, pp. 439–42, lists the stations in his day; cf. Grisar, *Das Missale*, pp. 116–20; Kirsch, *Die Stationskirche*, pp. 224–7; Saxer, 'L'Utilisation', pp. 936–86, 1031–3.

[35] Bernold, *Micrologus*, caps. 37, 56, cols. 1006C, 1018B.

[36] For processions, see Ben. can. caps. 16, 48, 50, 56–8, pp. 145, 153, 154, 155–6. There is evocation of a papal procession in Krautheimer, *Rome*, p. 278, and further discussion in Eichmann, *Weihe und Krönung*.

[37] Albinus, 10.1, p. 90.

with their triumphal words.[38] The papal character of the stations is illustrated by the custom whereby, if the pope were absent but in Rome, an acolyte took a specially prepared candle-wick for him to bless at the Lateran; such wicks were preserved, and at a pope's burial they were placed in a pillow under his head.[39]

In the mid-twelfth century, Benedict, a canon of St Peter's, recorded this and other, often long-established or revived, observances which served by solemn means as well as by trivial to cement the bond between pope, clergy, and citizens. On the fourth Sunday in Lent when the station was at S. Croce in Ierusalemme, the pope carried a rose wrapped in moss, which was the subject of his sermon; upon returning to the Lateran he presented it to the city prefect.[40] On the Sunday before Pentecost at S. Maria ad Martyres (the Pantheon) he preached on the Holy Spirit and roses were released from the ceiling in token of the Spirit's descent.[41] On other occasions, religion merged with revelry. After dinner on the Sunday before Lent, for example, there was a *ludus Carnelevaris*. The knights and footsoldiers of the city drank together; then the city prefect and the knights accompanied the pope from the Lateran to join the footsoldiers in the south-west of the city, 'so that in the place where the city had its beginning the delights of the body might on that day have an end'. They enacted a show before the pope, the purpose of which was to banish disputes from their midst. The account refers to the killing of a bear to symbolize the devil who tempted the flesh, of bullocks to symbolize their pride, and of a cockerel to symbolize their lusts; thus, they might live chastely and soberly, and keep a good Easter.[42] Other observances, again, were revels pure and simple. After Easter Vespers a choir sang before the pope as he took wine with his entourage.[43] On the Saturday following, all the Roman parishes joined in the mummery of the ancient *cornomannia*. They met the pope near the Lateran and, with each parish standing in a ring, they sang *laudes* in macaronic Latin and Greek. Then they returned to their localities for further mummery; a priest visited each house to place laurels on the hearth and give wafers to the children.[44] Finally there were observances that verged upon the superstitious. On Holy Saturday the archdeacon was responsible for preparing figures of lambs from pure wax which contained oil and chrism; on Low Sunday with the station at the Lateran, the pope distributed them in memory of the Exodus, in honour of the newly baptized, and as charms against spirits and thunder.[45] On the feast of St Peter and St Paul, the pope took charcoal from lamps over the saints' shrines for the archdeacon to distribute as a cure for fever.[46] The so-called *litania maior* on St Mark's Day (25 April) and the solemn procession on the feast of the Assumption of the Virgin (15 August) replaced ancient pagan festivals and were much frequented occasions.

---

[38] See Ben. can. caps. 19, 47, pp. 145–6, 153. For Gregory VII's Christmas procession of 1075, see *LP* 2. 282.

[39] Ben. can. cap. 34, p. 149.   [40] Ibid. cap. 36, p. 150.   [41] Ibid. cap. 61, p. 157.
[42] Ibid. cap. 7(5), p. 172.   [43] Ibid. cap. 7(3), p. 172, cf. cap. 23, p. 147.
[44] Ibid. cap. 7(1–2), pp. 171–2. [45] Ibid. caps. 43, 53, pp. 151, 155.   [46] Ibid. cap. 69, p. 158.

The Roman liturgical round was associated with a pattern of payments and perquisites in cash and kind that gave it material as well as religious and social significance. At the ancient ceremony of the *cornomannia*, the pope disbursed money to each archpresbyter, and every household gave at least one *denarius* when its hearth was decorated.[47] The largest and most regular payments were the *presbyteria* and *cenatica* made to the clergy from the pope downwards at many points in the liturgical year.[48] Occasional payments included those to the acolytes on Palm Sunday and to a wide range of clergy on Maundy Thursday.[49] At Eastertide the notaries who reported to the pope the number of baptisms in the city were duly rewarded.[50] When the papal station was at distant St Peter's, there was elaborate provision for clerical hospitality; during the Christmas vigil the cardinal-bishop of Albano gave the clergy a dinner.[51] Perhaps the most remarkable meal took place at Easter, when at the Lateran palace in a mimesis of the Last Supper the pope represented Christ, the prior of the basilica Judas Iscariot, and five cardinal-priests, five deacons, and the *primicerius notariorum* the other apostles.[52] As for the poor of Rome, such hope for a livelihood as they possessed arose from the alms of the pope and of the pilgrims who were attracted to the city by its patron saints and round of worship.

It is not possible to be sure which details of this picture hold good for the mid-eleventh century, although in all likelihood many of them do. A citizen of eleventh-century Rome lived against the background of an ancient and impressive liturgical round which spanned every level of life from the spiritual and sublime to the trivial and superstitious. For Roman clergy and laity, the stations, processions, carnivals, and shows were both an expression of religious fervour and a substitute for the *panem et circenses* of imperial times. They were the colour of everyday life; no doubt the Romans viewed them with a blend of pride, cynicism, and avarice. They were part of the air that men breathed; however dimly the state of the evidence allows the modern historian to view them, they are basic for comprehending the mentalities and loyalties of those who experienced them. They gave stability to papal Rome.

If the liturgical observances at Rome were mostly ancient, they were not static or uniform. Bernold's *Micrologus* illustrates how carefully the popes of the later eleventh century pondered changes, allowing some and disallowing others; liturgical order ranked high amongst their concerns.[53] More profoundly, the expeditions of Ottonian and Salian emperors from Germany to Rome and the succession of German popes from 1046 to 1058 were only two of the factors that led to the introduction into Roman churches of German liturgical practices. By *c.*1050 the so-called Romano-Germanic Pontifical, compiled in Mainz some ninety years earlier, was well established there.[54] Based largely upon Roman material it was adapted to the needs of the imperial church, and it came to Rome with a strongly German colouring. With limited facilities for book production in the city, the Roman church was used to

47 As n. 44.   48 e.g. Ben. can. caps. 7, 22, 58, pp. 143, 146, 156.
49 Ibid. caps. 37, 41, pp. 150, 151.   50 Ben. can. cap. 45, p. 152.   51 Ibid. cap. 14, p. 144.
52 Ibid. cap. 48, p. 153.   53 As n. 23.   54 *RGP*; for its arrival at Rome, see *RGP* 3.46–51.

obtaining liturgical books from north of the Alps,[55] and by the end of the eleventh century many were persuaded that the Romano-Germanic Pontifical represented ancient Roman usage as known to Pope Gregory the Great. But with characteristic conservatism the Lateran basilica persisted in its own ways,[56] and there were those at Rome who resented what they saw as German intrusion into Roman traditions. Liturgical change thus brought in its wake an increase of liturgical diversity, with attendant tensions.

In view of such openness to change, it is not surprising that individual Roman churches could from an early date in the eleventh century take measures of improvement which betokened a quickening of pastoral life. Soon after 1026, for example, the clergy of the basilica of SS. Apostoli instituted a *liber officialis*, or compendium of material for use in the parish.[57] It made cradle-to-grave provision for pastoral offices—baptism, marriage, penance, visitation of the sick, rites of the dead. It also aspired to raise the level of clerical life, proscribing simony, theft, and avarice but demanding chastity, residence, and attendance at synods. It sought to promote pastoral zeal in ways which foreshadowed the endeavours of greater reformers who emerged later in the eleventh century.[58] Another example is a stringent oath of commitment to a strict canonical life which echoed the Rule of St Benedict and which was taken by some Roman clergy before the middle of the eleventh century.[59]

From Hildebrand's earliest days at Rome, there were already voices there which insisted upon the weight and responsibility of the priestly office and which advocated a manner of life that was appropriate to it at its most demanding.

1.6 Roman Monasteries

There had been monasteries in Rome since ancient times, but it is hard to judge the condition of the monastic order there in the mid-eleventh century. The previous century had been eventful in Roman monastic history.[60] Alberic, prince of Rome, had been a patron of monastic reform, while Abbot Odo of Cluny (927–42) several times visited the city; in 936/7 he assisted Alberic in founding the monastery of St Mary's on the Aventine. Odo gave his attention to reforming the Latin monasteries of Rome; he is known to have taken in hand the extra-mural houses of St Paul's, St Lawrence's, and St Agnes's. St Paul's became the centre of his work at Rome, and St Mary's on the Aventine for a time shared an abbot with it in the person of a Cluniac monk called Baldwin. It is unlikely that Odo's reforms persisted after his death. But they served

---

[55] e.g. Pope Gregory V's request to the abbey of Reichenau when consecrating its Abbot Alawich at Rome in 998 that he send liturgical books: *Lib. cens.* cap. 24, 1.350.

[56] Peter Abelard, *Ep.* 10, *PL* 178.340BC, provides evidence for the continuation of its special observances into the 12th cent.

[57] Salmon, 'Un *libellus officialis*' and 'Un Témoin'.

[58] 'De onore sacerdotis: honor sacer grandis, quam gravis premitur pondus; scito per certum, orbem cunctum portat in dorsum': cited by Salmon, 'Un Témoin', p. 72.

[59] Werminghoff, 'Die Beschlüsse', p. 670 n. 4.

[60] There is a good survey of 10th-cent. Roman monasticism in Hamilton, *Monastic Reform*, nos. I–VI.

to establish a link between Cluny and Rome; moreover, they resulted in the Rule of St Benedict's at last being generally adopted in the Latin monasteries of the city.

The second half of the tenth century saw no such partnership as that of Alberic and Odo in reforming and founding monasteries. But Roman families were active in the field, and among the popes, the Tusculan Benedict VII (974–83) was an active monastic patron. His pontificate witnessed the foundation upon the Aventine of the monastery of SS. Bonifazio e Alessio in which Latin monks engaged in close contacts with monks of the Greek rite. Its days of greatness were under Abbot Leo (981–99), and it owed much to its association with the Emperor Otto III's aspiration for a 'renovatio Romani imperii'. A home of scholars, it for a time numbered among its monks two future martyr-bishops of the German eastward mission—Archbishop Adalbert of Prague and Bishop Bruno of Querfurt. In the eleventh century its glory quickly departed. Nevertheless, Greek traditions persisted at Rome, no doubt especially in monastic circles. They did so strongly enough for Pope Leo IX in 1053 to remind Patriarch Michael of Constantinople that the Greek rite was used there without disturbance.[61] The persistence of Greek worship was a reminder to all that Latin Christianity did not stand alone and that Greeks and Latins could practise their observances side by side. It is an aspect of Roman monastic and liturgical diversity that should not be overlooked.

The first half of the eleventh century saw no fresh monastic renewal at Rome. Perhaps because he took a low view of Roman monastic life, Abbot Odilo of Cluny (994–1049) avoided the city until the seeds of revival were sown with the Emperor Henry III's expedition of 1046. But when, while leaving the city in that year, a fall from his horse seriously injured him, he was first taken to the extra-mural monastery of St Pancras and then to that of St Mary's-on-the Aventine. There, he was tended, not only by Pope Clement II, but also by Lawrence, formerly archbishop of Amalfi and monk of Montecassino, a man learned in the Greek and Latin tongues.[62] According to Gregory's VII's biographer Paul of Bernried, Gregory's uncle was for a time abbot of St Mary's.[63] Such a monastery is likely to have been reasonably observant. Especially on the Aventine and the Palatine and also around St Peter's, as well as outside the city walls, there was probably a number of such houses, often small and in need of reform and restoration, but sometimes sound in their following of the Rule of St Benedict. Late eleventh-century pilgrims were particularly directed to six Roman monasteries, S. Cesareo in Palatio, S. Gregorio in Clivo Scauro, S. Maria and SS. Alessio e Bonifazio on the Aventine, S. Saba, and S. Pancrazio on the Aurelian Way.[64] At Rome as elsewhere, the monastic order was a familiar part of the ecclesiastical scene.

---

[61] Leo IX, *Ep.* 100.29, *PL* 143.764A.

[62] Sackur, 'Zur *Iotsaldi vita Odilonis*', pp. 120–1; for Lawrence, see Holtzmann, 'Laurentius von Amalfi', and U. Schwarz, *Amalfi*, pp. 47, 99–104.

[63] Paul of Bernried, cap. 9, p. 477.   [64] *Descr. eccles. Lat.* p. 554.

1.7 The Image of Rome

Rome in the mid-eleventh century presented a mixed image to those who lived there or who paid visits to the threshold of the apostles. Impoverished, underpopulated, and ruinous, its material desolation could be seen as matching its spiritual and moral condition before its reform was taken in hand. Peter Damiani's initial jubilation at the election in 1045 of Pope Gregory VI arose from what he described as the crushing of the thousandfold head of the venomous serpent of simony, which trafficked in spiritual gifts and offices; Rome had been as in the days of the flood, but now the dove had returned to the ark with the olive-leaves of peace.[65] Writing in the late 1070s but from long familiarity with Rome, Abbot Desiderius of Montecassino enlarged upon how the abuses with which Italy was rife had subverted the Roman church itself. By priestly negligence, simony had slowly crept upwards in the church; to compound the abuse, priests and deacons who should handle the Lord's sacraments that were entrusted to them with pure hearts and chaste bodies were marrying like laymen and establishing families. This worst and most damnable of customs had become particularly rampant in Rome from which the pattern of religion had of old been everywhere diffused by St Peter and his successors. Of such evils, Pope Benedict IX was, for Desiderius, the exemplar; for he followed the footsteps of Simon Magus, not Simon Peter. Rome had become a place of unbridled plunder, slaughter, and every abomination.[66]

Yet layer upon layer of Rome's history, visible in its monuments and remembered in its traditions, summoned men to a return to the past which also brought hope for the future.[67] Peter Damiani urged Gregory VI to revive the age of the apostles: 'Let the golden age of the apostles be renewed and, under your wise presidency, let the church's discipline blossom anew.'[68] Perhaps the most powerful traditional imagery was that of Rome, city of martyrs, and especially of those who had suffered there from the days of the apostles until Constantine in the early fourth century gave peace to the church:

> O far-famed Rome, mistress of the earth,
> Pre-eminent amongst all its cities,
> Red with the martyrs' roseate blood,
> White with the virgins' lilies fair.

Pre-eminent among the martyrs whom this tenth-century North Italian poem sung were the princes of the apostles St Peter and St Paul, martyred at Rome and buried in its basilicas that bore their names; they were respectively the bearer of the heavenly keys and the teacher whose zeal outdid all the philosophers.[69] They were followed by a long succession of popes who were martyrs and confessors; it continued up to Nicholas I (858–67).[70] If the list of saintly popes stopped abruptly with him, recent

---

[65] *Briefe*, no. 13, 1.143/11–15. [66] *Dial.* 3, Prol., pp. 1141–3.

[67] See Reekmans, 'L'Implantation monumentale'. [68] *Briefe*, no. 13, 1.144/1–2.

[69] 'O Roma nobilis, orbis et domina, | Cunctarum urbium excellentissima, | Roseo martyrum sanguine rubea, | Albis et virginum liliis candida:' (Traube, *'O Roma nobilis'*).

[70] See e.g. *De sancta Romana ecclesia*, Frag. B, in Schramm, *Kaiser, Rom, und Renovatio*, 2.131.

memory may have recalled the martyr-bishops Adalbert of Prague and Bruno of Querfurt who had been monks at Rome at the turn of the millennium.[71]

The early Christian martyrs had died under an empire which, because it was pagan, was subject to the power of demons. Yet its monuments remained as a witness to ancient political cultuses which had resonances in every age and society, including Christian ones. Every Roman was familiar with the temple of Peace and Latona in the Forum which recalled a cultus of Peace established in the Augustan age. Its near-synonym, Concord, was among the oldest personifications in Roman religion; at first it stood for harmony between civic parties, but it came to embody social harmony in the broadest sense. Concord, too, had its temples: that of Concord and Piety in the Forum, of Concord alone by the Triumphal Arch, and of Concord and Saturn not far from it. From Sulla to Antony, city conflicts had given rise to an association of *Pax* and *Concordia* as attempts were made to appease civil strife.[72] The conflicts between the later Carolingians kept the association alive in changing forms as a living part of social vocabulary.[73] It had deep resonances in the aims and aspirations of the eleventh-century papacy.

But it was through the memory of Constantine that Rome's imperial past was most forcibly and insistently brought home to eleventh-century observers and that its monuments were made to speak to them. On the Capitol, an equestrian statue, in fact of Marcus Aurelius, was believed to represent Constantine and was a perpetual reminder of his conversion.[74] Its location on the Capitol had a profound significance in the light of the legends of Constantine which were contained in the so-called *Actus Silvestri*.[75] This late fourth-century document, which circulated widely in several recensions, depicted Constantine as he was still universally regarded in the eleventh century—as the pious and right-thinking founder of the Christian empire. Having been the church's persecutor, after his conversion he became its protector; once the enemy of Christians, he became their friend. According to the *Actus Silvestri*, his former part in slaughtering Christians had occasioned his punishment by leprosy, to cure which the pagan priests of Rome with their headquarters on the Capitol had instructed him to bathe in the blood of human infants. Moved by their mothers' tears, Constantine had drawn back from this; a vision of St Peter and St Paul prompted him to recall the pope, Silvester I, from exile in the hope of being cleansed by humane means. If his hope was fulfilled, he would restore to the church all its buildings in the Roman empire and would himself worship the true God. After Silvester had explained the Christian faith to him, he did penance and confessed his sins; then the pope baptized him and healed his leprosy in the baths of the Lateran palace. Henceforth, the pagan Capitol gave way to the Christian Lateran as the religious centre of Rome.

[71] See above, 1.6.   [72] See *OLD* s.v. *pax, concordia*; P–W 4.830–5, 18.2430–6.

[73] Semmler, 'Ein Herrschaftsmaxime'.

[74] Adhémar, *Influences antiques*, pp. 207–16 and Plate 63; Brooke, *Twelfth Century Renaissance*, pp. 9–25 and Illustration 4.

[75] ed. Mombritius; for further discussion, see Cowdrey, 'Eleventh-century Reformers' Views of Constantine', pp. 68–9.

Still according to the *Actus Silvestri*, after his conversion Constantine went on to legislate in the Christians' favour. In the octave of his baptism, which was represented as having occurred at Eastertide, Constantine each day issued a law, and two others quickly followed. Most were fictitious, but all were programmatic for later ages. Thus, for example, the law of the fourth day conferred upon the pontiff of the Roman church the privilege that, throughout the Roman world, he was the head of the bishops as the emperor was head of the judges.[76] It was a recognition by the emperor of the pope's universal jurisdiction over the bishops. Constantine thereafter founded the basilicas of St Peter's and of the Lateran. Some 7,000 people followed Constantine's example by receiving baptism. At a meeting with the reluctant senate in the Basilica Ulpia, Constantine discussed the cult of idols. The upshot was that Christian bishops would henceforth enjoy the same privileges as pagan priests, although no religious compulsion was to be applied and conversion was to be voluntary. A measure of the importance of the legends of the *Actus Silvestri* for the Rome of Gregory VII is the care with which they were epitomized in the first recension of the *Descriptio ecclesiae Lateranensis*.[77]

Constantine the exemplary Christian emperor and Christian Rome as he had set it up were a key part of the image of papal Rome in the later eleventh century. Its two principal basilicas recalled his name. Gregory VII's Register provides reminders that the Lateran basilica was familiarly known as the Constantinian basilica.[78] In St Peter's, over the arch before the apse there was a mosaic of Christ in glory with the accompanying legend:

> Because with you as its leader the world rose in triumph to heaven,
> The victorious Constantine dedicated to you this temple.[79]

In accordance with this view of the past, the *Constitutum Constantini*, which was itself a probably eighth-century derivative from the *Actus Silvestri*, confirmed that all that was best in the ancient imperial past had been appropriated to the Roman church and its bishop. In the *Constitutum Constantini*, Constantine was made to proclaim that, when he was cleansed from his leprosy and was baptized, he had turned from the service of the demons to embrace the Christian faith. Recognizing Christ's commission 'You are Peter' he had resolved to exalt the see of Peter above his own empire and earthly throne. He conveyed to Pope Silvester I the Lateran palace and his earthly insignia, transferring to the shores of the Bosphorus the seat of temporal power and government. Old Rome was left to be the *urbs sacra*; it was not right that an earthly emperor should wield power where God the heavenly emperor had established the supremacy of priests and the headship of the Christian religion. The opening words of the *Constitutum Constantini* were programmatic:

[76] For the best edition of the laws, see Linder, 'Constantine's "Ten Laws" Series'.

[77] 3.543–5. The *Descriptio* took the legends of Constantine's conversion from the 'vita Sancti Silvestri', rather than from the *Constitutum Constantini*: p. 543.

[78] 3.10*a*, p. 268/12–13, 8.21, p. 559/5, 9.37, p. 631/6–7.

[79] Diehl, *Inscriptiones*, 1.340, no. 1752: 'Quod duce te mundus surrexit in astra triumphans, | Hanc Constantinus victor tibi condidit aulam.'

To the most holy and blessed father of fathers, Silvester, bishop of the city of Rome and pope, and to all his successors who shall occupy the throne of St Peter until the end of time, to the pontiffs and to all the most reverend catholic bishops, beloved of God, in the whole world who are made subject by this our imperial constitution to the most holy Roman church, both now and at all times past and future: grace, peace, love, longsuffering, mercy, from God and the Father Almighty, Jesus Christ his Son, and the Holy Spirit be with you all.[80]

It was in such unfettered freedom that the pope should henceforth preside over the worship and life of the Roman church so that it might be the head and centre of the government of the church universal. Beyond the miseries of Rome as it was in the present, the aspirations and the promises of the past—classical, scriptural, and Constantinian—were always alive and active.

Upon the evidence of the first recension of the *Descriptio ecclesiae Lateranensis*, as Gregory VII's generation saw matters the papal palace and basilica of the Lateran visibly embodied these promises.[81] Its author saw in the Lateran something more than a reminder of Constantine's past legacy to the papacy in terms of universal authority and of buildings that were appropriate for its exercise. The store of relics and precious objects at the high altar of the basilica and, still more, in the papal chapel of St Lawrence that was known as the *Sancta sanctorum* was an ever-present pledge of the divine power that resided in the apostolic see. Constantine had added to his generosity to Rome by sending them the wealth of relics that his mother Helena had gathered at Jerusalem. It included relics of the true cross which were preserved in the chapel of St Lawrence, together with Christ's sandals and the most precious of all the Lateran relics, the foreskin of Christ's circumcision. Above the main altar of the chapel was another object of the utmost sanctity—a portrait of Christ which, as it was believed, St Luke had designed although the face was the work of angels and not of human hands. Below the portrait were numerous relics of the Holy Land and of Christ's birth, life, death, and passion. Another altar of the same chapel contained the heads of the princes of the apostles, St Peter and St Paul, whose bodies rested in the basilicas that bore their names.

These are but examples of the multitude of holy objects which formed the treasure of the Lateran palace. They were more than memorials of a distant past; they made the eternal power of Christ and his apostles and saints tangibly present in the city that was the setting of papal rule and the centre of pilgrimage and devotion for devout men and women from every part of Christendom. For a worthy pope, they were a daily reminder of the resources that were latent in his see and of his obligation to make these resources effective both at Rome and to the ends of the earth.

1.8 The Crisis at Rome, 1044–9

This weight of history, tradition, and legend that had thus gathered about the church of Rome ensured that its predicament under the scandalous and ineffective Tusculan

---

[80] *Das Constitutum Constantini*, ed. Fuhrmann, lines 6–15, pp. 56–7.   [81] 3.542–55.

pope Benedict IX would not be indefinitely prolonged in an age that was alive with Christian aspiration to revive the pristine quality of the apostolic church. Its structures and its resources were more than sufficient to provide the basis for the thorough renewal of its life; hence the crisis in Roman affairs that occurred between 1044 and 1049. It set the papacy upon the path to a realization of its own position and prerogatives that would lead to its developed claim to ecclesiastical and political preeminence during the central Middle Ages.

By the autumn of 1044, Benedict IX's position had been undermined, partly by revulsion against a moral unworthiness which was somewhat exaggerated by the propaganda of later writers, but still more by his own ineffectiveness, by jealousy of the power of the Tusculan family, and by consequent restlessness amongst the Roman aristocracy.[82] In September, some of its number, apparently Crescentians of the Stephanian branch, drove Benedict from the city. By January 1045 he had returned to Trastevere, finding support among the Octavian faction of the Crescentians; but Roman forces resisted him. The Stephanians encouraged the Romans to set up Bishop John of Sabina as pope with the name of Silvester III. Benedict excommunicated him, and in March he recovered the Leonine city. Silvester withdrew to Sabina; a year later he renounced his claim to the papacy and resumed his bishopric, which he retained until he died in 1063.

Nevertheless, Roman faction had been stirred up and Benedict's position remained insecure. On 1 May 1045 he chose voluntarily to resign the papacy in favour of John Gratian, archpriest of St John *ante portam Latinam*; he himself retired to his family's possessions near Tusculum.[83] The new, and for the next eighteen months the only, pope seems to have undergone a form of election as well as making his arrangement with Benedict; he took the name of Gregory VI. From his hermitage at Fonteavellana, the austere and enthusiastic reformer Peter Damiani applauded his accession as heralding an end to simony, a return to the golden age of the apostles, and a reflowering of Christian discipline.[84] Gregory gained recognition in France by King Henry I.[85] He was, indeed, an old man of honourable reputation, and a friend of reformers. But it emerged that his accession to the papacy was in some way tainted by simony: perhaps he himself trafficked in money to secure it; more likely, his supporters used bribery to get him accepted by the Roman citizens and especially the Tusculans.[86]

The confused situation at Rome led to intervention from Germany, where Henry III had been king for seven years though he had not yet been crowned emperor. For

---

[82] Among many recent accounts of the crisis, with details of sources, see esp. Zimmermann, *Papstabsetzungen*, pp. 119–39; Herrmann, *Das Tuskulanerpapsttum*, pp. 151–65; Schmale, 'Die "Absetzung" '. The *Dictionnaire historique de la papauté* (ed. Levillain) provides articles on the popes concerned.

[83] Peter Damiani, *Briefe*, no. 72, 2.363/9–14.

[84] Ibid. nos. 3, 4, 13, 16, 1.107/12–14, 110/6–111/5, 142–5, 153–4. [85] *Ep.* 4, *PL* 142.575–8.

[86] See esp. *De ordinando pontifice*, ed. Anton, pp. 77/76–78/108; Peter Damiani (as n. 83) said that venality had happened, not that Gregory himself handled money.

that, he must come to Rome, where he needed to receive his crown from a pope whose authority and moral standing were beyond challenge. In Germany, moreover, he had been zealous to promote worthy, capable, and reliable men to be bishops and abbots, to hold church councils, and to extirpate moral abuses like simony and clerical unchastity. He is likely to have wished to discharge at Rome the responsibilities for ordering and cleansing the church that he had fulfilled at home. After preparations that began in 1045, he crossed to Italy in the autumn of 1046. On 25 October he held a synod at Pavia, at which he is said to have spoken and legislated against simony. His next major stop was at Piacenza, where between 28 October and 25 November he was met by Pope Gregory VI. Henry does not seem yet to have known about his alleged simony and he received him honourably; indeed, pope and king concluded a pact of intercession that looked like a pledge of mutual acceptance and co-operation.[87]

But Henry's policy towards Gregory soon changed. Perhaps Gregory expressed himself reluctant to perform Henry's imperial coronation in view of his marriage within the prohibited degrees to Agnes of Poitou; but it is more likely that Henry got word of Gregory's alleged simony. On 20 December Henry was present at a synod in Sutri which both Gregory and the sometime Pope Silvester III attended, as well as the clergy of Rome. Gregory was confronted with the accusation of simony. Whether as a result of synodal condemnation or, as was later said, by an act of self-deposition, he stood down from the papacy.[88] He was imprisoned and then dispatched to Germany, where he was placed in the custody of Archbishop Hermann of Cologne. Silvester's forfeiture of the papacy was confirmed.

On Christmas Eve a synod assembled at Rome, and Benedict IX was declared to have been deposed. By now Henry was clearly determined to have done with Roman factions and to install a German pope. At his instance, Bishop Suidger of Bamberg was chosen; there may have been a form of election by the Roman clergy and people, but he was undoubtedly Henry's nominee. On Christmas Day he became Pope Clement II, choosing the name of St Peter's supposed successor in the apostolic office; it was a token that the earliest days of the church were, indeed, returning. In St Peter's, he performed the imperial coronation of Henry and his wife Agnes of Poitou. Afterwards the Roman people added to the imperial title that of *patricius*, which had been in abeyance since 1012 under the Tusculan popes. As conferred by the Romans, it was a novelty which gave him new rights that as emperor he did not enjoy. He was not only protector of the Roman church but he gained fresh rights over papal elections; as Peter Damiani later put it, the emperor enjoyed a decisive authority in papal elections ('in electione semper ordinandi pontificis principatum').[89] He won the support of such figures as Peter Damiani and the octogenarian Abbot Odilo

---

[87] Hermann of Reichenau, *Chron. a.* 1066, pp. 680–2; see K. Schmid, 'Heinrich III. und Gregor VI.'.

[88] That he was deposed is indicated by Peter Damiani (as n. 83) and by *De ordinando pontifice*, pp. 80/174–7, 83/279–80.

[89] For the title *patricius*, see esp. Schramm, *Kaiser, Rom und Renovatio*, 1.229–34; Vollrath, 'Kaisertum und Patriziat'; and Martin, 'Der salische Herrscher'. For Peter Damiani's comment, *Briefe*, no. 89, 2.547/18–20.

of Cluny.[90] On 5 January 1047, pope and emperor together held a synod at Rome which legislated against simony.[91]

Clement's reign was short: he died on 9 October 1047. A period of urban strife led on 8 November to Benedict IX's resuming the papal office with the help of Marquis Boniface of Tuscany. But some of the Romans invited Henry III to name another pope. In December, he condemned Benedict and nominated a German, Bishop Poppo of Brixen, who took the name Damasus II. Accompanied by Marquis Boniface of Tuscany whom Henry placed under constraint to support him, he was established in Rome and consecrated on 17 July; but he died on 9 August. Gregory VI had died in Germany on 19 December 1047.[92] Benedict IX survived for long enough to make a brief bid to resume the papacy after the death in 1054 of the next German pope, Leo IX. But he died during the winter of 1055–6 at the monastery of Grottaferata which lay in Tusculan-dominated territory.

Even in reforming circles, the sequence of papal successions and depositions during the crisis years gave rise to conflicting judgements upon Henry III's actions. Many persons, like Peter Damiani and Abbot Odilo of Cluny, were approving. Others, especially if they had a knowledge of canon law, were critical even to the point of virulence. After Clement II's death, Henry consulted the Lotharingian Bishop Wazo of Liège about the next step; he received the reply that, while another pope survived, it was not for the emperor to fill the papacy, and that the supreme pontiff should be judged by God alone: he should recognize the still-surviving pope.[93] Wazo probably intended Gregory VI, not Benedict IX; although Marquis Boniface of Tuscany had wished to restore the latter.[94] More radical than Wazo's arguments were those of an anonymous writer, perhaps a French bishop, who, soon after Benedict IX's attempted resumption of the papacy in 1047, sent another prelate and his colleagues, evidently in Capetian France, a tract known to scholars as the *De ordinando pontifice*.[95] The anonymous author offered practical advice, citing canonical authorities, about appropriate attitudes towards Benedict IX, Gregory VI, and perhaps Damasus II. For him, Henry III was no exemplar of reform; he was *imperator ille nequissimus* whose marriage in 1043 to Agnes of Poitou was within the prohibited degrees and gravely sinful. No less iniquitous were his judicial proceedings with regard to the popes. He had acted against canonical authority and with tyrannical power, for God reserved to himself alone the deposition of high priests. Nor had the choice of popes anything to do with the emperor: it should be in the hands of Christian clergy backed up by Christian peoples, and the bishops of Christendom should be associated with their election and consecration. The three popes to whom the anonymous author cryptically refers—Benedict IX, Gregory VI, and Clement

90 Peter Damiani, *Briefe*, no. 26, 1.240/6–10; Sackur, 'Zur *Iotsaldi vita Odilonis*'.

91 *MGH Const.* 1.95, no. 49.

92 The date and month are established by a Mantuan calendar in Zaccaria, *Anecdotorum*, pp. 181–6; see Jounel, *Le Culte des saints*, p. 173–9.

93 Anselm of Liège, *Gesta*, 2.65, p. 228.   94 *Ann. Rom.* p. 333.

95 ed. Anton; the treatise was probably written between Dec. 1047 and Jan. 1048.

II—all got short shrift: Benedict's rule was from the first illegal because of simony, and although the rehabilitation of a deposed pope was possible, Benedict's unworthiness vitiated his position. Simony and a disorderly election made Gregory, too, an illegal pope who could not be restored in 1047. Clement was a mere shadow pope set up because he was prepared to countenence Henry's incestuous marriage. The *De ordinando pontifice* was exceptional if not idiosyncratic. But it shows what radical ideas about the making and unmaking of popes were canvassed in the later 1040s, and how the local and Roman basis of the papacy was being challenged by those who stressed its international signficance.

Henry III's choice of a pope to succeed Damasus II was a wise one, and it was effective in damping down such ultra-reforming misgivings. At a meeting of his court in Worms during November 1048, he named his kinsman Bishop Bruno of Toul. The sources make it clear that Bruno agreed upon the strict condition that his election should have the free consent of the Roman clergy and people. Thus, on the one hand, Henry secured another pope from an imperial see; on the other, Bruno distanced himself from the authority over papal elections that Henry had claimed in 1046. Bruno travelled to Rome in 1049 in the garments of a pilgrim, not a prince. On 12 February he was enthroned as Pope Leo IX after the canonical election upon which he had insisted at Worms.[96] His name was well chosen: the last Pope Leo had been established in 963 by authority of the Emperor Otto I after his coronation; but Leo I (440–61) was a famous pope of Christian antiquity who first clearly taught that in the pope St Peter himself exercised the fullness of power (*plenitudo potestatis*) that Christ uniquely gave to the prince of the apostles. Leo IX had no intention of falling out with the emperor whose choice he was. But like his first namesake he was concerned also to demonstrate the unique status of the Roman primacy, and to exercise its authority to the full.

In the years which followed the changes and controversies of the crisis years from 1044 to 1049, Leo and Henry generally established themselves in the eyes of posterity as a paradigm pope and emperor. Leo reigned until 1054. His canonical election made him acceptable to most contemporary reformers. By disowning the acts of Benedict IX and Gregory VI while proclaiming the succession of Clement II as providential, he legitimized the outcome of Henry III's Roman intervention so far as the papal succession was concerned. By his zeal against simony and clerical marriage, by the many councils that he held not only at Rome but also in Italy, Germany, and France, and by his reputation for sanctity which was attested by many miracles, he became and remained everybody's pattern pope. Even his disastrous military campaign of 1053 against the Normans of South Italy did nothing to diminish his stature.[97] Abbot Desiderius of Montecassino's retrospective eulogy was typically fulsome:

---

[96] The principal sources for Leo's succession are: *Anselme de Saint-Remy, Histoire*, caps. 10–11, pp. 212–15; Wibert, *Vita Leonis IX*, cap. 2.2, *PL* 143.486–8.

[97] *Epp.* 2, 75, *PL* 143.593B–594A, 699 CD.

A man in every way apostolic, born of royal stock, endowed with wisdom, pre-eminent for religion, outstandingly learned in all Christian doctrine, it was he who (in the words of scripture) 'began to call on the name of the Lord' (Gen. 4: 26). . . . By him all ecclesiastical affairs were renewed and restored, and a new light was seen to arise in the world.[98]

Henry, too, who reigned until 1056, established himself in almost all circles as an exemplary emperor who exhibited the virtues of Josiah the Old Testament king and of Constantine the Christian emperor.[99] Reform-minded writers came to play down the objectionable aspects of his intervention at Rome in 1046 by exaggerating Benedict IX's turpitude and by insisting that Gregory VI himself laid down the papacy rather than being deposed by Henry.[100] The legacy of the crisis of 1044 to 1049 was thus the establishment of two figures who embodied in the present the models that history and legend had for long built up: Leo IX was a pope who stood for the classic age of the papacy and for a truly apostolic order of affairs; Henry III had renewed the beneficent imperial rule that Constantine had practised after his conversion. They set the stage for the history of the decades during which Pope Gregory VII was the dominant figure in Christendom.

[98] *Dial.* 3, Prol., pp. 1142–3.

[99] Gregory VII was to become warm in his praise: *Reg.* 1.19, to Duke Rudolf of Swabia, 1 Sept. 1073, p. 32/1; 2.44, to Queen Judith of Hungary, 10 Jan. 1075, pp. 180/30–181/3; 4.1, to the faithful of St Peter in Germany, 25 July 1076, p. 190/16–18; 4.3, to the same, 3 Sept. 1076, p. 298/22–5; 7.21, to King Harold Hein of Denmark, 19 Apr. 1080, p. 497/26–30.

[100] Desiderius, *Dial.* (as n. 98); *Chron. Cas.* 2.77, pp. 320–2; Bonizo of Sutri, *Lib. ad amic.* 5, pp. 585–6; Bernold, *Chron. a.* 1046, p. 425.

Hildebrand

2.1 The Young Hildebrand

Not until the midst of the crisis of 1044–9 did Hildebrand clearly emerge in history as a young clerk of the Roman church.[1] Both his family background and the place and date of his birth remain obscure, despite much learned ingenuity in seeking to identify them. When pope, he referred to his education at Rome but never to his having been born there; it is likely, therefore, that he was born elsewhere.[2] He may have been a native of Sovana, a small town in South Tuscany some distance to the west of Lake Bolsena, and have been related to a local family, the Aldebrandini. Friends and foes alike alluded to his modest origins, especially on his father's side. But his childhood does not seem to have been a deprived one. Medical examination of his skeletal remains has indicated that, in his childhood, he was well nourished with ample protein and vitamin D; in his prime he stood some 163 cm. (5 feet 4¼ inches) tall; he was strongly built, and well exercised. He was used to riding a horse. His skull suggests Alpine/Mediterranean, not Lombard or Germanic, descent. Probably on his mother's side, he may have had relations, some of whom had borne his name, who had been long settled at Rome in the vicinity of the Palatine and the monastery of S. Gregorio in Clivo Scauro. He had a niece at Rome, and in 1084 his nephew Rusticus defended the Septizonium, which was in this vicinity, against Henry IV of Germany.[3] Attempts to link him with the Pierleoni and so to give him a Jewish

---

[1] For Hildebrand's own use of the spelling *Heldibrandus*, see Jasper, *Das Papstwahldekret*, pp. 35–6; cf. the notice of Gregory's election to the papacy: *Reg.* 1.1*, p. 2/14.

[2] The most important references in the Register to Gregory's early life are: *Reg.* 1.1*, notice of his election, p. 2/11–14; 1.19, to Duke Rudolf of Swabia, 1 Sept. 1073, pp. 31/35–32/33; 1.39, to the bishops and princes of Saxony, 20 Dec. 1073, p. 62/5–7; 1.79, to Archbishop Anno of Cologne, 18 Apr. 1074, p. 113/10–16; 2.44, to Queen Judith of Hungary, 10 Jan. 1075, pp. 180/30–181/3; 2.49, to Abbot Hugh of Cluny, 22 Jan. 1075, pp. 189/30–190/5; 3.10a, record of the Lent synod of 1076, p. 270/3–4; 3.21, to the Emir an-Nāṣir of Mauretania, (June 1076), p. 288/18–24; 4.11, to Count Robert of Flanders, 10 Nov. 1076, p. 311/11–12; 7.14a, record of the Lent synod 1080, p. 483/10–14; 7.23, to King William I of England, 24 Apr. 1080, p. 500/20–1.

[3] Hildebrand's Tuscan origins are alluded to in *LP* 2.282/1 ('natione Tuscus, de opido Raouaco, ex patre Bonizo'), cf. 2.360/34–6, where the reference is to Rovacum, near Sovana; similarly Paul of Bernried, cap. 1, p. 474/9–12. Benzo of Alba used Hildebrand's Tuscan origins to undermine his Roman credentials: 7.2, p. 671/23–32. Other main sources for Hildebrand's early life are: Peter Damiani, *Briefe*, no. 123, 3.403/22–404/16 (the monastery concerned is unidentified); Wenric of Trier, caps. 1–2, pp. 285/23–32, 286/10–20; Hugh of Flavigny, 2, p. 422/18–28 (where Hildebrand is said to have been born at Rome, to parents who were Roman citizens); Bruno of Segni, cap. 2, pp. 547/36–548/64; Beno, 2.4–12, pp. 376–80; Bernold, *Micrologus*, cap. 14, col. 986B; Bonizo of Sutri, *Lib. ad amic.* 5, pp. 587/27–588/10; *Annales Pegavienses*, p. 238/40–1 (which suggests that he was related to the Pierleoni); Paul of Bernried, caps. 1–11, pp. 474–8. For Hildebrand's modest social origins, see also Abbot Walo of Metz's letter to him,

connection have been unconvincing. Because Pope Leo IX made him subdeacon at an unknown date and because the canonical age for such promotion was 20 years, he is likely to have been born before 1029/34. Medical evidence, however, points to his having been between 65 and 75 years of age when he died in 1085, and probably about 70; this points to a date of birth *c*.1015.[4] If so, he may have been over 30 when the Emperor Henry III intervened at Rome in 1046, over 40 when he became archdeacon, and in his late fifties, perhaps about 58, when he was elected pope. At no juncture of his life for which there is significant evidence did he lack the appropriate years or experience.

While pope he repeatedly insisted that he had been educated at Rome 'ab infantia'; his claim to have been brought up in St Peter's household may imply that his earliest education was in a school attached to St Peter's basilica itself. But the papal palace at the Lateran also figures in his letters as 'apostolica aula'; and his education was certainly completed in the Lateran palace with boys from leading families from Rome and further afield.[5] While still 'in adolescentia' but before entering the papal service he was said to have become a monk; St Mary's-on-the-Aventine, a house rich in associations with figures like Abbots Odo of Cluny and Aligernus of Montecassino, was named as his monastery; an unnamed uncle was said to have been his abbot.[6] His letters as pope made no unambiguous reference to his monastic status, for his emphasis in them lay on his debt to the apostle St Peter; but his being a monk was widely attested by friends and, more especially, by foes.[7] Their testimony is sufficiently

---

Die Briefe des Abtes Walo, no. 1, pp. 52/16–53/2 ('vir de plebe', perhaps alluding to King David: Ps. 88: 20–1); William of Malmesbury, *De gestis regum*, 3.263, vol. 2.322 ('despicabilis parentelae'); Benzo of Alba, 6.2, p. 660/16–17 ('natus matre suburbana, de patre caprario'). For charters which may refer to Hildebrand's forebears, see Mittarelli and Costadoni, *Ann. Camal.* 1, Appendix, nos. 41 (975), 54 (994), cols. 96–8, 122–4. For Gregory's niece, see Paul of Bernried, cap. 32, pp. 487–8, and for his nephew Rusticus, *LP* 2.290/15–16, cf. Mittarelli and Costadoni, *Ann. Camal.* 3, Appendix, no. 86 (1096), col. 124. For a medical examination of Gregory's remains, carried out in 1984, see Fornaciari, Mallegni, and Vultaggio, 'Il regime', esp. pp. 41, 44, 46, 60, 67–70; Fornaciari and Mallegni, 'La ricognizione', esp. pp. 402–8.

4 His being made subdeacon, which was the lowest grade of major orders, is referred to by Desiderius, *Dial.* 3.1, p. 1143/28; Bonizo of Sutri, *Lib. ad amic.* 5, p. 588/8–10; Paul of Bernried, cap. 13, p. 478/26. Bernold's observation (as n. 2) that Gregory had been nurtured and instructed 'sub decem suis antecessoribus' does not make clear which ten popes were intended.

5 *Reg.* 3.21, p. 288/18–20, 4.11, p. 311/11–12. For the papal palace as *apostolica aula*, see *Reg.* 2.51, p. 194/13–17, 6.13, pp. 416/36–417/2.

6 Paul of Bernried, cap. 9, p. 477.

7 Gregory may have referred to his monastic state in *Reg.* 3.10a, p. 270/9–11, but the word *peregrinatio* could mean exile rather than the monastic life. In a privilege of 1078 for the monastery of Leno, he referred to St Benedict as *pater noster*: *QF* no. 150, p. 168/10, Hildebrand's alleged subscription of the Election Decree of 1059 as *monachus et subdiaconus* is a later interpolation: Jasper, *Das Papstwahldekret*, pp. 34–8, 111. In 1076, the propaganda of Henry IV of Germany arraigned Gregory as a 'false monk': *Epp. HIV* nos.10, 12, 13, pp. 62/1.7, 64/16, 68/29–31, cf. the decree of the synod of Brixen, (1080) ibid. Anhang C, p. 478/5. In biographies, see Wenric of Trier, caps. 1–2, pp. 285/26–7, 286/14–26, 38–287/1; Paul of Bernried, cap. 9, p. 477. In chronicles, Hildebrand's monastic state is noticed by Arnulf of Milan, 3.12, p. 182/2–3; *Chron. Cas.* 2.86, p. 355/14, 34; Hugh of Flavigny, 2, p. 422/22–3. Among propagandist works, see Bruno of Segni, cap. 2, pp. 547/36–548/2, 10–12; Rangerius of Lucca, *Vita s. Anselmi*, vv. 2285–8, p. 1205; Beno, 2.6, p. 377; Guy of Ferrara, 2, pp. 16–19; Peter Crassus, caps. 1,4,5, pp. 434/37–8,

weighty to be followed; if he was 30 or so years of age when his recorded career began in 1045–7, his early years at Rome provide an ample time for a noviciate and profession as a monk which would help to account for his early obscurity. Among his early mentors at Rome are mentioned Lawrence, exiled archbishop of Amalfi who was learned in Latin and Greek and the hagiographer of the first bishop of Florence, and John Gratian, the archpriest of the church of St John at the Latin Gate who in 1045 became Pope Gregory VI.[8] When John Gratian was pope, Hildebrand is said to have been his chaplain; by this time he was evidently in minor orders.[9]

Hildebrand shared Gregory VI's journey into exile in Germany—unwillingly, as he was to declare in 1080, no doubt because it separated him from the church of the princes of the apostles. He looked back to his sometime papal master as 'domnus papa Gregorius', showing that he retained a sense of personal attachment to him and implying that he held him to be guiltless of any grave offence such as simony.[10] He probably remained with him until his death in mid-December 1047. A letter of his own in 1074 establishes that he spent some time in Cologne, perhaps as a monk; an anecdote of Peter Damiani, if it is to be dated to this time, indicates a visit to Aachen, and there was a tradition that he was for a time at Henry III's court; if so, it may have been an opportunity to resolve any tensions which remained from Henry's treatment of Gregory VI. However, Hildebrand's own itinerary cannot be reconstructed in detail. According to Bruno of Segni, who heard him reminisce about this time, he engaged in study and practised Benedictine monasticism.[11] There was a later tradition that he became a monk at Cluny. But his own letters to Abbot Hugh of Cluny contain no reference to his monastic life there, and no Cluniac Necrology or similar source records him as a sometime Cluniac.[12] It is, however, possible that he stayed for a time

439/12–23, 443/12–13; Benzo of Alba, e.g. 2.8, 4.10, 6.2, 7.2, pp. 615/35, 626/35, 39–40, 660/16–17, 671/22–37. Hildebrand is also referred to as a monk in the anecdotes of Abbot Hugh of Cluny: Southern and Schmitt, *Memorials*, pp. 211/27–30, 213/19–21, and in the letter of the canonesses of Gandersheim to Pope Paschal II: Goetting, 'Die Gandersheimer Originalsupplik', p. 121/8–9. In the record of a *placitum* held near Chiusi on 16 May 1058, there is a reference to 'Domnus Illibrandus monachus, sanctae Romanae ecclesiae legatus': *I placiti*, ed. Manaresi, no. 405, 3.239–41. For his description as *monachus* in the inscription upon the bronze doors which were procured in 1070 for the basilica of St Paul-without-the-Walls, see Bloch, *Monte Cassino*, 1.143.

[8] Beno (as n. 3); see Holtzmann, 'Laurentius von Amalfi', and Laurentius . . . *Opera*, ed. Newton, pp. 1–13. Beno says of Hildebrand that, *derelicto monasterio*, he became associated with John Gratian and Lawrence: 2.6, p. 377.

[9] Bonizo of Sutri, *Lib. ad amic.* 5, p. 587/5–8.

[10] *Reg.* 7.14a, p. 483/11–12. In some circles, Gregory VI was long remembered for his sanctity and religion, e.g. Ralph Glaber, 5.26, pp. 252–3; William of Malmesbury, *De gestis regum*, 2.201–3, vol. 1.246–53.

[11] Sources as above, nn. 2–3. *Annales Palidenses*, a. 1047, p. 69, illustrates the growth of legend.

[12] For the tradition that Hildebrand was a Cluniac, see Bonizo of Sutri, *Lib. ad amic.* 5, p. 587/9–11; Otto of Freising (who said that he became prior of Cluny), *Chron.* 6.33, p. 484. For a recent argument that this tradition may be sound, see Fichtenau, 'Cluny und der Mönch Hildebrand'. But the lack of reference to Hildebrand as a Cluniac in Cluniac necrologies tells against this: Wollasch, 'Die Wahl des Papstes Nicholas I.'; Müssigbrod, 'Zur Necrologüberlieferung', p. 68 n. 24; id., 'Das Necrolog von Saint-Pons de Thomières', p. 82 n. 1. The remark in a Hildebrandine anecdote that Hildebrand was dear to Abbot Hugh 'ex antiqua cohabitatione' suggests that Hildebrand stayed at Cluny, perhaps after the death of Gregory VI, but it does not establish his profession there: Southern and Schmitt, *Memorials*, p. 211/29.

at Cluny as a visitor. Wherever he followed the monastic life, he seems to have done so with characteristic commitment; in 1080 he declared that it was unwillingly that, in the winter of 1048–9, he returned to Rome with Bishop Bruno of Toul, whom Henry III had chosen to succeed Pope Damasus II. For it was by summons of the future Pope Leo IX that Hildebrand was restored to the service of the Roman church which for the rest of his days was to be his overmastering concern.[13]

The 1050s were a decade of zealous service by Hildebrand both at Rome and, on the popes' behalf, in the church at large. He was by now a mature but by no means a senior or even a prominent Roman clerk. With hindsight, writers of a later generation, whether friend or foe, were prone to exaggerate his role. It is unlikely that, as Bonizo of Sutri alleged, he prompted Pope Leo IX to convene his reforming synod of April 1049; the story of the *Liber pontificalis*, improved upon by Bonizo, that on his death-bed in St Peter's, Leo entrusted Hildebrand with the administration of the Roman church, is suspect, since Hildebrand was travelling in France; a hostile cardinal's allegation that Hildebrand was a leader in engineering Leo's disastrous expedition of 1053 against the Normans and then the pope's captivity by the Normans is transparently fable.[14] At least until 1058/9, it was figures like Cardinals Humbert of Silva Candida and Boniface of Albano who were at the centre of Roman politics.[15] Nevertheless, Hildebrand when pope referred to Leo with respect and gratitude; Leo favoured him and employed him for tasks involving genuine responsibility. He did not always win approval. In a letter of 1074, he remarked that some at Rome still remembered Leo's chagrin at his strenuous defence of the church of Cologne, to which his experiences in exile had indebted him, against the claims of Archbishop Eberhard of Trier, who was Leo's metropolitan in his capacity as bishop of Toul.[16] But if, as is probable, Hildebrand's early championship of Patriarch Dominicus III of Grado/Venice in the ancient rivalry between his see and that of Aquileia occurred during Leo's lifetime, he and the pope were in this case of one mind; for in 1053 Leo reacted favourably to the tearful pleas that the patriarch made to him.[17]

At Rome, Hildebrand was given responsibilities at the patriarchal basilicas of St Peter and St Paul, the founder-apostles of the Roman church. Despite the allegations of financial malpractice that follow, it is impossible to dismiss Cardinal Beno's statement that Leo appointed him a guardian of the altar of St Peter; for a document of the South Italian monastery of Tremiti described him as treasurer ('ipochrisarius') of St

---

[13] *Reg* 7.14a, p. 483/12–16.

[14] Bonizo of Sutri, *Lib. ad amic.* 5, pp. 588/8–16, 589/27–9; *LP* 2.356a/12–17 (where Hildebrand was not necessarily present when Leo named him); Beno, 2.9, p. 379/20–9. For a story that Leo warned against Hildebrand's ever himself being elected pope, see *De episcopis Eichstetensibus*, cap. 37, p. 265.

[15] For their careers, see Hüls, *Kardinäle*, pp. 89–90, 131–4. In 1059 Peter Damiani still called them the eyes of the pope, though by now he named Hildebrand first among those whom Pope Nicholas II highly regarded: *Briefe*, no. 60, 2.205/3–8.

[16] *Reg.* 1.9, to Archbishop Anno of Cologne, 18 Apr. 1074, p. 113/10–16; the occasion may have been Leo's confirmation at his Roman synod of 1049 of Trier's primacy in Gallia Belgica: *Ep.* 3, *PL* 143.594–6.

[17] *Reg.* 2.39, to Doge Dominicus Silvius, 31 Dec. 1074, p. 175/18–22, 4.27, to the same, 9 June 1079, p. 342/3–11, 9.8 to the same, 8 Apr. (1081), p. 585/6–7; cf. Leo IX, *Ep.* 82, *PL* 143.727. For Leo IX's decision, see *Ep.* 32, *PL* 143.727.

Peter's, and the diatribe of the synod of Brixen (1080) alleged that he had been associated with the money-changers in the portico of St Peter's.[18] His connection with St Paul's-without-the-Walls was stronger, and involved him in a continuing association with monastic affairs. In 1050, Leo dispatched its abbot, Airard, to be bishop of Nantes while retaining his office as abbot. His reforming endeavours in the Breton march having proved ineffectual, his presence there is not attested after 1051. In 1059, he subscribed the Election Decree as 'episcopus et abbas Sancti Pauli'; he seems to have died in 1060. From 1050, Hildebrand was administrator ('economus, prepositus, provisor, rector') of St Paul's; he was never called 'abbas'. His official association with it lasted some twenty years. His attention to its business is illustrated by a letter of Pope Alexander II, dated 1 July 1066, in which he approved an agreement between Abbot Oderic of la Trinité, Vendôme, and Hildebrand in his capacity as archdeacon and *rector* and *economus* of St Paul's. It concerned the church of S. Prisca on the Aventine, which was to became a cell of Vendôme with twelve, or at least eight, monks. The agreement was accompanied by the status of 'external' cardinal ('dignitate cardinali') for Abbot Oderic, perhaps with the corollary that he would be cardinal-priest of that title. That Hildebrand concluded the agreement with the consent of the chapter of monks of St Paul's illustrates his close relationship with its monastic life. In 1070, the bronze doors which were made in Constantinople for St Paul's were said in an inscription to be of the time of Pope Alexander and of 'the lord Hildebrand, venerable monk and archdeacon'.[19]

During the pontificate of Leo IX's successor Victor II (1054–7), Hildebrand gained further experience of the everyday workings of papal government. The evidence of papal letters reveals him as being active in preparing such documents; he seems to have been effectively 'cancellarius et bibliothecarius' at the Lateran. Under Victor's successors, Hildebrand's name was largely absent from papal documents, no doubt by reason of his activities as archdeacon.[20]

Wenric of Trier later accused Hildebrand of wilfully abandoning monastic stability by touring the cities of Italy, Germany, and France, until there were few princes of his

[18] Beno, 1.9, p. 379/5–8; *Cod. dipl. Trem.* no. 64, 2. 197–8; *Epp. HIV* p. 478/7–9; Benzo of Alba, 7.2, p. 671/37–40. Hildebrand was also described as *apocrisarius*, in its other sense of ambassador or legate, by Peter Damiani, *Briefe*, no. 72, 2. 344/18.

[19] For Airard, see Leo IX, *Ep.* 38, *PL* 143.647C; Muratori, *Antiq.* 5.1042–4; Jasper, *Das Papstwahldekret*, p. 112/224–5; and for discussion, Guillotel, 'La Pratique', pp. 8–17, 33–40. For Alexander's II's letter of 1066, see *Cartulaire . . . de Vendôme*, no. 180, 1.311–13; for problems arising from the cardinalate, see Ganzer, *Die Entwicklung*, pp. 26–9, and Hüls, *Kardinäle*, pp. 212–13. According to Paul of Bernried, Hildebrand did much to restore the spiritual and material well-being of St Paul's: cap. 13, pp. 478–9. For Hildebrand's titles at St Paul's, see also *Cod. dipl. Trem.* no. 64, 2.197–9; Cappelletti, *Le chiese*, 17.430; Pflugk-Harttung, *Acta*, no. 153, 2.117–18. For the inscription on the bronze doors, see Bloch, *Monte Cassino*, 1.142–3. When pope, Gregory referred to his continuing concern for the *honesta et regularis regiminis ordinatio* of St Paul's: *Reg.* 1.52, to Archbishop Manasses I of Rheims, 14 Mar. 1074, pp. 79/20–80/1; see also *QF* no. 36, privilege (probably much interpolated) for St Paul's, 14 Mar. (?1074) (cf. the date of *Reg.* 1.52), pp. 20–8; *Reg.* 7.7 to Cardinal Richard of Marseilles, 2 Nov. 1079, p. 468/26–34.

[20] Victor II, *Epp.* 1–4, 7, 17–18, *PL* 143.803–11, 813–15, 829–34; Cappelletti, *Le chiese*, 17.430; Santifaller, 'Saggio', 1.162–3.

time whom he did not greet.[21] The element of truth in this stricture is that, especially during the 1050s, Hildebrand undertook missions on the papal behalf to regions far from Rome, which both extended his own acquaintance with prominent figures both ecclesiastical and lay, and made him widely known both directly and by reputation. These missions, rather than his activities at Rome, formed his principal business before he became archdeacon.

He was twice a papal legate in France. He was first dispatched by Pope Leo IX; in April or May 1054, he presided over a council at Tours. The occasion and purpose of this mission are incompletely known; there is direct evidence only of his dealings with Berengar, archdeacon of Tours, in respect of his eucharistic teachings. Berengar's own accounts of the proceedings provide the main evidence.[22] Hilde-brand emerges in a sympathetic light. His management of business seems to have been marked by orderliness and moderation. He sought to establish what Berengar's teachings actually were, rather than to pass premature judgement upon them. He began by holding private talks with him before he allowed a fuller examination by the archbishop of Tours and the bishops of Orleans and Auxerre and finally initiated a general debate in the council. Hildebrand had come prepared with a collection of marked passages about the eucharist in books by ancient authorities, and he was at pains to determine fairly whether Berengar's teachings were compatible with them. For his part, Berengar's response was to recall that Hildebrand had insisted upon the authority of Rome 'invincible in faith as in arms', but that he had not come down on either side; he therefore charged him with temporizing. The upshot of the delibera-tions was that Hildebrand reserved Berengar's case for audience at Rome, and turned to other business. But before the council ended, news came from Rome of Leo IX's death on 19 April. Hildebrand's legateship lapsed, and Berengar avoided an im-mediate testing of his teachings at Rome. There is one hint of other business that Hildebrand may have transacted at Tours: Abbot Geoffrey of Vendôme long after-wards referred to Hildebrand's goodwill to his abbey; because of its proximity to Tours, he may have had a decision at this council in mind.[23]

In February 1056, Hildebrand was back in France as the legate of Pope Victor II. He held a council at Chalon-sur-Saône which was attended by the archbishops of Lyons, Vienne, Tours, and Bourges, as well as by seven bishops and ten abbots who included Abbot Hugh of Cluny. The principal business was to resist simony; at least six bishops were deposed for this and other offences. The council gave rise to the widely diffused anecdote about Hildebrand, which he was himself telling at Rome by 1059, of how he convicted a French bishop—probably Hugh of Embrun—of simony by exhibiting his powerlessness to name the Holy Spirit when called upon to recite the *Gloria Patri*. Hildebrand was also concerned with more routine matters of local business. The council confirmed the possessions of the abbey of Saint-Pierre at

---

[21] *Epistola*, 2, p. 286/17–20.

[22] Berengerius, *Rescriptum*, 1.590–670, pp. 52–4; *Die Hannoversche Briefsammlung*, 3: *Briefe Berengars von Tours*, no. 87, *MGH Briefe*, 5.148–52.

[23] *Ep.* 1.18, *PL* 157.58D–59A.

Vienne and settled a bitter dispute over a church in favour of the canons of Romans. A letter of Pope Stephen IX, which must be dated soon after 18 October 1057, shows that Hildebrand dealt with business concerning Archbishop Aimo of Bourges, and that Stephen expected Hildebrand to return to Rome in the company of Archbishop Gervase of Rheims.[24] There is also later evidence to suggest a visit at this time to Tours, where Hildebrand saw to matters concerning its archbishop, Bartholomew, and was well received by the canons of Saint-Martin.[25] By such dealings, he was getting to know the French church and its clergy at first hand. Other anecdotes which Abbot Hugh of Cluny told in old age recalled his travels with Hildebrand during these years. They included a visit to Cluny itself as well as to another monastery, and made Hildebrand known amongst lay as well as ecclesiastical notables. Hildebrand's reputation for possessing supernatural powers to read men's thoughts, to foretell the future, and to see Christ himself in chapter at Cluny points to the impression of personal authority that he was beginning to create.[26]

In the years before he became archdeacon, Hildebrand also gained experience of German affairs. Much of it arose from the accession of two popes—Victor II, who was nominated at Mainz in November 1054 but who was installed at Rome after considerable reluctance only on 13 April 1055, and his successor Stephen IX who was quickly elected and enthroned in August 1057. Hildebrand was also associated with the events by which the infant Henry, born on 11 November 1050 to the Emperor Henry III and the Empress Agnes of Poitou, became king of Germany: he was elected at Tribur in November 1053, anointed and crowned at Aachen on 17 July 1054, and, on 5 October 1056 after Henry III's death, he succeeded him under his mother's regency.

So far as the papal succession is concerned, upon learning at Tours of Leo IX's death in 1054, Hildebrand no doubt quickly returned to Rome. According to the late evidence of the Montecassino Chronicle, the Roman authorities sent him to Germany where it was upon his insistence that a reluctant Henry III released a no less reluctant bishop of Eichstätt to become pope as Victor II. According to the Chronicle, Victor was reputed thereafter to have retained no liking for monks.[27] There is also a recollection of Hildebrand's part in bringing about Victor's succession in Benzo of Alba's story that, soon after Leo IX's death, three 'monks', Hildebrand with Cardinal-bishops Humbert of Silva Candida and Boniface of Albano,

---

[24] Those present are named in Mansi, 19.843, and *Cartulaire Saint-André de Vienne*, no. 54, pp. 264–6. The anecdote about simony was first recorded by Peter Damiani, *Briefe*, no. 72, 2.344–5, and was among the Hildebrandine anecdotes told in the early 12th cent. by Abbot Hugh of Cluny: Southern and Schmitt, *Memorials*, pp. 215–16, cf. p. 22; for other important citations, see Desiderius, *Dial.* 3.5, p. 1148; Paul of Bernried, caps. 16–17, pp. 479–80; Bonizo of Sutri, *Lib. ad amic.* 6, p. 592; Bruno of Segni, pp. 548–9. For Hildebrand and Bourges, see Stephen IX, *Ep.* 1, *PL* 143.870C; the matters concerned were not satisfactorily settled: Schieffer, *Die Entstehung des päpstlichen Investiturverbots*, p. 226.

[25] *Narratio controversiae inter capitulum S. Martini Turonensis et Radulphum eiusdem archiepiscopum*, *RHGF* 12.460A.

[26] Southern and Schmitt, *Memorials*, pp. 211–14.

[27] *Chron. Cas.* 2.86, pp. 335/1–16, 23–36; see also Bonizo of Sutri, *Lib. ad amic.* 5, pp. 589/39–590/33.

came to Henry III's court. Benzo's story is one of the testimonies for the assertion, made in and after 1076 by Gregory's adversaries, that, during Henry III's lifetime and so before 1056, Hildebrand swore in the presence of a number of bishops (according to the probable form of oath) that, so long as Henry III and his son lived, he would neither himself accept the papacy nor, as far as he was able, allow anyone else to accept it, without the king's consent. (Benzo of Alba implausibly represented Henry III as binding the 'monks' Hildebrand, Humbert, and Boniface by oath absolutely that they would never themselves become pope or play any part in a papal election.) In 1073, Gregory made it clear that he had once taken an oath of some kind in a letter to the Saxon bishops and princes, whom he told that, since God had so clearly manifested his will in his own recent election, he could not resist it on the grounds of the vow that he had once taken. An undertaking of this kind to the German rulers is best placed during negotiations in 1054–5 concerning Bishop Gebhard of Eichstätt; his acceptance of the papacy may have had as its condition a recognition of royal rights in papal elections in connection with which Hildebrand took an oath.[28]

Hildebrand's mission to Germany after the death of Leo IX is likely also to have been the occasion of another intensification of his commitment to the Salian royal house. This is suggested by an early letter of his as pope, in which he gave two reasons why he felt an especial responsibility for King Henry IV. As the first reason, he linked together his having himself 'elected Henry to be king' ('ipsum in regem elegimus') and Henry III's having treated him with especial honour amongst the Italians at his court; as the second, he recalled that, on his deathbed at Bodfeld, Henry III had commended his son to the Roman church in the presence of Pope Victor II.[29] To which step in Henry IV's king-making did Gregory refer when declaring that he had 'elected' him? It cannot be to his succession upon his father's death in 1056, for Pope Victor II, not Hildebrand, was then present. Nor is there evidence or likelihood that Hildebrand was in Germany when Henry was elected at Tribur in 1053. The possibility must be entertained that Hildebrand, who had the physique of a good horseman, travelled from Rome to Aachen by mid-July 1054 for the young king's anointing and coronation, which were performed by Hildebrand's acquaintance from his days of exile, Archbishop Hermann of Cologne. Hildebrand's 'election' may have taken the form of his joining in the universal cry, 'Fiat, Fiat. Amen', which followed the archbishop's asking the *populus* whether they would be subject to this prince and ruler, establish his kingdom with firm faith, and obey his commands.[30] Henry III's special favour to Hildebrand would have been shown at Aachen and during the

---

[28] Benzo of Alba, 7.2, p. 671/22–34. Gregory's oath was credibly cited in 1076 by the German bishops when they renounced obedience to him: Anhang A, *Epp. HIV* pp. 472/27–34. Other references to the oath occur in *Dicta cuiusdam*, p. 458/37–44; *Altercatio*, p. 170/17–18; Beno, 2.9, p. 379/2–4; Bernold of Constance, *Libelli*, 2, p. 35/20–6. Gregory's reference to his oath is in *Reg.* 1.39, 20 Dec. 1073, p. 61/35–8. On the oath, see Schmidt, 'Zur Hildebrands Eid'.

[29] *Reg.* 1.19, 1 Sept. 1073, to Duke Rudolf of Swabia, pp. 31/35–32/8.

[30] For the coronation order, see *RGP* 72.8–9, vol. 1.245–50.

protracted pope-making of Victor II.[31] The likelihood that Hildebrand became thus committed to Henry IV in his infancy must be remembered as a reason for his solicitude for him before and after he became pope.

It may have been Hildebrand's closeness to the German court that accounts for Victor II's employment of Hildebrand despite his part in bringing about his unwilling accession to the papacy. Hildebrand was a companion of Victor during his last journey to Tuscany. After visiting Florence and after being with Victor at his synod near Arezzo, he was at the pope's deathbed in that city on 28 July 1057.[32] Thereafter, business connected with the election of Pope Stephen IX again took him to Germany. With Henry III now dead and with the German kingdom under the Empress Agnes's regency, the election had occurred swiftly and without prior reference to the German royal court. According to the Montecassino Chronicle, Cardinal Frederick was asked by the Roman clergy who should be pope. He named five candidates, the first of them Cardinal Humbert and the fifth Hildebrand; but the Romans thought none of them appropriate and offered the papacy to Frederick. A suggestion that the election should be postponed until Hildebrand returned from Tuscany was overruled, and on 2 August Frederick was elected pope.[33] The impression of a swift and smooth election is probably a correct one. So far as notification of the German court was concerned, after the death of Henry III it was possible to take matters slowly. It was not until after 18 October, when Hildebrand helped with the procuring of a papal privilege of protection for the clergy of Lucca,[34] that he accompanied Bishop Anselm I of Lucca, the future Pope Alexander II whom he had first met during his recent visit to Tuscany, upon a legatine mission to Germany which took them *en route* to the troubled city of Milan.[35] The purpose in Germany of the legates was to bring official notice of the papal election and to secure a recognition of it which was critical because of possible German fear of the election of the brother of Duke Godfrey of Lorraine. The legates probably attended Agnes's Christmas court at Goslar; on 27 December, Hildebrand was certainly present when Gundechar, Victor II's successor as bishop of Eichstätt, was ordained at Pöhlde before a concourse of bishops and abbots.[36] Nothing is known about German reaction to the papal election, although there is nothing to suggest that Agnes did not acquiesce.

That Hildebrand's dealings in Germany were not restricted to the court and to such high matters is suggested by a memory that the canonesses of Gandersheim, to the west of Goslar, recorded half a century later. It appears that Henry IV's half-sister Beatrix, born in 1037 and abbess from 1044 to 1061, had recruited knights and had enfeoffed them with the abbey's lands. The community was thereby impoverished

---

[31] Later assertions that, in 1054, the Roman clergy and people were minded to make Hildebrand pope, and that he persuaded Henry III to renounce the Roman patriciate, may be discounted: e.g. Bonizo of Sutri, *Lib. ad amic.* 5, p. 589/32–8.

[32] Victor II, *Ep.* 18, *PL* 143. 831–4; Cappelletti, *Le chiese*, 17.428–31; *Chron. Cas.* 2.94, p. 353/4–6.

[33] *Chron. Cas.* 2.94, pp. 352–3.   [34] Stephen IX, *Ep.* 2, *PL* 143.871–2.

[35] Arnulf of Milan, 3.12, p. 182; Landulf Senior, 3.13, p. 82/25–39.

[36] Lampert of Hersfeld, *Ann. a.* 1058, p. 62/27–30; *De episcopis Eichstetensibus*, p. 246/7–18.

and appealed to the Empress Agnes, who in her turn appealed to Pope Victor II at Rome. Upon instructions from Victor's successor, Stephen IX, Hildebrand visited Gandersheim. Beatrix appeared before the young Henry, Agnes, and the German princes. They ruled that the knights should abandon their fiefs under the sanction of Beatrix's forfeiting her abbacy. The incident shows that Hildebrand was not without an opportunity for seeing at first hand the harmful results for ecclesiastical institutions which could accompany early Salian attempts to increase royal power in East Saxony.[37]

When Stephen IX died on 29 March 1058, Hildebrand had not yet returned to Rome. Before he died, Stephen ordered the Roman bishops, clergy, and people not to proceed to an election until Hildebrand was back. Stephen's reasons are not known, but they may have arisen from negotiations in progress with the German court about the conduct of future elections. Possibly, too, knowing himself to be mortally ill, Stephen had designated Bishop Gebhard of Florence to succeed him and had commissioned Hildebrand to secure German approval.[38] In any event, there had been important developments at Rome during Stephen's short pontificate which bore upon papal elections. One of the most eminent and articulate of reformers, Peter Damiani, had been brought from his hermit's cell at Fonteavellana to succeed two nonentities in the senior cardinal-bishopric of Ostia. Of the two other bishoprics most concerned with installing a pope, Albano was in the safe hands of Boniface, but Porto, for most of the 1050s in undistinguished hands, was filled during the summer of 1057 by John II, who was an active figure both before and after his secession in 1084 to the anti-pope. Stephen made Humbert of Silva Candida his *cancellarius et bibliothecarius*, and in 1057, according to the Montecassino Chronicle, he seems to have deemed Peter of Tusculum as well as Humbert to be *papabile*.[39] A concern of Stephen thus seems to have been a strengthening of the suburbicarian bishoprics. This may have been among the matters for which Hildebrand sought the goodwill of the German court.

In summary, however, up to the time of his becoming archdeacon, Hildebrand's prominence at Rome, though well established, should not be exaggerated. His expeditions to France and Germany on the papal behalf carried greater and more wide-ranging responsibility than his activities in the city. The result was to confirm his loyalties to both the authorities that the crisis years in papal history from 1044 to 1049 left with impressive exemplars: Pope Leo IX, to the service of whose canonically elected successors Hildebrand was committed, and the Emperor Henry III, to whose Salian family, as represented by the pious if irresolute Empress Agnes and by their infant son Henry IV, events had brought Hildebrand personally as well as politically

---

37 Letter of 1107/10 from the canonesses of Gandersheim to Pope Paschal II about a renewed granting of their lands as fiefs to knights, in Goetting, 'Die Gandersheimer Originalsupplik', pp. 120–3; for the date, see Schmidt, 'Hildebrand, Kaiserin Agnes und Gandersheim'.

38 Peter Damiani, *Briefe*, no. 58, 2.193/17–194/2; *Ann. Altah. maior, a.* 1058, p. 54; cf. the less reliable evidence of Lampert of Hersfeld, *Ann. a.* 1059, pp. 64–6.

39 As n. 33.

close. Time alone would show how the two claims upon Hildebrand's loyalty and concern would develop and interact.

2.2 Hildebrand as Archdeacon

2.2.1 Hildebrand Becomes Archdeacon

The date and circumstances of Hildebrand's appointment to be archdeacon at Rome are uncertain and obscure. Only on 14 October 1059 does his attestation of a charter which survives as an original provide an absolutely secure *terminus ante quem* by his subscription: 'Ego Heldebrandus qualiscumque archidiaconus sanctae Romanae ecclesiae consensi et subscripsi'.[40] The problem is the more difficult because evidence for the history of archdeacons at Rome up to 1059 is meagre in the extreme. The arraignment of Gregory VII by the synod of Brixen in 1080 including the allegation that he had seized the archdeaconship by simoniacally inducing a certain Mancius to part with it and by having himself been tumultuously made *economus*.[41] Colouring from stories of his tumultuous election to the papacy in 1073 seems likely. Nevertheless, papal charters yield traces of a Mancius who as early as 1044 was referred to as 'Peter the archdeacon also known as Mancius', and in both the papal and the imperial versions of the Election Decree of 1059 he attested as 'Mancius diaconus', although some texts of the imperial version called him archdeacon. In 1044 a Benedictus also appears as archdeacon and *vicedominus* of the Roman church, and in 1050 there was an archdeacon named Hugh.[42] One can say no more than that, up to the late 1050s, there was a succession of archdeacons who are likely to have been concerned only with routine liturgical and administrative tasks, and that at Nicholas II's first Roman synod Mancius, though probably not now known as archdeacon, was not in disgrace. The recent history of the office provides no clue as to when Hildebrand may have assumed it.

The problems surrounding his doing so are compounded by the crisis in papal affairs which followed Pope Stephen IX's death on 29 March 1058 and which provided no clear context for it. Stephen died at Florence. At Rome, Count Gregory of Tusculum, in evidently prearranged concert with Count Gerard of Galeria, acted quickly to secure on 5 April the election and installation of Cardinal-bishop John II of Velletri as Pope Benedict X. Hitherto his career had been reputable, but his choice of name followed that of the Tusculan popes of the recent past. For most of 1058, he resided in the Lateran palace and performed some, at least, of the duties of the pope. Upon his election, many from Rome, including Peter Damiani, fled to Florence, where Hildebrand joined them from Germany.[43] They agreed that Bishop Gebhard

---

[40] Nicholas II, *Ep.* 11, *PL* 143.1324–5.   [41] *Epp. HIV* Anhang C, p. 478/9–13.

[42] Zimmermann, *Papsturkunden*, no. 618, 2.1162/16–18; Leo IX, *Ep.* 38, *PL* 143.831c (for the false reference to Hildebrand as archdeacon, see Jasper, *Das Papstwahledekret*, p. 35 n. 119); Jasper, *Das Papstwahldekret*, p. 111/196.

[43] On 16 May 1058, Hildebrand was present at a *placitum* heard near Chiusi: *I placiti*, ed. Manaresi, no, 405, 3.239–41.

of Florence should be the next legitimate pope, although it was not until December that he was duly elected at Siena. Thereafter, he was escorted to Rome by Duke Godfrey of Lorraine. On 24 January 1059, he was enthroned in St Peter's; on 13 April, he began his synod at the Lateran during which his Election Decree was promulgated.

So far as Hildebrand's advancement to the post of archdeacon is concerned, in 1057 he had appeared in charters and official documents as subdeacon (or cardinal-subdeacon) of the Roman church, or with a title referring to his responsibilities at the basilica of St Paul's-without-the-Walls.[44] The few official documents which survive from 1058 yield no evidence save that, in the record of a *placitum* that he attended near Chiusi on 15 June, he appears as 'monachus, sanctae Romanae ecclesiae legatus'. As late as August 1059, documents associated with Pope Nicholas II's synods of Melfi and Benevento referred to him in terms, respectively, of his position at St Peter's and St Paul's, and as subdeacon.[45] In all but one of his letters which are likely to be of relevant date, Peter Damiani wrote of Hildebrand in a similar way; although it should be remembered that, for much of the summer and autumn of 1058, Peter withdrew to a monastery at Gamugno, outside Florence, where he suffered a prolonged illness, and so was on the fringe of affairs. Only from December 1059 did he regularly write of Hildebrand as archdeacon; until that time, he usually gave him no title at all, although, in a letter written in the second half of 1058, he referred to him as a subdeacon when he returned from Germany earlier in the same year.[46] Thus far, the evidence points to a date in the autumn of 1059.

Yet for a year and more before this time, sources occasionally refer to him as archdeacon. A letter which Peter Damiani wrote to him at a date which is unclear but arguably in the summer of 1058 twice uses the title archdeacon.[47] On 1 May 1059, the record of a debate in the Lateran basilica on the reform of canonical life in Roman churches opens with an address by Hildebrand, 'archdeacon of the apostolic see'.[48] Early in the same month, a charter of Pope Nicholas II for Bishop John of Siena, the authenticity of which is not suspect, named Hildebrand in its protocol and in his own subscription as archdeacon of the Roman church.[49] Moreover, the chronicle evidence of the Milanese writers Arnulf and Landulf Senior, and also of the *Annales*

---

[44] Victor II, *Ep.* 18, *PL* 143.834D; Cappelletti, *Le chiese*, no. 181, 1.257; Stephen IX, *Ep.* 2, *PL* 143.871B.

[45] Chiusi: as n. 43; Melfi: *Cod. dipl. Trem.* no. 64, 1.197–8; Benevento: *Chron. Vult.* no. 205, 3.98–100, at p. 98/23–4.

[46] *Briefe*, no. 58, 2.193/20–194/2. In the light of this letter, little credence can be given to Bonizo of Sutri's statement that Hildebrand was made deacon by Stephen IX: *Lib. ad amic.* 5, p. 590/28–9.

[47] *Briefe*, no. 63, 2.221/8–9, 225/5. The letter opens with a reference to Hildebrand's journey to the German court in 1057–8 during which he had benefited Peter; Peter contrasted his conduct at Florence when he had determined a lawsuit to the disadvantage of one of Peter's monasteries. The effectiveness of the contrast depended on close sequence in time and so to Hildebrand's return to Florence after Easter 1058; Hildebrand was not again at Florence until Nicholas II's visit of Nov. 1059–Jan. 1060. Peter joined them by Jan. 1060, and would have been unlikely then to have remonstrated with Hildebrand by letter: Nicholas II, *Epp.* 15–17, *PL* 143.1330–6.

[48] Werminghoff, 'Die Beschlüsse', p. 669/23.   [49] Pflugk-Harttung, *Acta*, no. 118, 1.84–5.

Romani, suggests that Hildebrand may have been archdeacon by 1058.[50] Such evidence is not compelling, but it is enough to leave open the possibility that Hildebrand became archdeacon soon after his return from Germany in the spring of 1058. A satisfactory resolution of the problem is impossible, although the balance of probability is in favour of a date in the summer or autumn of 1059.

2.2.2 Peter Damiani and Hildebrand

Invaluable evidence for the first ten or so of the fourteen or fifteen years of Hildebrand's archdeaconship is provided by the letters and poems of Peter Damiani, the cardinal-bishop of Ostia who was perhaps some eight to ten years his senior in age. The evidence presents difficulties, partly because Peter was a master of rhetorical skills and a repository of a prodigious if not always well ordered fund of biblical, natural, classical, dogmatic, and canonical learning, and partly because there is only scanty evidence for Hildebrand's side of their relationship and interaction. Thus, at the outset, Peter made it clear that Hildebrand had a powerful, if not a decisive, voice in his own promotion to his cardinal-bishopric;[51] but, whatever might be suspected, there is no word to establish whether or not Peter had a part in Hildebrand's becoming archdeacon.

Peter's letters testify to the decisive place that Hildebrand occupied in the counsels of Nicholas II, both as pope-elect and as pope. So late as the autumn of 1057, Peter addressed Hildebrand as one amongst other leading figures in the papal circle;[52] but probably in the second half of 1058 he wrote a letter jointly to the pope-elect and to Hildebrand in which he exclaimed to them both, 'You are the apostolic see; you are the church!'[53] In further letters from Nicholas's reign, Peter laid stress upon Hildebrand's personal qualities and official standing. The pope should consult him as 'a man of most sound and wholesome counsel', and Peter named him before Cardinal-bishops Humbert of Silva Candida and Boniface of Albano. He addressed Hildebrand as 'an unshakeable pillar of the apostolic see' and described him to the pope as 'a man of the greatest prudence'.[54] Peter creates a strong impression that Nicholas's short pontificate was the time when Hildebrand emerged as a figure of the highest stature at Rome.

As a letter-writer and preacher, and by the force of his personality, Peter was the outstanding mentor of his contemporaries in Italy and at Rome in matters of spiritual and moral weight. While there is little direct evidence of his impact upon the by now middle-aged and mature Hildebrand whether by attraction or by repulsion, it is likely to have been powerful. A general reading of Peter's letters makes clear the number of matters upon which there was common ground: examples are Peter's

[50] Arnulf of Milan, 3.12, p. 182/1–3; Landulf Senior, 3.15, p. 83/44–5; *Ann. Rom.* pp. 334/15–16, 27, 335/6.

[51] *Briefe*, no. 75, 2.377/1–2, cf. no. 57, 2.190/4–5.

[52] *Briefe*, no. 49, 2.62–77; although as addressed to Hildebrand, it opened with the words 'Gemino sedis apostolicae Hildeprando'.

[53] *Briefe*, no. 57, 2.165/8–166/8.

[54] *Briefe*, no. 60, 2.205/3–8, no. 63, 2.221/8–9, no. 72, 2.345/12.

lifelong campaign against simony and clerical incontinence and for the reform of clerical standards, and his solicitude for the Empress-mother Agnes in her penitential retirement at Rome. The level of biblical, dogmatic, and historical knowledge that Peter assumed in Hildebrand is striking; it establishes that Hildebrand was far from unlearned, and that their learning provided common ground for approaching present problems by way of the searching of the scriptures and of the Christian past. Occasionally, Peter addressed homiletic material to Hildebrand himself. In 1057 he was one of the recipients of a treatise on the days of creation and especially the sabbath, which Peter presented as a type of Christ as the focus of men's hope and love, in whose service they should lay aside all temporal desires and servile works.[55] In 1069, he addressed to Hildebrand a discourse on forty-day periods of abstinence and on the forty-two stations of the Israelites in the wilderness during their pilgrimage to the promised land. It emerged that Peter and Hildebrand had recently spoken together on the subject of fasting in secret, and that Hildebrand had abstained from leeks and onions because of his excessive fondness for them.[56] However attentively Hildebrand read Peter's more prolix treatises, there was evidently sustained dialogue between them; in general, Peter's writings are a reminder of the intense piety and asceticism, often propagated by such anecdotes as punctuated his discourses, which characterized clerical life in the Rome of Hildebrand's middle years.

Despite Peter's seniority by age and ecclesiastical rank, his letters from late 1058 depicted Hildebrand as a figure to whom he must defer and by whom he was directed. That his deference was not a matter of mere rhetorical convention emerges late in 1059 when Peter wrote to him about his legation to the city of Milan. As subdeacon, Hildebrand had several times been a legate; as archdeacon, he remained at the nerve-centre of papal authority, while it was the cardinal-bishop who served as Nicholas II's legate. Peter's experience at Milan led him to appreciate Hildebrand's wisdom and initiative in earlier requests, which Peter had neglected, that he should assemble, systematically ('nova compilationis arte') in a small book, the writings and acts of earlier popes which revealed the prerogatives of the Roman church ('privilegium Romanae aecclesiae'); for these were at issue in face of Milanese claims to autonomy. While there is no evidence that Peter ever compiled such a book (short and ordered treatises were scarcely his *métier*), he addressed to Hildebrand a full report on his vindication at Milan of Roman superiority and of the rightness of the Patarenes' campaign against simony and clerical incontinence; his report was liberally fortified with papal and canonical texts.[57] It was Hildebrand who was now setting the agenda.

In his prolonged pleadings for release from his episcopal duties so that he might return to the eremitcal life at Fonteavellana, Peter dwelt even more strongly upon Hildebrand's key position in papal circles. His draft letter of the second half of 1058

---

[55] *Briefe*, no. 49, 2.62–77; this may already have been a tacit complaint about his involvement in an active life as cardinal-bishop.

[56] *Briefe*, no. 160, 4.100–34; for the reference to leeks and onions, see p. 101/25–7.

[57] *Briefe*, no. 65, 2.228–47.

to the pope-elect and to Hildebrand, whom he depicted as the rod of God's wrath (*virga Assur*: Isa. 10: 5, 30: 31), contained the first of Peter's two references to Hildebrand as 'my holy Satan'. Peter evidently had in mind the Satan of the book of Job (1: 6–12, 2: 1–7), the chief officer of God's court who was God's agent in afflicting a righteous man with plagues from which he was eventually delivered. Hildebrand was the key figure in holding him to his episcopal duties; the letter ended with a prayer that God at whose command Herod's prison stood open for the escape of the great Peter of old (Acts 12: 7–10) would deliver the wretched Peter of today from Hildebrand's hands.[58] During Nicholas's pontificate, Peter wrote to the pope and archdeacon both separately and together with requests to be freed from his episcopal office.[59]

Very occasionally, Peter exhibited Hildebrand as presenting a kindly face to him, as when Hildebrand reassured him about a monk's dream that Peter had lost his sight: the dream did not presage Peter's own imminent death but that of his friend St Dominicus Loricatus.[60] However, tension between them, with allegations of hardness on Hildebrand's side, was manifest from an early date, and it seems to have increased with the years. In part, it seems to have stemmed from their representing views about the Roman church that, throughout the eleventh century, were persistently contrasting and hard to reconcile. Peter was a senior figure according to the model by which the cardinal-bishops, as the 'senate of the Roman church', were its keystone and leaders; as archdeacon, Hildebrand became at least *de facto* the overmastering figure amongst those who regarded the clergy of the city of Rome as the cardinals of its church, while the suburbicarian bishops were to be distinguished from them. But far more, the tension evidently resulted from the clash of two powerful personalities.

Tension was already manifest in the letter of 1058/9 in which Peter complained about Hildebrand's decision taken in Florence about a case concerning ownership of the land upon which was built one of Peter's monasteries: despite his original agreement of close friendship (*foederatae concordiae . . . iura*), Hildebrand had deferred to Peter's adversary, a certain Count Guido; like the apostle James when he was bishop of Jerusalem, the righteous man had gone astray.[61] In subsequent years, the literary sparring with Hildebrand in which Peter engaged may best be regarded as a kind of ritualized aggression—a rhetorically stylized confrontation which served to relax tension and facilitate collaboration. But Hildebrand seems sometimes to have stretched Peter's tolerance to the limit; in 1060 Peter accused him of unhelpful silence when dealing with him to his face and of denigrating him when speaking to others. In 1065, he complained to Pope Alexander II that Hildebrand, whom he described as both his 'hostile friend' and 'the greatest of his friends', would merely ridicule him if he spoke to him of the incapacitating illness from which he was suffering.[62] Peter's most vividly querulous characterization of Hildebrand was in a

[58] *Briefe*, no. 57, 2.162–90, esp. pp. 163/2, 167/1, 190/4–5.
[59] *Briefe*, nos. 72, 75, 79, 2.326–66, 375–7, 398–400.   [60] *Vita Rodulphi*, cap. 13, col. 1023BC.
[61] *Briefe*, no. 63, 2.220–5, esp. p. 225/1–8.   [62] *Briefe*, no. 75, 2.375–7, no. 122, 3.398–9.

letter of 1064 which he addressed to the pope and the archdeacon as 'to father and son'. Peter had offended them both in the last stage of the Cadalan schism by addressing without their knowledge a letter to Archbishop Anno of Cologne which contained a request that Anno should convene a synod to end the schism. Peter begged their mercy, and contrasted the manner of their approaches to him:

When sending your messages to me, you were pretty unevenly divided. One of you [Alexander] appeared to coax by the courtesy of fatherly goodwill, but the other [Hildebrand] to threaten alarmingly by hostile vituperation. One of you shone upon me like the sun with warm and splendid glow, while the other buffeted me like the raging east wind with violent blasts.

Peter cited the scriptural example of Rehoboam (1 Kgs 12: 8–24) to point a warning that it was by milder counsels that nations prospered and remained united; then he turned to a series of bizarre but pointed examples from the world of fable which demonstrated the effectiveness of mildness. Peter, who had produced the text of his letter to Anno, declared that he had made what restitution he could; why, then, must he still suffer persecution? Once again, Peter appealed to Hildebrand as 'my holy Satan', this time imploring him to allow time for Peter's stripes to heal.[63] Peter continued thereafter to harp on the gap between Alexander and his archdeacon. During Lent 1067 he urged the Empress-mother Agnes to return from Germany to Rome and so to please their lord the pope and the sustaining Hildebrand, who to her was a staff but to him a reed (cf. 2 Kgs. 18: 21, Isa. 36: 6, Ezek. 20: 6). Two years later, Peter wrote jointly to Hildebrand and to Stephen, cardinal-priest of S. Grisogono; while he addressed both as 'impregnable shields of the Roman church', he addressed Hildebrand as his lord but Stephen more cordially as 'dearest brother'.[64]

It is against the background of such letters that Peter's epigrams about Hildebrand must be read.[65] Peter ironically pointed up Alexander's deference to him:

Concerning the pope and Hildebrand:
    The pope I duly honour but, prostrate, I you adore;
    You treat him as lord, while he treats you as God.

So he proffered advice to those with business at Rome:

Concerning Hildebrand:
    If you would thrive at Rome, say this at the top of your voice,
    'More than the pope, I obey the lord of the pope.'

As regards himself, he reverted to Hildebrand's fierceness towards him:

Concerning Hildebrand again:
    May he who tames savage tigers and the bloody maw of lions
    Turn you, who until now have been to me a wolf, into a gentle lamb!

An epigram about Hildebrand's outstanding prudence ended with a twist that in physical size even he was Peter's inferior:

---

[63] *Briefe*, no. 107, 3.185.
[64] *Briefe*, no. 149, 3.554/8–14, no. 156, 4.74–9. Peter addressed both Hildebrand and Stephen as *dilectissimi* at 4.79/3.   [65] Lokrantz, *L'opera poetica*, nos. 17–18, 78–80, pp. 55, 68.

> Concerning Hildebrand, who although small in stature is evidently of great prudence
>> The measure of Sisyphus constrains him who subdues all things;
>> Willy-nilly, he before whom many tremble is ranged below me alone.

Another epigram to Hildebrand who had sent him a less than generous present may not be a comment upon an actual gift so much as upon Hildebrand's general parsimony with favours towards Peter:

> To the Roman archdeacon, who sent me a middle-sized fish:
>> No wonder if [St] Peter should always be stingy towards me,
>> Since the rivers bring forth middle-sized little fishes.

Whatever the tensions in their relationship, Peter continued to address letters to Hildebrand until 1069. In that year, a letter to him and to Stephen, cardinal-priest of S. Grisogono, contained a plea that they would help to recover from Pope Alexander II a precious book that the pope had neglected to return to Peter. Another long and laboured letter in which Peter followed the wanderings of the Israelites after the exodus through forty-two stations in the desert, shows that Peter and Hildebrand had been discussing such topics as personal abstinence.[66] From 1069, there is no evidence for contact by letter or otherwise between the two men. Peter seems to have become increasingly disenchanted with at least some aspects of the conduct of business at Rome;[67] silence may indicate that Peter distanced himself from Hildebrand in his final years as archdeacon. Nevertheless, as pope, Hildebrand expressed himself cordially about Peter. In his privilege for Fonteavellana of 1076, he said that he extended his protection to it 'from fear of God and from love for our most beloved son the lord Peter Damiani, cardinal of this Roman church'.[68]

Hildebrand's relationship with Peter Damiani was patently a complex one. There can be little doubt that Hildebrand had more in common with him than with Cardinal Humbert of Silva Candida, who until his death in 1061 was the only other figure at Rome whose writings survive in any quantity; there is little to suggest that Humbert was in any respect a major influence upon Hildebrand. With Peter, Hildebrand maintained an interaction which the former's letters show to have continued for more than ten years. They shared some objectives, but neither can be regarded as a disciple of the other. With regard to Peter, as to all others at Rome with whom he worked, Hildebrand was his own master both in ideas and in action. He had a mind of his own, and he charted his own course. But as pope, he looked back to Peter with affection and respect.

2.2.3 Hildebrand under Pope Nicholas II

As Peter Damiani's letters illustrate, Hildebrand was a regular and assiduous companion and adjutant of Nicholas II throughout his short but momentous pontificate. Later writers, both friendly and hostile, said that he took the lead in bringing about Nicholas's election at Siena and his establishment at Rome after the displacement of

---

[66] *Briefe*, nos. 156, 160, 4.74–9, 100–34.   [67] e.g. *Briefe*, no. 167, 4.234–7.
[68] *QF* no. 113, pp. 108–10, esp. p. 109/18–19.

his rival Benedict X.[69] So far as the course of events can dimly be discerned, this is an over-simplification. After his return from Germany with messages from the royal court, it was probably with the cardinal-bishops and others from Rome, in close concert with Duke Godfrey of Lorraine, that the initiative lay. But some leading cardinal-bishops distanced themselves from events at critical junctures: Peter Damiani spent Easter 1058 at Fonteavellana and, although he returned to Florence, from May to October he remained at his monastery of Gamugno; Humbert of Silva Candida and Peter of Tusculum in due course returned to Rome but found it hostile and headed for Montecassino.[70] Hildebrand, however, seems to have busied himself with the organization of victory on Nicholas's behalf. On 15 May 1058 his presence at S. Pellegrino, near Chiusi, when Duke Godfrey settled a lawsuit, testifies to his contact with the duke.[71] The hostile *Annales Romani* may preserve authentic memories of his zeal in organizing opposition at Rome to Benedict X, in making a first approach to the Normans by enlisting the aid of Prince Richard of Capua, and ultimately in securing Benedict's formal deposition by a synod in January 1059. At this time, Hildebrand built up links with some of the lay families which would thereafter be critical for his power in the city; in particular, the urban prefect Peter who had supported Benedict was deposed and replaced by Hildebrand's staunch adherent from Trastevere, John Tiniosus,[72] and the Pierleoni and Frangipani began to emerge as his allies.

On 13 April 1059, Nicholas II's Easter synod of 113 bishops, almost all of them Italian, met in the Lateran basilica. Its most celebrated business was the Election Decree which placed the initiative in the election of a pope in the hands of the cardinal-bishops; on the analogy of the metropolitan in an episcopal election, they represented the universal role of the apostolic see. The Election Decree built upon the role of the suburbicarian bishops in the election of Nicholas II. It also curtailed the claims of the German ruler, which had been strongly exercised by the Emperor Henry III. The electors at Rome were merely to show him honour and reverence according to the circumstances that prevailed at each election; of those circumstances, the electors were to be the judge.[73] However the Decree is interpreted, it is unlikely to have allowed the German ruler more than a right of consent to an already settled election. The discovery of a text of the Decree as issued in 1059 which included a list of subscriptions makes it virtually certain that Hildebrand did not subscribe.[74] The decree seems to have been mainly the work of the cardinal-bishops; Peter Damiani and Humbert were perhaps to the fore.[75] In default of direct evidence, it cannot be

---

[69] *Chron. Cas.* 3.12, p. 373/18–25; Bonizo of Sutri, *Lib. ad amic.* 6, p. 573/7–9; *Ann. Rom.* pp. 334/27–335/5; *LP* 2.279; Benzo of Alba, 7.2, pp. 671/45–672/11.

[70] *Chron. Cas.* 2.99, pp. 356–7.   [71] *I placiti*, ed. Manaresi, no. 405, 3.239–41.

[72] *Ann. Rom.* pp. 334–6; Benzo of Alba, 3.10, p. 626.40–3, 7.2, pp. 671/42–672/69.

[73] For the text, see Jasper, *Das Papstwahldekret*, pp. 98–119, esp. pp. 104/73–105/91.

[74] Jasper, *Das Papstwahldekret*, p. 111/201–3, cf. pp. 34–46. Hildebrand's subscription was added in the imperial version with the suspect designation *monachus et subdiaconus*.

[75] For Peter Damiani's part in drafting the *Narratio* of the Decree, see Woody, '*Sagena piscatoris*', pp. 36–8.

presumed that Hildebrand was involved or even that he wholly approved. Not only did he not subscribe it, but at no stage of his career, least of all with regard to his own election to the papacy, did he give a hint of commitment to its provisions. As a Roman clerk, he had no brief for the prerogatives of cardinal-bishops in such a matter as papal elections; given his contacts with the German court, the awkwardly inserted clause about the role of the German king is at least as likely to have understated as to have overstated what he was prepared at this time to have countenanced. The Roman aristocracy, rather than the German monarchy, had been the object of his recent hostility.

No less surprising than Hildebrand's low profile with regard to the Election Decree is his muted role when Berengar of Tours appeared in person to answer for his eucharistic teaching. A letter addressed to Hildebrand which Berengar brought with him and which he wrote in the name of Count Geoffrey *Martel* of Anjou claimed that Berengar had come at Hildebrand's own written prompting; it was an urgent appeal to Hildebrand to make good his temporization at Tours in 1054 by now defending Berengar's teaching.[76] In the event, Cardinal Humbert of Silva Candida took a strenuous lead against Berengar and drafted a profession of faith to be imposed upon him. It was theologically crude and extreme; although it drew upon the phraseology of Berengar's letter to Hildebrand, it formulated eucharistic teaching in terms that Hildebrand never himself adopted, even in his dealings as pope with Berengar at his Lent synod of 1079.[77] Hildebrand's questionings about the eucharist appear to have been brushed aside in favour of Humbert's certainties. Hildebrand's only known part in the hearing came at the end, after Humbert's profession had been put to him. According to Berengar's own account, he kept silent during most of the proceedings until he finally reproved the pope for having, as it were, thrown him to the beasts in the arena. He requested a further hearing, whether privately with the pope or with a small group of theologically competent bishops. Perhaps ironically, Nicholas suggested that he confide in Hildebrand.[78] At least Hildebrand might apply a little balm after the bruising that Berengar had suffered at Humbert's hands.

In a third matter which the synod of 1059 considered, Hildebrand played a larger part. On 1 May, a well-attended assembly which met under Nicholas's presidency in the Lateran basilica debated the manner of life of the clergy, especially in the city of Rome and in the surrounding dioceses which were directly subject to it. In a fervent address which he made as the spokesman of a group of observant superiors of religious houses and of their subjects, Hildebrand recalled that, in times past, many had committed themselves to a common life according to the pattern of the primitive church (Acts 2: 42–7, 4: 32–5); in obedience to it, they had totally alienated their

---

[76] *Die Hannoversche Briefsammlung*, 3: *Briefe Berengars von Tours*, no. 87, in *Briefsammlungen*, ed. Erdmann and Fickermann, *MGH Briefe*, 5.148–52.

[77] Cowdrey, 'The Papacy and the Berengarian Controversy', pp. 116–18; Montclos, *Lanfranc et Bérenger*, pp. 165–74.

[78] Berengerius, *Rescriptum*, 1.1078–127, esp. 1126–7, pp. 66–7.

belongings, either by distributing them to the poor or by leaving them to kinsmen or to churches. Some, however, had lapsed into the 'stubbornness of private property' ('ad praesumptionen peculiaritatis'), citing in justification certain chapters of the Emperor Louis the Pious's *Institutio canonicorum* of 816/17, the laxity of which Hildebrand severely censured. He urged the assembly to review and remedy the defective chapters, and likewise to review and amend the form of profession to the canonical life that was currently used at Rome. Thus, the contagion of lax standards might be kept from spreading to observant clergy. Nicholas II welcomed the proposal of Hildebrand ('filius noster'). The text of the *Institutio canonicorum* was scrutinized and the offending chapters were traced and condemned. The assembly, or at least its more rigorous members, declared that Louis the Pious had no right or power to change rules for the canonical life without the authority and agreement of the apostolic see 'because, although an emperor and a godly man, he was a layman'; nor might any bishop introduce a new regulation by his sole precept and judgement, especially when the authority of Pope Gregory the Great was ranged against it. The assembly went on to condemn the allocation of food and drink—four pounds of bread and six measures of wine daily for each canon—in the *Institutio canonicorum* as ministering to the excess of the Cyclopes rather than Christian temperance; it has been thought up, it was said, by clerks at Rheims, and it smacked of Gallic *gourmandise*.[79] The debate that Hildebrand initiated thus ranged widely and canvassed detailed reforms. He was taking up the theme of some of Peter Damiani's most powerful treatises.

The immediate result was not dramatic; there is no evidence for a tightening of the form of profession for canons at Rome. The encyclical letter *Vigilantia universalis* with which Nicholas followed the synod provided only that clerks should lead a common life in respect of eating, sleeping, and the common possession of the property of their churches; it did not proscribe all private property, but urged clerks to aspire to the fullness of the apostolic and common life.[80] Nevertheless, the debate that Hildebrand stimulated is a landmark in the spread of the regular canonical life.[81] If simony and clerical marriage were to be proscribed, the perils of poverty and loneliness were mitigated by upholding a disciplined and social life according to a biblical standard which had positive and attractive features. As for Hildebrand himself, his view of the debate that he stimulated does not emerge. But his zeal for a way of clerical life according to the norm of the primitive church of Jerusalem and his exhibiting it as a standard against which latter-day innovations and deviations must be judged were characteristic of his lifelong beliefs.

---

[79] Werminghoff, 'Die Beschlüsse', pp. 669–75; the account is incomplete. For the *Institutio canonicorum*, see *MGH Conc.* no. 39, 2.312–421; caps. 115, 116 and 120 were especially objectionable in Hildebrand's eyes.

[80] Peter Damiani, *Briefe*, no. 39, 1.379–84, no. 98, 3.84–97. For the oath, Werminghoff, 'Die Beschlüsse', p. 670 n.4. For *Vigilantia universalis*, Schieffer, *Die Entstehung des päpstlichen Investiturverbots*, p. 220/126–44.

[81] See Leclercq, 'Un Témoignage', esp. pp. 179–80.

In his address, Hildebrand described himself to the pope as 'the lowest servant of your holiness' ('minimum vestrae sanctitatis famulum').[82] The designation of himself as Nicholas's 'famulus' may be more than an expression of deference, for the few glimpses of Hildebrand's activities under Nicholas reveal him as remaining close to the pope, somewhat after the manner of the household archdeacon of a contemporary northern bishop. Nicholas himself was at Rome for his mid-April synods in 1059, 1060, and 1061; he seems to have remained in the city each year until about the end of May. Otherwise, he travelled in Central and South Italy, returning to Rome only for brief periods. Like other early reform popes, he retained his previous preferment; he was in Florence from early November 1059 until late January 1060, and he returned there before his death on 27 July 1061. For almost the whole of the pontificate, Hildebrand was in Rome when Nicholas was there, but otherwise he appeared only in localities where the pope also was. So far as is known, he was never Nicholas's legate; this role was performed by others, like Peter Damiani at Milan and Cardinal-priest Stephen of S. Grisogono in France and Germany. It seems to have been Nicholas's policy to keep him at his side, as also to travel with a large entourage of cardinal-bishops and other Roman clergy. Rome was left dangerously denuded.

After his speech at Rome, the next trace of Hildebrand's activities arose from his presence at the council of Melfi which Nicholas opened on 23 August 1059. At it, an attempt was made to reinforce the Election Decree and, in the vacuum left by the death of Henry III, to find a substitute for the papacy's dependence upon German support in an alliance with the newly settled Normans of Apulia and Capua, with whom it had been at enmity especially since the time of Pope Leo IX, who with imperial support, had fought the Normans and suffered military humiliation at their hands. The alliance was facilitated by the Normans' need to gain papal sanction for their conquests and for the authority of their rulers. At Melfi, Nicholas received an oath of fealty from Robert Guiscard, duke of Apulia and Calabria, and probably from Richard of Capua.[83] Robert Guiscard's oath bound him to help the Roman church in the defence and extension of the *regalia* and possessions of St Peter; if a pope should die, he would follow the admonition of the better Roman cardinals, clergy, and laity in procuring the election and installation of a successor 'to the honour of St Peter'. In effect, the duke underwrote the recent Election Decree. He also undertook to pay annually at Easter the sum of twelve *denarii* in Pavian money for every yoke of oxen in his land.[84] Hildebrand has sometimes been thought to have taken a leading part in effecting this reversal of papal policy, and his recent dealings with Richard of Capua to secure military support for Nicholas's establishment at Rome may have paved the way. But the critical figure at Melfi is more likely to have been Abbot Desiderius of

---

[82] Werminghoff, 'Die Beschlüsse', p. 671/3–4.

[83] According to the *Annales Romani*, Nicholas dispatched Hildebrand to Richard and conferred upon him the title of duke, thus securing his fidelity to the Roman church: p. 335.

[84] For Guiscard's commitment, see Ménager, *Recueil*, nos. 6–7, pp. 30–3. For Richard of Capua's presence, see his charter of 23 Aug. 1059 in Gattula, *Accessiones*, p. 161. For the background, see Cowdrey, *The Age of Abbot Desiderius*, pp. 112–13.

Montecassino.[85] The sole evidence for Hildebrand's presence at Melfi is a charter of the abbey of S. Maria at Tremiti which records the satisfaction of the pope, the Roman cardinals, and Hildebrand at the securing of Tremiti's monastic independence of Montecassino.[86] The most that this evidence conveys is that Hildebrand was actively present at the council, upon the first day of which the Tremiti charter is dated.

For Hildebrand's future dealings, the council was of the utmost consequence. In the long run, it established a relationship with the Normans of South Italy which, with many vicissitudes, was to colour the rest of his career as archdeacon and pope. It speedily had repercussions upon relations between the papacy and the German court. The Election Decree had drastically curtailed the part of the German ruler in papal elections; now, without consulting the German court, the pope received the fealty of the Norman rulers for lands over which the German kings claimed suzerainty. Not surprisingly, when Cardinal Stephen of S. Grisogono went as legate to Germany, the court declined even to receive him.[87]

During Nicholas's first stay at Florence, Hildebrand spent some, and perhaps all, of its three months' duration in the city or its vicinity. On 14 October 1059, his name occurs in a papal charter for the monastery of S. Pietro in Perugia; it is not certain whether the charter was granted at Rome or Perugia, but it is likely that pope and archdeacon passed through Perugia on their way to Florence.[88] It is one of several illustrations of Hildebrand's association with the current papal policy of fostering the monastic possession of tithes. It was probably on the same journey that Peter Damiani heard Hildebrand give an address at Arezzo in the pope's presence which was directed against the wrongful lay possession of ecclesiastical lands. Peter reminded Nicholas of Hildebrand's *exemplum* of a German count of high reputation among men: after his death some ten years before, a holy man had a vision of his inexorable punishment in hell together with past generations of his family. It was explained to the holy man that they were condemned to being successively forced down the steps of a ladder into a fiery abyss because an ancestor had seized land belonging to the cathedral of St Stephen at Metz which still remained in the family.[89] Peter Damiani thus showed that Hildebrand's role as archdeacon was by no means only administrative, but that he was an ardent and vocal advocate of reforms. Hildebrand's appearance in papal charters of 18 and 20 January 1060 establishes that he was then in the vicinity of Florence. The earlier charter was a confirmation of the property and privileges of the abbey of S. Andrea at Mosciano as they had been established by a panel consisting of Cardinal Humbert, Hildebrand, the bishops of Perugia and Roselle, and the archpriest of Florence. The second records the sequel to Nicholas's consecration of the basilica of S. Lorenzo at Florence in the granting of

---

[85] Cowdrey, *The Age of Abbot Desiderius*, pp. 115–17.
[86] *Cod. dipl. Trem.* no. 64, 2. 197–8, dated 23 Aug. 1059.
[87] Peter Damiani, *Briefe*, no. 89, 2.560/13–561/5. The date of Stephen's mission is debatable; it probably occurred in mid-1060.
[88] Nicholas II, *Ep.* 11, *PL* 143.1324–5.   [89] *Briefe*, no. 72, 2.346/1–19.

an immunity from all authorities save that of the bishop of Florence; again, the terms were established by a panel, this time of Humbert, Hildebrand, and the bishops of Perugia, Roselle, and Furconia.[90] Hildebrand's collaboration with Humbert to secure the rights of churches is notable, as is the evidence that he applied at Florence the principles that he had preached at Arezzo.

In April 1060, Nicholas was back in Rome for his annual synod. Hildebrand's presence is established by his subscription of two charters, both of which concerned monastic property. One arose from a case that Nicholas heard in the chamber of the Lateran palace in which the tithes of a *curtis* were judged to belong in perpetuity to the abbey of Leno; in the other, Nicholas vindicated the abbot of Farfa's possession of two *castella* in Sabina which a layman of the Ottavianeschi family had violently seized.[91] For the rest of Nicholas's pontificate, there is no evidence for Hildebrand's activities;[92] although when Nicholas II died at Florence, Hildebrand was in Rome.[93] The prolonged absences of Nicholas and his entourage are likely to have given his Tusculan and Crescentian adversaries a dangerously free hand to organize themselves. There may have been an awareness of tensions within the city that called for the presence of Hildebrand to deal with them.

2.2.4 The Cadalan Schism

Upon hearing of Nicholas's death, Hildebrand moved quickly to forestall civil strife at Rome by summoning an assembly of Roman clergy and laity to consider the succession. His initiative is a sign that, after the death on 5 May 1061 of Cardinal Humbert of Silva Candida, his position at Rome was quickly enhanced. There is no evidence of contact with the German court; for the third successive time, thoughts turned to a candidate for the papacy who was associated with the politically powerful Duke Godfrey of Lorraine, together with his wife, Countess Beatrice of Tuscany. This now occurred against the letter of the Election Decree of 1059, which incorporated the ancient canonical injunction that the papacy should first be offered to a clerk of the Roman church if there were a suitable candidate;[94] in 1061 there was no dearth of such candidates, and the decision to approach Bishop Anselm I of Lucca illustrates the prevailing pragmatism of the Roman clergy. Hildebrand seems himself to have gone to Lucca to talk to Anselm; by 1 October and so after considerable negotiation and arrangement under the protection of Prince Richard of Capua, and with the help of leading Romans like John Brachiuti, Leo son of Benedict, and Cencius I Frangipane, Anselm was formally elected and enthroned in the church of S. Pietro in Vincoli at Rome as Pope Alexander II by a procedure that Peter Damiani could exhibit as being generally conformable to the Election Decree.[95]

---

[90] Nicholas II, *Epp.* 16–17, *PL* 143.1332–6.

[91] Zaccaria, *Leno*, no. 18, pp. 104–6; see Constable, *Monastic Tithes*, pp. 87–8. *Reg. Farf.* no. 906, 4.300–2.

[92] Hildebrand's supposed subscription of a Montecassino document dated 24 May 1061 is a forgery by Peter the Deacon: Borino, 'Una sottoscrizione'; Meyvaert, 'A Spurious Signature'.

[93] *Chron. Cas.* 3.19, p. 385/15–21. [94] Jasper, *Das Papstwahldekret*, p. 104/80–3 and n. 28.

[95] *Chron. Cas.* 3.19, p. 385/15–21; *Ann. Rom.* p. 336, where Anselm is wrongly described as archbishop

Opposition to Alexander quickly developed. Even before his election, Count Gerard of Galeria and the abbot of S. Gregorio Magno in Clivo Scauri sent an embassy to the German court. Besides enjoying support in and around Rome from the Tusculans and Crescentians, they could rely upon the Lombard bishops, and their embassy to Germany was accompanied by the new imperial chancellor for Italy, Guibert, the future archbishop of Ravenna. The embassy took to King Henry IV the insignia of the Roman patriciate and asked for the choice of one of the Lombard bishops. The clear intention was completely to set aside the Election Decree and return to the practice of the Henry III's time whereby a strong initiative lay with the German ruler. At a meeting of the German court at Basel on 28 October 1061, Bishop Cadalus of Parma was elected pope; he took the name Honorius II.[96]

The course of the Cadalan schism was as follows.[97] Honorius's initial attempt in the autumn of 1061 to reach Rome was frustrated by resistance in Tuscany to his journey. Henry IV and his mother therefore commissioned Benzo, bishop of the Lombard see of Alba, to organize Honorius's cause and establish him at Rome. In 1062 and again in 1063, he was able to undertake expeditions which established the strength of his support in the city and issued in bloody fighting. But the fortunes of the rival popes did not mainly depend upon local forces. Alexander was helped a little by the Normans and much more by Duke Godfrey and Countess Beatrice. The critical factor was increasingly events at the German court. In April 1062, Archbishop Anno of Cologne, who had no commitment to Honorius, seized power by a *coup d'état*. At this time, Honorius's prospects of victory were favourable; but in May, Duke Godfrey appeared at Rome and, after difficult negotiations, induced Honorius to return to Parma and Alexander to Lucca, there to await a judgement of the German court. In October, a meeting of the court at Augsburg, for which Peter Damiani prepared his *Disceptatio synodalis*, left the question of the papacy undetermined, but Archbishop Anno of Cologne's nephew, Bishop Burchard of Halberstadt, was sent to Rome to adjudicate. He recognized the validity of Alexander's election without condemning that of Honorius. In January 1063, Duke Godfrey undertook to establish Alexander in Rome, and by 23 March he was resident at the Lateran. After Easter he held a synod of over a hundred bishops and abbots at which he excommunicated his rival and published a revised version of Nicholas II's encyclical of 1059, *Vigilantia universalis*.[98] But in May, Honorius strongly counter-attacked with his anathema against Alexander and by force of arms. At Rome he achieved considerable success in

of Milan; Peter Damiani, *Briefe*, nos. 88–9, 2.526/1–9, 586/2–7; Benzo of Alba, 2.4, 3.10, 7.2, pp. 614/ 23–6, 626/40–3, 672/22–43.

[96] *Ann. Rom.* p. 336; Benzo of Alba, 2.4, 7.2, pp. 614/23–8, 672/16–20; Bonizo of Sutri, *Lib. ad amic.* 6, pp. 594/33–595/11; Bernold, *Chron.*, a. 1061, pp. 427/39–428/7.

[97] The sources for the Cadalan schism upon which this paragraph mainly depends are: *Ann. Alt. maior, aa.* 1060–4, pp. 55–66; *Ann. Rom.* pp. 336–7; Benzo of Alba, 2.3, pp. 612–34 (for the date, see Lehmgrübner, *Benzo von Alba*, pp. 91–111); Bonizo of Sutri, *Lib. ad amic.* 6, pp. 594–6; Peter Damiani, *Briefe*, nos. 87–9, 2.504–72, no. 107, 3.185–8; Rangerius of Lucca, 1.121–36, pp. 1159–60. For a discussion see Whitton, 'Papal Policy', pp. 9–15.

[98] Schieffer, *Die Entstehung des päpstlichen Investiturverbots*, pp. 213–25.

establishing his power both in the Leonine city and the Castel S. Angelo and also around St Paul's basilica. Gradually, however, Duke Godfrey, with Norman support, gained ground in the city. Honorius found no effective support at the German court, where opinion increasingly turned to Alexander. By the end of 1063, Honorius's position at Rome was no longer tenable, and he returned to Parma. Peter Damiani's negotiations with Anno of Cologne led to a council at Mantua in 1064 at which Alexander was recognized as the rightful pope. To all intents and purposes, the Cadalan schism was at an end.

Hildebrand's part in the events of the schism is sparsely documented; such evidence as there is comes mainly from the vituperative writings of Benzo of Alba, the relevant parts of which were first written soon after the council of Mantua as tirades against Duke Godfrey of Lorraine and Archbishop Anno of Cologne. Their venom against Hildebrand is in itself testimony to the importance of his activity. Benzo exhibited him as Alexander's close and continuing associate and agent, applying to them such opprobrious nicknames as respectively Asinandrellus and Prandellus; he stigmatized Hildebrand as 'the Sarabaite'—one of those monks without a Rule who, in St Benedict's words, by their works remained committed to the ways of the world and by their tonsure lied to God.[99] According to Benzo, Hildebrand's stock-in-trade was intrigue, war, and the machinations that led to it. In 1061, he exhibited his involvement in simony by buying Norman support for Alexander's advancement to the papacy. In Rome, he recruited support from upstart and disreputable families like the Pierleoni and the Frangipani; outside it, he dealt with military figures like Godfrey of Lorraine and Richard of Capua. In 1062 and 1063, he was a ringleader in warfare at Rome against Honorius; as Benzo put it, he trusted not in God but in the multitude of riches; he preferred to conquer by shedding human blood rather than by the glorious deployment of the holy canons.[100] If he was Alexander's agent in war, so, too, in 1064 he had his share in his success.[101]

When every allowance is made for the hostility of Benzo of Alba who is the fullest source of information, it appears that Hildebrand's military endeavours at Rome during the Cadalan schism were not entirely successful. In 1062, Honorius's appearance at Rome led immediately to a rout of a force under Hildebrand's direction on the Campus Martius near the Leonine city; however, he was able eventually to recruit further fighters and, after bloody fighting, to confine Honorius's supporters to the Leonine city and the Castel S. Angelo. When Honorius returned to Rome in 1063, Hildebrand's Norman contingent suffered a serious defeat before Duke Godfrey of Lorraine came and restored the situation.[102] At no time did Hildebrand himself lead a successful military operation; as under Nicholas II, his principal contribution seems to have been the organization of eventual victory by securing sufficient aid

---

[99] e.g. 2.1, p. 612/38–9, 3.7, p. 624/36, 3.16, p. 629/3–4, 3.26, p. 632/16–18. For the term Sarabaite, see *Regula Sancti Benedicti*, 1.5–9, 1. 438–9.

[100] 2.2, p. 613/14–16, 2.4, p. 614/23–42, 2.8–9, pp. 615–16, 2.17–18, pp. 619–21, 3.16, p. 629/9, 3.24, p. 31/10–11.

[101] 3.27, p. 632/34–5.   [102] Benzo of Alba, 2.9, 17–18, pp. 616, 619–21; *Ann. Rom.* p.336.

from Tuscany and from the Normans. At least in the short term, his political judgement may sometimes have been at fault. He over-reacted against Peter Damiani's unauthorized *démarche* to Archbishop Anno of Cologne which proved to be a critical step towards the resolution of the Cadalan schism in Alexander II's favour. Hildebrand's fierce anger towards Peter stands in contrast to Alexander's mild and statesmanlike reaction.[103] Hildebrand's assessment of the political situation is nowhere expressly recorded. But he seems to have underestimated the papacy's need for support at the German court if Alexander's cause was to prevail, and to have failed to appreciate the changed climate of opinion in Germany after Anno seized power in 1062. In the longer term, however, Anno's fall from power early in 1066 showed the inadvisability of the papacy's placing complete reliance upon any single figure at the German court; to this extent, Hildebrand's reservations were justified. In maintaining the papacy's reform programme and in proclaiming it as a rallying call, Hildebrand may have had fuller success. Bernold of St Blasien later credited him with the major responsibility for the reissue, probably at Alexander's post-Easter synod in 1063 and in the presence of more than a hundred bishops, of the encyclical *Vigilantia universalis* which embodied the wide-ranging legislation of Nicholas II. Prudently, all reference to the procedure in papal elections was now omitted, but the proscription of simony and the provisions for its eradication were reinforced.[104] It was a signal that the papacy stood by Nicholas II's vision of a renewed church and of the means by which it might be realized.

The Cadalan schism sheds much light upon papal problems and dilemmas in the 1060s and into the 1070s. The years 1061–4 were a time of danger and uncertainty, during and after which guidelines were hard to find. The city of Rome was shown to be deeply divided: the count of Galeria, the Tusculans, and the Crescentians, who had sponsored Benedict X, were entrenched around it, and the *Annales Romani* indicate how widespread and long-lasting was resentment at Hildebrand's pursuit and humiliation of Benedict. The mustering of the two urban factions in this source, which Benzo of Alba confirmed, shows how many strategic points and localities they could still command. They appear as more numerous and effective than the newer families like the Pierleoni and Frangipani, strongest in Trastevere, upon whom Hildebrand depended. When it fell to him to organize papal support, he needed to look outside Rome for its recruitment. The papacy's new Norman allies provided only limited help. Of their leaders, Richard of Capua came and went; Robert Guiscard did not come at all; their own interests took priority over those of the

---

[103] Peter Damiani, *Briefe*, no. 107, 3. 285–8; see above, 2.2.2. Bonizo of Sutri's story that, early in 1064, Hildebrand told Anno of Cologne in Rome that kings had no rightful part in papal elections and refuted Anno's arguments about the German king's rights as *patricius*, is almost certainly fictitious: *Lib. ad amic.* 6, p. 596/5–17.

[104] Bernold, *Chron. a.* 1061, p. 428/5–12. In place of Nicholas II's clause about papal elections, the new version introduced the first three clauses of Nicholas's *Decretum contra simoniacos*: *MGH Const.* no. 386, 1.550–1; for the date, which may be 1059 rather than 1060, see Schieffer, *Die Entstehung des päpstlichen Investiturverbots*, pp. 61–2.

papacy. Norman troops and mercenaries fought for Alexander, but at critical moments they had to be put under other leadership, most effectively that of Duke Godfrey of Lorraine. Since three popes in succession had by now come from his family or from Tuscany, Godfrey and his wife, Countess Beatrice, were rightly seen as invaluable papal allies. Given its resources, its proximity to Rome and the papal patrimony, and its position in relation to communications with Lombardy and Germany, Tuscany with its ruling house provided resources which the papacy must safeguard. But who could know who the successors to Godfrey and Beatrice would be or what they would do? In any case, the Cadalan schism established that, despite the measures of Nicholas II's pontificate, the fortunes of the papacy in practice remained dependent upon the personalities, policies, and power of the German court. Not only did Honorius II owe his election to a meeting of it at Basel, but a shift in policy after Archbishop Anno of Cologne's *coup d'état* in 1062 facilitated the resolution of the schism in favour of Alexander II.

While the king was a minor, much would depend upon which over-mighty subjects predominated at court; the consequences of Anno's ascendency demonstrated that it was not inherently hostile to the reforming cause at Rome. But who could tell for how long Anno would hold power? More important still, the young King Henry was now, as the Niederaltaich chronicler wrote in 1062, 'beginning to be an adolescent'.[105] No one could doubt that his *adolescentia* would be decisive for the future. It was of the utmost importance for the papacy that he should emerge from it as a godly king and emperor after the pattern of his father, Henry III; using his pious if hitherto vacillating mother and all other means, the papacy might hope thus to find the protector that it needed. But the experience of the Cadalan schism raised two problems. First, would the duke of Lorraine, the mighty German prince who by marriage was strong in Tuscany as well and upon whom the papacy also relied, look favourably upon this use and consolidation of royal power? Secondly, if the young king was to be like his father in his religion and sense of duty, he must not be like him in exercising the power of *patricius* and in nominating the pope: it was by such an exercise of power that the anti-pope Honorius II had been chosen. Instead, he must be brought to accept the demand of the reformers that, by whatever process in point of detail, the Roman clergy and people should have the decisive voice in electing the pope. The papacy had one strong resource in seeking to bring this about: to receive imperial coronation, the young king must one day come to Rome; until he had done so, he could not show himself altogether intractable, and when he came to Rome, the papacy would have an opportunity to require his compliance. Or so it might hope.

The Cadalan schism laid bare how complex, uncertain, and vulnerable was the position of the reform papacy; it made clear its need for reliable allies; above all, it also showed how critical for its future would be the character and outlook of the German king Henry IV who was entering upon his *adolescentia*.

---

[105] *Ann. Altah. maiores*, a. 1062, p. 59: 'Rex igitur iam adolescere incipiebat.'

2.2.5 Hildebrand and Rome

Like his predecessors, Alexander II did not resign his earlier preferment upon becoming pope, but remained bishop of Lucca until his death. He imitated Nicholas II by seeking to spend a substantial part of the year in his Tuscan see. While no set pattern emerged, especially after the Cadalan schism was ended he tended to be at Rome for the early months of the year, with the annual post-Easter synod at the Lateran as the high point of his stay. At least in years for which substantial evidence survives, especially 1068 and 1072, he spent much of the second half of the year at Lucca. He never left Italy, although, like Nicholas II, he travelled in the central and southern parts of the peninsula.

Except in one major respect, Hildebrand's pattern of life under Alexander remained as it had been under Nicholas. As in Nicholas's reign, when the pope was at Rome, Hildebrand was also there, at the pope's right hand. Thus, he is known to have been at the post-Easter synods of 1065 and 1070,[106] and letters which he subscribed in 1065 and 1067 also attest his presence with Alexander.[107] He accompanied Alexander upon his travels in South Italy, and was his close associate in important business which brought him into contact with the Lombard and Norman princes. In August 1067, at a council in Melfi at which Hildebrand's presence is likely but not expressly attested, Archbishop Alfanus of Salerno laid a complaint against the Norman, William son of Tancred, that is, Robert Guiscard's brother, William 'of the Principate', and his *milites*, who had invaded the lands of his church. Although Alexander ordered their restoration, William proved contumacious and was excommunicated. A few weeks later, Alexander held a further council at Salerno, and Hildebrand played a leading part. It was attended by both Prince Gisulf of Salerno with his brothers Guy and John and Duke Robert Guiscard with his brother Roger, as well as by many Lombards and Normans. William had done penance, and at the council surrendered the disputed lands. A papal charter which Hildebrand subscribed confirmed the church of Salerno's possession of them.[108] In 1071, a far larger concourse of Roman and South Italian churchmen took place at Montecassino when Alexander consecrated Abbot Desiderius's new basilica; Hildebrand was present.[109]

But if Hildebrand accompanied Alexander when he was at Rome and when he was on his travels in the south, in sharp contrast to his employment under Nicholas II he is never known to have been with Alexander while he was at his other see of Lucca. It is apparent that the lesson of Nicholas's reign had been understood: given the restlessness of the Roman aristocracy and the uncertainty of Norman aid, it was unwise to leave Rome bereft of a firm guiding hand. During Alexander's more prolonged absences from Rome, Hildebrand's place was in the city, as his vicegerent. Several lines of evidence converge to show how closely Hildebrand became identified with

---

[106] 1065: *Ep.* 27, *PL* 146.1306–9. 1070: Mansi, 19.997–8; for the date, see JL 1.585.

[107] 1065: *Ep.* 29, *PL* 146.1309–10. 1067: *Ep.* 49, *PL* 146.1325–9.

[108] Alexander II, *Ep.* 54, *PL* 146.1335–7. At Capua, Alexander confirmed all the rights and possession of the church of Salerno: *Ep.* 55, *PL* 146.1337–9.

[109] Pantoni, *Le vicende*, p. 221/13–14.

Rome—its defence, administration, and jurisdiction, but also with its spiritual and reforming impact upon the church.

Friends and critics alike noticed Hildebrand's pre-eminence. Friendly comment may be illustrated by Archbishop Alfanus of Salerno's elegant ode *Ad Hildebrandum archidiaconum Romanum*. There is no clear clue to its date or occasion. However, the note of triumph suggests a date after the ending in 1064 of the Cadalan schism. Hildebrand's part in defending Alfanus's interests in August 1067 at the councils of Melfi and Salerno may have elicited it, whether as an expression of hope for his support or of gratitude after it had been given. Alfanus celebrated Hildebrand's especial fame and skill in law and government. He represented him as able so to wield the sword of St Peter that the hardness and violence of savage barbarians might be broken:

> Quanta vis anathematis!
> Quicquid et Marius prius
> quodque Iulius egerant
> maxima nece militum,
> voce tu modica facis.
>
> Roma quid Scipionibus
> ceterisque Quiritibus
> debuit mage quam tibi,
> cuius est studiis suae
> nacta iura potentiae?
>
> Qui probe quoniam satis
> multa contulerant bona
> patriae, perhibentur et
> pace perpetua frui
> lucis et regionibus.
>
> Te quidem potioribus
> praeditum meritis, manet
> gloriosa perenniter
> vita, civibus ut tuis
> compareris apostolis.

How great is the power of anathema!
> Whatever Marius and Julius once performed
> by the slaughter of multitudes of knights,
> that you perform by your lightest word.

And Rome—what more did it owe to the Scipios and the other Quirites
> than it owes to you, by whose earnest labours
> it has received the due rights of its power?

Duly, for they conferred many benefits upon their land,
> they are reckoned to enjoy perpetual peace
> in the regions of light.

Verily for you, who are endowed with more precious merits,
> there remains a life that is eternally glorious,
> so that you may be likened to the apostles, your fellow-citizens.

Whatever the occasion of the poem, there can be no mistaking that, while Hildebrand was still archdeacon, Alfanus recognized his unique authority at Rome and his outstanding capability.[110]

Hildebrand's critics, especially Wenric of Trier and Guy of Ferrara, later sought to strike a balance between what they regarded as the good and the bad aspects of Hildebrand's career, including his archdeaconship.[111] Wenric ascribed his promotion as archdeacon to his exceptional personal gifts, and said that his discharge of his duties won him fame and love throughout the world. Guy made much of the band of knights that he recruited, but suggested that he did this, not from vain glory, but for the good of the Roman church; he successfully defended it against its Norman and other neighbours, establishing peace and order in the lands of St Peter and protecting the poor and defenceless. Guy also presented an admiring description of Hildebrand's religious zeal and asceticism in a lavish and worldly environment: 'constant in fasting, devoted to prayer, and diligent in study, he made his body the temple of Christ.' He was unwearied in preaching to and instructing the people. Guy had himself observed his daily celebration of mass with the grace of tears that contemporaries admired as a mark of holiness. For Guy especially, it was possible to present Hildebrand as a Christian exemplar both in his strenuous external activity and in his spiritual life. On the debit side, Wenric placarded his high-handed and arrogant dealings with archbishops and bishops; he was excessively given to the deployment of money and of military might, and his personal image was disfigured by the parade and practice of earthly warfare. Guy elaborated his dedication to arms: from boyhood he had practised them, and in adult life he virtually led a private army. Together with Alfanus's ode, the balance of light and darkness which was struck by Wenric and Guy points Hildebrand's fame as a Roman figure, who was zealous in doing justice, in organizing and employing military force, and in exhibiting religious fervour.

Such contemporary evidence as can be collected confirms this picture. Hildebrand's involvement with doing justice and giving protection to the vulnerable is well documented. When Alexander was at Rome, he can be seen taking his key but subordinate place in the pope's entourage. Thus, at the post-Easter synod of 1067, a plea by Bishop William of Senigallia against Bishop Benedict of Fossombrone about the possession of a church was heard by Alexander in the Lateran palace; he did so with a large group of bishops and others, of whom Hildebrand was named first.[112] In 1069, Alexander dispatched Hildebrand from Rome to the monastery of Subiaco to put an end to vexations by its neighbouring lay lords and to restore its internal discipline. Accompanied by Abbot Desiderius of Montecassino, Hildebrand took a band of clerks and knights from the Lateran palace. He addressed the monks in chapter about

[110] Lentini and Avagliano, *I carmi*, no. 22, pp. 155–7. There may be a reference to the establishment of the Norman monarchy in England in 1066 in the phrase 'eas [Hildebrand's legal skills] timet | saeva barbaries adhuc | clara stemmate regio': lines 38–40. See also the praise of Hildebrand as archdeacon in *Die Briefe des Abtes Walo*, no. 1, p. 54/5–8.

[111] Wenric of Trier, caps. 1–2, pp. 285–7; Guy of Ferrara, 1.2, 2, pp. 534–5, 554–5.

[112] Mansi, 19.997–8.

the reasons for his coming and received the resignation of its aged abbot, Humbert, who admitted his faults and failures. Hildebrand insisted that the new election should take place according to the Rule of St Benedict but no monk of Subiaco was deemed suitable; the monks therefore elected as abbot John (1069–1121) of the family of the counts of Sabina, whom Hildebrand invested with his pastoral staff. Having restored the abbey's order and security, Hildebrand devoutly ascended to the Sacro Speco to which St Benedict had first withdrawn from the world.[113] Hildebrand also acted on Alexander's behalf when he was absent at Lucca. On 8 October 1072, he heard a plea arising from a long-standing dispute between the abbey of Farfa and the Roman monastery of SS. Cosma e Damiano *in Mica Aurea* about the possession of a church and its property. According to the record of the case, Hildebrand 'appointed a day upon which the abbots of both monasteries should be present to plead their case before him, acting on the pope's behalf (*coram se vicem papae gerenti*) in the Lateran palace, the bishops and cardinal-priests, the prefect with the judges and elders of Rome sitting with him'.[114] Together with his earlier experiences, the pleas and interventions in which Hildebrand is known to have taken part are likely to be only a few of those in which he participated. They must have made him familiar with the persons and problems of Italy from Turin and Venice to Salerno. They illustrate his position at Rome, and the Farfa plea of 1072, in particular, shows him deputizing at the Lateran for the pope whose successor he was soon to be.

In addition to Hildebrand's military expedition to Subiaco to repress its lay neighbours, his military role was commented upon at Milan in connection with his relations with the Patarenes there. Most graphically, Landulf Senior described him as being settled in the Lateran palace, from which he commanded the Roman militia as if he were a general.[115] His military organization at Rome seems to have been effective, for after the end of the Cadalan schism there was no sign of serious opposition to Alexander on the part of the Roman aristocracy. However, Hildebrand is likely to have been successful as much through restraint and moderation as through the exercise of military power. He acted with prudence. While archdeacon he seems already to have established the policy that for long stood him in good stead as pope, of risking no disturbance in the local balance of power. Despite his zeal against the holding by laymen of church lands, he made no systematic attempt to resume papal lands that had, over the centuries, fallen into the hands of local aristocratic families; whether friendly or hostile to the reform papacy, they were left alone.[116] In so far as he gained a reputation for restraining Norman incursions, he may have won their favour. Nor did he overdo his financial exactions; he used help that was willingly to hand from well-disposed families like the Pierleoni. In any case, as has been acutely observed, the domination by Pavia of the Italian money market reduced the scope for major

---

[113] *Chronicon Sublacense*, pp. 10–12.
[114] *Reg. Farf.* no. 1010, 5.9–11, see no. 1012, 5.16–17, for a further stage in the dispute when Gregory was pope.
[115] 3.15, p. 83/45–6.   [116] See Whitton, 'Papal Policy', esp. pp. 299–305, 308–9.

financial initiatives on behalf of the reform papacy.[117] If Hildebrand was restrained in his territorial and financial measures, he added to his reputation by using his military power to provide good justice. This is suggested by an anecdote that later circulated about how Hildebrand defended a poor man against the oppression of a powerful neighbour against whom Alexander had been reluctant to proceed; Hildebrand's bold anathema was followed by the oppressor's being struck dead by a thunderbolt.[118] It was not without reason that, according to Bonizo of Sutri, Cardinal Hugh Candidus recommended him for election to the papacy as one who had exalted the Roman church and freed the city of Rome.[119]

Of Hildebrand's religious life, there is only a little evidence to confirm the exemplary picture that Guy of Ferrara found it possible to present when exhibiting Hildebrand at best, although Peter Damiani's record of his giving up even leeks and onions bears out the account of his austerity of life. His continuing concern for monastic life in Rome is suggested by his continuing at least until the mid-1060s to be *rector* and *economus* of St Paul's-without-the-Walls.[120] A main concern of Hildebrand was to recruit from Italian monasteries monks who promised to follow him in the service of the Roman church, as in the leadership of other bishoprics and abbeys. At an unknown date when Hildebrand was at Salerno as a papal legate—it is the only occasion under Alexander when he appeared in this role, he secured the permission of the abbot of S. Benedetto for one of his monks, Peter, who later became bishop of Anagni, to become a papal chaplain.[121] It was at Hildebrand's suggestion that Alexander recruited from Montecassino a number of Abbot Desiderius's monks who served at Rome and elsewhere; they included Theodinus who became a deacon at the Lateran and in due course archdeacon, Aldemarius who became abbot of St Lawrence-without-the-Walls and Peter who became abbot of S. Benedetto at Salerno and a cardinal, perhaps 'external', at Rome.[122]

Between 1064 and 1073, the reputation that Hildebrand acquired and the records of his activity combine to indicate the leading position that he occupied and the multifariousness of his activities, at a time when the pope himself was for long periods in each year absent in his other see of Lucca.

2.2.6 Hildebrand and the Regions of Europe

When Hildebrand became pope in 1073, Abbot Walo of Metz congratulated him by writing that the Lord had caused one well versed in ecclesiastical duties to sit upon St Peter's throne; from that throne, the light of all virtues radiated through the world and upon it all things converged as, in a circle, the radii meet at the middle point that

---

[117] See Toubert, *Latium*, 1.573 n.2, 575 n.3, 578–9. Strictures by Hildebrand's critics upon his use of money are undoubtedly exaggerated: as above, n. 111; also Benzo of Alba, 2.8, p. 615/35–8, 7.2, p. 671/37–9; Beno, 2.9, p. 379/18–20; Arnulf of Milan, 4.2, pp. 206–7.

[118] Paul of Bernried, cap. 4, p. 475.

[119] *Lib. ad amic.* 7, p. 601/7–8.   [120] See above, 2.1.

[121] *De sancto Petro Anagniae*, cap. 4, p. 234AC. For this source, see Toubert, *Latium*, 2.806–29.

[122] *Chron. Cas.* 3.24, pp. 390–1; see further Cowdrey, *The Age of Abbot Desiderius*, pp. 64–5.

students of geometry call the centre.[123] In the middle decades of the eleventh century, there had been a great increase in the amount of ecclesiastical business from the localities of the church which was referred to Rome; in the vivid metaphor of Albert Hauck, the papacy acted upon the church at large 'like a magnet upon iron filings', attracting them and ordering them by the field that it created.[124]

Accordingly, Hildebrand was a prominent figure between 1064 and 1073 in many matters which involved the kings, leading churchmen, and monasteries of Europe. Partly because of his masterful personality and long experience, and partly because of his being usually present at Rome even when the pope was at Lucca, many looked to him as the figure through whom to transact business. For his own part, his zeal for reform and his familiarity with Germany, France, and Italy impelled him to concern himself with many persons and institutions in these regions and beyond. During these years his relationship with his papal master was a complex one. It is to the credit of both men that there is little evidence of personal tension or conflict between them; in all circumstances that can be observed, pope and archdeacon fulfilled their respective roles with mutual respect and regard. There is no evidence that Hildebrand was ever disloyal to Alexander or that he overstepped the proper limits of an archdeacon in relation to his bishop or of a senior Lateran cleric in relation to the vicar of St Peter. This is the more remarkable because the two men were very different: Alexander was by background a son of the Milanese upper aristocracy and the bishop of a major Tuscan see, whereas Hildebrand was of modest social origin and a lifelong clerk of the papal household at Rome. Alexander was no cypher; his personal stature and ecclesiastical statemanship were of a high order.[125] At a Rome where there was not, and for the rest of the eleventh century would not be, a homogeneity of opinion or approach even among reform-minded persons, his preference for quiet diplomacy, persuasion, and compromise stood in sharp contrast to Hildebrand's often rigorous and commanding approach. As it is the purpose of the present section to show, there were major issues in which their standpoints were contrasting. Their underlying community of purpose and mutual loyalty were strong enough to withstand the stresses.

A prime concern of both Alexander and Hildebrand was to foster in the kingdoms of Europe effective rulers who were at once patterns of Christian kingship to their own domains and reliable supporters of the apostolic see. They had a particular eye to Germany, where at Eastertide 1065 the young King Henry IV was declared to be of age: he must be prepared for prompt imperial coronation at Rome and, in the long run, nourished in the personal qualities and governmental responsibilities that the reform papacy demanded in a Christian ruler. Such was Alexander's own purpose; his leading agent was not Hildebrand but Cardinal Peter Damiani.[126] During Alexander's lifetime, no evidence emerges to indicate that Hildebrand's past

---

[123] *Die Briefe des Abtes Walo*, no. 1, pp. 51/16–51/7.
[124] *Kirchengeschichte Deutschlands*, 3.736.
[125] Schmidt, *Alexander II.*, presents a just estimate of an often underrated pope.
[126] See below, 3.1.2.

connections with the Salian royal house led to his active involvement by way of embassies to Germany or other diplomatic means. But in two letters of 1076, written after his first excommunication of Henry, Gregory VII declared that he had repeatedly admonished him:

While we still exercised the office of deacon, there reached us ill and most shameful tidings of the king's behaviour; on account of the imperial dignity and out of respect for his father and mother, and also on account of our hope and desire for his correction, we frequently admonished him by letters and by messengers to cease from his wickedness and, mindful of his illustrious family and rank, to shape his life in ways which befitted a king and, if God so disposed, an emperor-to-be.[127]

Hildebrand had evidently sought thus to reinforce the pope's endeavours to mould Henry as a virtuous king and emperor who was worthy of his family and inheritance.

In a similar way, Hildebrand supported Alexander in his dealings with King William I of England at the time of the Norman conquest of 1066, and with King Sweyn Estrithson of Denmark a little later. According to William's panegyrist, William of Poitiers, who wrote *c*.1073–4, as duke of Normandy, William sought Alexander's favour by informing him of his intention to invade England; in token of the pope's support, he received a banner ('vexillum'). Writing in the next century, Orderic Vitalis named Gilbert, archdeacon of Lisieux, as William's envoy, and decribed the banner as a 'vexillum sancti Petri'.[128] In 1080, as pope, Hildebrand reminded King William of the love and aid that he had bestowed while still archdeacon, and also of the criticism that he had undergone at Rome for supporting William when he caused so many homicides.[129] Under Alexander, the papacy was also in close and amicable contact with the Danish king with a view to securing the royal succession and to establishing a Danish metropolis.[130] Again, there was no contemporary reference to Hildebrand; but in letters of 1075 to Sweyn, Gregory recalled that, while he was still archdeacon, he and the king had been in touch by letters and messengers about the question of a Danish metropolis and other matters, and that they had reached a measure of agreement about them.[131] Pope and archdeacon appear to have acted in concert; nevertheless, the kings concerned were evidently in direct contact with them both.

Gregory's Register provides evidence of a similar situation with regard to an incident in the Spanish Reconquest. Late in Alexander's reign, a papal approval had been accorded to the Frenchman, Count Ebolus of Roucy, a son-in-law of Robert

---

[127] *Epp. vag.* no. 14, p. 34/7–14; *Reg.* 4.1, p. 290/16–20.

[128] William of Poitiers, 2.3, p. 154; Orderic Vitalis, 3, vol. 2.142; see also William of Malmesbury, *Gesta regum*, 3.238, vol. 2.299.

[129] *Reg.* 7.23, 24 Apr. 1080, p. 499/31–500/6; cf. Wenric of Trier, cap. 6, p. 294/19–24. An oblique reference by Gregory to a difference with Peter Damiani should not be assumed: although critical of Pope Leo IX's involvement in warfare, in 1065/6, Peter urged Henry IV to take the sword against Bishop Cadalus of Parma, the sometime anti-pope; he may have regarded the Norman conquest in a similar light: *Briefe*, no. 87, 2.504–15; no. 120, 3.384–92.

[130] Alexander II, *Ep.* 6, *PL* 146.1283; Adam of Bremen, 4.9, Schol. 72, 155, pp. 354, 446.

[131] *Reg.* 2.51, 25 Jan. 1075, pp. 192/31–3, 193/29–33; 2.75, 17 Apr. 1075, p. 238/26–31.

Guiscard who was well known at Rome, to campaign in Spain with a band of French knights. Upon the presumption that from ancient times the whole of Spain had been in St Peter's proprietorship, the lands that they captured were to be held as fiefs of the apostle. This was stipulated in a written agreement of which Hildebrand was the draftsman, and two papal legates, Cardinal-bishop Gerald of Ostia and the sub-deacon Rainbald, who were already in France were instructed to support Ebolus both in letters from Pope Alexander and by a mandate from Hildebrand ('legatione nostra').[132] Hildebrand evidently backed up Alexander's sponsorship of Ebolus by strong actions of his own.

It is in papal dealings with the Normans of South Italy and with the Lombards that the political stresses and strains to which Alexander's papacy was subject are most apparent. Nicholas II's alliance with the Normans at Melfi in 1059 was intended to furnish the reform papacy with permanent support; in 1061, Prince Richard of Capua's response to Hildebrand's call for aid at Rome must have seemed to be an earnest of effective protection in the years to come. But it was quickly apparent that neither the Normans of Capua nor those of Apulia could be relied upon very far. It was not in their interest. Once the papacy in 1059 had accorded the Norman princes the recognition that they needed, it had little further hold over them, save in the rare event that the succession of either a new pope or a new prince of Capua or duke of Apulia called for a renewal of fealty.[133] Both Norman leaders gave evidence of their unreliability. After Prince Richard captured the city of Capua in 1062, followed by Gaeta in 1063, his northward expansion directly menaced papal lands. In 1066, Alexander sought military aid against him from Henry IV of Germany, but in 1067 Duke Godfrey of Lorraine forestalled him by an expedition on Alexander's behalf.[134] At the same time, the depredations of Robert Guiscard's brother, William 'of the Principate', upon the lands of the church of Salerno put under strain relations between the papacy and the Hauteville family of Apulia. If the Normans of Capua and Apulia had a common interest in opposing the papal vassal William of Montreuil, they were deeply suspicious of each other. Under Alexander, a policy developed of 'divide et impera', tempered by a wish to maintain relations with all parties.

Hildebrand's own appraisal of this complex situation does not emerge, although his military organization of the papal lands was credibly interpreted as having been in part a defence against predatory Normans.[135] The point at which tensions developed seems to have been Hildebrand's relations with Abbot Desiderius of Montecassino. Although Montecassino was a bastion of the papacy in South Italy and its abbot was also a cardinal-priest of the Roman church, its interest lay not in the division of the Normans but in their unity and harmony.[136] Two pieces of evidence

---

[132] *Reg.* 1.6–7, to the legates, and to the French barons taking part, 30 Apr. 1073, pp. 8–12, esp. pp. 9/26–10/9.

[133] A point well made by Whitton, 'Papal Policy', esp. pp. 263–4.

[134] Amatus, *Storia*, 4.26, 5.1–19, pp. 199–200, 258–72. Bonizo of Sutri's unsupported story that Hildebrand invited Godfrey to intervene is improbable: *Lib. ad amic.* 6, p. 599/8–10.

[135] Guy of Ferrara, 1.2, p. 534/24–32.

[136] See Cowdrey, *The Age of Abbot Desiderius*, pp. 117–22.

suggest that Hildebrand's actions put his relations with Montecassino under strain. First, in an admittedly propagandist tirade against Prince Gisulf of Salerno, the Cassinese chronicler Amatus made the general observation that, by his lies, the prince was able to sow *grant discorde* between Abbot Desiderius and Hildebrand despite their being great friends.[137] Second, the Montecassino Chronicle relates how, at Alexander II's request and with the help of Robert Guiscard's nephew, Count Robert of Loritello, Abbot Desiderius in 1071 sought to reform the island monastery of S. Maria, Tremiti, in the Adriatic. His monk Trasmundus, son of the Lombard Count Oderisius II of Marsia, whom he left as abbot, quickly became an oppressive and cruel ruler of his monks, blinding three of them and tearing out the tongue of another. Desiderius recalled him to Montecassino, but Hildebrand espoused his cause, prevailing upon Desiderius to release him to become abbot of S. Clemente at Casauria and, soon afterwards, also bishop of Valva.[138] Whatever the truth of this story, it makes clearer Montecassino's memory of Hildebrand as intervening in its affairs, and indicates the lengths to which Hildebrand might go in support of one whom he saw as a reformer and perhaps also as a strong enough figure to establish order in a frontier area. Differences should not, however, be pressed too far. The evidence of Hildebrand's appearance with Alexander at the eclectic gatherings of Lombards and Normans at Melfi in 1067 and Montecassino in 1071 indicate that the two men maintained good mutual relations and that, whenever circumstances were favourable, they promoted pacification and harmony amongst the conflicting interests in South Italy.

Hildebrand's involvement with kings and lay rulers had its counterpart in his concern with the dealings of the apostolic see with leading metropolitans, who themselves sometimes looked to him for the promotion of their business at Rome. The exceptional case of Milan must be reserved for the next section; in general, Hildebrand showed no hostility towards legitimate and acknowledged metropolitan authority, which he was at pains to fortify in so far as it promoted papal interests. This had long ago been clear in his dealings with Venice/Grado, where he early championed the authority of the patriarchs in order to counterbalance those of Aquileia; in Denmark, he encouraged the establishment of a metropolitan see of Lund in order to provide the Danish kingdom with an organized and effective ecclesiastical structure.[139]

A further example of his desire while archdeacon to foster a vigorously governed metropolitan see which was confirmed in a proper relationship with the papacy is provided by Ravenna. Rome had an ancient claim to ecclesiastical and political lordship over Ravenna which arose from the sometime exarchate; although especially in Ottonian times the archbishops had resisted this claim, and the German emperors had exercised control of the see and province. After the death in 1072 of Archbishop Henry, who had incurred excommunication for his part in the Cadalan schism, his successor Guibert, who in the 1080s would become the Henrician anti-pope Clement III, came to the fore as a figure of whom Alexander and Hildebrand entertained an

137 *Storia*, 4.48, p. 219.   138 *Chron. Cas.* 3.25, pp. 392–3.   139 See above, 2.1, 2.2.6.

expectation that he would be a reforming bishop who would maintain obedience to and co-operation with the apostolic see. The main source for Guibert's accession to the see of Ravenna is Bonizo of Sutri, whose account contains much suspect detail. However, in view of the cordial letter which Gregory sent to Guibert three days after his own election as pope in expectation of their close collaboration, Bonizo's testimony that Hildebrand sponsored Guibert's promotion to Ravenna and his consecration at Rome by Alexander II in the last weeks of his life is evidently well founded.[140] Guibert of Ravenna was not the only metropolitan whose promotion at his instance Hildebrand lived to regret. The reform papacy had for long been concerned with the problems of the French see of Rheims. In a letter of 1074 to Archbishop Manasses I, Gregory recalled how, in 1069, he had favoured and consented to his promotion; three years later, Manasses himself recalled in a letter to Gregory that he had obtained his see by Gregory's intervention.[141] As archdeacon, Hildebrand was evidently concerned with the appropriate filling of key metropolitan sees.

That upon occasion he might be directly involved in the pope's decision about a metropolitan's request is indicated in a letter of Gregory in 1074 to Archbishop Gebhard of Salzburg. In 1070, a bull of Alexander II had allowed Gebhard to create a new diocese, that of Gurk, by dividing his own. Gregory reminded him that, when he had come to Rome and secured the pope's permission, Alexander had acted with Hildebrand's favour and approval ('me etiam favente atque assensum prebente'). Gregory had complied with Gebhard's request the more readily because he understood his motives to have been to promote religion and the salvation of many.[142] Such metropolitans evidently deserved his goodwill.

Perhaps more directly, two metropolitans, at least, regarded Hildebrand as the avenue by which it was appropriate for them to approach the apostolic see. One was Archbishop Siegfried of Mainz. Late in 1065 or early in 1066, he wrote to Hildebrand a characteristically obsequious letter which began with effusive thanks for his unfailing support and advocacy at the apostolic see. In what came very near to palm-greasing, he offered gifts to express his gratitude. Then he came to the point: he besought Hildebrand's good offices in smoothing the way for his own messengers to ask the pope for legates to a proposed Easter synod at which the recalcitrant Thuringians would be compelled to pay their tithes; failing the dispatch of legates, perhaps the pope would send a letter to the rebels. No evidence survives of a response from Rome, and owing to local circumstances the synod did not meet. However, in 1074, Siegfried still felt able to approach Gregory as one who, before he became pope, 'was always our right hand in all our business, never failing us or ours'.[143] This indicates that the archdeacon had, in some connections at least, been helpful.

---

[140] *Lib. ad amic.* 6, p. 600/22–38. For Guibert's oath to Alexander, see Deusdedit, *Coll. can.* 6.423, p. 599, and for Gregory's letter, *Reg.* 1.3, pp. 5–6. For a fuller discussion, see Ziese, *Wibert*, pp. 26–34.

[141] *Reg.* 1.52, pp. 78/33–79/5, see also 1.13, to Archbishop Manasses, 30 June 1073, p. 21/21–5: *Die Hannoversche Briefsammlung: IV. Schlussteil*, no. 107, *MGH Briefe*, 5.179/19–21. Papal relations with Rheims under Alexander II are illustrated by his *Epp.* 7, 5–16, 19, 21–3, 28, 37–42, 44–6, *PL* 146.1283, 1295–301, 1309, 1316–23.

[142] *Reg.* 2.77, 17 June 1075, pp. 240–1.

[143] *CU* nos.32–3, 40, pp. 61–4, 84/27–9.

Lanfranc, archbishop of Canterbury from 1070, also found it expedient to approach Hildebrand at a late and difficult stage of his endeavour to establish the primacy of his see over all the churches of the British Isles. He was well known and well thought of at Rome, which he had three times visited before his journey there in 1071 with Archbishop Thomas of York. Although the pope received Lanfranc with signal honour, he remitted the question of the primacy and other issues for settlement by an English council. The council of Winchester at Easter 1072 granted Lanfranc most, but not all, that he hoped for. In particular, King William did not allow Archbishop Thomas of York to take an oath to Lanfranc that would have firmly underpinned his promise of canonical obedience. Lanfranc therefore desperately needed a papal privilege to secure his primacy, and he wrote the pope a long letter in which he pressed for one to be granted.[144] He reinforced his plea by writing to Hildebrand, as well. Unlike Siegfried of Mainz, he wrote briefly; but he, too, recalled past favours. He asked Hildebrand to read the letter that he had written to Alexander, and pressed him for his good offices in securing an appropriately drafted privilege:

I ask and beg you to read it with due attention, so that you will securely grasp what the apostolic see should grant, and by its privilege confirm, to me and my church.[145]

No trace of a reply from Alexander exists, but Hildebrand's answer survives in Lanfranc's letter-collection; it is the only pre-papal letter of Hildebrand to have come down. Its brevity matched Lanfranc's, and its tone is difficult to judge. Upon the main issue it was curt: Lanfranc's plea for a privilege could not legally be granted unless he came to Rome again in person to discuss this and other matters. This was a canonically correct decision if, as is probable, Lanfranc's request for a privilege involved novel and not acknowledged rights of his see; Hildebrand wrote of messengers whom he hoped would reach Lanfranc with verbal messages which may have clarified his reasons for it. Hildebrand began his letter by expressing gratitude for the verbal messages of Lanfranc's messengers, and he ended it by referring to Lanfranc as 'a most dear son of the Roman church and a holy bishop'.[146] If he answered firmly, he was in no way discourteous. He gave no reason for supposing that he was taking a different view from Alexander's; probably he was seeking to be conciliatory and, as in the case of Archbishop Guibert of Ravenna, to do what he could as archdeacon to facilitate communication between the apostolic see and a metropolitan. That he was not opposed to Lanfranc's primatial claims is apparent from his first letter as pope to him, which was cordially expressed and implicitly conceded the claims.[147] It was Lanfranc who did not respond, or ever again come to Rome.

---

[144] Lanfranc, *Letters*, no. 4, pp. 48–57, esp. p. 54/104–6. For the background, see Cowdrey, 'Lanfranc, the Papacy and the See of Canterbury', pp. 464–73.

[145] Lanfranc, *Letters*, no. 5, pp. 56–9; in 1079 Gregory wrote to Lanfranc of 'the memory of our former love': *Reg.* 6.30, p. 443/25.

[146] Lanfranc, *Letters*, no. 6, pp. 58–9.

[147] Lanfranc, *Letters*, no. 8, pp. 64–7 = *Epp. vag.* no. 1, pp. 2–5; for further comment, see Cowdrey, 'Lanfranc, the Papacy and the See of Canterbury', p. 475.

Apart from the regions of Lombardy and Tuscany which remain to be discussed, Hildebrand's dealings alike with kings and lay princes and with metropolitans reveal him as acting in harmony with Alexander, and with remarkable pragmatism in discharging ecclesiastical business. He accepted the reality of metropolitan authority, and showed no intrinsic hostility even to Lanfranc's primatial aspirations, although he would not allow Lanfranc to take any short cut in establishing them. As the example of Ravenna especially shows, his aim was to bring the apostolic see and metropolitans into close and harmonious working in the interests of reform and good government.

2.2.7 Hildebrand and North Italian Reform Movements

Hildebrand's dealings especially between 1064 and 1073 with the reform groups and movements that were emerging in Lombardy and Tuscany require special consideration; they illustrate both his own deep commitment to them and his points of difference from Pope Alexander II. A major effect of the Cadalan schism was to demonstrate and to accentuate the polarization between many of the bishops and such popular movements as the Patarenes of Milan and other cities, which themselves found allies among the more austere and zealous of the monks. As a result, the Lombard bishops had mostly rallied to the anti-pope; the savage invective against Pope Alexander and Hildebrand in the writings of Bishop Benzo of Alba illustrates the fear and insecurity that impelled the bishops to solidarity with the anti-pope and with each other. Hildebrand was a particular object of Benzo's hostility, but hostility to him was indissolubly linked with hostility to Alexander. Yet pope and archdeacon were of contrasting backgrounds and temperaments. Alexander sprang from the Lombard aristocracy against whom the Patarenes reacted, and it is a misunderstanding to see him a founder, or even a sponsor, of the Patarene movement;[148] as pope, moreover, he remained bishop of a Tuscan see. To this extent, he had something in common with the established powers against which the more radical reformers campaigned. But Alexander was also a bishop from the lands of Countess Beatrice of Tuscany and her husband Duke Godfrey of Lorraine, upon whose support the reform papacy had been extensively dependent since the Emperor Henry III had died. He was also the pope whom all reforming circles at Rome supported. When dealing with the polarized affairs of Lombardy and Tuscany, he had little scope, and probably little desire, to favour an episcopate which held to the older ways of imperial Italy. In a charged situation where decisions had to be taken, he was almost inevitably in the end drawn to take decisions that suited the more radical reformers with whom Hildebrand was increasingly associated. A *modus vivendi* between pope and archdeacon was thus established which led sometimes to a convergence of actions and sometimes to mutual tolerance; there is no evidence of tension or dispute.

The actions of pope and archdeacon may be seen to have converged in two connections: in their dealings with the abbey of S. Michele della Chiusa near Turin and in those with the radical monastic reformers at Florence.

[148] See Violante, *La Pataria Milanese*, pp. 147–73.

In 1066, the strongly reform-minded Benedict was elected to be their abbot by the monks of S. Michele. According to Benedict's biographer William of Chiusa, Bishop Cunibert of Turin reacted forcefully by asserting his rights over the abbey and especially over abbatial elections. Benedict appealed to Rome and was heard at a Roman synod before an assembly of bishops and cardinals. In an address to them, Hildebrand is said to have taken his stand upon the principle of monastic exemption from episcopal authority, roundly condemning Cunibert for infringing St Peter's rights over a monastery that its founder had commended to his protection. By contrast, *pius papa Alexander* reproved Cunibert mildly as a son and fellow bishop: he should show proper solicitude for an abbot who had been duly elected and should have the grace to attend to his consecration. When Cunibert remained obdurate, however, Alexander himself consecrated Benedict and vindicated the abbey's rights against the bishop.[149] The incident disclosed more than a difference of personality and temperament between pope and archdeacon, for Hildebrand stood firmly upon the principle of monastic exemption and upon the consequent rights and duties of the Roman church. Yet there was no clash between the two men, and in face of Cunibert's obduracy Alexander finally took decisive steps in support of the monks which suited Hildebrand's case.

The approaches of Alexander and Hildebrand to the conflicts between the monks of Vallombrosa and the bishop of Florence, Peter Mezzabarba, were similar to those which they exhibited in the case of Chiusa. Once again, initially contrasting attitudes to a radical reform movement gave way to a convergence by which Alexander's eventual decisions fulfilled Hildebrand's purposes. Peter Mezzabarba succeeded Pope Nicholas II in his Tuscan see. He was the son of a wealthy Pavian family, and in 1061 was elected under Cadalan auspices in circumstances that led to allegations of simony. His election was strenuously opposed by the monks of Vallombrosa, whose strict Benedictine observance was combined, partly through the institution of *conversi* or lay brothers, with zeal by preaching and external activity to extirpate the spiritual and moral abuses of neighbouring clergy and laity. Hildebrand formed a close bond with the abbot of Vallombrosa, John Gualbertus. There is a conflict of testimony about the nature of their acquaintance. When John Gualbertus died in 1073, Gregory had become pope, and in a letter of condolence and eulogy which he addressed to the monks he said that he had never met John. On the other hand, John's first biographer, Andrew of Strumi, stated, from hearsay, that he had done so: at first he tested John's patience by sharp reproofs (this calls to mind Peter Damiani's reference to Hildebrand's harshness towards him); but when Hildebrand met John ('ad eius intuitu') he was so impressed that he forgot what it was in his mind to say, and they were henceforth joined by unshakeable brotherly love.[150]

---

[149] William of Chiusa, caps. 2–3, pp. 298–9. William's rather stylized account was written after Benedict's death in 1091, but is likely to contain authentic memories. Gregory set out his principles of monastic freedom and alluded to these events in *Reg.* 2.69, to Bishop Cunibert, 9 Apr. 1075, pp. 226–9, but eventually approved a final concord between bishop and abbot: *Reg.* 6.6, 24 Nov. 1078, pp. 406–7.

[150] *Epp. vag.* no. 2, pp. 4–7; Andrew of Strumi, *Vita s. Ioh. Gual.* cap. 61, p. 1092.

Alexander for long maintained reserve towards the monks' campaign against their bishop whom Duke Godfrey of Lorraine and his wife Countess Beatrice supported; in 1064 he wrote to the Florentine clergy and people that monks should keep to their cloister and not itinerate through villages and towns or preach to the people.[151] Early in 1067, Peter Damiani visited Florence and sought to mediate between the bishop and the rebellious citizens and monks; in a subsequent letter he urged the latter to put their case at Rome rather than to take the law into their own hands.[152] At a Roman synod, probably in 1067, John Gualbertus denounced Peter Mezzabarba as a simoniac and therefore a heretic; he offered to prove his point through an ordeal by fire. Opinion about the bishop was divided. According to Andrew of Strumi, most of the bishops supported Peter while most of the monks were against him; Hildebrand throughout helped and backed up the monks. According to a second, anonymous *Life* of John Gualbertus, Peter Damiani castigated the Florentine monks for their stand against their bishop, saying that they were like a biblical plague of locusts; but, like another Gamaliel (Acts 5: 34–9), Hildebrand openly and effectively vindicated them. Alexander himself would countenance neither the bishop's deposition nor the ordeal which John Gualbertus proposed. In early Lent 1068, John took matters into his own hands by staging a spectacular ordeal by fire at a monastery near Florence, S. Salvatore at Settimo, which was given widespread publicity. One of his monks, named Peter, thereby dramatically and decisively proved the bishop's simony. The Florentines were quick to inform Alexander and to ask for sentence to be passed at Rome. At his post-Easter synod, he readily decreed that Peter Mezzabarba should be banished from his see, and he sent Bishop Ralph of Todi, who was *persona grata* with the monks, to oversee the vacant diocese. Probably in 1072, the monk Peter who was the hero of the ordeal and by then abbot of Fucecchio, became also Boniface's successor as cardinal-bishop of Albano. The appointment must have had Alexander's concurrence if not his approval; it set the seal upon his eventual decision against Peter Mezzabarba, and it provided Gregory as pope with one of his most loyal and active collaborators at Rome.[153] Hildebrand's own part in the events of 1068 is not recorded, but his letter to the monks of Vallombrosa upon John Gualbertus's death expressed his admiration for their strict monastic discipline and impact upon the Tuscan church.[154] The effect of Alexander's decisions in and after 1068 was to confirm Hildebrand's bond with them and the stand which he had taken at the Roman synod of 1067.

---

[151] *Ep.* 120, *PL* 146.1046.   [152] *Briefe*, no. 246, 3.531–42.

[153] The main sources for events at Florence are: Andrew of Strumi, *Vita s. Ioh. Gual.* caps. 69–78, pp. 1094–1100 (for a critical edition of the letter of the clergy and people of Florence to Alexander II in cap. 75, see Miccoli, *Pietro Igneo*, pp. 147–57); *Vita Ioh. Gual. auct. anon.*, cap. 5, pp. 1106–7. The cross-currents in reforming opinion are illustrated by Abbot Desiderius of Montecassino's fully sharing Hildebrand's view: *Dial.* 3.4, pp. 1146–8. For the attitudes of Godfrey of Lorraine and Beatrice of Tuscany, see E. Goez, *Beatrix von Canossa*, pp. 70–1, 161–3.

[154] *Epp. vag.* no. 2, pp. 4–7; Andrew of Strumi recorded Cardinal Peter of Albano's testimony to Gregory's continuing spiritual debt to John Gualbertus; whenever Gregory celebrated mass and the grace of tears was denied him, the recollection of John served to renew it: *Vita s. Ioh. Gual.* cap. 85, p. 1102.

Hildebrand's dealings with the Patarenes of Milan were more prolonged than his dealings with the monks of Chiusa or Florence, and it is much harder to judge how he interacted with Alexander. Alexander may have been glad to leave much of the papacy's dealings in Hildebrand's hands, for he was himself also bishop of a see in the northern half of Tuscany and a native of Milan where the Patarenes were most active.[155] From the mid-1050s, the Patarenes strove with gathering zeal and militancy first against the marriage and concubinage of the clergy, but soon also and more characteristically against the 'heresy' of simony. Moreover, the church of Milan was proud of its distinctively Ambrosian traditions which, it was claimed, conferred upon it a virtual exemption in practice from Roman jurisdiction and sanctioned liturgical and penitential usages that differed from those current at Rome. The Patarenes, by reaction, readily invoked Roman authority to rectify what they saw as the abuses of the Ambrosian church. If much of their campaign against a corrupt ecclesiastical establishment and the social order in which it was rooted was violent and disruptive, they also sought constructively to establish exemplary centres of Christian devotion and simplicity upon the model of the primitive church of Jerusalem that Hildebrand commended in his allocution to Nicholas II's post-Easter synod in 1059. The Patarenes had a clear and articulate programme, and at Milan, they were well led especially after Ariald, the first of their leaders, in 1066 became a martyr for the cause. His associate leader, the higher-born, eloquent, and self-confident Landulf, had died a year before. From 1066, the sole leader was Landulf's brother, the layman Erlembald. His combination of fanatical religious zeal and charismatic military and mob leadership welded the Patarenes into a powerful and ruthless opposition to the proud separateness and corrupt conservatism of the Milanese clergy. Cutting across the lines of social class, especially in their leadership, but appealing especially to the Milanese populace, the Patarenes exemplified at their most articulate and militant the pressures for reform that were welling up in many Italian localities.

After Peter Damiani reported to him upon his Milanese journey in 1059, Hildebrand did not figure in sources relating to the Patarenes until 1065, when Ariald was urging Erlembald to take his late brother's place as their leader. The two Milanese went to Rome, where Alexander set the seal of his approval upon Erlembald's leadership by conferring upon him a banner of St Peter ('vexillum sancti Petri'). According to Landulf Senior, upon arriving at Rome Ariald had sought Hildebrand's help on account of his military leadership in the Lateran palace, but he declared that pope and archdeacon were of one mind in conferring the banner.[156]

On the other hand, Hildebrand may not have approved Alexander's sending to Milan in 1067 of the conciliatory legation of Cardinal Mainard of Silva Candida and

---

[155] The main sources for Milan and the Patarenes are the two chroniclers Arnulf and Landulf Senior (for the date of the latter, see Busch, '*Landulfi senioris historia*'), Andrew of Strumi, *Vita Arialdi*, and Bonizo of Sutri, *Lib. ad amic.*

[156] Arnulf of Milan, 3.15, pp. 189–90; Landulf Senior, 3.14–15, pp. 82–4; Andrew of Strumi, cap. 15, pp. 1059–60.

the Cardinal-priest John Minutus of S. Maria in Trastevere; if they sought to eliminate moral abuses, they also set their faces against the lay coercion of suspect clergy that Erlembald was accustomed to impose.[157] Indeed, Erlembald was quick to respond by himself going to Rome and, in view of the age of the temporizing archbishop of Milan, Guy, who had been consecrated in 1045, to raise the issue of the correct procedure in episcopal elections. He secured the agreement of many of Rome, and especially Hildebrand—'archidiaconus ille Hildeprandus', as Arnulf called him,[158] that the established procedure whereby, when a bishop died, the clergy and people of the vacant see requested the Italian king, that is, Henry IV, to appoint his successor, should be abandoned. Henceforth, there should be free canonical election by clergy and people; Hildebrand himself insisted that for such election, Roman consent was requisite. The issue of canonical election was thus thrown into sharp focus at Milan by Hildebrand's agency.

Upon returning to Milan, Erlembald secretly recruited a body of lay and clerical supporters who were upon oath to promote a free election as he understood it when Guy ceased to be archbishop. Guy got wind of the move, and late in 1070 or early in 1071 he decided to forestall Erlembald by resigning. He secretly dispatched his sub-deacon Godfrey to King Henry in Germany; Godfrey took Guy's staff and ring in order that he might be invested as his successor. But this secret, too, leaked out, and resentment at a high-handed action on Guy's part was compounded by rumours of Godfrey's simoniacal dealings at the king's court. He returned to a Milan which refused to receive an archbishop who was clandestinely appointed. According to the chronicler Arnulf, many at Rome joined Pope Alexander in condemning what had happened; Alexander dispatched a written judgement to Milan. Hildebrand's concurrence is not established but cannot be doubted.[159]

When Guy died in August 1071, he was a pitiable exile in the Milanese *contado*. The Milanese hoped to hold an election upon customary lines, and set Epiphany (6 January) 1072 as the date by which it should take place. Erlembald attempted to take the law into his own hands. Counselled by Hildebrand, he endeavoured to procure the election of a candidate acceptable to Rome. On 6 January, and still (according to Arnulf) upon Hildebrand's advice, in the presence of a Roman legate named Bernard he caused his supporters to elect a young Milanese clerk named Atto. No regard was given to the claims of the German king, Henry IV. The disregard of arrangements for an election that was more in accordance with custom caused an uproar among the cathedral clergy and the laity who supported them. They dragged Atto from a banquet that Erlembald had arranged in the archbishop's palace and forced him to renounce the see for ever. Hildebrand responded by ruling that, because it was made under duress, the renunciation was invalid.[160]

---

[157] Arnulf of Milan, 3.19, pp. 195–6; 4.2, pp. 206–7; cf. 3.23, p. 203.
[158] Mansi, 19.946–8; Arnulf of Milan, 3.19, pp. 195–6.
[159] Arnulf of Milan, 3.20, pp. 196–9.
[160] Arnulf of Milan, 3.23, p. 202–5; Landulf Senior, 3.29, pp. 94–5; Bonizo of Sutri, *Lib. ad amic.* 6, p. 599/16–33.

The conservatively-minded Milanese chroniclers Arnulf and Landulf Senior, who deplored the excesses of the Patarenes, represented Hildebrand as at this time dominating a weak Alexander; according to Arnulf, Alexander so feared Hildebrand that he would do nothing without him, thus reversing the Gospel precept that the disciple should not be above his master, while Landulf was still more forthright.[161] There can be no doubt that, in 1071 and 1072, Hildebrand's dealings with Erlembald were extremely close and that they led to actions upon Erlembald's part that Alexander may not have approved. Hildebrand's alliance with Erlembald would continue into Hildebrand's pontificate. But the distaste of the Milanese chroniclers for Erlembald may have led them to exaggerate their criticism of Hildebrand as his principal ally in the papal entourage, and it may be wrong to claim a radical division between pope and archdeacon. In 1065 it was Alexander who at Hildebrand's prompting gave Erlembald his papal banner, and at the Lent synods of 1072 and 1073 Alexander took firm measures which appear to have been upon his initiative and in which Hildebrand is likely to have concurred. The synod of 1072 followed up the Patarene election of Atto by recognizing him and anathematizing his rival, Godfrey; according to Bonizo of Sutri, Alexander took the lead in these decisions and sent a fatherly letter to Henry IV in which he urged him to lay aside his animosity towards the reform party at Milan and to accept Atto as archbishop.[162] Henry's response was to encourage the Lombard bishops who, early in 1073 at Novara, consecrated Godfrey; the consecrators thereby exposed themselves to excommunication.[163] At his Lent synod of 1073, Alexander excommunicated Godfrey with all his accomplices. Prompted (as it was said) by the Empress Agnes, Alexander also excommunicated a number of Henry's counsellors in Germany; in part, this was in response to Godfrey's consecration. Nevertheless, later in 1073, Atto, the Patarene candidate at Milan, was compelled to seek refuge in Rome.[164]

As in the cases of Chiusa and Florence, so in that of Milan, the outcome of events during the latter part of Alexander's pontificate seems to have been a substantial consensus with Hildebrand which set papal policies upon a line that Hildebrand would continue as pope; there was no occasion for him to introduce radical changes. But whereas at Chiusa and Florence, issues were largely resolved during Alexander's lifetime, at Milan the stage was set for one of the main problems of Gregory's early years as pope. There were rivals for the see. Godfrey, tainted with simony and excommunicated by the papacy, retained the support of the German king and the Lombard bishops; Atto, the Patarene candidate whom Hildebrand had done much to sponsor, was about to become a powerless exile in Rome. The issue of free canonical election was squarely posed, and, if Henry IV was not directly touched by excommunication,

[161] Arnulf of Milan, 4.2, pp. 206–7; Landulf Senior, 3.19, pp. 87–8.
[162] Arnulf of Milan, 4.2, p. 206–7; Bonizo of Sutri, *Lib. ad amic.* 6, p. 599/34–40; *Reg.* 1.11,15, pp. 18/8–13, 23–4.
[163] *Reg.* 1.12, to Bishop William of Pavia, 29 June 1073, p. 20/20–1.
[164] *Reg.* 1.15, to all the faithful in Lombardy, 1 July 1073, p. 24/9–16; Bonizo of Sutri, *Lib. ad amic.* 6, pp. 599/40–600/5; Arnulf of Milan, 4.4, pp. 208–9.

a group of his counsellors who stood close to his person had been anathematized at Rome.

2.2.8 Hildebrand's Election to the Papacy

By 1073, Hildebrand was in his fifties, and probably in his late fifties—a man of mature age and proven experience. Especially with regard to events at Florence and Milan, his purposes had prevailed in papal counsels; although differences of approach had sometimes been apparent, Alexander had eventually acted in accordance with them, and had done so with every appearance of goodwill. Despite the opposition that he had encountered, Hildebrand stood in the main stream of developments; his becoming pope would call for no major reorientation of papal policies. Behind his recent successes, he could draw upon a continuous experience in the affairs of the reform papacy since 1049, when he returned from Germany to Rome with Pope Leo IX. He had thereafter travelled often and widely in Italy, France, and Germany; as a result, he knew and was known by a vast number of churchmen and laity, both great and small. At Rome and in the lands of St Peter, he had been a diligent administrator, not least in the assiduous discharge of judicial business. When Alexander II, in particular, had been absent in his other see of Lucca, Hildebrand had effectively been his *alter ego* at Rome. His religious commitment and motivation, his austerity and regularity of life, and his sustained capacity for work of all kinds, won him widespread admiration. He was equally respected in older monastic circles such as those of Montecassino and Cluny, and among new and radical movements such as the monks of Vallombrosa and the Patarene zealots of Milan and other North Italian cities.

If Hildebrand derived strength from his association with the work of the reform popes since Leo IX, he also commended himself by his points of difference from them. The last seven popes had all come from away from Rome—from Lotharingia, Germany, or Tuscany: Hildebrand was Roman through and through, for since boyhood he had belonged to the Roman church and he had been brought up in St Peter's household. He thus met a prime requirement of canonical tradition: that, if possible, a pope should be elected from the clergy of the Roman church. Unlike his seven predecessors, Hildebrand was for most of his life a monk with whom the many monastic figures in Rome could identify themselves; for in his last years as pope, Alexander II promoted the Vallombrosan monk Peter Igneus to be cardinal-bishop of Albano and the Cluniac monk Gerald to succeed Peter Damiani, who died in 1072, as cardinal-bishop of Ostia, while the cardinal-priests included among their number Abbot Desiderius of Montecassino with the title of S. Cecilia and the enthusiastic but unstable Hugh Candidus with that of S. Clemente. Again, unlike his seven predecessors, Hildebrand was archdeacon of the Roman church, with no distant bishopric or abbey to retain; the apostolic see would have his undivided time and attention. In the early 1070s, with the city quiet, with Duke Godfrey of Lorraine having died in 1069, and with Henry IV in no position to exercise a decisive influence at Rome, everything pointed to Hildebrand as Alexander's successor in the event of his death. Alexander was probably Hildebrand's senior in age by only some five years, but no other pope since Benedict IX had reigned for more than five years. The likelihood that Hildebrand would succeed as pope one day, and perhaps soon, must for some time have been present in many minds.

In fact, Alexander died, it would seem suddenly, on 21 April 1073, which was the third Sunday after Easter.[165] The immediate sequel at Rome is set out in a record of Hildebrand's election which serves as a preface to his Register, in letters that he wrote during the next few days, and in his references to his election in later letters.[166] His early letters described how, upon Alexander's death, the Roman people was unwontedly quiet and left matters in his hands.[167] He took proper advice, and then laid down that, after a three-day fast with appropriate litanies, prayers, and almsgiving, a decision should be taken about how to proceed with the election of a new pope.[168] But on 22 April, when Alexander was buried in the Lateran basilica, there was a sudden popular tumult. With no opportunity to speak or to seek further advice, he was violently raised to the papal office.

Thus far Gregory himself. The record, which was clearly intended to publish the unanimity of the Roman clergy and people in the choice of Hildebrand, complements, rather than contradicts, his letters: whereas he set down the process whereby he was raised to the papal office, the record was concerned to publicize the solemn act, in the form of an address which the assembled people acclaimed with cries of 'Placet', 'Volumus', and 'Laudamus', by which Archdeacon Hildebrand became pastor and supreme pontiff. It took place during an orderly assembly on 22 April in the church where Alexander II had been enthroned—that of S. Pietro in Vincoli under the Esquiline, just north of the Colosseum, and so some two kilometres from the Lateran. The journey to it will have allowed order to be restored after the tumultuous events there. Those who, according to the record, elected Hildebrand and declared that he should henceforth and for ever be called Gregory were the cardinal clerks of the Roman church. However, there was no mention, as was provided for in the Election Decree of 1059, of an initiative by the cardinal-bishops which the cardinal clerks followed. The latter were understood as the domestic clergy of the Roman church, and listed in the ascending order of acolytes, subdeacons, deacons, and priests. They acted in the presence of bishops and abbots, with the consent of other clerks and monks, and with the acclamation of persons of both sexes and various grades. The record listed the qualities that fitted Hildebrand to be pope: he was religious, skilled in knowledge both sacred and secular, an outstanding lover of equity

---

[165] This Sunday was not a station day, and no inference can be drawn about where Alexander may have died. For the suddenness of his death, see Bonizo of Sutri, *Lib. ad amic.* 6, p. 600/35–8.

[166] The record appears as *Reg.* 1.1*, pp. 1–2. Gregory's relevant early letters are *Reg.* 1.1–4, pp. 3–7. Bonizo of Sutri's account is similar in character but unreliable in detail: *Lib. ad amic.* 7, p. 601/1–22. For later references in Gregory's letters, see *Reg.* 1.39, pp. 61–2; 2.49, pp. 75–6; 3.10a, pp. 270–1; 7.14a, p. 483; 7.23, pp. 499–502; *Epp. vag.* nos. 1, 54, pp. 2–5, 128–34.

[167] For the archdeacon's role, see Deusdedit, *Coll. can.* 2.109 (92), pp. 233–5.

[168] A three-day pause was enjoyed by Pope Boniface III's decree of 607: *LP* 1.316/3–7; cf. *Liber diurnus*, p. 212/31–2 (the role of the archdeacon according to this formula *De electione pontificis ad exarchum* should be noticed: p. 213/1–9).

and righteousness, strong in adversity but mild in prosperity, and he exhibited virtues like the sobriety, chastity, and hospitality that St Paul called for in a bishop (1 Tim. 3: 2–4). They were qualities that a well-disposed observer could claim to have been manifest during his archdeaconship. With such a candidate to hand, there could be no circumvention of a strict interpretation of canon law by looking outside the Roman church for a new pope. The record reclaimed the papacy for the clerks of the Roman church, and its place at the beginning of Gregory's Register was a challenging assertion of their view. With a candidate of Hildebrand's standing, it carried all before it, and it appears that Hildebrand was enthroned as pope in the church of S. Pietro in Vincoli.

How far the events of 22 April were planned before the tumult in the Lateran basilica began it is impossible to say. Bonizo of Sutri's story that the cardinal-priest Hugh Candidus took an initiative in the Lateran by proposing Hildebrand as a uniquely eligible candidate may well be true.[169] It can scarcely have been without Hildebrand's prior agreement that he was acclaimed under the name of Gregory, which recalled the most Roman of ancient popes and the first pope with a monastic background, although the matter may have been settled in the course of the journey to S. Pietro in Vincoli. Contemporaries were impressed by the unanimity of the election, which renewed the life of the church in its pristine days. In his letter of congratulation to Gregory, Abbot Walo of St Arnulf at Metz wrote:

We have been told that there was such agreement of the whole people to your election that in so great a multitude absolutely no one seemed to dissent. Whence, I ask, could there have been such unanimity and concord save by the prompting of the Spirit by whose inspiration of old the original company of believers was said to have one heart and one mind (Acts 4: 32)? . . . Thanks be to God, most excellent father, who so favoured your election that the church was not open to division.[170]

In his own letters, Gregory saw the suddenness and unanimity in which he was seized and forced into the papal throne as having the nature of an election *per inspirationem* which was self-authenticating as an act of God and as a demonstration of his irresistable will. At first, he recalled the liturgical texts of three weeks before, when during the *triduum sacrum* at the end of Holy Week there was a recollection of Old Testament prefigurations of Christ's sufferings. His forcible election was a trauma which stamped those sufferings upon his own life. Gregory manifestly had in mind John the Deacon's account of Pope Gregory the Great's reaction to his assumption of the papal office.[171] In the long term, Gregory interpreted his being seized upon by the Roman people as a constraint such as prophets like Isaiah and Jeremiah

---

[169] *Lib. ad amic.* 7, p. 601/5–11.   [170] *Die Briefe des Abtes Walo*, no. 1, p. 52/8–16.

[171] The main texts were Pss. 53: 5, 54: 5–6, 68: 3–4, Lam. 2: 11 = Jer. 31: 20; for a full discussion, see Schneider, *Prophetisches Sacerdotium*, pp. 27–8. For John the Deacon, see *Sancti Gregorii magni Vita*, 1.39–54, cols. 79–86, esp. col. 79BC and the citations of Ps. 68: 3 at cols. 83A and 85A; see also Gregory I's own advice about election to high office: *Reg. past.* 1.3–7, vol. 1, 136–55, esp. cap. 6: 'Quod hi qui pondus regiminis per humilitatem fugiunt, tunc vere sunt humiles, cum divinis indiciis non reluctantur.'

experienced by reason of their call unflinchingly to announce to all nations the right-eousness of God:

> Cry aloud, spare not, lift up your voice like a trumpet;
>> Declare to my people their transgression,
>> To the house of Jacob their sins (Isa. 58: 1).
>
> Cursed is he who does the work of the Lord with slackness;
>> And cursed is he who keeps back his sword from blood (Jer. 48: 10).

In the circumstances of 1073, the salient features of Gregory's election were that it was unanimous and unchallenged, that it followed the strict custom of the Roman church by promoting one of that church's own clerks, and that it had an overmaster-ing impact upon Gregory's own mind and sense of his papal responsibilities.

From the time of his first letters that he wrote as pope from the sickbed to which exhaustion consigned him, Gregory was securely established in office. From the day of his enthronement he exercised jurisdiction as pope, beginning his letters with the formula 'in Romanum pontificem electus.' He used the name Gregory, in due course assuming the numeral seven and so not repudiating his early Roman patron, Gregory VI.[172] In deacon's orders when elected, he was ordained priest at the first canonical opportunity—the Ember Wednesday after Pentecost (22 May). He was raised to the episcopate on 30 June, the Sunday after the feast of his especial patrons St Peter and St Paul.[173] From that Sunday, he used the title 'servus servorum Dei'. The steps by which he assumed the papal office were complete.

---

[172] Otto of Freising, *Chronica*, 6.32, p. 484/5–8. Otto made clear that Gregory VII chose his number rather than his name with Gregory VI in mind; Otto said that Gregory VI had been removed from the list of popes.

[173] *Chronica sancti Benedicti*, p. 203, which is to be preferred to Bonizo of Sutri's dating: *Lib. ad amic.* 7, p. 601/22–4; *Epp. vag.* no. 18, p. 50.

3

Pope Gregory VII and the German Kingdom and Empire

3.1 Background

When Gregory became pope in 1073, the German kingdom was entering upon an internal crisis which would have tested it to its foundations even if a conflict with the papacy had not supervened. For Henry IV's struggle with Gregory compounded another with the German princes, lay and ecclesiastical. The upheavals in Germany during the 1070s and 1080s, therefore, assumed the form of a three-cornered contest between pope, king, and princes, each party to which pursued aims and interests which did not fully correspond to either of the other's. From the very beginning of Gregory's pontificate, Germany as thus divided was at the centre of his concerns, and it remained so until his death in exile at Salerno in 1085. Before turning to the broader ecclesiastical and political issues that were involved, it is well to recall the depth of the personal commitment to the Salian royal family with which Gregory came to the papal office. For him as for most others, the Emperor Henry III, whom he had personally known, stood out as an exemplar of Christian rulership. Gregory felt a responsibility to bring his young son, whatever might be the aberrations of his youth, to rule in his father's likeness, in terms both of royal and imperial majesty and of the Christian virtues that beseemed it. The residence at Rome of the young Henry's devout mother, the Empress Agnes, was an added personal link. In April 1073, numerous considerations gave urgency to Gregory's concern for the young Henry. The faults of moral character for which he was already notorious must be remedied before they became ingrained and ineradicable. The recent excommunication at Alexander II's Lent synod of 1073 of some of the young king's counsellors was a reminder of the prevalence in the German church of simony. The coming to a head of the crisis in the church of Milan after the death of Archbishop Guy raised fundamental questions about the role of the German ruler not only in the churches of Italy but in ecclesiastical elections everywhere. The development of such problems in a German kingdom which quickly fell into civil war and division occupies so large a part in Gregory's pontificate that it must inevitably be the first aspect of it to be considered. Before turning to Gregory's involvement as pope in German history, a little must be said about some aspects of that history in Ottonian and early Salian times, about Henry IV's early years as king, and about the course of the German civil war in its first phase between 1073 and 1075.

3.1.1 Ottonian and Early Salian Kingship

A prime feature of Ottonian and early Salian rulership was its sacral character. It was eloquently set forth in the sermons of the churchmen and in the liturgical texts that they compiled. Henry III's chaplain Wipo, in his *Life* of Henry's father, the Emperor Conrad II (1024–39), made Archbishop Aribo of Mainz declare in his sermon at Conrad's royal coronation that all authority in this transitory world comes from the eternal God as its single source. In all reverence, a parallel could be drawn between the lordship of God and that of earthly kings. It was the church's duty to pray that, sinful man though he was, the king might keep his royal office pure and undefiled, and attain through affliction and temptation to a crown of glory:

You have yourself suffered wrongs, so that now you may know how to have mercy upon those who suffer wrongs. Divine mercy has not allowed you to be without discipline, so that you might learn through heavenly instruction how to rise to Christian rulership. You have come to the highest office; you are the vicar of Christ. Only one who imitates Christ is a true ruler.[1]

On this line of thinking the king participated in the kingship of Christ and had a sacral character which was expressed in the liturgy of his anointing and coronation. Of particular significance were the formulas of the Romano-Germanic Pontifical. 'Enkindle his heart to love your grace', prayed the archbishop, 'by this holy oil with which you have anointed priests, kings, and prophets, so that he may love righteousness and lead his people in its ways.'[2]

But the notion of sacral kingship should not be pressed too far. The king did not receive at his anointing the sacramental capacities of bishops and priests to ordain, to consecrate the eucharist, or to absolve. Moreover, the formulas of the Romano-Germanic Pontifical set limits to his legitimate concern with the holiest things. After his election, anointing, and coronation, the archbishop placed the king upon his throne with the following words:

Take and henceforth keep the place which hitherto you have held by paternal succession, and which is now in hereditary right committed to you by authority of Almighty God and our present gift—that is, by all the bishops and other servants of God. And as you see the clergy to stand nearer to the holy altars, so in appropriate places you should remember when it behoves you to grant them the greater honour. Thus may the mediator of God and man (1 Tim. 2: 5) strengthen you, the mediator of clergy and people, in this, the throne of royal power. May Jesus Christ our Lord, king of kings and lord of lords, cause you to reign with him in his eternal kingdom.[3]

The king was 'mediator cleri et plebis', and he had a superiority over clergy and people alike; his anointing set him apart from other men and gave him authority in and over the church. In this sense, he represented Christ, the mediator between God and man. Yet on account of the sacramental power that they had and that he lacked, he must know when to defer to the clergy. In this respect, the word *mediator* is best

---

[1] Wipo, *Gesta Chuonradi imperatoris*, cap. 3, pp. 21–3, cf. cap. 5, p. 26/14–27, *Tetralogus*, lines 11–22, p. 76.

[2] *RGP* 72.17, vol. 1.255/7–11.

[3] *RGP* 72.25, vol. 1.258–9.

translated 'governor'; the king had a mission to regulate society and to bring justice to all its parts. But he remained a layman; he must know when to hear and follow as well as when to order and command. Even pre-Gregorian texts raised deep problems in the relation between *sacerdotium* and *regnum*.

The German ruler did not aspire only to the dignity of king. Since Otto I's imperial coronation on 962, he had the expectation, expressed from 1045 in the title *rex Romanorum*,[4] that in due course he would receive imperial coronation at the hands of the pope in Rome. There, according to the Romano-Germanic Pontifical, the emperor would promise to be the protector and defender of the Roman church in all its necessities. Before he was crowned by the pope, the cardinal-bishop of Ostia would anoint the emperor-to-be, praying that he might prosper in his imperial duties so that, being appointed by God to rule the church ('in tua' [God's] 'dispositione constituto ad regendam aecclesiam tuam sanctam'), he might have free course to rule the people subject to him in righteousness and godly fear.[5] Yet with respect to the empire as well as to the kingdom, there was room for different views of the ruler's scope for legitimate action. Such formularies might justify Henry III in travelling to Rome in 1046 and, as *patricius*, in ordering the papacy much as he ordered the bishoprics of Germany. But it was also open for a strong pope to insist that the rule of righteousness could be ensured only when the emperor acted in proper obedience to the admonitions of the pope. And since the pope must grant imperial coronation, if strong and confident he could lay down his conditions.

The exalted phrases of preachers and liturgists are eloquent of how rulers were formally regarded and of the propaganda by which their claims were propagated; they should not give rise to anachronistic estimates of the formation of national consciousness, in Germany as elsewhere. In the mid-eleventh century, the terms *rex* and *regnum* turned upon the king as the superior of peoples who were joined to him and to each other by common loyalty and personal fealty rather than by a political or constitutional framework. In Germany, the peoples of the Rhineland and of the lands between it and the Slavonic region thought of themselves first and foremost as Saxons, Swabians, Bavarians, Franconians, or Lotharingians. They formed *gentes*, or even *regna*, which found an identity in the stem-duchies; even so, Saxony and Lotharingia, in particular, were divided by sub-loyalties into East and West Saxony and Upper and Lower Lorraine. Not until the mid-1070s, in the context of the civil wars of Henry IV's reign and of the letters that Gregory VII himself addressed to the Germanic regions as a whole, was there an appreciable sign of a common political awareness of a *regnum Teutonicum*, or *Teutonicorum*, or of a king who was envisaged as the ruler of an entity so designated.

Nevertheless, the king's lordship had for long impinged effectively upon the German stem-duchies, whose leaders attended his courts and through which he itinerated with especial solemnity at the beginning of his reign. Further, the king claimed authority over the *regnum Italicum*, which, however, did not become in

---

4 *MGH DDHIII* no. 134, p. 170/30 provides the earliest authentic occurrence of the title.
5 *RGP* 75.1,5, vol. 1.264.

German eyes a counterpart to the emergent *regnum Teutonicum*; rather, it was comparable to one of the *gentes* north of the Alps such as the Saxons or Swabians. Between 1032 and 1034, the kingdom of Burgundy (as distinct from the duchy) passed under Salian rule, but its remoteness and the difficulty of communication left it little amenable to Salian control. Although the Salian kings ruled over Germany, Italy, and Burgundy, it is important not to anticipate developments in the twelfth century: only then did the concept emerge of a triadic rule over the *regna* of Germany, Italy, and Burgundy, with a common ruler who was *rex* in respect of each and *imperator* in respect of all. In early Salian times, there were no such structures: the ruler was *rex*, and the object of his rule was a *regnum*, as the focus of personal loyalties and relationships; the imperial title represented an intensified form of this rulership, amplified by the ancient Roman, Carolingian, and Byzantine associations that world-chronicles were beginning to publicize by exhibiting the continuity of the imperial office over many centuries.[6]

In all lands, but especially in Germany, the church and its clergy were an essential resource of a king who was *mediator cleri et plebis*. It can be misleading to represent the relationship between king and church in such an institutional and fixed manner as is implied by the phrase 'imperial church system' (*Reichskirchensystem*). The relationship was not peculiarly imperial, but a variant, with German characteristics, of what was to be found in all western regions where kingship was established. It was not narrowly ecclesiastical, but its effects permeated the whole of society. Above all, there was no system; like rulership in all its aspects, the relationship was one of lordship over the wills and actions of men; there was a balance of forces in which all parties continually gained and yielded ground in matters great and small, while there were changes from reign to reign and contingency to contingency.[7]

In Germany, the most constant feature of the king's authority was that he could normally nominate, or at least approve the election of, the bishops of the German-speaking lands. He also enjoyed considerable power over the monasteries and abbatial elections; this power tended to increase because monasteries sought to escape from the pressures of their aristocratic neighbours by seeking royal protection. In the early eleventh century, the highest form of monastic *libertas* became that which was conferred by royal privileges. Moreover, bishops and abbots entered upon their offices by way of royal investiture. From the tenth century, the king handed them the staff that was the symbol of their pastoral charge; by the mid-eleventh century, he also conferred the ring which symbolized a bishop's marriage to his church. The king's use of the formula *Accipite ecclesiam*, to which Peter Damiani referred,[8] allowed for no distinction between the spiritual office and its temporal adjuncts; the totality of office was conferred by the king's hand.

The capacity of bishops and abbots for royal service was enhanced by the lavish endowment of the most favoured sees and abbeys. Not only did they acquire lands,

---

[6] See esp. Müller-Mertens, *Regnum teutonicum*; Von den Brincken, *Studien*.
[7] Reuter, 'The "Imperial Church System" '.
[8] *Briefe*, no. 140, 3.482/19–21.

markets, tolls, jurisdiction, and other sources of wealth, but in many cases whole counties came into their hands. Since clerics might not take part in the shedding of blood, much everyday administration was entrusted to lay advocates and other officials. But a major consequence of the acquiring of temporal rights was the reinforcement of the immunity of ecclesiastical lands from the interference of external authorities. Bishoprics and abbeys became the possessors of vast territorial powers which made their loyalty and services an indispensable support of the king and of public authority. With varying degrees of burdensomeness, they were obliged to perform the *gistum* and the *servitium regis*—the rendering to an itinerant king and his court of the hospitality and the provisions in kind that were essential to his style of life and to his ability to visit and oversee the localities over which he had lordship.

The bishops, in particular, were built into the fabric of royal government. Their role was complemented by the ramifications of the royal chapel.[9] Its traditional functions were to have custody of the king's relics and to conduct divine service, and also to see to the king's secretarial needs. But in its apogee under Henry III, it was the nerve-centre of the whole range of royal government. The personal connections of its members were even more serviceable to the king than its day-to-day activities. Its clerks were largely recruited from aristocratic families; it gave these families a stake in the prosperity of the king's rule while enabling him to keep abreast of what was happening in the localities. The services of its active members went far beyond religious and secretarial duties; they dealt with a wide range of administrative and diplomatic business, and in effect they became royal counsellors. Many of them held canonries in cathedrals throughout the kingdom, dividing their time between them and the royal service. Such an added link with the localities was the more valuable to the king because, in the early eleventh century, the cathedrals came to have an enhanced importance in the royal itinerary. The link between the king and the cathedrals was further strengthened by the practice whereby the king himself was granted a canonry in a number of cathedrals. He thus secured a part in the prayers and alms of cathedral chapters which were in process of becoming separate from their bishops' households. Royal chaplains also played a conspicuous part in palace chapels like those which Henry III established at Goslar and Kaiserswerth. The ablest or most favoured of the royal chaplains could in due course expect the reward of a bishopric. Such men supplied the king with powerful, competent, and reliable local agents who were trained in his service, who were conversant with his needs, and whose celibacy prevented them from establishing local dynasties. In all its facets, the royal chapel was an invaluable agency of royal support, government, and political control.

The early eleventh century saw the extension of such royal control to Italy. Italians as well as Germans served in the royal chapel, and many Germans became bishops in the provinces of Aquileia and Ravenna. Even in Lombardy, where German bishops were fewer, the king's control over episcopal elections was widely exercised and

---

9 Fleckenstein, *Die Hofkapelle*.

welcomed.[10] Royal power in Italy as in Germany was less of a system than has some-times been believed; it was nevertheless directed towards using the resources of the church in order to secure and to promote royal interests.

When, as with Henry III, there was a ruler of skill, energy, and judgement who at once used the resources of the church to make his rule more effective and promoted the well-being of the church by holding councils, advancing moral reform, and pro-moting men of spirituality and practical ability to bishoprics and abbacies, the German king's ends were well served by loyal churchmen. They served him as officials and administrators, not as feudatories. There were also advantages for the church, which enjoyed the benefits of peace and order, and which could expect that men of vision and competence would be promoted to high office in it. As always in medieval government, however, a royal minority deprived it of guiding authority and left it a prey to over-mighty subjects, episcopal as well as lay. If the minority were long, there was also the problem of how royal power might be revived after it, and of whether a new king would be able or willing to renew the rule of his forebears—and, indeed, of whether his subjects would wish or permit him to do so. Few biblical texts struck home more forcibly to medieval people than the words of the Preacher: 'Woe to you, O land, whose king is a child and whose princes eat in the morning' (Eccles. 10: 16).

3.1.2 King Henry IV's Minority and Early Years

The events and developments of Henry IV's minority and early years as king seri-ously weakened the position of the German monarchy as his father had left it. The young Henry became king in 1056 at the age of almost 6 years; he was declared of age when he was girded with the sword in 1065. He was at first under the regency of his 30-year-old mother, the Empress Agnes of Poitou. Her weak character and lack of political experience and judgement made her unsuited for the task, and she lacked kindred in Germany to whom she could turn for advice and support. After the death in 1057 of her first mentor, Pope Victor II who was also bishop of Eichstätt, she relied upon Bishop Henry of Augsburg whose high-handedness offended the young king and other bishops; scurrilous rumours circulated about his personal relationship with the empress.[11] Henry of Augsburg foreshadowed the over-mighty prelates who were to vie for domination throughout the 1060s. Agnes's regency witnessed some important promotions in Germany, both episcopal and lay. Among the upper clergy, in 1060 the see of Mainz received a new archbishop in Siegfried, who would rule it until 1084. In 1059, the duchy of Saxony was given to Ordulf Billung. There were three appointments to southern duchies. By 1059, Rudolf of Rheinfelden had become duke of Swabia and administrator of Burgundy. In 1060 he married the king's sister Matilda; after she died in the same year, he married Adelaide, sister of Bertha of Turin who was betrothed to the king. The marriage was quickly dissolved, but Rudolf had acquired the duchy and the royal connections that in 1077 would

---

[10] Pauler, *Das Regnum Italiae*, esp. pp. 164–73.
[11] Lampert of Hersfeld, *Ann. aa.* 1062, 1064, pp. 72–4, 92.

facilitate his election as anti-king.[12] In 1061, Count Berthold of Zähringen became duke of Carinthia, and Otto of Nordheim, a leading Saxon, became duke of Bavaria. These promotions left all the German duchies in the hands of men who were not directly of the royal family. Although Agnes could not have foreseen this, her ecclesiastical and ducal promotions brought to the fore some of her son's leading opponents in the 1070s and 1080s.

Agnes's regency ended abruptly in 1062. Archbishop Anno of Cologne was mainly responsible for the *coup d'état* at the island palace of Kaiserswerth, when he seized the young king and the royal insignia, carrying them off to Cologne;[13] he intended to be master alike of the king and of the kingdom. Henry himself made a plucky but vain attempt to escape from Anno by swimming to freedom in the Rhine. The experience at Kaiserswerth was calculated to confirm the suspicion of princes that Bishop Henry of Augsburg had already aroused in Henry, and to make him secretive, cunning, and self-reliant. As for his mother, her piety had already led her to take the veil. She spent a few years more in Germany to be near her son until he reached his majority, but from 1065 she followed the devout life of a *pauper et peregrina* in Rome, where Peter Damiani was her mentor.[14] She remained at Rome and in Italy until her death on 14 December 1077, though her concern to bring her son to a better mind in his public and private dealings several times led her to break her Roman seclusion by travelling to Germany.

After Anno's *coup d'état*, the dominant figures in Germany were Anno himself and his rival, Archbishop Adalbert of Bremen. In 1063, they were compelled to collaborate, but they were of incompatible characters, outlooks, and ambitions. The incompatibility was made the more damaging by what they shared—a concern to magnify the power and wealth of their respective sees.[15] Although not of noble birth, Anno represented the upward-thrusting ambition of the German princes, which he pursued with his own blend of egotism, ruthlessness, and nepotism. In 1059, he secured the see of Halberstadt for his nephew Burchard, and in 1063 he established his brother Werner as archbishop of Magdeburg. When Henry came of age, Anno had perforce to yield to Adalbert, whose outlook was royalist; although he was concerned to make his see the centre of a vast northern patriarchate and to spread his authority eastwards by missionary activity among the Slavs. The German lay aristocracy detested him; his quasi-ducal position in his see excited the especial hostility of East Saxon families like the Billungs. In January 1066, an assembly at Tribur brought about his fall from power. Archbishops Siegfried of Mainz and Anno of Cologne were his leading opponents; the assembly insisted that the king should either abdicate or remove Adalbert from his counsels.[16] In Saxony, Magnus Billung compelled him for a time to leave Bremen and to surrender many of his territorial acquisitions.

---

[12] See the comment of Frutolf, *a.*1057, p. 74/15–17.
[13] Lampert of Hersfeld, *Ann. a.* 1062, pp. 72–4; *Ann. Altah. maior. a.* 1062, pp. 59–60.
[14] *Briefe*, nos. 104, 124, 130, 144, 149, 3.141–58, 408–11, 434–6, 525–7, 546–54.
[15] Adam of Bremen, 3.34–6, pp. 370–3.
[16] Lampert of Hersfeld, *Ann. a.* 1066, p. 108/13–15.

He managed to return to court in 1069, and in 1072 the king for a while recalled Anno. But the archbishops' rivalry had been mutually damaging; after 1066 their power was never again what it had been. During and after Henry's minority, lay magnates, too, became prominent at court; for example, Otto of Nordheim, duke of Bavaria, was prominent alongside Anno of Cologne.[17]

Thus, in the ten years after Henry III's death, royal authority was enfeebled, while lay and ecclesiastical magnates behaved like over-mighty subjects. At the same time, the positions of lay and ecclesiastical magnates tended to be assimilated, so that they developed a common interest over against the king's. Even under the Ottos and the first two Salians, it had been from the king's point of view unfortunate that the granting of counties, markets, tolls, and other secular rights to bishoprics and abbeys in effect made their occupants less the supporters of the king who chose and promoted bishops and abbots, and more the peers and allies of the lay aristocracy whose members also possessed such rights. Bishops and abbots, dukes and counts, moved towards solidarity as a compact, aristocratic class of society over against the king. The circumstances of the minority favoured the consolidation of lands, the building of castles, the acquiring of jurisdiction, and the use of unfree *ministeriales* as serviceable officials, by which ecclesiastical and lay magnates established their power. A horizontal stratification of German society that was to become a feature of the twelfth century already became apparent. Before the major conflict of *sacerdotium* and *regnum* even began in earnest, the supports in society upon which the king depended were seriously weakened, while the princes were establishing themselves as a consolidated power in society.

Over-mighty subjects did not restrict their activities to Germany. A figure of especially disturbing augury was Godfrey the Bearded, from 1065 duke of Lower Lorraine, some of whose activities have already been noticed. He had been Henry III's most powerful and persistent opponent, and in 1047 he forfeited the duchy of Upper Lorraine. His marriage in 1054 to Countess Beatrice of Tuscany gave him the title of marquis of Tuscany and immense standing in Central Italy; in due course he added to his titles the marquisate of Fermo and the duchy of Spoleto. (It was partly to contain his power that Henry III betrothed his infant son Henry to Bertha, daughter of the count of Turin.) Godfrey's brother's accession to the papacy in 1057 as Stephen IX gave him consequence at Rome. This consequence grew during the Cadalan schism when the German court ill-advisedly supported Honorius II while Godfrey supported Alexander II. He was an astute politician and a fine soldier, whose attitudes towards the German court and the papacy were alike based on self-interest. But when he died in 1069, the Reichenau chronicler Berthold claimed that, by reason of his penances and alms, he was as it were a naked bearer of the naked cross ('ferme nudus nudae crucis baiulus').[18] Even before Henry IV's breach with Gregory

---

[17] *M* no. 23, p. 217/28–30.

[18] *a*.1069, p. 274/31–8. Berthold used a similar phrase of Hermann I 'of Baden', marquis of Verona and son of Duke Berthold of Carinthia when he became a monk at Cluny: *a*.1073, p. 276/3–5. His eulogy of Godfrey may be compared with Peter Damiani's reproof in *Briefe*, no. 154, 4.67–71.

VII, a prince, however concerned for his own advancement, who was regarded in Germany as having served papal purposes could, upon his death, be invested with a sanctity that reflected Christ's passion. A princely sacrality was conceivable, over against the king's.

After he came of age, Henry was active in seeking to revive and establish royal power. One of his first concerns was to undertake an Italian expedition, an object of which was the imperial coronation that Alexander II is credibly reported already to have mentioned at the council of Mantua.[19] It was mooted at the Easter assembly of 1065 when he became of age; at Pentecost it was postponed until the autumn, and in the event Archbishop Adalbert of Bremen saw that plans for that year came to nothing.[20] The main reason was that, if successful, an Italian expedition would bring advantage to his rivals Archbishop Anno of Cologne and Duke Godfrey of Lorraine. At Rome, however, hopes for an expedition remained high; the ever-enthusiastic Peter Damiani held out the expectation that Henry would soon be raised from the royal to the imperial dignity and triumph gloriously over all his foes.[21] In 1066, Prince Richard of Capua's campaign to the north of the River Garigliano posed a threat to papal lands that made Pope Alexander himself anxious for a German expedition. The Empress Agnes made one of her journeys to Germany in order to encourage it, and Henry renewed his preparations.[22] His Augsburg court at Candlemas 1067 was intended to advance them. But he was forestalled by Duke Godfrey of Lorraine, who was determined to keep Italian affairs in his own hands. Godfrey set off for Italy without the king, and mounted a successful campaign against the Normans.[23] Henry was thus denied both an imperial coronation that Alexander was anxious to perform, and an opportunity to assert his lordship in the Italian kingdom.

Not surprisingly, when Henry took in hand the restoration of royal power in Germany, he sought advisers of his own choice and making. Like many of the princes, his grandfather and father had already employed *ministeriales*—personally unfree but highly competent administrators who were the king's own men and oversaw his lands, rights, and castles in the localities where they served. After 1065 Henry increasingly used such men, whom he rewarded well.[24] They attracted resentment alike by their role as local agents and for the place that they often enjoyed at court; the chronicler Lampert of Hersfeld selected a certain Count Werner for conspicuously unfavourable notice.[25] The annalist of the Bavarian abbey of Niederaltaich, who was better disposed than Lampert towards the king, in 1072 complained bitterly that Henry despised his magnates and acted upon the advice of lesser men whom he had

---

[19] *Ann. Altah. maior. a.* 1064, p. 65/24–8.

[20] Letter of Anno of Cologne to Alexander II, Giesebrecht, *Kaiserzeit*, 3.1228–9, no. 4; *Chron. Cas.* 3.18, p. 385/1–6.

[21] *Briefe*, no. 120, 3.384–92, esp. p. 392/11–15.

[22] Amatus, 7.9, pp. 270–1; Peter Damiani, *Briefe*, no. 144, 3.525–7.

[23] Amatus, 7.9, pp. 270–1; *Chron. Cas.* 3.23, pp. 389–90.

[24] Such as Mazelin and Moricho: *MGH DDH IV* nos. 201–2, 205, 213. For Henry's use of *ministeriales*, see Bosl, *Reichsministerialität*, 1.12–16, 74–101.

[25] *Ann. aa.* 1063, 1064, 1066, pp. 88, 92, 106–8.

raised up. Thereby he offended against the principles of right social order, and his bishops, dukes, and princes withdrew from the affairs of the kingdom. The annalist named Dukes Rudolf of Swabia and Berthold of Carinthia as being especially offended.[26] In fact, Henry was doing upon his lands very much what his lay and ecclesiastical magnates had for some time past been doing upon theirs. But there were exaggerated fears that Henry might seek to establish a virtual autocracy by eliminating the princes who opposed him.[27]

With the help of his base-born assistants, Henry energetically built a network of royal lands and fortifications, especially in East Saxony and North Thuringia, but also in the middle Rhineland and along the lower Main. He was thus resuming the work of his father, who had also established a royal residence which was pleasantly situated at Goslar.[28] Goslar was on the lower slopes of the Rammelsberg whose silver mines, exploited since the late tenth century, provided a source of ready wealth. Henry IV's development of Goslar is graphically described in Abbot Norberto of Iberg's *Life* of Bishop Benno of Osnabrück. Henry III had brought this Swabian, of modest family, to Goslar and had used his talent for military organization. The *Life* describes his twofold role at Goslar in Henry's early years, as archpriest and as judge and administrator. He had outstanding skills as a builder and as an overseer of stock-rearing and agriculture. He was a stern exactor of royal dues and services. In 1068, Henry arranged his promotion to the see of Osnabrück.[29]

Using men like Benno as well as his *ministeriales*, who also were largely recruited from Swabia, Henry recovered lands lost during his minority, added to them, and built and garrisoned castles for the administration, defence, and subjection of his lands. With an exaggeration that reflects the bitterness of his Saxon and Thuringian contemporaries, Lampert of Hersfeld castigated this policy:

Henry furnished all the mountains and hills of Saxony and Thuringia with heavily fortified castles, and in them he placed garrisons. When they lacked the victuals that they needed, he allowed them to seize plunder from nearby villages and fields as though they were the lands of an enemy. Those who dwelt nearby he compelled to fortify these castles, to carry the necessary building materials, and themselves to toil as though they were slaves.

Of these castles, the strongest and most notorious was the Harzburg, only two hours' journey from Goslar; Henry used it as a burial place for his family. Lampert listed seven other especially hated castles, with the comment that Henry planned many more before the Saxon revolt of 1073 forestalled him.[30] Remote, inaccessible, and formidably defended, Henry's castles presented a challenge to local society which was regarded as being of an intensity unparalleled in earlier royal administration. They were tangible expressions of a royal and transpersonal power which the

[26] *Ann. Altah. maior. a.* 1072, p. 84.   [27] Bruno, caps. 60–3, pp. 274–7.
[28] Berges, 'Zur Geschichte'.   [29] *Vita Bennonis*, caps. 6–11, pp. 380–94.
[30] *Ann. aa.* 1071, 1073, pp. 152, 166, 194; cf. Bernold, *Chron. a.* 1072, p. 429/36–8; *a.* 1072, p. 275/39–40; Bruno, cap. 16, pp. 212–14. For Henry's activities, see esp. Fenske, *Adelsopposition*, pp. 13–45, 51–99; Leyser, 'The Crisis'.

Saxons, used to personal and patrimonial politics, did not understand and shrank from with fear and horror.

For as a Salian with a Franconian background, Henry had no roots in Saxony. All classes there opposed his policy but especially the aristocracy, and a fevered campaign of opposition developed. Henry was accused of preparing fortifications against the Saxons that he should have raised against the heathen Slavs who had dangerously recovered their strength, and he was censured for marrying his Swabian *ministeriales* to Saxon women of higher birth than themselves. In 1070 he came into open conflict with Otto of Nordheim when he countenanced charges of treason against him. Otto refused to stand trial by battle and his duchy of Bavaria was confiscated in favour of his son-in-law Welf IV. In 1071, Otto and his ally Magnus Billung were compelled to surrender. Next year, Archbishop Adalbert of Bremen's pleas led to Otto's pardon; but after the death of Duke Ordulf Billung, Henry's seizure of the family stronghold of Lüneburg, strategically placed on the River Elbe not far from Hamburg, and his garrisoning it with an élite force loyal to himself, added fuel to Saxon grievances. In 1073, rebellion broke out on a very serious scale. In June, the Saxon princes thought themselves insulted by the king's behaviour at a meeting of the court of Goslar. In July, at Hoetensleben, Otto of Nordheim joined Archbishop Werner of Magdeburg, Bishop Burchard of Halberstadt, Margrave Dedi of the Saxon Ostmark, and Count Hermann Billung as leaders of a conspiracy against the king. The South German dukes Welf of Bavaria and Rudolf of Swabia were also hostile to him. Henry's only reliable lay supporter was Duke Godfrey the Hunchback of Lorraine who had succeeded to the duchy upon his father's death in 1069. Faced by a Saxon revolt and with few supporters, Henry IV was thus in a weak political position in Germany when Gregory VII became pope.

Furthermore, in the years that followed his majority, Henry's personal reputation, as well as his political fortunes, fell to a low ebb. In 1066, he married Bertha of Turin, who proved to be one of the most admirable of medieval queens. But Henry established a reputation for depravity and promiscuity which, however much exaggerated by his enemies, was acknowledged to be well founded even by his posthumous biographer and eulogist. Disparagers of Archbishop Adalbert of Bremen, like Bruno the historian of the Saxon wars, accused him of encouraging the young king in his lusts. Bruno also made much of Henry's reputation for cruelty which he practised in despicable ways when pursuing his amours.[31] In 1069, Henry compounded his reputation for lust and cruelty when he allegedly declared Bertha to be so little attractive to him that he was unable to consummate his marriage. Following the example of Rudolf of Swabia who had put away her sister, he sought a divorce. Archbishop Siegfried of Mainz turned to the pope for help, but Alexander II set his face firmly against a divorce. At a council of Frankfurt in October, Cardinal Peter Damiani, as Alexander's legate, strenuously put the papal view, threatening that, if there were a

---

[31] *Vita HIV* cap. 2, pp. 414–16; *Ann. Altah. maior. a.* 1069, p. 78; Bruno, caps. 1, 4–15, pp. 194–6, 198–212.

divorce, Alexander could never contemplate Henry's imperial coronation; the German princes who were present concurred in his judgement. According to Lampert of Hersfeld, Henry replied, because he had no alternative rather than because he was persuaded by the legate's words, that 'If you are really fixed and determined in this matter, I must compel myself to shoulder as best I can a burden that I cannot shed.' He was perforce reconciled with his queen, who in 1071 promptly bore him the first of their sons.[32]

It was a grave matter for Henry that his conduct should thus be adjudged by Peter Damiani contrary alike to Christian law and to kingly honour ('ab nomine Christiano, nedum ab regio multum abhorrentem').[33] By chivalric, no less than by ecclesiastical, standards, he was unfitted to be king. He had disgraced the girdle of knighthood and the kingly probity that went with it. So he could be set aside as king. German chroniclers recorded that, for his treatment of his wife and for the ill fame of his dissolute youth, the princes attempted to deprive him of his kingdom.[34] In August 1073, when Archbishop Siegfried of Mainz and representatives of Archbishop Anno of Cologne met the Saxon rebels at Corvey in an attempt to pacify them, the Saxons cited, among other grievances, Henry's shameful treatment of the queen and other women; if Henry, they said, were judged by ecclesiastical laws, he must be deemed to forfeit his marriage, his girdle of knighthood, and his whole secular capability—how much more the kingdom![35] Several years before Gregory at Rome first proclaimed Henry's deposition and excommunication, it was thus being said in Germany that his personal character and conduct made him unfit to be king.[36] This was on top of his political treatment of his subjects, in which he was seen to have lived according to his own will; a king who had promised to be the Charlemagne of his age had shown himself to be its Rehoboam (1 Kgs 12: 1–20).[37]

Henry IV's domestic politics and private life combined to prevent him from establishing any such image of righteous kingship as his father had bequeathed and as the liturgy of a church required him to exhibit. While Henry was thus falling short of what was looked for in a king, the practice whereby, from Clement II to Victor II, the papacy had been ruled by German popes who retained their German sees, established a bond between the papacy and the German church which opened its horizons. The course of the Cadalan schism led in Germany to a fuller awareness of the reform papacy and its claims which is vividly illustrated by the changing standpoint of the Reichenau chronicler Berthold. In his first recension of the early 1060s, he was content to record Henry's assumption of the Roman patriciate, the election of Bishop Cadalus of Parma as the rightful pope, and the setting up of his rival, Anselm I of Lucca, as a usurper of the apostolic see. But in his second recension, written later in the decade, Alexander II was from the outset the rightful pope and Cadalus had

---

[32] Lampert of Hersfeld, *Ann. a.* 1069, pp. 115, 118–20; *CU* no. 34, pp. 64–6.

[33] Lampert of Hersfeld, *Ann. a.* 1069, pp. 118–20, esp. pp. 118/32–120/2.

[34] Bernold, *Chron. a.* 1068, p. 429/6–8; Berthold, *a.*1068, p. 274/6–9.

[35] *a.*1073, p. 198/12–20.   [36] Leyser, 'Early Medieval Canon Law', pp. 560–1.

[37] Lampert of Hersfeld, *Libellus de institutione*, 2, p. 353/25–8.

become the usurper. Berthold now applauded Alexander as a 'doctor catholicus' who strenuously resisted simony and clerical fornication; his right-hand man was Hildebrand, 'hereticis maxime infestus'.[38] Berthold illustrates the horror with which simony and clerical fornication were viewed in German reforming circles. He shows how figures like Peter Damiani were increasingly listened to in Germany; although he recorded a current opinion there that Peter treated too leniently those whom simoniacs had ordained.[39] He devoted a long section to Peter Igneus's ordeal at Florence in which he convicted his simoniacal bishop.[40] Germany was becoming open, not only to the reforming zeal that had been shown there under Henry III, but also to more advanced currents from Rome and Italy.

Henry's own ill-considered and unsuccessful ecclesiastical dealings served further to undermine his standing in Germany and to stimulate papal concern with German affairs. In 1066, under Anno of Cologne's influence, he tried to impose Anno's nephew Conrad upon the vacant archbishopric of Trier. When Conrad tried to take possession of his see, he was resisted by the burgrave, and a posse of knights hurled him from a rock to his death. The murder was unavenged, and a new bishop, Udo of the family of the counts of Nellenburg, was elected by the cathedral chapter. Anno of Cologne wrote querulously to the pope and sought vindication, but the consequence was humiliation for the king.[41] During the next few years, Henry tried to counterbalance the over-mighty prelates who had dominated his court by making episcopal appointments from his own circle, mainly upon the criterion of service-ability to himself.[42] Some examples are the worldly Benno II of Osnabrück, the young and ineffective Henry of Speyer, the ignorant but serviceable Hermann of Bamberg, and above all the simoniacal and greedy Charles of Constance. The result was a debasement of the episcopate.

The last of these appointments was particularly unfortunate. Berthold, whose abbey of Reichenau was in the diocese of Constance, told how, in 1069, upon the death of the praiseworthy Bishop Rumwold, the outcome of the open simony in which the king engaged was his nomination to the see of Charles, provost of his church on the Harzburg; in reply, the canons tried to secure the canonical election of one of themselves named Siegfried. In 1070, the king persisted in his attempts to impose Charles, who was able to establish himself in the see and to waste its possessions. The canons appealed to Alexander II, who forbade them to have any truck with Charles. He also instructed Archbishop Siegfried of Mainz, as metropolitan, not to consecrate Charles unless he purged his simony. Relying on Henry, Charles hung on to his see, and Siegfried of Mainz appealed to Alexander to defend him against the king's wrath. In 1071, Siegfried held a synod at Mainz; upon the canons' evidence,

[38] *a*.1061, p. 27/56–7 (from Bernold, *Chron. a.* 1061, p. 428/11–12), cf. *a*.1073, p. 276/8–9, where Hildebrand is referred to as *vir prudens, sobrius et castus*. For a clear distinction between the two recensions, see Dr I. S. Robinson's forthcoming edition.

[39] *a*.1066, p. 273/8–10, from Bernold, *Chron. a.* 1066, pp. 428/44–429/1.

[40] *a*.1067, pp. 273/19–274/4.

[41] The extensive source material is set out in Meyer von Knonau, *Jahrbücher*, 1.498–13.

[42] See esp. Fleckenstein, 'Heinrich IV. und der deutsche Episkopat'.

Charles was arraigned for his simony but not, Berthold complained, publicly deposed. Berthold launched a tirade against the simoniacal institution of bishops and priests, citing Pope Nicholas II's legislation against it. Local opposition to Charles was such that the king had eventually to abandon him and substitute for him a canon of Goslar named Otto.[43] It was a further humiliation for the king.

Berthold shows how, during the same critical years, Henry's interference with monasteries was no less objectionable and damaging. His own abbey of Reichenau provided a prime example. In 1069, after Abbot Ulrich I died, Henry imposed upon the monks Maginward, prior St Michael's at Hildesheim; the promotion was simoniacal. Within a year, Maginward was unwilling to sustain the king's further exactions and demands, and resigned. In 1071, Abbot Rupert of St Michael's at Bamberg acquired it, again simoniacally, only to suffer excommunication by Pope Alexander II and deprivation at his Lent synod of 1072.[44]

Berthold's account of events in the bishopric of Constance and the abbey of Reichenau illustrates how the king's dealings brought widespread obloquy upon himself, especially for the simony in which he engaged. The result was that Alexander II's pontificate saw a growth in recourse to Rome by German churchmen in matters both great and small. The greatest prelates made their way there. In 1068, Archbishop Anno of Cologne did penance for his association with the excommunicated Archbishop Henry of Ravenna and with the anti-pope, Bishop Cadalus of Parma.[45] In 1070, Anno visited Rome again; this time he was there with Archbishop Siegfried of Mainz and Bishop Hermann of Bamberg. They discussed many topics of individual and common interest, including Henry IV's power over the church and his episcopal appointments, and Siegfried's wish to resign his see and return to the monastic life by entering Cluny; his attraction to the religious life favourably impressed Archdeacon Hildebrand.[46]

The bishops' journeys to Rome were a warning to Henry IV that the papacy regarded his policy critically, and that it could bring its favours and its sanctions to bear. In 1073, at the very end of Alexander's pontificate, there were renewed warning signs when he summoned a number of German prelates to Rome on account of their carnal sins and of their simony; but only Bishop Werner of Strassburg made a positive response.[47] German chronicles and other sources are full of the potential for both conflict and collaboration between German prelates and the apostolic see which existed in the early 1070s.[48]

Two features of the situation in 1073, however, stand out. First, as a consequence of the political and ecclesiastical events of and after Henry IV's minority, the papacy

---

[43] Berthold, *a.*1071, p. 275/15–31; Lampert of Hersfeld, *Ann. a.* 1071, pp. 148–53; *CU* nos. 36–8, pp. 68–81.

[44] Berthold, *aa.* 1069, 1071, pp. 274/14–15, 375/30–1.

[45] *Ann. Altah. maior. a.* 1068, p. 74.

[46] *Reg.* 2.29, to Archbishop Siegfried of Mainz, 4 Dec. 1074, pp. 161–2.

[47] *Reg.* 1.77, to Countesses Beatrice and Matilda of Tuscany, 15 Apr. 1074, pp. 109/21–110/7.

[48] e.g. Berthold, *a.*1070, pp. 274/40–275/4; Lampert of Hersfeld, *Ann. a.* 1070, p. 122; Frutolf of Michaelsberg, *a.*1073, p. 82; *CU* no. 36, pp. 68–9.

was being ever more widely looked to as the source of jurisdiction, counsel, and direction. As Hauck remarked, 'everywhere within the German church, the ties of order began to be relaxed.'[49] Outwardly, everything looked much as it had been under Henry III, and during the crisis of the Saxon rising ideas of kingship such as were current in Ottonian and early Salian times remained strong in the minds even of rebel prelates. But Henry IV had so far failed to embody these ideas in his public life, and his private life compounded the condemnation which came from lay and ecclesiastical quarters alike. So he was ill-placed to withstand the accession to the papal throne of so formidable a figure as Hildebrand. His position was weakened at Alexander II's Lent synod in 1073, when according to Bonizo of Sutri the pope ex-communicated a group of his counsellors who, according to Bonizo, were 'seeking to separate him from the unity of the church'—probably by encouraging him in simo-niacal practices.[50] Excommunication was infectious, and for so long as Henry per-sisted in their company he placed himself outside the communion of the church. As Gregory wrote in 1074 to the Empress Agnes about Henry's predicament at this time:

Since he was placed beyond communion, the fear of divine wrath restrained us from ap-proaching him; as for his subjects, the daily necessity of meeting him bound them to his guilt.[51]

It was in such circumstances that, in Germany, Henry was confronted by the Saxon rising in 1073.

3.2 1073–5

3.2.1 The Saxon War

When Pope Alexander II died, Henry IV was preparing a campaign against the Poles; but, from July 1073, events in Germany itself demanded his full time and concern.[52] There began at Hoetensleben the Saxon rising that would for the next two years determine his fortunes and attitudes, compelling him to show deference to Gregory. The rising originated in a sworn association of various grades of the East Saxon aristocracy and free peasantry, and it involved both clergy and laity. Their common motive was fear in face of Henry's accumulation of material power in their neigh-bourhood and of the threat which they felt it to present to their liberty. Henry had foreseen no such eventuality as the rising. He was quickly forced to flee with the royal insignia from Goslar to the Harzburg, and thence for three days through dense forests to Eschwege and to the security of Hersfeld, in Hesse. The rising was a chal-lenge to his authority such as no medieval ruler could leave unanswered. He hoped to be reinforced by the army that he had summoned against the Poles. During the winter of 1073–4 he derived moral and material support from the citizens of Worms,

---

[49] *Kirchengeschichte Deutschlands*, 3.733.   [50] *Lib. ad amic.* 6, p. 600.

[51] *Reg.* 1.85, 15 June 1074, p. 121/28–31.

[52] The principal sources for the Saxon rising are Lampert of Hersfeld, *Ann.*, Bruno, and *Ann. Altah. maior.* which are hostile to Henry IV, and the *Carmen de bello Saxonico*, which is favourable. Meyer von Knonau provides the fullest narrative account; amongst discussions, see esp. Fenske, *Adelsopposition.*

whose fidelity he rewarded by a generous privilege.[53] It was to his advantage that the South German dukes, Rudolf of Swabia, Welf of Bavaria, and Berthold of Carinthia, whose loyalties would be critical during the Saxon war, were reluctant to countenance the violent measures adopted by the Saxons. Indeed, relations between the king and Rudolf of Swabia, in particular, had become surprisingly close after a meeting of the court at Worms in July 1072 at which Henry reached a compromise with the princes about ecclesiastical reform.[54] The dukes' restraint enabled Henry to return to Saxony in the autumn of 1073 and again in January 1074. The military forces that he commanded were mostly his own dependants and mercenaries. Insufficient to reduce the rebels to obedience, they sufficed to enforce negotiations which the Saxon leader Otto of Nordheim, to whom Henry promised the return of the lands that he had forfeited in 1070, was prepared to support. On 2 February 1074, a peace was concluded at Gerstungen on the River Werra in which Henry conceded the Saxons' principal demands for the dismantling of his new castles. But he forfeited none of his Saxon or Thuringian lands, and the peace did nothing to bring closer to each other the Saxons and the South German dukes. More seriously for the rebel cause, a rift emerged between the Saxon aristocracy and peasants, after Henry proceeded slowly with dismantling the Harzburg and levelled only its outer walls. At the end of March, the Saxon peasants took matters into their own hands by destroying the other buildings, plundering the church, desecrating its altars and relics, and violating the graves of Henry's firstborn son and younger brother.

The sacrilege offended the aristocracy and made its members fearful for their own possessions. The Saxon leaders, therefore, dissociated themselves from it, and sympathy for the king was forthcoming in all parts of Germany. When he kept Easter (20 April) at Bamberg, his position was already much strengthened; during his Christmas court at Strassburg he began to plan a major campaign against the Saxons to which Duke Rudolf of Swabia may already have pledged his support. In 1075, he gradually recruited an army to which most of the spiritual and lay magnates of the kingdom promised to send contingents. As is illustrated by the first of the five surviving letters which emanated in 1075 from Archbishop Werner of Magdeburg's household, the fears of the Saxon magnates grew. The archbishop pleaded with Archbishop Siegfried of Mainz to elicit from the king a commitment that Saxon grievances might be settled by judgement of the German princes rather than by war.[55] But Henry was deaf to such pleadings, for he enjoyed the firm support of Dukes Rudolf of Swabia, Berthold of Carinthia, and Godfrey of Lorraine. The Saxon peasantry mustered under the leadership of Otto of Nordheim, who was supported by Duke Magnus Billung, Archbishop Werner of Magdeburg, and—most strenuously among the bishops—Bishop Burchard of Halberstadt. For his part,

---

53 *MGH DDHIV* no. 267, according to which the citizens of Worms 'in maxima regni commotione maxima et speciali fidelitate nobis adhaesisse cognovimus'.

54 Vögel, 'Rudolf von Rheinfelden'.

55 Bruno, cap. 42, pp. 246–52; for comment on the early Saxon letters, see Kost, *Das östliche Niedersachsen*, pp. 21–93.

Henry assembled his army for a campaign which, on 9 June, led to his bloody but total victory at Homburg-on-the-Unstrut, which was followed by the humiliating surrender of the Saxon magnates. Duke Rudolf of Swabia played a leading part in the victory. Because of the king's uncompromising demands, renewed negotiations proved unfruitful. In the autumn, he prepared a new expedition, this time, significantly, without Dukes Rudolf of Swabia, Welf of Bavaria, and Berthold of Carinthia; they looked askance at Henry's intransigence and were concerned about the dangers, if he were successful, of revived royal power. Duke Godfrey of Lorraine emerged ever more strongly as Henry's most reliable ducal supporter. By the end of October, Henry's show of force was sufficient to bring the Saxon leaders to an unconditional surrender at Spier, south of Sonderhausen. Henry delivered them into the custody of princes loyal to himself, thus dispersing them not only throughout Germany but also in Italy and Burgundy. He rapidly undertook the rebuilding of his dismantled castles. By Christmas 1075, Saxon resistance was broken. Four letters from the archbishop of Magdeburg's household, dating from mid-June to December, illustrate the straits to which the Saxons were brought, but also their leaders' continuing pleas that the king, whose divine commission to rule they acknowledged,[56] would grant them a fair trial before the princes of the kingdom.[57]

Henry underlined his victory by keeping Christmas at Goslar. He secured from the assembled princes a promise that, in the event of his death, they would elect his son Conrad, who had been born in the troubled month of February 1074, in his stead. Those present may have recalled that, twenty-two years ago, the Emperor Henry III had caused Henry himself, while still an infant, to be acknowledged as the successor to the crown. Otto of Nordheim, who had urged moderation upon the Saxons before they ventured upon the disastrous campaign of the previous summer, was freed and the fiefs of which he had been stripped in 1070 were restored. He was given viceregal powers over the Saxons. Henry made other acts of clemency, as when he released from captivity so redoubtable an opponent as Bishop Burchard of Halberstadt, whom he had put into the charge of Bishop Rupert of Bamberg but received at court during the winter of 1075–6.[58] Henry evidently intended that Saxony should be transformed from a duchy into a region directly administered by the crown in which his old enemies would demonstrate their subjection by becoming obedient servants. The monarchy, made hereditary, was to be restored to the position in which Henry III had left it. Or such was Henry's hope; the continuing distance of the South German dukes made its fulfilment problematical.

3.2.2. 1073: The Quest for Concord between *Sacerdotium* and *Regnum*

When Gregory became pope, the prospects as he saw them for amending the life of the German church and kingdom were more favourable than might be expected in

---

[56] 'recordetur se coelestis regis vicem simul et nomine habere'.
[57] Bruno, caps. 48–9, 51, 59, pp. 256–64, 272–5.
[58] For this act of clemency, Henry received, if Erdmann's interpretation of the letter is correct, an expression of thanks from Bishop Hezilo of Hildesheim: *H* no. 32, p. 69; cf. Erdmann, *Briefliteratur*, pp. 145–9.

view of the condition into which it had fallen. The letter of congratulation which he received from Abbot Walo of Metz urged him to be zealous in promoting the moral reform of the church, and declared that all eyes looked to him to continue the work that he had begun as archdeacon:

But I would be foolish if I presumed to admonish you and to urge you on in your course, when with admirable zeal you are endeavouring things greater than our weakness can imagine. Like an eagle you soar above all lower things and seek to gaze upon the brightness of the sun itself.[59]

In fact, few of the German bishops and abbots similarly congratulated Gregory upon his accession, nor did they show themselves anxious to promote his objectives. Their thoughts had been turning to an initiative of their own. At a meeting in Worms during July 1072, at which the Empress Agnes and Abbot Hugh of Cluny, Henry's mother and godfather, had been present, leading German princes, including Duke Rudolf of Swabia, had come to an understanding with Henry about the promotion of ecclesiastical reform.[60] In view of this situation, in 1073 and 1074 Gregory wrote few letters to German bishops upon such matters as the extirpation of simony and clerical fornication. The main exception is a letter to his future supporter, Archbishop Gebhard of Salzburg, in which he reproved the archbishop's negligence in fulfilling the precepts of an earlier Roman synod, apparently Alexander II's synod of 1063, regarding clerical chastity, which he was urged to promote in his diocese by punishing transgressors and by diligent preaching.[61] If Gregory passed stringent legislation of his own at his Lent synod of 1074,[62] his Register includes no letters commending it to German clergy or laity. Gregory's endeavours in Germany at this time were differently directed. He looked to the Empress Agnes and to a well defined group of German and Italian bishops and princes to collaborate in securing the obedience of the king and the concord of *sacerdotium* and *regnum*. The model of the Emperor Henry III was in the forefront of his mind.

Within this framework, between Gregory's election in April 1073 and the crisis of July that began the Saxon rising in Germany, his relations with Henry already showed marked improvement. Henry's association with the counsellors whom Alexander II had excommunicated at his Lent synod of 1073 had infected him with a like condemnation;[63] Gregory did not, therefore, send Henry an official notice of his election to the papacy.[64] But during the spring and early summer, a number of figures emerged as potential mediators between pope and king. In Germany, where the southern dukes were disturbed by the onset of the Saxon rising, Dukes Rudolf of Swabia and Berthold of Carinthia were reconciled to Henry during March.[65] Henry

---

[59] *Die Briefe des Abtes Walo*, no. 1, p. 54/9–12. It must, however, be remembered that Walo sought Gregory's help in his own predicament at Rheims: see below, 5.3.3.1.

[60] Vögel, 'Rudolf von Rheinfelden'. [61] *Reg.* 1.30, pp. 50–1.

[62] Marianus Scottus, *Chron. a.* 1096 (1074), p. 560.

[63] *Reg.* 1.21, p. 35/4–9; 1.85, p. 121/24–31; 4.2, p. 293/34–7.

[64] Despite Bonizo, *Lib. ad amic.* 7, p. 601/20–2, the lack of confirmation in Gregory's letters makes it unlikely. See Borino, 'Perché Gregorio VII non annunziò'.

[65] *Ann. Altah. maior. a.* 1073, pp. 84–5; Lampert of Hersfeld, *Ann. a.* 1073, p. 172.

seems to have paid little attention to German bishops at his court who were ill-disposed to Gregory's election, nor did he countenance Italian bishops like Gregory of Vercelli who campaigned actively against the new pope.[66] That he may himself have shown preparedness to exhibit repentance and to do penance for the past transgressions for which his German subjects had blamed him is suggested by the description of him as 'humillimus', as well as 'illustrissimus', in a series of diplomas which began with three dated at his Pentecost court of 1073.[67] It would be rash to assume that this signalling of penitence was directed towards, or even known to, Gregory VII;[68] Henry had an eye to German princes who had been shocked by his youthful sins and simoniacal appointments, and who had sought to initiate better things at the Worms assembly of July 1072. They included some to whom Gregory looked as mediators with the king. Moreover, in the spring of 1073, a number of significant figures gathered about Gregory in Rome. Thus, the Empress Agnes and probably Bishop Raynald of Como and Countess Beatrice of Tuscany were there at or about the time of Gregory's episcopal ordination on 30 June; Dukes Godfrey of Lorraine and Welf of Bavaria may have been present as well.[69]

Six of Gregory's letters, written between May and September 1073, show how actively he thereafter sought the mediation of such German and Italian figures; three of these letters refer to earlier letters addressed to Gregory but now lost which indicate that, from the earliest days of Gregory's pontificate, lay figures like Dukes Rudolf of Swabia and Godfrey of Lorraine and bishops like Raynald of Como and Bruno of Verona were involved in discussions of Gregory's relations with Henry.[70] The six letters also shed light on Gregory's intentions. These were to promote what he called the concordant unity of *sacerdotium* and *regnum*, and to use his correspondents in order to promote it. As he wrote to Rudolf of Swabia:

Amongst your other gratifying words, what you have written manifestly upholds the principle by which the right order of the empire is indeed illustriously maintained and the strength

---

[66] Lampert of Hersfeld, loc. cit.; *Die Briefe des Abtes Walo*, no. 1, p. 53/6–16.

[67] *MGH DDHIV* nos. 258–60, 264–5, 267; see Vögel, 'Rudolf von Rheinfelden', pp. 17–19.

[68] Thus, *MGH DDHIV* no. 265, of 27 Oct. 1073, contains the *humillimus* formula but numbers among the king's *fideles* not only Archbishop Liemar of Bremen and Bishops Eppo of Zeitz and Benno of Osnabrück but also Count Eberhard, one of Henry's excommunicated counsellors, 'cuius consilium eo in tempore multum in nostra viguit curia'; this can scarcely have been intended for Gregory's eyes or knowledge.

[69] Agnes and Beatrice: Bonizo of Sutri, *Lib. ad amic.* 7, p. 601/24–5. Raynald of Como's recent journey to Montecassino with Agnes, and therefore his being in her company, is noticed in *Reg.* 1.1, p. 4/9–12. The reference in *Reg.* 9.3, p. 574/18–21, to Agnes, Raynald, and Welf of Bavaria as having been in Rome together may most plausibly be dated to 1073; Welf was at Este on 21 June: Mittarelli and Costadoni, 2, Appendix, no. 143, col. 246. The reference in *Reg.* 1.72, p. 104/5–7, to Gregory's meeting Godfrey of Lorraine at Rome may also refer to this period.

[70] The six letters are: (i) *Reg.* 1.9, to Duke Godfrey of Lorraine, 6 May 1073, pp. 13–15; (ii) 1.11, to Countesses Beatrice and Matilda of Tuscany, 24 June 1073, pp. 17–19; (iii) 1.19, to Duke Rudolf of Swabia, 1 Sept. 1073, pp. 31–2; (iv) 1.20, to Bishop Raynald of Como, 1 Sept. 1073, pp. 32–4; (v) 1.21, to Bishop Anselm II of Lucca, 1 Sept. 1073, pp. 34–5; (vi) 1.24, to Bishop Bruno of Verona (a former *magister scholarum* at Hildesheim), 24 Sept. 1073, pp. 40–1. The first, third, and fourth of these letters allude to earlier, lost correspondence, which underlines the intensity of Gregory's negotiations with this circle of advisers.

of holy church is secured: namely, that the priestly and imperial powers should be bound together in a unity based upon concord. For just as a man's body is governed by the earthly light of two eyes, so we well know that the body of the church is governed and illuminated by heavenly light when these two dignities maintain concord in true religion.

Gregory claimed strong personal reasons for seeking concord with Henry: first, the goodwill of the Roman church during Henry III's last years in securing his son's succession led Gregory to recall his own part in the infant king's election;[71] second, when Gregory had been in Germany, the old emperor had treated him with honour; and third, upon his deathbed Henry III had commended his son to the Roman church in the presence of Pope Victor II. Gregory well remembered that Henry IV was the son of Henry III, 'laudandae memoriae imperatoris'.

Therefore Gregory looked to the younger Henry to acknowledge his inherited responsibilities by striving to maintain the honour that he owed to God, by discarding childish fantasies, and by following the pattern of holy kings.[72] Gregory made clear to his correspondents how disturbed he was by Henry's evil conduct. Henry must be recalled to a love of the holy Roman church from which he had fallen away. More specifically, he must renew a lost peace with Gregory by making satisfaction to God for his association with evil counsellors. Gregory desired his salvation with unfeigned love; but, if he repaid love with hatred, Gregory must not shrink from due punishment, bearing in mind the prophetic word: 'Cursed is the man who withholds his sword from blood' (Jer. 48: 10). Henry must also show positive amendment of life. He must promote the welfare of the church, especially by increasing and protecting its goods, and he must uphold the dignity of kingship. Until Henry made satisfaction for associating with his excommunicated counsellors, Bishop Anselm of Lucca must not be invested with his bishopric by his hand. He must answer the demands of righteousness by duly attending to papal admonitions and advice. In his immediate circle, he must choose good counsellors and shun evil ones. By so doing, he would not only fulfil the kingly office that he already held, but he would show that he was fitted to come to Rome and receive the imperial dignity.

Gregory sought himself to do everything possible to bring Henry to a better mind. In May 1073, he intended promptly to dispatch envoys for this purpose. By September, he wished to take counsel at Rome with his most trusted collaborators—the Empress Agnes and the recipients of his letters. He hoped to bring Italy to a state of peace so that the way might be open for Henry to come to Rome. Thus, the path of concord as Gregory understood it might be pursued: he would propound his own demands, but he would also hear the counsels of others and accommodate them when possible. He would thereby promote the king's earthly prosperity and eternal glory. If he failed, he must himself be ready even for martyrdom; but he trusted for success in discharging the debt of charity that he owed all men. He was in good heart, for, as

---

[71] See Berges, 'Gregor VII. und das deutsche Designationsrecht', pp. 196–8.
[72] Gregory probably had in mind both Old Testament models like David and recent ones like the Emperor Henry III.

he told Bishop Raynald of Como, he had received tidings that Henry was beginning to heed the advice of good men.[73]

So it seemed to be. Within days of the dispatch of the last of the six letters, Gregory was overjoyed to receive from Henry a letter which, as he told the Patarene leader Erlembald of Milan, was full of pleasantness and obedience; he could recall no letter like it from a German king to himself or any of his predecessors. So impressed was he that, most exceptionally for an incoming letter, it was copied into his Register.[74] Henry's salutation tacitly acknowledged that Gregory, 'invested from heaven with the papal office', was pope not only by the fact but also by the manner of the election; for his part, he promised 'the most faithful performance of his due service'. He styled himself *rex Romanorum*, thus referring to his claim to the imperial dignity. Throughout his letter, he took up points made by Gregory in his six letters to prospective collaborators in reconciliation, and especially to Duke Rudolf of Swabia. The parallels are so strong that there can be little doubt that, in dire straits after the initial successes of the Saxon rising and in line with the *humillimus* formula of his recent diplomas, Henry claimed to seek peace in Germany and showed himself open to mediation by the princes and bishops whom Gregory trusted.

Henry expressed his acceptance of the doctrine of royal and papal authority that Gregory had propounded to Rudolf of Swabia who, as a close royal adviser, may have prompted Henry's submissive letter. *Regnum* and *sacerdotium* needed each other's help, and they should cleave indissolubly to each other: 'Thereby and not otherwise', Henry observed, 'can the concord (*concordia*) of Christian unity and the ordinances of true and unfeigned religion alike be preserved in the bond of perfect charity and peace.' Henry's possession of the *regnum* was a commitment to service ('ministerium') which was entered upon by divine permission. He acknowledged that he had not always given the priestly authority ('sacerdotium') the rights and honour that were its due, nor had he unsheathed the sword of justice that was entrusted to him against the guilty so readily as he should.[75] Borrowing the imagery of the prodigal son who, when he came to himself, returned both to God and to the father whom he had offended for absolution and restoration to grace (Luke 15: 17–24), Henry acknowledged that he had, indeed, sinned as Gregory indicated in his letters—from youthful impulses, from his headstrong lust for power, and by heeding evil counsellors. He accused himself of seizing church goods and, especially, of simoniacal dealings. He begged Gregory to guide him in setting matters right: 'But now, since we cannot restore the churches alone and without your authority, we earnestly entreat your counsel and advice upon these and all our other affairs; what you command in everything shall be observed!' He promised to send Gregory another letter by

---

[73] In an oath sworn to Gregory on 14 Sept., Prince Richard of Capua undertook also to swear fealty to Henry 'cum a te admonitus fuero vel a tuis successoribus': *Reg.* 1.21*a*, p. 36/16–17; this phrase also implies Gregory's expectation that Henry would be restored to communion.

[74] *Reg.* 1.29*a*, pp. 47–9 = *Epp. HIV* no. 5; *Reg.* 1.25, pp. 41–2.

[75] Henry avoided the possible implications of Gregory's phrase 'laicorum caput' which Gregory used only in his letter to Bishop Raynald of Como (*Reg.* p. 33/33–4) and which may not have come to Henry's notice.

faithful messengers; in 1076, Gregory was to recall that a second letter, now lost, did, indeed, follow. It was 'suppliant and full of all humility'; in it, Henry reinforced his promises of penitence and amendment.[76]

In the autumn of 1073, Gregory's letters to Erlembald of Milan show that the first of Henry's suppliant letters convinced him that the way was open for him to resolve the major problems of Italy and Germany.[77] He was the more confident because, as he said, Countesses Beatrice and Matilda of Tuscany, with others of Henry's greatest princes (Gregory probably had Duke Godfrey of Lorraine, Matilda's husband, particularly in mind) were seeking to establish unanimity between pope and king ('nostrum atque regis animum firmiter unire'). He was confident that Henry would fall in with his requirements about ecclesiastical issues. Even Henry's hitherto recalcitrant Italian chancellor Bishop Gregory of Vercelli had, or so Gregory believed, promised obedience to his wishes.

And so when, with both Henry's letters to hand, Gregory wrote on 20 December 1073 to the Saxon rebels, addressing his letter to Archbishop Werner of Magdeburg, Bishop Burchard of Halberstadt, Margrave Dedi of the East Saxon march, and the other princes of Saxony,[78] his purpose was to promote the Saxons' obedience to Henry and Henry's obedience to himself. He referred with emphasis to Henry as the Saxons' lord, and he deplored the discord ('discordia') and enmity between them with its consequences in homicides, arson, the plundering of the poor, and the devastation of the country. He payed little heed to the Saxons' grievances against the king. His immediate objective was an armistice; he had, he wrote, exhorted the king to suspend hostilities until he could himself send legates to investigate the causes of the conflict and pass a just judgement which would restore peace and concord. The Saxons were to respect a suspension of arms and were to set no obstacle to papal peacemaking. In the meanwhile, Gregory adopted a position of careful neutrality. The issue lay in the hands of God, and Gregory would give his favour to whichever party—the king or the Saxons—should be shown to be the victim of unrighteous violence. Although the exact phrase does not occur in it, the letter was, in effect, the first application of a criterion that would govern Gregory's later dealings with Henry and the German opposition in the three-cornered contest that rent Germany: 'cui parti magis iustitia favet'. He also laid down that the apostolic see should be acknowledged to be the final judge and arbiter. Gregory was committed to bringing peace and concord to the land; for, in his eyes, such was the requirement laid upon him by his papal office.

3.2.3. 1074: A Vision of Success

During the year 1074, Gregory sedulously maintained the collaboration with Countesses Beatrice and Matilda upon which he counted for his dealings with Henry

---

[76] *Epp. vag.* no. 14, pp. 36–7. Henry's second letter probably followed his Würzburg court in late Oct. and reached Gregory in mid-Dec. upon his return to Rome from South Italy.
[77] *Reg.* 1.25–6, pp. 41–4.   [78] *Reg.* 1.39, pp. 61–2.

IV as he adumbrated them in 1073. He began the year by exhorting Matilda to per-severance, and he said that he hoped for a visit to Rome by both ladies.[79] But there were problems. Matilda's marriage to Duke Godfrey of Lorraine had failed from the start, and the widening breach between them was disturbing for political no less than for personal reasons. Gregory wrote to dissuade her from taking the veil as a nun.[80] A note of reproof entered his letters. Matilda and her mother had not been as mild and helpful as they should in dealing with Bishop Werner of Strassburg, the one German bishop who had been penitent after Pope Alexander II's strictures; yet they had murmured against Gregory's apparent lenience towards Lombard bishops.[81] Gregory wrote more coolly still to Duke Godfrey, expressing disappointment that he had not kept his promise to help with the expedition to the East that Gregory planned.[82] But the countesses also did things that pleased and reassured him. When Abbot Thierry of Saint-Hubert-en-Ardenne, who was at odds with the duke, came to Italy in the summer with Bishop Hermann of Metz, the countesses showed him honour, and Matilda gave him a letter of commendation to Gregory.[83] By October, Gregory was once more placing his confidence strongly in the countesses; he told them that he discounted all rumours about them, and trusted them as he trusted no other princes.[84]

Gregory's letters of 1074 suggest that, in proper subordination to the Empress Agnes, the countesses had their place in an imperial structure with which, with Henry IV restored to grace and obedience, he aspired to complement his own papal authority. In March, he described the countesses as 'principes Romani imperii'.[85] In June, he greeted Agnes—'christianissima imperatrix'—as someone who had toiled strongly for the peace and concord of the universal church, and who had unweary-ingly pursued all that could bind papacy and empire in charity. Beatrice and Matilda had been her indefatigable aides, 'following you as disciples and faithfully imitating you as their lady and mistress'. The empress and they had renewed the church of the first Easter:

Therefore through you, we see a new example of an ancient gladness. Through you, I say, there often returns to our memory those women who of old sought the Lord in the tomb (cf. Mark 16: 5). For just as they came to the Lord's tomb with a marvellous zeal and charity before all his disciples, so you in devout love have visited the church of Christ, placed as it is in the sepulchre of affliction, before many—no! before all, of the princes of the earth. So that the church might

---

[79] *Reg.* 1.40, pp. 62–3; Gregory referred to another, lost letter that he had sent on 29 Dec. 1073 and to two letters from her. Gregory's greeting to Matilda as 'egregiae indolis puellae' echoes the biblical refer-ence to Zadok, not the priest but a military leader, as 'puer egregiae indolis' amongst King David's warriors (1 Chron. 12: 28).

[80] *Reg.* 1.47, 16 Jan. 1074, pp. 71–3; cf. 1.50, 4 Mar. 1074, pp. 76–7.

[81] *Reg.* 1.77, 15 Apr. 1074, pp. 109–11.

[82] *Reg.* 1.72, 7 Apr. 1074, pp. 103–4. For the planned expedition, see below, 7.1 and Cowdrey, 'Pope Gregory VII's "Crusading" Plans', pp. 29–31.

[83] *Chron. s. Hub. Andag.* cap. 25, pp. 583–4; *Vita Theod. abb. Andag.* cap. 25, pp. 51–2; *QF* no. 79, pp. 62–4.

[84] *Reg.* 2.9, 16 Oct. 1074, pp. 138–40; cf. *Epp. vag.* no. 5, pp. 10–13.   [85] *Reg.* 1.50, p. 76/23–7.

rise again to its proper state of liberty, you have striven with all your might, as if instructed by angelic responses, to urge others to the aid of a toiling church. Thus you can undoubtingly await the revelation of heavenly glory and eternal life which is in Christ Jesus (cf. 1 Pet. 4: 13). In the company of these godly women, you will by Christ's grace find our Saviour's presence and enjoy everlasting peace amongst the ranks of the angels.[86]

The immediate reason for the joy that Gregory thus expressed was that, partly through the Empress Agnes's mediation, Henry IV had been fully restored to the communion of the church; Gregory's longed-for concord of papacy and empire seemed to have been brought much closer. In December 1073, Gregory had hinted to the Saxon leaders that he might send legates to Germany;[87] in 1074, he did so by sending two cardinal-bishops, Gerald of Ostia and Hubert of Palestrina. At the same time, perhaps upon her own initiative rather than at Gregory's prompting, the Empress Agnes journeyed to Germany in the company of Bishops Raynald of Como and Henry of Chur.

Henry had kept Easter at Bamberg. Immediately afterwards, he travelled south to Nuremberg, where he met both Gregory's legates and his mother and a council took place on Low Sunday.[88] Gregory had planned a reforming council,[89] and the legates had a twofold purpose: to restore Henry to communion and thus to establish harmony between him and the Roman church, and to secure the obedience of the German bishops to the aims and methods of Gregory's ecclesiastical reforms. With the bishops, the legates had little success;[90] but, thanks largely to Agnes's journey and maternal mediation, Henry did penance to the legates who restored him to communion.[91] Henry seems to have accepted the requirement of the legates and of his own supporters that he would permit the return to their sees of certain refugee bishops; they probably included Adalbert of Worms and possibly Anno of Cologne and Atto of Milan. However, he reserved the right himself to hear their cases at a date that he would appoint.[92] This reservation was shrewd and to his advantage, for it signalled to the German bishops that he regarded them as being subject to his own, and not only to papal jurisdiction. To Gregory, he sent, along with lavish gifts, a written promise of obedience and amendment of life. He seems also to have hoped that his

---

[86] *Reg.* 1.85, 15 June 1074, pp. 121–3.   [87] *Reg.* 1.39, p. 62/13–18; see above, 3.2.2.

[88] For relations between Gregory and Henry in 1074–5, Erdmann's discussion in *Briefliteratur*, esp. pp. 225–81, remains fundamental. The sources for events at Bamberg and Nuremberg are partly the chronicles, esp. Berthold, *a.*1074, pp. 276–71; Lampert of Hersfeld, *Ann. a.* 1074, pp. 234, 250; Marianus Scottus, *a.*1096 (1074), p. 561; Bonizo of Sutri, *Lib. ad amic.* 7, pp. 601–2. Much may also be gathered from letters, esp. *Reg.* 1.85, pp. 121–2, 2.30, p. 163; *Epp. vag.* no. 14, p. 36; *Epp. HIV* no. 15, pp. 72–5 (for the dates, see Erdmann, 'Tribur und Rom', pp. 116–117); *H* no. 15, pp. 33–5; *M* nos. 40–1, pp. 240–6.

[89] For Gregory's retrospective reference to his intention to hold a German council, see *Reg.* 2.28, to Archbishop Liemar of Bremen, 12 Dec. 1074, p. 161/6–12.

[90] See below, 3.2.5.

[91] It is clear from *Epp. HIV* no. 15, that Agnes did not attend the Nuremberg assembly since Henry wrote to inform her about it. His greeting to her, 'Matri benedictionis et salutis', indicates that he thought her ultimately responsible for his readmission to communion. For her journey to Germany, see also *Vita Anselmi ep. Lucensis*, cap. 14, p. 17; Donizo, 1. 1230–6, p. 376.

[92] *Epp. HIV*, no. 15.

mother's solicitude would now help him towards the imperial coronation that he had for so long desired.[93] As for Henry's excommunicated counsellors, they promised the legates that they would make amends for their wrongful doings.

Henry's conduct at Nuremberg convinced Gregory of his penitence and amenability. Gregory had even in April shown signs of doubting whether simony could ever be eliminated from episcopal elections in Germany.[94] But he must have heartened when, at Eastertide, he consecrated at Rome the canonically elected Abbot Ekkehard of Reichenau.[95] Faced with the recalcitrance of the German bishops, Henry seemed to Gregory to be the principal means whereby they might be brought to obedience.

As for the Saxons, Gregory seems to have given their interests only a modicum of consideration. The sacrilegious destruction of the Harzburg contributed to their isolation.[96] In any case, by comparison with the prize of securing Henry's obedience, during 1074 the Saxon cause had little place in Gregory's concerns. A brief letter that he sent in October to Bishop Burchard of Halberstadt makes this plain.[97] Burchard had evidently sought Gregory's favour by deploring the lack of honour that his car-dinal-legates found in Germany, both at Nuremberg and upon their subsequent travels.[98] But, for Gregory, it was the bishops, not the king, who had failed in their re-sponse. In his letter to Bishop Burchard, he ascribed what had gone wrong to 'the princes and rich men of your country', not to the king. Without referring to political events, Gregory hoped that the flame of unanimity with himself would continually increase in Burchard's heart.

Towards Henry, Gregory's goodwill as established by the king's reconciliation to communion at Nuremberg waxed strongly during the rest of 1074. In December, it found expresson in two remarkable letters which Gregory, with the Empress Agnes at his elbow, wrote to Henry.[99] They were studded with such phrases as 'fili karis-sime', 'fili excellentissime', and 'gloriosus rex'. Gregory alluded to Henry's submis-sive letters,[100] with a reminder that the affairs of the church of Milan remained to be settled. But he also recalled how well disposed and amenable Henry had shown him-self to his legates at Nuremberg. Both his mother and they had testified to his zeal to extirpate simony and clerical fornication from his kingdom; at this, Gregory rejoiced exceedingly. Countesses Beatrice and Matilda also testified to Henry's friendship and unfeigned love. Gregory remembered Henry whenever he said mass at the apostles' tombs, and he exhorted him to seek good counsellors. As matters were

---

93 Such is the probable interpretation of the *res nostra* which Henry hoped would receive a *diu expecta-tum eventum: Epp. HIV* no. 15, p. 74/7–8, rather than Erdmann's reference to further action against the Saxons: *Briefliteratur*, p. 241.

94 *Reg.* 1.77, p. 110/5–7.

95 *Reg.* 1.82, 6 May 1074, pp. 116–118; Berthold, *a.*1073, p. 276/40–2.

96 For Henry's propaganda exploitation of the sacrilege, see Lampert of Hersfeld, *Ann. a.* 1074, p. 234/25–8; Bruno, cap. 35, pp. 238–41.

97 *Reg.* 2.12, 26 Oct. 1074, pp. 143–4.

98 The legates were back at Rome by Dec. 1074.

99 *Reg.* 2.30–1, pp. 163–8.   100 *Reg.* 1.29*a* and its lost sequel.

shaping, Gregory's vision for the collaboration of *sacerdotium* and *regnum* seemed to be assuming reality before his eyes; the right order of the world was taking shape. And so he could bring Henry into his most cherished plans for West and East alike. In his first letter, he desired him to add the sanction of royal authority in securing the obedience of Archbishop Siegfried of Mainz and his suffragans, and to send messengers who would testify to Gregory about their way of life. In his second letter, he told Henry of his renewed plans for an Eastern expedition, which he would himself lead, to relieve the Byzantine empire. He sought Henry's counsel and aid, for in the event of his departure he wished Henry to come to Rome and remain there as protector of the Roman church.[101] This bizarre wish shows that, in December 1074, Henry could scarcely have stood higher in Gregory's goodwill, trust, and favour. His vision of *concordia* between pope and German king seemed capable of realization.

3.2.4 1075: The Continuance of Hope

During the winter of 1074–5, neither Gregory nor Henry remained inactive. Henry's fortunes are relatively straightforward to follow. With the Saxon problem unresolved, he could not afford to distance himself from the ecclesiastical any more than from the lay princes of Germany; at his Christmas court in Strassburg, he began to recruit support for a military campaign that partly depended upon episcopal goodwill.[102] The German bishops were resentful of Gregory's high-handed proceedings against some of their number.[103] An ominously large group of them was at the Christmas court; with the benefit of hindsight, their attendance and their demeanour foreshadowed the meeting at Worms only thirteen months later, when almost all the German bishops withdrew their obedience from the pope. Henry was prudent in demonstrating his support for the bishops in face of Gregory's pressure.[104]

Gregory's policies and dealings are more difficult to follow, partly beause of the meagre and intractable state of the evidence but partly because he was himself exploring the prerogatives of the apostolic see and testing out the manner of their application. The so-called *Dictatus papae*, inserted into Gregory's Register between letters dated 3 and 5 March,[105] was probably in no sense made public, but its twenty-seven terse theses show some of the directions in which he was exploring the principles of papal authority.

His Lent synod at Rome, held from 24 to 28 February 1075, was of the utmost importance for his attitude to Henry and the German church. Unfortunately the record of it in his Register is essentially limited to a list of sentences passed against particular persons, although it was stated that other decrees were passed.[106] But

---

[101] For Gregory's Eastern expedition, see below, 7.1. Gregory planned to take Agnes and Matilda with him but to leave Beatrice to attend to his interests at home: *Epp. vag.* no. 5, pp. 10–13. His current sense of debt to the German royal family found further expression in his letter of 10 Jan. 1075 to Agnes's daughter, Queen Judith of Hungary: *Reg.* 2.44, pp. 180–2.

[102] Lampert of Hersfeld, *Ann. a.* 1074, p. 262; Berthold, *a.*1075, p. 277/17–22.

[103] See below, 3.2.5.

[104] See, e.g. *H* no. 17, p. 40/21–9.

[105] *Reg.* 2.55*a*, pp. 201–8; see below, 8.1.2.

[106] *Reg.* 2.52*a*, pp. 196–7.

three, interrelated matters require examination: the problem of Henry's counsellors, Gregory's measures against simony and other abuses, and whether, and if so in what terms, Gregory made a decree on the subject of lay investiture.

So far as Henry's counsellors are concerned, at his Lent synod of 1075 and for most of the year, Gregory showed restraint. At Nuremberg, his legates had merely received from them a promise of amendment, although in the letter of 1076 which he sent to the Germans to set out his reasons for excommunicating Henry he expressed himself a little more strongly, stating that he had summoned them to do penance and to make satisfaction for their simoniacal dealings.[107] At the Lent synod of 1075, their case seems to have been given priority: certain of Henry's counsellors whose crime had been that of advising simoniacal dealings were first among those whose sentences were recorded. Though not identified by name, their number was given as five; they were to be excluded from the church upon the condition that, if they failed to come to Rome by 1 June and make satisfaction, they would be deemed excommunicate.[108] The five were evidently those whom Alexander II had excommunicated in 1073. In his letter to the Germans of 1076, Gregory related that they had been obdurate in their wickedness, so that their sentence had stood and he had already warned the king to expel them from his household.[109]

It is not easy to determine how well informed Gregory was, or supposed that he was, about Henry's relationship with his excommunicated counsellors; moreover, Gregory seems to have regarded them as in a sense surrogates for Henry himself. In December 1074, he seems to have been confident that Henry had dismissed them; at least, he urged Henry to associate with himself in promoting ecclesiastical reform such counsellors as would guide him in righteous ways.[110] In his last extant letter to Henry before their breach in January and February 1076, which is to be dated 8 December 1075, the first subject that Gregory raised was Henry's evil counsellors. Gregory claimed not to be sure about Henry's current relationship with them. He therefore opened with a papal blessing that was conditional upon his showing proper obedience to the apostolic see. He showed that his doubts about Henry's conduct arose from unconfirmed reports that the king had knowingly associated with persons excommunicated by papal judgement and synodal decrees—that is, most recently at the Lent synod of 1075.[111] Only when he wrote his self-justifying letter to the Germans in 1076 did he retrospectively declare that, after his victory over the Saxons at the River Unstrut, Henry had broken his promise by taking his excommunicate counsellors back into his household and that he had returned to his evil actions in the church. By letters and by messengers Gregory had warned Henry that, amongst other things, he must put away his evil counsellors or himself face a judgement of excommunication. When summarizing his reasons for excommunicating Henry in February 1076, Gregory put first the king's unpreparedness to keep himself from the society of men who had been excommunicated for the sacrilege and crime of

---

[107] *Epp. vag.* no. 14, p. 34/27–34.
[109] *Epp. vag.* no. 14, pp. 34/34–35/5.
[111] *Reg.* 3.10, pp. 263/23–264/9.

[108] *Reg.* 2.52a, p. 196/16–20.
[110] *Reg.* 2.30, 7 Dec. 1074, p. 164/8–12.

simony.[112] There can be no doubt of Gregory's depth of feeling about the matter of Henry's counsellors, or of the importance of their case at the Lent synod of 1075 and, a year later, in bringing about Gregory's excommunication of the German king.

Gregory's zeal against simony as against the clerical fornication and concubinage that he associated with it had become noticeably more intense during the second half of 1074. One reason for this was that he saw in the attitudes of the German king and princes grounds for optimism that their co-operation would be forthcoming. In December, he told Henry that the testimony both of his mother and of his legates to Germany to his willingness utterly to extirpate simony from his kingdom and to make every effort to correct the deep-seated sickness of clerical fornication made him rejoice greatly.[113] A month later, Gregory wrote to the three South German dukes, trusting, as he said, in their faith and devotion, and urging them to help in enforcing the prohibition of simony and clerical fornication that he evidently intended to issue at his next Lent synod.[114]

That Gregory legislated stringently against both of these offences as well as against others is clear from his letters and from chronicle sources.[115] Thus, the Reichenau annalist Berthold introduced his extensive account of the synodal legislation by insisting upon the comprehensiveness of Gregory's determination to renew the ancient canons of the church:

At Rome, a synod was energetically convened during Lent to remedy by whatever means the numerous and monstrous matters of offence which were prevalent in our mother the church, and to do something towards renewing and legally enforcing the constitutions of the holy fathers which our latter-day practice had almost completely contradicted and annulled. . . . Therefore he decreed (*decrevit*) by apostolic authority, with the whole holy council affirming and agreeing, that the authentic rules of the holy fathers as rightly laid down by particular councils up to the present day should be given their proper force.[116]

In his letter of 8 December 1075 to Henry IV, Gregory looked back to the Lent synod in strikingly similar terms:

During this year, there assembled at the apostolic see a synod over which divine providence willed that we should preside; some of your own subjects were present at it. We saw that the order of the Christian religion had for long past been undermined and that the chief and

---

[112] *Epp. vag.* no. 14, pp. 36/18–38/31. Although the *commonitoriae epistolae* (p. 36/29) certainly included *Reg.* 3.10 and the reference may be only to this letter, it is possible that Gregory sent a subsequent letter or letters, now lost, so that *epistolae* should be translated in the plural; a later letter may have followed further tidings from Germany which confirmed that Henry was associating with the counsellors. In support of the hypothesis of another letter, it may be argued (i) that if *Epp. vag.* no. 14, p. 36/30–4, is a summary of *Reg.* 3.10, it is a loose one, and (ii) that 1 Pet. 5: 5 is not cited in *Reg.* 3.10.

[113] *Reg.* 2.30, 7 Dec. 1074, p. 163/23–8.

[114] *Reg.* 2.45, 11 Jan. 1075, pp. 183/18–184/25. For the development of Gregory's campaign, see below, 3.6.1.

[115] *Epp. vag.* nos. 6–11, pp. 14–27, with the Additional Note about their date on pp. 160–1. For chronicle sources, see esp. Berthold, *a.* 1075, pp. 277/23–278/5; Bernold, *Chron. a.* 1075, pp. 430/30–431/5; *Ann. Aug. a.* 1075, p. 127/50. For a discussion of Gregory's measures against simony and clerical fornication, see below, 8.7.9.

[116] Berthold, *a.*1075, p. 277/23–7, 34–6.

especial business of winning souls had for long fallen into decay and, by the prompting of the devil, had been trodden underfoot. Aroused by the peril and the manifest perdition of the Lord's flock, we had recourse to the decrees and teaching of the holy fathers, appointing nothing that was new or of our own devising; rather, we confirmed that, abandoning error, the first and only rule of church discipline and the well-tried way of the saints should be returned to and followed.[117]

Gregory's own retrospect of the synod and Berthold's account of it agree in referring to the wide range of its legislation, its religious and pastoral motive, its search for and reversion to good old law, and its rigour in renewing that law in its full force.

In his letters, Gregory wrote of the *decreta* both of himself and of earlier popes in connection with the synod, especially as it concerned the German church and the German king and kingdom.[118] He could scarcely any longer avoid taking up the law of simony, for the reissue in 1063 of the encyclical *Vigilantia universalis* required there to be a review of the current relaxation of canonical rules about simony in the light of older and better law.[119] Thus, in his letters written to German prelates after the Lent synod, he made much of his being prompted by 'the truly spoken decrees of the holy fathers' and used the phrase 'hoc Romanae ecclesiae decretum' to describe comprehensively the synodal decisions which were especially to be imposed upon the German clergy; he referred to decisions about simony and clerical fornication.[120]

More difficult to unravel are the decisions of the synod about the lay investiture of clergy with their churches, and especially the investiture of bishops by the handing over of their ring and staff; without the discovery of new evidence, it is impossible that a clear and satisfactory picture of whether, and if so, in what terms, Gregory passed an investiture decree in 1075 can emerge.[121] Nevertheless a tentative reinterpretation may be offered with due recognition of its limited and debatable evidential basis.

The firmest ground that there is comes from Gregory's own letters. In letters of 1077 and 1078, he wrote of a *decretum* about the single subject of lay investiture which was almost certainly associated with the Lent synod of 1075. In May 1077, he wrote to his legate in France, Bishop Hugh of Die, a letter which opens with the case of the bishop-elect of Cambrai, Gerard II (1076–92). Gregory wrote that Gerard had come to him in Italy and had acknowledged receiving the gift of the episcopate ('donum

---

[117] *Reg.* 3.10, (8 Dec.) 1075, pp. 265/27–266/8.

[118] The different significations of the noun *decretum* should be noticed. It usually meant a particular ruling on a single subject: see e.g. the record of the Nov. synod 1078, *Reg.* 6.5*b*, pp. 400–6. But it could also refer to a collection of such rulings like the encyclical *Vigilantia universalis*. In the *Collectio Lanfranci*, Nicholas II's version is headed *Sinodale decretum Nycholai papae*; in three MSS, Alexander's version is headed *Decretum Alexandri pape*: Schieffer, *Die Entstehung des päpstlichen Investiturverbots*, pp. 212–13.

[119] Schieffer, *Die Entstehung des päpstlichen Investiturverbots*, pp. 217–18, lines 71–88; Alexander's version incorporated Nicholas II's canon of 1060 against simony: *MGH Conc.* 1.549–51, no. 386. The circulation in Germany of Alexander's version of *Vigilantia universalis* is established by its presence in the *Codex Udalrici*: *CU* no. 24, pp. 48–50; see Schieffer, pp. 86–90.

[120] *Epp. vag.* nos. 6–7, p. 14/14, 9, p. 20/2–3. The phrase *hoc decretum* in these passages appears not to refer to a separate document but to the material that follows in the letters.

[121] For Gregory's developing view of lay investiture, see below, 8.8.

episcopatus') from Henry IV, but that he had pleaded in his own defence that he had lacked clear information about Gregory's decree ('decretum') which prohibited such an acceptance. Gregory had explained to Gerard how serious a matter it was to transgress a synodal decree ('synodale decretum') of the apostolic see.[122] Again, in March 1078, Gregory referred expressly to lay investiture in a letter to Bishop Huzmann of Speyer, who had received his pastoral staff from Henry IV so long ago as April/May 1075. Gregory feared that he had done this knowingly and rashly against a decree of the apostolic see ('contra decretum apostolicae sedis'); because Huzmann claimed to have had no certain knowledge of the decree before he was invested, Gregory now permitted him to perform the episcopal duties that had hitherto been inhibited, but when opportunity arose Huzmann must make satisfaction for his transgression before Gregory or his legates.[123]

Besides these instances, Gregory also referred to a _decretum_, apparently with relevance for the issue of investiture, to which he attached exceptional importance. In his letter of 8 December 1075 to Henry IV, he wrote of it immediately after the general comment on the legislation of his Lent synod which has already been noticed.[124] He introduced the subject of his _decretum_ by setting it in the context of a continuum of provision for the well-being of the church and of Christians which began with scripture, was perpetuated by the apostles, and had always been the basis of authentic ecclesiastical legislation:

Nor do we know that any other access to our salvation and to eternal life is open for Christ's sheep and for their pastors, except the one which we have learnt, in every page of the gospel and of other sacred writings, to have been pointed out by him who said, 'I am the door; by me if any man enters in, he shall be saved and shall find pasture' (John 10: 9), and to have been preached by the apostles, and safeguarded by the holy fathers. What some men, who set human prerogatives before those of God ('humanos divinis honoribus preponentes'), say is the insupportable burden and the immeasurable weight of this decree ('huius decreti'), but what we, rather, call in the strict sense a necessary truth and a light for recovering salvation, we had adjudged should rightly be received with devotion and put into effect, not only by you or by those in your kingdom, but by all the princes and peoples of the world who confess and worship Christ.[125]

In seeking to establish the subject of the _decretum_ to which Gregory here referred, two matters may confidently be eliminated. It was not simony in the immediate sense of trafficking in holy orders and ecclesiastical offices, for Gregory went on to make it clear that, in Henry's eyes, he had directly challenged legitimate royal prerogatives ('tuis honoribus obstaremus') and that Henry's violation of apostolic decrees ('apostolica decreta') had gone beyond simony to include the nomination of Tedald as archbishop of Milan and the irregular appointment of bishops of Fermo and Spoleto.[126] Nor can the _decretum_ have been concerned, at least primarily, with the issue of lay investiture, against which Gregory's legislative campaign developed only

---

[122] _Reg._ 4.22, 12 May 1077, pp. 330/27–311/9.   [123] _Reg._ 5.18, 19 Mar. 1078, p. 381/13–20.
[124] _Reg._ 3.10, pp. 265/27–266/8.   [125] _Reg._ 3.10, p. 266/8–20.
[126] _Reg._ 3.10, pp. 266/31–267/4, cf. p. 264/10–26. For the events concerned, see below, 3.5.1.

gradually and never assumed the universal and overwhelmingly urgent significance of which Gregory now wrote.

For a positive lead, it is necessary to return to Gregory's letter of 12 May 1077 which began with his comments on Henry IV's investiture of Gerard, bishop-elect of Cambrai. Gregory ended the letter by instructing Hugh of Die about an assembly which he was to hold in France. About its principal business, Gregory sounded the note of immediacy and urgency that he had sounded to Henry IV about the *decretum*. 'With unmistakable and resounding proclamation' ('manifesta et personanti denuntiatione'), he was to ensure the observance for the future ('deiceps') of canonical and apostolic authority in episcopal appointments by prohibiting any metropolitan or other bishop from consecrating anyone who had received the gift of the episcopate from a lay person. Moreover, no power or person whatsoever should any longer ('ulterius') involve himself in such business, on pain of incurring the anathema that 'the blessed Pope Hadrian in the eighth synod appointed and established for law-breakers of this kind and subverters of sacred authority.' Hugh of Die was to cause Hadrian's ruling ('capitulum') to be written down and read out to the whole assembly, which was to acclaim and confirm it. Gregory went on to say that he had himself placed upon record the authority of this decree ('post recensitam a nobis huius decreti auctoritatem'), after which action the particular matter of the investiture with bishoprics by lay hands had become reprehensible.[127] A comparison of Gregory's letter to Hugh of Die with that to Henry IV of 8 December 1075 leaves little doubt that the urgently important *decretum* of which he wrote to Henry was, or at least had as its core and centre, the *capitulum* that he associated with Pope Hadrian.

The reference was to canon twenty-two of the fourth council of Constantinople (869–70). This canon prohibited in general and absolute terms the intervention of any lay prince or magnate in any way whatsoever in the election or promotion of bishops; it also anathematized any lay figure who should contravene the exclusively canonical and ecclesiastical integrity of an episcopal election.[128] It would be hard to imagine a more trenchant or comprehensive statement than this canon offered of

---

[127] *Reg.* 4.22, pp. 333/18–334/8.

[128] *COD* pp. 182–3. The canon, with its anathema, may be translated as follows: 'In accordance with earlier councils, this holy and universal synod defines and decides that promotions and consecrations of bishops shall be made by the election and decision of the body (*collegii*) of bishops. It rightly enacts that no one of the lay princes or magnates shall involve himself in the election or promotion of a patriarch or met-ropolitan or any manner of bishop, lest there should arise any irregular or unseemly confusion or strife. It does this especially because it is not fitting that any of the mighty (*potestativorum*) or other laity should have any power in such matters. Rather, they should be quiet and mind their own business, until the elec-tion of a future bishop has been lawfully (*regulariter*) brought to a conclusion by the body (*collegium*) of the church. If, however, any lay person be invited by the church to assist and collaborate (*ad concertandum et cooperandum*), such a one may, so long as it be with due reverence, obey those who summon him, if he so desire; for in this way he may lawfully promote a pastor suitable for himself to the advantage (*salutem*) of his church.

'If any secular prince or magnate, or layman of another degree, should seek to act in contravention of a general (*communem*) and fitting and canonical election of the ecclesiastical order, let him be anathema, until he obeys and consents to what the church shall disclose itself to wish about the election and ordina-tion of its own bishop.'

what Gregory required, in theory and practice, in the election of bishops. The canon warrants, from Gregory's point of view, the eulogies that he expressed to Henry IV and later to Hugh of Die.

Despite its appositeness for their purposes, canon twenty-two had not hitherto figured among the authorities that eleventh-century reformers had invoked.[129] For even in their day, the standing of the fourth council of Constantinople as the eighth ecumenical council of the church was far from universally recognized. Moreover, Gregory strained history to the limit by describing its anathema, in his letter to Hugh of Die, as one that 'the blessed Pope Hadrian had in the eighth synod appointed and established'; Pope Hadrian II (867–72) was not personally present at the synod, although he sent legates to it.[130] Nevertheless, after Gregory's use of it in 1075, canon twenty-two quickly established its place in the principal canon-law collections of Gregory's partisans, who followed his version of its papal authority.[131] It found thereby at least something of the universal publicity that Gregory desired for it.

If the generality of its terms made it appropriate as a statement of what Gregory believed to be the pristine and authentic position of the church about elections, then upon the hypothesis that he reissued it at his Lent synod of 1075, it needed to be complemented by a decree or decrees directed specifically against the latter-day abuses that obscured it, such as the lay investiture of bishops before their consecration against which his own attitude was currently hardening. Into this context, the sole chronicle record of a decree against lay investiture at the Lent synod of 1075 can fairly easily be fitted. The Milanese chronicler Arnulf wrote that:

The pope held a synod at Rome and publicly ('palam') prohibited the king from thereafter ('deinde') having any right in giving bishoprics, and he debarred all lay persons from making investitures with churches. In addition, having proclaimed an anathema, he condemned

---

[129] Unless it underlies the royal clause of the Election Decree: Jasper, *Das Papstwahldekret*, pp. 104/ 84–105/91.

[130] For the council and for the 11th- and 12th-cen. view of its ecumenicity, see Dvornik, *The Photian Schism*, pp. 135–58, 309–45, 435–7; Kuttner, 'Liber canonicus', p. 391 nn. 21–2.

[131] See esp. Deusdedit, *Coll. can.* 4.18(16), pp. 409–10; Anselm of Lucca, *Coll. can.* 6.20, p. 276, with the title 'Ne quis laicorum principum vel potentum se interserat electioni vel promotioni episcoporum. Adrianus papa universali octave synodo presedens dixit'; Bonizo of Sutri, *Lib. de vita Christ.* 2.17, p. 42, with the title 'Quod nemo laicus interserat se electioni. Adrianus papa universali octave sinodo presidens dixit'. In addition, the chronicler Hugh of Flavigny cited most of canon 22 when he wrote about Gregory's proscription of lay investiture: 2, p. 412. Having dealt with the episcopal ordination in 1074 of Bishops Anselm II of Lucca and Hugh of Die, he passed to decrees that he believed Gregory to have issued against lay investiture at his Lent synod of 1074 or 1075, although he anachronistically cited decrees of Lent 1080: *Reg.* 7.14a(1), (2), p. 480/17–30. He then gave four canonical authorities: (i) canon 3 of the second council of Nicaea (757): *COD* p. 140/18–25; (ii) canon 22 of the fourth council of Constantinople (869–70), over which he wrongly asserted the presidency of Pope Nicholas I (858–67); (iii) canon 6 of the council of Nicaea (325): *COD* p. 9/7–12; and (iv) a canon, the number of which Hugh left blank, of a council of Antioch. It cannot be traced to any council of Antioch, but cf. *Canones apostolorum* 30: Mansi, 1.54; Hinschius, p. 29. Hugh's catena of citations may be compared with that given by Gerhoh of Reichersberg, when arguing for the exclusion of the lay power from the election or promotion of bishops; it included the first, second, and fourth of Hugh's authorities: *Comm. in Ps. LXIV*, pp. 451–2. The common material suggests the circulation of a collection of texts which included canon 22 of Constantinople IV.

('clamat') all the king's counsellors, and he threatened the king with the same unless in the near future ('in proximo') he should obey this ordinance.[132]

The public prohibition of the king from henceforth having any right in giving bishoprics is reminiscent of canon twenty-two, with an emphasis now placed upon the role of the king. The debarring of all laity from making investitures with churches may refer to a consequential decree of Gregory's which built upon Pope Nicholas II's ruling that no clerk should receive a church from lay hands ('per laicos') whether freely or for a price.[133] Arnulf also indicated that Gregory allowed Henry a period of grace within which he must obey his ordinance about his counsellors. It may be recalled that, in the winter of 1074–5, Gregory cherished hopes that Henry would mend his ways and merit imperial coronation at Rome.[134] With regard to episcopal elections, Gregory later implied that he had hoped for appropriate co-operation on Henry's part: as he was more powerful than other men in glory, honour, and strength, so he should also be more outstanding in his devotion in Christ.[135] Gregory's stance was not one of confrontation but of dialogue with a view to achieving peace and concord. He claimed not to have presented his legislation of Lent 1075 to Henry as a rigid and peremptory command. Using Germans who were present as intermediaries, he had sought to expound his own proposals for changing an evil custom—that of lay intervention in the process of making bishops. But he had left room for negotiation, and had invited Henry to discuss with competent subjects of his own ('quos sapientes et religiosos in regno tuo invenire posses') what modification might be possible within the bounds of canonical propriety.[136] Contrary to Arnulf's statement that Gregory sought answers to outstanding problems *in proximo*, Gregory said that the chance for discussion was not closed until Henry himself closed it by his interventions in the sees of Milan, Fermo, and Spoleto.[137] It must be concluded that Gregory did not regard the specific decrees of his Lent synod against such matters as lay investiture as coming into force, so long as Henry did not contravene them, until his concord had been secured.

---

[132] Arnulf of Milan, 4.7, pp. 211–12; cf. Landulf Senior, 3.31, p. 98. Arnulf's account gives rise to several difficulties. The reference to all the king's counsellors goes beyond the five of the official record in the Register: 2.52a, p. 196/11–13. Arnulf set the whole passage in the context of diplomatic contact between Henry and the South-Italian Normans which belong to the winter of 1075–6; it cannot, therefore, be assumed that Arnulf wrote soon after the synod of Feb. 1075 or that his account is not confused. He may have used reports of Patarene sympathizers with an eye to Milanese circumstances. However, the suggestion that Arnulf was writing about the Lent synod of 1076 encounters the difficulty that Gregory later mentioned a 'decretum nostrum contra investituram' of which Bishop Huzmann of Speyer should have been aware in the spring of 1075: *Reg.* 5.18, p. 381/13–20; cf. Hilpert, 'Zum ersten Investiturverbot.'

[133] Schieffer, *Die Entstehung des päpstlichen Investiturverbots*, pp. 222–3, lines 153–7.

[134] There is no reason to suppose that Gregory had Henry particularly in mind in his depressed letter of 22 Jan. 1075 to Abbot Hugh of Cluny: *Reg.* 2.49, pp. 188–90, esp. p. 189/20–5; during recent months, King Philip I of France, rather than Henry, had excited his criticism and anger: see below, 5.2.1.

[135] *Reg.* 3.10, p. 266/20–3.

[136] Gregory had left room for negotiation, although on a more confined basis, about the affairs of Milan in *Reg.* 2.30, to King Henry IV, 7 Dec. 1074, p. 164/13–26.

[137] *Reg.* 3.10, pp. 266/24–267/5.

If Gregory thus allowed Henry, so long as he believed him to be amenable, a generous interim during which he might proffer a constructive response, the corollary appears to have been that, should time prove that Henry or his bishops had all the time been disobedient to his decrees, these decrees must be deemed to have come into force from the time of their publication at the Lent synod.[138] During the winter of 1075–6, but only then, Gregory became rapidly persuaded of what had almost certainly always been the case—that Henry had never dismissed his excommunicated counsellors and had never intended to exhibit obedience to Gregory when his victory over the Saxons left his hands free to do otherwise.[139] Such being the position with the king and the German court, it is not surprising that, by 1077, Gregory took the view that the prohibition of lay investiture that he made in 1075 had been effective from the start.[140]

During most of 1075, however, his attitude towards Henry was completely otherwise. His letters establish that his cordiality towards Henry underwent no diminution whatsoever up to mid-September, when Henry's use of his victory over the Saxons and of his restored freedom of action at last became apparent. Until then, Gregory believed Henry to be in receipt of good and religious counsel, and to be active in promoting papal objectives of extirpating simony and clerical fornication. As regards lay investiture, Gregory gave no hint that he had issued any decree, still less that he regarded Henry as ignoring or defying it. Thus, in a letter of March to Bishop Burchard of Halberstadt, Gregory made it plain that his overriding, and perhaps his sole, concern with Saxon affairs was to secure the implementation of the measures against clerical unchastity of his legates of 1074 and his Lent synod of 1075. He made no reference to the Saxons' differences with the king, although he made plain his own lack of information about Saxon affairs.[141] When he wrote to the king on 20 July, he once more addressed him as 'fili carissime' and 'fili excellentissime'. He said that Henry retained his high regard because he resisted simony and clerical marriage; indeed, he anticipated even better things of him. He regarded Henry as his helper in filling the see of Bamberg, and he expressed confidence that Henry would proceed by the counsel of religious men.[142] In the same month, Henry, who was still on expedition in Saxony, sent Gregory a cleverly worded letter which was calculated to enhance Gregory's satisfaction and support. Henry argued that almost all the

---

[138] For Gregory's imposition of contingent sentences, cf. his decision at the Lent synod of 1075 that, if King Philip of France did not promise satisfaction and amendment to papal legates who would go to France, he would be deemed excommunicate: *Reg.* 2.52*a*, p. 196/20–2; also the record of papal dealings with Bishop Rainer of Orleans: *Reg.* 3.16, to Archbishop Richer of Sens, Apr. 1076, pp. 278–9.

[139] *Reg.* 3.10, pp. 263/26–264/4, *Epp. vag.* no. 14, to all the faithful in Germany, (summer 1076), pp. 36–7; cf. Berthold, *a*.1075, pp. 277/51–278/1.

[140] *Reg.* 4.22, pp. 330/27–331/9, 5.18, pp. 381–2.

[141] For Gregory's uncertainty about political affairs in Saxony, see *Reg.* 2.66, to Bishop Burchard II of Halberstadt, 29 Mar. 1075, p. 221/22–6; *Epp. vag.* no. 7, to Archbishop Werner of Magdeburg, (Feb. 1075), p. 16, illustrates his concern with ecclesiastical reform in Saxony. That the Saxon bishops knew about the legates' actions at Nuremberg is shown by *H* no. 15, pp. 33–5.

[142] *Reg.* 3.3, pp. 246–7.

German princes desired discord between pope and king, not peace.[143] Therefore he was sending to Gregory messengers whom he described as 'nobiles et religiosi', thus implying that the counsel which he was receiving was such as Gregory desired and would approve. They would bring a message that would be strictly secret to the pope, to the Empress Agnes, and to Countesses Beatrice and Matilda. When Henry returned from his Saxon expedition, he would send further messengers who would tell Gregory of his full purposes for the future, as well as of the reverence in which he held St Peter and the pope himself.[144]

When Henry's letter reached Gregory, the prevalence of fever had separated him from the counsellors upon whom he relied for a considered reply; but early in September, he answered cordially. He enlarged upon the benefit of the harmony of the Roman church and empire in avenging human sinfulness, and upon the good deeds and prayers by which some men sought to foster peace and concord between pope and king. Gregory was confident that Henry had begun to commit the business of the pope and of the whole church to sincere and religious men. With their counsel, Gregory was prepared—as he expressed it—to open to Henry the bosom of the Roman church and to receive him as lord, brother, and son. Such language can only refer to Henry's being welcomed to Rome for imperial coronation. In return, Gregory asked only for Henry's obedience to his admonitions, and for his rendering glory and honour to his Creator. Gregory then turned to the Saxons whom Henry had vanquished. He ranged himself entirely with the king. The Saxons had resisted him from pride and unjustly. Now, their pride was broken by the judgement of God; Gregory reinforced this point with biblical language about how the Maccabees had crushed their enemies.[145] Though Gregory's victory at the Unstrut was a matter for grief because of the spilling of Christian blood, it was a matter for rejoicing because it promoted the peace of the church. Gregory's message to the victorious king was the pious one that he should rather seek to defend God's honour and righteousness than to seek glory for himself.[146]

As Gregory saw matters less than six months before he excommunicated Henry, the Saxon rising was an act of human pride which God had justly punished by the agency of the king. Upon hearing of the Saxon defeat, he renewed his confidence in Henry as one who was now a Christian king and who, upon promise of due obedience, was fit to be admitted to the imperial title and office. He had ruled according to the spirit, if not yet according to the letter, of Gregory's programme at the Lent synod of 1075, including canon twenty-two of the fourth council of Constantinople.

---

[143] Henry took up Gregory's words in *Reg.* 2.31, p. 166/3-7.

[144] A fragment of Henry's letter is cited in *Reg.* 3.5, p. 251/21-31 = *Epp. HIV* no. 7, pp. 58-9. The messengers' names were given as Radbod and Adelpreth in *Reg.* 3.10, p. 267/26-8.

[145] Cf. 2. Macc. 5: 21, 43.

[146] *Reg.* 3.7, pp. 256-9. This letter contradicts Bruno, cap. 64, pp. 276-8, and Donizo, 1.1250-72, p. 377, that Henry's victory over the Saxons at once led to a worsening of relations between pope and king. In view of the dislocation of the order of letters in the third book of Gregory's Register, it should be noticed that *Reg.* 3.7 was dispatched at about the same time as *Reg.* 3.4, to Archbishop Siegfried of Mainz.

Upon such a tide of confidence and hope so far as the king was concerned Gregory was riding at least until the autumn of 1075.

3.2.5 1073–5: The Recalcitrance of the German Bishops

During the first three years of Gregory's pontificate, his relations with the German bishops were more tense and difficult than those with the German king. While the exigencies of the Saxon rising compelled Henry to court Gregory's favour and good-will, Gregory himself sought resolutely to promote the reform of the German church and especially of its higher clergy. Swabian chroniclers, who were well disposed to the pope, epitomized Gregory's intention as it was understood in Germany: 'Under Gregory's prudent guidance, priestly incontinence was checked not only in Italy but also in the regions of Germany; for what his predecessor had prohibited in Italy he zealously sought to prohibit in other regions of the catholic church.'[147] To the campaign against clerical fornication and concubinage must be added that against simony, especially amongst the higher clergy; as Berthold, in particular, implied, Gregory above all sought to promote reform by using the authority of the apostolic see of Rome as directly and resolutely as he believed the canonical tradition of the church to warrant and require.

From the outset, most of the German bishops met Gregory's endeavours with coolness, and increasingly with hostility. Gregory's disquiet was already apparent when, according to his Register, between 23 and 28 April 1073 he sent notices of his election to a number of churchmen, but none of them to a German.[148] The German bishops for their part showed extreme reluctance to have dealings with Gregory; some of them may even have counselled King Henry to resist his election to the papacy.[149] The bishops' coolness was a reaction to Pope Alexander II's zeal during his latter years when Hildebrand had been prominent in his counsels in summoning German bishops to Rome to answer for their carnal sins and simoniacal dealings. In April 1074, Gregory recalled to Countesses Beatrice and Matilda of Tuscany that of those who had been censured, only Bishop Werner of Strassburg had belatedly come to Rome; even so, while accepting his penitence Gregory did not as yet restore him to office.[150] Only Bishop Hermann of Metz earned his applause: a month before his comment upon Werner of Strassburg, Gregory answered a letter from Hermann with an acknowledgement of Hermann's abundant devotion to himself. Elsewhere Gregory expressed satisfaction at Hermann's visit to Rome in company with Abbot Thierry of Saint-Hubert-en-Ardenne; Gregory called him 'carissimus frater noster', and gave him apostolic authority to promote Bishop Hermann of Bamberg's repentance if that bishop were prepared to obey.[151]

---

[147] Bernold, *Chron. a.* 1073, p. 430/7–10; Berthold, *a.*1073, p. 276/12–14.

[148] *Reg.* 1.3, to Archbishop Guibert of Ravenna, pp. 5–6; 1.4, to the abbots of Cluny and of Saint-Victor at Marseilles, and to Archbishop Manasses of Rheims, p. 7; cf. *Epp. vag.* no. 1, to Archbishop Lanfranc of Canterbury, after 30 June 1073, pp. 2–5.

[149] See above, 3.2.2.   [150] *Reg.* 1.77, 15 Apr. 1074, pp. 109/21–110/7.

[151] *Reg.* 1.53, to Bishop Hermann of Metz, 14 Mar. 1074, pp. 80–1; 1.81, to Archbishop Udo of Trier, 6 May 1074, pp. 115–16; 1.84, to Bishop Hermann of Bamberg, 12 June 1074, pp. 119–20.

As for the German metropolitans, Gregory censured their lack of contact with the apostolic see and their disregard of its prerogatives. As early as November 1073, he seized the opportunity of a petitioner's coming to Rome and rebuked Archbishop Gebhard of Salzburg, who was later a staunch Gregorian, for having failed to write to him. He further rebuked him because, although he had attended a Lateran synod of Pope Alexander II—probably that of 1063—he had never obeyed its precepts about uprooting clerical unchastity; henceforth he must bear them due witness.[152] To Archbishop Anno of Cologne, Gregory wrote in April 1074 upon the more personal note of his own youthful visit to Cologne and Anno's services as papal chancellor. The rebuke was even more sharp. In the past, a bond of charity had joined Rome and Cologne. But charity had grown cold: apart from a recently dispatched letter (which does not now survive), Anno had made no approach to Gregory since he became pope. This was no mere omission: it was an offence. Making reference to the common dedication of their sees, Gregory threatened that 'if we find that you love St Peter's honour not as a whole but in part—at Cologne but not at Rome, you should look for our favour neither in whole nor in part'. However, the renewal of obedience would attract its due reward.[153]

Even more severely, Gregory rebuked Archbishop Siegfried of Mainz, the senior of the German metropolitan sees.[154] There was serious friction over two dioceses, Prague and the Moravian see founded at Olmütz in 1063, both of which formed part of Siegfried's province.[155] In the time of Pope Alexander II, Duke Wratislav II of Bohemia had requested and obtained the dispatch of papal legates to settle their relationship, thereby challenging the political rights of the king of Germany and the metropolitan rights of the archbishop of Mainz. So far as relations between Gregory and Siegfried are concerned, matters came to a head in March 1074. Siegfried wrote to Gregory in terms of exaggerated deference, protesting his service and his gratification that Gregory had become pope. Because of the ancient mother-and-daughter relationship of Rome and Mainz, he turned to Gregory with due deference ('velut membra ad caput') to make a complaint that, in Pope Alexander's time, Mainz had been denied its canonically appropriate rights. His suffragan Bishop Jaromir of Prague had been unjustly accused before Alexander by Bishop John of Olmütz. Short-circuiting the canonically proper procedure of an initial hearing before

---

[152] *Reg.* 1.30, 15 Nov. 1073, pp. 50–1.

[153] *Reg.* 1.79, 18 Apr. 1074, pp. 112–13. For Cologne's dedication to St Peter, see Leo IX's privilege for Archbishop Hermann (1052): *Ep.* 68, *PL* 142.687C.

[154] For the place in the German church of the see of Mainz, see Thomas, 'Erzbischof Siegfried I. von Mainz'.

[155] The sources for this dispute are numerous. See esp. *Reg.* 1.17, to Duke Wratislav of Bohemia, 8 July 1073, pp. 27–8; 1.38, to the same, 17 Dec. 1073, pp. 60–1; 1.44, to Bishop Jaromir of Prague, 31 Jan. 1074, pp. 67–8; 1.45, to Duke Wratislav, 31 Jan. 1074, pp. 68–9; 1.59, to his brothers Otto and Conrad, 18 Mar. 1074, pp. 86–7; 1.60, to Archbishop Siegfried of Mainz, 18 Mar. 1074, pp. 87–9; 1.61, to Duke Wratislav, 18 Mar. 1074, pp. 89–90; 1.78, to the same, 16 Apr. 1074, pp. 111–12; 2.6, to Bishop Jaromir of Prague, 22 Sept. 1074, pp. 133–4; 2.7, to Duke Wratislav, 22 Sept. 1074, pp. 135–6; 2.8, to Bishop John of Olmütz, 22 Sept. 1074, pp. 137–8; 2.53, decision of the Lent synod, 2 Mar. 1075, pp. 197–8; *CU* no. 40 to 'affusi, oramus et obsecramus', pp. 84–86/22 (see Erdmann, *Briefliteratur*, p. 250 n. 4); Cosmas of Prague, 2.27–31, pp. 120–7.

himself as metropolitan, Alexander's legates had suspended Jaromir from office, despoiled him of his goods, and delated him as a virtual excommunicate.

Gregory's reply was crushing. He wrote that unworthy reports had already reached him to which he would have given no credence had he not received Siegfried's letter: Siegfried had tried to divert the Bohemian dispute from settlement by the papacy to the scrutiny of his own will. Those who had thus advised him were ignorant of canonical traditions and the decrees of the fathers, and he should acknowledge his own intrepidity. More particularly, Gregory complained that when John of Olmütz first suffered vexation, Siegfried gave him no help. He took the matter up only after Gregory had sought to set matters right, and thus he had produced confusion. Gregory nevertheless claimed that he was now giving Siegfried only a gentle warning to venture no further along such lines as he was proposing. No patriarch or primate could reverse papal decisions. Siegfried should in no way strive against the Roman church, for as he well knew, without its clemency he could not retain his position. By God's help and by St Peter's authority, and in accordance with what the apostolic see had long since determined, Gregory would himself determine and implement whatever was right in the case of the Bohemian bishops.

The dispute about Prague and Olmütz made plain Gregory's claim to intervene directly or through legates in the affairs of the German church, despite the counter-claim of prelates like Siegfried of Mainz that ecclesiastical business should first and normally be discussed in Germany and only exceptionally be referred to Rome. As 1074 developed, Gregory began to make clear by deeds as well as by words that he intended to make good his claim. In May he wrote to Archbishop Udo of Trier and called upon him to defend the abbey of Saint-Michel at Verdun against the local bishop, Thierry: on papal authority he was to join with his suffragans Bishops Hermann of Metz and Pibo of Toul in order to rectify matters.[156] Gregory likewise asserted apropos the abbey of Reichenau that the apostolic see had a duty to oversee all churches and sacred places. In 1072, Pope Alexander II had brought about Abbot Rupert's deposition as a simoniac and intruder. Gregory wrote a letter proclaiming that he had now himself consecrated the canonically elected Abbot Ekkehard, whose goods and possessions he undertook to protect.[157]

More importantly, Gregory implemented a plan, conceived late in 1073 and given effect in the spring of 1074, to arrange a legatine council for the whole German church so that it might be reformed under direct papal authority and guidance. Gregory first mooted the dispatch of legates who would help to appease the Saxons' differences with King Henry. But after his Lent synod of 9–15 March 1074, at which he probably legislated against simony and clerical fornication,[158] he sent his legates Gerald of Ostia and Hubert of Palestrina with a wider commission. Their success in reconciling the king to the pope has already been noticed.[159] They were also

---

[156] *Reg.* 1.81, 6 May 1074, pp. 115–16.

[157] *Reg.* 1.82, 6 May 1074, pp. 116–18. It is noteworthy that Gregory did not refer to the king's part in Rupert's appointment.

[158] Marianus Scottus, *a.*1096 (1074), pp. 560–1.   [159] See above, 3.2.3.

commissioned to assemble in council the German bishops, abbots, and clergy, and with full papal authority 'to correct what needed correction in the German church and to supply what needed to be established in its religion'.[160] Such a council presented a challenge to the view of authority in the church that Siegfried of Mainz propounded to Gregory VII, and was an implementation of Gregory's counter-arguments.

On the side of church reform, the council achieved no lasting results, although it served to generate a volatile and troubled state of affairs in the German episcopate. The convening of the king's Easter court, which the legates attended, at Bamberg thrust to the fore its bishop, Hermann. Hermann's past made him objectionable to all shades of reforming opinion. He had become a bishop in 1065 through simony, and since the Saxon war broke out he had been the king's right-hand man in the affairs of the kingdom. In 1074, when Henry gave lands to his church by way of reward, he referred to him as someone 'qui in omni temptatione nostra fideliter adhesit'.[161] In 1075, Gregory's hopes for the king's restoration to communion and obedience made him willing to countenance Bishop Hermann's reconciliation and acceptance as bishop of Bamberg. Hermann himself had shown another side to his character by founding at Bamberg a church dedicated to St James in which he subsequently replaced regular canons by reformed monks. This was not to the liking of the canons of the cathedral who, in rallying to the defence of canons of St James, revived the allegations of simony to which Bishop Hermann was exposed.[162] In the early months of 1074, Gregory was exercised by these allegations which the canons of the cathedral had brought to his notice.

On 1 March, when the bishop was at Worms with the king, he received a letter from Gregory instructing him to present himself before the two legates on the Sunday after Easter (26 April). On Hermann's behalf, Meinhard, *scholasticus* of the Bamberg chapter, thereupon drafted a letter of masterly impudence by which the bishop sought both to evade judgement and yet curry Gregory's favour.[163] He professed his devotion and obedience to him, as well as belated gratification that he had become pope. Hermann asserted that he had wished to come to Rome; but he had been hindered, first by the needs of his own church of Bamberg, and then because he had reluctantly been drawn into the king's service. In this service, he had hoped to counteract the king's evil counsellors and to promote love and concord between king and pope. He pleaded that a dateline of 26 April was too close for him to answer charges against him, so he was sending a deacon to Rome who would explain matters to Gregory. Since he had to go on an embassy to Burgundy and France, he had decided also to fulfil a long-standing vow to visit the sanctuary of St James at Compostela. Then, said Hermann, 'when the saint's intercessions and your prayers

---

[160] *Reg.* 2.28, to Archbishop Liemar of Bremen, 12 Dec. 1074, p. 161/6–11.

[161] *MGH DDHIV*, no. 270; the evocative reference to Luke 22: 38 should be observed.

[162] For Hermann of Bamberg's activities and reputation, see Lampert of Hersfeld, *a.*1075, pp. 262–72, cf. Bruno, cap. 15, pp. 210–12. For his dealings over St James's at Bamberg, see esp. Hallinger, *Gorze-Kluny*, 1,353–6; Schieffer, '*Spirituales latrones*', pp. 22–30.

[163] *M* no. 40, pp. 240–2.

have brought me home, I will take steps for myself, so far as by God's help and your own I am able, to cut away the envy of my adversaries, so that my innocence shall no longer be burdened.' It is not known whether this letter was dispatched or received, or whether the deacon travelled to Rome. But by some means Gregory was brought to adopt the stance for which Hermann wished. By June he heard Bishop Hermann of Metz's pleas on his behalf and expressed the hope that, by the bishop of Metz's good offices, Hermann of Bamberg might be brought to obedience.[164]

Leading German churchmen took a different view. Despite Hermann's forecast to Gregory of his itinerary to Compostela, he was present at Bamberg for Henry's Easter court. As diocesan, it fell to him to preside at the pontifical ceremonies. Mindful of his simony and perjury, most of the bishops, with Archbishop Liemar of Bremen to the fore, rejected the baptismal chrism and the eucharistic elements that Hermann consecrated. In the later phrase of the Bamberg chapter, they were 'like the impure rags of a menstruous woman'. The bishops also spurned Hermann's ordinations.[165] However great the bishops' displeasure at papal intervention and at the sending of legates, they were not prepared to have dealings with a notorious simoniac of their own number. Towards the legates they were unco-operative. Liemar of Bremen later recalled that they had taken Siegfried of Mainz and himself aside, and had tried on their own authority to secure approval for a national synod. After consulting other German bishops, the metropolitans replied that it was a matter for the whole German episcopate; the legates rejoined that the archbishops should either comply or account for themselves in Rome at Gregory's November synod.[166]

The events of Eastertide 1074 piled paradox upon paradox. The king gave his bishops no support against the legates, upon whose good report to Gregory he depended for his own rehabilitation. The simoniacal bishop of Bamberg was treated with forbearance both by Gregory's legates in Germany and by Gregory himself at Rome. The legates castigated the German bishops who were most disposed to resist simony, and did so at the king's Easter court.

Although the legates remained in Germany for much of the year, they achieved nothing further of note; there was no prospect that they would convene the German council for which they had been sent.[167] Its collapse was due to the German bishops. When Bishop Burchard of Halberstadt reminded Gregory of the legates' lack of success in Germany, Gregory is more likely to have blamed the bishops than the king.[168] The king was the sole beneficiary of the events of Eastertide 1074. Restored to papal favour, he remained in Gregory's eyes the most likely agent of reform in the German church.

---

[164] *Reg.* 1.84, to Bishop Hermann of Bamberg, 12 June 1074, pp. 119–20.

[165] *M* no. 41, the cathedral chapter of Bamberg to a bishop, ?Embricho of Augsburg, ?May 1075, pp. 242–6; Bernard, *De damn. scis.* cap. (36), *MGH L. de L.* 2.43.

[166] *H* no. 15, Archbishop Liemar of Bremen to Bishop Hezilo of Hildesheim, late Jan. 1075, pp. 33–5.

[167] For the collapse of plans for a council, see Bonizo of Sutri, 7, p. 602. In June, the legates met Archbishop Anno of Cologne: *H* no. 46, p. 90/26–30. They may also have met Bishops Benno of Osnabrück and Burchard of Halberstadt: *Reg.* 2.12, 25, 66, pp. 143–4, 156–7, 221–2.

[168] *Reg.* 2.12, 26 Oct. 1074, p. 143/26–30.

In the autumn of 1074, Gregory used the opportunity of Henry's compliance to maintain the practice of direct intervention in German church affairs. In September, he renewed his dealings with Bohemia, and thus his opposition to the claims of Archbishop Siegfried of Mainz, by again summoning to Rome Bishop Jaromir of Prague and by promising papal help to Bishop John of Olmütz.[169] In October, he charged Bishops Werner of Strassburg and Burchard of Basle to decide on his behalf a dispute over the advocacy of Holy Cross at Woffenheim and to report back to him.[170] In November, Archbishop Anno of Cologne was to complete the two legates' investigation of the dispute about tithes between Bishop Benno of Osnabrück and the monastic houses of Corvey and Herford. Gregory seized opportunities to promote the moral reform of the church. Anno, who now stood high in papal favour, was to take steps throughout his province to enforce the chastity of clerks in major orders.[171] More significantly still for the future, in October Gregory wrote to a Count Albert and his wife—probably Count Albert of Calw and his wife Wiltrud—applauding the faithful witness of devout lay people. When so many higher and lower clergy had fallen under the devil's power, layfolk like themselves should stand firm in their faith. They should enforce whatever the apostolic see enjoined about bishops and priests who engaged in simony and fornication.[172]

From a German point of view, such actions were no doubt relatively minor irritants; it was in his preparations for the Lent synod of 1075 that Gregory caused major and dangerous offence to the German bishops. Preparations began some four months in advance, when on 16 October he wrote to Archbishop Udo of Trier, whom he approached as a faithful and diligent fellow-worker.[173] A leading clerk who was *custos* of the cathedral chapter at Toul, a see within Udo's province, had complained at Rome that his bishop, Pibo, had unjustly expelled him and deprived him of his prebend. In return, the clerk had accused his bishop of repeated simony, and of keeping a woman by whom he had a son in open fornication—unless the rumour was correct that he had married her in lay fashion. The clerk claimed that the bishop had half admitted the charges, only thereafter to visit the clerk with his wrath and with violence. Gregory took the clerk at his word. He charged Archbishop Udo, in concert with Bishop Hermann of Metz, to summon Pibo and to order him to reinstate the clerk. Udo was then to summon the clergy of Toul and investigate the moral charges against Pibo. He was to report his findings to Gregory before or during the next Lent synod. In itself, the procedure was unobjectionable: the pope referred a complaint to the competent metropolitan for local investigation. But Gregory's letter contained phrases which were gravely prejudicial to Pibo, and which showed what judgement Udo was expected to pass: Pibo was 'the so-called bishop', and even 'the bishop—no, the ex-bishop'. Gregory provided that, if Pibo were found innocent, the clerk should be duly punished; but, if he were found guilty, neither the pope nor the archbishop could 'allow the wolf to occupy the shepherd's place'.

---

[169] *Reg.* 2.6–8, 22 Sept. 1074, pp. 133–8.
[170] *Reg.* 2.14, 29 Oct. 1074, pp. 146–7.
[171] *Reg.* 2.25, 18 Nov. 1074, pp. 156–7.
[172] *Reg.* 2.11, 26 Oct. 1074, pp. 142–3.
[173] *Reg.* 2.10, pp. 140–2. For Gregory's earlier use of Udo, see *Reg.* 1.81, 6 May 1074, pp. 115–16.

Early in 1075, Archbishop Udo reported to Gregory. When the clerk brought Gregory's letter, Udo had at once decided that he could determine so grave a matter only in concert with a large number of his fellow bishops; that is, with a wider group than his own comprovincials of Metz and Verdun. When twenty and more were assembled—the occasion was probably the king's Christmas court at Strassburg—they expressed their unanimous revulsion against Gregory's manner of proceeding:

A new and unacceptable custom is being introduced into the church. To the prejudice of the bishops, a heavy and intolerable yoke is being placed upon us, to compel subjects in the name of obedience and under threat of excommunication by the device of putting certain questions to drag from them details of their private manner of life. Sons are being armed against fathers and standards of deference and duty are being overthrown. When matters were *sub judice* it was not fitting that papal interference should have gone so far as the degrading words 'ex-bishop' and 'wolf': even if the bishop deserved them, it would have been well to respect public seemliness and, still more, to pay due regard to the church by not bandying such words about. In their opinion [Udo continued] I should not do well to set a precedent by such unheard-of proceedings. They besought me not to hesitate in informing you of their unanimous plea, that especially in such unproven matters you would henceforth not issue such unwonted and harsh commands, by which respect to yourself might be damaged.

Thus the German bishops; caught between the upper millstone of a sometimes rashly interventionist papacy and the lower millstones of restless cathedral chapters and diocesan clergy, they foreshadowed the opportunist solidarity against Gregory that they were to show at Worms in January 1076.

Meanwhile, however, Archbishop Udo struggled to satisfy all parties. He went on to declare that he did not wish to be lax in obeying Gregory over such grievous matters. He had, therefore, duly summoned the bishop of Toul and the clerk to appear before him, and he had asked his two other suffragans, Hermann of Metz and Thierry of Verdun, to be assessors. Hermann of Metz had not been available within Gregory's deadline of his Lent synod of 1075. Otherwise, Udo had followed the stipulations of Gregory's letter to him. The clerk was first restored to his place at Toul; however, when challenged to testify to his bishop's face about the charges which he had laid against him, he kept an obstinate silence. Then the clergy of Toul proclaimed their bishop's innocence of them. On the king's behalf as well as his own, Bishop Benno of Osnabrück swore that Pibo's promotion in 1069 had not been simoniacal. The upshot was that it was the clerk whom Udo reserved for Gregory's judgement in view of his false allegations; after a further, private hearing, Udo dismissed Bishop Pibo in peace. He concluded his report to Gregory with this heartfelt plea:

This is the matter as it transpired. We beseech your excellency, to whom we have dedicated our honour and service, never again to burden us with anything like this. For we cannot bear it ourselves, and we cannot find others to share it.[174]

[174] *H* no. 17, pp. 38–41.

In connection with the Prague–Olmütz dispute, Archbishop Siegfried of Mainz had expressed his resentment of what he saw as undue papal inteference in the provincial order of the German church. Now, almost certainly under the king's eye at his Christmas court of 1074, a large part of the German episcopate had voiced its repugnance at such interference. In a case that Gregory had precipitately misjudged, a well-disposed archbishop's loyalty and service had been tested to the limit.

On 12 December 1074, Gregory wrote to Archbishop Liemar of Bremen a letter which was more peremptory and censorious than that which he had sent to Archbishop Udo of Trier.[175] It is likely to have done still more to disturb the German episcopate. Gregory announced his displeasure by omitting a salutation. He insisted upon Liemar's indebtedness to the Roman church; his insistence may indicate that, like his predecessor Adalbert, Liemar may have been made papal vicar over the Scandinavian kingdoms and may have been sent a *pallium* from Rome. Yet Liemar had proved himself the enemy both of the Roman church and of Gregory himself. With all his power he had resisted the endeavours of Gregory's two cardinal legates to hold a German national council. He had ignored their instructions that he should appear in Rome by the end of November. Gregory therefore summoned him to attend his Lent synod; in the meantime he suspended him from his episcopal office. In an outraged letter to Bishop Hezilo of Hildesheim, Liemar gave vent to his reaction.[176] He complained bitterly about his suspension; in his view, the suspension of a bishop was licit only if imposed by his brother-bishops in open synod. As for Gregory, Liemar wrote, '*Periculosus homo*: The man is a menace! He wants to boss bishops about at his pleasure as though they were his bailiffs. If they do not do all that he commands, then let them come to Rome on pain of suspension without a judgement!' Liemar added that he very well knew which of the German bishops—he probably had in mind Burchard of Halberstadt's report to Gregory about the legates' abortive endeavours at Nuremberg[177]—had, from bitter hatred of his lord the king whose help he was, put him into his present straits by their machinations. In fact, in his present strife he was labouring for the common good of all.

Eight days before Gregory wrote to Liemar, he had written more amicably to Archbishop Siegfried of Mainz.[178] Siegfried had been in touch with Gregory, and in his habitually fulsome way had professed his obedience: 'You well know, holy father, that no man on earth is more faithful to you than I am, or more zealous to obey your every command.'[179] Gregory referred approvingly to their long association, and to how Siegfried's sometime wish to retire to the monastery of Cluny was a proof of his devoutness. And yet the pope had heard that Siegfried had behaved otherwise than he himself would have wished; no doubt Gregory had in mind his collusion at Nuremberg with Liemar of Bremen. Gregory could not silently pass this over. He instructed Siegfried to come to his Lent synod at Rome; he was to bring six of his

---

[175] *Reg.* 2.28, 12 Dec. 1074, pp. 160–1.
[176] *H* no. 15, pp. 33–5.
[177] *Reg.* 2.12, pp. 143–4.
[178] *Reg.* 2.29, 4 Dec. 1074, pp. 161–2.
[179] *CU* no. 40 from *primum ecclesiae rationes*, pp. 86/23–87/16.

suffragans: Otto of Constance, Werner of Strassburg, Henry of Speyer, Hermann of Bamberg, Imbricho of Augsburg, and Adalbero of Würzburg. Of these, all save the last had received their bishoprics under Henry IV; Gregory was clearly concerned to remedy the objectionable appointments to which the king admitted in his *supplex epistola* of 1073. To counter Siegfried's plea of physical infirmity, Gregory allowed that, if he could not come to Rome, he should send representatives and should furnish Gregory with the findings of a diligent inquiry into the election and subsequent conduct of the six bishops.

Siegfried's reply survives.[180] It is larded with his habitual protests of obedience and service to Gregory. But greatly though he wished to visit him, ill-health precluded his coming to Rome. He had not had time to investigate the six bishops, and therefore had nothing that he could add to what Gregory already knew; although he had sent the bishops Gregory's letter with instructions to obey his commands. As regards resisting clerical unchastity and simony, Siegfried said that he was absolutely at one with Gregory.[181] But he added a plea that Gregory would proceed gently with the German bishops:

It will be a mark of papal clemency and fatherly discretion ('discretionis'), if when issuing commands about ecclesiastical matters to brother-bishops you take account of their actual circumstances and individual freedom of action, so that due discipline may be applied to the wandering and perverse while compassion and charity are not denied to those who are sick and in need of a doctor. When what is at stake has been established, censure and judgement should be so brought to bear that the measure of righteousness should not exceed the demands of papal discretion ('discretionis') and fatherly mercy.

For the moment at least, Siegfried pleaded in vain, for Gregory had already resolved to act sternly. On 11 January 1075, he wrote to the three South German dukes, and perhaps to other lay figures, sounding a note of urgency and calling for root-and-branch remedies.[182] Times were such as there had not been since the conversion of Constantine; Gregory therefore insisted upon the culpability of bishops who had set aside well-known laws and despised papal decrees. He referred especially to the need to prohibit those whose entry into holy orders had been tainted with simony from being allowed any office or ministry in the church, and those guilty of fornication from ministering at the altar. Since the time of Pope Leo IX, the church had been assiduous in publishing these rules, but few bishops had obeyed.[183] Therefore the

---

[180] *CU* no. 42, pp. 88–91.

[181] But see also his position, according to Lampert of Hersfeld, at the council of Erfurt in 1074: *Ann. a.* 1074, pp. 258–9.

[182] *Reg.* 2.45, pp. 182–5. According to the registered text, the letter was sent to Rudolf of Swabia and Berthold of Carinthia. Recipients' texts as cited by Deusdedit, *Coll. can.* 4.186 (107), p. 491, Hugh of Flavigny, 2, p. 491, and Paul of Bernried, cap. 39, p. 493, indicate that it was sent to others, including Welf of Bavaria: see Caspar's notes, *Reg.* p. 182.

[183] Cf. Archbishop Adalbert of Bremen's worldly advice to his clergy, 'Si non caste tamen caute', i.e. avoiding breaches of the bond of marriage: Adam of Bremen, Schol. 76, p. 364; and Gregory's complaint to Bishop Dietwin of Liège that clerical unchastity was a 'nefas . . . quod temporibus modernis inolevit ex taciturnitate pastorum': *Reg.* 2.61, 23 March. 1075, p. 216/10–12.

pope must employ new remedies: 'It seems much better that we should reinforce God's righteousness even by adopting new counsels, than that we should allow men's souls to perish because laws are ignored.' Gregory turned to the dukes as to all men of proven devotion, to urge that whether bishops spoke out or were silent they would not themselves accept the ministrations of simoniacs or fornicators. They should also act positively: 'Under the sanction of obedience you should seize every opportunity to publish and argue these things both at the king's court and in other places and assemblies of the kingdom, and prevent offending clergy, by force if necessary, from service at the holy mysteries.' The lay strike against the ministrations of offending clergy that had been facilitated by the encyclical of Nicholas II and Alexander II, *Vigilantia universalis*,[184] and promoted at Milan by the Patarenes was to be introduced into Germany and implemented by its greatest lay magnates. Gregory foresaw opposition, for he added that, if any thought that such action was beyond their competence, they should argue the matter with Gregory himself. To Rudolf of Swabia, Gregory added that he should himself make amends for past acts of his own that verged upon simony.

In summary, by the beginning of 1075 Gregory was applying a threefold pressure upon the German church in order to compel its reform. First, he sought to subject the bishops to the direct authority of the apostolic see, in derogation of their own ideas about ecclesiastical jurisdiction, by summoning to Rome bishops whom he suspected of offence, by sending legates to hold a national council under papal authority, and by using metropolitans to act as his directly commissioned agents. His Lent synods at Rome were his chosen forum for dealing with all business that he saw fit to summon. Second, he sought to use the lay structure of society to make good the deficiencies of the higher clergy in promoting his aims. He also entertained high hopes of the king. He envisaged both the princes and the king as agents of coercion upon disobedient clergy, and all assemblies, including the king's court, as forums in which pressure might be applied. Third, as the examples of Bamberg and Toul serve to illustrate, he sought to enlist cathedral chapters and their members, often at odds with their bishops on account of royal and episcopal exactions, to bring pressure to bear upon their bishops. So far as the upper clergy are concerned, the result was to draw most of the episcopate together in apprehension of Gregory and his demands. They were drawn for protection into a measure of solidarity with the king. The position of the lay princes was more ambiguous, since they had their own interests and ambitions which they pursued with little concern for papal demands. But collaboration with the pope had its attractions as a means of counterbalancing the power of the king. As the bishops tended to close their ranks against the pope while the princes tended to become his apparent allies, the king was necessarily drawn into a bond with his bishops. At least in the short term, a challenge to either was likely to appear as a challenge to both. But, in most of 1075, Gregory was at pains to prevent any such challenge from being presented.

---

[184] Schieffer, *Die Entstehung des päpstlichen Investiturverbots*, pp. 218–19, lines 100–4.

3.2.6 1075: Gregory VII's Attempts at Conciliation

Gregory's Lent synod of 24–8 February 1075 marked the high-water mark of his campaign to discipline German bishops and to reform the German church by direct and, as the German bishops saw it, autocratic methods. The official record of the synod is sparse, but it recorded sanctions against four German bishops: for his disobedience and pride, Liemar of Bremen was suspended from his episcopal office and excommunicated. Werner of Strassburg was suspended from his episcopal and priestly functions, Henry of Speyer was suspended, and so was Hermann of Bamberg unless he came and made satisfaction to Gregory before Easter. In addition, three Lombard bishops were punished—William of Pavia and Cunibert of Turin by suspension and Dionysius of Piacenza by deposition. The evidence of chronicles establishes that Gregory legislated stringently against simony and clerical incontinence, and commanded Christian laity not to accept the ministrations of clergy whom they saw to disregard papal standards.[185] Since the twenty-seven theses about papal power known as the *Dictatus papae* are inserted into the Register between items dated 3 and 4 March 1075, they are likely to have been compiled at about this time, in anticipation of Henry's coming to Rome later in the year for imperial coronation, to assert the prerogatives of the papacy in face of the claims of the German bishops, and to settle in the papacy's favour the relationship of papal and imperial authority.[186]

The chroniclers' references to the synodal decrees show that they were widely and emphatically published in Germany, so far as they were intended to take immediate effect. Gregory soon afterwards sent letters to Archbishops Siegfried of Mainz and Werner of Magdeburg.[187] They were skilfully drafted to be both trenchant and conciliatory. On the one hand, they showed a new comprehensiveness in bringing together Gregory's reforming demands and the means of their achievement: simony and clerical incontinence were to be ruthlessly extirpated; metropolitans should act as agents of papal commands; laymen should boycott the sacraments of offending clerks, 'so that those who are not corrected by the love of God and the honour of their office may be brought to their senses by the shame of the world and the reproof of the people'. On the other hand, these letters suggest a novel attempt by Gregory to meet the objections of German bishops to direct papal intervention which Siegfried of Mainz and Liemar of Bremen had forcibly expressed. Gregory placed his emphasis upon fraternal partnership rather than upon Roman command and superiority.[188] The German prelates were urged to show themselves his 'fellow-workers'; he hoped that the Roman church might rejoice in their collaboration as 'most dear brothers' and 'zealous fellow-workers'. Gregory struck a similar note of conciliation in a letter to Bishop Otto of Constance: because the bishop's messengers at the Lent synod had returned speedily, Gregory sent him a special account of its reforming decrees.[189]

---

[185] *Reg.* 2.52a, pp. 196–7. For chronicle references, see esp. Berthold, *a*.1075, pp. 277–8; Bernold, *Chron. a.* 1075, pp. 430–1; Marianus Scottus, *a*.1097 (1075), p. 560; *Ann. Aug. a.* 1075, p. 128.

[186] *Reg.* 2.55a, pp. 201–8; for further discussion, see below, 8.1.2.

[187] *Epp. vag.* nos. 6–7, pp. 14–17.

[188] See also *Epp. vag.* no. 9, pp. 18–20.   [189] *Epp. vag.* no. 8, pp. 16–19.

The letters suggest that Gregory sought in the late spring of 1075 to implement a policy of collaboration with the German bishops.

The note of conciliation occurs in other letters from Gregory to them. Towards the end of March, he treated with surprising mildness Bishop Dietwin of Liège of whose simoniacal dealings he had long been aware. He took account of Dietwin's extreme old age and of Bishop Hermann of Metz's assurance that the bishop's advisers were more to blame than he; Dietwin was merely urged to take thought for his own salvation, to make such amends as he could for his simoniacal dealings, and to institute resolute proceedings against his concubinous clergy.[190] He urged Bishop Burchard of Halberstadt, like all his fellow-workers, to intensify the struggle against unchaste clergy.[191] A similarly worded appeal to Archbishop Anno of Cologne insisted upon the right of the Roman church to prescribe new remedies for new offences, but Gregory nevertheless urged Anno himself to propagate papal decrees by way of his own provincial councils.[192] Writing to Archbishop Werner of Magdeburg, he called upon him to act as a new Joshua, sounding the trumpet of divine vengeance against the Jericho of his clergy's offences. Gregory went so far as to apply to the archbishop the Lord's prophetic commission to Jeremiah which he otherwise reserved for the pope: 'I have placed you today over peoples and over kingdoms, to root out and to destroy and to disperse and to scatter, to build up and to plant' (Jer. 1: 10).[193] In each of these letters, Gregory spoke with masterful urgency, yet he was at pains to respect the order of the German church as the German archbishops saw it, and so to reduce tension between them and Rome. He addressed the bishops as brothers and partners, studiously guarding against all suggestions that he could boss them about like his bailiffs.

As the year went on, much public opinion in Germany, particularly in the south, hardened against Gregory's programme of reform, and especially against his demand for the chastity of those in major orders. Resistance was strong amongst the parochial clergy. It was fomented by propaganda. In 1074, there had been written a pamphlet in defence of clerical marriage which was ostensibly written by a clerk named Ulrich to a pope named Nicholas; its readers would have recalled the reforming precepts that had emanated from the papacy of Nicholas II.[194] Gregory's use of the laity to spread his own propaganda and to coerce the clergy was an especial grievance.[195] In the second half of 1075, the misfortunes of two German bishops, in particular, illustrate the unrest in the German church. The first was Otto of Constance. Gregory used Otto's messengers of the Lent synod of 1075 to inform him of his

---

[190] *Reg.* 2.61, 23 Mar. 1075, pp. 215–16.

[191] *Reg.* 2.66, 29 Mar. 1075, pp. 221–2.

[192] *Reg.* 2.67, 29 Mar. 1075, pp. 223–5.

[193] *Reg.* 2.68, 29 Mar. 1075, pp. 225–6.

[194] *MGH L. de L.* 1.254–60. Its date and place of writing remain uncertain, but mid-1074 is probable. The reiterated complaints of lack of *discretio* on the pope's part (pp. 255/20–2, 26–8, 33–4, 256/32, 258/2, 260/8–11) may be significant; cf. Archbishop Siegfried of Mainz's use of the term, above, 3.2.5. The clerk who wrote the pamphlet may have had Siegfried's criticism of Gregory in mind.

[195] 'Girovagi sub specie religionis discurrentes, maximum ubique seminant discordiam. Papae decretum enorme de continentia clericorum per laicos divulgatur': *Ann. Aug. a.* 1075, p. 128.

decrees against simony and clerical unchastity. Later in the year, Otto duly responded by holding a diocesan synod which was well attended. His clergy resolutely rejected legislation to enforce chastity. Gregory responded by sending Otto a letter of censure for his failure to enforce the decrees of the apostolic see; he summoned him to his Lent synod of 1076 where he was to answer for this and for all other outstanding charges against him. He also wrote to all the clergy and laity of the *regnum Teutonicorum* against bishops who tolerated clerical concubinage: 'We charge you in no way to condone these bishops or to follow their precepts, even as they themselves do not obey the commands of the apostolic see or heed the authority of the holy fathers.'[196] The second bishop was the staunchly Gregorian Altmann of Passau. Seeking to enforce Gregory's decrees, he read them to a diocesan synod and met bitter resistance which included threats to his life. He persisted and held another synod on 26 December, but continued to encounter the implacable resistance of his clergy.[197]

If Gregory's reforming zeal thus excited hostility in German localities, in relation to German metropolitans his determination to secure the reform of the church continued to be tempered with conciliation and moderation. This was conspicuously so with regard to Archbishop Siegfried of Mainz. Gregory pursued with him the plan for a national synod of the German church; but leadership of it was now to rest, not with much-resented papal legates but with Siegfried himself as archbishop of Mainz. According to the Swabian annalist Berthold, Gregory himself instructed Siegfried to hold a general council ('universale concilium') at Mainz, whereupon Siegfried duly convened his suffragans for 17 August; being already disposed to disobey papal commands, the suffragans saw that the synod came to nothing.[198] Siegfried's report to Gregory survives.[199] He made his customary protestations of respect and dutifulness. He thanked Gregory as chief shepherd for arousing him to his pastoral responsibilities, and expressed his satisfaction that, while Gregory had taken an initiative that was proper for the apostolic see, he had also respected Siegfried's rightful position:

Your fatherly authority instructed us to assemble our fellow bishops on an appointed day and to hold a council by command of your apostolic commission ('ex apostolicae legationis mandato'). Whatever we found in our province and kingdom to be wrongly done or wickedly misdone or boldly presumed upon against the rules of ecclesiastical life either through the simoniac heresy or through any other cause, we should not hesitate to cut away with the sickle of righteousness.

Siegfried disingenuously commented that what Gregory had commanded was, indeed, fair and just, because canon law required twice-yearly councils to be held in every province of the church. But, to explain the abortiveness of the council, he

---

[196] *Epp. vag.* nos. 8–22, pp. 16–27 (the limited MS testimony to no. 11 may indicate that it did not circulate widely in Germany, perhaps on account of the crisis of Jan.–Feb. 1076); Bernard, *De damn. schis.* cap. 42, *MGH L. de L.* 2.45, see Erdmann, *Briefliteratur*, p. 274 n. 3.
[197] *Vita Altmanni*, cap. 11, p. 232; the events seem to relate to the year 1075. See below, 3.6.2.
[198] *a.*1075, p. 278/19–25; cf. Lampert of Hersfeld, *Ann. a.* 1075, p. 302.
[199] *CU* no. 45, pp. 97–100.

pleaded at great length that civil war made the holding of such assemblies in Germany for the present impractical. The bishops had suffered with everyone else; Siegfried gave it as an excuse for their non-attendance that 'their consequent penury prevented their coming to a church council, because to recover their goods they perforce went to the secular courts'. Furthermore, fear of the king prevented many from coming to a council. If those who lay open to the accusation of ecclesiastical crimes that Gregory wanted to be punished were added to those who dared not come from fear of the king, there would be scarcely enough bishops to pass judgement at any council that might assemble! On top of all this, in the divided state of Germany a council would become a cockpit for opposing parties. The German bishops, therefore, thought that a German council should be postponed until domestic peace was restored. Siegfried protested that he would, of course, always obey Gregory; after the Saxon campaign was over, he would at once send messengers to prove this. But he was sure that, at present, Gregory would see that a council was impracticable, and should be postponed until a time that Gregory saw to be ripe.

Berthold commented that the German bishops and clergy were, in fact, for the most part hostile to Gregory's reforming zeal, and Gregory well knew that this was the case. Replying on 3 September to Siegfried, Gregory dismissed the archbishop's arguments as mere pretexts which were unfitting for pastors of Christ's flock; he made an impassioned plea that Siegfried should consider first the welfare of men's souls. Specifically, Gregory declared himself anxious about the case of Bishop Werner of Strassburg, whose alleged simony Siegfried was to investigate and report upon directly to Gregory. The council should by no means be postponed, and Siegfried was resolutely to pursue the campaign against simony and clerical fornication.[200] Gregory's letter was brought to Germany by Bishop Henry of Chur. When it arrived in October, it was read to a council that Siegfried was holding at Mainz; since several bishops were present, it was clearly a provincial council. According to Lampert of Hersfeld, the clergy angrily rejected it and demonstrated their hostility to Gregory's campaign for moral reform.[201] What Gregory's next step might have been can be only a matter of speculation. The significant fact is that, hitherto at least in 1075, by envisaging a German council he had shown a concern for Siegfried's sensibilities about his own authority in the German church and a willingness to work with him that he had not shown in the previous year.

Gregory was still more accommodating in his dealings with Archbishop Liemar of Bremen. In 1074, Liemar had written hard words about Gregory as 'periculosus homo', and Gregory's sentencing of him at the Lent synod in 1075 to suspension and excommunication had been severe. But, like his master Henry IV who was for much of the year preoccupied with the Saxon rising and who was concerned to keep the way open for imperial coronation, Liemar needed Gregory's goodwill—in his case, in connection with the northern aspirations of his see. His need was highlighted by

---

[200] *Reg.* 3.4, pp. 248–50. [201] *a.*1075, p. 302.

the position of Bishop Rikwal of Lund. Rikwal was a fugitive clerk of the church of Paderborn who, in 1072, had become bishop of Lund; both Bishop Immad of Paderborn and Archbishop Adalbert of Bremen had excommunicated him. By 1075, Rikwal was concerned to salvage his position by securing release from both excommunications. It was an opportunity for Liemar to assert his metropolitan jurisdiction and, perhaps, his standing as papal vicar and legate in the North.[202] He therefore tempered his anger of 1074 and acknowledged Gregory's sentence of suspension.[203] Described by Bonizo of Sutri as 'vir sapientissimus et omnium artium peritissimus', he arranged for Bishop Immad of Paderborn twice to write to Gregory in his favour.[204] At first, he tried to secure a hearing by means of envoys, but when Gregory demanded that he come in person he complied. He travelled with an entourage that included Meinhard of Bamberg, the future Archbishop Wezilo of Mainz, and a clerk from Cologne named Widukind. The embassy satisfied Gregory that Henry IV was showing zeal and obedience to the pope in dealing with simony and clerical fornication. For himself, Liemar secured a full pardon and was restored to his office.[205]

The tribulations of Bishop Hermann of Bamberg reveal most clearly of all the movement in the middle months of 1075 towards conciliation and the relief of tension between the German king, the pope, and the German episcopate. At his Lent synod, Gregory had been as mild towards Hermann as he had been severe with Archbishop Liemar of Bremen: Hermann had merely been suspended from office unless he came to Rome and made satisfaction before Eastertide.[206] But the long-standing hostility to him of his cathedral canons persisted, with deep local roots in anger at the diversion of resources to new religious foundations and to the military needs of the king, and in resentment at the bishop's lack of consultation with them.[207] The principal source for the development of events is a letter written, probably in May, by the *scholasticus* Meinhard on the chapter's behalf to a bishop, probably Embricho of Augsburg, who was well disposed to Hermann.[208] It explained that, after Gregory summoned Hermann to the Lent synod, the canons had urged their bishop, if he trusted in his innocence, to go to Rome and free himself from the charge of simony. Archbishop Siegfried of Mainz had meanwhile come to Bamberg and, with Hermann's concurrence, had directed that two or three of the canons

---

[202] See below, 6.8. [203] Bonizo of Sutri, *Lib. ad amic.* 9, p. 616.

[204] Schmeidler, 'Ein Brief Imads von Paderborn'; *Dipl. Danic.* 1/2, no. 14, pp. 29–31.

[205] Bonizo of Sutri, *Lib. ad amic.* 7, p. 602, 9, p. 616; *Reg.* 3.3, to Henry IV, 20 July 1075, pp. 246–7.

[206] *Reg.* 2.52a, p. 196/27–8.

[207] *H* no. 81, p. 131, *M* no. 25, pp. 222–7, *M* no. 41, pp. 243–6.

[208] *M* no. 41. This letter was doubly one of apology: it sought to justify the chapter's action to a bishop who was well disposed to Hermann, and to argue that the chapter's proceedings against Hermann at Bamberg and at Rome were consistent with such German ideas of ecclesiastical jurisdiction as Siegfried of Mainz had expressed in his letters. (i) The canons wrote in answer to a letter alleging that they had acted precipitately; they claimed to have acted within the due bounds of ecclesiastical order: p. 242/25–32, cf. *M* 25, p. 223/15–20. (ii) They were at pains to show how the case against Hermann had been handled at Easter 1075; Siegfried of Mainz had himself approved proceedings at Rome: p. 243/1–29. (iii) At Rome, Gregory had been careful not to transgress German rights: p. 244/11–18. (iv) After relating what had happened, the canons insisted that their course of action had been canonically correct: p. 245/1–14.

should accompany him to Rome where he might canonically free himself from the charges against him. Hermann swore that, if he were not cleared, he would not again require his canons' obedience or claim episcopal oversight of them. Siegfried also travelled to Rome where, on Low Sunday (12 April) when Hermann's period of grace had expired, he took part in an assembly at which Gregory and the cardinals were accompanied by Bishops Adalbero of Würzburg and Hermann of Metz. At Gregory's urgent command, Siegfried delated Hermann of Bamberg as a simoniac. The assembly unanimously determined that, if Hermann came to Rome, he should receive a judgement which was not specified; if he were recalcitrant, Siegfried should, by papal command, instruct the clergy and people of Bamberg to deny him their obedience and to shun his communion and fellowship.

Hermann of Bamberg was some two days journey from Rome when he heard of this decision through a trusted agent whom (as the letter alleged) he had sent ahead to bribe favour at Rome. According to the letter, Hermann sent to Gregory some trusted members of his entourage to testify to his innocence. Gregory told them that Hermann must come to Rome and to papal judgement on pain of excommunication. Gregory's letters give his side of the affair.[209] Hermann had, indeed, stopped short in his journey to Rome and had sent messengers to corrupt its clergy by their gifts. He returned to Germany, saying that he would resign his see and enter a monastery. Some of the Bamberg clergy who were with Hermann had gone to Rome where, after long dealings with Gregory, they secured his letter of 20 April in which he described Hermann as an illiterate whose simoniac depravity had enslaved his church,[210] and whose recent outrage in seeking to bribe Roman clergy had brought upon him a papal sentence of condemnation. Gregory prohibited violation of the lands and goods of the see of Bamberg during its vacancy. To warrant his direct intervention, he introduced a novel argument which he evidently intended to counter German objections: he invoked the special relation to the apostolic see that Bamberg enjoyed because the Emperor Henry II had founded it in direct dependence upon it. He concluded his letter of 20 April by promising his protection to the lands and possessions of the see 'until Almighty God should by the mediation (*interventum*) of St Peter provide that church with a suitable pastor'.

Upon returning to Bamberg, Hermann took steps to restore his position. He made grants of lands to his lay adherents.[211] He also sought to give credibility to his penitential intentions by endowing the monasteries of Bamberg and by reviving his plan to go on pilgrimage.[212] This added fuel to the fire of his canons' anger against him. A letter of Provost Poppo and the *scholasticus* Meinhard to him set out the line of appeal

[209] (i) *Reg.* 2.76, to the clergy and people of Bamberg, 20 Apr. 1075, pp. 239–40. (ii) Further letters of 20 July 1075, *Reg.* 3.1–3, to the clergy and people of Bamberg, Archbishop Siegfried of Mainz, and King Henry IV, pp. 242–7.

[210] 'Unde quia quidam idiota predictam ecclesiam symoniacae perfidie heretica pravitate subversus invaserat, eam a iugo sacrilegae pervasionis illius provida consideratione liberare studuimus.'

[211] As emerges from *Reg.* 6.19, to the *ministeriales* of Bamberg, 17 Feb. 1079, pp. 430–1.

[212] *M* no. 25, cf. *Reg.* 3.1, pp. 243/5–9, 14–17, 23, 244/3, 22–9, 247/12–16.

that they proposed; it kept within the structure of jurisdiction that the German church had sought to defend against Gregory.[213]

But events had their own momentum. Archbishop Liemar of Bremen now made his journey to Rome in search of Gregory's favour, and the *scholasticus* Meinhard was associated with his visit. Provost Poppo, too, with some companions travelled to Rome with a letter, now lost, from the Bamberg chapter.[214] They did so with the knowledge and sanction of important persons of the king's court, and probably of the king himself.[215] In effect, Liemar's restoration to office was purchased at the price of Hermann's deposition. Given both Liemar's amenability to Roman judgement and the approval of the king's court for the mission from Bamberg, Gregory could now intervene in German affairs, not as an outside authority, but at the request of German churchmen and of the royal court. Archbishop Siegfried of Mainz could do little but concur.

Gregory communicated his total condemnation of the simoniac Hermann in three letters which were dispatched on 20 July in the wake of Liemar's visit.[216] He informed the clergy and people of Bamberg of their bishop's final and complete deposition—from his episcopal office for his simony and from his priesthood for his depredation of his church upon pretence of sanctity. Gregory also excommunicated him until he presented himself in person at Rome. Writing to Siegfried of Mainz, Gregory repeated his sentences of Hermann and charged the archbishop to help in securing 'the canonical election of a new bishop, so that you may show yourself to have made good your negligence with regard to the former simoniac'. To the king he wrote in cordial terms, approving Henry's supposed endeavours to curb Hermann's transgressions; like Siegfried, the king was charged to attend to the filling of the see in a befitting manner. Making no mention of legislation at his Lent synod about lay investiture, Gregory merely stipulated that the king should proceed 'by the counsel of religious men'. Gregory's studiously restrained language in effect left the king in a position himself to settle the future of the see.[217] Henry can scarcely have failed to notice the depth of the trust that Gregory was currently placing in him, or Gregory's lack of comprehension of the political and ecclesiastical realities of the German kingdom.

The summer of 1075 thus witnessed the spectacle of the pope and the king ostensibly collaborating in the deposition and disgrace of a simoniac bishop and in the election of his successor by a process which in Gregory's eyes must satisfy the principle of free election but which might in form and detail be a matter for generous accommodation. There was no swift response or result. For a short time after his return, Hermann continued to attempt to govern his see,[218] but he was compelled to withdraw to monastic retreat in the abbey of Münsterschwarzach; from there, he addressed to the king a querulous letter pleading to be restored to the royal favour

---

[213] *M* no. 25.　　　　[214] *Reg.* 3.1, p. 242/21–5.
[215] *H* no. 58, Poppo to the king's chancellor Adalbero, ?Aug. 1075, pp. 104–5.
[216] *Reg.* 3.1–3, cf. *H* no. 58.
[217] Cf. *Reg.* 3.7, to King Henry IV, early Aug. 1075, pp. 258/16–259/2.　　　　[218] *Reg.* 6.19.

and perhaps to his see of Bamberg.[219] He did so to no avail. The king delayed until 30 November, when he went to Bamberg and named Rupert, the provost of Goslar, to be the new bishop.[220] At the cost of finally abandoning Hermann, for so long his right-hand man in the crisis of the Saxon rebellion, Henry had been able to retain papal favour. But, by November, he had secured his principal goals in the defeat of the Saxons and in the freeing from papal sentence of Archbishop Liemar of Bremen.[221] Meanwhile, as Archbishop Gebhard of Salzburg was later to comment, there had been a remarkable show of concord between *sacerdotium* and *regnum*:

At that time, such concord prevailed between the German kingdom and the papacy, that everything done to depose one bishop of Bamberg and to substitute another was reckoned to be done under the command of and by obedience to the Roman pontiff.[222]

There were other developments in Henry IV's dominions which, in 1075, served to persuade Gregory that the king earnestly desired to promote the better order of the church. One was in Germany itself, and concerned the Swabian monastery of Hirsau. Hirsau was a proprietary monastery of the counts of Calw which had come under strong reforming influence in 1069, when Count Albert of Calw summoned from St Emmeram at Regensberg a monk named William to be its abbot.[223] William was resolved to free Hirsau from the yoke of temporal authority. To this end, he sought to promote monastic *libertas* in the highest form that was then current in Salian Germany by securing from Henry IV a royal diploma.[224] The change in Hirsau's status in 1075 and its progress towards *libertas* thus took place with Henry's co-operation, and it was brought directly to Gregory's notice when, towards the end of 1075, Abbot William travelled to Rome with Count Albert of Calw's concurrence in order to secure papal confirmation of the new arrangements as set out in Henry's charter.[225] The papal privilege which Gregory granted opened the possibility of Hirsau's in future being further reformed according to canon law rather than German law; at the same time, Gregory could express approval of the arrangements that Count Albert had already made and that had been confirmed by the king's seal.[226] As with the crisis over the see of Bamberg, so with regard to Hirsau Gregory could reflect that he was making progress towards his reforming objectives by way of an all-round collaboration and concord in which King Henry of Germany showed every sign of being amenable.

---

[219] *H* no. 2, pp. 17–19; see Erdmann, *Briefliteratur*, pp. 161–2. Erdmann dated the letter July/Nov. 1075.

[220] Lampert of Hersfeld, *Ann. a.* 1075, p. 324; Berthold, *a.*1075, p. 279/41–6. Berthold notes that Gregory soon restored Hermann to communion.

[221] See Bruno, cap. 15, pp. 210–12.   [222] *Epistola*, cap. 34, p. 279.

[223] See Cowdrey, *The Cluniacs*, pp. 196–208.

[224] *MGH DDHIV* no. 280; cf. *Vita Willihelmi abbatis Hirsaugiensis*, caps. 2–3, p. 212. For further details, see below, 3.6.3.

[225] *Vita Willihelmi*, cap. 4, p. 213.

[226] *QF* no. 88, pp. 71–3; see Cowdrey, *The Cluniacs*, pp. 199–201.

Even at the crisis point of Milan,[227] Gregory seems to have developed a comparable expectation of Henry's goodwill and compliance. There, too, no conflict developed until well after the conclusion in mid-1075 of the Saxon wars which freed Henry's hands. Of the rival candidates for the archbishopric, one, Atto, remained quietly at Rome with Gregory; while the other, Godfrey, resided at Milan.

Until Gregory's two legates in Germany restored Henry to communion at Nuremberg in the spring of 1074, his Register gives evidence of active and zealous concern for Milanese affairs. He showed unabated anger against the Lombard bishops who had consecrated Godfrey at Novara. He instructed the Countesses Beatrice and Matilda to shun them in matters spiritual and political. Archbishop Godfrey, too, was to be shunned: Bishop William of Pavia was to resist him and the bishops who had consecrated him, but to aid his Patarene opponents; on 1 July Gregory circulated a fervent letter to all the faithful of St Peter in Lombardy, charging them to shun Godfrey and resist him with all their power.[228]

Early in September 1073, when Gregory received Henry's *supplex epistola*,[229] there was a change in the climate of affairs. In his letter, Henry expressed preparedness to follow Gregory's directions in all church matters wherein he had erred, and he named first the Milanese church which was in error by his fault. He asked for its canonical correction by Gregory's apostolic discipline. Just before receiving Henry's letter, as part of his preparation for the concord of spiritual and lay powers, Gregory had told Bishop Raynald of Como that he might talk to the Lombard bishops but not have other fellowship with them.[230] Soon afterwards, he wrote to Erlembald about Henry's letters being 'full of sweetness and obedience, the like of which he could not recall that Henry or any of his predecessors had ever sent to a pope'. Several of Henry's leading subjects had vouched for his preparedness to obey Gregory so far as the Milanese church was concerned; Gregory would act to take advantage of the new situation.[231] He still urged bishops like Albert of Acqui and William of Pavia to assist Erlembald in the *bellum Dei* at Milan.[232] If he summoned all the Lombard bishops and abbots to his Lent synod of 1074 and renewed there his excommunication of Godfrey and recognition of Atto, he soon afterwards was at pains to reassure Countesses Beatrice and Matilda, who thought his treatment of the Lombard bishops to be unduly mild.[233] Thereafter, his letters show no signs of direct concern with Milanese affairs until the very end of 1075.[234] His silence may have been in part the

---

[227] See above, 2.2.7.

[228] *Reg.* 1.11, to Countesses Beatrice and Matilda, 24 June 1073, pp. 17–19; 1.12, to Bishop William of Pavia, 29 June 1073, pp. 19–20; 1.15, to the faithful to St Peter in Lombardy, 1 July 1073, pp. 23–5.

[229] *Reg.* 1.29a, pp. 47–9.

[230] *Reg.* 1.20, to Bishop-elect Anselm II of Lucca, 1 Sept. 1073, pp. 34–5.

[231] *Reg.* 1.25, to Erlembald, 27 Sept. 1073, pp. 41–2, cf. 1.26, to the same, 9 Oct. 1073, pp. 43–4.

[232] *Reg.* 1.27–8, to Bishops Albert of Acqui, and William of Pavia, 13 Oct. 1073, pp. 44–6.

[233] *Reg.* 1.43, to the suffragans of Milan and the abbots of Lombardy, 25 Jan. 1074, pp. 65–7; 1.77, to Countesses Beatrice and Matilda, 15 Apr. 1074, pp. 109–11; Arnulf of Milan, 4, pp. 208–9.

[234] i.e. until after Henry promoted Tedald to the see: *Reg.* 3.8–9, to Tedald with a covering letter to the suffragans of Milan, 8 Dec. 1075, pp. 259–63. The sparseness of registration in 1075 must be borne in

result of Erlembald's setbacks in 1074 and early 1075, culminating in Erlembald's death and the crippling of his cause at Milan.[235] But the critical factor was Henry's restoration to communion at Nuremberg, when he gave Gregory's legates an assurance that he would settle Milanese affairs in a manner acceptable to Gregory.[236]

Gregory's consequent goodwill is warmly expressed in a letter of 7 December 1074. He noticed that Henry had not yet settled the Milanese problem as his letters and promises had foreshadowed that he would. But his legates' reports when they at last returned to Rome had assured him of Henry's good intentions. He also referred to his own reiterated condemnation of Archbishop Godfrey: using his favourite device of proposing a dialogue, he said that if Henry could convince him by the words of righteous men that his sentence could be changed, he would listen. If not, he urged Henry to exercise his royal authority in correcting the Milanese situation.[237] There is no reason to doubt that Gregory hoped for Henry's collaboration over Milan as part of the concord that he sought between them. In any case, Gregory did not allow the city's affairs to undermine his confidence in Henry until the very last weeks of 1075.

3.3 From Worms to Canossa

3.3.1 Henry IV's Breach with Gregory VII

In view of the relaxation of tension between Gregory and Henry, and between Gregory and the German bishops, that marked most of 1075, it is not surprising that, as contemporaries saw matters, the breach effected by the bishops' renunciation of their obedience to Gregory at Worms on 24 January 1076 came suddenly, unexpectedly, and decisively: 'this was the day when the whole calamity under which we suffer began', wrote the chronicler Hugh of Flavigny. Hugh further noted that the appointment of Bishop Rupert of Bamberg, which took place on 30 November, had appeared to preserve a façade of goodwill between pope and king.[238] Yet tensions had been building up beneath the surface at least since September 1075. They are first apparent in a letter of Gregory to Countesses Beatrice and Matilda of Tuscany.[239] They had sent him a letter which does not survive about matters which he did not specify, though he expressed surprise at their having written it. For they well knew that Gregory had with him Henry's two messengers who some two months ago had brought him the king's letter,[240] of which he cited an excerpt, in which Henry insisted upon the secrecy of their mission save to himself, the Empress Agnes, and the countesses. Henry gave as his reason that almost all the German princes sought discord, not peace, between Gregory and Henry. Henry had promised in due course

---

mind. Gregory's letter to the Milanese priest Liutprand probably also dates from late 1075: *QF* no. 106, pp. 94–5.

[235] Arnulf of Milan, 4.9–10, pp. 214–17; Andrew of Strumi, *Vita s. Arialdi*, caps. 68, 78, pp. 1094, 1100; Bonizo of Sutri, *Lib. ad amic.* 7, p. 604.

[236] *Reg.* 3.10, to King Henry, (8 Dec.) 1075, p. 264/17–21.

[237] *Reg.* 2.30, to Henry IV, 7 Dec. 1074, p. 164.

[238] Hugh of Flavigny, 2, p. 431/6–23.

[239] *Reg.* 3.5, 11 Sept. 1075, pp. 251–2.

[240] *Epp. HIV* no. 7, pp. 58–9.

to send Gregory other messengers with fuller messages; he had assured his original messengers that he remained of the same mind as when he sent them. But now, Gregory complained, Henry had changed it. He had turned to the princes whom he had described as fomenters of discord. Whatever the countesses' request may have been, Gregory could not accede to it; the proper course was for Henry to revert to his former conduct.

The nature of Henry's supposed volte-face does not emerge. But it is likely to have concerned a return to his counsels of Duke Godfrey of Lorraine, Countess Matilda's estranged husband. If so, it should not be forgotten that his predecessor as duke had frustrated Henry's earlier plan to go to Rome for imperial coronation.[241] The present duke's connections with Tuscany remained considerable, and he was no friend of Gregory's. The last part of Gregory's letter advised Matilda about her attitude to him. Gregory was unsure about the reply that she should make to a communication from the duke, since he had openly broken a sworn promise to her. The subject of the promise is not stated; it may have concerned their personal relations, or it may have been of a political nature. Despite Godfrey's seeming unreliability, Gregory would approve any *modus vivendi* with him which Matilda might reach, so long as it was consistent with the traditional authority of the church; if not, he hoped that the charity binding himself with her would prevail. Whatever happened, he would be loyal to the two countesses.

Whatever the occasion of Gregory's letter, the last months of 1075 saw Henry, with his hands now freed in Germany from the Saxon revolt, embarking in Italy upon actions which Gregory would scarcely approve. Probably under advice from Duke Godfrey of Lorraine, he set aside plans for imperial coronation accompanied by such promises of obedient service as Gregory had looked for; instead, he sought in three ways to advance his power in Italy and to constrain Gregory from all sides.

First, in the north, he sought to settle the disputed archiepiscopal succession at Milan by promoting a fresh candidate of his own.[242] The defeat of the Patarenes and the death on 5 April 1075 of their militant leader Erlembald had led to a revival of Henry's support there. While he was preparing his Saxon expedition, he received an embassy from the city. Probably in early autumn, Henry dispatched Count Eberhard, one of the excommunicate counsellors to whom Gregory greatly objected. At Roncaglia, Eberhard held a meeting at which the Milanese were invited to declare their wishes about the succession. The outcome was that Henry ignored the existing rivals—Godfrey, whom he had himself caused to be elected and consecrated in 1071, and Atto, whom the Patarenes had set up in opposition and who had fled to Gregory at Rome. There succeeded instead a well-born Milanese subdeacon named Tedald who had served in the royal chapel and perhaps in the Saxon wars; the bishops of the province consecrated him. According to Bonizo of Sutri, Tedald was soon occupied in dealings with two of Gregory's future opponents—Archbishop Guibert of

---

[241] See above, 3.1.2.
[242] Arnulf of Milan, 4.8–5.5, pp. 212–24; Landulf Senior, 3.30–2, pp. 97–9; Bonizo of Sutri, *Lib. ad amic.* 7, pp. 604–6.

Ravenna whom Gregory had already threatened with suspension from office, and Cardinal Hugh Candidus whom Gregory had recently excommunicated.

Second, in the south Henry appears to have been in contact with the Normans. In late 1075, Count Eberhard together with Bishop Gregory of Vercelli who was Henry's Italian chancellor, was engaged in negotiations with the excommunicated duke of Apulia, Robert Guiscard. They seem to have sought to persuade him to receive investiture with his Italian possessions at Henry's hands. He evidently returned a diplomatic refusal,[243] but Henry's simultaneous activities at Milan and in Apulia were disquieting from a papal point of view, since they constituted a threat on two fronts.

Third, Henry also took the provocative action in Central Italy of appointing to the sees of Fermo and Spoleto bishops who were personally unknown to Gregory; he thus intruded in the affairs of the Roman ecclesiastical province; his action was the more offensive to Gregory because, during a recent vacancy of the see of Fermo, Gregory had committed its administration into the hands of the archdeacon pending an appointment to the see in which Gregory intended to respect Henry's interest.[244] All these steps indicate that, probably under the influence of Duke Godfrey of Lorraine, Henry was seeking to build up such a position in the Italian peninsula that he could hope to establish his imperial authority and claim his imperial title on terms that were his own, not Gregory's.

Gregory's initial reactions to these steps were remarkable for their restraint; at least in their public aspect they proceeded more from sorrow than from anger. If he knew about Henry's negotiations with Robert Guiscard, there is no evidence for his view of them. His response to Tedald's election at Milan was communicated in two letters which were apparently written upon hearing of it from supporters of his own through whom Tedald sought papal friendship and favour.[245] The first was addressed to Tedald himself. Gregory reminded him of Atto, who already had a claim to the see that Gregory could not neglect, as well as of Godfrey whose sacrilegious invasion of the see had led to his ruin. Gregory protested his affection for Tedald, whom he invited to come to Rome for the next Lent synod (14–20 February 1076), or, if he preferred, before it; it might thus be determined what course of action he should follow. Gregory went so far as to assure him that, if it transpired that he should withdraw papal support from Atto, he would further Tedald's promotion. Meanwhile, Tedald was to proceed no higher in holy orders; he should obey Gregory,

---

[243] Amatus, 7.27, pp. 320–1. See also the interpolation in Würzburg, Universitätsbibliothek, MS M ch q 33, fo. 49v: Lorenzo Valla, *De falso credita et ementita Constantini donatione*, ed. W. Setz, *MGH Quellen Geistesgesch.* 10 (1976), p. 26; according to it as to Amatus, Robert Guiscard refused fealty to Henry for lands that he held of the pope but expressed willingness to do it for other lands. His willingness may have been diplomatic; it elicited from Henry's envoys the convenient reply that they were not empowered to consider this.

[244] *Reg.* 3.10, to King Henry IV, (8 Dec.) 1075, p. 264/21–6; cf. 2.38, to Count Hubert and the people of Fermo, 22 Dec. 1074, pp. 174–5, esp. p. 174/20–4, where a suitable bishop was to be found 'cum nostra sollicitudine tum regis consilio et dispensatione'.

[245] *Reg.* 3.8–9, to the Milanese clerk Tedald, and to the suffragans of Milan, 8 Dec. 1075, pp. 259–63; cf. 3.10, p. 264/17–21. Tedald's approach to Gregory is apparently confirmed by Benzo of Alba's attack upon his faint-heartedness: 4.1, pp. 634–6.

and not trust in the king's protection, his own noble birth, or the help of the Milanese. Gregory's second letter was circulated to all the episcopal suffragans of Milan. Despite their past opposition to Gregory, he addressed them mildly and courteously. He sought their co-operation, and merely forbade any of them to promote Tedald in holy orders until he himself had come to a decision about him at Rome. As regards the sees of Fermo and Spoleto, his comments were terse and no less restrained; they referred only to the manner, and not to the fact, of Henry's appointments.

Gregory's restraint may partly be explained by the absence of simony from these events, but he seems also to have persisted in the quest for all-round appeasement of conflicts that he had adopted earlier in 1075. His use in his letter to Tedald of his favourite device of inviting Tedald to plead his own case suggests that, even in December, he had not abandoned his hope of dealing with Henry IV by way of a common progress towards *concordia*.

It is by way of the letters about Milan that the critically important and lengthy letter that Gregory addressed to Henry, probably on the same day, should be approached.[246] Gregory reviewed the present state of their relations. His disquiet was made apparent in the salutation, for he gave his blessing conditionally upon Henry's obedience to the apostolic see, 'as befits a Christian king'. He went straight to the heart of the issue, which was not Henry's dealings in Italy as such, but his association at home with persons excommunicated by the apostolic see and by synodal sentence. Gregory clearly intended political counsellors like Count Eberhard, who were under sanction from the days of Pope Alexander II and who were now involved in Italian affairs. If Henry was associating with them, his road to grace must once again be that by which he had travelled in 1074: he must banish excommunicates from his presence and compel them to do penance, while he must himself obtain absolution and forgiveness by due satisfaction.[247] Now, however, Gregory made no mention of sending papal legates for this purpose. He made Henry's way easy and unobjectionable: if he was indeed guilty, he should resort to a bishop in good standing, who would with Gregory's support impose a penance; then, with Henry's consent, the bishop should report in writing to Rome.

In Gregory's eyes, that was to make matters easy. He next reviewed Henry's recent conduct. It now appeared that, under colour of devotion, humility, and obedience, he had been resisting the church's decrees in matters wherein his compliance was necessary. Gregory touched first upon Henry's recent dealings at Milan, and at Fermo and Spoleto: in them, he should have shown greater respect to St Peter, the master of the church. Having enlarged upon the duty of obedience to St Peter, Gregory recalled the Lent synod of 1075 and its decrees. Gregory called upon Henry to obey them, but he also invited him to send competent and religious subjects of his own who might be able to persuade Gregory that his ruling might be tempered. Once again, Gregory invited a quest for *concordia*. He observed that Henry would have done well to have so proceeded before acting as he had latterly done:

[246] *Reg.* 3.10, pp. 263–7; it is dated 8 Jan. 1076, but Caspar's reasons for antedating it to 8 Dec. 1075, the same date as 3.8–9, are cogent: p. 263, n. 1.   [247] See above, 3.2.3.

Indeed, even if you had not been cautioned by us in so friendly a manner, it would have been only fair on your part first to have reasonably inquired of us how we had offended you or acted against your prerogatives, before you infringed papal decrees. But in truth, what regard you have for our admonitions and for the observance of righteousness, your subsequent actions and arrangements make clear.[248]

There is here a note of pain and of sternness, but Gregory ended his letter mildly, expressing confidence that Henry might even yet be brought to obey God's commandments. He reminded Henry of the debt that he owed to God for his victory over the Saxons, and he held before him the biblical examples of Saul, whose disobedience to Samuel after a military victory led to the Lord's rejecting him (1 Sam. 15), but also of David, whose humility met with a corresponding reward (2 Sam. 7). He expected his dialogue with Henry to continue. He concluded by saying that he had not answered all the points in Henry's letters to him; this may allude to Henry's earlier requests about his imperial coronation. He was sending back with the present letter Henry's two messengers of July, Radbod and Adelpreth, and also Udelschalk. He would declare his will more fully when these three messengers returned from Germany and reported on Henry's response to both his written and his verbal representations.

Gregory's letter calls for careful reading. It was not, in itself, an ultimatum, nor did it give evidence of Gregory's 'unconcealed hostility' to Henry.[249] When compared with the use that Gregory had made in recent letters to Germany about Saul's loss of God's favour through his disobedience to Samuel,[250] Gregory did not in this letter immediately threaten Henry with the fate of Saul; instead, he held up to him the two models of the disobedient Saul and the obedient David. Of itself, what Gregory wrote in this letter gives no grounds for the conclusion that Gregory was already holding out to Henry a threat of deposition because he despaired of him as ruler of Germany and Italy.

The verbal messages that Gregory sent by Henry's messengers had a different ring to them. Gregory himself wrote of a difference of tone in his written and verbal messages when, in the summer of 1076, he justified his sanctions of that year against Henry in a letter to all the faithful in Germany.[251] In December, he had sent Henry 'letters of admonition' ('commonitorias epistolas');[252] which reflected a desire that the king should respond to the call of apostolic mercy rather than expose himself to the rigours of apostolic severity. But his verbal messages spelt out in more threatening detail the consequence of disobedience, which included excommunication and deprivation of the kingly office. His continuing familiarity with his excommunicated counsellors involved him in their alienation from Christ, and he must show his repentence by abandoning them. Admonitions were fortified by threats:

[248] *Reg.* 3.10, p. 264/2–4. See the discussion of this letter, above, 3.2.4.
[249] See e.g. Hauck, *Kirchengeschichte Deutschlands*, 3.788; Haller, *Das Papsttum*, 2.386.
[250] *Reg.* 2.45, 11 Jan. 1075, to the South German dukes, p. 184/6–9; 2.66, 29 Mar. 1075, to Bishop Burchard of Halberstadt, p. 222/4–7; *Epp. vag.* no. 10, to the clergy and laity of the diocese of Constance, late 1075, pp. 24–7.
[251] *Epp. vag.* no. 14, pp. 36–9.
[252] The plural creates the possibility, but does not establish, that Gregory dispatched other, lost letters.

We also sent to him three religious men, faithful followers of his own, through whom we secretly admonished him to do penance for his sins which, shameful to say, were known to most men and noised abroad through many parts; for the authority of divine and human laws enjoined and commanded that on account of them he should not only be excommunicated until he had made due satisfaction but that he should also be deprived of his entire dignity as king without hope of recovery.[253] Finally, unless he excluded the excommunicates from associating with him we could come to no other judgement or decision about him than that he should be separated from the church and share the company of any excommunicates with whom he had chosen to have his part rather than with Christ (Acts 8: 21). However, should he be willing to heed our warnings and to amend his life, we called, and still call, God to witness how greatly we would rejoice for his salvation and honour, and with how much love we would embrace him in the bosom of holy church as one who, being set as a prince over the people (Isa. 3: 7) and having the rule of a most far-flung kingdom, it behoves to be the upholder of catholic peace and righteousness.

The severity of Gregory's verbal message did not pass unnoticed.[254] In the letters, his purpose was public and political; his verbal messages were those of a spiritual father whose concern was the private correction of an erring sinner. Not surprisingly, Henry understood them as an attack upon the roots of his kingship. Probably he had never intended to rid himself of the counsellors to whom Gregory objected on the grounds of their simony; it was not Italian but German affairs that principally led to the breach in 1076 between Gregory and Henry. In view of the relaxation of tension in 1075 which has been described, Carl Erdmann concluded that the Italian church, and especially events at Milan, were primarily responsible for it: 'It was not the structure of the Ottonian imperial church that made inevitable the clash with the Gregorian papacy, but solely its extension to Italy.'[255] In fact, Milanese affairs had been largely quiescent since the death of the Patarene leader Erlembald, and in his reaction to Tedald's election Gregory was surprisingly restrained and anxious to avoid a crisis. The heart of the problem was whether or not Henry would part with his German counsellors who were guilty of simoniacal dealings and who stood behind his episcopal appointments in Germany as in Italy, and whether the German bishops were still so far alienated from Gregory by his interventions in Germany, especially in 1074, that they would rally to the king if he rejected Gregory's demand that he dismiss his counsellors and do penance.

Henry held his Christmas court at Goslar; there, his position was strengthened in two major respects. Some who were present swore after his death to accept his infant son Conrad as king;[256] thus, the descent of the crown was confirmed in the Salian line. Further, Otto of Nordheim was freed from captivity and reconciled to the king;[257] the hostility of one of his most powerful adversaries was quietened. It was to

---

[253] Gregory's threats of excommunication were also referred to by Lampert of Hersfeld, *Ann. a.* 1076, pp. 342–4; Bernold, *Chron. a.* 1076, p. 432/3–6, and *De damn. schis.* cap. 7, p. 49. According to Bernold, Gregory gave Henry only until the next Lent synod to prove his penitence.

[254] Berthold, *a.*1075, p. 280/33–44.

[255] Erdmann, *Briefliteratur*, pp. 280–1.   [256] Bernold, *Chron. a.* 1076, p. 431/13–14.

[257] Lampert of Hersfeld, *Ann. a.* 1076, pp. 342, 356.

Goslar that Gregory's three messengers came with his letter and verbal messages. They arrived on 1 January, and their completion of the journey of 1700–1800 kilometres from Rome in some twenty-three winter days testifies to the urgency of their mission in Gregory's eyes. Henry received their messages as an ultimatum from Gregory to strip him alike of his earthly kingdom and of his eternal salvation. Faced with the demand that he declare his obedience to Gregory in time for tidings to reach Gregory's Lent synod, Henry angrily proceeded to extreme measures which were accentuated by the accumulated resentments of Gregory's pressure while the Saxon rising had compelled him to seem to submit. He demonstrated his rejection of Gregory's demands by publicly communing with his excommunicate counsellors. He convened an assembly of spiritual and lay princes to meet at Worms on 24 January, and so in time for its decisions to reach Gregory at his Lent synod.[258]

At Worms, there was a large attendance of bishops; besides the archbishops of Mainz and Trier, twenty-four bishops are known from the official acts of the assembly to have been present.[259] There were only a few lay princes, of whom the most notable was Duke Godfrey of Lorraine, who played a predominant part in compelling the bishops' obedience to Henry.[260] The presence of the royal household added a number of men with all to gain and nothing to lose by the adopting of the severest possible measures against Gregory. The virulence of feelings against him which had been built up in Germany by his zeal of the past two years against the king's lay counsellors and against so many of the bishops was played upon by Cardinal Hugh Candidus, whom Gregory had recently dismissed from Rome. He had been a leading figure in promoting Gregory's election to the papacy, and he was well versed in subsequent affairs at Rome. Smarting at his dismissal, he was restrained by no scruples in maligning both Gregory's public conduct and his private life.[261] He impugned his election and cast aspersions upon the propriety of his relations with Countess Matilda of Tuscany which must have tickled the ears of German churchmen who had been in receipt of Gregory's exhortations to promote clerical chastity. Henry and his propagandists were presented with an arraignment of Gregory that they were more than ready to exploit.

Henry may at first have intended that the assembly at Worms would proclaim Gregory's deposition and replace him by a new pope. If so, what happened fell short

[258] Lampert of Hersfeld, *Ann. a.* 1076, pp. 432/3–433/2; Bruno, caps. 65–7, pp. 278–84; Bernold, *Chron. a.* 1076, pp. 432/3–433/2; Bernold, *De damn. schis.* 3.7, pp. 49–50.

[259] *Quellen HIV* Anhang A, p. 470/4–13. The bishops present were: Archbishops Siegfried of Mainz and Udo of Trier; Bishops William of Utrecht, Hermann of Metz, Henry of Liège, Ricbert of Verdun, Pibo of Toul, Huzmann of Speyer, Burchard of Halberstadt, Werner of Strassburg, Burchard of Basel, Otto of Constance, Adalbero of Würzburg, Rupert of Bamberg, Otto of Regensburg, Ellinard of Freising, Ulrich of Eichstätt, Frederick of Münster, Eilbert of Minden, Hezilo of Hildesheim, Benno of Osnabrück, Eppo of Naumburg, Immad of Paderborn, Tiedo of Brandenburg, Burchard of Lausanne, and the Italian Bruno of Verona.

[260] Bernold described Godfrey as 'particeps immo auctor supradictae conspirationis': *Chron. a.* 1076, p. 433/10–11; Berthold said that he promised to escort Henry to Rome to set up a new pope: *a.*1076, pp. 283/20–2, 284/15–17.

[261] Lampert of Hersfeld, *Ann. a.* 1076, pp. 344–6.

of this intention. Henry's plan seems to have met criticism from the German bishops because it was against medieval ideas of a fair trial that a man should be condemned in absence, and because proceedings against a pope were unthinkable without the concurrence of the Roman church and of the Roman provincial bishops. It was agreed that Gregory should be, not that he had been, deposed; for no assembly of mainly German bishops, meeting in the Rhineland, could canonically pass sentence upon the bishop of Rome.

It was nevertheless vital for Henry that he should anticipate the sentence that Gregory was certain to pass against him at his Lent synod by depriving the pope of all authority, both legal and moral, to pass judgement. The Saxon chronicler Bruno recorded that each bishop present was compelled to subscribe to a written instrument in which he rejected Gregory as pope: 'I N. bishop of N. from this time and for the future deny Hildebrand my subjection and obedience, and I shall hereafter acknowledge him as pope neither in fact nor in name.' Some bishops subscribed willingly, but others did so reluctantly. Besides the imprisoned Burchard of Halberstadt, Hermann of Metz and Adalbero of Würzburg were amongst those who protested against the canonical impropriety of the proceedings. William of Utrecht was prominent in coercing the unwilling.[262] Some hoped soon to plead duress as a justification of their retraction of what they had signed.

Headed by Archbishop Siegfried of Mainz, the twenty-six bishops were named as senders of the long conciliar letter which set out to 'brother Hildebrand' the reasons for their willing or enforced disobedience.[263] They began by challenging the manner of his accession to the papacy. No doubt under Hugh Candidus's prompting, they arraigned him as an *invasor* who had notoriously and presumptuously seized it. If the bishops had at first turned a blind eye in hope that he would make things good by ruling well, the pitiful state of the whole of the church now cried aloud that the evil beginnings of his reign had been compounded by worse deeds and decisions. His pride and his itch for novelty had made him an agent of division and discord. He had sought to strip the bishops of their authority, and he had broken down the bonds of brotherhood in the church. The bishops recalled his having received accusations against some of them from their subjects while he denied their own authority:

You claim that, if a transgression of a subject of ours comes to your notice even by the merest rumour, none of us thereafter has any power to bind or loose save only yourself or whomever you specially authorize. How could anyone versed in sacred writings fail to recognize that such a view is beyond all reason?[264]

This alone would entitle the bishops to tell Hildebrand that he should no longer occupy the apostolic see.

But there was more. The bishops bandied allegations that, while the Emperor Henry III was still alive, Hildebrand had sworn never to allow anyone to become

---

[262] Bruno, cap. 65, pp. 278–80, which is the sole source for the text of the bishops' instrument; Lampert of Hersfeld, *Ann. a.* 1076, p. 346; Bernold, *De damn. schis.* 3.7, p. 50.
[263] *Quellen HIV* Anhang A, pp. 470–5.   [264] p. 472/17–21.

pope without the emperor's consent or his son's—whichever of them was ruler. They made the further allegation, which was probably not without some foundation, that he had once countered the ambition of a cardinal who had sought the papal office by swearing that, if other cardinals promised the same, he would never become pope.[265] On both these scores, the bishops branded him a perjurer. Next, by straining the meaning of the Election Decree of 1059, the bishops claimed that, by sponsoring and subscribing his name to it, Hildebrand had accepted that no one should become pope unless he were elected by the cardinals, approved by the people, and given the king's consent and approval.[266] Hildebrand's tumultuous accession to the papacy was, therefore, not only perjured but also illegal. Finally, the bishops arraigned Hildebrand for having filled the church with the stench of scandal by excessive familiarity with Countess Matilda of Tuscany ('de convictu et cohabitatione alienae mulieris familiariori quam necesse est').[267] It was, moreover, a particular affront to the episcopal order that, at the apostolic see, all judgements and decrees were promoted through women; indeed, the universal church was governed by a new senate of women. (The letter here intended Countess Beatrice and the Empress Agnes as well as Matilda.) At the same time, no remedy was made available for insults and injuries done to bishops whom Hildebrand abused with names like 'sons of whores'. Therefore the bishops repudiated Hildebrand:

Your accession was vitiated by gross perjuries; the church of God is exposed to the peril of severe storms by your misdeeds and novelties; you have besmirched your life and conduct by manifold disgrace. Accordingly, we renounce an obedience that we never promised you and will never show you. Because, as you have made publicly clear, none of us has hitherto been in your eyes a bishop, by the same token you will henceforth never be in any of our eyes the pope.

For his part, Henry IV not only confirmed his bishops' decision to renounce Gregory, but also invoked his authority as *patricius* which the Romans had given him early in his reign to oversee on their behalf the welfare of the Roman church. By virtue of it, he called upon him to stand down from the apostolic see:

Henry, king by the grace of God, to Hildebrand. Hitherto I have looked to you for whatever befits a father and, to the great chagrin of our own subjects, I have obeyed you in all things. But by way of return, I have received from you what is to be expected of the deadliest enemy of our life and kingship. For not only have you, in your arrogant presumption, snatched at all the hereditary honour that your see owes me, but you have gone much further: by your evil schemings you have sought to prise away from me the Italian kingdom.[268] And you have not been

---

[265] These allegations, and particularly the first, may have had some basis. An apparently independent reference to it occurs in Benzo of Alba, 7.2, p. 671; in a letter of 20 Dec. 1073 to the Saxon princes, Gregory himself referred to his not being able to maintain certain *concepta vota* when divine providence compelled him to accept the papacy: *Reg.* 1.39, p. 61/35–8. The occasion of an oath must have been Hildebrand's mission to Germany in 1054–5: see above, 2.1.

[266] It is highly unlikely that the bishops at Worms had a text of the Election Decree before them; in any case, Hildebrand had not himself subscribed to it: Jasper, *Papstwahldekret*, pp. 34–8, 82–5, 111.

[267] The phrase 'alienae mulieris' echoes Prov. 2: 6 and Ecclus. 9: 11–12. The presence at Worms of Matilda's estranged husband Duke Godfrey of Lorraine must be borne in mind.

[268] By his opposition to Henry's dealings over Milan, Fermo, and Spoleto.

content even with this! You have not feared to lay hands upon our most reverend bishops who are joined to us as most cherished limbs of ourself and, as they themselves say, against the laws of God and man you have vexed them with the most high-handed wrongs and the bitterest affronts. When in forbearance I paid no heed to all this, you instead took it for cowardice. You dared to rise up against me, the head, putting upon record what you very well know: to use your own words, that either you would die or else you would strip me of my soul and of my kingdom. I have determined that such arrogance should be curbed by deeds, not words. At their own request, I have held a general assembly of all the magnates of my kingdom. When I there made public all that I have ever kept silence about from fear and reverence, it was publicly declared by the sure words of those present—in what they actually wrote, you may hear them—that you can in no wise continue any longer to occupy the apostolic see. Because their decision is manifestly right and justified before God and man, I, too, add my assent. Every right to the papacy that you seem to have, I deny you; from the bishopric of the city whose patriciate is rightly mine by God's gift and by the sworn agreement of the Romans, I say—step down![269]

A German Gregorian later observed that Henry had sought to get rid of Gregory 'as no one would venture to sack his pig-man or goatherd from the care of the beasts entrusted to him'.[270] But, for all the rhetoric, Henry's message was more guarded than this suggests. The documents that emanated from Worms never employed the verb 'deponere', nor was a threat of deposition against Gregory expressly formulated. The model appears to have been the Emperor Henry III's eliciting in 1046 of Pope Gregory VI's self-dismissal from the papacy.[271] Henry IV called upon Gregory VII to forestall further action against him by proclaiming his own self-deposition.

To this end, Henry needed the active collaboration of the Romans. Therefore Henry's letter to Hildebrand was enclosed in another to the clergy and people of the Roman church in which he proscribed the monk Hildebrand as his enemy. He recalled the Romans' loyalty to himself in the past, and he called them to rise up against Hildebrand and to condemn him:

We do not say that you should shed his blood, for after his deposition life would be for him a severer punishment than death. We do say that, if he resists, you should compel him to step down. Thereafter you shall receive as pope another whom we shall choose by common counsel of all the bishops and of yourselves; the wounds that Hildebrand has inflicted upon the church, he will be both ready and able to heal![272]

Henry was at pains to ensure that the summons to Gregory to step down from the papacy and the promise that he would be replaced by a worthier pope should reach Rome by the Lent synod. He entrusted his documents to two bishops, Huzmann of Speyer and Burchard of Basel, who were accompanied by Henry's lay counsellor and agent Count Eberhard. *En route*, a main concern was to secure the adherence to Henry's plans of the Lombard bishops. At Piacenza on an unknown date, a large assembly of bishops and laity not only confirmed the decisions of Worms, but the

---

[269] *Epp. HIV* no. 11, pp. 62–4.
[270] Manegold of Lautenbach, *Ad Gebehardum*, cap. 25, p. 357/32–4.
[271] See above, 1.8.   [272] *Epp. HIV* no. 10, pp. 60–2.

bishops made a sworn compact to renounce their own obedience to Gregory. No doubt with a view to ensuring the utmost speed, Henry's letters were carried from Piacenza to Rome by a clerk of Parma named Roland who was accompanied by an unnamed servant of the king.[273]

In this precipitate way, Henry's onslaught against Gregory was launched. He had placed himself in a dangerously exposed position. Despite his claims in his letter to Hildebrand, at Worms he had the active backing of only a few lay princes apart from Duke Godfrey of Lorraine. As for the German bishops, not only had there been absentees from Worms but he could not count upon the long-term support even of some who had subscribed to the instrument by which they withdrew their obedience from Gregory. Some had acted under duress and were troubled in conscience by what they had done. If memories of Gregory's high-handed treatment of the German episcopate in 1074 were fresh in many minds, so was his greater flexibility in 1075. According to Lampert of Hersfeld, Bishops Adalbero of Würzburg and Hermann of Metz rejoined that the proceedings at Worms were no less irregular and uncanonical than anything that Gregory was alleged to have done. No bishop, let alone the pope, should be condemned in his absence, without proper accusers and witnesses, and without proof of his alleged crimes.[274] It further detracted from Henry's case against Gregory that, with whatever initial reluctance and coolness, the German bishops had for nearly three years unquestioningly acknowledged him as pope. Above all, Henry's attempt to justify his intervention in the Roman church upon the model of his father's in 1046 and upon his supposed rights as *patricius* was insecure. It was one thing for the old emperor, who was widely acknowledged to be a zealous reformer dedicated to the well-being of the church, to go to Rome in person and, with the support of the Romans themselves, to remedy notorious simony and corruption. It was a different matter for Henry IV, with his stained personal and political reputation, while remaining in Germany to attempt the displacement of so religious and respected a figure as Gregory. As Henry's letters tacitly acknowledged, only at Rome could Gregory be deposed and replaced; Gregory could count upon the loyalty of most Romans, clerical and lay alike. This was particularly the case after the episode at Christmas 1075, when his lay enemy Cencius had seized him during his celebration of mass and had caused him personal injury.[275] Tidings of this event may not have reached Henry by the time of the assembly of Worms and he cannot have calculated its full effect. But it compounded the improbability that either the Roman clergy or the Roman citizens would heed Henry's call to get rid of Gregory.[276]

---

[273] Berthold, *a*.1076, p. 282/33–9; Bernold, *Chron. a.* 1076, p. 433/1–4; Manegold of Lautenbach, *Ad Gebehardum*, cap. 25, p. 358/16–24; Bonizo of Sutri, *Lib. ad amic.* 7, pp. 606–7. At his Lent synod of 1078, Gregory deposed Bishop Roland of Treviso, who seems to have been the same Roland, saying that, to secure his see, he had been made a messenger in 1076 by guile and had not shrunk from making schism between *sacerdotium* and *regnum*: *Reg.* 5.14*a*, p. 369/13–20. He renewed his sentence against Roland in Lent 1080: *Reg.* 7.14*a*(3), p. 481/4–7.

[274] Lampert of Hersfeld, *Ann. a.* 1076, p. 346.

[275] See below, 4.7.

[276] For the possibility that, after the assemblies at Worms and Piacenza, Gregory sent Henry another,

3.3.2 Gregory VII's Lent Synod, 1076

Gregory's Lent synod opened on 14 February in the Lateran basilica, the church in which his own election to the papacy had occurred. It should also be recalled that the Lateran palace, of which the basilica was part, had amongst its most precious relics, in the papal chapel of St Lawrence, the heads of the apostles Peter and Paul; they were a pledge of the apostles' nearness to all that took place.[277] The synod was well attended; those present included Henry IV's mother, the Empress Agnes.[278]

Henry's messengers reached Rome on the day before the synod opened. The clerk Roland is likely immediately upon his arrival to have communicated to Gregory both Henry's written messages and his additional verbal threats.[279] On the first day of the synod, after the opening solemnities, Gregory caused the letters from Germany to be read aloud. The immediate result was uproar, in which Gregory barely restrained the Romans present from tearing the messengers limb from limb. There was no support for Henry's demand that Gregory be coerced into standing down from the papal office. Gregory adjourned the synod until the following day, ordering the records of ancient synodal decrees to be searched for past occasions when bold and disobedient men had publicly rebelled against God's supreme earthly representative. It was probably on 22 February that Gregory pronounced sentence upon Henry. Henry had addressed Gregory by his pre-papal name of Hildebrand with a command to stand down from the papacy; Gregory now addressed a personal appeal to St Peter, the apostolic patron of the Roman church, to vindicate his cause:

Blessed Peter, prince of the apostles, incline to us, we beseech you, your merciful ears; hear me your servant whom you have nurtured from infancy and to this day have delivered from the hands of wicked men who have hated, and do hate, me for my fidelity to you.[280] You are my witness as are, amongst all the saints, my lady the Mother of God and blessed Paul your brother, that your holy Roman church dragged me, unwilling as I was, to be its ruler; that I did not count it a thing to be snatched at to ascend your see; and that I would rather have finished my life in exile [i.e. in Germany or France as a monk] than have seized your holy place by worldly guile and for earthly vanity. And so I believe it to have been by your grace and by no works of mine that it was and is your good pleasure for Christian people entrusted personally to you to yield obedience personally to me through your authority committed to me. Likewise, by your grace, power is given me from God of binding and loosing in heaven and upon earth. Therefore, fortified by this confidence and for the honour and defence of your church, on behalf of God Almighty, Father, Son, and Holy Spirit, and by your power and authority, I deny

---

lost letter threatening him with excommunication and deposition if he persisted in his intransigence, see Guy of Ferrara, 1.3, p. 537/4–7.

[277] *Descr. eccles. Lat.* p. 547.

[278] For the date of the Lent synod, see *Reg.* 3.9, p. 262; *Epp. vag.* nos. 9–10, pp. 22, 24; Bernold, *Pro Gebhardo episcopo*, p. 109. Lampert of Hersfeld, *Ann. a.* 1076, pp. 342–3, postdates it by a week. For the official record, see *Reg.* 3.10a, pp. 268–71.

[279] The other main sources for the synod are: Lampert of Hersfeld, *Ann. a.* 1076, pp. 346–8; Bruno, cap. 68, pp. 284–6; Berthold, *a.*1076, pp. 282/35–283/19, with a reference to the Empress Agnes's presence; Bernold, *Chron. a.* 1076, p. 433/3–9; Bernold, *De damn. schis.* caps. 12–13, pp. 51–2; Hugh of Flavigny, *Chron,* 2, p. 435; Bonizo of Sutri, *Liber ad amic.* 7, pp. 606–7.

[280] Gregory's words here gained force from his seizure at Christmas by Cencius: see below, 4.7.

to King Henry, son of the Emperor Henry, who with unheard-of pride has risen up against your church, the government of the whole kingdom of the Germans and of Italy; I absolve all Christians from the bond of any oath that they have made or shall make to him; and I forbid anyone to serve him as king. For it is fitting that, because he has striven to diminish the honour of your church, he himself should forfeit the honour that he seems to possess. Finally, because he has disdained to show the obedience of a true Christian and has not returned to the God whom he forsook by communing with excommunicated men, by—as you are my witness—disdaining my advice which I sent him for his salvation, and by attempting to rend your church and separating himself from it, by your authority I bind him with excommunication. I so bind him with confidence in you, that the nations of the world may know and be convinced that you are Peter, and that upon you as the rock the Son of the living God has built his church, against which the gates of hell shall not prevail.[281]

In these words, which he was at pains to circulate in writing with a fervent covering letter 'to all who desire to be reckoned among the sheep that Christ commended to St Peter' (John 21:17),[282] Gregory invoked St Peter's authority first to deny Henry the exercise of his kingship, denying the binding force of all oaths that were taken to him, and then to excommunicate him for his disobedience. In the German and Italian kingdoms, the effect of the sentence was to suspend Henry from the exercise of his rulership; Gregory stopped short of declaring him deposed. Gregory's reasons for excommunicating Henry were set out in a significant order which probably reflects importance as well as time. First, Gregory named Henry's disobedience and his communing with his excommunicate counsellors. Second came his contempt of Gregory's fatherly advice as conveyed by his letters before and after he become pope. Third there was the virtual schism that Henry had brought about by the assemblies at Worms and Piacenza. Henry's persistence in familiarity with the counsellors whom Pope Alexander II had excommunicated was the touchstone of his recalcitrance as a ruler.

The German prelates who had set their names to the documents at Worms did not go unscathed. In the decrees of the Lent synod, their leader, Archbishop Siegfried of Mainz, was condemned for trying to tear the German bishops and abbots from their mother, the Roman church; he was suspended and excommunicated saving the contingency of a death-bed repentance. As for the archbishop of Trier and the twenty-four bishops, the synod distinguished those who had given their names to the documents willingly from those who had done so unwillingly. Deliberate and impenitent promoters of schism were to share Siegfried's suspension, though there was no mention of excommunication; there was also no mention of deposition. The unwilling were allowed until 1 August to make satisfaction to Gregory at Rome whether in person or by messengers, on pain of deprivation of their episcopal office from that date.[283] Gregory's graded sentence and his olive branch to unwilling signatories may have been the result of a penitent letter from some of their number that Gregory had already received.[284] It was, in any case, a master-stroke of moderation

---

[281] *Reg.* 3.10*a*, pp. 270–1. [282] *Reg.* 3.6*, 6, pp. 252–5.
[283] *Reg.* 3.20*a*, pp. 268–9. [284] Thus Bonizo of Sutri.

which gave wavering bishops a highway to reconciliation with Gregory. For the Lombard bishops who had sworn an oath against Gregory at Piacenza, there was no such hint of mercy, but only a stark sentence of suspension from every episcopal function and of exclusion from the communion of holy church.[285]

3.3.3 The Erosion of Henry IV's Position

At first, Henry's cause seemed to proceed from strength to strength.[286] He returned to Goslar and pressed ahead with the refortification of Saxony, where he met with no opposition from a despairing people. He was able to replace the deceased Anno as archbishop of Cologne by the complaisant Hildolf, a royal chaplain and canon of Goslar. But a first major setback came on 26 February, when his powerful lay supporter and principal mentor in his bid to condemn and replace Gregory, Duke Godfrey of Lorraine, died as the result of an assassination prompted by local Lotharingian hatreds. Lampert of Hersfeld described Godfrey as 'magnum regni Teutonici robur ac momentum'; and the shock of his loss was compounded by the shameful circumstances of his murder: he was stabbed in his buttocks by an assailant of inferior birth while he was at stool.[287] It was not only a political disaster but also a baleful portent. The need to regulate the ducal succession in Lorraine brought Henry to Utrecht for Easter (27 March). In preference to the nearest kinsman of the murdered duke, Godfrey of Bouillon, he appointed his own infant son Conrad, who was already the designated heir to the German kingdom. It was while he was at Utrecht that, on Easter eve, Henry received the somewhat belated tidings of Gregory's sentence upon him at the Lent synod. On Easter Sunday at mass, after Henry had been solemnly received at the cathedral, Bishop William of Utrecht made a public announcement of the papal sentence. He denounced Gregory as a perjurer, adulterer, and simoniac, and declared him to be an excommunicate.

Henry's own reaction was to intensify his propaganda campaign against Gregory in Germany and to pursue his plan to secure his replacement by an amenable successor. Like the propaganda material that had emanated from Worms, the new campaign was the work of Henry's master propagandist, Gottteschalk of Aachen. Its centre-piece was a letter, once again addressed to Hildebrand and ending with the summons, 'I Henry, king by God's grace, with all our bishops say to you, "Step down, step down!"'.[288] But it differed in many ways from the document prepared at Worms.[289] It was intended for the eyes neither of Gregory nor of the Romans; it was a propaganda flysheet for public circulation in Germany. It was longer and more considered. It substituted for the juristic and constitutional tone of Worms a moralistic and doctrinal one, aimed especially at the German bishops whose loyalties were uncertain. Harping upon Gregory's measures against them in 1074, it first arraigned

---

[285] *Reg.* 3.10*a*, p. 269.

[286] The main chronicle sources for the events of Jan.–Oct. 1076 are: Lampert of Hersfeld, *Ann. a.* 1076, pp. 348–82; Berthold, *a.*1076, pp. 283/20–287/6; Bruno, caps. 74–87, pp. 316–27.

[287] p. 348/15–20; Bernold, *Chron. a.* 1076, p. 433/10–12; Berthold, *a.*1076, p. 283/20–2.

[288] *Epp. HIV* no. 12, pp. 64–9.   [289] *Epp. HIV* no. 11, pp. 62–5.

Hildebrand because he had not scrupled to touch the rulers of holy church who were the anointed of the Lord, by which were meant the archbishops, bishops, and priests: he had trampled them underfoot like servants who do not know what their master is doing. By this means, he had gained favour with the common herd. On top of the offence of his own usurpation of the papal office—'Our Lord Jesus Christ called us to the kingdom (*regnum*), but he did not call you to the pontificate (*sacerdotium*)'— Hildebrand had also infringed Henry's own inviolability as king by the grace of God:

Me too, who although unworthy am hallowed to the kingship among the anointed, you have touched (cf. Ps. 104: 15); whereas the tradition of the holy fathers teaches that I should be judged by God alone and deposed for no crime unless (which God forbid) I should fall from the faith. . . . The true pope, St Peter himself, proclaims: 'Fear God; honour the king' (1 Pet. 2: 17); yet, because you do not fear God, you dishonour me whom he appointed.

Powerfully drafted though the letter was, it exposed some of Henry's weaknesses. The allusions to Gregory's measures of 1074 were directed against a position from which Gregory in 1075 had partly withdrawn in his bid to mend the bridges with the German episcopate. Whereas, when writing in January from Worms to Rome, Henry could claim the support of all the princes (he referred to a 'generalis conventus omnium regni primatum'), when writing at Easter to a German public which well knew the limited extent of his lay support, he could call upon Hildebrand to step down only 'by the judgement of all our bishops and by our own'. And for the bishops, Gregory had prepared an easy way of return to papal obedience.

Partly in order to arouse lay sympathy and support, at Utrecht Henry employed Gottschalk of Aachen to draft another propaganda manifesto against Hildebrand which he addressed individually to the German princes. By the diversity of salutations with which the letter began, Henry tacitly recognized the uncertainty of their loyalty.[290] He dwelt upon Hildebrand's impious monopolization of power:

Against God's will, he has usurped royal and priestly functions ('regnum et sacerdotium deo nesciente sibi usurpavit'). By so doing he has despised God's holy ordinance, which he willed to have its head and foundation in two things not one—in two things, I say: *regnum* and *sacerdotium*, as the Saviour himself gave us to understand during his passion by typically declaring two swords to be sufficient (Luke 22: 38). . . . How Hildebrandine madness has confounded this ordinance of God, you very well know, if you care to know. For according to his judgement no one is suffered to be a priest who has not begged it from his arrogance. Me too, whom God called to the kingship (although he did not call him to the priesthood), because he saw that I wished to reign by God and not by him and because he did not himself appoint me to be a king—me, I say, he sought to strip of the kingship; and he threatened to take from me my kingdom and my soul alike, although he gave me neither of them!

The purpose of this letter was to convene a further assembly of ecclesiastical and lay princes at Worms for Pentecost (15 May). At it, Bishops Altwin of Brixen, William of Utrecht, and Eberhard of Naumburg were to arraign Gregory, and steps were to be determined for securing his expulsion from the papacy and his replacement.

[290] *Epp. H IV* no. 13, pp. 68–73.

Even while Henry was at Utrecht, his cause was fraught by setbacks and ill omens which compounded the death of Duke Godfrey of Lorraine. An occasion which was intended to proclaim the solidarity of the German bishops with the king in the event exposed misgivings about their support for him at Worms. On Easter Sunday, Bishop Pibo of Toul jibbed at pronouncing Gregory's excommunication and secretly departed from Utrecht with Bishop Thierry of Verdun; William of Utrecht was left to condemn Gregory alone.[291] By an unfortunate portent, lightning struck, and fire largely destroyed, the church at Utrecht dedicated to St Peter, Gregory's especial patron, in which the dramatic events of Easter Sunday took place.[292] More seriously still, on 27 April, Bishop William of Utrecht died an agonizing death; many interpreted it as God's warning that he was not behind Henry and his supporters in their stand against Gregory.

Not long after these events at Utrecht, a group of princes led by the three southern dukes Rudolf of Swabia, Welf of Bavaria, and Berthold of Carinthia, with whom were associated Bishops Adalbero of Würzburg and Hermann of Metz, began to plot against the king. They revived the old charges of personal depravity and of misgovernment. Hermann of Metz and other princes released the Saxon captives whom the king had entrusted to their custody; in June, Bishop Burchard of Halberstadt, who in Lampert of Hersfeld's eyes was the critical figure for the military fortunes of the Saxons,[293] escaped and returned to his see. Thus, the Saxon rebellion, which seemed to have been ended by the battle on the Unstrut, now revived.

Henry's own plans were increasingly frustrated. In Italy, he found some support: an assembly at Pavia pronounced Gregory to be excommunicate, and it was probably at this time that the so-called imperial version of the Election Decree of 1059 was prepared.[294] But Henry's assembly at Worms, although quite well attended, was weakened by the absence of lay princes. It proceeded to no measures against Gregory, for of the bishops who were to have initiated them William of Utrecht was dead, Altwin of Brixen had been taken prisoner by Gregory's supporters, and Eberhard of Naumberg could not act alone. Henry's plan to get rid of Gregory was patently failing. He convened another assembly to meet at Mainz on 29 June (the feast of the apostles Peter and Paul). In the event, it was again mostly bishops who came; although Gregory's position was further discussed, no positive measures were taken against him. As the summer progressed, there was a gradual intensification of the Saxon rising. Otto of Nordheim, of late Henry's viceroy in Saxony, threw in his lot with the rebels, and Henry's counter-measures were unavailing. In September, the three South German dukes led an assembly at Ulm, where Bishop Altmann of

---

[291] Hugh of Flavigny, 2, p. 458. According to Hugh, there were present 'plures alii, qui etsi favebant regiis negociis, hoc tamen, quia sanctorum patrum obviabat decretis et sanctionibus repugnabat canonicis, aversati sunt.'

[292] *MGH DD HIV* no. 284.

[293] Lampert of Hersfeld, *Ann. a.* 1076, pp. 366/36–368/8: 'desperantibus iam reditum eius Saxonibus, repente, tamquam ab inferis vivus emergens, restitutus est.'

[294] Bonizo of Sutri, *Lib. ad amic.* 8, p. 609; Arnulf of Milan, 5.7, pp. 226/16–227/2. For the Election Decree, see Jasper, *Das Papstwahldekret*, pp. 82–119.

Passau attended as Gregory's legate, to organize resistance to the king in conjunction with the Saxons. They agreed that, on 16 October, there should be a further meeting in the Rhineland near Tribur, at which they hoped to settle the troubles that beset the German kingdom. Summonses to attend were sent all over Germany, and especially to the Saxons. At Ulm, Bishop Altmann of Passau restored to communion the hitherto wavering Bishop Otto of Constance.[295]

As for Gregory himself, even at the Lent synod of 1076 he was aware of the disquiet with their position of some German bishops who had joined Archbishop Siegfried of Mainz in renouncing their obedience to Gregory; he had shrewdly promised them such ready reconciliation as Otto of Constance found.[296] Otto's reconciler, Bishop Altmann of Passau, had written to the Empress Agnes at Rome for information about Gregory's sentence upon the king, thereby indicating his preparedness to be active in Gregory's cause.[297] At Rome, too, Abbot William of Hirsau was present after a period of grave illness at the Lent synod; the impact of its events converted him totally and permanently to Gregory's obedience and service.[298] The assurance of the loyalty of such churchmen as Bishop Altmann and Abbot William encouraged Gregory in the hope that others might be won to follow them.

The lines of Gregory's thought and activity up to the conclusion of Henry's meeting in October with the princes at Tribur–Oppenheim must mainly be sought by way of his suriviving letters.[299] After the death and burial at Verdun in February 1076 of Duke Godfrey of Lorraine, Gregory was particularly concerned with the loyalty of the Lotharingian ecclesiastical province of Trier which, with its suffragan sees of Metz, Toul, and Verdun, controlled the valleys of the Moselle and upper Meuse.[300] Except Thierry of Verdun, their bishops had been party to the proceedings at Worms; Gregory held all four guilty of association with the king and his designs. Nevertheless, to all save Pibo of Toul he addressed a letter saying that he considered their adherence to the 'schismatics' to have been unwilling. He urged them to make amends, which all three did in the course of the year: Hermann of Metz did so speedily, Udo of Trier travelled to Rome in June, and Thierry of Verdun did so later in the year.[301] Not surprisingly in the light of their earlier dealings, Gregory took a

---

[295] Bernold, *Pro Gebhardo*, cap. 5, p. 110/8–12; Berthold, *a.*1076, p. 286/25.

[296] See above, 3.3.2.

[297] Hugh of Flavigny, 2, p. 435.

[298] *Vita Willihelmi abbatis Hirsaugiensis*, caps. 4–6, 22, pp. 213, 219; Berthold, *a.*1075, p.281/13–36.

[299] The letters are: *Reg.* 3.12, to Archbishop Udo of Trier and Bishops Thierry of Verdun and Hermann of Metz, (Apr. 1076), pp. 273–4; 3.15, to the Milanese knight Wifred, (Apr.) 1076, p. 277; *Epp. vag.* no. 13, to Bishop Henry of Trent, (Mar.–July 1076), pp. 30–3; no. 14, to all the faithful in Germany, (summer 1076), pp. 32–41; *Reg.* 4.1, to all St Peter's faithful in the Roman empire, 25 July 1076, pp. 289–92; 4.2, to Bishop Hermann of Metz, 25 Aug. 1076, pp. 293–7; *Epp. vag.* no. 15, to all St Peter's faithful in the Roman empire, 29 Aug. (1076), pp. 42–3; *Reg.* 4.3, to all Christians in Germany, 3 Sept. 1076, pp. 297–300; 4.6, to Bishop Henry of Liège, 28 Oct. 1076, pp. 303–4; cf. 4.8, to the bishops of Tuscany, 1 Nov. 1076, pp. 306–7.

[300] Cf., in the longer term, *Reg.* 5.7, to Archbishop Udo of Trier and his suffragans, 30 Sept. 1077, pp. 356–8; *H* no. 33, pp. 69–72.

[301] Hermann: Hugh of Flavigny, 2, p. 641; Udo: Lampert of Hersfeld, *Ann. a.* 1076, p. 360; Thierry:

harder line with Pibo of Toul; he evidently remained unaware of Pibo's hesitation at Utrecht about Henry's position that had led him, with Thierry of Verdun, to avoid involvement in the renewed sentence against Gregory. Gregory for long sought to put pressure upon Pibo to secure his repentance;[302] after Tribur, he, too, did penance before Gregory's legates and travelled in person to Rome.[303]

In his letters, Gregory continued to express willingness that any of Henry's supporters who duly repented should be received back into the church.[304] A letter which he sent to Bishop Henry of Liège at the end of October illustrates how, even after his deadline of 1 August expired, he regarded the position of bishops who were compromised. Henry had inquired of Gregory whether *post mortem* prayers might be offered for Bishop William of Utrecht, who had died excommunicate. Gregory insisted upon the culpability against the ancient statutes of the church of those who, flouting these statutes and rending the unity of Christ's body the church, armed themselves with schismatic and heretical deceits, deliberately opposed themselves to the fathers, and knowingly held communion with excommunicates. With anyone who died impenitent for having subscribed to the act of schism at Worms and for deliberately holding communion with the excommunicate king, there was no place for communion in life or in death. But upon any deceased person who had not uncanonically communicated with the king, Gregory pronounced his absolution; he permitted prayers and alms on his behalf.[305] A few days later, he allowed that a Tuscan bishop, Rudolf of Siena, who had wittingly held communion with Henry and had compounded his offence by further disobedience, might after a time of penitential seclusion and abstention from communion hope for papal absolution.[306] Gregory's thoughts about the reconciliation of German bishops are likely to have been similar.

Despite Gregory's conciliation in offering penitent bishops an easy way of return, he encountered widespread criticism of his severity against Henry from persons who urged him to make peace with the king.[307] Earlier in 1076, he showed his concern for the loyalty of Bishop Henry of Trent, whose see was critically situated on the route northwards from Verona through the Brenner Pass to Germany.[308] The bishop had disregarded a message from Gregory, who was concerned to rebut suggestions that he had acted unjustly towards the king. It was such public misgivings that occasioned

---

Hugh of Flavigny, 2, p. 458. According to Lampert, after Tribur Thierry was the king's spiritual adviser at Speyer: p. 390.

[302] *Reg.* 3.12, pp. 273/29–274/12, cf. 4.2, p. 297/4–8.
[303] Berthold, *a.*1076, p. 287/23–9.
[304] *Reg.* 4.1, p. 291/13–21, 4.3, p. 300/1–5.   [305] *Reg.* 4.6, pp. 303–4.
[306] *Reg.* 4.8, to the bishops of Tuscany, 1 Nov. 1076, pp. 306–7.
[307] *Reg.* 3.15, p. 277/5–10; cf. his undated *Reg.* 3.14, to Patriarch Dominicus IV of Grado, pp. 275/30–276/6. For the division of German opinion in 1076, see Berthold, *a.*1076, p. 285/7–48.
[308] *Epp. vag.* no. 13; for the date see the note on pp. 30–1. Gregory's prediction that the feast of St Peter's Chains (1 Aug.) 'would not have passed before it is quite certainly made known to all men that the king was most justly excommunicated' probably does not foretell Henry's death or fall from power but, in the light of the decrees of Gregory's Lent synod (*Reg.* 3.10*a*, pp. 268/26–269/2), a desertion of the king by the German bishops in response to Gregory's period of grace until 1 Aug.

Gregory's widely circulated letter to all the faithful in Germany in which he sought at length to justify his actions and to demonstrate his willingness to welcome a duly penitent and obedient king.[309] His letter of 25 August to Bishop Hermann of Metz was likewise concerned to satisfy those who questioned the propriety of the excommunication of a king. In such letters, Gregory mounted a propaganda campaign which matched the zeal on Henry's behalf of Gotteschalk of Aachen. The battle for the loyalty of German public had begun in earnest.

As he developed his propaganda campaign, Gregory's attitude showed signs of modification and development. Henry's principal offence in retaining his excommunicate counsellors remained a recurring theme. But, by comparison with his impassioned sentence at the Lent synod in which he laid weight upon the suspension and excommunication of Henry and upon Henry's pride in rising up against St Peter and his vicar, the emphasis shifted to Gregory's desire for peace and to Henry's long-term and personal responsibility for the breakdown in relations between pope and king. In April, he told the Patarene leader Wifred of Milan that he sought peace with Henry, if only Henry would seek peace with God and amend what he had done to the peril of holy church and to the increase of his own damnation.[310] His manifesto to the Germans began with a long retrospect of Henry's behaviour over the years and of his own prolonged attempts, as archdeacon and as pope, to correct it. Gregory laid emphasis upon Henry's adherence to his excommunicate counsellors, and especially upon his having restored them to familiarity after his victory over the Saxons at Homburg-on-the-Unstrut. Even thereafter Gregory had still sought Henry's amendment of life and his establishment as an exemplary king. But Henry had proved contumacious, and in January 1076 he had undermined the loyalty to Gregory of the Italian and many German bishops. Gregory directed his remarks to Henry personally, and his letter ended with a prayer that God would turn Henry to penitence. If so, Gregory was ready, with the advice of his German supporters, to receive Henry back into the fellowship of the church.[311]

Gregory reiterated his readiness in July.[312] He insisted upon his own indebtedness to Henry's parents, the Emperor Henry III and the Empress Agnes,[313] whose example underlay his hope that Henry IV might even yet become an exemplary king. As pope, it was Gregory's duty to seek Henry's repentance; for their part, the Germans should seek his deliverance from the devil's grasp. But also in July, Gregory for the first time added an implicit threat of further, if unspecified, steps if Henry should prove deaf to such appeals: should he prefer the advice of his excommunicate counsellors, Gregory would not be behindhand in succouring a well-nigh collapsing church. Towards the king's supporters, Gregory sounded a corresponding note of firmness. If they repented, they should be received back into the church, but bishops and laity who openly adhered to the king and remained impenitent should be denied the communion and fellowship of the faithful.[314] The problem of Germans with wavering loyalties continued to exercise Gregory. By late August, he had received a

---

[309] *Epp. vag.* no. 14, pp. 32–41.
[311] *Epp. vag.* no. 14.
[313] *Reg.* 4.3, p. 298/22–5.

[310] *Reg.* 3.15, p. 277/5–10.
[312] *Reg.* 4.1.
[314] *Reg.* 4.1, p. 291/21–6.

letter—now lost—from the German bishops and dukes, in response to which he allowed any persons to be absolved whom he had excommunicated but who now were not afraid to shun the king.[315] Gregory was evidently concerned to guard against accusations of excessive severity and inflexibility.

He was also at pains to show that his actions were not directed by his own wilfulness and masterfulness. By drawing upon the widest possible fund of canon law and historical precedent, he sought to extend the German understanding of ecclesiastical law and jurisdiction which had made the Germans resistant to papal intervention. The bishops, in particular, were to be guided by the traditions to which Gregory believed both the pope and themselves to be subject. He did not return to the stark and sometimes overdrawn theses of the *Dictatus papae* but sought afresh to appeal to the traditions of a past that he was sure would uphold his manner of exercising the prerogatives of the apostolic see. When recording the decisions of the Lent synod of 1076, Berthold was careful to record how, before he passed sentence upon Henry, Gregory caused *synodalia statuta* to be searched for precedents in dealing with a disobedient ruler who had presumed to judge the apostolic see and to despise its commands.[316] Gregory later declared his trust that the archbishop of Trier and his suffragans 'shared his own faith and his knowledge of the books of the church fathers'.[317] Addressing the faithful in Germany, he invited anyone who thought his sentence upon Henry unreasonable to discuss it with him in the light of canonical precedent.[318] Most important of all, his letter to Bishop Hermann of Metz answered at length those who said that it was improper to excommunicate a king. Gregory referred them, with examples, to the words and deeds of the church fathers, in an endeavour to show that kings of old had been excommunicated, that kings were included in Christ's commission to Peter, 'Feed my sheep', and that the episcopal dignity was superior to the kingly.[319] Whereas in the *Dictatus papae* Gregory had sought to prescribe by apodictic statements that sometimes went beyond the evidence of the past as recorded and perceived by others, in the letter to Hermann of Metz Gregory sought to discover, educate, and persuade. In Hermann's case, his success was conspicuous: never again would Hermann seriously waver in his support for Gregory.

In the same letter to Hermann of Metz, Gregory reverted to the question of the king's excommunicate counsellors and his dealings with them. To Hermann's query about just who were the excommunicated bishops, priests, and laity whom Gregory deemed to be culpable, he somewhat brusquely answered that they were those who maintained communion with the excommunicate Henry—'si fas est dici rex'; they had not hesitated to impel the king to incur the wrath of God, and by himself communicating with the excommunicate simoniacs of his household Henry had not feared to incur excommunication and to transmit it to others.[320]

Given the strength of feeling in Germany that he had acted precipitately, Gregory became increasingly concerned lest Henry should be prematurely absolved by

---

[315] *Reg.* 4.2, p. 296/8–12.
[316] Berthold, *a.*1076, pp. 282/42–283/3.
[317] *Reg.* 3.12, p. 273/21–6.
[318] *Epp. vag.* no. 14, p. 30.
[319] *Reg.* 4.2, pp. 294/4–296/7.
[320] *Reg.* 4.2, pp. 293/28–294/3, cf. 4.1, pp. 290/12–291/12.

German bishops. He warned Hermann of Metz that no one should presume to absolve him, until Gregory had been informed by reliable witnesses of his due penance and satisfaction. It was for Gregory himself, together with the German bishops, to consider whether to absolve him.[321] This was another early hint, to match those in his general manifesto to the German people, that he and the Germans should deliberate together about Henry's future. Gregory's anxiety about the situation in Germany grew. He quickly became disturbed by rumours that Henry was seeking to divide him from his German followers. His fears increased that some in Germany might act too indulgently towards the king. He reinforced his insistence that he must himself, through legates if necessary, decide what was just and pleasing to God.[322] On 3 September another letter foreshadowed a development in Gregory's thinking that was perhaps forced upon him by tidings that the German princes were minded themselves to elect a new king.[323] Gregory began his letter with a retrospect to the Lent synod, commenting (as he said) upon why Henry had been excommunicated and deposed from the royal dignity ('cur sit anathematis vinculo alligatus et a regia dignitate depositus, et quod omnis populus quondam sibi subiectus a vinculo iuramenti eidem promissi sit absolutus').[324] Both the change in order to excommunication followed by deposition and the use for the first time of the verb 'deponere' are significant for the reconsideration and hardening of Gregory's position since the previous February.

He proceeded to set out what, in his view, must now be done. His guiding principle was that Christians should be moved by mercy rather than by justice. Let Henry's evil counsellors, who had infected him with their simony and provoked him into rending holy church, be removed far from him. Let him instead take good counsellors, who would respect the church and its law. If Henry would give suitable guarantees, Gregory was to be informed by suitable messengers, so that what should be done might be determined by common consent. Gregory reiterated that no one was to absolve Henry without the sanction of the apostolic see. But for the first time, Gregory also envisaged the possibility that Henry might not show obedience and that he might have to be replaced. If he did not return to God, let another be found for the government of the kingdom who would perform all that Gregory demanded and other things that were needful. After a prospective king had been elected, Gregory wished to be informed about his rank, person, and manner of life, in order that he might be satisfied as to his suitability.

An election by the princes was thus brought within the bounds of the discussion. The discussion was ceasing to be about what it had seemed to be since the Lent synod—a two-sided contest between pope and king. It was hardening into what it had already in effect been and would remain for the rest of Gregory's pontificate—a three-sided contest between pope, king, and princes in which all had partly conflicting interests. Amongst the princes themselves, too, there were divisions of interest

[321] *Reg.* 4.2, p. 296/8–22.   [322] *Epp. vag.* no. 14, pp. 42–3.   [323] *Reg.* 4.3.
[324] Perhaps through reflecting upon St Ambrose's sanction of 390 against the Emperor Theodosius: see *Reg.* 4.2, p. 294/19–23.

and opinion about what should be done. Such was the background to the negotiations in late autumn at Tribur and Oppenheim.

3.3.4 Tribur–Oppenheim

As they had arranged at Ulm a month earlier, in mid-October the German princes assembled at Tribur, a town to the south of Mainz and to the east of the Rhine.[325] With them as papal legates were Bishop Altmann of Passau who had been to the fore at Ulm, and also Patriarch Sigehard of Aquileia. Both were prelates of the imperial church, and so were more acceptable than Roman cardinals to Germans of the stamp of Siegfried of Mainz. Gregory used as his messenger to the assembly a German layman, Cadaloh, a monk who had formerly been a knight but was suffering from grave illness; Gregory imposed the journey upon him for the remission of his sins, and he died soon afterwards, evidently at St Blasien.[326] Such a messenger was calculated to impress upon the Germans the religious seriousness of Gregory's purpose.

The king encamped at Oppenheim, across the river and some seventeen kilometres to the south. He had a considerable body of supporters, but as had been the case ever since the assembly at Worms his lay and military entourage was unimpressive. If he had hoped to proceed by show of force, and this is far from certain, the number and power of those who joined the princes at Tribur made it impracticable for him to do so. Archbishop Siegfried of Mainz, who at Worms had led the bishops in withdrawing their obedience from Gregory, now defected from the king and took his place with the princes, together with his knights. There was also at about this time a damaging defection of bishops from the king; it included Henry of Liège, Frederick of Münster, Conrad bishop-elect of Utrecht, Huzmann of Speyer, and perhaps Werner of Strassburg and Burchard of Basel.[327] The surviving evidence does not suffice for a confident reconstruction of events at Tribur–Oppenheim. It is, however, clear that the king's position gradually weakened, and the defection of bishops was probably more a cause than an effect of this weakening. The course of events was complex. Deliberations began on 16 October, with long debates among the princes themselves. After ten days of intensive final negotiations, the parties dispersed on 1 November.

The narrative sources, all of which are anti-Henrician, give a false picture of unanimity among the princes who assembled at Tribur. The South German dukes and their supporters constituted an extreme though powerful wing of opinion; their aim was the immediate election of a new king who would replace Henry. Others, like Archbishop Udo of Trier, took a more moderate view. Desiring reform according to

---

[325] The principal narrative sources for Tribur–Oppenheim are: Berthold, *a.*1076, pp. 286/14–287/6; Lampert of Hersfeld, *Ann. a.* 1076, pp. 382–92; Bruno, cap. 88, pp. 326–31; Paul of Bernried, cap. 82, pp. 522–3. Amongst the many scholarly discussions, especial importance attaches to the debate in Germany during the 1930s and early 1940s; see the contributions by Brackmann, Erdmann, Haller, and Tellenbach reprinted in Kämpf (ed.), *Canossa als Wende*, and Baethgen, 'Zur Tribur-Frage'. For more recent work, see esp. Beumann, 'Tribur, Rom und Canossa', Schneider, *Prophetisches Sacerdotium*, pp. 172–87, Hlawitschka, 'Zwischen Tribur und Canossa'.

[326] Bernold, *Chron. a.* 1076, p. 433/18–22.   [327] Berthold, *a.*1076, p. 286/20–9.

the traditions of the Emperor Henry III, they were prepared to countenance Henry's continuing rule after his difference with the church had been settled.[328] At the time of Tribur, their position was the more compatible with Gregory's; it was with Udo and his comprovincial bishops that Gregory's contacts had for some time been strongest. Gregory is likely to have briefed his legates along the lines of his letter to the Germans of 3 September: if possible, Henry should be brought to repentance so that his excommunication and deposition might be withdrawn; if not, another king might be elected.[329] This is likely to have been agreeable to many of Gregory's sympathizers at Tribur; the legates are likely to have played a critical role in directing and concluding the negotiations both amongst the princes and between them and the king.

The increasing strength of the princes' opposition was such that Henry's overriding concern became to prevent a new election by the princes and so to seek reconciliation with Gregory whatever the cost. There are indications that, even during the debates at Tribur–Oppenheim, Henry might wish to travel to Rome in person and seek absolution from Gregory there.[330] But after long and tense debates amongst all parties, Henry was for the present denied this possibility. If the extreme party among the princes made concessions to their moderate peers by not proceeding to elect a new king, Henry was compelled to make humiliating and far-reaching concessions both to the princes and to the pope. He was compelled to permit the return to his see of Bishop Adalbert of Worms and so to abandon its citizens who had been among his most loyal supporters. He had to release the remaining Saxon hostages and to concede Gregory's central demand that he banish from his company his excommunicate counsellors.[331] In a letter addressed to all his magnates, Henry annulled everything that he decreed against Gregory at Worms. He promised due obedience to Gregory in all things, and he would make satisfaction for his inordinate actions. Henry's subjects were likewise to obey St Peter and his vicar; if they were excommunicated, they were to seek release from Gregory himself.[332] Henry agreed with the princes a

---

[328] This emerges, not only from the ending of the negotiations as presented by Berthold, but also from the fragment, hereafter referred to as the 'Königsberg Fragment', of a memorandum of events between mid-1076 and mid-1077 as recorded by an unknown bishop who transferred before Tribur from the Henrician to the princely party: Holder-Egger, 'Fragment', pp. 186–91. Erdmann's suggestion that the bishop may have been Otto of Constance is preferable to Holder-Egger's that he was Siegfried of Mainz, but his identity remains an open question. For Udo's abiding loyalty to Henry, see Lampert of Hersfeld, *Ann. a.* 1077, p. 289.

[329] On 31 Oct. Gregory told his Milanese followers that one source of his current afflictions was that, in Germany, 'symonaici cum Heinrico rege eorum decreta sanctorum patrum cum omni religione moliunter evertere'. His current appraisal of matters there was that 'De conspiratione autem hereticorum et regis, quomodo a catholicis episcopis et ducibus et multis aliis in Teutonicis partibus aperte inpugnetur, vos, qui illis prope estis, latere non credimus. Ad tantum enim numerum fideles Romanae ecclesiae pervenerunt, ut, nisi ad satisfactionem veniat rex, alium regem palam dicant eligere. Quibus nos favere servata iustitia promisimus promissumque firmum tenebimus': *Reg.* 4.7, p. 305/17–19, 23–30.

[330] Bruno, cap. 88, p. 328/25–6. Berthold's reference (p. 287/41–2) to the king's messengers' endeavour to persuade Gregory to allow Henry to come to Rome suggests that Henry may have sent a written request with the *Promissio*.

[331] See esp. Berthold, *a.*1076, p. 286/35–40. [332] *Epp. HIV* no. 24, pp. 72–3.

promise (*Promissio*) of personal obedience that he would dispatch to Gregory at Rome:

Urged by the counsel of my faithful subjects, I promise to the apostolic see and to you, Pope Gregory, that I will maintain due obedience to you in all things. Whatever infringement of the honour of your see or of yourself may seem to have arisen through me [probably a reference to the assembly at Worms] I will be at pains to set right by making proper satisfaction.

Because certain graver matters which I decreed against your see and your holiness are laid to my charge [probably a reference to Henry's plans to procure Gregory's expulsion from Rome and his replacement by another pope], at an appropriate time ('congruo tempore') I will either prove myself guiltless of them, with God's help, by the testimony of my innocence, or else in due course ('tum demum') I will willingly do penance for them.[333]

It was agreed that the king should be allowed a respite of a year after his excommunication, that is, until February 1077, within which he must be absolved by Gregory. But to this end, the princes stipulated that Gregory should be invited to come to Augsburg. The matter was to be ended in Germany, not at Rome.[334]

Such terms were far-reaching and humiliating for the king. Yet they did not amount to abject abasement, and he preserved some freedom of action. In his letter to his magnates, he most exceptionally referred to himself in the language of majesty ('mansuetudo nostra', 'nostra serenitas'), and in addressing his subjects he offered them the illustrious regard of his goodwill ('suae voluntatis gloriosam dignationem'). Even his promise of obedience to the papacy was made 'after the manner of our predecessors and forebears'. As regards the course of future events, in the *Promissio* the text of which Henry agreed with the princes, phrases like 'congruo tempore' and 'tum demum' made no commitment to a particular place or time. Henry made no commitment to a judgement by, or in the presence of, the German princes. The anonymous bishop of the 'Königsberg fragment' wrote only of a requirement that the king should show the pope 'debitam reverentiam', not 'oboedentiam'.[335] According to the text of the *Promissio*, Italy or Germany remained open as possible locations for Henry's exculpation. Nor was the king entirely bereft of political resources;

---

[333] *Quellen HIV* Anhang B, pp. 474–7. As it stands, the *Promissio* has a third paragraph: 'Now it would also beseem your holiness that you should not ignore the things noised abroad about you that are a source of scandal to the church, but, having removed from the public conscience this source of anxiety too, that you should establish through your wisdom the universal peace alike of church and kingdom.' The debate about its authenticity as part of the original *Promissio* has not been satisfactorily resolved. Brackmann and Erdmann defended, but Haller denied, its place in the original document. It remains difficult to believe that Henry would have included, or that the legates and princes would have permitted, a request that Gregory should exculpate himself in this way. The final clause may have been added for purposes of public propaganda, either in the late 1070s (Beumann) or in 1082: Cowdrey, *The Age of Abbot Desiderius*, pp. 237–8. The similar language in Lampert of Hersfeld, *Ann. a.* 1077, pp. 410/5–412/27, esp. pp. 410/16–17, 412/8–9, which reads like Gregory's response to the *Promissio*, should be noted as a difficulty to this view; but in 1082 a current version of Lampert's story about Gregory's self-exculpation at Canossa may have been adapted to refer to the Henrician case against Gregory.

[334] A date in early Feb. is attested by Berthold, Lampert, and Bruno. The unknown bishop's statement that the date set was the Epiphany (6 Jan.) is probably erroneous: Holder-Egger, 'Fragment', p. 189/5–8.

[335] 'Visum est ergo omnibus et iustum esse iudicabatur, quatenus regalis dignitas sacerdotali excellentiae debitam reverentiam exhiberet . . .': Holder-Egger, 'Fragment', p. 189/1–3.

according to Berthold, he was still powerful enough for the princes to fear reprisals after they had dispersed, and they swore mutual aid against future royal actions.[336]

It was another sign of Henry's resilience that he himself sent the text of the *Promissio* to Rome in the hands of a man of conciliation, Archbishop Udo of Trier.[337] Fearing—as Berthold said—the habitual chicanery of the king's advisers, the princes dispatched messengers of their own to Rome, in order to guard against Henry's deceitfulness and to arrange for Gregory's coming to Germany to settle its division ('dissensionem huiusmodi compositurus'). The princes also swore that, should Henry culpably remain excommunicate for more than a year, they would no longer have him as their king.

But Henry's single concern was now to become reconciled to Gregory. He withdrew to Speyer with *tutores* and *actores* designated by the princes, and with Bishop Thierry of Verdun as his adviser. The absence of royal diplomas between July 1076 and February 1077 suggests that the king refrained from public business. At Speyer, near the heartland of the Salian family inheritance and in whose cathedral his grandfather and father were buried, Henry embarked upon the life of a penitent.[338]

3.3.5 The Way to Canossa

Gregory probably received his first tidings of Tribur–Oppenheim not from official envoys from either camp but from Bishops Pibo of Toul and Huzmann of Speyer, and possibly others, whom Altmann of Passau as Gregory's legate sent to Rome for papal absolution. Gregory dealt somewhat severely with them: they were canonically reconciled, but they were confined to Roman monasteries until, at the Empress Agnes's plea, they were freed with the right to receive holy communion but not to perform episcopal duties.[339] The princes' envoys reached Rome before Henry's.[340] Berthold's dramatic story that, when Henry's *Promissio* was read out, the princes' envoys denounced it as having been falsified by Henry after it had been agreed, is unsupported by other evidence.[341] It is also implausible, for in a letter that Gregory soon afterwards dispatched to Germany, he showed no sign of shock or outrage at any such deception. Instead, he spoke of his many and great debates ('colluctationes') with the king's envoys and the arguments by which he resisted their words.[342] He had reason to be gratified, for on 31 October he had told his Patarene supporters that in Germany the fate of the king was in the balance and that he must keep his word whatever the outcome.[343] Now, matters were back in Gregory's control, and he could still

---

[336] Berthold, *a*.1076, pp. 286/44–5, 286/49–287/6.

[337] So Berthold, *a*.1076, p. 287/30–9; for Bonizo of Sutri, Udo was the messenger of the princes: *Lib. ad amic.* 8, p. 610/5–6. The difference illustrates his detachment.

[338] Henry's penitential withdrawal may have been part of Gregory's instructions to his legates; cf. his measures for bishops in *Reg.* 4.8, to the Tuscan bishops, 1 Nov. 1076, pp. 306–7.

[339] Berthold, *a*.1076, p. 287/24–9.

[340] Bonizo of Sutri's story about Udo's long imprisonment at Piacenza until permission for his release came from Speyer is uncorroborated and implausible in the light of Berthold: *Lib. ad amic.* 8, p. 610.

[341] Berthold, *a*.1076, p. 287/33–41.

[342] *Epp. vag.* no. 17, p. 48; cf. *Reg.* 4.12, to the German princes, late Jan. 1077, p. 312/27–33.

[343] *Reg.* 4.7, p. 305/23–31.

hope to succeed in his first preference of salvaging the Salian monarchy. He was arbiter; on the one hand, he disallowed Henry's plan of travelling to Rome for absolution there, but on the other, he rewarded the princes for their eventual moderation at Tribur with regard to Henry, who might now be reinstated as king, by agreeing to the princes' proposal of Augsburg as the place of his possible absolution.

Gregory declared his intention of coming to Germany in two letters to the faithful there, one of which instructed the princes about what they should do while the other extended an appeal for help to a wider audience.[344] Against the will and advice of his entourage at Rome but (as it later emerged) with the support of Countess Matilda of Tuscany and probably of Abbot Hugh of Cluny, the Empress-mother Agnes, and her brother Duke William of Aquitaine, he had decided to hasten to Germany.[345] By 8 January, he hoped to have reached Mantua in the far north of Matilda's duchy and on the route northwards to the Brenner Pass and so to Augsburg. The princes were to make preparations and to receive Gregory, and to make peace throughout the land. According to the account of events which Gregory wrote to the German princes after Canossa, his escort was arranged with envoys whom the princes sent to Rome. When Gregory left Matilda's lands, the same envoys were to meet him in good time for them to conduct him to the Brenner Pass, whence one of the South German dukes would escort him to Augsburg.[346] By 28 December, he had reached Florence, from where he deviated to Lucca before heading northwards to Mantua.[347]

For some time, Henry remained in seclusion at Speyer. The hostile annalist Berthold alleged that he readmitted to his confidence his evil counsellors, that he was visited by Lombards who incited him against Gregory, and that he cherished hopes of recruiting sufficient military forces in Italy to coerce Gregory into crowning him emperor if not to set up a new pope; only if such plans failed would he humble himself before Gregory and beg his absolution.[348] But there is nothing to confirm any of this. In all probability, Henry sought to circumvent the princes' plan for a general council at Augsburg where his own position would be in jeopardy, and to seek absolution by Gregory in order to win Gregory's goodwill and to salvage his own future as German king. As his self-presentation as 'humillimus' had preceded his restoration

---

344 *Epp. vag.* nos 17–18, pp. 46–51; Berthold, *a*.1076, p. 287/41–8.

345 *Epp. vag.* no. 19, pp. 50–2; Arnulf of Milan 5.8, pp. 227–8. Gregory's letter shows that his Roman advisers objected to the fact, not merely to the haste, of his Germany journey. See Borino, 'Le persone'.

346 *Reg.* 4.12, late Jan. 1077, p. 312: 'Sicut constitutum fuit cum legatis, qui ad nos de vestris partibus missi sunt, in Longobardiam venimus circiter viginti dies ante terminum, in quo aliquis ducum ad clusas nobis occurrere debuit, expectantes adventum illorum, quatinus ad partes illas transire possemus.' *Ad clusas* can hardly refer to the passes above Verona, for if he had arranged to enter Lombardy some twenty days before meeting his ducal escort, he would have wasted time there and then have been ill placed to travel the 280 km. or so to Augsburg in winter conditions by 2 Feb. The distance from the Brenner to Augsburg is some 160 km. For comparison, in Feb. 1053 the journey from Augsburg to Mantua took Pope Leo IX nineteen days; in Dec. 1049 he had travelled from Augsberg to Verona in a comparable time: JL 1.535–6, 544.

347 *QF* no. 122, pp. 120–3; *Vita Anselmi ep. Lucensis*. cap. 8, p. 15.

348 Berthold, *a*.1076, pp. 287/52–288/14.

to communion by Gregory's legates in 1074, so now a penitential pilgrimage would lead to his absolution by Gregory himself.[349] A pledge of Henry's singleness of purpose was the number of German bishops who, between Tribur and Canossa, sought to reach Gregory by their separate routes. Apart from Archbishop Udo of Trier, they included Archbishop Liemar of Bremen. Bishops Pibo of Toul, Huzmann of Speyer, Benno of Osnabrück, Eberhard of Naumburg, Werner of Strassburg, Burchard of Lausanne, and Burchard of Basel, also reached Gregory, as well as Henry's Italian chancellor Bishop Gregory of Vercelli. Two more German bishops, Rupert of Bamberg and Thierry of Verdun, fell captive on their way to Italy, respectively in the hands of Duke Welf of Bavaria and Count Albert of Calw. These bishops can scarcely have decided to seek Gregory without Henry's knowledge or even prompting. The king probably sought thereby to reassure Gregory of his own penitence and of his desire to promote the authority of the apostolic see in Germany. Gregory's goodwill could only be increased if his own reconciliation were accompanied by that of the bishops from the Rhine–Meuse area whom Gregory had especially cultivated and also by some of Henry's staunchest supports like Liemar of Bremen and Benno of Osnabrück. Gregory might look forward, if he visited Germany, to reuniting the German episcopate—those who had followed the king and those who had sided with the princes.

When Henry decided upon his winter journey to Italy, he set out with only a small following of, at most, some fifty men and women; its most important members were his queen, Bertha, and infant heir, Conrad.[350] If his bringing them on so arduous a journey seems harsh, he could not have left them in Germany as potential hostages, and their presence would help in securing assistance from Bertha's kindred in Savoy. Because the South German princes controlled the central Alpine passes, Henry had perforce to choose a western route. From Speyer he headed southwards, first to the lands of his friend Count William of Burgundy, and so to Besançon where he kept Christmas. According to Gregory, even before Henry entered Italy, he sent messengers to Gregory through whom he promised amendment of life and obedience for the future if he were granted absolution and papal blessing. Then, in the bitterest of winter conditions, for the chronicles unanimously testify to the winter of 1076–7 as of exceptional severity and duration, the royal party crossed the Jura to Geneva, and then travelled by the Mont Cenis Pass to Savoy. Lampert of Hersfeld, in particular, dwelt upon the rigours and perils of the journey. In Savoy, they met the queen's mother, Adelaide of Turin, with her son Count Amadeus. In Lombardy, many of the bishops rallied to Henry in the hope that he had come to recruit an army and coerce the pope by military force. But he continued his journey towards Rome through

[349] See above, 3.2.2.

[350] Besides Gregory's own letters, the principal sources for the encounter at Canossa are: Lampert of Hersfeld, *Ann. aa.* 1076–7, pp. 392–412; Berthold, *a.*1077, pp. 288/21–290/31; Bonizo of Sutri, *Lib. ad amic.* 8, pp. 609–10; Donizo, 2.1, lines 58–118, pp. 381–2; the 'Königsberg fragment', Holder-Egger, 'Fragment', p. 189/11–16. The episcopal author of the fragment said that Henry was guided by, and travelled to Italy with, a number of 'private advisers' ('cum privatis consultoribus'): p. 189/11–16. Among many modern discussions, see esp. Zimmermann, *Der Canossagang*.

Pavia, Piacenza, and Parma to Reggio, while the German bishops who were heading south continued by their several ways and with varying fortunes.

It is not known either when Henry learned of Gregory's whereabouts upon his northward journey or when Gregory discovered that Henry had entered Italy, although with a note of implied blame of the German princes, Gregory later observed that, if his escort to take him to Germany had arrived at the time and place agreed, he would have reached Germany before Henry's approach.[351] He must have been well on his way to Mantua. At Countess Matilda's urging, he returned to find security in her family castle and palace at Canossa.[352] Henry seems to have divested himself of his Lombard following at Reggio and to have established himself at Bianello, a few kilometres north of Canossa. From there, on about 21 January, he engaged through messengers in a long exchange with Gregory, who severely reproved him for his many transgressions. Countess Matilda took a prominent part in the negotiations, together with Countess Adelaide, Margrave Azzo II of Este, and Abbot Hugh of Cluny. According to Berthold, the latter, who was Henry's godfather, had been with him at Speyer and had to be released by Gregory from the ecclesiastical censure that his contact with Henry had implied.[353] Henry's advisers deemed Gregory's terms excessively severe, and a critical meeting took place in a chapel dedicated to St Nicholas, evidently at Montezane midway between Bianello and Canossa. Henry's pleas to Matilda led to her appealing strongly to Gregory on his behalf, with the support of Hugh of Cluny. On Wednesday 25 January, the feast of the Conversion of St Paul and a year and a day after the assembly at Worms, Henry, perhaps upon his own initiative, presented himself with a few companions before the inner gate of the castle at Canossa. In the bitter winter weather, he came fasting, unshod, and penitentially clad. For three consecutive days he thus appeared at the gate.[354] According to Gregory's own letter to his German supporters written a few days later:

Laying aside every regal adornment, he continued there before the castle gate in all wretchedness—barefoot and clad in wool. He did not cease with many tears to beg the help and consolation of our apostolic mercy, until he provoked all who were either there or in receipt of tidings of what was happening to such great mercy and pitying compassion, that they interceded for him with many pleadings and tears. For all marvelled at the unwonted harshness of our attitude; indeed, some complained that we were showing, not the strictness of apostolic authority, but a cruelty that was reminiscent of a tyrant's inhumanity.[355]

By the morning of Saturday 28 January, Gregory was persuaded of Henry's steadfastness in his penitence and promises of amendment. In response to the pleadings of all who were in the castle of Canossa, he absolved Henry and restored him to

---

[351] *Epp. vag.* no. 19, p. 51/1–2; cf. Bernold, p. 288/43–50.

[352] On Canossa as a fortress, see Tondelli, 'Scavi archeologici'.

[353] Berthold, *a*.1077, p. 289/13–14.

[354] Donizo supplies much of the topographical and chronological detail. No penitential significance attaches to the period of three days. Since it was the feast of the Conversion of St Paul, there may have been a reference to Paul's three-day fast at Damascus (Acts 9: 8–9).

[355] *Reg.* 4.12, to the ecclesiastical and lay princes of Germany, late Jan. 1077, p. 313/1–10.

the bosom of the church. According to Berthold, before Gregory celebrated mass, he received and reconciled not only the king but also other excommunicates. He gave the kiss of peace to the king and to five prelates—Werner of Strassburg, Liemar of Bremen, Burchard of Lausanne, Burchard of Basel, and Eberhard of Naumburg, and to other leading figures.[356]

As a condition of his absolution, Henry agreed to the terms of an oath (*iusiurandum*) to govern his future conduct. Without reference to the planned assembly at Augsburg, it began by preparing the way for a resolution of the divisions within the German kingdom:

> I, King Henry, with regard to the complaint and difference which the archbishops, bishops, dukes, counts, and other princes of the German kingdom maintain against me as do others who follow them in their difference, will, within the limit of time that the Lord Pope Gregory shall appoint, do either whatever is right according to his judgement or whatever makes for agreement according to his counsel, unless any insuperable impediment should hinder either me or him; when it is removed, I will stand ready to do whatsoever is called for.[357]

Accordingly, Henry promised that, if Gregory wished to cross the Alps or to journey elsewhere, Henry would furnish him with all possible security for himself, his entourage, and all who wished to travel with him. He also promised that he would consent to no hindrance to Gregory, and that he would aid Gregory against whoever might hinder him.

Henry promised fidelity to the terms of the *iusiurandum*, which was sworn to on his behalf of a number of persons. Berthold, who also referred to the part in the oath-taking that was intended for the Empress Agnes who had not yet arrived, named the German, Bishop Eberhard of Naumburg/Zeitz and the Italian, Bishop Gregory of Vercelli and others of Henry's *familiares*; Lampert of Hersfeld named the same bishops together with Margrave Azzo of Este and others, while Abbot Hugh of Cluny who as a monk could not swear added his sanction. The text of the *iusiurandum* which was preserved in the papal archives gave a list of those present which was fuller. It named a cross-section of the Roman church: Bishops Hubert of Palestrina and Gerald of Ostia (it should not escape notice that these were the legates who, early in 1074, had travelled to Germany and had restored Henry to communion), the priests Peter of S. Grisogono and Cono of S. Anastasia, the deacons Gregory and Bernard, and the subdeacon Humbert. *Ex parte regis* there were present Archbishop Liemar of Bremen (the senior German churchman at Canossa), Bishops Gregory of Vercelli and Benno of Osnabrück (respectively of the Italian and German churches), Abbot Hugh of Cluny, and 'many noble men'.

---

[356] The sources differ about the timing of the reconciliations of the bishops: Lampert of Hersfeld placed them early in the negotiations (pp. 402/12–404/3) while Berthold associated them with Henry's absolution (p. 290/4–15). They were probably the outcome of successive individual negotiations with Gregory which culminated in a general reconciliation together with the king.

[357] The *iuramentum* appears as *Reg.* 4.12a, pp. 314–15; for the Roman archival version with its list of witnesses, see Deusdedit, *Coll. can.* 4.421(161), p. 597, and Caspar's apparatus.

After the absolution of Henry and of other excommunicates, the pope celebrated mass. In all probability he gave Henry holy communion.[358] Thereafter, in a further powerful token of reconciliation, pope and king dined together. Gregory dismissed Henry with his blessing.

3.3.6 The Significance of Canossa

Gregory's encounter with Henry at Canossa was a unique event in that it cannot be fully explained in terms of current phenomena of eleventh-century life, whether religious or political; it stands alone in its purpose, character, and results. It was also complex, in that it brought together and fused into a single whole several different aspects of contemporary life, both religious and political.

One major aspect was religious and concerned the confrontation of two men, Gregory and Henry. Gregory's absolution of Henry at Canossa was the culmination of the long process by which, as archdeacon and as pope, Gregory had sought to bring the king to a right mind and manner of life, thus fitting him for the kingship and ultimately for the imperial office. As Gregory expressed it in his communiqué to the German princes immediately after his meeting with Henry, 'the king had humbled himself to do penance and had obtained the pardon of absolution' ('rex humiliatus ad paenitentiam absolutionis veniam impetravit'). As regards the future, Gregory bound himself in no way to the king, save that, in plain speech as was his custom, he told Henry that he might count upon his help, whether by way of justice or of mercy, in whatever conduced to his personal salvation and honour, so long as it might be done without peril to either of their individual souls.[359] By the phrase 'humiliatus ad paenitentiam', Gregory did not mean that Henry had been broken and laid low by being reduced to lasting shame and disgrace; rather, in Gregory's eyes, he had shown the salutary docility that was needful in all sinners before their restoration to communion.[360] Like the prodigal son of Christ's parable to whom Henry had referred in his submissive letter of 1073,[361] he had come to himself and to the ennobling virtue of Christian obedience by demonstrating his penitence before the vicar of St Peter and by acknowledging his authority as declared by scripture and tradition. Gregory's severity was made necessary, not only by Henry's long recalcitrance and by his presumption at Worms a year ago, but also by the unprecedented propaganda campaign

---

[358] Gregory's account to the German princes is ambiguous; his statement that 'relaxato anathematis vinculo in communionis gratiam et sinum sanctae matris ecclesiae recepimus' Henry (*Reg.* 4.12, p. 313/12–14) suggests but does not prove that he then received communion. Both Lampert of Hersfeld (pp. 410/27–412/27) and Berthold (p. 290/15–10) deny it, but they wrote after Forchheim and were concerned to undermine Henry's position. According to Lampert, Gregory saw the reception of communion as a kind of ordeal which Henry declined to accept because he preferred to await the judgement of a *generale consilium*; according to Berthold, Henry deemed himself unworthy, but Gregory perceived an underlying insincerity and untrustworthiness. Bernold implied, but did not say, that Henry took communion: *Chron. a.* 1077, p. 433/28–30. For Bonizo of Sutri, Henry's communion was a necessary part of his reconciliation to the church: *Lib. ad amic.* 8, p. 610/20–7.

[359] *Reg.* 4.12, pp. 311–14, esp. pp. 312/13–14, 313/26–314/4; *Epp. vag.* no. 19, p. 52/5–6.

[360] Cf. *Reg.* 4.8, to the bishops of Tuscany, 1 Nov. 1076, pp. 306/31–4, 307/11–16.

[361] See Henry's letter to Gregory of Aug./Sept. 1073, *Reg.* 1.29a, pp. 47–9, esp. p. 49/6–11.

both in Germany and at Rome by which Henry had proclaimed his actions to the world. The resonance of his manifestos in 1076 must be matched by the visible proof of sufficient penitence.

It is also likely that, for Gregory, Henry's privations on his journey across the Alps and at the gates of Canossa had the value of those undergone by the many pilgrims, including his own mother the Empress Agnes in 1065, who came to Rome on penitential journeys. Henry's experiences bear a striking similarity to those of Bishop Werner of Strassburg about whom Gregory wrote in 1074 to Countesses Beatrice and Matilda of Tuscany. Gregory began his letter to them by recalling that God, whom men are commanded to imitate, does not despise a heart that is contrite and humbled ('cor contritum et humiliatum'). He recalled that Werner's sins had besmirched the dignity of his episcopal office. Yet, alone of the German bishops immersed in carnal sins and in simony whom Pope Alexander II had summoned to Rome, Werner had come to the place of judgement in due humility and had fallen upon his face before Gregory to confess his sins. Under Alexander, probably at the Lent synod of 1073, he had experienced papal censure; at Gregory's synod, having reputedly shown his penitence and obedience by weariness, fastings, and journeyings, he had now sought papal mercy. Gregory's advisers had urged that he was, therefore, deserving of papal compassion. Gregory did not see fit to restore him fully to his episcopal dignity, but he had decided not to visit upon him full canonical rigour. It was a foreshadowing of Gregory's dealings with Henry, and the parallel was the closer because, later in his letter, Gregory in terms of reproof urged upon the countesses the duty of offering help and security to pilgrims like Werner.[362] In this letter to the countesses of Canossa, Gregory presented a model of the 'humiliatio ad paenitentiam' of a bishop which provided guidelines for that of a king. Far from being degrading or humiliating in the modern sense of the world, such penitential pilgrimages as Bishop Werner and King Henry made were invested with high religious value; they proved and exhibited the Christian qualities of those who undertook them, and they served to ennoble and exalt them. In 1084, an imperialist writer like Peter Crassus could attest this by his comment that Henry had at last come to Gregory in wonderful and unheard-of humility, deeming him to be a spiritual father.[363] As Gregory saw matters at Canossa, Henry had come to a right mind of which his austerities were proof to Gregory and to all Christians. As a spiritual father-in-God, Gregory had been compelled by such salutary humility to absolve the penitent king and to restore him to his place in the church, though not necessarily to the exercise of his kingship.

Even when viewed simply under its penitential aspect, however, the meeting at Canossa was more than one between two individuals—pope and German king. So far as Henry was concerned, Gregory proceeded to his restoration to communion not only on account of the king's own compunction but also because he himself was overcome by the supplications of all who were present.[364] A ritual of tearful pleading by

[362] *Reg.* 1.77, 15 Apr. 1074, pp. 109/17–110/22.
[363] Peter Crassus, cap. 6, p. 446/15–20.   [364] *Reg.* 4.12, p. 313/11–14.

the company of Christians present supervened. Furthermore, Lampert of Hersfeld noted how many German bishops and laity found their own way to Canossa, where they, too, suppliantly sought Gregory's pardon with bare feet and in penitential garb; Berthold wrote of the bishops and others whom Gregory reconciled and to whom he gave the kiss of peace along with the king as he prepared to celebrate the mass that was the culmination of the occasion.[365] Canossa was a collective, as well as an individual, occasion of penitential exercises and rituals.

In both these aspects, the ritual and the personal dispositions appropriate to penance merged with those appropriate to another familiar kind of self-humiliation, this time of a political nature—that which went by the Latin name of *deditio*. The word may be translated 'surrender' or 'capitulation', as conceded by persons, towns, or peoples to opponents whose strength they could not withstand; but, as with the word *humilitas*, it is necessary to understand it as expressing medieval, not modern, values and human dispositions. *Deditio* was an intensely personal matter. It required the visible acknowledgement of powerlessness before an adversary, and unconditional submission to his terms; these terms at his discretion might follow the rigour of justice (whether exercised as legal and social righteousness or as the right of the stronger), or the restraint of mercy and forgiveness. Such were the alternatives that Gregory envisaged when he told the German princes after Canossa that he would deal with Henry 'either with justice or else with mercy' ('aut cum iustitia aut cum misericordia'), and when, in the *iusiurandum*, Henry for his part promised eventually to implement either justice according to Gregory's judgement or else concord according to his advice ('aut iustitiam secundum iudicium eius aut concordiam secundum consilium eius faciam').[366]

Considered as an act of *deditio*, the meeting at Canossa witnessed a reversal of the roles in which the king and his adversaries had been placed fifteen months earlier after his victory over the Saxons on the Unstrut. Then, the *Carmen de bello Saxonico* which celebrated the king's victory told how the Saxon leaders had surrendered themselves to him with appropriate ritual gestures:

> Put off, proud people, your hardness of heart
> at this critical time!
> You and your posterity will surely now be destroyed,
> unless you yield your proud necks! . . .
> Or do you fear to submit your necks to a merciful king? . . .
> He will assuredly follow the ways of his ancestors:
> he will 'spare the submissive and subdue the proud'.
> Therefore all the Saxon men of valour humbly visited the king's camp
> as he approached with his army.
> Trusting no longer in arms and tricks and flight,
> with their weapons cast aside, with their proud necks bowed,
> and with bare feet,

[365] Lampert of Hersfeld, *Ann.* a.1077, pp. 402/12–404/3; Berthold, a.1077, p. 290/4–14.
[366] *Reg.* 4.12, p. 314/2–4, 4.12a, p. 315/3–5.

> They all with suppliant prayer surrendered themselves (*se dedunt*)
> without any condition. . . .
> Show to these who beseech you now or shall do so in the future
> what they may hope for from you, merciful king,
> if they surrender themselves (*se . . . dedent*) to you.[367]

At Canossa, Henry similarly surrendered himself unconditionally to the pope's justice or mercy. Other conventions of *deditio* were observed. There were protracted negotiations, and those whose role in human society it was to plead for mercy, women and monks, did so. The formality of the occasion is caught by the miniature in Donizo's *Life of Matilda*, in which the kneeling Henry seeks the support with Gregory of Abbot Hugh of Cluny and Countess Matilda as they sit in state: 'Rex rogat abbatem, Mathildim supplicat atque'.[368] It was by the pleas and the tears of such people as Hugh and Matilda that Gregory's stern resistance at Canossa was overcome. Also within the scope of the rituals of *deditio* were the final sharing of holy communion in the eucharist and of table-fellowship at dinner by which the healing of fractured human relationships was demonstrated.

Such being the collective overtones of the meeting at Canossa, it may be suggested that much of its uniqueness and significance lay in the fact that, in the critical events of 28 January, there was deliberately staged, not only an encounter of two men, Pope Gregory and King Henry, but also of two institutions, the holy Roman church and the kingdom of Germany and Italy. The considerable number of German bishops and laity who were involved should be borne in mind. The ordered lists of attestations to the *iusiurandum* to which Henry committed himself before he and his German companions received the kiss of peace—the clergy of the Roman church according to their order and rank, and representative figures of the German and Italian kingdom, epitomize such a meeting of collective bodies. It is not surprising that Donizo, a monk of S. Apollonio at Canossa, should have apostrophized Canossa in terms of 'a new Rome' when he looked back to the events of January 1077.[369] The taking of the *iusiurandum* in all the attendant circumstances was, therefore, a visible embodiment of the peace of the church and the concord of the kingdom which Gregory said that he had long sought and wished to go to Germany from Canossa the better to secure.[370] The mass and the dinner that followed the *iusiurandum* must have reinforced the symbolism of collective harmony under papal guidance which the *iusiurandum* was calculated to express.

For both Gregory and Henry, the meeting at Canossa and its outcome brought advantages but also left weaknesses. Especially in prospect, Gregory's position was a strong one. Every German metropolitan was now ostensibly on his side. With the king and so many bishops brought to obedience, he could aspire to be an effective arbiter in Germany by bringing about the reform of its church and the peace of its

---

[367] *Carmen*, 3.272–94, p. 188; the citation is from Virgil, *Aeneid*, 6.853.
[368] Donizo, fig. 7, facing p. 366.   [369] Donizo, 2.78, p. 381.
[370] *Reg.* 4.12, p. 313/19–26, cf. the address to all grades of the clerical and lay faithful in the German kingdom; p. 312/7–10.

kingdom. Although the timing of Canossa made it out of the question for him to reach Augsburg by 2 February as had been arranged, the terms of Henry's *iusiur-andum* gave promise of a national council which would promote Gregory's ends. The bishops would be the key to the situation, for those newly reconciled before or at Canossa would take their places alongside those who had already professed loyalty to Gregory and had made common cause at Tribur with the lay princes. Given a united episcopate, the princes might be expected to accept Gregory's judgement or arbitra-tion, and as at Tribur to accept that a penitent Henry might be their king. There was the prospect of a united *regnum Teutonicorum* which would facilitate the reform of the German church under Gregory's guidance without raising the problems of papal and episcopal authority that had fraught Gregory's earlier years.

But Gregory's position also had its weaknesses. So far as the king was concerned, his continuing obedience was far from assured; it was not long before Gregory was expressing misgivings about Henry's inactivity for good and about his presence as giving boldness to Gregory's North Italian enemies.[371] There was also dangerous uncertainty about Henry's political standing. Gregory candidly informed the German public that, at Canossa, he had finally settled nothing about Henry's possession and exercise of his kingly office.[372] Modern historians have increasingly recognized that their long debate as to whether in February 1076 Gregory did or did not depose Henry from the kingship arose from a *question mal posée*.[373] Even in his own mind, Gregory seems only over the next four years to have clarified the implications of his sentence. At his Lent synod he had first suspended Henry from the exercise of his kingship and freed his subjects from their oaths without expressly deposing him; he then excommunicated him. In September 1076, he presented his sentence in the reverse order and expressed himself more stringently; he spoke first of Henry's excommunication and secondly of his having been deposed from the royal dignity ('a regia dignitate depositus'). For the first time, Gregory envisaged the alternative of Henry's repentance and reinstatement or of a fresh election to the kingship by the princes that the pope would confirm.[374] At Canossa, Gregory had absolved Henry and restored him to the church's communion. Henry had shown himself *humilis* as Gregory understood the royal virtue of *humilitas* and thereby had met the cardinal requirement of a Christian king. Nevertheless, Henry's public standing as a king was left in suspense. It was not stated whether, in Gregory's eyes, the oaths of Henry's subjects were again binding. Only in 1080, when his second excommunication of Henry concentrated his thoughts, did Gregory resolve in his own mind the open question of how Henry stood. Only then did he reach the conclusion that 'seeing him humbled . . . I restored him only to communion but not to the kingship from which I

371 *Epp. vag.* no. 19, p. 52/10–22.

372 *Epp. vag.* no. 19, p. 52/5–9: 'victi eius humilitate et multimoda penitudinis exibitione, ab anathe-matis vinculo absolutum in gratiam communionis eum recepimus, de cetero nichil secum statuentes nisi quod ad cautelam et honorem omnium vestrum fore putavimus.'

373 The debate was led by Fliche and Arquillière; see their contributions as listed below in the Bibliography of Modern Authorities.

374 See above, 3.3.3.

had deposed him' in the Lent synod; nor had he restored the binding force of oaths taken to him.[375] But, from the point of view of the Saxons in particular, who since 1076 were again in open rebellion against Henry, the matter was settled. Gregory's words of September 1076 had been written, and Henry was deposed. Hence there became possible the foreshortening of history that the Saxon chronicler Bruno made in his book on the Saxon war. In 1076, Gregory 'by the counsel and consent of all condemned Henry by synodal judgement and, having deprived him of the name and office of king, struck him with the sword of his anathema'. Bruno then added Gregory's letter to Bishop Hermann of Metz of 1081, not that of 1076. At Canossa, Gregory did not restore the kingdom to Henry, and Bruno could mock Gregory's later dealings with Henry as evidence that the chair of St Peter had lost St Peter's constancy.[376]

Some in Germany who were not, like the Saxons, Henry's enemies may also have seen Gregory's treatment of him at Canossa in a different light than that which the pope intended. The resemblance between Henry's submission to the pope and the ritual of *deditio* by which secular rebels submitted to the king is likely to have been recognized and in some circles resented. Gregory's apparent assumption at Canossa of the king's role while the king himself figured as the outcast gave the occasion a shocking character.[377] In many German eyes, Canossa is likely to have been perceived as an act of enforced political submission which attracted sympathy towards the humiliated king and offence against the pope who used his spiritual position so to triumph over him. In Germany, the king had an opportunity to respond by seeking during the next years to renew the sacrality of Salian kingship and to recruit support by so doing.

If Gregory's treatment of Henry at Canossa may thus have offended some Germans, it also came to be regarded with reservations of a juristic kind in the mind and propaganda of at least one German bishop whose goodwill Gregory was concerned to retain. The 'Königsberg fragment' records the reaction of an unknown bishop who had reluctantly renounced Gregory at Worms but who had subsequently followed others in disowning his own act of weakness. At Tribur, he had seen it prescribed that, if Henry appeared before Gregory at Augsburg and was not proved innocent, he should make satisfaction according to the measure of his faults ('iuxta modum culpae satisfaciendo aecclesiae reconciliaretur'). But when he had craftily gone to Italy and intercepted Gregory, he had sought by force or guile to secure absolution on his own terms. As Gregory's own letter after Canossa made clear, Henry had coerced or deceived Gregory into effecting a reconciliation that was

---

[375] *Reg.* 7.14*a*, p. 484/10–15: 'Quem ego videns humiliatum multis ab eo promissionibus acceptis de suae vitae emendatione solam ei communionem reddidi, non tamen in regno, a quo eum in Romana synodo deposueram, instauravi nec fidelitatem omnium, qui sibi iuraverant vel erant iuraturi, a qua omnes absolvi in eadem synodo, ut sibi servaretur, precepi.' Cf. *Vita Anselmi ep. Lucensis*, cap. 16, p. 18, for a similar assessment.

[376] Caps. 68, 73, 90, 107, pp. 286, 296–316, 332, 354.

[377] See T. A. Reuter, reviewing Keller, *Zwischen regionaler Begrenzung*, in *EHR* 104 (1989), 980–1.

against the custom of the church, for Henry did not make such satisfaction as the Germans had required. Therefore in receiving Henry into communion, Gregory had left intact his suspension from the king's office. Writing with knowledge of Rudolf of Swabia's election as anti-king at Forchheim, the bishop could claim that Gregory's defective action at Canossa left open the way for the German princes unilaterally to elect a new king.[378] Evidently the king's arduous penitential journey that so deeply moved Gregory did not lead the bishop and those who thought like him to share Gregory's view that Henry's restoration to the kingship could be entertained. The way lay open for a revival of the plan of the South German dukes, suppressed after Tribur, to get rid of Henry as German king, whatever Gregory might wish. In view of the complexity of the German political situation, the manner of Gregory's reconciliation of Henry at Canossa tended further to polarize German divisions by dividing the parties that respectively supported the Salian monarchy and sought the election of an anti-king. Gregory's purpose of securing peace and concord by the exercise of his own arbitration was unlikely to be achieved.

For Henry, too, there were gains as well as losses in the reconciliation at Canossa. Tactically, his gains were considerable. By his journey from Speyer, he secured papal absolution before the elapse of a year and a day from the Lent synod of 1076 which was the princes' deadline as set at Tribur; he had deprived his German enemies of this reason for renouncing his lordship. Moreover, Gregory not only recognized him to be *rex*—he had done this even before Canossa;[379] but as the *iusiurandum* illustrates, at Canossa Gregory acted on the assumption that Henry exercised sufficient royal authority to facilitate the holding of a German assembly and to provide security for Gregory himself and for all those who travelled with, to, or from him.[380] Again, since September 1076, Gregory had placed excommunication first amongst his measures at the Lent synod against Henry;[381] he had spoken as though absolution were the key to a restoration to the kingship from which he had been deposed. Whatever the exact position about Henry's kingship in Gregory's eyes, and it is probable that he was himself far from certain about this, and whatever matters remained for resolution by a German assembly, at Canossa, to a significant degree Gregory acknowledged Henry to be a king in fact as well as in name. Henry had secured his purpose in going to Italy: he had headed off the hostile alliance of pope and princes that had threatened

---

[378] Holder-Egger, 'Fragment', pp. 188–9. The passage concerned is as follows: Henry with his private advisers 'domnum apostolicum ad prefinitum tempus et locum tendentem preoccupant. Ea quidem intentione, ut absolutionem suae voluntati magis quam rationi congruentem aut vi extorquerent aut ingenio elicerent. Sed nec spes eos omnino fefellit. Nam sive terrore sive dolo perpetratum sit, nescio, unum scio et salva Romana auctoritate dico, quia, si ita actum est, sicut nobis innotuit [see *Reg.* 4.12, p. 313/11–15], nequaquam aecclesiastico more reconciliatio illa processit, quippe quam nulla satisfactio precessit. Sic recepto in communionem regi de regni sententia nihil remissum est. Dum haec in Italia aguntur, iam anno transacto, ex quo regi regni gubernacula sinodali iudicio interdicta sunt, Theuthonici conventum facientes ducem Rodulfum in regem sibi elegerunt': p. 189/15–27.

[379] *Reg.* 3.15, p. 277/5, 4.1, pp. 290/14, 291/13.

[380] *Reg.* 4.12a, p. 315/7–16.

[381] *Reg.* 4.3, to the faithful in Germany, 3 Sept. 1076, p. 298/12–15.

him at Tribur. He had won a measure of tactical freedom to pursue his interests in Germany and Italy.[382]

Henry gained further tactical benefit from Gregory's reluctance to anticipate how matters might be settled if he came to Germany: as Gregory commented to the German bishops and princes from Canossa, 'ita adhuc totius negotii causa suspensa est'.[383] From the side of political theory, Gregory had not disposed of Henry's claim to the independence of his kingdom that he had propounded in his propaganda letters of 1076.[384] From that of practice, Henry had secured the placing of any future assembly upon a fresh and less dangerous footing. Gregory would not, as the programme of Tribur had envisaged, appear as Henry's accuser. He would come to Germany as an impartial judge and arbiter who sought to establish *pax* and *concordia* by uniting king, bishops, and princes—the cross-section of society that he addressed in a succession of letters[385]—in a reconciled and united *regnum Teutonicorum*.

Because Gregory had taken up this stance, there was little prospect of a viable alliance between Gregory and the anti-Henrican rebels emerging to threaten Henry. At best, Gregory would conciliate Henry's opponents so that they accepted him as king; at worst, they would pursue their hostility to Henry despite, not in pursuit of, the pope's policies and wishes. Meanwhile, the German opposition was divided between those who, like many in Swabia and the west of Germany, were receptive to Gregorian ideas, and those who, like the Saxons, stood mainly for local and political interests. These parties might sometimes work together, but there would be tensions and suspicions between them which would work to Henry's advantage while they weakened Gregory's leverage in Germany.

Yet Canossa also left the king with weaknesses. He had lost much of his support amongst the bishops who, he could tell Gregory in 1076 after the meeting at Worms, 'are united to me as members most beloved';[386] since some of them were also disenchanted with Gregory for the fact and the manner of his reconciliation of the king at Canossa, they had many common interests with the lay princes and might readily associate themselves with them against Henry and in favour of an anti-king.

Henry's role at Canossa was also in important respects a personal and political humiliation. This was not because it exposed him to public shame, for penance was an accepted part of religious discipline; penitential acts had been performed by biblical kings like David and Solomon and also by respected Christian rulers like Constantine, Theodosius I, and Louis the Pious.[387] It was damaging because it followed Henry's challenge in 1076 for the pope to stand down from the papal office

---

[382] 'Unoque facto duo peregit, scilicet et banni solutionem accepit et suspectum sibi colloquium apostolici cum adversariis suis ipse medius intercepit': *Vita HIV* cap. 3, p. 420/16–18.

[383] *Reg.* 4.12, p. 313/24–5.

[384] Esp. *Epp. HIV* no. 12, p. 66/4–7; no. 11, p. 62/22–3; see also the excerpts translated above, 3.3.3.

[385] *Reg.* 4.2,3,12; *Epp. vag.* nos. 14, 15, 17–19.

[386] *Epp. HIV* no. 11, p. 62/25–6.

[387] See e.g. the tract *De penitentia regis Salomonis*: Blumenthal, 'Canossa and Royal Ideology'. However, it is doubtful whether this tract bears directly upon events at Canossa: Märtl, 'Ein angebliche Text'. For the penances of rulers, see esp. Schieffer, 'Von Mailand nach Canossa'.

and his widely disseminated propaganda to this end throughout Germany and at Rome. In derogation of such strident challenge, Henry was compelled to accede to Gregory's demands about a ruler's proper humility and obedience. Like the Saxons in October 1075, he was brought to the straits of a *deditio* to his adversary.

Gregory's absolution of Henry gave him an added moral advantage by restoring his own policies to general credibility. By depriving Henry of his kingdom and excommunicating him, Gregory had exceeded the sanctions of earlier popes and bishops. Even so ardent a Gregorian as Bonizo of Sutri remembered that the sentence of February 1076 had struck the Roman world like an earthquake.[388] Half a century later, Henry's grandson Bishop Otto of Freising commented that:

I read and read again the records of Roman kings and emperors, and never do I find that before this anyone had been excommunicated or deprived of his kingdom, unless perchance someone might discern such an anathema when a bishop of Rome set Philip [the Arabian] with the penitents, or in Theodosius's being excluded from the fellowship of the church by St Ambrose on account of a bloody massacre.[389]

In 1076, much German opinion had put Gregory on the defensive against the charge that his excommunication of Henry was too severe.[390] At Canossa, however, his reconciliation of the penitent Henry, the sinner who came in humility for restoration to communion, seemed to many a proper exercise of the priestly office. Henry must now continue to show at least a measure of righteousness and obedience, or he risked forfeiting the loyalty of those who were committed to Gregory, and also of the many waverers whose support or acceptance both sides needed to secure.

So far as Germany was concerned, both pope and king therefore faced an uncertain future. The princes' invitation to Gregory at Tribur that he should come to Augsburg and settle German affairs left him with a settled purpose, safeguarded by Henry's *iusiurandum* at Canossa, to visit Germany with the full Petrine authority of his office. Canossa left Gregory and Henry in competition to establish right order in Germany in which each was concerned to explore and to maximize the authority of his office as he envisaged it. Each must promote his case both by propaganda and by well considered action.

After Canossa, both Gregory and Henry brought to the contest for authority in Germany and Italy a different, and in many respects a wiser, approach than they had shown before their breach in the winter of 1075–6. Gregory had grown in discretion. Stung, no doubt, by the propagandist calumnies fuelled by Hugh Candidus in 1076 about his political and personal relations with women and especially the *dévote* Countess Matilda of Tuscany, still in her prime and separated from her husband, Gregory gave no more pretext for mockery and gossip. Pious women played no such part as they had hitherto played in his plans, such as those for Henry's imperial coronation or for Gregory's eastern expedition in 1074. No longer did Gregory write

---

[388] *Liber ad amic.* 8, p. 609/12–13: 'postquam de banno regis ad aures personuit vulgi, universus noster Romanus orbis contremuit.'

[389] *Chronica*, 6.35, p. 490/25–30. Philip the Arabian was Roman emperor from 244 to 299, and Theodosius I from 379 to 395.   [390] See above, 3.3.3.

to Matilda in terms of personal closeness and familiarity; after Canossa and its immediate aftermath, only one letter of his to her survives, and his infrequent references to her, though sometimes cordial, were cautiously formal and diplomatic.[391] He had learned the lessons of caution and reserve. In his letters to Germany, too, there was a change. He became less concerned to write letters of admonition to individual bishops and to react piecemeal when they objected to his reforming aims and methods. He now more characteristically addressed all the faithful in the *regnum Teutonicorum*, both clerical and lay, and his constant objective was a papally controlled assembly which would bring peace to the land, stability to the monarchy, and reform to the church.

In response to Gregory's greater coherence of vision, Henry for the first time began to develop the positive skills of rulership, learning slowly but in many respects learning well. He began once more to invest the Salian monarchy with a sacral identity; he opposed to Gregory's papacy under the patronage of St Peter a monarchy under the patronage of the Blessed Virgin.[392] At Speyer in particular, he developed its pieties, and he attended to the care of the poor for which his panegyrist would one day honour him.[393] When sees and abbeys fell vacant, he began to appoint worthy men to rule them, so that the reproach of simony might be lifted from his rule.[394] Following in the tradition of his father, he sought to match Gregory's bid to be the source of peace in Germany by establishing the Salian monarchy as the leader in this role. He had the advantage that, whereas Gregory was at a distance—after returning to Rome in September 1077, he never again, so far as is known, travelled further north than Acquapendente in the papal patrimony, he was in Germany and could give tangible effect to his words. He could practise his newly discovered *métier de roi*.

After Canossa, Gregory and Henry both confronted an uncertain future with fresh skill and resource in the arts of rulership.

3.4 From Forchheim to the Second Excommunication of Henry IV

3.4.1 The Assembly at Forchheim

It was not until mid-September 1077 that Gregory returned to Rome. He had been determined to travel to Germany if circumstances had allowed; indeed, in March he entertained the idea of eventually travelling thence to Rome by a long detour through the Touraine.[395] Not only did Gregory refer to Henry as *rex*, but after Canossa he also envisaged his rehabilitation as king of the *regnum Teutonicorum* by an agreement

---

[391] The single surviving letter is *Reg.* 6.22, 3 Mar. 1079, pp. 434–5. After the immediate aftermath of Canossa, references to Matilda appear only in *Reg.* 6.12, privilege for the see of Pisa, 30 Nov. 1078, p. 414/22–4; 6.18, to Bishop Eberhard of Parma, 14 Feb. 1079, p. 430/10–12; 9.3, to Bishop Altmann of Passau and Abbot William of Hirsau, (Mar. 1081), p. 574/10–14; 9.11, to Abbot Desiderius of Montecassino, (May 1081), p. 589/3–8.

[392] See below, 3.4.3.

[393] For care for the poor, see *Vita HIV* cap. 1, pp. 408–12.

[394] See below, 3.4.7.

[395] *Reg.* 4.13, to Bishop Ralph of Tours, 1 Mar. 1077, p. 317/7–11, cf. *H* no. 107, p. 180/8–12.

with the German princes that he would himself mediate. On 9 June, a letter from
Gregory to Archbishop Nehemiah of Gran, in Hungary, opened with a clear statement of his purpose at that time:

We intended to cross into the kingdom of Germany in order that we might, with God's help,
arrange peace and concord between King Henry and the princes of the land.[396]

But it was never likely that Gregory's journey to Germany would take place, for no
one wanted it. The enmity to him of the Lombard bishops, which was fuelled by his
endeavours after Canossa to reform the North Italian church, made it virtually
impossible that he could reach any of the Alpine passes. During the first week of
February, Gregory almost certainly had further talks with Henry at Bianello with a
view to circumventing the bishops' hostility. A further assembly at Mantua was
mooted at which an understanding between Gregory and the Lombard bishops
might be attempted, but nothing came of it.[397] The encounter at Bianello was the last
occasion upon which Gregory and Henry met face to face. Henry did nothing to
facilitate Gregory's coming to Germany, but rather sought to assert his own kingly
authority in Italy by a series of judicial rulings. He also began his policy in the next
few years of securing his control over the eastern passes to Germany.[398] A plan of his
to secure the Italian crown, apparently at Pavia, may have failed through Gregory's
displeasure.[399] No less of a hindrance to Gregory's coming to Germany was the
princes' inability, and probably unwillingness, to provide Gregory with an escort.
Gregory's plan for a renewal of peace and concord between Henry and themselves
was little to their liking. Already at Tribur, the South German dukes had wished to
discard Henry and to elect a new king; they wished to keep their hands free to dispose
of the German monarchy in their own way. The revival of Saxon opposition to Henry
gave them every encouragement.

In Germany, events after Canossa moved swiftly.[400] Tidings of Canossa arrived
and circulated through Gregory's letter which was accompanied by a text of Henry's
far from welcome *iusiurandum*, together with such verbal messages as the messenger,
Radbod, may have carried.[401] In mid-February, Duke Rudolf of Swabia and his close
associates convened an assembly at Ulm which, on account of the shortness of notice
and the severity of the winter, was sparsely attended. It was decided to summon a
further assembly on 13 March at Forchheim, near Bamberg. This Franconian locality was significantly chosen: in 911, it had witnessed a royal election by which Duke
Conrad I of Franconia had been freely chosen to be king. At Ulm, it was probably
already envisaged that, with Henry in Italy, the business at Forchheim would likewise
be the election of a new king. The favoured candidate was Rudolf of Rheinfelden,

---

[396] *Reg.* 4.25, 9 June 1077, pp. 339–40; cf. 4.12, to the German princes (late Jan. 1077), p. 313/19–22.
[397] Donizo, 2.119–45, p. 381.
[398] See below, 3.4.3 and 4.4.
[399] Berthold, *a.*1077, p. 290/40–45; Paul of Bernried, cap. 86, p. 526.
[400] The principal chronicle sources for the assembly at Forchheim and events leading to it are: Berthold,
*a.*1077, pp. 291/44–292/30; Bruno, cap. 91, pp. 332–4; Paul of Bernried, caps. 88–90, 93–6, pp. 526–31.
[401] *Reg.* 4.12, 12a, pp. 311–15. For Radbod, see *Epp. vag.* no. 19, p. 52.

duke of Swabia; a new crown was already secretly commissioned for him at the Alsatian monastery of Ebersheimmünster, of which a kinsman of his was abbot.[402] The reasons why he was preferred to the more powerful Saxon leader Otto of Nordheim were probably, first, that Otto had a compromising record of collaboration with the king; second, that Rudolf had royal connections, his first wife having been Henry IV's sister Matilda and his second, Adelaide, the sister of Henry's queen, Bertha of Turin; third, that Rudolf was, therefore, closely connected to the Salian house as son-in-law of the Emperor Henry III and of the still-surviving Empress Agnes; and fourth that he had supported ecclesiastical reform, especially as patron of the monastery of St Blasien. As his letters about Germany in 1073–5 abundantly show, Gregory thought well of him, and his choice as king might be expected to find acceptance by him when it came to the point.[403]

The messenger Radbod returned to Italy with an invitation to Gregory that he seek some means of attending and that he treat with Henry to this end, which he proceeded to do.[404] The princes must have known that Gregory would be unlikely to come; their desire was to settle the problems of the German crown for themselves, using Gregory not to arbitrate in Germany but to give validation from Italy to what they themselves had already done. Gregory's immediate response was to send to Forchheim two legates, the Roman cardinal-deacon Bernard and Abbot Bernard of Saint-Victor at Marseilles. He sent with them a letter addressed to all those in Germany 'who are defending the Christian faith and religion'; in it, he sought to guide the assembly according to his own wishes.[405] He affirmed that, at Canossa, he had only freed Henry from excommunication; he had settled nothing further with him save what might conduce to the Germans' safety and honour. This was evidently an allusion to the *iusiurandum*, which had left open of the question of the kingship until Gregory should arbitrate. Gregory referred to the difficulty of his own present situation: he was outraged by the contumacy and opposition of the Lombard bishops; as for Henry, his merely negative obedience gave Gregory scant cause for rejoicing, for Henry's very presence in Italy emboldened the enemies there of the pope and of the apostolic see. He could not himself quickly find the means of coming to Germany, but with or without Henry's help he nevertheless remained resolved to do so. Meanwhile, his legates brought further, verbal counsel to the princes.

Immediately after the legates left Gregory, Count Manegold of Altshausen-Veringen, a messenger from Rudolf of Swabia and his circle, reached Gregory.[406]

---

[402] *Chronicon Ebersheimense*, cap. 26, p. 444. Henry caused the abbot of Ebersheimmünster to be expelled from his abbey.

[403] Jakobs, 'Rudolf von Rheinfelden und die Kirchenreform'; for Gregory's approval, see esp. *Reg.* pp. 19–21, to Duke Rudolf, Bishop Raynald of Como, and Bishop Anselm II of Lucca, 1 Sept. 1073, pp. 31–5, 2.45, to Rudolf, 13 Jan. 1075, p. 185/5–12, where Gregory referred to him as 'karissimum sancti PETRI filium'.

[404] *Epp. vag.* no. 19, p. 52/23–35.

[405] *Epp. vag.* no. 19, pp. 50–4.

[406] Manegold was a brother of the chronicler Hermann of Reichenau, whom Paul of Bernried described as 'magnus amator veritatis': caps. 89, 91, pp. 526–9.

The count's brief was to express encouragement for Gregory to cross the Alps, but to press Henry not to do so until he had sent ahead either Gregory or the Empress Agnes.[407] According to a source hostile to Henry, when Gregory sent the count to him with an envoy of his own, the cardinal-deacon Gregory, Henry disdained to offer Gregory the security that he needed in order to get to Germany. If so, Henry contravened his *iusiurandum* at Canossa. It is, however, unlikely that he so offended Gregory; he perhaps pointed out that he lacked the power. Count Manegold returned direct to Germany, but probably did not arrive before the assembly at Forchheim. But his mission achieved the ends for which it was no doubt intended: it neutralized Gregory's regret that, in 1076, the princes' delay in providing an escort had prevented his reaching Germany;[408] it fostered Gregory's goodwill towards the princes; and it forestalled both Gregory's and Henry's coming to Germany until the princes at Forchheim had themselves disposed of the German crown.

Therefore, despite Gregory's wish for postponement, at Forchheim the princes could proceed to an immediate election. The attendance was larger than at Ulm, but still not numerous. The prelates known by name to have been present are Archbishops Siegfried of Mainz, Gebhard of Salzburg, and Werner of Magdeburg, together with Bishops Adalbert of Worms, Adalbero of Würzburg, Altmann of Passau, and Burchard of Halberstadt. Dukes Rudolf of Swabia, Welf of Bavaria, and Berthold of Carinthia, together with Otto of Nordheim, were the leading lay figures; Duke Magnus of Saxony and Margrave Udo of Stade may also have been present.

It is difficult to reconstruct the course of events at Forchheim. It is likely that they opened on 13 March with the two papal legates reading Gregory's letter, and that, in order to establish the urgency of getting rid of Henry, the first day saw the ventilation by the princes of the grievances that had accumulated ever since Henry's minority. The gravity of Henry's offences is said to have surprised the legates. The sources differ about how Henry's position was regarded. The Swabian Berthold wrote that he was formally accused before and judged by the princes, who pronounced his deposition by their princely judgement. For Paul of Bernried, who followed a well informed source, Gregory had already deposed Henry at the Lent synod of 1076, although he also entertained the view that the princes passed sentence at Forchheim because they deemed him unsuitable for the kingship. The Saxon writer Bruno shared Paul of Bernried's opinion that Gregory had in 1076 passed a sentence of deposition. The truth seems to be that different but not incompatible views were advanced. According to the South Germans, Henry had offended against secular norms of kingship for so long and with such incorrigibility that the princes should proceed to his deposition; for the Saxons, Gregory had already deposed him by exercising the sanctions of the apostolic office.

Confronted by these arguments and being mindful of Gregory's unwillingness for decisive action to be taken before he could come to Germany, the legates were in a quandary about how they should react. At first, they kept to Gregory's commission

---

[407] For Agnes's position with regard to the royal succession, see *Reg.* 4.3, p. 299/26–37.
[408] *Epp. vag.* no. 19, p. 52/2–3.

that they should argue against an immediate election and for a deferring of the question of Henry's reinstatement as king. But in September 1076 Gregory had already envisaged a new election. Faced by the princes' arraignment of Henry and by their summary judgement upon him, the legates could do no more than place responsibility for an election at Forchheim entirely upon the princes. All that they would promise was that, if the princes deemed an election to be unavoidable, the pope would not openly resist it; according to the sources for the assembly at Forchheim, they came no nearer than this to consenting there to Rudolf's election. On their part, the princes were concerned to claim that Rudolf's election had papal authority; his letter of the previous September provided a basis for so doing. It was a burden of authority that Gregory himself was never to accept. Even in 1080, when again excommunicating Henry, Gregory insisted that, at Forchheim, the princes elected Rudolf for themselves, 'without my advice'.[409]

The preparation of a crown for Rudolf and the mission of Count Manegold leave little room for doubt that, whatever forms were observed at Forchheim, Rudolf's election was prearranged. On 14 March, a further meeting in the legates' lodgings concluded that only an immediate election could prevent a schism of the whole kingdom. Next day, the spiritual and lay elements in the assembly met separately to give it effect. Archbishop Siegfried of Mainz, who at Worms in 1076 had been the first among the prelates to renounce his obedience to Gregory, was now the first to cast his vote for Rudolf of Rheinfelden. Under the legates' guidance, efforts were made to keep the election free from simony by refusing to allow Rudolf to be asked to make promises to individual electors. But he promised two things in general: answering Gregory's critical demand, he promised that elections of bishops should be freely made by their own churches; and, building upon traditions already established in the complex history of German king-makings, he undertook that future kings should succeed by princely election, not by hereditary succession even in Rudolf's family.

Later propaganda would seek to associate Gregory directly with Rudolf's election. The story grew up that Gregory sent him a crown with the legend 'Petra dedit Petro, Petrus diadema Rodolfo'.[410] Contemporary sources give no hint of such papal complicity. During the 1070s, Gregory neither argued for nor encouraged elective kingship as envisaged at Forchheim. The princes presented Gregory with a *fait accompli*, and Germany with its first anti-king.

3.4.2 The Sequel to Forchheim in Germany

After Forchheim, both Rudolf and Henry were quick to court Gregory's favour. Rudolf sent him notice of his election in terms that sought to win his approval by insisting that, like Gregory himself when he became pope, he took the reins of

---

[409] *Reg.* 7.14a, p. 484/21–4, cf. 9.29, p. 613/6–9.
[410] For Gregory's complicity, see e.g. *Lib. de unit. eccles. cons.* 2.9, p. 220/26–30; Frutolf, *a.*1076, p. 86/15–16. For the crown, see Sigebert of Gembloux, *Chron. a.*1077, p. 364; cf. Otto of Freising, *Gesta Frederici*, 1.7, p. 142 (with the reading *Roma* for *Petra*).

government under constraint ('coactus') and by promising obedience to Gregory.[411] On 31 May, Gregory set out his reaction to Forchheim in two letters, one to his legates in Germany and the other to the faithful German clergy and laity.[412] It is significant that he seems to have made no direct approach to Rudolf which might have been construed as a recognition of his sole kingship as set up at Forchheim. His letters provide the only first-hand evidence of his intentions regarding Germany before his return to Rome in mid-September. He recalled that he had travelled northwards in order to establish peace in Germany to the honour of God and for the well-being of the church, but he had been prevented by the lack of safe-conduct across the Alps and had been diverted to Canossa. He remained committed to a German journey in the course of which, with the counsel of the faithful clergy and laity, he would examine the dispute ('causa') between the two *reges* Henry and Rudolf who now contested the kingdom. He would establish which of the two kings divine righteousness ('iustitia') favoured to govern it. The touchstone would be kingly obedience in word and deed. Gregory put forward his favourite model for priestly jurisdiction over kings: the dealings of Samuel with Saul in which, as Pope Gregory the Great had insisted, disobedience was shown to be tantamount to idolatry and caused kings to fall from their royal office and incur excommunication. For Gregory, this was more than a local, German matter. His intervention in Germany was part of his apostolic mission to settle the business of all the churches.[413] The fostering of peace and concord in Germany was critical, not only for this land, but for the universal church; to frustrate it would be to compass the destruction of the whole Roman empire.

Gregory's instructions to his legates were appropriately strong and positive. They were to call upon both kings now to make possible Gregory's journey to Germany so that he might himself hold a council that would both settle the issue of the kingship and bring about the peace, that is the reform, of the church and of Christian society. If either Henry or Rudolf set himself against the papal will and disobeyed the legates, the latter were told exactly what they must do: they should deny the guilty person the right to govern the kingdom and they should excommunicate him for his disobedience; that is, Gregory's sentence of February 1076 as then formulated against Henry should be strictly enforced against whichever of the rival kings now proved himself to be guilty. In the case of Gregory's enforced absence from Germany, the legates were themselves to assemble a council of all who could attend, and were to confirm the obedient king in the royal authority. As for the German faithful, they must resist whoever might oppose Gregory's coming to Germany. They were to enforce whatever sentence the legates might pass in his name, and they were to obey the king whom the legates approved. In a phrase that implicitly denied the finality of the

---

[411] *Reg.* 4.24, p. 337/8–26, 7.14*a*, pp. 484/24–485/5. See also Berthold, *a*.1077, p. 292/31–5; Paul of Bernried, cap. 98, p. 532; Bonizo of Sutri, *Lib. ad amic.* 8, p. 611. Sources favouring Henry said that Rudolf took the crown: Frutolf, *a*.1057, pp. 74/15, 76/11–13; *Chron. Ebersheimense*, cap. 26, p. 444/33–4.

[412] *Reg.* 4.23–4, pp. 334–8; cf. 4.25, to Archbishop Nehemiah of Gran, 7 June 1077, p. 338/17–32.

[413] Cf. *Dictatus papae* 21, *Reg.* 2.55*a*, p. 206.

election at Forchheim, such obedience was necessary in order that, as the consequence of an apostolic decision, the approved party might indeed 'obtain the royal dignity with honour (*honeste*) and bring help to a church that is now almost in collapse'.

As Gregory regarded matters, after Forchheim, Henry and Rudolf were both personally *reges*, though neither had, as yet, a full, clear, and final title to the royal dignity. The test of righteous obedience had still to be decisively applied. This should take place in a German council at which Gregory was present; but if he were prevented from coming to Germany, he commissioned his two legates to act in his name and as he would have acted.

Despite the restraint and balance of Gregory's instructions, his legates were drawn ever more closely into the wake of Rudolf of Rheinfelden and his princely supporters. They accompanied Rudolf upon his journey from Forchheim to Mainz where, according to a reliable source unwillingly, they gave their assent when, on 26 March, Archbishop Siegfried crowned him king.[414] It was not an impressive occasion. The coronation was the occasion of a riot by the citizens and of much bloodshed;[415] as a result, both Rudolf and Siegfried left Mainz in haste, never to return. During the early summer, the legates accompanied Rudolf on an itinerary through Swabia to Zürich. They seem to have made an attempt to implement Gregory's plans for the reform of the church.[416] But far more important than their own meagre steps towards reform was the implanting in Swabia of the canon-law collection that seems to have inspired them. It is likely that the legates had come to Germany armed with the so-called *Diversorum patrum sentente*. Its presentation of papal authority and of the position of the provinces and bishoprics of the church in relation to it was more conservative than Gregory had made in his *Dictatus papae*. Unlike the twenty-seven theses of the *Dictatus papae*, the *Diversorum patrum sentente* fitted in with the aspirations of prelates like Siegfried of Mainz and of South German friends of reform at centres like Reichenau. It became firmly implanted in Germany and was filled out by an Appendix of material that its reformers found congenial. The result was the growth in Swabia of a canon-law tradition that was trenchant, acceptable, and a major source for the propaganda on Gregory's behalf that became widely disseminated in the next few years.[417]

In political and military terms, however, Rudolf's Swabian itinerary did little to establish his royal authority. He used Saxon forces to lay siege to Augsburg whose citizens were loyal to Henry, but had to abandon the siege early in July upon news of Henry's return from Italy. Rudolf withdrew to Saxony. Unable to demonstrate his power in Swabia, it was soon apparent that, in Saxony, he had support only in its eastern parts. With Rudolf's journey to Saxony, the joint legatine activity of the two

---

[414] For the legates' unwillingness, see Frutolf, cap. 21, p. 88/8–10.

[415] *Lib. de unit. eccles. cons.* 2.9, p. 221/3–7; *Ann. Aug.* a.1077, p. 129/16–17; Frutolf, a.1077, pp. 88/12–18.

[416] Berthold, a.1077, pp. 293/21–294/2.

[417] See the text of and introduction to Gilchrist's edition of the *Diversorum patrum sentente*.

Bernards came to an end; only the cardinal-deacon accompanied him, while the abbot of Marseilles set out to return to Italy.

After separating from Rudolf, Abbot Bernard took further steps which did something to establish the anti-king's position in Swabia and more to promote Gregory's cause there. His immediate return to Italy was prevented when he was imprisoned by a partisan of Henry IV, Count Ulrich of Lenzburg. Probably in September, his release was secured by Abbot Hugh of Cluny, who wrote to Henry a sharp reminder of his obligation according to the *iusiurandum* at Canossa to ensure the free passage of Gregory's envoys in Germany.[418] In October, Abbot Bernard was at the monastery of St Blasien, where a confraternity agreement between it and Bernard's own abbey of Saint-Victor at Marseilles was dated by the regnal years of Pope Gregory and King Rudolf.[419] Thereafter, while awaiting an opportunity safely to resume his journey to Italy, he spent a year at the Swabian monastery of Hirsau. Its abbot, William, had become a fervent devotee of Gregory during a stay at Rome in the winter of 1075–6 when he was present at the first excommunication of Henry IV. At Bernard's prompting, during the next two years William adopted Cluniac Customs, in a modified form, at Hirsau, which was confirmed as a leading centre of monastic reform and of the extramural propagation of Gregory's cause. It also facilitated contacts between Abbot Hugh of Cluny and King Rudolf as well as other Swabian figures.[420]

Abbot Bernard used his year's stay at Hirsau to seek to secure for Gregory the active collaboration of the bishops of Upper Lorraine. Towards the end of 1077, he wrote to Archbishop Udo of Trier and his suffragans, Bishops Hermann of Metz, Pibo of Toul, and Thierry of Verdun.[421] He reproved them for tardiness in fulfilling Gregory's commands which, if Henry IV had prevented the abbot from communicating to them, they had received from his brother-legate. They well knew about the devastation of the church and kingdom which Henry had caused. Bernard arraigned Henry as a tyrant, as a fugitive from spiritual and temporal judgement, and as a hinderer of Gregory's peace-bringing purposes, who exhibited neither humility nor obedience but only cruelty. Bernard rehearsed what Gregory's intentions had been: he had hoped himself to come to Germany and, in concert with those best placed, to judge with equity between both kings. 'But he whom his conscience accused', Bernard continued, 'shrank from the judgement of the Holy Spirit—this man who did not cherish his kingdom in obedience, but oppressed it with arrogance, pride, and wickedness, whilst you looked on and did nothing!' Gregory himself had recently urged the Lotharingian bishops to shun a ruler who was disobedient;[422] let them now bestir themselves to name a day when they and as many as they could procure of their neighbouring princes might meet him as Gregory's legate to discuss the concord of

[418] Berthold, *a.*1077, pp. 297/40–298/4.   [419] *MGH Necr.* 1.327.

[420] See esp. the Prologue to the *Consuetudines Hirsaugienses*, *PL* 150. 927–30, and the *Epistola nuncupatoria, Proemium,* and *Praefationes* to Books 2 and 3 of the *Consuetudines Cluniacenses* of Ulrich: *PL* 149. 635–40, 643–4, 699–700, 731.

[421] *H* no. 33, pp. 69–72.

[422] In *Reg.* 5.7, to Archbishop Udo of Trier and his suffragans, 30 Sept. 1077, pp. 356–8.

the kingdom, the well-being of the church, and the defence of the poor and afflicted. In issuing this summons, Abbot Bernard avoided an absolute condemnation of Henry; but, in line with Gregory's admonitions, he reminded the bishops that, if Henry hindered their plans, he would forfeit their obedience, as would his rival Rudolf if he were to act likewise. Henry would suffer excommunication, and he would forfeit the kingship to his worthier rival.

Such was the aftermath of Forchheim in Swabia. In Saxony, the Cardinal-deacon Bernard acted with even less restraint. According to the chronicler Berthold, Rudolf of Rheinfelden had sought Gregory's counsel, and had merely been reminded of the pope's directions in the previous May.[423] Bernard went far beyond these directions by convening at Goslar on 12 November a meeting of Saxon bishops and lay princes. He foreclosed the matters that Gregory had studiously left open by renewing Henry's excommunication and prohibiting him absolutely from the government of the kingdom. He gave three reasons: first, Henry's disobedience and contumacy to-wards Gregory by having invaded the German kingdom during the past summer; second, his having denied Gregory the means of access to Germany in order that he might compose its divisions and calamities; and third, his spreading war and rapine through Swabia and elsewhere. By apostolic authority as legate, Bernard confirmed Rudolf in the German kingship and urged all the princes to obey him.[424] Henceforth, as Bruno's *Saxonicum bellum* abundantly illustrates, the Saxons could claim that Rudolf was king *apostolica auctoritate*;[425] Bruno could contend that, by papal authority, royal power no longer descended to anyone by inheritance but was a matter for free election, so that the *populus* (that is, the princes) could elect whomso-ever they would. In the election of Rudolf, the Saxons deemed Gregory to have been committed by the action of his legate. His continuing contention that the question of the kingship was in suspense was represented as vacillation and weakness on his part.

3.4.3 The Response of Henry IV

The Cardinal-deacon Bernard's sentence was prompted by Henry's reaction to Forchheim in deciding to return to Germany in early May 1077. Bernard's stricture that Henry had denied Gregory the means of access to Germany reads like a response to the royal actions that Henry had performed while he was still in Italy. Eight dip-lomas and similar items survive which record his emphatic judicial decisions and conferring of benefits there. Both their subject-matter and their phraseology made clear his insistence that he was king not only in name but also in fact and power. They were usually issued by him as 'divina favente clementia rex', and they bore his seal as 'rex invictissimus'; in one case he was even described as 'divina favente clementia Francorum et Langobardorum rex', a title with Carolingian undertones of divinely

---

[423] Berthold, *a.*1077, p. 302/32–6; *Reg.* 4.23–4.
[424] Berthold, *a.*1077, pp. 202/36–303/6; Bernold, *Chron. a.*1077, p. 435/2–6; Bruno, cap. 110, pp. 360–4.
[425] See the Saxon letters to Gregory in Bruno, caps. 107–8, 114, pp. 354–60, 372–6, and, on the elect-ive nature of the kingship for the future, cap. 91, p. 334/11–17.

sanctioned authority on both sides of the Alps.[426] Furthermore, Henry took energetic steps to secure control of the routes between Italy and Germany in the eastern
parts of the Alps. These routes were critical for Henry's long-term authority in both
kingdoms, for exits from the western and central passes were subject to control by his
South German enemies. They also mattered to Gregory if he was to come to
Germany, for hostile Lombard bishops threatened his access to more westerly routes.
Therefore, before he left Italy, Henry entrusted the county of Friuli, which since 976
had been associated with the duchy of Carinthia, to his *fidelis* Archbishop Sigehard
of Aquileia, who since Canossa had staunchly supported him. Those present when
Henry's diploma was drawn up included the Empress Agnes, as well as Queen Bertha
and Archbishops Tedald of Milan and Guibert of Ravenna and other German and
Italian bishops.[427] Henry complemented this measure by giving the duchy of
Carinthia to his loyal follower, Liutold of Eppenstein.[428]

Having thus secured his means of access to Germany, Henry travelled from
Villach to Salzburg, Regensburg, and Nuremberg, where on 11 June and with
Liutold's goodwill he further benefited the church of Aquileia by giving it the county
of Istria and the march of Carniola.[429] Two days later, he made substantial gifts to the
church of Brixen, at the south end of the Brenner Pass.[430] Henry's intention is clear:
the alienation of the South German dukes was to be made good by securing the
loyalty of German and Italian bishops whose sees were close to the more easterly
lines of communication.[431]

Henry's intention was not unnoticed by Gregory, who reacted prudently and with
moderation. When Sigehard died on 12 August and the clergy of Aquileia, without
reference to Henry or to Gregory, chose their archdeacon to succeed, Gregory
sought to induce them and the provincial bishops to ensure a truly free election
which would both safeguard Henry's legitimate interests and be approved by papal
legates.[432] However, before Gregory's letters were even written, Henry had disregarded the archdeacon and nominated Henry, a royal chaplain and canon of
Augsburg.[433] Gregory's immediate reaction does not emerge but it is unlikely to have
been very angry; he came to terms with the situation, and at his Lent synod of 1079
he received an oath of fealty and obedience from the new archbishop. It was based
upon the compromise of both accepting Henry's choice for the see and requiring the
archbishop to pledge loyalty and service to the pope.[434]

Henry returned to Germany not only as a king restored to communion but also as
a king who had given proof of his once more exercising the judicial and political

[426] *MGH DDHIV* nos. 286–91, 293–4.   [427] *MGH DDHIV* no. 293.
[428] *Die Chronik des Klosters Petershausen*, p. 110.
[429] *MGH DDHIV* nos. 295–6.   [430] *MGH DDHIV* no. 297.
[431] See the statement about Bishop Altwin of Brixen's loyalty in *MGH DDHIV* no. 304 (1078). For
Henry's determination to maintain his cause, see Arnulf of Milan, 5.10, pp. 231–2.
[432] *Reg.* 5.5–6, respectively to the clergy and people and to the suffragans of Aquileia, 17 Sept. 1077,
pp. 352–5.
[433] Berthold, *a*.1077, p. 301/27–9; *Ann. Aug. a*. 1077, p. 129/26–8.
[434] *Reg.* 6.17*a* (4), pp. 428–9.

functions of rulership. He could, therefore, quickly assemble an army and present a challenge to Rudolf and his electors. In their eyes, Henry thus fomented the great turmoil in the kingdom which the Cardinal-deacon Bernard was to deplore at Goslar.[435] At Regensburg, Henry's court was well attended from Bavaria, Bohemia, and Carinthia as well as by Archbishop Sigehard of Aquileia. It was made clear where Henry's main strength lay, and a military campaign against Rudolf was planned. In Germany as in Italy, Henry was determined to exercise the royal office and thus establish that he could bring law and order to the kingdom. A ruler who was the successor of the Ottonians and early Salians could scarcely do less. But while Henry was careful to offer Gregory no open challenge, he was disregarding the pope's purpose of himself coming to Germany to promote peace and concord while both kings awaited his adjudication in the matter of the kingship. Henry both exercised his kingship in action and sought to establish its credentials according to human law and Christian teaching. In effect, he renewed the political theory of the royal letters of 1076.[436] A bitter propaganda campaign against Rudolf as a new Pontius Pilate carried the implication that Henry was an *alter Christus*, while it was noised abroad that, in 1076, Gregory had condemned Henry *iniustissime*.[437] But so far as Gregory and the papal office were concerned, Henry was studiously non-polemical; he sought to win honour for the *regnum* without disparaging either the *sacerdotium* or Gregory himself. Henry's specific actions and his conception of monarchy may be considered in turn.

He at once acted vigorously. He held his Pentecost court in the Swabian city of Ulm. By the sanctions of Swabian law, he condemned the Swabian duke Rudolf, Dukes Berthold of Carinthia and Welf of Bavaria, and their Swabian supporters to death and to the forfeiture of their offices and fiefs.[438] In effect, he was pre-empting the decision about the kingship that Gregory had reserved for himself. He had already created a new duke of Carinthia; for the time being, he treated the duchies of Swabia and Bavaria as vacant, but in 1079 he gave Swabia to the Hohenstaufen, Frederick of Büren. He enfeoffed the bishops of Brixen and Augsburg with Bavarian lands, thereby reinforcing his control over the eastern Alps.[439] During the summer of 1077, he demonstrated that he could secure the election of his partisans to ecclesiastical offices at Augsburg, where his chaplain Siegfried became bishop, and at St Gall where the Eppensteiner Ulrich became abbot. Henry followed up these steps to

[435] See the statement of the unknown bishop in Holder-Egger, 'Fragment', p. 189/27–9: 'Regressus interim de Italia Heinricus nec parvam de sua absolutione gloriam reportans, maximam in regno commovit seditionem.'

[436] *Epp. HIV* nos. 12–13, pp. 64–73, Anhang A, pp. 470–5.

[437] *Die Chronik des Klosters Petershausen*, pp. 110, 112; Berthold, *a.*1077, p. 294/3–28; *Ann. Aug. a.* 1077, p. 129/13–14; the archbishop of Mainz's quarters at Forchheim were situated *in Pontii Pilati praedio*.

[438] Berthold, *a.*1077, p. 295/21–48; *MGH DDHIV* nos. 298, 306, and esp. 311, with its reference to 'dux Ruodolfus ob multas in nos regnumque nefandas praesumptiones omni divina et humana lege tam vitae quam rerum proscriptus et damnatus'.

[439] *MGH DDHIV* nos. 297, 304, cf. Berthold, *a.*1077, p. 298/41–6.

build up his power in South Germany by planning a military campaign in Saxony against Rudolf. It was a concern of his Trinitytide court at Nuremberg,[440] and of a subsequent visit to Mainz and the middle Rhineland.[441]

Henry was also at pains to reinvest his kingship with legal authority and Christian identity. He claimed that his measures against Rudolf and his adherents were undertaken in defence not only of human but also of divine law.[442] As king, he claimed a legal right and a public duty to vindicate himself against his enemies by disinheriting them and by depriving them of their offices and possessions.[443] He upheld the *dignitas imperii*.[444] His ceremonial crown-wearings, as at Ulm at Pentecost 1077, announced to his subjects that he had resumed his kingship and that it was, like his predecessors', fortified by sacral authority.[445] He acknowledged that it was his duty as king to establish the *stabilitas regni*; a means towards this was his care for the churches of God.[446] This was his justification for naming bishops and abbots, with whose worthiness for office he showed a novel personal concern. To monasteries, he offered a *regalis libertas* which corresponded to his kingly duty of providing for their security.[447] Perhaps most strikingly of all, he answered the papal claim that the authority of kings was exercised under the patronage of St Peter and the authority of his vicar by placing his kingship under the patronage of one greater even than St Peter—the Blessed Virgin Mary.[448] The most signal statement of this patronage was the reconstruction of the cathedral at Speyer which was undertaken between *c*.1080/1 and 1101/6. Speyer was the burial-place of many of the Salian family; in a diploma of 1101, Henry referred to it as 'our own special church of Speyer'.[449] Principally dedicated to the Virgin, the cathedral had already been constructed upon

---

440 Berthold, *a*.1077, p. 298/43–6, 299/29–31.

441 For the visit, see *MGH DDHIV* no. 298.   442 See above, n. 438.

443 *MGH DDHIV* no. 301: 'Lex est et ius gentium inimicos regis aperte deprehensos aperte communem totius regni persecutionem pati, ut, sicut periurii infamia sunt exleges, ita bonorum suorum omnium fiant exhaeredes, insuper tam ipsi quam possessiones eorum regali sententiae puniendi subiaceant. Iustum est enim, ut summa nequitia deprehensi summa vindicta multentur et regni domnum insequentes regni persecutionem patiantur. Haec sententia principum nostrorum iudicio super Ekbertum quondam marchionem dicta est, ut, quod in nos exercere non timuit, in se recipiat, videlicet ut in regno partem non habeat, qui nos integro regno privare laborabat.' The reference is to Ekbert II, margrave of Meissen; the date is 30 Oct. 1077.

444 *MGH DDHIV* no. 294: '. . . imperii dignitatem quae deo auxiliante per nos gubernatur . . .'

445 Berthold, *a*.1077, p. 295/26–48; Bernold, *Chron. a*.1077, p. 434/24–5.

446 *MGH DDHIV* no. 286: 'Si ecclesias Dei honoramus, ditamus et sublimamus regno nostro stabilitatem . . . per hoc adipisci non dubitamus.'

447 *MGH DDHIV* nos. 302, 308.

448 See the statements about the Virgin's patronage in *MGH DDHIV* nos. 296 (11 June 1077); 298 (1 July 1077): 'Saluti nostrae et regni consulere credimus, cum eam, per quam salus mundi credentibus apparuit, honorare studemus, sanctam videlicet dei genetricem virginem Mariam, quam in peccatis nostris propitiatricem, in peccatorum correptione sustentatricem, in regni et honoris nostri stabilitate fundatricem habemus', 306 (20 Mar. 1078): '. . . salutis auctorem in ea, per quam salus credentibus apparuit, honorare dignum duximus, videlicet dei genitrici virgini Mariae Augustensi aecclesiae nomine et dominatione principanti de nostra substantia illa bona conferendo, quae dilectus noster Sigefridus Augustensis episcopus petiit . . .'

449 *MGH DDHIV* no. 466 (10 Apr. 1101): 'in nostra speciali Spirensi ecclesia.' See also below, 3.5.5.

a massive scale by the Emperor Conrad II, who chose it for his burial-place. Henry intended to perpetuate it as the cathedral of the Salian house, and as a visible statement of the divine right of Salian kingship.[450]

Both the papacy of Gregory VII and the monarchy of Henry IV were advancing powerful and impressive claims in Germany to loyalty and service. Abbot Bernard of Marseilles had promoted Gregory's cause by building up the monastic centres of St Blasien and Hirsau and the study and dissemination of canon law, based upon the acceptable principles of papal authority whch were expressed in the *Diversorum patrum sententie*. Henry made headway in practising a style of kingship which both showed his surer grasp of his *métier de roi* and had a credible basis in political theory. The stage was set for a contest, alike in ideas and in the institutions of government, about who was to be the source of peace and order in German society which would continue for long after the lifetimes of the protagonists of the late 1070s.

For the present, the pattern of claims and loyalties was confused by the ambivalence of the princes. After Canossa and Forchheim, they increasingly professed disenchantment with Gregory because, unlike his legate at Goslar, he refused to give sole recognition to Rudolf and to discard Henry as king. Gregory clung to his view that the verdict of divine righteousness ('iustitia') had yet to be revealed as between the two kings. But Gregory and Henry were drawn ever more deeply into a contest about the credentials of the Salian monarchy in which the case of either party was skilfully presented. They were also drawn into a competition in practice about which should be the ultimate source of peace and concord in a Germany which was torn by feud, war, and deprivation and which was becoming increasingly war-weary.

3.4.4 Gregory VII at Rome, 1077–8

By August 1077, Gregory had accepted that at present no way was open for him himself to travel to Germany and there to compose its dissentions.[451] He returned to Rome, passing through Siena on 1 September. Despite the disappointment of his hopes, his attitude of restraint towards Henry IV was immediately made clear by his mild reaction to the king's filling of the see of Aquileia.[452] Gregory perhaps recognized the potential strength of Henry's position in Germany and the vulnerability of Rudolf's. He evidently still hoped that Henry might be won over to co-operation in his plans for general peace in the kingdom and for the reform of the church.

Gregory spelt out his position in his letter of 30 September to Archbishop Udo of Trier and his suffragans of Metz, Toul, and Verdun.[453] He recalled his long-standing anxiety about the disturbance and disorder of the German kingdom and about the perils of internecine domestic war. He enclosed copies of his letters of the previous May in which he set out his German policy,[454] and he renewed all the measures that

---

[450] The significance of Speyer for the Salian kings is well set out by Weinfurter, 'Herrschaftlegitimation'.

[451] Berthold, *a*.1077, p. 291/38–43: 'via sibi in partes Theutonicas ad tot discordias componendas non patuerit'; Arnulf of Milan, 5.20, pp. 231–2.

[452] As above, 3.4.3.   [453] *Reg*. 5.7, pp. 356–8.   [454] *Reg*. 4.23–4, pp. 334–8.

he had then prescribed for the avoidance of slaughter, arson, and the terrors of war, as well as for the just resolution of such problems as the kingship. It is a reminder of how central the establishment of peace and concord in Germany had become in Gregory's plans. He also sent the bishops a copy of Henry's *iusiurandum*,[455] 'in order that by reading it you can see how rightly and how humbly he behaved towards us on his part'. Not that all was well: Henry's *fideles* had captured two of Gregory's legates —Gerald of Ostia in Italy and Abbot Bernard of Marseilles in Germany, and Gregory had so far heard of no proper counter-measures by Henry. Henry had not directly broken his oath, but his inaction had involved him in some part of the responsibility. Yet Gregory remained well disposed towards Henry; he was not minded to overstep the demands of righteousness ('iustitia') by pressing the case against him. He reiter-ated his own, long-standing commitment to equity and to zealous action. He called upon the Lotharingian bishops, as well, to act strenuously. He did not specify in what way, but he may have known that Udo of Trier and Hermann of Metz had been engaged in attempts to mediate between Henry and Rudolf. There had been an armistice and a proposal for an assembly in the Rhineland which, in the absence of the rival kings, would look for a peaceful solution under the guidance of the papal legates.[456] It was evidence of the wish of many in Germany to keep in touch with both sides, to damp down conflict, and to seek an agreed solution to the disorder of Ger-many in a manner that avoided the extremer claims of any of the contending parties.

After Rudolf withdrew to Saxony, Gregory kept in direct touch with him.[457] As a result of Gregory's many contacts in Germany, representatives of both kings came to the well-attended Lent synod of 1078: Henry sent Bishops Benno of Osnabrück and Thierry of Verdun;[458] Rudolf's envoys travelled with difficulty and in disguise, and their names are not known. The chronicler Berthold enlarged upon the favourable hearing that Henry's bishops were given by many who were present. They pleaded Henry's cause by describing Rudolf's perjury and treachery to his rightful king; thus, they advanced the case that Henry had himself made against him in Germany. They did this to such effect that many pressed for Rudolf's immediate excommuni-cation. In a letter of 1083, Gregory implied that he had called upon the bishops who had elected Rudolf at Forchheim to justify their action on pain of their own and Rudolf's deposition.[459] However, in the end, Gregory maintained his impartiality. Since his own journey to Germany had proved impracticable, he planned to dispatch fresh legates who would convene a general assembly on his behalf. Perhaps he hoped thus to build upon the initiative of Udo of Trier and his fellow Lotharingian bishops. At the assembly, either a settlement and peace in Germany would be agreed, or else sentence would be passed by apostolic authority to determine which party—Henry's or Rudolf's—righteousness ('iustitia') favoured. Stern sanctions were passed against all who might seek to frustrate such a pacification.[460]

---

[455] *Reg.* 4.12*a*, pp. 314–15.   [456] Berthold, *a*.1077, pp. 300/40–301/9.
[457] Berthold, *a*.1077, p. 302/32–7.   [458] Berthold, *a*.1078, p. 306/17–18.
[459] *Reg.* 9.29, to all faithful clerks and laity, p. 613/6–13.
[460] *Reg.* 5.14*a* (6), pp. 370–1. For Berthold's account of the synod, see *a*.1078, pp. 306/17–309/34.

Gregory followed up his Lent synod with a letter in which he acquainted the faithful German clergy and laity with its many decrees. He urged upon them his plan for a general assembly which would resolve their country's problems.[461] He once again gave his prime intention as being that of promoting a 'reparatio pacis vestrae'. He repeated his wish to send new legates who would convene an assembly at a place convenient for both parties in order to achieve his objectives as defined at the Lent synod. The unnamed bearer of the letter was to co-operate with Archbishop Udo of Trier from Henry's side and with another, unnamed bishop from Rudolf's to set up the assembly. Gregory simultaneously sent Udo a personal letter with further instructions.[462] As soon as the two bishops had securely arranged the assembly, they, or Udo alone if his opposite number could not come, were forthwith to travel to Rome and escort Gregory's new legates to Germany. Gregory reiterated his charge that they should fully support whichever king righteousness ('iustitia') might vindicate. After the conclusion of the assembly, Udo was to establish a general truce of fifteen days. Finally, Udo was to urge Henry to ensure for Gregory's earlier legates, the two Bernards, a secure return to Rome if they so desired.

It is evident that, as a prelate who stood near to Henry and yet who sought the pacification of all parties, Archbishop Udo of Trier was currently the lynch-pin of Gregory's plans for Germany. He, not either of the two Bernards, was to arrange the German assembly. Gregory was sparing no effort to be, and to seem to be, impartial as between the two kings. Thus, despite Henry's proclamation and exercise of the kingship as his by direct divine authority and despite Henry's judicial condemnation of Rudolf, Gregory continued to regard him as at root faithful to the settlement at Canossa and to the *iusiurandum* that he had sworn there. In view of the arguments of Henry's episcopal representatives at the Lent synod of 1078, Gregory can scarcely have been unaware of his actions and attitudes. He was going to extraordinary lengths to be restrained, impartial, and conciliatory.

He seems to have behaved similarly towards Henrician bishops. Soon after the Lent synod, he wrote to one of their number, Huzmann of Speyer.[463] Huzmann had become bishop in April or May 1075, and Gregory indicated two faults that he found in him. He had knowingly and rashly been invested by the king against the decree of the apostolic see. Gregory had not, therefore, so far licensed him to exercise the episcopal office. Huzmann had claimed by messenger that he had not heard of the decree; Gregory now licensed him on condition that, when possible, he give an account of himself to the pope or his legate. Furthermore, Huzmann had shown laxity in opposing simony in his diocese. On this score, Gregory exhorted him to vigilance and zeal. By his mild line regarding each of Huzmann's faults, Gregory was offering him the fullest opportunity of proving himself. He was signalling a way of reconciliation to all in Germany who would respond. Conformably with this intention, Gregory began his letter to Huzmann with an unqualified greeting and apostolic blessing; he

---

[461] *Reg.* 5.15, 9 Mar. 1078, pp. 374–6.
[462] *Reg.* 5.15, 9 Mar. 1078, pp. 376–8.
[463] *Reg.* 5.18, 19 Mar. 1078, pp. 381–2.

ended with an assurance that right conduct for the future would win for Huzmann God's grace and mercy at the end of his life.

3.4.5 The German Reaction to Gregory VII's Plans in 1078 up to the Battle of Mellrichstadt

The course of events in Germany during the middle months of 1078 was not such that Gregory's renewed bid himself to bring peace and concord to Germany became likely to succeed. Henry IV kept Easter at Cologne. He there received news of Gregory's Lent synod. According to Berthold, he was disappointed that the measure of sympathy which he enjoyed at Rome had not led to Rudolf's excommunication.[464] He travelled to Mainz and from there convened a meeting at Fritzlar at which Saxon representatives would be present.[465] When it assembled, Archbishop Udo of Trier was prominent in Henry's support. Debate was acrimonious, but it was finally agreed that such a German assembly as Gregory intended would take place. Both sides would refrain from hostilities until it did. Henry seems, however, to have been determined to keep Rudolf away so that he could treat with those Saxon nobles who were least committed to the anti-king: by this means, Rudolf's position in Saxony might be undermined. Henry also took steps to strengthen his position in Lorraine. In concert with Bishop Thierry of Verdun, he undertook a campaign to apply pressure to Bishop Hermann of Metz whom he deemed too committed to Gregory. He also installed a loyal supporter, Thiepald, as bishop of Strassburg.[466]

As for the eastern Saxons who were most closely associated with Rudolf and hostile to Henry, they expressed their disenchantment with Gregory in a series of letters that are preserved verbatim in Bruno's *Saxonicum bellum*.[467] The Saxons concerned were implacably opposed to any such German assembly as Gregory desired. They made this clear in a letter of April 1078.[468] They insisted upon the finality and irrevocability of Gregory's condemnation of Henry in February 1076 and they enlarged upon their own fidelity to this condemnation despite the hardships that had ensued for them. In their eyes, Canossa had done nothing to restore Henry to the exercise of kingship. After Rudolf's election at Forchheim, the Saxons were astonished at Gregory's reaction of allowing that there were now two kings. Gregory had thereby himself brought about the very situation in Germany that he had claimed to be trying above all to bring to an end—division, dissension, and the devastation of civil war. They were especially shocked that he should place Henry's name before Rudolf's in his letters, and that it should be Henry who was asked to provide Gregory with an escort to Germany. Since Henry had been deposed and Rudolf duly elected, there was in any case no need for a general assembly to compose the division of the German kingdom; no such division existed.

---

[464] Berthold, *a.*1078, p. 309/38–47.   [465] Berthold, *a.*1078, p. 310/20–5.
[466] Berthold, *a.*1078, pp. 310–311/32.
[467] Bruno, caps. 108, 110, 112, 114–15, pp. 354–70, 372–8; for the dates, see Kost, *Das östliche Niedersachsen*, pp. 113–22.
[468] Bruno, cap. 108, pp. 354–60.

In further letters, the Saxons intensified their case. In October or November, another letter followed.[469] The Saxons made great play of Gregory's instructions of 31 May 1077 to his legates, the two Bernards, in which he had given them authority to pass judgement upon the two kings.[470] At Goslar in November 1077, the Cardinal-deacon Bernard had acted upon this authority by confirming Gregory's sentence of deposition and excommunication against Henry, and he had definitively recognized Rudolf as sole king. The Saxons called upon Gregory to stand fast by this decision. In a further letter of December 1078, they gave eloquent expression to their dismay at Gregory's vacillation and at his failure to stand by his sentence of February 1076.[471] The Saxon letters bear eloquent witness to the difference of intention and policy between Gregory and Henry's most militant German opponents.

Gregory had heard of the negotiations at Fritzlar when his legate returned to Rome in the early summer of 1078. Their inconclusive outcome led him on 1 July to address a letter to all in Germany who were not excommunicated;[472] it was to this letter that the Saxons' second letter was a riposte.[473] Gregory confirmed his determination to promote an assembly of the whole German people at which his legates would be present and which would determine whether righteousness ('iustitia') marked out Henry or Rudolf to be the rightful king. The proceedings at Fritzlar had revealed that some in Germany were at pains to frustrate plans for such an assembly. Gregory urged that they be ignored and that his plans should be put into effect.

But while this exchange of letters was taking place, the tide of civil war continued to rise; Rudolf was to the fore in raising it.[474] The upshot on 7 August was the bloody battle of Mellrichstadt, north of the River Main in East Franconia. Neither side could claim a military victory, but Rudolf's losses compelled him to return to East Saxony. His forces there and in South Germany became divided; for the present at least, Henry need not fear military challenge in the south.[475] He established himself in Bavaria, with Regensburg as his headquarters. It is an indication of Rudolf's worsened position in the south that Abbot Bernard of Marseilles decided to return to Gregory at Rome.[476]

3.4.6 Gregory VII and Germany in the Winter of 1078–9

The battle of Mellrichstadt left Germany more divided than before. Rudolf's principal military support was situated to the north and east of the critically important line of the River Main; Henry's was to its south. Rudolf was in the paradoxical position of depending militarily upon the East Saxons who were disenchanted with Gregory, while partly on account of his military losses and partly of his allies in the

---

[469] Bruno, cap. 114, pp. 372–6.
[470] *Reg.* 4.23–4, = Bruno, caps. 105–6, pp. 348–54.
[471] Bruno, cap. 115, pp. 376–8.
[472] *Reg.* 6.1, pp. 389–91.
[473] As n. 469.
[474] Berthold, *a.*1078, pp. 311/45–312/6.
[475] Bruno, caps. 96–102, pp. 340–6; Berthold, *a.*1078, pp. 312/7–313/4.
[476] Berthold, *a.*1078, p. 313/4–11.

Gregorian circles of Hirsau and Constance he was increasingly beholden to Gregory. Henry, on the other hand, was emboldened to intensify his claims to a kingship which did not depend for its authority upon the *sacerdotium* and which, unlike Gregory's papacy, could hold out to the Germans the prospect of a domestic pacification which had the guarantee of sufficient political sanctions. By thus further polarizing the situation in Germany, Mellrichstadt was a serious setback to Gregory's plans for a German assembly under his own guidance and control. The death on 11 November 1078 of Archbishop Udo of Trier during a siege of Tübingen by Henry's army deprived him of a valued agent in his search for pacification who, like a number of other German bishops, longed for an opportunity to serve harmoniously both pope and king. Gregory nevertheless remained sanguine that God would soon so work as to bring peace to the church.[477] For the present, he pinned his hopes upon a Roman synod that he convened for November; at it, he planned both to answer Saxon reproaches of his vacillation and to promote his own initiatives. When it assembled on 19 November, envoys of both German kings were present; each swore on his ruler's behalf that he had not guilefully impeded the holding by papal legates of Gregory's intended assembly.[478] According to the hostile but evidently well-informed chronicler Berthold, Henry's envoys again sought to secure Rudolf's immediate excommunication because he had invaded the kingdom, and their demand caused an impasse in the synod.[479] He also renewed his sentence of excommunication against whoever might culpably impede the meeting of a German assembly.[480]

The November synod also enacted stringent canons against many ecclesiastical abuses, including lay investiture, simony, and clerical unchastity. Berthold's full record of these canons shows how speedily they became known in his part of Germany; it indicates that Gregory directed them to the reform of the German church. His concern with Germany was, indeed, stated in the summary of the canon against Germans who held church lands conferred either by kings or by bishops who had acted under coercion.[481] Gregory seems to have had particularly in mind long-standing problems, especially at Bamberg, in which Henry was directly implicated.[482]

Gregory followed up his November synod by a letter which was designed to expedite a resolution of the contest for the German crown and so to open the way for civil peace and church reform. He addressed it to the well-disposed bishops, princes, clergy, and laity 'in the German and in the Saxon kingdom', that is, to supporters of both kings in the *de facto* balance of power after Mellrichstadt. It announced the pope's and the synod's intention of sending legates to Germany who would there convene an assembly and either establish an agreed peace or condemn whoever

477 *Reg.* 6.5, to Bishop Hermann of Metz, 22 Oct. 1078, p. 399/12–15.
478 *Reg.* 6.5*b*, 19 Nov. 1078, pp. 400/29–401/3.
479 Berthold, *a*.1078, pp. 313/50–314/7; Bernold, *Chron. a*.1078, p. 435/32–5.
480 *Reg.* 6.5*b*, p. 401/8–9.   481 *Reg.* 6.5*b*, p. 401/6–7.
482 *Reg.* 6.19, to the *ministeriales* of Bamberg, 17 Feb. 1079, pp. 430–1.

continued to foment division.[483] In December, he also wrote to Rudolf's supporter, Duke Welf of Bavaria, who had murmured against his supposed inconstancy; Gregory vindicated his German policy, insisted upon the power of righteousness ('iustitia') and the resolve of St Peter, and urged the duke to continue in the apostle's service.[484]

At Gregory's Lent synod of 1079, the matter of the two kings remained to the fore. On this occasion, Rudolf and the Saxons were at pains to ensure that their case was heard. In preparation, the Saxons sent Gregory a long letter for reading aloud at the synod, as Bruno put it, 'in case the lord pope could be aroused, if only by the mediation of the universal church, to the firmness and stability that beseemed the apostolic dignity.'[485] The letter took up the queries and doubts that had prevailed in November 1078 as to whether Henry should be excommunicated or not. Based upon bitter experience, the Saxons' case had been that Henry had been excommunicated both repeatedly and decisively. They recalled Gregory's sentence at Rome in February 1076, Henry's recalcitrance, and the patent hollowness of his penance at Canossa. Despite his *iusiurandum* his partisans had imprisoned and maltreated Gregory's legates; while Henry himself had spurned the warnings of many, including the Cardinal-deacon Bernard. Therefore, at Goslar in November 1077, Bernard had reiterated Gregory's own sentence of deposition and excommunication, and he had confirmed Rudolf in the German kingship. Henry's response had been to devastate the kingdom and ravage its churches, dividing bishops from their sees and misappropriating their goods to his own and his followers' use. At his synod in November 1078, Gregory had himself excommunicated all who invaded bishops' lands; Henry's seizures would by themselves suffice to number him and his followers among the excommunicated. The Saxons could only wonder at the hearing accorded to his spokesmen at the November synod. In Swabia particularly, Henry's oppressions had continued. In terms of the *iusiurandum*, he had perjured himself by hindering travellers to Rome, and he had been further excommunicated by Archbishop Siegfried of Mainz, his spiritual pastor, and seven other bishops, and then by Bishop Adalbero of Würzburg sitting with the Cardinal-deacon Bernard. Gregory should remember how often Henry with his followers had both merited and received condemnation. If he was not minded to renew the sentence of excommunication that had so often been passed, then at least let them not be admitted to communion at Rome or elsewhere until they had made satisfaction to the churches that they had ravaged. The impact of this letter was compounded by the coming to Rome, separately and after hazardous journeys, of the Cardinal-deacon Bernard and of two bishops, Altmann of Passau and Hermann of Metz. The bishops had been expelled from their sees, and they could add their testimony to what the Saxons had written.[486]

---

[483] *Epp. vag.* no. 25, pp. 64–7; cf. *Reg.* 5.15, to the Germans who were not excommunicated, 2 Mar. 1078, pp. 374–6.

[484] *Reg.* 6.14, 30 Dec. 1078, pp. 418–19. [485] Bruno, caps. 111–12, pp. 364–70.

[486] Berthold, *a*.1079, p. 316/40–5.

Yet by no means everything was working to Henry's disadvantage in Gregory's eyes. In the previous autumn, Abbot Hugh of Cluny's warning to Henry about his obligations under the *iusiurandum* had persuaded him to secure the release from captivity of Abbot Bernard of Marseilles; Gregory may have been thereby encouraged in his hope of calling Henry to due obedience.[487] At the Lent synod of 1079, Henry himself planned a skilful if last-minute *démarche* of which there is evidence in the record of a speech made by his envoy, apparently during its early stages.[488] The envoy professed to come from a suppliant king ('rex supplex') to inform Gregory of the imminent arrival of an embassy that would not be of a single, insignificant figure like himself; it would comprise a number of the greatest in the German kingdom, men of probity and religion. They would come to make peace between Henry's kingdom and Gregory's papacy ('ad componendam pacem inter ipsius regnum et sacerdotium vestrum'); Gregory should implicitly trust and Henry would rightly obey whatever Gregory and they might decide to be in the interests of Henry's kingship and the church's welfare. The envoy had himself come prepared to swear that he had been thus instructed by the king upon the advice of his princes; the more distinguished envoys to follow would do likewise, unless an insuperable obstacle kept them from reaching Rome. The envoy complained that he had heard of the irruption of Henry's enemies into the synod to the king's harm. He pleaded that, because of their hostility and hatred, they should not be heard; when Henry's main envoys arrived, what they said would in any case be refuted. The envoy urged that, since Henry was absent and wished to be obedient in all things, sentence should not be passed against him. The envoy evidently feared that Gregory would pass an immediate sentence in line with the anti-king's demands: he called upon the mercy of all sons of the Roman church to dissuade Gregory from passing such a sentence; the least of mankind should not be condemned without canonical proof against him, how much less a king!

The speech was eloquent, but not without its flaws. The final plea may not have impressed those who recalled that, in 1076, Henry had dared to arraign Gregory from distant Germany, and that Gregory had answered by condemning an absent king. Furthermore, the promise that the envoys to come would make peace 'inter ipsius regnum et sacerdotium vestrum' implied an equivalence and a separateness of the royal and priestly powers that Gregory would be unlikely to concede. It was a partisan, if more temperate, pleading of the case that Henry and his propagandists had been making for the kingship ever since the exchange of 1076.

It is not clear how events at the Lent synod developed. Not surprisingly in view of the political theory behind the envoy's address, the account in Gregory's Register does not refer to it;[489] although it may be subsumed amongst the many plaints ('inter multas proclamationes') with which proceedings about Germany began. The lengthy consideration of Berengar of Tours at the beginning of the synod may have been so arranged as to allow time for Henry's further envoys to appear. It is certain that they did not come during the synod; the Register refers to them but records the

---

[487] See above, 3.4.2.   [488] *MGH Const.* 1.552, no. 388.   [489] *Reg.* 6.17*a*, pp. 425–9.

oath taken on Henry's behalf as being expressed in the singular.[490] Like Berthold, the Register recorded Rudolf's envoys' diatribe against Henry which even Berthold allowed to be over-coloured; it moved many at the synod to call for an immediate papal sentence against Henry.[491] Berthold, however, said that the pleading of Henry's case by his envoy rallied the ever-present Henrician faction in Roman counsels.[492] Berthold is probably wrong in placing Henry's envoy's speech so late in the proceedings. But the synod was almost certainly divided in its sympathies. The sources are agreed that Gregory played for time and deferred passing any kind of sentence. According to Berthold, all sides agreed to Henry's being granted freedom from sentence until after Ascensiontide (2 May); his envoy promised that by then he would send an escort to bring Gregory's legates to Germany for matters to be settled there.[493] The envoys of both kings swore oaths on behalf of their masters. Besides providing an escort for Gregory's legates, Henry would obey them in all things ('dominus rex oboediens erit illis in omnibus secundum iustitiam et iudicium illorum'); although this phrase does not refer to an assembly, it clearly presupposed one.[494] The oath on Rudolf's behalf surprisingly envisaged a journey to Germany for an assembly by either Gregory or his legates. It is not certain whether Gregory cherished a hope of going himself, or whether the Saxons were seeking to curry favour. In either case, the terms of the oath conspiciously ignored the extremer points of the Saxon case against Henry and their strictures upon Gregory's indecision. King Rudolf would himself come to a German assembly or at least send suitable envoys. In the matter of the kingdom, he would obey the judgement of the holy Roman church, and he would duly assist the work of the pope and of his legates.[495] According to Berthold, Gregory excommunicated whichever king either had impeded an assembly during the past year or might impede one in the future.[496]

A significant feature of the Lent synod of 1079 was that, whereas Henry's spokesman adhered to the Salian view of the respective authorities of *regnum* and *sacerdotium* as formulated in 1076, Rudolf's spokesmen pleaded his case in a way that met Gregory's demands for royal obedience to kingly authority. The ground was being prepared for the renewed condemnation of Henry a year later. The result of Rudolf's pleading was a more even division of Roman opinion as between the two kings and, if Berthold is to be believed, the passing by the synod of something like a suspended sentence against Henry if he did not by 2 May provide an escort for Gregory's legates. Gregory, however, showed himself willing to trust the oath of Henry's legate that he would obey papal commands in all things.[497]

---

[490] *Reg.* 6.17a, p. 428/1–9; Berthold also wrote of Henry's *legatus* in the singular: *a*.1079, p. 317/1, 10.

[491] *Reg.* 6.17a, p. 427/16–25; cf. Berthold, *a*.1079, pp. 316/45–317/1; Bernold, *Chron. a.* 1079, p. 436/4–6.

[492] Berthold, *a*.1079, p. 317/1–4.   [493] Berthold, *a*.1079, p. 317/4–9.

[494] *Reg.* 6.17a, p. 428/1–9; Berthold, *a*.1074, p. 317/7–15.

[495] *Reg.* 6.17a, p. 428/10–24; Berthold, *a*.1079, p. 317/15–16.

[496] Berthold, *a*.1079, p. 317/16–18.

[497] *Reg.* 6.22, to Countess Matilda of Tuscany, 3 Nov. 1079, p. 434/25–31.

If, as is likely, Abbot Hugh of Cluny visited Rome early in 1079, his voice may have been added to those who counselled caution in deciding between the two kings, and may have fortified Gregory in the hope that Henry's word could be trusted.[498]

3.4.7 The Eclipse of Hopes for a German Assembly

Gregory lost no time before following up his Lent synod by sending legates to Germany. He chose two men of contrasting backgrounds, thereby signalling his purpose at once to hold to his own principles and to be conciliatory in his negotiations. They were Cardinal-bishop Peter of Albano, a tried champion of thoroughgoing ecclesiastical reform, and Bishop Ulrich of Padua, who was likely to be *persona grata* to Henry but who had recently been prominent at Rome for his opposition to the eucharistic teaching of Berengar of Tours.[499] These legates had left Rome by 3 March.[500] Their instructions were precise: they were to negotiate, first with Henry, a suitable place and time for an assembly to which further papal legates might come and deal with the problems of Germany; they were also to secure the restoration to their sees of bishops who had been expelled and to enforce the ecclesiastical rule that the excommunicated should be shunned. They were to attempt to pass no judgement as between the two kings.[501] It was a difficult commission to execute. The bishops expelled from their sees included such opponents of Henry as Altmann of Passau, Adalbero of Würzburg, and Hermann of Metz; measures to vindicate them would not encourage Henry to enter negotiations about other issues at stake. Rudolf and his party might well be suspicious that the legates were first to visit Henry, who was accorded more recognition than Saxon interests would allow. For his own part, Gregory can only have raised the temperature of conflict by a letter, widely circulated in Germany and Italy, in which he revived his call to the faithful to shun the ministrations of fornicating clergy, branded disobedience to the apostolic see as 'the sin of heathenism', and insisted upon obedience to apostolic precepts as the condition of entering the kingdom of heaven.[502]

In loyalty to his oath at the Lent synod of 1079,[503] Archbishop Henry of Aquileia arranged the safe conduct of the legates to Henry at Regensburg; they arrived there by Pentecost (12 May).[504] Berthold may have been correct in alleging that the

---

[498] Hugh's visit is made likely by a comparison of *Epp. vag.* no. 37, p. 92/29–30 with *Reg.* 8.2, p. 518/4–6; see Cowdrey, 'St Hugh and Gregory VII', pp. 182–3.

[499] For the legates, see Bernold, *Chron. a.* 1079, p. 436/6–10; Berthold, *a.*1079, pp. 318/39–319/4; Bonizo of Sutri, *Lib. ad amic.* 8, pp. 611–12. For Ulrich and Berengar, see below, 8.1.1.

[500] *Reg.* 6.22, to Countess Matilda of Tuscany, 3 Mar. 1079, p. 434/29–31.

[501] *Epp. vag.* no. 31, to Cardinal Peter of Albano and Bishop Ulrich of Padua, (July–Oct. 1079), p. 82/4–13; *Reg.* 7.3, to all the faithful in Germany, 1 Oct. 1079, pp. 462/33–463/10; Berthold, *a.*1079, pp. 318/42–319/4.

[502] *Epp. vag.* no. 32, to all the faithful of Italy and Germany, (1079), pp. 84–7. However, there were evidently Germany laymen who were open to answer such a call: *H* no. 34, pp. 72–4.

[503] *Reg.* 6.17a (4), pp. 418–9; see above, 3.4.3. Berthold regarded Archbishop Henry as a legate of Gregory's, but noted his commitment to King Henry: *a.*1079, pp. 318/39–43, 319/5–8.

[504] Berthold, *a.*1079, p. 330/8–10; *Reg.* 6.38, to Archbishop Henry of Aquileia, 16 June 1079, pp. 454–5.

archbishop deliberately retarded the legates' journey in order to win time for Henry.[505] Henry took steps to gain favour with Gregory by allowing Bishop Benno of Osnabrück to visit Rome on the business of his see, but also to seek Gregory's favour for himself.[506] In Germany, Henry had for some time endeavoured to undermine Rudolf's position by negotiating with Saxon nobles, particularly in talks held at Fritzlar, in Hesse, during February.[507] With Gregory's two legates, Henry proceeded slowly. At their Pentecost meeting with Henry at Regensburg, they managed to elicit from him a confirmation of his envoy's oath at Gregory's synod in February; Henry also consented to the convening of a German assembly.[508] But Ascensiontide had passed, and with it Gregory's deadline for the dispatch to Rome of an escort for the new and definitive legates who would hold the assembly.

While time was thus slipping away, Gregory was also in direct communication with Rudolf and his party in Saxony. He went to considerable lengths in recognizing their position. In late February 1079, he wrote urging 'King Rudolf and his followers' to fortitude in their struggle for Christian truth and for their own noble liberty. While he did not concede their claim that Rudolf should be regarded as the rightful and sole German king, he reminded them of what his synods in 1078 had decided 'about King Rudolf and Henry' and about the peace and concord of the kingdom. In due course, Bishops Hermann of Metz and Altmann of Passau would come and bring them up to date with Gregory's further decisions. Meanwhile, Gregory assured them of his steadfastness in providing for their needs.[509] In a further letter of March or April addressed to 'King Rudolf and all who with him are defending the Christian religion', Gregory expressed his sorrow at the continual ravaging of Germany by civil war. He alluded to frequent messages from 'Henry' whose personal envoys and highly-placed advocates sometimes promised complete obedience but sometimes craftily sought to bend Gregory to his support. For his part, Gregory was resolved to persist in the middle way of righteousness ('iustitia'). He hoped that his legates—an apparent reference to Peter of Albano and Ulrich of Padua—would reach the Saxons and explain his position.[510] In both letters, Gregory was concerned to secure the canonical filling of the see of Magdeburg, made vacant by the death after the battle of Mellrichstadt of Archbishop Werner and now at risk, as his legate Abbot Bernard of Marseilles had informed him, from the disorderly ambitions of local clergy. In Gregory's eyes, Magdeburg had become a focus of the key issues of his entire pontificate:

As right and order require, you should provide a steward who is pleasing to God with our consent and apostolic blessing and after public election by all good men, both clergy and laymen. For you yourselves know that it was neglect of the rulings of the holy fathers in appointing bishops which led to this present bloodshed and that, unless these rulings are respected, the outcome will be a multiplication of evils still worse than the former ones.[511]

---

505 Berthold, *a*.1079, p. 319/5–10.
506 *Vita Bennonis II*, cap. 17, pp. 408–9; Berthold, *a*.1079, p. 319/10–15.
507 Berthold, *a*.1079, pp. 315/37–46, 316/13–33.
508 Berthold, *a*.1079, p. 320/10–14.   509 *Epp. vag.* no. 26, pp. 66–9.
510 *Epp. vag.* no. 27, pp. 70–3.   511 *Epp. vag.* no. 26, p. 68/19–32, cf. no. 27, pp. 70/26–72/15.

After his Lent synod of 1079, Gregory was concerned to keep open his lines of communication with both sides in Germany and to maintain goodwill for his projected German assembly by offering each such encouragement as he could. But the hopes that he continued to cherish that Henry could be won to ways of obedience and the recognition that he accorded Rudolf as a king who was defending the Christian religion were building up an ever more manifest contradiction in his approach. In Germany, the conflict between Henry and the Saxons was growing increasingly bitter and intense. Prospects for an assembly at which the pope could sponsor peace and concord in the German kingdom became dimmer with every month that passed.

Their recession can be traced. At Regensburg, it had been agreed that preliminary negotiations should be resumed later in the year; neither king could afford to be seen actively to impede them. Probably in June, there was a gathering at Fritzlar to which, according to Berthold, Henry failed to give safe conduct to Duke Welf of Bavaria and the Swabian party. Many Saxons attended, but almost certainly not the anti-king Rudolf. Henry reluctantly acceded to a Saxon proposal for an exchange of hostages; however, it was not put into effect, and a further meeting at Würzburg was arranged.[512]

In mid-August, Henry with a strong party of his supporters met the legates there. Rudolf and the Saxons were deterred from entering so strongly Henrician a city. According to Berthold, Henry had himself contrived this situation in order to save his face with Gregory by a show of co-operation and obedience. He made a spirited defence of his position and conduct, and called for the excommunication of Rudolf and his followers. The legates reminded him of the provisional and restricted scope of their mission, and of Gregory's intention to send other legates to settle the problem of Germany. They also reminded him that he had put himself in jeopardy by associating with the citizens of Würzburg whose bishop had excommunicated them. The meeting at Würzburg had results which displeased both parties in Germany—the Saxons because Gregory's legates continued to recognize Henry in disregard of the legate Bernard's sentence at Goslar of now nearly two years ago, and Henry because the legates took no measures against Rudolf and the Saxons in spite of Henry's proscription of Rudolf under Swabian law.[513] According to Berthold, Rudolf was able to enhance his moral position by sending an embassy to Henry and calling upon him to desist from warfare and agree to the assembly that Gregory planned. Rudolf protested his own preparedness to abide by its decision and, if Henry was unwilling to agree, to punish him by force of arms. According to Berthold, this undermined the morale of Henry's army. It was in the interest of both sides to make a show of willingness to listen to Gregory and to welcome his arbitration.[514] But after the Würzburg gathering, there was no serious prospect of a German assembly upon anything like Gregory's terms.

512 Berthold, *a.*1079, p. 320/8–49.   513 Berthold, *a.*1074, p. 321/10–38
514 Berthold, *a.*1079, pp. 328/39–722/23.

During the second half of 1079, both sides pursued their causes by military and political means. Henry pressed ahead with plans, both material and propagandist, to secure the submission of the Saxons; there were fears that the Saxons might have to bid for terms.[515] Henry hoped to begin a campaign in Saxony at Christmas.[516] According to Berthold, Rudolf therefore returned to 'his own Saxony' and prepared to oppose Henry by arms.[517] Saxony continued to be ravaged by civil strife and violence. The summer and autumn saw various signs of Henry's confidence and good fortune. A diploma for his loyal supporter Bishop Burchard of Lausanne placarded Henry's condemnation of 'Duke Rudolf' at Pentecost 1077 'by every divine and human law'; it thus reiterated Henry's claim to exercise jurisdiction over him, whatever Gregory might claim or counsel.[518] This diploma and another for Bishop Ermenfrid of Sion, in the Valais,[519] illustrate the strengthening of Henry's control over routes to Italy. The marriage of the newly appointed duke of Swabia, Frederick of Büren, to Henry's only surviving daughter Agnes also improved Henry's position in South Germany.

It was the episcopal appointments of the rival parties that most clearly declared their respective intentions. Rudolf and the Saxons consulted their own interests but also sought to present themselves as choosing men who were acceptable to Gregory by means which could be construed as free canonical election. At Magdeburg, to which Gregory's attention had been drawn by his returning legate Abbot Bernard of Marseilles, one of his three favoured candidates, Hartwig, was elected and installed in early August 1079.[520] Soon afterwards, the Henrician Bishop Eberhard of Naumburg was replaced by Gunther, a canon of Magdeburg who had been disappointed of election there; Berthold presented his election, like Hartwig's, as being canonical.[521] He also recorded the promotion of Udo, a partisan of the Saxon opposition who became bishop of Hildesheim in succession to the temporizing Hezilo.[522]

---

[515] Berthold, *a*.1079, p. 325/19–24. See also *MGH DDHIV* no. 316, in which Henry safeguarded the property of the abbey of Niederaltaich from which he had secured finance; he at once affirmed his right thus to raise money and professed to do so within the rules of law and equity: 'Aecclesiarum iusta est haec consuetudo et sancta, ut ex hiis, quibus saepe habundant dei nutu, argenti vel auri thesauris indigentibus succurrant tempore necessitatis, quae tamen, ne detrimentum patiantur, recipere debent dignis commertiis. Quod inter nos et Altahensem aecclesiam actum est; nam ituri in expeditionem non habuimus omnia necessaria. Quae a dilecto abbate nostro Uvaltgero ex his, quae habuit Altahensis aecclesia in auro et argento, nobis mutuo sunt concessa. At nos de reditu incerti, de damno aecclesiae timidi, de salute animae solliciti praedium quoddam . . . in usus fratrum ibidem deo servitium [*sic*] in proprium tradendo firmavimus firmando tradidimus.' The diploma is dated 16 Aug. 1079. For Henry's expressions of pious kingship, see *MGH DDHIV* nos. 313–14, with their provision of prayers for those who fell *in publico bello*. For the possibility of a Saxon bid for peace, see *H* no. 29, pp. 64–7, with Erdmann's comments in *Studien zur Briefliteratur*, pp. 164–5.

[516] Berthold, *a*.1079, p. 323/19–24.   [517] Berthold, *a*.1079, p. 323/12–18.

[518] *MGH DDHIV* no. 311, which refers to 'dux Rodolfus ob multos in nos regnumque nefandas praesumptiones omni divina et humana lege tam vitae quam rerum proscriptus et damnatus'.

[519] *MGH DDHIV* no. 321, 30 Dec. 1079.

[520] *Epp. vag.* nos. 26–7, pp. 66–72; Berthold, *a*.1079, p. 323/46–8.

[521] Berthold, *a*.1079, p. 322/38–44.

[522] Berthold, *a*.1079, p. 323/44–6; for Udo, see esp. Goetting, *Die Hildesheimer Bischöfe*, pp. 295–314.

Henry, too, took care over episcopal appointments, but his new bishops were men who suited his claims to an unfettered exercise of kingly power, and he seems to have paid little regard to Gregory's requirements or reactions. In January 1079, he replaced Archbishop Udo of Trier, who had at once been well disposed towards himself and a key figure in Gregory's quest for peace in Germany, with a canon of Passau named Egilbert. Egilbert had been excommunicated by his bishop, Altmann, for his staunch advocacy of Henry. Friends and foes differed about whether his election was simoniacal. He for long reigned as a competent diocesan bishop, but his choice to succeed Udo expressed Henry's determination to go his own way.[523] At Cologne, also early in 1079, Henry appointed Sigewin, a canon of the cathedral who had belonged to the circle of Archbishop Anno II; he combined loyalty to the king with a reputation for piety.[524] In the south, Henry's appointments attracted stronger reforming censure. Especially objectionable was Norbert, provost of Augsburg, whom Henry appointed in 1079 to the see of Chur, which was situated just to the north of the central Alpine passes. Berthold enlarged upon Norbert's simony and especially on the scandal of his allegedly seeking episcopal ordination at the hands of the 'heretic', Archbishop Tedald of Milan.[525] Whereas Berthold praised the canonical propriety of the Saxon elections, he condemned Henry's appointments for their flouting of this propriety and for their disregard of Gregory's legislation against lay investiture, especially at his recent Roman synods. Both in Germany and, no doubt, in reports from Germany that Gregory received, the contrast between the dutiful King Rudolf and the contumacious Henry was being ever more sharply drawn.

During the second half of 1079, two of Gregory's letters illustrate his gathering difficulties in dealing with the German problem. While clinging to his plan to send new legates who would hold a definitive assembly, he was troubled by the conduct of his legates Peter of Albano and Ulrich of Padua; moreover, while Gregory avoided open criticism of Henry, the king's pursuit of his own interest was evidently troubling him. At some time after July, he addressed Peter and Ulrich.[526] He had received complaints about their conduct by which, he said, he was not convinced: one, clearly Peter, was reported to have behaved all too guilelessly, while the other, Ulrich, had been somewhat less than guileless![527] Gregory urged them to be circumspect, and to keep to their written and verbal instructions. They were not to pass judgement in the matter of the two kings, or of the bishops-elect of Trier, Cologne, or Augsburg whom Henry had nominated, or of those who had received investiture at lay hands. For all the urgency of Gregory's legislation at his November synod of 1078, it was not to be

---

[523] *Gesta Trev., Addit. et cont. I,* c. 11, p. 184/49–50; Berthold, *a.*1078, p. 314/7–11; *CU* no. 61, pp. 124–9. For Egilbert, see Erkens, *Die Trierer Kirchenprovinz,* pp. 96–122.

[524] Berthold, *a.*1079, p. 315/34–7.

[525] Berthold, *a.*1079, p. 323/25–35; *Ann. Aug. a.* 1079, p. 130/2.

[526] *Epp. vag.* no. 31, pp. 80–5; see also Berthold, *a.*1079, pp. 322/32–323/11.

[527] See *MGH DDHIV* no. 312, a diploma for the church of Padua dated 23 July 1079 which indicates that Ulrich used his legatine position to secure Henry's confirmation of his church's privileges; Berthold wrote that the legates were said to have come to Würzburg 'muneribus partim corruptis': *a.*1079, p. 3211/13–15; Bruno made a similar allegation: cap. 116, p. 378.

rigorously applied. The legates' tasks were to seek Henry's agreement for the holding of an assembly, for establishing peace in the German kingdom, and for restoring
to their sees the bishops who had been expelled. Gregory would in due course send
competent persons to settle these issues in concert with himself. The two legates
were to follow Gregory in maintaining impartiality. Nevertheless, Gregory referred
to two matters with which they should be actively concerned; in either case, Henry
was at fault from Gregory's point of view. The first concerned Abbot Ekkehard of
Reichenau, whom Bishop Eberhard of Parma had taken prisoner in 1077 and had released in February 1079 upon Gregory's demand; Henry had subjected Reichenau to
his partisan Abbot Ulrich of St Gall.[528] Gregory studiously avoided naming Henry
and represented the conflict as one between the two abbots. But the legates were told
to see that the invader was expelled. Second, in a postscript to the letter, Gregory
urged the legates to 'remember' Bishop Adalbert of Worms, whom Henry had driven
from his see.

In a letter of 1 October to the 'fideles sancti Petri' in Germany, Gregory still further revealed his unease about his German policy.[529] He sought to answer the complaints of infirmity of purpose ('secularis levitas') that some were said to be levelling
at him. He asserted his own steadfastness in their cause, reminding them of the
strength of partisan support for Henry amongst those who surrounded him at Rome
(the *Latini*, that is, spokesmen from the Roman ecclesiastical province); using a
phrase that recalled criticism of his steadfastness at Canossa, he said that they accused him, not of infirmity of purpose, but of excessive severity towards Henry.[530]
He sought to excuse his current legates from the allegations that were levelled
against them of acting beyond their instructions. He insisted upon his own firmness
in the cause of righteousness ('iustitia'), upon the limited scope of the legates' instructions, and upon his hope of sending other wise and appropriate legates to settle
German affairs. For the moment, however, he could say no more until his legates
brought him fuller tidings from Germany. Gregory's letter did nothing to stem the
Saxons' disenchantment with Gregory; a fifth Saxon letter gave expression to their
depth of feeling at what they interpreted as his weakness.[531]

Nor, when his legates returned towards the end of 1079, did their coming bring
him any comfort. Ulrich of Padua came first, and according to Berthold his main
concern was to win Gregory's sympathy for Henry and to play upon the loyalty to
him of the *Latini*.[532] What he said was, however, contradicted by a monk—perhaps
the Gisilbertus to whom Bernold referred[533] who had arrived as a legate from

---

[528] *Reg.* 6.18, to Bishop Eberhard of Parma, 14 Feb. 1079, pp. 429–30; *Casuum S. Galli contin. sec.*
p. 157.

[529] *Reg.* 7.3, pp. 462–3.   [530] *Reg.* 7.3, pp. 462/28–30, cf. *Reg.* 4.12, p. 313/7–10.

[531] Bruno, caps. 109–10, 116, pp. 360–4, 378.

[532] Berthold, *a.*1079, p. 322/34–52.

[533] Bernold, *Chron. a.* 1080, pp. 436/44–437/1, cf. *a.*1079, p. 436/13–14. It is not, however, clear
whether 'Gisilbertus religiossimus presbiter et monachus' was Rudolf's envoy in 1079: p. 436/13–14, or
in 1080: p. 436/22–3, or, conceivably, on both occasions.

Rudolf. According to Berthold, Ulrich withdrew to Padua in discomfiture. At Gregory's urgent summons, Peter of Albano also returned post-haste to Rome, and, still according to Berthold, he added his voice to those who contradicted Ulrich of Padua's advocacy of Henry. Gregory's legatine mission of 1079 thus ended in conflict between the two legates and in acrimonious debate at Rome. Until after the end of the year, Gregory's own outlook does not appear to have moved beyond that to which he gave expression in his letter of 1 October to the faithful in Germany. He shows no sign of having departed from his publicly proclaimed purpose of neutrality as between the two kings or from his intention to send suitable legates to discuss and to settle German affairs.[534] In any case, anti-Henrician circles in Germany are likely to have regarded this cautious letter as a summary of Gregory's position.[535] Gregory's second sentence against Henry at his Lent synod of 1080 came with as little forewarning as had his first sentence at the Lent synod of 1076.

3.4.8 Gregory VII's Lent Synod of 1080 and the Second Excommunication of Henry IV

Henry was determined if he could to pursue his enmity with Rudolf to a military conclusion and thereby to implement his own judicial sentence against Rudolf as a treasonable subject. Although he could not mount a military campaign in 1079, he never abandoned his intention of doing so. He spent Christmas at Mainz with a large company of spiritual and lay princes; he was able to assemble a considerable army from various regions of Germany. In mid-January he set out towards Saxony, where there were significant Saxon defections from Rudolf, including Hermann and Magnus Billung and Wipert of Groitsch, with numerous promises to Henry of support or at least neutrality. On 27 January, he encountered Rudolf's army at Flarchheim, near Langensalza in north-west Thuringia. Although there was a bloody battle, neither side gained a decisive military advantage. But Rudolf remained in possession of the battlefield, which in medieval warfare was deemed an indication of victory: Henry withdrew to Regensburg. On account of the depredations of his armies before the battle, Archbishop Siegfried of Mainz and Archbishop Gebhard of Salzburg, together with other bishops who were with them, renewed the sentence of excommunication against Henry.[536]

Both kings prepared to present their case to Gregory at the Lent synod which was to begin on 7 March. Henry's principal envoys were his partisans Archbishop Liemar of Bremen and Bishop Rupert of Bamberg together with an archdeacon named Burchard; according to Berthold, they came to Rome laden with gold to expend there on Henry's behalf. Henry also sent Bishop Ulrich of Padua, Gregory's

---

534 *Reg.* 7.3.

535 The letter circulated widely. It was almost certainly the letter which Berthold said was sent at the end of 1079 to the anti-king Rudolf and his supporters, rather than a separate letter that has been lost, for Berthold's précis corresponds closely to it: *a.*1079, p. 323/4–11. The letter was copied by Hugh of Flavigny: 2, p. 451.

536 Bruno, cap. 117, pp. 378–80; Berthold, *a.*1080, pp. 324/15– 325/47.

sometime legate to Germany, similarly laden; but his fate of being ambushed and killed *en route* was, for Berthold, a sign of God's judgement against him. Henry's selection of envoys does not suggest that he was in a mood for conciliation. There is no clear evidence as to whether or not Gregory gave them a hearing, either before or during the synod, although a later complaint by Henry suggests that he did not.[537]

A text has survived of the written deposition that Rudolf's envoy, whether the monk Gisilbertus or another, brought and that was submitted to the synod. Presented on behalf of 'King Rudolf and all his princes', it declared that Henry, whom Gregory had deposed from the kingdom by apostolic authority, had as a tyrant invaded the kingdom against the papal injunction. He had devastated it by fire, plunder, and the sword, had cruelly expelled bishops from their sees, and had distributed their property as fiefs to his supporters. Henry had perpetrated such numberless outrages against the princes of Rudolf's obedience because they would not obey him as king in face of Gregory's apostolic decree. Finally, the *colloquium* that Gregory had decided upon to determine justice and establish peace ('pro inquirenda iustitia et pace componenda') had not taken place through the fault of Henry and his supporters. Therefore they implored Gregory to perform on their behalf, or rather on that of the whole church, the justice that he had decreed against a sacrilegious destroyer of churches ('ut nobis, immo sanctae Dei ecclesiae, decretam sacrilegio pervasori ecclesiarum iustitiam faciatis').[538]

As for the message brought by Henry's envoys, the principal testimony is that of Bonizo of Sutri. According to him, they came to Rome 'according to a well-laid plan' as bearers of a proud and unheard-of commission: if the pope would excommunicate Rudolf without a judgement, Henry would pay him due obedience; if not, Henry would provide himself with another pope who would act according to his desire.[539] Henry himself later claimed that Gregory treated his envoys with infamous contempt and cruelty.[540] It may be that Henry demanded that his own repeated judicial condemnation of Rudolf by German law should be recognized by Gregory's immediate summary condemnation of him; it is less likely that Henry threatened Gregory with deposition if he did not comply. Not only does this depend on Bonizo's unsupported testimony, but Henry would have been imprudent to make such a threat unless he were free to undertake an Italian campaign; after the battle of Flarchheim he could not well leave Germany open to Rudolf's armies. Moreover, when Gregory gave sentence against Henry at his Lent synod, he referred to Henry's plan in 1076 to depose him but mentioned no such threat in 1080, although to have done so would have strengthened his case.[541]

---

537 Berthold, *a*.1080, p. 326/16–30 (Berthold's Annals break off at this point); Paul of Bernried, caps. 106–7, p. 538; Wenric of Trier, *Epistola*, cap. 8, p. 297; Huygens, 'Bérenger', pp. 392/62–393/74. *Epp. HIV* no. 17, p. 78/22–4, suggests that Henry's envoys may not have been granted a hearing if the reference is to the synod of 1080.

538 *MGH Const.* 1.554–5, no. 390.   539 Bonizo of Sutri, *Lib. ad amic.* 9, p. 612/13–19.

540 *Epp. HIV* no. 16, to the clergy and people of Rome, (1081), p. 76/5–7; cf. no. 17 (1082), p. 78/22–4.

541 For the reference to Henry's plan in 1076 to depose Gregory, see *Reg.* 7.14*a*, p. 484/7.

In proceeding somewhat suddenly to his second excommunication of Henry, Gregory seems not to have acted in response to any such single matter as the threat of deposing Gregory that Bonizo described. In passing his sentence, Gregory dwelt upon the long-term and incorrigible disobedience and contumacy by which Henry had already, through his deeds in Germany, brought renewed excommunication upon his own head. In effect, Gregory conceded the case of Rudolf's envoys, that by continually obstructing a German *colloquium*, Henry proved his own disobedience and stood condemned as the opponent of righteousness. He seems to have reacted to the reports of his returning legates, the Cardinal-deacon Bernard and, more especially, Cardinal-bishop Peter of Albano.[542] Bernold of St Blasien wrote that Rudolf was quick through his envoy to tell Gregory of his own victory at Flarchheim on 27 January, in which Gregory is likely to have seen the hand of God. Bernold also said that Gregory's own legates to Germany testified at the synod to Rudolf's unqualified obedience and to Henry's disobedience.[543] Paul of Bernried may also be correct in recording Gregory's belief that a vision of the Virgin required him to pass immediate judgement against Henry.[544] All these circumstances may have caused Gregory to make up his mind. It must be admitted, however, that the steps by which Gregory was brought to proceed as and when he did to a second condemnation of Henry do not fully emerge. But the sentence that he passed on 7 March was nothing if not impassioned and emphatic.

It took the form of an address and prayer not only (as in 1076) to St Peter, the prince of the apostles, but also to St Paul, the teacher of the nations;[545] Gregory thereby directed his words beyond his neighbours the *Latini*, whom he had several times declared to be well disposed to Henry, to the widest possible Christian audience. To the two apostles who were disciples and lovers of the truth he would declare the simple truth; thus, his brothers in the synod who heard him might the more readily trust him, as one who resisted the wicked and brought help to the faithful servants of the apostles. He had himself come unwillingly to the apostles' service—to holy orders, then with Pope Leo to their own church at Rome, and finally to his own occupancy of the papal office. In this office, they had chosen him to be their herald to the world; but the devil's own members had begun to rise up against him and to lay their hands upon him, even by shedding his blood.[546] Gregory cited the words of Psalm 2 which the earliest Christians had used of the chief priests and elders at Jerusalem in their hostility to the apostolic preaching, and he anticipated later passages in his address by adding those who abetted their recalcitrant rulers:

> The kings of the earth stood up,
>   and the princes *both secular and ecclesiastical with their*

---

[542] Not Abbot Bernard of Marseilles, who had died: *Reg.* 7.7, to the Cardinal-priest Richard, 2 Nov. 1079, p. 468/14–18.

[543] Bernold, *Chron. a.* 1080, p. 436/21–6.   [544] As n. 537.

[545] *Reg.* 7.14a(7), pp. 483–7.

[546] The reference to shedding his own blood is probably to the events of Christmas 1075: see below, 4.7.

> *courtiers and the commonalty* gathered as one,
> against the Lord and *you* his anointed.[547]

Even so they had endeavoured to rise against Gregory and to destroy him utterly by death or exile.

After this introduction, Gregory arraigned Henry 'whom men call king' as one who had raised his heel against[548] the apostles' own church. He dwelt upon the events of 1076, when Henry had conspired with German and Italian bishops to cast him down and enslave the church. By their own authority the apostles had resisted, and by their power had destroyed, his pride; he had thus been brought to seek absolution at Canossa. This Gregory had granted, because of his humility and promise of amendment. With a clarity of definition that hindsight now allowed, Gregory said that he had not, however, restored Henry to the kingship or commanded his subjects to observe the fealty from which he had absolved them. He had withheld them, because he wished himself to do justice and to make peace between Henry and the German bishops who had obeyed the apostolic see; by the oath (*iusiurandum*) of Canossa which the bishops of Vercelli and Osnabrück swore on his behalf, Henry had concurred. But these same German bishops and princes had quickly learnt that Henry was not keeping his promises. Despairing of him, they elected Duke Rudolf as king—but without Gregory's counsel. Rudolf sought Gregory's favour with an assurance that he had accepted the government of the kingdom under constraint, and he promised ready obedience to Gregory in all things.

Having thus set out why he was able to think well of Rudolf, Gregory turned to Henry. His account partly followed the record in the Register, but in its recognition of Henry's prolonged blameworthiness it seems to be deeply coloured by the recent reports of his legates. After Canossa, Henry had quickly begun to seek Gregory's help against Rudolf, and Gregory had promised his willing aid; but he must hear the case of both parties in order that he might know which of them righteousness ('iustitia') favoured. In a phrase that is not foreshadowed in any of Gregory's letters, he now observed that Henry, supposing that he could defeat Rudolf by his own military strength, had disregarded this answer. But by the winter of 1077–8, Henry knew that his hopes could not be fulfilled. Gregory made much of the Lent synod of 1078, when two bishops who were Henry's partisans, Thierry of Verdun and Benno of Osnabrück, came to Rome and asked Gregory to ensure righteousness ('iustitia') in his case—a request that Rudolf's envoys, from their side, approved. Gregory accordingly appointed that an assembly should be held in Germany, 'in order that at it either a peace might be agreed or else it might be determined to which king righteousness (*iustitia*) inclined.' For Gregory, this provided a kind of litmus test: the unrighteous party would be revealed by his unwillingness for such an assembly to take place; he had therefore solemnly excommunicated all (he here took up his opening paraphrase of Psalm 2), whether the agents of a king, duke, bishop, or anyone else,

---

[547] Ps. 2: 2–3, cf. Acts 4: 26. The words in italics are Gregory's interpolations.
[548] Cf. the reference of Judas Iscariot in John 13: 18.

'who by any device hindered the assembly from taking place'. Of this sanction, Henry and his partisans had by their own deeds fallen foul: they had incurred excommunication in circumstances that were apparent to all in the slaughter and devastation that ravaged almost the whole of Germany.

In passing sentence upon Henry, Gregory was thus renewing a sentence of excommunication from which he had absolved Henry at Canossa but under which he now recognized Henry already to have placed himself again by his own disobedience; as for Henry's deposition from the kingship and forfeiture of the oaths of his subjects, Gregory was reiterating sentences under which he had been placed in 1076 and from which he had never become free. Still addressing the apostles, he declared:

> ... I subject Henry, whom men call king, and all his supporters to excommunication and I bind them with the chains of anathema. And once again, on behalf of Almighty God and of yourselves, I debar him from the kingdom of the Germans and of Italy, and I take from him his entire royal power and office. I command that no Christian should obey him as king, and I absolve from the terms of their oaths all who have sworn, or shall swear, to him as master of the kingdom. May Henry himself and his supporters find themselves powerless in every military engagement, and may they win no victory during their lifetime.

Gregory also proclaimed the effects of his sentence so far as Rudolf was concerned. He acknowledged him to be the true king of the Germans (he did not name Italy, where Rudolf was king neither by inheritance nor by election), and he pronounced his absolution and blessing upon his loyal followers. He summarized his judgement upon the rival kings as follows: 'Just as Henry is rightly rejected from the dignity of the kingdom for his pride, disobedience, and falsehood, so the power and dignity of the kingdom are bestowed upon Rudolf for his humility, obedience, and truth.' With such clarity Gregory now perceived the sentence of righteousness ('iustitia') which had been unclear to him during the three years after Canossa but which the reports of his legates and, perhaps, his vision of the Virgin, had disclosed.[549]

Gregory ended with a peroration in which he vaunted the authority of the apostles whom he addressed and the power of their sentence upon Henry, for whom he nevertheless finally left a prospect of eternal salvation if he should, after this second excommunication, be moved to true penitence:

> So act now, I beseech you, most holy fathers and princes, that the whole world may understand and recognize that, if you can bind and loose in heaven, upon earth you can also withhold and grant to each, according to his merits, empires, kingdoms, principalities, duchies, marches, counties, and the property of all men. For you have often stripped from the wicked and unworthy their patriarchates, primacies, archbishoprics, and bishoprics, and awarded them to religious men. If you judge spiritual things, what powers should you not be believed to have over secular things? If one day you will judge the angels who are the masters of all proud princes, what can you not do with regard to their servants? Let kings and all the princes of the world now learn how great you are and what you can do; let them tremble to set at nought the

---

[549] It is significant that Gregory passed judgement upon Henry 'confidens de iudicio et misericordia Dei eiusque piissime matris semper virginis Mariae, fultus vestra [St Peter's and St Paul's] auctoritate': *Reg.* p. 486/10–12.

command of your church. As for this Henry, execute your judgement so swiftly that all may know him to fall and to be confounded not by chance but by your power! Nevertheless may it lead to his repentance, so that his spirit may be saved in the day of the Lord!550

The acts of the synod circulated in Germany, and in a letter that has been lost, Gregory communicated his sentence to the German princes.551 Gregory had staked everything upon the power of St Peter's anathema to disable Henry and to ensure the total victory of Rudolf in the struggle that divided the German kingdom.

3.5 Gregory VII and Henry IV, 1080–5

3.5.1 The Sequel in Germany to the Second Excommunication of Henry IV

After Gregory's hesitation since Canossa and after the suspension of judgement in his many letters, the force and decisiveness of his sentence at his Lent synod of 1080 must have occasioned general surprise. Henry lost no time in reacting with commensurate determination. Many of the bishops found themselves drawn or constrained to demonstrate their support for him. At Eastertide 1080, an episcopal assembly at Bamberg, the cathedral city of Bishop Rupert who had been one of Henry's envoys to the Lent synod, solemnly disowned obedience to Gregory and instituted a propaganda campaign against him.552 At Pentecost (31 May), the campaign was intensified by Henry's convening of an imperial synod at Mainz which was attended by nineteen bishops and many lay princes.553 The principal evidence for its proceedings is three letters, themselves well orchestrated, which were prepared for circulation in Germany and Lombardy; their authors were Bishop Huzmann of Speyer, Archbishop-elect Egilbert of Trier, and Bishop Thierry of Verdun.554 They presented the ills of the time as affecting both *regnum* and *sacerdotium*; Huzmann listed them, in this order, as the disturbance of the kingdom, the destruction of the kingly power, and the ruinous condition of the church. The bishops had assembled at Mainz in order to right these three wrongs, and the key to all of them was the elimination of 'Hildebrand'. Huzmann demanded his expulsion from the apostolic see and his replacement there:

550 The story in Bonizo of Sutri, *Lib. ad amic.* 9, pp. 6–17, Beno, cap. 7, p. 371, and Sigebert of Gembloux, *Chron. a.* 1080, p. 364, that at Eastertide 1080 Gregory further prophesied Henry's death or deposition from the kingdom, is insecure. It seems to be based upon a report circulating among Gregory's enemies which harked back to Gregory's authentic prophecy probably made in 1076 that 'the feast of St Peter (1 Aug.) will not have passed before it is quite certainly made known that the king was most justly excommunicated' at the Lent synod of 1076: *Epp. vag.* no. 13, p. 30; see above, 3.3.3. As current after 1080, the story extended this prophecy, which could plausibly have been claimed to be fulfilled in the falling away of support from Henry during the summer of 1076, into a far more rash foretelling of his death or deposition. It was probably one of the many propagandist stories that the Henrician party used after 1080 to discredit Gregory.

551 For the circulation of the synodal acts, see *Reg.* p. 479; for the lost letter, Wenric of Trier, *Epistola*, cap. 4, pp. 288/30–6, 289/36–9.

552 Gebhard of Salzburg, *Epistola*, cap. 15, p. 270/9–14.

553 Marianus Scottus, *Chron. a.* 1101 (1079), pp. 561/48–562/1; Sigebert of Gembloux, *Chron. a.* 1079 (1080), p. 364/16–17.

554 *CU* nos. 60–2, pp. 126–30; for no. 60, see also *MGH Const.* 1.117–18, no. 69.

We cannot imagine how this could be, unless the head of the poisonous serpent were wholly cut off, by whose poisoned breath these ills have hitherto been fanned. While the agent survives, how can the effects be eliminated? All those present at Mainz, both great and small, therefore decreed that Hildebrand, that crafty invader of the apostolic see, that accursed subverter of divine and human laws, should by God's help be wholly repudiated. Another more worthy than he should be elected to the apostolic see, who should gather what has been scattered and heal what has been broken, and who would like a good shepherd in holy church foster peace, not discord and wars.

This was a theme that all three bishops developed. 'Hildebrand', declared Thierry, 'who was called the head, the foundation, and the glory of the church, is now its tail, its ruin, and its shame.' He pilloried his deeds at the recent Lent synod:

Oh! the unheard-of arrogance of a man who boasts of himself above all boastfulness . . . and rends the unity of the church! . . . He has presumed to destroy the kingdom and its catholic king, . . . and to extol a spurious king while he envisaged and threatened the obliteration of a free and legitimate one to the point of extinguishing his very royal title. A heresy verily unheard-of in our days: perjury he calls fealty, and faith he turns into sacrilege!

The sharpest and most sustained indictment was Archbishop Egilbert's. He began his letter by declaring that it would be rash and mad to pass sentence upon a pope, and it would be iniquitous in any way to proceed against one who acted on St Peter's behalf as Christ's own messenger. But by just this token, it would be mortally dangerous to the church and an act of defiance to God, if one failed to resist a Hildebrand who, lacking the marks of peace and charity that Christ set upon his soldiers, did not merit even the name of Christian.

The bishops unanimously concluded that all Christians should renounce his obedience and join to elect a new supreme pontiff who would right what was wrong, restore what was broken down, and set at nought Hildebrand's example of mighty deeds.

These were brave words; composed under Henry's eye, they are likely to have accompanied the convening of the synod of imperial bishops at Brixen next month which took in hand Gregory's removal and replacement. But very soon, one at least of the dramatis personae at Mainz was having second thoughts; like many of the German bishops who were caught up in the clash between *regnum* and *sacerdotium*, he wanted nothing so much as to live peaceably with the head of both. Bishop Thierry of Verdun wrote to his archbishop-elect, Egilbert of Trier, explaining why he had not, when summoned, come to help in his consecration.[555] What was troubling him was the very point with which, after Mainz, Egilbert had begun his letter: it was presumptuous to pass sentence upon a pope. At Mainz, he had renounced Gregory only under extreme duress. But he had promised Gregory canonical obedience; moreover, at Verdun his own subjects had ostracized him and had denied him their obedience until he repented. He could not confer upon Egilbert a consecration that might be an execration. For the present, he could see no clear way ahead; one

---

[555] *CU* no. 63, pp. 130–3; for the circumstances, see Hugh of Flavigny, 2, pp. 458–9, 461.

pope had, indeed, been renounced by the German bishops, but no one had yet replaced him by way of legitimate election.

Given such scruples and hesitation, it is not surprising that most German bishops
did not come to Henry's synod in person but preferred to send representatives or
written messages.[556] In reading the shrill propaganda of the decree of the synod of
Brixen, it should be remembered that many who continued to favour Henry were far
from happy about his rejection of Gregory and his moves towards the schism that the
setting up of an anti-pope would create.

3.5.2 The Synod of Brixen

The synod of Brixen assembled on 25 June 1080 in a South Bavarian city whose
bishop, Altwin, was a loyal Henrician. Situated to the south of the Brenner Pass, it
was readily accessible for the bishops of North Italy and especially for those of the
province of Aquileia. The shrewdness of Henry's concern with this region since
Canossa was apparent. Henry was present with an army of both Germans and
Italians; he subscribed the decree of the synod after the bishops.[557] Of the bishops
present, most were Italians. Apart from Hugh Candidus, cardinal-priest of S.
Clemente at Rome who claimed to subscribe 'on behalf of all the Roman cardinals',
nineteen of the bishops who added their names were Italian and one was Burgundian.
Only seven were Germans, though they included Archbishop Liemar of Bremen and
Bishop Rupert of Bamberg who had been Henry's envoys to Gregory's Lent synod
of 1080.[558] Most of the nineteen German bishops who had assembled in Mainz at
Pentecost sent letters or envoys to express their condemnation of Gregory.

The synodal decree has as much the character of minutes as of a decree, for it
shows the development of debate as well as its conclusions. In its diatribe against
Hildebrand, it outdid even the German bishops at Mainz. It opened with a vehement
and unanimous complaint against the 'fierce madness of one Hildebrand, a false
monk, named Pope Gregory VII'. It wondered that the unconquered King Henry
had for so long suffered him to rage without restraint. It invoked the scriptural injunctions of St Peter and St Paul, apparently having in view Gregory's address to
these apostles when he condemned Henry at his Lent synod: the prince should not
bear the sword in vain; the king should not only be supreme but he should send his
officers to avenge the evil and to act for the praise of those who do well.[559] To fulfil
these apostolic injunctions, it seemed right to the king and his princes that the bishops should pass a judgement in preparation for the drawing of the temporal sword
against Hildebrand; the proper course was for the royal power to pursue him when
the bishops had first cast him down from his proud eminence.

---

[556] Decree of the synod of Brixen, in *Quellen HIV* Anhang C, p. 480/15–18; *MGH Const.* 1.118–20,
no. 70.

[557] For the decree, see *Quellen HIV* Anhang C. pp. 476–83.

[558] Bishop Benno of Osnabrück and Archbishop Guibert of Ravenna were present but did not subscribe.

[559] Rom. 13: 14, 1 Pet. 2: 13–14.

The decree went on to proclaim that no Christians who knew Hildebrand would fear to hurl the dart of condemnation against him. Unlike the corresponding document of 1076, it did not dwell upon the supposed scandal of Hildebrand's private life. Instructed once more, no doubt, by Hugh Candidus, it retailed his supposed offences of a public and ecclesiastical nature from early youth until his seizure of the papal office. A necromancer, a false monk, a frequenter of obscene shows, and a trafficker in money, he had usurped the archdeaconship at Rome, procured the murder of four popes, and used every device of force, terror, and uncanonical deceit to grab their office for himself. From such roots, the fruits of his recent actions had grown. The decree passed to the events that had culminated in the recent Lent synod: Hildebrand had compassed the death in body and soul of Henry, a catholic and peaceable king, and he had vindicated the perjurer and traitor Rudolf.

The decree concluded with a pronouncement by the bishops that differs significantly from the way of dealing with Gregory that was canvassed at Mainz and repeated at the beginning of the decree—that a condemnation by the bishops should be followed by the king's implementation of their sentence by the temporal sword. Instead, it was envisaged that Hildebrand, who had not been chosen by God but who had seized the papacy for himself by force, fraud, and bribery, should be canonically deposed and driven out. If upon hearing the call from Brixen he did not himself vacate the papal throne, he should then be condemned for all time. The key word was canonically ('canonice').[560] Here, Hugh Candidus's subscription on behalf of all the Roman cardinals was important. There was an implicit call for a further process by the Roman church which alone could depose him. It was hoped that, like Gregory VI, Hildebrand would remove himself by self-deposition from the Roman see that he had usurped. If not, the manner of his condemnation was left open. Similarly, if the decree foreshadowed a Roman expedition by Henry, it did not expressly mention it.

Nor did the decree of Brixen say who should succeed Gregory. This question received a whole day of discussion which was itself difficult and fraught. Rivalry between the metropolitans of Milan, Aquileia, and Ravenna may have been acute; evidence from Milan plausibly suggests that Archbishop Tedald may have been first canvassed, but that he declined.[561] In political terms, he would have been a powerful candidate, but the circumstances of his accession and his prolonged excommunication would have told against him. Eventually, Archbishop Guibert of Ravenna was chosen. He was also under Gregory's excommunciation, but his record as a moderately reforming prelate may have recommended him to the principles of the bishops and to the prudence of the king, who is likely to have taken the lead in choosing him. Henry's approach with regard to Guibert was cautious. At Brixen he made no recorded claim to act as *patricius* of Rome.[562] Guibert was henceforth described as

---

[560] ' . . . Hildebrandum . . . iudicamus canonice depondum et expellendum et, nisi ab ipsa sede his auditis descenderit, in perpetuum condempnandum'.

[561] Landulf Senior, 4.2. p. 99/32–6.

[562] *Lib. de unit. eccles. cons.* 2.6–7, 21, pp. 216–18, 237–8, does not associate the term *patricius* with Brixen; it does not appear in the text of the decree.

the *electus* to the papacy and was accordingly immantled; but although, according to
Bernold, his choice was in August confirmed at Mainz by Henry in concert with
some German bishops,[563] his position was that of one designated to follow Gregory
in due course and not of one who was definitively and canonically elected.[564] Until
Gregory had been canonically deposed at Rome, he could not be consecrated as pope,
nor did he as yet assume the papal name of Clement III. His position was provisional,
and he was exposed to the danger of a change of mind on Henry's part. Nevertheless,
the proceedings at Brixen declared Henry's intention, as soon as the situation in
Germany allowed, to follow his father's precedent of 1046 by making an expedition
to Rome where he would oversee the deposition of an unworthy pope and procure
the due election and consecration of one more worthy from whom he might at last
receive imperial coronation.

For all the rhetoric of the decree of Brixen, there is much evidence of doubt and
hesitation amongst German bishops upon whose goodwill Henry relied; the ambiguities of the decree reflect this doubt and hesitation. The scruples about the expulsion of a pope and the desire for peace and good relations with both pope and king
that underlay Bishop Thierry of Verdun's letter to his metropolitan were not
confined to him alone.[565] The conduct at Brixen of Henry's long-standing and faithful supporter Bishop Benno of Osnabrück as vividly described by his biographer was
no less ambivalent. Having already sought to mediate between Henry and Gregory,
he was described as an unwilling participant. He avoided association with the decree,
which does not bear his subscription, by the ruse of concealing himself beneath the
altar of the church where the synod took place, and of emerging and resuming his
seat only when proceedings were over. His intention was to be 'ever faithful to the
king but never disobedient to the pope'; in the long term, said his biographer, he succeeded in his purpose of keeping the friendship alike of both popes (Gregory and
Clement III) and of King Henry, following St Paul's precept: 'If possible, so far as in
you lies keep peace with all men' (Rom. 12: 18).[566]

Sources that were in general favourable to Henry reflected Benno's disquiet. The
German sense of hierarchy and due order which made its bishops resistant to
Gregory's excessive intervention in German church affairs now served to warn
against Henry's wielding the sword against Gregory. So royalist a source as the
Augsburg Annals condemned Henry's proceedings against Gregory as presumptuous and the designation of Guibert of Ravenna to be his successor as imprudent.[567]
It was an enduring opinion. After Henry's death, his eulogistic biographer commented upon the synod of Brixen by addressing a plea to Henry that he should refrain from attempting to remove the head of the church, lest in paying Gregory back
for his injuries he should fall into the trap of incriminating himself.[568]

---

563 Bernold, *Chron. a.* 1080, p. 436/32–3.
564 For Guibert's accession to the papacy, see Cowdrey, *The Age of Abbot Desiderius*, pp. 235–6. A similar view was independently expressed by Ziese, *Wibert*, pp. 55–64 and Heidrich, *Ravenna*, pp. 52–4, 56–8,
159–60.
565 See above, 3.5.1.   566 *Vita Bennonis II*, cap. 18, pp. 410–15.
567 *Ann. Aug. a.* 1080, p. 130/15–19.   568 *Vita HIV* cap. 6, p. 430/6–9.

As in 1076, so in 1080 there was a danger that Henry had reacted beyond his resources and beyond the limits of what his bishops and other followers would, in the
long run, support.

3.5.3 Gregory VII's Response to the Synod of Brixen

At the time of the synod of Brixen, Gregory was using the good offices of Abbot
Desiderius of Montecassino to restore relations between the apostolic see and the
Normans of South Italy. On 10 June, he received the fealty of Prince Jordan of
Capua, and on 29 June at Ceprano, Robert Guiscard, duke of Apulia, renewed his
vassalage to the apostolic see and to the pope.[569] Gregory seems to have been still at
Ceprano when, on 20 July, news reached him of the synod of Brixen.[570] He already
had upon his hands a major crisis in the affairs of the kingdom of León–Castile.[571]
Before returning to Rome, he immediately initiated plans for the expulsion of
Guibert from Ravenna (he had already excommunicated him at his Lent synod of
1078), and for his replacement by an archbishop who would be duly obedient to him.
His initial reaction was expressed in a letter of 21 July which he circulated from
Ceccano by messengers to the bishops of the Principate, Apulia, and Calabria—that
is, to all Italy south of the papal lands.[572] He saw in the synod of Brixen the direct operation of the devil: it was an assembly of Satan at which the bishops falsely so-called
were Satan's disciples. He began with an expression of invincible confidence:
inflamed by the devil's own pride, these bishops sought to confound the holy Roman
church; but, with God's help and under St Peter's authority, their presumption
would be turned to shame and confusion, while the apostolic see would receive glory
and honour. From the least to the greatest, and the greatest at Brixen was Henry IV
whom Gregory stigmatized as 'the head and originator of this pernicious council',
those responsible would experience St Peter's vengeance in body and soul. Gregory
derived strength from two historical precedents which he so presented as to show
how Henry's earlier outrages had been frustrated: the Cadalan schism, of which he
called Henry the fomenter, and the conspiracy of the Lombard bishops before
Canossa of which he made Henry the leader. The present 'incurable wound' of
Brixen showed how little St Peter's enemies had learnt to fear the sword of his wrath.

Then Gregory turned to Brixen itself. It had set up Guibert of Ravenna as its
Antichrist and heresiarch, and the participants were stained by their manner of life
and simoniacal background. Only submission to the justice and mercy of papal
authority could help them. Gregory ended a letter which was addressed to the
bishops of a region where such legends were current by alluding to the supposed fate
of Simon Magus when he opposed St Peter at Rome; he called upon the South Italian
bishops to give him every help in defending the Roman church.

---

[569] For Jordan's oath, see Deusdedit, *Coll. can.* 3. 289 (159), p. 396; for Robert Guiscard's, *Reg.* 8.1*a*,
c, pp. 514–16.
[570] For Gregory's presence at Ceprano on 20 July 1080, see *QF* no. 187, pp. 220–1.
[571] See below, 6.11.   [572] *Reg.* 8.5, pp. 521–3.

Such was Gregory's propaganda response to the synod of Brixen. He also called upon the Italians to join him in taking decisive coercive measures against Guibert. He addressed a letter to all the faithful of St Peter, both clerical and lay, in which he outlined a plan of campaign which he said was drawn up after negotiations with the Norman princes, including Robert Guiscard and Jordan of Capua, as well as with leading persons in the region of Rome and in Tuscany.[573] With their aid, he hoped in the cooler weather of September to mount a military campaign against Ravenna. He urged his followers to have confidence in the rapid destruction of his enemies and in the restoration of the peace and security of the church.

There is no evidence to suggest that the appeals that Gregory addressed to the Normans elicited from them any response. Two further letters which he addressed on 15 October respectively to the clergy and laity in the marches of Tuscany and Fermo and the exarchate of Ravenna, and to the clergy and laity of Ravenna,[574] showed that by then he was looking for forces from these regions to attack Guibert and to replace him by a new archbishop. His strictures upon Guibert were unabated, and he sought to justify direct Roman intervention at Ravenna by recalling the legendary collaboration of Rome with its patron saint, St Apollinaris, in the foundation of the see. In appointing a new archbishop, the church of Ravenna was to collaborate with a legation that Gregory would send of certain unnamed bishops—Roman cardinals or neighbouring bishops are clearly intended, of the archdeacon of Rome, and of other Roman deacons.

15 October was not a propitious date for Gregory to be planning military action; it saw in Italy a heavy military defeat of Countess Matilda of Tuscany's army, and in Germany the mortal wounding on the battlefield of Rudolf of Swabia. Nevertheless, on 11 December, Gregory made a third attempt to organize direct intervention at Ravenna, by addressing a fresh appeal to the clergy and laity of Ravenna and the Pentapolis, the march of Fermo, and the duchy of Spoleto. He referred to a clerk whose name was probably Raidolfus, and who had already been chosen to be archbishop of Ravenna—whether or not by the Roman legation to which he referred in October does not emerge. The recipients of his letter were urged to give Raidolfus every support against Guibert, the sacrilegious and reprobate destroyer of Ravenna.[575]

These plans for military intervention at Ravenna represented only one thrust of Gregory's plans after Brixen to promote the peace and security to which the letters referred. A contrasting approach is disclosed in a letter of 22 September to all his supporters in Germany.[576] Its tone was utterly different from the bellicosity of the letters by which he sought in Italy to elicit military action. To the Germans, he was silent about the use of force as about the position and iniquities of Guibert of

---

[573] *Reg.* 8.7, (summer 1080), pp. 524–5.   [574] *Reg.* 8.12, 13, pp. 531–4.

[575] *Reg.* 8.14, pp. 534–5; cf. *LP* 2.289/25–7. For the name Raidolfus, rather than Richard, see Holtzmann, 'Ein Gegner Wiberts'. The account in the *Liber pontificalis* suggests that Raidolfus was not a Ravennese but a Roman clerk: 2.289.

[576] *Reg.* 8.9, pp. 527–8.

Ravenna. Moreover, his diagnosis of the root cause of the afflictions of the church was a surprising one. He did not allude to Henry and his supporters; the root cause lay in the sins of Gregory himself and his supporters ('peccatis nostris exigentibus'). It was for their penance and amendment of life that he called; by this means, the German church might attain its long-desired peace. If Gregory's own adherents repented, they would quickly see an end of their adversaries' malice and the ruin of their cause. Already, some were returning to the church in penitence; they were marking out a path for all.

When Gregory wrote this letter, the question of the German crown was, in his eyes, settled in Rudolf's favour; the country was now blessed with an obedient and righteous ruler. As in 1076, so in 1080 he sought to offer an easy path to reconciliation.[577] It must start with the building up of his own followers in Christian righteousness; then his opponents could be won over, as well. All were to be united in a peace and security to be based upon repentance and righteousness as Gregory propounded them. Even after the death of Rudolf of Swabia, this would be a keynote of his appeals to Germany during the remainder of his pontificate. Rudolf's death would again involve Gregory in military and political appeals to the Germans. But his overriding concern would remain to urge them to follow the paths of repentance and righteousness. After Brixen, the possibility of a German assembly which had dominated Gregory's mind since Canossa no longer existed. His letter of 22 September 1080 adumbrated his future approach.

3.5.4 The Battle on the Elster

Unfortunately for Gregory's plans for warfare in Italy and for peace in Germany, the autumn of 1080 brought him setbacks in both regions. In Italy, Robert Guiscard was already showing himself to be more concerned with ambitions across the Adriatic than with the coercion of Gregory's Guibertine adversaries.[578] On 15 October, Henry IV's Lombard supporters inflicted a severe military defeat upon his absolutely reliable ally, Countess of Matilda of Tuscany, at Volta near Mantua;[579] soon afterwards, the loyal Gregorian Bishop Anselm II of Lucca was driven from his diocese.[580] Worst of all, in Germany, as the result of a battle also fought on 15 October, Henry's position was greatly strengthened by the death of the anti-king Rudolf of Swabia whom Gregory had so lately proclaimed as the German ruler upon whom the favour of God's righteousness rested. Both morally and militarily, the blow to Gregory and the benefit for Henry were great. Henry could mount no expedition to Italy until his Saxon opponents had been weakened. The Saxon chronicler Bruno described him as 'tireless in the labours of warfare', and in October he marched upon Saxony.[581] When denied access to Goslar, he ravaged Erfurt and made to deal

---

[577] See esp. *Reg.* 9.10, to Bishop Altmann of Passau, (1081), p. 587, for Gregory's willingness to ease the way to reconciliation for Henrician bishops, esp. Bishop Benno of Osnabrück.

[578] See below, 6.2.

[579] Bernold, *Chron. a.* 1080, p. 436/42–4; Bonizo of Sutri, *Lib. ad amic.* 9, p. 613/25–7 (misdated).

[580] *Vita Anselmi ep. Lucensis*, cap. 10, p. 16.

[581] For the battle, see esp. Bruno, caps. 121–14, pp. 386–95.

likewise with Naumburg. But he was brought to battle at Hohenmölsen, on the banks of the River Elster, a tributary of the Saale, to the south-east of Merseburg. In no small measure thanks to the military skill of Duke Otto of Nordheim, the Saxons had the better of a long and bloody battle; Bruno was able to enlarge upon how the battle on the Elster reversed the verdict of that in 1075 upon the Unstrut, another tributary of the Saale, when Rudolf of Swabia had led the victorious Henrician army: 'For all that the Unstrut, where we were vanquished, offended against us,' he wrote, 'the Elster gave us double recompense.' But during the battle on the Elster, Rudolf suffered two severe wounds, one of them resulting in the severance of the right hand with which he had sworn fealty to Henry. It seemed like a vindication of Henry's judicial sentence against him. His wounds proved mortal, and he was buried in Merseburg cathedral. Probably under the supervision of Bishop Werner, his tomb was quickly adorned with a life-size memorial plate of gilded and bejewelled bronze. Though represented naturalistically, he carried royal insignia—crown, orb, and sceptre. The inscription surrounding his effigy recalled, not his lineage or any papal sanction for his kingship, but his prospective utility to his German followers in peace and war; above all, it proclaimed the sacrificial character of his death:

King Rudolf, killed for the law of his fathers and rightly to be mourned, is buried in this tomb. If he reigned in a time of peace, there was not since Charlemagne his like as a king in counsel and with the sword. A sacred victim of battle through whom his people was victorious, he lies here. For him, death was life; he fell in the church's cause.[582]

Four spaces at the cardinal points in the inscription suggest that, on his anniversary, memorial candles were to be placed there; to this day, his mummified right hand is preserved in the cathedral as a relic.[583] But, for all the fine words of the inscription, no cultus or strong memorial tradition developed; in Germany at large, the victorious Saxon reversal of the defeat on the Unstrut was less regarded than the disaster of Rudolf's death. Hohenstaufen tradition had it that, when Henry IV soon afterwards stood by his rival's magnificent tomb, a bystander asked why he allowed one who had not been a king to lie buried in such regal honour; Henry replied, 'Would that all my enemies lay so honourably buried!'[584] It was a jest that Henry could afford to utter; it was as if the verdict of God had been given against Rudolf and for himself. Not until the following August could another anti-king be so much as elected. The Saxons were, indeed, far from defeated: they prevented Henry from keeping Christmas at his beloved Goslar,[585] and they rejected out of hand Henry's proposal that his son Conrad should become their king in return for a promise that he would himself never

---

[582] The inscription, the deciphering of which is not wholly clear, probably runs as follows: 'Rex hoc Rodulfus patrum pro lege peremptus | plorandus merito conditur in tumulo. | Rex illi similis si regnet tempore pacis | consilio gladio non fuit (*or*: ruit) a Karolo. | Qua vicere sui, ruit hic sacra victima belli: | mors sibi vita fuit; ecclesiae cecidit': see Sciurie, 'Die Merseburger Grabplatte'; Vogel, *Gregor VII. und Heinrich IV.*, pp. 239–43; Struve, 'Rudolf von Schwaben', pp. 471–4.

[583] For a story that the dying Rudolf sought to exculpate himself by shifting responsibility for his anti-kingdom to the bishops present, see Frutolf, *a.* 1080, p. 94/9–14.

[584] Otto of Freising, *Gesta Frederici*, 1.7, pp. 142–5.   [585] Bruno, cap. 125, pp. 394–5.

again set foot in Saxony. 'I have often seen a bad calf born to a bad ox', commented Otto of Nordheim; 'I have no desire for either the son or the father.' But Rudolf's death left the East Saxons divided even among themselves, and many of them were preoccupied with their local and family concerns.[586] They were seriously weakened, and it was safe for Henry to consider an expedition to Rome in which he could settle the score with Gregory.

3.5.5 Henry's First Expedition to Italy

The events of the winter of 1080–1 left both Gregory and Henry in circumstances of difficulty and uncertainty. Although Gregory sought to represent Rudolf's death in battle as nothing more than that of a king of blessed memory,[587] he had patently suffered a public setback to his belief that divine favour and righteousness were on his side. In 1081, serious fires at Bamberg and Mainz, cities that were associated with Rudolf's election as king, appeared to confirm God's sentence against Rudolf. Henry's Saxon enemies retained much of their military capability, for they had suffered fewer losses than Henry in the battle on the Elster. But negotiations which took place in February 1081 at Kaufungen, near Kassel, between bishops of both German parties showed signs of the Saxons' war-weariness and uncertainty about their political leadership. The main source is the Saxon chronicler Bruno. According to him, Henry initiated the negotiations in order to gain security in Germany while he embarked upon an Italian expedition. Each side nominated a group of five bishops to be its main spokesmen—for Henry, Archbishops Sigewin of Cologne and Egilbert of Trier and Bishops Rupert of Bamberg, Huzmann of Speyer, and Conrad of Utrecht, and for the Saxons, Archbishops Siegfried of Mainz, Hartwig of Magdeburg, and Gebhard of Salzburg, and Bishops Poppo of Paderborn and Udo of Hildesheim. The Saxons insisted upon the publicity of the negotiations; Archbishop Gebhard of Salzburg was their leading spokesman.[588] Bruno ascribed to him a long address, only the final part of which is likely to represent some of the archbishop's own words;[589] Bruno used the opportunity to present the general Saxon view of the rightfulness of their resistance to Henry. The speech ends with a challenge to the Henrician bishops either to show why Henry should rule the Saxons or else to allow the Saxons to prove that he should not rule at all. Whichever case prevailed, the Saxons urged their opponents no longer to harry them by fire and sword. Bruno said that Henry's party refused further debate, while the Saxons would not enter into a truce until mid-June when a fuller assembly might have been arranged. Anxious though they were for a suspension of hostilities, the Saxons would not ease Henry's way for an expedition to Italy. They were insistent upon the need for a new king who would duly protect them.

---

[586] See Fenske, *Adelsopposition*, pp. 77, 82.

[587] *Reg.* 9.3, to Bishop Altmann of Passau, (Mar. 1081), p. 574/1–3.

[588] *Lib. de unit. eccles. cons.* 2.9, p. 221/8–15.

[589] Bruno, caps. 126–8, pp. 394–403. For an analysis of Gebhard's speech, see Kost, *Das östliche Niedersachsen*, p. 103 n. 57.

If the death of Rudolf of Swabia left the Saxons leaderless and war-weary, Henry continued to exhibit increased confidence and competence as a ruler. He built upon the foundation that he had already been laying before 1080 to confirm his regality and to set it under the patronage of the Virgin.[590] On the eve of the battle on the Elster, he made fresh gifts to the cathedral at Speyer.[591] According to his diploma in its favour, they were virtually a votive offering to the Virgin:

Although we venerate the memory of all the saints, we should especially seek the patronage of the Ever-Virgin Mary, through whom alone the one Lord of all has pity upon all the faithful. In her mercy our fathers took refuge; under her protection we likewise seek refuge in the church of Speyer, which is particularly dedicated to her name in that of her Son.

With studied repetition of imperial titles, the diploma recalled that Speyer was the last resting-place of the Emperors Conrad his grandfather and Henry his father, as of his grandmother the Empress Gisela; it also referred to his own mother, the Empress Agnes. After the battle on the Elster and Rudolf's death, Henry soon visited Speyer.[592] The circumstantial evidence of the *Life* of Bishop Benno of Osnabrück makes it likely that Henry then charged him with the substantial rebuilding and completion of his grandfather's cathedral.[593] Henry confirmed the cathedral as a symbol of Salian piety and lordship. He set his dynasty more firmly than ever under the protection of the Virgin, the first of saints. It was his riposte to the Petrine claims of Gregory VII.

A further feature of Henry's diploma for Speyer was that its dispositions were made on the advice of archbishops—Sigewin of Cologne, Egilbert of Trier, and Liemar of Bremen, and bishops—Rupert of Bamberg, Otto of Regensburg, and Huzmann of Speyer,[594] four of whom were to represent him at Kaufungen.[595] Similarly in December 1080, four bishops were named as having prompted Henry's gift, made at Speyer, of a county to the Virgin in her church at Basel—Burchard of Basel, Huzmann of Speyer, Conrad of Utrecht, and Burchard of Lausanne.[596] Henry's better judgement in appointing and using competent bishops enhanced his standing as king and his resources to confront Gregory. It is particularly noteworthy that his bishops began to propagate in Germany the movement for the Peace of God which had spread widely in France and which promised relief to a war-weary and feud-ridden Germany.[597] Over the next decades, the movement would pass from the bishops' sponsorship to the king's and become a major factor in rallying public opinion to him.[598]

---

590 See above, 3.4.3.   591 *MGH DDHIV* no. 325, of 14 Oct. 1080.
592 *MGH DDHIV* nos. 326–7, of 6–7 Dec. 1080.
593 *Vita Bennonis II*, cap. 21, p. 420/26–30.   594 *MGH DDHIV* no. 325.
595 Bruno, cap. 126, p. 396.   596 *MGH DDHIV* no. 327.
597 See esp. the Peaces of Liège (1082): *MGH Const.* 1.603 n.1; Cologne (1083): *MGH Const.* 1. 602–5, no. 424; Bamberg (1085): *MGH Const.* 1.605–8, no. 425; Mainz (1085): Frutolf, 2.29, p. 98/15–19. For further discussion see Cowdrey, 'From the Peace of God'.
598 See esp. Henry's Peace of Mainz (1103): *MGH Const.* 1.125–6, no. 74.

By his manifestation of piety, by his almsgiving, by his appointment of and collaboration with more reputable bishops, and by his public sponsorship of internal
peace, Henry gradually built up in Germany a somewhat better image of his kingship.[599] Already, in the early 1080s, it began to assist him in the pursuit of his main
objectives in these years—the settling of his contest with the papacy of Gregory VII
and his reception of imperial coronation at Rome.

As for Gregory himself, despite the death of Rudolf of Swabia he began the year
1081 on a note of confidence and optimism. He held his Lent synod at Rome from 21
to 27 February.[600] It was less well attended than he hoped, and he suspended from
office 'certain bishops' whom he had summoned because neither they or their messengers came. They may have been German bishops whose transit was impeded by
Henry's blockading of their routes through Italy.[601] Nevertheless, there was a quite
numerous assembly. Gregory again excommunicated Henry and all of his supporters
who hardened their hearts to their excommunication. But, as in his letter to the
Germans after the synod of Brixen,[602] his keynote was mercy: those present were
urged to pray for the conversion of those who were astray. Gregory set no limit: 'We
seek the perdition of no man, but we desire the salvation of all men in Christ', he afterwards wrote.[603] As in 1076, so in 1081 the way to reconciliation was to be open.
Gregory did not exclude even Henry.

Nevertheless, Gregory did not cease energetically to promote his cause in Italy and
in Germany. In Italy, despite the setbacks of 1080 his hopes for a military expedition
against Guibert of Ravenna were still alive. A letter to Abbot Desiderius of
Montecassino, written early in February, revealed him to be unwarrantably sanguine
about Henry's supposed misfortunes: he had, he said, no sure tidings from Germany,
but almost everyone who came from it declared that Henry's position had never been
less happy. Gregory asked the abbot to discover Robert Guiscard's intentions with
regard to the Roman church. He alluded to a military expedition after Easter in
which Robert or his son might take part; if this were not possible, perhaps Robert
would send knights 'for the household militia of St Peter' ('in familiari militia sancti
Petri').[604]

Gregory set forth his plans for Germany in a letter of the next month to his loyal
supporters Bishop Altmann of Passau and Abbot William of Hirsau.[605] He thanked
them for reliable information about events in Germany and declared that, despite the
improbability of effective military support from his own party in Germany, he did
not unduly fear Henry's coming to Rome. No doubt remembering their defeat at
Volta in October, his main concern was the morale of Matilda of Tuscany's knights.
For her, a lack of effective South German support would be serious: she would be

---

[599] *Vita HIV* caps. 1,8, pp. 414/7–12, 439–41; although for persistent criticism of Henry's political
and personal behaviour, see *Die Briefe des Abtes Walo*, no. 8 (1085), pp. 80/17–81/18.

[600] *Reg.* 8.20a, record of the synod, pp. 543–4, cf. 9.3, to Bishop Altmann of Passau and Abbot William
of Hirsau, (Mar. 1081), p. 577/4–11.

[601] Bernold, *Chron. a.* 1080, p. 437/1–3.   [602] See above, 3.5.3.   [603] *Reg.* 9.3, p. 577/10–11.
[604] *Reg.* 9.4, (early Feb. 1081), pp. 577–9.   [605] *Reg.* 9.3, pp. 573–7.

compelled to make peace with Henry lest she lose all that she possessed. So Altmann and William should reassure her about what German help she might expect. Should Henry enter Lombardy, Altmann, who since 1076 had been Gregory's papal vicar in South Germany, should cause Duke Welf of Bavaria to swear fealty to St Peter and to provide the service that he had once promised in the presence of the Empress Agnes and Bishop Raynald of Como. Gregory pinned his hope upon Welf; by recruiting his aid and that of others, Altmann was to recover the loyalty of the Italians to St Peter.

Gregory urged that Germans who were faithful to the cause of Christian liberty should not be impelled by their tribulations to undue haste in electing a new king. There must be great care about his suitability; it was more important to make a right choice than a speedy one. Gregory evidently had no name to propose. His urgent concern remained that the Germans should intercede by prayers and alms that their enemies might be converted and return to the bosom of the church. As a king, the church could favour only someone who was as humbly devoted and useful ('utilis') to it as Gregory had hoped that Rudolf would be. Gregory indicated the kind of oath that would be required of him: he must swear fidelity to St Peter and to Gregory as his vicar, obedience to papal admonitions, and vigilance over papal lands and rights. As soon as their meeting was possible, a new king must swear a direct oath of fealty to Gregory that he would be a servant and a soldier of St Peter and of the pope ('miles sancti Petri et illius'). Gregory allowed Altmann latitude to vary the terms of the oath, so long as the essential features of unqualified fealty and obedience were preserved ('non tamen pretermisso integro fidelitatis modo et oboedientiae pro-missione').

During so troubled a time as the present, Gregory urged Altmann to show prud-ence and realism in implementing the church's disciplinary decrees. To ensure the sacraments for faithful Christians, Altmann should temper their rigour; the enforce-ment of full canonical order must be postponed until the time of peace that Gregory prayed would come soon. Yet where mercy was shown it must be under strict control: Gregory reproved the malice of unidentified 'Buggo', perhaps Bishop Burchard of Halberstadt, who had presumed upon special authority to absolve penitent Henricians. In a further letter to Bishop Altmann, Gregory charged him with advis-ing Archbishop Gebhard of Salzburg and other loyal bishops to be zealous in recall-ing those who had strayed from the truth by adhering to Henry and in welcoming fraternally those who might return. He strongly ('maxime') advised an approach to Bishop Benno of Osnabrück, whom he believed to be anxious to return.[606]

Gregory made a further endeavour to propagate his cause in Germany by the long letter, sent on 15 March 1081 and so sixteen days after his Lent synod, to Bishop Hermann of Metz, with the intention that it should circulate widely.[607] It was an exhortation to Hermann, who at this time needed reassurance about how to further the Gregorian cause in Germany,[608] that he should stand in the front rank of those

---

[606] *Reg.* 9.10 (1081), p. 587. Gregory referred to other letters of his to Altmann, which may have in-cluded *Epp. vag.* nos. 58–9, pp. 140–1.

[607] *Reg.* 8.21, pp. 544–63. [608] See Gebhard of Salzburg, *Epistola*, cap. 1, pp. 263–4.

defending the Christian religion with confidence in its eventual victory. Hermann had sought Gregory's confirmation that the apostolic see indeed had power to excommunicate a king like Henry, whom Gregory described as 'one who treated with contempt the law of Christianity, a destroyer of churches and of the empire, and a prime mover and adherent of heretics', and to absolve his subjects of their fealty. He marshalled the testimony of scripture, of the ancient popes and Christian fathers, and of historical precedent in order to demonstrate that this was so, and that papal power was immeasurably superior to kingly:

If the blessed Pope Gregory I, the most mild of doctors, decreed that kings who broke his decrees about just a single inn should be not only deposed but also excommunicated and damned eternally, who will hold us to account for deposing and excommunicating Henry, who was not only a despiser of papal judgements but also, so far as in him lay, a destroyer of his mother the church and a most greedy robber and savage destroyer of the whole kingdom and its churches—unless perchance it be another like himself?

Gregory put forward the pattern of humble and obedient kingship that he would have sought to disseminate if he had been able to come to Germany and settle the matter of the kingdom. Because he had not been able to come, faithful bishops were everywhere to propound it. In Lorraine, Hermann was both to do so and to perform episcopal duties in dioceses where bishops were excommunicated for their adherence to Henry.

Given so many uncertainties about both present and future, it is not surprising that friendly and hostile sources alike should testify to Henry's setting out for Italy in 1081 with an open mind about what his expedition might achieve. An attempt at accommodation with Gregory was not out of the question. Gregory himself placed it upon record that many of Henry's North Italian supporters were urging him to restore Henry to his favour.[609] When Henry passed through Pavia, the widely respected hermit, Bernard of Menthon, came down from his hermitage on the Great St Bernard Pass to warn Henry of the hazards of military action.[610] It might well be prudent for Henry to test Gregory's willingness to treat with him; given Gregory's weakness especially after Countess Matilda's defeat at Volta, it was not beyond possibility that he might be prepared to respond. The statements of the pro-Henrician *Liber de unitate ecclesiae conservanda*, written *c*.1091, that Henry went to Rome with the intention of recovering Gregory's favour and that only if he failed to do so would he seek his replacement by another pope who would love and preach peace,[611] may well contain a basis of truth. The Saxon chronicler Bruno also mentioned Henry's search for a solution which would leave Gregory as pope: according to him, Henry had in mind the possibility of in effect repeating Canossa by bringing Gregory, either by his own feigned penitence or by the use of force, to free him from excommunication. But, for Bruno, Henry's preferred solution was to expel Gregory from the

---

[609] *Reg.* 9.3, p. 574/3–4.
[610] *Alia vita sancti Bernardi Menthonensis*, 1.8, *AA.SS.Boll.* June 2, p. 1084BC.
[611] 2.7, 17, p. 217/45–218/20, 232/22–5.

papacy and to substitute Guibert of Ravenna.[612] The truth is probably that Henry travelled with his options open so that he could adopt whatever course might secure his ultimate aim of imperial coronation—either the installation of Guibert as pope or a rapprochement with Gregory.

Gregory was far from well placed to take up a rigid position. Apart from the religious motives which disposed him never finally to close the ways of mercy and forgiveness, it was increasingly clear that Gregory could hope for no immediate support from Robert Guiscard and the Normans. Robert was caught up in his plans across the Adriatic, which he crossed on 20 May when Henry was on the final lap of his journey to Rome. While protesting loyalty to Gregory, he had declined to help him. Gregory's doubts about the duke were further aroused, probably earlier in May, when Countess Matilda of Tuscany communicated a report that Henry was secretly negotiating with the duke about a marriage between the young prince Conrad and a daughter of the duke. It was also feared that Henry might grant the duke the march of Fermo, thus reviving papal fears of Norman encroachment upon and encirclement of the lands of St Peter. Nothing came of any such negotiations, but for Gregory the rumours about them were alarming.[613]

Henry's expedition to Italy in 1081 was ill prepared and ill conducted. He left Germany with only a small force and was in Verona by Easter (4 April). He marched by way of Milan and Pavia to Ravenna whence, accompanied by Archbishop Guibert, he left for Rome in early May. A letter from Gregory to Abbot Desiderius of Montecassino shows that the pope was well informed about Henry's progress.[614] Henry intended to reach Rome at about Pentecost (23 May); Benzo of Alba's account of the journey suggests that he may have hoped for imperial coronation on that day.[615] Gregory went on to tell Desiderius that both German and Lombard sources had declared Henry's host to be a small one, which he planned to augment at Ravenna and in the march of Fermo. Gregory did not think that he would succeed, or that he could even procure fodder and victuals for such forces as he had. In a sentence which hints at his having received tempting offers of negotiation and compromise, Gregory said that, if he had been prepared to countenance their wickedness, he might have been able to receive from Henry and from Guibert such ample services as no previous pope had enjoyed from the kings of Germany or the archbishops of Ravenna. But he despised equally their threats and their services. He concluded by urging Desiderius to continue steadfast as ever in his help to the papacy.

Gregory was incorrect in supposing that Henry might not be able to reach Rome. But he came poorly prepared and with too few troops. When he arrived, he found the Roman populace hostile and unresponsive.[616] He sent them a manifesto which was

---

[612] cap. 126, p. 394/28–35.

[613] *Reg.* 9.11, to Abbot Desiderius of Montecassino, (May 1081), p. 589/2–14; William of Apulia, 4.171–84, pp. 212–14; Anna Comnena, 1.13.8,10, vol. 1.50–1.

[614] *Reg.* 9.11, pp. 588–9.   [615] Benzo, 6, Praef. p. 656/25–8.

[616] *Epp. HIV* no. 17, p. 78/1–9; *Chron. Cas.* 3.49, p. 429/7–9, 20–2, 29–30; Benzo of Alba, 6, Praef. pp. 656–8; Bonizo of Sutri, *Lib. ad amic.* 9, p. 613/26–35.

brief, hastily drafted, and surprisingly restrained in its tone.[617] It began by referring to the events of 1046 when his father, Henry III, and the Romans had acted with mutual regard and helpfulness. He excused his own earlier lack of communication with them. With an excessive optimism that cannot have deceived the Romans, he claimed that, not by his own power but by God's, he had now annihilated his savage foes and that for the most part he had put in order the shattered components of the empire. He had come to receive from the Romans his rightful hereditary dignity of emperor. He was surprised that, upon his arrival, he was greeted by no embassy from the Romans. He excused his own failure to send envoys by recalling the shameful treatment that Gregory had meted out in Lent 1080 to his representatives— Archbishop Liemar of Bremen (who was not now with him), Bishop Rupert of Bamberg, and the archdeacon Burchard. He concluded with a plea that the Romans should understand his honourable motives in coming to Rome, and he called for a common search for a peaceful resolution of current discords:

> Whereas these subverters of peace and concord allege and noise abroad against us that the purpose of our coming is to diminish the honour of the prince of the apostles and to subvert the public welfare ('res publica') of you all, we say that they are merely telling their old story. We ourselves declare the truth to you in all faithfulness: it is altogether our will and resolve so far as in us lies to visit you in peace. Then we plan to take counsel, first and foremost with all of you and then with our other faithful subjects, so that the long-standing discord between *regnum* and *sacerdotium* may be resolved and all things return to peace and unity in Christ's name.

The manifesto was studiously reticent. It referred to Gregory's alleged crimes only obliquely, and it did not name or vituperate him. There was no mention of Guibert of Ravenna or of the possibility that he might replace Gregory. Henry kept open all the options with which he had set out from Germany, neither condemning Gregory nor commending Guibert. It was his own imperial coronation that he placed at the centre of the picture.

He made no progress towards it. On Pentecost eve, he camped in the Gardens of Nero, but the city was barred against him. Gregory was able to survey his camp from the security of the Castel S. Angelo. Bonizo of Sutri mocked at Henry's discomfiture when the Romans 'met him with lances not candles, armed bands not choirs of clergy, insults not acclamations, catcalls not applause'. At Pentecost itself, when he apparently hoped for coronation, Henry could enjoy only the simulacrum of a royal triumph and crown-wearing in his camp outside the city. Fearing the heat of summer, he left Rome before the end of June.[618]

Henry remained in Italy until, at earliest, December. By travelling and campaigning, he sought to improve his power there, especially at the expense of Countess Matilda of Tuscany.[619] While still at Rome, he issued two diplomas with a view to winning friends in her lands: in one, he responded to the tearful plea of Abbot Peter

---

[617] *Epp. HIV* no. 16, pp. 74–7.   [618] Benzo of Alba and Bonizo of Sutri (as n. 616).
[619] *Vita Anselmi ep. Lucensis*, cap. 20, p. 19; Donizo, 1, lines 200–8, p. 383.

of S. Eugenio in Pilosano, near Siena, and his monks that hunger and nakedness were keeping them from God's service, by confirming their possessions and tithes; in the other, he rewarded the citizens of Lucca by providing lavishly for their physical security and juridical liberty.[620] The Pisans, too, soon afterwards received a generous grant of rights and liberties.[621] From Siena on 10 July, Henry confirmed the possessions of the cathedral chapter at Arezzo in a diploma that spoke eloquently about the benefits of his royal justice.[622] During a visit to Lucca on 19–20 July, he not only favoured the nuns of S. Salvatore and conferred investiture upon the subdeacon Peter who had been elected bishop in place of the exiled Anselm, but also declared Matilda to be deprived of her lands and honours.[623] These measures were the more significant if Matilda had recently given her lands to St Peter in proprietary right by the hand of Pope Gregory.[624] Yet not all of Henry's actions were outright challenges to Gregory. He made the two major grants to the patriarchate of Aquileia of the sees of Trieste and Parenzo.[625] They not only represented an accession of power to his *fidelis* Patriarch Henry, but they also provided for his right to elect, invest with ring and staff, enthrone, and consecrate the bishops. The patriarch was thus to act on the king's behalf (*nostro iure, nostro more, nostra lege*); but the provision that the patriarch should invest may be significant: the diplomas did not directly challenge Gregory's decrees against lay investiture. Henry did not present Gregory with a frontal challenge, but sought still to keep his own options open.

3.5.6 The Propaganda Debate in Germany and the Election of an Anti-King

In Germany, the year 1081 saw a propaganda exchange which was characterized by the moderation of its ideas and by an underlying tone of longing for peace and agreement. On the Gregorian side, Archbishop Gebhard of Salzburg replied at length to Bishop Hermann of Metz's requests for material with which to confront the Henricians.[626] His first topic was the long-established Christian obligation not to hold communion with the excommunicated; he declared that breaches of this prohibition were the source of the current dissention and sedition in Germany. There could be no relaxation of this duty: even if sentences which had been imposed seemed precipitate or excessively severe, they must be upheld until dissolved by competent authority. Because of his insistence upon due order and deference to authority, Gebhard roundly condemned the German bishops' headstrong opposition to Gregory in 1080, especially as manifested in the assemblies at Mainz and Brixen. At Brixen, Gregory was not given even the semblance of a fair trial, and Gebhard arraigned Guibert of Ravenna for accepting designation to be the future pope. Gebhard also gave much discussion to oaths, particularly when they had been sworn unjustly or when they led to intolerable danger, and to the conditions under which

---

[620] *MGH DDHIV* nos. 333–4, dated 3 and 23 June 1081.
[621] *MGH DDHIV* no. 336.   [622] *MGH DDHIV* no. 335.
[623] *MGH DDHIV* nos. 337, of 379, 385; Rangerius of Lucca, *Vita*, 5.4805–10, p. 1257.
[624] *MGH Const.* 1.653–5, no. 444.
[625] *MGH DDHIV* nos. 338–9, both dated 20 July 1081.   [626] Gebhard of Salzburg, *Epistola*.

they ceased to be binding. He concentrated upon oaths taken by bishops: if their
oaths to the king and to God were in conflict, the latter must prevail. 'We have sworn
nothing,' Gebhard declared, 'except what we can rightly swear saving our order.' As
for Gregory, if as was alleged he had been excessively severe upon Henry IV and the
bishops of his party, the bishops should have sought redress by negotiation, not by
devastation and civil war. Gebhard also insisted that, at Worms in January 1076, the
bishops had been the authors of their own misfortune. Although right up to St
Andrewstide (30 November) 1075 concord had prevailed between the *regnum* and
the *summum sacerdotium*, at Worms the bishops had suddenly and unwarrantedly
turned upon the pope:

When, at the beginning of this affair, they first assembled at Worms where the whole calamity
from which we are suffering had its beginning, the lord pope had as yet issued no sentence of
excommunication or anathema against them. Without his knowledge and when he was thinking of no such thing, in as it were the first fruits of discord they renounced his authority with
proud and sullen boldness. This was the beginning of sorrows; this was the first leaven that
corrupted the whole lump of the church.[627]

If Gebhard thus wrote with studied moderation and sadness from the Gregorian
side, between October 1080 and August 1081 a temperate expression of opinion also
came from the side of the German bishops who had supported Henry since Gregory's
renewed sentence against him in 1080. It was written by Wenric, *scholasticus* of Trier,
to Gregory himself in the name of Bishop Thierry of Verdun.[628] Thierry had been
compelled to submit to Gregory by his own clergy, and he began by commiserating
with Gregory in his afflictions, by applauding his character and abilities from childhood until he ascended the papal throne and so ignoring the strictures of the synod
of Brixen to which Thierry could assert that he had not subscribed, and by acknowledging the justice and vigour of his actions as pope. He rounded off his epistle amicably: 'May matters always go well with you, the lord and truly most blessed pope.'

Nevertheless, while not directly associating himself with them, he throughout referred to the many and grave charges that others made against Gregory. The purpose
of his letter, which seems to have been indeed composed for Gregory's own eyes, was
to elicit his answer to them.[629] (In 1076, Gregory had been under similar pressure to
justify his actions against Henry to the Germans.[630]) Wenric placed emphasis upon
Gregory's exorbitant actions, as when he stirred up laymen against incontinent
clerks, and upon his reputation for countenancing and sponsoring physical violence,
not least upon the part of kings. Wenric noted the horror felt at Gregory's having
approved in 1074 the violence of the Patarene leader Erlembald, who trampled
underfoot the chrism that the Lombard bishops had consecrated.[631]

Wenric was severe in the criticism that he recorded of Gregory's actions, culminating at his Lent synod of 1080, in deposing Henry IV and in 'enthroning' Rudolf of

---

[627] cap. 33, pp. 278–9.   [628] Wenric of Trier. For Wenric's career, see Francke's introd., pp. 280–4.
[629] See Sigebert of Gembloux, *Catalogus*, cap. 160, p. 90.   [630] See above, 3.3.3.
[631] For the incident of the chrism, see Arnulf of Milan, 4.6, p. 210.

Swabia in his place. For Wenric, Henry was 'dominus meus rex'. It was unheard-of for a pope so lightly to divide kingdoms and to dispose of kings as though they were mere bailiffs. Wenric sharply questioned the character and suitability of Rudolf, whom he deemed to have been unworthy of the crown. Though Wenric did not directly refute Gebhard of Salzburg and, indeed, may not have known about his epistle to Hermann of Metz, he vigorously contradicted two of Gebhard's main contentions: he argued that, when imposed for the wrong reasons, sentences of excommunication were of no effect; and that Gregory had no right to absolve Henry's subjects from their oaths.

As regards issues arising from free elections, Wenric was more measured. He raised two such issues: whether ecclesiastical benefices should be free from secular law, and whether bishops should be admitted to their sees by the hand of the prince. With Gregory's aims he expressed a measure of sympathy, but he censured his methods as being ill-timed, violent, and conducive to public contention. Gregory had acted inconsistently: tolerant of Rudolf's excesses, he had been severe upon Henry's. Moreover, he had condemned bishops for nothing more than their loyalty to Henry. The history of the Maccabees, the letters of Pope Gregory the Great, and the writings of Isidore of Seville provided plenty of examples of priestly tolerance of spiritual appointments by lay rulers. Such ancient precedents served to emphasize the precipitateness of Gregory's measures against Henry.

Gebhard's and Wenric's writings indicate by their restraint an underlying desire on the part of many German churchmen on both sides for a relaxation of conflict, both in ideas and in political actuality. The debate centred, not upon high matters of *sacerdotium* and *regnum*, but upon such specific issues as the force of excommunication when unwarrantably imposed and upon whether or not subjects could be released from their oaths to the king. The terms of the German debate go far towards explaining Henry's concern to leave open the possibility of a rapprochement with Gregory whether by constraint or by agreement and his reticence about Gregory's supersession by Guibert of Ravenna. They also help to account for the slow progress that the Saxons and their Swabian allies made towards the election of a new anti-king in replacement of Rudolf of Swabia.

For the process of replacement was slow. Only after much skirmishing in Bavaria and East Franconia did a somewhat sparsely attended assembly of Saxons and Swabians at Ochsenfurt, near Bamberg, in early August 1081 elect Hermann of Salm. Of the family of the counts of Luxemburg and thus one of the leading dynasties of the German kingdom, Hermann like Rudolf could probably claim the descent from King Henry I (919–36) which was a touchstone of royal candidature. However, the procedure by which he was elected is not precisely known. The limitations of his power were soon manifest when, after some indecisive but destructive fighting, he withdrew to Saxony. There, on St Stephen's Day (26 December) 1081 at Goslar, Archbishop Siegfried of Mainz anointed him king.[632] In a show of support for

---

[632] Bruno, caps. 130–1, pp. 402–5; Bernold, *Chron. aa.*1081–2, p. 437. For Hermann's family, see Wolf, 'Königskandidatur', esp. pp. 44–50, 104–8.

Gregory, he eventually announced his intention to embark on an Italian expedition; in autumn 1081, he travelled from Saxony to Swabia, leaving Otto of Nordheim in charge of Saxony.[633] But neither Gregory's letters nor any other source provides evidence that Gregory was in any way involved in Hermann's election, nor can Gregory's concern with his plans and movements thereafter be documented. There is no evidence as to whether Gregory's support for Hermann's election was either sought or given.

3.5.7 Henry IV's Second Expedition to Italy

In 1082, Henry made a second expedition to Rome; but he did so earlier in the year than in 1081 and with better preparation. He arrived before the end of February with a larger army, and the manifesto that he sent before him to the Romans was longer and better thought-out.[634] He addressed his existing supporters and invited new ones: 'To all the Roman cardinals, clerks, and laity whether greater or lesser, as well those who have for long been faithful to him as those who would become so.' Its opening paragraph recalled Rome's ancient imperial eminence by appealing to *Romana auctoritas*—the prestige of Rome, which should always prevail by righteousness ('iustitia'); everywhere, its failures or its merits meant for its subjects either a hindrance or a help to right living. One obstacle alone impeded Rome's universal mission, and it was less the fault of the Romans than of a single man—the reference to Gregory was transparent—who should be a pattern for all but who had become an offence and a hindrance to all who honoured Rome's supremacy ('principatus') in matters of the catholic faith.

The manifesto turned to Henry's expedition of 1081 and to his expectation that, even though he came with few knights, he would find the Romans all faithful to him. Those whom he expected to be his friends he had discovered to be his enemies, when he came to them in the interest of simple righteousness ('pro mera iustitia') to make peace between *regnum* and *sacerdotium* by their counsel and according to apostolic authority. Henry was sure that they would have shown themselves the unfailing friends of righteousness that they truly were, had it not been for the machinations of 'this lord Hildebrand' ('illius dompni Hildebrandi'). When this man of violence had led the whole world into bloodshed and had armed brother against brother, was it surprising that he had also subverted his own city?

The church had often called upon Hildebrand to clear himself of the crimes alleged against him and to free it from offence ('scandalum').[635] But he had refused. Indeed, he had denied Henry's own envoys a hearing before himself and before the Roman clergy and people. Henry urged the Romans to do all in their power to make Hildebrand stand to justice for his crimes, whether at Rome or elsewhere; Henry

---

[633] Bernold, *Chron. a.* 1082, p. 437/35–7. [634] *Epp. HIV* no. 17, pp. 76–83.

[635] There may have been a reference here to the discussions of 1076 at Tribur–Oppenheim: see above, 3.3.4. The repeated use in this manifesto of the word *scandalum*, with its parallel in the Oppenheim *Promissio* in its longer form, suggests that the final clause of the *Promissio* may have been added in 1082 by Henry's propagandists in order to adapt the document for current use.

would guarantee him security and a fair trial. In effect, Henry now treated Gregory as Gregory had officially treated him during the three years after Canossa—as a ruler whose authority was in suspense until final sentence could be passed upon him. It was with the Romans that the final judgement must rest:

Behold! If God wills, we shall come to Rome at the time appointed. If Hildebrand pleases, let the matter be settled there; if he would rather come and meet us with our envoys, we agree to this, too. You yourselves also—as many of you as so wish—come, hear, judge! If he can and should be pope, we shall obey him; but if not, according to your sentence and ours let provision be made for someone else who would fit the church's needs.

The manifesto ended by dwelling upon the respective rights and duties of king and pope, which it was for the Romans to uphold. Hildebrand had upset the divine ordinance that, if the priest was to be protected, the king was to be obeyed; and God had appointed not one sword but two! (Luke 22: 38). God had made this clear in recent events: when Hildebrand had sought to depose Henry whom God had set up and maintained from childhood as king, God preserved him from Hildebrand and his partisans. For Henry was still reigning, although the Lord had destroyed his vassal Rudolf whom (as Henry claimed with exaggeration) Hildebrand had set up as king against Henry.

Having registered this point, Henry came to the crux of the manifesto. He reminded the Romans of their fidelity to his grandfather and father, the Emperors Conrad II and Henry III, and to himself until Hildebrand had subverted it. Let the Romans now not deny him the imperial office of his forebears, the stewardship of which his father had entrusted to the Romans—or let them explain their denial! For Henry had come prepared to fulfil all righteousness (cf. Matt. 3: 15) with the Romans, to yield all honour to St Peter, and to reward all who deserved reward. His final appeal to the Romans was that they should dissociate themselves from Hildebrand's oppression of the church and that they should cease to fight with him against righteousness:

No longer oppress the church for Hildebrand's sake, and no longer fight with him against righteousness! Let there be debate in the sight of the church: if it is right that you should have him as pope, defend him as a pope; do not defend him as a thief seeking places to hide.... It is wrong that he who calls himself 'servant of the servants of God' should by his power persecute God's servants.

The manifesto called upon Gregory now to show the humility that he had himself demanded of Henry at Canossa:

Let him not be ashamed to humble himself by taking away the universal stumbling-block ('scandalum') which he has set to all the faithful, through whose universal obedience he should be exalted.... Behold! small and great complain of the stumbling-block ('scandalum') that he has set, and beg for it to be taken away from them. Let him come with boldness. If his conscience be clean, he will indeed have glory.... We are ready to do nothing against you but everything with you, if only we may find you not unmindful of our own good deeds. Finally, we ask for nothing except for there to be righteousness in the place where, above all, righteousness should properly be found. We hope to find it among you; having found it, we are determined by God's mercy to reward it.

Events added to the urgency of Henry's pleas. On 21 February, Robert Guiscard captured Durazzo; he thereupon decided to attend to his interests in Italy. In April, he landed at Otranto and made for Rome; but, upon hearing that Henry had left for the north of Italy, he returned to Apulia. Of greater immediate impact than Robert Guiscard's return was the eastern emperor Alexius Comnenus's largesse to Henry IV that it prompted, as a means of undermining their common Norman enemy. Alexius sent Henry a first instalment of the gold and silks that he promised, together with letters of encouragement.[636] Henry was emboldened in his campaign to coerce Gregory.

Yet neither by his manifesto nor by his subsequent military activity does he seem to have made much impression upon the Romans. Throughout Lent, he laid siege to a Rome where the citizens showed no dispositon to receive him; he had to be content with ravaging the surrounding country. According to sources sympathetic to Gregory, when Henry's forces sought to create a diversion by kindling a fire in St Peter's basilica and distracting the Roman garrison, Gregory himself miraculously frustrated their stratagem by making the sign of the cross and thus extinguishing the fire. Henry had some minor successes in expeditions up the Tiber and especially near the imperial abbey of Farfa. His forces took prisoner Gregory's strong supporter, Bishop Bonizo of Sutri. He spent some time at Albano before returning to Rome after Easter. But, as in the previous year, he could not contemplate remaining there with an army during the malarious summer heat. With no prospect of a quick success, he withdrew early in the summer to North Italy. He left Guibert of Ravenna at Tivoli, from where he continued to harass the Romans.[637]

During the spring of 1082, Henry caused Gregory some damage. By arriving at Rome when he did, he made impossible the holding of a Lent synod. Moreover, his expedition placed Gregory under a financial strain that created difficulties within his own Roman circle. Early in May, a *conventus* of senior Roman clergy who included the cardinal-bishops of Porto, Tusculum, Palestrina, and Segni, debated whether church property might be mortgaged in order to raise money to resist Guibert in his attempts to seize the Roman see. They unanimously agreed that, in the light of ancient authorities and of the examples of holy men, the goods of the church should never be expended for secular purposes (*in militia seculari*); they should be reserved for the poor, for divine service, and for redeeming captives.[638] This debate should not be understood as evidence for serious opposition to Gregory as pope, for some who

---

[636] Anna Comnena, 3.10, 5.3.1–2, vol. 1.132–6, 2.13–14; Benzo of Alba, 6.4, p. 664; *Vita HIV* cap. 1, pp, 412/30–413/5 (where Alexius's gifts included a magnificent gold altar-piece for the cathedral of Speyer); Dölger, *Regesten*, nos. 1077, 1080.

[637] Bonizo of Sutri, 9, p. 613/35–40; Bernold, *Chron. a.* 1082, p. 437/22–35.

[638] For the *conventus*, see Zafarana, 'Sul "conventus" '. Gregory had himself insisted upon the traditional rule in dealing with other bishops: *Reg.* 5.20, to Bishop Rainer of Orleans, 24 Apr. 1078, p. 383/27–34.

took part, for example Bishop Bruno of Segni and the Cardinal-priest Bonussenior of S. Maria in Trastevere, remained unswervingly loyal to him until his death. But two conclusions may be suggested. First, the criticism at Rome of Gregory's use of church resources to finance warfare indicates that Henry's propaganda against Gregory's military dealings was well directed and found an echo in the city. Second, the record of the *conventus* made no mention of Gregory's resistance to Henry but only to Guibert of Ravenna, who, rather than Henry, had become the focal point of animosity among Gregory's supporters.[639] This may represent another propaganda success on Henry's part. His diversion of animosity from himself to the dispensable Guibert left open the possibility of his gaining Roman support for himself and so of achieving his aim of imperial coronation. This might be either by way of a reconciliation with Gregory or by the substitution of Guibert. Henry was astute in keeping his options open, for throughout 1082, so far as can be discerned, the Romans remained solidly loyal to Gregory. Neither Henry's arguments in his manifesto, nor his military activities, nor his command of Byzantine gold, seems to have seriously shaken their loyalty at this time.

3.5.8 Gregory VII and Henry IV at Rome in 1083

By the early months of 1083, the situation in Germany had become propitious for Henry to stay in Italy for a prolonged period in order to settle the issue of the papacy and to seek imperial coronation. The defeat of Margrave Liutpold II of Austria at the battle of Mailberg on 12 May 1082 by Duke Wratislav of Bohemia was a severe setback to the Gregorians of south-east Germany and especially to Gregory's legate there, Bishop Altmann of Passau.[640] Any hope that the new anti-king Hermann of Salm might cross the Alps to help Gregory was further eroded when the death on 11 January 1083 of Otto of Nordheim compelled him to return to Saxony.

In January, Gregory was in Benevento, perhaps in the hope of prevailing upon Robert Guiscard to bring him military support.[641] In 1083, Guiscard sent no such help; but he provided money, and in June he compelled Prince Jordan of Capua to abandon his entente with Henry and to make peace with himself.[642] Gregory no doubt took encouragement, for he always stood to gain from harmony between the Norman princes. On the other hand, early in 1083 there is the first clear evidence of a group of Romans abandoning Gregory and making contact with Henry.[643] Henry was encouraged to persist in his dual approach to Gregory—by way of negotiation as well as of military assault. In the winter of 1082–3, he brought to Italy Bishop Benno of Osnabrück, who spent a year and a quarter in sporadic negotiations with Gregory and others on Henry's behalf in an attempt (as Benno's biographer said) to create peace and concord between king and pope.[644]

---

[639] See Bonizo of Sutri, *Lib. ad amic.* 9, pp. 613–14; also the annotation to Donizo, p. 385 n. 14.
[640] *Vita Altmanni*, cap. 25, p. 236; Cosmas of Prague, 2.35, pp. 131–3.
[641] *QF* no. +210, which may be based upon a lost, genuine privilege.
[642] William of Apulia, 4.528–35, 5.106–20, pp. 232–3, 242–3.
[643] Lupus Protospatarius, *a.* 1083, p. 61.   [644] *Vita Bennonis II*, cap. 22, pp. 30/27–31/5.

In the spring, Henry also resumed his military option. As before, he concentrated his forces upon the Leonine city, but in addition he campaigned without success in the vicinity of the basilica of St Paul's-without-the-Walls. On Gregory's own admission, it was Roman negligence rather than German valour that, on 3 June, enabled Henry to occupy the Leonine city and to gain control of St Peter's. He established himself near St Peter's in the palace of the Caesars.[645]

Two diplomas testify to the confidence that Henry now felt.[646] The first, for the abbot of Farfa which was dedicated to the Virgin Mary, renewed his own devotion to her that had been manifest in his work at Speyer. With especial effect in a diploma issued in the shadow of St Peter's basilica, it lauded her as the highest of all the saints and, under Christ, the means of their sanctification. The second, for Archbishop Liemar of Bremen who was with Henry, named Henry as the son of Henry III, 'the second emperor'. Henry claimed to pursue a pattern of integrity and righteousness that his imperial forebears had handed down to him ('exemplum iusticie et honestatis a patribus nostris dive memorie augustis accipientes') by duly rewarding their faithful and righteous servants. Such a man was Liemar, whose long service in the Saxon wars and in his Italian campaigns he rehearsed, as well as referring to Liemar's service as a diplomat at Rome 'against Hildebrand, the subverter of the world' ('contra Hildebrandum pertubatorem orbis'). Dated, with brash hyperbole, 'at Rome after the capture of the city', it flaunted Henry's confidence in total victory. This confidence will not have been diminished by the arrival soon afterwards of further gifts, precious objects, and silks, which Alexius Comnenus sent to his 'most noble and most Christian brother', Henry.[647]

Gregory's reaction to Henry's military success is probably to be seen in an undated letter, preserved only in his Register; it may, therefore, not have circulated widely.[648] Gregory addressed it to all clergy and laity not bound by excommunication. Perhaps responding to Henry's call for 'debate in the sight of the church', he announced an earnest desire to hold a *generalis synodus* in a safe and secure place to which, whether friends or enemies, they might come from all the world. In the circumstances, he can scarcely have intended a gathering at Rome, which was neither safe nor secure. In effect, he was harking back to his plans of the late 1070s for a general assembly in Germany; but again, in 1083, neither Germany nor North Italy would have been feasible as a meeting-place. Perhaps he had in mind Montecassino: with the Norman princes now reconciled, there was hope for its security; Gregory may have remembered the concourse there in 1071 for the dedication of the new basilica.[649] Its purpose would be to publish where righteousness lay in the matter of the German kingship and to free Gregory from the charges that were laid against him:

---

[645] *Reg.* 9.35*a*, p. 628/4–15; poem *Venite cuncti populi*, in *MGH L. de L.* 1.433–4 (for its date, see Meyer von Knonau, *Jahrbücher*, 3.478 n. 13); *Vita HIV* cap. 6, pp. 430–3; Bernold, *Chron. a.* 1083, pp. 437/44–438/2. For the concentration of blame upon a bishop rather than upon a lay ruler, cf. Gregory's dealings at the same time in the county of Flanders: below, 5.2.2.

[646] *MGH DDHIV*, nos. 350–1.

[647] Anna Comnena, 3.10.2–5, vol. 1.133–6; Frutolf, *a.* 1083, p. 96/17–18.

[648] *Reg.* 9.29, pp. 612–13.

[649] See above, 2.2.5.

We intend to examine and, having unmasked by searching consideration, to drag before the face of the world from the secret caverns of his own equivocations, the man, whoever he is, who is the fount and source ('causa et auctor') of such great evils as for a long time past have been gathering and raging against the Christian religion. Moreover, his godlessness and unheard-of boldness have for long obstructed and frustrated the establishment of divine peace and true concord between the papal and royal authorities. In this synod, we wish with God's help to establish and confirm this peace as Christian zeal requires and demands. Accordingly, in this synod we intend by God's power, to the honour of St Peter, and according to the decrees of the holy fathers, to do what is right. Laying bare the wickedness of sinful men, we intend clearly to demonstrate the innocence of the apostolic see of the charges that are laid against it, concerning which some even of our own brethren are secretly murmuring.

The last phrase may be in part an allusion to the *conventus* of 1082. But Gregory's main concern was to meet the challenge of Henry's manifesto to the Romans, and perhaps also of an expanded and recirculated version of the Oppenheim *Promissio*. He sought to exculpate the apostolic see from the *scandalum* that it was alleged to have set to the church and to the world. He made only one condition: in accordance with the canonical principle of the *exceptio spolii*, by which no bishop who had been despoiled of his goods or expelled *vi et terrore* from his see should be accused, summoned, judged, or condemned until his goods were restored and he enjoyed peace,[650] Gregory required that, before all else at the synod, the goods of the Roman church of which it had been despoiled should, if it were judged to be right, be restored. Gregory probably had principally in mind the Leonine city and St Peter's.[651]

His letter continued with a paragraph of self-exculpation for his actions regarding Germany since Rudolf of Swabia's election as king. It reads like a reply to Henry's claim in the manifesto that God had protected him against Hildebrand's machinations and so made clear his favour: 'for', the manifesto had claimed, 'however unwilling he [Hildebrand] may be, we [Henry] still reign; whereas the Lord destroyed that knight of ours and perjurer [Rudolf], whom he [Hildebrand] set up as king over us.'[652] Gregory rejoined that Rudolf was made king by the Germans themselves, with no command or advice from him. He referred to an otherwise unknown synodal decree of his during the 1070s which provided that, unless the archbishops and bishops who had elected Rudolf at Forchheim could justify their action, they should be deposed from their sees and Rudolf from the kingship. As for who upset this ruling, Gregory declared that many of his hearers well knew the answer and that he himself could never forget. For if only Henry the so-called king—Gregory at last came out with his name—and his party had honoured their promised obedience to Gregory and to St Peter, Gregory confidently asserted that all the evils—the murders, perjuries, sacrileges, acts of simony, betrayals—would never have occurred. Gregory thus turned back on Henry and his party the acts of violence for

---

[650] For the text in the Pseudo-Isidorian Decrees, see *Isidori Praefatio*, cap. 6, in Hinschius, pp. 18–19; for fuller discussion, Cowdrey, 'The Enigma', esp. pp. 143–5, 148.

[651] If so, the *terminus a quo* for Gregory's letter is probably the capture of the Leonine city.

[652] *Epp. HIV* no. 17, p. 80/10–15.

which they alleged him to be answerable. Gregory concluded with an impassioned plea for all lovers of peace and concord who heard his letter that they would make possible the synod for which he was calling.

Henry's two diplomas and Gregory's call for a general synod represent the high-water mark of their public reactions to the fall of the Leonine city to Henry in June 1083. The summer was occupied by diplomacy and negotiation of a local kind. As in earlier years, Henry feared the summer heat at Rome and its attendant fevers. He built a small fortification on the Palatiolus, a hill to the east of St Peter's which looked across the Tiber to the Castel S. Angelo; at the end of June, he left Rome, leaving only a small garrison on the Palatiolus. On the eve of his departure, the vigil of St Peter (28 June), he accorded Archbishop Guibert of Ravenna a gesture of recognition, perhaps by allowing him to preside at mass in St Peter's.[653] But Guibert performed no papal functions: that must wait until he had been duly acclaimed by the Romans.

Henry proceeded by way of intrigue. After leaving Rome, he was able without the knowledge of Gregory or his close associates to reach an understanding with a small group within the papal service. Those concerned made a sworn agreement ('sacramentum') that, if Henry returned to Rome within a time not specified in the agreement but which the chronicler Bernold suggests to have been early in Advent (that is, after 3 December), they would compel Gregory, if he were alive and in Rome, to give Henry imperial coronation. If he were dead, or if he would not return to Rome and crown Henry within the time stipulated, they would elect a pope—no name was given, according to the canons. They would ensure that the new pope crowned Henry, and also that the Romans did fealty to him.[654] Less clandestine negotiations occurred, as well. Apart from whatever part Bishop Benno of Osnabrück may have continued to play, Abbot Hugh of Cluny attempted, probably at the end of June when Henry left Rome, to mediate between Gregory, who was in the city, and Henry, who left it for Sutri to avoid losing face if the abbot visited Gregory before visiting him. The surviving anecdote about Hugh's attempt suggests that Gregory was in a resolute mood: Hugh justified his insistence upon first meeting Gregory on the grounds that, when his motive was to create peace, the apostles would more readily forgive him for placing them second on his visiting list than would so severe a pontiff as Gregory! So he first visited Gregory, no doubt at the Lateran, and not Henry.[655]

Those who surrounded Gregory were more minded than he to seek a compromise. Bernold wrote of the Romans' war-weariness and of their openness to receive Henry's money and promises. With Prince Gisulf of Salerno as a conspicuous exception, many of them agreed with Henry that Gregory should convene a November synod at Rome which would seek to settle the matter of the kingship ('de causa regni'). Henry promised security to those coming and going, and Gregory sent

---

[653] Bernold, *Chron. a.* 1083, p. 438/2–8; Frutolf, *a.* 1083, p. 96/8–16.

[654] For the text of the *sacramentum*, see Cowdrey, *The Age of Abbot Desiderius*, p. 248/40–9.

[655] For Hugh's visit to Rome, see Reynald of Vézelay, *Vita s. Hugonis*, 4.26, cols. 903–4; Cowdrey, 'Two Studies', p. 29 n. 42.

letters to faithful bishops and abbots everywhere in which he summoned them to it.[656] Gregory evidently abandoned whatever plans he may have had for a general synod in a safe and secure place away from Rome.

Events at Rome gave him some encouragement. At a juncture in the summer's negotiations that cannot be determined, the garrison that Henry had left on the Palatiolus was wiped out by fever. A particularly serious casualty was its commander, Ulrich of Godesheim, who had for long been one of Henry's most trusted counsellors; Bernold described him as 'auctor huius scismaticae conspirationis et incentor'. The Romans razed Henry's fortification to the ground. Henry's reaction was to send Guibert back to Ravenna. He seems to have hoped that, since Guibert had found so little favour with the Romans, negotiations at Rome would now be easier with him out of the way.[657]

Prompted by the Romans and perhaps encouraged by the spectacle of a more amenable Henry, Gregory circulated widely his summons to a November synod at Rome.[658] Addressed to the archbishops, bishops, and abbots in France and Germany who remained faithful to the Roman church but not now to the laity as well, it breathed a different spirit from his earlier summons to a *generalis synodus*. The bitterly anti-Henrician tone was absent. Gregory was specific about place and time. He reproved his audience for tardiness in helping the Roman church. He vindicated his own integrity, but in broad terms; he asserted that both his own conscience and the scrutiny of religious men acquitted him of having failed to satisfy the demands of righteousness. The November synod would bring to a fitting conclusion the disputes and discord that had for long been rife between the apostolic see and the kingdom. Gregory confirmed that negotiations between his envoys and Henry 'the so-called king' had established sworn guarantees of safe conduct for all who attended the synod.

Before it was due to assemble, Henry returned to the vicinity of Rome. According to the sources sympathetic to Gregory that alone provide evidence,[659] Henry treacherously did all in his power to keep Gregory's supporters away. On or about 11 November, he captured and plundered the envoys of the German princes, thus committing an act of perjury that attracted hostile comment at Rome. Among others whom he imprisoned or maltreated was Cardinal-bishop Odo of Ostia whom Gregory had sent to talk to him; this is further evidence for continuing negotiations between Gregory and Henry. Henry was careful to prevent access to Rome for the staunch Gregorians Archbishop Hugh of Lyons, Bishop Anselm II of Lucca, and Bishop Raynald of Como. Nevertheless, the secret *sacramentum* of the Romans was still in force; Henry was, therefore, careful at least to seem willing to receive the imperial crown from Gregory and so to maintain a propaganda advantage among the Romans themselves.[660]

---

[656] Bernold, *Chron. a.* 1083, p. 438/8–15; Bernold's citation of the address of the letter as being to bishops and monks indicates that he referred to *Epp. vag.* no. 51, p. 122/6–7.

[657] Bernold, *Chron. a.* 1083, p. 434/25–29.   [658] *Epp. vag.* no. 51, pp. 122–5.

[659] *Reg.* 9.35a, pp. 617–8; Bernold, *Chron. a.* 1083, p. 438/21–31.

[660] Bonizo of Sutri, *Lib. ad amic.* 9, p. 614/2–8.

Not surprisingly, when the synod assembled in the Lateran on 20 November, it was sparsely attended. According to the meagre record in Gregory's Register, those present were mainly South Italians, with a few Frenchmen; the effect of Henry's tyranny had been to reduce the morale of the Roman citizens, and especially of the city officers, to a low ebb. The synod lasted for only three days, but it ended with a powerful and moving address by Gregory concerning the Christian faith and the fortitude which the times demanded. According to Bernold, Gregory was scarcely restrained at the synod from again excommunicating Henry by name; he excommunicated all who had in any way hindered those coming to Rome, whether upon pilgrimage or to visit the pope, thus implicitly including Henry. After the synod, Gregory seems to have addressed a letter widely to all the faithful, setting forth the afflictions of the Roman church and calling for sympathy and effective support.[661]

Soon after the synod ended, the time expired within which, according to the Romans' secret *sacramentum*, they would either compel Gregory to crown Henry or else elect another to be pope. The secret had been well kept, but those who knew of it at last disclosed it to Gregory and sought to play down its terms: they had undertaken, not that Gregory should solemnly anoint Henry but that he should merely give him a crown. Gregory absolved the participants from their oath; but Bernold, who is the principal source for these events, referred to further negotiations between the Romans and Henry of which it is hard to make sense: the Romans seem to have promised the king that, in line with their new construction of the *sacramentum*, he should either receive the imperial crown rightfully ('cum iustitia'), that is by some kind of agreement with Gregory, or else he should be content with a crown that Gregory would hand down from the Castel S. Angelo by means of a rod. Either way, they no doubt hoped to be free of their undertaking to Henry and to avoid further fighting in the city. When Henry tried to hold them to their oath, they resisted to the point of offering to demonstrate by judicial combat that they were no longer bound by it; there was some rallying of Roman support for Gregory. Henry, for his part, spent the winter near Rome, using both threats and promises to recruit strength for his cause.[662] His propaganda is illustrated by the tract known as the *Iudicium de regno et sacerdotio*, according to which an ordeal by water staged on 3 December by a group of Gregory's well-wishers including Abbot Desiderius of Montecassino repeatedly vindicated Henry.[663] A text of the Romans' *sacramentum* was appended to it.

The year 1083 ended with a Rome uncertain and fluctuating in its loyalties. Morale was low, while Gregory and Henry remained in confrontation with each of them having little idea of what steps he should take. If Frutolf's statement that Henry kept Christmas at St Peter's is correct, he must have achieved some military success in the Leonine city.[664] Once again, he confronted the Gregorian party across the Tiber,

---

[661] Bernold, *a.* 1083, p. 438/31–4; *Epp. vag.* no. 55, pp. 134–73; see also the longer version in *QF* no. 58, pp. 38–9, which probably dates from this time rather than 1074–5 as suggested by Santifaller.
[662] Bernold, *a.* 1083, p. 438/34–49.
[663] Cowdrey, *The Age of Abbot Desiderius*, pp. 247/1–248/39.
[664] Frutolf, *a.* 1084, pp. 96/30–98/2.

where the Castel S. Angelo remained a Gregorian bastion. Further money from Alexius Comnenus, which was intended for warfare against Robert Guiscard, became at Henry's disposal to recruit support among the Roman citizens.[665] But it was not only from Constantinople that Henry secured money. At the cost of incurring much odium, he extracted further contributions from churches and towns in Germany upon which he could bring pressure.[666] He needed either to bring matters at Rome to a speedy conclusion and so justify his exactions, or else to return to Germany quickly and prevent the growth of opposition.

3.5.9 Henry IV's Capture of Rome and the Setting up of the Anti-Pope Clement III

According to Bernold, during the winter of 1083–4 Henry finally abandoned hope of negotiating with Gregory about his imperial coronation so long as Gregory would not agree to the necessary canonical reconciliation and readmission to communion upon acceptable terms. He awaited Guibert of Ravenna's return to Rome so that he might replace Gregory as pope and then crown Henry. Some time after the end of January, Guibert left Ravenna.[667]

In February, Henry marched southwards through the Campania towards Apulia. Robert Guiscard was too cunning to offer battle, and Henry was able to traverse a large area and thus make a gesture of support for Alexius Comnenus in return for his financial subventions. It was a warning to Robert Guiscard that Henry would be dangerous if he permanently established himself in Rome, and that the Normans could not allow Gregory's cause to be defeated. For Henry's own morale, the march did suprisingly little. After his imperial coronation, Henry sent a remarkable account of events to Bishop Thierry of Verdun, who had emerged as one of his leading vicegerents in Germany.[668] Henry wrote of his despair that he would successfully conclude what he called his Roman business ('Romanum negotium') by entering the city; he had pondered an immediate return to Germany. In the light of Bernold's comments about his intentions, the dilemma that he felt seems clear: given Gregory's display of intransigence at his November synod, Henry could expect coronation by him, if at all, only upon terms that were unacceptably hard; in order to be crowned by a Guibert installed as anti-pope, he must first capture and subdue a Rome that seemed still to be largely loyal to Gregory. Henry told Bishop Thierry that he changed his mind about returning to Germany only when an embassy of Romans invited him to enter the city, promising him their total obedience.

The embassy was able to deliver the critical support within the city that it promised; the sums of money that Henry had received from Byzantium and from Germany had evidently done their work. Gregory's position had seriously deteriorated. Bernold disclosed that in due course he found it necessary to take forty hostages

---

[665] Bernold, *Chron. a.* 1084, p. 440/5–11; Dölger, *Regesten*, no. 1114.
[666] *Ann. Ratisbon. maior. frag. a.* 1084, pp. 87–8.
[667] Bernold, *Chron. a.* 1084, p. 439/34–7.   [668] *Epp. HIV* no. 18, pp. 82–5.

from Roman nobles who still held to him.[669] A crippling blow came in the spring, when some twelve or thirteen cardinals and many of the Roman aristocracy and local officials defected to Henry. They included Bishop John II of Porto who had been among Gregory's closest advisers, Peter the papal chancellor, and Theodinus the Roman archdeacon. Worse was to follow, when seventeen of the twenty-eight cardinal-priests eventually attached themselves to the anti-pope, and three of the seven Roman deacons.[670] Gregory is said to have taken the precaution of sending the other cardinal-bishops away from Rome to the Campania under the protection of Prince Gisulf of Salerno, no doubt with the intention of making them unavailable to perform their canonical functions, whether willingly or under duress, if Guibert were installed as pope and Henry were crowned by him.[671]

With the Romans' aid, Henry was able with unexpected ease to enter the city from the south on 21 March, which was the Thursday before Palm Sunday. With Archbishop Guibert, he occupied the Lateran palace.[672] To mark the occasion, Henry made a gift to his faithful supporter Bishop Burchard of Basel by a diploma issued 'in palatio nostro'.[673] Henry convened a synod in St Peter's which Gregory spurned his invitation to attend. After much debate, Henry himself accused Gregory of treason for raising up Rudolf of Swabia as king in his stead, and the synod declared Gregory to be disposed.[674] Henry set out to Bishop Thierry of Verdun the sequence of events:

Know that this Hildebrand has been deposed by the lawful judgement of all the cardinals and of the whole Roman people; our pope-elect Clement has been raised to the apostolic see by the acclamation of all the Romans, and on the holy day of Easter, we have been appointed and by consent of all the Romans consecrated as emperor, with the exultation of the whole Roman people.[675]

The ceremony took place in St Peter's, and the Romans acclaimed him as both *imperator* and *patricius*. It was later observed that Henry had emulated his father in 1046 by acting as *patricius* of the Romans, and that Guibert's adoption of the name Clement was a further allusion to the events of that year.[676] But unlike the events of 1046, those of Easter 1084 began a papal schism in which loyalties in Italy and far beyond were polarized for as long as the anti-pope lived.

A diploma which Henry caused to be hastily drafted not long after these events provides eloquent testimony to the fevered and violent events of the following days, during which his forces caused serious damage to the basilicas of St Peter and St Paul as well as in the diocese of Porto. Henry was quick to offer restitution to the basilicas and to his supporter, the cardinal-bishop of Porto. His expression of penitence for

---

[669] Bernold, *Chron. a.* 1084, p. 440/12–13.
[670] Beno, 1.1, 2.2, 3.10, pp. 369–70, 375, 394.
[671] Beno, 1.1, pp. 369/30–370/5.   [672] Bernold, *Chron. a.* 1084, p. 440/9–13.
[673] *MGH DDHIV* no. 356.
[674] For the synod, see Benzo of Alba, 6.6, 7, Prol., pp. 666/29–34, 669/25–33.
[675] *Epp. HIV* no. 18, p. 84/6–11. For these events, see also Bernold, *Chron. a.* 1084, p. 440/15–18.
[676] For the term *imperator et patricius* see *MGH DDHIV* no. 453, p. 612/20, and the next note; *Lib. de unit. eccles. cons.* 2.16, 21, pp. 218/11–20, 238/16–17.

the violence may have mitigated the resentment that was evidently caused.[677] But the diploma is a reminder that, in 1084, the Germans as well as the Normans who were soon to come to Gregory's aid behaved with traumatic violence at Rome. The campaigning and ravaging enabled Henry to secure control of areas as critical as the Septizonium, the Palatine, and the Capitol. But in the melée of violence that followed his coronation, Henry's position cannot be envisaged as either triumphant or secure.

Henry's substantial successes compelled Gregory to take refuge in the Castel S. Angelo, which remained unconquered as did the Tiber Island which defended the river-crossing further south. Despite the defections and Henry's control of both the Lateran and St Peter's, his position was not desperate. All save one of the cardinal-bishops remained loyal to him; they included figures of the stature of Odo of Ostia, Peter of Albano, and Bruno of Segni. Cardinal-priests who remained loyal included the senior of their number, Abbot Desiderius of Montecassino, with all the resources that his abbey commanded, and the canonist Deusdedit. Many of the Roman aristocracy remained loyal, and with control of the Castel S. Angelo and the Tiber Island, Gregory could hope to victual his forces in the city. The Henricians made their own propagandist attempts to justify the events of Holy Week and Easter.[678] But the credentials of the anti-pope Clement III could be challenged. They were powerfully attacked by Archbishop Gebhard of Salzburg to Bishop Hermann of Metz. His benediction as pope was vitiated because it was performed, not as canonical propriety demanded by the cardinal-bishops of Ostia, Albano, and Porto, but by two of his suffragans as archbishop of Ravenna—Bishops Heribert of Modena and Constantine of Arezzo, both of whom Gregory had in any case suspended from office in 1081. Gebhard could argue that such men's ministrations proclaimed Guibert to be, not the Roman patriarch, but a reprobate heresiarch. Gebhard intended his letter for wide circulation; he ended with a warning to every Christian to guard against bowing his head to Antichrist and against adoring the image that Nebuchadnezzar had set up; whoever did so would bind himself by the most deadly anathema which bound the heresiarch himself.[679]

These were stronger words than Gebhard had uttered at Gerstungen. They reflect the gravity which, in the eyes of Gregory's more earnest supporters, the creation of schism superadded to all that had gone before.

3.5.10 The Final Stages in Italy

In the skirmishing that took place in Rome after Easter, the German excesses for which Henry had felt the need to express penitence provoked a reaction in which

---

[677] *MGH DDHIV* no. 453; for its authenticity and date, see Gawlik, 'Analekten', pp. 499–9, and *MGH DDHIV* 3.746.

[678] *Dicta cuiusdam.*

[679] *CU* no. 69, pp. 141–2; see also Bonizo of Sutri, *Lib. ad amic.* 9, p. 614/15–23, and Bernold, *Chron. a.* 1084, p. 440/18–40.

Gregory's partisans were able to claim some success.[680] Moreover, by dispatching to him Abbot Jarento of Saint-Bénigne at Dijon and some cardinals, Gregory was now able successfully to summon Robert Guiscard to his aid. Robert had lately defeated his own rebels in Apulia; he had good reason to break an imperial hold upon Rome that, for so long as it lasted, would have presented a threat to his rear during future campaigns across the Adriatic. The Montecassino Chronicle indicates that Abbot Desiderius, who must have left Rome, perhaps as one of the cardinals who accompanied Jarento, sent a messenger to Rome 'to announce to the pope [Gregory] his deliverance, and to the emperor [Henry] the coming of the duke [Robert Guiscard]'.[681] This may best be construed as an attempt by Desiderius to forestall further bloodshed at Rome by prompting Henry to leave the city before Gregory's Norman allies began military action. If so, Desiderius's plan only half succeeded. On 21 May, Henry left the vicinity of the city and headed north; after his long absence he was concerned to return to Germany and attend to his position there, and he had no interest in a campaign against the Normans. A series of diplomas marks his journey: Sutri on 23 May, Borgo S. Valentino on 24 May, Pisa on 5 June, and Verona on 17–18 June.[682] His letter to Bishop Thierry of Verdun said that he hoped to keep the feast of St Peter and St Paul (29 June) at Regensburg and thereafter to meet Thierry at Augsburg. He seems to have had high expectations that many in Germany would rally to his obedience, not only among the Saxons but also in South Germany: he even named Archbishop Gebhard of Salzburg and also a Count Albert, by whom he may have meant Albert of Calw, the neighbour of Hirsau. His intention to seek the consolidation of the German church in obedience to the papacy of Clement III was, accordingly, signalled by his being accompanied to Germany by Cardinal-bishop John of Porto.

By the time that the Normans reached Rome, Henry had already reached Siena. The Normans had nothing to fear from him, and Rome lay open to their fury. The sources differ about what happened. The Montecassino Chronicle briefly follows a source which, though apparently circumstantial, gave an artificial version of events: Robert Guiscard came by night to the church of SS. Quattuor Coronati to the east of the Colosseum; upon the advice of the *consul Romanorum* Cencius, head of the Frangipani family, he adopted the diversionary tactic of starting a fire; while the citizens were extinguishing it, he swiftly freed Gregory from the Castel S. Angelo and at once conveyed him to Montecassino. A different picture, which did not thus conceal the savagery of the Norman sacking, emerges in Bernold and—the best source for these events—Geoffrey Malaterra. Having rescued Gregory from the Castel S. Angelo, Robert Guiscard restored him to the Lateran. After encountering further Roman hostility, the Normans ravaged and burnt much of the city. By the conventions of the time, the Normans probably felt justified in sacking the city because

---

[680] The principal sources for this section are: *Epp. HIV* no. 18, pp. 82–5; Bernold, *Chron. aa.* 1084–5, pp. 440/40–441/6, 34–9; *Chron. Cas.* 3.53–4, pp. 434–6; William of Apulia, 4.527–66, pp. 232–4; Geoffrey Malaterra, 3.34–7, pp. 77–80; Hugh of Flavigny, 2, pp. 462–3; Bonizo of Sutri, *Lib. ad amic.* 9, pp. 614–15; Donizo, 2.217–18, p. 384; Landulf Senior, 3.33, p. 100; Guy of Ferrara, 1.20, pp. 548–50; *LP* 2.290.

[681] 3.53, p. 435/2–3.   [682] *MGH DDHIV* nos. 359–66.

many of its citizens had resisted and not surrendered. When the sacking was ended, the Normans, with Gregory in their train, set about the recovery of papal lands outside the city as far to the north as Sutri and Nepi.[683]

Gregory kept St Peter's Day (29 June) at Rome, and at about that time, according to Bernold, he passed canonical sentence upon Guibert and Henry, together with their supporters. But Robert Guiscard could not dislodge the anti-pope from Tivoli, to the east of Rome, to which as in 1082 he had withdrawn when Henry travelled north. Especially because Norman depredations must have hardened many at Rome in hostility to the pope who had summoned their perpetrators, Clement remained as a threat to Gregory. In July, Robert Guiscard left for the south; Gregory and a considerable group of loyal followers left with him.

Rome remained a divided as well as a devastated city. Gregory was far from lacking supporters there, and in the south he had the powerful if volatile backing of the Normans as well as of churchmen like Abbot Desiderius of Montecassino. The anti-pope was by no means in a commanding position. A very large number of cardinals and other Roman churchmen had, it is true, gone over to him. But Henry's forces, as well as the Normans, had earned a reputation for violence. Moreover, Henry had now secured his principal object of imperial coronation; Clement could no longer count upon his active intervention. Never again would Henry come near Rome. Clement was in the Lateran early in November, and he is said to have kept Christmas in St Peter's. That he could do so is an indication of the strength of Roman feeling against Gregory. But in mid-1085, the still active Gregorian party enforced his withdrawal to Ravenna, which he is not known to have left until 1087. Rome became in effect *terra nullius*; not until 1094 would either a pope or an anti-pope establish himself there for any considerable time.

Gregory reached Salerno in June, having probably visited Montecassino on the way. Since Robert Guiscard wished Gregory solemnly to consecrate his new cathedral of St Matthew at Salerno, it was to his advantage to give him due honour and prestige. Gregory evidently preached at Salerno openly and incisively, for a story retailed by Paul of Bernried tells how a local hearer said within himself, 'Behold! the author of warfare and seditions; after disturbing the whole world, he has come to harass this city.' For such thoughts, he was struck dumb, and was healed only after receiving Gregory's forgiveness.[684] For Gregory, the struggle with Henry and against his anti-pope was far from over. He held a synod at Salerno which renewed his sentence against them and all their followers. The sentence was not intended to be unheard or ineffective. Gregory seems to have sought military and material support by writing powerful letters to France.[685] He sent two of his senior and most loyal cardinals, Odo of Ostia and Peter of Albano, to Germany and France respectively to announce and

---

[683] Matilda of Tuscany wrote to Henry's German opponents: 'Sciatis domnum papam iam recuperasse Sutrim atque Nepe. Barrabas latro, id est Heinrici papa, iste quoque aufugit': Hugh of Flavigny, 2, p. 463.

[684] cap. 124, pp. 545–6; the words attributed to the *rusticus* echo Acts 17: 6, and are clearly legendary.

[685] e.g. the identically worded *Epp. vag.* no. 55, p. 134–7, and Santifaller, *QF* no. 58, pp. 38–9.

to implement it. With Peter travelled another ardent Gregorian, Abbot Jarento of Saint-Bénigne at Dijon, who was, it is said, entrusted with a letter to Sisenand, the Castilian governor of the city of Coimbra in Portugal, and also Prince Gisulf of Salerno. They travelled by sea to Saint-Gilles and then by land to Cluny before dividing upon their respective business. Gregory's two major legates were entrusted with a letter to all the faithful that ranks among the most forceful and moving that Gregory ever wrote.[686] He justified the whole course of his life and actions, calling upon Christians everywhere to rally to the defence of St Peter and the Roman church. It was also a task of the legates to raise money for the recovery of Gregory's cause. Peter of Albano and Gisulf of Salerno were to revive for the apostolic see a payment of one penny from every household which he believed that Charlemagne had assigned to it throughout the whole of France; there were to be centres for collection at Aachen, le Puy, and Saint-Gilles.[687] On 5 April 1085, Peter received from Count Peter of Substantion the gift to the apostolic see and to Gregory and his canonically elected successors of his county and of the bishopric of Maguelonne, together with an annual *census* of an ounce of gold.[688]

Gregory's hopes came to rest above all upon his supporters in Tuscany and beyond the Alps. Robert Guiscard was an old man in a hurry to pursue his adventures against the Byzantines; in October 1084, he returned across the Adriatic, leaving Gregory with a refuge at Salerno but not with a base for a prospective return to Rome. But Countess Matilda of Tuscany had proved her resilience and reliability. On 2 July 1084, her forces won a resounding victory over his enemies at Sorbaria, near Modena, thus weakening Henry's Lombard allies. To Gregory and his supporters, it brought unexpected and heart-warming encouragement.

3.5.11 The Final Stages in Germany: Debate

Gregory VII's last encyclical from Salerno and his dispatch to Germany of Cardinal-bishop Odo of Ostia proclaimed his invincible determination to carry on the struggle against Henry. Henry returned to the Germany from which he had been absent for three years with a matching resolve. The final months of the struggle between them was anything but an epilogue to the main drama; it was a continuation of it which was not resolved or even scaled down. Gregory remained constant in his determination to assert the rights of St Peter:

Ever since by God's providence mother church set me upon the apostolic throne, deeply unworthy and, as God is my witness, unwilling though I was, my greatest concern has been that holy church, the bride of Christ, our lady and mother, should return to her true glory and stand free, chaste, and catholic. But because this entirely displeased the ancient enemy, he has armed his members against us in order to turn everything upside down. . . . So, now, my dearly beloved brothers, listen carefully to what I say to you. All who in the whole world bear the name of Christian and truly understand the Christian faith know and believe that St Peter, the

---

[686] *Epp. vag.* no. 54, pp. 128–35.
[687] *Reg.* 8.23, pp. 565–7; see Caspar's notes and Vogel, 'Gregors VII. Abzug', p. 343.
[688] *GC* 6, inst. no. 11, pp. 349–50.

prince of the apostles, is the father of all Christians and their first shepherd after Christ, and that the holy Roman church is the mother and mistress of all the churches. If, then, you believe and unshakeably hold this, I, such as I am, your brother and unworthy master, ask and command you by Almighty God to help and succour your father and mother, if through them you would have the absolution of all your sins, and blessing and grace in this world and the world to come.[689]

Such was the message that Odo of Ostia brought to Germany. As for Henry, few rulers in human history have been more subject than he was to the fluctuations of fortune. The years between his imperial coronation at Rome in 1084 and the death of his rival for the German kingship, Hermann of Salm, in September 1088 were the most fortunate of his long reign. Until her death at the end of 1087, he was supported by his wife Bertha who, despite his despicable treatment of her in the early years of their marriage, had shared the rigours of his winter journey to Canossa and the triumph of his imperial coronation. In 1074, she had borne his eldest surviving son Conrad who, in 1087, was crowned king at Aachen; in 1086, she gave him another son, Henry, who would twenty years later succeed him. If these two sons would be the agents of reversals of fortune, such tragic episodes were in the future. As for Henry himself, he had shown himself resilient; bitter experience and native shrewdness had taught him to rise to the demands of his regality as he saw it. His letter of 1084 to Bishop Thierry of Verdun illustrates both his grasp of detail and of planning ahead, and his ability to form a good working relationship with a well-chosen agent.[690] When he returned to Germany, Henry received a triumphal reception; a poem survives, probably from Freising, which solemnly greeted the return of the triumphant Caesar to his *Teutonica patria* and proclaimed the church's expectation of the benefits that his return would bring.[691] But his Saxon opponents were in some disarray. Otto of Nordheim's death in 1083 had left them without a lay leader of their own, and the anti-king Hermann of Salm disposed of few forces. Leadership was effectively distributed between Archbishop Hartwig of Magdeburg, Bishop Burchard of Halberstadt, and the Margrave Ekbert II of Meissen. Many Saxon magnates were primarily intent upon consolidating their own lordships, and to this end were sometimes prepared to come to terms with Henry. Therefore, in a weary land torn by feuds and wasted by devastation, Henry now seemed to many, at least for a time, to promise the surest hope of the peace for which they ardently yearned.[692]

During the remainder of 1084, Henry seemed able to fulfil this promise. He travelled widely, which was in itself a sign of his power. At some date after 7 August, he set out from Regensburg for the key city of Augsburg, which he recaptured from Duke Welf of Bavaria. He returned to subdue some of his other Bavarian enemies. The autumn saw him in the Rhineland, where the see of Mainz was vacant after the death in February of the exiled Archbishop Siegfried. To succeed him, Henry

---

[689] *Epp. vag.* no. 54, pp. 132/28–134/13.
[690] *Epp. HIV* no. 28, pp. 82–5.
[691] *Ann. Aug. a.* 1084, p. 131; Meyer, 'Ein Gedicht', pp. 257–8.
[692] Bernold, *Chron. a.* 1085, p. 444/16–22.

nominated Wezilo, a learned man who had proved his competence and loyalty to Henry in Italy but who was also a promoter of monastic reform; the anti-pope Clement III dispatched his *pallium* from Rome. There was now a Henrician of manifest personal stature in the principal German see. Wezilo's was the first in a number of appointments to German sees of men who commanded respect.

Before the year was out, Henry had appointed Frederick II of Bohemia to succeed the faithful Henry as patriarch of Aquileia, Erpo to be bishop of Münster, and Henry to be bishop of Paderborn. At Metz in October, he even secured the temporary submission of Bishop Hermann. In a letter to his subjects in Westphalia, Henry insisted upon his own role as an effective upholder of public righteousness (*iustitia*) when he insisted upon the payment of tithes to Bishop Benno of Osnabrück.[693] Henry kept Christmas at a well-attended court in Cologne, to which a number of Saxons seem to have come;[694] at about the same time, Egilbert was at last consecrated archbishop of Trier. Henry could look back upon the year 1084 with satisfaction, and towards the year 1085 with solid confidence.

In face of these developments, Gregory's legate, Cardinal-bishop Odo of Ostia, had arrived in Germany some months after Henry's return in a heroic endeavour to rally the flagging Gregorian cause. He first made for the parts of Swabia that were most firmly controlled by Duke Berthold II of Zähringen who, with Duke Welf IV of Bavaria, provided political leadership and protection for the Gregorians of South Germany. Odo also had the collaboration of the reformed Swabian monasticism that was centred upon the abbey of Hirsau. With such support, he scored an initial success. The see of Constance was effectively vacant through the prolonged absence of Bishop Otto, whom Gregory had excommunicated in 1080. On 21–2 December, Odo held a synod at Constance at which there was elected and consecrated as bishop a monk of Hirsau named Gebhard, who was a brother of the duke of Zähringen. Gebhard was an exemplary monk and staunch Gregorian who would serve Odo well in Germany when Odo became Pope Urban II. At the same synod, Odo raised to the priesthood another strong Gregorian, the chronicler Bernold, giving him authority on behalf of the papacy to reconcile penitent schismatics.[695]

Odo soon afterwards visited Reichenau, a monastic centre of the Gregorians on Lake Constance, which was associated with Hirsau while not following its Customs; Odo received its confraternity and addressed the monks in chapter.[696] From there, he went to St Blasien, a key centre of the Hirsau connection, and dedicated a church.[697] Odo thus consolidated the bonds with the Gregorian papacy of the leading Swabian centres of monastic reform and expansion.

---

[693] *Epp. HIV* no. 19, pp. 84–7. In view of the problems attaching to the date of no. 20, pp. 86–9, it is not here used as evidence of Henry's intention to hold a synod at Mainz in Nov.; see, however, Erkens, *Die Trierer Kirchenprovinz*, p. 51.

[694] *Ann. Sax. a.* 1085, p. 721.

[695] Bernold, *Chron. a.* 1084, p. 441/39–46; id. *Libelli*, 11, p. 144–5.

[696] *MGH Lib. conf.* 1.230, facs. 151 B1–4.   [697] *GP* 2/1, p. 269, no. *2.

Henry made no direct bid to counteract Odo's activities in Swabia but concentrated upon Saxony, where he believed that many people desired peace and might be won to seek it from him.[698] An exploratory meeting of Saxons at Gerstungen which was convened with a view to considering peace with the king seems to have been abortive.[699] But on 20 January 1085, another meeting at Gerstungen and Berka the two sites probably represent the camps of the different parties embarked upon a fuller discussion which the sources referred to as a *colloquium*. It took the character of a search for peace and concord such as Gregory had earlier propounded. Henry thought it diplomatic to stay away, while Odo of Ostia, though present, came as an observer rather than as a major participant. There was a large attendance of laymen who were eager for peace, but the debate was between German bishops who deployed canonical, rather than political, arguments.[700]

Nevertheless, it had a political purpose. The initiative in convening it seems to have rested with Henry at his Christmas court.[701] Its purpose in his mind was to show that he was clear of the moral and legal objections that hostile German bishops urged against him, and so to establish that he was fully entitled to rule. Memories of Gregory's criterion after Canossa of a rightful ruler remained strong: that appropriate persons should assemble to test upon canonical authority to which of two sides righteousness (*iustitia*) inclined.[702] To such a test, Henry and his party now felt that they could confidently appeal.

The course of the *colloquium* on 20 January went far to vindicate their confidence. The alignment of parties was a powerful one. Archbishop Wezilo of Mainz and Gebhard of Salzburg were the protagonists; each was supported by a formidable array of prelates: Wezilo by Archbishops Sigewin of Cologne, Egilbert of Trier, and Liemar of Bremen, with numerous suffragans; Gebhard by Archbishop Hartwig of Magdeburg and most of the Saxon bishops. It was agreed at the outset that there would be no pronouncements of a generalized or of a personal and propagandist kind; the debaters would keep strictly to scriptural and canonical authorities, without addition, subtraction, or tendentious glossing.[703] Gebhard of Salzburg opened by rehearsing proof-texts from Pope Gelasius I and from the ancient synods of Nicaea and Sardica to justify Gregory's sentence against Henry and to insist upon the duty of avoiding all dealings with the excommunicate king and his adherents. In reply Wezilo of Mainz took the unexpected, and tactically effective, step of citing in Henry's defence the Pseudo-Isidorian rule of the *exceptio spolii*, that a person despoiled of his possessions must have them restored before legal proceedings against

---

[698] *Epp. HIV* no. 19, p. 86/1–3.   [699] *Ann. Path.* pp. 99–100.

[700] The principal sources for the *colloquium* at Gerstungen–Berka are: (i) Odo of Ostia's subsequent account: *Die Regensburger Rhetorischen Briefe, Anhang,* no. 5, in *Briefsammlungen,* ed. Erdmann and Fickermann, *MGH Briefe,* 5.375–80. (ii) From the Heinrician side: the later accounts in *Lib. de unit. eccles. cons.* 2.18, pp. 234–5 and Frutolf, *a.* 1085, p. 100. (iii) From the Saxon side: *Ann. Sax. a.* 1085, pp. 721–2; *Ann. Magd. a.* 1085, pp. 176–7.

[701] *Ann. Rat. maior. a.* 1085, p. 88/20–8.

[702] Frutolf, *a.* 1085, p. 88/20–5.   [703] Odo of Ostia (as n. 700), p. 376/12–18.

him can begin, to which Gregory had himself appealed at Rome after Henry's seizure in 1083 of the Leonine city.[704] His argument ran that, before Gregory first sentenced Henry to deposition and excommunication in 1076, the revolt of the Saxons and Swabians had robbed him of much of his kingdom; therefore Gregory's sentence was from the outset canonically void. To this argument which he had not anticipated, Gebhard managed only a feeble riposte. The *colloquium* broke up leaving the Henricians the tactical victors. But there had been no meeting of minds, and each side was hardened in its own position.

The discomfiture of the Gregorians was intensified when their party gathered separately upon the following day. Bishop Udo of Hildesheim, his brother Count Conrad of Reinhausen, and their kinsmen Count Dietrich of Katlenburg were accused of having negotiated clandestinely with Henry. They admitted that they had, but they denied any intention of joining his party. A brawl followed, in which Dietrich and a similarly named relative were killed. The bishop and his brother Conrad fled and submitted to Henry. The incident made painfully apparent the tensions and divisions that rent the Saxons and that made loyalties uncertain and shifting.

Confronted by the double setback of Archbishop Gebhard's tactical defeat in the canonical argument and of the brawl which led to Bishop Udo of Hildesheim's secession, Cardinal-bishop Odo of Ostia felt compelled to emerge from the position of an observer. Two letters of his show how he sought to recover some of the ground that the Gregorian cause had lost and to counter Bishop Udo's defection.

He addressed the first letter as an encyclical to all godly men who wished to defend the Christian faith and religion.[705] He wrote with the authority of a legate of the holy Roman church with whom were associated the archbishops, bishops, abbots, and godly men in Saxony. It was drafted as an explanation to powerful and friendly individuals of what had happened at Gerstungen–Berka in the debate between the Gregorian party and as Odo put it the adversaries of God's holy church; it was an exposure of the falsity of the self-proclaimed victors. In fact, Odo argued, Archbishop Wezilo had travestied the text about the *exceptio spolii*, and had won no dialectical victory. But, first, he focused attention upon the main point that the Gregorians had been concerned to establish: the duty of abstaining from communion with those known to have been excommunicated by Gregory VII.[706] At Gerstungen–Berka, the Gregorians had duly produced Gregory's letters, and they had demonstrated from holy scripture (Matt. 16: 19, John 20: 22–3) the authority of the apostles, and through them the bishops, to bind and to loose in Christ's name. Should they be challenged, their sentences could only be tested by due process; they could not be simply declared void. Nor did Odo allow an argument in defence of Henry based upon the *exceptio spolii*. Where Gebhard of Salzburg had faltered, Odo now provided a long

---

[704] See above, 3.5.8.   [705] As n. 700.

[706] The reference was to the excommunication in *Reg.* 7.14a (7), pp. 483–7, as circulated in Germany in the lost letter referred to by Wenric of Trier, cap. 4, pp. 288–9.

and ingenious reply in which he set himself to show that Archbishop Wezilo's citation of it was inappropriate and mendacious. He had provided the name neither of
the book that he cited nor of the authority that he excerpted. In fact, coming from the
compiler Isidore's Preface, it was merely his opinion; it was not an authoritative
decree of a pope or council. Not only had the Henrician party misrepresented its
authority; they had tendentiously abridged it. Isidore's opinion referred only to the
case of a bishop; the Henricians had concealed this limitation and had unwarrantably
extended it to laity and so to the king. When the plea was thus extended, Odo argued,
the result was absurd: any man whose ox or ass happened to have been stolen could
claim to be immune from spiritual sanctions, no matter how grave his offence. Odo
claimed that such considerations represented a victory for the Gregorians in the
battle of authorities that was the heart of the debate at Gerstungen–Berka. The argument of Wezilo and his friends was a fraudulent invention which had no support in
scripture or in the fathers of the church; for despite all his industry as a compiler,
Isidore was not to be numbered among the latter. By the same token that the devil was
the father of all lies, the Henrician spokesmen could be dubbed the fathers of their
own fictions.

It was a powerful *ad hominem* riposte. No doubt it was eagerly read by Odo's own
party in Germany. But it may be doubted whether it persuaded many who had
welcomed Wezilo's interpretation of the *exceptio spolii*,[707] for it cut the ground from
beneath all Gregory's measures against Henry IV, and was too useful to be lightly
abandoned.

Odo's second surviving letter, written in February and in his own name as a papal
legate, was addressed to Bishop Udo of Hildesheim.[708] Despite Udo's secession,
Odo addressed him cordially as a fellow bishop and most dear brother. He recalled
their recent sharing of communion at Gerstungen–Berka. But, using a biblical refence
that Gregory had often made his own, he deplored Udo's having fallen into the
'crime of idolatry' of which the prophet Samuel had spoken (1 Sam. 15: 18). Udo had
thrown in his lot with those who had been sentenced and excommunicated by the
apostolic see and by the pope who, in catholic truth, presided over it. Odo urged him
to meet himself and Bishop Burchard of Halberstadt for a private talk. He might have
full hope of forgiveness. As an alternative, he might come to the synodical discussion
that Odo planned to hold at Goslar during the coming Lent. He concluded with the
warning that, if Udo persisted in his obduracy, he would share the condemnation of
the party that he had embraced.

Characteristically mild and conciliatory though Odo's letter was, it was ineffectual
in recalling Udo to the Gregorian obedience. Indeed, although at Gerstungen–Berka
he had been numbered with the Gregorians, his loyalty may for some time have been
wavering.[709] He joined Henry IV at Frizlar, and was loyal to him for the rest of his

---

[707] See *Lib. de unit. eccles. cons.* 2.18, p. 235/8–11.
[708] *H* no. 7, pp. 25–7.
[709] *H* no. 28, pp. 63–4, which shows him in touch with Bishop Conrad of Utrecht.

reign. Henry had further successes in winning Saxons to his obedience.[710] In general, his hold upon the German episcopate was intensified. On 2 February, Archbishop Wezilo of Mainz consecrated Bishops Siegfried of Augsburg and Ulrich of Chur.

3.5.12 The Final Stages in Germany: Confrontation

In fact, the parties in Germany were rapidly becoming polarized and going their separate ways. The times were past for such debates as those at Gerstungen in 1081 and in January 1085, when the two sides confronted each other with arguments or with canonical proof-texts from the Bible or ancient Christian authorities. During the month or so before Gregory died, both parties held assemblies of their own which were intended to placard and to put into effect their own programmes and claims to obedience.

Cardinal-bishop Odo of Ostia did not, therefore, in the event, hold his 'synodical discussion' (*synodale colloquium*) at Goslar in Lent.[711] Each side convened a *generalem synodem* which would declare upon the authority of its respective pope what ought to be done. When Henry IV convened such a gathering at Mainz, Odo sought to anticipate it at Quedlinburg, where the anti-king Hermann of Salm kept Easter (20 April); the synod met in Easter week.[712] It was attended by, besides Archbishop Gebhard of Salzburg, Archbishop Hartwig of Magdeburg and his suffragans, and Saxon bishops, like Burchard of Halberstadt, from the ecclesiastical province of Mainz. No bishops from elsewhere attended in person, though those of the Swabian sees of Würzburg, Worms, Strassburg, and Constance sent representatives. The anti-king was present with a number of laymen. The *acta* of the synod were set out in four-teen canons. In them, Odo's prime concern was to vindicate the Gregorian view of the Roman primacy and its claims, which were under challenge from Henricians determined to compel the reversal of Gregory's excommunication of Henry. The synod listened to and affirmed the ancient decrees which forbade anyone to review or to reverse a papal judgement. When a clerk from Bamberg protested that Roman pontiffs had not inherited but invented such a primacy, he played into the synod's hands: a layman spoke up to remind him of Christ's own words, that a disciple is not above his master (Matt. 10: 23–4, Luke 6: 40). This being so, the synod asserted, who could deny a like superiority in the vicar of St Peter, whom all catholics revered as master and lord?

The synodal decrees turned to Wezilo of Mainz. Citing decrees of Popes Innocent I, Leo I, Pelagius I, and Gregory I, the synod branded as null and void his own con-secration, and all other ordinations of clergy and consecrations of buildings in which he was involved. It anathematized him and those of his party who twisted the *exceptio spolii* by arguing that laymen despoiled of their property were immune from ecclesi-

---

[710] *Ann. Sax. a.* 1085, pp. 722–3; *Ann. Magd. a.* 1085, p. 177.

[711] *H* no. 7, p. 26/29–30.

[712] Bernold, *Chron. a.* 1085, pp. 442/17–443/21; cf. *Dictatus papae* 16, *Reg.* 2.55a, p. 205. Bernold's full account should be compared with the independent text of the *acta* in *MGH Conc.* 1.651–3, no. 443.

astical judgement and that excommunicates could be received back into communion without proper reconciliation. Wezilo's defence of Henry at Gerstungen–Berka was thus rejected.

Next, the synod considered the reconciliation of schismatics, and its rulings were stern. No one excommunicated by a bishop who was himself in good standing could be restored to communion unless he were duly absolved. (Odo's commissioning of Bernold indicates the arrangements that he understood to be appropriate.[713]) Nor might those excommunicated for sacrilege, a penalty which many will have incurred in the plundering and arson of the civil wars, be restored unless by due process of reconciliation, even if they had long since made restitution for what they had despoiled. Six further canons enforced discipline and morality according to the strictest Gregorian standards, by demanding clerical chastity and punishing simony and the lay appropriation of tithes. The promotions in holy orders that Cardinal Odo had performed at Constance, including that of Bishop Gebhard, were confirmed. The rigour of ecclesiastical discipline was especially manifest when the marriage of the anti-king Hermann of Salm was called in question on grounds of consanguinity, although the case was not judicially pursued because no lawful accuser was present. Finally, a series of anathemas was pronounced, with candles burning, against the enemies of the Gregorian cause—against Guibert the heresiarch and subverter of the apostolic see; against three eminent Roman apostates who had come to Germany as the anti-pope's legates: Hugh Candidus, John II the ex-cardinal-bishop of Porto, and Gregory VII's sometime chancellor Peter; and against leading German prelates: Archbishop Wezilo of Mainz and Liemar of Bremen, the lately defected Bishop Udo of Hildesheim, and all their accomplices.

By enacting such a body of canons, Cardinal-bishop Odo's synod at Quedlinburg went far to meet the challenge of Gregory's final encyclical from Salerno. There was no mitigation of the reforming demands that Gregory had always addressed to Germany, and the claims which he made as regards papal primacy and universal obedience were unswervingly maintained. But the splendid façade probably disguised division and dissatisfaction amongst many who took part in the synod. The hostile observations later made by the anonymous author of the *Liber de unitate ecclesiae conservanda* are illuminating.[714] He noted that Odo offended many bishops by raising the matter of the anti-king's marriage and by, it was alleged, requiring him to put away his wife. If those who were present welcomed Odo's zeal in rallying the forces who for one reason or another were opposed to Henry IV, many had not gone along with his demands for moral reform and especially for the restitution of church property. The canons thus concealed much disagreement. Such disagreement was endemic, and had already been revealed when Abbot William of Hirsau had written to the anti-king Hermann, urging him and his followers to obedience to Pope Gregory, to unremitting hostility to simony, clerical incontinence, and lay investiture, and to disregard of the evil examples of Saxon bishops who were tolerant of clerical

---

[713] See above, 3.5.11.   [714] 2.22, p. 239.

transgressions. The letter elicited a fierce reply to Abbot William from the prelates and clergy of Saxony in which they impugned his inordinate zeal:

Moses and Isaiah [*recte* Jeremiah] were ordered to rule a multitude but refused, the one pleading his inexperience and the other his youth (Exod. 3: 11, 4: 10; Jer. 11: 6); yet you, in your boldness, like a false apostle usurp an office which by virtue of your order you do not have: the law commands that fathers should be honoured (Exod. 20: 12), but you dishonour your fathers —for, by way of consecration, bishops beget abbots; abbots do not beget bishops! . . . Ponder what has been written: 'Whoever proudly despises his brother or tries to disfigure him is an outcast from the bond of charity.'[715] Now whoever is a stranger to charity is a stranger to the Lord, for the Lord is charity. Be an imitator of the Lord so that, just as he created all things by his word, you, too, may do nothing without the word, that is, without reason. Put a finger to your mouth![716]

So great was the gap of sympathy and comprehension between the Gregorian reformers of Swabia and the Saxon bishops and clergy who were their nominal allies against Henry. Quedlinburg did nothing to bridge the gap, and it is not surprising that Saxon defections to Henry should apparently have continued.[717]

When Henry's general synod met at Mainz, it was carefully set up to demonstrate that, since Gregory VII had been disposed of, the German church had been given new order and vitality under the energetic and beneficent leadership of Clement III as pope and Henry IV as emperor.[718] Henry was its driving force ('praecipue auctor huius synodi'); but beside him stood Clement who, as the Hersfeld anonymous observed, sponsored the synod in the metropolis of Mainz in order to promote the catholic faith and the peace and concord of the churches. What Gregory had failed to provide for Germany by masterful interference, Henry and Clement would provide by harmonious co-operation. The synod, which met in the second week after Easter, was well attended. There were present as Clement's legates the three Roman figures whom Odo of Ostia proscribed at Quedlinburg—Hugh Candidus, John of Porto, and Peter the chancellor; although, unlike Odo, none of the legates assumed the presidency. Three archbishops were there—Wezilo of Mainz, Egilbert of Trier, and Sigewin of Cologne; Liemar of Bremen was absent but promised to accept whatever was decided. Sixteen bishops came from Lorraine, Franconia, Bavaria, and Swabia; others were represented. There was a large lay attendance.

The business of the synod was no less comprehensive than that at Quedlinburg. Gregory VII was again condemned and declared to be deposed, while Guibert of Ravenna's accession to the papacy was confirmed. Hermann of Salm was declared to be a traitor and enemy of the peace, while his followers were excommunicated. German bishops who had disobeyed the summons to the synod—no fewer than two

[715] The source of the quotation is unknown.

[716] *H* nos. 18–19, pp. 41–6; the passage translated occurs at p. 46/7– 26.

[717] *Ann. Sax. a.* 1085, pp. 722/40–773/23. For an analysis of Saxon and other German attitudes, see Leyser, 'The Crisis of Medieval Germany', esp. pp. 424–43.

[718] The sources for the synod of Mainz are listed and discussed by Meyer von Knonau, *Jahrbücher*, 4.543–50; the most illuminating is the *Lib. de unit. eccles. cons.* 2.19–22, pp. 235–40.

archbishops, Gebhard of Salzburg and Hartwig of Magdeburg, and thirteen bishops were named—were deposed from their sees and excommunicated. A start was made to the process of replacing them by loyal but at the same time reputable substitutes. The Hersfeld anonymous wrote in theologically Cyprianic terms of the establishment of an 'episcopatus unus et indivisus'. The synod followed the lead that Bishop Henry of Liège and Archbishop Sigewin of Cologne had set while Henry was in Italy of proclaiming the Peace of God; but now it covered the whole empire. A new order was proclaimed which would not only provide a united and effective church owing obedience upon mutually acceptable terms to Pope Clement III; it would also answer under imperial authority the war-weary yearnings of the Germans from end to end of the kingdom for peace and security. Finally, the synod sought to buttress the power of the realm by raising Duke Wratislav II of Bohemia to royal rank as king not only of Bohemia but also of Poland. He was to be a king within the German realm; according to a Bohemian source, Henry with his own hand placed a royal circlet upon his head.[719]

Held in consecutive weeks and only a month or so before the death of Gregory VII, the rival synods of Quedlinburg and Mainz indicate the balance at that time in the struggle for mastery of the German church. For the time being, Henry was in the ascendant, with an intelligible programme and with gathering support. The Gregorians were in deepening difficulties which were compounded because, upon Gregory VII's death, Odo of Ostia's legatine authority lapsed. They were divided between the disparate groups in Saxony and Swabia; in Saxony, where their main military strength lay, there was also internal division and resentment. Hermann of Salm was not only the merest shadow king, but his matrimonial position was questionable upon strict canonical criteria. Time alone would show whether the renewed harmony of *regnum* and *sacerdotium* that Henry was striving to build rested upon sure foundations and whether he could extend his successes by subduing his German enemies, or whether the Gregorian papacy had in figures like Cardinal-bishop Odo of Ostia the reserves of spiritual power and political skill to bring about the revival of its fortunes from the nadir which they had reached in the exile of Gregory VII to Salerno.

From a Gregorian point of view, the signs in Germany as in Italy were not unhopeful. On the one hand, despite Henry IV's show of strength and support at Mainz, doubts about Henry's personal and kingly qualities had not been laid to rest, and some expressons of loyalty to him were not securely based.[720] On the other hand, in some areas of Germany, and especially in Swabia and Bavaria, during the past twelve years Gregorian ideas and ideals had taken a hold which was indelibly to determine the religious outlook of these areas for centuries to come. Upon certain aspects of this Gregorianization some comments may next be made.

---

[719] Cosmas of Prague, 2.37, p. 235/1–8.
[720] The example of Abbot Walo of St Arnulf, near Metz, is instructive: *Die Briefe des Abtes Walo*, nos. 8–9, pp. 78–84.

3.6 Gregory VII and the German Church

Gregory's political dealings with King Henry IV and with the episcopate and princes inevitably occupy the centre of the stage when his impact upon Germany is under discussion. In important respects, however, his impact must also be studied in more narrowly ecclesiastical terms. The purpose of this section is to do so with respect to four developments that were of lasting importance in German history.

3.6.1 The Campaign against Simony and Clerical Unchastity

For both theological and practical reasons, clerical simony and clerical marriage and fornication were resisted by virtually all those who in the later eleventh century sought the renewal of Christianity and the raising of the standards of the Christian life. Gregory's commitment to their extirpation, both before and after his elevation to the papal office, is beyond question. He expected his legates, and still more the archbishops and bishops, to be unremitting against them. Yet in Germany as else-where beyond the Alps, his direct and energetic action was confined to relatively brief periods. It developed somewhat slowly; it was intensively sustained only during brief campaigns; and it occupied a limited place amongst the active concerns of his later years.[721]

The slowness with which it developed in 1073 and early 1074 can partly be put down to his travels in South Italy from July to December 1073, but it was also a result of his distant relations with the German episcopate. This is suggested by a letter of November 1073 to Archbishop Gebhard of Salzburg. The letter arose from the chance of an individual's petition to Gregory at Rome. Gregory seized the opportunity to rebuke Gebhard for having neglected to make contact with him. He had also neglected to enforce the rules about clerical chastity which had been promulgated at a Roman synod at which he had been present; Gregory seems to have had in mind Alexander II's synod of 1063 after which his version of the encyclical *Vigilantia universalis* had circulated. Gregory urged Gebhard to be zealous in enforcing such papal rules upon his clergy.

Even during 1074, Gregory's campaign developed slowly.[722] The year witnessed the legatine mission to Germany of the Roman cardinal-bishops Gerald of Ostia and Hubert of Palestrina; by means of it, Gregory sought to promote the amendment both of King Henry IV and of the German bishops and church, especially in respect of clerical chastity.[723] The legates returned to Rome without holding the council that might have taken in hand the moral reform of the clergy, although it might have brought episcopal and clerical opposition to Gregory's aspirations to a head; such direct action as they took against clerical concubinage was ineffectual. If, as is probable, Archbishop Siegfried of Mainz's synod of Erfurt is to be dated to October 1074,

---

[721] See Mirbt, *Die Publizistik*, pp. 266–70. For Gregory's campaign against clerical unchastity, see also Cowdrey, 'Pope Gregory VII and the Chastity of the Clergy'.

[722] Lampert, *Ann. a.* 1074, pp. 256–60, confuses events of 1074 and 1075.

[723] *Reg.* 2.66 to Bishop Burchard of Halberstadt, 29 Nov. 1075, p. 221/13–19.

one metropolitan, at least, was not entirely deaf to the legates' promptings that he should take his clergy in hand. The chronicler Lampert of Hersfeld stated that Siegfried did not consider the time to be ripe for the uprooting of the established custom of clerical marriage; he temporized by giving his clergy a stay of six months during which they might voluntarily adopt a life of chastity and thus relieve both himself and the pope of the need for further action. But at length, at what was probably the provincial synod which he held in distant Westphalia, he presented the clergy with the stark alternative of forswearing marriage or abandoning the service of the altar. There was heated debate after which the synod dissolved into disorder. A faction threatened Siegfried with deposition and death, whereupon he promised to request the pope to temper his stringent requirements. After other business, the reconvened synod broke up with its tensions unresolved; Siegfried retired to Heiligenstadt, also in Thuringia, where he repeatedly censured those who had disturbed his synod.[724]

Siegfried's subsequent exchange of letters with Gregory tends to confirm that something like what Lampert described had indeed occurred. In December, Gregory summoned him and his suffragans to his Lent synod at Rome. In his letter of excuse from attending on grounds of ill-health, Siegfried ended with a promise of obedience to whatever Gregory commanded, especially with regard to clerical chastity and the simoniac heresy. But, perhaps with his undertaking at Erfurt in mind, he pleaded with Gregory to temper zeal with discretion by applying discipline to the perverse and obstinate but by showing charity to those who were weak and in need of a physician.[725] Siegfried also wrote to all the bishops and senior clergy of his province, reporting upon all that had happened—the lack of success of Gregory's legates in opposing clerical concubinage, the scandal and infamy that had ensued. Siegfried's suffragans were to send to him any clergy who were now recalcitrant; Siegfried confirmed that the rigour of Gregory's rulings must stand.[726]

For the rest, Gregory's letters to Germany about clerical marriage and simony which can be securely dated to 1074 are few in number. They were forcibly expressed, yet they show no consistent line of action. In October, he dispatched two letters which must be read together. To Bishop Burchard of Halberstadt, he acknowledged the legates' failure to bring about 'what the Christian religion demanded and still demands', blaming the active resistance of most of the German bishops. In his other letter, which was probably addressed to Count Albert of Calw and his wife, he urged two lay persons to hold fast to all that they had learnt from the apostolic see about bishops and priests who were guilty of simony or fornication.[727] Gregory did not specifically refer to any decree or writings of his own pontificate and his requirement did not go beyond that of his predecessors in 1059 and 1063, when they forbade

---

[724] The source for the synod of Erfurt is Lampert of Hersfeld, *Ann. a.* 1074, pp. 258–60.

[725] *Reg.* 2.29, to Archbishop Siegfried of Mainz, 4 Dec. 1074, pp. 161–2; *CU* no. 42, p. 91/3–13.

[726] *Mainzer Urkundenbuch*, no. 343, 1.239.

[727] *Reg.* 2.11–12, to Count Albert and his wife, and to Bishop Burchard of Halberstadt, 26 Oct. 1074, pp. 142–4.

anyone to hear the mass of a priest whom they knew to keep a concubine or living-in woman.

Gregory did not altogether bypass the German archbishops. A month later, he wrote to Anno of Cologne with the primary purpose of dealing with a matter of business about tithes which was left over from the legates' visit. He concluded his letter by urging Anno to require all in major orders throughout his whole province to live in chastity.[728] However, it was to the laity that Gregory principally looked. In January 1075, he addressed the South German dukes, Rudolf of Swabia, Welf of Bavaria, and Berthold of Carinthia, with an appeal for concerted action. He castigated the German archbishops and bishops for choosing to ignore the sacred canons which prohibited the ministrations of clergy guilty of simony or fornication. Almost all had disregarded papal admonitions, whether in councils or by legates and letters. He therefore called upon the laity positively to prevent the officiating of guilty clergy, using force if necessary.[729] By thus seeking to mobilize lay resistance to offending clergy, Gregory was, from one point of view not innovating, for at Milan and throughout Central Italy such measures had for long been applied.[730] But no pope had enjoined them upon the laity in lands north of the Alps. Gregory was aware that, to the Germans, they would have the appearance of novelty and must be defended by energetic propaganda.[731]

Gregory's Lent synod of 1075 was the occasion of firm legislation against simony and clerical unchastity, and it was followed by sustained and resolute action to make it effective in Germany which took no account of Archbishop Siegfried of Mainz's plea for moderation. The Swabian annalist Berthold, in particular, wrote of Gregory's attempt to assemble and give due sanction to the measures against simony and clerical fornication that were dispersed amongst the rulings of former times.[732] In the changed ecclesiastical climate of the year 1075, Gregory sought and expected more collaboration from the German bishops than he had found in 1074, and he planned to work through them rather than through legates of his own.[733]

Letters that Gregory almost certainly dispatched to Germany after the Lent synod of 1075 convey the urgency with which he urged bishops to act.[734] Letters to Archbishops Siegfried of Mainz and Werner of Magdeburg and to Bishop Otto of Constance have survived; there may have been others.[735] These letters were not entered in Gregory's Register, a fact which may indicate the pressure under which

---

[728] *Reg.* 2.25, 18 Nov. 1074, pp. 156–7.

[729] *Reg.* 2.45, 11 Jan. 1075, pp. 182–5. [730] See below, 4.2.

[731] *Reg.* 2.45, p. 184/13–16: 'Multo enim melius nobis videtur iustitiam Dei vel novis reaedificare consiliis, quam animas hominum una cum legibus deperire neglectis.'

[732] *a.* 1075, p. 277/23–37. Gregory himself wrote of the *statuta* and *decreta* which were enacted in 1075 on the authority of past tradition: *Reg.* 2.62, to Archbishop Sigehard of Aquileia, 23 Mar. 1075, p. 217/14–18.

[733] See above, 3.2.6.

[734] For the date of *Epp. vag.* nos. 6–11, see the note in *Epp. vag.* pp. 160–1.

[735] *Epp. vag.* nos. 6–8, pp. 14–19. That they circulated in Germany is confirmed by Berthold, *Ann. a.* 1075, p. 277/38–44 where a slightly different text is cited which included a prohibition of the improper use of tithes and a blessing upon the obedient and penitent.

the papal clerks were working. But other letters to German bishops were soon registered. On 23 March, Gregory reproved Bishop Dietwin of Liège for his prolonged
complicity in simoniacal dealings; he was to correct them, and also to admonish and
discipline the concubinous clergy of his diocese.[736] On 29 March, Gregory wrote to
three more German prelates, maintaining his requirement of the enforcement of
clerical chastity. He reminded Bishop Burchard of Halberstadt of his predecessors'
decrees about it which he had in due course ('deiceps') published by letters and messengers; he called upon the bishop to renew his zeal and to mobilize the laity in a boycott of the ministrations of disobedient clergy. Archbishop Anno of Cologne was to
convene a council of his brother-bishops which would promote clerical chastity, and
in this letter he added a reminder of the papal prohibition of simony. He also urged
Archbishop Werner of Magdeburg to strenuous endeavour in the campaign for
clerical chastity.[737] In the sequel to his Lent synod, Gregory was evidently concerned
to make direct use of German metropolitans and other bishops to press the demand
for clerical chastity upon a reluctant episcopate and upon a clergy that was largely
hostile or at best indifferent.

The hostility of the German clergy was apparent in a campaign of propaganda in
defence of clerical marriage, the main themes of which Lampert of Hersfeld summarized in terms of its invoking biblical assertions that chastity was appropriate for
some but not all (Matt. 19: 11–12, 1 Cor. 7: 9), and of its warning that men who were
compelled to live the life of angels for which they were not fitted would lapse into the
grossest indecencies. If Gregory persisted in requiring universal chastity of the
clergy, many would desert their priesthood rather than their marriages; then it would
have to be seen where a pope for whom men were not good enough would find angels
to govern the congregations of the church.[738] Between 1074 and 1079 there began to
circulate a propagandist *Epistola de continentia clericorum*, purportedly addressed by
the saintly Bishop Ulrich of Augsburg (923–73) to a Pope Nicholas. In Ulrich's lifetime there was no pope of this name, but the ascription recalled Pope Nicholas II and
his measures of 1059–60 against clerical marriage. The letter expressed fear that an
absolute sentence against clerical marriage would serve to undermine papal authority and credibility. It advanced arguments similar to those which Lampert recorded,
adding historical examples such as the legend of Paphnutius, a martyr-figure and
bishop who was himself unmarried and who had allegedly persuaded the council of
Nicaea (325) to allow married clergy the liberty of abstaining from their wives or not
at their own discretion. Its message was that the pope should cease compelling those
whom he should merely warn, lest by imposing a command of his own devising he
should be found to have set himself against the Old and the New Testaments.[739]

---

[736] *Reg.* 2.61, p. 215–16.

[737] *Reg.* 2.66–8, pp. 221–6.   [738] *Ann. a.* 1074, pp. 256–9.

[739] Pseudo-Udalricus, *Epistola*; for the legend of Paphnutius, see Cassiodorus, *Hist. eccles. trip.* 2.14,
pp. 107–8. The letter was written before Gregory's Lent synod of 1079: Bernold, *Chron. a.* 1079, p. 436/
1–4; it may have been known at the council of Constance in 1075. For its date and origin, see esp. Robinson,
'Bernold von Konstanz und der gregorianische Reformkreis', pp. 178–80.

During 1075, Gregory nevertheless insisted upon his campaign in Germany to extirpate the simoniac heresy and to enforce the chastity of the clergy. The bishops—they were probably very few in number—who attempted to offer a measure of co-operation encountered the determined resistance of their clergy. Gregory continued to regard Siegfried of Mainz as the lynch-pin of his endeavour to impose reform without tarrying for any. In July or August, Siegfried wrote him a letter which began by promising the obedience of a son to a father and of a subject to his ruler. He acknowledged Gregory's command that he hold a council and bring the sickle to the simoniac heresy and to every other transgression of ecclesiastical righteousness; he added a recognition of his canonical obligation to hold such councils twice a year. But he pleaded both the general disruption of the German kingdom and the prevalence of feuds which would surely erupt if those at odds came together at a council: for such reasons, the wisest heads among his advisers advised him to delay until the Lord himself demonstrated his favour by restoring peace to the land. Nevertheless, Siegfried would regard Gregory's word as final, although he concluded with a strong hint that, in his own opinion, a council would best be postponed.[740]

In his personally dictated reply which he sent by the hand of Siegfried's southern-most suffragan Bishop Henry of Chur,[741] Gregory would have none of this. Siegfried's arguments savoured of man, not of God. The archbishop must show himself a shepherd, not a hireling, by taking immediate action. Gregory pointedly held before Siegfried the example of Eli the priest (*sacerdos*) who had perished at Shiloh after he had failed to rebuke the fornication of his sons and other abuses of the priestly office (1 Sam. 2: 22–4, 27–35, 4: 16–18). Siegfried should put aside the craven advice of his entourage and at once convene a council so that battle might be immediately joined against the forces of iniquity.[742] At Mainz in October, Siegfried accordingly held a council at which he announced Gregory's demand that priests abandon either their wives or their ministration at the altar. Their response was a riot in which Siegfried was lucky to get away with his life.[743]

Bishop Otto of Constance, too, a suffragan of Siegfried whose diocese comprised the heartlands of Swabia, felt the force of Gregory's censure. In the latter half of 1075, he, like Siegfried, held a synod. It was well attended. At it, the assembled clergy, perhaps mindful of the legend of Paphnutius, rejected the canon of the council of Nicaea about clerical chastity.[744] Gregory's response was severe in the extreme. He castigated Otto because, in spite of his earlier letters to Siegfried of Mainz and to himself, and despite the rulings of Popes Leo the Great and Gregory the Great of which Gregory reminded him, he had relaxed the reins of lust for those in major

---

740 *CU* no. 45, pp. 97–100.

741 Lampert of Hersfeld, *Ann. a.* 1075, pp. 300–1. Erdmann's objection to Bishop Henry as the bearer of *Reg.* 3.4 is scarcely warranted, since Lampert may have placed his own interpretation upon it: *Studien zur Briefliteratur*, p. 274 n. 1.

742 *Reg.* 3.4, 3 Sept. 1075, pp. 248–50.   743 Lampert of Hersfeld, *Ann. a.* 1075, pp. 302–3.

744 Bernard, 2.42, p. 45/24–8. For canon 3 of Nicaea, see *COD* p. 7. For the date of Otto's council, see Erdmann, *Studien zur Briefliteratur*, p. 274 n. 3.

orders and had allowed them to keep or to take women. He was to come to the next Lent synod at Rome and answer for his disobedience to and contempt for the apostolic see. In an accompanying letter to Otto's clerical and lay subjects, Gregory further accused him of disobedience and rebellion. He informed them of Otto's summons to Rome and released them from the duty of obedience to their bishop even if they were bound by oath, for so long as he persisted in rebellion against God and the apostolic see. He wrote yet another, brief letter for circulation to all the clergy and laity of the German kingdom, prohibiting obedience to all bishops who tolerated the keeping of women by clerks.[745]

After the sequence of events in Germany which led from Worms to Canossa, Bishop Otto of Constance remained under pressure to amend the lives of his clergy. In January 1076, he was among the majority of German bishops who, at Worms, withdrew their obedience from Gregory; but, in October, he was able to benefit from Gregory's preparedness to ease the return of such bishops and to secure from Bishop Altmann of Passau his restoration to communion though not to his episcopal functions. Otto nevertheless resumed these functions, and in 1077 Gregory's legates the Roman cardinal-deacon Bernard and Abbot Bernard of Saint-Victor at Marseilles held an assembly at Constance during which, by papal authority they inhibited his actions and, in accordance with Gregory's prohibitions at his Lent synod of 1076, condemned the simony and incontinence that were rife among the clergy of his diocese. They emphasized the duty of the laity to shun the ministrations of incontinent clerks. They also proclaimed a stop to local procedures whereby clergy evaded charges of simony and sought to introduce a ready means whereby clerks suspected of heresy might be accused by clergy and laity. These events were described by Berthold of Reichenau whose abbey lay within the diocese of Constance, and they suggest that Gregory was concerned through his legates to maintain his campaign against simony and clerical incontinence. But it may be doubted whether the legates' measures had significant effects upon the diocese or its bishop whom, in 1080, Gregory deposed and excommunicated for his continued tolerance of married clergy. Indeed, Berthold admitted that, after 1077, most of the incontinent and simoniacal clergy returned to their former ways.[746]

From this time, Gregory did little, whether by directly addressing German bishops and laity or through his legates, to confront the problem that they presented. In 1076, he dispatched to Flanders the kind of letter that in 1075 he had addressed to Germany, urging its lay rulers to mobilize both clergy and laity against married priests and simoniacal bishops.[747] At his November synod of 1078 and his Lent synod of 1079, he renewed at Rome his general condemnation of simony and clerical fornication.[748] It seems to have been after the Lent synod that Gregory circulated his brief but

---

[745] *Epp. vag.* nos. 10–11, pp. 22–7.

[746] Berthold, *a.* 1077, pp. 293/21–294/8; Bernold, *Pro Gebhardo episcopo*, pp. 109–11.

[747] *Reg.* 4.10–11, to Countess Adela of Flanders, and to Count Robert of Flanders, 10 Nov. 1076, pp. 309–11.

[748] *Reg.* 6.5*b*, pp. 401/20–1, 405/24–406/3; Bernold, *Chron. a.* 1079, p. 436/1–4.

pungent letter to all the faithful in Germany and Italy in which he prohibited those in major orders who were guilty of fornication from entering a church until they had mended their ways and insisted that, if they did not repent, no one should accept their ministrations, 'for their blessing is made a curse and their prayer a sin'.[749] At this stage, Gregory did not renew his call to the laity in 1075 to take positive coercive action against offending clergy; he only called upon them to boycott their ministrations. It was as if he apprehended the need not to throw further fuel upon the fires of civil disorder in Germany.

For with the gathering civil war and schism there, Gregory's zeal for the moral amendment of the clergy in respect of fornication and simony gave place to his wider concern to promote the *pax et concordia regni* and the welfare, in the broadest and most positive sense, that might be established under the direction of the pope and with the co-operation of an obedient king. After such general peace and concord were established, the correction of the clergy might follow as part of the general righteousness that would prevail. Gregory's perspective was apparent in his pastoral letter to Germany of September 1080, dispatched between the synod of Brixen in June and the death of the anti-king Rudolf of Rheinfelden in October. Gregory gave new force to his conviction that men must wait upon the providence of God, whose just judgement upon men was apparent in the long affliction of the church and in the gathering force of tyrannical persecution. Yet by moral renewal the time might be hastened when the foemen's wrath would be stilled and the church might receive its long-desired peace and security. Gregory therefore called upon the bishops to be zealous in searching out and extirpating prevalent evils according to the precepts that they had received from the Roman church—Gregory referred to such precepts in general without naming clerical fornication or simony; and he called upon the laity to swell the tide of those who were already repenting and returning to the bosom of the church.[750]

Gregory was increasingly compelled to turn from specific moral abuses to take account of the need for peace and concord in the kingdom. It is one of the ironies of his dealings with Germany that, after 1077 and especially after 1080, he became in effect compelled to adopt the priorities that Archbishop Siegfried of Mainz had advocated in 1075 and that Gregory had then brushed aside: civil war and local feud must be settled before such specific evils as clerical fornication and simony could be addressed. During Gregory's last years, Gregory's legates in Germany became increasingly perplexed about where they stood in respect of his campaign against clerical wrongs. In 1081, he answered the inquiry of his legates Bishop Altmann of Passau and Abbot William of Hirsau in terms that virtually paraphrased Siegfried of Mainz's letter of 1075:

As for your question about priests, we answer that, as matters stand, on account both of the disturbance of the peoples and of the death of good men—I mean because there are very few who perform for faithful Christians the offices of the Christian religion, for the present you

---

[749] *Epp. vag.* no. 32, pp. 84–7.   [750] *Reg.* 8.9, 22 Sept. 1080, pp. 527–8.

should bear with the situation and temper the rigour of the canons. Such matters may more suitably be discussed and the canons upheld in a time of peace and tranquillity, which by God's grace we hope will come soon.[751]

But Gregory was writing to churchmen who were of a different stamp to Siegfried of Mainz. Altmann of Passau and William of Hirsau were profoundly committed to Gregory and to his concerns for the church. Sporadic though Gregory's own active campaigning against clerical fornication and simony may have been, his concern for their extirpation passed both to them and to the canonical and monastic institutions that they represented. These institutions transmitted them to the twelfth century. Moreover, the cathedral school of Constance, the see of Bishop Otto and then of Bishop Gebhard, produced in teachers and alumni like Bernard and Bernold men for whom the moral reform of the clergy as Gregory had initiated it was a major issue.

Thus, in the short run, the campaign against clerical fornication and simony that Gregory promoted with urgency in 1075 was, by the mid-1080s, overlaid and retarded because of Gregory's more widely defined aims for the peace and concord of the German church and kingdom. It became largely submerged in the unresolved contest for authority in the German church between Gregorians and Henricians. In the long run, however, Gregory's standards of clerical morality found lasting and able champions amongst regular canons, monks, and publicists. Each of these groups calls for brief comment as allies that Gregory found and used in the German church.

3.6.2 Bishop Altmann of Passau and the Canonical Life

It was not only by coercive sanctions that attempts were made during the central Middle Ages to raise the standards of the clergy. Sanctions had their complement in attempts positively to establish a pattern of life to which non-monastic clergy should aspire. Hence there followed the many-faceted promotion of the so-called canonical life amongst the clergy which found its prime inspiration in the Jerusalem church as depicted in the Acts of the Apostles 2: 44–7, 4: 32–4:

And all who believed were together and had all things in common; and they sold their possessions and goods and distributed them to all, as any had need. And day by day, attending the temple together and breaking bread in their homes, they partook of food with glad and generous hearts, praising God and having favour with all the people.

Now the company of those who believed were of one heart and soul, and no one said that any of the things which he possessed was his own, but they had everything in common. And with great power the apostles gave their testimony to the resurrection of the Lord Jesus, and great grace was upon them all. There was not a needy person among them, for as many as were possessors of lands or houses sold them, and brought the proceeds of what was sold and laid it at the apostles' feet; and distribution was made to each as any had need.

The canonical life for the clergy typically involved keeping a common table and a common dormitory, as well as the holding in common of all or most property. It

---

[751] *Reg.* 9.3, p. 576/20–7; cf. *CU* no. 45, pp. 99/27–100/11. See also Altmann's fragmentary letter to Gregory: *Epp. vag.* no. 58, pp. 140–1.

facilitated the living of a chaste life both by the physical circumstance of a communal regime and, perhaps more important, by warding off the human and emotional isolation which, more even than sexual continence, represents the hardship of the celibate life. By imposing poverty and the community of possessions, it also diminished the scope for simoniacal dealings. By establishing a structure of authority in cathedral and collegiate churches which had much in common with that of a monastery, it placed the clergy under supervision and discipline. But, unlike the monastic life, that of canons was primarily directed towards pastoral work amongst the laity and the promotion of higher standards in the church at large. The ideal of the canonical life was eminently compatible with Gregory VII's purposes in revitalizing the church. It was no innovation of the late eleventh century, for it had centuries of history behind it which included such legislation of the Carolingian period as the Rule of Bishop Chrodegang of Metz (*c.*755) and the *Institutio canonicorum* of Aachen (816). Its appeal to Gregory was already manifest in 1059, when, as Archdeacon Hildebrand, he sought to establish in Roman churches a stricter interpretation of the canonical life than the *Institutio canonicorum* embodied.[752] The encyclical *Vigilantia universalis* propagated the common life of the clergy as the corollary of its condemnation of incontinence and simony.[753] In the late eleventh and early twelfth centuries, the canonical life gained coherence, and therefore usefulness for reformers like Gregory, by the gradual spread of the Rule of St Augustine, the earliest reference to which occurs at Rheims in 1067.

In the later eleventh century, regular canons became of especial prominence in several regions of Germany in Alsace, in the region of the middle Elbe and especially the diocese of Halberstadt, but first and most signally in Bavaria. Their outstanding patron there was Bishop Altmann of Passau (1065–91). Together with his metropolitan, Archbishop Gebhard of Salzburg, Altmann was pre-eminent for his loyalty to and service of Gregory VII in a region where clergy and laity alike were predominantly Henrician in their loyalty. Both by his fidelity to the Gregorian cause and by his fostering of the regular canons, Altmann was outstanding among the Gregorians of Southern Germany.[754]

By origin not a Bavarian but a Westphalian, he had been a royal chaplain under the Emperor Henry III, upon whose death he had remained in the service of the Empress Agnes; he was an outstanding figure among the devout clergy whom Agnes gathered about herself.[755] As bishop of Passau, he was concerned to build stone churches and to provide them with chaste and instructed clergy. He responded from deep conviction to Gregory's call to bishops to deal firmly and immediately with clerical

---

752 See above, 2.2.3.

753 caps. 1–4, 9, Schieffer, *Die Entstehung des päpstlichen Investiturverbots*, pp. 214–23.

754 For the background to and course of the introduction of the canonical life in Germany, see esp. Siegwart, *Die Chorherren* and Classen, 'Gerhoch of Reichersberg'. Recent literature is reviewed by Weinfurter, 'Neuere Forschung', and 'Reformkanoniker und Reformepiskopat'.

755 The principal source for Altmann's career is the *Vita Altmanni*, written at Göttweig *c.*1125–41 with late 12th-cent. additions. For his early years, see caps. 2–5, pp. 229–31.

incontinence and simony. He conducted a prolonged campaign by both exhortations and threats to bring his canons and parochial clergy to abandon their wives. Like Siegfried of Mainz and Otto of Constance, he eventually convened a council at Passau, probably in late 1075, at which he read out Gregory's letters which enjoined clerical continence. Like the other bishops he encountered hostility but he confirmed his own unyielding position. Soon after, on St Stephen's day (26 December) which was the patronal festival of his cathedral, he again proclaimed Gregory's demands, thereby provoking a tumult from which he barely escaped alive.[756]

During the years that followed, Altmann was compelled to seek refuge in Saxony, while his clerks at Passau retained their wives; according to his *Vita*, they did so with the active connivance of King Henry IV. He became increasingly active in Gregory's service. In 1076, he served as a legate in the negotiations at Ulm and Tribur–Oppenheim.[757] In 1079, he visited Rome for the Lent synod, and stayed for some time with Gregory. As his friend Bishop Anselm of Lucca had done in 1074,[758] he resigned his see to Gregory because he had received it from a lay hand; he accepted it back with reluctance. At this time, Gregory named him along with Bishop Hermann of Metz and Abbot Ekkehard of Reichenau as persons from whom the anti-king Rudolf of Swabia and his Saxon followers might learn more of Gregory's dealings about the German kingdom. By 1081, Altmann was serving in Germany in a permanent legatine capacity after the manner of Anselm of Lucca in Lombardy and Hugh of Die and Amatus of Oloron in France ('vicem nostram in Teutonicis partibus prudentiae tuae commisimus'). Among his concerns were the reconciliation of penitent ex-supporters of Henry IV; after Rudolf of Swabia's death, Gregory sent Altmann and Abbot William of Hirsau instructions about German affairs, including the election of a new anti-king. Fragments of letters from Gregory in the appendix to Altmann's *Vita* illustrate his being in close touch with Gregory about both the overall furtherance of the liberty of the church and the details of how to regard the holy orders of persistently sinful clergy and the status of certain priests who were unwittingly ordained by an excommunicated bishop.[759]

Altmann's close and sympathetic contact with Gregory and his manifest concern for the moral standard of the clergy combined to add force to his pioneering endeavours to propagate the canonical life in Bavaria. His biographer remarked that as in some places he destroyed the service of the devil, in others he established the service

---

[756] *Vita Altmanni*, caps. 11, 17, pp. 232–3, 234. The council at Passau is undated, but is probably 1075 rather than 1074: reasons for the later date are that (i) it was preceded by a long campaign on Altmann's part; (ii) Altmann read out Gregory's letters, in the plural; (iii) Gregory's campaign gained full intensity in Germany only in 1075.

[757] See above, 3.3.4.

[758] For Altmann's friendship with Anselm of Lucca, see Bernold, *Chron. a*. 1091, p. 452/27–31.

[759] *Vita Altmanni*, caps. 13–14, p. 233; for Altmann's having received his staff and ring by messenger, cap. 5, p. 230/39–41. For his visit to Rome in 1079, see also *Epp. vag*. no. 26, pp. 68–9. For his legatine activities in the 1080s, see *Reg*. 9.3, to Bishop Altmann of Passau and Abbot William of Hirsau, (Mar. 1081), pp. 575–7; 9.10; to Bishop Altmann of Passau, (1081), p. 587. For further contacts with Gregory, *Epp. vag*. nos. 58–60, pp. 140–3.

of Christ.[760] Already *c.*1071 and with the patronage of the Empress Agnes, he established a regular canonical life at the suburban church of St Nicholas at Passau; its canons received privileges from Popes Alexander II (1073) and Gregory VII (1075) as well as, in 1074, a diploma from King Henry IV. In June 1076, Henry drove Altmann from the city and reinstated the clerks whom he had expelled from St Nicholas. As soon as Henry left, the canons seized it back and cleansed the church with brooms and holy water; but they were soon once more expelled. The first provost, Hartmann, became a chaplain of the anti-king Rudolf of Rheinfelden and fled to the monks of St Blasien, becoming their prior.[761] Also *c.* 1071, Altmann undertook the reform of two houses of secular canons in his diocese St Florian, where the canons were said to have been 'mindful of their wives and of worldly gain but neglectful of the service of God', and St Pölten, the clergy of which were 'dedicated to drunkenness, gluttony and lust'; in either case he substituted regular canons.[762] The canons of St Florian and St Pölten became concerned with diocesan matters of a quasi-archidiaconal kind.[763]

Despite the resistance that his reforming zeal provoked, Altmann retained a measure of authority in some parts of his diocese. In 1083, he developed a hermitage which he had established eleven years before at Göttweig into a house of regular canons. Unlike St Nicholas at Passau, the proximity of which to the city left it vulnerable to its enemies, the remoteness of Göttweig made it not only an exemplar of clerical life but also a place of refuge for persecuted adherents of Gregory VII, both clerical and lay.[764] The early 1080s also witnessed the foundation in the diocese of Passau of a house of regular canons at Reichersberg, which was placed by its lay founder under the authority of the cathedral of Salzburg.[765]

In the long term, the most important foundation for regular canons in Bavaria during the lifetime of Gregory VII was Rottenbuch, in the diocese of Freising. Rottenbuch was founded in 1073 by Duke Welf of Bavaria in association with Bishop Altmann of Passau. Like Göttweig, its situation was remote; after Pope Urban II's charters of 1090 and 1092 it became the principal centre of the canonical life in Bavaria.[766]

In Gregory VII's lifetime and after, the houses of regular canons ensured a strong witness to the strict standards of clerical life that they both proclaimed and exemplified. Their association with so strongly Gregorian a figure as Altmann of Passau helped to constitute them an effective witness to Gregory's spiritual, moral, and

---

[760] *Vita Altmanni*, cap. 8, p. 231/27–9.

[761] *Vita Altmanni*, cap. 8, p. 231; Bernold, *Chron. a.* 1091, p. 452/22–7; Alexander II, *Ep.* 145, *PL* 146.1417–18; *QF* no. 98, pp. 82–5; *MGH DDHIV* no. 273. On Hartmann, see Jakobs, *Der Adel*, pp. 113–15, 267.

[762] *Vita Altmanni* cap. 9, pp. 231–2.

[763] Haider, *Passau—St Florian—St Pölten*, pp. 36–49.

[764] *Vita Altmanni*, caps. 25–9, pp. 236–8. At the wish of its canons, Göttweig in 1094 became a monastic house. Altmann was buried there in 1091.

[765] Classen, *Gerhoch of Reichersberg*, pp. 66–71.

[766] For the history of Rottenbuch, see Mois, *Das Stift Rottenbuch*.

political objectives. More articulately than any other circle in Latin Christendom, the regular canons of Bavaria cherished and perpetuated Gregory's memory. In 1128, the regular canon Paul of Bernried wrote a *Life* of Gregory which was couched in terms of warmest praise, not least for his campaign in Germany against simony and clerical incontinence.[767] Another regular canon, Gerhoh of Reichersberg, continued to write admiringly of Gregory into the 1160s; from 1121 to 1123, he was a canon of Rottenbuch.[768] Another leading Gregorian polemicist, Manegold of Lautenbach, was a canon of Rottenbuch from 1085 to *c*. 1094, holding there the office of *decanus*. Thereafter, he became the first prior of the house of regular canons at Marbach in Alsace.[769] Both as a burgeoning institution and through the succession of writers and propagandists that they produced, the regular canons were and remained a vital means whereby Gregory's aspirations for the church were transmitted to South Germany, and especially to Bavaria.

3.6.3 Hirsau and German Monasticism

During Gregory VII's lifetime, his purposes in Germany were also advanced by profound developments in the monastic order, especially in Swabia. More than in the case of the canonical life, Gregory eventually set his mark upon them by steps that he took. The most relevant developments for the study of Gregory were three of the successive new directions in the monastic life which have been called 'young-Cluniac'.[770] This designation is acceptable in so far as it epitomizes the common factor of newly introduced monastic Customs which, indirectly or directly, were derived from the abbey of Cluny which lay outside the realms of Henry IV. The key German monasteries were Siegburg, St Blasien, and Hirsau, all of which became centres of networks of houses which spread over wide areas of Germany. In broadest terms, they had the somewhat paradoxical result of propagating in Germany a concept of ecclesiastical liberty upon a Cluniac model, while also representing the monastic interests, both spiritual and temporal, of the upwards-thrusting dynastic families of Germany whose competition with the monarchy of Henry IV was an aspect of the social changes that were transforming the Germany of Henry's day.[771] Hitherto, for example, the highest liberty that a German monastery could enjoy was to be directly subject to the king whether directly or through an imperial bishop; now, a road to monastic liberty opened up which partly or entirely bypassed the king. Step by step, the 'young-Cluniac' forms of monasticism opened the way for Gregory's notion of liberty to impinge upon Germany.

---

[767] Paul of Bernried.

[768] For Gerhoh's estimate of Gregory, see esp. *De inv. Antichristi*, caps. 19–20, pp. 315–30; also Classen, *Gerhoch of Reichersberg*, pp. 55–6.

[769] For Manegold's strong defence of Gregory, see his *Contra Wolfelmum Coloniensem* and *Ad Gebehardum liber*.

[770] Despite the many criticisms to which it has been subject, Hallinger, *Gorze-Kluny* remains the fundamental study of German monasticism in the tenth and eleventh centuries.

[771] For a contemporary observation that the German *principes* took the initiative in bringing to Germany monks from across the Alps, see Lampert of Hersfeld, *Ann. a.* 1071, pp. 154–7.

At Siegburg, near Cologne, Cluniac Customs were introduced indirectly *c*.1068/ 70 by Archbishop Anno of Cologne.[772] The version that was imported was that of the monastery of Fruttuaria, near Turin, which William of Volpiano had founded in the early years of the eleventh century. As Fruttuaria had developed, it established close relations with both papacy and empire while escaping major burdens and obligations to either; for it was free from all obligation to external lordship and owed neither *census* to Rome nor military or other service to the empire. This lack of obligation was in part the consequence, but even more the foundation, of a strong hostility to the simoniac heresy, whether in religious or political connections.[773] Anno brought monks from Fruttuaria when returning from a journey to Rome. His journeys involved him in a significant circle of people. Fruttuaria was highly regarded by the Empress Agnes.[774] To the most powerful family of its region belonged both Bertha, wife of Henry IV, and Adelaide, wife of Duke Rudolf of Swabia. Personal links were present between those promoting ecclesiastical change in Germany and both the papacy and newer monastic trends. The bringing of monks from Fruttuaria to Siegburg had no dramatic results. Siegburg soon lost contact with Fruttuaria, and it remained an episcopal monastery which tended towards neutrality in the contest between Gregory and Henry. But Anno's actions showed that initiatives were possible and gave an example of monastic reform for dynastic families to imitate.

The independent abbey of St Blasien, which was situated to the north-east of Basel, had a long association with the family of Rudolf of Rheinfelden.[775] It, too, adopted the Customs of Fruttuaria but without there being any immediate change in its constitutional status. The critical occasion seems to have been the meeting of the German court at Worms in July 1072. The dramatis personae were significant: the Empress Agnes was present at a reconciliation of Rudolf of Rheinfelden with Henry IV; Abbot Hugh of Cluny was there, and leading roles were played by Archbishop Anno of Cologne who had recently introduced Fruttuarian Customs at Siegburg and Archbishop Siegfried of Mainz who was soon to contemplate himself entering Cluny as a monk. Rudolf of Rheinfelden's association with the new dispensation at St Blasien was probably a factor in 1077 in marking him out as anti-king. In his annal for 1083, Bernold, who from *c*.1085 to 1091 was a monk of St Blasien, named it with Hirsau and All Saints' at Schaffhausen, with their dependencies and their regular discipline, as exemplary monasteries in the German kingdom which attracted many to a life of evangelical perfection and charity.[776]

---

[772] For Anno and Siegburg, see the *Vita Annonis*, caps. 21–7, pp. 476–8; Lampert of Hersfeld, *Ann. a.* 1075, pp. 330–3. The fullest modern study is Semmler, *Die Klosterreform von Siegburg*; see also Jakobs, 'Rudolf von Rheinfelden'.

[773] For its charter of 1005 from Abbot William's relation, the Italian king Arduin, see *MGH DD Arduin*, no. 9. For Fruttuaria in general, see Jakobs, *Der Adel*, pp. 242–53.

[774] See Agnes's letter to Abbot Albert and the monks of Fruttuaria, probably of 1062, in Giesebrecht, *Geschichte der deutschen Kaiserzeit*, 3.1226, no. 1.

[775] Lampert of Hersfeld, *Ann. a.* 1072, pp. 160–3, gives the background. For St Blasien, see esp. Jakobs, *Der Adel*.

[776] *Chron. a.* 1083, p. 439/17–32.

Hirsau itself eventually, although not from the outset of its eleventh-century rehabilitation, adopted Customs from Cluny itself.777 Situated to the north-west of Tübingen, it was founded in 830 but in 1049 was virtually refounded by Count Albert of Calw at the behest of his uncle Pope Leo IX. Albert retained his proprietorship of the monastery, but in 1065 introduced monks from Einsiedeln. In 1069 he deposed the abbot who was then appointed. He replaced him by the outstanding figure in Hirsau's history, William, who was abbot from 1069 to 1091. William came from the monastery of St Emmeram at Regensburg and brought its Customs with him. The next four years were to be a critical period in Hirsau's history.

The events of these years are hard to disentangle and the subject of continuing debate among historians.778 So far as they directly bear upon Gregory VII, two documents are of the utmost importance: Henry IV's diploma for Hirsau, commonly known as the Hirsau Formulary, which is dated at Worms on 9 October 1075 and which confirmed dispositions made at Hirsau by Count Albert on the previous 14 September, and a privilege of Gregory VII which may be of earlier date but which is probably of some four or five weeks later.779

The Hirsau Formulary is a long and complex document. Its main provisions are:

Count Albert surrendered Hirsau and its possessions upon the altar of its patron saint Aurelian to God, St Mary, St Peter, St Aurelian, and St Benedict 'in potestatem et proprietatem'. He recognized the abbots as the sole administrators of the monastery and its possessions. The count with his posterity thus abdicated all proprietary rights ('Dehinc omni potestate, servitio, iure et proprietate predicti monasterii . . . sese omnino abdicavit').

In the event of an abbatial vacancy, the monks were to enjoy free power of electing and instituting a successor according to the Rule of St Benedict.

After such free election, the new abbot should be put in office by self-investiture: he should receive his pastoral staff from the altar of St Aurelian by the hand of the dean or another senior monk of Hirsau, who acted both as the first member of the monastic community and on behalf of the patron saint.

While the rights of the diocesan, the bishop of Speyer, were not mentioned, the provision that the abbot should be ordained *canonice* may tacitly have preserved his right, if in good standing, to perform the blessing of the abbot.

The monks might choose at their advocate any member of the count's family whom they judged suitable; otherwise they might choose whomever they thought

---

777 On Hirsau, see esp. Jakobs, *Die Hirsauer*, and his articles 'Die Cluniazenser und das Papsttum', 'Rudolf von Rheinfelden', 'Das Hirsauer Formular', and 'Eine Urkunde und ein Jahrhundert'. Jakobs gives full references to the extensive literature.

778 For a summary, see Cowdrey, *The Cluniacs*, pp. 196–210; I would now place less reliance than I did then upon the *Vita Willihelmi abbatis Hirsaugiensis*.

779 *MGH DDHIV* no. 280; *QF* no. 88, pp. 71–3.

fit. At the abbot's petititon, the advocate should receive his *Bannleihe* ('bannum legitimum'), or authority to exercise judicial powers, from the king.

Referring to an earlier papal privilege, whether of Alexander II or of Gregory is not stated, the Formulary provided that, in order that Hirsau should enjoy the perpetual protection of the Roman church ('sub Romanae aecclesiae mundiburdio et maiestate semper stabiliatur et defendatur') against kings or others who might contravene this charter ('testamentum hoc'), the abbot would annually pay one bezant at Rome in guarantee that its provisions would be inviolable.

The purpose of the Formulary was summed up in a programmatic declaration about the abbot:

Let him, after he had been ordained canonically and without the exercise of lordship or impediment by any person, thereafter perform the ministry that he has received according to his power and knowledge; let him as a free man serve God alone according to his order; and let him in every way have free power within and without to dispose in Christ of all matters that have been committed to him.

This guarantee of the free power of the abbot was a remarkable pronouncement to have figured in a royal diploma of King Henry of Germany which bore the date 9 October 1075. The king directly surrendered none of his own rights over the church, for Hirsau was a dynastic monastery; therefore, in the ceremony of the abbot's self-investiture at the altar of St Aurelian, the proprietary rights of the count of Calw, not those of the king, were set aside. Moreover, the provision about the royal *Bannleihe* asserted royal jurisdiction and authority even over a dynastic monastery. Yet, by setting his seal to the diploma, Henry signalled to the public in Germany and to Gregory at Rome his openness to consider fresh departures with regard to the monastic order in Germany.[780]

As soon as the royal seal was placed upon it, Abbot William travelled from Worms to Rome in order to secure the corroboration of a papal privilege and probably also to negotiate further on the king's behalf about the understanding for which Gregory hoped.[781] Gregory promptly granted a privilege. It is likely that, when he did so, the train of events which led to his warning letter to Henry IV of 8 December 1075 had not begun. On the contrary, Gregory is likely still to have maintained the goodwill towards the king to which he gave expression early in September when he looked for the increase of peace and concord between himself and the king whom he hoped to welcome in Rome 'as lord, brother, and son'.[782] The terms of the Hirsau Formulary with its concessions to all parties and the report of the king's disposition at Worms that Abbot William gave at Rome may even at this late hour have encouraged

---

[780] See esp. the remarks of Schneider, *Prophetisches Sacerdotium*, pp. 131–3.

[781] For his journey, see Berthold, *a.* 1075, p. 281/13–36 (for his knowledge of the Hirsau Formulary, see Jakobs, 'Das Hirsauer Formular', p. 87 n. 15); *Vita Willihelmi abbatis Hirsaugiensis*, caps. 2–4, pp. 212–13.

[782] *Reg.* 3.7, 10, pp. 256–9, 263–7; see above, 3.2.4.

Gregory to believe that Henry was minded to listen to papal counsels and Roman ideas of relations between *sacerdotium* and *regnum*.

Gregory's privilege for Hirsau fits well into this context.[783] It was brief. Its main provisions were introduced by a reference to the annual payment of a gold bezant in respect of which Count William's liberality to Hirsau ('sue liberalitatis institutionem') was underpinned by papal protection. Gregory's provisions were twofold:

> He took Hirsau and its possessions entirely under the safeguard and protection of the apostolic see ('sub sancte apostolice sedis tuitione et protectione'). Significantly addressing Abbot William in the vocative case and thus, perhaps, taking up the position of the abbot as expressed in the Hirsau Formulary, Gregory described his present privilege as confirming that, under the wings of St Peter and St Paul, the abbot and his successors should have free and absolute possession and use of the monastery and its possessions ('libere et absolute possidenda et regulariter atque utiliter ordinanda').

> Gregory confirmed the regulations and the forms of immunity and liberty which Count Albert set out in the text of his conveyance and caused to be sealed with the king's seal ('Constitutiones quoque et immunitatis et libertatis modos, quos prefatus comes, illustris Adelberthus, scripto sue tradicionis inseruit et regio sigillo imprimi curavit, . . . diligenter observandos statuimus . . .').

While a reference to an earlier royal diploma cannot be ruled out, it is likely that the reference is to the Hirsau Formulary of 1075. All the evidence indicates that the events of September and October 1075 effected a radical change in the constitutional situation of Hirsau which made it desirable for Abbot William to seek papal as well as royal confirmation. At the end of the Formulary, a record was made of the count's conveyance ('traditio'), that is of his handing over of proprietorship, in the presence of seventeen named witnesses. Berthold referred to the witnesses who, according to Swabian law, testified to the absolute passing of proprietorship from Count William

---

[783] In the last two items listed above, n. 7, Jakobs has recently argued that *QF* no. 88 should be dated with or soon after *Reg.* 2.11, to Count Albert of Calw and his wife, 26 Oct. 1074, pp. 142–3, and 2.14, to Bishops Werner of Strassburg and Burchard of Basel, 29 Oct. 1074, pp. 146–7. This has the attractive result of eliminating the need to postulate a lost papal privilege to which the Hirsau Formulary refers (p. 361/17–19), and it eases the problem that the privilege refers to St Aurelian alone while the Formulary refers also to St Peter as a patron of the monastery. But the latter difficulty is more apparent than real, since St Aurelian is given prominence in several passages of the Formulary (pp. 359/37–9, 360/17, 362/17). The reference in the privilege to Abbot William as holding Hirsau and its possessions 'libere et absolute possidenda et regulariter atque utiliter ordinanda' seems to look back to the drastic measures of Sept.–Oct. 1075 rather than to any earlier arrangements. Furthermore, it is improbable that, in 1075, Gregory provided Abbot William with a new privilege that has been lost, since in 1095 Pope Urban II used *QF* no. 88 as the model for his privilege: *Ep.* 129, *PL* 151.402–4. Urban followed the pattern of Gregory's privilege ('nos . . . bonae memoriae praedecessoris nostri Gregorii formam sequentes'). Gregory's text was changed into a full confirmation of Count Albert's dispositions in the Hirsau Formulary: 'Constitutionis [sic] quoque immunitatis, et libertatis modos, quos praefatus comes illustris Adelbertus scripto suae traditionis inseruit, . . . diligenter statuimus, uti nec de promissis quidlibet negligatur, nec de vetitis quidlibet praesumatur.'

to the saints of Hirsau, and the *Vita Willihelmi* wrote in similar terms.[784] The statement of Gregory's privilege that William enjoyed Hirsau and its possessions 'libere et absolute possidenda' strongly suggests that the situation created by the Hirsau Formulary was already established: Hirsau was not only subject to papal protection but it had also been transferred from Count Albert's proprietorship into that of St Aurelian, with Abbot William exercising plenary authority.

A further, surprising feature of Gregory's privilege remains for comment. To the second provision, which confirmed the regulations and the forms of immunity and liberty which Count Albert set out, the rider was added: 'those, that is to say, which are not against canonical sanctions, so that nothing of what is permissible may be omitted and nothing of what is forbidden may be imposed' ('. . . hos dumtaxat, qui canonicis sanctionibus non obsistunt, ut nec de permissis quidlibet negligatur nec de vetitis quidlibet irrogetur'). The count's provisions were to be subject to a scrutiny which might both enhance Hirsau's position still further and exclude features which proved objectionable to the church's law. Hirsau's constitution was to be based upon sure foundations as Rome understood them rather than as Germany did. The norm was to be canon law, not German law. Hirsau's liberty was to be liberty in a Roman sense. In effect, Gregory claimed *carte blanche* to make of Hirsau whatever he would.

He did not now particularize further. If the drafting of Gregory's privilege is correctly placed between Gregory's letters to Henry IV of September and December 1075, Gregory hoped that a well-disposed German king might soon come to Rome, and may have counted upon his being amenable to suggestions about ecclesiastical liberty which were more in line with current Roman thinking than the attempt of the Hirsau Formulary to provide something for everyone. It is impossible to know which canonical sanctions Gregory reserved the possibility of invoking. Perhaps he had in mind the Rule of St Benedict upon a strict interpretation, since the requirement that the abbot should receive his staff from the altar of St Aurelian went beyond the principle stated elsewhere in the Hirsau Formulary that abbatial elections should be conducted 'iuxta predictam libertatem et sancti Benedicti regulam'; the Rule said nothing of such a ceremony. Probably, however, Gregory had in mind the reconsideration in which he seems to have been engaged since early in 1075 of the involvement of lay princes and magnates in the making of bishops; these had included such matters as investiture, and Gregory may have wished to reconsider all aspects of lay power in respect of monasteries and their abbots.[785]

At this juncture, it is unlikely that Gregory's own ideas of what was permissible or desirable in Germany were precisely articulated. They were certainly in process of drastic revision. A little over a year earlier, he had been so far willing to tolerate the state of affairs from which the Hirsau Formulary delivered Hirsau as to recognize the hereditary advocacy of the counts of Eggisheim at Holy Cross at Woffenheim as Pope

---

[784] As n. 781.

[785] See above, 3.2.4, with especial reference to the principle enshrined in canon 22 of the fourth council of Constantinople, and to Gregory's offer of dialogue with Henry: *Reg.* 3.10, p. 266/24–32.

Leo IX had done.[786] Gregory's privilege for Hirsau seems to be the first evidence that Gregory was abandoning his toleration of German practice and that, by late 1075, he aspired to introduce into Germany what he by then believed were the norms of canon law. Abbot William's visit to Rome with the Hirsau Formulary in his hand may well have seemed to present Gregory with an opportunity for refashioning a German monastery, perhaps with Henry IV's agreement, as his active ally, by introducing Roman ideas about monastic liberty. If so, his own privilege for Hirsau marks a kind of half-way house between his arrangements of 1074 for Holy Cross at Woffenheim and his privilege of 1080, in which he entrusted All Saints' at Schaffhausen to Abbot William of Hirsau for thorough reform on the model of Cluny's liberty.[787] The importance of the events centring upon Hirsau in September–October 1075 lay in the possibilities that they left open for introducing into Germany Gregory's own conception of monastic liberty as it was taking shape.

These possibilities were forthwith extended by a fortuitous development. No sooner had Abbot William received Gregory's privilege and made ready to depart for Hirsau than he was stricken down by a severe illness that kept him in Rome for some five months and from which he eventually recovered only, as it seemed, by special divine grace.[788] He cannot have left the city until about Eastertide 1076. He must, therefore, have been there throughout the period when Gregory's relations with the German king deteriorated and when, at his Lent synod of 1076, Henry was excommunicated.

William's sickness and the concurrent political events had the effect of turning him into an out-and-out partisan of Gregory VII and into an activist in his cause against Henry. Hirsau's political stance was correspondingly transformed. As early as Pentecost 1077, Abbot William welcomed there the anti-king Rudolf of Swabia; for almost a year, Hirsau was the headquarters in Germany of Gregory's legate, Abbot Bernard of Marseilles.[789] In 1081, Gregory commissioned William, in collaboration with Bishop Altmann of Passau, to oversee the election of a new anti-king in succession to Rudolf of Swabia, and William sought thereafter to be Hermann of Salm's mentor on Gregory's behalf.[790] In the extended obituary that Bernold of St Blasien gave William, he described him as 'in causa sancti Petri ferventissimus'.[791]

It was at Abbot Bernard of Marseilles's instance that Hirsau looked to Cluny.[792] During his stay, he advised Abbot William to look to it for a model of internal

---

[786] *Reg.* 2.41, to Bishops Werner of Strassburg and Burchard of Basel, 29 Oct. 1074, pp. 146–7.

[787] *Reg.* 7.24, to Abbot William of Hirsau, 8 May 1080, pp. 502–5.

[788] Berthold, *a.* 1075, p. 281/27–35.

[789] Bernold, *Chron. a.* 1077, p. 434/21–3; Berthold, *a.* 1077, p. 298/4–9; *H* no. 33, pp. 69–72; William of Hirsau, *Cons. Hirsaug.* Prol. col. 927.

[790] *Reg.* 9.3, to Bishop Altmann of Passau and Abbot William of Hirsau, (Mar. 1081), pp. 573–7; *H* nos. 18–19, pp. 41–6.

[791] *Chron. a.* 1091, p. 451/13–16; see also Paul of Bernried, cap. 118, p. 543, where Altmann of Passau, Ulrich of Zell, William of Hirsau, and Siegfried of Schaffhausen are listed *quadrigae quatuor praecipui rectores* who promoted Gregory's cause by their canonical and monastic institutions.

[792] The principal sources for this paragraph are Ulrich's *Antiquiores consuetudines Cluniacensis monasterii* which he prepared for Abbot William of Hirsau, and William's own *Consuetudines Hirsaugienses*. For

monastic discipline. The change from the Customs of St Emmeram was thus instituted in 1079. On his return journey from Hirsau to Rome, Abbot Bernard called at
Cluny and persuaded Abbot Hugh to respond to Hirsau's request. Contact was
established by a monk of Cluny, Ulrich of Zell, who had been Abbot William's con-
frère at St Emmeram and whom Abbot Hugh sent on a diplomatic mission to King
Henry IV and to a major German prelate.[793] Ulrich visited Hirsau on his outward
and return journeys to the German king.[794] On his first visit, he spoke at length to
Abbot William about Cluny's Customs which William asked him to write down.
William also sent three successive pairs of monks to Cluny where they observed the
Customs at first hand. William secured Abbot Hugh's goodwill to prune, change, and
augment Cluny's Customs to suit the needs of his own community and its circum-
stances; he eventually drew up his own body of Customs.

By such a route, Hirsau came under the direct influence of Cluny with respect to
its internal monastic life. But, so far as can be seen, Abbot William did not go on to
seek, nor did Gregory VII press him to make, any change in Hirsau's own constitutional position. Gregory issued no new privilege to advance upon the position that
had been reached in the Hirsau Formulary; Urban II's privilege of 1095 shows that,
far from its terms being revised as Gregory had foreshadowed that they might be,
they were allowed to stand.[795] But in two respects, one direct and one indirect,
Gregory was able to benefit from Hirsau's large measure of assimilation to Cluny.

First, he used the direct opportunity which it presented (and which was extended
by the spread of Hirsau's monastic influence) to propagate in Germany his own conception of monastic liberty as exemplified in Cluny itself. Early in 1079, he had already commiserated with the monks of Saint-Victor at Marseilles for the long
absence of their abbot, Bernard, who had been based upon Hirsau. Gregory expressed a desire so to establish a monastic union between their house and the basilica
of St Paul at Rome 'that, as Cluny has now for a long time done, it may specially
cleave to the apostolic see and rejoice in the special help and blessing of this [the
Roman] church'.[796] In May 1080, Gregory wrote a letter to Abbot William of Hirsau
about the monastery of All Saints' at Schaffhausen which, as Gregory recalled, was
already *iuris apostolicae sedis* in return for an annual *census*. The circumstances were
that, in 1079, upon the death of the founder, Count Eberhard of Nellenburg, his son
and successor Burchard summoned Abbot William to reform All Saints'. William

---

the historical material, see the *Epistola nuncupatoria* and the Prologues to the three books of Ulrich's
Customs: *PL* 149.635–40, 643–4, 699–700, 731, and the Prologue to Abbot William's Customs: *PL*
150.927–30.

[793] Thus Ulrich, col. 731A. The king must have been Henry rather than Rudolf of Swabia, who spent
most of 1079 in Saxony. William of Hirsau said that Abbot Hugh had sent Ulrich to Swabia *pro causa
monasterii*: col. 929 BC; cf. Ulrich, col. 643A.

[794] After his first visit to Hirsau, William had asked Ulrich not to return there: Ulrich, col. 731B; this
may hint at William's disapproval of Ulrich's journey to Henry.

[795] *Ep.* 129, *PL* 151.402–4.

[796] *Reg.* 6.15, 2 Jan. 1079, pp. 419–20; cf. *QF* no. 173, privilege for Saint-Victor at Marseilles, 4 July
1079, pp. 199–206.

did so, sending a group of monks from Hirsau, and himself holding the abbacy along with his own for some two years. In January 1080, Burchard met the abbot and surrendered his own rights as proprietor and advocate, constituting All Saints' a free monastery. In his letter to Abbot William which followed Burchard's dispatch of messengers to Rome, Gregory expressed his pleasure that Burchard had renounced all the secular power that he had claimed over the monastery and had allowed it to be free ('liberum esse'). Wishing to provide for the future sacrosanctity of the place ('perpetuam illic sanctitatis stabilitatem providere cupientes'), Gregory committed the monastery to Abbot William on his own behalf ('nostrae sollicitudinis vicem') for the oversight of its internal régime and, above all, to ensure that an abbot was canonically elected. By extinguishing the rights of all secular powers, he defined the liberty of Schaffhausen in the most thoroughgoing terms:

No bishop, king, duke, or count, and no person whatsoever whether great or small, is to presume to claim for himself in this place any rights of proprietorship ('aliquas proprietatis conditiones') whether by hereditary right, or advocacy, or investiture, or of any kind of power that might infringe the liberty of the monastery. No one may invade, diminish, or alienate the ornaments or possessions of the church. Let it be as safeguarded from every secular power and as peaceful in the liberty of the Roman see, as it is laid down that the monasteries of Cluny and Marseilles should remain.

Gregory dealt in a correspondingly radical manner with the advocacy of Schaffhausen: the abbot might choose as advocate whomever he would; if an advocate proved not to be serviceable ('utilis') to the monastery, the abbot should replace him. There was no question of the royal *Bannleihe*. Gregory went so far as to declare null and void a privilege of his predecessor Alexander II, who he said had been deceived, by which Count Eberhard of Nellenburg and his family had been recognized as hereditary advocates with the right of appointing the abbot and administering the monastery's property. As for episcopal offices such as ordinations and consecrations, if the diocesan, the bishop of Constance, were in discord with and disobedient to the apostolic see, the abbot might have recourse to any well-disposed alternative.[797]

Gregory's letter about Schaffhausen, which Abbot William caused to be published in many places including a diocesan synod at Constance,[798] rather than any document that Gregory dispatched to Hirsau itself after 1075, embodied his ultimate formulation of the liberty of a German monastery. It may be construed as indicating what lay behind Gregory's aspiration in his Hirsau privilege of that year 'that nothing of what is permissible may be omitted and nothing of what is forbidden may be imposed'. Only after a long and radical process of rethinking did Gregory arrive at the conclusion that the liberty of a monastery as guaranteed when it was in a state of direct subjection to Rome consisted in the absolute exclusion of all manner of outside proprietorship, power, and jurisdiction, and of all claims of secular lordship

---

[797] *Reg.* 7.24, to Abbot William of Hirsau, 8 May 1080, pp. 502–5, cf. *QF* no. 184, with the date 3 May 1080, pp. 216–19. Alexander II's privilege does not survive. For the Nellenburg family and its monastic foundation, see Hils, *Die Grafen von Nellenburg*, esp. pp. 82–6.

[798] See *Reg.*, p. 505 n. 2; I have been unable to follow up this reference.

whether exercised by bishops or by the king and lay princes or families. It also implied exemption from the spiritual claims and authority of the diocesan bishop if he were not concordant with and obedient to the apostolic see of Rome.

Expressing this concept of liberty which was, for Gregory, archetypically realized at Cluny, the letter about Schaffhausen embodies the view to which Gregory eventually came. It was a far cry, not only from the position of Alexander II, but from his own in 1074 in the case of the Holy Cross at Woffenheim. It was a programmatic statement of Gregory's view of monastic liberty, and when in 1082 Abbot William and the new abbot of Schaffhausen, Siegfried, reformed the Habsburg family monastery of Muri, making it for a few years a cell of St Blasien, the advocacy was dealt with as at Schaffhausen in 1080 rather than as in Hirsau in 1075.[799] Nevertheless, it was to remain exceptional in practice. As Pope Urban II's privilege of 1095 for Hirsau shows, even there the dispositions of the Hirsau Formulary remained intact. Into the twelfth century, the Hirsau Formulary, not the Schaffhausen letter, remained of decisive importance for the constitutional position of the German monasteries.[800] Otherwise stated, the Schaffhausen letter was more significant as an epitome of Gregory's aspirations for the monastic order than as a measure of practical reform.

Gregory's purposes in Germany were also forwarded in a second but indirect way by Hirsau's indebtedness to Cluny. In 1075, the Hirsau Formulary already referred to Count Albert of Calw's purpose that, so far as possible, there should always be available at Hirsau a refuge for all Christ's poor ('quod prout posse suberit cunctis Christi pauperibus beneficium semper illic patefiat receptaculum').[801] This purpose seems to have involved more than the dispensing of monastic aid to the materially poor and to the spiritually penitent. It foreshadowed Hirsau's becoming, like the houses of regular canons in Altmann of Passau's Bavaria, a haven for persecuted Gregorians. In the letter that the Cluniac monk Ulrich dispatched with his Customs, he made three points to Abbot William that encouraged him to proceed in such a direction.[802] First, as regards his own monastic community, Ulrich approved of William's practice of recruiting only spiritually and physically fit men with strong adult vocations; his community was to be equipped as a powerful religious centre. Second, Ulrich also approved the dismissal of unsuitable monastic servants and the recruiting of others from noble and free stock who came voluntarily and for religious reasons. Ulrich ventured the suggestion that such men should not remain outside the cloister, but that according to their capabilities they should be given a place and a role within the monastic community. Third, recruits for the monastery and its activities should be sought out and compelled to come in. Ulrich held up before William the example of the new Cluniac house at la Charité-sur-Loire which stood near a public highway. It gave hospitality to all who passed by and retained many of its visitors for

---

[799] *Acta Murensia*, no. 10, pp. 32–4. For Muri, see esp. Jakobs, *Der Adel*, pp. 49–65. Muri regained its status as an abbey in 1086.

[800] See Cowdrey, *The Cluniacs*, pp. 210–13.

[801] *MGH DD HIV* no. 280, p. 360/9–10.

[802] cols. 635–40, cf. Book 2, Prol. cols. 699–700.

its permanent service and for that of the Cluniac body. In so doing, like Elijah whom God fed by means of ravens, it never lacked the resources to support its work. Hirsau had the advantage of being supported by a rich count and his religious wife; 'let us not believe', Ulrich wrote, 'God to be so localized that what he has done in France he cannot repeat in the territory of Speyer!'

From the initiative of Abbot William as thus encouraged by his Cluniac mentors, there rapidly grew the exemplary monasticism that the chronicler Bernold eulogized. It corresponded to the monastic *sanctitas* that Gregory aspired to foster. Bernold followed closely the model that Ulrich had commended to Abbot William. He noticed that the reformed houses were full to the seams with recruits from the noble and the learned classes of society who had converted to seek evangelical perfection in the monastic life. The monastic duties, including external ones, were performed, not by seculars, but by brothers of the monastery: 'the more noble they were in the world, the more they wish to busy themselves in the basest of offices, so that those who in the world were counts or margraves now reckon it to be the height of pleasure to serve the brothers in the kitchen or bakery and to feed their swine in the fields.' Hospitality was continuously and generously made available to the *pauperes Christi* and to guests according to their need.[803]

Within the monasteries, the recruiting of laymen in large numbers led to the multiplication of *conversi* or lay brothers who formed part of the monastic community. Outside, it facilitated a campaign of preaching and propaganda for a church animated by Gregorian standards of moral and spiritual life. The Augsburg Annals complained of *girovagi* who, under colour of religion, ran about sowing the greatest discord everywhere.[804] To the anonymous monk of Hersfeld who, in 1092/3, wrote the most effective of the Henrician tracts of the period, those who disseminated the message of Hirsau were fomenters of schism and division, and foremost of the enemies of the ecclesiastical unity that he sought to conserve. The division that Hirsau brought into the monastic order by adopting alien dress and Customs spilled over into the body politic. Those who transgressed the boundaries and conventions set by good monastic tradition were destroying *sacerdotium* and *regnum* alike, while giving themselves out to be alone the true church and the custodians of righteousness.[805]

Nowhere did the programme that animated the monks of Hirsau and the monasteries that were influenced by it find more forceful expression than in Abbot William's letter of admonition to the anti-king Hermann of Salm after his election in 1082. The hopes that William entertained of him were strong: through him, the light of truth and righteousness that had been extinguished might be rekindled; the dilapidated state of the church might be restored; and, by the hammer of his just rule, an age of iron might be beaten into an age of gold. William's precept for the anti-king

---

[803] *Chron. a.* 1083, p. 439/20–32.
[804] *Ann. Aug. a.* 1075, p. 128. For *girovagi*, see the *Regula Sancti Benedicti*, 1. 10–11, 1. 438–41.
[805] *Lib. de unit. eccles. cons.* 2.38, p. 266, cf. 2.42, pp. 274–5.

was one of obedience: he should not refuse to devote himself with due reverence to the service of the lord pope. He was to seek the extirpation of the scandal of the simoniac heresy and of clerical incontinence, and he was himself to obey canonical rules when giving ecclesiastical offices ('et vos ipse in dandis ecclesiasticis potestatum investituris devitatis praevaricari').[806] William even warned Hermann against the laxity of the anti-Henrician bishops of Saxony amongst whom he was sojourning. He concluded with a fervent call upon Hermann to collaborate with Gregory VII in extirpating clerical incontinence:

Be heedful, therefore, my son, and acknowledge how gravely you will offend against God and the obedience that you owe the lord pope, and how gravely you will distance yourself from the prayers, indeed from the communion, of all Christ's faithful, if you do not by the terror that you inspire impose the lock of a most rigorous barrier against their most obscene and bestial delights.[807]

Driven by Abbot William's zeal, Hirsau and its monastic connection became one of the most potent disseminators in Germany, and especially Swabia, of Gregory VII's ideals and programme for the church and for the transformation of German society.

Not surprisingly, Abbot William's zeal was answered with outraged rejection by the Saxon bishops and clergy.[808] But in large areas of Swabia around Lake Constance and the upper Rhine, the reformed monasticism of Hirsau, Schaffhausen, and St Blasien found wide support among lay princes opposed to Henry IV who rallied the loyalties of their own dependents. A Swabian opposition formed around the families of Rheinfelden, Zähringen, and Welf. Lesser families like the Nellenburgs and Habsburgs adhered to it. Despite Henry IV's military successes in Swabia which drove the anti-king Rudolf to Saxony, and despite the power to the south and west of the Rhine of Henrician bishops like Otto of Strassburg, Burchard of Basel, Burchard of Lausanne, and Ermenfrid of Sion, Gregory's cause found upholders who were not only open to be his political allies against Henry IV but who also to a greater or lesser extent shared his religious outlook. Gregory found allies in secular and church offices alike. After 1080, Duke Frederick of Hohenstaufen was matched as anti-Henrician duke by Berthold of Rheinfelden. In 1084, Gebhard, brother of Burchard of Zähringen, who had been a monk at Hirsau, became bishop of Constance in succession to the Henrician Otto.[809] Abbot Ekkehard of Reichenau, brother of Count Burchard of Nellenburg, became firm in his Gregorian loyalty. Through such connections, a Gregorian opposition to the Salians emerged in Swabia which ensured the continuance of Gregory's cause there.

Alike in the religion and in the political field, Hirsau and its monastic associates transmitted, and in considerable measure implemented in South Germany, Gregory VII's purpose of establishing the supremacy of papal authority and its permeation of church and society.

---

[806] For the meaning of this phrase, see Jakobs, *Die Hirsauer*, pp. 207–13.
[807] *H* no. 18, pp. 41–3. [808] *H* no. 19, pp. 43–6.
[809] Bernold, *Chron. a.* 1084, p. 441/39–46.

3.6.4 Bernold of St Blasien and the Propagation of Gregory VII's Aims

A feature of the contest in Germany between Gregory VII and Henry IV was the waging by the supporters of both of a skilful and determined campaign of ideas which Carl Erdmann memorably described as representing the beginning of modern political propaganda. In Erdmann's opinion, Henry's decision in January 1076 to bring about Gregory's expulsion from the papal throne led to its unleashing. Henry's own clerks produced skilfully drafted manifestos on his behalf by which his case was not only communicated to Rome but was also disseminated in Germany in an arraignment of the 'false monk Hildebrand' which set out the ecclesiastical and ethical case against him.[810] Henry made an appeal to German public opinion which superimposed a conflict of ideas upon that of armies, and which called forth the skills of *literati* in the service of both parties. It was no one-sided conflict; perhaps the most effective piece of propaganda was the pro-Henrician tract *De unitate ecclesiae conservanda* which a monk of Hersfeld wrote early in 1090s.[811] But in Henry's German manifesto of 1076, there was already a challenge to Hildebrand as to one who had incurred the anathema that the apostle Paul pronounced upon those who preached 'another gospel'.

And so St Paul, when he spared not even an angel from heaven if he preached new things, did not exclude you as well, when you teach new things upon earth. For he said: 'If either I or an angel from heaven shall preach anything save what we have preached to you, let him be anathema' (Gal. 1: 8).[812]

It was a challenge to defend Gregory against the preaching of novelty to which Gregory's supporters amongst the canons and monks of Bavaria and Swabia were well placed to respond by vindicating his fidelity to Christian faith and tradition. It would exceed the bounds of this study of Gregory to give a full account of their endeavours to justify his words and deeds.[813] However, the work of one of them, Bernold of St Blasien, may serve to illustrate their zeal in Gregory's cause.

Bernold was born *c.*1050, the son of a priest;[814] like others in the mid-eleventh century, this circumstance quickened his concern about the morality of the clergy and the standards that should inform it. He was educated in the cathedral school at Constance, where his revered teachers were Albert who died a monk in 1079 and Bernard, later *scholasticus* of Hildesheim.[815] Another profound influence upon him seems to have been Henry IV's unsuccessful attempt in 1069–71 to impose upon the

---

[810] *Epp. HIV* nos. 10–13, p. 60–73. See Erdmann's seminal study, 'Die Anfänge'.

[811] It should, however, be remembered that this tract survives only in an early 16th-cent. printed edition and that nothing is known about its dissemination.

[812] *Epp. HIV* no. 12, p. 66/26–9.

[813] The fullest surveys are Mirbt, *Die Publizistik*, Carlyle and Carlyle, *A History*, and Robinson, *Authority and Resistance*.

[814] See the priest Alboin's remarks in *De incont. sac.* 2, p. 12/21–2. For Bernold, see esp. Robinson, 'Zur Arbeitsweise' and 'Bernold von Konstanz und der gregorianischen Reformkreiz', to both of which articles I am deeply indebted in the present section.

[815] Bernold, *Chron. aa.* 1079, 1088, 436/17–19, 448/8–9.

see his simoniacal clerk Charles.[816] After Gregory VII's excommunication in 1075 of Bishop Otto of Constance, the still youthful Bernold became a dedicated and well-instructed advocate of the Gregorian cause. In 1079, he attended Gregory's Lent synod at Rome at which he witnessed Gregory's condemnation of the eucharistic teaching of Berengar of Tours; he also became acquainted with Bishop Anselm II of Lucca. During his legatine journey in Germany, Cardinal Odo of Ostia in 1084 ordained Bernold priest and appointed him papal penitentiary for the reconciliation of excommunicated clergy. Bernold became the close associate of Bishop Gebhard III of Constance whom Odo also ordained; Bernold probably took part in the synod of Quedlinburg in 1085. Soon afterwards he became a monk of St Blasien but *c.*1091 he transferred to All Saints' at Schaffhausen, where he died in 1100. During his latter years he was in close and cordial contact with the canons of Rottenbuch.[817] Thus, a lifetime of study and propaganda in the Gregorian interest culminated in his association with the centres of canonical and monastic life which were most active in promoting that interest in South Germany.

The foundation of Bernold's learning was his intensive study of the abundant texts of canon law and historical precedents which were available to him at Constance.[818] His most-studied collection was the so-called Dionysio-Hadriana which both represented papal authority and carried the historical cachet of association with the Carolingian reforms. The annotation of texts which he and like-minded students undertook shows how he both identified the material that he himself later used and provided other polemicists like Manegold of Lautenbach with authorities without which their work would have been less effective. Bernold also provided the material for, if he did not himself draft, such programmatic decrees as those of the synod of Quedlinburg which announced the Gregorian model of church life in Germany even when its proponents were militarily beleaguered. As his work progressed, Bernold was at pains not only to garner canonical material but also to seek to harmonize it in a Gregorian sense; his grasp of the need to resolve apparent contradictions foreshadowed the *Sic et non* of twelfth-century early scholasticism.

As early as the mid-1070s, when he was only some 25 years of age, Bernold began to produce and to circulate literature in Germany which was designed to justify Gregory's dealings and to propagate his aspirations. His *De incontinentia clericorum* of 1075–6 comprised an exchange of letters with a priest, Alboin, about Gregory's decrees on clerical chastity. His defence of the rightness of Gregory's campaign was reinforced by a warning of the fate that overcame Bishop Henry of Trier whose mortal sickness synchronized with Gregory's excommunication of him at his Lent synod of 1075.[819] His *Apologeticus* of 1076 or soon after was unusual by being in form a tract rather than a letter. He extended his debate with Alboin to a wider audience of

---

[816] See above, 3.1.2.   [817] Bernold addressed his *De presbyteris* to the 'dominis ac diligentissimis in Christo fratribus apud Reitenboch apostolicae vitae formam fideliter servantibus' and referred to their 'huius vitae legitimum certamen': p. 142/18–20.

[818] See Autenrieth, *Die Domschule von Konstanz.*

[819] *De incont. sac.* 5, pp. 25/40–26/12.

those who needed to be convinced that 'in his decrees, our pope has departed little—no, not at all—from the fathers of the past'. Bernold vindicated Gregory's decrees against both simony and clerical incontinence, and he began his treatise by citing in full Gregory's 'decretal epistle' of 1075 to Bishop Otto of Constance.[820] In a third work, *De damnatione scismaticorum*, Bernold exchanged letters with his teachers Albert and Bernard about Gregory's Lent synod of 1076, defending the authority of the pope to pass the sentence that he had passed and discussing the validity of the sacraments of guilty clergy. The exchange of letters faced up to questions that were asked about Gregory's exercise of his powers but was strong in its condemnation of the German bishops who had withdrawn their obedience to him at Worms, and it upheld Gregory's sentence upon Henry IV and his supporters. Bernold's works ensured that Gregory's programme and actions would not only be publicized but would also be shown to have abundant and weighty canonical justification. He provided a vitally important counter-measure to the manifestos in Henry's support which his own clerks and apologists were disseminating. If his work lacked the rhetorical skill of the Henrician manifestos, he wrote clearly and intelligibly; his massive knowledge of canonical and historical sources and his transparent conviction of the rightness of Gregory's actions added authority to what he wrote in the minds of those who were willing to hear his message.

Bernold's vindication of papal authority was firm but judicious; it was calculated not only to hold but also to extend public support for Gregory.[821] The element of firmness lay in his insistence on the power of the keys by virtue of which Peter and his successors could bind in heaven and upon earth. Yet Bernold was careful to explain that the popes fulfilled their office not only by the exercise of power but also by the persuasiveness of their preaching, and their words had the sanction of the Holy Spirit.[822] An important feature of Bernold's work was that, from the point of view of the Christian who was puzzled about whom he should obey, he established a clear hierarchy of authority within the church. Of especial force was the section *De fontibus iuris ecclesiastici* in his *De excommunicatis vitandis*.[823] Prime among the sources of law were the apostles, after whom came the popes who were their successors in their power as in their preaching. Next followed ecumenical councils and then provincial councils, and finally there were the accredited fathers and doctors of the church. Over the whole structure, the popes were now supreme, and they had the power to judge apart from a synod.[824] Where necessary, they might exercise direct authority over any person, clerical or lay; and they claimed prior obedience over all other prelates ('apostolicae sedi principaliter ab omnibus obediendum esse').[825]

Nevertheless, Bernold was careful to maintain a judicious balance as regards papal authority. On the one hand, because of his power to bind and to loose, the pope might

---

[820] *Epp. vag.* no. 8, pp. 16–19, cited *Apol.* cap. 1, pp. 60–1.
[821] On this subject, see Weisweiler, 'Die päpstliche Gewalt'.
[822] *Apol. rat.* cap. 8, p. 97/2–5; *De excomm. vit.* cap. 29, p. 125/6–15; *Apol.* cap. 6, p. 66/14–17.
[823] pp. 123–41.   [824] *De damn. scis.* cap. 5, pp. 48/44–49/5.
[825] *Apol.* caps. 23–4, pp. 87–8.

digress from and if necessary change existing canons; Gregory VII was right to challenge the aberrations of local custom. On the other hand, Bernold insisted that, in practice, Roman pontiffs habitually followed and maintained ancient customs, unless urgent and reasonable cause compelled them to depart from them.[826] Papal authority was by no means beyond criticism. In his writings about the events of 1076, Bernold accepted that, following the example of Peter himself when Paul resisted him to his face (Gal. 2: 11–14), popes had sometimes been admonished by their subjects. Bernold argued that Gregory VII himself had repeatedly offered to appear before a council at Rome or elsewhere in order to justify himself in face of allegations that he had come by the papacy improperly.[827] Having thus established Gregory's openness, Bernold went on to provide a fervent justification of his steps at his Lent synod of 1076.

Bernold followed Gregory in his insistence that, in human society, the *sacerdotium* is altogether superior to the *regnum*. In the obituary notice of Gregory in his Chronicle, he singled out for especial praise Gregory's determination that the ecclesiastical order should not lie in subjection to lay hands, but should excel it alike in holiness of conduct and in the pre-eminence of its authority; he referred the inquirer who sought warrant directly to Gregory's letters.[828] Bernold was elsewhere insistent that Roman pontiffs might judge and depose emperors and princes, just as they might exercise jurisdiction over the patriarchs of the church.[829]

Within the parameters that he thus set for papal authority, Bernold took active as well as scholarly steps to promote Gregory's cause. In the area of canon law, it is likely that he compiled the so-called 'Swabian Appendix' to the compilation *Diversorum patrum sententie* which Gregory's legates Cardinal-deacon Bernard and Abbot Bernard of Marseilles brought to Germany in February 1077.[830] The Appendix was concerned mostly with the burning topic of excommunication and its consequences, and culminated with titles on the excommunication of kings and other powerful men and the deposition of kings. Like Bernold's *Apologeticus*, the Appendix and the foregoing compilation circulated in Germany, and was used by such Gregorian writers as Bernard of Hildesheim, Archbishop Gebhard of Salzburg, and Manegold of Lautenbach.[831]

In his *Chronicon*, too, Bernold showed total commitment to Gregory's purposes for Germany. Bernold presented Gregory's lay supporters, both men and women, in the terms that he himself used: they were *milites* or *fideles sancti Petri*, and their commitment was to the *servitium sancti Petri*. Especially after 1080 when Archbishop

---

[826] *De excomm. vit.* caps. 58–60, pp. 140–41; *Apol.* cap. 20, pp. 84–5.

[827] *De damn. scis.* cap. 3.2, 11, pp. 47/39–42, 51/21–33.

[828] a. 1085, pp. 443/44–444/13: 'quod illum latere non poterit, quicumque eiusdem apostolici regestum diligenter perlegerit'. For Bernold's use of the word *regestum*, see Robinson, 'Zur Arbeitsweise', p. 60.

[829] *Apol. rat.* cap. 8, p. 97; *De sol. iur.* caps. 4–5, pp. 147–8.

[830] See above, 3.4.2. The 'Swabian Appendix' comprises caps. 316–30 of Gilchrist's edition of the *Diversorum patrum sententie*: pp. 180–96. For the question of authorship, see ibid. pp. xxvii–xxxii; Autenrieth, 'Bernold von Konstanz und die erweiterte 74-Titelsammlung'.

[831] See Robinson, 'Bernold von Konstanz', pp. 181–2.

Guibert of Ravenna was designated for the papacy by Henry IV, Bernold's world was polarized between Gregory, 'the most dedicated builder of the Christian religion and the most energetic defender of the church's liberty',[832] and Guibert the heresiarch and apostate. If Henry IV, 'the former king', shared his condemnation because he was his patron and adherent, from 1082 until 1088 Bernold introduced each new annal by recording where King Hermann kept the Christmas festival. In his value judgements as in his time references, Bernold sustained an intensely Gregorian framework of contemporary history. His frequent obituary notices of persons of his own outlook had the succinctness and eulogy of entries in a martyrology; the vocabulary of martyrdom came readily to his pen. In obituaries of opponents or of bishops tainted by simony, Bernold highlighted their often sudden and miserable deaths and lack of absolution. In his latter years when writing step by step with events, Bernold wrote history in order to propound a thoroughly Gregorian world-view.

His lifelong purpose of promoting the chastity of the clergy was likewise no merely academic exercise. He seems to have undertaken his journey to Rome in 1079 in order to secure Gregory's own condemnation of the treatise of Pseudo-Ulrich, *De continentia clericorum*, and the legend of Paphnutius by which it sought to provide canonical justification for the clergy in keeping their wives. He stimulated a revival of Gregory's own dispatch of letters against clerical unchastity in Germany and Italy.[833] Bernold was present at Gregory's condemnation of the eucharistic teachings of Berengar of Tours and wrote a tract against Berengar which propagated in Germany the eucharistic teaching that, in 1079, Gregory publicly championed.[834] Bernold's most widely circulated work in Germany was his *Micrologus*, the writing of which was facilitated by his first-hand observation in 1079 of Roman liturgical usages. In it, Bernold sought in detail to disseminate in Germany the customs of the local Roman church. They were to be universally followed; local customs, however hallowed, which diverged from them must be set aside and papal directives must be implemented.

Bernold's life of study, exegesis of ancient texts and authorities, and propaganda both in words and deeds, illustrates how profoundly and effectively Gregory's cause was propagated by his followers in South Germany. Their commitment was, in many cases, absolute and unwavering in all the vicissitudes of fortune. By his writings, Bernold enabled them to feel that it was well founded in the traditions of the Christian past, which he made available through his annotation of manuscripts and by his dissemination and discussion of appropriate precedents. Through the networks of the regular canons and the new monasticism with which he was in touch, his propaganda entered deeply into the public consciousness at a deeper level than political events. Through such committed propaganda, continued in successive

---

[832] *a.* 1085, p. 444/5–6: 'Erat enim catholicae religionis ferventissimus institutor, et aeclesiasticae libertatis strennuissimus defensor.' Guibert was 'Guibertus heresiarcha': p. 444/13–16.

[833] *Chron. a.* 1079, p. 436/1–4; Berthold, *a.* 1079, p. 317/36–41; *Epp. vag.* no. 32, pp. 84–7.

[834] *Chron. a.* 1079, p. 435/43–6; Huygens, 'Bérenger de Tours', pp. 378–87; Weisweiler, 'Die vollständige Kampfschrift'.

generations by writers like Manegold of Lautenbach, Paul of Bernried, and Gerhoh of Reichersberg, Gregory's cause took deep root in the religion of South Germany despite the vicissitudes of the last years of his life and despite his death in exile.

3.7 Conclusion

Gregory's purposes with regard to the German church and kingdom underwent profound changes during his pontificate. At the outset, his prime concern was to bring the young King Henry IV to a better mind. He sought to instruct him in the religious, political, and moral qualities that, in his view, were called for in one who succeeded his father, Henry III; thus, Gregory might be able soon to proceed to Henry IV's imperial coronation at Rome, which Henry also desired. Only the constraint of events arising from the German civil wars, which Gregory had not caused and which he could not control, led to Gregory's eventual recognition of Rudolf of Rheinfelden as German king and to his countenancing of elective kingship. So far as the German church was concerned, the campaign against clerical simony and incontinence, which Gregory's letters suggest that he particularly directed to Germany, developed slowly during the early months of his pontificate, but reached its peak in 1075 after his Lent synod of that year. Save for a brief period after his synod of 1079, although the elimination of these 'heresies' remained one of Gregory's objectives, he did surprisingly little in an active way to continue the campaign that he had energetically undertaken in 1075. It had perforce to take second place to wider and deeper purposes which he formed in response to the turmoil in the German kingdom which began in the early months of his pontificate and which was renewed after 1077.

More than anything else, his standing concern with regard to a Germany that, from 1073, was rent by civil war and that, from 1077, was divided in its loyalties between two kings, was to promote a German national assembly which would bring peace and concord to the land. Gregory hoped himself to come to Germany in order to hold such an assembly; if this was not possible, he hoped to work through legates who would represent the fullness of papal authority. Before his first breach with Henry IV at the beginning of 1076, Gregory already regarded the bringing of peace to the German kingdom upon papal initiative as one of his objectives; the course of Cardinal-bishop Odo of Ostia's German itinerary in 1084–5 suggests that it remained active, through the medium of widely attended assemblies under legatine authority, to the end of his pontificate. By his insistent quest for an assembly, Gregory posed deeply and permanently the question of which authority, *sacerdotium* or *regnum*, was not only the ultimate but also the direct source of justice, peace, and order in German society, and of whether the kingdom had a power which was subordinate to that of the papacy or one which was comparable and complementary to it. Gregory's sentences of excommunication and deposition against Henry IV and his claim of the right to decide in a divided kingdom as to which of the rival kings satisfied the demands of righteousness constitute only one aspect of his conception of the superiority of the *sacerdotium*. This superiority was not only a matter of such occasional juridical exercise; it was also one of which authority provided for the peace and concord of the kingdom. As such, it involved a claim to determine the standing basis upon which men should conduct themselves towards each other. Gregory's long quest for a national assembly under his own authority cast the pope, not the king, as the source of peace and order in society.

It was, therefore, virtually impossible that it should take place, for no party in Germany wanted it or was prepared to support it. As at Forchheim, the princes opposed to Henry IV wished to hold the initiative in electing a new king at their own time and in their own way; Henry IV replied by asserting his own regality and, ultimately, his own right to be the source of peace and justice in his kingdom. When Gregory died in 1085, Germany although war-weary was divided between the loyalties and the claims to authority that were exemplifed by Odo of Ostia's assembly at Quedlinburg and Henry IV's at Mainz. There was no prospect of building bridges or of taking such common national counsel as Gregory had sought. Gregory's cherished hopes for an assembly of the whole German kingdom under his own auspices had always been unrealistic, and the division of Germany in 1085, with Henry for the time being in a position of considerable strength, stood in manifest contradiction of them.

Yet Gregory had won many able and committed disciples, especially among the canons, monks, and publicists of South Germany. Their aspirations for a revitalized ecclesiastical order were well rooted in German soil, both through association with the German princes who opposed Henry IV and in movements for church reform which were established and widespread. Their readiness to accede to Gregory is best seen in figures like Abbot William of Hirsau and the monk Bernold of St Blasien, who themselves visited him in Rome and responded at first hand to his personality and zeal. In Germany, Gregory's charisma was strong in winning the loyalty of the many who, for religious or political reasons, were predisposed to follow him. No less, Gregory also repelled many, such as Archbishop Liemar of Bremen, who regarded his interventions as a threat to their own position and canonical rights. Such men looked, rather, to the regality, in symbol and in the practice of kingship, which Henry IV after 1077 had some success in establishing. Both by attraction and by repulsion, Gregory left an indelible mark upon a Germany which was in any case in a time of crisis. He could find devoted allies and agents: he was, however, not able to bring about a resolution of any of its problems. They were not patient of resolution by the means that he envisaged.

Gregory VII and the Kingdom of Italy

4.1 The Kingdom of Italy

The kingdom of Italy may be understood as that part of the Italian peninsula which lies to the north of a line from Terracina in the south of the Roman Campania to a point on the Adriatic coast just south of the River Sangro. With Germany and Burgundy, it formed one of the three kingdoms over which the Salian king Henry IV reigned. It was the expectation of German kings that they would receive the Italian crown at Pavia, Milan, or Monza before they proceeded to imperial coronation at Rome. They also retained claims to lordship over Southern Italy which found recognition even by Gregory VII, as when in September 1073 Prince Richard of Capua swore fealty to Gregory, he acknowledged his duty, with appropriate reservations, to swear fealty to Henry IV, as well.[1] There was, in effect, a papal and royal condominium in the South; but, given the problems of distance and communication, it was only occasionally, and usually when the king himself visited the South, that the royal claim became of practical significance.

A host of factors—economic, political and historical, and not least the need for imperial coronation by the pope at Rome, made his lordship over the kingdom of Italy up to and including Rome a vital interest for a German ruler such as Henry IV. It was not an interest that it would have entered the head of an eleventh-century pope radically to challenge. Without the Emperor Henry III's intervention at Rome in 1046 and its sequel in the accession of Leo IX to the papacy in 1049, there would have been no reform papacy; while the prerogative of performing an imperial coronation gave the pope a trump card with regard to both ecclesiastical and political affairs in Germany. It also had a bearing upon North Italy; since the German king's access to Rome lay through it and since papal influence there was considerable, a German king who had not been imperially crowned could not afford entirely to alienate the pope; although it might be expedient, as in 1046, for the king to get rid of a weak or unworthy pope, or, as in 1084, for him to seek to substitute a more amenable one.

The complexities of the ecclesiastical structure of the kingdom of Italy must also be borne in mind. Its provinces cut across regional and political divisions. There were three organized church provinces. In the north-west, that of Milan comprised, besides the archbishopric, seventeen bishoprics in Lombardy and Liguria; Pavia, an exempt see depending directly upon Rome, formed an enclave within it. To its east, disposed around the northern end of the Adriatic from Mantua, Verona, and Padua to Trieste, lay the province of Aquileia; it also included the bishopric of Como, a city

---

[1] *Reg.* 1.21a, p. 36/16–18.

to the north of Milan which controlled the approaches to the St Gotthard and Septimer passes as Verona controlled the road to Brenner. In addition to the patriarchal see, the province comprised five bishoprics in Istria and ten in the march of Verona and in Lombardy; Trent, which was nearer to the Brenner than Verona, was subject ecclesiastically to Aquileia, but since 1027 it was part of Bavaria and so of the German kingdom. Stretching southwards from Ferrara and the Po estuary was the province of Ravenna. Eleven of its bishoprics, including the important crossroads see of Bologna, lay in Romagna; the four bishoprics of Modena, Parma, Piacenza, and Reggio/Emilia extended across the north of the margraviate of Tuscany into Lombardy. The province extended so far to the west that the ancient monastic centre of Bobbio lay within it. Although part of the province of Ravenna, much of the Romagna was assigned by the imperial privileges of 962 and 1020 to the lands of St Peter.

South of the province of Ravenna there was no organized church province; for the description of the region extending down to the southern border of the kingdom of Italy as a Roman ecclesiastical province has little medieval warrant and can be misleading. Rather, there was in the centre of Italy an aggregation of some sixty-four bishoprics, many of them very small, which were immediately subject to the jurisdiction of the bishopric of Rome. Many of them were situated in the lands of St Peter in the narrower sense of the region between Acquapendente and Terracina; there were thirteen in Roman Tuscany and ten in the Roman Campagna. The Pentapolis contained twelve more, and some eleven others were scattered near these regions. But there were also two areas which lay outside the papal lands as conceded in 962 and 1020 and over which the king could assert certain claims: in the duchy of Spoleto there were eight bishoprics, and in the southern part of Tuscany ten more which included Florence, Lucca, Pisa, and Siena.[2]

There was also the city of Rome itself, with its own ecclesiastical organization and suburbicarian bishoprics.[3] This complex ecclesiastical structure and its political context made it necessary for Gregory VII to deal with different regions in different ways.

4.2 Central Italy

An inquiry into Gregory's dealings in the kingdom of Italy may conveniently begin with the bishoprics (except Pavia) over which the bishop of Rome exercised direct jurisdiction in this capacity. There are two reasons. First, although there is a dearth of surviving evidence, the proximity of these bishoprics and the manifest concern that Gregory felt for them makes it probable that their business occupied much of the time of the pope and his immediate entourage. The historian must not become so preoccupied with Gregory's activities in matters of wider importance that he

---

[2] G. Schwartz, *Die Besetzung*, remains a useful guide to the complexities of the ecclesiastical organization of the kingdom and to the succession of bishops. The numbers given above are of sees which are likely to have had bishops during Gregory's pontificate; they cannot be more than approximate.

[3] See above, 1.5.

overlooks the local and routine matters that were his daily concern. Second, many of the claims and methods that Gregory pursued in relation to the kingdoms of Germany and Burgundy, as well as to the lands beyond them, had been formed and tested in Central Italy.

For almost the whole of his pontificate, Gregory enjoyed a considerable degree of support or at least acceptance there. Up to the installation of Clement III as anti-pope in 1084, Gregory encountered little open resistance in the lands of St Peter that were nearest to Rome. In the Roman Campagna, indeed, there was general episcopal loyalty even after 1084 to the Gregorian cause, especially from those bishops who had a monastic background. In Roman Tuscany, as well as in the Pentapolis and in Umbria, a number of bishoprics after 1084 showed less settled loyalties; even before that date, Bishop Bonizo of Sutri, who after Gregory's death wrote his *Liber ad amicum* in his defence, gained no recognition at Sutri and at Massa Maritima Henry was able to secure the election of a friendly bishop.[4] To the north and east, in bishoprics where the king had a recognized stake, Gregory faced a more delicate position. Between 1076 and 1080, his dealings with Henry IV met with criticism to which Gregory and his supporters made reference without precisely declaring its source. In the winter of 1076–7, he made his journey towards Germany against the counsels of almost all his advisers except Countess Matilda of Tuscany.[5] In October 1079, Gregory told his German supporters that 'However many *Latini* there are, all save a tiny few applaud and defend Henry's cause, and accuse me of excessive harshness and mercilessness towards him'; the Swabian chronicler Berthold confirmed the strength and persistence of such sentiments.[6] The criticism is likely to have come, at least in part, from clergy and laity of Central Italy who, after 1084, showed Guibertine sympathies.

Gregory seems to have responded by showing caution and moderation in his dealings with the bishops of the region and with royal business which impinged upon them. An example is his dealings with Bishop Rudolf of Siena. On 1 November 1076, Gregory informed five Tuscan bishops that Rudolf had gone illicitly to Henry IV and had communicated with him, thereby incurring an excommunication from which he had lightly asked to be released. Gregory called upon his brother bishops to excite him to proper penance so that his restoration to communion might be permitted. As with German bishops in 1076, Gregory offered him a road to restoration; in the following September, he went further by employing him, together with Bishop Rainer of Florence, to oversee the canonical election of a bishop of Volterra.[7] Gregory showed a tactful blend of firmness and moderation when dealing with such an erring bishop and enlisting his collaboration.

Until his breach with Henry IV in 1076, Gregory showed comparable moderation and restraint in accommodating the king's claims and interests which suggest that he took account of a prevailing loyalty to Henry in much of Central Italy. Two examples

---

4 Schwartz, *Die Besetzung*, pp. 261, 263.   5 *Epp. vag.* nos. 17, 19, pp. 48/1–2, 50/26–8.
6 *Reg.* 7.3, p. 462/28–33, cf. 4.12, to the German princes, Jan. 1077, p. 313/1–10. For a similar statement in Berthold, see *a*.1079, p. 317/1–4.
7 *Reg.* 4.8, 5.3, pp. 306–7, 350–1.

illustrate Gregory's caution. In 1073, the strongly reform-minded Anselm II was elected bishop of Lucca. Anselm engaged in a prolonged consultation with Gregory as to whether he should receive investiture at the king's hands. Gregory's reiterated advice to the reluctant Anselm was that he should refrain from receiving investiture until Henry had made amends for his contact with his excommunicate counsellors and was restored to peace with Gregory.[8] In the spring of 1074, this condition was satisfied when Gregory's legates visited Germany. According to the chronicler Hugh of Flavigny, Anselm came to Rome in December for ordination by Gregory, but while he was there messengers from Henry requested Gregory to follow custom by post-poning ordination until Anselm, and also Hugh, bishop-elect of Die in the kingdom of Burgundy, had not only been elected bishop but had also received royal investi-ture. Gregory turned to the cardinals for advice which, in Hugh of Flavigny's opin-ion wrongly, favoured acceding to the king's request. Gregory therefore agreed to defer Anselm's ordination until the king had invested him, but he proceeded with that of Hugh of Die.[9] Gregory seems to have acted with prudent regard to political reality. In Burgundy, Henry's power was weak; therefore Gregory proceeded with the ordination of Hugh of Die. In Central Italy as at Rome, there was sufficient recog-nition of Henry and his claims for Gregory to act accommodatingly by permitting investiture before consecration.

A second example of Gregory's sensitivity to royal claims is provided by the filling in 1074 and 1075 of the bishoprics of Fermo and Spoleto. In December 1075, Gregory's anger at Henry's nomination of bishops to these sees was a major factor in his sudden disenchantment with the king.[10] But twelve months earlier, Gregory's careful provisions for the filling of the see of Fermo had included an express inten-tion of consulting the king about the election; a new bishop was in office by June 1075, apparently by agreement.[11] When the see again became vacant and Henry himself filled it together with Spoleto, Gregory did not object to this high-handedness on the grounds that it was intrinsically inadmissible, save in a conditional aside, 'if, however a church can be handed over or given by a man'.[12] Stung, no doubt, by Henry's not reciprocating his own courtesy of December 1074, he objected that, in derogation of the canonical rule that a bishop should ordain only those who were approved by and known to their ordainer, Henry had given the two churches to clerks unknown ('ignoti') to him.[13] Since the next bishop of Fermo was named Wolfgang, it appears

[8] *Reg.* 1.11, to Countesses Beatrice and Matilda of Tuscany, 24 June 1073, pp. 18/29–19/4; 1.21, to Anselm, bishop-elect of Lucca, 1 Sept. 1073, pp. 34–5.

[9] Hugh of Flavigny, 2, pp. 411/35–42, 50–412/9. For Anselm's later rejection of his investiture, see *Vita Anselmi ep. Lucensis*, cap. 4, p. 14.

[10] *Reg.* 3.10, to King Henry IV of Germany, 8 Dec. 1075, p. 264/21–6. See above, 3.3.1.

[11] *Reg.* 2.38, to Count Hubert of Fermo and all its clergy and people, 22 Dec. 1074, p. 38/20–4. A bishop named Peter was in office in June 1075: Schwartz, *Die Besetzung*, p. 234.

[12] A possible reference to *Vigilantia universalis*, cap. 6: Schieffer, *Die Entstehung des päpstlichen Investiturverbots*, pp. 222–3/153–7.

[13] As n. 10. The canon-law text that Gregory seems to have had in mind is *Decreta Leonis papae ad Anastasium episcopum Thessalonicensem*, caps. 2–5, Hinschius, p. 619.

that Henry put forward a German who was his own partisan.[14] As at Lucca Gregory was prepared to countenance royal investiture, so at Fermo he was prepared to allow the king a voice in the choice of bishops, so long as those chosen were known to him as the canons demanded.

In fact, Gregory's insistence that bishops whom he would ordain should be approved by and known to him can be illustrated from his Register as a normal and standard requirement. At Lucca, Anselm was known to Gregory as a learned and discreet man.[15] In Corsica, Gregory in 1082 required information about the election and the person of a bishop before he would ordain him.[16] At Volterra in 1077, Gregory set out more fully the stages of an election there: first, a candidate should be established in the pope's eyes as being 'utilis et idoneus' in accordance with canonical requirements; second, his election should be duly performed by the clergy and people of his prospective church and confirmed on the pope's behalf; third, the duly elected candidate should be sent to the pope for ordination.[17] In Gregory's eyes, papal consecration to the episcopate was more than an exercise of jurisdiction; it established a personal bond which was cemented by the pastoral care upon which Gregory set high importance.[18] Gregory's oversight of the many bishoprics of Central Italy was so exercised as to foster relations of friendship and loyalty between Gregory and the bishops. His consecration in the first year of his pontificate alone of two Sardinian and three Central Italian bishops is a reminder of the close and regular contact that episcopal appointments established between Gregory and the bishoprics that were directly subject to his jurisdiction.[19]

Gregory's official and personal involvement in episcopal appointments was reinforced by other means whereby his authority was promoted in Central Italy. There can be no doubt that the bishops, clergy, and laity of the many bishoprics of this region usually provided a numerically preponderant element in his Lent and November synods at Rome.[20] The records of them are sparse, and only occasionally were matters of business from Central Italy recorded in the Register, as when, in Lent 1078, Abbot Berard I of the imperial abbey of Farfa was threatened with excommunication and deposition for an unspecified cause, or as when the moral transgressions of leading lay figures were considered.[21] But like royal crown-wearings in

[14] He was excommunicated by Gregory in 1079: *Reg.* 6.17a, p. 429/14. For his name, see Schwartz, *Die Besetzung*, pp. 234–5. The next bishop of Spoleto was named Rudolf, so may also have been a German: Schwartz, p. 240.

[15] *Reg.* 1.11, pp. 18/29–19/11, cf. *Vita Anselmi ep. Lucensis*, cap. 2, pp. 13–14.

[16] *Reg.* 9.28, to Cardinal Hermann of SS. Quattro Coronati, pp. 611/32–612/4.

[17] *Reg.* 5.3, pp. 350–1. Gregory made no reference to lay investiture, perhaps because, although the king had been restored to communion at Canossa, the kingdom was in suspense.

[18] As in the case of Anselm of Lucca: *Reg.* 1.21, p. 35/13–16, see also *Vita Anselmi ep. Lucensis*, cap. 3, p. 14. As the case of Bishop Hugh of Grenoble shows, the bond was not limited to Central Italian bishops directly subject to the papacy: Guigo, *Vita sancti Hugonis*, 2.7–8, 3.10, cols. 767, 769.

[19] *Reg.* 1.85a, p. 123.

[20] See e.g. *Reg.* 2.52a, p. 196/10–15; 3.10a, p. 268/10–14; 5.14a, p. 368/34–41; 6.17a, p. 425/17–23; 7.14a, p. 480/4–9.

[21] *Reg.* 5.14a(7), (8), (12), p. 371/6–16, 28–31.

the courts of lay rulers, the synods provided occasions for regular contact between the pope and leading clerical and lay figures. A great deal of local business of which record does not survive is likely to have been transacted at them both formally and informally.[22] Their impact upon local churches may best be seen in the *Ordo officiorum* of the cathedral of Volterra, compiled in the next century. It records six rulings by Gregory, three of them made in Roman synods. His pastoral concern is illustrated by his wish to eradicate false penances, and to ensure that those in grave sin confessed to true pastors who would guide them to amend their whole lives. Gregory was concerned to secure the due observance of feasts and fasts, including the commemoration of earlier popes.[23]

Over the region of Central Italy at large, Gregory's vigilance was an active one, both to secure order and also to fulfil the pastoral commission of his office. In connection with a local dispute at Roselle, he propounded a principle which underlay his actions both there and in the wider sphere of Germany: it belonged to the papal office to recall to concord those who were in discord with each other. The churches of Roselle and Massa Maritima were, therefore, set a time within which they must agree about disputed possessions and respect past papal rulings.[24] For routine purposes, such as the collection of revenue, the papacy in Gregory's day evidently had agents at large; thus, when he gave certain possessions of the Roman church at Rimini to the local monastery of St Peter and St Paul, the annual rent of twelve pence was to be paid to the agents ('actionarii') of the apostolic see.[25] Especially in Tuscany, monasteries and houses of regular canons were given privileges which demonstrate Gregory's confidence in them as centres of religious reform and political influence.[26]

Gregory further secured his purposes in Central Italy by the sending of legates. In his Register, his dispatch early in 1075 of the abbots of two Roman monasteries, Gepizo of SS. Bonifazio e Alessio and Maurus of S. Saba, is unusually well documented. His commission to them spoke of the pope's need in practice to entrust the care that he had for the whole church to trusted sons who represented locally the fullness of his authority. Writing about their legation to the clergy and people of Montefeltre and Gubbio in the Pentapolis, he urged each church to act under the

---

[22] e.g. *Reg.* 3.13, to the clergy and people of Roselle, (Apr. 1076), pp. 274/26–8, 35–275/5.

[23] *De sancti Hugonis actis liturgicis*, caps. 58, 64, 114 = 134, 136, 138, 262, pp. 79, 84, 129–30, 149, 81–2, 153, 221. Caps 114 = 134 and 138 contain material enacted in general synods; with cap. 221, cf. *Reg.* 6.5*b*, p. 401/29.

[24] *Reg.* 3.13, pp. 274–5, cf. *QF* no. 84 for an earlier confirmation by Gregory of the possessions of Massa Maritima. For the settlement of other disputes, see *Reg.* 2.17, to Abbot Sigebald of S. Salvatore at Perugia, 13 Nov. 1074, pp. 149–50; judgement relating to the abbey of S. Michele a Marturi, Florence, 28 Aug. 1077, *QF* no. 140, pp. 155–7 (Gregory passed through Florence in Aug. 1077.)

[25] *QF* no. 154, pp. 178/31–179/1.

[26] Privileges for monasteries recorded in *QF* include S. Maria nell'Isola di Gorgona (dioc. Pisa), 28 Jan. 1074 (no. 61); Camaldoli, 20 Mar. 1074 (no. 70); S. Ponziano at Lucca, 25 Apr. 1074 (no. 78); Fonteavellana, 23 Mar. 1076 and 4 Apr. 1080 (nos. 113, 182); S. Michele in Borgo at Pisa, 10 Aug. 1077 (no. 139); S. Felicità at Florence, (1078) (no. 146); S. Salvatore di Settimo (dioc. Florence), 10 Jan. 1078 (no. 149); St Peter and St Paul at Rimini, 25 Mar. 1078 (no. 154); S. Zeno at Pisa, 2 Mar. 1081 (no. 197); S. Salvatore at Fucecchio (dioc. Lucca) 9 May 1085 (no. 218). For regular canons, the cathedral chapter of S. Florido at Città di Castello, 19 Feb. 1079 (no. 164).

legates' oversight in electing a new bishop, and to prevent the spoliation of their churches by presenting their churches' treasure and ornaments for the legates' inspection. The legates' ultimate destination was the march of Fermo. There, they were to recover the goods that the bishop of Pesaro had foolishly alienated, and they were to settle lawsuits between the bishop and his local adversaries. The legates were to warn Rainer, a member of the family of the dukes of Spoleto and of the counts of Camerino, to perform proper penance for an act of fratricide, on pain of his case's being settled by Gregory himself. (It ultimately came up at a Roman synod.)[27] Gregory evidently used legates for the local discharge of his business in Central Italy with a comparable commission to that which he imposed in dealings with more distant regions of Christendom.

If Gregory looked for the obedient service of bishops and legates, he required with urgent insistence that his directions should be enforced both by the concurrent application of the spiritual sanctions and pressures of all grades of the clergy and by the physical coercion of the faithful laity. Thus, for example, in instructing his legates of 1075 about righting the wrongs of the church of Pesaro, he insisted that all possible force should be brought to bear upon wrongdoers:

Resolutely commanding the bishops, the counts, and all the faithful of St Peter, call upon them faithfully to help the bishop of Pesaro to defeat them by bringing spiritual and secular aid according to what is needful. Above all, you are most sternly to chastise those who after payment of money do not fear to go on keeping land in violence and pride; you are to intervene and restore the goods of the church to the bishop.

Gregory's mobilization of the laity deserves particular notice. Habitually resorted to when need arose, it indicates that Gregory's use of the German laity to coerce sinful clergy was not a novel expedient, so much as the extension to Germany of a usage that was well established in Central Italy as a means by which popes defended their interests.[28]

It was at the northern limits of Central Italy that Gregory most strenuously asserted his authority and duty to rule effectively. His attempt to call out the laity in 1080 in order to coerce Archbishop Guibert of Ravenna will be noticed later.[29] A standing concern of Gregory was to secure the obedience, reform, and good order of the churches of Corsica and Sardinia. As early as October 1073, Gregory wrote to the judges of Sardinia and expressed his especial care for their island.[30] It was a care that he was to work through his Central Italian suffragans in order to promote. In

---

[27] *Reg.* 2.40–1, 46, 48, 5.14*a* (7), pp. 177–8, 185–6, 188, 371.

[28] For appeals to clergy and laity to add their sanctions to Gregory's or his legates' rulings, see *Reg.* 2.38, to Count Hubert and all the clergy and people of Fermo, 22 Dec. 1074, p. 175/1–6; 2.46, to Gregory's legates in the march of Fermo, 13 Jan. 1075, p. 186/8–17 (cited); 2.7, to named laity and to the laity in general of the county of Chiusi, 13 Jan. 1075, p. 187/22–35; see also below, nn. 32, 34. It should be appreciated that, in Central Italy, there was a long tradition of calling upon the laity to coerce simoniacal clergy; see Goez, 'Reformpapsttum', pp. 225–8 and n. 121.

[29] See above, 3.5.3 and below, 4.6.

[30] *Reg.* 1.29, to the judges of Sardinia, 14 Oct. 1073, pp. 46–7; 1.41, to Judge Orzoccor of Cagliari, 16 Jan. 1074, pp. 63–4, 1.85*a*, p. 123.

September 1077, as he returned to Rome from his journey to Canossa, he wrote to the bishops, clergy, and consuls of Corsica with an energetic assertion of papal authority over all local churches. Since his multifarious commitments prevented him from personally visiting every part of the church, he must use agents to represent his authority and to provide for the salvation of the people and the common good. He therefore commissioned Landulf, the bishop-elect of Pisa, to be the permanent vicar of the apostolic see in Corsica.[31] He followed this letter by another to the Corsicans, in which he reminded them of the papal proprietorship of their island, and also of the sacrilege and spiritual peril of those who had withheld their due subjection and obedience. The Corsicans must repent and return. He gave those who were well disposed a double assurance: there was in Tuscany an abundance of noble laymen who were ready and willing to come to their military help and defence; and he was sending Landulf of Pisa as bishop and upholder of the rights and interests of St Peter.[32] In 1078, Gregory gave Landulf and his successors a privilege in which he promised papal protection against the enemies of his church, recognized that he had come to his see in a canonical manner with consecration at his own hands, and entrusted Pisa with a papal vicariate over Corsica.[33]

In October 1080, Gregory reverted to the problem of Sardinia. He praised the judge of Cagliari for his respectful reception of his legate, Bishop William of Massa Maritima, and reminded the judge of the authority of St Peter and his vicar. He said that Normans, Tuscans, Lombards, and even Germans had importuned him to sanction their incursions into Sardinia, but he had in the past forbidden them and for the future would do so by both secular and spiritual means.[34] Exercising his authority through Tuscan bishops, Gregory stated the universal and particular claims of the papacy, and his determination by all means, both spiritual and secular, to enforce his rulings and his purposes.

All in all, Gregory both had and deserved a high degree of success in securing the loyalty of the churches of the Central Italian region. His ways of doing so were various, but prominent among them was the exercise of effective pastoral care. He showed moderation in advancing and in exercising his claims to authority; this was not least apparent, during the early months of his pontificate, in his recognition of the corresponding claims of the German king and in his seeking accommodation with him, as in the cases of Lucca and Fermo. Gregory's balance of firmness and moderation was the more prudent in view of the support that Henry IV seems to have possessed in the region. It won him a high degree of acceptance for an exercise of authority that was firm, moderate, and statesmanlike. He knew the region from boyhood, and showed a sureness of touch in its affairs that he did not so conspicuously exercise in relation to regions north of the Alps.

---

[31] *Reg.* 5.2, to the bishops, clergy, and consuls of Corsica, 1 Sept. 1077, pp. 349–50.
[32] *Reg.* 5.4, to all clergy and laity in Corsica, 16 Sept. 1077, pp. 351–2.
[33] *Reg.* 6.12, to Bishop Landulf of Pisa and his successors, 30 Nov. 1078, pp. 413–14.
[34] *Reg.* 8.10, to Judge Orzoccor of Cagliari, 5 Oct. 1080, pp. 528–30; for a reference to Gregory's earlier dealings about Sardinia with Duke Godfrey of Lorraine, see *Reg.* 1.72, 7 Apr. 1074, p. 104/5–7.

4.3 Lombardy

It is not surprising that, in face of Gregory's claims and the sanctions by which he sought to enforce them in the bishoprics of Central Italy which were subject to his direct spiritual jurisdiction, he should face widespread and bitter opposition amongst the bishops of North Italy who were apprehensive of intensive papal intervention in this region as well. Nowhere was opposition more sustained than in Lombardy, most but not quite all of which comprised the province of Milan, with its proud Ambrosian tradition and claim to virtual autonomy from Rome. Gregory himself regarded Lombardy as a coherent region,[35] and its bishops in the province of Milan and beyond collectively represented his most implacable foes in Italy.[36] For Gregory's ardent partisan Bishop Bonizo of Sutri, they were 'the headstrong (*cervicosos*) bishops of Lombardy, who did not know how to bear the gentle yoke of the Lord'.[37]

The major centre of Lombard hostility to Gregory was the metropolis of Milan; in the reforming and militant movement of the Patarenes, the deeply divided city provided him with some of his most favoured allies.[38] From his early months as pope, the rival claims to the see of Henry IV's candidate Godfrey and of Atto, who took refuge at Rome, ensured that, as pope, Gregory should continue to be deeply concerned with its affairs. The Lombard bishops were the especial object of his wrath, on the grounds that by consecrating Godfrey they defended and fostered there the heresy of simony, for which Godfrey had been condemned and excommunicated. In Gregory's eyes, they had become the open assailants of the Roman church and the precursors of Antichrist. He instructed Countesses Beatrice and Matilda of Tuscany to have no communion or other dealings with them. Bishop William of the exempt see of Pavia was likewise to avoid them, and also to give every support to the catholic party at Milan—that is, the Patarenes.[39] Gregory also wrote an encyclical letter to all the faithful of St Peter, particularly in Lombardy, in which he arraigned Godfrey as one who had presumed to buy the church of Milan like a common slave-girl, thereby seeking to prostitute the bride of Christ to the devil and to separate her from the catholic faith.[40] In these letters, Gregory rested the weight of his accusation entirely

---

Gregory was also concerned to enforce upon the archbishop of Cagliari and the clergy the canonical requirement that, according to the custom of the Roman church, they should shave their beards. Local idiosyncrasies were not permissible.

[35] e.g. *Reg.* 1.15; to the faithful of St Peter in Lombardy, 1 July 1073, p. 23/19–21, 30.

[36] *Reg.* 1.20, to Bishop Raynald of Como, 1 Sept. 1073, p. 34/15; 1.77, to Countesses Beatrice and Matilda of Tuscany, 15 Apr. 1074, p. 110/23; 3.14, to Patriarch Dominicus of Venice, (Apr.) 1076, p. 275/30–3; 8.5, to the bishops of South Italy, 21 July 1080, p. 522/15–22.

[37] *Lib. ad amic.* 6, p. 595/11, 7, p. 605/25–7.

[38] For a general summary, see Cowdrey, 'The Papacy, the Patarenes and the Church of Milan'. The Patarene leader Erlembald is most strikingly portrayed by Andrew of Strumi, *Vita s. Arialdi*, cap. 15, pp. 1059–60.

[39] *Reg.* 1.11, 24 June 1073, p. 18/8–28; 1.12, 29 June 1073, pp. 19–20.

[40] *Reg.* 1.15, 1 July 1073, pp. 23–5.

upon Godfrey's simony; he made no reference to the matter of lay investiture, nor did he name the king.

During the remainder of 1073, Gregory repeatedly displayed his enthusiastic support for the Milanese Patarenes, and especially for their lay leader Erlembald. He made Erlembald his confidant in matters relating to all parts of Italy and beyond. He reported to Erlembald—with a rejoicing that Erlembald will not have shared—the receipt of Henry IV's letter, 'full of sweetness and obedience', in which the king acknowledged his guilt that the church of Milan was 'in error' and requested Gregory to correct it according to canonical propriety. Messengers passed frequently between Milan and Rome.[41] Gregory called on bishops whom he believed to be well disposed to rally to Erlembald's support; he entertained especial hopes of Bishop Gregory of Vercelli who was Henry IV's chancellor for Italy, Albert, bishop-elect of Acqui, and William of Pavia.[42]

No doubt in the light of Henry IV's conciliatory letters of 1073 and the mission of Gregory's legates to Germany in 1074 who restored the king to communion,[43] Gregory in the latter year moderated his campaign against the Lombard bishops and looked for reconciliation with them, as well. In January, he summoned all the suffragans of Milan (but not Godfrey himself) to his Lent synod, together with all the abbots of Lombardy. The terms of his summons were studiously mild: obedience or disobedience to it would disclose which, or perhaps it would be all, of them were faithful soldiers of Christ who were committed to his service.[44] Unfortunately, little record of the Lent synod survives, especially so far as the Lombard bishops are concerned; according to the Milanese chronicler Arnulf, however, Gregory publicly acclaimed Atto as archbishop of Milan—without royal approval, which angered Henry, and in the absence of the Ambrosian clergy and people which was evidently resented by Milanese conservatives like Arnulf.[45] But Gregory was afterwards widely accused of undue mildness. He wrote to the Countesses Beatrice and Matilda a letter of reassurance. He had restored Dionysius of Piacenza and the other Lombard bishops to none of their episcopal functions save to the power when necessary of confirming children. He saw himself as steering a middle course of justice and mercy: as he put it, he was keeping the reins of the whole business in his own hands so that no one need despair of pardon for the reformed or of punishment for the obstinate. He understood that, because of their love of and regard for the Roman church, they had murmured against his lack of strictness, but he was gladly giving them an answer consistent with the affection that bound them to him. He referred to other critics, as well, and of the variety of their judgements of him: some thought that he was cruel but others that he was too mild with respect to the same causes and actions.[46]

---

[41] *Reg.* 1.25–6, 27 Sept. and 9 Oct. 1073, pp. 41–4; cf. 1.19*a*, Henry IV to Gregory VII, (Aug./Sept. 1073), pp. 47–9 = *Epp. HIV* no. 5, pp. 54–7.

[42] *Reg.* 1.26, pp. 43/37–44/2, 1.27–8; 13 Oct. 1073, pp. 44–6.   [43] See above, 3.2.3.

[44] *Reg.* 1.43, 25 Jan. 1074, pp. 65–7.

[45] Arnulf of Milan, 4.4, pp. 208–9; cf. *Reg.* 2.30, to King Henry IV, 7 Dec. 1074, p. 164/13–17.

[46] *Reg.* 1.77, 4 Apr. 1074, p. 110/23–39.

Gregory's impression of moderation when dealing with the Lombard bishops was in no way matched at Milan by Erlembald and his Patarene militants, who remained confident of Gregory's favour. Erlembald treated the rites of the Lombard bishops as null and void. Thus, at Easter 1074, when the Henrician archbishop Liemar of Bremen was similarly dishonouring the sacraments of Bishop Hermann of Bamberg, he trampled underfoot the chrism that one of them had consecrated for the city, and postponed the Easter baptisms until other chrism could be procured. The conservative Milanese chronicler Arnulf complained that Erlembald's many violent deeds made the people more obedient to him—partly from simplicity, partly for money, and partly because his crimes went unpunished. But he also implied that Erlembald's power was precarious: he only seemed (*videretur*) to dominate his fellow-citizens. This is confirmed by the Patarene sympathizer Andrew of Strumi, who let slip that, in Erlembald's days, many Milanese were left desolate of the sacraments, and by Bonizo of Sutri, who credibly said that Erlembald was thrown on the defensive: 'the number of the faithless daily grew, while that of the Patarenes diminished'. It was the *capitanei*, the leading social class of the city and its environs, whom the chronicler Landulf Senior said were driven from the city, who were most determined to get rid of Erlembald and all that he represented. Erlembald made too many enemies in Milan itself for his cause to be sustained.[47]

By December 1074, Gregory had become uneasy that Henry IV, who otherwise seemed to be obedient, had still not settled the affairs of Milan as he had promised in his two submissive letters of 1073, although he remained persuaded of Henry's essential goodwill. He pressed Henry for a resolution of the problem of Milan: if Henry could send him holy and wise men who would explain how the Roman church's reiterated decrees excommunicating Archbishop Godfrey and recognizing Archbishop Atto might be changed, Gregory would concur. If he could not, Gregory besought Henry freely to restore to the Roman church its rightful prerogative. Then, at last, Henry might know that he held his royal power rightly, for he would be directing the loftiness of his dominion to Christ the king of kings, in order to effect the restoration and the defence of his churches.[48] Gregory evidently looked to Henry for the abandonment of Godfrey and the recognition of Atto, and for his collaboration in the moral reform of the see of Milan.

Despite this note of urgency, Gregory's preparations for his Lent synod of 1075 appear to have remained studiously low-key so far as Italian affairs were concerned. In the case of the see of Fermo, he was prepared, in a letter of 22 December, to allow an episcopal election to proceed 'with the counsel of the king', and he postponed Anselm of Lucca's ordination until he had been invested.[49] In Lombardy itself, there is no evidence for a general summons of all bishops such as Gregory had issued a year earlier. Gregory's only summonses that survive are addressed to individual bishops

---

[47] Arnulf of Milan, 4.5–6, pp. 209–11; Landulf Senior, 3.30, pp. 96/31–97/10; Bonizo of Sutri, *Lib. ad amic.* 7, p. 604.

[48] *Reg.* 2.30, 15 July 1074, pp. 163/17–23, 164/13–21.   [49] See above, 4.2.

who were to attend for special reasons: Bishop Cunibert of Turin because of a dispute with the abbey of S. Michele della Chiusa, and Bishop William of Pavia about the problem of his sister's marriage.[50] As in 1074, so in 1075 there is little evidence about the business of the Lent synod with regard to Italy. According to the official protocol, Gregory suspended the two Lombard bishops whom he had individually summoned, and he deposed Bishop Dionysius of Piacenza whose dealings with the monasteries of his city had recently attracted Gregory's adverse attention.[51] The account of the synod in the Milanese chronicle of Arnulf raises serious difficulties of interpretation. As drafted, its terms are not expressly specific to Milan or to Lombardy, and even so it is unlikely that Gregory issued an immediately effective prohibition of lay investiture.[52]

Whatever Gregory may or may not have done at his Lent synod, the year 1075 saw two major reverses to his interests at Milan as he saw them, both of which left him uncertain in his response. The first flowed from the accident that, on 30 March, a disastrous fire, the second in four years, swept through much of Milan, destroying or damaging many churches including the 'winter church' or cathedral. To the medieval mind, such things did not occur by chance. Many Milanese deemed it to be God's punishment for the sins and excesses of the Patarenes. Erlembald was unabashed and persisted in his ways of violence; at Easter, he again tried to enforce his own will with regard to the seasonal liturgy. He elicited a powerful opposition of knights and citizens. It gathered reinforcements from the countryside. A sworn association undertook to vindicate righteousness ('iustitia') and the honour of St Ambrose, and to receive the archbishop whom King Henry had sent, that is, Godfrey. In bloody skirmishes, Erlembald was killed and his corpse dishonoured. His clerical aide, Liutprand, who had helped him to subvert the city's Easter observances, was brutally mutilated by the cutting off of his nose and ears. The Patarenes were put to rout. Many of the surviving Patarenes fled to Cremona and neighbouring cities. At Milan, the Patarene movement receded into the shadows for twenty years.[53]

At Rome, Gregory heard of the defeat of his Patarene friends with horror and dismay. He failed to grasp that the Patarenes' collapse was virtually complete. His faith in their cause survived. Later in 1075, he wrote a fervent letter to the priest Liutprand, whose mutilations had been calculated to disqualify him from exercising his priesthood, to assure him that his scars were, in truth, the glorious badges of martyrdom. Gregory urged him to stand fast in Christian witness and took him into immediate papal protection.[54] Especially after his breach in February 1076 with

---

[50] *Reg.* 2.33, to Bishop Cunibert of Turin, 12 Dec. 1074, pp. 169–70; 2.35–6, to Bishop William of Pavia, and Countess Matilda of Este, 16 Dec. 1074, pp. 35–6.

[51] *Reg.* 2.52a, pp. 196/28–197/2; for Bishop Dionysius, see also 2.26, 27 Nov. 1074, pp. 158–9. It should be noticed that Gregory's pre-synodal letters to the bishops of Turin and Piacenza opened with the formula *salutem et apostolicam benedictionem* which was expressive of his recognition: cf. 1.43, p. 66/1–7.

[52] See above, 3.2.4.

[53] Arnulf of Milan 4.8–10, pp. 212–17; Landulf Senior, 3.30, p. 96/28–97/38; Bonizo of Sutri, *Lib. ad amic.* 7, pp. 604/35–605/15.

[54] *QF* no. 106, pp. 94–5; cf. Peter Crassus, *Def. Hen. IV*, 4, p. 439/23–7.

Henry IV, Gregory continued to write about political matters to Patarene knights as cordially he had formerly written about them to Erlembald.[55] From the chronicler Berthold's account of the Lent synod of 1078, it would seem that Gregory then caused to be recited a list of the miracles which had been performed at the tomb of Erlembald, 'who three years before had suffered from righteousness' sake'. His deeds at Milan were commemorated at length, and he was celebrated as a martyr and saint.[56] But, in truth, Gregory's chosen supporters at Milan had collapsed and the Patarenes had lost their significance.

Gregory's second major reverse in 1075 came when, after his victory over the Saxons but while Gregory still entertained hopes for his co-operation, Henry arbitrarily set aside the two rivals for the see of Milan, Godfrey who had never securely established himself there and Atto who had taken refuge at Rome. His choice for the see was a young Milanese subdeacon of his own chapel named Tedald, who was said to have done him good service in the field against the Saxons.[57]

At least so far as his letters reveal it, Gregory's reaction was surprisingly muted, partly because Tedald approached him with a view to recognition. In December 1075, Gregory summoned Tedald to Rome at or before his Lent synod of 1076; he urged the Lombard bishops meantime to refrain from promoting Tedald in holy orders.[58] The breach between Gregory and Henry followed almost immediately, and Gregory's fury at the actions of the German and Italian bishops at Worms and Piacenza transformed his policies from the moderation of those of 1075. But his first reaction to Tedald's nomination had been, at least publicly, mild.

Against the background of Gregory's further relations with Henry, the long-term effects in Lombardy of the defeat of the Patarenes and the nomination of Tedald were threefold. First, Tedald ensured for Henry a continuing measure of support at Milan. The Lombard bishops quickly ordained him bishop, and he was able to secure some support in the city. In October 1076, Gregory assured his Patarene friends there that the power of St Peter would now overcome Tedald as it had overcome his predecessors Guy and Godfrey.[59] Given Patarene weakness, this did not happen; for Gregory, Tedald of Milan was bracketed with Guibert of Ravenna at the head of those in North Italy whom he most deprecated. At some earlier stage, Gregory

---

55 *Reg.* 3.15, to Wifred, knight of Milan, (Apr.) 1076, pp. 276–7, 4.7, to Henry, Arderic, and Wifred, 'fidelibus sanctae apostolicae sedis legitimis filiis Mediolanensis ecclesiae', 31 Oct. 1076, p. 305.

56 Berthold, *a.* 1077, pp. 305/24–306/4.

57 See above, 3.3.1. The sources give differing details of Tedald's succession. Landulf Senior said that the Milanese sent four candidates to Henry whom he rejected, naming Tedald instead: 3.32, p. 99. According to Bonizo of Sutri, the Milanese *capitanei* elected Tedald at Henry's command, whereupon Henry invested him: *Lib. ad amic.* 7, pp. 605–6. Arnulf said nothing of Henry's rejection of Milanese candidates but only that he promoted Tedald 'proprio . . . indulgens arbitrio'. He also said nothing about an election, although Tedald was received 'a clero et populo': 5.5, pp. 222–4. No one seems to have pressed the claim of Godfrey, although Arnulf implied that he was still alive. According to Bonizo, Tedald had been present when Godfrey was consecrated at Novera in 1073: *Lib. ad amic.* 6, 7, pp. 600, 605.

58 *Reg.* 3. 8–9, 8 Dec. 1075, pp. 259–63, cf. 3.10, p. 264/17–21. For a fuller discussion, see above, 3.3.1.

59 *Reg.* 4.7, p. 305/30–4. For Tedald's reception for a time at Milan, see Arnulf of Milan, 5.5, p. 224/4–6.

pronounced against Tedald an anathema which he renewed and intensified at his
Lent synods of 1078, 1079, and 1080.[60] According to a Milanese source at the synod
of Brixen in 1080, Henry IV first wished to offer the papacy to Tedald, whose name
stands first among the episcopal attestations of the synodal decree.[61] With his military past, he came to the fore in Henry's Italian expeditions of the early 1080s; in 1083,
his troops were active in operations at Rome. Bernold listed him among the *capita
scismaticorum* who died in 1085.[62] Milan continued, through Tedald, to bring support to Henry IV and to be, in the eyes of Gregory and his party, the see of a notorious Henrician archbishop.

Second, however, by one of the most remarkable paradoxes of Gregory's pontificate, the defeat of his Patarene protégés at Milan also led to an upsurge of Milanese
opinion in his favour. The evidence is provided by the chronicler Arnulf, the
spokesman for the conservative, upper-class ecclesiastical and social establishment
in Milan as seen in its better aspects. He had always known that, in the church of his
city, reform was called for. But he could not abide the lay aggressiveness of the
Patarenes, and he was repelled by the support that Erlembald found at Rome:

We do not resist you, O Roman lieges, since our master St Ambrose says: 'I desire in all things
to follow the church of Rome.' We are one with you in faith; with you, we abjure all heresies.
But it seems right to us that the law of the church should be taught by a doctor of the church,
and not by an unskilled layman ('sed videtur nobis ratum, ut ius ecclesiasticum doctor
exhibeat ecclesiasticus, non ydiota laycus').[63]

Once Erlembald had gone, Arnulf could be shocked by the high-handedness of
Henry and his Milanese supporters when they imposed Tedald upon the church:

In short, this archbishop was received by a clergy and by a people which was, as ever, avid for
some new thing. The self-same bishops who had consecrated Godfrey now consecrated him.
A wonderful thing indeed, and unheard-of in times past, that, when one bishop had been
chosen for a city and another consecrated, yet a third should intrude himself![64]

Arnulf abandoned his former solicitude for the king. By a conversion that he likened
to that of St Paul on the road to Damascus, he turned, fully and conscientiously, to
Gregory. In this, he was not alone; he was one of a deputation of the upper clergy and
laity of Milan who, early in 1077, went to Gregory at Canossa. Encouraged, no
doubt, by the public example of a king 'humiliatus ad paenitentiam', they similarly
sought absolution from Gregory for their resistance to Rome and for their slackness
in the cause of reform. Gregory seized his opportunity by sending to Milan the
Cluniac, Cardinal Gerald of Ostia and Bishop Anselm II of Lucca, who was a

[60] *Reg.* 5.14a(1), p. 369/4–8, 6.17a(5), p. 429/11–13, 7.14a(3), p. 481/4–9. The date of Gregory's first,
unrecorded sentence against Tedald is uncertain; it may have post-dated Tedald's contact with Henry at
Pavia after Canossa: *MGH DDHIV* no. 293.

[61] Landulf Senior, 3.32, p. 99/32–4; *Quellen HIV* Anhang C, p. 480/30.

[62] Benzo of Alba, 6, Praef., pp. 657/29–31, 658/50–4, Landulf Senior, 3.32, pp. 41/46–100/11; *MGH
DDHIV* nos. 338–9, 350. For Tedald's death, Bernold, *Chron. a.* 1085, p. 443/35–40.

[63] Arnulf of Milan, 3.15, p. 190/9–14.   [64] Ibid. 5.5, p. 224/1–6.

Milanese of the leading family of da Baggio. They preached to the citizens and then absolved and blessed all those who would hear them.[65]

And yet, third, despite, or perhaps because of, the military valour of Tedald in Henry's cause and the conversion of Arnulf and his like to Gregory's obedience and loyalty, Milan, which at the outset of Gregory's pontificate had been a nerve-centre of his dealings with Henry, after 1077 became a no man's land of little significance. Tedald never sufficiently established himself there. His support at the synod of Brixen for a Ravennese anti-pope had adverse consequences. Milan and Ravenna had long vied with each other for ecclesiastical precedence. After Archbishop Guibert of Ravenna had been possessed of the papacy, partly by Milanese arms, he made it a prime concern to assert and confirm Ravenna's privileges.[66] This provides a probable explanation of the Milanese chronicler Landulf Senior's curt dismissal of Guibert as 'out of his wits and rich in the devices of the Greeks' and of his taking his story no further: disenchantment with an emperor who sponsored an anti-pope from Ravenna was profound.[67] Yet while the militarily strong Tedald was alive, Gregory's sympathizers at Milan could not hope for superiority. He died on the same day in 1085 as Gregory himself. Only thereafter was the way open for the diplomatic skills of Pope Urban II to make headway in consolidating the city's loyalties in a way favourable to the papacy.[68]

Milan occupies a large place in the historiography of Gregory's pontificate. In Arnulf and Landulf Senior, it had eloquent chroniclers. The choice of Guy, Godfrey, Atto, and Tedald as its archbishops raised problems about episcopal elections and the relative rights in them of local church, king, and pope. The Patarenes and their lay leader Erlembald provide a striking and accessible example of a popular religious movement in its social as in its spiritual aspects. Their rise, dominance, and eclipse form one of the dramas of medieval history. It must not, however, be overlooked that similar if less well-documented groups existed in other cities, and that there was coming and going amongst them. Those in cities like Cremona and Lodi helped others in need; the few sympathetic bishops performed ordinations for and generally encouraged reforming groups in churches other than their own; monastic figures like, until his death in 1073, John Gualbertus at Vallombrosa were warmly supportive.[69]

Gregory's letters and privileges show that he encouraged reforming groups wherever he could, to the extent of directly intervening through legates. Lodi, Cremona, and Piacenza offer glimpses of his concern. At Lodi, he had a high opinion of the bishop, Opizo. In 1075, he wrote to the people of the city in praise of their zeal against simony and priestly fornication and to encourage support for the bishop in his

---

[65] Ibid. 5.8–9, pp. 227–31; *Vita Anselmi ep. Lucensis*, cap. 17, p. 18.
[66] Clement III, *Epp.* 2–3, *PL* 148.828–31.   [67] 3.32, p. 99/32–6.
[68] Cowdrey, 'The Papacy, the Patarenes and the Church of Milan', pp. 41–7; id., 'The Succession of the Archbishops of Milan'.
[69] Bonizo of Sutri, *Lib. ad amic.* 6, pp. 594, 597–9, 7, pp. 602, 605; Andrew of Strumi, *Vita s. Ioh. Gual.* cap. 78, p. 1100.

promotion of reform.[70] It was Gregory's ideal scenario, if in a tiny city. At Cremona, Arnulf was a less satisfactory bishop whom, in 1078, Gregory deposed for his simony.[71] Probably a year earlier, Gregory had brought help to those clergy and people at Cremona who loved righteousness ('clero et populo Cremonensi iustitiam diligenti') by accepting for St Peter, and giving his own protection to, the church of S. Agatha. He endowed its caritative work for the poor for so long as its hospital ('xenodochium') remained under the control of the church.[72] Thus, he sought to establish a nucleus of true religion. At Piacenza, Gregory also looked for, and thought that he could find, a body of clergy and laity upon whom he could depend. It is far from clear either in what ways or how far Bishop Dionysius was culpable or what form the undoubted opposition to him in his city took. In April 1074, Gregory went out of his way to single him out as a Lombard bishop about whose correction or penalty he was concerned.[73] In the following November, he wrote him a fraternal letter. Dionysius had himself sent the simoniacal Abbot Regizo of S. Savino to Rome for correction, and he had resigned his office to the pope. To safeguard the monastery's goods, Gregory provided that, until the monks could elect a new abbot and subject to the rights of the church of Piacenza ('salvo tuae ecclesiae iure'), Regizo should retain custody of the abbey. In all this, Gregory counted upon Dionysius's own co-operation for the well-being of the monks. But Gregory's legates who brought the letter were also themselves to adjudicate in another dispute involving Bishop Dionysius and what appears to have been a reform-minded coalition of the abbot of S. Sepulchro with the city church of Piacenza ('plebemve Placentinam') and a subdeacon named Bonizo who may have been the future bishop of Sutri and Piacenza. The legates were to restore peace so that, after much litigiousness, the monks and the bishop might alike return to the due service of God. Gregory also wrote to the monks of S. Savino about their new election, and urged them to pray constantly for the recovery and safety of the Roman church.[74] Gregory's temperateness and his hope for all-round appeasement were quickly frustrated. At his Lent synod of 1075, he deposed the bishop.[75] He straightaway wrote to those of a right mind in the city ('universis catholicis Placentinae ecclesiae') enlarging upon the disarray of their church and the incorrigibility of their bishop. He absolved from their oaths those who owed him fealty and called for outright opposition to him of the most determined kind. Gregory would himself see that all the faithful of St Peter should come to their aid in expelling the wolf and choosing a shepherd. As citizens of God ('cives Dei') they should be strong, for God was with them. He specially absolved any who should die in defence of righteousness ('pro defensione iustitiae').[76]

Gregory's clarion call for militant public action at Piacenza had no recorded result. There was no new election, and Dionysius regarded himself as bishop until his death

---

[70] *Reg.* 2.55, 3 Mar. 1075, pp. 200–1.   [71] *Reg.* 5.14*a*(2), p. 369/9–12.
[72] *QF* no. 124, p. 124.
[73] *Reg.* 1.77, to Countesses Beatrice and Matilda of Tuscany, 15 Apr. 1074, p. 110/23–7.
[74] *Reg.* 2.26–7, 27 Nov. 1074, pp. 158–9.   [75] *Reg.* 2.52*a*, p. 197/2.
[76] *Reg.* 2.54, 5 Mar. 1073, pp. 198–9.

in 1082/5. Not long after Bonizo became bishop of his native city under Pope Urban II, a rising of his opponents there drove him from the city with appalling physical injuries.[77] As at Milan, so at Piacenza and probably in other Lombard cities, Gregory's attempts to recruit support met with limited success, and a balance of contrasting interests led to stalemate.

It was not only among the reformist clergy and people of the Lombard cities that Gregory sought, but largely failed to find, effective and long-term allies. He seems to have entertained hopes that, amongst the lay nobility, Adelaide (died 1091), countess of Savoy and mother of Henry IV's queen, Bertha, would join the pious ladies, like the Empress Agnes and Countesses Beatrice and Matilda of Tuscany, to whom he looked for friends and allies. Adelaide was a strong-willed woman whom Peter Damiani had long ago addressed as a new Deborah and a 'virago Dei'; she was a prospective ally in the struggle against concubinous clergy, and a protector of the 'vere thalamus Iesu', the monastery of Fruttuaria.[78] Her son, Count Amadeus II, was among those whom Gregory hoped to recruit for his eastern expedition of 1074.[79] In 1073, Gregory sought Adelaide's protection for the monasteries both of Fruttuaria and of S. Maria della Chiusa; the latter monastery, in particular, was exposed to the hostility of Bishops Gregory of Vercelli and Cunibert of Turin.[80] A year later, Gregory acceded to Adelaide's request that he should offer papal protection to her own monastic foundation of S. Maria de Pinerlo, near Turin.[81] However, in the contest between Gregory and Henry IV, Adelaide's position seems to have been detached. According to Lampert of Hersfeld, Adelaide drove a hard bargain with her son-in-law to facilitate his passage through her lands on his way to Canossa where she was one of those who pleaded with Gregory for Henry's absolution.[82] Her younger daughter, also named Adelaide (died 1079) was married to the German anti-king Rudolf of Swabia; in 1080, at the time of the synod of Brixen, Henrician attempts to recruit her support for the king's party seem to have failed, and in 1082 her stance seems to have been that of a mediator.[83] Turin was simply too far from Rome, her family connections were too complex, and her local interests were too pressing, for her to give Gregory the help for which he initially hoped; although she never acted in a way that was hostile to his interests.

Perhaps the most permanently reliable help that Gregory found in Lombardy came from monasteries of the older Benedictine tradition. His active concern to secure such help is suggested by a letter of 1073 about the monastery of S. Maria di

77 Schwartz, *Die Besetzung*, p. 191.   78 *Briefe*, no. 224, 3.295.

79 *Reg.* 1.46, to Count William of Burgundy, 2 Feb. 1074, p. 70/17–21.

80 *Reg.* 1.37, to Countess Adelaide, 7 Dec. 1073, pp. 58–9; see also 2.33, to Bishop Cunibert of Turin, 14 Dec. 1074, pp. 169–70; 2.69, to Bishop Cunibert of Turin, 10 Apr. 1075, pp. 226–9; 6.6, general letter, 24 Nov. 1078, pp. 406–7; William of Chiusa, caps. 12, 14, p. 205a–b. According to William, Cunibert 'ex bonis initiis malos eventus habuit': cap 2. p. 298a/46–7.

81 *QF* no. 74, pp. 53–6. Gregory referred to Adelaide as 'carissima sancti Petri filia'.

82 *Ann. a.* 1077, pp. 396/5–21, 404/4–11; *Reg.* 4.12, to the Germans, (Jan. 1077), p. 313/15–18.

83 Benzo of Alba, 4.13, 5.9–13, pp. 646/49–647/3, 653–5.

Butrio (dioc. Tortona). He refused the request of its abbot-elect that he should confirm a privilege of his predecessor Pope Alexander II which he pronounced to be suspicious on grounds of poor Latinity and defective canonical authority. He postponed the issue of a privilege of his own until the vacant see of Tortona had been filled; much would depend on whether it was filled canonically. He also had reservations about the personal suitability of the abbot-elect. Gregory evidently counted upon the monastery of S. Maria either to reinforce the virtues of a good bishop or to resist one who was uncanonically elected; he was also concerned to ensure the monastic competence of a new abbot.[84]

The history of the abbey of S. Michele della Chiusa, Gregory's defence of which against Bishop Cunibert of Turin has already been noticed,[85] suggests that, here at least, Gregory found monastic support. The life of its abbot from 1061 to 1091, Benedict, from start to finish exhibits him as a wholehearted and valiant Gregorian in his resistance to simoniacal bishops and to a schismatic king.[86] Benedict suffered much at their hands, and especially at those of Bishop Cunibert of Turin.[87] He was in touch with more distant monastic centres: he received encouragement from Abbot Hugh of Cluny, and having visited Gregory at Rome, probably in 1082, he went on to Montecassino, thus exciting the anger of Henry IV.[88] Abbot Benedict stands out as perhaps the most consistent and effective Gregorian among the bishops and abbots of Lombardy.

Lombardy was of major concern to Gregory throughout his pontificate. It was the heart of Henry IV's kingdom of Italy; its bishops were intensely hostile to him and they showed solidarity in their militant opposition. The succession of archbishops in its metropolis of Milan was a central issue in Gregory's dealings with Henry IV, and the ingrained prevalence there of the 'heresies' of simony and clerical marriage and incontinence, together with Milan's claims to virtual independence of Roman intervention, added to the urgency of his concern. At Milan itself, the effect of Gregory's actions was to open up the church and city to outside influences of various kinds. However, his alliance with the extreme faction of the Patarenes and their eclipse in 1075 ensured that loyalties at Milan did not coalesce or find any point of focus; the city remained deeply divided. Throughout its province, Gregory found allies and sympathizers, especially among Patarene groups but also in some of the older Benedictine monasteries like S. Michele della Chiusa. Yet the resistance of the bishops, and the reserve of lay rulers and of many of the aristocratic classes, set limits to Gregory's ability actively to enlist Lombard sympathies and loyalties. The considerable number of Lombard bishops who added their names to the decree of Henry IV's synod of Brixen in 1080 testifies to the resistance that Gregory continued to encounter.[89]

[84] *Reg.* 1.33, 28 Nov. 1073, pp. 53–4.
[85] As n. 80.
[86] William of Chiusa, *Vita*.
[87] *Vita*, caps. 9–11, pp. 203*b*–204*b*.
[88] *Vita*, caps. 11, 12, p. 204*b*/4–11, 52–61.
[89] *Quellen HIV* Anhang C, pp. 480–3.

4.4 Aquileia, Grado, and Venice

With regard to both its ecclesiastical and its general history, the north-eastern region of Italy which comprised the march of Verona and Aquileia presents problems of extreme complexity.[90] Historically, Aquileia was the major city there. It owed its pre-eminence to the Roman emperors from Augustus to Diocletian; although he made it subject to the *vicarius Italiae* at Milan, Diocletian declared it to be 'Roma secunda, maxima Italiae urbs, Italiae emporium'; he designated it as the metropolis of Venetia and Istria. But after 568, the Lombard invasions forced its bishop to flee to the island of Grado, some ten kilometres to the south. Whereas the Lombards occupied Aquileia, Grado, together with a coastal strip along the northern Adriatic from Venice to Istria, remained part of the Eastern Roman Empire. The political division of the region was reflected in an ecclesiastical division, which was compounded by the so-called 'schism of the Three Chapters' which arose from the second council of Constantinople in 553 and nagged on. The details of the schism are of no relevance to the study of Pope Gregory VII. But the amalgam of political and ecclesiastical factors left rival patriarchs at Grado (*Aquileia nova*) and Aquileia; the title of patriarch first occurs in the mid-sixth century. According to canonical propriety, however, the legitimate successor of St Hermagoras, the legendary first bishop and pupil of St Mark the Evangelist who founded the see of Aquileia, was undoubtedly the patriarch of Grado.

From Carolingian times through the Saxon to the early Salian period, the emperors did not agree; they followed the practice of ancient Rome by favouring Aquileia. Aquileia had formed part of the Lombard kingdom which Charlemagne took over. With its province, it became vital for the defence of the West against marauding Avars and Hungarians. By the eleventh century, the settlement and Christianization of the Hungarians had rendered this function otiose. But the city of Aquileia and its province mattered increasingly to the later Saxon and Salian emperors because of its control of communications between Germany and Italy: not only did a pass lead through Tarvis to Carinthia but, because the sees of Verona and Mantua were suffragan to Aquileia, it was also important in relation to the Brenner. So it is no surprise that, in 1027, a Roman synod dominated by the Emperor Conrad II, with Pope John XIX at his side, should have acceded to the request of the formidable Patriarch Poppo of Aquileia that the claims of Grado should be nullified, or that, in 1062, Henry IV of Germany should have confirmed the subjection of the church of Grado to the patriarch of Aquileia.[91] From Carolingian times, the emperors extensively built up the territorial lordship of the patriarchs of Aquileia especially in Friuli, but also in Istria and Carniola.

It is also no surprise that the mid-eleventh-century popes should have taken a contrary view. At a Lateran synod in 1024, Pope John XIX with no German emperor to

---

[90] Schmidinger, *Patriarch und Landesherr* remains the best guide; see also Herrmann, *Das Tuskulanerpapsttum*, pp. 89–101.

[91] *MGH Const.* 1.82–4, no. 38; *MGH DDHIV* no. 98.

prompt him had already ruled in favour of Patriarch Ursus of Grado. In 1044, Pope Benedict IX vindicated the status quo of 1024 against the ruling of 1027 by acknowledging the bishop of Grado to be 'Gradensis ecclesiae nove Aquileiae patriarcha' but his rival to be merely the bishop of Friuli (*Foroiuliensis presul*).[92] In 1053, Pope Leo IX confirmed Benedict's decision. He established a tradition of the acceptance of the claims of Grado by the reform popes which persisted unbroken well into the twelfth century. In his letters as pope, Gregory VII looked back to his own complicity in Leo's confirmation.[93]

As pope, Gregory was presented with the virtually impossible task both of seeking to recruit for his purposes the powerful patriarchs of Aquileia whose goodwill was courted by Henry IV because of the communications between Italy and the north which ran through their province, and also of remaining loyal to the powerless patriarchs of Grado to whose claims he was committed by long papal tradition and by his own espousal of Grado's cause from the time of Pope Leo IX. It is not surprising that he never settled upon a viable, let alone a successful, course of action.

Two things may be said at the outset. First, throughout the march of Verona and Aquileia as well as the lands of Venice, there is no evidence that Gregory could anywhere count upon the intercessory, reforming, or political support from the monastic order that he found in at least some monasteries in other regions of Italy. He is known to have issued no privilege for a monastery there, and his letters are barren of reference to the monastic order. Second, with regard to Aquileia itself, even at his most conciliatory he neither conceded to the see the title of patriarchate nor to its ruler the title of patriarch.

Nevertheless, during the reign of Patriarch Sigehard (1068–77), he seems to have had hopes of securing co-operation from Sigehard and his suffragans. He made this clear with regard to a suffragan of Aquileia when, in September 1073, he wrote to the new bishop of Verona, Bruno (1072–76/80), a German who had been *magister scholarum* at Hildesheim. Bruno had written to Rome claiming an established right for the bishop of Verona to receive a *pallium*. Gregory commended his expressions of love and service to St Peter, but required him to come to Rome in person and establish his claim. Gregory went out of his way to proclaim his own desire to respect the rights of other churches: 'As we desire due honour to be paid by other churches to the Roman church, so we desire ourselves to uphold the proper right of each church.' Gregory also told the German occupant of so strategically placed an Italian see that he wished to declare to his face his sincere love for the German king, and his solicitude for him if only he would put aside childish ways and follow the pattern of holy kings. Bruno duly received not only a *pallium* but also the bonus of a horse-cloth of state ('naccus') and of a papal privilege as warranty.[94] Gregory needed friends, and he would go a long way to conciliate them.

92 Zimmermann, *Papsturkunden*, nos. 561–2, 618. 2.1057–63, 1159–64.
93 Leo IX, *Ep*. 82, *PL* 143.727; for Gregory, see above, 2.1.
94 *Reg*. 1.24, to Bishop Bruno of Verona, 24 Sept. 1073, pp. 40–1, 1.85*a*, p. 123/18–20.

In 1074–5, Gregory made a strong attempt to win the whole province of Aquileia, as headed by Patriarch Sigehard, for his political and reforming purposes. Early in 1074, he wrote to Sigehard ('Sicardo Aquilegiensi fratri et coepiscopo') what seems to have been a personal letter in which he bewailed the oppressions of the rulers of this world, the failings of the clergy, and the consequent irreligion of the people at large. Short though the notice was, he summoned Sigehard, with all his suffragans, to his imminent Lent synod.[95] Nothing emerges about the bishops' response, although it may be inferred that it was not significant from Gregory's action a year later when, after his Lent synod, he wrote cordially to Sigehard, although using the same form of address, and informed him of his decrees against clerical unchastity and simony. Gregory urged Sigehard both to implement them in his own diocese and to admonish his suffragans by word or in writing to do likewise.[96] While never countenancing Sigehard's patriarchal status, Gregory earnestly sought his co-operation as metropolitan in furthering his own purposes as pope.

In 1076, Gregory's show of goodwill seemed to bear fruit. After Easter, Sigehard joined a group of German ecclesiastical and lay princes who drew together against the excommunicated Henry IV; together with Bishop Altmann of Passau, he served as Gregory's legate during the negotiations at Tribur–Oppenheim.[97] But when Henry was restored to communion at Canossa, Sigehard loyally supported him and facilitated his return journey to Germany. In 1077, Henry rewarded him with the grants of counties and jurisdiction in Friuli, Istria, and Carniola which formed the basis of Aquileia's temporal lordship for generations to come, and in 1081 Henry granted to the church of Aquileia the bishoprics of Trieste and Parenzo.[98] Against the background of Gregory's unpreparedness to concede its patriarchal status, it was a demonstration of how much the see of Aquileia stood to gain by adhering to the Salian king.

Nevertheless, when it came to choosing Sigehard's successor, Gregory continued to show himself to be remarkably flexible. Immediately after the patriarch's death on 12 August, the clergy and people of Aquileia elected as his successor their own archdeacon; they acted without reference to either Gregory or Henry, perhaps with the intention of breaking the line of German patriarchs. They sought Gregory's approval of what they had already done. Gregory reacted promptly. From Rome, he wrote to the clergy and people laying down two principles about episcopal elections: first and foremost, in avoidance of all simony the bishop should be such a man, and should be so elected, that he came to office not as a thief and robber but as a pastor

---

95 *Reg.* 1.42, to Archbishop Sigehard of Aquileia, 2 Jan. 1074, pp. 64–5; the personal and cordial tone of the letter should be compared with the more formal summons of the bishops and abbots of the Milanese province which Gregory sent on the following day: 1.43, pp. 66–7.

96 *Reg.* 2.62, to Archbishop Sigehard of Aquileia, 23 Mar. 1075, p. 217. When compared with Gregory's almost simultaneous letters to German archbishops: *Epp. vag.* nos. 6–7, pp. 14–17, Gregory was studiously mild in his requirement of the province of Aquileia. While he envisaged ecclesiastical sanctions on married or concubinous clergy, he made no mention of coercive sanctions to be applied by the laity.

97 For Tribur–Oppenheim, see above, 3.3.4.

98 *MGH DDHIV* nos. 293, 295–6, 338–9; see above, 3.4.1,3.

who entered by way of the door; secondly, Gregory had no desire to deny or hinder whatever belonged to the service and due fealty of the king ('quod ad servitium et debitam fidelitatem regis pertinet'). Therefore, if the election at Aquileia had been rightly and canonically conducted, Gregory would confirm it; but before he did so, the legates who brought his letter must be assured that the person chosen was suitably qualified and had been regularly elected. If not, there must be a fresh election; if so, Gregory would defend the person elected with his full authority. Gregory also wrote to all the suffragans of the see of Aquileia, even though many of them 'had departed in schismatic wickedness from the unity of the church'. He informed them of the archdeacon's election and sought the co-operation of them all in implementing his directions to the clergy and people of Aquileia. He exhorted even those who were in schism and under anathema to collaborate with their brethren who remained in the bosom of the church in completing the process of election. So far, in 1077, Gregory was prepared to go in the direction of compromise and accommodation.[99]

But from Germany, Henry IV had forestalled matters by naming as patriarch a royal chaplain and canon of Augsburg named Henry, who was the brother of one of the Henrician suffragans of Aquileia, Bishop Ellenhard of Pola.[100] Nothing more was heard of the archdeacon; Gregory's current anxiety not to press matters to an issue with Henry IV led him to accept the *fait accompli*. At his Lent synod of 1079, Gregory received from Henry of Aquileia an oath of fidelity and obedience to himself and his successors; according to the chronicler Berthold, Henry preceded his oath by testifying that his election had been canonical and that he had known nothing of a papal prohibition of lay investiture.[101] He remained for a time in Gregory's favour, for in June Gregory acceded to his request for the personal right to wear his *pallium* on two special feast-days. Gregory gave as his reasons that, in keeping with his oath, he had assisted the papal legates to Germany, Bishops Peter of Albano and Ulrich of Padua, and that he had laboured hard 'ad componendam pacem'.[102]

It was a house of cards. In 1080, the synod of Brixen showed how little Gregory could rely on Henry and his suffragans. Henry himself subscribed to its rejection of Gregory as *Henricus patriarcha*. Five of his suffragans also subscribed; they included Roland of Treviso who distinguished himself by adding that he did so *libentissime*, and Sigebodo of Verona who, like both his metropolitan and his predecessor, was unmindful of Gregory's gesture to his see in respect of the *pallium*.[103] Indeed, the sole suffragan of Aquileia upon whom Gregory could unreservedly depend was Raynald (1061–92) of the far western see of Como; a sometime chaplain of the Empress Agnes, he was a long-standing agent and adviser.[104] Otherwise, Gregory

---

[99] *Reg.* 5.5–6, 17 Sept. 1077, pp. 352–5. [100] Schwartz, *Die Besetzung*, p. 41.
[101] *Reg.* 6.17a(4), pp. 428–9; Berthold, *a.* 1079, pp. 317/43–318/2. Berthold's statement that Gregory proceeded to confer on Henry the ring and staff 'et caetera Aquiliensis patriarchatus insignia' can scarcely be correct as it stands, since Gregory never recognized the patriarchate.
[102] *Reg.* 6.38, to Archbishop Henry of Aquileia, 16 June 1079, pp. 454–5.
[103] *Quellen HIV* Anhang C, pp. 482–3. For Roland, see above 3.3.1, 2.
[104] See above, 3.2.2, and *Reg.* 6.39, to Bishop Raynald of Como, 21 June 1079, pp. 455–7.

found little political and ecclesiastical support of a reliable kind in the march of Verona and Aquileia.

He fared no better at Venice, the history of which provides a far from simple subplot to that of Aquileia. In political terms, Venice and its dependencies along the Adriatic littoral lay outside the kingdom of Italy. Venice was important for its position to the west of Aquileia and near the northern border of the Romagna; it was even more important for its potential as a channel of communication between the western and eastern empires. Venice desired to be independent of both Germany and Constantinople, but it also desired to be in amicable contact with both. By contrast to his letters about Aquileia, Gregory VII regularly used the title patriarch when referring to the leading ecclesiastic of the Venetian lands, Dominicus IV Cervoni, of whom he used the terms patriarch of Venice and of Grado synonymously. He could do so because, since the mid-ninth century, all the patriarchs of Grado had been Venetians. Venice had always supported Grado's claims to be the true successor of Aquileia—*Aquileia nova*, whose patron saint was St Mark. But, in 827, by an act of 'sacred theft' Venice brought from Alexandria the relics of St Mark. Venice preempted Grado's claim to be the city of St Mark, for the evangelist now rested in Rialto and had never rested at Grado. With the body of the saint in the doge's palace and, by the late eleventh century with the basilica of St Mark under construction, Venice could aspire to control the patriarchate. This provided one reason for tension in the time of Gregory VII between Venice and the patriarch. It gave rise to another: the patriarch aspired to fulfil his historical role, underwritten by the papacy, as metropolitan of a province of the western church, while Venice, under the leadership of its doge, sought to use the patriarch in order to reinforce its urban development as it safeguarded its independence and pursued its political interests in the Adriatic. Gregory was confronted with the twofold necessity of seeking to reconcile and unify all interests in the city, and of seeking to direct Venice's external dealings into ways that suited his own interests with regard to both Germany and Constantinople. He made great efforts to contend with an impossibly difficult nexus of problems.

Gregory quickly showed that he appreciated the usefulness of Patriarch Dominicus as an intermediary with the Byzantine court. Having received an embassy from the Emperor Michael VII Ducas (1071–8), he expressed an intention of employing Dominicus, whom he describes to the emperor as 'confratrem nostrum Dominicum patriarcham Venetiae, Romane ecclesiae et imperio vestro fidelissimum', to convey his reply.[105] In the spring of 1076, Gregory expressed his gratitude to the patriarch for his profession of obedience to the Roman church, as well as for his amazement and grief at the recent and hateful acts against Gregory of the Lombard and many German bishops at Worms and Piacenza.[106] The patriarch had good reason for adhering to Gregory, who in 1074 had done his best to secure from the Venetians the rehabilitation of his poverty-stricken patriarchate. Gregory had written to Doge Dominicus Silvius (1071–84) and the people of Venice, reminding them of the

[105] *Reg.* 1.18, to the Emperor Michael, 9 July 1073, p. 29/22–30.
[106] *Reg.* 3.14, to Patriarch Dominicus of Grado, (Apr.) 1076, pp. 275/25–276/5.

dignity of the patriarchal title which was shared with only four other sees (Alexandria, Antioch, Constantinople, and Jerusalem). He dwelt upon the material indigence of the last and the present patriarch, whose worldly goods would scarcely support the least of bishops; indeed, the patriarchs had been minded altogether to desert Grado. Gregory appealed to the Venetians to treat them with proper veneration and generosity.[107] This took no account of the tensions between the city and the patriarchate, and it is unlikely that anything came of it. The doge was little interested in the patriarch's wider claims; moreover, he became increasingly anxious about the expansion in the Adriatic of Gregory's Norman allies. His reaction in February 1076 of assuming the title *dux Dalmatiae* offended Gregory, who told the patriarch that such presumption neither could nor should succeed.[108]

Gregory did not allow the deterioration of the position at Venice to proceed without a comprehensive attempt to reverse it. During his journey from Canossa in 1077, he resolved upon an attempt to order relations both externally between the patriarch and neighbouring bishops and also domestically within the ecclesiastical and civic life of the Venetians. He wrote first to 'Dominicus, patriarch of Grado, and the other bishops of Venice', dwelling upon the number of matters that needed to be ordered by papal solicitude. He was, therefore, sending on his behalf the trusted Roman cardinal-deacon Gregory who would carry out with them a thoroughgoing rehabilitation of ecclesiastical life and Christian institutions.[109] Then he wrote to the doge and people of Venice, adding to his salutation a hint of menace in the words 'si oboedierint'. He began with blandishments, praising their tradition of filial devotion to the Roman church and the liberty which they derived from the ancient stem of Roman nobility. But for their recent behaviour he rounded on them with unexpected force. They had fallen from rectitude and put themselves outside the church by receiving and communicating with excommunicates. They had made themselves the ministers and slaves of Satan. Gregory did not specify their offences, but he seems to have learned of dealings with Henry IV and his agents during the year between Worms and Canossa. Gregory treated Venice much as he was currently treating Milan. He sent the cardinal-deacon Gregory to Venice as he sent Cardinal-bishop Gerald of Ostia and Bishop Anselm II of Lucca to Milan: to impose penance, to absolve from excommunication, and to restore the Venetians to communion. Thereafter, with the counsel of the patriarch and his comprovincial bishops and with the aid of the doge and people, the cardinal-deacon would see to the well-being of the churches and the ordering of the Christian religion.[110] There is no evidence about the upshot or even as to whether the cardinal-deacon was received at Venice, but it is hard to believe that Gregory's comprehensive *démarche* was in any respect effectual. That it was not is suggested by a final letter that Gregory sent in April 1081 to the doge and people of Venice, 'to those, that is, who do not communicate with the

---

[107] *Reg.* 2.39, 31 Dec. 1074, pp. 175–6.

[108] *Reg.* 3.14, p. 276/11–14. The textual problems of this letter as noted by Caspar should be borne in mind.

[109] For Gregory, see Hüls, *Kardinäle*, p. 249.   [110] *Reg.* 4.26–7, 9 June 1077, pp. 340–3.

excommunicated'. He warned them to keep clear of the excommunicated and the snares that they laid. Gregory seems still to have had in mind dealings with Henry IV and his partisans, perhaps in the context of Henry's negotiations, present or prospective, with Byzantium. It also emerges from the letter that the Venetians did not wish wholly to break with Gregory. They had prompted his letter by making an unspecified request of him which he could not at present consider, although he would do so when he could. He concluded with a plea for all-round charity and justice.[111] It was essentially a holding letter, which reflects on the one hand the Venetians' pragmatic purpose of keeping their hands free while preserving contact with all sides, and on the other Gregory's lack of ability or opportunity to deal effectively with the manifold problems that Venice posed.

Throughout the march of Verona and Aquileia and the territory of Venice and Istria, Gregory did not command the allies and sympathizers who might have enabled him to take initiatives of a religious or political kind with any prospect of effectiveness. The region was critical for communications between Italy and Germany, and to a lesser extent with Constantinople. Gregory showed himself well aware of the constraints that the situation imposed, and he showed appropriate prudence and moderation, especially with regard to the patriarchs of Aquileia. He was at least successful in avoiding any major infringement of his own interests or of longer-term papal appraisals of the ecclesiastical and political order in the region.

4.5 Tuscany

Tuscany in the mid-eleventh century comprised a large area of Central Italy extending from a small region north of the River Po around Mantua southwards to the River Arno and thence the west of the Apennines to the northern limits of the papal patrimony. Between *c.*1027 and 1052, the margraviate of Tuscany, and lordship over this area, were in the hands of Count Boniface II, of the house of Tuscany–Canossa, whose castle at Canossa was to be the scene of the meeting between Gregory VII and Henry IV in January 1077. During Ottonian and early Salian times, the rise of the lords of Canossa had been smooth and well founded; they owed much to the emperors but also were the recipients of papal favours. The long connection between the houses of Lorraine and Tuscany was established in 1037 by Count Boniface's marriage to Beatrice, daughter of Duke Frederick II of Lorraine, who was related both to the Salian royal family and to Pope Leo IX. Two years after Boniface's murder in 1052, Beatrice married Duke Godfrey the Bearded of Lorraine whom the Emperor Henry III had deposed from his duchy. In 1055, during his Italian expedition, Henry took Beatrice and her daughter Matilda as prisoners to Germany; but a year after Henry died in 1056, Beatrice was able to return with her husband and with Matilda in the company of Pope Victor II. Godfrey and Beatrice set about the rehabilitation of their power in Lorraine and Tuscany. With a view to consolidating the

---

[111] *Reg.* 9.8, 8 Apr. (1081), pp. 58–5.

link between these regions, just before Duke Godfrey died in 1069, the young Matilda was married to Godfrey's son, Duke Godfrey the Hunchback (duke of Lorraine from 1069 until 1076). The marriage proved unhappy and a son died in infancy; by 1073, when Gregory became pope, Matilda had for some time been separated from her husband. But since 1069, Beatrice had moved ever closer to the papacy of Alexander II; from 1071 she associated Matilda with her rule, in order to prepare her for her own future political role.

In the early years of the connection between the houses of Lorraine and Canossa, the centre of power lay in and around the cities of Lucca and Florence. There, as elsewhere in Tuscany including the vicinity of Canossa, the early eleventh century was a period of remarkable monastic foundation; the examples of Vallombrosa and Camaldoli illustrate a reforming fervour which antedated the revival of the papacy in its various stages, which formed part of a disseminated quest for reform to which the reform papacy in due course responded, and which fostered many links in both directions between the papacy and local centres of more fervent religion in the localities of Tuscany. Relations between the papacy of Alexander II and Vallombrosa, which culminated in 1068 with the ordeal by which Peter Igneus convicted the bishop of Florence of simony and in the appointment of Peter to be cardinal-bishop of Albano, may serve as an illustration.[112]

During the pontificate of Gregory VII, when the leading political figures were the Countesses Beatrice (until her death on 18 April 1076) and Matilda, the most important area of their lordship was what became known then, and throughout the twelfth century, as the Matildine lands. Their heartland lay between the middle Po valley around Guastalla and Ferrara in the north, and, in the south, the northward-facing valleys of the Apennines between the Rivers Taro and Reno. The principal urban centres were Mantua, Reggio/Emilia, and Modena; Mantua, in particular, became a centre of court life in a lordship that lacked political cohesion and organization; by and large, Beatrice and Matilda had a precarious hold over the towns, which were restive under their rule. For many decades, the house of Canossa had followed Tuscan custom by founding monasteries.[113] Its foundations included Polirone, Nonantula, S. Prospero at Reggio, and Frassinoro, as well as a house of regular canons at Canossa which Beatrice and Matilda transformed into the monastery of S. Apollonio. Such foundations added to the religious fervour of the region. Their situation at strategically and economically important places on rivers and roads made them important for comital power; but their foundation, endowment, and protection constituted a heavy and continuing charge upon the rulers' resources.

The burgeoning of religious life in many localities of Tuscany was noticed by the reform papacy. Gregory's letter of 1073 to the monks of Vallombrosa upon the death of their abbot, John Gualbertus, provides but one example of his awareness of what was happening.[114] But the salient feature of his early dealings with Tuscany was the close and personal bond which he established with Countesses Beatrice and Matilda.

---

[112] See above, 2.2.7.   [113] See esp. Goez, 'Reformpapsttum'.
[114] *Epp. vag.* no. 2, pp. 4–7.

It would be crass to follow Gregory's detractors at Worms in 1076 and at Brixen in 1080 by alleging that there was impropriety of an emotional, let alone of a carnal, nature in Gregory's relations with them, indiscreet and even intemperate though his utterances to and about them at times undoubtedly were. His concern sprang from the pastoral care of individuals with whom he dealt that has been too little appreciated. No doubt the piety and religious zeal of the countesses also weighed with him. But a critical factor seems to have been the parallels, which existed between the rulers of the house of Canossa and the Salian royal family. Countess Beatrice and the Empress-mother Agnes were of comparable age; they were fervent in their piety and in their preparedness to be of service to Gregory; Gregory looked to them to guide their respective children, Countess Matilda (born *c.* 1046) and the young King Henry (born 1050), who were also much of an age. However, whereas Matilda was docile and responsive to Gregory's admonitions, Henry, for whose upbringing from infancy Gregory was closely concerned,[115] was, for all his politic protestations of repentance and amendment, ultimately recalcitrant in face of papal and parental promptings. Until the deaths of Beatrice in 1076 and Agnes in 1077, Gregory's urgent purpose was to work by means of Beatrice and Matilda as of the Empress Agnes to recall Henry to the devoutness of his late father, to true and lasting repentance, and, ultimately, to admittance to his imperial title and duties.

Although no evidence survives for any meetings between Hildebrand and either of the countesses before he became pope, after April 1073 he was quick to enlist them for his purposes. Countess Beatrice was among those to whom his Register records the dispatch of news of his election, and she was present in Rome at his episcopal ordination.[116] On 24 June 1073, a letter to both countesses made clear their central place in his perspectives and plans; he was perhaps encouraged by a recent profession of goodwill from Matilda's husband, Duke Godfrey of Lorraine, to whom Gregory confided his plan for sending to King Henry of Germany religious men who would bring him to a right mind and therefore to papal favour. He cautioned the countesses to have no communion or dealings with the simoniacal bishops of Lombardy. He also took up and made more explicit than in his letter to Duke Godfrey his hope that Henry might be recalled to his Christian duties and thereby be made fit to receive an imperial crown.[117] On 1 September, Gregory sent a group of letters in which he announced plans for talks at Rome in which Duke Rudolf of Swabia, Empress Agnes, Countesses Beatrice and Matilda, Bishop Raynald of Como, and others would discuss the king's restoration to communion and consequent promotion to the empire.[118] Henry's obedient letter, which arrived soon afterwards, encouraged Gregory to hope that the king was amenable to papal guidance.[119]

---

[115] *Reg.* 1.19, to Duke Rudolf of Swabia, 1 Sept. 1073, pp. 31–2; *Epp. vag.* no. 14, p. 34/7–26.

[116] *Reg.* 1.4, 28 Apr. 1073, p. 7; Bonizo of Sutri, *Lib. ad. Amic.* 7, p. 601/24–5.

[117] *Reg.* 1.9, to Duke Godfrey of Lorraine, 6 May 1073, pp. 13–15; 1.11, to Countesses Beatrice and Matilda, pp. 17–19. See above, 2.2.7.

[118] *Reg.* 1.19, to Duke Rudolf of Swabia, pp. 31–2; 1.10, to Bishop Raynald of Como, pp. 32–4; 1.21, to Anselm, bishop-elect of Lucca, pp. 34–5; cf. *Vita Anselmi ep. Lucensis*, 4, p. 17.

[119] *Reg.* 1.29*a*, pp. 47–9 = *Epp. HIV* no. 5, pp. 54–7.

From the start, Gregory wrote to the countesses in terms of personal warmth and Matilda attended his Lent synods in Rome.[120] From December 1073, he singled Matilda out for expressions of affection and personal admonition that he reserved for her alone. A letter of 3 January 1074, in which he exhorted her to perseverence, shows that she had initiated a correspondence in which she had protested a love of St Peter which Gregory compared to that of the vessel of election, St Paul (Acts 9: 15), for Jesus Christ; Gregory confirmed his hope that Matilda and her mother would visit Rome.[121] Soon afterwards, Gregory sent Matilda, as his beloved daughter in Christ, a long letter of spiritual direction. He dissuaded her from taking the veil after the failure of her marriage and encouraged her in the frequent reception of holy communion. He renewed his special commendation of her to the Lord's Mother; in a passage that echoed his advice to Henry IV, he urged her to demonstrate repentance and contrition at the Virgin's feet.[122] In another letter, Gregory called upon Beatrice and Matilda to do justice on his behalf between the bishop and count of Roselle. He used the opportunity to express his especial confidence in them amongst all the princes of the Roman empire. Reinforcing his admonition of Matilda not to abandon the world, he pressed upon them the claims of an active life of charity and good works:

Your charity knows and, I think, fully understands that in all your activities I seek the honour of God and your salvation. Therefore I say with the Prophet, 'Offer the sacrifice of righteousness and hope in the Lord' (Ps. 4: 6), and, 'Judge the orphan and defend widows, and come and reason with me, says the Lord' (Isa. 1: 17–18). From love of God, then, I place before prayers, fastings, vigils, and all other good works whatsoever, the help for the wretched and aid for the oppressed which spring from love of our neighbour; with the Apostle I do not hesitate to set true charity before all other virtues (1 Cor. 12: 13). For if this, the mother of all virtues, which compelled God to come from heaven to earth and bear our wretchedness, did not guide me, and if there were someone who in your stead would help wretched and oppressed churches and serve the universal church, I would be at pains to advise you to leave the world and all its cares. But because you do not, as many princes do, reject God from your palace but, rather, by the sacrifice of righteousness you invite him to enter it, we ask you and counsel you as most beloved daughters to bring the good which you have begun to a perfect end (cf. Phil. 1: 6). Neither human favour, nor love of money, nor desire for vain glory, should cast a shadow upon your sacrifice. For a man sells something great for a trivial price, who serves God with his eye upon this life.[123]

Like others who served Gregory faithfully, the countesses did not escape his reproof.[124] But in a letter which he addressed to the Empress Agnes near the end of his first pontifical year thanking her for her zeal for peace between Henry IV and the

[120] *Reg.* 1.11, pp. 18/8, 19/18–20. For Matilda at Rome, see Cosmas of Prague 2.31, pp. 126–7 (1074); Bonizo of Sutri, *Lib. ad amic.* 7, p. 602/33–46 (1074), p. 605/23–4 (1075).

[121] *Reg.* 1.40, pp. 62–3.

[122] 'Pone itaque finem in voluntate peccandi et prostrata coram illa ex corde contrito et humiliato lacrimas effunde': *Reg.* 1.47, 16 Feb. 1074, pp. 71–3, esp. p. 73/29–30, together with Autenrieth, 'Der bisher unbekannte Schluss'. Matilda may have wished to take the veil at Rome with the Empress Agnes: *Reg.* 1.85, to Empress Agnes, 15 June 1074, pp. 122/27–123/2.

[123] *Reg.* 1.50, 4 Mar. 1074, pp. 76/27–77/14.

[124] *Reg.* 1.77, to Countesses Beatrice and Matilda, 15 Apr. 1074, pp. 109–11.

church, he was fulsome in his praise for them. They had followed Agnes 'as disciples faithfully imitating their lady and mistress', and he compared them with the faithful women at Christ's tomb. Gregory especially commended Agnes's solicitude for Matilda.[125] Accordingly, throughout 1074, the countesses were prominently in Gregory's mind. They figured in his plans for a military expedition to discipline the Normans and to aid the beleaguered Eastern Christians at Constantinople. In the earlier phase of his plans, he counted upon the participation of Beatrice with her daughter Matilda and her son-in-law Duke Godfrey of Lorraine.[126] In the December phase, when Gregory planned himself to be *dux et pontifex* of an eastern expedition, leaving a supposedly obedient Henry IV to protect the apostolic see, he proposed to take with him the Empress Agnes and Countess Matilda, leaving Countess Beatrice, who was currently in Germany, in the west so that she might safeguard their common interests.[127] Before Beatrice went to Germany, Gregory had reiterated his unshakeable trust in the countesses despite murmured allegations against them. He invited them to Rome and confided in them about several matters.[128] Throughout 1075, they remained his close confidantes.[129]

Gregory continued to address Matilda, in particular, in terms of warmth, as his 'most beloved and loving daughter' ('charissime plena dilectione filia').[130] Unsurprisingly, the assembled German bishops who renounced their obedience to Gregory at Worms in January 1076 concluded their letter to 'brother Hildebrand' with the personal allegation which the chronicler Lampert of Hersfeld knew and rebutted, that he had as it were filled the whole church with the stench of gravest scandal by his intimacy and cohabitation with a 'strange woman' ('de convictu et cohabitatione alienae mulieris') (cf. Prov. 2: 16, Ecclus. 9: 11–12). They appended the general allegation that all the judgements and decrees of the apostolic see were promoted by women, while the universal church was governed by 'this new senate of women' ('hunc feminarum novum senatum').[131]

While Countess Beatrice lived, Gregory took no apparent notice and continued to treat her and her daughter as close advisers and confidantes, especially with regard to his proposed journey to Germany, for which he depended upon safe conduct through their lands.[132] In January 1077, his meeting with Henry IV took place at

---

[125] *Reg.* 1.85.

[126] *Reg.* 1.46, to Count William of Burgundy, 2 Feb. 1074, p. 70/23–5, cf. 1.72, to Duke Godfrey of Lorraine, 7 Apr. 1074, pp. 103/27–104/5.

[127] *Epp. vag.* no. 5, pp. 10–13. For Beatrice's journey to Germany, see *Reg.* 2.9, to Countesses Beatrice and Matilda, 16 Oct. 1074, p. 139/19–23, 2.30, to King Henry IV, 7 Dec. 1074, pp. 163/28–164/2.

[128] *Reg.* 2.9, pp. 138–40.

[129] *Reg.* 2.30, pp. 163–5, 3.5, to Countesses Beatrice and Matilda, 11 Sept. 1075, pp. 251–2, 3.8, to the Milanese clerk Tedald, 8 Dec. 1075, p. 260/26–33; cf. Lampert of Hersfeld, *Ann.*, *a.* 1080, pp. 399/32–400/10. For the persistence of criticism of Gregory's use of women as agents in church affairs, see *Lib. de unit. eccles. cons.* 2.36, p. 263/14–30.

[130] *Epp. vag.* no 5, p. 12/3–4.

[131] *Quellen HIV* Anhang A, p. 474/10–15; cf. Lampert of Hersfeld, *Ann.*, *a.* 1077, p. 400/10–20.

[132] *Epp. vag.* no. 13, to Bishop Henry of Trent, (Mar.–July 1076), p. 32/2–5; *Reg.* 4.2, to Bishop Hermann of Metz, 25 Aug. 1076, p. 297/8–15; *Epp. vag.* no. 19, to all the faithful in Germany, (Feb.–Mar. 1077), pp. 50/26–52/1.

Matilda's castle of Canossa and in her presence. During Gregory's subsequent travels in Italy, she accompanied him, 'like another Martha'.[133] But thereafter, Gregory's letters record only one exchange of letters between pope and countess: early in 1079, she approached him about a variety of Lotharingian and German affairs; he replied to her as 'dilecte in Christo filiae', but his letter was terse, businesslike, and not manifestly of his own dictation.[134] His former familiarity had undoubtedly occasioned scandal, and the intermissions of correspondence may have been calculated to avoid it. They may have discussed the matter at or after Canossa, and the scandal was evidently reduced: at Brixen in 1080, the synodal decree ascribed many turpitudes to Hildebrand but made no allusion to a liaison with Matilda.[135] In effect, Gregory handed over his former role as friend and mentor of Matilda to Bishop Anselm II of Lucca. But, in truth, after Canossa the world had changed. The two senior ladies, the Empress Agnes and Countess Beatrice, were removed from the scene by death. Gregory no longer envisaged the speedy grooming of Henry IV for the imperial dignity, but sought himself to bring peace and order to Germany by direct intervention. As regards German affairs, Matilda remained important for her Lotharingian connections and for the position of her Italian lands across lines of communication. But the constellation of personal relations which Gregory had cherished in his early years as pope had vanished irrecoverably.

In face of Henry IV's expeditions to Rome in the early 1080s, Matilda demonstrated that her devotion to Gregory and his cause in Italy was in no way diminished. At an unknown date, but perhaps as early in 1080, she visited Rome and, at the Lateran palace in Gregory's presence, allegedly gave her lands, whether in Italy or in Lorraine, to the church of St Peter.[136] In 1082, she came to Gregory's aid by having the treasure of the church of S. Apollonio at Canossa melted down and the precious metals sent to Gregory at Rome to provide for the city's defence against Henry IV.[137] According to the *Life* of Bishop Anselm of Lucca, she fought valiantly for the Gregorian cause 'like a new Deborah';[138] a woman had proved faithful and strong when men had failed. She suffered a grave setback when, on 15 October 1080, Henry IV's Lombard supporters routed her army at Volta, near Mantua, thereby making it impossible for her to hinder Henry's passage through North Italy to Rome.[139] In

---

[133] *Reg.* 4.12, to the German princes, late Jan. 1077, p. 313/15–18. For Matilda's travels with Gregory after Canossa, see Donizo, 2.167–70, p. 383.

[134] *Reg.* 6.22, 3 Mar. 1079, pp. 434–5. In 1078 Gregory referred in a privilege to Matilda as 'serenissimam filiam nostram': 6.12, to Archbishop Landulf of Pisa, 30 Nov. 1078, p. 414/20–4. In May 1081, there is a reference in the Register to a letter from Matilda to Gregory, though not to any reply: 9.11, to Abbot Desiderius of Montecassino, p. 589/3–8.

[135] *Quellen HIV* Anhang C, pp. 476–83.

[136] No contemporary record of the original gift survives, but there is a detailed reference in its renewal in 1102, which was carved on marble in a crypt of St Peter's on the Vatican: *MGH Const.* 1.653–5, no. 444. For the date of Matilda's original gift, see Overmann, *Gräfin Mathilde*, pp. 143–4; the Matildine lands are listed on pp. 1–40.

[137] Donizo, 2.300–3, p. 385 and n.

[138] *Vita Anselmi ep. Lucensis*, caps. 11, 20–1, pp. 16, 19–20.

[139] Bernold, *Cron. a.* 1080, p 436/42–4; Bonizo of Sutri, *Lib. ad amic.* 9, p. 613/25–7.

1081, Henry accused her of treason to himself and sentenced her to the forfeiture of all her lands.[140] Only in Lorraine could the sentence be directly implemented, but in Italy Henry ravaged her lands, and privileges that he issued in favour of her cities of Lucca and Pisa are landmarks in the history of their independence.[141] Gregory recognized that Matilda's effective usefulness to him as an ally depended upon her receiving support from his party in Germany.[142] But after the installation of the anti-pope Clement III at Rome and Henry's imperial coronation by him, she re-emerged as an indefatigable and successful champion of the Gregorian cause. She wrote to the Germans warning them of Henry's imminent return to Germany bearing Gregory's seal which he had stolen, and enlarged upon Henry's misdeeds and propaganda.[143] On 2 July 1084, the overwhelming victory of her army over Henry's in the battle of Sorbaria did much to sustain the flagging morale of Gregory's partisans everywhere during his exile in Salerno.[144] After Gregory's death, she was an active leader of the Gregorian party who sought to vindicate his cause at Rome itself and elsewhere in Italy.[145]

No less important for Gregory VII's cause than Matilda's indefatigable military support were the theological and propagandist endeavours which she inspired in her circle of followers. She was herself concerned to provide liturgical books, as well as sacred vessels, which would facilitate impressive worship in the monasteries of her lands. Her appropriation of monasticism to serve Gregory's purposes is illustrated by her gifts to St Peter after Canossa of the monasteries of Polirone, S. Apollonio at Canossa, and Frassinoro; Gregory committed Polirone to Abbot Hugh of Cluny for the introduction of Cluniac Customs and Frassinoro to la Chaise-Dieu.[146] She appears to have promoted the export of the 'giant bibles' which made more readily available for study the complete text of the scriptures; by their visual magnificence, they declared the authority of the church as Gregory envisaged it.[147] By biblical studies that Matilda directly commissioned, Gregory's spiritual preoccupations were developed and propagated. The tracts on the Song of Songs and on the Virgin Mary for which Matilda asked the *grammaticus* John of Mantua are especially significant, for they suggest that she persisted in heeding the spiritual guidance that Gregory gave her in 1074.[148] The former of these tracts reinforced Gregory's

---

[140] No chronicle evidence survives, but there are references in *MGH DDHIV* nos. 373, 379, 385; see Overmann, *Gräfin Mathilde*, pp. 232–8.

[141] *MGH DDHIV* nos. 334, 336, cf. 337.

[142] *Reg.* 9.3, to Bishop Altmann of Passau and Abbot William of Hirsau, (Mar. 1082), p. 574/10–16.

[143] Hugh of Flavigny, 2, p. 463; Donizo, 2.200–3, p. 383.

[144] *Vita Anselmi ep. Lucensis*, caps. 23–4, pp. 20–1; Bernold, *Chron. a.* 1084, p. 441/7–11; Donizo, 2.343–65, pp. 386–7.

[145] See Cowdrey, *The Age of Abbot Desiderius*, pp. 183, 186, 189, 199, 202–7, 210, 240–2. Bonizo of Sutri eulogized Matilda's warlike qualities in *Lib. ad amic.* 9, p. 620/8–13.

[146] *QF* nos. 125*–127*, 130, pp. 125–7, 132–5; Hugh of Flavigny, 2, pp. 443–4.

[147] Donizo, 2.1370–1, pp. 405–6. For giant bibles and biblical propaganda, see Fichtenau, 'Neues zum Problem', Brieger, 'Bible Illustration', and Robinson, 'The Metrical Commentary'.

[148] For the text of John of Mantua's tracts, see the edition by Bischoff and Taeger with an important introduction; also Cantelli, 'Commento al Cantico'.

admonition that she should not take the veil but should, while following a life of prayer, remain active in the world as an obedient Christian prince. John of Mantua acknowledged that the Song of Songs envisaged a life of contemplation, and he set forth in order the steps by which Christians might progress in it. But the needs of the time rendered the active life appropriate for her: in face of the evidence of the power of Antichrist in the world, it was for her to resist *consilio et armis* the decline from which the church was suffering.[149] Writing between spring 1081 and autumn 1083 when her fortunes were at a low ebb after the defeat of her forces at Volta, John assured her that 'you will be proclaimed throughout the centuries as happy and blessed, if you persevere as manfully as you have begun against the heresy that serves the Antichrist'.[150] As Gregory had exhorted Matilda to the regular receiving of holy communion, so John took pains in his polemical passages against Berengar of Tours to urge her to be a careful and instructed communicant.[151] Gregory's commendation of devotion to the Virgin has its complement in John's exegesis, made at Matilda's urgent request, of the Marian passages in the first chapter of St Luke's Gospel.[152]

Besides caring for Matilda's spiritual life and for the political action that should spring from it, John also practised a mode of biblical commentary which has been appropriately described as 'political allegory'.[153] By means of it, the literal and still more the figurative interpretation of scripture was directed towards the public eulogy of Gregory and his cause. Current events were interpreted in the light of scripture in order to achieve this end. In circles where Gregory's intentions were well known and approved, his ecclesiastical and political aspirations were to be firmly set upon a biblical foundation. In his commentary on the Song of Songs, John of Mantua interpreted the strife of his own day between Gregorians and Henricians, in the light of St Paul's words in 2 Thessalonians 2: 3,8, as an eschatological contest between the forces of truth and the precursors of Antichrist. In such a contest, the champions of catholic truth would become all the stronger and would win through to victory. Matilda should, therefore, persist in valiant strife. She would prove herself to be well advanced upon the way of contemplation by her very engagement in the action that befitted one who was appointed by God to exercise temporal authority.[154] That comparable ideas were widely and popularly disseminated in Matildine circles is suggested by contemporary poems which took the struggle of Christ with Leviathan into the streets.[155]

Amongst the bishops of Tuscany, Gregory had an indefatigable, able, and dedicated supporter, in another mentor of Matilda, Bishop Anselm II of Lucca. After Anselm's scruples about his investiture by Henry IV and his withdrawal to be a monk perhaps at Saint-Gilles, Gregory in 1075 recalled him to his see. With Gregory's

---

[149] John of Mantua, pp. 26/6–8, 19–28, 65/1–19. John sums up at pp. 154/29–155/21.
[150] Ibid., p. 65/19–21. [151] Ibid., pp. 46–9, esp. 49/17–24.
[152] Ibid., pp. 156–82. [153] Robinson, ' "Political Allegory" '.
[154] Esp. John of Mantua, pp. 35/30–36/12, 51/32–52/25, 63/24–65/25, 79/34–80/14, 91/25–92.26.
[155] e.g. Lokrantz, *L'opera poetica*, no. D 7, pp. 153–5, cf. pp. 21–2, 206–8. The poem is preserved in a Polirone MS.

reluctant concurrence, Anselm as bishop continued to wear his monastic habit, as a token that, along with the episcopal office which, according to his biographer, he discharged exemplarily as preacher, teacher, and visitor of his diocese, he sought to embody the standards of the monastic and canonical life. He regarded himself as a monk of the Cluniac abbey of Polirone.[156]

As a city, Lucca was not disposed to welcome as its bishop so radical a reformer as Anselm. By and large, its clergy and people were religiously and morally of good repute, but in an old-fashioned way. They had gladly supported the temperate and judicious Pope Alexander II who, as Bishop Anselm I of Lucca, had retained the see after becoming pope and who regularly came there. But there is no evidence at Lucca for any such popular movement as the Patarenes of Lombard cities, and the fervent monks of Vallombrosa founded no houses there. Lucca was free from the urban strife that vexed other cities on account of religious issues. Politically, too, it was quiet. Yet there was an undercurrent of hostility to the house of Canossa which had been gathering since the days of Matilda's father, Count Boniface. In his skilfully drafted diploma of 1081, which has been justly described as the Magna Carta of the city's later freedom, Henry IV made play of the harshness of recent comital exactions. In conjunction with religious resentments, aspirations for urban independence led many at Lucca to resist the reforming endeavours of Anselm II, especially since after 1077 he was increasingly the loyal associate and mentor of the countess.[157]

During his years of residence in Lucca, Anselm made it his consistent endeavour to reform the life of the cathedral chapter of S. Martino. His predecessor, Pope Alexander II, had treated the chapter with conspicuous caution: although he consecrated the rebuilt cathedral, undertook to reorganize the chapter, and was concerned with raising moral standards, he made no attempt to introduce a common life. This was despite a strong direction by Pope Leo IX, confirmed by Pope Victor II, that such a way of life, free from unchastity and simony, should be adopted. Soon after he became bishop, Anselm II sought to impose a common life upon the cathedral clergy; their reluctance was not diminished by Anselm's willingness himself to practise full community of property with them, or by his seeking the support of Countess Matilda.[158] By late 1076, Gregory VII was actively giving Anselm his backing. On his way to Canossa, he visited Lucca and sought in person to persuade the canons to comply with their bishop's requirements. But his promptings had no lasting effect, and in August 1077 he wrote to them to forbid their entering the cathedral or enjoying their canonries and prebends until they made satisfaction for their simony and resistance to reform.[159] In November 1078, he called expressly for the

---

[156] *Vita Anselmi ep. Lucensis*, caps. 5, 40, pp. 14–15, 24.

[157] *MGH DDHIV* no. 334, esp. p. 438/29–30. For developments at Lucca, see Schwarzmeier, *Lucca*, esp. pp. 13, 66–71, 400–12.

[158] Leo IX, *Ep.* 55, *PL* 143.671–2; Alexander II, *Epp.* 105–7, *PL* 146.1388–95. For Anselm, see *Vita Anselmi ep. Lucensis*, caps. 6–7, p. 15. For the cathedral and its canons, see esp. Kittel, 'Der Kampf' and Giusti, 'Le canoniche di Lucca'.

[159] *Vita Anselmi ep. Lucensis*, cap. 8, p. 15–16; *Reg.* 5.1, to the canons of S. Martino at Lucca, 11 Aug. 1077, pp. 348–9.

living of a common life, but again to no effect. There seems to have followed some kind of judicial hearing by Gregory at Rome. In October 1079, he excommunicated the disobedient canons and ordered their expulsion from the city. In 1080, Cardinal Peter of Albano who acted on Gregory VII's behalf, held a council at S. Ginese, near S. Miniato, which was attended by several bishops, including Anselm; at it, he pronounced a further sentence of excommunication against the disobedient canons.[160]

In this critical year, Peter of Albano's sentence left Lucca deeply divided between, on the one side, a conservative majority of the cathedral clergy and the leading figures of the city and countryside, and, on the other, Bishop Anselm and his reforming circle which included a minority of cathedral clergy such as the *primicerius* Bardo and the archpriest Lambertus, together with a small group of like-minded persons who enjoyed the support of the countess. Later in 1080, the former party, led by a canon and subdeacon named Peter, expelled Anselm and his followers from the city. In 1081, when Henry IV gave the city its privilege, Peter was named as bishop of the city, which became effectively Guibertine. Anselm took refuge at Mantua on the other side of the Apennines, with the countess.[161]

From 1081 until his death in 1086, the exiled Anselm redoubled his zeal in the service of the countess and, above all, of Gregory VII. The sometime bishop of Lucca, in effect, found a new and fuller role as papal vicar. Whereas he had once been Gregory's mentor in teaching him resistance to lay investiture, he now, according to his biographer, set out to be Gregory's meticulous disciple and imitator:

Before all else, this was the continuous object of his zeal: that he should imitate his most holy master Pope Gregory in all things, so that he should not differ from him in the slightest detail. He always attributed to Gregory's merits anything that he did.[162]

His care for Countess Matilda, which his biographer likened to the care which the dying Christ charged the beloved disciple to bestow upon the Virgin (John 19: 26–7), was intended to provide her with spiritual guidance according to the teachings of Gregory.[163] In return, Matilda added Anselm to the number of those from whom she commissioned biblical commentaries. He responded with a work on the Psalms of which there survive only two fragments of fierce polemic against Henry IV and Guibert of Ravenna. He also commented upon the book of Lamentations, with its message of penitence and resilience in face of disaster.[164] After Gregory's death, he wrote a forceful polemic against Guibert's propagandist attempts to win over Matilda and her circle.[165]

[160] *Reg.* 6.11, to the canons of S. Martino at Lucca, 28 Nov. 1078, pp. 412–13; 7.2, to the clergy and people of Lucca, 1 Oct. 1079, pp. 460–1. For the synod of S. Ginese, see *Vita Anselmi ep. Lucensis*, cap. 8, p. 16; Rangerius, *Vita Anselmi*, lines 1803–1910, pp. 1195/3–1197/20.

[161] *Vita Anselmi ep. Lucensis*, caps. 9–11, p. 16.

[162] *Vita Anselmi ep. Lucensis*, caps. 31–3, pp. 22–3, citation on p. 22/42–5; Paul of Bernried, cap. 111, p. 540; Bernold, *Micrologus*, cap. 17, col. 988B.

[163] *Vita Anselmi ep. Lucensis*, caps. 12, 30, 35, pp. 17, 22, 23. For the prayers that Anselm composed for Matilda's use, see Wilmart, 'Cinque prières'.

[164] Paul of Bernried, cap. 112, p. 541; *Vita Anselmi ep. Lucensis*, cap. 26, p. 21.

[165] *Liber contra Wibertum*, esp. p. 527/16–27; *Vita Anselmi ep. Lucensis*, cap. 21, p. 20. On the *Liber*

From 1081, Anselm served Gregory as his papal vicar in Lombardy. While he was unable himself ever to visit that region, he ministered to Gregorian supporters who came to him at Mantua.[166] He persisted in his zeal for the dissemination of the canonical life, in commendation of which he wrote a lost tract.[167] Surviving letters suggest that he was active in seeking to rally support for Gregory in distant parts of Europe; thus, probably in 1085, he wrote to King William I of England urging him to bring military aid to the Roman church in its peril, and to Bishop Hermann of Metz, whom he praised for his steadfastness and encouraged in further service to the Gregorian cause.[168] His sermon *De caritate* illustrates the force and eloquence with which he proclaimed in Tuscany the duty of defending the Roman church and re-called supporters of the anti-pope by offering them a way of repentance and recon-ciliation.[169] His most signal and enduring service to Gregory was the compilation, at his request, of his collection of canon law, which was particularly important because it set out the canonical justification for using coercion against those who were obstin-ate in schism.[170]

Anselm's was one of the three names that Gregory put forward in his final testa-ment as his own possible successor in the throne of St Peter. His present to Anselm of a mitre may signify that he was Gregory's preferred candidate.[171] His death at Mantua on 18 March 1086 supervened. But the presence at his deathbed of Bishops Heribert of Reggio, Benedict of Modena, and Ubald of Mantua is a reminder that the circle of Countess Matilda and Bishop Anselm of Lucca remained a major element in Gregory's following.[172]

Gregory's cultivation of close relations with Countess Matilda, Bishop Anselm, and their circle was not his only recourse in seeking to harness for the reform papacy the religious zeal that was especially manifest in Tuscany. He looked as well to the cathedrals, houses of regular canons, and monasteries wherever he could hope for a response from them. Florence, Fiesole, and Pistoia were, as dioceses, consistently loyal to him. Florence, in particular, engaged his attention. On his way to Canossa at the end of 1076, he issued a privilege for its cathedral by which, at the request of Bishop Rainer, he confirmed the dispositions of Rainer's predecessor Bishop Gerard, who became Pope Nicholas II, for the cathedral and its community of regu-lar canons ('canonica'), which Gebhard had placed under papal protection. When returning from Canossa, Gregory took much trouble in adjudicating in a dispute

---

contra Wibertum, see Märtl, 'Zur Überlieferung', and for what may be part of Anselm's earlier letter to Guibert, Somerville, 'Anselm of Lucca and Wibert of Ravenna'.

[166] *Vita Anselmi ep. Lucensis*, cap. 24, pp. 20–1.

[167] *Vita Anselmi ep. Lucensis*, caps. 31–3, pp. 22–3; Bonizo of Sutri, *Lib. de vita chris.* 5.77, p. 204/25–6.

[168] *H* nos. 1, 21, pp. 15–17, 50–2.

[169] Pásztor, 'Motive dell'ecclesiologia'; text on pp. 96–104.

[170] Anselm of Lucca's *Collectio canonum*, ed. Thaner, is an edition of Books 1–10 and part of Book 11; for Book 13, see Pásztor, 'Lotta per le investiture', pp. 405–21. Chapter headings of all thirteen books are printed in *PL* 149.485–534. For the problems that the collection presents, see Fransen, 'Anselm de Lucques canoniste?'

[171] *H* no. 35, p. 75/9–17; Paul of Bernried, cap. 111, p. 540.

[172] *Vita Anselmi ep. Lucensis*, cap. 41, p. 25.

between the canons and the monks of S. Michele a Manturi about certain obla-tions.[173] With Bishop Rainer's concurrence, Gregory was active in protecting and fostering other Florentine houses.[174] He likewise issued privileges for those in other Tuscan cities.[175] He remained in touch with Vallombrosa; its monks, too, received a papal privilege, now lost.[176]

For the monastery of S. Salvatore at Fucecchio, of which Cardinal Peter of Albano was abbot from before 1071 until at least 1078,[177] Gregory issued his last known priv-ilege from Salerno shortly before he died. He placed it under direct papal protection and greatly strengthened its position against its diocesan, the bishop of Lucca.[178] Gregory's relations with Fucecchio had been such as to illustrate the problems with which the Tuscan lay aristocracy presented him. Fucecchio was founded in the tenth century by the Cadolingi family, one of whom, William Bulgarelli, had been respons-ible for the coming of the Vallombrosan Peter of Albano to be its abbot. William's son Ugiccio had disregarded his example of lay piety, and at his Lent synod of 1078, Gregory threatened him with excommunication if he did not cease his depredation of the see of Lucca.[179] Probably in 1081, Gregory wrote to Abbot Peter of Fucecchio and Prior Rudolf of Camaldoli in order to explain why he could not absolve Ugiccio while he remained impenitent; he charged them to pray for the count and work for his genuine repentance. Within a few months, they seem to have brought it about, for Ugiccio once again favoured the reform party.[180] After the defeat of Matilda's army at Volta, the position of all the Tuscan monasteries became difficult; Gregory's priv-ilege of 1085 for Fucecchio, which predated Matilda's military victory at Sorbaria, was a striking demonstration that his authority in Tuscany had not altogether faded, and that even from exile in Salerno he could do something to help and encourage his Tuscan supporters.

Loyalties in Tuscany remained divided, not least in the towns. But the resolve and resources of Countess Matilda in respect of military power, and the dedication and energy of the exiled Bishop Anselm II of Lucca as Gregory's papal vicar, testify to the resilience of the Gregorian cause throughout the vicissitudes of the 1080s. Matilda and Anselm were totally committed to Gregory in purpose and in activity. Their circle was well organized to provide both propagandist and military support. Its ser-vices were comparable to those which Gregory received from his partisans in South Germany.

---

[173] *QF* nos. 122, 28 Dec. 1076, pp. 120–3, 140, 28 Aug. 1077, pp. 155–7.

[174] *QF* nos. 146, for the nunnery of S. Felicità at Florence (1078), pp. 159–61; 149, for the abbey of S. Salvatore de Settimo, 10 Jan. 1078, pp. 165–7.

[175] e.g. at Pisa, *QF* nos. 139, for the monastery of S. Michele in Borgo, 10 Aug. 1077, pp. 153–5; 197, for the monastery of S. Zeno, 2 Mar. 1081, pp. 227–9.

[176] *QF* no. *7, p. 2, cf. *6 p. 2, concerning a privilege for the monastery of S. Salvi at Florence.

[177] Miccoli, *Pietro Igneo*, pp. 113–23.

[178] *QF* no. 218, 9 May 1085, pp. 265–7.

[179] *Reg.* 5.14a(8), p. 371/14–16.

[180] *Epp. vag.* no. 43, pp. 104–7; *IP* 8.482, nos. 2–3.

4.6 Romagna and Emilia

Whereas Matildine Tuscany furnished Gregory with his surest and most durable support in the kingdom of Italy, the ecclesiastical province of Ravenna was, for the most part, at best indifferent to Gregory and at worse hostile and critical. At least during the latter half of Gregory's pontificate, the archbishop of Ravenna, Guibert, became prominent among Gregory's opponents and from Easter 1084 was anti-pope as Clement III. The province of Ravenna was of the utmost strategic significance. Ravenna itself was situated on the Adriatic coast, at the south of the estuary of the River Po. The backbone of the province was a sequence of ten bishoprics spaced along the vital line of communication, the Emilian Way. To the west, four of them, Piacenza, Parma, Reggio, and Modena, straddled the Matildine lands. Moving eastwards, there followed, in the Romagna, Bologna, Imola, Faenza, Forli, Forlimpopoli, and Cesena. Other suffragan sees, notably Ferrara, lay in or near the Po estuary. Romagna broadly corresponded to the exarchate of Ravenna; in 754, the Frankish king Pepin III gave Ravenna, together with the cities and castles of the exarchate, inalienably into the power of St Peter and the jurisdiction of the Roman church and the pope.[181] The popes had, therefore, a title to regard it as part of the papal patrimony. But Ravenna was never effectively subjected to their authority, and its archbishops engaged in a prolonged rivalry with the popes. The German emperors, and especially Otto III, used their own lordship over Italy to confer upon the archbishops extensive rights and jurisdiction of their own over bishoprics, monasteries, and forests, both in and to the south of the exarchate.[182]

When Gregory became pope in 1073, he did so with high hopes that the long and deep ecclesiastical and political tension would be quickly resolved. Since Henry III's visit to Rome in 1046, the two archbishops of the period, Hunfrid (1046–51) and Henry (1052–72), had, indeed, both suffered papal censure—Hunfrid that of Leo IX for detaining lands which the Roman see claimed to be its property, and Henry for adhering to the anti-pope Cadalus of Parma. The new archbishop, Guibert, was the son of a prosperous family from Parma. He had been imperial chancellor for Italy from 1058 to 1063, but he had been an apparently well-disposed attender at Nicholas II's Roman synods of 1059 and 1060, and there is no compelling evidence that he compromised himself in Roman eyes during the Cadalan schism.[183] One of Pope Alexander II's last acts before his death was himself to ordain Guibert bishop at Rome with the concurrence of Archdeacon Hildebrand. Guibert took an oath of fealty to Alexander and his canonically elected successors; he promised, among other things, an annual visit to Rome, whether in person or through an envoy, on the feast-day of St Peter and St Paul (29 June).[184]

---

[181] *LP* 1.442, 446, 450–3. The history of relations between Rome and Ravenna is well set out by Jordan, 'Ravenna und Rom', pp. 193–4.

[182] Esp. *MGH DDOIII* nos. 418, cf. 341, 416, 419.

[183] For Guibert, see esp. Köhnke, *Wibert von Ravenna*, Ziese, *Wibert von Ravenna*, Heidrich, *Ravenna*.

[184] Bonizo of Sutri, *Lib. ad amic.* 6, p. 600/16–38; for the text of the oath, see Deusdedit, *Coll. can.* 4.423 (162), p. 599.

Archbishop Guibert figured prominently among those to whom, according to Gregory's Register, he sent individual tidings of his election. Gregory said that he looked forward to their close and continual co-operation. Reversing customary protocol, he referred to himself in the first person singular and to Guibert in the honorific second person plural. Reminding Guibert of the charity which he had pledged to the Roman church and to his own person, he besought the prayers of him and of his suffragans. Pope and archbishop should seek to join their churches in such concord and charity, that peace and perfect love should bind their hearts in one.[185]

Gregory was, indeed, quick to assert St Peter's rights over a city in Romagna. On 1 June 1073, he wrote to Count Guy of Imola about a claim of certain citizens of Imola, made directly to him, that, despite his recent oath to the pope, Guibert had sought to subject the Imolans by oath to his own jurisdiction. Gregory urged the count to support the citizens against such demands, but also to safeguard St Peter's rights, by working for peace and concord amongst all concerned.[186] Gregory was evidently concerned to uphold the ancient Roman claim that Ravenna was immediately subject to the pope. Nevertheless, his relations with Guibert appear to have been amicable. He not only summoned him to the Lent synod of 1074 but he accorded him the precedence over other Italian metropolitans that Pope Clement II had accorded to the archbishops of Ravenna. If due allowance is made for the partianship of chroniclers who wrote after the Guibertine schism had begun, there is no evidence for conflict between pope and archbishop at this time.[187] Indeed, Guibert promised support for Gregory's proposed military campaign against the Normans that was to follow in the spring.[188] When, early in 1075, Gregory summoned Guibert to the next Lent synod, he addressed him as *frater karissime* and claimed him as an ally in his defence of the Christian religion.[189] It is not clear whether or not Guibert attended,[190] but only after Canossa can even the beginnings of difference between Gregory and Guibert be demonstrated. Even so, Guibert's presence in 1077 at Henry IV's court in Pavia is not of itself evidence for anti-Gregorian activity.[191]

Real animosity began with the Lent synod of 1078. Just before it, Gregory addressed a letter not only to Guibert and all his suffragans, but also to all bishops and abbots 'in the march of Fermo and Camerino, in the Pentapolis, and in the regions of Emilia and Lombardy'. He addressed them collectively and not as individuals, and withheld his greeting and blessing on account of their presumption ('temeritas')

---

[185] *Reg.* 1.3, 26 Apr. 1073, pp. 5–6; cf. 1.10, to Count Guy of Imola, 1 June 1073, p. 16/20–7 where Gregory referred to his initially good opinion of Guibert's *fraterna caritas et sacerdotalis honestas.*

[186] *Reg.* 1.10, pp. 16–17.

[187] Bonizo of Sutri, *Lib. ad amic.* 6, p. 600/31–5, 7, p. 602/26–35; *Vita Anselmi ep. Lucensis,* cap. 18, p. 19; cf. Ziese, *Wibert von Ravenna,* pp. 35–8.

[188] Bonizo of Sutri, *Lib. ad amic.* 7, pp. 602/36–603/6.

[189] *Reg.* 2.42, 4 Jan. 1075, p. 179.

[190] In the absence of supporting evidence, little credence can be given to Bonizo of Sutri's statement that Guibert failed to attend and therefore, *ob periurii crimen,* was suspended: 7, p. 605/16–18. There is no evidence for Guibert's attitude towards the Lombard bishops' renunciation of Gregory at Piacenza in 1076.

[191] *MGH DDHIV* no. 293.

against St Peter and the Roman church. The likely explanation of such language is that Guibert and the bishops of a wide region were complicit in some such general exercise of lordship in contravention of Pepin's gift as Gregory had complained about when it occurred locally at Imola in 1073. Gregory declared to all who were summoned that he was willing to temper justice with mercy. At the synod, he excommunicated and suspended both Archbishop Tedald of Milan and Guibert 'for their unheard-of heresy and pride towards this holy catholic church'.[192] This, again, most naturally refers not to dealings with Henry IV or to political plots with other bishops against Gregory, but to the archbishops' insistence upon and exercise of their metropolitan rights in ways which Gregory deemed incompatible with prerogatives and rights of the apostolic see. A similar reference seems to underlie the terms in which Gregory wrote during November 1078 to 'all the Ravennese both greater and lesser', probably intending the province as well as the city of Ravenna. Referring to Guibert as 'the man who is now said to be bishop of the church of Ravenna', Gregory accused him of having wasted a once rich and religious church by tyrannical depredation and of having marred it by his irreligious life. Gregory alleged that, at the recent November synod, he had irrevocably deposed him from his see and had forbidden his subjects to have any contact with him.[193] Guibert's crime was that he had made the claims of Ravenna as great as those of Rome, and had exercised his authority as though he had full disposal of the resources of his church. There Gregory seems to have let matters rest, for he gave no directions for the election of a successor. At his Lent synod of 1079, he probably made no further reference to Guibert.[194]

At his Lent synod of 1080, Gregory renewed his sentence of deposition, *iam plerumque datum*, against Tedald 'the so-called archbishop of Milan' and Guibert of Ravenna. He gave no sign of having fresh gravamina against either of them.[195] But in June at the council of Brixen, Henry IV, who perhaps sought first to establish Tedald as his prospective anti-pope, prevailed upon Guibert to accept this role.[196] Thereafter, Gregory regarded him as an opponent, not only with respect to the papal patrimony, but also in the context of his struggle with the German king. The story of Gregory's attempt in 1080 to replace him by a loyal archbishop and of his uneasy cliency of Henry IV has already been told.[197] So far as relations between Rome and Ravenna are concerned, three matters remain for further comment.

---

[192] *Reg.* 5.13, 28 Jan. 1078, pp. 366–7; 5.14*a*(1), 17 Feb.–3 Mar. 1078, p. 369/4–9. Despite Gregory's reference in the latter source to an *olim iam factum anathema* involving both archbishops, there is no reliable evidence for an earlier sentence against Guibert, and *Reg.* 8.12, p. 532/2–4 with 8.13, p. 533/16–24 refers only to one synodal sentence, that of 1078.

[193] *Reg.* 6.10, 26 Nov. 1078, pp. 411–12; cf *LP* 2.285/25–7. For the recorded decrees of the Nov. synod, see *Reg.* 6.5*b*, pp. 400–6; they contain no direct or indirect evidence for a sentence regarding Ravenna, although *LP* refers to a renewing of the anathema.

[194] Berthold, *a.* 1079, p. 317/27–8, is not elsewhere supported; the decrees of the Lent synod of 1079 make no reference to Guibert of Ravenna, although a number of bishops, including Tedald of Milan, were condemned: *Reg.* 6.17*a*, pp. 425–9, esp. 429/11–16.

[195] *Reg.* 7.14*a*(3), 7 Mar. 1080, p. 481/4–7.   [196] See above, 3.5.2.

[197] See above, 3.5.3, 5, 7–9.

First, at Ravenna Guibert continued to show himself a moderate but active reformer of his church. For example, in 1081 he encouraged the clergy of his cathedral to adopt a common rule of sleeping, eating, and praying which was not unlike that which the reform popes had promoted at Rome and Bishop Anselm II at Lucca.[198] Guibert was no worldly and scandalous prelate but, like Liemar of Bremen and others, a reformer of a non-Gregorian stamp; he became caught up in events with which it was beyond his capability to cope.[199]

Second, Gregory's aim, especially in 1080, in dealing with Ravenna and its province should not be misunderstood. Once he had determined to install a new archbishop, his overriding concern was to restore the city and region to its proper place, as he saw it, in the papal patrimony.[200] His relevant letters never named Henry IV; they alluded to the king's interests only indirectly and in so far as Gregory sought to eliminate all claims to and exercise of lordship and jurisdiction which contravened the rights of St Peter as Pepin III had determined them. Ravenna was to be restored to its unique and rightful position as the special daughter of Rome.[201] According to the foundation legend of the church of Ravenna, St Peter had himself sent its patron St Apollinaris to be its first bishop; Gregory's new archbishop was to stand in a similarly direct relationship to himself.[202] Gregory repeatedly castigated Guibert for his offences against papal rights as he had envisaged them since 1078:[203] despite his oath of 1073, he had devastated the spiritual and temporal resources and goods of his see and had usurped papal prerogatives.[204] Gregory was, therefore, determined to restore Ravenna to its pristine liberty under papal lordship as part of the patrimony.[205] To this end, he summoned the military strength of both the Norman vassals of the apostolic see and the bishops and laity of the papal patrimony according to his idea of its proper extent.[206] Gregory's struggle with Guibert of Ravenna seems to have been pre-eminently one for the rehabilitation of the papal patrimony; only secondarily and as a consequence did he envisage it as part of his struggle with Henry IV.

Third, Gregory's attempt of 1080 to vindicate papal claims that Ravenna was part of the patrimony by organizing military forces to subdue it and to impose a new archbishop was followed *c.*1085 by Guibert's writing a tract which delated Gregory as a man of war. Known only from fragments and references in the works of Bishops Guy of Ferrara and Anselm II of Lucca,[207] it evidently circulated in north-eastern Italy. 'What Christian', Guibert asked with regard to Hildebrand, 'ever instituted so many wars or killed so many men?'[208] Even while a youthful monk, he had recruited and

[198] Rubeus, *Historiarum Ravennatum*, pp. 307–8.

[199] See his obituary in Ekkehard of Aura, *a.* 1100, p. 162/14–21; Ekkehard heard him say that he wished that he had never accepted the title of pope.

[200] *Reg.* 8.7, 12–14, pp. 524–5, 531–5. [201] p. 533/30–2, cf. p. 534/1–5.

[202] pp. 531/20–5, 532/36–533/6, 535/13–16; cf. *Reg.* 6.10, p. 411/12–16 for an earlier reference to this theme.

[203] pp. 531/25–39, 533/7–15, 535/20–1. [204] pp. 533/16–26.

[205] pp. 532/5–19, 533/32–5. [206] pp. 525/6–17, 531/15–19, 534/25–30.

[207] Guy of Ferrara; Anselm of Lucca, *Liber contra Wibertum*.

[208] Guy of Ferrara, 1.15, p. 545/25–6.

paid his own war-band (*satellitium*) under colour of the defence and freedom of the Roman church; he had always studied and waged warfare, setting children against parents, knights against kings, and servants against masters, and destroying the peace of the church in the whole world.[209] Moreover, he had done what was unheard-of in a bishop or pope by condemning an emperor. Guibert repeatedly arraigned him for fomenting war in Germany through his setting up of Rudolf of Rheinfelden against Henry IV, thereby destroying the loyalties that bound society, unleashing rapine, arson, and all manner of evils, and setting an evil example to all. Christians should not teach men to start wars; they should urge them to bear injuries rather than to avenge them.[210] By 1085, Guibert had built up a general polemic against Gregory, who was by now his rival pope, as a warrior who had everywhere subverted the peace of Christendom and had set a pattern of violence. He took up the propaganda of Henrician bishops in Germany.

As he finally developed it, Guibert's polemic may, therefore, have been more the result of his travels with Henry's court with its sophisticated propaganda resources than of what he learnt from scholarly circles in Ravenna. The notion that there was, in the eleventh century, a 'Ravenna law school' which was ahead of the rest of North Italy in the study of the Roman civil law has been damagingly criticized.[211] More-over, such documents which have been associated with it as the so-called 'Ravenna forgeries' which purported to establish the emperor's right to choose the pope as well as the territorial claims of the church of Ravenna, and the *Defensio Heinrici IV regis* which goes under the name of Peter Crassus, may have little to do with the church or province of Ravenna.[212]

It was less in Ravenna itself than in parts of its province nearer to the Matildine lands that the most effective propaganda against Gregory was conducted, especially in his latter years. Some of it was of a popular kind, as is suggested by a poem, some-times unwarrantably ascribed to 'Peter Crassus', which celebrated King Henry IV's victory at Rome in 1084 and the discomfiting of the 'malicious Hildebrand' who had recklessly seized the apostolic see and polluted the world. The poem especially plac-arded his unblushing alliance with his 'evil partner' Matilda and his bribery of the whole world with money. Its local, Emilian origin is suggested by its naming the

---

[209] Guy of Ferrara, 2, p. 554/7–11, 16–19.

[210] Guy of Ferrara, 1.6, pp. 538/42–539/1, 1.7, pp. 539/34–540/7, 1.8, p. 541/14–18, 1.15, p. 545/25–37.

[211] The view was first suggested by Ficker, *Forschungen*, 3.110–21, and strongly argued by Jordan, 'Der Kaisergedanke', and 'Ravenna und Rom'; for criticisms, see Robinson, *Authority and Resistance*, pp. 80–3 and Heidrich, *Ravenna*, pp. 148–50.

[212] The 'Ravenna Forgeries' are edited by C. Märtl, *Die falschen Investiturpriveligien*; she concludes that they may have originated anywhere in North Italy at a date between the 1080s and the early years of the 12th cent.: pp. 52–95. The *Defensio Heinrici IV regis* appears to have been by a lay writer named Peter who was versed in Roman civil law and who wrote for another person named Crassus. It was completed, and probably entirely written, with a view to presentation at an imminent council, probably Guibert's Roman synod of Mar. 1084: cap. 7, p. 453/32–3, cf. caps. 4, 5, 7, pp. 438/13–16, 442/21–3, 448/44–6. It is addressed to King Henry. Its author may have come from anywhere in imperial Italy, although Ravenna is not very likely: Robinson, *Authority and Resistance*, pp. 75–83; Heidrich, *Ravenna*, pp. 148–55.

'diabolical society' of laymen upon whom Gregory had vainly depended. From his struggles with them, Henry had emerged as victor and had destroyed the subversive movement of the Patarenes.[213]

More comprehensive and sophisticated was the tract *De scismate Hildebrandi* which the Guibertine Guy, bishop of Ferrara by 1083, composed early in 1086; he wrote at the prompting of the anti-pope Clement III after hearing debates at Ravenna at which the case for and against Gregory had been argued with passion.[214] The purpose of the tract was to rally the whole church to Clement, but it owes its effectiveness to its setting out the *sic et non* of Gregory's credibility as pope. Guy had observed Gregory at first hand during his Lent synod of 1080, and, in his first book, he presented a powerful case in his favour. He applauded the austerity of his life and his pastoral concern for others, and he argued the case for the validity of his election to the papacy. He did not spare Henry IV a full arraignment of his supposed personal vices and simony, from which Hildebrand had laboured to convert him. He gave a defence of Gregory's warfare against Henry, as of his campaign against incontinent clergy. He was especially eloquent in his refutation of the picture of Gregory as a man of bribery, violence, and bloodshed. Time and again he contradicted Clement III's own allegations against Gregory, and he drew heavily upon texts of early Christian writers and upon the events of early church history to adduce warrant for Gregory's actions. In a second book, however, which had the form of a dialogue between an inquirer and a master, Guy set himself, in response to his own case for the defence, to present an irrefutable condemnation of the errors that Hildebrand had everywhere spread. He had, in truth, become pope in defiance of Pope Nicholas II's Election Decree. Guy now arraigned Gregory's warfare against Henry IV as a gross abuse of power which had stained the papacy with homicide, bloodshed, and indiscriminate violence. Guy refuted the contention which he ascribed to Gregory that the sacraments of schismatics were null and void. He ended by concluding that, now that Gregory was dead, Clement III should be recognized as pope even though the manner of his election might be deemed to have been irregular. Since Guy's tract survives in only a single manuscript, it cannot be assumed to have circulated widely. But it provides evidence for the debates that took place in north-eastern Italy during and after Gregory's latter years and of the balance of arguments that inclined many to turn away from him.

In the light of such debates as Guy of Ferrara engaged in, it is not suprising that Gregory should have been widely rejected and Clement widely recognized in Romagna and in Emilia. By 1084, three of the dioceses adjacent to that of Ravenna— Bologna, Faenza, and Ferrara, certainly had Guibertine bishops and the fourth, Imola, probably had.[215] Sigefried of Bologna, whom Gregory excommunicated at his Lent synod of 1079,[216] is the only Romagnan bishop, apart from Guibert of Ravenna

---

[213] Ed. E. Dümmler, *MGH L. de L.* 1. 433–4; see Heidrich, *Ravenna*, pp. 151–3.
[214] Guy of Ferrara.
[215] For surveys of the dioceses of Romagna and Emilia, see Schwartz, *Die Besetzung*, pp. 151–99; Heidrich, *Ravenna*, pp. 107–18.   [216] *Reg.* 6.17a(5), p. 429/11–14.

himself, whom Gregory is known to have censured by name; this indicates the limited efficacy of his power there. Outside Romagna, he showed some caution even at Piacenza, where, in 1067, the Patarenes had already expelled for a time the recalcitrant Bishop Dionysius. As pope, Gregory was at first conciliatory towards him, but in 1075 he pronounced his deposition. In February 1076 it was at Piacenza that the Lombard bishops, including Dionysius, followed their German brothers by withdrawing their obedience from Gregory. At Brixen in 1080 and in subsequent years during Henry's expeditions to Italy, Dionysius was a staunch Henrician.[217] In the Emilian sees, Bishop Eberhard of Parma was an imperialist,[218] as was Humbert of Modena;[219] while at Reggio, the imperialist Gandulf was opposed by the Gregorian Heribert who was at the deathbed of Bishop Anselm II of Lucca.[220] To the east of the Matildine lands, Gregory found little lasting support, even in those dioceses over which the papacy had an ancient claim to recall. On the other hand, it was an indication alike of Guibert of Ravenna's strength in his province and of his weakness at Rome that, in 1084, his papal consecration in the Lateran was performed, not by Roman cardinal-bishops, but by his own suffragans.[221]

4.7 The Church and City of Rome

For Gregory's dealings with Rome itself and with its immediate surroundings, there is a dearth of evidence. Only a handful of his letters and privileges shed light upon them. Amongst chronicles, the *Annales Romani*, which record something of Hildebrand's archidiaconate, have a gap from 1073 to 1116.[222] The *Liber pontificalis* noticed only Cencius Stephani's seizure of the pope at Christmastide 1075 and Henry IV's and Robert Guiscard's dealings at Rome in Gregory's latter years. Bonizo of Sutri's *Liber ad amicum* is somewhat more concerned with Roman events, but it is partisan and tendentious. Evidence from chronicles and writings which originated further afield is sparse and difficult to interpret. Nor was there considerable building or other public work at Rome during Gregory's pontificate which might illuminate the course of events or the resources at his command.

The paucity of evidence is, perhaps, not fortuitous or merely the consequence of Gregory's being able to deal with local affairs by administrative action that left little or no written record. With regard to the ecclesiastical and civil affairs of Rome and its region, his approach seems to have been one of *quieta non movere*.[223] Unlike Pope Leo

---

[217] Bonizo of Sutri, *Lib. ad amic.* 6, pp. 598/12–14, 600/22–5, 7, p. 606/35–9, 9, p. 613/5–9; *Reg.* 2.26, to Bishop Dionysius of Piacenza, 27 Nov. 1074, pp. 158–9, 2.52a, p. 197/2; Benzo of Alba, 6. Praef., p. 658/48–9, cf. 4.2, 11, pp. 636, 645.

[218] Donizo, 2.338–41, p. 386; Bernold, *Chron. a.* 1085, p. 443/35–7.

[219] Bonizo of Sutri, *Lib. ad amic.* 9, p. 614/15–23.

[220] For Gandulf, *Reg.* 6.17a(6), p. 429/17–21; Donizo, 2.338–41, p. 386; Bernold, *Chron. a.* 1085, p. 443/35–7. For Heribert, Bernold, *Chron. a.* 1085, p. 443/35–7; *Vita Anselmi ep. Lucensis*, cap. 41, p. 25.

[221] See above, 3.5.9.

[222] See Whitton, 'The *Annales Romani*'.

[223] I follow here the conclusions of Whitton, 'Papal Policy in Rome,' to which I am greatly indebted in this section.

IX before him and Pope Urban II afterwards, he made no express reference to the *Constitutum Constantini* as a warrant for the temporal possessions of the apostolic see in Italy or at Rome.[224] Nor can it be convincingly shown that he envisaged, much less implemented, a policy of recovering local lands of the Roman church which for generations had been undisturbed in the hands of lay families. Guy of Ferrara did, indeed, reckon it to Gregory's credit that, after becoming pope, he instituted and resolutely pursued the guarding, defending, and recovering of towns, villages, enceintes, and castles, and that he recruited a band of knights through whose military power he upheld the rights of the Roman church against the Normans and other predatory neighbours.[225] But, while such activity after 1073 cannot be ruled out, it cannot be extensively documented.[226] As archdeacon and executive at large of the apostolic see, Hildebrand had been active, not so much in recovering its ancient lands and rights, as in correcting recent dispossessions and depredations of churches in the region of Rome.[227] As pope, it is only in connection with his extravagant 'Crusading' plan of 1074 that he can be seen doing anything of the sort: in the spring, an objective of his military organization was to overawe the turbulent Normans.[228] He was acknowledged to have the right of building, fortifying, and garrisoning strong points in small towns whose citizens were expected to support any garrison of knights, while the citizens were at all times liable to provide the pope free of payment with services of a military, advisory, and judicial nature.[229] But Gregory seems normally to have relied for the regulation of local affairs less upon armed force than upon the authority of the papal office, upon the dispatch of writ-like missives which tersely conveyed his will,[230] and upon the expressions of authority and the personal contacts that were possible at his Lateran synods.

Like all ecclesiastical rulers of his age, Gregory felt himself to be under an especial obligation to safeguard the property and rights of the patron saint of his see—in his case, St Peter himself. At his November synod of 1078 in particular, he forbade the misappropriation or concealment of the property of St Peter wherever situated and the omission of services that were due.[231] It was perhaps to implement such a

---

[224] See Cowdrey, 'Eleventh-century Reformers' Views'. [225] 1.2, p. 534/21–34.

[226] Cardinal Beno's reference in 1084 to 'Centius iudicum primicerius cum aliis iudicibus, et cuncti milites signa banda gestantes' refers to the ordinary police arrangements of the city: 1.1, p. 369/26–7; cf. Otto of Freising, *Gest. Fred.* 4.77, p. 672/20–2. There are, however, two clear references to Gregory's seeking to recruit knights from bishops further afield: *Epp. vag.* no. 13, to Bishop Henry of Trent, (Mar.–July 1976), p. 32/2–6; in 1078, Gregory thought of recruiting knights from Archbishop Manasses I of Rheims: *RHGF* 14.612E.

[227] See above, 2.2.5.

[228] Bonizo of Sutri, *Lib. ad amic.* 7, pp. 602–4; Amatus, *Storia*, 7.12, pp. 303–4.

[229] Deusdedit, *Coll. can.* 3.201(149), p. 360.

[230] *Reg.* 1.66, 20 Mar. 1074, pp. 95–6; Gregory enjoined the monks and lay dependents of the monastery of S. Quirico in Antrodoco to recognize as their lord Bishop Rainer of Rieti to whom Gregory had given their monastery, 'alioquin iram nostrae malivolentiae seu excommunicationis vinculum non evadetis'.

[231] 'Si quis predia beati Petri apostolorum principis ubicunque posita in proprietatem suam usurpaverit vel sciens occultata non propalaverit vel debitum servitium exinde beato Petro non exhibuerit, recognoscat se iram Dei et sanctorum apostolorum velut sacrilegus incurrere. Quicumque autem in hoc

safeguarding of St Peter's possessions and rights that there was drawn up the long inventory of papal possessions and sources of income that the cardinal-priest Deusdedit included in the canon-law collection that he compiled before 1087.[232] He listed territorial possessions that secular rulers had granted to the apostolic see, its patrimonial estates, and tributes that were due to it from foreign rulers and lands. The intention was manifestly to place upon record the ancient rights and possessions of the Roman church in so far as they could be documented, rather than to facilitate any new departure in administration; it remained for Pope Urban II to introduce new arrangements on the model of his former monastery at Cluny. Probably, though not demonstrably, the oversight of papal finances under Gregory was in the hands of his successor as archdeacon, Theodinus, until his defection in 1084.

Within such limitations as are suggested by Deusdedit's inventory, Gregory was at pains to husband the resources of the Roman church both locally and in the church at large. The scarcity of evidence for changes in the proprietorship or leasing of lands near Rome probably indicates that such transactions were few in number and conventional in form.[233] There seems to have been no active market in land, and no papal policy of resumption of lands or leases. However, Gregory clearly had a system of agents ('actionarii') who collected revenues and dues in Central Italy.[234] Further afield, Gregory showed some concern for the *census* from monasteries which, though individually often small, cumulatively represented a significant part of the income of the Roman church. Probably in 1075, he sought to enlist the service of Bishop Hugh of Die to ensure their regular payment from French monasteries;[235] the inference is that such *census* were often paid only sporadically if at all, but that they were capable of being exacted when those who owed them were properly motivated or, more hopefully, when there was an agent to oversee their collection and forwarding. Occasionally, Gregory stood to benefit appreciably from fresh donations, as when, in 1077, Count Bernard of Besalú provided that seven religious houses should pay *census* to Rome totalling 32 *solidi* a year.[236] In general, however, Gregory was concerned to confirm existing arrangements or, when new *census* were stipulated, to follow established lines. Only some one in five of Gregory's privileges for monasteries mentioned money; Gregory's dealings with them lend no colour to the allegation

---

crimine deprehensus fuerit, eandem hereditatem beati Petri legitime restituat et poenam quadrupli de propriis bonis persolvat': *Reg.* 6.5*b*(11), p. 405. In 1076, Gregory equated Norman depredation upon the goods of the church with the outrages of simoniacs against law and religion: *Reg.* 4.7, to his partisans in Milan, 31 Oct. 1076, p. 305/14–19.

[232] *Coll. can.* 3.184–289, pp. 348–96; see Zema, 'Economic Reorganization', pp. 145–7; Sydow, 'Cluny und die Anfänge', pp. 38–9. Deusdedit drew upon papyrus *acta* and other records not only at the Lateran but also at a *turris chartularia* near the church of S. Maria Nova where papal records were held: Ehrle, 'Die Frangipani'; R. Schieffer, 'Tomus Gregorii papae'.

[233] Deusdedit recorded the lease of a *castrum* at Albinium, in the county of Narni: *Coll. can.* 3.201 (149), p. 360. In 1078, the gift to the Roman church of a *castrum* at Morcicchia in the duchy of Soletto, merited record in Gregory's Register: 6.5*a*, pp. 399–400. cf. Deusdedit, *Coll. can.* 3.259 (149), p. 376. For the bequest of a *curtis* to the Roman church by a son of Count Gerard of Galeria, see below, n. 250.

[234] *QF* no. 154, pp. 178/1–179/1.   [235] *Epp. vag.* no. 12, pp. 28–9.

[236] *Lib. feud. maior*, 2.16–17, no. 501.

that, as pope, he was a dedicated financier (*Finanzmann*) or that he was preoccupied with increasing the income of the Roman church.[237]

More profitable than monastic *census* were, perhaps, the financial dues which were owed by lay princes, as when, in 1077, Bernard of Besalú commended his county to St Peter and promised an annual tribute of a hundred gold mancuses.[238] But, as with monastic *census*, such payments were an exceptional rather than an established feature of Gregory's arrangements.[239] Another source of income was Peter's Pence, which were owed by the rulers of a number of countries to the Roman church. Only with regard to England is there evidence as to whether or not they were forthcoming during Gregory's papal years. His predecessor, Alexander II, had pressed upon King William I their status as an annual payment ('pensio').[240] In 1074, Gregory called upon the king to be attentive to the *ius sancti Petri* as it should be collected in England, but in 1080 it transpired from the exchange between pope and king about the latter's alleged obligation to fealty that there had of late been negligence; William promised to send Peter's Pence as soon as possible and probably sought to honour his promise. The potential contribution of Peter's Pence from England to papal revenues at Rome should not be underestimated; according to Archbishop Lanfranc of Canterbury's records, the Romescot liability of East Kent alone amounted to almost 4,000 pence.[241] But the scanty evidence makes possible no estimate whatever of the income of Gregory's papacy from local and general sources. One can only surmise that it was adequate for ordinary times but that, as was shown by Pope Stephen IX's plans for a campaign against the Normans, exceptional circumstances would call for exceptional measures.[242]

To a considerable degree, Roman officials and agents are likely to have been remunerated by the fees and considerations which they received for documents issued, favours procured, and services rendered. Reports of the large sums of money that, in 1075, Bishop Hermann of Bamberg considered it useful to lay out at Rome 'ad explendos Romanae cupiditatis hiatus' must, no doubt, be treated with some reserve.[243] But the execution of business is likely to have brought officials income which it was in their interest to safeguard and which there is no evidence that Gregory challenged or sought to regulate. The Lateran itself was supported by renders in kind and in cash from Roman churches and monasteries.[244] Perhaps more valuable for the Roman church and for its representatives up to the pope himself was

---

[237] See Fabre, *Étude sur le Liber censuum*, pp. 68–71.

[238] As n. 236; cf. Count Peter of Substantion's *census*: above, 3.5.10.

[239] See Erdmann, *Die Entstehung*, pp. 204–5; Eng. trans. pp. 221–2.

[240] *Ep.* 139, *PL* 146.1413; cf. Deusdedit, *Coll. can.* 3.269, p. 378.

[241] *Reg.* 1.70, to King William I, p. 102/18–24, cf. Deusdedit, *Coll. can.* 3.270, p. 378; Lanfranc, *Letters*, no. 39, pp. 131–3. For evidence of its payment and of the East Kent assessment, see *The Domesday Monachorum*, p. 80; *Calendar of the Manuscripts . . . of Wells*, 1.17.

[242] *Chron. Cas.* 2.97, p. 355; Amatus, *Storia*, 3.50–2, pp. 166–8, 170. In 1082, Gregory resorted to exceptional measures of expending church property in order to finance his defence of Rome against Henry IV: see above, 3.5.7.

[243] *M* no. 41, p. 244/19–23; cf. *Reg.* 3.3, to King Henry of Germany, 20 July 1075, p. 247/1–7.

[244] See Gregory's privilege for St Paul's-without-the-Walls: *QF* no. 36, esp. pp. 27/38–28/15.

the wealth that accrued from the offerings of pilgrims, and especially from those who completed penitential pilgrimages. When, in 1075, Gregory imposed penance upon the pilgrim Count Simon of Crépy, he assigned part of the money which Simon paid to his own use and part to the support of 'two most religious men' who were currently at Rome.[245] It is a vivid example of how Gregory was able to provide hospitality for his supporters who resorted to him for counsel and edification. He was, however, scrupulous in not accepting penitential payments from those of whose amendment he was not assured, even when he was himself in dire financial need.[246] Gregory's insistence at his November synod of 1078 upon the regular presentation of oblations by the laity when they attended mass may have brought income to the churches of Rome as well as in other places where it was observed.[247]

Upon the available evidence, it is not possible to form more than an impression of the state of papal finances under Gregory VII; but it is likely that, until the final crisis of Henry IV's Italian expeditions, he did not find it difficult to maintain the religious, administrative, and economic life of the apostolic see in fair equilibrium, if on a largely hand-to-mouth basis.

If Gregory made no major changes in the finances and administration of the Roman church, he seems also to have made no major challenge to its religious condition. There are, indeed, two respects in which he was said by Bonizo of Sutri to have extirpated radical abuses, particularly in the first year or so of his pontificate. First, having claimed that the sons and kindred of concubinous priests were a prime cause of Roman unrest, Bonizo alleged that Gregory quickly gave all Roman clergy the choice between living a common life with no individual property or of renouncing all claim to support from the goods of the church and abstaining from clerical functions. Many, according to Bonizo, opted for withdrawal into private life so that, with their families, they became the pope's enemies.[248] Such a reform would have been in keeping with Hildebrand's allocution to the Roman synod of 1059, with attempts by popes like Nicholas II and Alexander II to sponsor regular clerical life at Rome, and with the precepts of these popes' encyclical *Vigilantia universalis*. It has further been claimed that a Vatican manuscript, lat. 629, includes a Rule for regular clergy which Gregory sponsored, in 1074 or perhaps in 1078. After a decree upon the liturgical use of the Psalms, it imposed a strict regime of fasting and abstinence, and provided for a common life from which private property was stringently excluded. But there is good reason for doubting Gregory's responsibility for anything except the opening liturgical decree.[249] The document does nothing to confirm Bonizo's statement;

---

[245] *Vita beati Simonis com. Cresp.* cap. 3, col. 1213C. It is an interesting possibility that one of the beneficiaries was Abbot William of Hirsau in his sickness: see above, 3.6.3.

[246] *Reg.* 9.23, to Count C., (1082), p. 605/4–10.

[247] *Reg.* 6.5*b*, pp. 402/31–2, 406/4–9.

[248] *Lib. ad amic.* 7, p. 603/17–23.

[249] For the supposed Rule, see Morin, 'Règlements inédits'. The arguments of Dereine, 'La Prétendue Règle' remain decisive against Gregory's responsibility for anything but the opening section. See also Bardy, 'Saint Grégoire VII et la réforme canoniale'; Leclercq, 'Un Témoignage'; and Schmidt, 'Die Kanonikerreform in Rom'.

while it is not, in principle improbable that Gregory fostered the common life among Roman clergy, there is no further evidence that he did so.

Second, Bonizo claimed that, in 1074, Gregory took radical and successful steps to remedy grave disorder in the basilica of St Peter. A body of over sixty lay sextons ('mansionarii'), who were married or concubinous, provided night-and-day supervision of the basilica and effectively controlled and exploited all altars save the principal one. They pretended to be priests and cardinals, deceiving pilgrims into accepting their ministrations and, especially during the hours of darkness, they engaged in all manner of robberies and outrages. With great difficulty, Gregory expelled the sextons and installed reputable priests. As for the high altar, the cardinal clergy celebrated masses there before dawn for their own financial gain; Gregory strictly regulated the service of this altar to eliminate this abuse.[250] There is no inherent improbability in Gregory's instituting some such reforms which had precedents earlier in the eleventh century;[251] but there is no confirmation of Bonizo's highly coloured account which is made suspect by his insistence that, at so early a date, Archbishop Guibert of Ravenna fished in the troubled waters at Rome which the reforms provided. On Bonizo's evidence alone, it would be rash to conclude that, even briefly, Gregory took in hand a searching reform of the Roman clergy who from an early date were in any considerable number thereby rendered hostile to him.

Moreover, for all his desire to secure liturgical uniformity in the Latin church at large on the basis of the Roman rite, at Rome itself Gregory made no thoroughgoing attempt to resolve the diversity of use that characterized its many churches. The fullest evidence for his liturgical concerns, particularly at Rome, is provided by Bernold of St Blasien, who visited the city in 1079 and wrote his *Micrologus* after 1086. It is supplemented by the decree on the recitation of the Psalms which is prefixed to his supposed Rule for the clergy. The Volterra chapter-book testifies to the prominence of liturgical material among the rulings that Gregory circulated to churches under his direct jurisdiction.[252] It emerges that Gregory had a number of objectives in liturgical matters at Rome which are likely to have won him local approval. In his decree on the recitation of the Psalms, he declared his purpose of restoring the ancient custom of the Roman church, especially by reverting to the status quo before German elements had crept into its worship.[253] Bernold referred to Gregory's lifelong assiduity to seeking out and implementing whatever was best in the apostolic traditions that governed liturgical practice.[254] Such a reputation may

---

[250] *Lib. ad amic.* 7, pp. 603/23–604/2; cf. Paul of Bernried, cap. 26, p. 484.

[251] See above, 1.5.

[252] On liturgical matters, see esp. Elze, 'Gregor VII. und die römische Liturgie'. For material in the Volterra chapter-book, see *De sancti Hugonis actis*, caps. 58, 64, 114, 134, 138, pp. 79, 84, 129–30, 149, 151–3, 221.

[253] Morin, 'Règlements inédits', p. 179/1–13: 'Romani autem diverso modo agere ceperunt, maxime a tempore quo teutonicis concessum est regimen nostrae aecclesiae. Nos autem et ordinem Romanum et antiquum morem investigantes statuimus fieri nostrae ecclesiae sicut superius praenotavimus, antiquos imitantes patres.'

[254] '. . . qui sub decem suis antecessoribus, a puero Romae nutritus et eruditus, omnes apostolicas traditiones diligentissime investigavit, et investigatas studiosissime in actum referre curavit. Hunc ergo

have commended Gregory strongly, not only to Bernold, but also to many in Rome. One, at least, of Gregory's specific concerns is likely to have enlisted favour there: he insisted upon the due commemoration everywhere of all Roman popes and martyrs.[255] All in all, for Gregory the usage of the Roman church was to be the standard for universal imitation following a liturgical conservatism that sought to exclude what was not ancient and to promote what was believed to be the usage of Pope Gregory the Great.[256] Such a preference for Roman tradition is likely to have been favoured by many Roman clergy, in so far as it was intended to reassert the supremacy of the Roman church in liturgical matters and to clear away the accretions of foreign, and especially German, traditions since Ottonian times.

If Gregory made bold statements about insisting upon Roman norms, in matters of detail he prudently made changes piecemeal and gradually. One innovation that he made illustrates the sensitivity of local opinion: when he instituted a summer fast in the octave of Pentecost, opinion at Rome was and remained divided, with many doubting the canonical propriety of such a change.[257] Other legislation seems to have been less controversial, as when he also imposed a strict fast in the first week of Lent.[258] So far as can be perceived, Gregory was content to leave the worship of the Roman churches little disturbed, while he enunciated traditional principles that may have been congenial to many clergy and laity. In the Roman church, he preferred peace and concord to change and contention.

His behaviour towards the city of Rome seems to have been similar. A twelfth-century memory that, in the early 1080s, Gregory curtailed the ceremonies of the *cornomannia*, at which money was distributed among the citizens, 'after the costs of war increased',[259] suggests that, for most of his pontificate, Gregory tolerated such things to continue undisturbed, thus avoiding resentment on the part of the populace at large.

He seems to have had his reward for such inaction in the habitual acceptance of his rule as pope by most of the clergy and citizens of Rome, or at least in their compliance. His letters occasionally refer to the *Romani*, by whom he seems to have meant the inhabitants of the city and its environs, including those who were directly in the papal service.[260] Upon this evidence, it is clear that relations were, indeed, not

doctorem religione et auctoritate praecipuum, imo apostolicam traditionem per ipsum in consecrandis mysteriis potentissimum imitari decrevimus': *Micrologus*, cap. 14, col. 986B. For the limitations of Bernold's understanding of what he found in Rome, see Van Dijk and Hazelden Walker, *The Origins*, pp. 49–50, 74, 248–9.

[255] *Micrologus*, cap. 43, col. 1010A; cf. *Reg.* 6.5b, p. 401/29, which suggests that this provision was among those made *pro restauratione sanctae ecclesiae* (p. 400/27) at the Nov. synod of 1078; cf. Mansi, 19.385.

[256] *Micrologus*, caps. 5, 14, 17, 43, 56, cols. 980CD, 986B, 988B, 1010AB, 1018BC.

[257] *Micrologus*, cap. 25, col. 997B–D, cf. cap. 43, col. 1000A.

[258] *Micrologus*, cap. 24, col. 995C.

[259] Ben. can. cap. 7 (1–2), pp. 171–2, esp. p. 171b/28–9.

[260] See esp. *Reg.* 6.17, to Abbot Hugh of Cluny, 2 Jan. 1078, p. 423/16–18. Gregory referred to the inhabitants of the peninsula, esp. of its northern and central parts, as *Italici*: *Reg.* 1.19, p. 32/3, 2.31, p. 166/27; 2.32, p. 168/24, 7.14a, p. 484/5; 9.3, p. 574/5,26; or *Latini*: *Reg.* 7.3, p. 462/28.

altogether easy. In January 1075, he wrote to his confidant Abbot Hugh of Cluny that those amongst whom he lived, the *Romani*, Lombards, and Normans, were as he often told them, worse than Jews and pagans.[261] It was against the counsel of most of his entourage, whom he identified as *Romani*, that, at the end of 1076, he travelled northwards towards Germany.[262] In the summer of the same year, Bishop Hermann of Metz had been concerned about the attitude towards Gregory of the *Romani* and the Normans.[263] Yet as late as May 1081, while Gregory was concerned about the effect upon the *Romani* of a withdrawal of Norman aid for the papacy, he was also confident that the *Romani et qui circa nos* were entirely loyal and serviceable.[264] In the event they for long afterwards withstood Henry IV's appeals to them.[265] Over the years they caused him anxiety, but he was able to keep them loyal by his prudent counsels of *quieta non movere*.

With more demonstrable success, for his dealings with them are somewhat better documented than with the generality of the *Romani*, Gregory recruited and kept the loyalty and service of almost all of the cardinals of the Roman church up to the major defection of 1084.[266] Historians have underestimated Gregory's skill in dealing with them, for they have followed uncritically the strictures of Cardinal Beno's letter in which he listed the defectors of 1084 and claimed that, from the earliest days of his pontificate, Gregory banished the cardinals, that is, the cardinal-priests and Roman deacons with other city clergy, from his counsels because he preferred persons of unsuitable background.[267]

It should first be noticed that, even in 1084–5, the list of cardinals who remained loyal to Gregory to and beyond the end of his pontificate is at once more numerous and more distinguished than that of those who defected to the anti-pope Clement III. Among the bishops, the sole defector was the aged John II of Porto.[268] Beno named eight defecting priests: Leo of S. Lorenzo in Damaso, then *archipresbyter cardinalium*, Beno himself, who was priest of SS. Martino e Silvestro, Hugh Candidus of S. Clemente who, alone among the cardinals, had defected from Gregory long ago, John of uncertain title, Peter II of S. Grisogono the papal *cancellarius et bibliothecarius*, Atto of S. Marco, Innocent of uncertain title, and Leo of S. Lorenzo in Lucina; and three deacons: the archdeacon Theodinus, John of S. Maria in Domnica, and

---

[261] *Reg.* 2.49, 22 Jan. 1075, p. 189/25–7.

[262] *Epp. vag.* no. 17, p. 48/1–2: 'postponentes pene omnium fidelium nostrorum consilia'; no. 18, p. 50/1: 'contra voluntatem et consilium Romanorum'; no. 19, p. 50/26–8: 'contra voluntatem pene omnium fidelium nostrorum, excepta carissima et fidelissima beati filia videlicet Mathilde.'

[263] *Reg.* 4.2, to Bishop Hermann of Metz, 25 Aug. 1076, p. 293/22–4.

[264] *Reg.* 9.11, to Abbot Desiderius of Montecassino, p. 589/8–14.

[265] See above, 3.5.5, 7–9.

[266] This and the next four paragraphs are based on Fürst's analysis of the cardinals: 'Gregorio VII', pp. 26–7, supported by data from Hüls, *Kardinäle*.

[267] Beno, 1.1–2, pp. 369–70; see esp. the allegation that 'Postquam aliunde ascendit, a consilio removit cardinales sacrae sedis. Cum quibus personis consilia sua diebus et noctibus habuit, Roma vidit et audivit': p. 370/12–13; cf. 2.12, p. 380.

[268] Beno, himself a cardinal-priest, did not mention John of Porto who was outside his usage of the term cardinal. For John of Porto's activities on Clement's behalf, see above, 3.5.12.

Crescentius.[269] By contrast, as against one defecting bishop, six remained loyal: Odo of Ostia, Peter of Albano, Hubert of Palestrina, Hubald of Sabina, Bruno of Segni, and John of Tusculum. As against eight defecting priests, seven were loyal: Desiderius of S. Cecilia, Rainer of S. Clemente, Bonnussenior of S. Maria in Trastevere, Deusdedit of S. Pietro in Vincoli, Benedict of S. Pudenziana, Herimannus of SS. Quattro Coronati,[270] and Richard of uncertain title. Beno's three defecting deacons are matched by three loyal ones: Damian, Gregory, and Oderisius.

It is not only in point of numbers that the lists of cardinals indicate Gregory's retention of substantial support. Of the twelve defectors who are known by name, only two of the deacons are known to have taken office after 1073, while all of the eight defecting priests appear to have been in office before that date, as was the episcopal defector John of Porto. If most of the defectors were not of Gregory's appointment, a large number of the cardinals who took office in his time remained loyal: three bishops, five priests, and perhaps two known deacons; as did two bishops, one priest (the powerful Desiderius of S. Cecilia, abbot of Montecassino), and one deacon who were in office by 1073. Gregory was well served by many cardinals, both to those whom he inherited from his predecessors and still more by those whom he himself brought to office. Even Bishop John of Porto was for long prominent in his service.[271]

If Beno's list of defecting cardinals calls for critical comment, his allegation that Gregory neglected to attend to the counsels of the cardinals is no less misleading. Many of those whom he promoted were men of high calibre and profound loyalty. This was especially so in the case of the bishops. Gregory's outstanding appointment was that of Odo of Ostia, whom he recruited in 1079, perhaps by direct negotiation at Rome with Abbot Hugh of Cluny whose grand prior he had been.[272] Upon becoming pope in 1088 as Urban II, Odo made an uncompromising assertion of his commitment to continue Gregory's aims as pope.[273] Hubert of Palestrina served Gregory as legate and was with him at Canossa. John Minutus, whom Gregory promoted from being cardinal-priest at S. Maria in Trastevere to the bishopric of Tusculum, maintained his loyalty by taking part in the raising to the papacy of Victor III and Urban II. Bruno of Segni went on to be abbot of Montecassino and an effective propagandist for the reform papacy. Appointments to the rank of priest during Gregory's pontificate included Rainer, the future Pope Paschal II, who replaced the apostate Hugh Candidus at S. Clemente, Deusdedit of S. Pietro in Vincoli whose *Collectio canonum*, dedicated to Pope Victor III, was intended to demonstrate that the Roman church was the head and recourse of all the churches and to provide guidance

---

[269] Beno, 2.2, p. 375/12–15, raised the number of cardinals to thirteen but added no new name.

[270] See Gregory's eulogy of Hermann of SS. Quattro Coronati: *Reg.* 9.28, (1082), p. 611/16–31.

[271] 'Iohannes Portuensis episcopus, qui intimus fuerat secretis Hildebrandi': Beno, 1.6/17, p. 371; 'morum honestate et religione vir praeclarus': Paul of Bernried, cap. 69, p. 512.

[272] See Cowdrey, 'St Hugh and Gregory VII', p. 182.

[273] 'De me porro ita credite, sicut de beatissimo Gregorio; cuius ex toto sequi vestigia cupiens, omnia quae respuit respuo, quae damnavit damno, quae dilexit prorsus amplector': *Ep.* 1, *PL* 151.284A.

for all Christians,[274] Herimannus of SS. Quattro Coronati, later bishop of Brescia, where he was a pillar of Gregorian principles in Lombardy,[275] and Abbot Richard of Saint-Victor at Marseilles, by 1078 priest of an uncertain title, who was active on Gregory's behalf in Spain. The services of cardinals whom Gregory inherited must be added. Bishops Peter of Albano and Gerald of Ostia were conspicuous as legates and promoters of the most rigorous Gregorian principles, while Bishop Hubald of Sabina survived to give his support to both Gregory's successors Victor III and Urban II. Among the priests, Desiderius of S. Cecilia was a frequent counsellor and agent of Gregory, and succeeded him in the papal office as Victor III. These examples suffice to establish Gregory's success in recruiting, using, and retaining the loyalty of a large and varied group of cardinals. Not only did they serve him well and often with manifest commitment, but their number included his three successors in the papal office. Others who survived Gregory actively provided continuity between his pontificate and those of his successors through all the vicissitudes of the years which followed his death at Salerno.

Even if it be granted that Gregory thus retained the support of many cardinals individually, it might still be claimed that he failed to make good use of the resources which they potentially offered him as an organized group, or college. Gregory's pontificate was a time of slack water in the momentous transformation of the cardinals which took place in the later eleventh century from being liturgical assistants to being a college with many responsibilities. In the days of Pope Nicholas II and of the Election Decree of 1059, they already began to show a corporateness and a development of functions which was built upon only after Gregory's death, partly in the entourage of the anti-pope Clement III but also in that of Pope Urban II. In particular, the Election Decree marked the emergence of the cardinal-bishops into what Cardinal Peter Damiani had called 'the senate of the Roman church'. By his insistence upon the pope's personal prerogative as vicar of St Peter and by his own masterful exercise of papal power, especially in his dealings with Henry IV of Germany, Gregory set back the corporate development of the cardinals of the Roman church, thereby depriving himself of the benefits that such a continued development might have brought in restraining his more extravagant actions and in assisting his more prudent ones.

While it is true that there was no advance in the corporate standing or activity of the cardinals during Gregory's pontificate, such a construction of his dealings misunderstands the state of the Roman church in his time. With the death in 1072 of Peter Damiani, the coherent group of cardinal-bishops which had characterized the early years of the reform papacy was finally dissolved. Despite the quality and loyalty of the bishops whom Alexander II and Gregory himself appointed to the suburbicarian sees, they no longer showed, nor were they perceived of possessing, any

---

[274] 'Hoc itaque opus vestrae paternitati dedicavi, quod non solum sanctae apostolicae sedi sed omni ecclesie et omni clerico profuturum putavi': *Coll. can. Prol.* p. 5/12–14.

[275] See Guerrini, 'Un cardinale gregoriano'; and for his relation to Gregory, Paul of Bernried, cap. 34, p. 489.

marked cohesion. The very title of cardinal-bishop passed from general currency; it
was not, for example, used in Gregory's letters.[276] Rather, his letters reflect a practice whereby the term *cardinales* was restricted to the priests and other members of
the Roman clergy; it was in such terms that the protocol of Gregory's own election
was framed and registered.[277] The reaction among the Roman clergy against the
standing of the cardinal-bishops was by no means negative or inarticulate. In the
prologue to his *Collectio canonum*, the cardinal priest Deusdedit wrote with vituperative if partly veiled hostility of the Election Decree of 1059 which assigned the
leading role in papal elections to the cardinal-bishops.[278] Deusdedit conspicuously
cited Pope Stephen III's Electoral Decree of 769 which provided for the choice of
one of the cardinal-priests or cardinal-deacons.[279] It says much for Gregory's circumspection that he could both retain Deusdedit's loyalty to the end and also use to
good effect the services of the Roman bishops of whose prerogatives Deusdedit was
critical.

Differences among the Roman clergy were not limited to constitutional arrangements; they also involved fundamental principles of authority. It is remarkable that
Gregory, who held such strong views about the pope's personal authority as he canvassed in his *Dictatus papae*,[280] should have been tolerant of such principles as
Deusdedit expounded in his comprehensive and learned collection. Deusdedit gave
little place to the pope's personal authority, but made him the spokesman of a *sancta
Romana ecclesia* in which, as a corporate entity, the prerogatives of the apostolic see
were embodied; it was in the Roman church, rather than in the pope himself, that its
primacy was vested.[281] Deusdedit's views were probably shared by a number of the
cardinal-priests and especially by those who, like Cardinal Beno, deserted Gregory in
1084.[282] Very different views were being canvassed at Rome, whether by figures like
Bishop Odo of Ostia who based papal authority upon Christ's commission to the
apostles of whom Peter was the chief,[283] or by canonists within the Roman church
like the cardinal-priest Atto of S. Marco or outside it like the compiler of the
Diversorum patrum sententie or Anselm of Lucca. Gregory himself seems to have

---

[276] In Gregory's single reference in the Register to *coepiscopis nostris cardinalibus*, the word *et* was in-
terlined in a contemporary hand between the latter two words: *Reg.* 1.16, p. 26/17.

[277] *Reg.* 1.1*, pp. 1/16–2/5; above, 2.2.8.

[278] 'Preterea antiquum ordinem electionis seu consecrationis Romani pontificis et cleri eius huic opere
inderere libuit. Nam quidam olim in dei et sanctum patrum sanctionibus contemptum ad sui scilicet
ostentationem et adscribendam sibi ventosam auctoritatem, quae nullis canonicis legibus stare potest,
scripserunt sibi novam ordinationem eiusdem Romani pontificis, in qua quam nefanda quam deo inimica
statuerunt, horreo scribere: *qui legit intellegat*': *Coll. can. Prol.* pp. 4/30–5/4; the last phrase, which perhaps alludes to Pope Victor III's having subscribed, as Abbot Desiderius of Montecassino, the Election
Decree of 1059, cites Matt. 24: 15. For a similar view of the Decree, see Deusdedit, *Liber contra invasores*,
cap. 11, p. 310/12–25, and for Deusdedit's prescriptions for papal elections, *Coll. can. Capitula libri primi*,
pp. 13/20–14/24, and the references there set out.

[279] *Coll. can.* 2.161, p. 268.   [280] *Reg.* 2.55a, pp. 201–8, esp. caps. 2–19, 23–5, 27.

[281] See Blumenthal, 'Fälschungen bei Kanonisten' and eadem, 'Rom in der Kanonistik'.

[282] e.g. Beno, 1.1–7, pp. 369–72.

[283] See Odo's letter, *H* no. 7, esp. 26/3–10, *Die Regensburger rhetorischen Briefe*, no. 5, *MGH Briefe*, pp.
376/23–377/26.

been poised between differing views. His own election to the papacy in 1073 was on a basis that Deusdedit could have approved, but in his final testament he counselled a choice of successor from three bishops—Anselm of Lucca, Odo of Ostia, and Hugh of Lyons—all of whom were open to objection upon Deusdedit's principles; none was a cardinal-priest or deacon of the Roman church.[284]

When there were such differences of opinion, and such half-submerged tensions, among the bishops and cardinals of the Roman church, Gregory did well to leave alone the internal structure and functioning of the Roman church. He deserves credit for his prudence in tolerating differences of opinion and in doing nothing that would exacerbate them. His wisdom is confirmed by the deep and debilitating divisions that emerged among his followers in the immediate sequel to his death.[285] Gregory's prudent inactivity with regard to the Roman cardinals as a group may be judged to have been opportune, and to have contributed to his long enjoyment of the support of most of the clergy and people of Rome.

It should not be forgotten that a principal part of the cardinals' business remained liturgical. Gregory's bonds with them were the stronger because, whenever he was at Rome, he was their leader throughout the church's year in a round of worship in the basilicas and churches of the city. Because it followed an ancient routine, it is rarely alluded to in the sources used by historians; but, with a pope of Gregory's religious fervour, there can be little doubt that it was of critical importance in sustaining loyalty and regard for Gregory both among the cardinals who were leading liturgical figures and among the remaining clergy and people. Not only was Gregory by upbringing and sentiment the most Roman of popes, but there are hints that he had the marks of sanctity that most commended eleventh-century bishops to their flocks. When presenting the case in Gregory's favour, Guy of Ferrara extolled him as a man of many charities who protected the poor and needy. He mixed freely and easily with all sorts and conditions of men without compromising his own spiritual and moral life. He exhibited the marks of devotion that proclaimed the true priest; in particular, when celebrating the masses that he daily said, he had the grace of tears which won especial admiration.[286] Gregory's devotion at mass was widely noted; stories circulated that it was answered by heavenly approval, so that the Holy Spirit was seen to settle upon him in the likeness of a dove.[287] Gregory's pastoral care and tact when dealing with his Roman flock were also remembered. An anecdote for long circulated that, when away from the city, he knew that a leading Roman cleric had committed adultery. Rather than cause his close friend the embarrassment of knowing that he was aware of his lapse, he sent Abbot Hugh of Cluny to offer penance and reconciliation. 'Thus', the story ran, 'the pope exhibited the skill of a good father, who both took care to correct his son and also dissimulated his knowledge of his fault, lest his

---

[284] *H* no. 35, p. 75/9–17. [285] See Cowdrey, *The Age of Abbot Desiderius*, pp. 185–206.
[286] Guy of Ferrara, 1.2, pp. 534–5.
[287] For Gregory's grace of tears, see also Paul of Bernried, cap. 32, p. 487–8; Andrew of Strumi, *Vita s. Ioh. Gual.* cap. 85, p. 1102; for the dove, *Chron. Cas.* 3.54, pp. 435–6; Paul of Bernried, caps. 30–1, pp. 486–7.

son be tormented by sadness upon sadness.'[288] It is evidence of Gregory's reputation for exercising in his own diocese the pastoral care that he is known to have extended to visitors like Count Simon of Crépy and Bishop Hugh of Grenoble. Gregory's pastoral skills, and the recognition which they gained, should not be overlooked as a reason for Roman loyalty to him.

The loyalty is impressive in view of the deep-seated tensions in the city, as well as among the clergy, with which Gregory had to contend. Perhaps the most dangerous was that which centred upon the succession of city prefects. During his first four years as pope, Gregory had no more trustworthy ally than the prefect Cencius son of the prefect John. In the days of Pope Alexander II, the prefectship had been in contention between this Cencius, son of a John Tiniosus who had held the office under Pope Nicholas II, and another Cencius, son of a prefect Stephen of the Crescentian family who had held office before John Tiniosus. Under Alexander II, the Roman citizens had themselves rejected Cencius Stephani and had given the office to his rival Cencius Johannis. Cencius Stephani had by 1073 gained a reputation for all manner of violence and crime, including the murder and robbery of his own godfather; for this, Alexander had excommunicated him but, it was said, had lifted the sentence at Hildebrand's instance. Cencius had also actively supported the anti-pope Honorius II, and the Castel S. Angelo, which he controlled was a bastion of the Cadalan party. Bonizo of Sutri contrasted the two Cencii as respectively embodying the hopes of all good and of all evil men.[289] In 1073, Cencius Johannis, whom Gregory reputedly forbade from entering a monastery because he needed his active service in the city, was securely in office as city prefect, while Cencius Stephani was prominent among the Roman nobles and others who were hostile to Gregory.

Cencius Stephani seems to have supported Cardinal Hugh Candidus in his promotion of Gregory in the papal office. However, Gregory and he were quickly at loggerheads, although Gregory continued to exercise restraint and mercy. In 1074, Cencius Stephani took advantage of Gregory's serious illness to falsify the will of a third Cencius, son of Count Gerard of Galeria, of which he was the executor. He took for himself a *curtis* and all save two hundred pounds of a legacy that the testator intended for the Roman church. When Gregory recovered, he compelled Cencius Stephani to provide hostages for good behaviour and to restore the *curtis* to the Roman church.[290] He did no more than was necessary to meet the basic demands of justice. Probably early in 1075, Gregory again treated him with mercy. The city prefect Cencius Johannis resolved to curb his practice of levying tribute from those who crossed the Tiber near his fortress. The prefect imprisoned Cencius Stephani and condemned him to death, but apparently after the pleading of Countess Matilda of

---

[288] *Alexandri monachi Cantuariensis Liber ex dictis beati Anselmi, Miracula*, cap. 30, in: Southern and Schmitt, *Memorials*, pp. 218–19.

[289] For the two Cencii, see esp. *Ann. Rom.* pp. 335–7; Bonizo of Sutri, *Lib. ad amic.* 7, pp. 603–4; Paul of Bernried, caps. 45–8, pp. 498–500; Berthold, *a.* 1076, pp. 281/42–282/19, *a.* 1077, pp. 290/47–291/11, 304/34–305/25; Bernold, *Chron. a.* 1077, p. 434/31–4.

[290] Bonizo of Sutri, *Lib. ad amic.* 7, p. 604/11–20; cf. Arnulf of Milan, 5.6, p. 224/7–9; Lampert of Hersfeld, *Ann. a.* 1076, p. 344/9–14.

Tuscany and of other Roman nobles, Gregory extended clemency, requiring him only again to give hostages, to swear amendment upon the tomb of St Peter, and to surrender his fortress.[291]

Gregory's tempering of justice with mercy elicited no response from Cencius Stephani who, at Christmas 1075, perpetrated an act of extreme violence against Gregory as he performed the religious rites of the season. Cencius's outrage attracted widespread and enduring attention in friend and foe alike in both Italy and Germany.[292] This attention is largely to be explained by the synchronism between Cencius's outrage and the rapid deterioration during the winter of 1075–6 of relations between Gregory and Henry IV of Germany which led to their sentences upon each other. The suddenness of the breach between Gregory and Henry renders more than improbable the allegations of later writers that Cencius acted in collusion with persons outside Rome, whether Henry himself, Duke Robert Guiscard, or Archbishop Guibert of Ravenna. His attempted coup was a local Roman event. Cencius's objective is not clear: did he intend to kill or banish Gregory and replace him by another pope, or did he intend to humiliate him and so force him into submission to himself and his faction in the Roman lay aristocracy? The lack at this time of a readily conceivable replacement and Cencius's opportunist manner of acting make the second possibility the more likely one.

The course of events is sufficiently clear. Late on Christmas Eve, Gregory was celebrating mass, as was customary, at the altar of the manger in the church of S. Maria Maggiore. A sudden torrential deluge limited public attendance. Cencius Stephani, who had allies living nearby, seized the opportunity to go there with a band of horsemen and drag Gregory from the altar. Gregory, who sustained a wound that seems to have been bloody rather than severe, was taken to Cencius's stronghold in Parione. Early on Christmas morning, when the weather had improved, a large body of Roman citizens went in urgent quest of Gregory, whom they delivered from Cencius's captivity. Gregory was able to return to S. Maria Maggiore and complete the interrupted mass of the night before. He then proceeded in triumph to the Lateran, demonstrating his unimpaired authority by processing crowned.[293] While he thus projected to future propagandists an image of victory through martyrdom, Cencius was humiliated. The Romans razed to the ground the fortress in which he had detained Gregory. Further stories circulated about Gregory's magnanimity and forbearance in dealing with him when he feigned penitence. He was compelled to flee the city to a castle outside Rome, probably at Palestrina where the Crescentian family had been traditionally strong. From there, he ravaged papal lands and possessions,

[291] Bonizo of Sutri, *Lib. ad amic.* 7, pp. 603/13–18, 605/20–24; Paul of Bernried, cap. 47, p. 499.

[292] The principal sources for the events of Christmas 1075 and their sequel are as follows: (i) Italian. Gregorian: *LP* 2.282/14–27; Bonizo of Sutri, *Lib. ad amic.* 7, p. 606/7–15; *Ann. Cas. a.* 1075, pp. 1418–19; Arnulf of Milan, 5.6, pp. 224–5. Anti-Gregorian: Beno, 1.8, pp. 372/23–373/2. (ii) German. Gregorian: Lampert of Hersfeld, *Ann. a.* 1076, p. 344; Berthold, *a.* 1076, pp. 281/42–282/19; Bernold, *Chron. a.* 1076, pp. 431/17–433/3; Paul of Bernried, caps. 48–57, pp. 499–505.

[293] Gregory processed 'coronatus et cum omni laude episcoporum atque cardinalium': *LP* 2.282/ 20–1.

and he was excommunicated at Gregory's instance by Bishop Hubert of Palestrina. After Canossa, Cencius curried favour with Henry IV by capturing near St Peter's at Rome Gregory's loyal supporter Bishop Raynald of Como, whom he took to Henry at Pavia. The king was himself newly freed from excommunication and had no wish to court its reimposition; he therefore delayed in arranging to meet the excommunicated Cencius. When he at last did so, Cencius suddenly died of a tumour in his throat.[294]

Such a death was, in the eyes of Gregory's partisans, the just reward of iniquity. Another death followed in the summer of 1077 which enabled them to proclaim the glory of martyrdom in Gregory's cause. Before Gregory returned to Rome in September, Stephen, a brother of Cencius Stephani, slew the city prefect Cencius Johannis, of whose actions during recent months nothing is known although he is likely to have resisted Gregory's assailants. The Roman people dragged Stephen from his castle and lynched him; they also killed or expelled from the city many of his followers. Cencius Johannis was buried in a marble tomb at St Peter's. At the Lent synod of 1078, Gregory caused the miracles that were performed there to be recounted. The synod acknowledged that, like Erlembald, the Patarene leader at Milan, Cencius had deserved and been granted the heavenly crown of martyrdom.[295]

There can be no doubt that these events between 1075 and 1078 strengthened Gregory's prestige and position in the city of Rome. The family and party of his implacable lay opponent were reduced to powerlessness. It seems to have been now that the Crescentian stronghold of the Castel S. Angelo passed into Gregory's control, so that it could be his resort in the crisis of his final years at Rome. In face of the attack upon him at Christmas 1075, there is no reason to doubt the assertion of the *Liber pontificalis* that the *Romani* were outraged against Cencius Stephani, for their ready and overwhelming action led to Gregory's being freed from captivity. His immediate return to the Lateran was a timely triumph, for it left the Roman clergy and people unreceptive to the summons that Henry IV would soon address to them to get rid of the false monk Hildebrand.[296] In the murdered city prefect Cencius Johannis, the Gregorian following found a martyr-saint whose tomb and miracles were a potent reminder of divine favour upon those in the city who supported Gregory. It was reinforced by the contrasting memory of the melancholy death of his namesake Cencius Stephani who had risen against Gregory.

Throughout and after these events, Gregory appears to have had the advantage of the powerful support of the Frangipani family. As long ago as 1061, their head, another Cencius, had helped Hildebrand to promote the election of Pope Alexander II.[297] In 1084, this Cencius re-emerged and, according to the good evidence of the Montecassino Chronicle, assisted Robert Guiscard in his forceful reduction of the

---

[294] Bonizo, *Lib. ad amic.* 8, pp. 610/37–611/; Arnulf of Milan, 5.6, p. 225/5–8; Berthold, *a.* 1077, pp. 290/47–291/11; Bernold, *Chron. a.* 1077, pp. 433/48–434/2.

[295] Bonizo of Sutri, *Lib. ad amic.* 8, 9, pp. 611/17–24, 620/3–5; Berthold, *a.* 1077, pp. 304/23–305/28; Bernold, *a.* 1077, p. 434/31–4; Paul of Bernried, cap. 92, p. 529.

[296] See above, 3.3.1, 2.   [297] See above, 2.2.4.

city.[298] After Gregory's death, Cencius worked closely with Abbot Desiderius of Montecassino in his attempts to hold together the Gregorian cause.[299] He is likely to have used his resources in the vicinity of the Colosseum and elsewhere to give stability to Gregory's rule throughout his pontificate and to keep dissident elements in check.

Such factors as the elimination of Cencius Stephani, the martyrdom of Cencius Johannis, and the support of Cencius Frangipani ensured that, until the pressure of Henry IV's Italian expeditions began to tell as from 1082, Gregory had no more discernible problems with the loyalty of the Romans. His second excommunication and deposition of Henry IV in 1080 evoked no manifestation of hostility in the city. Apart from the long-since alienated Hugh Candidus, no Roman figure attached his name to the decree of the synod of Brixen.[300] As late as May 1081, Gregory could express total confidence in the loyalty of the *Romani*.[301] Only as from 1082 did strains and stresses begin to appear as both sides poured money into the city and preparations for war imposed an unprecedented burden upon papal finance. The contest for the loyalty of the Romans merged with the wider struggle between Gregory and Henry.[302] Rome became and remained a divided city, and the division hardened with the installation in 1084 of the anti-pope Clement III. Until and after his death, Gregory nevertheless retained an appreciable following in the city upon which his two successors, Victor III and Urban II, would be able, if with much difficulty and long struggle, to build.[303]

4.8 Conclusion

In the kingdom of Italy and in the church and city of Rome, Gregory's intentions, actions, and degree of success showed differences from region to region. This was partly a response to a variety of geographical, historical, and political factors, and partly a result of the degree and character of the support or hostility that he elicited. For the most part, Gregory showed prudence and insight in his appreciation of differing situations. When a cautious and accommodating approach was called for, as for example in his dealings with Aquileia and Venice, Gregory showed a moderation and willingness to settle for what he could hope to achieve which were statesmanlike and conducive to his advantage. In Lombardy, by contrast, the recalcitrance of the Lombard bishops and the militancy of the Patarenes led Gregory into a stance of confrontation and zealous partisanship in regional affairs. His alliance with the

---

[298] See above, 3.5.10.

[299] *Chron. Cas.* 3.66, pp. 449/10–11, 450/14–19; see also Bloch, *Monte Cassino*, 1.82–8.

[300] *Quellen HIV* Anhang C, p. 480/26–9: 'Ego Hugo Candidus sancte Romane ecclesie presbyter cardinalis de titulo sancti Clementis regionis tertie urbis huic decreto a nobis promulgato assensum prebui et subscripsi vice omnium cardinalium Romanorum.' The final claim lacked all substance.

[301] *Reg.* 9.11, to Abbot Desiderius of Montecassino, p. 589/12–14.

[302] See above, 3.5.8–10.

[303] See Cowdrey, *The Age of Abbot Desiderius*, pp. 177–217.

Patarenes failed with their collapse in 1075 and showed how fragile had been his over-enthusastic embracing of their cause. In Tuscany, too, he found allies who seemed to meet his own requirements of lay figures and of churchmen. In this case, however, Countess Matilda, Bishop Anselm II of Lucca and their circle, and the monasteries of the region offered him well-founded support of the kind for which he looked, and served him well in all the vicissitudes of his pontificate. Even in Tuscany and Lombardy, there is evidence of Gregory's concern to temper justice with mercy and to seek peace and agreement where they could be found.

At Rome itself, Gregory was for most of his pontificate successful in maintaining his position by ways of moderation, of not raising contentious issues in religious or civic terms, and of not pressing the more radical aspects of his rule. He showed skill in holding together possibly disparate elements, and seems to have relied more upon the force of his personality and example and upon the exploitation of such incidents as his own captivity at Christmas 1075 than upon potentially unsettling change and reorganization of the church or city. He kept life going on in a way that was generally acceptable.

5

Gregory VII and France

5.1 Introduction

The dramatic events of the struggle between Gregory and Henry IV of Germany should not obscure either the magnitude or the permanence of Gregory's concern for the right ordering of church and society in France.[1] Approximately one-third of his surviving letters, both within and outside his Register, relate to it.[2] He became pope with an extensive knowledge of French persons and French affairs; not only had he travelled there,[3] but especially under Pope Alexander II the papacy was much concerned with France. Whether upon business or as pilgrims, Frenchmen great and small were frequent visitors to Rome who kept the Lateran palace well informed about what was going on in all parts of their country.

Despite Gregory's sustained concern with French affairs, no such main theme as his relations with Henry IV of Germany serves to give his dealings structure and coherence. It will emerge that his contacts with King Philip I were, with one brief exception, restrained and low-key, not confrontational and dramatic. He had many dealings with French magnates and lesser laity, but he sought to direct them in furtherance of his political designs only seldom and mostly in the early months of his reign. The two main designs concerned Spain and Constantinople. Within days of his election to the papacy, he wrote to his legates in France and to French *principes* such as Count Ebolus of Roucy (dept. Aisne) who were planning military expeditions into Muslim Spain which had been proposed under the oversight of Alexander II's papacy; Gregory was mainly concerned to ensure due respect for the

---

[1] It is not easy to determine the limits of France for the purpose of this chapter. To the south, lands beyond the Pyrenees will be reserved for the discussion of Spain at 6.11. In the west, the counties of Brittany and Flanders, which extended to the estuary of the River Scheldt, are included; but consideration of the province of Rouen, which was virtually coterminous with the duchy of Normandy, will in general be reserved for section 6.9 on the Anglo-Norman lands:. To the north, the diocese of Cambrai presents a problem since it was ecclesiastically part of the province of Rheims but much of it was politically subject to the king of Germany; it is included in this chapter. In the north-east, the county of Champagne was firmly French, but further south, the limits of the French kingdom roughly followed the Rivers Saône and Rhône, although especially between Mâcon and Lyons they ran some distance to the west. Although the kingdom of Burgundy (as distinct from the duchy) and its constituent the county of Provence were politically part of the empire, they were largely Romance-speaking and their ecclesiastical orientation was towards France; they come firmly within the scope of this chapter. The see of Lyons, in particular, played a critical role in the affairs of the French church. Gregory VII himself was pointedly silent about Henry IV's authority in the kingdom of Burgundy.

[2] Gaudemet, 'Grégoire VII et la France', pp. 214–16. Of many studies of Gregory and France, my principal indebtedness is to Fliche, *Le Règne de Philippe I*, id., *La Réforme grégorienne*, and id., *La Réforme grégorienne et la reconquête chrétienne*, and Becker, *Studien zum Investiturproblem*.

[3] See above, 2.1.

rights of St Peter over conquered lands.[4] Early in 1074, Gregory solicited the collaboration of French magnates at the beginning of his plans for an expedition to the
East which would relieve Constantinople. He reminded Count William of Upper
Burgundy of his solemn promise made at Rome under Pope Alexander to supply
military help for the service of St Peter and of a similar promise made by Count
Raymond of Saint-Gilles; Gregory now called upon him to join an expedition which
would pacify the Normans of South Italy and relieve the threatened city of Constantinople.[5]

Such military and political demands upon Frenchmen were exceptional. Most of
Gregory's dealings in France centred upon particular individuals or contingencies.
Although some of them ran on for months or even years while many of them reflected
his general concerns for church and society, they depended to a large extent upon his
own reactions to individual persons and situations, which could be unpredictable
and unexpected whether for their violence or for their restraint. Gregory's contemporaries and agents were no less liable to be disconcerted than the modern observer.
For, as far as France is concerned, Gregory seldom declared set objectives or modes
of action; his activities with regard to France cannot be interpreted in the light of his
own statements to anything like the extent that is possible with regard to Germany.
He responded much more in France than in Germany to persons and circumstances
as he encountered them.

This is not to say that his attitudes to persons or problems did not develop and
change; his dealings with the French king and his view of lay investiture are examples
of matters in which it will be possible to show signal modification and growth. But,
in most aspects of his concern for France, his flexible and even pragmatic approach
contrasts sharply with the rigour and would-be consistency of his most important
legate in France, Hugh, bishop of Die and (from 1082/3) archbishop of Lyons.
Given Gregory's flexibility and unpredictability, his aims and methods in France
must be deduced from his particular actions and attitudes. The springs of his activity were anything but systematic or consistent. They arose from deep but personally
conceived convictions about the application of the Christian religion to social and
individual life, both in the church and in the whole of human society. He applied to
human affairs no neatly formulated code of dogma, morality, or church order.

This is partly an expression of Gregory's own powerful personality. But it also ex-
presses a general feature of law in western society during Gregory's lifetime to which
he was especially well attuned and which is critical for an understanding of his outlook. He lived and worked before the refinements of legal thought and practice which
characterized the twelfth and thirteenth centuries took effect. By and large, the time
had not become ripe for the detached and objective application to precisely ascertained circumstances of settled rules and procedures of canon, civil, or feudal law.
The awarding of due punishment for admitted and proven transgressions, or the

---

[4] *Reg.* 1.6–7, 30 Apr. 1073, pp. 8–12. Any expeditions had little if any result.
[5] *Reg.* 1.46, 2 Feb. 1074, p. 69–71; cf. 1.49, to all Christians prepared to help Constantinople, 1 Mar.
1074, pp. 75–6; 2.3, to Count William of Poitou, 10 Sept. 1074, pp. 126–8.

objectively equitable resolution of conflicts about rights or property, were only partly and even secondarily the business of those who did justice. More important by far, and the first priority of rulers and judges, was the restoration, or at least the easing, of fractured relations, loyalties, and obligations which should bind neighbours to each other and which should create the good order of society as a whole. The principal purpose of justice and of executive action was not to apportion rights and things, but to reconcile men to each other. To accomplish such reconciliation, large concessions might be made in enforcing the strict demands of the law and in seeking to win alienated or erring men to harmony and truth. The twin concepts of peace and concord dominated the pursuit of justice, alike in the constitution of human societies and in the most actual contingencies of everyday life. Peace was envisaged, not just as an absence of strife and contradiction, but as the creation of harmony and the fostering of common well-being in soul and body; concord was the agreement and mutual deference that men supplied in order to open the way for such peace.

Many of Gregory's letters might be cited by way of illustration. One is his letter of spring 1079 to Abbot Hugh of Cluny after Bishop Landeric of Mâcon complained to Gregory that the Cluniacs had seized certain rights ('iura') of his church which his predecessors had possessed without disturbance. Gregory first proposed to Hugh that, if this were so, he should restore the situation either by allowing Mâcon undisturbed possession or by making a suitable exchange; what mattered was less the restoration of the status quo with regard to the rights in question than the achieving of whatever resolution would restore good relations between the men and societies concerned. If it proved impossible thus to settle the matter ('causam componere'), Gregory's legates should take the problem up; thus, the lawsuit ('lis') might find a fitting end and no disagreement should remain between the parties to it. 'For', Gregory concluded, 'without concord (*concordia*), we declare that religious devotion has no worth, nor is any work, however good it may seem, anything at all'.[6] More than to satisfy distributive justice and to determine what exactly belonged to whom, Gregory sought to re-establish a pattern of human relations, duties, and loyalties. For thus the ends of peace and justice in human society might be secured.

Especially between the first and second excommunication of Henry IV, when Gregory had wished to travel to Germany and hold a national assembly, his talk had been of establishing peace and concord there and of restoring a stable pattern of human relationships between a rightful king and his subjects. In France, Gregory envisaged his task in similar terms. But whereas in Germany there was a strong monarchy which increasingly responded by Henry IV's purpose of himself being the source of peace through the reassertion of his royal authority, in France monarchy was weaker and would develop comparable claims more slowly. It could not, if it wished, challenge Gregory in theory or in practice. Thus, in France, he was able to advance his claims and methods throughout his pontificate without encountering radical and effective opposition. He could act as circumstances seemed to demand without raising profound issues of *sacerdotium* and *regnum*.

[6] *Reg.* 6.33, 14 Apr. 1079, pp. 446–7.

His dealings with France may best be considered overall in terms, first, of the lay persons in France with regard to whom he acted, second, of his dealings with the church and clergy of the French-speaking lands, and third, of the objectives which his human contacts and particular actions seem to disclose.

5.2 Gregory VII and the French Laity

5.2.1 The King

Gregory's dealings with King Philip I of France were in many respects similar to those with King Henry IV of Germany, for there was much in common about their backgrounds, ages, and behaviour during their early years as kings. They were much of an age: as the third ruler of the Salian house, Henry had become king in 1056 when aged 6; he was therefore 23 years old when Gregory became pope. Philip, who was the fourth king of the Capetian line, became sole king in 1060 at the age of 8; when Gregory became pope he was aged 21. Both had married by 1073; in 1066 Henry had married Bertha of Turin and in 1071 Philip had married Bertha of Frisia. Although the matrimonial behaviour of both kings gave rise to scandal and criticism, both marriages remained intact until after Gregory's death in 1085. In both cases, Gregory as pope felt that both by virtue of his office and as an older man he had a duty to bring a young king to the acceptance of marital probity and responsibility, with due regard for the frailty but also for the potential docility of younger men.

As a Capetian, Philip had a lineage and pedigree which Gregory recognized and respected. His letters show that, throughout his pontificate, he maintained a regard for the Capetian family which was comparable to that with which, at least initially, he viewed the Salians of Germany. He did not name any Capetian of the past as an exemplary ruler after the stamp of Henry III in Germany. But he praised the French kingdom as an entity not only for its pre-eminence in wisdom, religion, and power, but also for its devotion to the Roman church.[7] The Capetian line had hitherto been exemplary. Its kings had won the highest renown and glory in the eyes of God as of men throughout the world. They were a pattern for the young Philip to imitate. He, for his part, had declined sadly from the ways of his ancestors and had dragged down his kingdom from its past excellence. Although Gregory never expressly drew the parallel between the two men, like Henry of Germany he had grievously offended by the private and public sins of his youth in which he had become hardened: in a moment of particular anger, Gregory listed the despoiling of churches, the adulteries, the most wicked plunderings, the perjuries, and the manifold crimes for which he had often reproved him.[8] In Philip's case as in Henry's, Gregory had been concerned if possible to elicit repentance and amendment of life so that he might win

---

[7] The letters which principally declare Gregory's attitude to the house of Capet are: *Reg.* 1.35, to Bishop Roclin of Chalon-sur-Saône, 4 Dec. 1073, pp. 56–7; 1.75, to King Philip, 13 Apr. 1074, pp. 106–7; 2.5, to the archbishops and bishops of France, 10 Sept. 1074, pp. 129–33; 2.18, to Count William VI of Poitou, 13 Nov. 1074, pp. 150–1; 8.20, to King Philip, 27 Dec. 1080, pp. 542–3.

[8] *Reg.* 2.5, p. 131/4–7; for Gregory's dealings with Henry IV, cf. esp. *Epp. vag.* no. 14, p. 34/7–26.

God's favour and so enjoy a prosperous kingship. Gregory aspired to win him for partnership with himself in restoring the fabric of Christian society:

The power of Christian princes should join with us in the camp of the heavenly king for the command of the forces of Christianity ('ad custodiam christianae militiae'). Therefore, as you are the single and undivided heir of the renown and glory before God and men of those whose successor in the kingship you are, we strenuously exhort you to imitate their virtues and, by pursuing with all your power the righteousness of God, to defend and restore the churches as far as in you lies.[9]

Gregory was above all concerned to define and establish a right pattern of human relationships which corresponded to his ideal picture of Philip's forbears; particular events and problems, however important in themselves, should be handled with rigour or with restraint according to how far Gregory's main purpose was served.

It is not surprising that Gregory should have begun by treating Philip with studied restraint. Not that Gregory was in any doubt about his culpability: a letter of December 1073 shows that he considered him to be in the forefront of those kings who through simony oppressed and enslaved the churches of their realms.[10] He was concerned for the see of Mâcon in Burgundy, which was an outlying royal bishopric and so of great importance for the king. In his letters about Mâcon, Gregory was circumspect: he did not allege that Philip had, as yet, behaved simoniacally there. Indeed, Landeric, the archdeacon of Autun, had freely and canonically elected to be its bishop. But Gregory feared that Philip would demand payment before Landeric occupied the see. So he wrote to a bishop who was *persona grata* to himself and who also had the king's ear, Bishop Roclin of Chalon-sur-Saône, saying that, unless the king allowed bishops in general to be freely admitted to their sees, the whole of France would be subject to anathema. Gregory also instructed the metropolitan, Archbishop Humbert of Lyons, to attend to Landeric's consecration; but, in April 1074, it was Gregory himself who performed Landeric's consecration at Rome.[11] The whole process of his election, consecration, and taking up of his see was thus contrived and accomplished without the king's effective intervention for good or ill.

Personal relations were preserved. Gregory's restraint towards the king was encouraged by Philip's prudent dispatch to Rome of his chamberlain Alberic with promises that he would amend his private life and maintain right conduct in episcopal elections.[12] Philip's intercession with Gregory for the suspended Bishop Roger of Châlons-sur-Marne, though ineffectual, signalled a preparedness to keep in touch with Gregory by letters and messengers.[13] While the sequel to Landeric of Mâcon's consecration cannot be documented, once he had been received by his church Gregory expressed no objection to the king's investing him. It was necessary to seek concord and good relationships. So long as Gregory could eliminate simony and lay

9 *Reg.* 1.75, p. 107/16–22.   10 *Reg.* 1.35, p. 56/14–20.
11 *Reg.* 1.35–6, to Bishop Roclin of Chalon-sur-Saône, and to Archbishop Humbert of Lyons, 4 Dec. 1073, pp. 56–8; 1.76, to Archbishop Humbert of Lyons, 15 Apr. 1074, pp. 107–8; 1.85*a*, summary of Gregory's first papal year, (28 June 1074), p. 123.
12 *Reg.* 1.35–6.   13 *Reg.* 1.56, to Bishop Roger, 17 Mar. 1074, pp. 83–4.

intervention from the making of a new bishop and secure free canonical election and consecration, he was himself probably prepared at this stage of his pontificate to tolerate, as in the case in Italy of Bishop Anselm II of Lucca, royal investiture.

At Beauvais, Gregory showed a similar restraint towards Philip. With the king's connivance, some citizens had offended against their bishop and had been excommunicated by Gregory, who, however, revoked his sentence at the bishop's request. In April 1074, Gregory wrote to the king, from whom he had received letters promising obedience. He required the king to make amends but threatened no sanction; his main concern was to instruct him in the duties of a Christian ruler.[14]

If the first twelve months of Gregory's pontificate were in this way a time of appeasement between the papacy and the Capetian king, the period between September and December 1074 saw a brief but violent crisis. The evidence for it is mainly to be found in three letters from Gregory—to the archbishops and bishops of France; to William, sixth count of Poitou and eighth duke of Aquitaine; and to Archbishop Manasses I of Rheims.[15] As often in Gregory's pontificate, the crisis broke suddenly and apparently unheralded. It seems to have been prompted, not by the endemic problems of simony or by royal encroachments upon established rights and property, but by occasional and less deeply rooted acts of violence. In all of the letters, Philip's principal offence was said to be his unheard-of savagery in robbing foreign merchants, especially Italians, who were travelling to a fair in France. Gregory also instanced violent treatment in France of pilgrims *en route* for Rome. One suspects an orchestrated campaign of atrocity stories mounted at Rome by some who wished to end Gregory's moderation towards Philip. Gregory reacted with the utmost severity. He did not seize upon the prevalence of simony in Philip's France but upon social disorder. Especially in his lengthy letter to the bishops, he fulminated against the private warfare, slaughter, and arson which were associated with a free-for-all of mindless anarchy. In a crescendo of anger, he arraigned Philip as the fount of his country's chronic disorder. 'Of these things', he told the bishops, 'your king, who should not be called king but tyrant, at the devils' instigation is the head and cause.' To the count of Poitou, Gregory wrote that, by his crimes, Philip seemed to outdo not only Christian but even pagan princes. He told Manasses of Rheims that the harassing of foreign merchants was 'the unheard-of evil, the detestable crime, of Philip king of France—no, rather ravening wolf, unjust tyrant, and enemy of God and of the religion of holy church'.

He urged the French bishops to show themselves to be shepherds not hirelings; they were to take the most strenuous action to correct him. They should invite him to repent and amend his life. If necessary, upon pain of forfeiting their own offices they should put all France under interdict. Should this fail, Gregory would seek by all means ('modis omnibus') himself to wrest the kingdom of France from Philip's possession. This implied material as well as spiritual sanctions. In his letter to the count of Poitou, Gregory urged that the voice of the French laity should be added to

---

[14] *Reg.* 1.74–5, to the clergy and people of Beauvais, and to King Philip, 13 Apr. 1074, pp. 105–7.
[15] *Reg.* 2.5, 18, 32, to Archbishop Manasses I of Rheims, 8 Dec. 1074, pp. 168–9.

the bishops'. If the king listened, Gregory would respond with due charity. If not, at his Roman synod Gregory would excommunicate him and he would assuredly strip of their possessions both the king himself and all who showed him the honour and obedience which were due to the king. Gregory reiterated to the archbishop of Rheims his threat to oppose Philip by every power and means ('viribus et modis omnibus'); he announced the coming to the archbishop's parts of France of legates with whom the archbishop should co-operate. At his Lent synod of 1075, Gregory so far implemented his threats as to stipulate that, if Philip did not satisfy the legates who would come to France of his penitence and amendment, he would be deemed to be excommunicate.[16]

Such was the crisis that suddenly erupted between Gregory and Philip of France. During months when Gregory's relations with Henry IV of Germany seemed to have become both more friendly and more co-operative than before,[17] he was threatening Philip with the sanctions of excommunciation and dispossession of his kingdom that, in February 1076, he was to visit upon Henry. In the latter months of 1074, amongst the kings of Europe it was Philip not Henry who was the prime target of Gregory's wrath. As in others of the crises of Gregory's pontificate, anticlimax followed. There is no evidence to suggest that the excommunication of Philip was ever deemed to have become effective, or that legates discussed with him the allegations that led to it. Nothing is known about how Gregory's wrath about the harassment of merchants and pilgrims was appeased, although it is likely that Philip prudently took steps to ensure that there would be no further cause for such complaint.

An apparent consequence of the crisis of 1074–5 was that Gregory and Philip took the measure of each other. Gregory had pressed hostility to Philip beyond all reason and upon an issue—the harassment of merchants—that was not, in itself, central to relations between the papacy and France. There is no evidence for any response on the part of either bishops or lay magnates to any of Gregory's three letters. The qualification and relative mildness of his synodal sentence against Philip suggests that he knew that he must draw back; he lacked the leverage in France to act directly upon Philip, and there was no assurance that the king would be receptive to the admonitions of papal legates. The prudence of Gregory's retraction became clear over the next two years. The year 1077, in particular, was a watershed in the attendance of bishops at the Capetian court.[18] Until that year, they had been assiduous attenders, and between 1060 and 1077 churchmen were regularly subscribers of royal charters. After 1077, they attended seldom and their subscriptions became few. The change is probably to be explained by the increasing effectiveness of Gregory's legates, especially Bishop Hugh of Die, in bringing his standards to bear upon French bishops through personal contacts, reinforced by the effective sanctions of their councils and visitations. It would now be pointless for Gregory to pre-empt legatine action by the indiscriminate use of such direct appeals to French bishops and magnates as he made in late 1074.

---

[16] *Reg.* 2.52a, p. 196/20–2. [17] See above, 3.2.3.
[18] Lemarignier, *Le Gouvernement royal*, pp. 144–7.

As for the king, he gained something from the exodus of bishops from his court by placing renewed emphasis upon the conception of the *dignitas regia* which fore-shadowed ideas of an impersonal and dynastic crown.[19] (The parallel with Henry IV's response to Gregory in the late 1070s is apparent.) Yet, in real terms, his relat-ively weak position within France with regard to both bishops and lay feudatories made it impolitic for him to harbour resentment against Gregory. He did well to lie low. So long as he did so, after 1077 as before, he could to a large degree still count upon the traditional loyalty of the bishops and upon the strength of the fealty which bound French lay society to the crown. Provided that he lived quietly, he could hope to continue many of his practices in using and exploiting the church, including those which were simoniacal in papal eyes. His best policy with regard to the papacy was to remain inconspicuous while reassuring Gregory by occasional expressions of defer-ence and goodwill.

In sharp contrast with Henry IV of Germany, Gregory's dealings with Philip after the Lent synod of 1075 found scant mention in Gregory's letters and in other sources. The early date at which the dearth of evidence begins tells against its being only a by-product of Gregory's preoccupation with Germany; the cooling off and reserve seem from 1075 to have been matters of deliberate policy. They seem to have operated on both sides. Philip was at pains to secure Gregory's favour or at least tolerance. In 1076, Gregory referred approvingly to Philip's opposition to the notoriously venal Bishop Rainer of Orleans.[20] In May 1077, Gregory was not with-out hope that Philip might co-operate with his legate Bishop Hugh of Die in con-vening an ecclesiastical council.[21] Later in the year, when Gregory called upon Hugh of Die to investigate moves to elect a bishop of Chartres, he noted that Philip had twice sought papal approval for the choice of a monk of S. Eufemia in Calabria named Robert, who was known to Gregory and who, though not definitively elected by the church of Chartres, had strong support there. Robert had told Gregory that he would not receive the gift of the episcopate from the king, but Gregory made no ad-verse comment to Hugh upon the king's initiative.[22]

The incident is typical of the studied moderation with which Gregory seems to have treated Philip. By 1077–8, Gregory's prohibition of lay investiture was in force so far as France was concerned. But Gregory perplexed his legate Hugh of Die by his lack of reaction to his complaints against the king. After the council of Autun in 1077, Hugh informed Gregory that Bishop Ivo of Senlis had been invested by the king before ordination by 'that heresiarch of Rheims' in direct defiance of Gregory's in-junction. Bishop Robert of Auxerre, ordained when under canonical age, had not received investiture but he had won royal favour by way of royal courtiers. The king's opposition had fortified the opposition of the 'heretics' at Autun who resisted the

---

[19] For the king's claims especially after 1077, see *Recueil des actes de Philippe I[er]*, nos. 85–7, 90–1, pp. 222/11–15, 225/14–18, 227/20–7, 233/3–17; cf. *RHGF* 14.615AB, no. 80.

[20] *Reg.* 3.16, to Archbishop Richer of Sens, Apr. 1076, p. 278/16–22.

[21] *Reg.* 4.22, to Bishop Hugh of Die, 12 May 1077, pp. 331/29–332/13.

[22] *Reg.* 5.11, to Bishop Hugh of Die, end of 1077, p. 364/6–15.

election of the 'most religious' Gebuin to the see of Lyons. Hugh of Die was no less vociferous against Philip when he wrote to Gregory about his council of Poitiers in January 1078. He complained of the duplicity of the king who in letters had commended Hugh and his plans as legate, but who had assiduously prohibited both Count William VI of Poitou and the bishops of the royal demesne from attending the council. Hugh also accused the king of blatant simony in connection with the archiepiscopal see of Tours.[23] All these complaints produced no discernible reaction from Gregory. Indeed his mildness led Hugh to complain to him that 'those who once did not presume to sin even in trifling matters are now practising a lively traffic with the tyrant in churches committed to them'.[24] Gregory's apparent procrastination led the legate to keep alive language about the king as tyrant which the pope had long since abandoned. In 1079, Gregory condemned, but without specific comment about King Philip, the royal investiture of the bishop of Chalon-sur-Saône.[25] In 1081, when his legates Hugh of Die and Amatus of Oloron suspended Norman bishops who had not come to their council, probably that of Saintes, Gregory excused the bishops because the reason was not disobedience but fear of the French king; yet there is no sign of animus, let alone sanctions, against Philip himself.[26] Gregory soon afterwards blamed Count Fulk *le Réchin* of Anjou and the count of Tours, and also the canons of Saint-Martin at Tours, but not King Philip, for expelling Archbishop Ralph of Tours from his see.[27] In 1083, he was aware that King Philip, as well as Count Robert of Flanders, had borne a reponsibility for promoting the simoniacal Lambert to the see of Thérouanne. He went so far as to urge the count if necessary to break his oath of fealty to his king; yet he is not known to have issued any warnings to Philip, let alone to have proceeded to sanctions against him.[28]

In the 1080s as at the outset of his pontificate, Gregory had not abandoned his hope of shaping Philip's kingship according to what he represented as the good pattern of his Capetian forbears. When, in 1080, Archbishop Manasses of Rheims was finally deposed and a successor had to be elected, Gregory dispatched a series of letters which show how, in his view, an election to so critical a see should be conducted. First, he wrote to the clergy and people of Rheims, enjoining them to make a free election under the eye of the legate Hugh of Die; then he addressed the most powerful local magnate, Count Ebolus of Roucy, who should provide effective temporal protection ('modis omnibus adiuvare'). Next, he wrote to the suffragan bishops of Rheims who should bring their concurrence. Lastly he approached the king, who should withdraw his favour from Manasses and duly support whomever the process of free election should have substituted. He would thereby at last justify Gregory's

---

[23] *RHGF* 14. 613–16, nos. 79–80. [24] *RHGF* 14.616B, no. 80.

[25] *Epp. vag.* no. 30, to Bishop Hugh of Die, (Apr.–May) 1079, p. 78/20–80/2.

[26] *Reg.* 9.5, p. 579/31–6.

[27] *Narratio controversiae inter capitulum S. Martini Turonensis et Radulphum eiusdem urbis archiepiscopum*: *RHGF* 12.459–61; *Epp. vag.* no. 52, pp. 126–7.

[28] *Epp. vag.* nos. 45, to Count Robert of Flanders, (1082), pp. 108/31–109/2; 46, to the clergy and people of Flanders and especially Count Robert, (1082), p. 112/13–17; *Reg.* 9.33, to Archbishop Hugh of Lyons, (1083), p. 620/18–21.

long patience: 'Act, therefore, and now that you have become a man in years, see to it
that we should not seem without avail to have spared the sins of your youth, or in vain
to have expected your amendment.'[29] As well by the order as by the substance of
these four letters, Gregory took the opportunity of the election at Rheims to show
that his attitude to the office and person of the Capetian king had not changed from
that of his early months as pope. He also made clear what had become, in the course
of his pontificate, his view of a king's proper place with respect to an episcopal election. The king was the authority who should accept and implement, without a ceremony of lay investiture, the free and preceding decision of clergy and people as
confirmed by the authority of comprovincial bishops.

Provided that this procedure was followed in the key matter of episcopal elections,
Gregory was prepared to be restrained and flexible in dealing with the day-to-day
shortcomings of the Capetian king.

5.2.2 Lay Magnates

For the magnates of the French-speaking lands Gregory used the word *principes*
which he also used of their German peers. In view both of the weakness of Capetian
power outside the small royal demesne and especially south of the River Loire, and
of the virtual eclipse of Salian power in the kingdom of Burgundy and especially
Provence,[30] the loyalty and co-operation of the French *principes* were critical for
Gregory. By and large, the number of his surviving letters to them is disappointingly
small; however, they provide clues from which his purposes regarding them may be
reconstructed.

It must be noticed at the outset that the stock and nobility of French magnate
families in the provinces were as critical for Gregory as those of the Capetian family
in respect of the kingdom itself. Dynastic integrity and continuity were a major concern. In Capetian France, Gregory's dealings with William VI, count of Poitou, and
VIII, duke of Aquitaine (1058–86), provide the best example. Gregory approached
William not only as a great feudatory but also more personally, as the brother of his
close confidante at Rome, the Empress Agnes, 'whom we love as a mother'. A critical
situation arose in 1074, when William took as his third wife Hildegard, daughter of
Duke Robert of Burgundy, to whom he was related within the prohibited degrees of
kinship. A provincial synod, under Gregory's legate Amatus of Oloron and Archbishop Gozelin of Bordeaux, was forcibly disrupted, and Gregory acted directly.
Despite Agnes's pleading, he insisted upon an immediate separation. Such a union,
he wrote, arose from the lust of the human heart; to renounce it safeguarded both the
count's own salvation and the excellence of stock ('generositas') which had always
marked his line. For the nobility of a family ('nobilitas generis') was gravely debased
when offspring were begotten otherwise than in lawful marriage. Gregory ended by

---

[29] *Reg.* 8.17–20, 27 Dec. 1080, pp. 538–43, esp. p. 543/15–17.
[30] After the death in 1032 of King Rudolf III of Burgundy, charters of Saint-Victor at Marseilles were
occasionally dated 'nullo nobis alio rege solo Christo Domino in perpetuum': *Cartulaire de Saint-Victor*,
nos. 526 (1038), 527 (1074), 1.520–1.

assuring William that 'the Roman church has always loved your house—you and your whole lineage (*prosapia*)—with such singular and outstanding charity that it could not suffer your lying in such great danger'.[31] In 1079, Gregory similarly praised Count Centullus of Béarn, in the south of Gascony, for his religion and good government, but warned him that all might be jeopardized by his marriage to a kinswoman. Centullus duly separated from his wife Gisla who took the habit at Cluny and *c.*1080 was prioress of Marcigny; as a penance the count founded the Cluniac priory of Sainte-Foi de Morlaas.[32] No less detrimental to the integrity of a family than marriage within the prohibited degrees was the abandonment of a wife during her lifetime and the taking of another woman. In 1082, Gregory rebuked an unidentified French count for such a transgression. Hitherto, Gregory had regarded the count as the superior of kings, as well as other princes, in respect of righteousness and uprightness of conduct; now, man's ancient enemy had renewed in him the first deceit by which he had caused Adam's expulsion from paradise on account of a woman.[33] Gregory also expressed his belief that the integrity of a family stock and righteousness of personal and public life were required of princes when, in 1081, he exhorted Count Theobald of Blois to abstain from contact with excommunicates: he was to be so mindful of the last judgement 'that your nobility (*nobilitas*) which has been exalted by God's divinity above other men should not be made soft by earthly cares and pleasures and thereby lose the power of spiritual desire'. As Theobald expected fidelity from his own subjects, so he should himself act in fidelity to the God who had created and redeemed him.[34] In distant Brittany, the bishops were to take special steps to correct the matrimonial lawlessness ('de incasta copulatione') of greater laymen.[35]

In the kingdom of Burgundy, where there was to all intents and purposes no royal power, the dynastic integrity of the lay magnates was even more important. Gregory's view of its princes was most clearly shown in relation to Count Raymond of Saint-Gilles and his family. At his Lent synod of 1076, he excommunicated Raymond for his marriage to a near kinswoman, and also a *comes Forensis* who was perhaps the count of Forcalquier; in November 1078, he repeated his sentence upon Raymond.[36] The second excommunication of Henry IV in 1080 and Henry's counter-measures at the synod of Brixen left Gregory and the magnates of the kingdom of Burgundy well aware of an increased need for mutual agreement and support. The first evidence came on 23 December 1080, when Gregory wrote to Count Raymond and to his son Count Bertrand.[37] He addressed them as 'nobiles comites' and reminded them of the

[31] *Reg.* 2.2–3, to Bishop Isembert of Poitiers and to Count William VI of Poitou, 10 Sept. 1074, pp. 125–8. For William's close dealings with Gregory in founding the Cluniac abbey of Montierneuf at Poitiers, see Villard, *Recueil*, pp. 3–6, nos. 2–6.

[32] *Reg.* 6.20, 25 Feb. 1079, pp. 431–2; *GC* 1, instr. p. 161, no. 6. See Wischermann, *Marcigny-sur-Loire*, pp. 111, 176–7, 367–9.

[33] *Reg.* 9.23, pp. 603–5.   [34] *Reg.* 9.9, 28 Apr. 1081, pp. 585–7.

[35] *Reg.* 2.1, to the bishops and abbots of Brittany, 28 Aug. 1074, pp. 124/33–125/10.

[36] *Reg.* 3.10*a*, p. 269/20–1; 6.5*b*, p. 401/12. For Raymond's marriages, see L. and J. Hill, *Raymond IV de Saint-Gilles*, pp. 8–12.   [37] *Reg.* 8.16, pp. 537–8.

former love of their house for St Peter and of its fidelity to him; this had brought them widespread fame and outstanding honour and glory. Gregory knew that the two counts imitated their forebears in respect both of nobility of lineage and zeal for virtue ('parentum vestrorum sicut nobilitatis lineam ita quoque probitatum studia vos imitari cognovimus'). He particularly looked for their support of the rightfully elected Archbishop Dalmatius of Narbonne against his simoniacal rival Peter whom they were to resist *modis quibus potestis*, that is, by force if necessary.

The demands of dynastic integrity were sometimes reinforced by direct oaths of loyalty and service to St Peter on the part of both French and Burgundian princes. In connection with his proposed expedition to help Eastern Christians, Gregory early in 1074 reminded Count William of Burgundy that he and Count Raymond of Saint-Gilles had solemnly sworn upon the tomb of St Peter at Rome that they would come armed if need be to fight in defence of St Peter's interests ('pro defensione rerum sancti PETRI').[38] Later in the year, Gregory appealed directly to Count William VI of Poitou for active support against King Philip I; for William was 'one who truly loves St Peter and ourselves', so that he shared Gregory's sorrow at the king's spiritual danger and would join other well-disposed French princes to seek his amendment.[39] After the events of 1080, Gregory's claims upon a prince of the kingdom of Burgundy were more closely defined: taking no account of any claim on the part of the Salian king, Gregory received a direct oath of fealty to St Peter and himself. On 25 August 1081, Gregory received from Count Bertrand, son of Raymond of Saint-Gilles, a personal oath of immediate fealty; Bertrand also commended all his hereditary principality ('honor') to the pope, surrendering to his lord Pope Gregory all churches in his power and promising to see that they were ordered according to divine law.[40] Bertrand followed it with a letter in which he promised to be as good as his word. He addressed Gregory as 'sublimissime domine et princeps totius orbis terrae' and described himself as Gregory's *servus*. He declared himself deeply afflicted and pained by the recent injustice to Gregory of an unjust judge ('de iniustitia, quam actenus passus estis ab iniquo iudice, ita sum afflictus, quasi corpore et mente flagellis maximis verberatus'); he evidently meant the sentence of Henry IV at the synod of Brixen. He then referred to the affairs of the abbey of Saint-Pierre at Montmajour. Its abbot, Bermundus, had been driven out for sodomy and other unspeakable crimes; Bertrand sent to Gregory a new abbot, William, who had been canonically elected, so that he might receive his abbey from the pope's hand together with a confirmation and renewal of the abbey's privileges. Bertrand ended by alluding to his own recent oath by which he had abandoned, for love of God and St Peter and Abbot Richard of Marseilles and Gregory himself, all bishoprics and abbeys in his lands.[41]

Count Bertrand's preparedness to show such obedience to Gregory had a parallel in the very last days of Gregory's life. In April 1085, Count Peter of Substantion and Melgueil, whose principality was on the French side of the River Rhône, made a gift

---

[38] *Reg.* 1.46, 2 Feb. 1074, pp. 69–71. [39] *Reg.* 2.18, 13 Nov. 1074, pp. 150–1.
[40] *Reg.* 9.12a, b, pp. 589–91. [41] *Reg.* 9.29a, pp. 614–15.

to the Roman church *per allodium* of all his lands and of the bishopric of Mague-lone.[42] The occasion of the gift was the legatine journey from Salerno of Cardinal Peter of Albano, into whose hands Peter delivered it. Peter was to receive the county back as a papal fief in return for an annual *census* of an ounce of fine gold. The elec-tion of bishops was for the future to take place freely. While the motives behind the gifts of Counts Bertrand of Provence and Peter of Substantion are nowhere stated, it is likely that, on both sides of the River Rhône, there was a sense that Gregory must be supported lest the power of Henry IV of Germany and of his anti-pope should penetrate and grow. Gregory seems to have sought to establish a band of papal fiefs and specially privileged abbeys, like Saint-Victor at Marseilles, which would spread along the coast of the Mediterranean from Provence to Northern Spain. Count Peter may also have been moved by Gregory's last encyclical from Salerno and by Cardinal Peter of Albano's eloquence in Gregory's cause.[43] If so, there was an interesting fore-shadowing of how, ten years afterwards, princes would respond to the papal prepara-tion for the Crusade.

Especially in the Capetian kingdom, Gregory looked to lay princes for moral and material aid which was brought to bear in direct obedience to his own requests and requirements. Some examples may be given. In November 1074, Gregory imposed sanctions of interdict and excommunication upon Bishop Isembert of Poitiers. He sent a copy of his sentence to Count William VI of Poitou and charged him with en-suring that the demands of righteousness were implemented ('Tibi vero, Guilielme comes, iustitiam committo tractandam').[44] In December 1080, he called upon Counts Raymond and Bertrand of Saint-Gilles by all means ('modis omnibus') to help Archbishop Dalmatius of Narbonne to secure his see; they were to resist his simoniacal rival Peter by whatever means they could bring to bear ('modis quibus potestis resistite').[45] In France during the same month, Gregory wished to facilitate the election of a successor to the deposed Archbishop Manasses I of Rheims. He called upon Count Ebolus of Roucy to resist Manasses with all his power ('pro mag-nitudine tua') and likewise to support his duly instituted successor. He sounded the note he often sounded in his latter years, that just as Ebolus would suffer no slackness in his own *fideles*, so he should be ready in the service of St Peter, who bore respons-ibility for the whole church ('ad quem spectat totius ecclesiae causa').[46] A similar obligation arose from the defence of monasteries which were under papal protection; for example, in 1079 Gregory urged it upon the *principes* of the region of Bourges in respect of the abbey of Déols.[47]

---

[42] *GC* 6, instr. pp. 349–50, no. 11, cf. p. 354, no. 15.   [43] *Epp. vag.* no. 54, pp. 128–35.

[44] *Reg.* 2.23–4, to Bishop Isembert of Poitiers and to Archbishop Gozelin of Bordeaux and Count William VI of Poitiers, 16 Nov. 1074, pp. 155–6.

[45] *Reg.* 8.16.

[46] *Reg.* 8.18, 27 Dec. 1080, pp. 539–40; cf. 9.9, to Count Theobald of Blois, 28 Apr. 1081, pp. 586/36–587/2; *Epp. vag.* nos. 46, to the clergy and people of Flanders, (1082), p. 112/17–21; 54, (July–Nov. 1084), p. 132/9–22.

[47] *Reg.* 6.28, 20 Mar. 1079, pp. 440–1; cf. the letter of the same date to the monks of Déols, 6.27, p. 439.

Gregory called upon French *principes* whenever necessary to assist the work of his legates. Count Theobald of Blois was deemed to be especially serviceable in this respect. In 1077, when Gregory directed Hugh of Die to hold a council in the province of Rheims, he noticed that, if King Philip should fail to provide support, the count had promised to help with its summoning and would facilitate its business. In 1081, Gregory wrote of the testimony of Hugh of Die and others to the count's zeal for the concerns of the Roman church.[48] If Gregory looked for comital help in great matters, he also solicited it in small. Thus, he looked to Count William of Poitou for help in vindicating the property rights of one of Gregory's clerks whose goods had been accorded papal protection.[49]

To at least one French count, Gregory consistently showed an intransigent face, showing little hope that he could bring to bear on him a salutary influence. In 1074, Gregory wrote to Archbishop Ralph of Tours, rebuking him for associating with Count Fulk *le Réchin* (1067/8–1109) of Anjou, who had been bound by excommunication in the days of Pope Alexander II for imprisoning his brother Count Geoffrey *le Barbu*.[50] Hugh of Die later stated that he for long ('diutino tempore') remained so bound;[51] there is no evidence that Gregory freed him or that he sought directly to bring him to amendment. In 1081–2, Fulk was openly at loggerheads with Archbishop Ralph of Tours, and in collusion with the canons of St Martin and the monks of Marmoutier sought to drive him from his see. In 1081, Ralph appears to have sought a sentence against Fulk from Gregory at Rome.[52] Gregory evidently remitted the matter to the bishops of the province of Lyons, for in 1082 an assembly of bishops excommunicated Fulk for his cruel persecution of the church of Tours; they did so 'by authority of St Peter and of the primate and legate Hugh'.[53] Having thus stimulated a sentence in France, Gregory warned the clergy and people of Tours and Angers to have nothing to do with the excommunicate count.[54] Gregory still made no approach of which there is trace to Fulk himself.

Instead, he seems to have concentrated upon seeking the support of Fulk's political rivals in order to contain his power and influence. In 1081, Gregory encouraged the election to the see of le Mans of Hoel, a Breton who enjoyed the favour of Fulk's adversary King William I of England.[55] Gregory's cold-shouldering of Fulk probably combined with his willingness to countenance the claim of the Breton see of Dol to a metropolitan status which challenged the position of the see of Tours to rally the counts of Brittany to Gregory. In 1077, they were quick to profess full assent to

---

[48] *Reg.* 4.22, 12 May 1077, p. 332/8–13, 9.9, to Count Theobald of Blois, 28 Apr. 1081, p. 586/4–8. For Hugh of Die's favourable opinion of the count, see his account of his council of Meaux (1081): *RHGF* 14.787–8, no. 10.

[49] *Reg.* 6.32, to Bishop Isembert of Poitiers, 13 Apr. 1079, p. 445/25–33.

[50] *Epp. vag.* no. 3, (after 9 Mar.), 1074, pp. 8–9.

[51] *RHGF* 14.791, no. 13. The letter is dated 1094.   [52] See *Reg.* pp. 605 n. 1, 606 n. 3.

[53] *RHGF* 12.613–14, no. 11.

[54] *Reg.* 9.24, (1082–3), pp. 605–6; cf. *Epp. vag.* nos. 48, 52, pp. 116–17, 126–7.

[55] *Epp. vag.* no. 48, to Archbishop Ralph of Tours, (1082), pp. 116–17; cf. Orderic Vitalis, 4, vol. 2.300–3.

Gregory's proscription of lay investiture as well as other simoniacal elements in epis-copal elections.[56] In May 1078, Gregory wrote to a number of Breton counts, seek-ing their support for the dispatch of Breton clergy and laity to a council at which his legate Hugh of Die would settle the problems which had arisen from the succession of 'Archbishop' Evenus of Dol.[57] The first of the counts whom Gregory then ad-dressed, Hoel II, was greeted by Gregory as a 'gloriosus princeps' when Gregory urged upon him the duty of respecting, restoring, and protecting monastic prop-erty.[58] Like the king of England and duke of Normandy, the Breton princes were to be honoured and fostered as rivals to Fulk and as potential promoters of papal pur-poses in their region of France.

Further still to the north, Gregory's dealings with Count Robert I *le Frison* of Flanders (1071–93) are more than usually open to study because of the large number of letters to or about him that survive.[59] In real life, Robert was not conspicuous for dedication to either the religious or the political objectives of the Gregorian papacy. Like Fulk of Anjou, he came to his principality through bitter and unscrupulous family conflict: he gained power by the battle of Cassel in which his young nephew Arnulf, the legitimate heir, was killed.[60] Concerned to expand and to consolidate his own territory, he exploited the popes' struggle with Henry IV of Germany to serve his own ends; his conduct towards the churches of his county progressively deterior-ated. But in 1076, Gregory entertained high hopes of winning him as a champion in the struggle against clerical fornication and episcopal simony. He wrote to his mother Countess Adela and to the count himself, proscribing clerical fornication in terms more characteristic of his campaign in Germany than of any campaign that he had addressed to France.[61] To the count, he added a vehement condemnation of simoniacal bishops; they were to be treated as Christ's enemies, and no obedience was to be paid to them. Gregory's letter incidentally discloses how he had prepared for him to have a mentor at his elbow: Gregory had for some time maintained in the Lateran palace a clerk, Ingelrannus, who was a canon of Saint-Omer and whom he described as the 'communis fidelis' of the pope and the count.[62] The count should often read over Gregory's letter with Ingelrannus and with other 'lovers of truth' ('veritatis amatores') and thereafter instruct and incite all clerks and laity in the way of truth.

It came as a shock to Gregory when, in November 1078, he learned from Ingelrannus and others that his legate Hubert and Bishop Hugh of Langres had, as a result of 'the machinations of the count's enemies', excommunicated Robert. Their

---

[56] *Reg.* 4.13, to Archbishop Ralph of Tours, 1 Mar. 1077, pp. 316–17.

[57] *Reg.* 5.22–3, to the subdeacon Hubert and the monk Teuzo, and to Breton counts, 22 May 1078, pp. 385–8.

[58] *Epp. vag.* no. 56, (1073–84), pp. 136–7.

[59] Flemish affairs are well discussed by Robinson, 'The Friendship Network', esp. pp. 18–19.

[60] Wenric of Trier may have had Robert, among others, in mind when he wrote of Gregory's support of tyrants who made their way to the throne through blood: cap. 6, p. 294/19–26.

[61] *Reg.* 4.10–11, 10 Dec. 1076, pp. 309–11.

[62] For Ingelrannus, see *Chron. mon. Watinensis*, cap. 26, p. 172.

reason probably arose from the situation in the see of Thérouanne after the death in 1078 of Bishop Drogo and with the succession of Bishop Hubert. Gregory's perplexity about the situation was probably compounded by other events of 1078. At the house of regular canons at Watten which staunchly upheld Gregory's campaign against clerical fornication and simony, a privilege recently granted by Gregory was called in question and had to be declared authentic by Ingelrannus. Moreover, after the abbot of Bergues-Saint-Winoc was deposed as a simoniac by the council of Poitiers in January 1078, the monks enjoyed Count Robert's protection in electing a successor whom Bishop Hubert opposed. Ingelrannus accompanied the new abbot to Rome for consecration there, and may have reported to Gregory favourably about the count's recent conduct. Whatever impression Gregory may have received, he was anxious to safeguard comital authority and goodwill. He ordered Bishop Hugh of Die to correct any wrong judgement that Hubert and the bishop of Langres might have passed, or at least quickly to restore the count to grace after the manner of the good shepherd of the Gospel who quickly sought and restored a sheep that was lost. He roundly rebuked Hugh of Langres for acting *ultra vires* and without authority from Hugh of Die. Almost a year later, he addressed Hubert in similar terms of reproof.[63]

Gregory's preparedness to think well of Robert was unimpaired, but it again came under severe test in and after 1082. Gregory became aware that, in the previous year, Bishop Hubert of Thérouanne, whose reputation for simony was known to the pope, had resigned his see; Robert had forthwith imposed upon the see a successor, Lambert, who was publicly notorious for his simony.[64] Robert was party to the very simoniacal dealings against which Gregory had urgently warned him in 1076; unlike the incident of 1078, the circumstances of the filling of the see of Thérouanne were well known to him. For he came under a double pressure to take stern measures. On the one hand, at the synod of Meaux in October 1082, his legates Hugh of Lyons and Amatus of Oloron excommunicated Robert for his offences and for subjecting to rigorous imprisonment five clerks who wished to present their case against him at a Roman synod. On the other hand, Lambert was raised through the succession of holy orders by three bishops who were themselves under suspension; strongly supported

---

[63] *Reg.* 6.7, to Bishop Hugh of Die, 25 Nov. 1078, pp. 407–8; *Epp. vag.* no. 24, to Bishop Hugh of Langres, (*c*.25 Nov. 1078), pp. 62–5; *Reg.* 7.1, to the subdeacon Hubert, 23 Sept. 1079, pp. 459/29–460/6. Gregory's privilege for Watten is *QF* no. 136, 28 Apr. 1077, pp. 142–4; for events there and at Bergues-Saint-Winnoc, see esp. *Chron. mon. Watinensis*, caps. 18–28, pp. 170–5.

[64] In probable order of time, Gregory's relevant letters about Count Robert are: *Epp. vag.* nos. 45–6, to Count Robert of Flanders, and to the clergy and people of Flanders especially Count Robert of Flanders, (1082), pp. 108–13; *Reg.* 9.13, to Count Robert, (1083), pp. 591–2; 9.33–5, to Archbishop Hugh of Lyons, to Count Robert, and to all the bishops and *principes* of Flanders, (1083), pp. 619–27; *Epp. vag.* no. 47, to Count Robert, (1083), pp. 114–15; *Reg.* 9.36, to Count Robert, (1083), pp. 628–9. Arguments that the last letter might be dated to 1084, e.g. by Borino, 'Può il Reg. vat. 2', pp. 394–402, esp. pp. 399–401, must be considered in the light of the circumstance that the next and final letter in the Register, 9.37, was written as an immediate response to news of King William I of England's imprisonment of his brother in 1082 and is likely to date from 1082–3. There is no need to challenge Caspar's dating of 9.36 as *Ende 1083* in the absence of other internal or external evidence for 1084.

by the count, Lambert had forcibly possessed himself of the see in violent and bloody scenes during which many clerks, including Ingelrannus, were dispossessed of their goods and expelled from the city. The circle of clerks who were Gregory's chosen agents was thus, at least for a time, broken up.

There followed an interlude in which, having thus been established in his see by Count Robert, Lambert was himself set upon by his rivals and cruelly mutilated.[65] It seemed that the tables might be turned: with the support of the count, Lambert complained of his injuries at Rome, where Gregory absolved him and remitted the issue of dealing with the culprits to his legates Hugh of Lyons and to the more moderate and judicious Hugh of Cluny. But Lambert before long utterly alienated Gregory by wholeheartedly adhering to the pope's rival, Archbishop Guibert of Ravenna. Lambert thus disappeared from history.

From first to last in his dealings with Count Robert, Gregory referred to him with courtesy and unwavering recognition. He addressed him as *nobilis*; in the most admonitory of his letters, which he addressed to the Flemish bishops and *principes*, he spoke of them as 'serving under Robert, the most noble count', ('sub R. comite nobilissimo militantibus'). Gregory had loved Robert, and if he did not now spurn his salutary warnings, he would again love him 'as our most beloved son'.[66] Gregory consistently appealed to Robert's pre-eminence in good works among the *principes* of France and to the need that his example should continue. At the most tense point of their relations, he expressed confidence that Robert would heed the rulings of his legate Hugh of Die/Lyons. He was aware that the account of events which he received by letter from Count Robert was different from what the clerk Ingelrannus told him face to face. Indeed, Robert had written things to the apostolic see which were not fitting. But Gregory expressed his concern to keep Robert within the church, and he hoped one day to convince him in conversation alike of the ignorance of his current advisers and of the authority and discernment of the Roman church.[67]

In the longest and most remarkable of his letters relating to Flanders, which he addressed to all the Flemish bishops and *principes*,[68] Gregory enlarged upon the divine commission by which he acted. He told the bishops, in particular, to urge the count to penance and restitution within forty days. It is significant that, throughout his letter, Gregory concentrated his wrath upon Bishop Lambert, a member of Antichrist for whom he expressed no word of hope. The count was his associate who could be won to a rightful way of life; the bishops were, therefore, collectively and individually to contend for his soul much as, in 1076, Ingelrannus was commissioned to instruct him. Although Gregory threatened the ultimate sanction of excommunication against the count and his clerical and lay servants if he were intransigent, his immediate message was one of friendship: 'I have said many things to him in letters', he told Robert's subjects, 'just as I say them now to you; because I loved him greatly.'

---

[65] *Reg.* 9.31, to two lay assailants of Lambert, (1083), pp. 617–18.
[66] *Reg.* 9.35, pp. 622/28–9, 623/10–13, cf. 626/29–35.
[67] *Reg.* 9.33, p. 620/5–9, 9.34, p. 621/12–18, 9.35, p. 623/35–9.
[68] *Reg.* 9.35.

Therefore the bishops were to deliver to him the homily on obedience that Gregory developed at remarkable length. Even when Lambert apostatized to Guibert of Ravenna and Gregory reflected that he had stored up wrath for himself with Robert's help and comfort ('L. inimicus Dei et invasor Teruanensis aecclesiae, ope et sustentatione tua adhuc sibi iram Dei thesaurizet'), Gregory looked for Robert to come to a right mind. He regretted that his misguided purpose had deflected a man whom good report had everywhere commended to become a public danger to his country ('ex corde dolemus, quod virum, quem bona fama passim commendaverat, mala nunc intentio ad commune periculum illius patriae retorqueret'). Let Robert now cut Lambert off as a putrifying member and, instead, let him support Gerard who had been canonically elected, 'so that as by one candidate you offended God you may by another commend your righteousness to God himself and to St Peter'.[69]

Gregory's perspective upon events in Flanders led him to concentrate blame upon the reprobate bishop and to leave intact the good character and effective rule of the lay prince.[70] Gregory never abandoned his confidence that Count Robert might be won for his own purposes, and he did nothing to undermine him in his public office.

5.3 Gregory VII and the French Church and Clergy

The record of Gregory's dealings with King Philip I of France and with the lay princes of the French-speaking lands is meagre, especially when it is compared with the number and weight of his letters to similar persons in Germany. This was, no doubt, a consequence of the political weakness of the Capetian monarchy and of the greater princes of France and Burgundy. In these lands, Gregory had proportionately more to do with churches and churchmen, and his letters to them survive in considerable numbers. His letters to the clergy most fully disclose his aspirations for the spiritual and social life of France.

5.3.1 The Hearing of French Churchmen at Rome

A large number of Gregory's letters concerning France arose from petitions for help or justice which, throughout his pontificate, came to Rome at the instance of the petitioner.[71] Such petitions sometimes related to great men and great matters; more

---

[69] *Reg.* 9.36.

[70] Cf. Gregory's contemporary estimate of the respective culpability of Archbishop Guibert of Ravenna and King Henry IV: see above, 3.5.7.

[71] The following letters have been particularly considered in this connection: *Reg.* 1.32, to Bishop Araldus of Chartres, 27 Nov. 1073, pp. 52–3; 1.36, to Archbishop Humbert of Lyons, 4 Dec. 1074, pp. 57–8; 1.67, to Bishop Gerald of Sisterton, 21 Mar. 1074, pp. 96–7; 1.68, to Bishop Froterius of Nîmes, 22 Mar. 1074, pp. 97–9; 1.73, to Bishop Isembert II of Poitiers, 12 Apr. 1074, pp. 104–5, 2.15, to three bishops, 11 Nov. 1074, pp. 147–8; 2.20, to Archbishop Richer of Sens, 15 Nov. 1074, pp. 147–8, 2.20, to Archbishop Richer of Sens, 15 Nov. 1074, pp. 152–3; 4.20, to Bishop Josfred of Paris, 25 Mar. 1077, pp. 326–8; 6.24–5, to Bishop Amatus of Oloron, and to Abbot Arnald of Saint-Sever, 8 Mar. 1079, pp. 436–8; 6.32, to Bishop Isembert of Poitiers, 13 Apr. 1079, pp. 445–6; 6.33, to Abbot Hugh of Cluny, 14 Apr. 1079, pp. 446–7; 9.15, to Bishop Hugh of Die, 4 Dec. (1081), pp. 594–5; 9.19, to Archbishop Hugh of Lyons, (1082–3), pp. 599–600; *Epp. vag.* nos. 35, to Archbishop Ralph of Tours, (1073–9), pp. 90–1, 63, to Archbishop Ralph of Tours, (1073–85), pp. 144–5; 64, to Archbishop Ralph of Tours, (1073–85), pp.

often, they concerned persons or institutions of middling or of lower standing and matters that were local or even trivial in substance. Such petitioning was clearly not a novelty in Gregory's pontificate; some petitions which came to him concerned matters that had already been active under Alexander II, and as archdeacon, Gregory will have been familiar with the procedure. For servicing the pope's handling of petitions, the papal clerks had by 1073 developed an epistolary form which, if not set or stereotyped, had become fairly consistent. Papal answers were brief. They often opened with a phrase like 'Pervenit ad aures nostras', or 'Pervenit ad nos', thereafter setting out the petition that had been made and by whom. There followed the pope's decision, which tended not to settle the matter but to remit it for settlement locally by a stated agency. Letters of this character occur both in and apart from Gregory's Register. While there is no means of ascertaining what their total number may have been, those which survive may, on account of their *ad hoc* nature, be only a small part of the total that were dispatched.[72]

Petitioners came to Rome from widely scattered parts of France and Burgundy. They must incidentally have provided the pope and his entourage with invaluable intelligence about what was happening in France and about the loyalties and doings of many who were and were not well disposed to Gregory. Some examples will illustrate how particular and how various the petitions were. The abbot of Saint-Laumer at Blois complained that his monks had taken advantage of his absence on pilgrimage to Jerusalem in order to elect someone else. The cathedral chapter at Mâcon complained about the long vacancy of their see, alleging that the French king was hindering an election. A priest of Saint-Martin at Cruis, near Forcalquier, a church in St Peter's proprietorship, complained that the bishop of Sisteron had acted violently against its goods and clergy. Archbishop Ralph of Tours, a repeated complainant, said that he and his retinue had been waylaid by violent men belonging to the diocese of Archbishop Richer of Sens. It was said that Hugh IV of Lusignan, a local lord, had seized the property of a clerk of Gregory himself, also named Hugh, who had been bequeathed the property by his late brother Rorgo *de Coequo*. A knight complained to Gregory that, having duly put away a wife whom he had wrongfully married, he had unjustly been made to separate from her lawful successor.

In view of the detailed and particular nature of such petitions, it is not surprising that Gregory seldom settled them himself, although he might indicate what seemed to him a possible solution or might take collateral action in order to facilitate one. He himself gave two reasons for his not giving decisions: he was seldom sufficiently informed of the circumstances; more important, it would be unjust for him to pass judgement unless both parties were present.[73] His custom was to remit the petition to an appropriate authority in France for decision. Sometimes he prescribed a named metropolitan or diocesan bishop or a group of bishops; towards the end of his

144–5; 64, to Archbishop Ralph of Tours and Bishop Eusebius (or Geoffrey) of Angers, (1073–85), pp. 146–7.

[72] This is of significance in attempting to estimate the total number of Gregory's letters.

[73] *Reg.* 9.19, p. 599/25–8.

pontificate he favoured a metropolitan acting in concert with a diocesan. He might also choose a provincial or legatine council, or else one or more of his legates in France. Or, exceptionally, he might name a favoured lay prince, like Count William VIII of Poitou. Sometimes Gregory's letter was addressed to the person against whom complaint had been made, usually a bishop; if so, he was instructed to take appropriate steps to set matters right. More often, Gregory chose a neutral figure or authority who was to proceed as Gregory directed. In either case, there must be no delay. If the matter were settled, the upshot must immediately be reported to Gregory in writing. If it were not, both parties were to come to Rome where Gregory would settle the matter in proper form. Gregory was concerned that, in all such proceedings, justice should be tempered with mercy and that mercy should particularly be remembered. He was as much concerned to bring about the reconciliation of the parties as to secure the settlement of the matter at issue between them.

Gregory's clerks used a similar form of letter when Gregory himself initiated the summons of a bishop, abbot, or other person, together with his adversaries, to come to Rome. He preferred to deal with such business at his regular Lent or occasional November synods; alternatively or as a follow-up, he set terms for appearance at Rome on 1, or more rarely 30, November. Gregory was far from desirous of acting alone; when in doubt, he early showed that he liked to take the advice of the Roman clergy, bishops, and cardinals before he made up his own mind.[74] Moreover, when business was transacted at a Roman synod, the decisions reached could be approved and publicly applauded by the whole assembly.[75] They had the authority of the apostolic see and of the Roman church, as well as of the pope himself.

Gregory particularly summoned to Rome from France business that related to places of special political importance. Orleans was situated on the River Loire in the southern tip of the royal demesne. It was the theatre of prolonged strife amongst factions of its clerks, and between its bishop and one of the factions.[76] The issues had been ventilated at Rome in the days of Pope Alexander II, and the French king was involved in ways that were consistent with papal purposes. A clerk named Eurard was notorious for his irregularities of behaviour and for his violence against the cathedral clergy. In February 1075, Gregory ordered both him and his adversaries to come to Rome by 1 November so that their quarrel might be equitably settled. Eurard was an accomplice of his simoniacal bishop, Rainer. In April 1076, Gregory summoned him to Rome by 1 November to give an account of himself. This

---

[74] *Reg.* 1.16, to Bishop Gerald of Ostia, 1 July 1073, p. 26/14–23. The consultation need not have been, as Caspar suggests (n. 3) at an otherwise unrecorded synodical gathering but at such an assembly as Hildebrand attended on 8 Oct. 1072: see above, 2.2.5.

[75] *Epp. vag.* no. 4, to Archbishop Ralph of Tours, (after 9 Mar.), 1074, pp. 8–9.

[76] For Gregory's dealings with Orleans, see *Reg.* 2.52, to Eurard a clerk of Orleans, 28 Feb. 1075, pp. 194–5; 3.16–17, to Archbishop Richer of Sens, and to Bishop Rainer of Orleans, Apr. 1076, pp. 278–80; 4.9, to Archbishop Richer of Sens, 2 Nov. 1076, pp. 307–8; 5.8–9, to Archbishops Richer of Sens and Richard of Bourges and their suffragans, and to Bishop Rainer of Orleans, 6 Oct. 1077, pp. 358–61; 5.14, to the clergy and people of Orleans, 29 Jan. 1078, pp. 367–8, 5.20, to Bishop Rainer of Orleans, 24 Apr. 1078, pp. 383–4; 6.23, to the clergy and people of Orleans, 5 Mar. 1079, pp. 435–6.

summons, like that of 1075, was ignored; by 2 November Rainer had not come to Rome. Gregory therefore wrote to his metropolitan, Archbishop Richer of Sens, summoning Richer to attend the Roman synod which Gregory planned for 1077, bringing with him Rainer and his various opponents at Orleans, with the clerk Eurard prominent among them. But Gregory's journey to Canossa overtook events. On his return to Rome, he had to admit to the bishops of the provinces of Sens and Bourges that his attempts to get Rainer to Rome had come to nothing; he left it to the bishops publicly to pronounce a papal sentence of deposition upon Rainer if he remained contumacious. They were also to assist the canonical succession of a clerk, Sanzo, whom Gregory sent to them as his own choice for the see whom, on the strength of Sanzo's showing at Rome, both St Peter's counsel and Gregory's own recommended. But Sanzo's election further divided the clergy of Orleans. Gregory rejoined that he had both examined the cases of both sides and questioned Sanzo himself before the Roman bishops ('coram episcoporum nostrorum presentia diligenter perscrutari fecimus'); he provisionally commended Sanzo to the church of Orleans. In April 1078, Gregory referred the still recalcitrant Bishop Rainer to the synodal judgement of his legates Hugh of Die and Hugh of Cluny; but even in March 1079, Rainer had not been finally condemned and Gregory again announced his purpose of sending legates to settle the future of the see of Orleans. There, the evidence fails. But it is clear that, on the one hand, Gregory had repeatedly sought to regulate the affairs of a politically sensitive see by summoning its clergy to Rome; and that, on the other, he could not settle them by this means. He had to invoke both the bishops of neighbouring provinces and the intervention of his own legates. Even so, he seems never to have achieved his aims; Sanzo succeeded to the see, but into the 1090s his position remained fraught and insecure.[77]

The city and see of Poitiers were at the political centre of the lands of Count William VIII of Poitou, to whom Gregory looked as a principal friend among the French princes. In 1074, events there gave him especial concern, and he therefore sought to draw its local business to Rome.[78] The earliest evidence in his letters for problems at Poitiers concerns a liturgical dispute between the canons of Saint-Hilaire-le-Grand and those of the cathedral about how and where the patronal festival of St Hilary should be celebrated. The Lent synod at Rome in 1074 had decided in favour of the cathedral canons, and Gregory required their rivals to accept the synodical judgement. But the latter were quick to bring to Rome another complaint—that the bishop, Isembert II, was behaving oppressively against a monastery at Noiallé which was rightly theirs. Gregory required that the matter be settled at a provincial synod; if it were not, the bishop and canons should present themselves at Rome on 1 November for the case to be considered in Gregory's presence. But by September,

---

77 Yves (Ivo) de Chartres, *Correspondance*, nos. 51, 53, 1.206–11.

78 For Poitiers, see *Reg.* 1.54, to the canons of Saint-Hilaire, 16 Mar. 1074, pp. 81–2; 1.73, to Bishop Isembert, 12 Apr. 1074, pp. 104–5; 2.2–4, to Bishop Isembert, to Count William, and to Archbishop Gozelin of Bordeaux, 10 Sept. 1074, pp. 125–9; 2.18, to Count William, 13 Nov. 1074, pp. 150–1; 2.23–4, to Bishop Isembert, and to Archbishop Gozelin and Count William, 16 Nov. 1074, pp. 155–6.

Gregory was persuaded that Isembert's conduct was going from bad to worse. He had sent his knights forcibly to break up an assembly in Poitiers at which the legate Amatus of Oloron and the metropolitan Gozelin of Bordeaux were seeking to deal with the problem of Count William's marriage within the prohibited degrees; Isembert was to answer before Gregory at Rome by 30 November on pain of deposition. By 13 November, Gregory was so far reconciled towards the count as to seek his support against King Philip I. But on 16 November, Gregory already suspended and excommunicated Isembert on account of his accumulated transgressions; he now summoned him to the Lent synod of 1075 for final trial and sentence. Gregory committed the ecclesiastical affairs of the see of Poitiers to Archbishop Gozelin of Bordeaux; matters of public justice, including the grievances of the canons of Saint-Hilaire, he entrusted to the count.

Events at Poitiers attracted Gregory's careful consideration at Rome. But he took care to reinforce the authority in Poitou of the metropolitan and the count; in the event, the settlement of local issues proved to be best left in local hands. For after 1075, events seem to have quietened down so far as the bishop was concerned.

The situation at Tours, downsteam of Poitiers on the River Loire, was very different. The Touraine, of which it was at the centre, formed part of the lands of Count Fulk *le Réchin* of Anjou, with whom Gregory was always at loggerheads. Its archbishop, Ralph, was probably not by conviction much of a Gregorian; indeed, his accession in 1072 had allegedly been marred by simoniacal transactions with the king.[79] But from early days he looked to Gregory for help and guidance, even in small matters. Gregory regarded him as a serviceable agent whom he should guide and favour. Ralph's numerous contacts with Rome included a number of hearings of business at Gregory's Roman synods and at his November deadlines.[80]

As early as Lent 1074, a Roman synod had discussed Archbishop Ralph's association with the excommunicated count of Anjou and had considered the possibility of his own excommunication and deposition; Ralph was summoned to Rome by 1 November to make satisfaction. At Rome, he secured Gregory's goodwill, and the question of his association with Fulk ceased to be troublesome. Four letters of Gregory which were dated 15 November included orders to the abbot of Beaulieu-lès-Loches to attend the Lent synod of 1075 unless he yielded proper obedience to

---

79 *RHGF* 14.615, no. 80; cf. *Narratio controversiae inter capitulum S.Martini Turononsis et Radulphum eiusdem urbis archiepiscopum*: *RHGF* 12.460D.

80 The relevant letters of Gregory are: *Epp. vag.* no. 3, pp. 8–9; *Reg.* 2.19–22, to Archbishop Richard of Bourges, to Archbishop Richer of Sens, to Abbot Stephen of Beaulieu, and to the knight Hugh of Sainte-Maure, 15 Nov. 1074, pp. 151–4, 4.5, to the bishops of Brittany, 27 Sept. 1076, pp. 301–3; 4.13, to Archbishop Ralph of Tours, 1 Mar. 1077, pp. 316–17; 5.17, report on decisions about French bishops, 9 Mar. 1078, p. 380; *Epp. vag.* nos. 22, to the clergy and people of Tours, (after 9 Mar. 1078), pp. 58–9; 23, to Archbishop Ralph of Tours, (summer 1078), pp. 60–3; 33, to Archbishop Ralph of Tours, (1079), pp. 86–9; 37, to Archbishop Ralph of Tours, (1078–9), pp. 92–5; *Reg.* 7.15, to the bishops of Brittany and the clergy and people of the province of Tours, 8 Mar. 1080, pp. 488–9; *Epp. vag.* no. 48, to Archbishop Ralph of Tours, (1082), pp. 116–17; *Reg.* 9.24 to the clergy and people of Tours and Angers, (1082–3), pp. 605–7; *Epp. vag.* no. 52, to the canons of Saint-Martin at Tours, (1082–3), pp. 126–7. For events in 1082–3, see also the *Narratio, RHGF*, 12.459–61.

his archbishop, and a knight named Hugh of Sainte-Maure was to do likewise unless he restored property to the church of Tours that he had unjustly seized. Gregory was evidently concerned to foster good relations with Archbishop Ralph. In 1076, this became further apparent when the question of the jurisdiction of the archbishop of Tours over Brittany became acute. Ralph had already raised it at Rome, and in 1077 Gregory canvassed the possibility that Ralph and the bishop of Dol—Gregory tactfully used the title bishop rather than archbishop—might be invited to put their respective cases before the apostolic see. In 1078, relations between Gregory and Ralph were threatened when Bishop Hugh of Die, who had in the past several times expressed high regard for Ralph, now complained against him to Gregory in highly coloured terms. In the interests of King Philip of France, Ralph, whom Hugh described as being beyond the pale ('pestis et dedecus sanctae ecclesiae'), had violently disrupted Hugh's legatine council at Poitiers in January. Hugh had suspended him, and he had appealed to Rome.[81] At his Lent synod in 1078, Gregory deemed Hugh's case against Ralph to be unproven. He restored him to office and remitted his case to Hugh for more thorough and considered investigation. Gregory afterwards several times in letters reminded Ralph of the kind and paternal treatment that he had received at Rome. In 1080, at his Lent synod, Gregory gave long and careful consideration to the constitutional relations between the sees of Tours and Dol. He sought a compromise which left the archbishop of Tours with jurisdiction over the Breton bishops but which allowed the bishop of Dol to wear the *pallium*. Once more, a Roman synod gave Archbishop Ralph a decision which made his loyalty to Rome worthwhile. By such means, Gregory could offset the recalcitrance of the count of Anjou, win the support of a French metropolitan, and preserve the conditions for advancing papal purposes in the Loire valley and adjacent regions.

Gregory showed like circumspection in a further crisis at Tours which is known from the somewhat fanciful *Narratio controversiae* written later by the canons of Saint-Martin, of which the French king was titular abbot, and from letters of Gregory to the clergy and people of Tours and Anjou and to the canons of Tours. King Philip allegedly caused Archbishop Ralph to be expelled from his see by the counts of Anjou and Tours after he had failed to answer at the king's court for his deference to Gregory's legates Amatus of Oloron and Hugh of Die. Ralph sent a clerk to Rome, where Gregory publicly heard his plea on St Peter's day (29 June).[82] He dispatched his two letters in Ralph's strong support. But he confined his strictures to the already excommunicated Count Fulk of Anjou rather than to the French king, thus avoiding a major confrontation. Ralph was back in office by 1084.[83] Over a politically sensitive area, Gregory remained vigilant to the end, dealing with business at Rome on principal occasions of the Roman year and showing tact and moderation.

---

[81] For Hugh's letter to Gregory, see *RHGF* 14.615–16, no. 80; for his earlier relations with Archbishop Ralph, *RHGF* 14.777–8, nos. 1–4.

[82] Thus the *Narratio*, p. 459C; if so, military circumstances at Rome point to 1082 rather than 1083.

[83] *GC* 14.69.

Gregory also used his Roman synods, or summonses to Rome at other solemn occasions, to deal at the apostolic see with miscellaneous business, whether or not there were political implications. Especially in the early years of his pontificate before his legates were fully deployed in France, he sometimes sought to resolve local but troublesome disciplinary matters. Thus, for example, Abbot Ivo of Saint-Denis was to come to Rome by 30 November 1075 so that Gregory could be satisfied that allegations of simony against him were groundless.[84] Gregory also sought to resolve disputes between religious houses. By 1074, Abbot Arnald of Saint-Sever's differences with the monastery of Saint-Croix at Bordeaux about a church at Soulac had become a regular item of the agenda at Roman synods; Gregory set 1 November as the term for its resolution, if necessary at Rome.[85] He sought likewise to settle rifts between bishops and their churches; in 1075, he counselled Bishop Hugh of Die that his dispute over property with members of his church should be settled synodically at Rome.[86] Gregory's Roman synods were pastoral as well as judicial in conception, and a summons could have a wider, moral and religious purpose. In August 1074, Gregory told the bishops and abbots of Brittany that his care for all the churches compelled him to summon them all to his Lent synod of 1075, where they might join others of their order in taking thought for right Christian standards of which Brittany stood in especial need.[87]

When business came to Rome, Gregory commanded the sanction of an oath taken upon the tomb of St Peter himself. Its form and setting as a solemn act before the Roman church are set out in the oath prescribed in 1076 for the simoniacal Bishop Robert of Chartres. Robert vowed to abdicate his see without delay or damage to his church if and when a papal legate came to Chartres. In 1077, he notwithstanding resisted a legate's attempt to depose him. In 1081, Gregory again used the sanction of an oath sworn over St Peter's tomb in connection with Chartres. Another bishop, Gosfred, with the support of his uncle Bishop Josfred of Paris thus purged himself from accusions of simony before Gregory commended him to his clergy and people.[88] In 1077, Gregory exacted from another simoniacal bishop, Stephen of le Puy, an oath such as that taken by Robert of Chartres.[89] During the Lent synod of 1078, Archbishop Manasses of Rheims was required to take an oath over St Peter's body; he would obey further summonses and judgements of the apostolic see and he would answer to its legates. But, as in the case of Robert of Chartres, the oath was

[84] *Reg.* 2.64–5, to Abbot Ivo of Saint-Denis, and to the monks of Saint-Denis, 25 Mar. 1075, pp. 219–20.

[85] *Reg.* 1.51, to Abbot Arnald of Saint-Sever, 14 Mar. 1074, pp. 77–8.

[86] *Reg.* 2.43, to Bishop Hugh of Die, 5 Jan. 1075, pp. 179–80.

[87] *Reg.* 2.1, 28 Aug. 1074, pp. 124–5. The awareness of Breton *principes* of Gregory's measures concerning lay investiture and simony may indicate that Gregory's summons did not go entirely unanswered: *Reg.* 4.13, to Archbishop Ralph of Tours, 1 Mar. 1077, p. 316/26–33.

[88] *Reg.* 3.17*a*, pp. 282–3, cf. 4.14–15, to the clergy and people of Chartres and to Archbishop Richer of Sens and his suffragans, 4 Mar. 1077, pp. 317–19, 9.16, to the clergy and people of Chartres, (end 1081), pp. 395–7, cf. 9.32, to Bishop Hugh of Die, (1082/3), p. 619/16–31.

[89] *Reg.* 4.19, to all the bishops and clergy of France, 23 Mar. 1077, pp. 325–6.

forgotten upon Manasses's return to France, and Gregory duly rebuked him.[90] The sanctions that Gregory commanded at Rome were impressive, but even oaths over St Peter's body could not be relied upon after those who took them returned home.

5.3.2 Gregory VII's Use of Legates

To relieve the burden of work that was attracted to Rome as well as to provide and to enforce fair justice backed by adequate sanctions, Gregory needed to reinforce his authority by using legates. While he employed them widely in the church, it was in France that their activity was most intense. His letters set out his conception of their role and duties.

His fullest exposition is in his commendation of Bishop Amatus of Oloron as legate which in June 1077 he addressed to all grades of society in Narbonne, Gascony, and Spain. He asserted that, from its earliest days, the Roman church had been accustomed to send legates to all regions of the Christian world. Thus, the pope could entrust to legates business with which he was unable to deal in his own presence. Legates were not merely administrative agents. They shared in the papal duty of preaching salvation and promoting virtue throughout all churches, as well as of instructing the world in sound doctrine. A papal legate was, therefore, to be received as though the pope himself, or rather St Peter whose vicar the pope was, were present.[91] In other instructions to legates and references to them, Gregory reinforced this view. In 1078, he addressed Bishop Hugh of Die and Abbot Hugh of Cluny as his most beloved brothers who were prudently to balance the claims of mercy and justice:

Act wisely and let all your deeds be in charity, so that the oppressed may find you their prudent defenders while the oppressors may acknowledge you to be lovers of righteousness.[92]

In 1080, he conceded to the recalcitrant Archbishop Manasses of Rheims that a legate in France might offer better justice than was possible at Rome: the archbishop might state his case in the presence of Hugh of Die and other religious men in his own land ('patria'), where there could be an adequate presence of accusers and defenders; to come to Rome would involve labours and difficulties, and a lack of accusers and defenders there might leave little hope of justice.[93] Nor was the pope always well placed to settle cases at Rome. In the turmoil of the year 1082, Gregory admitted to Hugh of Die that he had neither the knowledge nor the time to keep track of the relatively minor pleas that French churchmen addressed to Rome; he needed a legate's collaboration.[94]

---

[90] *Reg.* 5.17, report on decisions about French bishops, 9 Mar. 1078, pp. 378–9, cf. *RHGF* 14.782AB, no. 9, *Reg.* 7. 12, to Archbishop Manasses of Rheims, 3 Jan. 1080, pp. 475–7.

[91] *Epp. vag.* no. 21, pp. 56–9.   [92] *Reg.* 6.3, 22 Aug. 1078, pp. 395/32–396/2.

[93] *Reg.* 6.12, 3 Jan. 1080, p. 47/1–7.

[94] *Reg.* 9.32, pp. 618/30–619/1, 12–15: 'Noverit itaque prudentia tua, quia multa tanquam a nobis deferuntur et scripta et dicta nobis nescientibus; multa etiam subripi possunt minus ad singula intentis, utpote divisis ad plurima et intentis ad maxima, quibus vehementer artamur.... Super hoc ergo indubitanter cognoscas, quia perperam acta sive subrepta dampnamus, iuste acta et diffinita firmamus et a te firmanda et statuenda mandamus.' Cf. *Reg.* 4.22, to Bishop Hugh of Die, 12 May 1077, p. 353/1–8; Gregory wished

There was, of course, nothing new in the dispatch to France and elsewhere of legates who might hold synods; before becoming pope Gregory had himself visited France in such a role.[95] But after, 1073, he was concerned to develop the work of his legates in France. He was quick to recall to Rome Cardinal-bishop Gerald of Ostia and the Roman subdeacon Rainbald who had been Alexander II's legates.[96] After his legation to Germany in 1074, Gerald returned to France as legate and in January 1075 held a synod at Poitiers.[97] But it was of critical importance for the future that in the autumn of 1073, when he returned to Rome, Gerald took with him Hugh, the newly elected bishop of Die in the kingdom of Burgundy, who had been chosen to replace the simoniacal bishop Lancelin.[98] Gerald commended him warmly to Gregory.

5.3.2.1 Hugh, Bishop of Die and Archbishop of Lyons

Hugh stayed at Rome until the next Lent, a guest of Gregory at the Lateran palace where a fellow-resident was Bishop Anselm of Lucca; the two young bishops-elect established a close friendship. In both cases, the issue of lay investiture arose: whereas Gregory conceded that Anselm's consecration might be postponed until King Henry IV had invested him, he gave no such liberty in the case of Hugh, whom he ordained priest and bishop before he returned to his see.[99] It was a landmark in Gregory's hardening attitude towards lay investiture.

Gregory's letters concerning Hugh's return to Die already manifested the ambivalence of attitude that would always mark the pope's dealings with his legate. When commending Hugh to Count William of Die and to all members of the church there, Gregory made stringent and uncompromising demands for the strictness of the new bishop's ministry: he had warned Hugh to show no weakness in extirpating simony and lay control of churches. But early in 1075, a letter bearing in the Register the caption *Dictatus papae* urged Hugh to be patient and restrained in recovering the lands of his see, and to defer to the pope's moderating authority:

It seems to us that, because the sons of your church wish to make restitution to you as regards the church's goods, you should receive and absolve them, on condition that after sworn guarantees certain of them should promise to come with you to ourself at Rome—that is, by God's will to take part in a synod, in order that there they may perform whatever seems to us to be rightful. For we are better pleased that you should for a time be blamed for mercy, than that from an excess of severity you should incur the hatred of your church. You should certainly show due regard for your sons, that they are raw and untrained, and you should arouse them to better things little by little; for no one all at once reaches the heights, and high buildings are erected in stages ('quia nemo repente fit summus et alta aedificia paulatim aedificantur').[100]

---

a wide variety of business to be dealt with at a legatine council in France, 'quatenus in eis nostra deinceps possit solicitudo et longa fatigatione sublevari.'

[95] See above, 2.1.   [96] *Reg.* 1.6, 30 Apr. 1073, pp. 8–10.
[97] *Chronicon Malleacense*, p. 406.   [98] Hugh of Flavigny, 2, p. 410.
[99] Hugh of Flavigny, 2, pp. 411–12; cf. Berthold, *Ann. a.* 1078, pp. 306/43–307/15.
[100] *Reg.* 1.69, to Count William and all the faithful of Die, 23 Mar. 1074, pp. 99–100; 2.43, to Bishop Hugh of Die, 5 Jan. 1075, pp. 179–80, with p. 180/10–15; cf. *Reg. Greg. I.* 5.58, 9.219, 11.56, vols. 1.356/60–9, 2.787/129–788/135, 2.962/26–8.

Gregory had in mind the letters of Pope Gregory the Great, for whom pastoral understanding in dealing with rude peoples was always to be brought to bear as a counterweight to canonical severity.

During the years that followed, Hugh proved himself a devoted agent of Gregory VII in France who remained loyal to his master to the end; he and his friend Anselm II of Lucca were two of the three bishops whom Gregory commended upon his death-bed as his possible successors.[101] But in temperament, personality, and manner of action, Gregory and Hugh exhibited differences as well as similarities. Whereas Gregory was always seeking for what should be the principles of action within the church, Hugh showed total assurance about them. Gregory approached clergy and laity pastorally and with a presumption of a need to be merciful; Hugh insisted upon rigour and upon the strictest demands of justice. Both men laboured unwearyingly for the implementation of Christian righteousness, but whereas Gregory aimed at peace, concord, and reconciliation, Hugh was prompt to coerce and to punish. Thus, from the beginning to the end of their association, there was a dialogue of contrasts between Gregory at Rome and Hugh in France.

Hugh was no exception to the rule that Gregory's legates were seldom permitted to act alone; Gregory saw to it that Hugh normally acted upon great occasions or in great matters with a second, or even a third, legatine figure at his elbow who might exercise a moderating influence. From time to time he was active in both the kingdom of France and in that of Burgundy. Except for the diocese of Cambrai, which was part of the church province of Rheims, he was not directly concerned with the affairs of even that part of Germany west of the River Rhine which went by the name of Gallia. Though he was never intensively concerned with the south-west of France, there was no territorial delineation of spheres between him and Bishop Amatus of Oloron who was mainly active there; at times, Hugh and Amatus acted in concert, with sometimes the one and sometimes the other taking the lead.[102]

The most conspicuous feature of Hugh's legatine activity was the series of ecclesiastical councils upon which he embarked almost as soon as he became bishop of Die and which continued until his translation in 1082/3 to the archbishopric of Lyons. The councils in which he was solely or jointly involved were held at Anse (late 1075), Dijon (January 1076), Clermont (August 1076), Autun (September 1077), Poitiers (January 1078), possibly Bordeaux (October 1079) and Toulouse (late 1079), then Lyons (February 1080), Avignon (February 1080), Bordeaux (October 1080), Saintes (January 1081), Issoudun (1081), perhaps Poitiers (1081), Meaux (1081), and Meaux again (October 1082).[103] This impressive sequence should not arouse the supposition that Gregory prepared for Hugh a role which was ready-made; nor should his activities be too neatly categorized. Together with Amatus of Oloron in

---

[101] *H* no. 35, p. 75/9–16.

[102] For Gregory's legates in France, see esp. T. Schieffer, *Die päpstlichen Legaten*, pp. 88–139. The fullest study of Hugh of Die remains Lühe, *Hugo von Die und Lyon*.

[103] For councils in France, see Mansi, 20.481–588 and Hefele–Leclercq, 5.135–6, 217–32, 267–8, 281–3; they should be used in the light of Schieffer, *Die päpstlichen Legaten*. For a possibility that Hugh held further councils at Brioude, Autun, and Dol in 1085/6, see Pontal, *Les Conciles*, p. 187.

the south of France, Anselm II of Lucca in Lombardy, and Altmann of Passau in South Germany, Hugh is often described as a 'standing legate' or 'permanent legate'. But these are modern terms of art, with no equivalent in Gregory's own vocabulary or in that of his contemporaries.[104] Gregory seems in fact to have employed the four bishops in ways appropriate to the needs of different regions and their respective circumstances. Their powers changed and developed. Moreover, even Hugh of Die was never accorded such thoroughgoing powers as in 1071 Pope Alexander II had ascribed to Archbishop Lanfranc of Canterbury.[105] Indeed, the chronicler Hugh of Flavigny may have been correct when he wrote of Alexander's legate in France, Cardinal Gerald of Ostia, in terms that would have fitted Hugh of Die in his early years.[106] Only gradually did Gregory's principal legates like Hugh of Die emerge as having distinctive functions.

The vocabulary in which Gregory's letters spoke of Hugh suggests that there was development. Gregory's early references to Hugh as a son, '(dilectus) filius noster',[107] soon gave way to terms expressive of brotherhood and collegiality, '(con)frater, co-episcopus'. Especially during the spring of 1077, Gregory referred to Hugh's role in terms of a personal representation of the pope, whether with a general validity ('cui vices nostras in Galliarum partibus agendas commisimus', or the like),[108] or in relation to a specific matter ('cui vicem nostram dedimus').[109] Such phrases quickly gave way to habitual descriptions of Hugh as holding an office, whether as *vicarius noster*,[110] or as *legatus noster* (more occasionally, *apostolicae ecclesiae legatus*).[111] From the latter months of 1077, Hugh was described by others as papal *vicarius*.[112] This movement from a more personal to a more official mode of expression might be dismissed as merely a matter of words, if Gregory's dealings with Hugh did not fall into three stages with which the changes in vocabulary broadly correspond.

The first stage extended until just after Canossa. Gregory seems at the start to have been uncertain about what would be the timing and other details of the dispatch of legates to France, and in particular about how and by whom the cases of King

---

[104] See e.g. Anselm of Canterbury's reference to 'reverendus archiepiscopus Lugdunensis, HUGO nomine, fungens in Gallia legatione apostolica': *Proslogion, Prooemium, Opera*, 1.94.

[105] Lanfranc, *Letters*, no. 7, p. 62/41–4.

[106] '. . . ad Gallias destinavit, et vices suas ei per Franciam et Burgundiam commisit': 2, p. 410; cf. Gregory's own early description of Cardinal Gerald of Ostia and the subdeacon Rainbald as 'in legatione Galliae constituti': *Reg.* 1.6, to Gerald and Rainbald, 30 Apr. 1078, p. 8/33–4.

[107] *Reg.* pp. 213/10, 214/9; *Epp. vag.* p. 28/21–2.

[108] *Epp. vag.* p. 28/22–4; *Reg.* pp. 321/12–13, 324/18–19, 325/26–7, 333/5.

[109] *Reg.* pp. 328/13, 387/25–6, 393/25–7.

[110] *Reg.* pp. 321/17, 433/15, 439/32–3, 440/30, 458/3, 476/8–9, 477/3, 492/5, 496/4–5.

[111] *Reg.* pp. 378/29, 409/4, 538/27–8, 596/7, 604/34, 618/1, 623/16; *Epp. vag.* p. 49/15; as early as 1076, Hugh acted 'in legatione nostra': *Reg.* p. 269/27. When writing to Gregory, Hugh spoke of himself in such terms as 'suae sanctitatis inutilissimus servus Hugo humilis presbyter Diensis': *RHGF* 14.613DE, 615A. To French churchmen he usually wrote as 'Romanae ecclesiae legatus': *RHGF* 14.777CE, 778B, 787A, but once as 'apocrisiarius': *RHGF* 14. 778C.

[112] See e.g. the references to Hugh in the letters of Bishop Amatus of Oloron: *RHGF* 14.764A, 765CD, 767C.

Philip and Bishop Roger of Châlons-sur-Marne might be dealt with.[113] For the most part, Hugh's early activities were limited to Burgundy and to France south of the River Loire. His three earliest synods were held there; little is known about them, although at his Roman synod in Lent 1076 Gregory confirmed Hugh's legatine decisions in general terms.[114] Even when allowance is made for the scanty registration of Gregory's letters in 1076, references in the Register to Hugh up to March 1077 are meagre in the extreme.[115] The only other reference is a non-registered letter which Gregory addressed to the abbots and religious superiors of France. Gregory assigned to Hugh the task of collecting the annual taxes (*census*) that French churches owed to St Peter. Although Gregory did not say how they were to be collected, he probably regarded the onus as being upon the superiors to send their taxes to Hugh rather than upon Hugh to travel round and collect them.[116] The period up to March 1077 was little more than a prelude to Hugh's activities in France upon Gregory's behalf.

There followed a second, transitional stage in the spring of 1077. After Canossa, Gregory was much concerned with French affairs;[117] but his use of Hugh of Die, though more manifest, was sporadic and still territorially restricted. On 1 March, he wrote to Archbishop Ralph of Tours in connection with the settlement of the relation between the sees of Tours and Dol. Gregory extended the hope that, if he were able to visit Germany, he might return by way of France and visit Ralph; alternatively, he might see that appropriate persons were sent who could discuss and settle the matter. Despite Hugh of Die's close relations with Archbishop Ralph, Gregory did not name him; only on 31 May did he tell King William I of England that he had decided to send his legates Hugh of Die, the subdeacon Hubert, and (if he were recovered from illness) the monk Teuzo to investigate the problem.[118] Gregory used Hugh of Die in two other connections: in Burgundy, he was to investigate the dispute of the canons of Romans with Archbishop Warmund of Vienne;[119] and he was to supervise the election of a new bishop in the exempt see of le Puy.[120]

But, in March 1077, Gregory was studiously careful to avoid a major involvement of Hugh of Die in the province of Rheims, where he still entertained hopes of

---

[113] *Reg.* 2.32, to Archbishop Manasses of Rheims, 8 Dec. 1074, p. 169/1–6; 2.55*a*, report of the Lent synod of 1075, p. 196/20–5; 2.56, to Archbishop Manasses of Rheims, 4 Mar. 1075, p. 210/2–6. One man whom Gregory considered sending was Abbot Hugh of Cluny: *Epp. vag.* no. 23, to Archbishop Ralph of Tours, (summer 1078), p. 60/11–15.

[114] *Reg.* 3.10*a*, p. 269/25–8. The principal evidence for the early synods is Hugh's letters of summons to Archbishop Ralph of Tours and his suffragans: *RHGH* 14.777–8, nos. 1–3; Hugh of Flavigny, 2, pp. 415–16, where the order of the synods is confused.

[115] Apart from *Reg.* 1.69, 2.43, only 2.59, to the monks of Romans, 9 Mar. 1075, pp. 212–14; 3.10*a*, record of the Lent synod of 1076, p. 269/25–8.

[116] *Epp. vag.* no. 12, (1075), pp. 28–9.

[117] *Reg.* 4.13–20, 1–31 Mar. 1077, pp. 316–29.

[118] *Reg.* 4.13, to Archbishop Ralph of Tours, 1 Mar. 1077, pp. 316–17; 4.17, to King William I, 31 Mar. 1077, pp. 322–3.

[119] *Reg.* 4.16, to the clerks of Romans, 21 Mar. 1077, pp. 320–1.

[120] *Reg.* 4.18–19, to the canons of le Puy, and to the bishops and clergy of France, 23 Mar. 1077, pp. 324–6.

collaboration with his *confrater* Archbishop Manasses. When matters came to his attention in which he wished to temper the archbishop's heavy-handed decisions, he sent an agenda of inquiries not to Hugh, but to Bishop Josfred of Paris.[121] Josfred was to investigate whether Manasses had passed too hard a sentence upon Walter, the castellan of Douai, and whether a canon of Douai had been over-severely treated by his chapter. More sensitively, he was to find out whether Manasses had been excessively severe and had acted *ultra vires* in his treatment of members of the monastery of Saint-Remi at Rheims. And Gregory was shocked to hear of the cruelty of the citizens of Cambrai in burning alive a popular religious leader, Ramihrd, who had campaigned against clerical fornication; Josfred was to report on this. Most strikingly of all, Gregory concluded his letter by entrusting to Josfred the task of informing all bishops throughout France that the ministrations of clerks guilty of fornication must everywhere be rigorously stopped. Gregory wrote to the bishop of Paris the kind of letter that he would soon be writing to Hugh of Die as legate. He referred to Hugh in his letter only in passing: should the abbot of Saint-Remi be found culpable and should he disobey Bishop Josfred, one course of action among several might be that the abbot should present himself before Hugh of Die 'cui vices nostras commisimus', or another legate who might hold a synod in France. At this stage, Gregory did not seem to envisage Hugh as exercising in practice an extensive legatine commission in most of France, or as being more than one legate, albeit perhaps the senior, amongst others.

The course of events which led to the third stage, of Hugh's becoming definitively Gregory's *vicarius* and *legatus* in France, arose suddenly and somewhat fortuitously. In May 1077, when Gregory was at Ficarolo on the River Po, there came to him Gerard, the bishop-elect of Cambrai. In a long letter to Hugh of Die,[122] Gregory explained that Gerard had been duly elected by the clergy and people; but then, as he said in ignorance both of Gregory's legislation at the Lent synod of 1075 and of his excommunciation of Henry IV of Germany a year later, he received from Henry the *donum episcopatus*. Because of Gerard's demonstration of humility ('humiliatio') and, still more, of his canonical election, as well as of the good report of him that Gregory had received from other bishops, he was disposed to be merciful to him. But to avoid wider misunderstanding of his mercy, Gerard was to make his situation publicly clear by purging himself by oath before Hugh of Die together with his metropolitan, Archbishop Manasses of Rheims, and other comprovincial bishops. To this end, Hugh was if possible to convene a council in the province of Rheims ('in partibus illis'), with the concurrence of King Philip of France. If the king would not concur, the council might meet at Langres. Gregory anticipated the cordial co-operation of its bishop, Hugh, whose see was just over the border in the church province of Lyons; Gregory also expected support from Count Theobald of Blois. Hugh was to associate with himself Bishop Hugh of Langres in convening a synod where he thought fit.

[121] *Reg.* 4.20, 25 Mar. 1077, pp. 326–9. Gregory did not describe Josfred as his legate.
[122] *Reg.* 4.22, 12 May 1077, pp. 330–4.

Gregory went on to set out its agenda in a way that recalls his letter of 25 March to Bishop Josfred of Paris. But the role of the French king in the appointment of bishops made it inappropriate that Gregory should work through someone who was not only bishop of Paris but also prominent in the royal chancery;[123] Gregory therefore now enlisted the aid of Hugh of Die. First and foremost, Hugh was to deal with Bishop-elect Gerard of Cambrai, who was to confirm by oath what he had said to Gregory at Ficarolo; he was also to purge himself of complicity in the burning of Ramihrd—a matter which Gregory had hitherto referred to the bishop of Paris. This done, Hugh of Die and Manasses of Rheims were to consider Gerard's consecration. The problem of Cambrai led Gregory now to involve Hugh in the affairs of the northern province of Rheims. Gregory went on to list further problems for which, among others, Hugh of Die was to seek a final solution at his synod. Some had arisen in provinces other than Rheims. In that of Sens, Hugh was to attend to the deposition and replacement of Bishop Robert of Chartres and to the problem of the abbacy of Saint-Denis.[124] In that of Bourges, there was the problem of the see of Clermont.[125] In the exempt see of le Puy, Hugh was to see to the election of a new bishop.[126] First upon Gregory's list was a long-standing problem within the province of Rheims— the fate of Bishop Roger of Châlons-sur-Marne.[127] Furthermore, Hugh of Die was to tackle abuses which were rampant throughout France. Gregory made no express mention of the clerical fornication which he had addressed in his letter to Bishop Josfred of Paris. But Hugh was to issue a general interdiction of the simony of which Bishop-elect Gerard of Cambrai had confessedly not been guiltless in his time as archdeacon. And Hugh was to announce throughout France in the most emphatic terms that, upon pain of forfeiting their office, metropolitans and bishops might not lay hands upon anyone who had received from a lay person the *donum episcopatus*.

Gregory's letter was a clarion call to Hugh, if possible with the collaboration of Archbishop Manasses and of the French king, but if not by whatever means Hugh saw fit, to proclaim Gregory's most stringent demands against simony and lay invest-iture, and to settle if he could, on the pope's behalf, local issues that had been long outstanding in various parts of the French church. Hugh must have felt reinforced in his authority later in 1077, when Gregory confirmed the strong action that he had taken at Chartres in dismissing a young and unworthy candidate, Gosfred, and urged Hugh to pursue a resolution of the situation at Chartres according to the prescrip-tions of his general letter of instructions.[128]

Hugh of Die's summons to Archbishop Ralph of Tours with his suffragans and clergy shows that he decided to hold his council at Autun, which was also in the

---

[123] *Recueil des actes de Philippe I*er, pp. LVI–LVII; Josfred (Geoffrey of Boulogne) acted as chancellor in 1075–7 and *c.*1081–5.

[124] *Reg.* 4.14–15, to the clergy and people of Chartres, and to the bishops of the province of Sens, 4 Mar. 1077, pp. 317–19; 2.64–5, to Abbot Ivo of Saint-Denis, and to the monks of Saint-Denis, 25 Mar. 1075, pp. 219–20.

[125] Hugh of Flavigny, 2, p. 413.   [126] *Reg.* 4.18–19.

[127] *Reg.* 6, to Bishop Roger of Châlons, 17 Mar. 1074, pp. 83–4; 2.56, to Archbishop Manasses of Rheims, 4 Mar. 1075, pp. 209–10.   [128] *Reg.* 5.11, to Bishop Hugh of Die, (late 1077), pp. 363–5.

province of Lyons but in the lands of the well-disposed Duke Hugh of Burgundy.[129]
It met from 10 to 17 September. Hugh thereafter sent a verbal report to Gregory but
received no reply. Before the end of the year, he therefore sought further instructions. His account of the council, though incomplete, makes it clear that he had acted
with the zeal and rigour that Gregory had seemed to require of him in impressing
upon the French episcopate the need for amendment of past ways and for future
obedience.[130] He had visited severe sanctions upon three prelates about the ordering
(*ordinatio*) of whose churches he now sought Gregory's decision—Rheims, whose
archbishop (later in his letter Hugh called him 'haereticus Remensis') had not attended the council, Bourges, the precise transgression of whose archbishop does not
emerge,[131] and Chartres, whose too-young bishop had been deposed. For the rest,
Hugh's rigour had been directed against bishops who had come by their office in improper ways. Bishop Radbod of Noyon had been forced to abandon the see that he
had simoniacally acquired. Hugh reported to Gregory upon Bishop Ivo of Senlis,
whom King Philip I had invested and Archbishop Manasses of Rheims had ordained
in defiance of Gregory's written instructions about royally invested bishops; upon
Bishop Robert of Auxerre, a youth who, while he had not received royal investiture,
had come by his see through currying favour at court; upon Archbishop Richer of
Sens, who had insulted Gregory's authority in the person of his legate; and upon
Archbishop Gozelin of Bordeaux, whom Hugh had suspended from his episcopal
and then from his priestly functions in view of a long history of contumacy. With
regard to all eight of these bishops, whether Hugh had sentenced them or not he
humbly besought Gregory's advice and directions. The evidence of a later letter from
Archbishop Manasses of Rheims to Gregory established that, at Autun, Hugh legislated as forcibly as Gregory had instructed him against bishops who received from
lay hands the *donum episcopatus*.[132] But strongly though Hugh proclaimed such papal
demands as subjects of general legislation, his particular actions as a legate were anything but those of a plenipotentiary. In practice, he referred major cases to Gregory
for final or sole decision.

   Hugh concluded his letter to Gregory about the council of Autun by referring to
another council that he had convened at Poitiers, in the lands of the friendly Count
William VIII of Poitou, for 15 January. The principal source for this council is another letter that Hugh afterwards wrote to Gregory.[133] Hugh added substantially to
his gravamina against French bishops and abbots. In his eyes, the villain of the occasion was Archbishop Ralph of Tours, hitherto co-operative, but now 'pestis et
dedecus sanctae ecclesiae', who under royal pressure sought violently to disrupt the

---

[129] *RHGF* 14.778, no. 3; cf. Hugh of Flavigny, 2, pp. 414–16.

[130] *RHGF* 14.613–14, no. 79; cf. Manasses's report to Gregory about his excommunication at Autun:
H no. 107, pp. 178–82.

[131] On 6 Oct. 1077, after Hugh's sentence, Gregory asked Archbishop Richard of Bourges to act with
Archbishop Richer of Sens and their suffragans against Bishop Rainer of Orleans: *Reg.* 5.8, pp. 358–9.

[132] *RHGF* 14.611E, no. 76.

[133] *RHGF* 14.615–16, no. 80. Count William of Poitou seems in fact to have supported Hugh of Die at
the council.

council; Hugh resurrected the charge that Ralph's accession to office had been tainted by simony. When Hugh suspended Ralph from office, he appealed to Rome, as did his principal accomplice, Bishop Silvester of Rennes; Hugh consigned him to a papal sentence of which he was confident: 'because he appealed to the apostolic see, where he claimed that he had been purged by his simony, we dispatched him to the apostolic see and left him to be deposed by your judgement.'

As regards others, because Abbot Ermenger of Bergues-Saint-Winoc was a proven simoniac, Hugh deposed him. But most of the bishops who were named were, like Ralph of Tours, referred to Gregory for judgement: Archbishop Hugh of Besançon and Bishops Agino of Autun and Isembert of Poitiers who had absented themselves from the council without proper excuse; Bishops Guy of Beauvais and Radbod of Noyon who were simoniacs; and Ralph, who had invaded the see of Amiens, together with those who had consecrated him—Bishops Helinand of Laon, Theobald of Soissons, and Ivo of Senlis. Although Count Fulk appeared before Hugh at the council, the legate left the question of his absolution, too, for Gregory's decision. More stringently even than at Autun, Hugh legislated in general for the amendment of the French church. A series of ten surviving canons opened with a prohibition that bishops or any inferior clerks should receive the gift of a bishopric or any ecclesiastical preferment from the king or other lay persons. Hugh went on to deal with both simony in general and clerical concubinage; thus, Gregory's aspirations for the renewal of the French church were fully covered.[134]

The consequence of Hugh's flurry of rigorous action at the councils of Autun and Poitiers was that many French prelates travelled to Rome for Gregory's Lent synod of 27 February to 3 March 1078. Hugh of Die himself followed not long after.[135] There were bridges to be rebuilt between pope and legate. Hugh had already ended his report to Gregory on the council of Poitiers by expressing his fear that Gregory would set aside his own zeal and rigour by a mildness that would both undermine the legate's authority in France and encourage King Philip in the very trafficking in sees that Gregory was concerned to extirpate:

Let your holiness be on your guard lest it should any longer be so tauntingly thrown up against us that simoniacs or criminals of every sort who are suspended, deposed, or even excommunicated by us, freely run off to Rome; that where they should experience a fuller rigour of righteousness they come away with mercy of a sort according to their own wishes; and that those who once did not venture to transgress in even the lightest matters nowadays practise a most ready trafficking with the tyrant [King Philip] in the churches committed to him.

Gregory's rulings at his Lent synod fulfilled Hugh's worst fears. A memorandum bearing the date 9 March 1078 announced the spirit in which Gregory had dealt with the French bishops:

Because of the custom of the holy Roman church whose unworthy servant we are is to tolerate and even to overlook some matters, we have followed the moderation of prudence rather than the rigour of the canons when, not without heavy toil, we have discussed the cases of the

---

[134] Mansi, 20.498–9; for canon 1, see Beulertz, *Das Verbot*, pp. 5–6, no. 3.
[135] *Reg.* 5.22, to the subdeacon Hubert and the monk Teuzo, 22 May 1078, p. 386/10–19.

bishops of France and Burgundy who were suspended or excommunicated by our legate Bishop Hugh of Die.

In particular, Hugh's sentence upon Manasses of Rheims seemed not to have been awarded in accordance with the authority ('gravitas') and customary mercy of the Roman church; therefore, subject to Manasses's taking an oath, Gregory restored him to his order and office.[136] As for Archbishop Hugh of Besançon, the letters by which he had been summoned to Poitiers had been concealed from him by his own clergy; he, too, was restored to office save that, if Hugh of Die thought fit, he should purge himself by oath. Gregory restored the interdicted Archbishop Richer of Sens to office on condition that he explain himself to Hugh of Die. Gosfred of Chartres had not been properly accused and had been tried in absence; he was, therefore, restored until Hugh of Die should try him by due process. Archbishop Richard of Bourges had abandoned his church in a fit of anger and not by synodal judgement; he recovered his staff and ring on condition that he clear himself before Hugh of Die. As for the villain of the piece at Poitiers in Hugh of Die's eyes, Archbishop Ralph of Tours, he had been accused in circumstances of the utmost irregularity; he was to receive every opportunity to justify himself so that, if he were innocent, the charges against him might be buried.[137] While the final details of the proceedings against these bishops were often left to Hugh of Die for settlement, Gregory overturned in the interests of mercy a wide range of decisions that his legate had taken from zeal for justice. Many French bishops had found in Gregory at Rome a sovereign defence against legatine rigour in their own land.

It is not surprising that Hugh of Die should not have held another council until at earliest the autumn of 1079,[138] and that, at the councils of Bordeaux and Toulouse, he should have presided jointly with Bishop Amatus of Oloron. Yet from early in 1078, and perhaps from even before Hugh's visit to Rome, Gregory expected that he would take a lead in convening another council under his own leadership to deal comprehensively with French affairs; the principal item would be the problem of Archbishop Manasses of Rheims.[139] Hugh at first convened a council at Troyes but cancelled it; another assembled at Lyons in January/February 1080, when Manasses failed to appear and Hugh sentenced him to deposition. Gregory approved Hugh's sentence and confirmed it at his own Lent synod at Rome; yet he continued to hold out to Manasses an opportunity for mercy and reconciliation until his final deposition at the end of the year.[140]

---

[136] For Manasses's later comment see *RHGF* 14.782DE. [137] *Reg.* 5.17, pp. 378–80.

[138] There is some evidence that he suffered a period of serious illness at about this time: Hugh of Flavigny, 2, p. 421.

[139] *Reg.* 5.20, to Bishop Rainer of Orleans, 24 Apr. 1078, pp. 383–4; 5.22–3, to the subdeacon Hubert and the monk Teuzo, and to the counts of Brittany, 22 May 1078, pp. 385–8; 6.2, to Archbishop Manasses of Rheims, 22 Aug. 1078, pp. 391–4; *Epp. vag.* no. 30, to Bishop Hugh of Die, (Apr./May 1079), pp. 76–81; *Reg.* 6.40, to Count Boso of la Marche, 28 June 1079, pp. 457–8; 7.12, to Archbishop Manasses of Rheims, 3 Jan. 1080, pp. 475–7.

[140] *Reg.* 7.20, to Archbishop Manasses of Rheims, 17 Apr. 1080, pp. 495–6; 8.17–19, to the clergy and people of Rheims, to Count Ebolus of Roucy, and to the suffragans of Rheims, 27 Dec. 1080, pp. 538–41.

Gregory involved Hugh in other business, as well. When, in the late spring of 1079, he encouraged him to hold the council of Lyons to deal with Manasses, he added other matters—the current dispute between Archbishop Gebuin of Lyons and Abbot Hugh of Cluny, and the problems of the churches of Chalon-sur-Saône and Langres. He began his letter by acknowledging that Hugh of Die had sought to serve God faithfully with all the love of his heart.[141] Both before and after Hugh became archbishop of Lyons at Gregory's urgent desire, since he looked for one who would indeed be a soldier of Christ and a defender of righteousness for which he would desire to undergo even death in the body,[142] Gregory entrusted Hugh with business in different parts of France.[143] He was especially to be concerned with affairs in the distant county of Flanders, on account both of its importance as a marcher area between France and Germany, and of Gregory's consequent desire for good relations with Count Robert; Hugh was charged to hold a council there. In 1079, Hugh advised Gregory about suitable candidates for the archbishopric of Arles; Gregory also used him to assist Bishop Amatus of Oloron with strife between monasteries at Bordeaux and to deal with continuing problems of the abbey of Bourg-Dieu at Déols.[144]

During the early 1080s when Gregory was hard-pressed at Rome by Henry IV of Germany, it was more difficult than ever for him to keep track of events in France. His letters to Hugh of Die/Lyons illustrate the problems which petitioners from France did not cease to bring to him at Rome. Hugh must, therefore, serve as his eyes and ears in France. Thus, when the clerks of Autun complained to him against the monks of Saint-Benoît-sur-Loire at Fleury who were asserting claims over the monastery of Saint-Simphorien at Autun, Gregory could not trace at Rome his earlier letters to Hugh nor could he recall the matter. Therefore he remitted the case to Hugh for further investigation and for him to confirm whatever had been rightfully decided.[145] But ample room for friction between pope and legate still remained. At the end of 1081, Bishop Josfred of Paris appeared in Rome with his nephew Bishop Gosfred of Chartres; they complained that, probably during his council at Issoudun in March, Hugh of Die had without due canonical process excommunicated and deposed Gosfred. When a report that Gregory urgently secured from Hugh differed

---

[141] *Epp. vag.* no. 30, pp. 76–7.

[142] *Reg.* 9.18, to Bishop Hugh of Die, 24 Oct. (1081), pp. 598–9.

[143] As bishop of Die: *Reg.* 6.7–9 to Bishop Hugh of Die, to Archdeacon Hubert of Thérouanne and others, and to Archdeacons Ernulf and Hubert of Thérouanne and others, 25 Nov. 1078, pp. 407–10; 7.16, to Bishop Hurbert of Thérouanne, 26 Mar. 1080, pp. 489–91. As archbishop of Lyons: *Reg.* 9.13, to Count Robert of Flanders, (1083), pp. 591–2; 9.31, to two knights of Thérouanne, (1083), pp. 617–18; 9.33–5, to Archbishop Hugh of Lyons, to Count Robert of Flanders, and to Flemish bishops, upper clergy, and princes, (1083), pp. 619–27.

[144] Arles: *Reg.* 6.21 to the clergy and people of Arles, 1 Mar. 1079, pp. 342–4. Bordeaux: *Reg.* 6.24–5, to Bishop Amatus of Oloron, and to Abbot Arnald of Saint-Sever, 8 Mar. 1079, pp. 436–8. Déols: *Reg.* 6.27–8, to the monks of Déols, and to the princes of the region of Bourges, 20 Mar. 1079, pp. 439–41.

[145] *Reg.* 9.32, to (Arch)bishop Hugh of Die/Lyons, (1082–3), pp. 618–19; cf. *Epp. vag.* no. 44, to Bishop Hugh of Die and Abbot Richard of Marseilles, (1081–2), pp. 106–9, when the legates (or one of them) should settle issues that had come to Gregory from south-west France.

materially from the bishops' testimony, Gregory allowed Gosfred to purge himself of any wrongdoing by an oath upon St Peter's tomb and restored him to his see. Upon learning that Hugh demurred, Gregory rebuked him for excessive severity and for unfilial inconsideration of the predicament of the Roman church:

If divine mercy has allowed Gosfred a time of respite, you will clearly understand that it was far less blameworthy so to proceed than it was for you to have extended the hand of rebuke in judicial censure of your mother [the Roman church]. It would have become you, and it would have seemed more fitting, at such a time as this when she is undergoing such tribulations to have ministered to her as a son the kindnesses of consolation in imitation of God and with a good conscience, rather than by sending her such matters and bothering her with such trifles, thus adding distress to distress and multiplying not sharing her burdens.[146]

Gregory nevertheless addressed this letter to 'his most beloved brother and fellow bishop', and Hugh's zeal to join the many French churchmen who attended Gregory's November synod of 1083 may have restored his credit in Gregory's eyes.[147] It says much for the mutual regard and forbearance of both men that, despite such differences of temperament and behaviour, the bond of collaboration and service remained strong to the very end of Gregory's life.

5.3.2.2 Bishop Amatus of Oloron

Amongst Gregory's other legates in France, Amatus of Oloron stood closest to Hugh of Die/Lyons in duty and function. Amatus was bishop of Oloron, like Die a small and rather remote see, from ?1073 to 1089, and from 1089 to 1101 he was archbishop of Bordeaux. Like the young Hugh of Die, the new bishop of Oloron seems to have come to Gregory's attention through Cardinal Gerald of Ostia when he returned from France to Rome in 1073; but unlike Hugh, Amatus seems never to have met Gregory face to face. Under Pope Alexander II, Amatus had already been associated with Gerald in visiting sanctions upon Bishop Isembert of Poitiers. After Gerald's departure, Amatus acted as Gregory's legate; in concert with Archbishop Gozelin of Bordeaux, he held a provincial council in 1074 at Saint-Maixent near Poitiers in order to consider the matrimonial position of Count William VI.[148]

Nothing more is heard of Amatus's service of Gregory until the intensification of Gregory's interest in French affairs after Canossa. Then, Gregory commissioned him to be legate in Gallia Narbonensis (in traditional terms, approximately the region bounded by the Rivers Garonne, Tarn, and Rhône), Gascony to the west, and Spain to the south. For service in Spain, Gregory associated with him Abbot Frotard of Saint-Pons at Thomières.[149] At this time, Gregory referred to Amatus as 'cui et vicem nostram ad partes illas dedimus',[150] thus echoing phrases that he had lately

---

[146] *Reg.* 9.32, p. 619/16–31; the echo of Gal. 6: 2 should be noted.

[147] Bernold, *Chron. a.* 1083, p. 438/28–31.

[148] *Reg.* 2.2, to Bishop Isembert of Poitiers, 10 Sept. 1074, pp. 125–6; cf. 1.73, to the same, 12 Apr. 1074, pp. 104–5; see above, 5.2.2.

[149] *Epp. vag.* no. 21, to the Christians of Narbonne, Gascony, and Spain, (*c.*28 June 1077), pp. 56–9; *Reg.* 4.28, to the kings and lay princes of Spain, 28 June 1077, pp. 343–7, esp. p. 346/22–34.

[150] *Reg.* p. 346/23–4; see also pp. 471/39–472/1.

used of Hugh of Die. In future references in his letters to Amatus, which are fewer than those to Hugh, Gregory called him 'legatus noster',[151] but never 'vicarius noster'; thus, it cannot be assumed that Gregory himself in this sense equated Amatus with Hugh. In his own letters, Amatus referred to his office as 'sanctae Romanae ecclesiae legatus', though once as 'domini papae Gregorii VII gratia Dei vicarius'.[152] When subscribing documents arising from councils at which he presided he used such phrases as 'vicarius Romanae urbis', 'sanctae Romanae ecclesiae vicarius', and simply 'vicarius';[153] thus, at least in a conciliar context he thought of himself as a papal 'vicarius', although suitors called him 'legatus Romanus'.[154]

In 1077 and 1078, Amatus's legatine activities appear to have centred upon Catalonia, where in 1077 he held councils at Gerona and Besalú and in 1078 another at Gerona.[155] French bishops from Gothia and from the county of Toulouse attended these councils. In 1077, his attempt to hold a council at Gerona was disrupted by Archbishop Guifred of Narbonne, who was excommunicated at the subsequent council of Besalú which was attended by the bishops of Agde, Elne, and Carcassonne.[156] At Gerona in 1078, he passed a number of stringent canons, particularly against simony and clerical incontinence; they included a requirement that simoniacal clergy should be reordained.[157] At his November synod of 1078, Gregory confirmed the sentence of excommunication that Amatus had imposed.[158]

Until this time, Amatus seems to have acted within the commission that Gregory gave him in 1077. But from the spring of 1079, he ceased to be particularly concerned with Gothia or Spain; instead, apparently in obedience to a lost directive from Gregory, his attention turned to a wider area of western France. Part of his concern was with the churches of the whole of Aquitaine.[159] This first became clear in March 1079, when Gregory directed Amatus, in concert with Bishop Hugh of Die, to settle a dispute at Bordeaux between the monasteries of Sainte-Croix and Saint-Sever.[160] His letters heralded a long collaboration between the two legates in holding councils. When they were jointly held in Aquitaine, the usual arrangement was that Amatus presided while Hugh was an assessor, as at Bordeaux (October 1079 and October

---

[151] *Reg.* pp. 437/21–2, 471/38–9, 616/10; *Epp. vag.* p. 108/1.

[152] *RHGF* 14.669D, 670AC, 676BE. He attested the canons of the council of Gerona (1078) as 'Amatus episcopus sanctae Romanae ecclesiae legatus his synodalibus gestis vice domini mei papae subscripsi': Mansi, 20.520B.

[153] *RHGF* 14.765C, 766B, 767D.   [154] *RHGF* 14.769A.

[155] For Amatus's councils, see Mansi, 20.518–20, 551–2, 577–80, 581–8; Hefele–Leclercq, 5.280–3; for comment, see esp. Schieffer, *Die päpstlichen Legaten*, pp. 110–15, 122–30, 135–6.

[156] *Lib. feud. maior*, no. 501, 2.16–17.

[157] Canon 11, Mansi, 20.519; see Saltet, *Les Réordinations*, pp. 207–8, and Schebler, *Die Reordinationen*, pp. 239–41.

[158] *Reg.* 6.5*b*, p. 401/10–11.

[159] 'Amatus, S.R.E. legatus, Ellorensiumque humilis episcopus, iussu et vice domni papae Gregorii VII, ob ecclesiarum Dei correctionem in Aquitaniae partes directus': *RHGF* 14.763–5, no. 1, 12 Oct. 1079.

[160] *Reg.* 6.24–5, to Amatus of Oloron, and to Abbot Arnald of Saint-Sever, 8 Mar. 1079, pp. 436–8; for the council of Bordeaux, see *RHGF* 14.763–5, no. 1. *Reg.* 6.20, to Count Centullus of Béarn, 25 Feb. 1079, pp. 431–2, may refer to Amatus as diocesan bishop rather than as legate.

1080) and Saintes (January 1081). At the council of Issoudun (March 1081) in the north of the county of Marche, Hugh took precedence despite its location within the duchy, perhaps because little of the agenda concerned Aquitaine.[161] At the council of Meaux in Champagne (late 1081), Hugh presided while Amatus assessed. Only after Hugh became preoccupied by his translation to Lyons did Amatus hold councils in Aquitaine on his own—at Charroux (November 1082) and Saintes (October 1083).

From the beginning of 1079, Gregory treated Amatus's authority as extending further north than Aquitaine.[162] In November 1079, Gregory instructed him to hold a council in Brittany at which he would thoroughly overhaul the penitential practice of the region and attend to other matters concerning the cure of souls.[163] Amatus's surviving correspondence with Archbishop Ralph of Tours shows that his authority covered that province. He claimed by papal disposition to have a duty of visiting Ralph's diocese and of making appropriate arrangements for the well-being of the church.[164] Amatus twice summoned Ralph and his suffragans to his council at Bordeaux in 1080; in his second letter, he called on Ralph to bring to justice two re-calcitrants who disobeyed the legate's orders—the simonical Abbot Gervasius of Saint-Savin (dioc. Poitiers) and a layman who had revoked his willingness to dissolve his uncanonical marriage.[165] Amatus was evidently concerned with disorders that Gregory himself was anxious to abate. Amatus and Hugh of Die even summoned bishops from Normandy to their council of Saintes and sought to impose sanctions for non-attendance.[166] In 1081, Gregory involved Amatus marginally in his final dealings with Archbishop Manasses of Rheims.[167]

Amatus's far-flung exercise of legatine authority in the provinces of Tours and Rouen cut across the primatial authority that Gregory VII in April 1079 vested in the archbishop of Lyons over the ancient region of Gallia Lugdunensis.[168] Gregory seems to have been oblivious to the conflict of jurisdictions to which Archbishop Gebuin of Lyons referred in a letter of 1080 to Archbishop Ralph of Tours and Bishop Eusebius of Angers. Gebuin said that when he had discussed the privileges of his see with Gregory at Rome, Gregory had made no ruling about Amatus; he had

---

[161] See Schieffer, *Die päpstlichen Legaten*, pp. 126–7.

[162] *RHGF* 14.671–2, nos. 8–9.

[163] *Reg.* 7.10, to the bishops and princes of Brittany, 25 Nov. 1079, pp. 471–2, *RHGF* 14.670, no. 6. There is no evidence that Amatus held a council in Brittany.

[164] 'Venientibus ergo nobis, omnipotente Domino annuente, vestro concilio qui auctoritatis simul et religionis ecclesiasticae caput honorabilius statis, indictio constituatur, quatenus causa Dei, sanctaeque ecclesiae status, ubi manet, confirmetur; ubi dolet, confortetur; ubi periit, restauretur': Bishop Amatus of Oloron to Archbishop Ralph of Tours, *RHGF* 14.670A.

[165] *RHGF* 14.669–70, nos. 5–7. The respect that Amatus thought to be due to a papal legate in the Touraine is illustrated by the *Narratio controversiae inter capitulum S. Martini Turonensis et Radulphum eiusdem urbis archiepiscopum*: *RHGF* 12.459–61. His instruction to Ralph of Tours to come to the council of Bordeaux (1080) 'with all the privileges of your church' suggests that Amatus used the prospect of the confirmation of papal privileges as an incentive for attendance: *RHGF* 14.671B, no. 6.

[166] *Reg.* 9.5, to Bishops Hugh of Die and Amatus of Oloron, (1081), pp. 579–80.

[167] *Reg.* 7.20, to Archbishop Manasses of Rheims, 17 Apr. 1080, pp. 495–6.

[168] *Reg.* 6.34–5, to Archbishop Gebuin of Lyons, and to the archbishops of Rouen, Tours, and Sens, 20 Apr. 1079, pp. 447–52; see below, 5.3.3.2.

only asked Gebuin to co-operate with Hugh of Die if he should hold a council in the provinces of the Lyons primacy. It was only by hearsay that Gebuin had learnt before leaving Rome that Amatus had been given legatine authority in the province of Tours.[169] In the face of this situation, there seems to have been circumspection all round. At the ensuing council of Bordeaux, business arising within Gebuin's sphere of influence seems to have been avoided. At Saintes in 1081, Amatus and Hugh of Die suspended from office the Norman bishops who failed to attend, but Gregory intervened to withdraw this sentence.[170] For the rest, apart from his participation in the council of Meaux, Amatus's activities seem to have been largely confined to the heartland of his legateship in south-west France, where such decisions as Gregory heard of met with his approval.[171] Amatus does not appear to have raised or pressed any major issues. It must have made for harmony when Hugh of Die acceded to the primacy of Lyons, thus placing it in the hands of someone with whom Amatus was familiar and sympathetic.

5.3.2.3 Abbot Hugh of Cluny

It will be apparent from Gregory's use of his principal legates in France, Hugh of Die/Lyons and Amatus of Oloron, that he seldom left them to work alone but normally required them to collaborate with at least one other legate. The figure whom Gregory employed most often apart from these two bishops was Abbot Hugh of Cluny. Most of the abbot's legatine or quasi-legatine responsibilities were intended to be exercised in conjunction with Hugh of Die; he seems never to have acted with Amatus of Oloron.[172] So far as Hugh of Die is concerned, Gregory seems to have been aware of a need to provide for a moderating influence: as Gregory himself assumed at Rome the role of a merciful reviser of such rigorous decisions as Hugh of Die made at his councils of Autun and Poitiers, so he employed Hugh to counterbalance the bishop's severity as he went about the pope's business in France.

From the earliest stage of his pontificate, it was in Gregory's mind to enlist Abbot Hugh's services. While Cardinal Gerald of Ostia was legate in France, his having been grand prior of Cluny combined with Gregory's wish for Cluny's intercessory and diplomatic help to lead Gregory to associate Abbot Hugh with Gerald in matters of legatine business. In 1074, Hugh was among the group of possible legates whom Gregory planned to employ in France.[173] Another was Hugh of Die, and in 1076 the two men were already acting together at Gregory's behest to advise politically and direct spiritually Count Simon of Crépy in his quarrel with King Philip of France and in his burgeoning vocation to monasticism.[174]

---

[169] *RHGF* 14.671–2, nos. 8–9. [170] *Reg.* 9.5.

[171] *Reg.* 9.30, to Cardinal Richard of Marseilles, (1082–3), p. 616/8–13; *Epp. vag.* no. 49, to Hugh and the other clerks of Sainte-Radegonde at Poitiers, (1082), pp. 118–19.

[172] The evidence strongly suggests that Abbot Hugh's presence at or after the council of Saintes in 1081 had no actual or virtual legatine character.

[173] *Reg.* 1.62, to Abbot Hugh of Cluny, 19 Mar. 1074, pp. 90–1, esp. p. 90/33–5; *Epp. vag.* no. 23, to Archbishop Ralph of Tours, (summer 1078), p. 60/11–15.

[174] *Vita beati Simonis com. Cresp.* cap. 3, cols. 1213C–1214A.

It was, however, with respect to Hugh of Die's dealings with Archbishop Manasses of Rheims that Gregory most urgently and persistently required Hugh of Die to work in association with Hugh of Cluny. In May 1077, Gregory instructed Hugh of Die to hold a council in France, if possible with the collaboration of Manasses and other French bishops. Gregory strongly urged his legate on his behalf to associate with himself Hugh of Cluny, especially because of his competence rightly and firmly to settle the problems of the see of Clermont, but also with a view to other business. Gregory paid tribute to the abbot's qualities:

We trust in the mercy of God and in his own manner of life that no one's pleadings, and no one's favour or friendship, and no manner of acceptance of persons, will avail to divert him from the path of righteousness.[175]

Hugh of Cluny did not, in fact, attend the councils of Autun or Poitiers to extend a restraining hand. Nevertheless, in 1078 and 1079, Gregory named the abbot as a legate in conjunction with Hugh of Die and on occasion with a third legate, in relation to Bishop Rainer of Orleans, to the see of Dol, and to Archbishop Ralph of Tours.[176] As relations between Hugh of Die and Manasses of Rheims grew more strained and Manasses's claims became more extravagant, Gregory became ever more concerned to use Hugh of Cluny as a moderating influence upon both parties. When Hugh of Die went to Rome early in 1078, Gregory already reiterated that Hugh should associate Abbot Hugh with him in a further council which would consider the problems of Manasses of Rheims and other French bishops.[177] A few weeks earlier in his Lent synod, Gregory had also urged Manasses himself, as part of his rehabilitation after Hugh of Die's sentence at Autun, to seek purgation in France from the charges outstanding against him in the presence of Hugh of Die and Hugh of Cluny, 'quibus in his vicem nostram dedimus'. In August 1078, Gregory confirmed this recommendation in a letter to Manasses himself, while inviting the two Hughs to consider grievances that Manasses had expressed in a recent letter to Gregory.[178] A letter of self-justification that Manasses addressed to Hugh of Die late in 1079 included the claim that, at Rome in 1078, Gregory had conceded to him that he might be judged in France by Hugh of Cluny alone; because the summons that he received to the projected council at Troyes was made jointly by Hugh of Die and Hugh of Cluny, he and his entourage of clergy had been prepared to come. By a like token, Manasses would not come to Lyons, because the name of Hugh of Cluny did not appear in his summons.[179]

At the beginning of 1080, Gregory nevertheless strongly urged Manasses to attend the council of Lyons, where his freedom from guilt might be established, not

---

[175] *Reg.* 4.22, to Bishop Hugh of Die, 12 May 1077, p. 333/9–17.

[176] *Reg.* 5.20, to Bishop Rainer of Orleans, 24 Apr. 1078, pp. 383–4; 5.22, to the subdeacon Hubert and the monk Teuzo, 22 May 1078, pp. 385–6; *Epp. vag.* no. 37, to Archbishop Ralph of Tours, (1078–9), pp. 92–5.

[177] *Reg.* 5.22.

[178] *Reg.* 6.2–3, to Archbishop Manasses of Rheims, and to Bishop Hugh of Die and Abbot Hugh of Cluny, 22 Aug. 1078, pp. 391–6; cf. *RHGF* 14.611–12, no. 76.

[179] *RHGH* 14.782, 785BD, no. 9.

only by Hugh of Die but also by the legate Cardinal Peter of Albano and Abbot Hugh; Gregory hoped that they might attend, and so supply a moderating and counterbalancing weight if such were called for.[180] It is not known whether or not the cardinal and the abbot were present at the council of Lyons. However, in April when Gregory made a last attempt to persuade Manasses to purge himself by oath, he named the monastery of Cluny as well as la Chaise-Dieu as places to which Manasses might retreat for consideration, and Hugh of Cluny, if he were available, was a person before whom as well as before Hugh of Die Manasses might purge himself.[181] Almost to the last, Abbot Hugh was made out to be a potential agent of papal mercy and restoration.

In 1083, when Hugh of Die had been translated to Lyons and when Gregory was directing him towards Flemish affairs, Gregory continued to associate Hugh of Cluny with him in order to secure the acceptability of his legatine intervention. He described the two Hughs as jointly his legates when dealing with laymen who had brought violence to bear upon the suspended Bishop Lambert of Thérouanne. When he wrote to the archbishop about the calling of a synod to settle the affairs of the same diocese, he told the archbishop to act in concert with Hugh of Cluny, for the reason of diplomacy that Hugh of Lyons was mistrusted by the king of France. In an accompanying letter to Count Robert of Flanders, Gregory recognized that Hugh of Lyons was also mistrusted by the count; lest his mistrust should impede the discharge of necessary business, Gregory deemed it prudent to associate with the archbishop 'that grave and famous man (*gravem et illustrem virum*) the abbot of Cluny'.[182]

The consistent evidence of Gregory's letters from 1073 to 1083 is that he greatly valued Abbot Hugh of Cluny as a salutary check upon Hugh of Die/Lyons, both as a man of sober judgement who carried authority in French affairs, and as a man of mercy and reconciliation whose characteristic style of action was no less necessary than Hugh of Die/Lyons's zeal and rigour. Nevertheless, except in the early matter of Count Simon of Crépy, there is no firm evidence that the two Hughs ever in fact acted together to implement Gregory's directions. Given Gregory's repeated expressions of confidence in the abbot and the emphasis that Gregory laid upon the mercy and prudence for which the abbot stood, it is unlikely that the lack of actual collaboration was a result of Gregory's own purposes. While there is no specific evidence, it is likely that Hugh of Die skilfully avoided implementing Gregory's directions that he should work closely with the abbot. Differences of temperament and outlook, and also the ancient differences between the Burgundian bishops and the abbots of Cluny about Cluny's liberty, may have resulted in Hugh of Die's already showing something of the antipathy towards the abbot which became publicly manifest in the sequel to Gregory's death.[183]

[180] *Reg.* 7.12, to Archbishop Manasses of Rheims, 3 Jan. 1080, pp. 475–7.
[181] *Reg.* 7.20, to Archbishop Manasses of Rheims, 17 Apr. 1080, pp. 495–6.
[182] *Reg.* 9.31, to two laymen at Thérouanne, (1083), pp. 617–18; 9.33–4, to Archbishop Hugh of Lyons, and to Count Robert of Flanders, (1083), pp. 619–22.
[183] For relations between the two Hughs immediately after Gregory's death, see Cowdrey, *The Age of Abbot Desiderius*, pp. 187–8.

5.3.2.4 Other Legates in France

Throughout his pontificate, Gregory employed in France a number of other persons whom he described as 'legati'. They varied considerably in standing. Some were in the most official sense legates who, rather like the 'missi dominici' of Carolingian times, had recognized judicial and administrative roles *vice* the pope himself.[184] But these shaded off into papal emissaries of lower personal rank who, while commissioned by the pope and answerable to him, could also act in an ancilliary way to a papal vicar like Hugh of Die/Lyons. Apart from the three legates who have already been discussed, it is likely that almost all were, as the three leading figures were not, in some sense members of the Roman church itself.[185]

Some of Gregory's legates were humble clerks. The one most continuously used was the subdeacon Hubert, whom Gregory referred to as 'dilectus filius noster'.[186] Sometimes, Hubert travelled alone, particularly in and beyond the north-western parts of France; besides his many dealings in the Anglo-Norman lands, in 1076 he passed a sentence of excommunication upon Archdeacon Hubert of Thérouanne.[187] Like Hugh of Die, his serviceability did not prevent his receiving the occasional rebuke from Gregory, as when in 1079 Gregory reproved his delay in returning to Gregory at Rome.[188]

At other times, Hubert journeyed and acted in concert with other legates. When Gregory became pope in 1073, Hubert was travelling, probably in or beyond France, with an otherwise unknown deacon named Albert who was also a Roman clerk.[189] When Hugh of Die's legatine activities expanded in 1077, Gregory proposed that both should go to Brittany and establish the true situation about the see of Dol; a year later, Hubert was to report about it at a council which Hugh of Die and Hugh of Cluny would hold.[190] In 1078, Gregory committed the resolution of remaining doubts about the accession to office of Archbishop Ralph of Tours to Hubert who

---

[184] As envisaged by Gregory in *Dictatus papae* 4, *Reg.* 2.55a, p. 203/1–3.

[185] Archbishop Warmund of Vienne has been asserted to have acted as a papal legate in the province of Rheims during the later 1070s: Huyghebaert, 'Un légat de Grégoire VII'; but the evidence cited does not establish that he intervened as a legate. In a letter to Gregory, Archbishop Manasses of Rheims accused him to Gregory of claiming to be a legate although he was not one: *RHGF* 14.611B, no. 76. Warmund may have presumed upon the association with Hugh of Die that Gregory established in *Reg.* 4.16, to the clerks of Romans, 21 Mar. 1077, p. 321/10–19. In reply to Manasses, Gregory did not refer to Warmund as having legatine authority: *Reg.* 6.2–3, to Archbishop Manasses of Rheims and to Bishop Hugh of Die and Abbot Hugh of Cluny, 22 Aug. 1078, pp. 394/1–13, 395/5–14.

[186] *Epp. vag.* pp. 60/19, 90/4.

[187] *Reg.* 4.10, to Countess Adela of Flanders, 10 Nov. 1076, p. 309; 7.16, to Bishop Hubert of Thérouanne, 26 Mar. 1080, pp. 489–91.

[188] *Reg.* 7.1, to the subdeacon Hubert, 23 Sept. 1079, pp. 458/29–459/7.

[189] *Reg.* 1.8, to the clerk Hubert and the deacon Albert, 30 Apr. 1073, pp. 12–13; that both were clerks of the Roman church is established by the phrase '. . . sancto PETRO, cuius filii et legati estis': p. 13/10–11. For Hubert's presence in England in 1072, see *Councils and Synods*, 1/2, pp. 601–4, no. 91/III; Hubert is likely to have been still engaged upon business in the Anglo-Norman region with which Pope Alexander II had entrusted him.

[190] *Reg.* 4.17, to King William I of England, 31 Mar. 1077, pp. 322–3; 5.22, to the subdeacon Hubert and the monk Teuzo, 22 May 1078, pp. 385–6.

would act in concert with Hugh of Die and a clerk of Besançon named Wighard.[191] In conjunction with Bishop Hugh of Langres, Hubert also in 1078 pronounced a sentence of excommunication upon Count Robert of Flanders; Gregory considered it to have been passed *ultra vires* because they acted without the knowledge of either Gregory or his vicar Hugh of Die, who was to investigate the matter.[192] The incident reveals that a papal clerk like Hubert might be subject to the oversight of Hugh of Die as papal vicar.

Hubert sometimes also acted with another figure, Teuzo, whom Gregory also described as 'legatus noster',[193] he was a monk of an unknown monastery, and his evident closeness to Gregory suggests that he was from Rome. The two co-operated in business arising in Brittany and Normandy.[194] Teuzo was also present at Hugh of Die's councils of Autun and Poitiers. In his report to Gregory on the latter, Hugh described how Teuzo had nearly been lynched during the violence, and he described Teuzo as his 'most faithful fellow-labourer in the Lord' who would report to Gregory more fully on the business of the council.[195] Teuzo here appears as Hugh of Die's right-hand man and messenger. Like Hubert, Teuzo seems also to have acted in close dependence upon Hugh as Gregory's vicar. Another clerk of a similar stamp was the Roman subdeacon Roger who was to act with Hugh of Die and Hugh of Cluny in the matter of Bishop Rainer of Orleans.[196]

Gregory also employed in France Roman cardinals of higher rank and personal standing. One was the 'external' cardinal, Abbot Richard of Saint-Victor at Marseilles. By May 1078, he was already a cardinal-priest of unknown title and entrusted with legatine authority in Spain.[197] There is some indication that, when Amatus of Oloron's sphere of legatine activity was redefined, the abbots of Saint-Victor supplied the vacuum not only in Spain but also in parts of the south of France. Before Richard became abbot, Gregory's enhancement of Saint-Victor's standing by a monastic union with the Roman monastery of St Paul's-without-the-Walls was coupled with a plea for practical assistance. Gregory's association of Richard's brother and predecessor Abbot Bernard with Amatus of Oloron in dealing with the matrimonial position of Count Centullus of Béarn suggests that Gregory envisaged help in France as well as Spain.[198] In 1079, Gregory sent Richard to Spain as legate for a second time; at the time of his journey, the monks elected the cardinal to be their abbot.[199] While he was mainly concerned with Spanish affairs, there are signs that

---

[191] *Reg.* 5.17, 9 Mar. 1078, p. 380/14–27; *Epp. vag.* no. 23, to Archbishop Ralph of Tours, (summer 1078), pp. 60–3. The Wighard of the second letter may have been the *legatus Diensis episcopi* of *Reg.* p. 380/20.

[192] *Reg.* 6.7, to Bishop Hugh of Die, 25 Nov. 1078, pp. 407–8; *Epp. vag.* no. 24, to Bishop Hugh of Langres, (c.25 Nov. 1078), pp. 62–5; *Reg.* 7.1.

[193] *Reg.* p. 322/23.   [194] *Reg.* 4.17, 5.22, 7.1.   [195] *RHGF* 14.614D, 615D, 616A.

[196] *Reg.* 5.20, to Bishop Rainer of Orleans, 24 Apr. 1078, pp. 383–4.

[197] *Reg.* 5.21, to Abbot Hugh of Cluny, 7 May 1078, p. 384/22–7.

[198] *Reg.* 6.15, to the monks of Saint-Victor, 2 Jan. 1079, pp. 419–20, esp. p. 420/23–8; 6.20, to Count Centullus of Béarn, 25 Feb. 1079, pp. 431–2.

[199] *Reg.* 7.6, to King Alphonso VI of León–Castile, 15 Oct. 1079, pp. 465–7; 7.8, to Cardinal Richard of Saint-Victor, and to his monks, 2 Nov. 1079, pp. 468–70.

Gregory also directed him towards France. In 1081, when Gregory renewed the
privileges of Saint-Victor, he also entrusted to his care the important monasteries of
Saint-Pierre at Montmajeur and Nôtre-Dame at la Grasse.[200] In 1082, he referred
the case of an unnamed French count to a synod at which either of his legates, Hugh
of Die or Richard of Marseilles, might be present.[201] At about the same time, he
instructed Richard about the affairs of the house of regular canons of Saint-Sernin
at Toulouse.[202] Such references add some credibility to the chronicler Hugh of
Flavigny's statement that, in the years before his death, Gregory was concerned to
establish a number of what the chronicler called 'vicarii' in the Christian world;[203]
Richard may have inherited Amatus of Oloron's original sphere of activity on both
sides of the Pyrenees.

The greatest figure who came to France from Rome as a legate was Cardinal-
bishop Peter of Albano. He came on two occasions. In 1080, he came alone with a special commission to defend the liberty of Cluny against the claims of its neighbouring
bishops.[204] Four years later he came again from Salerno as a bearer of Gregory's last
encyclical; this time he was accompanied as legate by Prince Gisulf of Salerno, the
only layman whom Gregory ever so employed.[205] If, as is probable, the final letter in
the eighth book of Gregory's Register refers to this mission, their commission embraced the whole of Gallia, probably including not only France but also Germany
west of the Rhine.[206] Gregory began his letter with a succinct statement of his
legates' position in relation to himself. He then required them to collect the annual
payment of a penny from every French household that Charlemagne had supposedly
established.[207] A tangible result of Peter of Albano's mission was the donation to the
apostolic see of the county of Substantion and Melgueil as a papal fief.[208]

Gregory's legates in France do not lend themselves to easy classification, for with
regard to them as in much else Gregory's practice responded to changing circumstances and needs. Nevertheless, there is a broad distinction to be drawn between the
three major figures Hugh of Die, Amatus of Oloron, and Hugh of Cluny, all of whom
were Frenchmen holding local ecclesiastical office, on the one hand, and, on the
other, the Roman clergy and their associates of whatever rank. By and large, the first

---

[200] *QF* nos. 198–9, 201, pp. 229–32, 234–7; *Reg.* 9.6, to Cardinal Richard of Saint-Victor, (18 Apr.
1081), pp. 581–3; 9.29*a*, Count Bertrand of Arles to Gregory VII, (1081), pp. 614–15.

[201] *Reg.* 9.23, pp. 603–5.

[202] *Reg.* 9.30, to Cardinal Richard of Saint-Victor, pp. 615–17

[203] 'Deinde confirmavit vicem suam potestatemque ligandi et solvendi omnibus vicariis suis, sicut ipse
per orbem constituerat': 2, pp. 466/13–14.

[204] See Cowdrey, *The Cluniacs*, pp. 51–7, and id. 'Cardinal Peter of Albano's Legatine Journey'.

[205] Bernold, *Chron. a.* 1084, p. 441/34–9; Hugh of Flavigny, 2, p. 464; *Epp. vag.* no. 54, to all the faithful, pp. 128–35.

[206] Since the collecting points for the tax referred to in the letter were Aachen, as well as le Puy and
Saint-Gilles.

[207] 'Vobis commissa negotia non latent et iam vos ita acsi nostra, immo quia nostra ibi in vobis prae-
sentia est, cuncta digne peragite': *Reg.* 8.23, to Bishop Peter of Albano and Prince Gisulf of Salerno,
(?1084), pp. 565–7.

[208] See above, 5.2.2.

group served Gregory continuously throughout much of his pontificate, while (with the exception of Hubert) the second served him for an occasion or for shorter periods. But neither group is internally homogeneous; every legate had his distinctive manner of service. In the first group, even Hugh of Die and Amatus of Oloron disclose points of difference: Hugh on the whole showed continuity in his sphere of activity while that of Amatus was redefined; Amatus's legatine authority lacked the intensity of Hugh's, and Amatus held fewer councils upon his own unshared authority. Yet Hugh of Die and Amatus of Oloron had in common that they became legates at an early age, and that, upon appointment, they were bishops of insignificant dioceses, from which they were later promoted to archbishoprics. Both stand in contrast to Hugh of Cluny, who was older in years and the abbot of one of the greatest abbeys in Western Christendom. Gregory seems to have intended him to represent his own mercy and habitual show of moderation over against the zeal and impetuousness of Hugh of Die, in particular. The Roman clerks, and especially those who were humble subdeacons and deacons, provided Gregory with more amenable agents than bishops with their own authority and standing or the abbot of Cluny with his universal prestige and multifarious concerns. Moreover, the Roman clerks, especially in so far as they worked with the greater legates, could keep Gregory informed about these legates as about other French affairs.

Because Gregory's use of legates was flexible and unstereotyped, and because it developed in answer to circumstances and experience, it was well adapted to meeting the needs of the pope for local agents which Gregory set out when he initially commended Amatus of Oloron for service in Spain and southern France.[209]

5.3.3 Primates and Metropolitans

5.3.3.1 *Archbishop Manasses I of Rheims*

Gregory's purpose, which was intensified from 1077, of making the apostolic see as it were universally present in France by the dispatch of legates inevitably led to difficulties with the prelates in France who claimed primatial or metropolitan standing. It should not be presumed that Gregory had a set purpose of undermining their authority or of denying them a standing of their own. On the contrary, so long as they were obedient to papal directions when given and so long as they furthered papal aspirations for the church, Gregory sought to clarify, uphold, and even increase their authority as part of the traditional framework of the church. As in other respects, Gregory was willing to encourage as well as to command, and to treat mildly and with forbearance even the recalcitrant, if he saw hope of winning them even imperfectly for his purposes. It was not only towards King Philip I of France that Gregory was, for most of the time, restrained and patient.

Of no one are these considerations truer than of Archbishop Manasses I of Rheims (*c.*1069–80), who presented Gregory with the most prolonged, severe, and

[209] *Epp. vag.* no. 21, pp. 56–9.

intractable problems that he encountered among the archbishops of France.[210]
Relations between the two men began with some cordiality and, until a very late date,
continued to be governed by moderation on Gregory's part. Manasses was one of the
select few who are named in Gregory's Register as receiving individual notice of his
election to the papacy, with an accompanying request for moral and practical help in
bearing the burden of the papal office.[211] Gregory's letter to Manasses is not
recorded in full, but his concluding words to Archbishop Guibert of Ravenna are
likely to indicate his message to another powerful metropolitan:

> Do not doubt our desire to join the Roman church with that over which you, by God's grace,
> preside in such concord ('concordia') and, in so far as we may be able having regard to the com-
> mon dignity of us both ('cum communi utriusque honore') with such universal love ('omni-
> moda caritate'), that in our souls the bond of peace and the fulness of love ('coniuncta pax et
> plena dilectio') may ever be combined.

To perpetuate such a bond, messengers communicating mutual gladness and consolation should often pass between pope and metropolitan.[212]

Gregory meant such words to be taken seriously as defining his relationship with
metropolitans whose wearing of the *pallium* and obligation frequently to come to
Rome embodied a participation in the apostolic office which was no less well founded
than the participation of papal legates. As in other aspects of papal activity, Gregory
laid weight upon a seeking of concord which would issue in peace and love. As a matter of mutual concern, the possibly conflicting dignity ('honor') of both pope and
metropolitan must be duly safeguarded on both sides. But the matter of central concern was not any structure of ecclesiastical offices but a personal complex of human
relationships. In the interests of peace and concord among men and the restoration
of fractured harmony, the strict demands of justice might be tempered or even set
aside. Dangerous issues might not be pressed; when they emerged, both sides might
be reluctant to produce situations of crisis or to engage in decisive action.

In the case of Manasses of Rheims, it was not until the second half of 1077 that serious difficulties began to be manifest. Soon after Gregory became pope, Manasses's
oppression of the abbey of Saint-Remi at Rheims provoked exchanges between pope
and archbishop the interpretation of which must not be prejudiced by later events.[213]
They exhibit Gregory as being anxious both to deal resolutely with the monks' complaints against their archbishop and to restore sound canonical and human relationships all round.

Abbot Herimar of Saint-Remi had died in December 1071, since when Manasses
sought to keep the abbey vacant and to enjoy the free disposal of its property. Many
verbal and written communications had passed in both directions between the apostolic see and the archbishop and the monks. In June 1073, Gregory sought to bring

---

[210] The basic account of Gregory's dealings remains that of Fliche, *Le Règne de Philippe*, pp. 417–22;
but his account should be read in the light of Robinson, '*Periculosus homo*', esp. pp. 125–7, and id. 'The
Friendship Network', esp. pp. 16–18.

[211] *Reg.* 1.4, cf. 1.1–3, pp. 3–7.   [212] *Reg.* 1.3, p. 6/19–27.

[213] On the events of 1073–4, see *Die Briefe des Abtes Walo*, pp. 22–6, together with pp. 51–71, nos. 1–5.

matters to a head. He called upon Manasses to promote the canonical election of a new abbot and to desist from harassing the persons and the goods of the monks, on pain of provoking papal severity and wrath. Gregory dispatched his letter and the monks of Saint-Remi who carried it by way of Cluny; he required Abbot Hugh to give the monks refuge, and to forward the letter by a suitable messenger who was to report back to Gregory about Manasses's response.[214]

At an unknown date but probably soon after receiving Gregory's letter, Manasses gave the abbey into the charge of Abbot Walo of St Arnulf at Metz, who had lately written to Gregory in warm congratulation upon his election to the papacy. No doubt Manasses sought thereby to win favour with Gregory. But it was not long before Manasses and Walo were at loggerheads.[215] Their antagonism was bitter and protracted. Walo presented himself before Gregory at his Lent synod of 1074, to which a letter from Manasses (now lost) was also publicly read. Gregory sought to be conciliatory to all parties. He allowed Walo the choice of keeping or of resigning the abbacy of Saint-Remi; whatever Walo did, Manasses was to provide for the future of the abbey only with his agreement and advice. At the end of the synod, Gregory also wrote to Manasses. He did so in terms of warm friendship and favour; he reminded Manasses that he had so strongly promoted his candidature for the archbishopric that his own reputation as pope was at stake in whatever Manasses might do.[216] Gregory declared himself to be relieved that Manasses had preferred so religious a figure as Walo to the abbacy of Saint-Remi, but he recognized that Walo might find it difficult to rule two houses. If so, Manasses should, indeed, collaborate with him in electing a new abbot at Rheims according to the Rule of St Benedict. Gregory also wrote to Walo's Lotharingian bishop, Hermann of Metz, who had sent him a letter. Gregory made clear his expectation that Walo would return to Metz, but only after he had assisted in the election of his successor at Rheims.

Unfortunately for Gregory's attempt during his Lent synod to secure all-round conciliation and justice, Abbot Walo frustrated it by finally deciding after he had embarked upon his journey northwards that he could not bear even to look once more upon the face of Archbishop Manasses.[217] He therefore returned to Metz leaving Gregory's business unfinished. It was thus not by Manasses's action that Gregory's plans failed to mature, while Walo's letters show that his bitter vendetta with Manasses continued unabated.

The scanty evidence that survives shows that, from his side, Gregory persisted throughout 1074 in a critical recognition of Manasses's standing and rights as metropolitan of the province of Rheims, and that Manasses responded with a measure of co-operation. During the acute stage in the last months of 1074 of Gregory's hostility

[214] *Reg.* 1.13–14, to Archbishop Manasses of Rheims, and to Abbot Hugh of Cluny, 30 June 1073, pp. 21–3.

[215] *Reg.* 1.52–3, to Archbishop Manasses of Rheims, and to Bishop Hermann of Metz, 14 Mar. 1074, pp. 78–81; *Die Briefe des Abtes Walo*, nos. 1–4, pp. 51–67.

[216] Cf. Manasses's reminders to Gregory of his part in his becoming archbishop: *H* no. 107, pp. 179/16–21, 180/22–181/3.

[217] *Die Briefe des Abtes Walo*, no. 2, p. 60/6–10.

to King Philip I of France, Gregory addressed Manasses first among the northern French archbishops and bishops upon whom he called to convene a national council and to impose upon the king whatever sanctions might be necessary.[218] In due course he wrote to Manasses individually, beginning his letter with a reminder of Manasses's debt to the Roman church and to himself and with a veiled complaint that Manasses had not visited Rome. Gregory hoped that the king had mended his ways; if not, Gregory reiterated his purpose of taking drastic action. He looked for Manasses's collaboration with himself and with his legates:

If our legates, as we expect, come to your parts to act with you and with your help in these matters [the position of the king] and many others about which you have written to us [in a lost letter], you should receive them for St Peter's sake and love them for our own; thus, you will be able to prove in these matters, too, with how great love you cleave to the prince of the apostles and to us.[219]

Gregory clearly continued to envisage Manasses as someone who was at least potentially amenable to papal purposes and who might prove willing to work harmoniously with the pope and with his legates. Early in 1075, Gregory continued in much the same strain. He rebuked Manasses for negligence in not responding to the complaints of the clergy of Châlons-sur-Marne against their bishop, Roger III, but sought to work through Manasses as metropolitan as well as through his legates in order to apply sanctions. Gregory also commissioned Manasses to compel his allegedly simoniacal suffragan, Bishop Radbod of Noyon, to submit a dispute with Bishop William of Utrecht to Manasses's own synodal jurisdiction.[220] Again, Gregory showed his preparedness to act through Manasses as metropolitan of his province.

Unfortunately, a two-year gap follows in the evidence for Gregory's dealings with Manasses; in part, Gregory's preoccupation with German affairs may account for this. The next item in the Register which concerns Manasses is Gregory's lengthy letter of 25 March 1077 to Bishop Josfred of Paris in which Manasses was alleged to have behaved in several matters with undue severity.[221] Gregory reacted to complaints brought to Rome by Manasses's subjects. They included two monks of Saint-Remi at Rheims, who alleged that a lately appointed abbot, Henry of Homblières, had been imposed upon their community simoniacally and uncanonically. Henry had been introduced in the vacuum left by Abbot Walo of Metz's failure to play the role which Gregory had assigned to him. Although Gregory referred in his letter to a possibility that Manasses had improperly impeded the monks in their right of appeal to the apostolic see, he reacted cautiously. He merely hinted at the possibility of an overall investigation of the grievances against Manasses ('. . . de his et de multis aliis aptioris loci et temporis opportunitatem conveniendi eum Deo auxiliante

---

[218] *Reg.* 2.5, to the archbishops and bishops of France, 10 Sept. 1074, pp. 129–33; see above, 5.2.1.
[219] *Reg.* 2.32, to Archbishop Manasses of Rheims, 8 Dec. 1074, pp. 168–9.
[220] *Reg.* 2.56, to Archbishop Manasses, 4 Mar. 1075, pp. 209–10; 2.58, to Archbishop Manasses, 5 Mar. 1075, pp. 211–12.
[221] *Reg.* 4.20; see above, 5.3.2.1.

prestolantes'); he prescribed, in the meantime, a complex process of investigation, culminating in a possible hearing at Rome in November, of the question of whether Archbishop Manasses or Abbot Henry was, indeed, culpable. His only immediate requirement of Manasses was that he should release the two monks from the sentence that he had passed upon them.[222]

The development of Hugh of Die's legatine authority in France during 1077 inevitably led to a conflict with Manasses's claims for the traditional authority of his see as the archbishop regarded it. Gregory himself probably intended no frontal challenge, nor did he in 1077 or at any other time countenance the charges of simony and of scandal in his private life that Manasses's adversaries sought to establish against him.[223] When, in May 1077, Gregory built upon his intention of initiating measures in France, he did so by providing that Hugh of Die should act collaboratively with Manasses of Rheims and his comprovincial bishops with respect to the election and consecration of Bishop Gerard of Cambrai and, by implication, with other business;[224] he did not set his legate to oppose them.

Nevertheless, the legate was soon engaged in conflict with the archbishop. Hugh of Die's eventual written report to Gregory upon the council that he held at Autun, outside the province of Rheims, is important not only for its reference to the sanction of excommunication that Hugh passed against Manasses who failed to attend, but also for showing that for some time past Hugh had established links with a circle at Rheims, centred upon some of its cathedral clergy, of men who were bitterly hostile to the archbishop. Its leader was another Manasses, now provost of the cathedral, who would be archbishop of Rheims from 1096 to 1106. Hugh also named Bruno, *scholasticus* and then chancellor of the cathedral, who in 1084 founded la Grande Chartreuse. Hugh described the provost Manasses as his 'friend in Christ', also disclosing that, at his council of Clermont in 1076, he had restored him to his office which he had surrendered because he had come by it simoniacally. Hugh commended Manasses and Bruno to Gregory as men who had suffered for the name of Christ and who would be his ready collaborators. Hugh was evidently concerned to marshal support amongst the senior clergy of Rheims against an archbishop whom he dubbed 'the heretic of Rheims'.[225]

Soon after the council of Autun, Archbishop Manasses, too, wrote to Gregory with his account of events.[226] A surprising feature of his letter of self-justification is the restraint of his references to Hugh of Die. He spoke respectfully of him, but presented him as the catspaw of his own kinsman Bishop Hugh of Langres who was the legate's *consiliarius* and *magister*. About the bishop of Langres, Archbishop Manasses was anything but restrained. He accused the bishop of universal notoriety in respect of sexual promiscuity, not only with young women but, by innuendo, with young

---

[222] *Reg.* 4.20, pp. 327/26–328/21.

[223] For accusations of simony, see Hugh of Flavigny, 2, p. 415/42–4; Guibert de Nogent, *Autobiogr.* 1.11, pp. 62–7. For allegations of sexual misconduct, see *Die Briefe des Abtes Walo*, no. 3, p. 62/20–4.

[224] *Reg.* 4.22, to Bishop Hugh of Die, 12 May 1077, pp. 330–4.

[225] *RHGF* 14.613–14, no. 79.

[226] *H* no. 107, pp. 178–82.

men as well. He it was who, at Autun, orchestrated a conspiracy of the archbishop's enemies against him. He clearly intended the same group as Hugh of Die commended to Gregory as his friends. He added the name of Bishop Helinand of Laon, whose preferment to the see of Rheims Manasses reminded Gregory that he had himself prevented when, in 1069, he put forward Manasses himself.[227] He also added the name of Count Ebolus of Roucy whom he delated as a persistent ravager of the goods and lands of the see of Rheims. But, once again, the leader was the provost Manasses, who was a kinsman of Count Ebolus. The archbishop castigated him as a vile buffoon ('vilissimus scurra') whose offences included incest with his sister, a nun and abbess. Archbishop Manasses claimed that he had sent a sufficient excuse for his non-attendance through his archdeacon: he had himself stood in dread of being seized by his enemies; correspondence with Gregory himself led him to look forward to meeting the pope face to face during his travels; his suffragans had been well represented at Autun; in any case, he had not been summoned to Autun to answer for any offence. He therefore appealed to Gregory against both his own excommunication and the derogation of his rights as metropolitan when the bishops of Die and Langres (neither of them, it should be remembered, bishops of his province) consecrated Bishop Gerard of Cambrai. For good measure, he hinted that Gerard had promised simoniacal gifts to Bishop Hugh of Langres. Manasses ended by protesting the service and loyalty to Gregory of the French bishops, whom he distanced from Gregory's *bêtes noires*, their Lombard brethren:

So, most reverend father, I beseech your clemency to deliver us from this levity and pride. We are not Lombards ('Langobardi non sumus'); we always bow our necks to your jurisdiction like loyal men and servants ('ut fideles et servi'). Allow us to appear in your presence and, meanwhile, until we come to you, permit me to be free from such an excommunication as is unheard-of in our times. May your holiness prosper, most reverend father.

According to a later account of events which Manasses addressed to Hugh of Die, he soon afterwards appealed at Rome in person against Hugh's sentence at Autun.[228] He must have arrived some days before Christmas 1077. His absence in Rome must have precluded his attendance at Hugh of Die's council at Poitiers in mid-January 1078.[229] Manasses claimed that both he and Gregory expected Hugh to appear in Rome, as indeed he did later in the spring; at Gregory's command, Manasses awaited his coming for some eleven weeks. Thus, at the Lent synod of 27 February to 3 March, Manasses was able, a little artificially, to claim the moral high ground. Reversing the situation as Manasses had described it to Gregory in his letter, Manasses was now present in person while Hugh was represented by his clerks. After a sharp debate in the synod, it was agreed that Hugh had acted rashly and excessively at Autun. Manasses pleaded that he should never again be subjected to Hugh's justice; Gregory allowed that, if need arose, he should appear before Hugh of Cluny. In

---

[227]	For Helinand, see Guibert de Nogent, *Autobiog.* 3.2, pp. 270–3.
[228]	Manasses of Rheims to Hugh of Die, *RHGF* 14.782A–C. The letter dates from late 1079.
[229]	Hugh of Flavigny, 2, p. 418/16–18.

return for this concession, Gregory required Manasses to promise attendance at a council held in France ('in partibus Galliarum') if he were summoned by a papal legate or by papal letters.

Gregory's own memorandum of his dealings with Manasses and other French bishops during the synod is broadly in line with this account.[230] He was far from treating them like Lombards. He studiously relaxed his legate's severity by following what he said was Roman custom in tolerating or even disregarding some matters, and by using the restraint of prudence rather than the severity of the church's law. He restored Manasses to the exercise of his office and order, subject to his swearing an oath over the body of St Peter that it was not from pride that he had disregarded Hugh of Die's summonses to his synods; as Manasses later told Hugh of Die, he was to promise obedience for the future to papal summonses, even though they involved appearing before a legate. Moreover, Manasses had to swear to be a good custodian of the lands and goods of the church of Rheims.

The oath which Gregory prescribed for Manasses to take showed by implication wherein he perceived the archbishop's weaknesses to lie, and therefore the kind of matters that might still require rectification before a legate: they were not in the areas of simony or sexual laxity, but had to do with a personal pride that might lead him to disregard or to disobey incongenial papal requirements whether communicated directly or through a legate, and with a material rapacity that placed at risk the lands and treasure of the see of Rheims. Gregory seems to have been confident that Manasses's oath would guarantee his future good conduct. But a dangerous ambiguity remained. Using a set formula, Manasses swore in certain circumstances to appear before the pope's legate ('ante legatum suum').[231] Manasses therefore claimed that he need appear only before Abbot Hugh of Cluny, whereas Gregory had certainly intended no such restriction. Gregory was soon envisaging a further French council at which Hugh of Die would collaborate with Hugh of Cluny harmoniously to settle a range of matters relating both to Manasses and to other French bishops.[232] It would foster the peace and concord that Gregory sought in public affairs. But he expected that in all business, including that concerning Archbishop Manasses of Rheims, the two legates would act together.

The ambiguity latent in Gregory's ruling at Rome about Manasses came into the open during the summer of 1078, when the long period of dialogue began which led to Manasses's deposition in December 1080. Manasses approached Gregory by letter about a miscellany of matters with regard to which he sought direct papal support.[233] He opened and closed his letter by reminding Gregory of his recent serviceability to him in connection with Countess Matilda of Tuscany's interests in

[230] *Reg.* 5.17, 9 Mar. 1078, pp. 378/25–379/15.

[231] For the text of the oath, see *Reg.* p. 379/5–15.

[232] *Reg.* 5.22–3, to the subdeacon Hubert and the monk Teuzo, and to the counts of Brittany, 22 May 1078, pp. 385–8.

[233] *RHGF* 14.611–12, no. 76. The range of possible dates is between Manasses's return from Verdun after Pentecost (27 May) 1078: p. 611B, and Gregory's letters in response: *Reg.* 6.2–3, to Archbishop Manasses, and to Bishop Hugh of Die and Abbot Hugh of Cluny, 22 Aug. 1078, pp. 391–6.

Lorraine.[234] At Gregory's own prompting, he had himself restored to the countess all the lands that her late husband, Duke Godfrey of Lorraine, had held of him. He promised to help with their future defence and to do whatever the countess requested to oppose her rivals in Lorraine, Duke Godfrey of Bouillon and Count Arnulf of Chigny. At Pentecost 1078, he had travelled to Verdun and confirmed these arrangements with Bishop Thierry who was attending to the countess's interests. Moreover, Manasses had recently been willing to dispatch to Rome, in company with Bishop Josfred of Paris, some knights whom Gregory had besought; but upon receiving a further request from Gregory, Manasses had diverted them to protect Countess Matilda's interests in Lorraine.

This record of recent service enabled Manasses stoutly to protest his loyalty to Gregory ('ego fidelis vester et per omnia ecclesiae iura vobis obedire paratus'). He instanced two grievances of his own which Gregory should himself correct. First, falsely pretending to be a papal legate, Archbishop Warmund of Vienne had intervened in the province of Rheims to depose priests and to restore them to office. Second, while Manasses had been at Rome with Gregory, two of his suffragans, the detested Helinand of Laon with Theobald of Soissons, had consecrated Bishop Ralph of Amiens who, Manasses did not neglect to add, had received the gift of the episcopate from a layman (he meant from the king), in defiance of Gregory's own decree against lay investiture which Hugh of Die had promulgated at Autun.[235]

Manasses then broached, although in brief and almost cryptic language, the most important topic in his letter. He asked Gregory to uphold the privileges of his see as they had been granted by earlier popes to earlier archbishops,[236] and therefore what he also called the *privilegium* that Gregory had conferred at Rome—that, whether he was formally accused of an offence or not, he should answer either to the pope himself or to his legates who were clerks of the local Roman church, but not to legates who were corrupt men and who held offices on the north side of the Alps.[237] Such men had behaved shamefully towards him; he therefore also asked Gregory that he, who could himself by right summon the bishops of all France, should be permitted recourse to Gregory alone and should be exempt from all kinds of legatine summons until next Easter (1079), when he would again visit Gregory. In addition, he must himself in his capacity as archbishop now investigate many wrongs that had occurred during his recent stay at Rome. Should complaints come to Gregory about these investigations, he urged Gregory to delay consideration until both he and the pope were together at Rome. Manasses clearly sought to evade any intervention by Hugh

---

[234] For the background, see Meyer von Knonau, 2.656–7; Erkens, *Die Trierer Kirchenprovinz*, pp. 27–33. For the Matildine lands in Lorraine see Overmann, *Gräfin Mathilde von Tuscien*, pp. 37–9, 146, 193–210.

[235] Neither Manasses nor Gregory referred to a third consecrator.

[236] Manasses perhaps had in mind Pope Hadrian I's privilege of *c.*775: Flodoard, *Hist. Rem. eccles*, 2.17, p. 463. For local tradition at Rheims, see Sot, 'Le Mythe'.

[237] Strictly interpreted, Manasses's letter excluded Hugh of Cluny as well as Hugh of Die from acting as a papal legate in business relating to Manasses. But his animus arose from Hugh of Die's sentence at Autun: cf. *RHGF*, 14.4782A.

of Die; such complaints were not to be the business of French episcopal legates such as he.

His main request being thus made, Manasses turned to his own local enemies at Rheims. Count Ebolus of Roucy had recently been to Rome where he had protested loyalty to Gregory; Provost Manasses had not been to Rome but, in concert with Ebolus, he did not cease to ravage the church and destroy local peace. Archbishop Manasses asked Gregory to act firmly against both of them. A final grievance which Manasses put to Gregory was that Hugh of Die had suspended at his council of Poitiers his suffragan, the aged Bishop Drogo of Thérouanne;[238] Manasses urged Gregory to restore the bishop to office in view of his closeness to death.

Gregory was not deceived by the tendentiousness of Manasses's letter. He was aware that the plea for business to be settled by himself at Rome was an attempt at evasion: 'indutias querit ut superfugiat'.[239] Manasses wanted no truck with legates and especially with Hugh of Die. He was asking Gregory to dispense in his case with the help of such legates as Gregory had declared it to be needful for the pope to employ.[240] Gregory nevertheless began his letter to Manasses amicably. Manasses might confidently request of the apostolic see whatever was genuinely needful for his office and consonant with sound tradition. Gregory said that he was well disposed to Manasses both from brotherly love and because of the pleas of his own supporters who also commended Manasses to him—Gregory perhaps meant Countess Matilda and her Lotharingian adherents. But Manasses must understand that, for the good of the whole church, Gregory could not at present accede to his wishes.

Gregory seized at once upon Manasses's request that he be deemed answerable only to Gregory himself and to his legates who were native Romans whenever his archiepiscopal actions were called in question. He rejected Manasses's claim to be subject only to such papal legates as were born or educated at Rome or who were clerks of the Roman church in a local sense. This was a gross infringement of the rights of the Roman church which a wealth of historical examples warranted; Manasses had no grounds for pleading that his was a special case. Nor could Gregory accept a limit upon the pope's sovereign right to vary privileges granted to other churches. The rights of the church of Rheims were, indeed, negotiable at a proper time in face-to-face consultation between Manasses and Gregory. But meanwhile, Gregory reiterated the position which he said was established at Rome during the last Lent synod, that matters involving Manasses were to be settled by Hugh of Die and Hugh of Cluny acting jointly on the pope's behalf. Gregory therefore summarily referred all the requests in Manasses's letter for settlement by the two legates; he included that concerning Provost Manasses and Count Ebolus of Roucy, although he seems to have accepted at face value the archbishop's submission that they were acting with illicit violence against himself and his church. Gregory ended his accompanying letter to his legates by urging them to foster all-round reconciliation: 'Act manfully and wisely and let all your deeds be in charity (cf. 1 Cor. 16: 13–14), so that

---

[238] *RHGF* 14.616AB, no. 80.   [239] *Reg.* 6.3, p. 395/29–31.
[240] See his letter about the legatine mission of Bishop Amatus of Oloron: *Epp. vag.* no. 21, pp. 57–9.

oppressors may find you prudent in defence and the oppressed may acknowledge you to be lovers of righteousness.'[241]

Manasses was not inactive in his own province; no doubt he wished to show all concerned that the French church could operate responsibly upon its own terms. In April 1079, he held a council at Soissons which was attended by at least seven other bishops of his province. The choice of Soissons showed that Bishop Theobald was restored to obedience, while a provincial council would provide an opportunity for dealing with the grievances to which Manasses had referred in his letter to Gregory.[242] But he also came under pressure to attend a council that Hugh of Die planned to hold, first unsuccessfully at Troyes in the late summer or early autumn of 1079,[243] and then in fact at Lyons in January/February 1080. A major source for these events is a very long and repetitive letter that Manasses sent to Hugh in early January 1080 to justify his refusal of the legate's summons to Lyons.[244] Manasses stood by his contention that, at Rome in Lent 1078, Gregory had conceded that, during councils held in France, whereas Hugh of Die should decide the cases of other men, Hugh of Cluny alone should pass judgement upon him. Manasses had obeyed his summons to Troyes where he had gone with a posse of abbots, clerks, and knights, because it had been issued in the names of both Hugh of Die and Hugh of Cluny. Having travelled to Troyes, he was given no proper explanation of the adjournment of the planned council, and he had fully discharged his duty by the fact of his having attended.

Gregory thought otherwise. When he heard that the council had not met, he charged Hugh of Die to hold a further council at which a major item of business would be a careful examination of the case of Manasses. Gregory had evidently now been more deeply impressed than ever before by the accusations that were outstanding against him. He did not specify what they were, but they are likely to have included the plundering of church lands and treasures at Rheims of which he was accused from start to finish of Gregory's dealings with him.[245] Gregory was also giving more credence than before to the allegations of Provost Manasses and his friends.[246] He made no mention of Abbot Hugh of Cluny, probably because Cluny's dispute with its neighbouring bishops was *sub judice*.[247] If the case against Manasses were judicially proven, Hugh of Die was to pass strict sentence; Gregory showed no sign of acknowledging the restriction that Manasses claimed. Even if the case were not established, Gregory now regarded his ill-repute in France and Italy to be such that he must purge himself by the supporting oaths of six other bishops. If he could

---

[241] *Reg.* 6.3, pp. 395/32–396/2.

[242] Mansi, 20.501–4; Hefele–Leclercq, 5. 248; *Recueil des actes de Philippe Ier*, no. 94, pp. 242–5.

[243] The date is uncertain. On 28 June, Gregory referred to a council to be held *proxime*: *Reg.* 6.40, p. 458/2–6. Time must be allowed for news of its non-occurrence to have reached Gregory at Rome, for Gregory to have further instructed Hugh of Die, and for Hugh to have arranged the council of Lyons.

[244] *RHGF* 14.781–6, no. 9. The letter was written after news of an event on 24 Dec. 1079, probably near Chiny in Lower Lorraine, reached Manasses.

[245] *Reg.* 1.13, p. 21/32–7, 7.20, p. 496/14–16, 20–3, 8.17, p. 538–9.

[246] *RHGF* 14.783A.   [247] See above, 5.3.2.4.

thus purge himself, he might remain peacefully in the possession of his church and dignity.[248]

In his letter to Hugh of Die, Manasses in due course offered three 'canonical excuses', as he called them, why he need not appear at the council of Lyons which Hugh of Die proceeded to convene. First, the summons made no mention of Hugh of Cluny. Second, even if it had done so, Manasses need not answer at Lyons, which was outside the kingdom of France. Third, conditions of warfare made the journey from Rheims to Lyons impracticably hazardous. Manasses went on to complain that, in the course of three weeks, he had received two very different letters of summons to Lyons. The first required him to answer the accusations of Provost Manasses and his party. But Manasses claimed that he and his namesake had already made their peace. It embraced all the archbishop's former foes at Rheims save two—Bruno who was a foreigner from Cologne, and one Pontius whose testimony had been discredited at the Lent synod of 1078. It is apparent that Hugh's second summons was written after he received Gregory's letter and that Hugh rehearsed its requirements. Manasses reiterated that he was faced by no credible accusers. As for the six bishops, there was insufficient time for him responsibly to recruit them from his far-flung province, even if there were six good men and true to be found. Alluding to Gregory's reproach that his ill-repute was well known in France and Italy, Manasses retorted that his good name had already been vindicated at the Lent synod of 1078.

Manasses also argued at length that having at this synod exempted him from Hugh of Die's judgement, Gregory could not without self-contradiction now make him subject to it. But he offered an olive branch. He offered to welcome Hugh of Die in the spring of 1080 to a council of the French kingdom at a place of the legate's choice—perhaps Rheims or Soissons or Compiègne or Senlis. There, with the collaboration of the French king, Manasses would help Hugh of Die by way of pacification to settle the affairs of the French church. 'It is better that, by acting more mildly and not exceeding justice, you should secure the advantage and honour of the Roman church throughout France than by exasperating France you should hinder its justice and subjection to the Roman church.' If, however, Hugh of Die should persist in his obstinacy ('pertinacia') and should arbitrarily suspend or excommunicate him, Manasses made a show of ancient papal and patristic citations to suggest that the power of the keys over the church would be destroyed:

I proclaim that, if you excommunicate me, the prerogative of St Peter and of the lord pope, that is the power of binding and loosing, will fail. . . . The prerogative of Peter does not stand, wherever judgement is not based upon his equity.

In this challenge to Hugh of Die about his legatine jurisdiction over him, Manasses threw down the gauntlet to Gregory's most cherished principles of papal authority. The issue was starkly posed: did or did not Petrine authority as exercised by the pope whether directly or through his legates prevail over the customs and distinctive loyalties of the church within the kingdom of France?

[248] *Epp. vag.* no. 30, pp. 76–9. The date should be emended to (1079, late summer or autumn).

A letter which Gregory wrote to Manasses on 3 January 1080, and therefore before he can have heard of the contents of Manasses's letter to Hugh of Die, shows that Manasses had, indeed, also written to Gregory.[249] The letter is lost, but from the points that Gregory took up it may be supposed that it included only some of the material deployed in his letter to Hugh of Die. Neither now or at any time did Gregory himself take up with Manasses the fundamental issues of papal versus regional authority that it posed; it is unthinkable that Gregory would have let them pass if Manasses had expressly put them to him. Instead, the focus remained upon the specific allegations of Manasses's local adversaries at Rheims and upon the scandal to which his supposed excesses there gave rise.

Gregory's letter studiously combined firmness with moderation. It opened with a rebuke, not for challenging papal authority, but for persisting for so long in bringing ill repute upon himself and his church and for evading judgement—Gregory again used the phrase 'iudicium subterfugere'—when he should have dispelled the cloud of suspicion from himself and from his church. It was to dispel it that Gregory still aimed. He reiterated from their correspondence of mid-1078 that Manasses could be allowed no privilege of being judged only by the pope in person. In reply to Manasses's latest letter, he said only that he should accept a legatine judgement, and he scouted Manasses's excuse that he could not travel to Lyons because of the dangers of the journey: Archbishop Gebuin of Lyons and Bishop Hugh of Langres would certainly make good provision for his security. Manasses should, therefore, go to Lyons in order to be cleared of his ill repute. To ease matters, Gregory hoped that this might be done, not only by Hugh of Die, but also by Cardinal Peter of Albano. This would have gone far to meet Manasses's wishes: he had already expressed preparedness to be judged by Hugh of Cluny, and Gregory commented that he could look to him for mercy as well as for justice; by implication, the involvement of Peter of Albano would meet Manasses's declared willingness to accept as legate a clerk of the Roman church, and here was a cardinal-bishop! If Manasses nevertheless did not go to Lyons, Gregory reserved the right to confirm whatever sentence his legates might pass upon him. He ended by urging Manasses to reflect that better justice was to be expected from them in a land ('patria') where plenty of suitable accusers and defenders would be to hand, than at Rome where they would be in short supply. If Manasses knew that he was guilty with regard to the particular accusations outstanding against him, let him cease his prevarications and free his soul by due penance. Gregory's underlying thought was that a sinner should be 'humiliatus ad paenitentiam' and thus restored by the grace of obedience.[250]

Manasses did not present himself at Lyons and Hugh of Die pronounced him deposed. At his Lent synod of 7 March, Gregory, as he was committed to doing, confirmed the sentence. A month later, Gregory wrote to inform Manasses of the confirmation.[251] He showed no anxiety to be rid of Manasses; on the contrary, even now his keynote was mercy—as he told Manasses, an excessive mercy beyond the

---

[249] *Reg.* 7.12, pp. 745–7.   [250] See esp. the language of *Reg.* 8.17, pp. 538/33–539/1.
[251] *Reg.* 7.20, 17 Apr. 1080, pp. 495–6, cf. 8.17, pp. 538–9.

custom of the Roman church. He prescribed for Manasses a course by which he might even yet ward off the sentence. He gave him until Michaelmas (29 September) still to purge himself by the oaths of six bishops; he gave as examples his suffragans Ursio of Soissons, Helinand of Laon, Gerard of Cambrai, and Roger of Châlons-sur-Marne, making it clear that such paragons of ecclesiastical virtue were not requisite as Manasses had alleged to be so in his letter to Hugh of Die.[252] Not without irony, Gregory conceded that Manasses need not be subject to the rigours of a journey to Rome; he might purge himself of his ill repute nearer home before Hugh of Die and Hugh of Cluny, or if the latter were unavailable, Amatus of Oloron. Despite talks that Gregory must have had with Hugh of Die, Gregory made no mention of deeper issues of Petrine authority in the church. He merely made three immediate conditions of a practical kind: he must fully restore the property of Provost Manasses, Bruno, and their associates who had accused him; he must himself keep away from Rheims until Ascensiontide (21 May); and under Hugh of Die's supervision as regards what chattels he took, he should make a spiritual retreat at Cluny or at la Chaise-Dieu. This was Manasses's final chance. If he disdained it, Gregory would make his deposition final and irrevocable.

Manasses made no use of his opportunity, but it was only at the very end of 1080 that Gregory finally rejected him.[253] He then rehearsed to the clergy and people of Rheims the stipulations that he had made in April; far from demonstrating obedience and humility by making a monastic retreat, Manasses had flouted Gregory's condition that he keep away from Rheims and had quickly returned to invade its church and to devastate its lands.[254] The clergy and people were to proceed to a canonical election which would be subject to the approval of Bishop Hugh of Die. Gregory asked Count Ebolus of Roucy, who had for so long pressed Gregory to take action against Manasses,[255] now to shun his 'pestifera amicitia' and to provide protection for a free election. He absolved the suffragans of Rheims from their obedience to Manasses. No doubt because Rheims was the place of royal coronations and because the loyalties of the French bishops were deeply bound up with the king, Gregory called on King Philip to withdraw his friendship from Manasses and to add his sanction to the free election of a new archbishop.

It was believed in the twelfth century that Manasses fled to King Henry IV in Germany;[256] in any case, he now vanished from history. It was not until 1083 that a new archbishop, Raynald I (1083–96), was elected;[257] after his death, the Provost Manasses who had led the opposition at Rheims to Manasses I reigned for ten years as Manasses II. Both these archbishops were willing and active collaborators with the popes of their day, Urban II and Paschal II. The change of ecclesiastical climate at

---

[252] *RHGF* 14.784A–C.

[253] *Reg.* 8.17–20, to the clergy and people of Rheims, to Count Ebolus of Roucy, to the suffragans of Rheims, and to King Philip I, 27 Dec. 1080, pp. 538–43.

[254] Cf. Guibert de Nogent, *Autobiog.* 1.11, p. 64.   [255] *RHGF*, 14.612A.

[256] Guibert de Nogent, *Autobiog.* 1.11, p. 64.

[257] Bishop Halinard of Laon's candidature for the see should be placed before, not after, the reign of Manasses I.

Rheims probably owed at least as much to Hugh of Die as to Pope Gregory VII. Gregory had been slow to break with Manasses I; he had expressed his difference with the archbishop mainly in terms of his local acts of violence and of the ill repute into which these actions brought him in the church at large. In Gregory's dealings with Manasses, the conflicting claims of papal and archiepiscopal authority were never sharply defined or even, perhaps, fully recognized. As between Hugh of Die and Manasses, they came to the centre of the picture; while Hugh was able to mobilize at Rheims, where Pope Leo IX's energetically organized council of 1049 was well remembered,[258] a group of clerks and laity which included such figures as the future Archbishop Manasses II and the future Prior Bruno of la Grande Chartreuse. Hugh of Die used them effectively to remove Manasses I despite Gregory's clinging to a hope of mercy and conciliation. Pope Urban II, himself a pupil of Bruno and a canon of Rheims until *c.*1067, inherited the loyalty of this party and achieved an agreement with the see of Rheims that always eluded Gregory.

5.3.3.2 *Primacies in France*

When writing to Gregory in 1078, Archbishop Manasses of Rheims referred to himself as having the right to convene the bishops of all France (. . . 'qui totius Galliae episcopos debeo convocare').[259] The claim to primacy at which Manasses thus hinted was one that Gregory never expressly discussed at length in surviving evidence; he neither acknowledged or denied it. However, when in 1074 he called upon the archbishops and bishops of northern France to resist King Philip, he first addressed Manasses of Rheims, thereby according him an undefined seniority.[260] In 1078, Manasses was seeking a clarification of the rights of Rheims, by a confirmation both of earlier papal privileges and of the archbishop's exemption from any judgement not given by a Roman pontiff or a clerk of the Roman church. Gregory was not prepared to settle the matter definitively, but he held out the possibility of future face-to-face talks if circumstances became favourable.[261] As an aspect of his mercy towards Manasses, Gregory never foreclosed upon the possibility of such talks. Given Manasses's recalcitrance, they did not take place; but it was no radical departure in papal policy when, in 1089, Pope Urban II's privilege for his former church of Rheims included a confirmation of Archbishop Raynald's primacy over the whole province of Belgica Secunda. More unexpectedly, Urban conceded to Raynald the right that Gregory had withheld from consideration with Manasses—that Raynald should owe subjection and obedience to no one save the Roman pontiff, and that judgement of causes relating to him should be settled by the Roman pontiff alone.[262]

On the one hand, Urban followed the usage of the popes of his day, already apparent when Amatus of Oloron's duties in France were stated in terms of the ancient province of Gallia Narbonensis, by defining Raynald's sphere of authority in terms of a province of Roman Gaul. There is no reason to suppose that, whatever he may

---

[258] See the testament of Provost Ulrich of Rheims (1075): *GC* 10, instr. no. 24, pp. 27–9.
[259] *RHGF* 14.611D.   [260] *Reg.* 2.5, p. 130/2–4.   [261] See above, 5.3.3.1.
[262] *Ep.* 27, *PL* 151.309–11; but cf. Hugh of Lyons's explanation to Bishop Lambert of Arras of the respective rights of primates and legates: *RHGF* 14.791–2, no. 14 (1094).

have made of Manasses's claim in respect of the 'totius Galliae episcopos', he would have declined to define Manasses's authority in terms of a primacy of Belgica Secunda if he had returned to his favour. On the other hand, Urban's acceptance of the archbishop of Rheims's right of direct access to papal justice in all cases went far beyond what it is likely that Gregory would ever have conceded. But it may be doubted whether, in 1078, Gregory knew anything of the traditions of Rheims, or whether there was any record of them in Roman archives; Urban will have known of them from his days as a canon of Rheims. An agreed statement of the primatial status of Rheims was possible only by way of compromise between a pope like Urban who had such knowledge and an archbishop like Raynald who was heir to Hugh of Die's success in recruiting a papal party amongst the clergy of the local church.

Gregory's confirmation in 1079 of the primacy of the church of Lyons over the province of Gallia Lugdunensis, that is over Lyons, Rouen, Tours, and Sens, in favour of Archbishop Gebuin of Lyons, was, by contrast, readily conceded to the archbishop.[263] It is commonly suggested that Gregory confirmed the primacy of Lyons in order to resist the claims for his see of Archbishop Manasses of Rheims, that he deliberately established a rival primacy to Rheims in a see outside the kingdom of France, that by investing Lyons with primatial status he conferred upon it a fresh honour, and that its primacy conferred only honour and not tangible authority. None of these statements can be established upon the basis of the evidence.

Gregory did not set out from the kind of political considerations that such statements imply. The documents relating to Lyons and Rheims disclose the guidelines that Gregory claimed to follow. First and foremost, as pope Gregory acknowledged a duty to establish and to implement the traditional rights and prerogatives of major sees as laid down by his papal predecessors and to confer them upon archbishops whose election was canonical and whose way of life was worthy.[264] Second, the humble and obedient service that subordinate metropolitans owed to a primate was to be discharged subject in all respects to the honour and authority of the apostolic see.[265] Third, the privileges claimed by a see should never hinder the proper working of the ecclesiastical structure but should promote the good of the church. Popes could, therefore, from time to time set up or dismantle papal vicariates like that once vested in Arles and likewise ecclesiastical primacies, by transferring authority from one see to another.[266] Fourth, the privileges of a see were specific to itself; in every case they must be established and interpreted in the light both of the records of its past and of the circumstances of the present time.[267] There was no overall model of a primacy.

---

[263] *Reg.* 6.34–6, to Archbishop Gebuin of Lyons, to the archbishops of Rouen, Tours, and Sens, and to the canons of Lyons, 20 Apr. 1079, pp. 447–53; for the date and recipient's text of 6.34, see *QF* no. 171, pp. 196–8. In all matters relating to primacies in France, I am indebted to Fuhrmann, 'Studien zur Geschichte mittelalterlicher Patriarchate' and to Villard, 'Primatie des Gaules', although I differ considerably from Villard's conclusions about the primacy of Lyons.

[264] *Reg.* 6.34, pp. 447/25–447/29.   [265] *Reg.* 6.34, pp. 448/29–449/6.
[266] *Reg.* 6.2, to Archbishop Manasses of Rheims, 22 Aug. 1078, p. 393/7–22.
[267] *Reg.* 6.2, p. 393/22–4.

Gregory's confirmation in 1079 of the primacy of Lyons is well documented.[268] His privilege was issued at the request of Archbishop Gebuin, who had come to Rome with some of his canons to request confirmation of the standing ('dignitas') that earlier popes had accorded to their church; however, no earlier popes were specified. In his covering letter to the archbishops of Rouen, Tours, and Sens, Gregory repeated that he had confirmed the decrees of earlier popes. He, too, cited no examples; Gebuin's subsequent testimony that Gregory toiled far into the night when preparing the privilege suggests that warrant for it had to be laboriously worked out.[269] Gregory ultimately copied verbatim two papal documents that provided, not historical precedents, but reasons why there should be a graduated church hierarchy that included primates, as part of a more extended hierarchy of angels and men. Within it, metropolitans should show to primates the humble reverence for which they looked in their own provincial bishops. As regards the principles of a Christian hierarchy, he excerpted a letter of Pope Gregory the Great to the bishops of Gaul about their duty to the papal vicar Bishop Vergilius of Arles.[270] About the place of primates, he turned to a Pseudo-Isidorian letter attributed to Pope Anacletus.[271] Gregory associated the canons of Lyons with their archbishop. They were to surrender into Gebuin's hands all offices and goods that they had come by simoniacally or in other wrongful ways. For the confirmation of the traditional pre-eminence of Lyons amongst the churches of France must henceforth be matched by its being a pattern of religion. By pre-eminence, Gregory had in mind the intrinsic privileges of the church of Lyons; there is no hint of the comparative rank of Lyons with other churches or of an attempt to confront the claims of Rheims or of any other see.

It is, moreover, clear that in the mid-1070s the primacy of Lyons was already acknowledged even in distant parts of Gallia Lugdunensis. In 1076, while Gebuin's predecessor Humbert was still in office, documents in a cartulary from Marmoutier tell how its abbot was in contention with the abbot of Saint-Pierre de la Couture, both houses being in Maine, over a church at Sablé. When Archbishop Ralph of Tours passed judgement, he declared himself willing to defend his judgement 'before our primate the archbishop of Lyons' or if need be before the pope. At the council of Poitiers in January 1078, Archbishop Gebuin of Lyons authorized Bishop Arnald of le Mans to hallow the church at Sablé.[272] Not only was the title of primate which Gregory confirmed in 1079 already well known, but the principle of hierarchy upon which he based it was acknowledged in France.

Gregory's confirmation is significant on account of the interaction that followed amongst pope, primate, and legates. Archbishop Gebuin had come to office in 1077

---

[268] See n. 263.   [269] *RHGF* 14.671B, no. 8.

[270] *Reg.* 6.35, pp. 450/22–451/9, from *Reg. Greg. I*, 5.59/1–19, vol. 1.357–8, via *Decreta Bonifacii papae*, Hinschius, p. 703/17–30.

[271] *Reg.* 6.35, pp. 451/10–452/2, from *Epistola Anacleti secunda*, cap. 26, Hinschius, pp. 79/21–80/6.

[272] *Cartulaire manceau*, 2.69–77, nos. 5–6; cf. *RHGF* 14.669, no. 4, which dates from 1080; the reference to litigation 'apud Lugdunensem primatem et caeteros primores Pictavensis concilii' should be noted.

with the support of Hugh of Die. He was elected at the council of Autun, after which Hugh petitioned Gregory to send his *pallium* by the hand of Bishop Gunthard of Valence so that Hugh might confer it upon him; in face of local Burgundian opposition fortified by King Henry IV, his absence if he went to Rome would endanger his church.[273] At the council of Poitiers in January 1078, however, Gebuin lost credit with Hugh of Die when he supported Archbishop Ralph of Tours and Bishop Silvester of Rennes, the two bishops whom Hugh severely blamed for the tumultuous course of the council.[274]

The survival of a number of letters relating to Ralph of Tours makes it possible to see something of the tensions of Gebuin's primacy.[275] A cause of them was the troubled history of the abbey of la Couture. In 1073, King William I of England had captured Maine in which it lay. He deposed its abbot, Raynald, and replaced him by its prior, Juhel.[276] In 1078, Raynald secured release from the harsh imprisonment to which the king had subjected him. He sought reinstatement from his bishop, Arnald of le Mans, who turned for counsel to his archbishop, Ralph of Tours. The two prelates found themselves acutely embarrassed, not least because they feared that Raynald might take his case to Rome. In a letter to Arnald, Ralph recalled that Arnald had given Juhel his abbatial benediction in full knowledge that Juhel had received investiture with his abbacy at the lay hands of King William; although Ralph knew that this was wrong, he had turned a blind eye. If Gregory got to know about it, he would accuse the two prelates of treason against himself ('rei, ut ita dicam, apostolicae maiestatis teneamur'). It would be best if possible to avoid being summoned to Rome.[277] But the problem did not rest so easily. When Archbishop Gebuin of Lyons travelled to Rome to secure his privilege, Abbot Raynald went with him.

When, soon after his return, Gebuin wrote to Ralph of Tours about his journey, he could say that it had gone well for himself. Looking back to the council of Autun, he reported that the bishop of Valence had quickly brought from Rome his *pallium*. But he had soon gone to Rome himself, had re-established himself in Gregory's favour after the contretemps of the council of Poitiers, and had been granted his privilege of 20 April. At Gregory's command, Gebuin sent it to Ralph to be copied by him and by each of his suffragan bishops. Having thus displayed his primatial authority over the province of Tours, Gebuin gave Ralph what must have been the unwelcome task of solacing his fellow-delinquent at Poitiers in the eyes of Hugh of Die, Bishop Silvester of Rennes. Silvester's clergy had petitioned Gebuin for their bishop to be allowed to administer confirmation; but, as he had been inhibited by a papal legate, Hugh of Die, Gebuin could not, as primate, release him without a personal hearing of his

---

[273] *RHGF* 14.614BC, no. 79.   [274] *RHGF* 14.615A–E, no. 80.

[275] *RHGF* 14.667–8. Villard, 'Primatie des Gaules', shows the incorrectness of some of the dates there given, although not all of his revisions can stand.

[276] Probably not before 1076, when Juhel was still prior of la Couture: *Cartulaire manceau*, p. 75, no. 5.

[277] *RHGF* 14.667–8, no. 1. On this letter, see Villard, 'Primatie des Gaules', p. 425 n. 18. However, since Ralph wrote with urgency and asked for a reply by 7 Dec., its date is probably late Nov. 1078. This would leave insufficient time for the two journeys by Gebuin to Rome which Villard postulates.

case.[278] Such were the terms upon which Gebuin saw the authority of primates and legates as being related to each other.

Gebuin at much the same time wrote as primate to Archbishop Ralph of Tours and to a group of bishops and other churchmen from his province and beyond. He said that they had sent Abbot Raynald of la Couture to him for justice to be done after his sufferings at the hands of the king of England; clearly, Ralph's hope that matters might be hushed up had not been fulfilled. Gebuin had taken the abbot to Rome, where Gregory had upheld him. Gregory had also discussed with Gebuin what should be done about his opponents who had disregarded Gregory's decree against lay investiture. Gebuin in his letter gave directions to the group of churchmen in the pope's name ('auctoritate apostolica et nostra'): Juhel, whom he reviled as an accursed adulterer who had climbed into his father's bed (Gen. 49: 4), and his faction were to be anathematized; Bishop Arnald of le Mans who had performed his benediction should be tried and if appropriate suspended from office; the monks of la Couture were to be placed under interdict until the 'maledictus adulter' Juhel was expelled and Raynald restored to office.[279] Gebuin thus celebrated his return from Rome by a confident display of primatial authority, exercised in answer to detailed papal instructions in circumstances where the spheres of primates and legates were suitably defined.

This pattern of harmonious authority was quickly shattered. First of all, the vindication of Abbot Raynald and the anathematization of his rival Juhel placed the well-meaning but weak and vacillating Archbishop Ralph of Tours in a difficult position towards his good friend and suffragan Bishop Arnald of le Mans. Arnald had quickly written to Ralph expressing a sense of betrayal by him. In reply, Ralph tried to distance himself as far as he could from Gebuin's decisions. More important, he alluded to a fresh and unexpected factor in the situation. During 1079, another of Gregory's legates, Amatus of Oloron, had been expanding his area of concern northwards; Gebuin's letter had been closely followed by a letter from Amatus inviting him to his council to be held at Bordeaux. It appeared that neither of Gregory's agents, Gebuin of Lyons or Amatus of Oloron, knew what the other was doing. Ralph described himself as being left in a quandary. But his advice to the bishop of le Mans was that he should be patient under his suspension until the whole matter of la Couture could be further discussed at the forthcoming council.[280]

Archbishop Gebuin of Lyons was no less astounded to hear of Amatus of Oloron's intervention in the western part of his jurisdiction. He was quick to write about it to Archbishop Ralph of Tours and Bishop Eusebius of Angers. He recalled that, when Gregory had received him so kindly at Rome in the spring, he had made no allusion to Amatus of Oloron; rather, when conferring his privilege, he told him to assist Hugh of Die if Hugh should ever hold a council in any of his provinces. Gebuin hinted that he had nevertheless before he set out for Rome heard rumours of

---

[278] *RHGF* 14.668, no. 2. Since Gebuin refers to his privilege as having been granted and as being ready to be copied, the letter must date from after 20 Apr. 1079 and, indeed, from after Gebuin's return to Lyons.
[279] *RHGF* 14.668–9, no. 3. [280] *RHGF* 14.671–2, no. 9.

Amatus's legation to the province of Tours. In his perplexity, he sought Ralph's and Eusebius's advice, for he wished neither to diminish the rights of the church of Lyons nor to contravene papal instructions.[281]

For Gebuin, the year 1080 proved inauspicious. It began with the routing of his challenge, as leader of other Burgundian bishops, of the liberty of Cluny and to the vindication of Cluny both by Cardinal Peter of Albano and by Gregory himself at his Lent synod.[282] Worse was to follow in April, when, at the instance of King William of England whose goodwill Gregory deemed indispensable to himself, Gregory reversed his rulings as communicated by Gebuin about the affairs of la Couture. He wrote to Bishop Arnald of le Mans restoring him to his episcopal functions from which Gebuin had suspended him. He absolved and restored to office Abbot Juhel but declared Abbot Raynald to be an ambitious and perjurious invader whom Bishop Arnald was to evict from the abbey. Gregory insisted that both Hugh of Die and Amatus of Oloron concur in Juhel's restoration.[283]

In the course of the year, the legate Amatus of Oloron insisted on his jurisdiction over the province of Tours. Amatus wrote to Archbishop Ralph in cordial terms but he persisted in the assumption of his right to visit his province. He twice summoned the archbishop and his suffragans to his second council of Bordeaux in October.[284] Gebuin nevertheless held fast to his authority over the province of Tours. In 1080, he praised Archbishop Ralph fulsomely, perhaps excessively so, for maintaining the humble devotion that his predecessors had shown to their mother church of Lyons, and he asked Ralph on his behalf to oversee the election of a suitable monk from Marmoutier to be abbot of Savigny (dioc. Lyons).[285]

It can scarcely be denied that, by the early 1080s, Gregory's empowerment of his legates Hugh of Die and Amatus of Oloron, together with his confirmation of the primatial rights of the see of Lyons right across the middle of France, had produced confusion and a conflict of authorities. In 1082/3, the promotion of Hugh of Die, at Gregory's strong wish,[286] to succeed Gebuin as archbishop of Lyons did much to clear up the confusion. This was clear when, perhaps during Archbishop Hugh of Lyons's attempt to reach Gregory's November synod of 1083, the primacy of Lyons was exercised collegiately by his own suffragan bishops in order to protect Archbishop Ralph of Tours from his local enemies; they suspended from office Bishop Geoffrey of Angers and excommunicated Count Fulk of Anjou and the monks of Marmoutier. The sentence against the count was passed 'ex auctoritate

[281] *RHGF* 14.671, no. 8.   [282] See above, 5.3.2.4.

[283] *Reg.* 7.22–3, to Bishop Arnald of le Mans, and to King William I, 24 Apr. 1080, pp. 499–502; 9.5, to Hugh of Die and Amatus of Oloron, (1081), pp. 579–80. The reference to *legatus noster* in *Reg.* 7.22, p. 499/12, is to Gebuin of Lyons not Amatus of Oloron: Schieffer, *Die päpstlichen Legaten*, pp. 122–3; cf. also the reference to the *legatio* of Gebuin in *RHGF* 14.672A.

[284] *RHGF* 14.669–71, nos. 5–7. The bishops of the province of Tours were to bring their privileges to Amatus for confirmation, thereby illustrating an important aspect of the establishment of a legate's authority; lack of legatine confirmation would diminish their reliability.

[285] *RHGF* 14.672–3, no. 10.

[286] *Reg.* 9.18, to Bishop Hugh of Die, 24 Oct. (1081/2), pp. 598–9.

beati Petri atque domini Hugonis primati et Romane ecclesiae legati'. In a concluding address to all the bishops, clergy, and laity of the province of Tours, the bishops
called for full support to be given to the church and to the archbishop of Tours.[287]
This firm statement, together with the vigour with which Archbishop Hugh combined the roles of primate and papal legate, prepared the way for Pope Urban II to
vindicate the primacy of Lyons over Gallia Lugdunensis at the council of Clermont
in 1095.[288]

5.3.3.3 French Metropolitans

Gregory's manner of dealing with primacies according to circumstances and on their
individual merits was paralleled in his dealings with French and Burgundian metropolitans. His principal demands upon them were obedience to papal directives and
co-operation in the general purposes of the papacy. When these were forthcoming,
Gregory both upheld metropolitans in their authority and used the resources of their
churches as they might have expected. There is no evidence that Gregory intended
to reduce or to inhibit their authority by his use of legates. Indeed, his tempering of
Hugh of Die's sentences upon French metropolitans at his councils of Autun and
Poitiers suggests that he was concerned to reinforce it.[289] Similarly, Gregory's recognition of the primacy of the see of Lyons seems, upon Pseudo-Isidorian principles,
to have been intended to reinforce rather than to check the authority of primatial and
metropolitan sees.

Especially during his early years, Gregory was much concerned to uphold metropolitan authority. He was at pains to secure the restoration to his duties of
Archbishop William of Auch who was under censure from Pope Alexander II's time,
and if possible to clear him of allegations that were current against him. He insisted
upon his suffragans' duty of obedience to him unless plausible charges could be laid
against him before Gregory at Rome.[290] In a dispute between the monks of Saint-
Hilaire at Poitiers and their bishop, Isembert, the first recourse for justice should be
to a provincial council of Archbishop Gozelin of Bordeaux. When Gregory eventually summoned Isembert to Rome, he was careful also to summon his archbishop because only by the involvement of local churchmen could a fair hearing be ensured.[291]

---

[287] *RHGF* 14.673–4, no. 11.

[288] *Ep.* 45, *PL* 151,438–9. I have not followed Villard in accepting as genuine Gregory VII's supposed
privilege of 6 Mar. 1077 conferring on the see of Vienne a primacy over the seven provinces of Vienne,
Bourges, Bordeaux, Auch, Narbonne, Aix-en-Provence, and Embrun: *QF* no. +134, pp. 139–41; cf.
Villard, 'Primatie des Gaules', pp. 429–39. The question of the primacy of the see of Sens was not raised
on any side in the surviving evidence, despite its well-established roots, e.g. Pope John VIII's privilege of
876: *Ep.* 15, *PL* 126.660; even when Gregory confirmed the subjection of Sens to the primacy of Lyons in
1079 there was no reference to it. In 1095, Urban II insisted that Archbishop Richer of Sens acknowledge
the primacy of Archbishop Hugh of Lyons: *Ep.* 45, *PL* 151.438–9.

[289] *Reg.* 5.17, 9 Mar. 1078, pp. 378–80; see above, 5.3.2.1.

[290] *Reg.* 1.16, to Cardinal Gerald of Ostia, 1 July 1073, pp. 25–6; 1.55, to the suffragan bishops of Auch,
16 Mar. 1074, pp. 81–3.

[291] *Reg.* 1.73, to Bishop Isembert of Poitiers, 12 Apr. 1074, pp. 1–4–5; 2.2, to the same, 10 Sept. 1074,
pp. 125–6; 2.4, to Archbishop Gozelin of Bordeaux, 10 Sept. 1074, pp. 128–9.

In accordance with this principle, Gregory might refer a matter for settlement by a metropolitan of a province, as when Archbishop Richer of Sens was to avenge acts of violence which occurred when a laymen of his diocese ambushed Archbishop Ralph of Tours.[292] Gregory's first recourse in protracted proceedings against Bishop Rainer of Orleans was to charge Archbishop Richer of Sens to exercise his metropolitan authority, reinforced by papal sanctions if necessary. When Gregory summoned Rainer to Rome, he kept Richer informed and requested his collaboration if the matter were heard there. But Rainer provided to be contumacious, and Gregory resorted to calling for joint action by Archbishops Richer of Sens and Richard of Bourges together with their suffragans.[293] Gregory similarly called upon two metropolitans, Richard of Bourges and Ralph of Tours, to settle a quarrel between the monasteries of Bourg-Dieu at Déols and Saint-Sulpice.[294] In such cases, Gregory sought to secure the complementary exercise of his own authority and that of the metropolitans whom he involved according to the circumstances and to the progress of individual cases.

The problems of two metropolitan sees in particular required Gregory's more prolonged attention, and in either case his actions were pragmatic and calculated to promote the effective exercise of an archbishop's authority. At Narbonne, the scandalous Guifred had been in office for some half a century when Gregory became pope. At his Roman synods, Gregory repeatedly pronounced sentences of excommunication or deposition upon Guifred and suffragans who colluded with him.[295] Yet at the very end of Guifred's life, Gregory sought to build upon a good report from Abbot Bernard of Marseilles about Guifred's twin brother, Bishop Berengar of Gerona, in order to bring about Guifred's own belated repentance.[296] At his Lent synod of 1080, however, Gregory deposed and excommunicated Bishop Peter of Rodez who had usurped the see after Guifred's death.[297] Later in the year, Gregory rejoiced in the free election to the see of Narbonne of Dalmatius, abbot of la Grasse, and sought the support for him of Count Raymond of Saint-Gilles and his son Bertrand. Gregory again passed sentence upon Peter at his Lent synod of 1081.[298] With Dalmatius's succession, Gregory could hope that the see and province of Narbonne would be better ordered.

Gregory had also to contend with the centuries-old dispute about whether the see of Dol was rightfully an independent metropolis of Brittany, or whether it and the

---

[292] *Reg.* 2.20, to Archbishop Richer of Sens, 15 Nov. 1074, pp. 152–3.

[293] *Reg.* 3.16–17, to Archbishop Richer of Sens, and to Bishop Rainer of Orleans, Apr. 1076, pp. 278–80; 4.9, to Archbishop Richer of Sens, 2 Nov. 1076, pp. 307–8; 5.8–9, to Archbishops Richer of Sens and Richard of Bourges, and to Bishop Rainer of Orleans, 6 Oct. 1077, pp. 358–61.

[294] *Reg.* 2.20, to Archbishop Richer of Sens, 15 Nov. 1074, pp. 152–3.

[295] *Reg.* 3.10a, Feb. 1076, p. 269/10–12; 5.14a(5), Feb.–Mar. 1078, p. 370/7–10; 6.5b, Nov. 1078, p. 401/10; 6.17a, Feb. 1079, p. 429/11–12.

[296] *Reg.* 6.16, to Bishop Berengar of Gerona, 2 Jan. 1079, pp. 422/27–423/2.

[297] *Reg.* 7.14a(3), p. 481/4–9.

[298] *Reg.* 8.16, to Counts Raymond and Bertrand of Saint-Gilles, 10 Dec. 1080, pp. 537–8, 8.20a(1), p. 544/6–9.

other Breton sees should be subject to the metropolitan authority of Tours.[299]
Gregory established direct contact with Brittany in 1074 when, as an expression of
his pastoral concern for churches in remote areas of Christendom, he summoned its
bishops and abbots to his Lent synod of 1075.[300] He thereby probably unwittingly
encouraged the Bretons in the view that the authority of Tours could be bypassed;[301]
in September 1076, the church of Dol sent to Gregory at Rome a youth named
Gilduin with the request that Gregory ordain him bishop ('pontifex'). Gregory was
convinced of the gross turpitude of the bishop, Juhel, whom Gilduin was intended to
replace. While he deemed Gilduin to be unacceptable because he was under the
canonical age, with the consent of the Breton delegation he consecrated one of its
number, Ivo or Evenus, abbot of Saint-Melaine (dioc. Rennes), to be their archbishop
('vobis in patrem et archiepiscopum consecravimus'). Gregory was aware that the
archbishop of Tours contested Dol's claim to metropolitan status. In a letter to the
Breton bishops, he took account of this, studiously using the term *episcopus*, not
archiepiscopus, of Evenus. He said that he had consecrated him and given him the
pallium only provisionally, until the claims that Archbishop Ralph of Tours had already advanced for his see could be properly taken into account. If reason and justice
demanded that Dol be subject to Tours, Gregory must uphold the rights of Tours
('nos quidem sanctae Turonensi ecclesiae ius suum conservari et debitam subiec-
tionem a Dolensi ecclesia exhiberi volumus'); however, Gregory would allow Evenus
and his canonically elected successors the use of the *pallium*. But if the metropolitan
rights of Dol were vindicated, the Breton bishops would owe obedience to it. Until
the matter was definitively settled, the Breton bishops were to be subject to Evenus
as if he were archbishop.[302] Gregory reinforced his ruling by a letter to King William
I of England, whose Breton campaign of 1076 included an unsuccessful siege of Dol.
Gregory referred cautiously to Dol as 'the principal see of the province of Brittany'.
He enlarged upon the iniquities of Bishop Juhel and sought William's aid to expel
him; he commended the newly consecrated Bishop Evenus.[303]

　　Not surprisingly, Archbishop Ralph of Tours reacted strongly to so considerable
a countenancing by Gregory of the Breton case as was implied by the consecration of
Evenus and the conferring of the *pallium*. Immediately after Canossa, Gregory wrote
to him a letter in which he insisted upon the provisional character of his actions and
upon the care and circumspection with which he intended to proceed to a definitive
decision. He might himself come to France or if not he would send competent legates

---

　[299] *Reg. Inn. III*, 2.79, vol. 2.150–71; this letter with its footnotes offers a conspectus of the dispute between Tours and Dol which Pope Innocent III definitively settled in favour of Tours. See also the section
Acta varia in causa Dolensis episcopatus ex archivis ecclesiae Turonensis in Martène and Durand, *Thes. nov.
anec*. 3.850–988.
　[300] *Reg.* 2.1, to the bishops and abbots of Brittany, 28 Aug. 1074, pp. 124–5; for the reaction of the
Breton princes, see 4.13, to Archbishop Ralph of Tours, 1 Mar. 1077, p. 316/26–34.
　[301] Thus, in 1078, Gregory could respond to the claim of the Bretons that their region enjoyed an ancient right of special papal protection which had been allowed to lapse: *QF* no. 153, pp. 174–5.
　[302] *Reg.* 4.4–5, to the clergy and people of Dol, and to the Breton bishops, 27 Sept. 1076, pp. 300–3.
　[303] *Epp. vag.* no. 16, to King William I, (1076, after 27 Sept.), pp. 44–7.

to investigate; if these plans yielded no solution, he would summon to Rome both Ralph and the bishop of Dol for a thorough examination of their case.[304] Gregory soon afterwards assured King William, whose plea in favour of Juhel he politely but firmly set aside, that he would send to Dol a high-powered legation of Hugh of Die, the Roman subdeacon Hubert, and (if his health permitted) the monk Teuzo, which would look into the matter of the episcopal succession.[305] In 1078, Evenus of Dol appeared in Rome when Hugh of Die was also there. In Gregory's two consequent letters, he conceded to Evenus the title *archiepiscopus* but referred an inquiry into the circumstances of his succession to a general council in France which Hugh of Die and Hugh of Cluny would hold. Gregory called on Hubert and Teuzo to see that the Breton clergy and laity as well as King William were properly represented at the council.[306]

Gregory did not, however, thus procure progress in France. At his Lent synod in Rome of 1080, there was a long and laborious discussion of the problems centring upon Dol. Gregory reported on it both to the Breton bishops and to the church of Tours. He had made, not a definitive settlement, but the best accommodation that he could then manage ('quam iustius potuimus'). Archbishop Ralph of Tours had pleaded that his church had been denied its rights over Brittany as enshrined in papal documents proving that Brittany owed subjection to Tours as its spiritual mother and metropolis. The bishop of Dol ('Dolensis episcopus'), on the other hand, had produced no such papal warrant for his own case, while his arguments had been unpersuasive. Nevertheless, Gregory said that Evenus claimed to have left at home his best proof-text; Gregory therefore deferred a decision until legates should complete the hearing locally in France. He left open an alternative: if the Bretons could produce authority for their freedom from Tours, they should continue unmolested in the enjoyment of their liberty; but if they could not, they must perpetually acknowledge Tours to be their mother-church and metropolis. In the latter event, Evenus might continue to wear the *pallium*, but the right would not pass to his successors.[307]

The bull of Pope Innocent III which in 1199 at last made a secure papal decision in favour of Tours provides evidence that Amatus of Oloron considered the dispute at his council of Saintes in 1081. The case for Dol was poorly presented by a clerk of that see who came up with no satisfactory papal warrant and who argued feebly. Amatus therefore confirmed Gregory's ruling of 1080 for the contingency of a failure of the Breton case.[308]

Gregory's concern in a difficult and obscure dispute with regard to which he had to feel his way was to do everything possible to establish and to secure the respective rights of Tours and Dol according to the demands of historical precedent and of

---

[304] *Reg.* 4.13, pp. 316–17.

[305] *Reg.* 4.17, to King William I, 31 Mar. 1077, pp. 322–3.

[306] *Reg.* 5.22–3, to the subdeacon Hubert and the monk Teuzo, and to three Breton counts, 22 May 1078, pp. 385–8.

[307] *Reg.* 7.15, to all the bishops of Brittany and to the clergy and people of the province of Tours, 8 Mar. 1080, pp. 488–9; it is likely that separate copies were sent to the two groups that are named.

[308] *Reg. Inn. III*, 2.79, vol. 2.164–5.

current needs both legal and pastoral. He had an acute sense of a duty to establish and secure the rights of the churches concerned; in pursuit of this duty, he showed patience, restraint, and an unwearying concern for an equitable outcome which he was not able definitely to achieve. He was also at pains to secure the concurrence and harmony with each other of all the persons concerned.

5.4 Gregory VII's Objectives in France

On the basis of the foregoing study of Gregory's dealings with the French king, lay magnates, and clergy, an attempt may be made to clarify his objectives with regard to the French-speaking lands of France and Burgundy. His objectives were here not profoundly determined by the vicissitudes of his relationship with the monarchy. In Germany, his conflict with King Henry IV was the guiding theme of his pontificate; but in the kingdom of Burgundy, Henry's power was weak and could be largely ignored, while in France Gregory was in acute conflict with King Philip I for only a brief period in 1074–5. Thereafter he showed remarkable restraint towards the king, and even a willingness to turn a blind eye to his actions and excesses as when he sought to impede Hugh of Die in his conduct of the council of Poitiers. In France and Burgundy, the leading theme, constant in its underlying principle but changing in Gregory's perception and application of it, is the freeing of churches of all kinds and at all levels from forms of lay intervention which contradicted traditional and canon-ical righteousness as Gregory interpreted it.[309] The way was well prepared for Gregory, in particular by the widespread movement over the past two centuries for privately-held churches and ecclesiastical property to be transferred from lay to monastic ownership.[310] Gregory's inroads upon lay power over churches was well prepared for, and there were many in France to whom they were far from unexpected or unwelcome.

5.4.1 The Extirpation of Simony

Gregory's concern to purge the French church from simony in head and members, as well as the difficulties that he was to encounter, became apparent in his dealings in the duchy and kingdom of Burgundy during the early years of his pontificate. In 1073, the election of Landeric of Autun as bishop of Mâcon elicited from Gregory a forthright condemnation of King Philip I of France because he exacted payments from bishops before they were admitted to their bishoprics. He declared that his care of all the churches as well as the destruction that simoniacal practices brought upon particular churches impelled him to impose severe sanctions. Yet the hope that the king might be amenable to better counsel led him to defer an immediate sanction.[311] If simony was to be deplored in a king, it was to be punished in archbishops; it occa-

---

[309] See Hugh of Flavigny's summary of Gregory's aims: 2, p. 423/3–22.
[310] See e.g. Mollat, 'La Restitution des églises privées'; Diener, 'Das Verhältnis Clunys zu den Bischöfen'.
[311] *Reg.* 1.35, to Bishop Roclin of Chalon-sur-Saône, 4 Dec. 1073, p. 56/14–26; see above, 5.2.1.

sioned the downfall of an archbishop of Lyons and an archbishop of Vienne. The downfall of Archbishop Humbert of Lyons came relatively slowly. Gregory at first entrusted to him the consecration of Bishop Landeric of Mâcon and only later undertook the consecration himself at Rome. When Gregory informed Humbert and his suffragans of this action, he still expressed his expectation that Humbert would be his zealous collaborator in correcting all abuses.[312] But in 1076, by the agency of the strongly Gregorian Bishop Hugh of Langres, Humbert was expelled from his see as a simoniac. In 1077, Gebuin, archdeacon of Langres, succeeded Humbert as archbishop during Hugh of Die's council at Autun.[313]

In the province of Vienne, the downfall of Archbishop Herman came more dramatically. Gregory anounced his concern to extirpate simony especially at the lower levels of church life in connection with the accession of Bishop Hugh of Die. Announcing to Count William of Die that he had consecrated Hugh at Rome, Gregory said that he had himself charged Hugh to be rigorous in opposing simony as a means to eliminating lay claims upon parish churches:

> Amongst all other things, we carefully admonished him [Hugh] to stand with all the power at his command against the simoniac heresy, and not to consecrate churches in his diocese or to allow divine service to take place in churches that had been otherwise consecrated unless as is canonically correct they had first been absolutely freed from lay hands to secure both their own legal independence ('suo iuri') and his episcopal oversight.

Gregory soon found it necessary to temper Hugh's zeal against lay subjects who showed only qualified willingness to yield to him their ecclesiastical goods.[314] At Romans, with which town as well as with the church of Vienne Hugh of Die had youthful connections,[315] Gregory found it even less straightforward to promote his ends. In March 1075, he was satisfied that a model of ecclesiastical order and freedom was being established by the clerks of Saint-Barnard, a collegiate church of which the provostship was held by Archbishop Herman of Vienne. In answer to the clerks' request, Gregory both confirmed the standing of Saint-Barnard itself as enjoying the *libertas Romana* of a church directly subject to the apostolic see, and at the request of Hugh of Die he granted a like status to a daughter-house which it was establishing and in which a regular canonical life would be observed. A year later, Gregory considered himself to have been deceived about the clerks' good intentions. At his Lent synod of 1076, he excommunicated its provost, Archbishop Herman, who had been justly deposed for simony, perjury, sacrilege, and apostasy. He had not ceased to harass the church of Vienne, and Gregory placed the church of Vienne as well as that of Saint-Iréné at Lyons, of which the archbishop was also the superior, under interdict until Herman was no longer their ruler. The clerks of Romans were put under

---

[312] *Reg.* 1.36, to Archbishop Humbert of Lyons, 4 Dec. 1073, pp. 57–8; 1.76, to Archbishop Humbert of Lyons and his suffragans, 15 Apr. 1074, pp. 107–8.

[313] Hugh of Flavigny, 2, pp. 415/47–416/3.

[314] *Reg.* 1.69, to Count William of Die, 23 Mar. 1074, pp. 99–100, 2.43, to Bishop Hugh of Die, 5 Jan. 1075, pp. 179–80.

[315] *Reg.* 2.59, to the clerks of Romans, 9 Mar. 1075, pp. 212–14, at p. 214/8–11.

interdict until they made amends for expelling the regular canons from their church. In 1077, Gregory wrote again to the clerks of Saint-Barnard, who were still under excommunication. They were to cease claiming the *libertas Romana* which Gregory had so lately confirmed as a reason for excluding the new archbishop and ex-officio provost, Warmund, and they were to submit to the judgement of Hugh of Die as papal vicar.[316] Events at Romans show how a simoniacal archbishop might be got rid of by Gregory's direct action and how Hugh of Die as Gregory's vicar might seek to rectify a corrupt situation. But they also show how easily Gregory might, at least initially, be deceived and how his attempts to promote amendment might be turned against him.

In the relatively few cases in which it is possible further to document Gregory's zeal against simony in France, his attention was likewise often directed to individual sees. An early example, which shows similarities with his dealings at Vienne, is the see of le Puy which was directly subject to the apostolic see. The course of events there is hard to follow, but in April 1074 the see was disputed by two rivals, each of whom bore the name Stephen. Neither of them had an unobjectionable record but one, whom Gregory described as bishop-elect, won the pope's approval because he believed him to have expelled a predecessor who was a simoniac and an invader of the see. The bishop-elect had further pleased Gregory by promising obedience to the Roman church, thereby recovering a favour which he had somehow forfeited. Gregory required him to return to Rome before assuming office, but in the meantime the clergy and people of le Puy were to help him banish every stain of the simoniac heresy from their church and so render pure service to Christ and his Mother who was their patron saint. Gregory was quickly disenchanted with the bishop-elect: he was first excommunicated by Gregory's legates Hugh of Die and the subdeacon Hubert; then Gregory himself condemned him at his Lent synod of 1076 for simony and homicide. Hugh of Die again condemned him at his council of Clermont. In 1077, Gregory ordered the canons of le Puy to disown their simoniacal bishop and to elect a successor. Gregory seized the opportunity to communicate by letter the fate of a simoniacal bishop to all the bishops of France. Hugh of Die was commissioned to settle matters at le Puy on Gregory's behalf.[317] The affair of le Puy shows how difficult it was for the pope to secure reliable assessments of the true state of affairs in a French bishopric, how he reacted to events rather than directing them, but also how he sought to use a situation as it developed to promote his anti-simoniac zeal widely in France.

The case of Bishop Rainer of Orleans had similar features. From the days of Pope Alexander II, his see was notorious at Rome for the simony of its bishops.[318]

---

[316] *Reg.* 2.59, 3.10*a*, record of the Lent synod of 1076, p. 269/12–20, 4.16, to the clerks of Romans, 21 Mar. 1077, pp. 320–1.

[317] *Reg.* 1.80, to the clergy and people of le Puy, 13 Apr. 1074, p. 114, 3.10*a*; record of the Lent synod of 1076, p. 269/23–24; 4.18–19, to the canons of le Puy, and to all French bishops and clergy, 23 Mar. 1077, pp. 324–6; 4.22, to Bishop Hugh of Die, 12 May 1077, p. 333/1–8; Hugh of Flavigny, 2, pp. 413, 417.

[318] *Epp.* 19, 23, *PL* 146.1298D, 1300–1.

Gregory's concern as pope with Orleans was first focused upon an incorrigible clerk named Eurard whom Alexander had already disciplined for his irregular acquisition of ecclesiastical office.[319] It transpired that Eurard had acted collusively with Bishop Rainer, who had not only associated with him while excommunicate but who had also engaged extensively in simony, not least in connection with the provostship of the cathedral at Orleans. At least in 1076, Rainer was also opposed by King Philip I, and he had enemies among the canons of the cathedral. Yet Rainer's case confirms how difficult it was for Gregory to bring effective sanctions to bear on a simonical bishop. Gregory tried everything. In 1076, he charged the metropolitan, Archbishop Richer of Sens, through whom he sent Rainer a letter of warning, if necessary to compel the bishop's obedience by the sanction of excommunication; Rainer was himself to appear before Gregory at Rome by 1 November. But on 2 November, Gregory wrote to Richer of Sens to say that Rainer had not appeared; unless he could show good reason why, he would suffer deposition. Both Richer and Rainer were to come to the Lent synod that Gregory planned to hold in Lent 1077. Events in Germany prevented this, but next October Gregory extended his campaign in France against Rainer rather as he had extended that against Stephen of le Puy.[320] He informed the archbishops of Sens and Bourges with all their suffragans of Rainer's crimes, which included wholesale trafficking in archdeaconries and abbeys. Since Rainer had failed to come to Rome, his brother bishops were to assemble and to try him. They were to replace him by a certain Sanzo. But nothing came of this, either; a further setback was that charges of immorality were levelled against Sanzo. Therefore, in 1078, Gregory tried to deal with the case by his legates: Rainer was to appear before Hugh of Die, Hugh of Cluny, and the subdeacon Roger at a legatine council. Finally, in 1079, Gregory planned to send legates to Orleans itself. It seems all to have produced little result. Rainer continued to vex the church of Orleans, while Sanzo became established, with the king's support, only in 1096, when he proved vulnerable to charges which included long-term simony.[321] Nothing could better illustrate the intractability of simony in France, where in connection with the church of Cambrai Gregory was forced to acknowledge that the sale of altars was well-nigh universal and endemic.[322]

As the example of the abbey of Saint-Denis illustrates, similar problems might arise when dealing with an abbot. As in the cases of the bishoprics of le Puy and Orleans, Gregory's concern with Saint-Denis arose from the laying of information at Rome by local people. Abbot Ivo I was accused of having come by his office simoniacally, that is by the intervention of money. Gregory reacted cautiously, giving

---

[319] *Reg.* 2.52, to Eurard clerk of Orleans, 28 Feb. 1075, pp. 194–5.   [320] *Reg.* 4.19.

[321] *Reg.* 3.16–17, to Archbishop Richer of Sens, and to Bishop Rainer of Orleans, Apr. 1076, pp. 278–80; 4.9, to Bishop Richer of Sens, 2 Nov. 1076, pp. 307–8; 5.8–9, to Archbishops Richer of Sens and Richard of Bourges and their suffragans, and to Bishop Rainer of Orleans, 6 Oct. 1077, pp. 358–61; 5.14, to the clergy and people of Orleans, 29 Jan. 1078, pp. 367–8; 5.20, to Bishop Rainer of Orleans, 24 Apr. 1078, pp. 383–4; 6.23, to the clergy and people of Orleans, 5 Mar. 1079, pp. 435–6; Yves de Chartres, *Correspondance*, nos. 51, 53–4, 59, pp. 206–11, 212–27, 232–9.

[322] *Reg.* 4.22, to Bishop Hugh of Die, 12 May 1077, p. 332/28–31.

credence to one of the monks who spoke well of his abbot; but he could not allow
what had become a matter of public defamation to pass unsettled. If the legates
whom he purposed to send to France in 1075 could come to Saint-Denis, they were
to deal with the case; if not, Abbot Ivo was to come to Rome by 30 November. The
abbot was meanwhile to retain cure of souls over his monks, whom Gregory urged to
shun schism and discord. But the matter was not quickly composed. In 1077, Saint-
Denis was among the troubled places in France which he commended to the legatine
attention of Hugh of Die; it seems that Ivo had no difficulty in warding off any
sanctions.[323]

Many of Gregory's actions against simony in France and Burgundy thus arose
piecemeal from individual cases which were reported to him. When dealing with
them, he met with differing degrees of success: he achieved most in Burgundian sees
like Vienne and Lyons from which royal power was remote, but less in a bishopric like
Orleans or an abbey like Saint-Denis which were nearer to the heart of Capetian
France. There, Gregory had difficulty with enforcement. He encountered, not so
much positive resistance, as an ingrained inertia which made it hard to change the
ways in practice of bishops and abbots. Moreover, Gregory showed no disposition for
most of his pontificate to press matters to an issue with the king of France.

He endeavoured to combat simony in France by two other means. One was
through the activity of his legates who acted on his behalf in their councils and in the
localities of France. Hugh of Die and Amatus of Oloron, especially, legislated against
it at their councils and sought opportunities of counteracting it.[324] This was perhaps
Gregory's most effective line of action. But he also sought to make progress in out-
lawing simony by the dissemination of his letters. An example is the attempt to
circulate to all French bishops and their clergy his sentence of 1077 upon Bishop
Stephen of le Puy. In part, he sought to reinforce the action of his legate Hugh of Die
and to publish it as an example. For le Puy was a much-frequented sanctuary of the
Blessed Virgin; publicity for Gregory's letter would cut off the offerings of the faithful which Stephen had allegedly diverted to supporting his own apostate and proud
offences against God. The circulation of the letter would serve to placard the heinous
concomitants of simoniacal dealings.[325] In 1079, Gregory again sought to make propaganda against simony in his privilege which confirmed the primacy of Lyons over
Gallia Lugdunensis.[326] Archbishop Gebuin of Lyons had succeeded the simoniacal
Humbert, and Gregory intended that the privilege, with its proscription of simony
on the part of a prelate, should be disseminated across France through the provinces
which were subject to Lyons.[327] Gregory included in the privilege an exposition of
the teaching of Pope Gregory the Great: amongst those whom he excluded from suc-
ceeding to the primacy in future were those who were elected or promoted by means
of gifts. Gregory specified three kinds of gifts: those by way of the hand ('a manu')

---

[323] *Reg.* 2.64–5, to Abbot Ivo of Saint-Denis, and to the monks of Saint-Denis, 25 Mar. 1075, pp.
219–20, 4.22, p. 333/1–8.

[324] See above, 5.3.2.2,3.

[325] *Reg.* 4.19.

[326] *Reg.* 6.34.

[327] *RHGF* 14.668, no. 2.

when money passed, those by way of service ('ab obsequio') as when men sought ecclesiastical office by deference to the powerful, and those by way of the tongue ('a linguo'), as when a man by himself or through a subordinate made special pleas for office.[328] Such forms of gift especially concerned the courts of kings and great men, and it is hard not to see a message which Gregory sought to transmit as widely as possible across the French kingdom to all French clergy. He sought to counteract simony by drawing upon the prestige of Pope Gregory the Great as a mentor and teacher; his privilege also contained the warning that those who did not enter upon their preferment by the door should forfeit not only a major office such as the primacy but also all claim to suitability for any office in the church.[329]

5.4.2 The Question of Lay Investiture

One reason for the limited amount of attention that Gregory gave to simony in his letters to France and Burgundy is that, in his purpose to eliminate lay power over churches, he increasingly concentrated upon the lay investiture of all grades of clergy with their bishoprics, abbacies, benefices, or other preferments.[330] Lay investiture involved a symbolic act by which a layman handed over to a cleric the symbols of his office—in the case of a bishop or abbot, his pastoral staff and ring. More important than the symbolic act was the transaction that it symbolized—the passing from the king or lay magnate to the bishop or abbot of the gift of his bishopric or abbacy. Gregory focused above all on the *donum episcopatus* when it represented the king as the source of episcopal office.

Gregory's concern with and hostility to lay investiture developed greatly between 1073 and *c.*1080. As the example of Bishop Anselm II of Lucca demonstrates, he did not at the beginning of his pontificate see it as being in itself a major issue; his misgivings about it seem to have been aroused during his dealings at Rome in 1074–5 with regard to Anselm's promotion to the Tuscan see of Lucca and with Hugh's promotion to the Burgundian see of Die, both of them within the realms of King Henry IV of Germany.[331] Until this time, Gregory does not appear to have been rigorous with regard to the kingdom of France. In dealing with the election of Bishop Landeric of Mâcon, in December 1073 he was concerned to ensure that the French king should renounce simony; if this were done, he showed no objection to Landeric's being invested with his see, as in all probability he was.[332]

Whatever the manner in which Gregory may have directly or indirectly referred to lay investiture at his Lent synod of 1075,[333] it was not until the spring of 1077 that any response may be detected in French-speaking regions. The first response came

---

[328] *Reg.* p. 448/11–17; cf. Gregory I, *Hom. XL in Evang.* 1.4.4, col. 1092.

[329] *Reg.* p. 448/21–9.

[330] The modern discussions of lay investiture to which I am most indebted are Scharnagl, *Der Begriff der Investitur*, Schieffer, *Die Entstehung des päpstlichen Investiturverbots*, and Beulertz, *Das Verbot der Laieninvestitur*.

[331] See above, 5.3.2.1.

[332] *Reg.* 1.35, to Bishop Roclin of Chalon-sur-Saône, 4 Dec. 1073, pp. 56–7.

[333] See above, 3.2.4.

from the unexpected direction of Brittany, and in connection with the Breton wish to assert the metropolitan status of the see of Dol.[334] In a letter to Archbishop Ralph of Tours, Gregory said that the *principes* of Brittany, from which he had summoned bishops and abbots to his Lent synod of 1075, had turned against an ancient and evil custom; they had shown reverence for papal authority 'by no longer wishing either to exercise the lordship of investiture or to seek financial advantage in the ordaining of bishops' ('ulterius in ordinandis episcopis nec dominium investiturae tenere nec pecuniae commodum quaerere velle').[335] From the Breton side, the reference to Gregory's concerns of the Lent synod of 1075 was a transparent attempt to sway him in favour of the ecclesiastical independence of Brittany from Tours. From Gregory's side, the noteworthy point is that investiture did not stand in isolation: he equated it with the exercise of lay lordship, and he associated it with simony.

The problem of investiture soon afterwards also arose in connection with an episcopal election at Cambrai. Cambrai formed part of the ecclesiastical province of Rheims, but the city and much of the diocese were politically subject to the German king.[336] As Gregory set matters out in a letter of May 1077 to his legate Bishop Hugh of Die, the new bishop, Gerard II (1076–92) had come to Gregory in Italy and had confessed that after election by the clergy and people of his diocese, he had received the *donum episcopatus* from King Henry IV. Gerard had justified himself by claiming that he had heard neither of Gregory's *decretum* of 1075 nor of his excommunication of Henry in 1076. Gregory did not admit ignorance as an excuse; Gerard was to resign the *donum* which he had wrongfully received into Gregory's hands. But because canonical election had preceded his investiture, Gregory was prepared to be merciful. Lest others should cite Gerard's example as a precedent for claiming undeserved mercy, Gerard was to swear before Bishop Hugh of Die, Archbishop Manasses of Rheims, and other bishops of his province, that before his investiture ('ante acceptionem illam et, ut dicitur, investituram episcopatus') he had, indeed, not heard of Gregory's decree or of the German king's excommunication.[337]

Gerard's public disavowal was, in itself, tantamount to a proclamation and confirmation of the decree of 1075 in the province of Rheims. But in further instructions to his legate, Gregory showed that he intended the decree as published in 1075 and as enforced in the case of Gerard of Cambrai to be placarded in the kingdom of France with the utmost publicity and force. Hugh of Die was to hold a council, as Gregory hoped with the counsel and consent of King Philip I.[338] At it, he was before all else publicly to prohibit in ringing tones ('congregatis omnibus et in conventu residentibus manifesta et personanti denunciatione interdicat') such errors as Gerard of Cambrai had fallen into. Henceforth, canonical and papal authority was to be upheld when bishops were appointed. No metropolitan or bishop might lay hands upon one

---

334 See above, 5.3.3.3.

335 *Reg.* 4.13, to Archbishop Ralph of Tours, 1 Mar. 1077, p. 316/26–33.

336 For Cambrai's position, see Kéry, *Die Errichtung des Bistums Arras*, pp. 226–41.

337 *Reg.* 4.22, to Bishop Hugh of Die, 12 May 1077, pp. 330/29–331/28; *Gesta episc. Camerac., cont.*, pp. 497–8; *Chron. s. Andreae Cam.* 3.1, pp. 539–40.

338 *Reg.* 4.22, pp. 331/29–332/4; the 'Quapropter' with which the passage opens should be noted.

who had received the gift of episcopate from a lay person ('qui a laica persona donum episcopatus susceperit') on pain of forfeiting his (the consecrator's) office; no power or person was henceforth to involve himself in the giving or receiving of the episcopal office. For the last provision, Gregory invoked the sanction imposed by canon twenty-two of the fourth council of Constantinople (869/70);[339] Gregory ordered this chapter to be publicly read to and acclaimed by the whole of Hugh's projected council.

There could afterwards be no shadow of an excuse for those who, after Gregory in 1075 had renewed the decree of Constantinople and its concomitant legislation ('qui post recensitam a nobis huius decreti auctoritatem'), had received investiture with a bishopric from the hand of secular lords or powers, or for the bishops who had presumed to lay hands upon such persons. Hugh of Die was to see that all who since Lent 1075 had offended against the decree should present themselves to Gregory and account for what they had done.[340]

The full force of Gregory's instructions to his legate must be taken. The case of Bishop Gerard of Cambrai drew from him a statement of the illicitness of lay investiture throughout the kingdom of France for which he required the utmost publicity. Because Gerard was invested by Henry IV of Germany, Gregory was able diplomatically to avoid direct reference to the French king, for whose concurrence he seems to have hoped through persuasion rather than confrontation. Whatever Gregory may have said at his Lent synod of 1075, in 1077 the canonical authority to which he appealed was the 200-year old one of canon twenty-two of the fourth council of Constantinople. This canon made no reference to lay investiture as such. Thus, on the one hand, Gregory's use of it as an authority for its prohibition was an application of the principle that it enshrined for which Gregory himself was responsible. But, on the other hand, the canon of 869/70 proclaimed the underlying requirement that laymen of every rank should have no part whatsoever, save retrospectively and by ecclesiastical permission, in the promotion of a bishop. It was this express canonical requirement that henceforth lay at the centre of Gregory's intentions for the French church, even when lay investiture was made the subject of legislation and other forms of proscription.

After these events, Gregory maintained his condemnation of lay investiture with conviction and vigour. At Rome, he legislated at least twice in Roman synods to prohibit it, not in any single region, but universally. In November 1078, he penalized clerks who received bishoprics, abbeys, and lesser churches from lay hands; in March 1080, he repeated this prohibition in stronger terms and extended his censure to laymen who conferred, as well as to clerks who received, lay investiture.[341] But his

---

339 See above, 3.2.4.   340 *Reg.* 4.22, pp. 333/18–334–8.
341 *Reg.* 6.5*b*(3), p. 403/11–19; 7.14*a*(1–2), pp. 480/14–481/3. According to Berthold, *a.* 1078, pp. 308/51–309/7, Gregory also condemned both laity and clergy who were involved in the conferring of greater and lesser churches. This statement is not confirmed in Gregory's Register or elsewhere, and it raises serious difficulties; see Schieffer, *Die Entstehung des päpstlichen Investiturverbots*, pp. 167–70. For the decrees and their dissemination, see also Beulertz, *Das Verbot der Laieninvestitur*, pp. 6–9, nos. 4–6.

prime target in ending the practice was undoubtedly the French-speaking lands. He
followed up his letter of 1077 to Bishop Hugh of Die by at least two prohibitions in
general terms. In 1079, his privilege for Archbishop Gebuin of Lyons, which
confirmed the primacy of his see and which was intended for wide circulation, forbade the see not only to simoniacs but also to any who 'acceded to the see through the
secular power (*per secularem potestatem*), that is, by the gift or confirmation of any lay
person who seems to resist holy religion and to come into contradiction with the pure
and authentic authority of the holy fathers';[342] an allusion to the *decretum* of the
council of Constantinople (869/70) which, in his letter to Hugh of Die, Gregory
made the basis of his opposition to lay investiture, is probable. In the same year, Hugh
of Die reported to Gregory that a candidate for the episcopate had invaded the see of
Chalon-sur-Saône by way of receiving investiture from King Philip I ('per saecularem potestatem, id est regiam investituram'). Not only did Gregory declare the
bishop to be deposed from all power over and claim to his church, but he urged Hugh
in very strong terms to proscribe lay investiture; at all his councils, Hugh was to excommunicate those who ignored the decree which Gregory had passed against lay
investiture at his November synod of 1078 and who had received investiture with
churches at the hands of any layman.[343]

   As for Hugh of Die, he had not been behindhand in implementing Gregory's instructions to him in 1077. At his council of Autun, for which no canons survive, it is
known from the letter of Archbishop Manasses of Rheims to Gregory of the following summer that Hugh published and confirmed Gregory's decree ('vestrum ecclesiasticum decretum') as adumbrated in his letter to Hugh. Manasses complained
to Gregory that two of his own suffragans, Helinand of Laon and Theobald of
Soissons, had irregularly consecrated Bishop Ralph of Amiens; they had heard the
legislation at Autun, yet they had consecrated a bishop who had acquired the *episcopii
donum* from a lay person—Manasses meant, but did not say, the king. Gregory instructed his legates Hugh of Die and Hugh of Cluny to investigate the matter; if the
charges against Ralph of Amiens were true, they were to punish severely his having
received lay investiture; this was so that others might fear to imitate his evil example.[344] In his own, delayed report to Gregory on the council of Autun, Hugh of
Die had already accused Manasses of complicity in lay investiture: Bishop Ivo of
Senlis, whom the king had invested, had been ordained by 'the heresiarch of Rheims',
whom Gregory in his letter of 1077 had prohibited from such action.[345] The force of
Hugh's charge was reduced by Gregory's mild reception of Manasses at Rome,[346]
and Gregory refrained from taking specific steps against the king in anticipation of
his stronger ruling at his Lent synod of 1080. However, at his council of Poitiers in
January 1078, Hugh of Die enacted a strict canon that no clerk should accept the

---

[342] *Reg.* 6.34, p. 448/17–21.   [343] *Epp. vag.* no. 30, pp. 78/20–80/2.
[344] *RHGF* 14.611BC, no. 76; *Reg.* 6.2, to Archbishop Manasses of Rheims, 22 Aug. 1078, p. 394/3–13;
6.3, to Hugh of Die and Hugh of Cluny, 22 Aug. 1078, p. 395/8–19.
[345] *RHGF* 14.614A, no. 79; *Reg.* 4.22, to Bishop Hugh of Die, 12 May 1077, p. 334/3–8.
[346] *Reg.* 5.17, 9 Mar. 1078, pp. 378/31–379/15.

donum episcopatus or of any inferior ecclesiastical grade from the hands of king, count, or layman; laymen who resisted canonical decrees by violently holding on to churches would bring an interdict upon those churches.[347] By such means the decree against lay investiture was widely disseminated in France.

There is some evidence that Gregory's concern to have done with lay investiture registered itself there. In the problems that arose over the abbey of la Couture, Archbishop Ralph of Tours feared Gregory's anger, amongst other reasons, because Bishop Arnald of le Mans had blessed Abbot Juhel who had received the *donum regiminis* from the lay hand of King William I of England. By branding this blessing as in truth a malediction, Archbishop Ralph indicated that he was in fundamental sympathy with Gregory's opposition to lay investiture; he also feared that, if the matter came before Gregory, he would deem both archbishop and bishop to have acted treasonably against himself ('rei, ut ita dicam, apostolicae maiestatis teneamur').[348] When King Philip I proposed that Abbot Robert of S. Eufemia in Calabria should succeed in the see of Chartres, Robert at the end of 1077 came to Gregory and explained that he had refused to accept the *donum episcopatus* that the king had offered him;[349] he had evidently heard about the prohibition that Gregory was seeking to enforce. At an unknown date, a privilege of Gregory for the monastery of Saint-Pierre-de-Joncel (dioc. Béziers) provided that no future abbot should be installed by anyone's fraud or craft whether by investiture or by worldly power ('cuiuscumque obreptionis astutia sive per investituram sive per saecularem potestatem').[350]

The strength of Gregory's general denunications of lay investiture and their dissemination by his letters and legates, especially the energetic Hugh of Die, tell against any suggestion that, in his dealings with France and Burgundy, Gregory made it a matter of only marginal concern. It emerges as a prime means by which, especially after 1077, he sought to free churches, both great and small, from lay lordship and control, in implementation of canon twenty-two of the fourth council of Constantinople.

5.4.3 The Problem of Free Elections

Gregory's concern to extirpate simony from France and Burgundy was increasingly subsumed in his measures against lay investiture which were directed towards securing that the *donum episcopatus* should be conferred by clerical and not by lay hands, and should thus be free from lay involvement. In their turn his steps to this end found their full development in his requirement that there should be free and canonical elections to bishoprics and abbacies. As with lay investiture, his campaign to secure free elections developed markedly during his years as pope.[351]

---

347 For the best text, see Beulertz, *Das Verbot der Laieninvestitur*, pp. 5–6, no. 3.
348 *RHGF* 14.667–8, no. 1.
349 *Reg.* 5.11, to Bishop Hugh of Die, (late 1077), pp. 363–5.
350 *QF* no. 29, pp. 15–16, esp. p. 16/2–4.
351 For the concept and history of free elections, see esp. P. Schmid, *Der Begriff der kanonischen Wahl*.

The problem was an active one from the beginning of his reign. Initially, his intentions were, first, to exclude or at least to minimize the substantive intervention of external authorities, and especially lay authorities, and second, to secure that an election was conducted according to the best canonical model. Thus, in an abbatial election of Saint-Remi at Rheims, the role of Archbishop Manasses was to be limited to giving counsel and consent so that the convent of monks might elect their ruler according to the Rule of St Benedict.[352] In the election of Bishop Landeric of Mâcon, the bishop was to be elected by the unanimous consent of clergy and people; the king might subsequently add his assent, provided that the gift of the episcopate took place freely, that is, without simony.[353] Similarly, after he had consecrated Bishop Hugh of Die, Gregory expressed gratification that his election had taken place with the unanimous consent of his flock, although he reproved Count William of Die for his subsequent interference with the property and clergy of the local church.[354]

That the election of a bishop should be the act of the clergy and people of his see was from first to last the bed-rock of Gregory's notion of a free election. The protracted problem of the succession to the see of Orleans, in the south of the Capetian royal demesne, shows that, after Canossa when Gregory's concern with French affairs was intensified, he was placing greater emphasis upon free election in terms of his conception of Christian liberty. After instructing the clergy and people to elect a new bishop and pastor and to allow no place for simony to creep in, he reminded the electors that Christ alone had suffered and died for them; they were to uphold his liberty and to allow no one to impose upon them either the yoke of iniquity or any lordship ('dominium') which would be to the perdition of their souls. To ensure such liberty, Gregory moved towards a more active role for the papacy, exercised both directly and through comprovincial bishops and papal legates. At the outset, the archbishop of Sens and his suffragans were to collaborate in securing a free election. Later in 1077, Gregory introduced his legate, Hugh of Die. He studiously refrained from directly censuring King Philip I, although he was alleged to have offered a candidate the *donum episcopatus*. He built upon the papal action in difficult elections that he had taken in the early days of his pontificate.[355] His vicar Hugh of Die was to visit Orleans, whether in person or through an agent. He was to determine the wish of all parties and to report to Gregory so that, whether a free and canonical election of the present candidate proved possible or whether an alternative course of action was required, Gregory himself might ensure that the duties of the pope and of the local church were duly performed.[356]

---

[352] *Reg.* 1.52, to Archbishop Manasses of Rheims, 14 Mar. 1074, pp. 79/15–80/1; cf. *Regula sancti Benedicti* 64.1–2, 2. 648–9.

[353] *Reg.* 1.35, to Bishop Roclin of Chalon-sur-Saône, 4 Dec. 1073, pp. 56/30–57/5. A distinction between the *consensus* of the clergy and people and the *assensus* of the king cannot be sustained, since Gregory uses *consensus* of the king in 1.36, to Archbishop Humbert of Lyons, 4 Dec. 1073, p. 58/3–4.

[354] *Reg.* 1.69, to Count William of Die, 23 Mar. 1074, pp. 99–100.

[355] See his dealings with Die and Mâcon: *Reg.* 1.69, 76.

[356] *Reg.* 4.14–15, to the clergy and people of Orleans, and to Archbishop Richer of Sens and his suffragans, 4 Mar. 1077, pp. 317–19; 4.22, to Bishop Hugh of Die, 12 May 1077, p. 333/1–8; 5.8, to

In Provence, the exercise of resolute papal action to secure the election of a suitable candidate is apparent in 1079, when Gregory censured the clergy and people of Arles for their delay in electing a new archbishop. He dispatched there a bishop from the neighbouring province of Aix, Leodegar of Gap, who was to oversee a canonical election of a clerk of Arles who should have the written testimony of Gregory's vicar, Hugh of Die; if, as Gregory expected, there was no suitable clerk of that church, the clergy and people were to promise Leodegar that they would receive as their pastor whomever Gregory should consecrate and send.[357] Gregory thus adopted a procedure which he was to promulgate generally at his Lent synod of 1080. Upon the death of a bishop, a successor should be canonically chosen at the instance of a visiting bishop who should be dispatched by the pope if a metropolitan were being elected, or by the metropolitan if a bishop were being elected. Banishing all secular ambition, fear, or favour, the clergy and people would thus elect for themselves a pastor according to God's will with the assent of the apostolic see or of their metropolitan. An election that was in any way vitiated would be null and void; all power of election would devolve upon the discretion of the apostolic see or of the metropolitan.[358]

In 1079–80 Gregory was in effect working towards establishing a practice which did justice to two canonical principles. One was that the election of a bishop should be by the clergy and people of his church, who should in the first instance seek to elect a clerk of their own church if one were found suitable but who if there were no such suitable candidate might thereafter look elsewhere.[359] The second was that the process of election should be such that the voices of churchmen should be decisive and exclusive, so that the gift of the episcopate came from their hands alone; such was the principle which was enshrined in canon twenty-two of the fourth council of Constantinople.[360]

Gregory's synthesis of these canonical principles in his dealings with Burgundy and France is apparent in the two major elections of the early 1080s. In the kingdom of Burgundy, royal power was a negligible factor. Therefore, upon the death of the Archbishop Gebuin of Lyons, Gregory called upon Hugh of Die as his legate to ensure that the see should be filled by 'a true soldier of Christ and defender of righteousness'. In the first instance, canonical propriety must be respected by looking for

Archbishops Richer of Sens and Richard of Bourges and their suffragans, 6 Oct. 1077, pp. 358–9; 5.11, to Bishop Hugh of Die, (late 1077), pp. 363–5; 5.14, to the clergy and people of Orleans, 29 Jan. 1078, pp. 376–8.

[357] *Reg.* 6.21, to the clergy and people of Arles, 1 Mar. 1079, pp. 432–4.
[358] *Reg.* 7.14*a*(6), p. 482/19–32.
[359] For the canonical background, see Cowdrey, *The Age of Abbot Desiderius*, pp. 189–90.
[360] See above, 3.2.4. There is an apparent incompatibility between the two principles, in so far as the first gave the lay *populus* as well as the *clerus* a place in elections, while the second was expressed in terms of the clerical order. In Gregory's interpretation, the inconsistency was eased because (i) in the local church, the *populus* was understood as concurring in a decision taken by the *clerus*, in accordance with the maxim 'docendus non sequendus populus'; and (ii) canon 22 was understood in terms of authorities external to the local church. The election of bishops by cathedral chapters was of course, a later development.

a suitable clerk of that church. If no such could be found, Gregory prescribed that, by request of his brother-bishops and by way of election by the members ('filiis') of the church of Lyons, Hugh should himself be translated from Die to fill the see.[361] Thus, Gregory's purpose for the see might come to pass. Such exercise of papal authority and initiative found acceptance by prominent lay princes in southern France during Gregory's last years.[362]

In Capetian France, Gregory's elaborate arrangements at the end of 1080 for the election of a successor to the deposed Archbishop Manasses of Rheims are tantamount to being Gregory's definitive statement of how an episcopal election should in practice be conducted when the power of the king must be taken into account.[363] Gregory simultaneously dispatched four letters which are remarkable both for their contents and for the order in which they appear in his Register. First, he called upon the clergy and the people of Rheims to elect by common counsel amongst themselves but also with the counsel of Bishop Hugh of Die an archbishop who would deliver their church from false pastors and restore its ancient liberty. The prescription of free election by clergy and people was common to all four letters. In his third letter, Gregory called upon the suffragan bishops of Rheims to assist its clergy and people in the election, adding that he would himself confirm by papal authority whomever the *pars melior* of them should elect with Hugh of Die's approval. It was a feature of canon twenty-two of the fourth council of Constantinople that it permitted churchmen at their discretion to call upon lay persons to assist and collaborate when an election had been made. In his second letter, Gregory called upon the local magnate Count Ebolus of Roucy to support by all means ('modis omnibus'), that is by force if necessary, the duly elected bishop. Fourthly and very significantly lastly, Gregory sought the aid of King Philip I, who was in no way to impede a canonical election but who was to demonstrate his coming of age in the Christian religion by supporting whomever was duly chosen. Canonical tradition as Gregory interpreted it allowed him to find for the king a recognized if subordinate role in the filling of a see which gave him no part in the conferring of the *donum episcopatus* and which excluded simony, but which nevertheless recognized his regality as Gregory viewed it. It also, by implication, excluded lay investiture. Such was the paradigmatic character of Gregory's last major dealing with the French church, except in Flanders, which is recorded in his Register.

5.4.4 The Enforcement of Clerical Chastity

In view of Gregory's intentions for the church in general, there can be no doubt of his concern to eliminate from France and Burgundy all manifestations of clerical

---

[361] *Reg.* 9.18, to Bishop Hugh of Die, 24 Oct. (1081), pp. 598–9.

[362] For Provence, see *Reg.* 9.12a, b, oath and donation of Count Bertrand II, pp. 589–91, and for the county of Substantion–Melgueil, see above, 5.3.2.4. For abbatial elections, see 9.6, to Abbot Richard of Marseilles and his successors, 18 Apr. 1081, pp. 581–2; 9.29a, Count Bertrand of Arles to Gregory, (1081), pp. 614–15.

[363] *Reg.* 8.17–20; see above, 5.2.1.

marriage, concubinage, and fornication, or that his legates in France were active in promoting clerical chastity. Yet, in his letters, Gregory referred to it in French contexts with surprising infrequency and restraint. There is no evidence for any such concerted attack in France as he made in Germany in 1074–5. He seems never to have addressed to French bishops any such intensive correspondence demanding the exercise of their authority against simony and clerical incontinence as he addressed to German and Italian metropolitans and other bishops. The single exception is his letter of 1077 to Bishop Josfred of Paris. After charging him to inquire into a number of precise matters that had arisen in the province of Rheims, Gregory concluded with an admonition to start a campaign against clerical fornication which was similar to that which he initiated in other lands after his Lent synod of 1075. By papal authority, Josfred was to call upon his brother bishops throughout the whole of France to impose an absolute ban upon the ministrations of clerks who would not cease from the ways of fornication. Josfred was himself to embark upon a general preaching campaign, and he was to visit severe penalties upon bishops who were either slack to join in, or who were themselves guilty of simony or fornication.[364] But Gregory's perfervidly expressed paragraph stands out for its exceptional character so far as France is concerned. An incidental remark in a letter of 1081 to his legates Hugh of Die and Amatus of Oloron shows that they had used French knights to coerce priests guilty of fornication as well as of simony.[365] Otherwise, when sending instructions to these legates, Gregory made no general reference to clerical fornication but concentrated upon simony, lay investiture, and lay involvement in ecclesiastical elections.[366]

Gregory's few references, in a French context, to the question of clerical chastity as addressed to particular persons were restricted in date to 1076–80 and in region to the small north-western region of France which comprised Flanders and Hainault. In November 1076, he wrote to Countess Adela and to Count Robert of Flanders in order to insist that clerks who persisted in fornication should not minister at the altar but should be expelled until they repented; rulers should endeavour to see that only chaste clerks were permitted to officiate.[367] In the following year, one matter which Bishop Josfred of Paris was to investigate was the fate of a priest of Cambrai, Ramihrd, who was said to have been burned alive for preaching that unchaste priests should not say mass but should be boycotted by the laity.[368] In 1080, in answer to a complaint made at Rome by his subjects, Gregory rebuked Bishop Hubert of Thérouanne for his connivance in clerical unchastity.[369] The restriction of such evidence to a region bordering upon Germany links it with Gregory's earlier campaign in Germany.

---

[364] *Reg.* 4.20, 25 Mar. 1077, pp. 328/35–329/15.

[365] *Reg.* 9.5, p. 580/20–3.

[366] See esp. *Reg.* 4.22, *Epp. vag.* no. 30. There is no evidence that *Epp. vag.* no. 32, to the faithful of Italy and Germany, (1079), pp. 84–7, had a parallel text addressed to France.

[367] *Reg.* 4.10–11, 10 Nov. 1076, pp. 309–11.

[368] *Reg.* 4.20, p. 328/22–34, cf. 4.22, p. 332/16–22.

[369] *Epp. vag.* no. 41, to Bishop Hubert of Thérouanne, (late 1080), pp. 102–3.

It is probably not accidental that the diocese of Cambrai, politically in part subject to King Henry IV, was to the fore in the only propaganda campaign in France at this time which is known to have expressed hostility to Gregorian measures to enforce clerical chastity. Two letters survive from what appears to have been a fairly widespread reaction to Bishop Hugh of Die's measures at the council of Autun in September 1077.[370] The first was addressed by a circle at Cambrai to the motherchurch of Rheims and to all in its province; its recipients were urged to be strong in upholding the public liberty of the clergy. The circle at Cambrai did not initiate the chain of letters which is thus illustrated but amplified a letter from an unnamed neighbouring region, perhaps Flanders,[371] which sought resistance to a recent and novel decree as promulgated by papal legates, probably at Autun.[372] The Cambrai letter complained about aspects of what was called 'the oppressiveness of the Romans' ('Romanorum importunitas') who interfered with everything. They diminished the king's authority—an apparent reference to King Philip I's role in episcopal elections; they excommunicated metropolitans—Archbishop Manasses of Rheims was so treated at Autun; under show of religion but in truth from ambition, they deposed and raised up bishops; they summoned frequent councils; and they imposed outlandish judgements ('peregrina iudicia'). The council of Autun was held by venal impostors—Hugh of Langres whose life and character were known to all,[373] and Hugh of Die, who save for his name was known to none. As it was understood at Cambrai, they had ruled that no one should hold two offices or more than one prebend, and that the sons of clerks should not be promoted or ordained. More objectionably still, whereas the custom of Cambrai was that clerks who had taken no vow of continence might be married to one wife, the legates had broadened former legislation about married priests to include the whole clerical order.[374] Citing the legend of Paphnutius,[375] the Cambrai letter sought to provide warrant for the marriage of all clergy. In face of such unheard-of burdens as were now being imposed, the writers felt isolated. Their own bishop, Gerard, had concurred in the rulings of

---

370 *Cameracensium et Noviomensium clericorum epistolae.*   371 See *Reg.* 4.10–11.

372 A reference to Autun, rather than to Boehmer's suggestion of Poitiers in Jan. 1078, is virtually certain. (i) There are no grounds for supposing that any of the legislation referred to was not part of the lost canons of Autun. (ii) The reference to a *decretum*, in the singular, and to its novelty suggests knowledge of only the earlier council. (iii) The reference to both Hugh of Langres and Hugh of Die as leaders suggests Autun, where they are known to have collaborated. (iv) The gibe about Hugh as 'Diensem, ut dicunt, episcopum, cuius praeter nomen nulla est nobis cognitio' is plausible as a comment on Autun but not Poitiers, by the time of which Hugh was well known. (v) The reference to both deposing and making bishops suits Autun: *RHGF* 14.613–4, no. 79. (vi) If the reference is to Autun, the Cambrai letter may be dated late 1077, leaving time for the series of letters which began perhaps in Flanders and led to the Noyon letter which was written before Archbishop Manasses of Rheims's return from Rome in late spring 1078.

373 This, like the penultimate sentence of the Noyon letter, hints at the scandalous character of Hugh of Langres which Archbishop Manasses of Rheims described to Gregory: *H* no. 107, pp. 178/28–179/8; see above, 5.3.3.1.

374 Boehmer cites canon 9 of the council of Poitiers: Mansi, 21.499; but it may have been anticipated at Autun.

375 See above, 3.6.1.

Autun by banning married clerks, and he had pleaded that he could not go against Hugh of Die whose blessing and reconciliation he had received.

The Cambrai circle therefore invited other churches to state their opinion and bring their support. Only a reply from the church of Noyon has survived. It opened as the Cambrai circle might have wished with an exhortation both in adversity to hope for better things and in keeping the faith manfully to resist the adversaries who came against them. The letter from Noyon was careful not to justify clerical marriage in general, but it stoutly defended the ordination of the sons of clerks and condemned as too stringent the prohibition of holding more than one office. Its authors would not, however, go further, for among other, unstated reasons they preferred to await the return from Rome of Archbishop Manasses of Rheims, whose excommunication at Autun was said to have been over-hasty, and the outcome of envy not of righteousness.

The caution of the reply from Noyon is significant, and suggests that much would turn on how Manasses fared at Rome. In the event, like other bishops whom Hugh of Die sentenced at Autun and Poitiers, he found mercy at Gregory's hands, to the discomfiture of Hugh of Die. In the province of Rheims, Gregory will have been seen as distancing himself from his legates; and he did not commission his legates to renew the general campaign against fornication. So far as can be seen, the campaign of the circle of Cambrai melted away when Gregory's mercy was set in contrast with his legate's excessive rigour. As Gregory pursued his campaign against simony and lay investiture, the stage was set for him to move towards the culmination of his reforming endeavours in France which was represented by the unresisted deposition of Archbishop Manasses of Rheims and the carefully balanced arrangements for the free election of his successor.

5.4.5 Peace and the Defence of the Unprotected

A major factor in disposing the French clergy to look to Gregory, at best with attention and a will to collaborate but at worst with not more than a negative resistance to his interventions, was the assiduity with which he applied the moral and practical resources of the apostolic see to the defence of the vulnerable and to the furtherance of public peace. Amongst the vulnerable were the French clergy and monks; in a society where temporal protection was restricted and uncertain, the exercise of papal authority both directly at Rome and locally through legates and councils made it a matter of prudence as well as of duty for many churchmen to give active or passive recognition to papal authority as wielded by Gregory.

As in Germany, so in France Gregory saw in the state of public disorder a challenge to promote peace and concord which the apostolic see must answer. In 1074, he set out the state of France as he saw it to all the archbishops and bishops of the kingdom.

A long time has already elapsed since the kingdom of France, once renowned and very powerful, began to be wrenched from its state of glory and, as evil customs multiplied, to be denuded of its many marks of virtue. Truly, in these days both its high honour and the whole face of its righteousness seem to have fallen, when laws are neglected and all righteousness is trampled

underfoot, and when all that is foul, cruel, pitiable, and intolerable is there both done with impunity and by being accorded licence is now made into a custom. For many years, since royal
power among you faded, there has been no law and no authority to prohibit or punish wrongful acts. Men who are at enmity have fought each other to the limit of their power as if by some
common law of nations, and have prepared arms and forces to avenge their own wrongs. Given
such disturbances, if slaughter, arson, and all the rest that warfare brings with it are rampant,
one should indeed grieve but not greatly wonder. For now, all men are filled with evil will as
with an epidemic disease and, with no one to challenge them, they regularly commit horrend-
ous and execrable crimes. They think nothing of committing perjuries, sacrileges, and incest,
or of betraying one another. As nowhere else, fellow-citizens, neighbours, and brothers seize
each other from greed for gain. Extorting all their goods from them, they cause them to end
their lives in abject wretchedness. They cast into prison pilgrims to and from Rome as opportunity offers; they afflict them with torments more grievous than any of the heathen, often
demanding from them a ransom greater than their possessions.[376]

When due allowance is made for the exceptional crisis in Gregory's relations with the
French king that elicited this outburst, it provides the essential background for the
many respects in which Gregory sought to intervene in France in order to promote
peace and to protect persons and institutions, both great and small, that he deemed
to be vulnerable.

Local disputes were often referred to him at Rome. In 1074, for example,
Archbishop Ralph of Tours prompted a letter from Gregory to a knight, Hugh of
Sainte-Maure near Chinon, who had seized goods of his church. If he was guilty,
Gregory ruled that he must make satisfaction to the archbishop; if he had a grievance
against the archbishop, let them both appear at a Roman synod.[377] The account in the
Register of Gregory's Lent synod of 1076 shows that he sought to enforce justice
upon the simoniac, Archbishop Herman of Vienne, who, although deposed, was vex-
ing or occupying churches at Vienne, Romans, and Lyons.[378] In 1079, Gregory wrote
to Count Boso of la Marche about his persistent ravaging of a church belonging to the
see of Jerusalem and referred the case, if necessary, to the authority of his legate
Hugh of Die.[379]

Gregory was sometimes concerned with the settling of local disputes which
threatened peace and for the bringing of the parties to a state of concord. When
Archbishop Ralph of Tours complained to him that he and his men were suffering
violence from a certain Lanzelin who was a subject of Archbishop Richer of Sens,
Gregory reminded Richer that he should have dealt with such a matter without papal
prompting, but that he should now be resolute to bringing to bear whatever sanctions
were necessary to restrain Lanzelin.[380] In 1079, Gregory's legates Amatus of Oloron
and Hugh of Die were to compose a prolonged discord between the abbeys of Sainte-
Croix and Saint-Sever at Bordeaux about the possession of a church.[381] Gregory was

[376] *Reg.* 2.5, 10 Sept. 1074, p. 130/14–32, cf. 1.75, to King Philip of France, 13 Apr. 1074, pp. 106–7.
[377] *Reg.* 2.22, 15 Nov. 1074, p. 154.   [378] *Reg.* 3.10*a*, p. 269.12–17, 22–3.
[379] *Reg.* 6.40, 28 June 1079, pp. 457–8.   [380] *Reg.* 2.20, 15 Nov. 1074, pp. 152–3.
[381] *Reg.* 6.24–5, to Bishop Amatus of Oloron, and to Abbot Arnald of Saint-Sever, 8 Mar. 1079, pp.
436–8.

also concerned to prevent violence against those who were travelling to and from Rome, whether as merchants, pilgrims, or on business.[382]

Monasteries stood in especial need of protection. Because of their conspicuous role in eleventh-century society, protection extended to them won prestige and influence for those who extended it. Gregory acknowledged an urgent responsibility towards those monasteries which had been committed to the especial proprietorship of St Peter ('cui monasterium speciali et proprio iure subiectum est'). On occasion, Gregory sought to mobilize aid over a wide area in order to secure the peace of such a monastery. An especially good example is Saint-Pierre at Montmajour (dioc. Arles). In 1079, Gregory called upon all the ecclesiastical and lay magnates of Provence to abstain from their sacrilegious invasion of its goods. Time was to show that Montmajour's troubles were more deep-seated; in 1081, Count Bertrand of Provence reported upon his expulsion of the grossly sodomitical abbot Bermundus and his replacement by an abbot upon the advice of Archbishop Gebuin of Lyons. The count renewed his commitment to defending monastic liberty, and Gregory entrusted Montmajour into the hands of Abbot Richard of Saint-Victor at Marseilles.[383] Thus, Gregory arranged for a measure of both lay and monastic oversight. In 1080, Gregory reacted similarly to complaints from the monks of Aurillac (dioc. Clermont) which its founder, Count Gerald, had commended to St Peter. Archbishop William of Auch was to vindicate its possession of a church that had been seized by the monks of Pessan in his diocese on pain of interdict from their sacrilege. More extensively, all Christians in the three provinces of Bourges, Narbonne, and Bordeaux were to rally to Aurillac's defence against a variety of lay and monastic persons who were infringing its rights and possessions; Gregory especially named Berengar, *vicomte* of Carlat.[384] Gregory also took churches into papal protection on terms which brought St Peter's sanctions to bear upon their lay neighbours. Thus, in 1081 in a letter addressed 'to all who are faithful to God and St Peter', he gave such protection to the church of Maskarans (dioc. Poitiers) in return for an annual *census*, promising that whoever abstained from harassing it out of love for St Peter would enjoy the apostle's help, forgiveness, and blessing.[385]

Such intervention on favour of the peace of churches which were of the *proprium ius sancti Petri* is an intense example of the protection that Gregory extended to many greater and lesser monasteries by means of his privileges. Some were given to large centres like Cluny and la Chaise-Dieu.[386] In Cluny's case, Gregory spectacularly defended its liberty and security by specially dispatching his legate, Cardinal-bishop

---

[382] These were the occasion of Gregory's sharp contention with King Philip of France in 1074: see above, 5.2.1; also *Reg.* 9.13, to Count Robert of Flanders, (1083), p. 592/12–15.

[383] *Reg.* 6.31, to all the archbishops, bishops, princes, clerks, and laymen in Provence, 31 Mar. 1079, pp. 444–5; 9.29a, Count Bertrand of Arles to Gregory, (1081), pp. 614–15, *QF* nos. 198–9, pp. 229–32.

[384] *Reg.* 7.18–19, to Archbishop William of Auch, and to all in the provinces of Bourges, Narbonne, and Bordeaux, 12 Apr. 1080, pp. 492–5.

[385] *Reg.* 9.7, 28 Apr. 1081, pp. 585–7.

[386] Cluny: *QF* no. 107 (1075/6), pp. 95–100; la Chaise-Dieu: *QF* no. 181 (1080), pp. 210–12.

Peter of Albano.[387] Like Saint-Victor at Marseilles, Cluny was itself entrusted with the protection of the rights of other houses, some of them belonging to the 'proprium ius sancti Petri'.[388] It is difficult to assess how far Gregory's promises of protection, reinforced as they were by the work of legates like Hugh of Die and Amatus of Oloron, of the French and Burgundian metropolitans, and of monastic leaders like Hugh of Cluny and Richard of Marseilles, were more effective in practice than those of earlier popes. Perhaps the most eloquent testimony to their prestige is the alacrity with which lesser people in various parts of France sought Gregory's protection for their churches. Such a man was the obscure knight named Isaac who sought protection for all the property, both movable and immovable, of the small monastery of Sainte-Marie at Voormezele (dioc. Thérouanne).[389] Again, in 1078, Abbot Benedict of Sainte-Croix at Quimperlé took advantage of Gregory's conviction that he should renew the lapsed papal duty of protection over Brittany to secure a papal privilege protecting the possessions of his monastery; on at least one occasion, Gregory intervened with Count Hoel of Brittany in order to urge him to restore and safeguard them.[390] Such examples suggest that Gregory's concern to be a source of peace in France was sometimes recognized and appreciated.

A number of Gregory's more urgent endeavours to afford protection against violence and oppression were directed towards helping those groups, often of middling clergy, which were his allies in particular churches against recalcitrant archbishops and bishops, and towards counteracting the clerical and lay groups that opposed them. In the resulting feuds, there was little by way of local defence for Gregory's allies, who were vulnerable to reprisals against their goods and persons.

In the early days of his pontificate, Gregory was concerned, with the help of Abbot Hugh of Cluny, to rectify Archbishop Manasses of Rheims's violence against the monks of Saint-Remi whose persons he was alleged to have subjected to cruel and shameful captivity and whose temporal goods he was alleged to have plundered.[391] Later in his dealings with the archbishop, Gregory was in touch with the group opposed to the archbishop whose number included the cathedral provost Manasses and the chancellor Bruno. One of the group, named Fulcuius *Monoculus*, visited Gregory at Rome.[392] In 1080, it was amongst Gregory's conditions in the archbishop's final chance for amendment of life that he should make full restitution of the property of Provost Manasses and his circle and should refrain from making inroads upon the resources of his church.[393]

---

[387] See above, 5.3.2.4.

[388] *QF* nos. 108–9 (Montierneuf and Gigny), (1075/6), pp. 100–4.

[389] *QF* no. 23d, p. 8; the date is unknown.

[390] *QF* no. 153, pp. 174–6; *Epp. vag.* no. 56, to Count Hoel of Brittany, (1073–84), pp. 136–7.

[391] *Reg.* 1.13–14, to Archbishop Manasses of Rheims, and to Abbot Hugh of Cluny, 30 June 1073, pp. 21–3.

[392] Bruno of Chartreux, *Ad Radulphum, cognomentum Viridem, Remensem praepositum*, cap. 13, in *Lettres des premiers Chartreux*, 1.74–7; the incident is not dated, but is probably from the time of Gregory. Fulcuius is probably the poet Fulcuius of Beauvais: ibid. pp. 256–7.

[393] *Reg.* 7.20, to Archbishop Manasses of Rheims, 17 Apr. 1080, p. 496/14–23.

Likewise, at other places Gregory sought to mobilize sanctions against the assailants of those whom he deemed his allies. At Orleans, the clerk Eurard was their persistent persecutor and the leader ('dux et auctor') of a faction that ravaged the church's goods and harassed its clergy; he was to answer at Rome and, with his followers, he was threatened with anathema. At Chartres, Gregory blamed Bishop Robert and his brother Hugh, perhaps a layman, for wrongs against the church and clergy; he called upon Archbishop Richer of Sens and his suffragans to seek prompt redress. At Lille, Gregory was determined to use his legate Hugh of Die to remedy the injuries done by the provost and canons against his messenger Ingelrannus and Lambert, a canon who had complained at Rome against his deprivation. At Thérouanne, Gregory called upon the bishops of Flanders to intervene against Count Robert who was responsible for sacrilegious depredations of church property and of savage atrocities against the clergy in the wake of the banishing of Bishop Lambert. In addition, he responded strenuously against other lay figures who behaved similarly, apparently Count Eustace of Thérouanne and the *subdefensor* Oilardus of Quesques; they were to appear before Gregory's legates Hugh of Lyons and Hugh of Cluny. Gregory also sought to protect his injured supporters. He defended the canons of Sainte-Croix at Orleans against their bishop and the clerk Eurard, naming a certain Joscelin and especially a clerk named Benedict who had been his messenger. At Lille, the canon Lambert needed special protection, and in Flanders, Gregory indicated by name the clerks who were most at risk—at Thérouanne, the provost, the dean, the archdeacon, a deacon who may have been the Ingelrannus who was especially conspicuous among Gregory's agents, and an abbot.[394]

In such cases of local violence, Gregory possessed an impressive detailed knowledge. Those who supported him had direct access to him at Rome, and he called upon both his legates and the provincial episcopate to come to their assistance. His sanctions were spiritual as well as material, and the prestige which attached to St Peter as prince of the apostles could be brought to bear. In programme at least, Gregory was able to publish his purpose of bringing peace and order to troubled places in France, and to win recognition for the papacy upon his own terms.

Gregory was also concerned after his own fashion to promote peace and concord in France by means of the lay power. His awareness of the consequences of public

---

394 The principal sources for this paragraph are: Orleans. *Reg.* 2.52, to the clerk Eurard, 28 Feb. 1075, pp. 194–5; 3.16–17, to Archbishop Richer of Sens, and to Bishop Rainer of Orleans, Apr. 1076, pp. 278–80; 4.9 to Archbishop Richer of Sens, 2 Nov. 1076, pp. 307–8; 5.8–9, to Archbishops Richer of Sens and Richard of Bourges and their suffragans, and to Bishop Rainer of Orleans, 6 Oct. 1077, pp. 358–61; 5.14, to the clergy and people of Orleans, 5 Mar. 1079, pp. 435–6. Chartres. *Reg.* 4.15 to Archbishop Richer of Sens and his suffragans, 4 Mar. 1077, p. 319. Lille. *Reg.* 6.26, to Provost Fulcard and the canons of Lille, 14 Mar. 1079, pp. 438–9. Flanders. *Reg.* 9.31, to the (*subdefensor*) O(ilardus) and (Count) E(ustace) of Thérouanne, (1083), pp. 617–18, 9.33–5, to Archbishop Hugh of Lyons, to Count Robert I of Flanders, and to the bishops of Cambrai, Noyon, and Amiens, (1083), pp. 619–27; *Epp. vag.* no. 47, to Count Robert of Flanders, (1083), pp. 114–15. *Reg.* 9.35, which is of Gregory's own dictation, is of first importance as a statement of his idea of papal authority as brought to bear upon a local situation.

disorder and his sense of a ruler's responsibilities in face of it found expression in his exasperation in 1074 with King Philip I.[395] They were also manifest in his dealings with French dukes and counts who wished to abandon their earthly principalities and enter monasteries. In 1079, he rebuked Abbot Hugh of Cluny for admitting to the cloister Duke Hugh I of Burgundy.[396] The incident has been widely misunderstood; Gregory's censure was not directed against the fact of admitting such a lay ruler to the cloister, but against the attendant circumstance that the duke had failed to make due provision for the peace and security of the church and of his subjects. So far as the church is concerned, light is shed on Gregory's reasons by correspondence between Archbishop Manasses of Rheims, Bishop Hugh of Die, and Gregory himself in 1080. Manasses gave as a reason for his failure to attend Hugh's council of Lyons the turbulence of the duchy of Burgundy which made it unsafe for him to travel; he alluded to the recent captivity of Count William I of Nevers and his son, Bishop Geoffrey of Auxerre.[397] As regards Burgundian society, Gregory accused the abbot of Cluny of leaving countless Christians with no protector:

Behold! Those who seem to fear or love God flee from Christ's battle, put aside their brothers' safety, and seek rest as though loving only themselves. The shepherds flee, as do the dogs, the defenders of the flock; wolves and robbers attack Christ's sheep while no one resists. You have taken or received the duke into rest at Cluny, and brought it about that a hundred thousand Christians lack a guardian.

This number included the most vulnerable members of society—the poor, widows, orphans, clerks, and monks.

Yet by becoming a monk, Duke Hugh had imitated Count Simon of Crépy,[398] whose monastic conversion Gregory welcomed with enthusiasm. The difference was that, upon Gregory's direction, Simon delayed until he had made peace with King Philip of France and had restored order to his region—until, as his biographer put it, 'pax et concordia confirmantur'.[399] This phrase may serve as an epitome of Gregory's purpose for French as for German society. It was a purpose that princely entry into a monastery, and even to the eremitical life, should serve and not contradict; then it became praiseworthy. By his work for Gregory, Simon of Crépy abundantly served it after his monastic conversion.[400]

---

395 *Reg.* 2.5; see above, 5.2.1.

396 *Reg.* 6.17, to Abbot Hugh of Cluny, 2 Jan. 1079, pp. 423–4. For Duke Hugh's sound rule, see Richard, *Les Ducs de Bourgogne*, pp. 13–16; for the monastic conversion of lay princes, see also Cowdrey, 'Count Simon of Crépy's Monastic Conversion', and below, 11.4.

397 *RHGF* 14.782D; also Gregory's rejection of such an excuse in *Reg.* 7.12, to Archbishop Manasses of Rheims, 3 Jan. 1080, p. 476/3–18. In this letter, Gregory significantly told Manasses that he could have safe conduct through Burgundy from the episcopal—not lay princes'—retinues of Archbishop Gebuin of Lyons and Bishop Hugh of Langres.

398 *Vita beati Simonis com. Cresp.* cap. 6, col. 1216D.

399 Ibid. caps. 3–4, cols. 1213C–1214B.

400 Ibid. cap. 11, cols. 1219–20.

5.5 Conclusion

In sharp contrast to his dealings with Germany, Gregory never came into prolonged and open conflict with the Capetian monarchy or with any major element in the French church, whether secular or monastic. Gregory pursued his campaign against lay investiture which he subsumed in an endeavour to exclude lay control altogether from ecclesiastical appointments great and small, more resolutely in France than in any other part of Latin Christendom; yet during and after his pontificate, no sustained 'investiture contest' or even 'investiture controversy' broke out in France.

The key to the paradox is that, with regard to France, Gregory's purposes ripened slowly. Only after Canossa did his principal legates and papal vicars in France, Hugh of Die and Amatus of Oloron, become powerfully active, and only after this juncture did his resistance to lay investiture and to lay intervention in ecclesiastical elections become sharply expressed and focused. Furthermore, Gregory's main impact in these matters was not prolonged. After the deposition at the end of 1080 of Archbishop Manasses of Rheims, he was preoccupied by his renewed struggle against Henry IV of Germany. Apart from the county of Flanders which was close to Henry's German kingdom, only between 1077 and 1080 were major issues of French origin at the forefront of his concern.

At all times, but particularly during these years of special concern, Gregory's approach to French persons and problems was, in general, moderate and restrained. These adjectives are especially appropriate for his dealings with the most conspicuous of the French churchmen whom he sought to discipline, Manasses of Rheims. They also apply to his dealings with the king, save for the atypical episode in 1074 which was occasioned by the harassment of Italian merchants and which did not throw into relief major issues of *sacerdotium* and *regnum*. After Canossa, Gregory showed no tendency to challenge the king but seemed not to notice or to press grievances that he might well have had in view of the king's ecclesiastical dealings. During the critical years from 1077 to 1080, Hugh of Die's rigour and severity against French bishops at his ecclesiastical councils, especially those of Autun and Poitiers, stood in striking contrast to Gregory's mercy and moderation towards bishops who came to him at Rome. Few French bishops had cause for seeing in Gregory Archbishop Liemar of Bremen's 'periculosus homo' who treated bishops as though they were his bailiffs. The year 1078 had been described as witnessing the 'Canossa' of the French bishops who flocked to Rome and were reconciled.[401] Especially when the large number of German bishops who were at Canossa is borne in mind, there is much truth in this description. French bishops learnt that a mercy was to be found from Gregory at the Lateran which might not be forthcoming if they stayed at home. The merciful Gregory stood in welcome contrast to the severe Hugh of Die. Nor was it only bishops who had been bruised by legatine severity who came to value Roman justice and equity. Gregory's letters afford evidence of French clergy and laymen, both great and small, who found through recourse to Gregory at Rome the

---

[401] Schwarz, 'Der Investiturstreit in Frankreich', p. 300; Becker, *Studien zum Investiturproblem*, p. 67.

provision or at least the initiation of a justice and protection that answered to their needs.

Gregory's moderation in practice also precluded the outbreak of major conflicts of a political nature between Gregory and the French monarchy and French princes. The potential for conflict was strong, especially after, in 1077, Gregory proclaimed and gave wide publicity to the binding force in France of the principle that underlay canon twenty-two of the fourth council of Constantinople, which withdrew episcopal elections from lay hands save in so far as ecclesiastical authorities might initiate and permit their obedient and subservient concurrence.[402] Given the prevalence of royal actions that could be deemed simoniacal, of lay investiture, and of royal initiative in episcopal elections, a headlong clash of pope and king could have developed— the more so because of the zeal of Hugh of Die as Gregory's legate. But two groups of Gregory's letters of the 1080s show that Gregory was careful not to allow the potential for strife to develop but that he sought a concord which, while not fully securing his objectives, established a *modus vivendi* between the papacy and France which lasted for two centuries after his death.

The first is the group of letters by which, in 1080, Gregory sought to provide for the election of a successor to the deposed archbishop of Rheims,[403] with regard to whom Gregory had for long shown restraint and patience. The letters show how Gregory sought to implement in practice the canonical position as he derived it from such canonical precedents as that set by the fourth council of Constantinople. Above all, the new election must be freely made by the clergy and people of Rheims, and under the eye of the legate Hugh of Die. Gregory addressed the king last of all, as was appropriate in the light of canon twenty-two of Constantinople; yet he also wrote in terms of respect and restraint, placing emphasis upon what a well instructed king was rightly to be invited to do, both in respect of repelling the obdurate Manasses and of assisting the election of his successor. Gregory made no explicit reference to simony or to lay investiture, and did not in so many words proscribe the new archbishop's receiving his see at the hands of the king. Philip was to do nothing that would impede his canonical election and succession, but he was to help whomever the more faithful and religious persons in the church of Rheims might elect. Above all, Gregory invoked the Petrine sanction which Philip was to bear in mind:

Above all else, strive to make into your debtor St Peter, in whose power reside both your kingdom and your soul and who can bind and loose you both in heaven and upon earth, and strive worthily to deserve not his condemnation for your negligence and disregard of the truth, but rather by his favour to deserve his eternal help for your diligence and performance of righteousness.

In his expressed hope that Philip was leaving behind him the evil ways of his youth for the paths of righteousness, Gregory foreshadowed the twelfth-century papal recognition of the Capetian king as 'rex christianissimus'; it was an approval that the Capetians, for their part, would find it useful to cultivate. Gregory did not press the

---

[402] *Reg.* 4.22, pp. 333/18–334/8; see above, 5.4.3.   [403] *Reg.* 8.17–20.

extremer implications of canonical precedents in ways that threatened the Capetian monarchy or materially undermined the loyalty of its bishops. Gregory's pontificate ended with an equilibrium between the papacy and the Capetian monarchy which would later be strained, not least by Philip I in his later years, but which would not be broken until the age of Pope Boniface VIII and King Philip IV. France would witness no such head-on clashes with the papacy as would ensue in Germany and in England.

The second group of letters is those which Gregory sent in 1082–3 to Flanders with reference to Count Robert I and the see of Thérouanne.[404] Not only did he in effect turn a blind eye to King Philip I's involvement save in so far as he urged Count Robert to break his fealty to the king if the path of righteousness should so require, but he sought to guide the count, whom he knew to be deeply culpable for his violent intervention at Thérouanne, towards the acceptance of a canonical election which would expunge his earlier faults and promise amendment for the future:

We urge your excellency to receive honourably and as is fitting Gerard, the canonically elected bishop who has entered the church of Thérouanne by the door, that is, through Christ, and by showing him the reverence that is due to a shepherd to give him your counsel and aid [the 'consilium et auxilium' that were due from a subject to his lord]; so that, as by one candidate [Lambert] you offended God you may by another [Gerard] commend your righteousness to God himself and to St Peter.[405]

From his side, Gregory thus stated a view of the place of the lay ruler in episcopal elections which accorded with his prescription for the election at Rheims in 1080 and with the *Fürstenspiegel* which he had set out to Count Robert's subjects in 1083.[406] From the Flemish side, nothing was done to fracture relations with the papacy, with which a *modus vivendi* was consolidated which was similar to that between the papacy and the Capetian kingdom. In the long term, Gregory was again setting the stage for harmony and collaboration, notably in the response which the Flemings under Count Robert II made in 1095 to Pope Urban II's call to the Crusade.

If Gregory's generally diplomatic handling of relations with such lay rulers as King Philip I and Count Robert I of Flanders damped down potential conflict and achieved a degree of concord between them and the papacy, his dealings with French churchmen on the whole told in the same direction. French churchmen, great and small, became habituated to looking to Rome for justice and for mercy. Papal legates might sometimes be vexatious and interfering, but they were also agents of a papal power which could offer a justice that was unattainable in France itself. The high-and-dry inertia of a Manasses of Rheims looked old-fashioned and stagnant by comparison with the zeal and purpose of a Hugh of Die or an Amatus of Oloron. At the same time, personally weak metropolitans like Ralph of Tours or Gebuin of Lyons were by no means reluctant to have a measure of papal backing and approval. Gregory thus built bridges between the papacy and the French church which would for long survive.

---

[404] See above, 5.2.2.   [405] *Reg.* 9.36, p. 629/23–9.   [406] *Reg.* 9.35.

Of particular significance were the bishops whose outlook Gregory was able to form because they spent protracted periods with him at Rome. Thus, Bishop Hugh of Die, whose work there and at Lyons continued until he died in 1109, was profoundly influenced by his early stay at Rome in company with Bishop Anselm II of Lucca. Upon returning to France, he administered his own small diocese in a way that Gregory praised at his Lent synod of 1076, mentioning especially his recovery of tithes, first-fruits, and churches from lay hands; such exemplary work in his diocese was no less pleasing to Gregory than the beginnings of his work as a legate.[407] Hugh of Die and Lyons's work was, at a diocesan level, continued by Hugh, bishop of Grenoble from 1080 to 1132.[408] His *Life*, which was written by Prior Guigo I of la Grande Chartreuse, provided for the twelfth century a pattern of a bishop who embodied and perpetuated Gregory's aspirations for the French church. Hugh's qualities were early recognized by Hugh of Die; he shared the legate's concern to win from lay hands churches, tithes, and cemeteries, as well as to do away with clerical marriage and simony. At Hugh of Die's council of Avignon in 1080, he was canonically elected to the see of Grenoble and ordained up to the grade of the priesthood. According to Guigo's *Life*, he refused episcopal ordination by Archbishop Warmund of Vienne on account of his simony.[409] He therefore resorted to Gregory at Rome; while there, he underwent some kind of spiritual crisis through which Gregory gave him pastoral guidance. Upon returning to his diocese, he maintained close touch with the abbey of la Chaise-Dieu, where he was professed as a monk, and later with Chartreuse, founded in his diocese in 1084 by the Bruno who as a canon of Rheims had opposed Archbishop Manasses. The combination of an association with eremitical monasticism, such as that of Chartreuse, with exemplary pastoral ministration in the diocese, became a powerful and enduring element in French ecclesiastical life.[410] By such deep-flowing currents Gregory's work was perpetuated in France, where his studied moderation had won him willing hearers.

[407] *Reg.* 3.10a, p. 269/25–8.

[408] Guigo, *Vita sancti Hugonis*, esp. caps. 1.4–3.11, cols. 765B–770A; see Cowdrey, 'Hugh of Avalon', esp. pp. 48–9.

[409] The charge of simony against Warmund is improbable and has not been satisfactorily explained; there may be confusion with his predecessor Herman.

[410] See Cowdrey, 'The Carthusians and their Contemporary World', and id. 'The Gregorian Papacy and Eremitical Monasticism'.

6

Gregory VII and the Periphery of Latin Europe

6.1 Introduction

In April 1075, Gregory dispatched a group of six letters to destinations in eastern and northern Europe—to Duke Gésa of Hungary who was the cousin and rival of King Solomon, to Duke Wratislav of Bohemia, to the Bohemian people, to Duke Boleslav II of Poland, to Prince Isjaslav of Russia, and to King Sweyn Estrithson of Denmark.[1] They were written with diverse situations and purposes in view; yet, taken together, they provide an exceptionally full conspectus of Gregory's approach to the kingdoms and principalities that surrounded Germany, North Italy, and France—the nearer kingdoms to which his concern was particularly directed.

Gregory set out the grounds for his concern in clarion tones to the king of Denmark. Perhaps with the example of Pope Gregory the Great especially in view, he wrote that:

Amongst our predecessors it was a matter of law and custom that, by sending caritative embassies, they taught the way of the Lord to all nations, that they rebuked all kings and princes whenever they deserved to be accused, and that they invited all men by lawful disciplines into eternal blessedness. For the law of the Roman pontiffs has won more lands than the emperors'. 'Their sound has gone out into all lands' (Ps. 18: 5, Rom. 10: 18), and Christ has ruled as emperor those whom Augustus ruled. But now, kings and chiefs of the world have become scorners of the church's law when they should, rather, have upheld righteousness and defended that law. They have gathered together (Ps. 2: 2) to inflict so many outrages upon the church and to fall into such disobedience, which according to Samuel is similar to idolatry (1 Sam. 15: 23), that our embassies have almost come to a stop because they appear virtually fruitless; wherefore we direct our words in prayer alone to the Lord of kings and the God of vengeance.[2]

By reason of his office, the pope had a commission to shepherd all the peoples of the earth, whether or not they lived within the boundaries of the Roman empire at the apogee of its prosperity. The Roman church was in the fullest sense the universal mother; every land was subject to St Peter, who was so named after the unshakeable rock which breaks the gates of hell and destroys all that resist it with adamantine

---

[1] *Reg.* 2.70, to Duke Gésa of Hungary, 17 Apr. 1075, p. 229–30; 2.71–5, to Duke Wratislav II of Bohemia, 17 Apr. 1075, pp. 231–2, to the people of Bohemia, 17 Apr. 1075, pp. 232–3, to Duke Boleslav II of Poland, 20 Apr. 1075, pp. 233–5, to King Isjaslav of Russia and his wife, 17 Apr. 1075, pp. 236–7, to King Sweyn II of Denmark, 17 Apr. 1075, pp. 237–8.
[2] pp. 237/30–238/8.

strength.[3] It behoved all kings and princes to make St Peter their friend and debtor, so that they might enjoy his blessing in this world as in the next.[4] In the pope, they should hear the voice of St Peter; as for their own offices, they should regard them as a stewardship from God which should be exercised in remembrance that God would finally call them to account.[5]

Gregory's six letters suggest that his concerns with far-flung peoples was three-fold—political, judicial, and pastoral. Politically, Gregory sought to foster among the nations something like a balance of power: more distant peoples were to be established in their independence from outside political supremacy and in the habit of obedience to the papacy; by such means, the power especially of the Salian monarchy in Germany might be kept within bounds. Thus, Gregory's gravamen against King Solomon of Hungary was that, when his kingdom was rightly subject in a specially close way to the lordship of St Peter, he had made himself subject to the German king and from being a king ('rex') had become a kinglet ('regulus'). Even while Gregory's expectations of Henry were favourable, he was concerned that Henry's power to the east should be contained.[6] To King Sweyn of Denmark, Gregory enlarged upon the deficiencies of other kings than himself; in Denmark, he aspired to see a very strong kingdom guided by the wisdom of an exemplary king who showed proper reverence to the mother of all the churches; the king of a distant realm was, by strong and righteous rule, to compensate for the unreliability of rulers who were nearer to Rome.[7]

Closely allied to his political concern, Gregory had a judicial one, similar to that which he expressed in the late 1070s with regard to Germany, of promoting peace and concord wherever matters of justice were at issue and men were at odds with each other. He introduced his intention for Hungary to Duke Gésa in these terms:

If it belongs to our office to ensure for all men their rights and to compose peace and establish concord among them, how much more does reason demand and expediency require that we should sow charity amongst prominent men whose peace or hatred affects the many. Therefore it is our business, and godly solicitude dwells in our heart, that, if we are able, we should make peace between you and your kinsman King Solomon, so that justice may be maintained on both sides and that each may be content with his due. May each not transgress the bounds of justice or exceed the measure of good custom. Thus, peace may come to the illustrious kingdom of Hungary, which has hitherto been strong and independent ('quod hactenus per se principaliter viguit') so that there has been a king ('rex') and not a kinglet ('regulus').

Likewise, the duke of Poland was above all else to observe the rule of charity by restoring to the prince of Russia the property that he or his men had stolen.[8] By moderating in disputes within and between kingdoms and principalities, the papacy was to be the fount of justice, peace, and concord.

But, above all, Gregory's concern was a pastoral one, 'to teach the way of the Lord to all nations'.[9] He was to follow the precedents set by Pope Gregory the Great of old and Pope Alexander II more recently in seeking to propagate the faith within

---

3 p. 230/17–23.   4 pp. 231/27–30, 235/11–20, 236/28–36.
5 pp. 233/3–18, 233/33–234/14, 235/1–10.   6 p. 230/11–13.
7 p. 238/1–22.   8 pp. 230/1–14, 235/21–30.   9 p. 237/31.

universal horizons. He explained to the people of Bohemia that, by virtue of his office, the pope owed a general debt to faithful and unfaithful Christians alike: he must confirm the faithful in their good intentions and he must see that the unfaithful returned to faith in the Creator and accepted the punishment due for past sins.[10] In discharging this debt, Gregory had the advantage that people from the ends of the earth as from nearer regions came to the apostolic see on pilgrimage and on business; like the visitors referred to in his letters, they came in a receptive frame of mind.[11] Gregory was also assiduous in sending far and wide the 'caritative embassies' of which he spoke to the king of Denmark. They were the messengers ('legati') of the law of Christianity; whatever specific charges might be given to them, their task was to confirm proper loyalty and to promote true religion in the lands to which they came.[12] The results of the movement of pilgrims and messengers to and from Rome must be remembered whenever Gregory's dealings with distant lands are under consideration.

In both ends and means, these dealings varied greatly from region to region, yet Gregory's letters of April 1075 establish a common background against which they must be discussed.

6.2 South Italy and Sicily

Of the peripheral lands of eleventh-century Europe, South Italy and Sicily were nearest at hand to the papacy. They were relatively distant from sources of external control: although the German emperors retained a claim to suzerainty it could seldom be brought to bear; with the loss of Bari to the Normans in 1071, Byzantine rule was at an end; between 1071 and 1091, the Normans carried out the conquest of Sicily from the Muslims. From the Lombard and Norman rulers both ecclesiastical and political who vied for control, Gregory felt the need for both spiritual and material support.[13] Immediately upon becoming pope, he looked most conspicuously to the Lombards. The first letter in his Register is addressed to Abbot Desiderius of Montecassino; after informing him of his election, Gregory sought from the abbot and his monks the prayers that might have availed to free him from the burden of the papal office, but which might now protect him from its dangers. The second letter is addressed to Prince Gisulf II of Salerno (1052–77), whom he asked to procure similar prayers from Abbot Leo of La Cava and the other monks of his lands. He urged both abbot and prince to come to Rome, for the church stood in need of their counsel and service.[14] In the summer of 1073, at Benevento and in the presence of Abbot

---

[10] p. 232/19–23.   [11] pp. 236/21–8, 238/12–18.

[12] pp. 230/23–5, 234/25–35, 237/4–14, 238/13–18.

[13] For a fuller discussion and bibliography of the subject-matter of this section, see Cowdrey, *The Age of Abbot Desiderius*; for the general situation in South Italy, see esp. pp. xxviii–xxxii, and for the main stages of Gregory's dealings, esp. pp. 122–76.

[14] *Reg.* 1.1–2, to Abbot Desiderius of Montecassino, and to Prince Gisulf of Salerno, 23 Apr. 1073, pp. 3–5. These were the only letters to be dated on the day after Gregory's election.

Desiderius and of other cardinals who were travelling with him, Gregory concluded a treaty with Prince Landulf VI of Benevento (1038–77) in which, following the formula for the oath of a 'procurator patrimonii sancti Petri', Landulf forswore infidelity to the Roman church and to the pope upon pain of forfeiting his office by papal sentence.[15]

The loyalty of the Lombard princes was to be complemented by that of their Norman rivals who, at Melfi in 1059, had done fealty to the papacy for their lands and so had been made papal allies.[16] That Gregory did not send notice of his election to Robert Guiscard, duke of Apulia and Calabria, may have been the consequence of a false rumour which reached Rome that Robert Guiscard had died at Bari. Instead, Gregory dispatched to Robert's wife Sichelgaita a letter of which the Cassinese historian Amatus preserved the gist.[17] Gregory expressed his condolences upon the death of the duke whom he described as 'lo karissime fil de la sainte Eglize'. He urged Sichelgaita to see that his son should receive from the church's hand the possessions that Robert Guiscard had held from Pope Alexander II. When Robert, who was unwell, saw the letter, he thanked the pope and promised his faithful service. No doubt he was mindful of his own need both to secure from a new pope the confirmation of his fiefs and to ensure the eventual succession of his son by Sichelgaita, Roger, rather than Bohemond, his elder son by his former wife Alberada. At Capua in September, Gregory received the fealty of Prince Richard (1058–78). Richard's oath carried the condition that he should also swear fealty to Henry IV of Germany when called upon to do so by Gregory or his successors, subject to his fealty to the Roman church; Gregory was evidently concerned to safeguard Henry's claims to condominium with the pope over South Italy.[18]

Gregory's early dealings with the Lombard and Norman rulers, which involved his absence from Rome between July and December 1073,[19] illustrate his underlying purpose, which continued through his pontificate, of securing a peaceful and harmonious South Italy whose rulers supported the Roman church by due loyalty and by the provision of services both spiritual and military. On 27 September 1073, Gregory wrote to Erlembald of Milan that his stay at Capua was serving this end. The Normans—he clearly had in mind Richard of Capua and Robert Guiscard—who before had been seeking a unity that would have prejudiced public order and the good of the church, could now obtain peace subject to Gregory's aproval. With Richard of Capua's recent oath in view, Gregory was sanguine that, to the major benefit of the church, his influence upon the Norman princes would bring them into humble submission and habitual reverence to himself.[20]

Such had been the aspiration of the papacy since Pope Nicholas II came to terms with the Normans in 1059. But, given the political tensions and conflicts of South

---

[15] *Reg.* 1.18a, 12 Aug. 1073, pp. 30–1.
[16] See above, 2.2.3.
[17] Amatus, *Storia*, 7.8, p. 298.
[18] *Reg.* 1.21a, 14 Sept. 1073, pp. 35–7.
[19] JL 1.600–2. Gregory was at Capua from at least early Sept. to mid-Nov.
[20] *Reg.* 1.25, 27 Sept. 1073, p. 42/8–16. For Guiscard's continuing recognition of a need to renew his fealty to Gregory in return for his lands, see *Reg.* 2.9, to Countesses Beatrice and Matilda of Tuscany, 16 Oct. 1074, p. 139/13–19.

Italy, it repeatedly proved necessary for the papacy to fall back upon a policy of 'divide et impera'. As pope, Gregory found himself under the same necessity, above all on account of the ambition and unreliability of the most powerful of the Norman rulers, Robert Guiscard, who relied upon the papacy to legitimate his conquest but was unwilling to satisfy its expectations of obedience and service. In August 1073, Gregory sought a meeting with him at S. Germano near Montecassino. Robert Guiscard assembled a large army. Gregory and he eventually came to Benevento, where negotiations in which Abbot Desiderius was the intermediary broke down on a point of protocol: who should visit whom? The historian Amatus wrote of the discord, ill-will, and anger that were left between them.[21] It was to compensate for this breach that Gregory hastened to consolidate his position with Richard of Capua, and the hope that he expressed to Erlembald of Milan that a rapprochement with Robert Guiscard might follow was unfulfilled. For the rest of the 1070s, 'divide et impera' remained the order of the day, although Gregory never abandoned the hope of rapprochement.

In 1074, Gregory sought to set Robert Guiscard under both spiritual and material constraint. He was the more concerned to do so because after the extinction in 1073 of the ruling house of Amalfi, Robert Guiscard sought to secure control there in opposition to Gregory's ally, Prince Gisulf of Salerno;[22] while in February 1074, Norman attacks upon the duchy of Benevento led to the death of Pandulf, son and heir of Prince Landulf with whom Gregory had recently concluded a treaty.[23] At his Lent synod of 1074, Gregory excommunciated and anathematized Robert Guiscard and all his accomplices.[24]

For some weeks before he passed this spiritual sentence upon Robert Guiscard, Gregory had also been planning to bring material coercion to bear upon him. In the early days of 1074, he asked Countess Matilda of Tuscany to accompany her mother Countess Beatrice to Rome on business which proved to include measures against Robert Guiscard.[25] A month later, Gregory explained his intentions in a letter to Count William of Upper Burgundy, whom he called upon to furnish an army for the defence of the property of St Peter according to an undertaking that he had made in the time of Pope Alexander II. William was to transmit Gregory's call to Count Raymond of Saint-Gilles (whom he referred to as the father-in-law of Prince Richard of Capua), to Count Amadeus of Savoy, and to others who might be responsive. Count William's messenger was to travel to Gregory by way of Countess Beatrice of Tuscany, who with her daughter Matilda and her son-in-law Duke Godfrey of Lorraine was collaborating in the enterprise. Gregory declared his purpose to be twofold: with no intention to shed Christian blood, it was primarily to overawe the

[21] Amatus, *Storia*, 7.9, pp. 298–9.

[22] Amatus, *Storia*, 8.7–8, pp. 348–9, according to which the Amafitans sought to give their city to Gregory who refused it; cf. U. Schwarz, *Amalfi*, pp. 58–9.

[23] *Chron. s. Benedicti*, p. 303; *Ann. Benev.*p. 181; for the date, see Meyer von Knonau, 2.340.

[24] *Reg.* 1.85*a*, p. 123/25–8; Bonizo of Sutri, *Lib. ad amic.* 7, p. 602.

[25] *Reg.* 1.40, to Countess Matilda of Tuscany, 3 Jan. 1074, pp. 61–3; cf. 1.46, to Count William of Upper Burgundy, 2 Feb. 1074, p. 70/21–5.

Normans into obedience to righteousness ('iustitia'); but Gregory was confident that
the knights whom he already had to hand would suffice to deal with the rebellious
Normans, and he hoped that, secondarily, his expedition might proceed to
Constantinople and bring help to the beleaguered Byzantines against harassment by
the Saracens.[26]

The aid for which Gregory hoped was slow to materialize; he particularly chided
Duke Godfrey of Lorraine for not fulfilling his promise.[27] But at some time after 9
May, Gregory felt ready to proceed with his plan.[28] He found some support.
Countess Matilda of Tuscany, Marquis Azzo II of Este, and Prince Gisulf of Salerno
had been at Gregory's Lent synod; Matilda and Gisulf, at least, seem to have stayed
on at Rome. Archbishop Guibert of Ravenna, too, remained with Gregory and had
promised that after Easter he would mount a large expedition against the Normans
but also against the counts of Bagnorea, to the north of Rome. Gregory also placed
high hopes in the help of Prince Richard of Capua, with whom the Cassinese chronicler Amatus wrote that Gregory at this time established firm friendship and alliance.
But Amatus made it clear that Gregory's principal resource was the Countesses
Beatrice and Matilda. Amatus adopted a tone of irony and mockery. Because
Gregory found no help from men, he turned to that of women. The countesses
promised to field a force of 30,000 knights, 500 of whom would be Germans. Gregory
replied that 20,000 would suffice, since Richard of Capua would collaborate. But the
countesses insisted that overwhelming forces were necessary, and Gregory allowed
himself to be persuaded by them.[29]

The facts of Gregory's campaign were more prosaic. Gregory moved north from
Rome to meet the Tuscan forces. (It is not clear that Archbishop Guibert had any part
in detemining the direction of the march, and he seems to have returned to Ravenna.)
In the week after Pentecost, two of Gregory's letters, with the dating 'Data in ex-
peditione', show him to have been, on 12 June, at Monte Cimino between Sutri and
Viterbo and, on 15 June, at S. Flaviano which is to the south-east of Lake Bolsena and
on the road northwards from Viterbo.[30] Amatus named Monte Cimino as the mustering point of the army, but Bonizo of Sutri named S. Flaviano. The expedition
ended in fiasco before it could achieve anything. Three reasons were given. First, according to Amatus, Gisulf of Salerno failed in his role of paymaster: willing though
he was to compass the destruction of Robert Guiscard, he distributed only contemptible rewards—'Indian girdles and bands and cheap cloths, fit only for girding
women and equipping servants or for adorning walls'. Second, again according to
Amatus, the Pisan contingent in the Tuscan army recalled old grievances against
Gisulf of Salerno, for whose safety Gregory had to send him secretly to refuge in
Rome. Third, according to Bonizo of Sutri, a sudden insurrection stirred up by

---

[26] *Reg.* 1.46. For Gregory's military plans of 1074, see Cowdrey, 'Pope Gregory VII's "Crusading" Plans'.
[27] *Reg.* 1.72, 7 Apr. 1074, pp. 103–4.
[28] 9 May is the date of Gregory's last letter before leaving Rome: *Reg.* 1.83, pp. 118–19.
[29] Bonizo of Sutri, *Lib. ad amic.* 7, pp. 602–4; Amatus, *Storia*, 7.12, pp. 303–4.
[30] *Reg.* 1.84–5, pp. 119–23.

Gregory's enemies in Lombardy called Countesses Beatrice and Matilda back to Tuscany. With none of his objectives fulfilled, Gregory had perforce to return to Rome, where he fell ill. He sought abortively to deal with Robert Guiscard by way of negotiation: the duke answered his summons to Benevento, bringing a strong retinue, but Gregory was unable to attend. During the summer, Robert Guiscard allied himself with Duke Sergius of Naples against the principality of Capua. This prompted the mediation of Abbot Desiderius of Montecassino and led to a reconciliation, albeit short-lived, between Robert Guiscard and Richard of Capua.[31] Robert Guiscard needed to keep a channel of communication open with Gregory, for Gregory had not yet invested him with his fiefs.[32] But Gregory's plan for an expedition to South Italy had come to nothing, and in his later military preparations of 1074 there was no mention of the Normans.[33] The political situation in South Italy eluded his control.

The winter of 1074–5 saw Gregory in dejection about South Italian affairs. He confided to Abbot Hugh of Cluny that 'I convict those amongst whom I live, I mean the Romans, Lombards, and Normans, of being, as I often say to them, worse even than Jews and pagans'.[34] At his Lent synod of 1075, Gregory again excommunicated Robert Guiscard, together with his nephew Robert of Loritello, for their invasion of the property of St Peter.[35]

The breach between Gregory and Henry IV of Germany during the winter of 1075–6, however, in the long run favoured a rapprochement between Gregory and the Normans as a matter of common self-interest. In the latter months of 1075, Henry already sought but in vain to enlist the friendship of Robert Guiscard. He dispatched to him Bishop Gregory of Vercelli and his counsellor Count Eberhard with an invitation that he should receive his lands as a royal fief. Robert Guiscard received the envoys politely but firmly refused. Ignoring ideas of papal and German condominium, he recalled how he had captured his lands from the Byzantines and had made himself and his lands subject to St Peter and his vicar. He was himself a bulwark against the pride of the Greeks and the violence of the Saracens. Therefore he could not permit Henry to invest him with any of his own conquests; however, he might be prepared to do so in respect of lands that Henry might in future bestow—subject to his fealty to the church. Robert Guiscard made clear his need to keep intact his bond with the papacy, which was near at hand, and to remain independent for the time being of Henry and his designs; although he left the door open for future negotiations if Henry's power in Italy were to increase.[36]

---

[31] Bonizo of Sutri, *Lib. ad amic.* 7, pp. 602–4; Amatus, *Storia*, 7.12–17, pp. 303–10.

[32] *Reg.* 2.9, to Countesses Beatrice and Matilda of Tuscany, 16 Oct. 1074, p. 139/13–19.

[33] *Reg.* 2.31, to King Henry IV of Germany, 7 Dec. 1074, pp. 165–8; 2.37, to all the faithful, 16 Dec. 1074, p. 172.

[34] *Reg.* 2.49, 22 Jan. 1075, p. 189/25–7.   [35] *Reg.* 2.52a, p. 197/2–4.

[36] Amatus, *Storia*, 7.27, pp. 320–1. According to an interpolation in Lorenzo Valla, *De falso credita et ementita Constantini donatione*, p. 26 n. 58, Robert Guiscard refused fealty to Henry for lands that he held of the pope but expressed willingness to do it for other lands. His expression of willingness may have been diplomatic; it elicited from Henry's envoys the convenient reply that they were not authorized to consider this.

In fact, neither Robert Guiscard nor Richard of Capua stood to gain from German intervention in South Italy, for if successful it could only threaten their own power and freedom of action. Henry's breach with Gregory at the beginning of 1076 gave the Normans an incentive to seek agreement with each other and with Gregory in order to maintain the status quo. Gregory had still greater and more immediate reason for promoting the reconciliation and mutual goodwill of the two Norman leaders. He began to exhibit a more conciliatory attitude towards the twice excommunicated Robert Guiscard and to underwrite the diversion of Norman energies towards the capture of Sicily from the Saracens. In March 1076, he informed Archbishop Arnald of Acerenza of his pleasure that Robert Guiscard's brother, Count Roger of Calabria and Sicily, had sought papal blessing and absolution from the excommunication under which he had fallen in 1074 as Robert Guiscard's supporter. If Roger proved truly penitent, the archbishop should lose no time in absolving him as also the knights who were about to campaign with him in Sicily. The archbishop should also make it clear through Roger that the gates of mercy were always open to Robert Guiscard himself, and that Gregory was willing to admit him to familiarity as a son of the Roman church; though if he were recalcitrant, Robert Guiscard could expect no licence from the Roman church further to communicate with Roger.[37] In a letter sent soon afterwards to the Milanese knight Wifred, Gregory rejoiced that the Normans had recently talked with him about making peace. With an apparent reference to Robert Guiscard's brush-off of Henry IV's envoys, Gregory observed that the Normans wished to have St Peter alone, after God, as their lord and emperor. Peace could already have been made if Gregory had been prepared to concede all that the Normans had wished; he hoped soon, to the benefit of the Roman church, to recall them firmly and permanently to their fidelity to St Peter.[38]

There was no speedy reconciliation, for on the Italian mainland the Normans pursued their own interests with scant regard for Gregory's. Robert Guiscard and Richard of Capua came together, but in agreement that Richard should help Robert to conquer Salerno while Robert should help Richard to capture Naples; their collaboration extended to razzias into the Roman Campania.[39] In October 1076, Gregory wrote to his Milanese allies of his anger, saying that he would never condone the sacrilegious invasion of papal lands.[40] In the winter of 1076–7, Robert Guiscard's siege and capture of Salerno deprived Gregory of a cherished political ally; although Robert permitted Prince Gisulf to leave Salerno honourably. Upon Gregory's return from his itinerary in North Italy, Gisulf joined him at Rome, where he remained in papal service until his death in 1091.[41]

In the long term, the Norman overrunning of the principality of Salerno removed a source of strife from South Italy and simplified its politics from a papal point of

---

37 *Reg.* 3.11, 14 Mar. 1076, pp. 271–2.   38 *Reg.* 3.15, (Apr.) 1076, pp. 276/29–277/4.
39 Amatus, *Storia*, 7.28–9, 8.22, pp. 322–3, 361–2.   40 *Reg.* 4.7, 31 Oct. 1076, p. 305/14–24.
41 For the siege and capture of Salerno, see Amatus, *Storia*, 8.14–30, pp. 354–71; William of Apulia, 3.412–64, pp. 186–9. For somewhat differing accounts of Gisulf's journey to Rome, see Amatus, *Storia*, 8.30–1, pp. 371–2; William of Apulia, 3.457–64, pp. 188–9.

view, not least because the powerful Lombard figure, Archbishop Alfanus of Salerno, adhered to the Normans just before the city fell.[42] In the short term, Gregory's relations with the Normans remained uncertain and ambivalent. He followed the path of division and sanctions rather than pursuing his ultimate objective of uniting them. An exacerbating factor was the continuing predations of the Normans, not least upon papal lands. The death on 18 November 1077 of Prince Landulf of Benevento, who left no surviving son, gave Robert Guiscard an opening on 19 December to lay siege to that city, thereby presenting Gregory with a direct challenge. Gregory was as powerless to bring military help to Benevento as he had been to Salerno, but at his Lent synod in 1078 he imposed spiritual censures on the Normans. The official record gave no names, but Gregory collectively excommunicated all Normans who were endeavouring to invade the lands of St Peter in the march of Fermo and the duchy of Spoleto; he went on to proscribe those who were besieging Benevento, those who sought to invade and to plunder Campania, Maritima, and Sabina, and those who were endeavouring to ravage the city of Rome itself. Any bishop or priest who performed divine service for Normans who were excommunicated was punished by perpetual exclusion from the priestly office.[43]

Another death which brought major consequences was that on 5 April 1078 of Prince Richard of Capua; it represented the first disappearance of a top-ranking Norman leader since the treaty of Melfi in 1059. During the prince's terminal illness, Gregory's sanctions against the Normans at his Lent synod had the desired effect of dividing them. No doubt with a view to securing a smooth succession after his father's death, which excommunication might have placed at risk, Richard's son Jordan hastened to Rome in the company of his uncle Count Ralph of Caiazzo and secured absolution. Before Prince Richard died, he restored to St Peter his own conquests in the Campagna, as a step towards also receiving absolution. Robert Guiscard was put at a disadvantage. Not only did Jordan connive at a widespread revolt of his Apulian and Calabrian vassals, but he abandoned the siege of Naples and compelled Apulian troops to leave Benevento. The setback for Robert Guiscard left him less of a threat to papal interests and eased the way for a *rapprochement* between him and Gregory.

In the late 1070s, several factors contributed to making such a 'rapprochement' likely. First, despite his politic reconciliation with Gregory when his father's death was in prospect, Prince Jordan of Capua quickly established himself as a violent and unreliable figure who threatened ecclesiastical interests both at Rome and at Montecassino. On 21 April 1079, Gregory expressed his disenchantment in an outraged letter to him which opened without greeting or blessing and which listed three causes of offence: Jordan had compelled his stepmother to remarry against her will; he had recently ('nuper') hindered and robbed an unnamed bishop who was on his

---

[42] Amatus, *Storia*, 8.17, pp. 357–8.

[43] For events in this and the next paragraph, see Amatus, *Storia*, 8.32–5, pp. 372–4; *Chron. Cas.* 3.45, p. 423; *Ann. Cas. aa.* 1077–8, pp. 1420–1; *Ann. Benev. a.* 1077, p. 181. For Gregory's sanctions, *Reg.* 5.14*a*, caps. 9,11, p. 371. Amatus said that Robert Guiscard was excommunicated by name.

way to Rome; and still more recently ('novissime') he had entered, plundered, and violated the church of St Benedict at Montecassino.[44] Gregory followed this letter with two more which referred only to the third of these offences. He rebuked Abbot Desiderius of Montecassino for his failure to punish so great an outrage, placing his abbey under an interdict but also promising further steps on its behalf. He quickly lifted the interdict because the feast of the Ascension was approaching, and urged the monks to pray for Jordan's repentance. The Montecassino Chronicle gave the substance of Gregory's letters but identified the plunder, as Gregory did not, as money deposited at the abbey by Bishop Dodo of Grosseto (Roselle).[45] Whatever the precise nature of these happenings, the effect of Gregory's anger was to isolate Jordan of Capua. Robert Guiscard returned from Calabria and prepared to attack him. Jordan sought to open peace talks, thus providing Abbot Desiderius of Montecassino with an opportunity to resume his attempts to reconcile all parties in South Italy.[46]

Desiderius's return to papal favour and to the centre of the diplomatic stage was a second factor which facilitated better relations between Gregory and Robert Guiscard. In the mid-1070s, the breach between Gregory and the duke seems to have distanced the abbot from the papacy, since he could not afford to fall out with so powerful and generous a neighbour as Robert Guiscard. But by 1079, Berengar of Tours could observe that Desiderius was a prominent figure at the Lateran ('summae tunc in palatio auctoritatis').[47] He once more became a channel of communication between Gregory and the Normans.

Thirdly, Gregory and Robert Guiscard had an element of common interest with regard to Byzantium. Papal and ducal policies had for some years run along parallel lines. Since 1073, Gregory had been in touch with the Emperor Michael VII Ducas (1071–8) with a view to promoting the unity of the eastern and western churches.[48] Robert Guiscard, too, was concerned to foster relations with Michael, partly to offset the danger that Byzantium represented by providing an asylum for rebels against his authority, and partly because he increasingly aspired to win the empire for himself. In 1074, he secured a foothold by negotiating with Michael a marriage alliance by which he agreed to dispatch to Constantinople his infant daughter who was betrothed to Michael's son. The interests of both Gregory and Robert were, therefore, adversely affected when, in October 1078, Michael was deposed and succeeded by Nicephorus III Botaniates (1078–81).[49]

The years 1077 to 1080 thus witnessed the elimination of Prince Gisulf II of Salerno as an independent papal ally and as a cause of friction between Gregory VII and Robert Guiscard. The veteran Prince Richard of Capua had been succeeded by

---

[44] *Reg.* 6.37, pp. 453–4. See Tirelli, 'Osservazioni', pp. 999–1001; Hoffmann, 'Zum Register', p. 104.

[45] *Epp. vag.* pp. 72–7, nos. 28–9; *Chron. Cas.* 3.46, p. 424.

[46] *Chron. Cas.* 3.45, pp. 423–4; William of Apulia, 3.617–87, pp. 198–202, Cuozzo, 'Il "Breve chronicon" ', pp. 171, 223–8.

[47] Huygens, 'Bérenger de Tours', p. 400.   [48] See below, 7.1.

[49] For the alliance, see William of Apulia, 3.501–2, p. 190, cf. p. 306; Amatus, *Storia*, 7.26, pp. 318–20; Anna Comnena, 1.10.3, 12.2, vol. 1.27, 43, 171; see Dölger, *Regesten*, no. 1003. For a fuller account, see Von Falkenhausen, 'Olympias'.

the weak and volatile Jordan, who was predatory by disposition but who bowed to an effective show of military strength. In Byzantium, Gregory and Robert Guiscard had a common hostility to the Emperor Nicephorus III Botaniates. And in Italy, Robert Guiscard had no reason to welcome further intervention by Henry IV of Germany, whose claims to lordship over him he had evaded and whose excommunication and deposition Gregory again proclaimed at Rome on 7 March 1080. Abbot Desiderius of Montecassino was to hand as a negotiator who could hope, in the interests of both his abbey and of the papacy, to rehabilitate the arrangements of the treaty of Melfi whereby the Norman duke of Apulia and the Norman prince of Capua were established as allies and protectors of the apostolic see, while both were also patrons of Montecassino.

The reconstituting of the papacy's alliance with the Normans came quickly. Building upon the recent negotiations between Robert Guiscard and Jordan of Capua, and also upon Robert Guiscard's success in quelling his Apulian rebels, Desiderius went to Gregory at Rome, probably before the Lent synod of 1080, to raise the question of Robert Guiscard's absolution.[50] At the synod, Gregory's decrees were appreciably more moderate than those of recent years. He threatened with excommunication those who might invade or despoil the part of the march of Fermo which was not yet overrun, Spoleto, Campania, Maritima, and Sabina, the county of Tivoli, the monastery of Montecassino with all its possessions, and also Benevento. But he also promised legal redress by himself or his local agents to those Normans who might feel themselves to be justly aggrieved by the inhabitants of those lands; if justice were denied them, they might take proportionate steps to avenge their own wrongs.[51] Negotiations with the Normans followed in which Gregory used not only Desiderius but also Count Simon of Crépy, who was currently living in Rome as a hermit.[52] Assisted by other cardinals, Desiderius eventually freed Robert Guiscard from excommunication.[53]

Early in June, Gregory judged the time to be ripe for him to travel to South Italy. On 10 June at Ceprano, he took an oath of fealty from Prince Jordan of Capua.[54] Probably after journeying further south, he returned to Ceprano by 29 June. He took a similar oath from Robert Guiscard, and invested him with the land that his predecessors Nicholas II and Alexander II had granted him. As for the lands that he had seized unjustly—Gregory named Salerno, Amalfi, and part of the march of Fermo—Gregory promised his acquiescence, saying that he trusted Robert Guiscard so to behave to the honour of God and St Peter that both he and Gregory might suffer no danger to their souls.[55] Gregory's concessions to the Normans at his

---

[50] *Chron. Cas.* 3.45, p. 424.   [51] *Reg.* 7.14a(4), p. 481.

[52] *Vita beati Simonis com. Cresp.* cap. 13, cols. 1220D–1221B. Simon is said to have travelled with 'a most holy man' who is unidentified but may have been Abbot Desiderius.

[53] *Chron. Cas.* 3.45, p. 424.   [54] Deusdedit, *Coll. can.* 3.289 (159), p. 396.

[55] William of Apulia, 4.16–32, 69–70, pp. 204, 206, 311–12; Anna Comnena, 1.13.6–7, vol. 1.48–9; Bonizo of Sutri, 9, p. 612; Romuald of Salerno, *a.* 1080, p. 191. For Robert Guiscard's fealty and investiture, *Reg.* 8.1a–c, pp. 514–17; a variant text of 1a is preserved in a Bible of the Roman basilica of St Paul's-without-the-Walls: Deér, *Das Papsttum*, p. 32.

Lent synod and to Robert Guiscard at Ceprano are a measure of his anxiety to secure their alliance after his renewed breach with Henry IV of Germany.

He was unreservedly confident that the two Norman princes would now serve his purposes. When, in mid-summer, he summoned all the faithful of St Peter to his campaign at Ravenna, he began:

Both by ourselves and by our legates, we have had talks with Duke Robert, Jordan, and the other most powerful leaders of the Normans, who have unanimously promised that, as they are sworn to do, they will supply help for the defence of the holy Roman church and of our own honour against all men.[56]

It was not only from lay magnates that Gregory sought support. Upon hearing of Henry IV's synod of Brixen and of the choice of Archbishop Guibert of Ravenna to be anti-pope, he also turned to the bishops of the Principate, Apulia, and Calabria, that is, of the Normans' lands, to seek their energetic support against the enemies of the Roman church.[57]

Gregory had other reasons for feeling confident of Robert Guiscard's collaboration. They seemed to be continuing upon convergent courses in respect to Byzantium. There appeared at Bari a Greek who gave himself out to be the Emperor Michael VII, deposed in 1078, whom both Gregory and Robert Guiscard had looked upon with favour.[58] They both now accepted that he had returned, and Gregory sent a letter in his favour to the Apulian and Calabrian bishops. He urged them to back Robert Guiscard's military measures in support of 'Michael's' claim to the imperial throne.[59] Furthermore, Robert Guiscard began to implement plans, conceived after his capture of Salerno in 1077, to begin the rebuilding of the cathedral there. In September 1080, Gregory was able to congratulate Archbishop Alfanus, who was now a staunch Norman ally, upon the uncovering of the body of St Matthew, the city's patron saint. Gregory declared that he, too, saw in the relics of the apostle and evangelist a pledge of his own victory in the church at large, which he hoped to accomplish with Norman help.[60] The apparent concurrence of papal and Norman interests did not, however, persist. During the winter of 1080–1, Robert Guiscard began to reassess the situation in Byzantium. He sent an envoy there, ostensibly to seek redress for the injury done to the daughter whom he had betrothed to Michael VII's son when she was placed in a convent, but in fact to seek the alliance of the rising figure of Alexius Comnenus, at this time grand domestic and exarch of the west.[61] It was apparent that the duke would assist Gregory's plans only in ways that suited himself.

---

56 *Reg.* 8.7, p. 525/10–15, cf. 9.4, to Abbot Desiderius of Montecassino, (early Feb. 1081), p. 578/4–7. For the Ravenna campaign, see above, 3.5.3.
57 *Reg.* 8.5, 21 July 1080, pp. 521–3.
58 Anna Comnena, 1.12.6–10, vol. 1.44–6; Lupus Protospatarius, *a.* 1080, p. 60; William of Apulia, 4.162–70, p. 212; Romuald of Salerno, *a.* 1080, p. 191.
59 *Reg.* 8.8, 18 Sept. 1080, pp. 526–7.
60 *Chron. Cas.* 3.45, p. 423; *Reg.* 8.8, 18 Sept. 1080, pp. 526–7.
61 Anna Comnena, 1.15.2, vol. 1.53–4.

Gregory was slow to come to terms with so unpalatable a truth. He persisted in his hope of drawing Robert Guiscard into his military plans in Northern and Central Italy. Probably in early February, he tried to use Abbot Desiderius of Montecassino's good standing with the duke in order to ascertain—as he put it—how well disposed towards the Roman church the duke still was. In a letter, he requested the abbot to ascertain whether, if Gregory were forced to call a military expedition after Easter 1081, Robert Guiscard would promise aid either personally or through his son. If no expedition took place, Gregory wished to be informed how many knights Robert Guiscard would be willing to furnish for the pope's service ('in familiari militia sancti Petri'). Desiderius was also to sound the duke about whether he would devote Lent, when Norman knights customarily refrained from warfare, to military action led by Gregory himself or by his deputy, in order to subdue those vassals of the papal lands who were rebellious and to confirm the loyalty of the remainder. Gregory also asked Desiderius to remind Robert Guiscard to restrain his nephew Robert of Loritello from invading papal lands.[62] Gregory's mind was evidently still set upon his plans of 1080. His letter seems to have been written in vain, for, apart from a brief notice in the Beneventan Annals that, perhaps early in 1081, Robert Guiscard made an expedition to Tivoli which he may have intended as a gesture of help for Gregory,[63] there is no record of action by Desiderius or reaction from Robert Guiscard. As in 1074 so in 1080–1, papal plans for direct military campaigns proved abortive.

As the year 1081 went on, Gregory's ability to command military support in South Italy for his plans in the north and in the papal lands was further eroded. Robert Guiscard became increasingly preoccupied with his ambitions in the Byzantine empire. In April, when he was making preparations at Brindisi, his envoy returned from Constantinople, denouncing the *soi-disant* Emperor Michael as an impostor and reporting on the seizure of the Byzantine throne by Alexius Comnenus (emperor 1081–1118).[64] Robert Guiscard was determined to press on with his designs across the Adriatic before Alexius could consoldiate his position. After charging the guardians of his son Roger not to deny the papacy any aid that they could bring, in May he crossed the sea; during the summer, the Normans captured Corfu, Vonitza, and Valona, and laid siege to Durazzo.[65] By thus leaving Italy, Robert Guiscard once again demonstrated how little he could be counted upon to help the papacy at Gregory's behest and convenience.

The year 1081 also saw King Henry IV of Germany's first expedition to Italy.[66] Gregory sought Robert Guiscard's aid, but Robert's overseas plans were too important for him to respond.[67] Henry, too, angled for the duke's support, as he had done in 1075. As then, so now Robert Guiscard seems to have talked but to have been too circumspect to make any commitment. Gregory heard of these negotiations. In May 1081, he told Abbot Desiderius of written intelligence that he had received from

---

[62] *Reg.* 9.4, pp. 577–9; cf. William of Apulia, 4.66–8, p. 206.
[63] *a.* 1080, p. 181; cf. *Chron. Cas.* 3.58, p. 438.   [64] Anna Comnena, 1.15.1–6, vol. 1.53–6.
[65] Anna Comnena, 1.14.1, 4 and 3.12, vol. 1.51, 53, 128–42; William of Apulia, 4.177–284, pp. 214–16.
[66] See above, 3.5.5.   [67] Anna Comnena, 1.13.10, vol. 1.51.

Countess Matilda of Tuscany: Henry had made a compact ('placitum') with the duke that the king's son should marry the duke's daughter, and that the duke would hold the march of Fermo from the king. Such an arrangement would have followed up Henry's diplomacy in 1075. Desiderius was to investigate the truth of such rumours and to come to Gregory as soon as possible. But Robert Guiscard was careful to enter upon no commitment to Henry; he also kept in contact with Gregory.[68]

For Robert Guiscard's fortunes across the Adriatic were not such that he could afford to prejudice his position with Gregory as re-established at Ceprano in 1080. He had increasingly to reckon with the military and diplomatic skill of the new Byzantine emperor, Alexius Comnenus. Alexius took energetic steps to counter Robert Guiscard. In the summer of 1081, he made an armistice with his eastern enemies the Seljuk Turks, and even solicited their aid as mercenaries against the Normans. He also embarked upon negotiations with Henry IV in order to tie Robert Guiscard down in the west, promising him large financial subsidies for his campaigns in Italy. He fomented revolts against Robert Guiscard in South Italy and sought the support against him of Archbishop Hildebrand of Capua. He improved his situation in the Adriatic by a treaty with Venice, which gave him naval support in return for commercial concessions.[69] All this pressure indirectly told in Gregory's favour by compelling Robert Guiscard to give more attention to Italian affairs, and also to Henry IV as the dangerous ally of his Byzantine enemy. After a hard-fought victory near Durazzo on 18 October, which in effect gave him control of Illyria, Robert Guiscard notified Gregory of his success. Gregory replied with a letter reminding him of his debt to St Peter and of his duty to defend St Peter's interests.[70]

Henry IV's expedition to Italy in 1082 was better planned and more sustained than that of 1081.[71] Henry's more resolute action in Italy, together with his link with Alexius Comnenus and the resulting spectre of a Byzantine-supported rising in South Italy, continued to compel Robert Guiscard to devote more of his attention than he would have wished to Italian affairs. Instead of pressing home the advantage that the fall of Durazzo to him on 21 February 1082 gave, he decided to secure his rear in Italy. Leaving most of his army behind with Bohemond in charge, in April he landed at Otranto with a handful of followers. With an eye to preventing a junction of Henry's forces with the Apulian rebels, he headed for Rome. But it became clear that Henry had returned northwards to confront Matilda of Tuscany. So, for the remainder of 1082 and throughout 1083, Robert Guiscard remained preoccupied in the south, with neither the immediate incentive nor the opportunity to intervene militarily in the papacy's favour.[72] Nevertheless, on 16 April 1083, Gregory deemed it timely to grant to Alcherius, whom Robert Guiscard had appointed archbishop of Palermo, a privilege in which he rejoiced that, 'by the labour and zeal of our son the

---

[68] Anna Comnena, 1.13.10, vol. 1.51; William of Apulia, 4. 169–84, pp. 212–14; *Reg.* 9.11, pp. 588–9.

[69] Anna Comnena, 3.10–11 and 4.2.2–3, vol. 1.132, 146–7; Dölger, *Regesten*, nos. 1067–70.

[70] *Reg.* 9.17, pp. 597–8.   [71] See above, 3.5.7.

[72] For the main events, see William of Apulia, 4.458–527, pp. 228–33; Lupus Protospatarius, *a.* 1082, p. 61; Romuald of Salerno, pp. 194–5; Geoffrey Malaterra, 3.34, pp. 77–8; *Ann. Benev. a.* 1082, p. 182.

illustrious Duke Robert' ('gloriosi ducis ROBERTI'), the church of Palermo had been restored to the Christian faith from Saracen domination and paganism. Gregory confirmed to Palermo its ancient metropolitan status in Sicily and to its archbishop the right to wear the *pallium*.[73] But, however much Gregory may have welcomed the rehabilitation of organized church life in Sicily, Robert Guiscard's commitment to the papacy, though genuine, came low in the duke's scale of priorities. Nevertheless, he was back in Italy and at odds with Henry IV; for Gregory, that could not but be comforting.

Under pressure from Henry IV, it was the Normans of Capua rather than those of Apulia who presented Gregory with immediate difficulties. The measure of the problem is indicated by the Montecassino Chronicle, according to which most of the Lombards of South Italy ('omnes fere istarum partium homines') reacted to Henry's presence in 1082 near Rome by conspiring against 'the Normans', who therefore decided that the prudent course would be reconciliation to Henry; if he were to secure Rome he would be in a position to expel them from all their lands. The reference is likely to have been to those Normans who were subject to the volatile Prince Jordan of Capua, since Robert Guiscard was set upon an anti-Henrician course. The Chronicle goes on to relate how, after negotiating directly with Henry, 'the Normans' called upon Abbot Desiderius to accompany them to the king; they were prompted, not only by considerations of their own security, but also by a desire arising from their fidelity to the Roman church to promise peace between pope and emperor. But when Gregory heard of their actions, he excommunicated Henry and all his adherents. 'The Normans' therefore turned from their earlier love and service of Gregory to political and spiritual revulsion from him.[74]

Other evidence confirms and adds precision to the Chronicle's account. William of Apulia recorded that, because he feared the loss of his principality, Jordan did fealty to Henry, gave his son as a hostage, and supplied him with money.[75] For the first time since Henry III's days, a Norman prince had expressly recognized German lordship over South Italian lands. Gregory's letters show that he responded by excommunicating Jordan as a perjurer against St Peter and himself by reason of his fealty to Henry. He dispatched Prince Gisulf of Salerno as an intermediary to win back the loyalty of the *magister militum* Sergius VI of Naples and his subjects from giving aid and comfort to Jordan of Capua. He also wrote to Archbishop Hervey of Capua and to all the bishops of the Principate in order to confirm their loyalty and to reinforce the excommunications that he had proclaimed. Gregory advised the bishops to allow those who were under intolerable pressure to flee to the lands of the *gloriosus dux* Robert Guiscard or of his brother Count Roger I of Sicily, or else to himself at Rome. But they were to encourage those who possessed the necessary fortitude to stand their ground.[76] In 1082, Henry thus brought about once again the state of

---

[73] *QF* no. 212, pp. 252–4.   [74] *Chron. Cas.* 3.50, pp. 430–1.

[75] William of Apulia, 5.110–17, p. 242; cf. *Ann. Benev. a.* 1080, p. 181; Geoffrey Malaterra, 3.35, p. 78.

[76] *Reg.* 9.26, to Archbishop Hervey of Capua and other bishops of the Principate, p. 609; 9.27, to Archbishop John of Naples, pp. 610–11.

affairs that seemed in 1080 to have been overcome—division between the Normans of Capua and of Apulia.

There ensued a period of turmoil which profoundly affected both the principality of Capua and the abbey of Montecassino.[77] The summer of 1083 saw events turning rather more in Gregory's favour. In June, Robert Guiscard overcame the main centre of rebel resistance to himself at Cannae; he went on to harass Prince Jordan of Capua into making peace with himself.[78] Unity of a sort between the two Norman rulers was restored. Robert Guiscard also aided Gregory by sending to Rome 30,000 gold *solidi*, thus doing something to offset the financial subvention that Henry was receiving from Byzantium.[79] Henry passed the winter of 1083–4 in the vicinity of Rome; perhaps as a gesture to Alexius Comnenus, he campaigned briefly in Apulia. His entry into Rome in March 1084, followed by his imperial coronation by the anti-pope Clement III, prompted Robert Guiscard to respond. Gregory sent Abbot Jarento of Saint-Bénigne at Dijon with some cardinals to seek his help. As a completed and consolidated Henrician victory at Rome would hamstring him in his primary concern of developing his fortunes across the Adriatic, he responded by coming to Rome with a considerable force. Henry prudently left the city on 21 May, and, when the Normans arrived, it lay open to their fury and predation.[80]

When Robert Guiscard left Rome in July, Gregory had perforce to accompany him in view of Norman violence in the city and its effect upon the morale and loyalty of its inhabitants. They travelled by way of Benevento to Salerno.[81] Historians have been misleading when they have represented Gregory's progress to Salerno with Robert Guiscard as a shameful journey to near-captivity, and his final months as a time of weakness and bitterness. While allowance must be made for partisan prejudice, that was not the view of contemporaries, nor is it what is to be expected. William of Apulia said that Robert Guiscard conducted Gregory to Salerno 'with great honour'.[82] He had every reason to make Gregory's journey free, solemn, and dignified; for he looked forward to the papal consecration of the new cathedral of St Matthew at Salerno, which Gregory performed in July, soon after his arrival.[83] A cowed or a humiliated pope would have added nothing to the dignity of such an occasion. Moreover, the occasion was marked by a ceremony of reconciliation between Robert Guiscard and Jordan of Capua.[84] At Salerno, Gregory could take encouragement from the renewed concord of his Norman vassals.

The duke did not, however, delay for long before reverting to his overriding concern—his campaign across the Adriatic against Byzantium. He was a septuagenarian with no time to lose. Moreover, since his return to Italy, the Normans had suffered reverses in Thessaly, a Greek and Venetian fleet had taken Durazzo, and in October

77 See Cowdrey, *The Age of Abbot Desiderius*, pp. 155–65.
78 William of Apulia, 4.528–35, 5.106–20, pp. 232–3, 242–3.
79 Lupus Protospatarius, *a.* 1083, p. 61.   80 See above, 3.5.10.
81 *Ann. Benev. a.* 1084, p. 182; Geoffrey Malaterra, 3.37, p. 80; *Chron. Cas.* 3.58, p. 438.
82 William of Apulia, 4.557, p. 234; Hugh of Flavigny, 2, pp. 465–6, 470–1.
83 William of Apulia, 5.122–4, p. 242, cf. 5.255–67, p. 250.
84 Lentini and Avagliano, *I carmi*, no. 53, lines 9–10, p. 216; see William of Apulia, p. 243 n. 2.

1083 Castoria had also been lost. So, in the autumn of 1084, he left Italy for the last time.[85] As Bernold claimed, at Salerno Gregory remained steadfast unto death in the defence of righteousness.[86] But, if his spiritual and moral zeal remained undiminished, the divided purposes of the Normans left him without military or political resources to match it by effective action.

In truth, the Normans of South Italy upon whom the papacy set its reliance in the days of Pope Nicholas II were not dependable as papal vassals and allies. Alike in South Italy and Sicily and across the Adriatic, their first and overriding concern was to secure land, plunder, and power for themselves. The lands of St Peter were not proof from their aggressiveness. If the popes, and Gregory most of all, sought to promote their unity in order to command their services, they all too often had to fall back upon a tactic of fomenting division in order to counter threats to papal interests. As the events of 1080–1 made clear, they were not willing to contribute their knights to papally led military expeditions in regions where they had no interests. Their one major response to a call for help nearer home was Robert Guiscard's march to Rome in 1084, when they subjected the city to one of the gravest sackings of its history and rendered Gregory's position there untenable. Yet, for all their unreliability, Gregory gained considerable advantage from the very fact that they were in South Italy. There were strict limits beyond which their unreliability did not go. At no time did the strongest leader, Robert Guiscard, show a firm disposition to respond positively to the approaches of Henry IV of Germany, whose victory in Italy would have threatened Norman independence and interests. Indeed, Robert Guiscard was a useful ally when Jordan of Capua temporarily accepted Henry's lordship. On balance, the Normans were far too much concerned for their own position to have truck with a powerful German overlord.

They were seldom of positive help to Gregory and, as the three excommunications of Robert Guiscard show, they often caused him grave problems. Yet by their presence in South Italy, they ensured that Gregory would never have a major enemy on his southern border. Their conquest of Sicily gave Gregory a hope of reconstituting Christian life and order in a long-lost province of the church.

6.3 The North-East Adriatic

To the north of Epirus where the events connected with Robert Guiscard's campaign against the Byzantine empire mainly occurred, lay two kingdoms with which Gregory VII, like his papal predecessors, was actively concerned. The southernmost was the Serbian kingdom at this time known as Zeta, approximately corresponding to modern Montenegro, with its ecclesiastical centre at Antivari (Bar), and, to its north-west, the kingdom of Croatia and Dalmatia, with its ecclesiastical centre at Spalato (Split). A third major church was that of Ragusa (Dubrovnik) which lay on the Serbian side of the political border; while the metropolis of Spalato claimed it as a suffragan see, the Serbs championed its independence.

---

[85] William of Apulia, 5.121–53, pp. 242–4. [86] *Chron. a.* 1085, p. 444/2–4.

In the late eleventh century, the Dalmatian region was of concern to both the German and the Byzantine authorities, as well as to the Venetians in the north and the Normans to the south. During the tenth and earlier eleventh centuries, there had been considerable conciliar and papal concern with the region; two features of it had been the problem of establishing a regular metropolitan and diocesan organization, and a conflict between Latin and Slavonic (Glagolitic) liturgical usages.[87] For many reasons, Dalmatia was a region with which Gregory was bound to become involved.

His primary concern was with the Croatian kingdom which, to the north, had common frontiers with the south-east German marches and with the kingdom of Hungary, and over which Byzantine suzerainty was at best nominal. Between 1058 and 1073/4, it was ruled by King Peter Krešimir IV. Gregory's first recorded dealings occurred in 1074, during the vacuum of power left by this ruler's death. Tidings reached Rome that the citizens of Ragusa had imprisoned their bishop, Vitalis, who had, in fact, already been excommunicated by a legate of Pope Alexander II, and that the citizens had irregularly elected a successor. In a letter to them, Gregory reacted much as he might have done to a matter arising within the Roman 'ecclesiastical province': he announced that he was sending Archbishop Gerald of Siponto as his legate to investigate what had happened; the imprisoned bishop was to be released, and the legate was to do justice in his case as in other needful matters. If his action were ineffectual, both the former bishop and his successor-elect were to appear before Gregory at Rome on pain of the excommunication of all who disobeyed.[88] The immediate upshot is unclear, but in due course the legate replaced Vitalis by a new bishop named Peter; he also, in November 1075, held a synod at Spalato which was concerned with the general well-being of the Dalmatian churches.[89]

Political developments in the Croatian kingdom quickly gave Gregory an opening for more wide-ranging intervention. Peter Krešimir died without leaving a direct heir in the established line of King Trpimar; his nephew Stephen was deemed unfit to rule and entered a monastery. In the obscure events that followed, a ruler named Slavac became established in the central region of the kingdom, where he seems to have championed the Slavonic liturgy; to the north, power was secured by a duke, Demetrius Zwonimir, who until his violent death in 1089 was a warm supporter of the Gregorian papacy. The situation invited external intervention. It was probably, though not demonstrably, with Gregory's knowledge that a Norman adversary of Robert Guiscard, Count Amicus of Giovinazzo, in 1074–5 undertook a campaign in Croatia which eliminated Slavac without producing more positive results.[90] Early

---

[87] For the history of Croatia in the late 11th cent., see Šišić, *Geschichte der Kroaten*, 1.220–319. For councils in Dalmatia and for an outline of events, see Waldmüller, *Die Synoden in Dalmatien*, esp. pp. 25–94; for other recent surveys, see Šanjek, 'La Réforme grégorienne en Croatie', Spremić, 'Gregorio VII e gli Slavi del sud', and Košćak, 'Gregorio VII e la Croazia'. These items provide fuller bibliographies of sources and secondary authorities, many of which have not been available to me.

[88] *Reg.* 1.65, 20 Mar. 1074, pp. 94–5.

[89] *Cod. dip. Croat.* 1.136, no. 107.   [90] As n. 89.

in 1075, Gregory himself attempted to procure an intervention. He wrote to King Sweyn Estrithson of Denmark about 'a certain most opulent province by the sea, not distant from us, which contemptible and mean heretics are holding'. He probably had in mind Croatia, and was exercised about the prevalence of the Slavonic liturgy; he invited the Danish king to send one of his sons with a military force for the papal service there.[91] But Sweyn was already dead, and nothing came of this approach.

Later in the year, Gregory took the decisive step of sponsoring the advancement of Demetrius Zwonimir to be king of Croatia and Dalmatia.[92] He sent further legates to Croatia—Abbot Gebizo of SS. Bonifazio e Alessio at Rome and Bishop Folcuin of Fossombrone. The settlement of the kingdom which they were commissioned to sponsor is set out in three undertakings that the new king made which were recorded by Deusdedit in his collection of canons.[93] At a synod which met in the church of St Peter at Spalato, Demetrius Zwonimir was invested as and appointed ('constitutum') king of Croatia and Dalmatia by the unanimous election of the assembled clergy and people. He received a standard ('vexillum'), sword, sceptre, and crown, and he promised faithfully to fulfil the commands that he should receive from the pope. In a series of specific clauses, he made undertakings which expressed both the obligations of obedient kingship as Gregory conceived them, and the salient benefits of the Christian oversight which Gregory aspired to provide in distant regions. Demetrius Zwonimir would be loyal to the apostolic see; he would implement everything that the apostolic see or its legates might determine; he would maintain justice especially to churches; he would enforce celibacy upon all clergy in major orders; he would protect the poor, widows, and orphans; he would institute among the laity a proper marriage discipline; he would prohibit the slave trade; and he would ensure the observance of lawfulness and equity in all things.[94] Second, in return for kingdom that he had been granted, Demetrius Zwonimir promised an annual payment to St Peter at Eastertide of 200 Byzantine *solidi*, and he gave to the apostolic see the monastery of St Gregory called Varna with all its treasure as a hospice for the papal legates whom Gregory evidently envisaged as a frequent means of contact between the apostolic see and the Croatian kingdom. Third, as king by the grace of God and by gift of the apostolic see, Demetrius Zwonimir took an oath of fidelity to Gregory and his lawful successors, whom he promised to receive and obey as he would their legates, if they should ever come to his kingdom. In 1079, Gregory demonstrated his continuing commitment to these arrangements when he wrote to a knight named Wezelin who, despite his having promised fidelity to St Peter and the pope, had rebelled 'against him whom papal authority had set up as king in Dalmatia'. Wezelin was to

---

[91] *Reg.* 2.51, 25 Jan. 1075, p. 194/11–17; for the reference as being to Croatia rather than South Italy, see Šišić, *Geschichte der Kroaten*, 1.269–73; Mandić, 'Gregorio VII e l'occupazione veneta', p. 464.

[92] See, besides the literature indicated in n. 1, Deér, *Papsttum und Normannen*, pp. 14–15, 52–8, 60.

[93] *Coll. can.* 3.278, pp. 383–5; cf. Demetrius Zwonimir's self-denigration in *Cod. dip. Croat.* 1.180, no. 139 (1083).

[94] For similar legislation by Alexander II's legates in 1060, see Waldmüller, *Die Synoden in Dalmatien*, pp. 57–8.

desist from his rebellion against Demetrius Zwonimir, which was tantamount to rebellion against the apostolic see itself. If he had a grievance against the king, he should come to Gregory for justice, rather than rebelling against him to the injury of the apostolic see.[95]

The Serbian kingdom of Zeta was critical in view of the relationship to the Byzantine empire, of which, at least in theory, it formed part. In 1078, an initiative of its king, Michael (1051–81), led to at least the adumbration of a relationship between it and the apostolic see similar to that which was established with Croatia. Gregory wrote to Michael about a difference between written requests conveyed through another papal legate, named Peter, and those made in a letter from the king himself; the difference made it impossible for Gregory to settle an outstanding dispute. The dispute clearly once again concerned the church of Ragusa, over which the Croatian see of Spalato claimed jurisdiction while King Michael championed its independence. Gregory requested the sending to Rome of Bishop Peter of Michael's metropolis of Antivari, of the bishop of Ragusa, and of other suitable envoys through whom a canonically just solution to the dispute might be found. By this means, Gregory said that he might be made aware of the rights of Michael's kingdom ('tuique regni honor a nobis cognosci'). This would clear the way for Gregory to hear Michael's plea as a most dear son of St Peter, which was for the gift of a banner ('vexillum') for himself and for the grant of a *pallium* for the archbishop of Ragusa.[96] The letter indicates that King Michael wished to commend his kingdom to the apostolic see on the lines of the kingdom of Demetrius Zwonimir, and that Gregory was minded to accede to his request.

The events of the mid-1070s in Dalmatia were important as providing Gregory, before he was confronted by the election of an anti-king in Germany, with a model of elective kingship which was validated by the investiture of a king with a papal banner ('vexillum') and by his taking an oath of fidelity and obedience to the apostolic see. It should be observed that this model resulted from Gregory's reaction to situations as they presented themselves to him in the kingdoms of Croatia and Zeta, rather than from his deliberate imposition of a form of elective and dependent kingship that he had antecedently formulated. To a large degree, he acted within lines set by past precedents. In Croatia after the death without heir of King Peter Krešimir and the military defeat at Norman hands of the liturgically suspect Slavac, Gregory was concerned to establish the suitability of Demetrius Zwonimir as the most powerful and religiously acceptable duke to succeed to the rule of a long-established kingdom. The situation was in many respects similar to that in 751, when Pope Zacharias decided upon the suitability of the Carolingian Pepin III to receive election to the Frankish kingdom. The symbolism of Demetrius Zwonimir's promotion to the kingship was, indeed, forceful: he was invested by the conferring of a papal banner ('vexillum') and chosen ('constitutus') by the acclamation in synod of the clergy and people. Yet the investiture, like its sequel in the annual payment that Demetrius Zwonimir promised

---

[95] *Reg.* 7.4, 7 Oct. 1079, pp. 463–4.
[96] *Reg.* 5.12, to Michael *Sclavorum rex*, 9 Jan. 1078, p. 365.

to Rome and the oath which he took to the pope, followed the pattern of the Norman rulers of South Italy in 1059.[97] Demetrius Zwonimir's continuing to acknowledge the terms of his coming to the kingship, like King Michael of Zeta's wish for himself to receive a papal *vexillum* to underpin a rule that he had exercised for some twenty-seven years, suggest how largely Gregory's dispositions met the need of the rulers themselves for the reinforcement of their kingship.[98] Perhaps the most novel aspect of Gregory's dealings was his expectation that he might henceforth control the religious and political life of the region through legates for whom a residence in Spalato was permanently provided and endowed.

Apart from the contacts already noticed, there is evidence of only one direct papal intervention in Dalmatia during the remainder of Gregory's pontificate: after November 1078, a papal legate, a Roman cardinal by the name of John, held a synod at Nin, in Croatia.[99] As for the kings of the region, they pursued their own interests, but during Gregory's lifetime they found them to be congruous with his own. Demetrius Zwonimir of Croatia, who was loud in his protestations of loyalty to the terms of his oath of 1075/6, was concerned to ward off the pressures of Alexius Comnenus and, still more, of the Venetians; therefore, after Robert Guiscard had renewed his own fealty to Gregory in 1080, Dalmatian forces helped the duke by land and sea in his campaigns across the Adriatic.[100] In the kingdom of Zeta, there is no suggestion that King Michael's son and successor Bodin (1082–1101) wavered in his support of Gregory. But after Gregory's death, Bodin petitioned the anti-pope Clement III to confer a *pallium* upon Archbishop Peter of Antivari.[101] How Gregory himself regarded the long-term dynastic futures of the two kingdoms does not emerge.

6.4 Hungary

The Hungarians owed their conversion to Christianity to their ruler Stephen I (997–1038), the first of the Árpád dynasty, who in 1000 by papal sanction received a royal crown. Gregory VII's letters concerning Hungary show him to have been concerned, through all the vicissitudes of his dealings with Henry IV of Germany, to build upon the events of the year 1000 as he interpreted them in order to maintain the independence of Hungary from constitutional subjection and political clientship to the king of Germany. The Hungarian kingdom and its church were to be directly subject to Rome. Gregory's concern was the greater because, when he became pope, the king of Hungary, Solomon I (1063–74), owed much to Salian support and was married to Henry IV's sister Judith/Sophia. At least until 1081, Gregory's letters

[97] See above, 2.2.3.

[98] Demetrius Zwonimir was under challenge from the Venetians, whose doge, Domenicus Silvio, in Feb. 1076 claimed the title of 'dux Dalmatiae': *Cod. dipl. Croat.* 1.137, no. 108; cf. Mandić, 'Gregorio VII e l'occupazione veneta', p. 462.

[99] See Waldmüller, *Die Synoden in Dalmatien*, pp. 93–4.

[100] William of Apulia, 4.135–7, 300–4, pp. 210–11, 220–1.

[101] Kehr, 'Papsturkunden in Rom', no. 7, pp. 148–9.

show that he was in frequent contact by letters and messengers with leading laity and churchmen in Hungary.

His claims with respect to Hungary were challenging and clear. They are best set out in a letter of October 1074, when an approach from the king elicited a rebuke to the king for an 'ill-advised undertaking' ('incauta conditio') in which he had gravely offended St Peter. Gregory insisted that he should have known from the elders of his nation that (as Gregory construed the events of 1000) King Stephen had offered and devoutly handed over his kingdom to the Roman church in full right and authority to be its own possession. When, in 1044, King Henry III of Germany had defeated the Magyars in the battle of the River Raab, he had acknowledged St Peter's lordship by sending to Rome the Hungarian crown and royal lance. Yet, as Gregory had heard, Solomon had recently so far departed from kingly duty and rightfulness as to receive his kingdom as a gift ('in beneficium') from the king of the Germans. If this were true, Solomon must immediately correct his error: he could not long remain king unless he acknowledged his royal dignity to be a gift of the apostolic, not of the kingly majesty ('apostolicae, non regiae magestatis beneficium'). But Gregory ended on a hopeful note: if Solomon did right and lived as befitted a king, then he would enjoy the motherly love of the Roman church and the friendship of Gregory himself.[102]

Such was Gregory's construction of Hungarian political life; the reality was more complex. King Solomon I was the nephew of his predecessor Béla I (1060–3); upon his succession under German auspices, Béla's sons Gésa/Joas and Ladislas had become dukes. There ensued a prolonged family feud from which, by the end of 1074, Gésa emerged victorious. Solomon remained a factor in Hungarian politics until he disappeared from history in 1083. But Gésa reigned as king until his own sudden death in April 1077, when he was succeeded by his brother Ladislas (1077–95).[103]

As pope, Gregory's first known contact with a Hungarian figure was with Duke Gésa, whose renewed pressure upon King Solomon in 1072 had impelled him towards Henry IV of Germany. Gésa turned for allies to the Poles and to Gregory. Gregory replied to his approach by warmly commending his zeal for the apostolic see and by expressing his own goodwill and preparedness to help him. He named Marquis Azzo III of Este, as one especially beloved to him amongst the princes of Italy, as a faithful intermediary if Gésa should wish to make contact.[104] During 1074, Gésa built up his pressure upon Solomon until he defeated him in battle at Mogyród. Solomon, in desperation, looked ever more urgently to his German brother-in-law, promising him the cession of cities and the payment of tribute; but such help as Henry IV was able to marshal was to no avail.[105] It was tidings of Solomon's promises to Henry that elicited Gregory's letter of October 1074 to Solomon,[106] with its rebuke for his concessions to Henry.

---

[102] Reg. 2.13, 28 Oct. 1074, pp. 144–6.
[103] For Hungarian history, I follow Hóman, Geschichte, 1.272–92, and the relevant annals of Meyer von Knonau.
[104] Reg. 1.58, 17 Mar. 1074, pp. 85–6.
[105] Lampert of Hersfeld, Ann. a. 1074, pp. 250–3, 254–7.   [106] Reg. 2.13.

Gregory's letters of 1075 to Hungarian recipients are of the utmost significance for his conception of royal authority and of the purpose of papal intervention in the affairs of a Christian kingdom. He wrote first to Solomon's queen, Judith, whom he addressed not as the sister of Henry IV but as the daughter of the Empress Agnes. Gregory enlarged upon the personal reasons which, on top of the debt that he owed to all Christians through the universality of his papal office, led him to love her as though she were his own human sister: the affection that the Emperor Henry III and the Empress Agnes had shown him in his own early days; the devotion and solicitude that Agnes was now showing him in his during her religious retreat at Rome; Judith's own life-long upholding of the qualities of her own imperial breeding while she lived among a savage and unknown people ('inter asperam et incognitam gentem'). Gregory commiserated with her in the adversities with which he knew her to be bearing, and he promised help in matters which she had pressed upon him through her mother. But his main message was that she should continue steadfast in all the qualities that her imperial background should equip her to bring to her situation. The qualities that Judith inherited from her Salian imperial stock were to continue to benefit the uncultivated people over whom she was queen.[107] It was a vain hope on Gregory's part, for, in 1074, Judith had taken refuge with her brother in Germany, while her husband was reduced to virtual powerlessness. There were no means by which Judith could any longer be effective in promoting Gregory's ends in Hungary.

During the spring of 1075, Gregory also twice wrote to Gésa.[108] It does not emerge whether Gregory knew of negotiations with Byzantium through which Gésa, perhaps in 1075, received a crown from the Emperor Michael VII Ducas;[109] however, he addressed him as duke, not king. But in March, he approached him in terms which suggest that he was aware of his striving for the Hungarian crown and that he wished to counsel him accordingly. Gregory wrote that, although Gésa might not have received an earlier letter,[110] he was exercising the charity by which he admonished kings and princes as his sons, and that he desired for Gésa the honour and glory that were the counterpart of righteousness. He insisted upon Hungary's independence: like other distinguished kingdoms, it should remain in a state of proper liberty and should be subject to no king of another kingdom but only to the holy and universal mother, the Roman church. Because Gésa's cousin Solomon had unlawfully ('usurpative') received the kingdom of Hungary from the German king, not from the Roman pontiff, divine judgement—Gregory clearly had in mind Solomon's defeat by Gésa at Mogyród—had inhibited his lordship ('dominium eius, ut credimus, divinum iudicium impedivit'). Now, therefore, effective rule had passed to Gésa; for the time being ('interim'), Gregory exhorted him to care for the churches and to be zealous for religion, obeying the legates of the Roman church whenever

---

[107] *Reg.* 2.44, 10 Jan. 1075, pp. 180–2.
[108] *Reg.* 2.63, 23 Mar. 1074, pp. 218–19, 2.70, 17 Apr. 1075, pp. 229–30.
[109] M. Mullett, in Shepard and Franklin (eds.), *Byzantine Diplomacy*, pp. 230–1, 233; Gésa's inclusion in the Byzantine 'family of kings' found permanent record on the crown of St Stephen.
[110] Probably *Reg.* 1.58.

they came. Then St Peter's intercessions would enable Gésa to enjoy prosperity in this life and in the next.

Almost a month later, Gregory again wrote to 'Duke' Gésa; this time, his declared purpose was to compose peace and establish concord in Hungary, and to restore charity amongst its leaders, whose peace or hatred affected all its people. Thus, Gregory sought to reconcile Gésa and his cousin Solomon, whom Gregory was careful to describe as king. A measure of justice might thereby be achieved all round, in a prosperous Hungarian kingdom which had customarily enjoyed independence under a king ('rex') and not a kinglet ('regulus'); Gregory drove the point home by again denouncing Solomon's submission to the king of Germany. Because God had foreseen this injury to St Peter, he had, by the judgement of battle, transferred power in the kingdom to Gésa. Gregory reminded Gésa of the irresistable power of St Peter. He invited him to ask for whatever he desired from the Roman church (Gregory seems to have meant appropriate support in his coming to terms with a Solomon who had duly renounced his submission to Henry IV of Germany, not the conferring of the Hungarian crown upon himself); Gregory urged Gésa to demonstrate his obedience by appropriate good actions. Gregory's messengers were charged to deliver further, verbal messages.

When, after his sudden death, Gésa was succeeded as king by his brother Ladislas, the coming to office of the new king appeared to Gregory in a somewhat different light. Gésa had advanced towards the kingship after a victory in battle which was a sign of the transfer to him of God's favour; Ladislas had become king by the peaceful election of his subjects. Gregory quickly wrote, not to Ladislas, but to Archbishop Nehemiah of Gran (Esztergom), whose messenger had come to him before he left Rome at the end of 1076 in the hope of establishing in Germany a peace and concord which, it may be noticed, was similar to that which he aspired to create in Hungary; he hoped that German pacification might have repercussions there.[111] Gregory must have heard of Ladislas's election from another source. His response to it was to charge the archbishop with summoning the bishops and princes of Hungary to a meeting and then with reporting upon the new king's intentions and devotion to the apostolic see; Gregory would do what pertained to him ('quod ad nos attinet'), by which he seems to have meant the conferring of the kingdom upon Ladislas on St Peter's behalf, and he would promote the welfare of the king and his kingdom. He sent further instructions verbally by his messenger. He thus took the first, cautious steps to promote the welfare of the Hungarian kingdom through the king whom the Hungarians had elected.

Although Gregory to this extent recognized Ladislas as king from the time of his election, and although King Solomon disappeared from his calculations so far as they are known, he was slow to proceed towards complete acceptance. The probable reason was that Ladislas made no positive approach about receiving his kingdom from the apostolic see. But in March 1079, after earlier attempts at effective com-

---

[111] *Reg.* 4.25, 9 June 1077, pp. 339–40.

munication had failed, Gregory wrote to Ladislas of whom he said that he had heard good reports of his willingness duly to serve St Peter and to obey the pope 'as befitted a free-born son' ('ut liberalem filium decet'); Gregory thus acknowledged Ladislas's freedom from subjection to other kings. Indeed, Ladislas conformed to the pattern of the best kings by exemplifying both a pattern of righteousness in his way of life and also the lineage of nobility in his blood ('servando tam in moribus normam iustitiae quam etiam lineam nobilitatis in sanguine'). Yet Gregory looked for more: he invited him to prove by deeds what he had hitherto attested only by words. Gregory had a specific request to make: he renewed his plea for Ladislas to provide a haven for three counts and their knights who had been unjustly exiled; Gregory did not say by whom, but those responsible may have been Bavarians rather than Hungarians. He urged Ladislas to increase his generosity towards them 'because of fidelity to St Peter and of our own commendation of them' ('ob fidelitatem beati Petri nostramque commendationem'); Gregory thus invoked his own idea of the proper relationship between the king of Hungary and the apostolic see. He next reminded Ladislas of the marks of Christian kingship in general: an unswerving pursuit of righteousness; protection of widows, orphans, and pilgrims; the resolute and active defence of churches; and the like. Finally, Gregory asked Ladislas to take all possible steps to maintain effective communication with him.[112] The letter was eloquent of Gregory's concern to draw Ladislas closer to the apostolic see, both in moral commitment and in everyday practice.

Some two years later, Gregory further pursued this end by writing to Ladislas's queen, Adelaide, who was the daughter of Rudolf of Swabia, the late German anti-king. His letter is unique in being certainly penned by his own hand.[113] Amongst other spiritual advice, Gregory offered a pattern for a Christian queen which was the counterpart of his counsel to Ladislas about Christian kingship. Adelaide should always seek to attract the heart of her husband ('domini tui') the king, whom Gregory described as his own dearest son, to the fear and love of God, and she should have an especial care for churches, the weak, and the unjustly oppressed. Both directly and through his queen, Gregory was concerned to fortify Ladislas in freedom from other lordship and in obedience to himself.

After Gregory's death, Ladislas's reign was far from unblemished from a Gregorian point of view, for in 1091 he recognized the anti-pope Clement III and entered negotiations with Henry IV of Germany.[114] Yet, in most respects, he was remembered as a zealous Christian king who was the second king of Hungary to merit canonization. It was during his reign that King Stephen I was raised to the altar; such measures as those of the council of Szabolcs (1092) served to raise the standard of the Hungarian church; and the foundation of the see of Zagreb (1092) was a major step forward in ecclesiastical organisation. The reign of St Ladislas provides evidence that Gregory VII's aspirations for Hungary were partly but not entirely achieved. His extremer claims to Petrine lordship over Hungary were warded off without being

---

[112] *Reg.* 6.29, 21 Mar. 1079, pp. 441–2. [113] *Reg.* 8.22, (1081), pp. 564–5.
[114] Ziese, *Wibert*, pp. 161–3, 214–15.

denied, but so was the subjection of Hungary to German control. The Árpád dynasty in which Gregory recognized a true lineage of blood was established as a Christian family, and in Stephen I and Ladislas Hungary produced sainted kings to hallow the kingdom. If the Hungarian kings did not perform fealty to the papacy after the positive manner of their Croatian neighbours whose kingdom they would soon absorb, and if Gregory had to accept the ruler whom the Hungarians elected rather than the ruler whose rights were established by his adjudication, at least Hungary came to have a ruling dynasty, springing from a Christian ancestor, such as was prominent among Gregory's desiderata for the kingdoms of Europe.

6.5 Bohemia

During the pontificate of Gregory VII, Bohemia's situation was in many respects the opposite of that of Hungary. Whereas Hungary formed a separate kingdom with its own ecclesiastical organization, Bohemia was subject to German rule. Politically, it had been subjected to German suzerainty in 950 by the Emperor Otto I; after the see of Prague was established in 967 and given papal approval in 973, it became part of the province of Mainz. Although the Latin liturgy predominated, its Slav counterpart was widely used. From 1061 to 1092, the duke of Bohemia was Wratislav II, whose family traced its descent from the legendary Přemysl. In 1068, his brother Jaromir/Gebhard became bishop of Prague, but the two brothers were divided by a prolonged quarrel. Wratislav transferred his residence from the Hradčany, which was the seat of the bishopric, to Vyšehrad in the southern part of Prague where he built a stone castle and several churches. In 1063, the position of the see of Prague was diminished by the foundation of the see of Olmütz, in Moravia.[115]

Gregory lost little time before seeking to advance papal control over the Bohemian duchy and church, which bulked large in his Register between the summer of 1073 and the spring of 1075.[116] He adopted the method of a direct approach to Duke Wratislav. He sent legates of his own—the Cardinal-deacons Bernard and Gregory; in July 1073, he praised Wratislav and his brother Conrad duke of Brünn and Otto duke of Moravia for receiving them honourably. They had done so in face of much resistance, especially from Bishop Jaromir of Prague, whom Gregory described as once his friend but now an associate of Simon Magus in his resistance to St Peter. Wratislav and his brothers were urged to bring together the legates and Bishop Jaromir, who would thus have an opportunity both of accepting the legates' decisions and of having any well-grounded grievances resolved by them. If the bishop were recalcitrant to this, Gregory would not only confirm existing sanctions against him but proceed to severer measures. Thus, both Jaromir and, through him, many others would learn the weight of papal authority.[117] Gregory's opening letter to Bohemia

---

[115] For the background, see, besides the relevant annals of Meyer von Knonau, Bosl (ed.), *Handbuch der Geschichte der Böhmischen Länder*, 1.228–30; Vlasto, *The Entry of the Slavs*, pp. 86–113.

[116] For a full list and discussion of Gregory's letters, see above, 3.2.5.

[117] *Reg.* 1.17; cf. Cosmas of Prague, 2.30, pp. 125–6.

affords a prime example of how he sought to resolve conflict and foster peace and concord under the ultimate sanction of papal censure; it provides the keynote for Gregory's future dealings with the duchy.

At the end of the year, he took a further step in cultivating Wratislav's obedience to and dependence upon Rome. After praising the evidences that he had provided of devotion to the apostolic see, he renewed Alexander II's exceptional gift to him of the right to wear a mitre, which had itself confirmed a grant to Wratislav by Pope Nicholas II in return for an annual *census* of a hundred silver marks. By means of the mitre, Gregory hoped to link the duke closely with the apostolic see, and tacitly to counterbalance his commitment to the German kingdom. Gregory acknowledged that the work of his legates in Bohemia had come to a standstill, but he confirmed what they had done and hoped soon to build upon it.[118]

In his quarrel with Jaromir of Prague, Wratislav had little alternative but to exhibit co-operation with Gregory. Gregory himself quickly sought to resolve upon his own authority the question of the sees of Prague and Olmütz. In January, he allowed Bishop Jaromir of Prague the benefit of the canonical *exceptio spolii* and restored his possessions.[119] He summoned both Jaromir and Bishop John of Olmütz to Rome by mid-April, and hoped that Duke Wratislav might also be able to come.[120] In March, Gregory prepared the way for his own adjudication by requiring Dukes Otto of Moravia and Conrad of Brünn to refrain from attacks upon the see of Olmütz, by brushing aside Archbishop Siegfried of Mainz's claims as metropolitan to jurisdiction, and by sending another cordial letter to Duke Wratislav in which he declared the nullity of any steps that Siegfried might take against the duke.[121]

During Holy Week, Gregory was able to inform the duke that he had restored a duly penitent Jaromir to the see of Prague, and he asked the duke to receive the bishop with brotherly affection. Thus personal relationships were to be restored; as for the dispute between the sees of Prague and Olmütz, Gregory remitted a decision to a future Roman synod which both bishops and their representatives should attend, together with representatives of Wratislav himself. Pending a decision, the bishop of Olmütz should hold the territory that was in dispute between the two bishops. Gregory also provided for the settlement, at Rome if necessary, of the differences between Wratislav and Jaromir arising from the collegiate church and castle that Wratislav established at Vyšehrad.[122]

It emerges from three letters that Gregory dispatched on 22 September 1074 that the problems of Bohemia could not be so readily brought to harmony as Gregory wished. He complained to Bishop Jaromir that he had abused the indulgence shown to him in the spring by alleging Gregory's sanction for further wrong that he had done to Bishop John of Olmütz. Moreover, Gregory had come to see that Jaromir's

---

[118] *Reg.* 1.38. For Nicholas II's grant of the mitre, see Deusdedit, *Coll. can.* 3.279 (150), p. 385.

[119] *Reg.* 1.44.   [120] *Reg.* 1.44–5.   [121] *Reg.* 1.59–61.

[122] *Reg.* 1.78. According to Cosmas of Prague, Countess Matilda of Tuscany, who was related to Jaromir on his mother's side, successfully interceded with Gregory on Jaromir's behalf at his Lent synod: 2.31, pp. 126–7.

allegations against Duke Wratislav over the Vyšehrad were mendacious. Jaromir was to make good the harm that he had done to both duke and bishop; otherwise, he must appear at Rome in person or through representatives. He was also to desist from his vendetta against Wratislav, and above all from excommunicating his men. To the duke himself, he wrote cordially, thanking him for sending the *census* of a hundred marks which he owed in return for his mitre; Gregory welcomed what he regarded as evidence of the duke's deepening loyalty to the apostolic see. Wratislav had also done what was called for on his part to seek peace with Bishop Jaromir, whose conduct Gregory severely censured; the duke should now bring to bear upon Jaromir all sanctions that might lead him to right the wrongs that he had committed against the duke and against John of Olmütz. Gregory sent a third letter to John, promising papal support but urging him to desist from self-help.[123]

At his Lent synod of 1075, Gregory once more considered the 'lis et discordia' between the bishops of Prague and Olmütz, in the presence of them both. The synod attempted an adjudication between them which Gregory sought to enshrine in a written final concord which was reached in full awareness of the impossibility of getting to the bottom of the dispute between them. While leaving open the possibility of further investigation within a time-limit of ten years, Gregory simply ruled that all possessions in dispute between the two sees should be equally partitioned between them.[124] A few weeks later, Gregory wrote to Duke Wratislav, first of all urging him to admit his nephew Frederick, who was provost of Brünn and whom he described as a 'fidelis' of the Roman church, to his rightful inheritance ('beneficium'); thus he would meet the claims both of natural kinship and of reverence to the apostolic see. Second, he was to foster in his duchy the bond of peace, especially between himself and his brothers Dukes Conrad and Otto, and between the bishops of Prague and Olmütz, 'for just as those who give place to discord and disputes are undoubtedly the sons of the devil, so those who devote themselves to peace are called the sons of God'. Gregory accompanied this letter by a pastoral letter to all the Bohemians, in which he exhorted them to follow the Christian life and especially to seek mutual peace and the values and virtues that are proper for Christians.[125]

From the fourteen letters that Gregory wrote to Bohemia before April 1075, a clear picture emerges of Gregory's expectations for the duchy. He made no express reference to Bohemia's relation to the German crown and did not say anything to provoke a bid for independence from it. But ecclesiastically, he overrode the claim of Archbishop Siegfried of Mainz to exercise metropolitan jurisdiction and sought to settle ecclesiastical disputes by the immediate imposition of papal authority. Politically, he sought to perpetuate his predecessors' conferring of a mitre upon the duke in return for an annual *census* and thus to render the Přemyslid dukes morally obedient to papal authority. Within Bohemia, Gregory's intention was to seek the resolution of discord and disputes and the fostering of peace and concord. His prime purpose was to bring lay and ecclesiastical rulers to a habit of mutual loyalty and

---

[123] *Reg.* 1.6–8.   [124] *Reg.* 2.53.   [125] *Reg.* 2.71–2.

collaboration; disputes over rights and possessions were not to be pressed to the limit but settled by compromise in order to facilitate the harmony of human relationships. Thus the peace of God might be established among men and promoted throughout the land.

It was a noble vision, but it had all too little foundation in reality. While Duke Wratislav was at loggerheads with his brother Bishop Jaromir of Prague, it suited him to curry favour with Gregory, to the extent of paying his *census* to Rome. But after Gregory's breach with Henry IV of Germany in January 1076, Wratislav's loyalty to his German suzerain took precedence. Gregory is known to have written only once more to Bohemia. In January 1080, he answered an approach from Duke Wratislav by reproving his dealings with excommunicates, by whom he evidently meant Henry and his supporters, and also his remissness in securing the well-being of the churches in his lands. He treated the duke to a long homily on a ruler's duties and especially upon the need to pay proper regard to papal admonitions. Wratislav had invited back to Bohemia Slav monks whom his predecessor Spytihnév II had expelled; Gregory dismissed his request for the Slav liturgy to be used in his duchy. Gregory would not at once send the legate whom Wratislav requested, but he would consider sending a deputation later in the year, and he asked Wratislav to send Provost Frederick of Brünn or another person named Felix to prepare the way.[126]

Nothing is known of the upshot, but from 1075 Wratislav was a staunch supporter of Henry IV of Germany. His forces were regularly made available for Henry's battles and campaigns, and Henry rewarded him with gifts of land—in 1075, with the Saxon Ostmark, and in 1076 with Meissen. At the synod of Mainz in 1085, Henry IV elevated Wratislav to the personal, though not the hereditary, rank of king of Bohemia and Poland, crowning him with his own hand, while in 1086, Archbishop Engelbert of Trier crowned Wratislav at Prague.[127] In the long term, Gregory's cultivation of Duke Wratislav and his attempts to bring papal authority to bear in his duchy were wholly frustrated.

6.6 Poland

In comparison with Hungary and Bohemia, Poland plays only a small part in Gregory's known dealings with eastern Europe.[128] During his pontificate, it was ruled by two princes of the Piast house, Boleslav II 'the Bold' (1058–79) and Ladislas I Herman (1079–1102). Boleslav was an energetic and capable ruler whose policies were consistently anti-German. He was also much concerned with the organization of the Polish church, and in 1075/6 set up a new see for Mazovia at Płock. Yet for all the apparent compatibility of their interests, there is no evidence that Boleslav looked

---

[126] *Reg.* 7.11, 2 Jan. 1080, pp. 473–5.

[127] Lampert of Hersfeld, *Ann. aa.* 1075, pp. 284–5, 292–3, 308–13, 1076, 340–3, 370–5, 1077, 394–5; Bruno, caps. 36–40, 95, 117, 121, 123, pp. 140–5, 338–41, 380–3, 388–9, 392–3; Cosmas of Prague, 2.37–8, pp. 134–41.

[128] For Poland, see esp. Vlasto, *The Entry of the Slavs*, pp. 128–33.

positively to Gregory, while only one letter to him from Gregory survives; Gregory is not known to have been in touch with any other Polish figure. Gregory dispatched his letter to Boleslav in April 1075. He praised the care for the church in his lands through which he had in effect been a good servant of St Peter. But he expressed concern for the order of the Polish church. He had good reason, for the metropolitan see of Gnesen had not recovered from devastation by the Bohemians in 1036, and Cracow which had become the ducal capital had not effectively replaced it. Gregory expressed anxiety about the lack of a clearly established metropolis, about the consequent disarray and uncanonical conduct of such bishops as there were, and about the need for more bishops to be introduced if there was to be proper oversight of so large a country. He was, therefore, sending legates to Boleslav for whom he sought support in building up the church so far as they could and in referring to Gregory such matters as they could not themselves settle. Gregory also asked Boleslav to restore to the 'king of Russia', Isjaslav, money that he had seized from him.[129]

Nothing is known of a sequel to this letter, and there is no reason to suppose that Gregory had a direct or even indirect part in Boleslav's assumption at Gnesen in 1076 of a royal title and crown.[130] Three years later, the martyrdom of Bishop Stanislas of Cracow cast a shadow upon Boleslav's reign. Under his indolent and weak successor, Ladislas, there was no known contact between Gregory and Poland.

6.7 Russia

In 1075, the complex politics of eastern Europe provided Gregory with a brief opportunity for intervention in the affairs of Kievan Russia, which had suffered many disorders since the prosperous reign of the Grand Prince Jaroslav (1019–54).[131] After his death, his three eldest sons, Isjaslav/Demetrius, Svjatoslav, and Vsévolod, at first ruled jointly, but their coalition proved unstable. After many vicissitudes, in 1068 Isjaslav, who was married to a Polish wife, Gertrude, a lady of profound Latin piety, was driven out, but he was reinstated in 1070 with Polish help. In March 1073, Isjaslav and Gertrude were again expelled from Russia; this time, Duke Boleslav II of Poland did not help them but negotiated with Svjatoslav. Early in 1075, Isjaslav sought help at Mainz from Henry IV of Germany;[132] but Henry provided no effective help. In desperation, Isjaslav turned to Gregory VII at Rome, whither he dispatched his son Jaropolk/Peter. It was no doubt Jaropolk who complained to Gregory about Boleslav of Poland's seizure of money belonging to Isjaslav; in asking Boleslav for it to be restored, Gregory prudently made no reference to wider issues of Russian politics.[133] But Jaropolk secured from Gregory a letter addressed to

---

[129] *Reg.* 2.73, 20 Apr. 1075, pp. 233–5.   [130] Lampert of Hersfeld, *Ann. a.* 1077, p. 394–5.

[131] For Russia, Meyer von Knonau continues to provide invaluable information on events and sources. See also Vlasto, *The Entry of the Slavs*, pp. 287–91; Ziegler, 'Gregor VII. und den Kijewer Grossfürst Isjaslav'; Meysztowicz, 'L'Union de Kiev avec Rome'; Murjanoff, 'Über ein Darstellung'; Ziese, *Wibert*, pp. 164–7.

[132] Lampert of Hersfeld, *Ann. a.* 1075, pp. 262–3, 300–1.

[133] *Reg.* 2.73, p. 235/21–30; see above, 6.6.

Isjaslav/Demetrius 'king of the Russians' and to 'the queen his wife'.[134] Gregory said that, after professing due fidelity ('fidelitas') to the prince of the apostles, Jaropolk had asked that he might himself receive the kingdom ('regnum') of the Russians from Gregory's hands as a gift of St Peter, and he had claimed his father's permission to do so. Gregory promised Isjaslav St Peter's protection and papal assent to all his rightful petitions. He said that he was sending two legates, one of whom was well known to Isjaslav as his friend and companion. Isjaslav should co-operate with them in all that they were instructed to do.

Gregory's letter was not without short-term effect. Isjaslav's rival Svjatoslav died in 1076. Perhaps because he felt it wise to please Gregory in the aftermath of Henry IV's penance at Canossa, Boleslav II of Poland helped his brother-in-law to re-enter Kiev on 15 July 1077; Isjaslav's subsequent part in a Polish campaign against Bohemia helped to place pressure on one of Henry IV's staunchest allies. In Russia itself, there was some evidence of a communication of Gregory's way of thinking in the prayers and illuminations that were inserted in the so-called 'Codex Gertrudianus'—the devotional book in which Gertrude recorded her continuing reverence for St Peter and solicitude for the pope. A remarkable illumination embodied the thought of Gregory's letter by showing her son Jaropolk/Peter and his wife Kunigunde/Irene of Orlamünde being supported by their respective patron saints, while Christ himself placed crowns upon their heads.[135]

But Isjaslav's rule in Kiev was short-lived; in October 1078, he was killed in a skirmish occasioned by continuing family dissentions. He was succeeded by his brother Vsévelod (1078–93), while an appanage was created for Jaropolk. Jaropolk's devotion to St Peter remained strong enough for him to complete his father's plan to build in Kiev the only church in early Russia which is known to have been dedicated to him. But Jaropolk was murdered in 1086. Vsévelod proved to be a weak ruler, and his daughter Eupraxia in 1089 became the second wife of Henry IV of Germany. There is, however, no evidence of Russian dealings with the anti-pope Clement III.

It is difficult to see any strength in Gregory VII's dealings with the Russian princely family. Isjaslav's démarche to him in 1075 was the desperate bid of an exile who was prepared to try anything in order to grasp at a return to power. His Polish wife was deeply pious and kept to her Latin upbringing and loyalties; the marriage for a time gave St Peter an unwonted place in Russian religious awareness. But there is no sign of any looking to Rome amongst Russian churchman, nor did Gregory make approaches to them of which evidence survives. It is not known what, if anything, his legates of 1075 achieved. When set in the context of Gregory's other letters of 1075 to eastern Europe, his response to Isjaslav and Gertrude shows his alacrity, when opportunity seemed to present itself, to assert the direct lordship of St Peter over eastern lands, to invoke the titles of king and queen and to confer crowns, and to

---

[134] *Reg.* 2.74, 17 Apr. 1075, pp. 236–7; cf. Deusdedit, *Coll. can.* 3.276 (150), p. 381.

[135] See Meysztowicz, 'Manuscriptum Gertrudae', esp. no. 90, pp. 154–5; Murjanoff, 'Über ein Darstellung'. The codex is now Cividale, Museo archeologica, MS 136. Gertrude's devotion to St Peter was, no doubt, the reason for Jaropolk's unusual baptismal name.

receive the fealty or fidelity of their rulers at least in the words of an appropriate formula. But his negotiations produced no tangible or enduring political result in
Russia, nor did they make any impact upon relations between the Latin and the eastern churches.

6.8 The Scandinavian Kingdoms and Iceland

Gregory's dealings as pope with the Scandinavian kingdoms of Denmark, Sweden,
and Norway took place in the aftermath of the endeavours of Archbishop Adalbert of
Hamburg–Bremen (1043–72) to develop his jurisdiction over northern Europe to
the extent of establishing a northern patriarchate, and in the shadow of the hostility
towards Gregory of his successor Archbishop Liemar (1072–1101).[136] Before 1072,
papal support for Adalbert's plans had been qualified and ineffectual; under King
Sweyn Estrithson (1044–74/6), direct contacts between Denmark and the apostolic
see had increased. Thus, under Alexander II, there was a papal request that Sweyn
and his successors should regularly send Peter's Pence to Rome; they were to be presented, not as hitherto at the altar of St Peter's basilica, but in person to the pope and
his successors.[137] Visits, actual or projected, to Rome by Danish bishops including
Egino of Lund suggest the preparation of the ground for evading the jurisdiction of
Hamburg–Bremen, and for making Lund the Danish metropolis.[138] At an uncertain
date but perhaps in 1072, King Sweyn sought to provide for the royal succession in
Denmark by sending Magnus, his son by one of his concubines, to Rome for royal
consecration, but the boy perished during the journey.[139] In letters which Gregory
addressed to Sweyn in 1075, he recalled that, while he was still archdeacon, he and
the king had been in cordial touch by letters and messengers about setting up a
Danish metropolitan see and about other matters, and that promises about them had
been exchanged. Gregory made it clear that it was open for Sweyn to commit himself
and his kingdom more closely to St Peter, but he left the initiative with Sweyn;
neither now nor later did he press a claim to sworn fidelity or any similar bond.[140]

When he became pope, Gregory seems to have held high expectations of Sweyn,
for he was the only king to whom, according to his Register, official notices of his
papal election was sent.[141] Yet contacts between Gregory and Denmark were slow to
develop; and, during Gregory's pontificate, plans for a Danish metropolis proceeded
no further. Two matters help to explain these delays. First, in 1074, Gregory seems
to have intended the legates whom he dispatched to Germany in March, Cardinal-
bishops Gerald of Ostia and Hubert of Palestrina, when they had concluded their
business there to travel to Denmark.[142] There, they were to discuss with the king, for

---

[136] For a fuller account of Gregory's dealings with Scandinavia, see Cowdrey, 'The Gregorian Reform
in the Anglo-Norman Lands and in Scandinavia'.
[137] *Ep.* 6, *PL* 146.1283.
[138] Adam of Bremen, 4.9 and Schol. 115, pp. 444–7, read in the light of Gregory's letters as below, n. 140.
[139] Adam of Bremen, Schol. 72, pp. 354–5.
[140] *Reg.* 2.51, 25 Jan. 1075, p. 193/29–33, 2.75, 17 Apr. 1075, p. 238/21–8.
[141] *Reg.* 1.4, 28 Apr. 1073, p. 7.   [142] For their mission to Germany, see above, 3.2.3.

the honour of his kingdom ('pro honorificentia regni tui'), the subject of a metropolis and other topics that had been broached in Pope Alexander's day. But on account of the disordered state of Germany, the journey had seemed too dangerous, so the legates had returned to Rome. Gregory lost little time before writing to Sweyn with a request that he send messengers from Denmark with whom he might pursue discussions.[143]

As regards the establishment of a Danish metropolis, a second factor which caused delay was the diplomacy of Archbishop Liemar of Bremen. In 1074, Liemar did his best to frustrate the mission of Gregory's legates in Germany; in January 1075, Gregory suspended him from his archbishopric and summoned him to his Lent synod at Rome.[144] Liemar failed to attend; therefore Gregory excommunicated him.[145] But, for all his hostility to a legatine council in Germany, Liemar had always favoured ecclesiastical reform. Above all, he wished to implement the traditional claims of Hamburg–Bremen in northern Europe.[146] So he tried to relax the tension between Gregory and the German church. After the Lent synod, he acknowledged the sentence that was passed upon him and sent envoys to Gregory; then he set out in person for Rome to seek restoration to office.

In preparation for his journey, he asked Bishop Immad of Paderborn to write to Gregory on his behalf.[147] Immad's letter helps to explain why the plan for a Danish metropolis was for so long postponed. He gave an adverse account of a certain Rikwal who, in 1072, had succeeded Egino as bishop of Lund. Immad said that Rikwal was a clerk and sometime canon of Paderborn who for ten years had been a wanderer and fugitive. He had contumaciously refused to return to Paderborn; therefore Immad had excommunicated him. He had then fled to the Danes whose lands, Immad reminded Gregory, were by ancient right subject to the see of Hamburg–Bremen. Immad had written to Archbishop Adalbert, whose summons to return to Paderborn Rikwal ignored; Adalbert, too, passed sentence of excommunication. But now at last, Immad concluded, after so many delays—perhaps because he feared to lose his Danish bishopric—Rikwal had promised to return and to make satisfaction. Immad's purpose in writing to Gregory in these terms seems clear: as Rikwal's bishop, he wished to restore his subject's position; but he also wished to persuade Gregory that Liemar's own restoration, and perhaps also his confirmation as papal vicar and legate in the north, were called for, in order that he, too, might absolve Rikwal from the excommunication that his predecessor Adalbert had decreed.

Immad did not suggest that Rikwal should be deposed from the see of Lund, which he retained until his death in 1089. And in the event, Immad's letter did little to help Liemar, whose purposes for his see, so far as they depended upon Gregory's

---

[143] *Reg.* 2.51, pp. 193/29–194/7.

[144] *Reg.* 2.28, to Archbishop Liemar of Bremen, 12 Dec. 1074, pp. 160–1.

[145] *Reg.* 2.52a, p. 196.

[146] To this end, he may have prepared for submission at Rome a dossier of six forged papal privileges underlining the claims of the archbishops of Hamburg–Bremen to be papal legates and vicars in the North: Seegrün, *Das Erzbistum Hamburg*, pp. 83–100.

[147] Schmeidler, 'Ein Brief Bischof Imads'; *Dipl. Danic.* no. 14, pp. 39–31.

goodwill, were frustrated after 1076 by his unswerving adherence to Henry IV. The principal importance of Immad's intervention seems to have been its impact upon Gregory. His further correspondence with the Danish kings gives no hint that he blamed Sweyn for making Rikwal a bishop or for giving him protection. But after being told of Rikwal's record, Gregory never again referred to the plan for a Danish metropolis, which was revived only after Rikwal's, and therefore Gregory's, deaths. Only the king could provide for the day-to-day welfare of his churches, and it was now necessary to work through the kings directly and regularly. So, in his letters to Sweyn of 1075, Gregory threw open for the king's suggestions the ways in which co-operation might develop. He praised Sweyn fulsomely, and asked him to say, through his own messengers and through Gregory's, how the authority of the Roman church might best be brought to bear. Gregory was encouraged by his understanding that Sweyn might be minded to help the Roman church by military support against its enemies; in particular, an unnamed Danish bishop had indicated that he might be willing to send a son with an army to intervene in a land which was probably Croatia.[148]

From 1075, Gregory's objectives in Scandinavia became fully apparent. They showed restraint, given that, especially with the postponement of a plan for a Danish metropolis, the ecclesiastical organization of Scandinavia remained rudimentary. He made no mention of Peter's Pence, and still less of any obligations which might be associated with the liability to pay them. To Sweyn of Denmark, he was content to write only in general terms of the godly devotion through which he knew Sweyn to be resolved to commit his kingdom to the prince of the apostles and to the king's desire to be fortified by St Peter's authority. In letters to kings of Denmark, Norway, and Sweden between 1077 and 1081, Gregory concentrated upon impressing on them a pattern of righteousness that would foster prosperous kingship. Royal dynasties were to recognize their sources in Christian exemplars; where possible, the divisiveness of the ancient succession rights within royal clans was to be remedied by their limitation to a single son who would follow his father.

In Denmark, Gregory built up the posthumous image of Sweyn Estrithson as an ideal Christian ruler. In November 1077, he praised Sweyn to his son and successor Harold Hein (1076–80) as a king who had always and in all respects displayed to St Peter an unfeigned reverence through service and obedience; as a son of the Roman church, he was second to almost no other king. During his lifetime, he had, indeed, been stained by grievous carnal sins, but they would be purged by his own repentance and by memorial prayers and alms.[149] In April 1080, and so only some six weeks after

---

[148] *Reg.* 2.51,75; for Croatia, see above, 6.3. The date of Sweyn's death presents a problem. It is variously indicated in the sources as having occurred in 1074 and 1076, but there are strong reasons, especially in the *Anglo-Saxon Chronicle, a.* 1076, and Icelandic sources, for preferring the later date: Seegrün, *Das Papsttum und Skandinavien*, pp. 84–5 (suggesting 28 Apr. 1076); Saxo Grammaticus, 1.236–7 n. 34. It cannot be presumed that Gregory sent his letters of 1075 after Sweyn's death, or that Sweyn cannot have received them.

[149] *Reg.* 2.51, pp. 193/35–194/7.

the second excommunication of Henry IV of Germany, Gregory carried eulogy to the limit. Omitting any reference to Sweyn's sins, he now commended him to his son as an immaculate model of kingly excellence. He had been second to no king of his time: 'His surpassing virtues', Gregory asserted, 'so shone out above all other kings that we ranked him above them all, not excepting even the Emperor Henry III who adhered so closely to the holy Roman church; and we considered that we should embrace him in a unique love'.[150] From such a paragon of kingship, Gregory wished a dynasty to descend. In the earlier letter, Harold was urged dutifully to attend to his father's commemoration. In the second, he was urged so to imitate his father that a royal stock should patently be established ('quatinus inde possis ornamenta virtutum propagando educere, unde videris nobilissimi sanguinis lineam trahere'). When Gregory heard that Harold's brothers were seeking the aid of King Olaf III of Norway to compel Harold to divide his inheritance, he called upon Olaf to procure their peaceful and honourable submission, '[ne] regni status labefactetur aut dignitas'.[151] In Sweden, to a similar end Gregory proposed that Kings Inge I and Halstan who already shared power should live in brotherly concord and love, and should remember the good deeds and reputation of their father King Stenkil (1060–6).[152]

In his attempts directly to promote the well-being of the Scandinavian churches and their clergy, Gregory approached the kings of all three kingdoms. The Swedish kings were to secure respect and obedience for priests and especially bishops.[153] Harold of Denmark was first to see that churches were protected and then to ensure reverence for the priestly order; he was to seek to eradicate superstition and witchcraft.[154] Gregory also sought the kings' help in fostering liturgical and pastoral correctness and zeal, and in promoting Roman standards and uses. In the short term, he requested the dispatch to Rome of bishops or of other mature and prudent clergy who might bring information about their kingdoms and return with written and verbal advice and commands. Thus, in 1079, he asked Harold to send a Danish clerk.[155] A year later, he similarly asked King Inge of Sweden for a bishop or suitable clerk; a pastoral letter to Sweden in 1081 establishes that a bishop—it may have been Rodulvard of Skara[156]—made the journey.[157] To secure longer-term results, Gregory sought from the kings of Norway and Sweden the dispatch of young nobles for a period of training at the Lateran palace in the Latin language and in Roman standards of religion and discipline.[158] Especially in the circumstances of the 1080s,

---

[150] *Reg.* 5.10, 6 Nov. 1077, pp. 361–3; 7.21, 19 Apr. 1080, pp. 497–502. For Sweyn's character, see Adam of Bremen, 3.12,54, pp. 338–40, 396–8; Saxo Grammaticus, 11.7, vol. 1.58–60.

[151] *Reg.* 6.13, 15 Dec. 1078, pp. 415–28; cf. Saxo Grammaticus, 11.10, vol. 1.69–73.

[152] *Reg.* 9.14, (1081), pp. 592–4. For Stenkil, see Adam of Bremen, 3.15–16,53, 4.30, pp. 344–7, 394–7, 474–5.

[153] *Reg.* 9.14, p. 593/24–8.   [154] *Reg.* 7.21, p. 498/8–35.

[155] *Reg.* 7.5, 15 Oct. 1079, p. 465/15–19.

[156] See Oppermann, *The English Missionaries*, pp. 128, 130, 136–7.

[157] *Reg.* 8.11, 4 Oct. 1080, pp. 530–1, 9.14, p. 593/5–8.

[158] *Reg.* 6.13, pp. 416/34–417/2 (Norway); 9.24, p. 594/3–9 (Sweden).

it may be doubted whether any such youths were trained at Rome. But Gregory's intention shows how, with the postponement of the plan for a Danish metropolis, he sought to train young Scandinavians both for circumstances as they were and, perhaps, against the contingency of the plan's being revived.

Gregory's last and most important letter to Denmark was written two days after the death of King Harold Hein, its principal addressee.[159] Harold was succeeded by his brother, the energetic and warlike Cnut II (1080–6), who strenuously resumed his father's policies in building up royal power.[160] Cnut's reign illustrates both the effectiveness and the limitations of Gregory's impact upon Denmark. Cnut seems to have paid some attention to Gregory's letter. Denmark became a place of refuge for hard-pressed German Gregorians: in 1085, Archbishop Hartwig of Magdeburg, Bishop Burchard II of Halberstadt, and the anti-king Hermann of Salm all fled thither.[161] The hagiographical tradition that rapidly grew after Cnut's murder in a local quarrel credited him with having done many of the things that Gregory pressed upon Scandinavian kings. He built and endowed churches, notably at Roskilde, Dalby, and Lund. He promoted respect for Christian worship and he instituted fasts according to the general discipline of Christendom. He secured the levying and payment of tithes. He protected the rights of bishops and clergy, and he cared for the vulnerable members of society. His hagiographers presented Cnut as the 'gloriosus rex et protomartyr Danorum'; thus far, the Christian image that Gregory proposed in Sweyn Estrithson was established in one of his sons.

Yet there were limitations. Cnut had become king after his brother Harold by family arrangement, not by the kind of hereditary title that Gregory recommended; for towards the end of his life, Sweyn is said to have secured the oaths of his leading subjects that his many sons should succeed each other in order as kings of an undivided inheritance.[162] Five of his sons in the event succeeded each other. The records of Cnut's reign and cultus do not emphasize obedience to the apostolic see or refer to the need for communication with it. The cultus, in particular, developed in the hands of Anglo-Saxon monks of insular training and outlook. The Danish clergy looked for and found a patron saint who would suit their domestic needs in Denmark and guarantee their position in Danish society. The cultus of St Cnut found them a guarantor at home who diminished their need to look to Rome. If Gregory's admonitions in his pastoral letters to some extent prepared the way for the establishment of St Cnut as the royal patron of Denmark, the springs of his cultus lay within Danish society and its institutions. Gregory's admonitions yield important evidence for his wishes and policies, but their immediate practical consequences in shaping the eleventh-century Scandinavian kingdoms were marginal.

---

[159] *Reg.* 7.21, to King Harold of Denmark and to its bishops, princes, clergy, and people, 19 Apr. 1080, pp. 497–8.

[160] The hagiographical sources for Cnut's reign are collected in *VSD*, pp. 60–176.

[161] *Ann. Magd. a.* 1085, pp. 178. For the political circumstances, see E. Hoffmann, 'Knut der Heilige', pp. 560–3.

[162] Saxo Grammaticus, 11.11, vol. 1.73–3; William of Malmesbury, *De gestis regum*, 3.261, vol. 2.319.

The pastoral aspect of Gregory's concern for far-off northern regions which was evident in his wish to provide for well trained clergy and to protect the weak finds further illustration in his single known dealing with the church in Iceland. According to the *Hungrvaka* saga, which dates from the thirteenth century but embodies older, reliable material, in 1082, Gregory arranged for Archbishop Hartwig of Magdeburg to ordain to the episcopate a clerk named Gizurr. Gizurr had been educated and ordained priest in Saxony (it is not known where). From 1082 until 1118, he was bishop of Skálholt in the south of Iceland; according to the saga, he ruled well 'as both king and bishop in the land'.[163]

6.9 The Anglo-Norman Kingdom

As in the Scandinavian kingdoms, so in the Anglo-Norman lands Gregory had as a major objective the establishment of a strong royal dynasty which would visibly stem from an exemplary Christian king, and in which the crown would descend from father to eldest son.[164] For no contemporary secular ruler did he profess a higher regard during his lifetime than for William, duke of Normandy from 1035 and king of England from 1066 until his death in 1087. In Gregory's eyes, England and Normandy comprised a single *regnum*,[165] since they were subject to a ruler who personally had kingly rank. It must, however, be remembered that the two parts of his dominion were ecclesiastically separate: Normandy was virtually conterminous with the province of Rouen which was part of the French church; it was and remained wholly separate from the two English provinces of Canterbury and York.

In 1080, Gregory reminded William of the support which, as archdeacon, he had given to William's invasion of England and advancement to the kingly dignity; he had already acted upon a confidence in William's personal virtues and serviceability to the church which subsequent events had served to confirm.[166] Pope Alexander II had likewise held William in high regard as a Christian king.[167] Yet, when he became pope, Gregory's dealings with William were somewhat slow to develop. Soon after his consecration, Gregory wrote amicably to Lanfranc without mentioning the king.[168] Later in 1073, there were even signs of tension between Gregory and the Norman kingdom. Gregory wrote again to Lanfranc, censuring him sharply for allowing Bishop Herfast of Elmham to challenge the exemption that Pope Alexander had granted to the abbey of Bury St Edmunds and to vex its abbot, Baldwin, whom Alexander himself had ordained priest. Lanfranc had been complicit in a direct

---

[163] *Hungrvaka*, caps. 4–5, in Helgason, *Byskupa Sogur*, 1/83–90, Eng. trans. in *Stories of the Bishops of Iceland*, pp. 45–50; cf. *Dipl. Danic.* nos. 36–7, 43, pp. 80–3, 91. For Gizurr, see Kuttner, 'St Jón of Hólar', esp. pp. 368–70, 374–5.

[164] For further discussion, see Cowdrey, 'Pope Gregory VII and the Anglo-Norman Church and Kingdom', id., 'The Gregorian Reform in the Anglo-Norman Lands and in Scandinavia', id., 'Lanfranc, the Papacy, and the See of Canterbury', and id., 'The Enigma of Archbishop Lanfranc'.

[165] See e.g. *Reg.* 5.19, to King William, 4 Apr. 1078, p. 381/22. When writing to Gregory, William styled himself 'gratia Dei Anglorum rex et dux Normannorum': Lanfranc, *Letters*, no. 39, p. 130/1–2.

[166] *Reg.* 7.23, 24 Apr. 1080, pp. 499/31–500/11.

[167] Lanfranc, *Letters*, no. 7, pp. 60–3.   [168] *Epp. vag.* no. 1, pp. 2–5.

affront to papal authority. Gregory asked him to warn King William, whom he described as 'a most dear and special son of the holy Roman church', to give Herfast no credence, for the king's own royal credibility in Gregory's estimation was at stake. If Herfast were recalcitrant, both he and Baldwin should come to Rome for Gregory to determine their case. Direct approaches to Rome were also possible, for, soon afterwards, Gregory wrote to Bishop Remigius of Lincoln who had consulted him about a clerk who was guilty of homicide.[169]

Only in April 1074 did Gregory's dealings with King William begin to take firm shape, and they did so upon an initiative by the king, who had sent an expression of sorrow at Alexander's death and joy at Gregory's accession, together with an inquiry about Gregory's own well-being. Gregory wrote separate letters to the king and to Queen Matilda, who had also sent a letter;[170] clearly William was in search of more cordial relations with Gregory. Gregory, for his part, praised William for his duty and devotion to the Roman church. He exhorted him to persist in obedience and righteousness, and to set the honour of God before all earthly concerns. After telling William of his own storm-tossed and careworn predicament, Gregory turned to two practical matters in which he evidently wished to incite William to greater generosity. In Normandy, a privilege for Saint-Étienne at Caen about which William had written to Gregory 'was for the salvation of his soul'; he should attend to the advice of Gregory's legates about canonical points, and if the terms of the privilege seemed over-generous on William's part, he should remember the reward that God and St Peter would return for his generosity to St Stephen.[171] In England, Gregory asked William to collect Peter's Pence with the vigilance and thoroughness that he would apply to his own revenues and thus, again, make St Peter his debtor.

During the next four years, the scanty evidence suggests that relations between Gregory and William remained amicable but did not significantly develop. Their first known contacts concerned the see of Dol. Despite their differing interests, Gregory presented William as a ruler of exemplary justice and desire for concord whose desires and interests Gregory would go far to promote.[172] From 1078, however, Gregory made a number of interventions in Anglo-Norman affairs which can scarcely have been in themselves welcome to William but which by 1080 led to a

---

[169] *Reg.* 1.31, to Archbishop Lanfranc, 20 Nov. 1073, pp. 51–2; 1.34, to Bishop Remigius of Lincoln, 2 Dec. 1073, p. 55.

[170] *Reg.* 1.70–1, to King William, and to Queen Matilda, 4 Apr. 1074, pp. 100–3.

[171] The privilege referred to presents a difficulty. In 1068, Pope Alexander II issued a privilege to Abbot Lanfranc and his successors for Saint-Étienne: *Ep.* 57, *PL* 146.1339–41; but Gregory VII is not known to have done so. In 1074, negotiations either for a revision of Alexander's privilege or for the granting of a new one seem to have been in progress, but if so they came to nothing. In the light of recent problems over Bury St Edmunds (*Reg.* 1.31, cf. Alexander II, *Ep.* 81, *PL.* 146.1363–4 (1071)), William may have raised difficulties about the exemption of Saint-Étienne from episcopal authority. Two versions survive of William's own charter for Saint-Étienne confirming its possessions, one dating from 1066/77 and the second from 1081/7; but they raise no issues which might have been raised with the papacy or influenced by its directives: Musset, 'Les actes', no. 8, pp. 59–65, cf. no. 30, p. 142.

[172] *Epp. vag.* no. 16, pp. 44–7; *Reg.* 4.17, to King William, 31 Mar. 1077, pp. 322–3, esp. 323/6–19. For the problem of Dol, see above, 5.3.3.3.

statesmanlike definition of the concord prevailing between them. Gregory became concerned about the archbishops of Rouen and Canterbury. At Rouen, Archbishop John had suffered a debilitating stroke which for the last two years of his life left him without the power of speech. As early as 4 April 1078, Gregory wrote to William that the see was, in effect, devoid of a pastor. Praising William for his care of the church, Gregory nevertheless outlined a plan for the well-being of the see of Rouen. His legate should come and assess the archbishop's condition; if necessary, he should either persuade him to resign or, in extreme circumstances, proceed to the canonical election of a new archbishop. Unsurprisingly, especially if William had word of Gregory's recent synodal legislation about canonical election and investiture, nothing happened: John remained archbishop until his death on 9 September 1079.[173] In March 1079, Gregory rebuked Lanfranc of Canterbury for not having travelled to Rome during his own pontificate; Gregory's letter to him included the suggestion that fear of the king might have been a deterrent: the king might even be setting himself against Gregory in some novel way, and Lanfranc was to admonish him about his attitude to the apostolic see.[174] A month later, Gregory's privilege for the see of Lyons confirmed its primacy over the province of Rouen.[175] Whether or not Gregory had consulted William about this matter is not known, but, especially in view of Archbishop John's incapacity, William may not have shown himself to be in concurrence.

For these and for other reasons which will be noticed later, relations between Gregory and William became strained. Gregory was also displeased with his legates to the Anglo-Norman land. In September 1079, he wrote to the subdeacon Hubert rebuking his failure to come to Rome, whither he was to repair for consultations. The monk Teuzo had been over-zealous in his dealings with William, despite William's shortcomings. One example of them which Gregory gave was his obstruction of the visits to Rome of bishops and archbishops. Gregory referred to the claims of ancient friendship and to his own forbearance hitherto; but if William did not relax his attitude, he would feel the wrath of St Peter.[176]

By April and May 1080, Gregory's atitude to William had become far more cordial. His letters made clear his need to rally the goodwill of other kings after his second excommunication of Henry IV of Germany, and he no doubt wished to compel his renewal of the papal alliance with the Normans of South Italy by a cordial and perhaps militarily no less concrete alliance with the Normans of the north. Gregory offered William the olive-branch of the reinstatement of Bishop Arnald of le Mans and of the absolution of Abbot Juhel of la Couture.[177] He sent William notice of these events with a long covering letter addressed to the king as 'excellentissimi fili'. He

---

[173] *Reg.* 5.19, to King William I, 4 Apr. 1078, pp. 382–3. On John's illness, see Orderic Vitalis, 3.3, vol. 3.18–21.

[174] *Reg.* 6.30, 25 Mar. 1079, pp. 443–4.

[175] *Reg.* 6.34–5, 19 Apr. 1079, pp. 447–52; see above, 5.3.3.2.

[176] *Reg.* 7.1, 23 Sept. 1079, pp. 458–60.

[177] *Reg.* 7.22, to Bishop Arnald of le Mans, 24 Apr. 1080, p. 499; cf. 7.23, to King William, 24 Apr. 1080, p. 501/22–9; see above, 5.3.3.3.

reminded William of his own services to him from his days as archdeacon. Approaching him 'tanquam dilectissimo filio et fideli sancti PETRI et nostro', he addressed him as a jewel among princes ('gemma principum') from whom should stem a distinguished line of kings; he would enjoy prosperity himself, and he would be a beacon for others:

Now, therefore, my son most beloved and ever to be embraced in Christ, since you see your mother [the church] to be so greatly afflicted and since an imperative necessity of coming to our aid presses upon you, I wish you to be such, and I warn you in true and unfeigned charity for your honour and salvation, that you show obedience in all ways. Thus, as with God's help you have deserved to be a jewel amongst princes, so you may deserve to be a standard of right-eousness and a pattern of obedience for all princes of the world. So, without doubt, in the glory that is to come you will be a prince among princes, so that until the world ends princes will be saved by your example. Even though some of them are not willing to be saved, your own reward will be in no wise diminished. Not only so, but in this world, too, an increase of victory, hon-our, power, and majesty will be granted from heaven to you and to your heirs.[178]

Gregory was soon after able to emphasize the hereditary prosperity of William's kingship, for tidings reached him of the temporary reconciliation to him of his eldest son, Robert Curthose.[179] Gregory lost no time in writing letters to King William, to Queen Matilda (who had written to him, probably in joy at her son's reconciliation to his father), and to Robert Curthose himself.[180] Gregory reminded William of the proper relation between the papal and the royal power. For the good order of the world, God had appointed both dignities, the different and graduated functions of which were as the sun and moon. Popes must one day present kings before God's judgement seat; popes must, therefore, have continual oversight of kings, and kings must return prompt obedience to popes. Upon Robert Curthose he enjoined filial duty. He should always remember with how strong an arm and with what public renown his father had won all that he possessed from the hand of his enemies. He did so knowing that he would not live for ever; he strove so manfully in order that he might pass on his possessions to his heir. Therefore Robert should honour his father and his mother, putting far from him the advice of wicked men and following his father's will in all things.

Thus Gregory sought to consolidate the Norman royal line as between father and son. Throughout his correspondence with the Norman royal family, he was also con-cerned to associate the queen with the formation of a royal stem. As a daughter of the count of Flanders, she brought to William a nobility of birth which was requisite for his family. In 1074, he referred to her as noble by blood and nobler in her virtues; she should be instant in conveying to her husband things meet for his soul.[181] In 1077, he

---

[178] *Reg.* 7.23, p. 499–502.
[179] Orderic Vitalis, 5.10, vol. 3.110–13. For Count Simon of Crépy's part in bringing about the recon-ciliation, see *Vita beati Simonis com. Cresp.* cap. 11, col. 1219CD. For relations between Robert and his father, see C. W. David, *Robert Curthose*, pp. 17–41, esp. pp. 27–31.
[180] *Reg.* 7.25–7, 8 May 1080, pp. 505–8. Gregory's recognition of the love with which Matilda adhered to God's servants ('fideles') (p. 507/17–19) may allude to the role of Count Simon of Crépy in the recon-ciliation.   [181] *Reg.* 1.71, p. 103/7–8.

prayed for absolution for the king, for the queen, and for all their most noble sons.[182] The family reconciliation of 1080 thus included a place for Matilda as a source of virtues to her husband.[183] In the first half of 1080, Gregory in these ways expressed his confidence in the royal stock of the Anglo-Norman kingdom; he no doubt did so the more readily since, once the early problem of their consanguinity had been over-come, William and Matilda were the only royal pair in Christendom whose marital relationship and fidelity embodied his own standard in this respect. If their eldest son Robert Curthose remained dutiful, the Norman royal family would be a paradigm of how it should be in all kingdoms.

After such an affirmation of the Conqueror's regality, negotiations which oc-curred later in 1080 placed the concord and friendship between Gregory and William upon a clearer footing. The evidence for them is preserved, not in Gregory's letters, but in two items of Lanfranc's letter-collection.[184] When the legate Hubert returned from his visit to Gregory at Rome, he approached the king in England through Lanfranc with a twofold verbal request from Gregory: on the pope's behalf, Hubert urged ('admonuit') the king to do fealty to Gregory and his successors, and to ensure that Peter's Pence were more diligently collected. The note was one of in-vitation, not of direction. In William's masterly reply which probably came from Lanfranc's hand, the king declined to do fealty ('fidelitatem') which he himself had never promised and which his Anglo-Saxon precedessors could not be shown to have performed; but he acknowledged recent laxity in collecting Peter's Pence, and he promised that he would quickly dispatch what was owing. He ended by assuring Gregory of his loyalty: 'Pray for us and for the well-being of our kingdom, for we loved your predecessors and we wish to love you sincerely above all men and obedi-ently to hear you.'

Gregory had the wisdom to take William at his word; he did not again raise the issue of fealty. A concord based upon prudent compromise and genuine friendship ensued. There is evidence that William and Lanfranc took steps to ensure the due rendering in future of Peter's Pence.[185] Gregory's subsequent attitude in practice to William found expression in a letter of 1081 in which he ordered his legates Bishops Hugh of Die and Amatus of Oloron to withdraw their sanctions against Norman bishops who had failed to attend their council. Gregory allowed that, in some mat-ters, William did not conduct himself as dutifully ('ita religiose') as Gregory would wish. But he did not destroy or sell the churches of God, and he endeavoured to pro-mote peace and justice amongst his subjects. When approached by 'certain enemies

---

[182] *Reg.* 4.17, p. 323/26–32.   [183] *Reg.* 7.26.

[184] Lanfranc, *Letters*, nos. 38 (Lanfranc to Gregory VII) and 39 (William I to Gregory VII), p. 128–33. Since Lanfranc was directly involved, the events concerned must have followed the king's return to England after the council of Lillebonne at Pentecost (31 May) 1080: Orderic Vitalis, 5.5, vol. 3.24–5. They are not likely to have been an immediate sequel to *Reg.* 7.21, 19 Apr. 1080, which was brought to William by his own messengers: p. 501/27–8. They may have followed *Reg.* 7.25–7, 8 May 1080, in which a visit by the legate Hubert was assumed: p. 507/31–2.

[185] For William, see the mandate in *Calendar of the Manuscripts of the Dean and Chapter of Wells*, 1.17; for Lanfranc, *The Domesday Monachorum*, p. 80. See also Urban II, *Epp.* 4, 23, *PL* 151.286–8, 305–6.

of the cross of Christ' whom Gregory did not identify, William had had nothing to do with them. He caused priests to surrender their wives and laymen their tithes. In sum, he showed himself more worthy of approval and honour than other kings. It was, therefore, reasonable to handle his regime with a certain mildness and to be indulgent towards his subjects' lapses. The legates were not to trouble him further without Gregory's express leave. 'For it seems to us that he may be more effectually won for God by gentle moderation and a show of reason than by the austerity or severity of righteousness.'[186]

Gregory acted in such a spirit when, a year or so later, William imprisoned his half-brother Bishop Odo of Bayeux. Gregory wrote to Archbishop Hugh of Lyons (as Hugh of Die had by then become) in severe condemnation of such an arrest of a bishop.[187] But to the king himself he wrote more gently, recalling their long friend-ship ('amicitia') and their common devotion to St Peter. He pleaded reasonably for Odo's release, citing such examples of respect by monarchs of episcopal rights as that of the religious Emperor Constantine at the council of Nicaea.[188] Gregory's moder-ation paid dividends. In 1085, a letter to William from Bishop Anselm II of Lucca suggests that, as seen by one of Gregory's closest supporters in the straitened cir-cumstances of his last months, William's loyalty held firm so that he could be looked to for military help.[189]

Gregory's fostering in the Anglo-Norman kingdom of a Christian royal stock stemming from an exemplary ruler and within which the royal inheritance passed from father to eldest son was in line with his hopes for the other kingdoms of the peri-phery of Latin Europe and especially the Scandinavian. His unsuccessful request for William's fealty also had parallels elsewhere, notably in the north Adriatic lands. If Gregory's aspirations for England and Normandy were similar in this respect to those which he held in other peripheral regions, they perforce differed in so far as William's domains comprised ancient and well-organized church provinces led by archbishops of ecclesiastical and political stature. Gregory was concerned to bring the three provinces of William's realms into regular contact with and proper obedi-ence to Rome. To this end, his use of legates such as the subdeacon Hubert was of but secondary importance; they were little more than messengers with a limited power to negotiate; even greater men like Bishops Hugh of Die and Amatus of Oloron were effectively limited to this kind of role in relation to Normandy.[190] Gregory sought to establish direct relationships especially with the three archbishops.

---

[186] *Reg.* 9.5, pp. 579–80.					[187] *Epp. vag.* no. 53, pp. 128–9.

[188] *Reg.* 9.37, pp. 630–1. The reasons for Odo's imprisonment in 1082 are far from clear, but chron-iclers wrote of his sending money to Rome and recruiting knights for an expedition: *Anglo-Saxon Chronicle, a.* 1082; William of Malmesbury, *Gesta regum.* 3.277, vol. 2.334; *Chronica monasterii de Hida,* in *Liber monasterii de Hyda,* p. 296; Orderic Vitalis, 7.8, vol. 4.40–5. Odo may have planned to intervene at Rome in Gregory's defence against Henry IV of Germany. From Gregory's point of view, Odo's plans would have been comparable with the aid to which he had alluded to the king in 1080: *Reg.* 7.21, pp. 500/26–501/3, and to the aid that he had earlier looked for from French prelates like Archbishop Manasses of Rheims: see above, 5.3.3.1.

[189] *H* no. 1, pp. 15–17.					[190] See above, 5.3.2.1, 2.

As Gregory was aware, there were limits to what he could achieve. In this connection, too much should not be made of King William's resistance to the exercise of papal authority. The Canterbury monk Eadmer later drew up a list of the Conqueror's supposed rules which limited dealings of the English church with the papacy upon a Norman model.[191] Although there was a measure of truth in it, especially in respect of the king's unwillingness to let archbishops and bishops travel to Rome, Eadmer's picture is exaggerated in the light of developments in the 1090s and 1100s. William neither did nor could place a ring-fence about the Anglo-Norman church in order to isolate it from the papacy. More important in limiting contacts was the factor of physical distance and difficulty of travel. Most important of all were the reserve and inertia of Anglo-Norman prelates themselves in face of mounting papal demands and would-be interventions.

Archbishop Lanfranc of Canterbury (1070–89) was consistently unresponsive to Gregory's approaches. His coolness is the more remarkable when compared with his sympathy with the aims and co-operation in the purposes of the reform papacy from Leo IX to Alexander II. It seems partly to be explicable by Archdeacon Hildebrand's role in 1072 when Lanfranc was denied the papal privilege that he sought in order to reinforce the primacy of the see of Canterbury over that of York unless he came again to Rome.[192] Perhaps more important, Lanfranc is likely to have been put off by Gregory's protracted unwillingness to condemn the eucharistic teachings of Berengar of Tours, by his apparent disregard of Lanfranc's own anti-Berengarian tract which he sent to Rome, and by what he saw as the ineffectiveness of Gregory's eventual condemnation of Berengar in 1079.[193]

It did not pass unremarked in England that, on becoming pope, Gregory sought to perpetuate Alexander II's good relations with Lanfranc and that a letter that he almost immediately wrote confirmed his intention; indeed, Gregory's expressed desire that Lanfranc should correct the marital aberrations of the Irish and of others 'in Anglorum insula' tacitly acknowledged his claim to primacy over all of the British Isles.[194] But Gregory was soon writing to Lanfranc in terms of reproof,[195] and in 1079, he rebuked him for failing in his duty to pay 'ad limina' visits to Rome, urging him to come without further delay.[196] In 1080, part of the legate Hubert's commission was that he should reiterate this requirement. He seems to have brought an even stronger letter from Gregory that has not survived. But Lanfranc replied evasively and almost impertinently; he professed devotion and service, but cast doubt upon the

---

[191] *Hist. nov.* 1, pp. 9–10. [192] Lanfranc, *Letters*, nos. 56–9.

[193] Lanfranc, *Letters*, nos.4, 46, 49, pp. 56–7, 142–51, 158–9; see below, 8.11.

[194] 'Nec minori eum [Lanfranc] amoris diligentia palpandum curavit Gregorius Alexandri successor, multa illius consilio transigens, multa etiam domesticis suis ignota, illius conscientiae communicans. Sermonis huiusce veritati assistit epistola in initio papatus Angliam directa, quae inter epistolas Lanfranci reperitur': William of Malmesbury, *Gest. pont.* 1.42, p. 66; *Epp. vag.* no. 1, pp. 2–5 = Lanfranc, *Letters*, no. 8, pp. 64–7.

[195] *Reg.* 1.31.

[196] *Reg.* 6.30. Gregory referred in it to earlier, perhaps verbal, messages summoning Lanfranc to come to Rome.

need for him to present himself in person.[197] In 1082, when Lanfranc had still not come, Gregory wrote even more insistently. Out of pride or carelessness, Lanfranc had for too long abused his patience. Neither old age nor distance was an admissible excuse. Gregory gave him four months notice to come by 1 November and purge his disobedience. The penalty for non-appearance would be suspension from office.[198] But Lanfranc still did not come.

Gregory had no greater success in imposing his will upon William Bona Anima, archbishop of Rouen (1079–1110). After his failure to expedite the canonical election of a successor to the ailing Archbishop John,[199] Gregory was displeased to hear reports that William, John's eventual successor who since 1070 had been abbot of Saint-Étienne at Caen, was the son of a bishop; he informed his legate Hubert that, if this were the case, he would never consent to his promotion. William was, indeed, the son of Bishop Radbod of Séez;[200] yet nothing further emerges about the setting aside of this impediment.[201] However, probably in 1081, Gregory wrote to Archbishop William and expressed his displeasure at the insufficiency of a letter that the archbishop had sent. Gregory reproved him for not having yet come 'ad limina apostolorum', and also for slackness in meeting his legates in France. He reminded him of the canonical requirement that an archbishop should be prompt in securing his *pallium*. Failure to comply would be to risk severer sanctions.[202] The sequel is not known, though it is improbable that William, any more than Lanfranc, travelled to Rome; but Gregory is not known to have proceeded further against either of the archbishops.

When writing to Archbishop William, Gregory observed that, since he became pope, he could not recall having seen a single Norman bishop at Rome.[203] In 1079, he had attempted to remedy this by instructing his legate Hubert that, from each of the three English and Norman provinces, he should on St Peter's behalf command and invite at least two bishops to attend his Lent synod in 1080 or, failing that, to come to Rome immediately after Easter.[204] That no Normans came is clear from Gregory's later letter to the archbishop of Rouen,[205] and in 1081 he tempered the sentence of his legates Hugh of Die and Amatus of Oloron against Norman bishops who had failed to attend their own synod.[206] It is improbable that any English bishops responded to Gregory's summons, either.[207]

[197] Lanfranc, *Letters*, no. 38, pp. 128–31. Lanfranc's references to Gregory's letter suggest that it contained arguments additional to those in *Reg*. 6.30.

[198] *Reg*. 9.20, pp. 600–1.   [199] *Reg*. 5.19.

[200] *Reg*. 7.1, p. 459/26–8. For William Bona Anima, see Orderic Vitalis, 3.4, vol. 2.26–8, 68–71, 254–5. According to Orderic, the first choice for the see, made by 'the king and many others', was Guitmund, monk of la-Croix-saint-Leufroi and later bishop of Aversa: 4, vol. 2.278–81.

[201] Although the precedent of Thomas of York in 1071 suggests that it might have been reserved for resolution at Rome: Eadmer, *Hist. nov.* 1, p. 11.   [202] *Reg*. 9.1, pp. 568–9.

[203] p. 568/15–20.   [204] *Reg*. 7.1, p. 460/7–13.   [205] *Reg*. 9.1.

[206] *Reg*. 9.5, p. 579/21–6. The most likely explanation for the exception of Archbishop William of Rouen from the legates' sanction is that he had duly excused his absence.

[207] If, in 1082, William of St Calais, bishop of Durham, visited Rome with the king's leave to seek Gregory's approval for the establishment of a monastic chapter in his cathedral, the visit may have been

Despite all this reserve and lukewarmness, the prestige of the papacy throughout the Anglo-Norman lands as the see of St Peter and in England as the place from which Pope Gregory the Great had initiated the conversion of its people must be kept in mind as a factor which determined human loyalties. For King William I— otherwise William the Bastard, who had seized the English crown upon the battlefield of Hastings, Gregory's underwriting of his kingship and dynasty as a royal line blessed by God was an essential guarantee of his regality. Yet the long disregard by the archbishops and bishops of the Anglo-Norman lands of Gregory's orders, which were based upon strong canonical authority, that they come to Rome and the ineffectiveness in practice of Gregory's sanctions however forcibly expressed, can only have undermined papal authority and have reinforced the inertia of most prelates so far as papal injunctions were concerned. The erosion of papal authority in Normandy and England since Gregory succeeded Alexander II partly explains Lanfranc's willingness after 1084 to enter upon an exchange of letters with partisans of the anti-pope Clement III who seem to have included Gregory's vehement and long-standing opponent Cardinal Hugh Candidus, and subsequently to receive three letters from Clement himself.[208] Lanfranc deprecated Guibertine attacks upon Gregory and the practice of referring to him as Hildebrand, and it is unlikely that either he or the English kingdom, even under King William II, positively broke with the Gregorian papacy or made any kind of commitment to Clement. But it is a further indication of the attrition of Gregory's authority that, when the Conqueror died in 1087, he did not in the end leave his whole lands to his eldest son Robert Curthose who received only Normandy, but left England to his second son William Rufus, and that Lanfranc, if perhaps not altogether willingly, executed King William I's final dispositions about the succession.[209]

6.10 Ireland

After his initial willingness as pope to countenance at least tacitly Lanfranc's claims to primatial authority over the Irish as over the rest of the British Isles,[210] Gregory pursued such a line no further. Nevertheless, the welfare of the Irish did not cease to concern him. At a date after 1074 which cannot be ascertained, he wrote a pastoral letter to the most powerful of the kings of Ireland, Toirdhealbhach Ó Braian, king of Munster, and to all Irish prelates, magnates, and Christians. He sought to commend to the Irish the universal authority of St Peter and of his vicar, as well as to emphasize

calculated by the king as a gesture to moderate Gregory's displeasure with the Anglo-Norman bishops: *De iniusta vexatione*, p. 91; see Cowdrey, 'Lanfranc, the Papacy, and the See of Canterbury', pp. 495–6.

[208] Lanfranc, *Letters*, no. 52, pp. 164–7 (the *terminus a quo* should be amended to 24 Mar. 1084, when Clement was enthroned at Rome and took his papal name, and the *terminus ante quem* probably to before May 1085, when Hugh Candidus was in Germany); Liebermann, 'Lanfranc and the Antipope'. Lanfranc probably knew Hugh Candidus at first hand during his travels in 1049 with Pope Leo IX, who brought Hugh from Remiremont to Rome for the papal service: Bonizo of Sutri, *Lib. ad amic.* 5, p. 588/18–25: see Hüls, *Kardinäle*, pp. 158–9.

[209] *Acta Lanfranci*, p. 290, cf. Eadmer, *Hist. nov.* 1, p. 25.   [210] See above, 6.9.

the duty of all Christians to show reverence and obedience to the Roman church. He urged any of the Irish who might need his aid to have recourse to him for a sure answer.[211] The letter belongs to an ancient genre of papal letter which featured citations from the Old Testament scriptures and sought to excite the loyalty of powerful kings in distant regions.[212] It is the kind of letter that Gregory may have chosen to write when visiting pilgrims happened to provide a channel of communication. It should not be taken to imply any particular statement about local issues such as the see of Canterbury's primatial authority, but to be an expression of Gregory's concern for the religious welfare and oversight of distant peoples to the ends of the earth.

6.11 Christian Spain

Gregory showed a profound concern for what he called the 'regnum Hyspaniae', combined with an awareness of the complexity of its political and ecclesiastical life.[213] His concern sprang from a view of Spanish history which comprehended the entire Christian era from both a political and a religious point of view. These two aspects were closely associated in his mind, but may be considered consecutively.

During the first half of his pontificate, Gregory twice advanced apparently sweeping claims to papal superiority over the Spanish kingdom. In both cases, he addressed groups of laymen. In April 1073, he reminded French nobles who might be minded to fight in Spain against the Saracens that the kingdom of Spain had from of old appertained to St Peter ('proprii iuris sancti PETRI fuisse'); although it had been long occupied by pagan Saracens, it still legally belonged to no mortal man but to the apostolic see; Gregory adduced the canonical principle that what had once legally passed into the proprietorship of churches might be forcibly wrested from their use, but it could never by lapse of time escape from their lawful title unless it were by proper concession. When in 1077 he commended new legates to the kings, counts, and other nobles of Spain, he was more insistent. By ancient title-deeds, the kingdom of Spain had passed to St Peter and the Roman church 'in ius et proprietatem'. The vicissitudes of history and the negligence of former popes had obscured this proprietorship: because of Saracen occupation, the Roman church was denied the benefits that arose from its rights; indeed, the very memory of the facts and of Roman proprietorship had faded. Now that God was vouchsafing victory over the Saracens, neither silence on Gregory's part nor Spanish ignorance should prevent the restoration of the true order of things.[214]

---

[211] *Epp. vag.* no. 57, pp. 138–41.

[212] e.g. Pope Vitalian's letter of 665 to King Osuiu of Northumbria: *Ep.* 5, *PL* 87.1004–5.

[213] Among the histories of Spain and the Spanish church, good surveys are provided by Fernandez Conde (ed.), *Historia de la Iglesia en España*, 2/1, and Linehan, *History and the Historians*. Kehr's studies as listed in the Bibliography of this book remain fundamental. Among monographs and articles, see esp. P. David, *Études historiques*; Reilly, *The Kingdom of León–Castile*, and the essays in id. (ed.), *Santiago, Saint-Denis, and Saint Peter*; and Bishko, 'Fernando I'. Papal documents are usefully assembled by Mansilla, *La documentación*.

[214] *Reg.* 1.7, to all nobles minded to go to Spain 30 Apr. 1073, p. 11/20–7, 4.28, to the kings and lay magnates of Spain, 28 June 1077, pp. 345/35–346/16.

It is far from clear which ancient authorities Gregory was alleging. He may have had in mind the *Constitutum Constantini*, according to which the Emperor Constantine handed over to Pope Silvester I 'all the provinces of Italy and of western regions', although this is far from certain.[215] It has rightly been pointed out that Gregory's conception of papal superiority over lay rulers owed much to the protection for long extended to monasteries and churches, and that subjection to the 'ius sancti Petri' involved a spectrum of consequences which must be defined according to the circumstances of each particular case.[216] Nevertheless, it is clear that, at least at the beginning of his pontificate and with an eye to north-eastern Spain, Gregory could envisage St Peter's legal proprietorship of Spanish lands in a strict sense. In his letter of 1073, he wrote of Count Ebolus of Roucy, who planned to enter Spain and to wrest lands from the Saracens, as having made a written compact with the papacy according to which he would hold reconquered lands directly of St Peter; other French campaigners in Spain were warned that they would do better not to enter Spain at all than to go upon any other presupposition.[217] But no such claims to direct Petrine proprietorship without reference to Spanish kings and rulers appear again in Gregory's letters. Gregory's expectations and requirements became increasingly flexible and pragmatic, as he learnt by experience how to deal with fragmented political authority in a distant country with which communication was not easy, from which accurate information was hard to obtain, and over which the papacy had few effective sanctions, whether temporal or spiritual.

It is noticeable that Gregory increasingly appealed first and foremost, not to any special status of Spain with respect to the papacy, but to the universal authority of St Peter and the Roman church over the kingdoms of the whole world.[218] The duties of Spanish rulers were those of rulers everywhere, and were defined in respect of God himself rather than of the Roman see: they were to be his faithful ministers in upholding righteousness;[219] they were to show proper humility and obedience in response to the demands of the Christian religion;[220] above all, their minds should be upon the last things, and upon how transitory and lowly was earthly rule by contrast

---

[215] *Das Constitutum Constantini*, lines 261–70, pp. 93–4. In favour, (i) the omnibus phrase 'occidentialium regionum provincias, loca et civitates' might warrant Gregory's acceptance of the commendation of lands in Spain and also in southern France; (ii) the phrase 'pragmaticum constitutum' may underlie Gregory's 'ex antiquis constitutionibus' (*Reg.* p. 345/38); and (iii) Gregory's appeal to the Spanish to follow the 'statuta christianissimorum principum' agrees with his appraisal of Constantine (*Reg.* pp. 559/5, 631/7–8). But (i) Gregory never in any of his letters expressly refers to the *Constitutum Constantini*; (ii) Gregory refers to rulers and their enactments in the plural and so had more than one legal warrant in mind; and (iii) Spain does not appear amongst the endowments listed in *Das Constitutum Constantini*, lines 203–8, pp. 85–6.

[216] Fried, 'Der päpstliche Schutz'. [217] *Reg.* 1.7, pp. 11/27–12/3.

[218] St Peter's universal authority: *Reg.* 1.63, to King Sancho I Ramírez of Aragon, 20 Mar. 1074, p. 92/10–13; 7.6, to King Alphonso VI of León–Castile, 15 Oct. 1079, p. 465/34–8; universal mission of the Roman church: *Reg.* 4.28, pp. 343/25–344/3.

[219] *Reg.* 4.28, p. 344/21–4.

[220] *Reg.* 4.28, pp. 344/38–345/13, 346/35–347/17; 7.6, p. 466/4–8, 9.2, to King Alphonso VI, (1081), p. 571/1–8.

with the glory that would follow.[221] Especially as addressed to King Alphonso VI of León–Castile, increasingly the most powerful of the Spanish kings, Gregory's comments upon the basis of rulership were such as he addressed to kings everywhere: kings held the reins of government ('regni gubernacula') as a divine stewardship, and as a trust imposed by Christ.[222]

With regard to St Peter's bond with the Spanish kingdoms and principalities, Gregory's emphasis was less upon the claims that St Peter might impose than upon the benefits that he would confer upon his faithful servants: he would advance them to the fullness of kingship and give them victory over their adversaries in this world and everlasting joy in the next.[223] It was with the rulers of Spain as with those of, for example, Denmark and England:[224] however earnestly Gregory might invite and urge them to subject themselves and their kingdoms to St Peter, it was, in general, a matter for them to decide in what ways they would serve him. In practice, Gregory was content to accept what they offered, so long as it expressed due loyalty and service on their part.

In Spain, this was conspicuously the case with the principalities that appear to have been most specifically commended to St Peter. The origins of the commendation of the kingdom of Aragon are difficult to discern. It is certain that, in 1068, King Sancho I Ramírez (1063–94) went to Rome and, as he later expressed it to Pope Urban II, 'handed over myself and my kingdom to the power of God and of St Peter'.[225] Gregory believed, probably correctly, that Sancho's father, King Ramiro I (1035–63), had already made his kingdom tributary to the apostolic see.[226] But Sancho confessed to Urban II that he had not translated his intention of serving St Peter into action so fully as he ought.[227] The limitations emerge in documents from the papal side. In his privilege of 1071 for the abbey of San Juan de la Peña, Pope Alexander II referred only to Sancho's having submitted himself, with no mention of his kingdom, to papal authority ('dignitas'), and to the restoration to the papacy of monasteries that had for long been alienated from it ('monasteria sue ditionis diu alienata Romane ecclesie propria iure tenenda reddidit').[228] Gregory VII maintained a like reserve. In 1074, he praised Sancho's _fidelitas_ to the prince of the apostles, where the thought seems to have been one of personal devotion; its basis was not a recent act of commendation but the sonship of the Roman church and the concord and friendship with the pope that Spanish kings had exhibited of old.[229]

In 1075, Gregory again addressed King Sancho in terms of his own wish to benefit the kingdom rather than of any special obligation to obedience on the king's part.

---

[222] _Reg._ 1.83, to King Alphonso VI of León–Castile, 9 May 1074, p. 119/17–19, 4.28, p. 345/26–34, 7.6, p. 467/4–11; cf. _Epp. vag._ no. 65, to King Sancho Ramírez of Aragon, (1076/85), pp. 146–7.

[223] _Reg._ 1.63, p. 92/10–15, 7.6, p. 467/12–20.   [224] See above, 6.8.9.

[225] Ewald, 'Die Papstbriefe', no. 2, pp. 359–60.

[226] _QF_ no. 215, (1084/5), pp. 258–60. For Ramiro I, see his last testament in _Cart. de San Juan de la Peña_, no. 159, 2.199; but he did not name the saints to whom he entrusted the custody ('baiulia') of his son and kingdom.

[227] As n. 225.   [228] Mansilla, _La documentación_, no. 4, pp. 7–9.

[229] _Reg._ 1.63, pp. 91/32–92/8, 92/10–15.

The occasion was the succession of bishops in the see of Jaca (Huesca). King Sancho had consulted Gregory about it and had indicated his wishes; the aged and infirm bishop of Jaca, Sancho (1056–76) travelled to Rome to discuss it there. Gregory wrote to the king and stated that the bishop had proposed the names of two possible successors. Gregory rejected both on the grounds that, although they were personally suitable, they were the sons of concubines, whose ordination would be contrary to the canons. Gregory prescribed a course of events whereby Bishop Sancho should continue in office for at least a further year so far as his spiritual functions were concerned, seeking assistance in their exercise from his comprovincial bishops; he should delegate other business to a competent clerk. If his health were restored, he should continue as bishop; if not, a report should be sent to the apostolic see so that the see of Jaca might be appropriately filled.[230]

In 1076, King Sancho added Navarre to his realms. In the same year, he disregarded Gregory's instructions about the see of Jaca;[231] instead, he appointed his brother, García, to the see. But García quickly turned against the king, although he enjoyed Gregory's lasting goodwill. At the very end of his pontificate, Gregory issued a privilege in García's favour, confirming the boundaries and rights of his see. He made no reference to King Sancho by name, although he referred to King Ramiro I's having made himself and his kingdom tributary to St Peter.[232] Gregory's goodwill towards García is an indication of his lasting disfavour towards the king. After 1076, Gregory is known to have addressed only one letter to King Sancho, in which he described his kingship as a stewardship held directly from God and did not emphasize Petrine claims. Gregory's commendation in his letter of Bishop Raymond of Roda was so phrased as to express his wish to continuing contact with the king through the bishops of his realm.[233] But, after 1076, claims to a special bond between Aragon and the papacy, though surviving, received little discernible emphasis by Gregory.

A similar pattern concerning a ruler's obligations to the papacy, combined with a concern for monasteries and for payments to Rome, marked Count Bernard II of Besalú's dealings. No evidence of Gregory's intentions with regard to Besalú survives, but in December 1077, at a council of Besalú held by Bishop Amatus of Oloron,[234] the count, upon the legate's advice, expelled and replaced the simoniacal abbots of his county. To this extent, he was a willing reformer. He issued a charter in which he made three specific provisions: he listed the payments ('census') to be paid to St Peter in respect of seven religious houses; should an abbot be irregularly elected or a simoniac, he was to be expelled by papal authority; and Bernard promised that he and his heirs would pay a personal *census* of 100 gold mancuses so that he might be the special knight or servant ('peculiaris miles') of St Peter.[235] No mention was made of any commendation of the county, nor, indeed, is there evidence that any of these *census* were paid to Rome during Gregory's days. Even when Spanish rulers commended

---

[230] *Reg.* 2.50, to King Sancho I of Aragon, 24 Jan. 1075, p. 191/1–6. [231] *Reg.* 2.50.
[232] *QF* no. 215, pp. 258–60. Gregory associated Ramiro I's sons with his initial gift, but not by name.
[233] *Epp. vag.* no. 65, (1076/85), pp. 146–9. [234] For the circumstances, see above, 5.3.2.2.
[235] *Lib. feud. maior*, no. 501, 2.16–17.

themselves to St Peter, little was done from the papal side to formulate and impose conditions; rulers responded as best suited their interests and opportunities.

Gregory's concern with Spain was, however, more strongly informed by his understanding of its religious than of its political and proprietary history. His construction of its religious past led him to make demands upon all concerned with the affairs of Spain which were clearly formulated and insistently imposed at every stage of his pontificate. It was most fully articulated in letters which he sent in March 1074 to all of the Spanish kings—Sancho I Ramírez of Aragon, Alphonso VI of León–Castile, and Sancho IV of Navarre.[236] Gregory traced Spanish Christianity from its beginnings in St Paul's intention of travelling there (Rom. 15: 24, 28); St Peter and St Paul had dispatched from Rome seven martyr-bishops who implanted in Spain the order and liturgy of the Roman church.[237] There had thus been an initial concord in matters of religion between Spain and the city of Rome. But there ensued the catastrophes of the Priscillianist and Arian heresies and of the Visigothic and Saracen invasions; Spain was thereby torn from Roman religious observance and reduced to temporal desolation. It was for present-day Spanish kings, following the example of the better of the kings of the past,[238] to remedy this age-long decay by receiving the Roman liturgical order and no other, and by banishing the rites of Toledo and of other localities which had their origin in Hispanic heresy; they were to follow the faith of St Peter as did the other kingdoms of the west and north. Gregory repeatedly called upon kings to promote the Roman rite.[239] Moreover, Count Ebolus of Roucy's first concern according to the pact that he had made with the papacy in prospect of his Spanish expedition was with the correction of the spiritual error into which Spanish Christians had fallen.[240] Gregory charged successive legates with doing all in their power to extirpate the Hispanic rite and to establish the Roman; and it was a prime charge upon the Spanish episcopate to participate in such a campaign in every feasible region of the peninsula.[241]

Gregory's determination to exercise pastoral supervision over Spain was principally manifest in his dispatch of a series of legates whose spheres of activity were sometimes defined in terms of Spain alone but sometimes of parts of south-west France as well.[242] In 1077, he expressed his view of legates with reference to his sending of Bishop Amatus of Oloron to these regions:

---

[236] *Reg.* 1.63, 1.64, to Kings Alphonso VI of León–Castile and Sancho IV of Navarre, with all the bishops of their lands, 19 Mar. 1074, pp. 92–4.

[237] For the legends of the seven bishops, see *AA. SS. Boll. Mai.*, 3.440–4.

[238] For the ancient concord and friendship of Spanish kings with Roman popes, see *Reg.* p. 92/6–9; cf. Gregory's references to papal admonitions to bishops and their response: pp. 93/26–94/2.

[239] *Reg.* 7.6, pp. 465/38–456/8, 9.2, p. 570/26–41; cf. Gregory's praise for King Ramiro I of Aragon, who 'primus in regno sui quasi alter Moises abiecta Toletane illusionis superstitione legem ac consuetudines Romanas recepit': *QF* no. 215 (1084/5), p. 259.

[240] *Reg.* 1.6, to the legates Gerald of Ostia and the subdeacon Rainbald, 30 Apr. 1073, pp. 9/26–10/9.

[241] *Reg.* 3.18, to Bishop Simeon of Oca-Burgos, May 1076, pp. 283–4, with its conclusion: 'Procura ergo, ut Romanus ordo per totam Hyspaniam et Gallitiam et ubicunque potueris in omnibus rectius teneatur.'

[242] For legates in Spain, see esp. Säbekow, *Die päpstlichen Legaten*, pp. 12–17; P. David, *Études historiques*, pp. 348–59.

Matters which the governor and ruler of the Roman church cannot deal with by his own presence he can entrust on his behalf to legates, and through them proclaim the precepts of salvation and integrity of life to all the churches established throughout the world.[243]

Under Pope Alexander II, Cardinal Hugh Candidus had already been active in Spain, first from *c*.1065 to 1068 and again from 1071, when Alexander's privilege for San Juan de la Peña applauded his work in restoring the Christian order, resisting simony, and promoting the Roman liturgy.[244] Hugh nevertheless fell foul of accusations of simony by Abbot Hugh of Cluny and his monks on account of his dealings in southern France; but he retained Gregory's confidence, and he had been a prime supporter of Gregory's elevation to the papacy. In the spring of 1073, Count Ebolus of Roucy and other French lords were considering military expeditions to Spain. Gregory as pope moved quickly to charge Alexander's legates in France, Cardinal Gerald of Ostia and the Roman subdeacon Rainbald, to heal the breach between Hugh Candidus and the Cluniacs. He again directed Hugh Candidus to Spain, and confirmed his instructions to the other legate and to the abbot of Cluny to send to Spain with Ebolus of Roucy and other Frenchmen such persons as would promote papal purposes there.[245] There is no evidence as to the immediate sequel, whether in the form of French expeditions or of activity on Hugh Candidus's part. But Gregory's instructions to Gerald and Rainbald, and an accompanying order that they should return to Rome, were forestalled by the legates' crossing into Spain, where Gerald deposed for simony Bishop Munio of Oca—an action that Gregory later confirmed.[246] Gerald was back in Rome by Easter 1074.

King Alphonso of León–Castile was sufficiently impressed by Gerald's work that, in 1077, he asked Abbot Hugh of Cluny to secure from Gregory his return to Spain as legate.[247] But Gregory was employing Gerald elsewhere, and in June 1077 he commissioned Bishop Amatus of Oloron and Abbot Frotard of Saint-Pons de Thomières. He prepared the way for them by two programmatic letters.[248] Amatus's legatine commission embraced Gallia Narbonensis, Gascony, and Spain; in 1077 and 1078, his own activities centred upon Catalonia, while Frotard became particularly concerned with Aragon. In León–Castile, Gregory from this time used the resources of Saint-Victor at Marseilles. One of its monks named Richard, who was the brother of its abbot, Bernard, was already a Roman cardinal-priest. In May 1078, Gregory sent Richard on a mission in Spain which bore little, if any, result.[249] In October 1079, Gregory dispatched him for a second time; during his journey to Spain, the monks of Saint-Victor elected him abbot in the stead of his deceased brother, and in confirming the appointment Gregory made him also abbot of the Roman monastery

---

[243] *Epp. vag.* no. 21, pp. 56–9.   [244] As n. 228.   [245] *Reg.* 1.6–7.
[246] *Reg.* 1.16, to Bishop Gerald of Ostia, 1 July 1073, pp. 25–6, 1.64.
[247] *Recueil des chartes . . . de Cluny*, no. 3441, 2.553 (incorrectly dated 1070).
[248] *Reg.* 4.28; *Epp. vag.* no. 21.
[249] *Reg.* 7.6, p. 467/21–7. It would, however, be reading too much into Gregory's words to describe Richard's first mission as a complete failure; cf. *Reg.* 8.3, to King Alphonso, 27 June 1080, p. 519/14–15, which refers to a positive report by Richard on the king's obedience.

of St Paul's-without-the-Walls.[250] Richard was prominent in the events of the crisis of 1080 but continued to enjoy Gregory's favourable opinion.[251] A last mission was planned from Salerno in 1084, when Gregory wished Abbot Jarento of Saint-Bénigne at Dijon to travel to Portugal.[252]

Gregory's early papal dealings with so trusted a legate as Gerald of Ostia show how closely he sought to supervise and control his legates in Spain. He expressed surprise at Gerald's delay, without excuse, in returning to Rome; he was to come as quickly as possible, so that Gregory might know what he had been doing and might direct his future dealings.[253] When Gregory learned that Gerald had crossed into Spain already, he became still more insistent: whenever a Roman legate held a synod in distant parts, he should at once return to Rome and report upon what he had done, or at least send a competent messenger, so that the pope might ratify or amend it; how else might Gregory be able to deal with appeals and other consequential business that were directly addressed to Rome?[254] His close supervision of legatine decisions in Spain was apparent in 1074, when he confirmed Gerald's and Rainbald's excommunication and deposition of Spanish bishops. Gregory also received from Spanish bishops who attended his Lent synod at Rome written undertakings that they would uphold Hugh Candidus's conciliar rulings of 1068 about liturgical matters.[255]

Gregory sometimes sought to settle Spanish matters himself without legatine intermediaries. This was especially the case with regard to the see of Oca, when Bishop Munio appealed to him against the legates' sentence of deposition. He convinced Gregory that, as regards the Roman liturgical order, he was of one mind with the bishops who had been at Gregory's Lent synod. Gregory reserved other charges against him for more informed consideration at a later Roman synod, and in the meantime asked King Alphonso VI to restore him to his see.[256] The king evaded the request. In 1075, the see of Oca was transferred to Burgos, and Simeon remained bishop. Simeon prudently wrote a cordial letter to Gregory protesting his wish to be a true son of the Roman church. Gregory took him at his word, and in 1076 charged him with promoting the Roman liturgy throughout Spain.[257] Simeon retained Gregory's trust for the rest of his life.[258] However, he was too old to be in contention for the archiepiscopal see that Alphonso planned to establish after his conquest of Toledo, which took place in 1085. In 1081, Gregory sought to guide Alphonso's choice of a prospective archbishop. He disallowed an unnamed candidate on grounds of deficient literacy and advised the king to make his choice on the basis of sterling human qualities rather than of nobility of birth.[259] In the event, Alphonso's choice of

---

[250] *Reg.* 7.6, 7.7–8, to Cardinal Richard, and to the monks of Saint-Victor, 2 Nov. 1079, pp. 468–70.
[251] See above, 5.3.2.4.   [252] See above, 3.5.10.   [253] *Reg.* 1.6, p. 10/25–7.
[254] *Reg.* 1.16, pp. 25/17–26/6. Gregory's censure in 1074 of Abbot Hugh of Cluny's tardiness in coming to Rome was the sharper because Spanish matters were involved: *Reg.* 1.62, to Abbot Hugh of Cluny, 19 Mar. 1074, pp. 90/33–91/5.
[255] *Reg.* 1.64, pp. 93/26–94/12.   [256] *Reg.* 1.83.   [257] *Reg.* 3.18.
[258] *Reg.* 9.2, p. 571/1–4. For Burgos, see esp. Serrano, *El obispado de Burgos*, 1.286–329, 3.36–71.
[259] *Reg.* 9.2, p. 571/5–23. Gregory's careful outlining of a canonically correct procedure whereby a candidate should first be sought from the clergy of the local church establishes that provision was being

Bernard, a Cluniac monk who was archbishop from 1086 to 1126 and who, under Urban II, became papal legate in Spain and Narbonne,[260] was an admirable one from a Gregorian point of view.[261]

The situation which arose in Catalonia after the death in 1076 of Count Raymond Berengar I illustrates the gap between Gregory's aspirations and his achievements in the political affairs of Spanish principalities. The count had provided for the succession to be shared by his sons Raymond Berengar II, named *cabeza de estopa* (1076–82) and Berengar Raymond II, named *el fratricida* (1076–96). The brothers soon quarrelled. In 1079, Gregory took advantage of a good report by Abbot Bernard of Marseilles upon Bishop Berengar of Gerona to instruct the bishop with a view to composing the strife ('discordia') between the brothers.[262] With the assistance of suitable abbots, clerks, and laymen, Berengar was first to seek to restore peace. Should the brothers refuse, upon papal authority he was next to impose a truce until envoys of Gregory's own might determine the matter. If they persisted in disobedience, Gregory prescribed a test which was similar to that which he was applying to the rival kings in Germany: whichever of the brothers was found to be a peacebreaker would suffer excommunication with all its spiritual and temporal consequences; but the other should possess the whole inheritance with full apostolic blessing and its benefits both here and hereafter. Either by sending messengers or by appealing in person at Rome, Berengar was to report to Gregory upon any rulings that were made.

Some effort seems to have been made to carry out Gregory's intention, for in 1079 and again in 1080 the brothers made pacts in which they divided the inheritance, but without lasting result.[263] In 1082, Raymond Berengar II was assassinated, it was supposed with his brother's complicity; his brother eventually died on the First Crusade upon which he had embarked as a penance. As in Aragon, so in Catalonia, Gregory was not able to secure the implementation of his guidance and directions.

During Gregory's pontificate, the most powerful and successful ruler in Spain was King Alphonso VI of León–Castile. He had succeeded to the kingdom of León. A period of strife with his elder brother, King Sancho II of Castile, led to a period of exile among the Moors of Toledo, but the assassination of Sancho in 1072 enabled him to return and consolidate his power over both kingdoms. A principal means by which he consolidated his position was by association with the monks of Cluny and

made for a new election at Toledo, rather than for the recognition of the archiepiscopal status of an existing see.

[260] Urban II, *Ep.* 64, *PL* 151.346.

[261] For Bernard, see esp. Rivera Recio, *La iglesia de Toledo*, 1.125–96.

[262] *Reg.* 6.16, 2 Jan. 1079, pp. 421/27–422/26.

[263] I have not adopted Kehr's suggestion that *Reg.* 8.16, thought by Caspar to be addressed to Counts Raymond and Bertrand of Saint-Gilles, 23 Dec. 1080, pp. 537–8, was in fact addressed to the Catalonian counts: (i) Narbonne, the see where Gregory sought intervention, was more accessible to the counts of Saint-Gilles than to those of Barcelona; and (ii) even with due allowance for diplomatic language. Gregory's statement that 'parentum vestrorum sicut nobilitatis lineam ita quoque probitatum studia vos imitari cognovimus' (p. 527/18–19) ill fits the recent history of the house of Barcelona. See Kehr, 'Das Papsttum und der katalanische Prinzipat', pp. 31–2.

their abbot, Hugh of Semur.[264] Alphonso believed that their intercessions had brought about his freedom from imprisonment at Burgos by his brother Sancho in the time of their strife. In return for this deliverance and for a continuing place in Cluniac intercessions, he in 1077 doubled the annual *census* of 1,000 gold pieces that his father, King Ferdinand, had assigned to Cluny.[265] From 1076, Alphonso had permanently at his court a Cluniac monk, Robert, who was his principal adviser in ecclesiastical matters.

Alphonso's building up of his power undoubtedly involved a potential clash between his claims and those of the Gregorian papacy. Until 1077, Gregory gave expression to the claim that the kingdom of Spain belonged to St Peter and the papacy 'in ius et proprietatem'.[266] In that year, Alphonso took to using the title of 'imperator totius Hispaniae', which implied a claim to his own overlordship of the whole peninsula.[267] It is impossible to know how aware, if at all, Gregory and Alphonso were of the claims that the other was advancing. Gregory, however, showed signs of discretion and moderation. After 1077, he did not again use the phrase 'in ius et proprietatem', nor did either he or Abbot Hugh of Cluny refer to Alphonso's imperial title, whether to acknowledge or to deprecate its use. Alphonso, for his part, showed himself to be a champion of the Roman liturgy. As early as 1074, bishops from his lands who were at Rome during and after Gregory's Lent synod convinced the pope of the king's good intentions.[268] At home, Alphonso met with resistance from devotees of Hispanic practice. Stories, apocryphal but revealing, survive of how, in April 1077, he staged a judicial duel between a Castilian champion of the Roman liturgy and a Mozarabic champion of the Hispanic; although the latter won, Alphonso declared himself in favour of the Roman rite. Again, when a Hispanic service-book survived an ordeal by fire, Alphonso is said to have kicked it back into the flames with the words, 'At the will of kings, the horns of the law are bent.'[269] Such stories illuminate the background against which, in the same year, Alphonso hoped for the collaboration of both Rome and Cluny in promoting the Roman liturgy.[270] In 1080, at the council of Burgos, this liturgy won definitive acceptance in Alphonso's realms.[271]

Despite Alphonso's predilection for the Roman liturgy, Gregory's relations with him and his kingdom were subject to vicissitudes which resulted from the distance of Spain from Rome and the consequent room for misunderstanding at Rome of what was happening there. In the autumn of 1079, Alphonso stood very high in Gregory's favour. This is clear in a letter to the king in which Gregory commended to him his legate, Cardinal Richard, upon his return to Spain.[272] Addressing Alphonso as his 'most dear son in Christ, the glorious king of Spain', Gregory applauded his bond of

---

[264] For a fuller discussion of the Cluniacs in Spain, see Cowdrey, *The Cluniacs*, pp. 214–40.
[265] *Recueil des chartes . . . de Cluny*, nos. 3441, 3509, 4.551–3, 627–9.
[266] *Reg.* 4.28, pp. 345/35–346/1.
[267] For the development of the title *imperator*, see Cowdrey, *The Cluniacs*, p. 225 n. 1.
[268] *Reg.* 1.64, pp. 93/26–94/4, 1. 83.
[269] *Chron. Burgense*, p. 309; *Crón. Najerense*, p. 273.
[270] *Recueil des chartes . . . de Cluny*, no. 3441, p. 553.
[271] Fita, 'El concilio nacional' and 'El monasterio toledano'.   [272] *Reg.* 7.6.

faith and devotion with St Peter, whom he represented as having authority over all lands with no special mention of Spain. Gregory dwelt upon Alphonso's zeal in correcting the rooted religious error of his country. He urged him to persist in it by collaboration with the legate Richard, and thereby to maintain concord and unity with the apostolic see. To reinforce their bond, Gregory sent Alphonso the gift of a golden key in which was enclosed a fragment of St Peter's chains, so that the king might be kept the more mindful of St Peter's blessings towards him.

When Cardinal Richard arrived in Alphonso's kingdom, probably in the spring of 1080, he was deeply shocked by two happenings there against which he reacted with the utmost revulsion. After the death of his first wife Agnes of Aquitaine who had produced no heir, Alphonso had married Constance of Burgundy who was a niece of Abbot Hugh of Cluny but who was related to Agnes in the fourth degree, so that the marriage was canonically objectionable. Further, in order to consolidate the position of the abbey of Sahagún as a religious centre of his kingdom, Alphonso had replaced its abbot, Julian, by a Cluniac monk named Robert who had been serving as his ecclesiastical adviser. Some of the monks of Sahagún were affronted by this substitution and left their abbey in protest.

Richard lost no time in reporting these happenings to Gregory in a letter which does not survive. It was evidently written in the strongest terms, which moved Gregory to a comparably strong reaction. Gregory's reaction is the more remarkable when it is remembered that King Henry IV of Germany's synod of Brixen, which declared Gregory deposed from the papacy and selected Guibert of Ravenna to be his successor, met on 25 June. On 27 June, from Ceprano where he was restoring his relationship with the Norman leader Robert Guiscard, Gregory dispatched three letters about the Castilian crisis as he apprehended it.[273]

To Abbot Hugh of Cluny, he sent the text of Cardinal Richard's letter so that he might read for himself about the offence against religion ('impietas') which had arisen from the disobedience ('presumptio') of his monk Robert.[274] Like Simon Magus of old,[275] Robert had risen up against St Peter and had placed the salvation of hundreds of thousands of people at risk; Gregory was convinced that Robert had been exposing them to contamination by the Hispanic rite. Gregory felt sure that Abbot Hugh would deplore Robert's disobedience as much as he did, and he expressed a confidence in the abbot because, apparently, it had been cemented by their recent meeting at Rome and the clearing up of past misunderstandings.[276] He urged

---

[273] *Reg.* 8.2–4, to Abbot Hugh of Cluny, to King Alphonso VI of León–Castile, and to Cardinal Richard, 27 June 1080, pp. 517–21.

[274] Gregory appears to have had in mind the provisions against monastic 'praesumptio' in the Rule of St Benedict, caps. 69–70, with its overtones of self-assertion and of acting without proper authorization by the abbot.

[275] For Simon Magus, see Cowdrey, 'Simon Magus in South Italy', pp. 77–86. *Reg.* 8.2 does not imply that Robert was a simoniac in the specific sense of having purchased his office; his offence was that he had risen up against St Peter.

[276] On the interpretation of *Reg.* 8.2, p. 518/2–12, see Cowdrey, 'St Hugh and Gregory VII', pp. 182–3, as developed in 'Cluny and Rome', p. 263.

the abbot to excommunicate, recall, and strictly punish Robert. Hugh should also warn King Alphonso, whom Robert had deceived, of the wrath of St Peter that he had provoked by dishonouring the legate and by preferring falsehood to truth—that is, by preferring the Hispanic to the Roman way of worship. If Alphonso did not make due amends, he must expect himself to be excommunicated, while Gregory would mobilize against him the faithful of St Peter in Spain. Should Alphonso still persist, Gregory would consider himself coming to Spain and instituting severe measures against him ('dura et aspera moliri'),[277] as an enemy of the Christian religion. Hugh, for his part, was to recall his monks who were at large in Spain; he was to use his influence to ensure that no ordinance was issued in Spain that did not have the sanction of Gregory's legate.

Gregory enclosed a letter which Abbot Hugh was to forward to King Alphonso. It opened in terms of eulogy for the excellence of his kingship as the legate Richard had reported upon it after his first legatine mission. But now, Gregory had learnt of the harm that the devil was doing to him and to all who depended upon him for their eternal salvation. The devil's agents were the false monk Robert and his own ancient helper, an abandoned woman; by the latter, Gregory can only have meant his second wife, Constance, in the light of her consanguinity with his first wife, Agnes. Gregory urged Alphonso at once to put from him these two partisans of error and to obey his legate Richard. He particularly insisted that, on pain of excommunciation, he should put away his new wife, for the eugenic reason that his carnal posterity by a tainted marriage could not but be debased ('inutilem et reprobam'). But he also reported that he had ordered 'the most wicked monk Robert' to be called back to Cluny for penitential punishment; he was sure that Abbot Hugh would comply, 'for we walk in the same path, with the same mind, and by the same spirit'. A third letter, to the legate Richard, was much shorter. It commiserated with him in the reverses that his letter showed him to have suffered; Gregory exhorted him to persist in his endeavours. Gregory also informed him of the rigorous steps that he had taken to secure Robert's return to Cluny and his being subjected there to severe discipline.

Uncertainty surrounds the fate of these letters; it does not emerge whether Abbot Hugh forwarded the letter to King Alphonso, and it is improbable that the king saw it. It may even be that some or all of the letters were not dispatched from Rome in the first place. It is, however, clear that, having written his querulous report to Gregory, Cardinal Richard took prompt steps to relieve the crisis; the worst may have been over in Spain even before Gregory's letters were drafted. The monk Robert, who had done much to occasion the crisis by his supposed compromise with the Hispanic rite, had been replaced as abbot of Sahagún by another Cluniac, Bernard of Sédirac, apparently by 24 April 1080.[278] If Robert was recalled to Cluny, he did not stay there for long, but was soon back in Spain where he continued to enjoy Alphonso's favour.[279] By the late spring of 1080, and perhaps as early as April, King Alphonso and Cardinal

---

[277] Gregory adapted the phrase 'dura et aspera' of the *Regula Sancti Benedicti* 58.8, vol. 2. 628–9.
[278] Fita, 'El concilio nacional', no. 5, pp. 349–51.
[279] For his later presence in Spain, see Cowdrey, *The Cluniacs*, p. 238 n. 3.

Richard held the council of Burgos, at which the king finally accepted the Roman rite as the universal observance of his realms.[280] On 8 May, Alphonso confirmed the privileges of Sahagún in the presence of Cardinal Richard and confirmed Bernard as its abbot.[281] Within weeks, the ecclesiastical position in Spain had been restored to equilibrium from Gregory's point of view.

He registered his satisfaction in a letter that he sent to King Alphonso in 1081.[282] Above all, he expressed gratification that the liturgical order of the Roman church, the mother of all the churches, had been received by the churches of Alphonso's realms according to ancient usage; for Gregory's investigations had persuaded him of the heretical tendencies of the Hispanic rite. By turning from it, Alphonso had chosen St Peter for his patron and had shown an authentically royal care for the salvation of his subjects. Gregory's letter indicates that, in order to explain matters, Cardinal Richard and Bishop Simeon of Burgos had travelled to Gregory at Rome. In token of his devotion to St Peter, Alphonso had sent, presumably by their hands, a lavish gift which no doubt was his return in the gift-exchange which Gregory had begun in 1079 with his sending of a fragment of St Peter's chains. Whatever Alphonso's gift was, Gregory assured for it a conspicuous place at Rome where visitors would see it, and it elicited from him a particularly fulsome papal blessing. As regards Alphonso's requests about his second marriage and about the abbey of Sahagún, Gregory preferred to answer verbally through Cardinal Richard and Bishop Simeon. Alphonso was also to seek the guidance of the cardinal and of other godly men about the canonical choice of a suitable archbishop of Toledo when it fell into Alphonso's hands.

In the event, these issues were peaceably resolved. Despite the problem of consanguinity and Gregory's earlier harsh comments, Alphonso was able to retain Constance as his queen. Towards Sahagún, Gregory was munificent: in 1083, Abbot Bernard travelled to Rome, where he received from Gregory a privilege which placed the abbey under papal protection on the model of Cluny itself; as Cluny was a beacon of Roman liberty in France, so Sahagún should be in Spain.[283] In 1086, Abbot Bernard became archbishop of Toledo; his long and fruitful archiepiscopate combined the interests of the Gregorian papacy with those of Cluny and of the kingdom of León–Castile.[284]

In some respects, Gregory was conspicuously successful in promoting his purposes in Spain. By 1080, the Roman rite was accepted in the major principalities and kingdoms of Christian Spain; although the Hispanic rite was never completely eliminated, the main centres of ecclesiastical and political authority were committed to the usage that, in Gregory's eyes, represented the expulsion of error and signalled the obedience of rulers and their peoples to the claims of St Peter. Other factors than Gregory's insistence had helped towards the victory of the Roman rite: the Spanish

---

[280] For the date of the council, see ibid., p. 237 n. 1.
[281] Fita, 'El concilio nacional', no. 6, pp. 351–6.
[282] *Reg.* 9.2.　　　[283] *QF* no. 209, pp. 243–6.
[284] See Abbot Hugh of Cluny's letter to Bernard: Cowdrey, 'Two Studies', no. 4, pp. 145–9.

involvement of monastic centres north of the Pyrenees like Saint-Pons de Thomières, Saint-Victor at Marseilles, la Chaise-Dieu, and above all Cluny; the growth of pilgrimage to Santiago de Compostela, foreign participants in which preferred to find ministrations with which they were familiar; the similar preferences of French princes and knights who came to Spain in order to fight the Saracens. But Gregory's directives, implemented by the zeal of his legates, registered his authority with all those involved, whether Spanish or not. Furthermore, Gregory's dealings with León–Castile concluded with his offering advice about the establishment of an archbishop of Toledo which King Alphonso victoriously entered on the day of Gregory's death (25 May 1085). The rehabilitation of an archiepiscopal see gave the church in Alphonso's lands a basis for the structured organization that Gregory hoped for in the churches of distant lands. In Bernard of Sédirac, its first archbishop with whom Gregory had favourable dealings when he was abbot of Sahagún, Toledo had a leader who ranks among the outstanding churchmen to have emerged during Gregory's pontificate and who continued to implement his intentions for the church for long after his death.

Politically, Gregory was less successful. The rulers who proved most amenable, like Count Bernard of Besalú and King Alphonso VI of León–Castile, served Gregory on their own terms and to their own advantage; politically, they took more from Gregory than they gave to him. He was unable to make good his initial claim, upon any interpretation of it, that the kingdom of Spain belonged to St Peter in a special way 'in ius et proprietatem'. In Catalonia, he was unable satisfactorily to compose the feud between the sons of Count Raymond Berengar I. In the kingdoms of Navarre and Aragon, which were joined from 1076 in the hands of King Sancho Ramírez I, Gregory virtually lost contact with the king, although he maintained his authority with leading bishops. In León–Castile, Gregory was able eventually to claim that he had cemented the loyalty to St Peter of King Alphonso VI and of his kingdom. But he did so at the cost of tolerating his second, uncanonical marriage which challenged both Gregory's understanding of canon law and his deepest convictions of what constituted a stable and useful dynasty. He was constrained to define St Peter's claims to superiority in such terms as he used of every kingdom upon earth.

But for all the balance that must be struck, Gregory's pontificate was decisive so far as Spain was concerned in bringing the Christian parts of the peninsula more closely under papal authority and guidance than at any time since the Muslim conquest of the eighth century. As the Reconquest continued, it was certain to lead to a Spain which was overwhelmingly Roman in its Christian observance and papal in its loyalty. There, as well as all round the periphery of Latin Christendom, Gregory made his mark in fostering Christian kingdoms and principalities, and in securing a hearing for the authority and purposes of the apostolic see of Rome.

Gregory VII and the World Beyond Latin Christendom

7.1 The Byzantine Church and Empire

To enter into the frame of mind in which Gregory VII regarded the Byzantine empire and church calls for an effort of imagination. It should be recalled that the single most traumatic event in relations between east and west in Christendom has been the capture and sacking of Constantinople in 1204 by the Latin forces of the Fourth Crusade, which lay far in the future. In the late eleventh century, there was little sense of alienation, let alone of separation, between Latin and Greek Christianity. Gregory and his circle at Rome regarded Constantinople, the capital of the Byzantine empire and one of the four ancient patriarchates of the east, as the city of its founder, Constantine the Great (died 337). After Constantine became sole emperor, he fixed his capital at Byzantium on the Bosphorus; having rebuilt the hitherto insignificant town, he established it anew as Constantinople. Thereafter over the centuries, layer upon layer of pious legend in the west represented Constantine as the most religious emperor.[1] To cite only the older sources that were the most influential in the late eleventh century, the *Actus Silvestri* celebrated his conversion to Christianity and the baptism that he was alleged to have received at Rome; it especially praised his exaltation of papal prerogatives in Christian church and society.[2] The *Constitutum Constantini* drew upon the *Actus Silvestri* to commemorate Constantine's pious transfer of the centre of temporal rule from Rome to Constantinople and his setting up of the Lateran as the papal palace from which the church universal should be governed.[3] The *Constitutum Constantini* was widely publicized through its inclusion amongst the Pseudo-Isidorian Decrees, where it was set in the context of Constantine's supposedly exemplary behaviour at the council of Nicaea (325), when, amongst other things, he proclaimed the superiority of bishops to human jurisdiction: 'You can be judged by no one, because you are reserved for the judgement of God alone and you are, indeed, called gods (Ps. 81: 6); therefore you cannot be judged by men.'[4] Yet other legends told how Constantine had sent to Rome the relics of the holy cross that his mother Helena had discovered at Jerusalem, together with a wealth of other relics, with which he endowed the Roman church and especially the Lateran palace and basilica.[5] As the city of the most pious Constantine,

---

[1] See fuller discussions in Cowdrey, 'Eleventh-century Reformers' Views of Constantine', and id., 'Pope Urban II and the Idea of Crusade'.

[2] For the *Actus Silvestri*, see above, 1.7.   [3] *Das Constitutum Constantini*, ed. Fuhrmann.

[4] Hinschius, pp. 248–9.   [5] See esp. the *Descr. eccles. Lat.*

Constantinople was firmly and favourably established in the daily consciousness of the eleventh-century papacy.

The events of Pope Leo IX's pontificate when, in 1054, Cardinal Humbert and Frederick of Lorraine made their journey to Constantinople as papal legates which ended in the laying of mutual anathemas by the legates and the patriarch, Michael Cerularius, did little to dissipate this basic goodwill.[6] The anathemas left no visible long-term scar upon memories at Rome, and least of all on the young Hildebrand's; although he must have learned at Rome of what had happened. Instead, the legates' mission served to focus and to sharpen Rome's perception of its relationship with, and responsibility towards, Constantinople. In the letters which were prepared at Rome before the legates set out, there was a clear expression of the relationship between the churches as being one of mother and daughter.[7] On Rome's part, this was not only a claim to superiority and authority but also the acknowledgement of a duty to care and to aid. Nor were all the legates' impressions unfavourable. If they got on badly with the patriarch, they fared better with the emperor, Constantine IX Monomachus. It was an advantage that, in the words of the papal accreditation that the legates took with them, he was 'the successor of the great Constantine in blood, name, and empire'.[8] When Humbert later recalled his talks with him, the 'ortho- doxae memoriae imperator' as he called him, he said that they confirmed his own ob- servation that, in the east, neither the emperor nor laymen in general disposed of churches or of ecclesiastical ordinations and resources. The easterns did not fall into the western offence of simony, and in important respects their churches enjoyed true freedom.[9] Humbert's observations were in line with the pristine freedom of the church as apparent in Pseudo-Isidorian stories about the first Constantine at the council of Nicaea. Along with the prevailing unfavourable Roman perceptions of Byzantium,[10] there were thus some favourable ones; it was possible for them to be built upon later in the eleventh century.

So far as Gregory himself is concerned, the disciplinary, dogmatic, and liturgical differences between Greeks and Latins presented remarkably little obstacle. In con- trast to Cardinal Humbert's passionate condemnation of the eastern custom which required the generality of priests to be married,[11] Gregory made no allusion to it. On dogmatic issues, he was content to observe that the Constantinopolitan church was at variance with Rome ('dissidens a nobis') about the double procession of the Holy Spirit from the Father and the Son. He hoped to win Constantinople to harmony with Rome; but although, at a time of personal depression, he declared that the devil himself was at work in turning the eastern church from the catholic faith, he never gave a hint of condemning it outright on grounds of hardened and obstinate

---

[6] For these events, see Hussey, *The Orthodox Church*, pp. 129–38.

[7] See esp. Leo IX's letter to Patriarch Michael Cerularius and Archbishop Leo of Ochrida, caps. 23–36, Will, *Acta et scripta*, pp. 78–83.

[8] Will, *Acta et scripta*, pp. 86, 88.   [9] Humbert, *Adversus simoniacos*, 3.8, pp. 206–7.

[10] See e.g. Leo IX's letter to the eastern churchmen, caps. 5–22, Will, *Acta et scripta*, pp. 67–78.

[11] For Humbert's strictures on the marriage of eastern clergy, see Will, *Acta et scripta*, pp. 147–50, 153–4. Pope Leo IX drew upon Humbert's arguments in his *Ep.* 105 *bis*, PL 143.781–2.

heresy.[12] In marked contrast with his condemnation of the Slavonic and Hispanic liturgies, he made no suggestion that the Greek liturgy was radically objectionable, still less that it must urgently be abandoned. He was, indeed, scathing in his comments upon the Greeks when they themselves condemned as if it were heretical the Armenian use of unleavened bread in the eucharist; he roundly deprecated the levity of the Greeks, both in impugning the holy Roman church, the mother of all the churches, and in defending their own use of leavened bread while contumaciously condemning the Latin use of unleavened bread. Yet while defending strenuously the Latin custom, Gregory neither found fault with nor rejected the Greeks' use of leavened bread as such, for he recalled St Paul's dictum that to the pure all things are pure (Titus 1: 15): 'Nos verum azimum nostrum inexpugnabili secundum Deum ratione defendentes ipsorum fermentatum nec vituperemus nec reprobamus sequentes apostolum dicentem mundis esse omnia munda.' Again, the contrast with the strictures upon the east of Cardinal Humbert is remarkable.[13] Nor, in his dealings with the eastern emperor, did Gregory assert or imply that any of the theses that he formulated in his *Dictatus papae* of 1075 had any bearing—least of all thesis 12, that popes may depose emperors.[14] The burden of proof rests upon those historians who would claim that the *Dictatus papae* has any special reference to Byzantine affairs, whether ecclesiastical or political. While Gregory deplored the temerity ('temeritas') of the Greeks,[15] to a remarkable extent his attitude to them was conciliatory, though marked by a determination to use all means at his disposal to win them over to what was, in his eyes, a proper concord with and obedience to the Roman church in faith and practice.

Gregory's accession to the papacy occurred at a time when Byzantium desperately needed friendship and help. The year 1071 had been one of disaster, particularly on account of the defeat of its army by the Seljuk Turks at the battle of Manzikert. Thereafter, the Seljuks were able to overrun Asia Minor and establish principalities there; the defeated emperor, Romanus IV Diogenes, was dethroned in favour of Michael VII Ducas (1071–8). In the summer of 1073, Michael dispatched to Gregory two Byzantine monks bearing written and verbal messages which Gregory judged to exhibit his goodwill and devotion towards the Roman church. Michael

---

[12] *Reg.* 2.31, to King Henry IV of Germany, 7 Dec. 1074, p. 167/1–2; 2.27, to all the faithful, esp. to those across the Alps, 16 Dec. 1074, p. 173/8–11; 2.49, to Abbot Hugh of Cluny, 22 Jan. 1075, p. 189/14–19, where Gregory declared that 'Circumvallat enim me dolor immanis et tristitia universalis, quia orientalis ecclesia instinctu diaboli a catholica fide deficit et per sua membra ipse antiquus hostis christianos passim occidit, ut, quos caput spiritualiter interficit, eius membra carnaliter puniant, ne quandoque divina gratia resipiscant.' For earlier consideration in papal circles of the question of the double procession, see Peter Damiani's letter to Patriarch Constantine III Lichoudes of Constantinople (1059–63): *Briefe*, no. 91, 3.1–13; its good-tempered tone should be observed.

[13] *Reg.* 8.1, to Archbishop Gregory of Tsamandos, 6 June 1080, p. 513/1–20; cf. Peter Damiani's opinion as expressed in a letter of *c.*1052 to Archbishop Henry of Ravenna: *Briefe*, no. 41, 2.1.1–2. At the Lent synod of 1079, the opponents of Berengar's eucharistic teaching appealed to Greek as well as to Latin fathers in support of their view: *Reg.* 6.17*a*, pp. 426/26–427/3. For Humbert's views, see his tracts in Will, *Acta et scripta*, pp. 93–126, 136–50.

[14] *Reg.* 2.55*a*, pp. 201–8.   [15] *Reg.* 8.1, p. 513/19–20.

evidently canvassed substantial proposals, probably about the dogmatic and litur-gical matters at issue between the churches and perhaps also about the possibility of military support for Byzantium from the west. Some matters were, in Gregory's view, of too great weight to be pursued through the two monks; he replied to Michael that he had taken steps to send ('ad vos studuimus mittere') a trusted intermediary, Patriarch Dominicus IV of Venice/Grado, to confirm the seriousness of Michael's intentions in respect of them. From his side, Gregory used the vocabulary of seeking concord and peace that he so often used of resolving problems in the west: he desired to renew the ancient ecclesiastical concord between the Roman church and her daughter of Constantinople (the language used in 1053–4 came naturally to his mind); he also hinted at a wider purpose of seeking peace, so far as in him lay, with all the churches of the east. He commented that, as the concord that had at first sub-sisted between Roman popes and eastern emperors had been to the advantage of the apostolic see and of the empire, so the later cooling of mutual charity had harmed both sides. It was a diplomatic invitation to the emperor to explore further the secur-ing of both ecclesiastical and political advantages. Gregory gave the bearer of the letter further verbal messages, and invited Michael to reply.[16]

It does not emerge whether the patriarch of Venice travelled to Constantinople, nor is it known whether or how Michael replied by any channel. Gregory's con-tinuing solicitude is, however, apparent in his so-called 'Crusading' plans of 1074.[17] These plans were elicited, not by any further official Byzantine approach, but by the unsolicited reports of humble people, both eastern and western, about the depreda-tions and atrocities of the Seljuk invaders of Asia Minor. Early in 1074, Gregory was, in any case, planning an armed expedition with the primary purpose of overawing the Normans.[18] In a letter to Count William of Burgundy, he expressed the hope that the expedition might perhaps have the further usefulness of Gregory's crossing with it to Constantinople in aid of the cruelly afflicted Christians of the east who were eagerly seeking his help against the Seljuks.[19] Soon afterwards, an eyewitness, evid-ently western, of Saracen atrocities returned from the east and added his testimony about the devastation and slaughter that the Seljuks were committing up to the very walls of Constantinople. Gregory used the eyewitness as the bearer of a general sum-mons to Christians which made no mention of the Normans but called on them to be ready to lay down their lives for their brethren by bringing military aid to the east.[20]

Gregory's military expedition assembled but came to nothing without even leav-ing Italy. By September 1074, Gregory had so far relegated his plans as to tell Duke William of Aquitaine that military help for the east seemed no longer to be needed, since rumour had it that the eastern Christians had themselves abated the ferocity of the heathen there.[21] But by early in December, Gregory was again referring to east-

---

[16] *Reg.* 1.18, to the Emperor Michael VII Ducas, 9 July 1073, pp. 29–30. For Patriarch Dominicus's earlier activity as an intermediary between Constantinople and western circles, see Peter Damiani, *Briefe*, no. 91, 3.1–2.

[17] See further Cowdrey, 'Pope Gregory VII's "Crusading" Plans'. [18] See above, 6.2.

[19] *Reg.* 1.46, 2 Feb. 1074, pp. 69–71. [20] *Reg.* 1.49, 1 Mar. 1074, pp. 75–6.

ern Christians who were imploring his help in their desperate plight against the Seljuks. He reported to King Henry IV of Germany that he had already issued a general call for Christians to defend their religion ('legem Christi') against the heathen and to lay down their lives for their brethren. He claimed that many both in Italy and beyond the Alps had already responded; more than 50,000 men were preparing themselves to the extent of asking Gregory to be the general and bishop ('dux et pontifex') of the expedition and to lead it as far as the Lord's sepulchre at Jerusalem. Gregory was the more minded to respond, because he believed that the Constantinopolitan and other eastern churches were ready to accept Roman adjudication amongst their diverse opinions. He wished, when he travelled east, to leave Henry to protect the Roman church—no doubt he had particularly in mind the danger of Norman encroachments on the lands of St Peter.[22]

Nine days after writing to Henry, Gregory issued a summons to an overseas expedition which was especially directed to those beyond the Alps. The purpose was to aid Christians in the Constantinopolitan empire which the devil was seeking himself to turn from the catholic faith, while in his members the Seljuks he was slaughtering its people like cattle. He gave verbal instructions through whoever carried his summons about where those who responded should muster.[23] A messenger *en route* northwards with the summons was commissioned to show it to Countess Matilda of Tuscany. With the Empress-mother Agnes who had already volunteered, she was invited to accompany the expedition to the east, while her own mother, Countess Beatrice, like Henry IV of Germany, was to attend to Gregory's interests at home.[24]

There is no evidence to suggest what plans Gregory may have made to assemble and victual the ships for so large a host. In any case, his plans quickly proved fruitless. In January 1075, he wrote in a mood of deep pessimism to Abbot Hugh of Cluny on account of their frustration. He took up the language of his general summons in December by expressing his grief that at the devil's prompting, the eastern church was falling away from the catholic faith; those whom the devil was himself killing spiritually, his members, the Seljuks, were punishing carnally through their continuing slaughter.[25] The implication of Gregory's letter was that eastern churchmen had themselves rebuffed Gregory's pursuit of a concord based upon the faith of St Peter.

Nevertheless, Gregory was unwavering in his support for the Emperor Michael VII, despite diplomatic expedients on the latter's part which might be expected to have alienated Gregory, if indeed he knew of them. One Byzantine démarche was the sending of a crown to King Gésa of Hungary, despite Gregory's claims with regard to his kingdom.[26] Nor was Gregory perceptibly disturbed when, in 1074 and therefore when he was urgently concerned to help Byzantium, Michael concluded a treaty of friendship and fraternity with Robert Guiscard whom Gregory excommunicated at his Lent synod of that year; Robert's adolescent daughter Olympias was betrothed to Michael's infant son Constantine and was in 1076 sent to Constantinople, where

[21] *Reg.* 2.3, 10 Sept. 1074, pp. 126–8.   [22] *Reg.* 2.31.   [23] *Reg.* 2.37.
[24] *Epp. vag.* no. 5, pp. 10–13.   [25] *Reg.* 2.49, 22 Jan. 1075, p. 189/14–19, as cited in n. 12.
[26] See above, 6.4.

she received the name Helen.[27] When, in October 1078, Michael was deposed and succeeded by Nicephorus III Botaniates (1078–81), Gregory speedily excommunicated Nicephorus at his November synod.[28] Gregory's predilection for Michael persisted until 1080 when, rather suspiciously soon after Robert Guiscard's oath to Gregory at Ceprano, a Greek who was alleged to be Michael himself appared at Bari.[29] Robert Guiscard was prompt in taking up his cause and sought Gregory's support. Gregory gave it strongly in a letter to the bishops of Apulia and Calabria. He recalled the unjust deposition of Michael, 'the most glorious Constantinopolitan emperor', from the summit of imperial power ('ab imperialis excellentiae culmine') and took up Robert Guiscard's request for the help of the faithful to restore him. The knights who responded were to be steadfast in their loyalty to Michael, while the bishops were to provide for their proper spiritual preparation for the campaign and to confirm their loyalty to the duke and the emperor with whom they would cross the sea.[30]

The apparent coincidence of papal and Norman interests was short-lived. During the winter of 1080–1, Robert Guiscard reassessed the situation. He sent an envoy to Byzantium, ostensibly to oversee his daughter's welfare, but in fact to seek the alliance of the rising figure of Alexius Comnenus, at this time grand domestic and exarch of the west. In the spring of 1081, when Robert Guiscard was still making preparations for his expedition, his envoy returned. He denounced the *soi-disant* Michael as an impostor, reported on Alexius Comnenus's seizure of the Byzantine throne, and assured Robert Guiscard that Alexius was taking good care of his daughter.[31] Robert Guiscard, however, was soon pursuing ambitions of his own across the Adriatic.[32] In view of their recently renewed alliance and of Gregory's need for defence against Henry IV of Germany, Gregory found it necessary to give Robert Guiscard a measure of support. When, late in 1081, Robert Guiscard won a victory over Alexius Comnenus's army at Durazzo, Gregory sent his congratulations, saying that he saw in the Norman success a token of St Peter's patronage and an earnest of greater things to come.[33]

Alexius Comnenus, for his part, gave increasing diplomatic and financial aid to Henry IV. Probably in 1081, Gregory subjected him to the excommunication that had bound his predecessor Nicephorus Botaniates, although the terms do not survive.[34] From this time, direct evidence for Gregory's dealings with Alexius Comnenus and with Byzantine affairs in general is lacking. But in 1089, after Robert

[27] See above, 6.2, and, for a fuller bibliography, Cowdrey, *The Age of Abbot Desiderius*, p. 133 n. 96.
[28] *Reg.* 6.5*b*, 19 Nov. 1078, p. 400.
[29] Anna Comnena, 1.12.6–10, vol. 1.44–6; Lupus Protospatarius, *a.* 1080, p. 60; William of Apulia, 4.162–70, p. 212; Romuald of Salerno, *a.* 1080, p. 191; Cuozzo, 'I "Breve Chronicon"', pp. 171–2.
[30] *Reg.* 8.6, 25 July 1080, pp. 523–4.   [31] Anna Comnena, 1.15.2–6, vol. 1.53–6.
[32] See above, 6.2.   [33] *Reg.* 9.17, to Robert Guiscard, (1081, after 18 Oct.), pp. 597–8.
[34] If Gregory's admonition to the doge and people of Venice to avoid dealings with excommunicates: *Reg.* 9.8, 8 Apr. (1081), p. 585/15–20, referred to the Byzantines, Gregory's excommunication must have been in force by that date. But the generality of the reference makes it likely that it referred to supporters of Henry IV of Germany. According to Anna Comnena, Alexius made an attempt by letter to secure Gregory's support against Robert Guiscard: 3.10.1, vol. 1.122–3.

Guiscard's death in 1085, Urban II revoked Alexius's excommunication and entered into renewed negotiations about the union of the churches.[35] The conclusion which these events suggest is that, although after 1081 Gregory was drawn some way into hostility towards Alexius Comnenus, he made no radical departure from his earlier plans to foster the concord of the churches and to bring help to the threatened Christians of the east. Such were Gregory's consistent objectives in his dealings with Byzantium.

7.2 The Armenian Church

The only eastern church other than that of Constantinople with which Gregory is known to have had direct dealings is the Armenian. He set out with a marked prejudice against its doctrinal orthodoxy but, as with the Byzantines, he showed goodwill in seeking its amendment. As early as 1074, his expectation that all the eastern churches were prepared to listen to what the Petrine faith of the Roman church might determine amongst their various opinions included an express reference to the Armenians; he deemed almost all of them have diverged from the Catholic faith, no doubt, in the case of the Armenians, by falling into monophysite error about the duality of the divine and human natures in the incarnate Christ.[36] Direct dealings with the Armenians appear to have come only some four and a half years later, and then by chance. An Armenian impostor named Macharus had come to Italy where he had sought to win notoriety by the ascetic excess of wearing irons, and he had thereby collected a good deal of money for himself. Gregory had himself heard him and branded him as a heretic, whereupon he had fled to South Italy. Macharus's activities had alarmed the catholicos of the Armenians, Gregory II Vkayaser (1065–1105), whom Gregory VII called archbishop of Tsamandos (Zamanti) in Cappadocia.[37] The Armenians were subject to the same Seljuk pressures as the Byzantines, and the

---

35 Urban's releasing of Alexius from excommunication through legates is referred to by Bernold, *Chron. a.* 1089, p. 450/12–13. For the negotiations about union in that year, see esp. Holtzmann, *Beiträge*, pp. 59–105.

36 *Reg.* 2.31, to King Henry IV of Germany, 7 Dec. 1074, pp. 166/32–167/5.

37 The title *archiepiscopus Simandensis* that is used in Gregory VII's letters of the Catholicos Gregory II has no equivalent or confirmation in Armenian sources. The recent centre of the Armenian catholicate at Ani fell in 1064 to the Seljuk Turks; Gregory II's election in the following year took place at Tsamandos, west of Mitylene, but he did not for long reside there. Especially from 1074, when he visited Constantinople, he travelled widely, leaving to others his formal duties as catholicos. Several Armenian sources record a visit to Rome in or about 1074, but they give no details. Such a visit might account for Gregory VII's special mention of the Armenians in *Reg.* 2.31, but a number of considerations make it improbable: (i) it is not easy to account for Gregory VII's unfavourable comments on the Armenians in 1074 by comparison with his sympathetic attitude in letters of 1080 if Rome had already met and learned from Gregory II in 1074: *Reg.* 2.31, cf. 7.28, to Archbishop Roffrid of Benevento, (1080), pp. 509–10; 8.1, to Archbishop Gregory of Tsamandos, 6 June 1080, pp. 510–14, as discussed below; (ii) Gregory VII's letters of 1080 give no hint of a past visit to Rome by the catholicos and imply that he was not personally known there; (iii) in 1080, Gregory VII seems to have owed his information about Armenian Christianity largely to the Armenian priest John who had lately arrived; (iv) uncertainty in the drafting of Gregory's letters of 1080 about the catholicos's title would be harder to account for if he had earlier come to Rome; (v) some Armenian sources are silent about a visit to Rome by Gregory II at any date. Nothing is known about

catholicos was no doubt anxious not to forfeit papal favour. To undo the damage caused by Macharus, he sent to Rome a priest named John who satisfied Gregory of his own orthodoxy and of that of most of the Armenians. Gregory in effect reversed his judgement of 1074. He charged Archbishop Roffrid of Benevento, to whose region Macharus had fled, to apprehend the impostor and, in concert with Abbot Desiderius of Montecassino and his own comprovincial bishops, to examine him; they were to deal with him according to whether they found him to be penitent, docile, or obdurate.[38]

Gregory took advantage of the opportunity presented by the catholicos's returning messenger, John the priest, to send to him, as his 'beloved brother in Christ', a letter which he wrote with the intention of establishing common ground and of fostering concord.[39] He began by stating what attitudes of mind were proper for him as pope: in face of those who separated themselves from the body of Christ, he inevitably felt vehement grief; but with such as were of sound doctrine and kept the unity of the faith, he rejoiced with saving agreement and unspeakable joy. So far as the Armenians in particular were concerned, he had been led to believe that, in certain ways, they had diverged from the apostolic faith. He named three matters in particular: their use of an unmixed chalice in the eucharist, their practice of making chrism from butter instead of from balsam, and their adhering to the errors for which the council of Chalcedon (451) had deposed and condemned the heresiarch Dioscorus, patriarch of Alexandria—that is, for denying the two natures in Christ.[40]

Gregory said that the catholicos's envoy had reassured him on these three points. Nevertheless, he asked the catholicos to send him under seal a statement of his faith on these points and on others which might be at issue; indeed, he should regularly send letters to the apostolic see. Gregory particularly asked him to confirm the adherence of the Armenian church to the faith of the first four ecumenical councils —Nicaea (325), Constantinople I (381), Ephesus (431), and Chalcedon (451)— whose deliberations popes from Silvester I to Leo I had confirmed. Gregory also cited at length a letter of Pope Gregory I to the eastern churches in which he also affirmed the faith of the fifth ecumenical council, Constantinople II (553), at which the so-called 'Three Chapters', which were favourable to Nestorius and open to the objection that they unduly separated the two natures of Christ, were condemned.[41] It was a tactful way of seeking assurance that the Armenians had kept to an acceptable path after the council of Chalcedon. Gregory went on to make it clear that he

Gregory II's whereabouts in 1080. For a résumé of his life with full references to the sources, see Kapoian-Kouymjian, 'Le Catholicos Grégoire II'; also the discussion by Halfter, *Das Papstum und die Armenier*, pp. 113–21. (I am indebted to Professor R. W. Thomson for guidance as regards the Armenian background.)

[38] *Reg.* 7.28.   [39] *Reg.* 8.1.

[40] At Chalcedon, Dioscorus was deposed and excommunicated for his association with the monophysite heresy of Eutyches. He was also condemned by later ecumenical councils: Constantinople III (680–1), Nicaea II (787), and Constantinople IV (869–70), *COD* pp. 125, 135, 161, 163, 182. Gregory's singling out of Dioscorus may also have been because of his contumacy at Chalcedon: see Deusdedit, *Coll. can.* 1.36(24), p. 46; Anselm of Lucca, *Coll. can.* 3.92, p. 173.

[41] For Gregory I's letter, see *Reg. Greg. I*, 1.24, vol. 1.32/355–77.

would not want to press issues of a dogmatic nature if the Armenians would make certain relatively modest concessions. Thus, he expressed unease at their adding to the chant *Sanctus Deus, sanctus fortis* the words 'Qui crucifixus es pro nobis'. But he did not challenge them on the grounds of monophysite or theopaschite implications; he asked the Armenians to omit them in deference to the scruples of other Christians, for St Paul's charitable reason, that Christians should avoid offending each other about matters which, although of weight for themselves, were objectionable to others (Rom. 14: 19–24). By such a generous concession, Gregory argued, the Armenians could demonstrate their sense of and solidarity with the faith of the universal church. Finally, Gregory alluded favourably to the Armenians' use of unleavened bread in the eucharist, for which the Greeks had the temerity to attack them. Gregory concluded his letter with a prayer for the catholicos that God, the source of all that men rightly know and feel and believe, would more abundantly illuminate his mind, directing him in the way of prudent understanding and preserving him in the concordant unity of the faithful ('in concordi fidelium unitate').

Gregory's encounter with the Armenians provides evidence for his own rule of faith as based upon the authoritative traditions of the church.[42] It also illustrates how far he was prepared to go, subject to his insistence upon the authority of the apostolic see as speaking with the voice of St Peter, in seeking common ground with another church and its head and spokesman. His presumption was that harmony and collaboration could be established, and that a quest should be made to establish good relationships upon a basis of peace and concord. With the Armenians as with the Byzantines, Gregory sought to secure Christian unity by discussion and agreement, rather than by command and coercion.

7.3 Islam

Gregory's perception of and attitude to the Muslims and their religion were far from simple or uniform. In the Tuscany even of his day, the cruelty of the Saracens ('crudelitas Saracenorum') and the terror that they struck were still part of the public memory.[43] In Gregory's mind, the memory was revived by stories of the slaughter and devastation of current Seljuk attacks upon the Byzantine empire. There was also the disturbing fact that Africa, which in the eyes of contemporary cosmographers represented one third of the earth, had long since been lost to Muslim domination. On the other hand, during the three decades or so after 1060, the Normans reconquered Sicily from its Muslim emirs. The same period witnessed a succession of campaigns against Muslims in Spain by French adventurers and by Christian rulers. In his incidental references to the Muslims, Gregory often expressed aversion to them. He bracketed them with Jews and pagans; at best, they followed their religion and its law such as they were, but this was of no avail for the salvation of their souls,

[42] It may be compared with the statement of faith made by a newly elected pope as prescribed in Deusdedit's *Coll. Can.*: see *Liber diurnus*, ed. Foerster, pp. 429–31.

[43] *QF* no. 61, for the monastery of S. Maria nell'Isola di Gorgogna (dioc. Pisa), 18 Jan. 1074, p. 40.

nor did God grant them the warrant of such miracles as those by which he often attested the truth of the Christian religion. At worst, Muslims were the ungodly haters of Christians; in Spain, Gregory feared that grave danger threatened a Christian people which laboured under the great hatred of the ungodly Saracens ('christianam gentem quae in partibus illis magno impiorum Sarracenorum odio laborare dinoscitur').[44]

Gregory did not distinguish clearly between different ethnic groups of Muslims. He did not name the Seljuk Turks as a distinctive people or mark them off from the Arabs; he referred to all alike by the ancient designation of Saracens. Nevertheless his hostility to the Seljuk assailants of Byzantium was especially intense, because eastern Christians were suffering more than any others through unceasing savagings by Saracens ('nimium afflicti creberrimis morsibus Sarracenorum'); the imagery was that of wild animals after their prey.[45] Gregory so far identified the Seljuks as to call them a 'gens paganorum' who slaughtered Christians like cattle; they were, therefore, enemies of God and members of the devil.[46]

In the case of the Muslims of Sicily, Gregory's language was markedly less extreme. In 1076, when he understood that Count Roger of Calabria and Sicily was seeking reconciliation with the church, he charged Archbishop Arnald of Acerenza to oversee the penances of Roger and those of his knights who might be minded to fight 'against the pagans', that is, the Muslims of Sicily. But he also voiced a concern that he was soon to articulate more clearly to Christians in North Africa, that Christians should take proper thought for the good name of their own religion ('Christiani nominis culturam') in the eyes of pagans; to this end, they should refrain from major offences and thereby deserve victory over their enemies.[47] In 1083, when Gregory issued his privilege to Archbishop Alcherius of Palermo in which he confirmed the ancient rights and possessions of his see and conferred upon him the *pallium* of a metropolitan, he expressed rejoicing that the see of Palermo, which on account of men's sins had for so long been subjected to the power and falsehood ('perfidia') of the Saracens, should now have been restored to the Christian faith.[48] Gregory said nothing about Christians' attitudes or conduct towards the Sicilian Muslims. But, in the light of his letter of 1076, his concern seems to have been that the two religions should quietly coexist, and that Christians should by their faith and works win their religion a good report in Muslim eyes.

Gregory's comments in his letters upon the Saracens in Spain suggest a deeper

---

44 See *Reg.* 2.9, to Countesses Beatrice and Matilda, 16 Oct. 1074, p. 139/5–9; 6.16 to Bishop Berengar of Gerona, 2 Jan. 1079, p. 421/30–4; *Epp. vag.* no. 54, (1084), pp. 130–3.

45 *Reg.* 1.46, to Count William of Burgundy, 2 Feb. 1074, pp. 70/29–71/2.

46 *Reg.* 1.49, general summons to defend Constantinople, 1 Mar. 1074, p. 75/14–19; 2.31, to King Henry IV of Germany, 7 Dec. 1074, p. 166/14–20, 26–32; 2.49, to Abbot Hugh of Cluny, 22 Jan. 1075, p. 189/14–19.

47 *Reg.* 3.11, 14 Mar. 1076, p. 271/25–272/7; cf. 3.20, to the clergy and people of Bougie, (May/June 1076), pp. 286/19–287/15.

48 *QF* no. 212, 16 Apr. 1083, p. 253.

hostility than those which he passed upon the Saracens in Sicily, but they were less outraged than what he had to say about the Seljuk assailants of eastern Christians. Lands in Spain that French warriors might recover would be justly seized back from pagan hands.[49] For the Christian people who lived under Muslim rule were, Gregory believed, notoriously vexed by the great hatred of the ungodly Saracens.[50] And more deep-seatedly, the Saracen invaders had played a harmful and active part in alienating Spain from its originally close relation to the apostolic see: they had further debilitated, both spiritually and materially, a Spain already rent by Christian heresies, and had bent it to the service of their own infidelity and tyranny.[51] The righting of such damage was part of the justification of the Christian reconquest that Gregory supported. He looked forward to the ecclesiastical reorganization of captured lands: as in Sicily he rejoiced in the renewed metropolitan status of the see of Palermo, so in Spain he was concerned for the worthy filling of the see of Toledo when it could be recaptured.[52] So far as his own letters and privileges are concerned, Gregory had nothing good to say of the Muslims in Spain, and he did not, as in Sicily, urge Christians to moderate their behaviour in warfare before them. Yet there is one piece of indirect evidence that, in Spain, he sought the conversion of Muslims to Christianity. By his order, and at the repeated urging of Abbot Hugh of Cluny, a sometime Cluniac monk and later hermit named Anastasius spent time during Gregory's pontificate preaching Christianity to the Saracens, but without effect.[53]

Some of Gregory's most interesting dealings with a region under Muslim domination arose from his contacts with the Christians of North Africa who formed a significant element in the population of Ifriqiya—approximately the present-day Algeria and Tunisia.[54] Such Christians followed the Latin rite, and, at least from time to time, their bishops looked to Rome for help and guidance.

The reform papacy's concern with African Christians was already apparent in 1053, when Leo IX responded to an approach by sending letters to Archbishop Thomas of Carthage and to other African bishops named Peter and John.[55] Leo deplored the shrinking of the number of bishops from over 200 in the ancient heyday of the African church to a mere five in his own day. But he was glad that the Roman church had been approached about a bishop who had exceeded his powers. He confirmed that no African bishop should ordain or depose another bishop, or convene a provincial council, without the concurrence of the archbishop of Carthage. Leo seized upon the occasion to insist upon the pope's right to settle difficult cases that arose in all other churches in the world. He insisted upon the upholding of due

---

[49] *Reg.* 1.7, to French barons, 30 Apr. 1073, pp. 11/27–12/3.

[50] *Reg.* 6.16, to Bishop Berengar of Gerona, 2 Jan. 1079, p. 421/32–4.

[51] *Reg.* 1.64, to Kings Alphonso VI of León–Castile and Sancho IV of Navarre, 19 Mar. 1074, p. 93/13–17; 4.28, to the kings and magnates of Spain, 28 June 1077, p. 346/3–7.

[52] *Reg.* 9.2, to King Alphonso VI of León–Castile, (1081), p. 571/5–23.

[53] Galterius, *Vita s. Anastasii*, cap. 5, col. 429.

[54] On Africa, see esp. Courtois, 'Grégoire VII et l'Afrique', and Hettinger, *Die Beziehungen des Papsttums*.

[55] *Epp.* 83–4, *PL* 143.727–31.

order and hierarchy among the bishops of a particular region. Leo's firm emphasis upon papal authority and upon the proper structuring of the church led to the inclusion of the two letters in a small dossier upon such subjects which was compiled in connection with the visit of Leo's legates to Constantinople in 1054. As pope, Gregory VII seems to have been familiar with Leo's two letters.

They did much to set the guidelines for Gregory's contrasting reaction to two incidents in African churches that came to his notice. The first, in 1073, concerned the church of Carthage, from whose archbishop, Cyriacus, Gregory received a report that he had refused to perform uncanonical ordinations, even though he was commanded to do so by the Hurasanid emir 'Abd al-Ḥaqq (1059–95) who was supported by a dissident faction within the Christian community. The emir had subjected Cyriacus to imprisonment and to beatings. Gregory replied in letters of his own dictation to the clergy and people of Carthage, and to the archbishop himself.[56]

In his letter to the clergy and people, he drew extensively upon New Testament texts in order to encourage them to imitate Christ in his sufferings and death. He urged that, laying aside all simulation, they should revere Cyriacus as their spiritual father, and he pleaded that they should fear nothing that might happen to them through being subject to Saracen coercion ('inter arma Saracenorum positis'), that they should shun envy and strife amongst themselves, and that they should be properly subject to the higher powers, especially to those who ruled them as Christians in the name and place of Christ. Gregory reproved those who had accused their archbishop before the Saracens and had thus caused him to experience in himself the false accusations and suffering of Christ. He made a fervent appeal to them to repent. He used some restraint because of the distance of Carthage from Capua from where he was writing and because of his imperfect briefing about what had been at issue. But he called for a setting right of the situation lest he be constrained to proceed to a sentence of anathema.

To the archbishop, Gregory replied in commendation of his steadfastness and in exhortation that he maintain his witness, if necessary, to the point of death:

> But thanks be to God, that being set in the midst of a corrupt and crooked people, the constancy of your faith so became known as a shining light to all (cf. Phil. 2: 15), that, being brought before the king's audience, you determined rather to be afflicted by manifold torments than, at the king's command, to perform ordinations against the holy canons. But how much more precious still would have been the confession of your religion, if after the beatings that you have suffered, you had attained by the demonstration of their error and by the preaching of the Christian religion to the pouring out of your very life itself!

In this spirit, Gregory urged Cyriacus to persevere in his witness for the true welfare of the African church.

These events at Carthage are in sharp contrast with others at Bougie, some 350 km. to the west, which came to Gregory's notice in 1076. In the latter case, Gregory was well pleased with the local Christian church, and he was no less gratified by the

---

[56] *Reg.* 1.22–3, 15 Sept. 1073, pp. 36–40.

goodwill expressed by the Muslim ruler, the Hammadite emir an-Nāṣir (1062–1089/90). In May or early June 1076, Gregory wrote to the clergy and people of the church at Bougie, who had sent their newly elected archbishop, Servandus, to Rome for consecration. This Gregory gladly performed, and he provided him with such instruction and training for his office as time permitted. Gregory then sent him back to his people, whom he exhorted so to receive and obey him that the Saracens amongst whom they lived would mark their faith and charity, and would be provoked by their good works to emulate rather than to despise the Christian faith.[57]

Servandus's consecration gave Gregory an opportunity to promote the setting up of such an ecclesiastical province in Africa as Leo IX had envisaged. He quickly wrote to Archbishop Cyriacus of Carthage, deploring the fact that, even with Servandus's return, Africa would lack the three bishops who were required to perform episcopal consecrations. He therefore urged Cyriacus to attend to the canonical election of a third bishop whom he should send to Rome, and who would thereafter share the burden of ruling the African church.[58]

It is not known what, if anything, the sequel to this letter may have been. But before the end of 1076, Gregory wrote to the emir an-Nāṣir, who had petitioned Gregory for Servandus's consecration.[59] The emir had clearly been anxious to win Gregory's favour, for he had both sent him gifts and freed Christian prisoners with the promise that he would free more. Gregory said that he saw in these acts the prompting of their common God, and he went to remarkable lengths in affirming the beliefs that they shared:

God, the creator of all, without whom we can do or even think nothing that is good, has inspired your heart; he who enlightens every man who comes into the world (John 1: 9) has enlightened your mind in this purpose. For Almighty God, who wills all men to men be saved and none to perish (cf. 1 Tim. 2: 4), approves nothing in us more fully than that, after his love for God, a man should love his fellow men and that what he would not have done to himself he should do to no one else (cf. Matt. 7: 12). Such charity as this, we and you owe to our own more particularly than to other peoples; for we believe and confess one God, albeit in a different way, and we daily praise and revere him as the creator of the ages and the governor of this world. For as the Apostle says, 'He is our peace, who makes both one' (Eph. 2: 14).

From this expression of a basic community of faith, Gregory proceeded to more tangible matters. He had, he said, discussed an-Nāṣir's goodwill with a number of the Roman nobility, who had been duly impressed. Two of them, Alberic and Cencius who had a lifetime association with Gregory in the Lateran palace,[60] wished to send men of their own to the emir in order to express their respect and to talk about ways

---

57 *Reg.* 3.20, pp. 286–7; I here follow Hettinger's modification of Caspar's dating: *Die Beziehungen des Papsttums*, pp. 158–9.

58 *Reg.* 3.19, June 1076, p. 285.

59 *Reg.* 3.21, pp. 287–8. The letter bears no date, but must be of 1076 because it was written in the same year as *Reg.* 3.19–20: p. 387/28. It was probably sent some time after these letters, because time must be allowed for Gregory's discussions with a number of Roman nobles and for the decision of Alberic and Cencius to dispatch their own envoys: p. 238/16–24.

60 For these figures, see above, 2.1.

in which they might be useful to him. The purpose of Gregory's letter was to commend these men and to ask that they might be favourably heard. Gregory gave no hint as to the nature of the business to be discussed, but it may have concerned mercantile, rather political, links between Rome and Africa.[61] Gregory concluded his letter with a blessing upon an-Nāṣir that resumed his earlier favourable estimate of the emir's religion:

For God knows, that we love you sincerely ('pure') to the honour of God, and that we desire your welfare ('salutem') and prosperity in the present life and in that to come; and we beseech with our heart and lips that, after long continuance in this life, God will bring you into the blessedness of the bosom of the most holy patriarch Abraham.

It was a blessing that Gregory extended to Christians,[62] but it also expressed the common veneration of Abraham by Christians and Muslims. Yet, in view of Gregory's statement in 1084 that the Saracens' religion is of no avail for salvation,[63] it would be hazardous to conclude that Gregory had a considered belief in the possibility of the emir's being saved as a Muslim. It would also be unwarranted to read Gregory's words as a prayer for the emir's conversion to Christianity, which would have been undiplomatic and is neither explicit nor implicit in Gregory's words.

Gregory, in fact, seems to have been little concerned with the conversion of Muslims, least of all in the context of a largely Muslim society. His thoughts centred not upon them, but upon Christian minorities who should witness to their faith in face of them. Where Muslims were militarily or socially hostile, Christians should remember the precepts of the gospel and should witness fearlessly with an acceptance of sufferings and death upon the model of Christ. If Muslims were amicable, it behoved Christians so to believe and live that their faith gained respect in Muslim eyes. In his letter to an-Nāṣir, Gregory went remarkably far towards acknowledging that Muslims and Christians worshipped the same God. But modern missionary ideas were foreign to Gregory's mind, which envisaged the witness of Christians, not usually the conversion of pagans. In his concern to be diplomatic in his letter to an-Nāṣir, Gregory was drawn beyond the habitual limits of his thinking. Nevertheless, as made only some twenty years before the preaching of the Crusade, his expression of goodwill to the emir is remarkable.

---

[61] For the suggestion that the contacts were of a mercantile nature, see Lopez, 'A propos d'une virgule', and Hettinger, *Die Beziehungen des Papsttums*, pp. 176–86.

[62] Cf. *Reg.* 5.21, to Abbot Hugh of Cluny, 7 May 1078, p. 385/21–5; 7.8, to the monks of Saint-Victor at Marseilles, 2 Nov. 1079, p. 469/28–30.

[63] *Epp. vag.* no. 54, pp. 130–3.

8

Gregorian Ideas

8.1 Introduction

Gregory VII's letters disclose him to have been a man of cultivated mind, particularly with respect to the study and knowledge of the Bible; he was also versed in some of the Christian fathers, especially Pope Gregory the Great whom he evidently regarded as a model in the discharge of the papal office.[1] During his lifetime at Rome, he was associated with men of learning in biblical and patristic literature and in church and secular history; it is necessary to instance only Cardinals Humbert and Peter Damiani before he became pope and the cardinal-priest Deusdedit of S. Pietro in Vincoli afterwards. He was also in touch with such learned circles as those of Countess Matilda of Tuscany, which included Bishop Anselm II of Lucca, and of Abbot Desiderius of Montecassino with the vast intellectual resources of that abbey both at Montecassino and in Rome. Gregory could and did draw upon large stores of thought and learning when it suited his purposes to do so. Yet he was not himself of a speculative turn of mind, nor did his grasp of Christian truth owe much to dogmatic inquiry or reflection. Furthermore, his thought was in no way systematic. Like all popes upon their accession, he made, with undoubted conviction, a comprehensive profession of acceptance of the historic faith of Christianity.[2] But deep reflection on its dogmas was not his *métier*. Whatever might have been the case had he not been called to the service of the Roman church, he was perforce the man of action who was concerned with the multifarious issues raised by the church and the world in which he lived, taking them as they arose and developed.

It is commonly stated that, from the time of his becoming pope, he acted upon a number of sharply defined and clearly formulated principles of papal action. Such a view is misleading; the presuppositions upon which he acted were subject to change and adaptation. In one conviction he never wavered: since the pope was the vicar of St Peter, the authority that Christ had conferred upon St Peter in the New Testament had devolved upon him absolutely and by hereditary and inalienable right. As a consequence, he had functions and duties that he must needs perform. Upon this, he was adamant; upon all else, he was surprisingly flexible, feeling his way and therefore perplexing both rigorous collaborators like Hugh, bishop of Die and archbishop of Lyons, and cautious and steady-minded ones like Abbot Hugh of Cluny. His zeal, moral force, and religious conviction, however, ensured that he

---

[1] Useful guidance is provided by the index of citations in *Reg.* pp. 644–50, and *Epp. vag.* pp. 169–70.
[2] For a paradigm statement of faith, see *Liber diurnus*, ed. Foerster, pp. 429–31 = Deusdedit, *Coll. can.* 2.110, pp. 235–7.

should retain to a remarkable degree the loyalty and service of a wide variety of men and women.

By way of introduction to a study of Gregory's conception and discharge of the papal office in the context of Christian truth as he apprehended it, it may be useful to consider three topics which illustrate his manner of thinking and the processes by which he arrived at dogmatic conclusions and practical decisions.

8.1.1 The Berengarian Controversy

Before he became pope, Gregory had been for long concerned with the controversy surrounding the eucharistic teaching of Berengar of Tours.[3] He had shown more reluctance than most of his contemporaries to adopt a firm stance. He had not associated himself with the extreme formulation of realist doctrine which was drafted by Cardinal Humbert and which Berengar had been compelled to accept in 1059.[4] If Lanfranc of Canterbury sent to Rome a copy of his *De corpore et sanguine Domini* as Pope Alexander II requested,[5] there is no evidence that Gregory at any time paid attention to his arguments or adopted his conclusions; he seems to have kept a remarkably open and uncommitted mind. At an earlier stage of his career, he had his own collection of ancient texts about the eucharist on the basis of which he hoped that a conclusion about Berengar's teaching might be established.[6] But, rather than insisting upon any particular form of words or doctrinal argument, he had always sought to promote further discussion and to see what might be said on all sides of the question. Thus, while there is no evidence that Gregory shared Berengar's understanding of the eucharist, Berengar was able to look to him as someone sympathetic from whom, if from anyone, he could expect a fair hearing; although he also regarded him as something of a temporizer who had not given him the support that he deserved.[7]

At Rome, there seems to have been no further official consideration of Berengar's teaching during Alexander II's pontificate, although there were informal discussions on the basis of which Berengar cherished hopes of a more sympathetic hearing than he had received during the lifetime of Cardinal Humbert.[8] After Gregory became pope, Berengar's case remained quiescent until 1078, largely upon Gregory's insistence, while Berengar looked forward to further talks at Rome. The principal evidence is a letter that Berengar wrote to Gregory between 1075 and 1078.[9] He addressed Gregory cordially: 'To Pope Gregory, who is to be received with all reverence in Jesus Christ, Berengar sends every possible offering of love unfeigned'; and in the letter he thrice called him 'pater optime'. He thanked Gregory for having sent a letter (now lost) in his support to Bishop Hugh of Die. He claimed to have complied with Gregory's injunction to keep silent when challenged about his eucharistic

---

3 See above, 2.1, 3. For Gregory and Berengar, see esp. Montclos, *Lanfranc et Bérenger*, and Cowdrey, 'The Papacy and the Berengarian Controversy'.

4 Huygens, 'Bérenger', pp. 372/73–107, 374/132–375/155.

5 Lanfranc, *Letters*, no. 4, pp. 56–7.   6 See above, 2.1.   7 See above, 2.2.3.

8 See Cowdrey, 'The Papacy and the Berengarian Controversy', pp. 120–1.

9 *Briefe Berengars*, no. 89, pp. 154–5.

teaching 'quantum oportebat', thus implying that there had been occasions when he had spoken.[10] He cherished hopes of soon having a chance of presenting his case to Gregory at Rome, though privately and not before hostile judges; Berengar clearly wished to avoid a repetition of his experience at Rome in 1059.[11] In the event, Berengar travelled to Rome in the mid-winter of 1077-8 and stayed for about a year. His memoir of his stay, written soon after his return to France as a kind of 'historia calamitatum', is a valuable if highly partisan source for it.[12]

Berengar's months in Rome were marked by lively debate about his opinions, in the course of which points of view were expressed which show how divided current churchmen were, at Rome as well as elsewhere. A calm and measured treatise, perhaps by a disciple of Berengar rather than by himself, put the case for his teaching.[13] Another Berengar, perhaps Bishop Berengar of Venosa, addressed to Gregory VII an energetic rebuttal, expressing confidence that what Pope Gregory I had taught about the eucharist his namesake would, by divine purpose, confirm.[14] Bishop Bruno of Segni referred to philosophical disputes in which Berengar of Tours led his audience to impossible conclusions,[15] while Peter the Deacon much later referred to his irresistable power of argument.[16] Berengar himself was later to take another Cassinese monk, Alberic, to task for having at this time shared his point of view but for turning his coat in 1079.[17] Gregory himself gave Berengar's future his consideration; a letter of 7 May 1078 to Abbot Hugh of Cluny reveals that, in answer to the abbot's inquiry, Gregory sent him verbal information about his own opinions and intentions regarding Berengar.[18] Regrettably, there is no hint as to what Gregory said.

Berengar's memoir sheds light upon events during the last months of 1078. It opens with a meeting of bishops in the Lateran on 1 November, and so in advance of the November synod that assembled on 19 November. Berengar cited a profession of faith that was prepared for the earlier meeting:

I profess that, after the consecration, the bread on the altar is the true body of Christ, which was born of the Virgin, which suffered on the Cross, and which is seated at the right hand of the Father, and that the wine on the altar which is afterwards consecrated is the true blood that flowed from Christ's side.[19]

While this profession was patient of an orthodox construction, it could also be taken in a sense that Berengar could accept; therefore he welcomed it. Gregory, he said, caused it to be read in ringing tones so that all present might hear, and the pope approved it although in cautious terms: it should suffice as a statement of faith, particularly for simple Christians 'to whom milk should be given rather than solid food' (cf. Heb. 5: 11–14). He assured the assembly that Berengar was no heretic but that he

---

[10] e.g., perhaps, at the council of Poitiers (1075): Lanfranc, *Letters*, no. 46, pp. 142–51; Somerville, 'The Case against Berengar of Tours'.

[11] See above, 2.2.3.   [12] Huygens, 'Bérenger', pp. 388–403.

[13] Matronola, *Un testo inedito.*   [14] Morin, 'Bérenger contre Bérenger.'

[15] *Exp. in Levit.* cap. 7, col. 404C.   [16] *De viris illustribus*, cap. 21, col. 1033AB.

[17] Meyvaert, 'Bérenger de Tours', pp. 331–2.   [18] *Reg.* 5.21, p. 384/27–9.

[19] Huygens, 'Bérenger', p. 388/4–9.

based his teaching on good written tradition. Berengar said that Gregory recalled discussions at Rome in Peter Damiani's lifetime, when Peter with Gregory's support had disagreed with Lanfranc of Canterbury's pronouncements about the eucharist —an apparent but not a certain reference to Lanfranc's *De corpore et sanguine Domini*.

Berengar commented that Gregory seemed by his address to have quietened the folly of those who deemed him a heretic. He claimed that Gregory did this the more effectively because, before the All Saintstide meeting, he canvassed widely among the regular and secular clergy of all grades a catena of excerpts from Augustine, Jerome, Ambrose, and other fathers of the church. No doubt it was the same as, or similar to, the patristic anthology that he had brought to Tours in 1054.[20] Berengar gave names of those who went along with his own view of the eucharist ('mecum sentientes') as drawn from these passages: Bishop John of Porto, Bishop Bruno of Segni, Bishop Ambrose of Terracina, Cardinal Atto of Milan, Cardinal Deusdedit, Peter the papal chancellor, the French clerk Fulco, the learned Tethbaldus, a monk named Bonadies, and many others. It should be observed that Berengar did not claim that either Gregory or these associates fully assented to his teachings or that there was an identity, as opposed to a compatibility, of view. Rather, in the light of the newly-prepared profession, they regarded Berengar's teachings as being intrinsically acceptable when set against the background of early Christian authorities.

According to the memoir, at the end of the assembly Gregory offered to have Berengar confirm his profession by an oath to be taken in its hearing. If the assembly wished, the oath might be supported by an ordeal of hot iron, presumably to establish his sincerity in taking it, which would be undergone by a member of his circle of supporters. But on the evening before the ordeal was to take place, Abbot Desiderius of Montecassino unexpectedly visited Berengar to tell him that Gregory had cancelled both the oath and the ordeal. According to Berengar, Gregory's volte-face was the result of an intervention by hostile persons who urged the necessity of a more public ventilation of the eucharistic controversy in the Lent synod of 1079. Berengar heaped blame and vituperation upon Bishops Ulrich of Padua and Landulf of Pisa.[21]

For events at the Lent synod which opened on 11 February, Berengar's memoir must be set against the perfervidly anti-Berengarian record in Gregory's Register.[22] It opens with a reference to a sermon on the body and blood of Christ; the preacher is not named. When it was delivered, most of those present were said to have held, with full warrant from the Greek and Latin fathers, that the bread and wine in the eucharist were changed *substantialiter* into Christ's body and blood, while others blindly advanced a figurative view. The summary of the Berengarian view is partly

[20] See above, 2.1. The patristic material most valued by Gregory is illustrated by his citations of Ambrose, Gregory the Great, and John Chrysostom in his advice on frequent communion to Countess Matilda of Tuscany: *Reg.* 1.47, 16 Feb. 1074, pp. 72–3. Gregory may have taken the citations from his anthology.

[21] For these events, see Huygens, 'Bérenger', pp. 388–93.

[22] *Reg.* 6.17a, pp. 425–7; cf. *LP* 1.285–6.

erased and manifestly incomplete.[23] The words erased suggest that the scribe was making a garbled attempt to record Berengar's view that, to safeguard the doctrine of the resurrection, the real presence of Christ's risen body was to be located in one place at the Father's right hand in heaven; it could not be dispersed in innumerable scattered fragments upon earthly altars.[24]

Next, now offering a clearer sequence of events, the official record stated that, when Berengar's case began to be dealt with and before the council assembled for its third session (13 February), the Berengarian party 'ceased to strive against the truth'. The reason given was a sudden and dramatic manifestation of the Holy Spirit.[25] This was unexplained, but it suggests some such miraculous vindication of the anti-Berengarian party as was later the subject of discussion, perhaps a sign at an early-morning mass that the adverb *substantialiter* must be adopted.[26] Whatever happened, Berengar, 'huius erroris magister', now confessed his long-standing fault, and asked and received a papal pardon. He made a profession embodying the word *substantialiter* and expressing the view of the eucharist that had been so dramatically vindicated.[27] In conclusion, Gregory charged Berengar not to teach or dispute with anyone about the body and blood of Christ, unless it were to recall to true belief those whom his teachings had led astray.

Not surprisingly, Berengar's memoir presents a different picture. It makes no reference to debate during the Lent synod. Having described the intervention, and the subsequent ill fates, of the bishops of Padua and Pisa, Berengar retailed how Gregory sank so low ('usque eo . . . deiectus est') as to permit the profession of faith prepared for All Saintstide 1078 to be expanded into that of 1079 with its inclusion of the adverb *substantialiter*.[28] On Gregory's behalf, Bishop Landulf of Pisa brought the revised profession to Berengar. He still hoped to equivocate, and set out his position at length. In this hope, he read and accepted the new profession upon oath. His enemies proceeded to try and wrest from him a declaration that he shared their interpretation of it. He silenced them by an oblique allusion to a recent interview with Gregory: he said that the pope had summoned him and, in the presence of Bishop John of Porto, had assured him that not only was he himself confident that Berengar's teaching was compatible with Christian tradition but he had sought and received confirmation

---

[23] 'Quidam vero cecitate nimia et longa perculsi figura tantum se et alios decipientes quibusdam cavillationibus conabantur astruere.' After *tantum*, the words 'quae substantiale illud corpus in dextera patris sedens esse' are erased.

[24] See Berengar, *Purgatoria epistola contra Almannum*, in Montclos, *Lanfranc et Bérenger*, pp. 530–5, esp. 530/6–8, 534/76–80; *Briefe Berengars*, no. 87, pp. 151/31–152/3.

[25] 'Nempe sancti Spiritus ignis emolumenta palearum consumens et fulgore suo falsam lucem diverberando obtenebrans noctis caliginem vertit in lucem.'

[26] Peter the Deacon much later retailed a story of Theodemarius, a Cassinese monk, who at a time not stated said mass and at the consecration saw the bread become flesh; when Gregory was told, he rejoiced and compelled Berengar and his followers to renounce their heresy: *Ortus et vita*, cap. 48, pp. 71–2. A source hostile to Gregory wrote of his failure to procure such a miracle, perhaps with the intention of defeating a tradition that one had occurred: Beno, 1.4, *MGH L. de L.* 2.370–1.

[27] *Reg.* 6.17a, pp. 426/15–427/19, cf. 3.17a, p. 281.

[28] For a comparison of texts, see Montclos, *Lanfranc et Bérenger*, p. 231.

that this was so through a vision of the Blessed Virgin to one of his *familiares*. Berengar thought that he had thus escaped, but Gregory again disappointed him by a volte-face. He made the unprecedented demand that Berengar should prostrate himself and confess that he had hitherto been in error by not adding the word *substantialiter* to his assertion that the consecrated bread and wine were the body and blood of Christ. By an admission that Berengar retrospectively condemned as sacrilegious, he confessed his error. He pleaded in mitigation that he had done so not only from fear of death but also because he had in mind an episode at a time unspecified, when Abbot Desiderius of Montecassino and a Cassinese monk Petrus Neapolitanus, whom he greatly respected, had intimated to him Gregory's own wish that he should retreat for Gregory's lifetime to a place of quasi-imprisonment; then Gregory might be freed from the allegation that he himself went along with Berengar's reading of traditional Christian texts and from the need to vindicate his own right belief.[29]

What, then, is to be concluded about Gregory's approach to the Berengarian problem? He manifestly adopted a more tentative and even sympathetic approach to Berengar than did his papal predecessors from Leo IX to Alexander II. This moderation is understandable in one who was brought up, as they were not, in Rome with its caution and conservatism in liturgical and dogmatic matters. There is no suggestion that anyone in Rome understood Christ's words of institution in any but a literal sense. But the Christian tradition as the young Hildebrand gathered it together in 1054, or as Pope Gregory canvassed it before All Saintstide 1078, provided only a catena of New Testament and patristic passages that had never been ordered or synthesized in an agreed and satisfactory formula embodying realist and excluding figurative language. Gregory seems to have for long acted towards Berengar much as he did in other liturgical and sacramental matters: not by trying to establish and impose a single ruling but by exploring which varieties of usage were and were not acceptable in the light of traditional authorities. His guiding principle seems to have been that which he formulated in 1075 about practices relating to ordination; 'The holy and apostolic see is accustomed to tolerate many things once their warrant has been considered, but never to depart from the concord of canonical tradition in its decrees and constitutions.'[30] Up to the Lent synod of 1079, he was at all times concerned to examine sympathetically whether Berengar's view of the eucharist, however unfamiliar and imperfect, could be deemed intrinsically acceptable in the light of biblical and patristic authorities. Up to this time, Gregory did not abandon the hope that, even though Berengar's opinions differed from his own and from those generally current, and even though they were more like milk for babes than meat for grown men, they might still be within the limits that Christian tradition established. For his part, Berengar no doubt made too much of Gregory's preparedness, especially during the winter of 1078–9, to hear him with sympathy and to incline towards his views. But Berengar's exaggeration was part of the price of Gregory's long and

---

[29] For these events according to the memoir, see Huygens, 'Bérenger', pp. 393–403.
[30] *Reg.* 2.50, to King Sancho I of Aragon, 24 Jan. 1075, p. 191/24–6.

patient search for agreement. Another part of the price was Gregory's exposure, after his second excommunication of Henry IV of Germany in 1080, to the unjust claim of his imperialist enemies that he himself was a Berengarian.[31]

The most difficult question of all about Gregory's attitude to Berengar remains to be put: why, during his Lent synod of 1079, did he shift his ground so drastically, cease to hesitate, insist upon the past error of Berengar's eucharistic doctrine, and demand that he accept the adverb *substantialiter*? The meagre evidence makes it impossible to do more than pose a hypothesis. It is that, for the first time in conciliar proceedings about Berengar in which Hildebrand/Gregory was directly involved, at the Roman synod of Lent 1079 the soteriological aspect of the Berengarian controversy was a central issue. It may have brought home to Gregory some implications of Berengar's teaching that he had not hitherto appreciated.

A novel feature of the profession that Berengar was compelled to make in 1079, besides the word *substantialiter*, was the introduction of vocabulary expressing Christ's redemptive work, both in general and in the sacrament: 'verba nostri Redemptoris, vivificatricem carnem, pro salute mundi oblatam'. It is surprising that this development had been for so long delayed; Berengar had often argued that his figurative interpretation of the eucharist was necessary in order to safeguard the effectiveness of Christ's redemptive work. He had done so on the grounds that, as St Augustine had taught, after Christ became obedient to death upon the Cross his body was raised to immortality and impassibility at the Father's side. Christ's risen body could not suffer the fragmentation upon earthly altars that a realist interpretation of the eucharist required; if it did, the heavenly integrity of Christ's body upon which the Christian hope of salvation depended would be destroyed.[32]

Upon the garbled evidence of Gregory's Register, such an argument seems to have been part of the Berengarian statement at the Lent synod of 1079.[33] It may be suspected that, in Gregory's eyes as in those of most present, neither dialectic nor traditional texts destroyed Berengar but the threat that he was seen to present to human salvation. The Lent synod of 1079 may have been the occasion when, with the confirmation of whatever miracle its official record in Gregory's Register may hint at, the connection between the unqualified reality of Christ's presence in the eucharist and the hope of human salvation was officially recognized and expressed in the widely circulated profession that Berengar was compelled to make. Not least as it was borne in upon Gregory's own mind, it may have been decisive in bringing about an absolute condemnation of Berengar's teaching. Berengar returned to Tours, having acquired for himself letters of safe-conduct and protection in Gregory's name

---

[31] Decree of the synod of Brixen, in *Quellen HIV* p. 480/19–21; letter of Egilbert, bishop-elect of Trier (June 1080), *CU* no. 61, p. 128/23–7.

[32] For Berengar's argument on this matter, see esp. his *Purgatoria epistola contra Almannum*, in Montclos, *Lanfranc et Bérenger*, pp. 531–5, esp. p. 534/76–80; his memoir, Huygens, 'Bérenger', pp. 398/223–399/250; and his *Rescriptum contra Lanfrannum*, 2.2708–94, 3035–81, 3.740–65, pp. 175–7, 184–5, 210–11.

[33] See above, n. 23.

in which the pope was made to describe him as 'filius noster karissimus Berengarius sacerdos' and as 'Romanae ecclesiae filius'.[34]

Gregory's long dealings with Berengar illustrates the gradual and sometimes painful development of his thought and action, especially when a dogmatic issue was involved. The resolution of such issues was not his *métier*; while there is no doubt of his profound respect for biblical and traditional authority, the concern to foster concord which characterized many of his dealings made him ready and anxious to hear and make all possible concessions to differing approaches. When the time for decision came, dialectic and ancient authorities were of far less weight than current pastoral and religious needs; a miraculous disclosure of God's will was, more than anything else, the immediate basis for decision. Once God's will was manifest, Gregory was steeled for firm and drastic action. But the long process by which his thinking developed was perplexing to his friends, and it gave his enemies an opportunity to question the rightness of his belief to the point of accusing him of heresy.

8.1.2 The *Dictatus papae*

That much of Gregory's thinking was exploratory and developing, rather than established and decided, is also to a surprising extent confirmed by the twenty-seven theses about papal authority which are inserted into Gregory's Register between documents dated 3 and 5 March 1075.[35] They are generally referred to as the *Dictatus papae*, 'the dictation of the pope', although the title, which is decorated by flourishes with the pen which are rare in this workaday manuscript and which is in a slightly later scribal hand, is shared with four letters in the early part of the Register.[36] Since the *Dictatus papae* has a place in what is almost certainly the original register of the papal chancery, its authenticity as a document emanating from, and almost certainly drafted by, Gregory himself cannot be seriously questioned. Yet, given the importance of the theses proposed and the forthrightness with which they are expressed, it is puzzling that they should have remained largely unused and unnoticed in subsequent years both by Gregory and by his friends and foes. They were in no sense published, even though the Lent synod which ended on 28 February would have provided a forum for their proclamation and discussion. They left little mark on future letters of Gregory, whether registered or not; where allusions to them may be suspected, there was a tendency to tone them down and to adhere more

---

34 *Epp. vag.* nos. 72–3, pp. 156–7. For Berengar's subsequent fortunes and activities in relation to the papacy, see Cowdrey, 'The Papacy and the Berengarian Controversy', pp. 136–8.

35 *Reg.* 2.55a, pp. 201–8. In this section, I owe a great debt to Fuhrmann, '*Quod catholicus non habeatur*' and 'Papst Gregor VII. und das Kirchenrecht', and to R. Schieffer, 'Rechtstexte des Reformpapsttums'. I have not accepted as evidence for Gregory VII's ideas the so-called '*Dictatus* of Avranches': Mordek, '*Proprie auctoritates apostolice sedis*', and Wojtowytsch, 'Proprie auctoritates apostolice sedis'; the reasons for regarding it as having been formulated after 1085 as given by Kempf, 'Ein zweiter *Dictatus papae* Gregors VII.?' are compelling.

36 *Reg.* 1.47, to Countess Matilda of Tuscany, 16 Feb. 1074, p. 71; 2.31, to King Henry IV of Germany, 7 Dec. 1074, p. 165; 2.37, to all the faithful of St Peter, 16 Dec. 1074, p. 173; 2.43, to Bishop Hugh of Die, 5 Jan. 1075, p. 180.

closely to biblical or canonical precedents.[37] Popes from Victor III to Innocent II in their letters and official documents provide only occasional parallels with them; when they do, the succinctness and challenge of their wording are reduced.[38] No chronicle or similar source refers to the *Dictatus papae*. In the polemical literature of Gregory's lifetime and after, very few echoes or allusions can be found. This is particularly surprising in the writings of Gregory's opponents such as Beno and the cardinals who defected in 1084, since Gregory's uncompromising claims for his authority would have provided them with excellent targets for criticism.[39] Another surprising fact is the rarity with which the *Dictatus papae* was cited in eleventh- and twelfth-century canon-law collections. Deusdedit, Anselm of Lucca, Ivo of Chartres, and Gratian were among those who passed it by completely. It was included at length in two collections, both of south-western French origin: the *Liber Tarraconensis* (1085/90), and the *Collection in Seven Books* (c.1100).[40] Throughout canonical literature, citation of, or even reference to, particular theses does not occur. Both in the papal entourage and in the church at large, the *Dictatus papae* attracted little notice. The possibility must be reckoned with that it was never intended by Gregory to do so.

A clue to its origins may be provided by Cardinal Peter Damiani's letter of 1059 to Archdeacon Hildebrand, as Gregory then was, about Milanese affairs. Peter remarked that Hildebrand had often asked him to work through the decrees and official deliverances of the Roman popes and diligently abstract whatever seemed to be particularly relevant to the authority of the apostolic see ('quicquid apostolicae sedis auctoritati spetialiter competere videretur'); he should assemble it in a small book which was systematically arranged ('nova compilationis arte').[41] The *Dictatus papae*, all of whose theses refer to the authority of the apostolic see, seems to be related to this desire. So far as is known, neither Peter Damiani or anyone else responded before 1075 to Hildebrand's request. The *Dictatus papae* reads like Gregory's own attempt to sketch out headings under which ancient material might be sought, assessed, and arranged. In a sense, Gregory's lifelong quest to establish the prerogatives of the apostolic see was a reverse counterpart to his quest for authorities in respect of Berengar's eucharistic teaching. In Berengar's case, he early furnished himself with an apparatus of ancient texts on the basis of which he sought a conclusion that he found only in 1079. The *Dictatus papae* suggests that he had in his mind a series of trenchant yet only provisionally formulated theses about papal prerogatives which he was concerned to warrant, and if necessary to modify, when he had been presented

---

[37] One may compare e.g. the treatment of the indefectibility of the Roman church, in the light of Luke 22: 32, in *Dictatus papae* 22 with that in *Reg.* 8.1, to Archbishop Gregory of Tsamandos, 6 June 1080, p. 513/10–14.

[38] For examples, see Fuhrmann, '*Quod catholicus non habeatur*', p. 286 n. 74.

[39] The indexes to the three volumes of *MGH L. de L.* contain no references to the *Dictatus papae* as a whole or in detail.

[40] For the MSS concerned, see Gilchrist, 'The Reception of Pope Gregory VII', pp. 44–5, 56–7, 199–200. The influence of Bishop Amatus of Oloron may be suspected but cannot be established.

[41] *Briefe*, no. 65, 2.229/10–15.

with the relevant ancient texts. If this is so, Gregory's letter to Bishop Hermann of Metz in March 1081 represented a major step forward in the process which superseded the *Dictatus papae*.[42] Based much more firmly on ancient precedents and texts, it presented a more nuanced and rounded picture of papal authority. Unlike the *Dictatus papae*, it achieved a wide circulation and was regarded as authoritative by papalist writers and canonists into the twelfth century. The *Dictatus papae* is of the utmost importance as illustrating a stage in the development of Gregory's mind; it must not be interpreted as expressing his characteristic and final position, which must be sought in the letters of his last years as pope.

The tentativeness that lies behind the apparent assurance of the *Dictatus papae* is apparent from a number of the theses as formulated in it. In the case of so fundamental a proposition as *Dictatus papae* 1, 'That the Roman church is the foundation of the Lord alone', it is remarkable that, in his letters and pronouncements, Gregory made little reference to this claim. In other theses, Gregory seems to have been exploring claims which, as he drafted them, it would have been hard to substantiate from the canonical tradition. This is conspicuously the case with the most radical of all the theses put forward, that it was licit for the pope to depose emperors (*Dictatus papae* 12). Gregory seems to have been able to adduce only the formal and generalized sanction-clauses at the end of letters of Pope Gregory the Great.[43] Others were also insecure so far as the availability of express warrant was concerned. *Dictatus papae* 2, that only the Roman pontiff is rightly called 'universalis', in applying the epithet to the pope himself went beyond Pope Leo IX's edict at the council of Rheims in 1049 that only the bishop of the Roman see should be called 'primas' and 'apostolicus' of the universal church; no regard was paid to the strong and express deprecation by Pope Gregory I of the title 'universalis' as used of the pope.[44] *Dictatus papae* 11 that 'this name', that of pope, is unique in the world, overlooked the use of the title up to the eighth century for many others than the bishop of Rome.[45] Despite the support that was claimed, *Dictatus papae* 23, that a canonically elected pope is undoubtedly made holy by the merits of St Peter, could not be given traditional warrant in the sweeping terms in which it is formulated. The claim of *Dictatus papae* 5, that the pope can depose persons in their absence, could find exceptional justification in the case of Dioscorus at the council of Chalcedon, but as a general rule it fitted uneasily with Gregory's habitual carefulness to ensure the presence of the accused to hear the case against them.[46] *Dictatus papae* 24, that by papal command and licence

---

[42] *Reg.* 8.21, 15 Mar. 1081, pp. 544–63. For its dissemination, see *Reg.* pp. 544–6 and, in canon-law texts, Gilchrist, 'The Reception of Pope Gregory VII'.

[43] Cf. *Reg.* 4.2 to Bishop Hermann of Metz, 25 Aug. 1076, p. 294/16–19; 8.32 to Bishop Hermann of Metz, 15 Mar. 1081, p. 550/8–18.

[44] Anselm of Saint-Remy, *Histoire*, cap. 27, p. 240; *Reg. Greg. I*, 8.29, vol. 2.552/56–553/2. Cf. *Diversorum patrum sententie*, cap. 24: 'Ne universalis quisquam vocetur'; ed. Gilchrist, pp. 114–15.

[45] See Niermeyer, *Mediae Latinitatis Lexicon Minus*, s.v. *papa*.

[46] For Dioscorus, see above, 7.2. For Gregory and the presence of the accused, see e.g. *Reg.* 1.63, to King Sancho I of Aragon, 20 Mar. 1074, p. 91/17–24; 2.4, to Archbishop Gozelin of Bordeaux, 10 Sept. 1074, p. 129/2–19; 3.16, to Archbishop Richer of Sens, Apr. 1076, p. 278/16–22; 5.17, memorandum on French affairs, 9 Mar. 1078, p. 380/14–27; 9.19, to Archbishop Hugh of Lyons, (1082–3) p. 599/25–33.

subjects might accuse their superiors, was also difficult to support from older material. In such respects, the *Dictatus papae* went beyond positions which were adopted in the 1070s by those even among Gregory's supporters who were versed in canon law; the difference between the collection known as the *Diversorum patrum sententie* and the *Dictatus papae* is especially instructive.[47] Perhaps most important of all in rendering the *Dictatus papae* unsuitable for long-term use as it stood as a basis for the claims of the *sacerdotium* was a tendency throughout to sharpen the point of the theses advanced to an extent that made them vulnerable to criticism. They were also too stark and uncompromising to suit Gregory's own sense of the need for circumspection and for the tempering of extremes in order to suit papal claims to the realities of actual situations. It is not surprising that Gregory himself did not run the risk of building on them and that they were brought but seldom to the attention of friend and foe.

Neither is it surprising that attempts to postulate a specific *raison d'être* or historical context for the *Dictatus papae* have been inconclusive. Broadly speaking, such attempts have explored three possibilities. First, it might have been either a table of contents for a planned but not completed canonical collection about the papal primacy, or else an index for such a collection which was made but which has been lost.[48] The case for such a hypothesis is that Gregory is known from the letter to him of 1059 from Peter Damiani to have desired such a collection; that there is a similarity of form and expression between the *Dictatus papae* and the chapter headings of such canonical collections as those of Deusdedit and Anselm of Lucca; and that express reference to supporting canonical authorities is made in *Dictatus papae* 23. Arguments against are that most of the clauses read like free-standing attempts to define papal prerogatives; that the deliberate sharpening of the point of many clauses in the light of Gregory's own vision of papal authority tends to set them at a distance from possibly supporting canonical material rather than to invite its being collected around them; and that the *Dictatus papae* lacks order and arrangement, both overall and in an individual clause such as *Dictatus papae* 7, where four large and disparate items are lumped together in a way that would make the orderly presentation of canonical material difficult.

Second, it has been argued that the *Dictatus papae* was formulated as the agenda for negotiations about reunion between the Greek and Latin churches.[49] In favour of this, Gregory was concerned with such union during the early years of his pontificate, and the disappointment of his hopes by the beginning of 1075 may have led him at that time to reflect radically upon papal prerogatives in relation to

---

[47] Cf. *Diversorum patrum sententie*, caps. 7, 9, and *Dictatus papae* 24, cap. 13 and *Dictatus papae* 5, and cap. 24 and *Dictatus papae* 2. For the *Diversorum patrum sententia*, see above, 3.4.2.

[48] For the former view, see esp. K. Hoffmann, *Der* Dictatus papae *Gregors VII.*, esp. pp. 13–18; for the latter, Borino, 'Un ipotesi sul "Dictatus papae"'.

[49] This was strongly argued by Gauss, 'Die Dictatus-Thesen' and eadem, *Ost und West*, esp. pp. 57–67; for the supposed concern of the *Dictatus papae* with eastern matters, see also Koebner, 'Der Dictatus papae'.

Byzantine affairs.[50] In any case, a substantial number of the clauses of the *Dictatus papae* may seem relevant to relations between the papacy and the Byzantine church and empire. Yet at no stage of his dealings with Byzantium did Gregory place such emphasis upon the prerogatives of the Roman church as he laid throughout the *Dictatus papae*. When he excommunicated the Emperor Nicephorus III Botaniates who was in his eyes a usurper, there was no hint of a sentence of deposition by the pope. In fact, Gregory's approach to Byzantium was always in terms of concord rather than confrontation, so that any such emphasis upon papal prerogatives as contained in the *Dictatus papae* would have been inappropriate for his purpose. Both past relations between east and west as recorded by history and the canonical tradition, and also current dealings with Byzantium, may have coloured the formulation of some clauses of the *Dictatus papae*, but there is no reason to ascribe to Byzantine affairs a central significance in determining its origin and character.

Third, the *Dictatus papae* has been regarded as having specifically been directed towards Gregory's Lent synod of 1075, perhaps as the basis for a papal allocution; Gregory may have intended to set out in it the prerogatives of the apostolic see in relation to the churches and lay rulers of east and west, with a view to promoting decrees which would implement them.[51] But despite attempts to discern an underlying plan in the *Dictatus papae*, it is too formless a document for it to be readily envisaged as the basis of an address. Nor did it allude to what seem to have been the most pressing matters at the synod, such as free elections, simony, and clerical fornication. Above all, its juridical character does not conform to what is known of Gregory's allocutions on such occasions, which were sermon-like, with references to the Bible rather than to canonist tradition, and which were fervent and hortatory in tone.[52] Nothing in the form or the content of the *Dictatus papae* would seem to suit the spoken word as Gregory used it.

If any context suits the *Dictatus papae*, it is Gregory's expectation in the early months of 1075 that an amenable and obedient Henry IV of Germany might soon come to Rome and receive the imperial coronation that he had so long desired.[53] Such a visit to the apostolic see would have given Gregory the opportunity to require as a *quid pro quo* for coronation a recognition by both Henry and the German church of the prerogatives of the Roman church as Gregory understood them. It would have resolved the problems that had existed between Gregory and the German church and kingdom ever since his accession to the papacy. On the one hand, Gregory could have instructed Henry in the place of the imperial dignity in relation to papal authority and have provided sanctions against Henry's relapsing into the sins and offences of his youth; on the other, he could have impressed upon the German church his own concept of papal authority as opposed to that which Archbishop

---

[50] See above, 7.1.   [51] Koebner, 'Der Dictatus papae', esp. pp. 66–9, 88–92.

[52] Such allocutions are best illustrated by Gregory's sentence against Henry IV in 1076 and 1080: *Reg.* 3.10*a*, pp. 270–1; 7.14*a*, pp. 483–7; and his allocution in praise of Cluny in 1080: *Epp. vag.* no. 39, pp. 96–9. Allocutions by Gregory sometimes seem to lie behind decrees of his synods, e.g. his decree of 1080 on false and true penances: *Reg.* 7.14*a*(5), pp. 481–2: see below, 8.1.3.

[53] See above, 3.2.4.

Siegfried of Mainz and other metropolitans had been propounding.[54] Acceptance of such provisions as the *Dictatus papae* enshrined might have been made the condition for Henry's imperial coronation. There is much in the *Dictatus papae* which is consonant with such a hypothesis. As regards the place of an emperor, the papal claim to depose emperors, which was suddenly advanced and which Gregory showed no sign of directing towards Byzantium, would have sounded a warning against evil conduct to Henry. *Dictatus papae* 8, that only the pope might use imperial insignia, would have been a timely reminder of the superiority of the *sacerdotium* at the very highest level of human society, as would *Dictatus papae* 9, that all princes must kiss the feet of the pope and his alone. With regard to the possibility of Henry's lapsing into his old ways, the incompletely drafted *Dictatus papae* 6, 'Quod cum excommunicatis ab illo inter caetera nec in eadem domo debemus manere', reads like a reminder of Henry's own persistent associating with his excommunicated counsellors; the unique departure into the first person plural ('debemus') may suggest an intention of requiring some kind of adherence to the substance of the *Dictatus papae* by Henry's entourage. *Dictatus papae* 27, that the pope can release from their fealty the subjects of wicked men, was a reminder of the sanctions of which he disposed against a ruler who persisted in disobedience. As for the German church, a long list of clauses can be assembled which may have been intended to refute claims for it such as were entertained by Siegfried of Mainz during the past three years.[55]

The relevance of much of the *Dictatus papae* to Henry's coming to Rome for imperial coronation is sufficient to warrant the suggestion that it may have been in Gregory's mind during its formulation, and the failure of any such visit to take place may help to explain why the *Dictatus papae* was not further developed or used. But a number of clauses have little or nothing to do with this contingency,[56] and the document as a whole does not read as if it was exclusively directed towards it.

The conclusion must be that the *Dictatus papae* remains an enigma so far as the circumstances of its compilation are concerned. Despite the forthrightness of its language, it is too exploratory in character and too loosely attached to past traditions and to contemporary received opinions, even Gregory's own, for it to provide a considered, final, and definite statement of Gregory's conception of papal authority. Yet the fact of its inclusion in the Register invests it with a significance greater than would attach to a mere personal memorandum. It renders it a testimony to one stage of the continuing process whereby Gregory sought to establish the prerogatives and *modus operandi* of the papal office. Neither too much nor too little should be claimed for it.

8.1.3 Gregory VII's Roman Synods of 1078–80

Whereas the Berengarian controversy and the *Dictatus papae* have for long attracted historians' attention as key topics for the study of Gregory's aims and methods, less attention had been paid to his Lent and November synods at the Lateran. Yet it may

---

[54] See above, 3.2.5. [55] Esp. caps. 3–5, 7, 13–14, 16, 18, 20–1, 24–5.
[56] Esp. caps. 1–2, 10–11, 15, 17–18, 22–3, 26.

be argued that, more than the *Dictatus papae*, their records declare Gregory's aspirations for the church through the exercise of papal authority whilst also demonstrating his most urgent concerns in seeking the renovation of the church in head and members. More than any other single source, they show the heart of Gregory's conception of the papacy, not least because they show the papal office in action. They also further demonstrate that Gregory's concern with and understanding of current problems were subject to continual growth, development, and change.

His best-attested synods so far as the general well-being of the church is concerned were those held between his return to Rome after his North Italian travels in 1077 and his final breach with Henry IV of Germany in 1080. The records suggest that, in these central years of his pontificate, he sought what might be called the overall moral rearmament of Latin Christendom. Now above all he sought to realize the aim that he expressed in his last encyclical: 'My greatest aim has been that holy church, the bride of Christ, our lady and mother, should return to her true glory and stand free, chaste, and catholic.'[57] It was not that, in 1078–9, Gregory acted upon a formulated and balanced programme of renovation; rather, he gathered together, augmented, and intensified what had, for the most part, already been matters of concern during his early years. Thus, he aspired to implement what he saw as the principal demands, both spiritual and moral, of the Christian religion in the age during which he lived.

The November synod of 1078 stands out as the first occasion upon which Gregory reinforced his customary Lent synod by a second in the autumn.[58] He did this partly in response to political developments—the seizure of power in Byzantium by the Emperor Nicephorus III Botaniates and, in the west, Henry IV of Germany's military advantage after the battle of Mellrichstadt and Gregory's need thereafter to secure oaths from representatives of Henry and of Rudolf of Swabia that they would not impede Gregory's planned assembly in the German kingdom. But in the official record in Gregory's Register, the purpose of the synod was recorded in terms that were unprecedentedly comprehensive: it was summoned 'for the renewal (*pro restauratione*)' and 'for the benefit (*ad utilitatem*) of holy church'. This purpose was reinforced in the record of the Lent synod of 1079, which was convened 'for the honour of God and for the building up (*hedificationem*) of holy church, and for the well-being (*salutem*) of men in body and soul';[59] the breadth and coherence of purpose stands in contrast to the piecemeal and restricted objective which was ascribed to the Lent synods of 1078 and 1080, 'in which Gregory, confirming apostolic decrees, corrected many things that needed correction and confirmed those that needed confirmation.'[60] In November 1078, Gregory seems to have intended a renewal of the Christian religion in Latin Christendom which had no parallel since Nicholas II's synod of 1059, with his encyclical *Vigilantia universalis*.

---

57 *Epp. vag.* no. 54, pp. 132–3.
58 For the official record, see *Reg.* 6.5*b*, pp. 400–6. In the rest of this section, the abbreviation *cap.* indicates the *capitula* of Gregory's synods and *decr.* the *decreta*.
59 *Reg.* 6.17*a*, p. 425/19–21.   60 *Reg.* 5.14*a*, p. 368/39–41; 7.14*a*, p. 480/9–11.

In the Register, the business of the November council of 1078 was recorded with exceptional fullness, especially when it is borne in mind that the records of Gregory's synods were always far from complete. Thirty-three *capitula* of items of business discussed were listed, followed by thirteen *decreta* which embodied pronouncements which were made at the end of the proceedings with the authority of the pope and of the synod. The *decreta* were circulated and recorded with exceptional completeness and publicity. The Swabian annalist Berthold of Reichenau copied them in their entirety in his long and approving account of the synod.[61] In canon-law collections far into the twelfth century, they were accorded a notice which far exceeded any other record of Gregory's pontificate, so that they represent Gregory's major contribution to the medieval canon law.[62] Gregory himself propagated the measures of his synods against clerical fornication in a letter which he circulated widely in Germany and Italy; in it, besides proscribing the acceptance of the ministrations of unchaste clergy, Gregory strongly enjoyed obedience to papal precepts.[63] Not only was the business of the November synod of 1078 exceptionally comprehensive, but its *decreta* circulated widely and attracted notice and record.

Several of the *decreta* appear to bear traces of Gregory's justification of them during synodal proceedings. In some cases, this was by way of biblical or ecclesiastical warrant: the condemnation of simoniacal ordinations was brought home by citing Christ's statement that those who do not enter by the door are thieves and robbers (John 10: 1) (*decr.* 5); and the requirement that Christians should bring appropriate offerings to mass was supported by God's word through Moses, 'No one shall appear in my sight empty' (Exod. 23: 15) as well as by good ecclesiastical tradition (*decr.* 13). Alternatively, decrees were reinforced by the statement of an underlying moral principle, as when episcopal simony was condemned on the grounds that, as a bishop received the episcopate freely, so he should freely confer subordinate offices (*decr.* 4), while the lay appropriation of tithes was castigated as an example of the sin of sacrilege which leads to eternal damnation (*decr.* 7).

It would be misleading to reduce to a system or programme the business of the November synod of 1078; yet it is sufficiently wide-ranging to allow it to be set out in a way which indicates Gregory's principal concerns at this stage of his pontificate. In some respects Gregory urgently renewed the concerns of his early years as pope. This is above all true of his campaign against simony and clerical fornication. So far as simony is concerned, Gregory now extended his campaign to proscribe all the forms of it that Pope Gregory the Great had set forth. Addressing primarily the bishops, he imposed suspension from their office upon those who sold ecclesiastical offices, such as prebends, archdeaconries, and provostships, within their dioceses; while ordinations that were in any way simoniacal—Gregory followed Gregory the Great by for the first time in his pontificate specifying not only those in which money passed but also those which were conferred in return for favours or services

[61] Berthold, *Ann. a.* 1078, pp. 314–15.
[62] For details, see Gilchrist, 'The Reception of Gregory VII', esp. pp. 70–1, 223–4.
[63] *Epp. vag.* no. 32, pp. 84–7, cf. Berthold, *Ann. a.* 1079, p. 317/36–41.

(*decr.* 5)[64]—or that were uncanonical, in the sense that they infringed the right of free election by clergy and people followed by the approval of the rightful consecrator, were declared invalid (caps. 9, 11, *decr.* 4,5). Gregory's insistence upon clerical chastity was also related to a bishop's duty of vigilance: any bishop who tolerated fornication or incest among his clergy was to be suspended (caps. 12, 28, *decr.* 12).

Gregory insisted strongly upon the responsibility of the bishops in their diocese for the pastoral and material well-being of the church. They were warned against false ordinations (cap. 13). At least in the case of dioceses immediately subject to Rome, he insisted upon the proper liturgical commemoration of past popes (cap. 20).[65] As a means of raising clerical standards and to facilitate the study of scripture and canonical sources, all bishops were to establish in their churches schools for instruction in the liberal arts (cap. 31). They were straitly charged to safeguard the landed and movable property of their churches (caps. 29–31), and they were to impose no burdensome or improper services upon monasteries (cap. 26, *decr.* 10). Abbots, for their part, were not to retain tithes and other dues (cap. 25, *decr.* 9). Both bishops and abbots were required to keep within the acknowledged bounds of order and discipline when dealing with priests and monks from outside their jurisdiction, while bishops were not arbitrarily to deal with penitents who came to them from other dioceses (caps. 24, 27). All this legislation amounted to an attempt in detail to impose proper order upon the church under papal authority. Gregory was particularly concerned to regulate points of jurisdiction and administration which gave rise to strife and recrimination, or which carried the danger of the loss of church property.

He was also anxious to restrain what he regarded as the excesses of lay intervention in church affairs. He took the major step of making the first general condemnation of lay investitures of which express record survives; he noted that they were widespread and productive of much disturbance in the church to the detriment of the Christian religion. He addressed his condemnation to the clergy: no clerk was to accept investiture of a bishopric, abbey, or church, from an emperor, king, or any person whether man or woman, on pain of the investiture being by papal authority invalid and of the clerk's himself being excommunicate (cap. 8, *decr.* 3). To further safeguard church property, Gregory addressed the laity directly, both by prohibiting the lay ownership of tithes (caps. 26, 32, *decr.* 7), and by seeking to secure from depredation church lands and especially those of St Peter (caps. 1, 7, 23, 32, *decr.* 1, 2, 11).

Another main concern was the religious and moral discipline of the laity. Gregory instituted a reform of false penances by requiring penance to be awarded according to the gravity of the offence and, when grave sin was committed by a layman, such as a knight, merchant, or official of a lord, whose avocation could not be followed without falling into sin, he must abstain from his avocation during his time of penance

---

[64] Gregory I, *Moralium libri*, 9.34, 53, *PL* 75.888–9, *XL Homiliarum in evangelia libri duo*, 1.4.4, *PL* 76.1091–2.
[65] Cf. *De sancti Hugonis actis liturgicis*, cap. 262, p. 221.

(caps. 14–15, *decr.* 6). Gregory legislated about fasting (cap. 21, *decr.* 8) and about the presentation of due offerings at mass (cap. 33, *decr.* 13), as well as about consanguinity as a bar to marriage (cap. 21). He also enacted that Jews should not be set in authority over Christians (cap. 22).

Such measures indicate Gregory's determination to proceed with renewed energy with the raising of everyday standards of Christian life, both in the dioceses directly subject to Rome and in the church at large.[66] He sought to exercise papal authority through a synod which itself took part in the process of legislation and which added a corporate sanction of its own. Gregory's method at a synod was less the proclamation of general principles of papal action than the identification of what he saw as specific instances of sin, abuse, irregularity, or maladministration, and to mobilize the bishops, in particular, to reorder the church in respect of them so that the level of the whole should be raised to what he saw as acceptable standards.

Between the November synod of 1078 and the Lent synod of 1080, Gregory took up a number of the matters about which he acted during the earlier synod and developed his position with regard to them. Three subjects in particular reveal how his thought and action were being shaped and developed as his pontificate progressed.

In the case of simony (*decr.* 5), Gregory was concerned to explain clearly to a wide public the broader approach that he had introduced. He chose the opportunity of his privilege for the see of Lyons, which he confirmed as the primatial see of Gallia Lugdunensis.[67] The middle section is an expansion of this decree. Gregory enlarged upon the threefold nature of simony to which he had referred in 1078 ('a manu', 'ab obsequio', 'a lingua'), and drew more fully on the writings about it of Pope Gregory the Great. He similarly expanded his condemnation of anyone who might come to the see of Lyons by the improper favour of the secular power—whether by way of its gift or even by its confirmation.[68] He repeated in a stronger form the sanction which the decree passed on those who entered not by the door but otherwise, as thieves and robbers. The primatial see of Lyons and its archbishop were to stand as exemplars in France of the free and morally purified state of the church which Gregory aspired to bring about.

Second, Gregory was at pains to develop his legislation against lay investiture as adumbrated in November 1078 (*decr.* 3). In 1078, he directed his sanction only against clerks who received investiture from lay hands; he said nothing about the laymen who conferred it. His legislation of March 1080 was both more stringently expressed and directed equally against the clerks and the laymen who were involved. In repeating his earlier condemnation of bishops, abbots, and other clerks, he now enlarged upon the moral offences of which they were guilty—not only the sin of ambition, but also the far graver reproach of disobedience which was tantamount to idolatry (1 Sam. 15: 23). Having spoken thus to clerks, he turned to laymen of all

---

[66] A distinction between sees directly subject to Rome and others is made in caps. 20, 30, and *decr.* 9.

[67] *Reg.* 6.34, 19 Apr. 1079, pp. 447–9; the section that follows *decr.* 5 of 1078 is p. 448/11–29.

[68] Gregory may have had in mind canon 22 of the fourth council of Constantinople: p. 448/17–21; see above, 3.2.4.

ranks from emperor downwards. The same penalties of deposition and forfeiture of
rank which applied to the clergy were visited upon laymen as well. Gregory expressly
branded their practice of investing clerks with their benefices as a derogation of the
proper liberty of the church ('ecclesiae propriam libertatem'), and he excluded
them from every blessing in body or spirit until they should have made proper
amends.[69]

Third, Gregory's decrees about false and true penances provide evidence that his
thinking and actions underwent profound change between 1078 and 1080, in a direction that was to settle the revision of penitential discipline in the west during the
next century.[70] His decree about penance in November 1078 was patently of a provisional nature. It began by defining false penances as those which were not imposed in
proportion to the gravity of the transgression according to the best authorities of the
past; Gregory clearly had in mind the tariffed penances as they had been settled over
past centuries. He ruled that anyone whose avocation in life could not be followed
without sin—he instanced knights, merchants, and officials, and who fell into grave
sin, could not do true penance unless he laid aside his avocation and followed the
counsel of religious men about his way of life; lest such a penitent fall into despair, he
should meanwhile perform good works so that God might enlighten his mind
regarding penitence (*decr.* 6). The decree was in major respects unsatisfactory: it
offered no definition of true penance; it did not deal with the problem of excessively
large penances which left no room for the amendment of other sins, which were
unduly burdensome for the penitent and his family, and which, therefore, were
admittedly liable to push men to despair.[71] It is clear that, during the next year,
Gregory was at pains to reconsider, not only how penance was being imposed, but
also the guidelines that should determine the church's penitential discipline. In
November 1079, he wrote to all the clergy and laity of Brittany about a synod that his
legate, Bishop Amatus of Oloron, was to hold there. A main concern was to be the
rectification of the lax practice regarding penances which he said that earlier popes—
no doubt he had particularly in mind his predecessors before 1046—had tolerated
through incompetence and negligence, so that false penances had abounded. His
injunctions to the Bretons read like the application of a fresh approach that was of
general applicability. He reiterated his rigorous ruling of the previous November
that those who fell into grave sin—he named homicide, adultery, and perjury, and
who continued to practise avocations which themselves could scarcely be followed
without sin, could not exhibit the fruit of true penance; they must lay them aside save

---

[69] *Reg.* 7.14a(1)(2), pp. 480–1.

[70] On the character of, and changes in, the medieval penitential system, see C. Vogel, *Le Pécheur et la
pénitence*, esp. pp. 15–36. The older works by Müller, 'Der Umschwung', and Anciaux, *La Théologie du
sacrement de pénitence*, esp. pp. 15–36, remain useful. For further discussion of Gregory and penance, see
Cowdrey, 'The Reform Papacy and the Origin of the Crusades', and id., 'Pope Gregory VII and the
Bearing of Arms'.

[71] For an example of a severe penance, see that which, at Gregory's behest, the Roman cardinals imposed in 1073 upon Peter Raymundi, son of Count Raymond Berengar I of Barcelona, for the murder of
his stepmother: Kehr, 'Das Papsttum und der katalanische Prinzipat', no. 7, pp. 80–1.

in so far as the counsel of religious men allowed them to continue.[72] But Gregory added two considerations of his own about penance: the reason for his ruling was that a penance was fruitless if a penitent continued in his fault or in another of comparable seriousness; and, more profoundly, if a man wished to perform proper penance, he must return to the foundation of faith in his baptismal promise, by renouncing the devil and his works and by believing in God and following his commandments.[73] Gregory was moving towards an insistence that account must be taken of all grave sins, and that outward penance must be accompanied by inner conversion of life.

At his Lent synod of 1080, Gregory established a new decree which went far to establishing these two points as the basis of future penitential discipline.[74] The decree reads as though it recapitulated an impassioned allocution on penance by Gregory himself. The decree now began with a statement of Christian teaching. All who sought salvation must shun false penances, for just as false baptism does not cleanse from original sin, so false penance does not cancel sins committed after baptism. Gregory turned to the true penance which a sinner must perform on the advice of religious men, if he would have a sure pardon of his sins. The mark of true penance was that a man who had sinned gravely should turn wholly to God; laying aside all his iniquities, he should continue steadfastly in the pursuit of good works. Gregory drove home the need for personal conversion and for the amendment of all of a man's sins by citing the word of the Lord by the prophet Ezekiel: 'If the ungodly shall turn from all his iniquities and keep every one of my commandments, he shall surely live and not die' (Ezek. 18: 21). Gregory interpreted his requirement that a man do penance for all his sins as requiring, as he had required in 1078, that he take full account of those arising from his avocation; but he insisted more strongly upon the need for recourse to wise and religious pastors, who could point out surely the way of truth and salvation. The peril of despair could be avoided by the seeking of informed guidance, which would take proper account of the fundamentals of the Christian life.

The effect of Gregory's reconsideration of penance between 1078 and 1080 was to give a new profundity and direction to thought and practice concerning it. He summoned clergy and laity alike to reflect upon the renewal of human life in baptism and upon the use of penance to maintain the integrity of one's baptismal state. He insisted on inner conversion. Avoiding the extremes of the excessive concentration upon a single moral offence to the neglect of others and of the light and careless evasion of true penitence by merely nominal penalties, he insisted on inner conversion and the balanced and complete turning from all sins which were to become the themes of twelfth-century thought about penance. The decrees of Gregory's Lateran synods during the middle years of his pontificate suggest how profoundly his ideas about penitential discipline and practice were changing , and how wideranging was his concern for the pastoral and moral renewal of the church and of the individual Christian.

---

[72] Peter Raymundi's penance is a guide to what Gregory had in mind.
[73] *Reg.* 7.10, 25 Nov. 1079, pp. 471–2.   [74] *Reg.* 7.14*a*(5), pp. 481–2.

8.2 The Sources of Christian Authority

The undertone of quest and development that can be observed in much of Gregory's thought and action must be set against the background of the certainty which he derived from the traditions and formularies of the apostolic see of Rome. *The Collectio canonum* of Cardinal Deusdedit preserves, from the *Liber diurnus* of the Roman church, a text of the solemn profession of faith and commitment that a new pope placed upon the tomb of St Peter:[75] It is likely that Gregory himself made a profession that was not necessarily identical but that followed its lines when he became pope in 1073. In form, it was a personal address to St Peter, in the second person singular, as prince of the apostles and bearer of the keys; it makes clear that the personal and direct relationship in which Gregory was to feel that he stood to St Peter was no personal idiosyncrasy but an expression of a current Roman understanding of the papal office.[76]

The profession spoke of an integrity of the faith ('verae fidei rectitudinem') which, from Christ as its author, descended through biblical and ecclesiastical tradition: it passed from Peter and his fellow-apostle Paul, and through Peter's own disciples and successors, to each new pope, who must keep it with unswerving fidelity in mind and body ('totis conatibus meis usque ad animam et sanguinem custodire'). He would safeguard the Christian faith in respect of the Trinity and the Incarnation of Christ and of the other doctrines of the church of God as enshrined in the acts of the ecumenical councils ('universalibus conciliis') and in the written decree of popes and approved doctors of the church; in particular, he promised to preserve inviolate and to the letter ('ad unum apicem') all the decrees of the seven ecumenical councils which the profession enumerated: Nicaea (325), Constantinople I (381), Ephesus (431), Chalcedon (451), Constantinople II (553) and III (680–1), and Nicaea II (787). He also promised the utmost fidelity to the decrees of his predecessors among the popes:

All the canonical decrees of the apostolic popes my predecessors, and whatever they have synodically decreed or approved, I will most diligently and vigorously confirm and defend undiminished; just as they decreed them, I will maintain them in full force. Whatever or whomever they condemned or rejected, I condemn and reject with a like judgement. I will keep unimpaired the discipline and rites of the church as I received them and as I found them canonically handed down by my predecessors. I will preserve undiminished the goods of the church and I will attend to their undiminished custody. I will diminish or alter nothing in the tradition that I find to be delivered and preserved by my most authoritative predecessors; I will admit no novelty, but zealously and as their true disciple and follower ('sequipeda') I will maintain and reverence with every effort of my mind whatever I have found to be canonically handed down.

The profession recognized that the pope might encounter problems, and it imposed restraint upon his reaction to them:

---

75 The best text is in *Liber diurnus*, ed. Foerster, pp. 429–31; see also Deusdedit, *Coll. can.* 2.110 (93), pp. 235–7.

76 e.g. Gregory's excommunications of Henry IV: *Reg.* 2.66, 29 Mar. 1075, pp. 270–1; 7.14*a*, pp. 483–7.

If there should come to light things contrary to canonical discipline, I will correct them with the counsel of my household ('filiorum meorum consilio'), or else—unless they constitute a grave offence against the Christian religion—patiently bear with them with your intercession and that of your most blessed fellow-apostle Paul.

But the profession quickly reverted to uncompromising language:

I will by God's help uphold the sacred canons and the canonical dispositions of the popes as the directives of God and of heaven, in the knowledge that, at the divine judgement-day, I must render a strict account to God and to you [St Peter], over whose most holy see I now preside by God's grace and by your patronage, and whose place, with your intercessions, I occupy.

Gregory's understanding of the sources of Christian authority was similar to that embodied in the profession; the similarity is evidence of how deeply Gregory's outlook was derived from the familiar and common assumptions of his Roman environment. He gave expression to his understanding in his letters of 1075 to the diocese of Constance about the duty of extirpating simony and of promoting clerical chastity. He claimed to be implementing 'the words of the gospels and of the apostles, the decrees of authoritative councils, and the principles of distinguished doctors': the apostle Paul had charged Christians not even to eat with fornicators and adulterers or other such vicious men (1 Cor. 5: 11), while the prohibition of clerical marriage was founded upon rulings by Popes Leo I and Gregory I. When writing to Bishop Burchard of Halberstadt on the same lines, Gregory insisted that the rules which he was proposing had been laid down by the holy fathers; he added that they were to be kept with the greater reverence because they had done so not of their own volition but by the inspiration of the Holy Spirit.[77] For Gregory, there existed a continuum of authority, under the guidance of the Holy Spirit, through both biblical and ecclesiastical tradition. As he told the bishops and abbots of Brittany, it was for him to see that, in all the churches, the instructions of the faith and the precepts of holy scripture were rightly upheld.[78]

More even than the form of profession indicated, Gregory laid weight upon scriptural authority. There seem to have been several reasons. First, the New Testament included epistles of St Peter and St Paul, the founder-apostles of the Roman church, upon which Gregory drew extensively.[79] Second, the gospels provided the proof texts upon which Gregory was urgently concerned to base his own claims as vicar of St Peter: Matt. 16: 18–19, in which Christ named Peter as the rock upon which his church would be built and committed to him the keys of the kingdom of heaven; Luke 22: 32, in which Christ gave Peter the assurance that his faith would not fail and charged him to strengthen his brothers; and John 21: 17, in which Christ commissioned Peter to 'Feed my sheep'.[80] Third, Gregory's formation as a monk seems to

---

[77] *Epp. vag.* nos. 8–11, pp. 16.28; *Reg.* 2.66, 29 Mar. 1075, pp. 221–2.

[78] *Reg.* 2.1, 28 Aug. 1074, p. 124/15–18; cf. 3.10, to King Henry IV of Germany, (8 Dec.) 1075, p. 266/8–14.

[79] For Gregory's scriptural citations, see the indexes in *Reg.* pp. 643–8 and *Epp. vag.* p. 169. For a fuller discussion of Gregory's use of scripture, see Arquillière, *Saint Grégoire VII*, esp. pp. 222–60.

[80] For Gregory's citation of these texts, see *Reg.* pp. 645–6.

have accustomed him to turn to the holy scriptures, not only as a source of external precepts, but also as a means through meditation and reflection of underpinning Christian action by a foundation in Christian doctrine.[81] Thus, he urged the community at Vallombrosa to lay a scriptural foundation for its collective and individual activities:

Let your mind meditate daily upon the lessons of the holy scriptures by which the assertions of the heretics are confuted and the faith of holy church is defended against the members of the devil who are trying to overthrow the Christian religion by their manifold devices; let your mind stand upright to the confusion of evil men in the liberty wherein it is wont to stand.[82]

A very large part of Gregory's citations, alike of scripture and of Christian authors,[83] was made, not verbatim, but from his own cultivated memory of them. He frequently sharpened or redirected them in order to add authority to his own statements and rulings; for example, his frequent citation of Samuel's words to Saul about the duty of obedience (1 Sam. 15: 22–3) was usually so made as to accentuate the precept of obedience.[84] Gregory also added to the authority of his letters by opening with long expositions of the Christian faith which drew extensively upon the epistles of St Peter and St Paul; Gregory's intention was evidently add to the apostolic authority of his statements and to give his rulings and arrangements added justification. Thus, in 1073, when he urged the clergy and people of Carthage 'to lay aside all quarrels' ('simultate deposita': cf. 1 Pet. 2: 1, 'deponentes . . . simulationes') 'and to obey their archbishop as their spiritual father', he opened with a long consideration of Christian patience and obedience, in which he drew heavily on the epistles of St Peter and St Paul. In 1079, when he sent legates to Spain, he set the context of their mission by addressing to the Spanish kings and magnates an exposition of the Christian religion which was similarly couched in scriptural language.[85] Gregory was concerned to establish a Christianity which rested upon conviction as well as upon command.

His attitude to the ecclesiastical tradition which he saw as extending that of holy scripture was similar to that expressed in the profession of faith as preserved by Deusdedit; the remarks about tradition which are scattered through his letters are best understood in its light. Gregory claimed that the statutes of the Roman church did not depart from the only right path, which was that of the 'holy fathers'.[86] By holy fathers, Gregory meant primarily his own predecessors in the papal office. It was for him to confirm and establish what they had decreed, for they had not acted by their own will but by the inspiration of the Holy Spirit.[87] It is consistent with this

[81] For the monastic use of scripture, see esp. Leclercq, *The Love of Learning*, pp. 13–21, 87–105.

[82] *Epp. vag.* no. 2, (1073, after 12 July), pp. 6–7.

[83] For Gregory's citation of early authors and councils, see *Reg.* pp. 649–50.

[84] For Gregory's citations, see *Reg.* p. 644 and *Epp. vag.* p. 169; for comment, see Arquillière, *Saint Grégoire VII*, pp. 234–5.

[85] *Reg.* 1.22–3, pp. 36–49; 4.28, pp. 343–7.

[86] *Reg.* 1.12, to Bishop William of Pavia, 29 June 1073, p. 20/27–9.

[87] *Reg.* 2.66, to Bishop Burchard II of Halberstadt, 29 Mar. 1075, p. 222/9–12; 6.34, to Archbishop Gebuin of Lyons, 19 April 1079, pp. 447/25–448/4.

view that his citations of early Christian writers were preponderantly made from popes—Julius I, Innocent I, Leo I, Gelasius I, Anastasius II, Hormisdas, and above all Gregory I. By the same token, he seldom cited Greek or Latin doctors who had not been popes. John Chrysostom and even Augustine of Hippo were each cited only in one letter; Ambrose, famous for his excommunication of the Emperor Theodosius, was cited in but three letters.[88]

Like the formula of profession, Gregory attributed high authority to the ecumenical councils of the church. His principal pronouncement about them was in his letter of 1080 to the Armenian catholicos, Gregory of Tsamandos. Gregory requested from him a confirmation that his church shared the faith of the first four councils, 'which were approved by the holy fathers'—here, Gregory seems to have meant by the phrase leading doctors like St Athanasius and St Cyril of Alexandria—'and confirmed with apostolic authority by the Roman pontiffs Silvester, Leo, and others'. Gregory made a long citation from Pope Gregory I in which he gave comparable authority to the fifth council, Constantinople II, which had upheld Christological orthodoxy against Nestorian opinions.[89] The emphasis which Gregory placed upon the first four councils may probably be accounted for, partly because of their special importance in laying down the Trinitarian and Christological doctrines which he wished to be assured that the Armenians accepted, and partly because of a diplomatic preparedness on his part to invoke only councils held before the Armenians consolidated a separate ecclesiastical identity after Chalcedon. In one major respect, Gregory went beyond Deusdedit's formula. When dealing with the issue of lay investiture, he recognized the fourth council of Constantinople (869–70) as the eighth ecumenical council, claiming the authority of Pope Hadrian II for a decision that it made.[90] The claim was a striking application of the principle expressed in part of *Dictatus papae* 17, that no chapter should be regarded as canonical without the pope's authority.[91]

Gregory's sense of the continuity of tradition from holy scripture through the fathers and councils of the church to his own day led to his repeatedly affirming a purpose of upholding the law as it had come down to him from an immemorial past as a timeless whole, but which had sometimes been obscured or overlaid by neglect or error. He gave a carefully nuanced statement of his purpose with regard to it in a letter which he sent to King Henry IV of Germany just before their first breach; he had particularly in mind his legislation at his Lent synod of 1075:

Seeing that the state of the Christian religion had now for a great time been undermined and that its true responsibilities for winning souls had for long fallen into neglect and, by the devil's prompting, had been trampled underfoot, . . . we returned to the decree and teaching of the

---

[88] See the lists of references in *Reg.* pp. 649–50, and *Epp. vag.* pp. 169–70. Gregory revealingly commented that Ambrose was 'licet sanctus non tamen universalis ecclesiae episcopus', i.e. pope: *Reg.* 8.21, to Bishop Hermann of Metz, 15 Mar. 1081, p. 554/11–15.

[89] *Reg.* 8.1, 6 June 1080, pp. 511/27–512/20.

[90] *Reg.* 4.22, to Bishop Hugh of Die, 12 May 1077, pp. 333/27–334/3.

[91] *Reg.* 2.55a, p. 205/8–9. For the number of ecumenical councils, see above, 3.2.4.

holy fathers. We established nothing novel and nothing of our own devising ('nichil novi, nichil adinventione nostra statuentes'), but we determined that, leaving aside all error, the first and only rule of ecclesiastical discipline and the well-tried path of the saints should be restored and followed.[92]

If Gregory's prime concern was in this way to rediscover and to enforce authentic law, he also claimed authority to devise new means of implementing what old law sought to achieve. It is important not to interpret Gregory's statements in terms of positive legislation or of dispensation from established rules which belong to later historical epochs; and it is easy to read too much into Gregory's own actual or re-ported words. When, in *Dictatus papae* 7, he formulated a claim that the Roman pontiff had a sole right of making new laws, he was careful to preface it by saying that he did so 'for the necessity of the time',[93] and he associated the pope's right with others—assembling new churches, making an abbey from a house of canons and vice versa, and dividing a rich see or uniting impoverished ones—which were specific and seldom exercised. In a pronouncement which is possibly, but far from certainly, attributable to him, there is an insistence that custom must be subject to the test of truth:

If perchance you plead custom, due attention must be paid to the Lord's words, 'I am the truth and the life' (cf. John 14: 6). And certainly, to borrow a saying of St Cyprian, any custom, how-ever ancient and widespread, must be altogether made subject to truth, and a usage which is contrary to truth must be done away with.[94]

In interpreting this pronouncement, due attention must be paid to the prevailing medieval idea of the openness of custom to revision when it became necessary to establish custom upon a firm basis of law.[95] Thus, in 1077, in the matter of the elec-tion of a new archbishop of Aquileia, Gregory gave clear expression to his view of the superiority of law to custom and of the need to correct evil custom by insisting upon the implementation of good law. With regard to the key issue of episcopal elections, an ancient and well-known rule had been laid down by Christ himself: a true shepherd must enter by the door (John 10: 1–2), that is, by free election of clergy and people without lay impediment from outside. Neglect and evil custom had eroded and vitiated the true rule of Christ, which it was Gregory's concern to renew and to restore ('innovare et restaurare').[96] He made no new departure:

[92] *Reg.* 3.10, (8 Dec.) 1075, pp. 265/29–266/8. For similar statements, see 2.66, to Bishop Burchard II of Halberstadt, 29 Mar. 1075, p. 222/9–12; 2.67, to Bishop Anno of Cologne, 29 Mar. 1075, pp. 223/31–223/1; 2.68, to Archbishop Werner of Magdeburg, 29 Mar. 1075, p. 226/4–7; 5.5, to the clergy and people of Aquileia, 17 Sept. 1077, p. 353/21–7; *Epp. vag.* no. 10, to the clergy and laity of Constance, (late 1075), p. 24/32–4.

[93] *Dictatus papae* 7, 'Quod illi soli licet pro temporis necessitate novas leges condere': *Reg.* 2.55a, p. 203.

[94] *Epp. vag.* no. 67, p. 151; see Ladner, 'Two Gregorian Letters', pp. 225–42. For the problem of authorship, see Somerville with S. Kuttner, *Pope Urban II*, pp. 53–5, 300.

[95] See esp. Isidore of Seville, *Etymologiarum*, 2.10.2: 'Consuetudo autem est ius quoddam moribus in-stitutum, quod pro lege suscipitur, cum deficit lex'; cf. 5.3.2–4.

[96] It is significant that the verb *reformare*, with its suggestion of novelty and initiative, is seldom used by Gregory; in his letters, it occurs only at *Reg.* pp. 300/30, 303/1, 422/1, 451/33 (cited from Pope Gregory I), 532/10, 582/4–5.

We are trying to introduce nothing novel, nothing of our own devising ('nichil novi, nichil nostris adinventionibus superinducere conamur'); we are seeking only what the salvation of all men and their necessity duly demand: that in the ordination of bishops, according to the universal understanding and consent of the holy fathers, the authority of the gospel and of canonical tradition should above all maintained.[97]

Gregory, in fact, followed the convention of his age by accepting that the enormous variety of rules from papal, synodical, and other sources which were inherited from the past constituted a kind of common law of the church. It was binding in so far as it did not contradict the law as stated by popes and universal councils, was consistent with the church's dogmatic and moral teachings, and served the utility of Christian life.[98] Whenever these tests were not satisfied, or when custom needed to be refined in the form of law, the pope had both a right and a duty to make law.

If the pope's prime duty was thus to renew and restore old, or rather, timeless law, there were four kinds of contingency in which he might take an initiative of his own. The first was prudential: upon grounds of rational calculation and expediency, he might, in particular circumstances, tolerate and sanction anomalies in order to achieve a greater good; although he might never make general enactments that ran contrary to the letter or the spirit of authentic tradition ('Solet enim sancta et apostolica sedes pleraque considerata ratione tolerare, sed nunquam in suis decretis et constitutionibus a concordia canonicae traditionis discedere'). When Gregory formulated the statement, he indicated the negative limits of its operation by insisting upon the inviolability of the rule that defect of birth was a bar to episcopal ordination.[99] Its proper operation was illustrated when he instructed his legates in France, Bishops Hugh of Die and Amatus of Oloron, to refrain from enforcing against lay knights who co-operated in the coercion of priests who were guilty of fornication or simony the rule that laymen should surrender tithes that they held.[100]

Second, in a similar spirit of seeking the well-being of the church without being unduly inhibited by past rulings, Gregory insisted that some rulings, even when embodied in papal privileges, were formulated with regard to particular circumstances of subject-matter, person, time, and place, and that circumstances could so far alter as to render them obsolete. If, on the one hand, papal privileges must not infringe the authority of authentic tradition, on the other they must conduce to the welfare ('utilitas') of the church. Thus, Archbishop Manasses of Rheims might not appeal to the primacy of the see of Arles as set up by Pope Gregory I and acknowledged by many of his successors, since the rights of the see had been lawfully rescinded by papal authority.[101] Moreover, Gregory himself could quash a privilege even of his

---

[97] *Reg.* 5.5, to the clergy and people of Aquileia, 17 Sept. 1077, pp. 352–4.
[98] See Kuttner, 'Liber canonicus', esp. pp. 390–7.
[99] *Reg.* 2.50, to King Sancho I of Aragon, 24 Jan. 1075, pp. 190–2.
[100] *Reg.* 9.5, (1081), p. 580/20–34; cf. his stringent decree about the lay possession of tithes at his Nov. synod of 1078: *Reg.* 6.5*b* (7), pp. 404–5. Gregory's advice about dealings with King William of England in the earlier part of the letter to his legates should also be noticed.
[101] *Reg.* 6.2, 22 Aug. 1078, p. 393.

immediate predecessor Alexander II, because it contained provisions which he deemed to run counter to better and more ancient authority.[102]

Third, the pope might devise new means ('consilia') of upholding what he apprehended to be the righteousness ('iustitia') of God which gave authority to all law, whenever the prevailing circumstances of the time seemed to place in peril both the souls of men and the integrity of the law ('Multo enim melius nobis videtur iustitiam Dei vel novis reaedificare consiliis, quam animas hominum una cum legibus deperire neglectis'). Gregory invoked this liberty when he sought to encourage in South Germany the lay opposition, by force if necessary, to the ministrations of clergy guilty of simony or fornication which had hitherto operated to the south of the Alps.[103] Fourth, in a similar connection, Gregory went so far as to claim, not only the right to employ new means of enforcing the law, but also the capacity in new circumstances to make new law, thereby adding to the body of law that he inherited from the past. His most express statement of such a claim arose from his determination to enforce clerical chastity in the German church. It was cautiously formulated, not in respect of the theoretical prerogatives of the Roman church, but of the special needs of a particular time:

It has always been permissible, and it will always be permissible, for this, the holy Roman church, to devise against newly arising abuses new decrees and remedies which, since they issue from reason and authority, no judgement of men can rightly reject as being invalid.[104]

Such papal law-making did not interrupt or stand superior to, but continued and revitalized, the continuum of rightful ecclesiastical authority which arose from the holy scriptures and continued through the deliverances of popes and councils, under the guidance of the Holy Spirit, up to the present time. Such were the basis and also the limitations of papal authority with regard to matters of law within the Christian church.

8.3 The Authority of the Papacy

In 1083, Gregory began a letter to the clerical and lay magnates of Flanders by what is probably his most considered statement of how he envisaged papal authority as it rested upon his shoulders:

Although we are a sinner and unequal to bearing so great a burden, the charge and care of all the churches (cf. 2 Cor. 11: 28) have nevertheless been entrusted by God to our mean self. For the Lord Jesus Christ appointed St Peter to be the prince of the apostles, giving him the keys of the kingdom of heaven and the power of binding and loosing in heaven and upon earth. Upon him he also built his church and committed his sheep to him to be fed (cf. Matt. 16: 18–9, John 21: 17). From this time [i.e. when Christ commissioned Peter], this principate and authority have passed through St Peter to all who have succeeded to his throne, or who will

---

[102] *Reg.* 7.24, to Abbot William of Hirsau, 8 May 1080, p. 504/6–15; cf. 9.19, to Archbishop Hugh of Lyons, (1082/3), pp. 599/37–600/7.

[103] *Reg.* 2.45, to the South German dukes, 11 Jan. 1075, pp. 182–5.

[104] *Reg.* 2.67, to Archbishop Anno of Cologne, 29 Mar. 1075, p. 224/1–5.

succeed to it until the end of the world, by divine privilege and by hereditary right ('Ex quo tempore principatus ille et potestas per beatum P. successit omnibus suam cathedram suscipientibus vel usque in finem mundi suscepturis divino privilegio et iure hereditario'). By reason of our own succession to his chair, it is incumbent upon us by inescapable necessity to help all who are oppressed and to fight, even to death if it should be necessary, against the enemies of God in defence of righteousness until they are converted with the sword of the Spirit, which is the word of God (Eph. 6: 17).[105]

As for the apostolic see as an institution, it possessed an authority which was constant from age to age, and which was universal in respect both of all the churches ('omnium ecclesiarum princeps') and of all peoples ('communis mater, omnium gentium magistra et domina'). Gregory's predecessors in the papal office had taught the way of the Lord to all nations, and the law of the Roman pontiffs had extended to more lands than that of the Roman emperors.[106] Within this context of the authority of the pope and of the Roman church, Gregory presented his authority under two, complementary aspects, a masculine and a feminine. They were represented by the fatherly figure of St Peter, with whom Gregory often associated St Paul, and by the motherly figure of the holy Roman church or the apostolic see. (The Latin words 'ecclesia' and 'sedes' are both feminine in gender.)

St Peter was the universal father and lord of all churches, lands, and individual Christians. He was the 'princeps apostolorum'—the prince, or chief, of the apostles who was a figure of authority, command, and judgement.[107] His authority rested upon Christ's words to him in the New Testament (Matt. 16: 18–19, Luke 22: 32, John 21: 17). The authority of a prince merged with the no less masculine but more caring roles of father and shepherd. Thus, Peter was the rightful father and shepherd ('patrem et pastorem') of the whole of France.[108] When counselling Countess Matilda of Tuscany, Gregory wrote of Peter as both her father and the prince of heaven.[109] As regards Gregory himself, he was constantly aware that he had been brought up in a household in the Lateran of which Peter was 'paterfamilias'.[110] In relation to himself as pope, Peter was lord and father; but when he acted upon Peter's behalf, Gregory himself acted paternally and pastorally towards those who were subject to him.[111]

Even more emphatically and habitually, Gregory wrote of the holy Roman church, or of the holy and apostolic see, as the mother of all—the 'communis mater' who raised up sons in Christ in all parts of the world, and who was the mother of all

[105] *Reg.* 9.35 to the bishops and princes of Flanders, (1083), pp. 622/32–623/7; cf. 8.1, to Archbishop Gregory of Tsamandos, 6 June 1080, p. 513/7–14.

[106] *QF* nos. 58, 79, pp. 38, 62; *Reg.* 2.75, to King Sweyn II of Denmark, 17 Apr. 1075, pp. 237/30–238/1.

[107] *Reg.* 2.25, to Archbishop Anno of Cologne, 18 Nov. 1074, p. 157/12–14; 3.10*a*, Lent synod of 1076, pp. 270–1.

[108] *Reg.* 8.23, to Bishop Peter of Albano and Prince Gisulf of Salerno, (1084), p. 566/23–4.

[109] *Reg.* 1.47, to Countess Matilda of Tuscany, 16 Feb. 1074, p. 73/19–22.

[110] See above, 2.1.

[111] *Reg.* 1.77, to Countesses Beatrice and Matilda of Tuscany, 15 Apr. 1074, p. 110/29–31; 9.8, to Doge Dominicus Silvius of Venice, 8 Apr. (1081), p. 585/15–20.

churches and peoples.[112] Gregory laid especial emphasis upon the Roman church which was the mother of all the churches throughout the world however distant, and which would be so to the end of time.[113] As mother, the Roman church was no mere symbol or emotional focus; its role was active and all-pervading as the active centre of Christian unity and as the source of authentic faith and discipline. In 1081, Gregory proclaimed this with especial force and clarity near the beginning of his justification of his pontificate to Bishop Hermann of Metz. He appealed to the age-long recognition by Christian fathers and by general councils that the Roman church was the universal mother. As such, it both upheld faith and religion and, as head and mother, dealt with major business from all the churches.[114] Gregory had especially claimed its duty to deal with major business in his early dealings as pope with the church of Milan. Thus, he told the Lombard faithful that, when the Roman church as mother of the Lombard churches and mistress of all Christendom heard of the simoniacal succession at Milan of Archbishop Godfrey, it took steps to assemble a council at Rome to discharge its duty as such.[115] Gregory afterwards told the Lombard bishops that they owed obedience to the Roman church as to a mother; just as it was 'hard (*durum*) for them to kick against the pricks' (cf. Acts 9: 5) by over-coming ingrained but excessive local loyalties, so it was 'bitter' ('asperum') when they opposed the Roman church, which they should also obey as a mother.[116] Filial duty as to a mother was particularly incumbent upon archbishops and their sees. For archbishops, the legal constraints of canonical duty were supported by sanctions of family affection and gratitude as of sons to their mother.[117] Loyalty to the Roman church as mother was a facet of the liberty ('libertas') which its sons should cherish: writing in 1081 to the clergy and people of Ravenna about an election to replace the apostate Archbishop Guibert, Gregory urged them to act filially in concert with him to rescue Ravenna; thereby they would promote the motherly liberty of the Roman church and thus be its free sons.[118]

In matters of church order, doctrine, and liturgical observance, the mother's authority of the Roman church was no less far-reaching than in matters of jurisdiction and canonical obedience. In great matters and in small, national or local churches should follow the lead of their mother at Rome. Gregory advanced this plea

[112] See e.g. *Reg.* 1.29, to the judges of Sardinia, 14 Oct. 1073, p. 46/27–32; 4.28, to the kings and magnates of Spain, 28 June 1077, p. 343/25–33; 5.13, to Archbishop Guibert of Ravenna and his suffragans, 28 Jan. 1078, p. 366/20–4; 7.5, to King Harold Hein of Denmark, 15 Oct. 1079, pp. 464/26–465/1; 9.9 to Count Theobald of Blois, 28 Apr. 1081, p. 586/4–8; *Epp. vag.* no. 55, to all the faithful (?1084), pp. 134–7.

[113] *Reg.* 8.1, to Archbishop Gregory of Tsamandos, 6 June 1080, p. 513/7–10.

[114] *Reg.* 8.21, 15 Mar. 1081, pp. 548/26–549/12; it is characteristic of Gregory's use of supporting texts that none of the citations from early popes which follow on pp. 549–50 refers to the maternal quality of the Roman church.

[115] *Reg.* 1.15, 1 July 1073, p. 24/9–19.

[116] *Reg.* 3.9, 8 Dec. 1075, p. 263/2–5. The movement of Gregory's thought from the conversion of St Paul to the language of *Regula sancti Benedicti*, cap. 58.8, should be observed.

[117] See esp. *Epp. vag.* no. 23, to Archbishop Ralph of Tours, (summer 1078), pp. 60–1; *Reg.* 6.30, to Archbishop Lanfranc of Canterbury, 25 Mar. 1079, p. 443/21–8, 32–6.

[118] *Reg.* 8.13, 15 Oct. 1080, p. 534/1–8.

with especial force when seeking to secure liturgical conformity between the Spanish and the Roman churches. Having dwelt upon the centuries-long deviation of Spain, Gregory urged upon the kings of León–Castile and Navarre 'as true offspring' that 'even after long deviations they would at last follow their true mother, the Roman church, in which they would find the pope to be their brother, by receiving the order and office of the Roman church'. Again, Gregory told Bishop Simeon of Burgos that 'the Roman church wishes you to know that she does not wish to feed the children that she nurtures in Christ with different breasts or with different milk, but that, according to the apostle, they may be one and that there shall be no division among them (cf. 1 Cor. 1: 10); otherwise she would be called not mother but divider.' In Spain, therefore, the order of the Roman church as mother of all must be observed in its pristine quality.[119] Elsewhere, Gregory imposed a similar requirement even in a relatively minor matter. When he insisted that the clergy of Sardinia should shave their beards, he urged them to follow the custom of the holy Roman church, 'the mother of all the churches and especially of yours'.[120] The obligation to follow Rome went far beyond legal duty; it was as the bond between good sons and their mother.

Gregory associated the fatherhood of St Peter and the motherhood of the Roman church to especial effect in the last encyclical that he circulated in 1084 from Salerno:

All who in the whole world bear the name of Christian and truly understand the Christian faith know and believe that St Peter, the prince of the apostles, is the father of all Christians and their first shepherd after Christ, and that the holy Roman church is the mother and mistress of all the churches. If, then, you believe and unshakeably hold this, such as I am, your brother and unworthy master, I ask and command you by Almighty God to help and succour your father and mother, if through them you would have the absolution of all your sins, and blessings and grace in this world and in the world to come. [121]

The balance of and complementarity between St Peter as father and the Roman church as mother of all Christians is a distinguishing feature of Gregory's representation of the authority of the papacy.

The balance that Gregory thus established was of critical importance on account of the differing views that were current throughout his pontificate among his own closest supporters about the residence, credentials, and daily exercise of ultimate authority in the church. At Rome, Cardinal Deusdedit, in particular, placed such authority in the Roman church as a collectivity of which the pope was the mouthpiece and agent; while an equally learned canonist like Bishop Anselm II of Lucca gave far greater weight to the personal authority of the pope himself.[122] It was always important for Gregory to retain the goodwill and co-operation of all points of view while holding fast to his own view of the prerogatives of the vicar of St Peter.

---

[119] *Reg.* 1.64, to Kings Alphonso VI of León–Castile and Sancho IV of Navarre, 19 Mar. 1074, p. 93/17–21; 3.18, to Bishop Simeon of Burgos, May 1076, p. 284/7–11, 9.2, to King Alphonso VI of León–Castile, (1081), p. 570/27–30.

[120] *Reg.* 8.10, to Judge Orzoccor of Cagilari, 5 Oct. 1080, p. 529/9–15.

[121] *Epp. vag.* no. 54, to all the faithful, (1084), pp. 134–5.

[122] On the differing views, see further Cowdrey, *The Age of Abbot Desiderius*, pp. 99–102, also Blumenthal, 'Fälschungen bei kanonisten' and 'Rom in die Kanonistik'.

The *Dictatus papae* provides evidence of the balance of his own thinking, at least as in the early months of 1075.[123] Most of its theses are concerned with the prerogatives of the Roman pontiff. However, three theses—*Dictatus papae* 1, 22, 25—are concerned with the *Romana ecclesia*. *Dictatus papae* 1 advanced the claim, for which it is difficult to find an express parallel elsewhere in Gregory's letters, that the Roman church was founded by the Lord alone. The claim was repeated by Deusdedit;[124] its prominent place in the *Dictatus papae* may have been intended to make clear Gregory's recognition of this Roman point of view. *Dictatus papae* 22 reverted to the prerogatives of the Roman church, in order to assert its indefectibility: 'The Roman church has never erred nor, as scripture witnesses (cf. Luke 22: 32), will it ever err.'[125] Gregory accordingly claimed in 1081 that the Roman church had a superiority over all other churches in respect both of teaching and warranting the Christian faith and of exercising jurisdiction:

Just as they [other churches] received its [the Roman church's] teaching for the confirmation of faith and for instruction in holy religion, so too they received its judgements. By doing this, they agreed and were concordant with one spirit and one voice that all major matters and weightier business, and in addition the judgements of all the churches, should be referred to it as mother and head. There never could or should be an appeal against it, or a revision or refutation of its judgements, by anyone at all.[126]

Accordingly, in *Dictatus papae* 26, no one might be accounted a catholic who was not in agreement ('non concordat') with the Roman church; once again, Gregory's statements elsewhere show that he had in mind matters both of faith and of jurisdiction.[127]

Gregory sought to relate the authority of the Roman pontiff to that of the Roman church, which he thus so carefully balanced, by claiming that authority in the church was granted to St Peter *principaliter*; the adverb should be understood in all of its three shades of meaning—primarily and before all others, directly and without intermediary, and as befits a *princeps* with authority to command. Commenting upon Matthew 16: 18–19, Gregory said that:

The holy fathers received and upheld with great reverence this institution of the divine will, this foundation of the oversight of the church, this privilege which was principally ('principaliter') delivered and confirmed to St Peter as prince ('princeps') of the apostles by heavenly decree. They called the holy Roman church the universal mother, both in their general councils and in their other decrees and decisions.[128]

---

[123] *Reg.* 2.55a, pp. 201–8.

[124] *Coll. can.* 1.61, p. 63: 'Haec vero sacrosancta Romana apostolica ecclesia non ab apostolis, sed ab ipso domino salvatore nostro primatum optinuit.' Nevertheless, the possibility remains that one reason for Gregory's not using the *Dictatus papae* may have been that its emphasis on the Roman pontiff may have been objectionable to Roman clergy like Deusdedit whose goodwill he could not afford to forfeit.

[125] *Reg.* 3.18, to Bishop Simeon of Oca-Burgos, May 1076, p. 284/2–7, confirms the biblical reference.

[126] *Reg.* 8.21, to Bishop Hermann of Metz, 15 Mar. 1081, p. 549/6–12.

[127] *Reg.* 7.24, to Abbot William of Hirsau, 8 May 1080, pp. 504/21–505/4; cf. 7.6, to King Alphonso VI of León–Castile, 15 Oct. 1079, p. 466/8–16.

[128] *Reg.* 8.21, pp. 548/26–549/6.

No less definitely, Gregory insisted that Christ had named Peter personally as the rock upon which he founded his church. It was also to be remembered that the Roman church was itself consecrated by the martyr-blood of Peter and Paul.[129] Petrine authority was, therefore, the basis upon which that of the Roman church was established.[130] Gregory above all appealed to Christ's words according to Matthew 16: 18–19 in order to assert that this was so. But he also cited Christ's promise to Peter, 'I have prayed for you that your faith may not fail; and when you have turned again, strengthen your brethren' (Luke 22: 32), in order to add to an authority to exercise universal rule and jurisdiction a personal commission to maintain the integrity of Christian faith and worship throughout Christendom; it was through Peter's faith that the duty of securing the right belief of all the churches was vested in the Roman church, and not vice versa. The same promise secured the pope personally from the danger of falling into heresy despite a view to the contrary that was being canvassed in the late eleventh-century Roman church; for Gregory, in what reads like a deliberate rebuttal of this view, no heretic had ever ruled the Roman church nor, by the Lord's ordinance, would any do so until the end of time.[131] Further it was to Peter himself ('specialiter') that, in John 21: 17, Christ committed the pastor's duty of feeding his sheep.[132] By his use of these gospel passages, Gregory insisted upon the pope's personal authority while respecting the corporate prerogatives of the Roman church.

Gregory's understanding of the papal office is succinctly expressed in his habitual use of the title vicar of St Peter. He never described himself as vicar of Christ; although this title had ancient authority and some currency in the eleventh century, it was not regularly used by the popes before the thirteenth century. Nor did any contemporary apply the title to him.[133] Gregory's use of the title is best explained by his own epitome of his authority which he formulated towards the end of his pontificate to the bishops and princes of Flanders, to whom he declared that, until the end of

---

[129] *Reg.* 3.10*a*, Lent synod 1076, 14–20 Feb., p. 271/5–7; cf. 1.22, to the clergy and people of Carthage, 15 Sept. 1075, p. 37/5–6; 1.64, to Kings Alphonso VI of León–Castile and Sancho IV of Navarre, 19 Mar. 1074, p. 93/21–5.

[130] *Reg.* 2.70, to Duke Gésa of Hungary, 17 Apr. 1075, p. 230/26–8; 1.72, pastoral letter to the Bohemians, 17 Apr. 1075, p. 233/11–14; 4.2, to Bishop Hermann of Metz, 25 Aug. 1076, pp. 294/24–295/5; 8.21, to Bishop Hermann of Metz, 15 Mar. 1081, p. 548/16–18; 9.35, to the bishops and princes of Flanders, (1083), p. 622/34–7. The use of the word *principaliter* in the first two letters cited should be noticed.

[131] *Dictatus papae* 22, *Reg.* 2.55*a*, p. 207, 2.31, to King Henry IV of Germany, 7 Dec. 1074, p. 167/5–15; 3.18, to Bishop Simeon of Oca–Burgos, May 1076, p. 284/2–11; 8.1, to Archbishop Gregory of Tsamandos, 6 June 1080, p. 513/7–14. For the possibility that the Roman church might need to judge a heretical pope, see Ullmann, 'Cardinal Humbert'.

[132] *Reg.* 1.15, to the faithful in Lombardy, 1 July 1073, p. 24/34–6; 3.10, to King Henry IV of Germany, (8 Dec.) 1075, pp. 264/29–265/10; 4.2, to Bishop Hermann of Metz, 25 Aug. 1076, pp. 294/24–295/1; 8.21, to Bishop Hermann of Metz, 15 Mar. 1081, p. 548/16–18; 9.35, to the bishops and princes of Flanders, (1083), p. 622/34–7.

[133] For the title vicar of Christ, see Maccarrone, *Vicarius Christi*. The sole reference to Gregory as *Christi vicarius* is that of Prior Guigo I of la Grande Chartreuse, *Vita sancti Hugonis*, 2.7, PL 153.767B; Guigo wrote in the mid-1130s.

time, Christ's commission to Peter as expressed in the Petrine texts of the gospels would pass through Peter 'by divine privilege and hereditary right' to all who succeeded Peter in his throne.[134] By divine privilege, Gregory understood primarily the sanction of Christ's words to Peter in the gospels; by hereditary right, he seems in the light of current liturgical usage to have understood the consequent devolution not by linear succession amongst men but by direct divine endowment, upon whoever should succeed to Peter's throne, of the rights, duties, and burdens that arose from Christ's commission to Peter.[135]

If God imposed such a task upon the pope, he also provided the means of bearing and fulfilling it. Such is the background against which it is appropriate to understand the much-discussed thesis 23 of the *Dictatus papae*: 'That the Roman pontiff, if he be canonically ordained, is undoubtedly made holy by the merits of St Peter.'[136] In this thesis of the *Dictatus papae* alone, Gregory indicated his canonical authority: it was a tradition initiated by Bishop Ennodius of Pavia (died 521). The relevant passage in Ennodius's writings made two points that bear particularly upon Gregory's assertion: first, that Peter 'dispatched to those who followed him an enduring endowment of merits with an inheritance of innocence' ('cum haereditate innocentiae'); and secondly, that, even though a man whom the summit of the papal dignity elevated were himself lacking in good things won by his own merit, they would be sufficiently furnished by his predecessor, St Peter.[137]

As Gregory understood the tradition which Ennodius established, the holiness that was implanted in a canonically ordained pope had two aspects, an official and a personal. On the official side, the pope, however personally unworthy he must be by reason of being human, was invested through his office with the identity of Peter, so

---

[134] *Reg.* 9.35.

[135] Cf. *Reg.* 4.7, to the faithful in Milan, 31 Oct. 1076, p. 303/13–16; also, for the concept of hereditary right in terms of the conferring of an office by divine authority and by transmission through bishops, the words of the archbishop to a newly crowned king in the Romano-Germanic Pontifical: 'Sta et retine amodo locum, quem hucusque paterna successione tenuisti, hereditario iure tibi delegatum per auctoritatem Dei omnipotentis et presentem traditionem nostram, omnium scilicet episcoporum ceterorumque Dei servorum': *RGP* 1.258; see above, 3.1.1. This conception of hereditary right may be influenced by the biblical law of the Levites: 'non habebunt sacerdotes et Levitae . . . partem et hereditatem cum reliquo Israhel, . . . et nihil aliud accipient de possessione fratrum suorum; Dominus enim ipse est hereditas eorum' (Deut. 18: 1–2).

[136] 'Quod Romanus pontifex, si canonice fuerit ordinatus, meritis beati Petri indubitanter efficitur sanctus testante sancto Ennodio Papiensi episcopo ei multis sanctis patribus faventis, sicut in decretis beati Symachi pape continetur': *Reg.* 2.55a, p. 207/3–7. For comment, see esp. Ullmann, '*Romanus pontifex*'.

[137] Gregory had in mind Ennodius's *Libellus adversus eos qui contra synodum scribere praesumpserunt*, written to defend the actions of the so-called Palmary Synod of 502 in defence of Symmachus. The most relevant passage is as follows: 'Non nos beatum Petrum, sicut dicitis, a domino cum sedis privilegiis vel successores eius peccandi iudicamus licentiam suscepisse. Ille perennem meritorum dotem cum haereditate innocentiae misit ad posteros. Quod illi concessum est pro actuum luce, ad illos pertinet quos par conversationis splendor inluminat. Quis enim sanctum esse dubitat, quem apex tantae dignitatis adtollit, in quo si desint bona adquisita per meritum, sufficient quae a loci decessore praestantur. Aut enim claros ad haec fastigia erigit, aut eos qui eriguntur illustrat': *Libellus*, cap. 14, ed. Vogel, p. 52; cf. Hinschius, p. 666.

that he acted as if he were Peter and by Peter's grace.[138] Since he was Peter's vicar, the powers that Christ conferred upon the prince of the apostles were renewed and perpetuated in him. From Ennodius's time to Gregory's, this view of the pope's official sanctity was widely maintained; it was strongly propounded by Cardinals Humbert and Peter Damiani.[139] It is significant of Gregory's acceptance of it that, in his understanding, the fulness of Petrine authority came to him, not with his election and enthronement although he exercised papal jurisdiction from that time, but from the day of his episcopal ordination 'at the body of St Peter', that is, at St Peter's basilica and in the presence of his relics which were the continuing pledge of his powers. It was, accordingly, by God's grace and by virtue of Peter's power to bless and to bind and loose that Gregory could tell the Germans in 1076 that he hoped to come to them 'and profit you in all things'.[140] Only from the date of his episcopal consecration did Gregory open his letters with an 'apostolic' blessing or begin his frequent practice of concluding them with a prayer to God which called down blessing upon their recipients.[141] Only after his full entry upon his Petrine inheritance could he objectively claim and dispense the blessing that came from Peter's merits. By a like token, because the pope's official sanctity enabled him to draw upon the resources of Peter to confer an effectual blessing, he could impose an anathema which bound and inhibited both spiritually and materially. Most momentously, by virtue of his apostolic power he could give to or withhold from a king material prosperity in this life and above all victory in warfare, and thus impose a sanction to bring him to penitence.[142]

For Gregory, the official sanctity of a duly ordained pope had a necessary corollary in his personal sanctity. Gregory derived it from the words of Ennodius, in which he was concerned to refute the suggestion that Peter and his successors had any licence to sin.[143] In 1081, Gregory took up Ennodius's assertion that Peter left to his successors an enduring endowment of merits when he declared that popes who were duly ordained were made better ('meliores efficiuntur') by the merits of Peter; his contrast with the deterioration of conduct in Saul and David after they became kings establishes that he meant better personally and morally.[144] As for Ennodius's claim that the deficiencies of a pope who was, after all, a sinful man, were made good when he was raised to the papal office by Peter's merits, Gregory expressed the same confidence in a letter of 1074:

[138] *Reg.* 3.10a, Lent synod 1076, 14–20 Feb. 1076, p. 270/11–15.

[139] The sources are fully surveyed by Ullmann, '*Romanus pontifex*', pp. 230–45.

[140] *Epp. vag.* no. 18, to all the faithful in Germany, (Dec. 1076), pp. 50–1.

[141] Up to 29 June 1073, Gregory began his letters with the phrase 'salutem in domino Iesu Christo'; from 30 June, he changed to 'salutem et apostolicam benedictionem': *Reg.* pp. 19, 21. For the concluding prayers (*Schlusswünschen*) of Gregory's letters, see below, Table at end of 8.4; the first example is in *Reg.* 1.15, to the faithful in Lombardy, 1 July 1073, pp. 24/34–25/2.

[142] *Reg.* 5.14a(6), record of the Lent synod 1078, 27 Feb.–3 Mar. 1078, p. 371/1–5; 5.15, to the German kingdom, 9 Mar. 1078, p. 376/4–10; 6.1, to the German kingdom, 1 July 1078, p. 390/17–21; 7.14a(7), record of the Lent synod 1080, 7 Mar. 1080, p. 486/20–7.

[143] As n. 137.

[144] *Reg.* 8.21, to Bishop Hermann of Metz, 15 Mar. 1081, p. 561/1–13.

Although our own merits do little to commend our prayers to God, they are helped by the goodness ('pietas') of Peter whose servant we are; we therefore trust that they are not altogether vain in the sight of the Lord.[145]

As vicar of St Peter, the pope was invested with a sanctity which was both official and personal, and which was attested by the claim that, of the bishops who had succeeded Peter in the Roman see, 'almost a hundred' were reckoned among the most holy of men ('inter sanctissimos').[146]

Gregory's way of regarding the holiness of the pope illustrates the combination of distance and closeness in which he believed that he stood in relation to Peter. The distance was apparent in his awareness of being the chosen servant and steward of Peter, with whom he sometimes associated his fellow-apostle Paul; it was by Peter's grace and authority, not by any right of his own, that he performed the duties of his papal office.[147] He was a sinner to whom, unworthy though he was, the papal authority had been entrusted.[148] Yet Gregory could move quickly from such an expression of distance from Peter to one of close identification with him, as in his last letter to King Henry IV of Germany before their breach early in 1076:

Because in [Peter's] chair and government we, such as we are a sinner and unworthy, by divine disposition act on behalf of his power, he himself assuredly receives whatever you send to us, whether in writing or by word of mouth. While we are reading the letters of the alphabet or hearing the words of those who speak, [Peter] himself discerns by piercing investigation the frame of mind from which the messages come.[149]

Similarly, Gregory told the people of Bohemia that he felt the more bound to discharge his duty of admonishing them in proportion to their own diligence in listening to St Peter in his admonitions.[150] More directly still, he told the Countesses Beatrice and Matilda of Tuscany of his confidence that their love for him shone true, when the servant was loved through Peter and Peter was loved in his servant.[151] The closeness in which Gregory stood to Peter is a commonplace of his letters, so that he spoke of 'having the favour (*gratia*) of St Peter and our own'.[152] In 1076, when answering the queries of Bishop Hermann of Metz, he likewise prayed that St Peter might answer through him, because Peter often received honour or suffered injury in the person of his servant Gregory.[153]

---

[145] *Reg.* 1.85, to the Empress Agnes, 15 June 1074, p. 122/33–6; cf. 3.10*a*, record of the Lent synod 1076 (14–20 Feb. 1076), p. 270/11–14.

[146] *Reg.* 8.21, p. 560/2–5.

[147] As n. 145; also *Reg.* 2.15, to Archbishop Humbert of Lyons and other bishops, 11 Nov. 1074, p. 148/3–7; 3.10, to King Henry IV of Germany, (8 Dec.) 1075, p. 263/26–8; 3.10*a*, record of the Lent synod 1076, (14–20 Feb. 1076), p. 270/2–15; 7.14*a*(7), record of the Lent synod 1080, 7 Mar. 1080, pp. 483/17–19, 486/17–19.

[148] *Reg.* 5.21, to Abbot Hugh of Cluny, 7 Mar. 1078, p. 385/21–5.

[149] *Reg.* 3.10, p. 265/4–10.   [150] *Reg.* 2.72, 17 Apr. 1075, p. 233/5–10.

[151] *Reg.* 2., 16 Oct. 1074, p. 138/31–2.

[152] *Reg.* 1.66, to the monks and lay tenants of SS. Quirico and Giulitta in Antrodoco, 20 Mar. 1074, p. 96/9; 2.60, to Bishop Otto of Constance, 13 Mar. 1075, p. 215/6.

[153] *Reg.* 4.2, 25 Aug. 1076, p. 293/24–7.

Such expressions of closeness to St Peter have led some historians to speak of Gregory's 'Petrine mysticism'. However, the term is to be rejected, partly because of Gregory's own sense of personal unworthiness and of being Peter's servant, but still more because, in all of its familiar significations, the word mysticism is foreign to Gregory's religious and mental outlook. It is appropriate, instead, to represent Gregory as being totally committed, as vicar of St Peter, to Peter's service and to the commission which was entrusted to the pope 'by divine privilege and hereditary right', as Gregory understood these terms. By this route, Gregory established his own total and abiding identification with Peter's role in the church and in the world as it was defined by Christ's words to him in the gospels.

8.4 The Religious Outlook of Gregory VII

Gregory's view of the world in which he was called upon to exercise the authority and office of St Peter was firmly based upon his understanding of the Christian scheme of creation, redemption, and the last things; without an understanding of his depth and comprehensiveness of religious conviction, there can be no just appraisal of his thought. His conviction was formed by his familiarity with the Bible, as is apparent from his disclosure of it in his letters. Especially important are the letters in which he set forth his scheme of belief, in whole or in part, and in the concluding prayers (*Schlusswünschen*) with which he rounded off some thirty-eight of his letters.[154] His concluding prayers were also rich in phrases taken from liturgical collects, and illustrate the importance of the liturgical round of the Roman church in shaping and sustaining Gregory's ideas.

The concluding prayers, in particular, testify to Gregory's understanding of the goodness of creation. God is the creator and ruler of all things, from whom all good things come.[155] Elsewhere, Gregory referred to God who created man in his image and redeemed him by his precious blood.[156] Similarly, Jesus was he through whom all things were made and who rules all things.[157] It was not by chance that Gregory chose for the motto in the rota of many of his privileges the words of Psalm 144: 9: 'Your mercies, Lord, are over all your works.'[158] Deeply as Gregory shared the *mépris du monde* which was a mark of eleventh-century spirituality, his absorption of the biblical and liturgical tradition sustained him in a view of the goodness of the created order and of the possibility of its redemption through the mercy of God.

---

[154] For expositions of faith, see esp. *Reg.* 1.22, to the clergy and people of Carthage, 15 Sept. 1073, pp. 37/1–38/14; 4.18, to the kings and lay magnates of Spain, 28 June 1077, pp. 344/8–345/34; 6.13, to King Olav III of Norway, 15 Dec. 1078, p. 416/1–25; for a list of the concluding prayers, see the Table at the end of this section.

[155] See esp. the phrase from the collect for the fifth Sunday after Easter: 'a quo bona cuncta procedunt': *Reg.* pp. 91/16, 168/1, 259/3, 292/13, 363/17, 420/29, 442/30–1, 565/24–5.

[156] *Reg.* 9.9, to Count Theobald of Blois, 28 Apr. 1081, p. 587/1–2 (the echo of the canticle *Te Deum laudamus* should be observed).

[157] *Reg.* 2.29, to Abbot Hugh of Cluny, 22 Jan. 1075, p. 189/8–9; cf. John 1: 3.

[158] See the plates at the end of *QF*.

Gregory accordingly expressed his faith in the redemption in language that he derived from the First Epistle of St Peter, who was the rock upon whom Christ built his church, and from the epistles of his fellow-apostle St Paul. He proclaimed Christ's sacrificial death for mankind, and also the consequent duty of all Christians to live, and if necessary to die, in conformity with Christ's death. Gregory thus sounded a note of universalism, that Christ's redemptive work was sufficient to redeem the whole creation:

According to the purpose of the will of the eternal Father (cf. Eph. 1: 5), and with the co-operation of the Holy Spirit of God, [Jesus Christ] was made man for the salvation of the world and was born of a pure virgin. He reconciled the world to God through his death, cancelling our sins by the redemption which is by his blood. Having overcome death in himself, he made us alive with him and revived us, as well, in a living hope and to an inheritance which is unfading, undefiled, and incorrupt (cf. 1 Pet. 1: 4). In him, as we trust in his mercy, eternal salvation and life are prepared for you, if however you keep firm faith in him to the end (cf. Heb. 3: 6), believing, as the apostle Paul says, that in him dwells all the fullness of the godhead bodily (cf. Col. 2: 9).[159]

Gregory was far from entertaining any Manichean duality of good and evil, or from holding a view of the absolute reprobateness of any human being.

Gregory insisted upon the urgency of reflection upon the last things of death, judgement, heaven, and hell. He especially reminded his correspondents of the nearness of death to the individual and of the last judgement to the human race; in his last encyclical from Salerno, he added that the precursory time of Antichrist was fast approaching.[160] Such thoughts were especially requisite in kings and lay magnates, whom he frequently admonished that they should so pass through things temporal that they finally gained things eternal.[161] They were to remember both the misery and fragility of the human condition and that they must stand before the heavenly judgement of Peter and Paul, at which they must render a detailed account of their stewardship of their earthly rule. Thus, he reminded the kings and lay magnates of Spain that:

You yourself know and daily observe how fleeting and frail is the life of mortal men, and how deceiving and deceitful is a hope in things present. For, like it or not, we are ever hastening to our end; yet, although we are subject to so certain a danger, we can never foresee when death is round the corner, nor can we ever for long hold on to anything that is sought after or possessed in this present life and world. Always be mindful, therefore, of the latter end to which you will come, and with how much affliction you will make your wretched exit from this world and return to the decay of earth and to the squalor of the dust, and of how you must render account of your doings in a strict inquiry: fortify yourselves against such future perils.[162]

---

[159] *Reg.* 6.13, p. 416/9–20.

[160] e.g. *Reg.* 2.72, to the people of Bohemia, 17 Apr. 1075, p. 233/10–18; 2.73, to Duke Boleslav II of Poland, 20 Apr. 1075, p. 235/1–5; *Epp. vag.* no. 54, pp. 132–5.

[161] This is the predominant theme of Gregory's concluding prayers; he cited the collect for the fifth Sunday after Pentecost at *Reg.* p. 232/3–4: 'qui te faciat per bona transire, ut mereatis addipisci aeterna.'

[162] *Reg.* 4.28, 28 June 1077, p. 345/13–34; among other examples, see 1.38, to Duke Wratislav II of Bohemia, 17 Dec. 1073, p. 61/4–8; 2.51, to King Sweyn II of Denmark, 25 Jan. 1075, p. 193/17–28; 7.15, to King William I of England, 8 May 1080, p. 503/11–16.

Gregory also wrote to bishops in similar terms.[163]

The time before men came to their encounter with the last things was for them both individually and collectively one of an internal and external struggle between good and evil which transcended merely human affairs. For every man was always subject to the lordship of either God or the devil, or, as Gregory more commonly expressed it in terms of the Christian religion, all were members either of Christ or of Antichrist. The touchstone of their loyalty was their obedience or disobedience to the will and commandments of God, not those of men, and whether they preferred God's honour to their own, putting his righteousness before temporal gain.[164] Those who failed this test had chosen the part of the devil, or Satan, or Antichrist; Gregory used these terms synonymously. Of the power of the devil in this world, Gregory had no doubt. Especially in the perilous times of Gregory's struggle with Henry IV of Germany, as Antichrist the devil was everywhere working in his own members; as a result, few men could be found who preferred God with his honour and precepts to secular ease and the favour of earthly princes.[165] Thus, almost the whole world was placed in the power of the evil one.[166] There had been no such hapless time for the church since it found its freedom in the fourth century under the Emperor Constantine who, in the understanding of Gregory's age, had delivered it from the tyranny of the pagan emperors who had subjected it to the power of demons.[167] Gregory stigmatized those who opposed him as pope by describing them as members of the devil who were in revolt against him to the point of seeking his blood.[168] Such thoughts contributed to the sense which he expressed throughout his pontificate of being himself as it were at sea in a storm and in peril of shipwreck, and of the church as being similarly imperilled.[169]

Gregory's sense of the perils in which he and the church stood as a result of the workings of the devil was, however, more than offset by his confidence, which remained unshaken to the end, in the victorious power of Christ which was deployed against the devil. As he told the citizens of Piacenza when he informed them of the deposition of their bishop, Dionysius:

[163] e.g. *Reg.* 1.84, to Bishop Hermann of Bamberg, 12 June 107, p. 120/20–8; 2.61, to Bishop Dietwin of Liège, 23 Mar. 1075, p. 216/4–8, 24–8; 8.1, to Archbishop Gregory of Tsamandos, 6 June 1080, p. 513/25–34.

[164] *Reg.* 4.2, to Bishop Hermann of Metz, 25 Aug. 1076, p. 295/10–17; 4.27, to Doge Domenicus Silvius of Venice, 9 June 1077, p. 342/11–22; 8.21, to Bishop Hermann of Metz, 15 Mar. 1081, p. 557/11–19.

[165] *Reg.* 4.1, to all the faithful in the Roman empire, 25 June 1076, pp. 289/20–290/3; cf. *Epp. vag.* no. 54, to all the faithful, (1084), pp. 132–5.

[166] *Reg.* 1.9, to Duke Godfrey of Lorraine, 6 May 1073, p. 14/20–1; 2.1, to the bishops and abbots of Brittany, 28 Aug. 1074, p. 124/29–33; 3.15, to the knight Wifred of Milan, (Apr.) 1076, p. 277/17–19; Gregory had in mind 1 John 5: 19.

[167] *Reg.* 2.45, to the South German dukes, 11 Jan. 1075, p. 183/1–5; *Epp. vag.* no. 54, pp. 132–5.

[168] *Reg.* 7.14*a*, record of the Lent synod 1080, 7 Mar. 1080, p. 483/19–23; 8.5, to the bishops of South Italy, 21 July 1080, pp. 521/32–522/5.

[169] e.g. *Reg.* 1.3, to Archbishop Guibert of Ravenna, 26 Apr. 1073, pp. 5/28–6/16; 1.70, to King William I of England, 4 Apr. 1074, pp. 101/30–102/11; 4.6, to Bishop Henry of Liège, 28 Oct. 1076, p. 304/22–9; *Epp. vag.* no. 51, to the archbishops, bishops, and abbots of France and Germany, (summer 1083), pp. 122–5.

Wherefore do you, the citizens of God, take comfort; for God is with us. Even though there stand against us the fortified cities of the land of Canaan and the gigantic bodies of the sons of Anak (cf. Num. 13: 29, 34), our leader Jesus as our companion-in-arms advances undaunted into the land of promise. For he, too, is a giant to run his course (cf. Ps. 18: 6), who says, 'Take heart, for I have overcome the world' (John 16: 33).[170]

Throughout the vicissitudes of the early 1080s, Gregory expressed his confidence in victory, assuring his followers that better times would come soon because the cause of Christ must triumph.[171]

The antagonistic services which men might yield to Christ and to the devil divided them into two solidarities, which were widely acknowledged by his followers, at least in Italy.[172] Over against the body of Christ, of which Christ was head and his true followers were members, was the body of the devil whose members were the members of Antichrist. Gregory explained the division in his second apologia to Bishop Hermann of Metz:

In sum, it is more appropriate that any good Christians whatsoever should be accounted kings than that evil princes should be so. For the former by seeking the glory of God forcefully rule themselves, but the latter by seeking not the interests of Jesus but their own (cf. Phil. 2: 21) are at enmity with themselves and tyrannically oppress others. The former are the body of Christ the true king, but the latter are the body of the devil. The former so command themselves that they may reign eternally with the true emperor; the latter so wield power that they may perish with the prince of darkness, who is king over all the children of pride (cf. Job 41: 25).[173]

The two solidarities, and especially that of the body of Christ, persisted beyond this life. Thus, Christians who remained faithful to the end of their lives would be numbered with those who will judge the devil and his members, while they themselves will reign eternally with Christ.[174] Meanwhile, their warfare was directed against members of the devil who were trying by their manifold devices to overthrow the Christian religion.[175] For Gregory regarded his adversaries as members of the devil who had risen up against him.[176] Especial condemnation was appropriate for spiritual and temporal rulers who disobeyed. A recalcitrantly simoniac bishop had, in

---

[170] *Reg.* 2.54, 3 Mar. 1075, pp. 198–9; cf. *Reg.* 3.15, to the knight Wifred of Milan, (Apr.) 1076, p. 277/121–29.

[171] *Reg.* 6.5, to Bishop Hermann of Metz, 22 Oct. 1078, p. 399/10–15; 8.4, to Abbot Richard of Marseilles, (27 June 1080), p. 521/2–10; 8.8, to Archbishop Alfanus of Salerno, 18 Sept. 1080, p. 526/26–38; 8.9, to the faithful in Germany, 22 Sept. 1080, pp. 527/35–528/1,10–18; 9.5, to Bishops Hugh of Die and Amatus of Oloron, (1081), p. 580/31–4; 9.8, to the doge and people of Venice, 8 Apr. (1081), p. 585/20–6; *Epp. vag.* no. 51, to the faithful in France and Germany, (summer 1083), pp. 122–5.

[172] See e.g. the poem included among Peter Damiani's verses: Lokrantz, *L'opera poetica*, no. D7, pp. 153–5, esp. stanza 12, cf. pp. 21–2, 206–8.

[173] *Reg.* 8.21, 15 Mar. 1081, p. 557/11–29; cf. 4.2 to Bishop Hermann of Metz, 25 Aug. 1076, p. 295/10–18; 9.3, to Bishop Altmann of Passau and Abbot William of Hirsau, (Mar. 1081), p. 575/10–13.

[174] *Reg.* 3.15, to the knight Wifred of Milan, (Apr.) 1076, p. 277/32–6.

[175] *Epp. vag.* no. 2, to the community of Vallombrosa, (after 12 July 1073), pp. 6–7.

[176] *Reg.* 7.14*a*, Lent synod 1080, 7 Mar. 1080, p. 483/21–3; 8.4, to Abbot Richard of Marseilles, 27 June 1080, p. 520/33–5; 8.5, to the bishops of South Italy, 21 July 1080, pp. 521/32–522/2.

Gregory's eyes, made himself a member of the devil and involved his accomplices in the devil's service.[177] No less decisively, Gregory divided kings and princes according to their conduct. A good ruler was a member of Christ;[178] but demons dominated and reduced to servitude to themselves rulers who did not live in a godly manner ('religiose') and who did not duly fear God in whatever they attempted.[179]

As good Christians were members of Christ, so the wicked were members of Satan or of Antichrist. Gregory never identified any of his own lay adversaries, or those of the Christian religion, with Antichrist. If the devil himself sought to turn the Christians of the east against the catholic religion, the Seljuks who were slaughtering eastern Christians like cattle did so as members of the devil; Gregory did not identify them outright with demons.[180] In the context of the uncertainties about the German kingdom after Canossa and Forchheim, a reprobate king disclosed himself to be a member of Antichrist, not Antichrist himself.[181] The same was true of a reprobate bishop like Lambert of Thérouanne.[182] Gregory's reprobate adversaries the Lombard bishops, who were guilty of the consecration of Archbishop Godfrey of Milan, were 'the precursors of Antichrist and henchmen of the ancient enemy', and 'ministers of Satan and heralds of Antichrist'; they were not themselves identified with Antichrist.[183] The extreme case was Archbishop Guibert of Ravenna. After the synod of Brixen in June 1080, Gregory was immediately provoked in a torrent of anger at his complicity in a papal schism to describe the synod as 'an assembly of Satan', which set up for itself Guibert, the devastator of the holy church of Ravenna, as 'Antichrist and heresiarch'. But this was exceptional. In his propaganda letters against Guibert of the following autumn which were addressed to Ravenna and the exarchate, Gregory did not repeat his identification of Guibert with Antichrist, but spoke of him as an imitator of his father the devil.[184] In his considered pronouncements, Gregory saw the devil working in history as Antichrist in anticipation of the last time;[185] he did not normally identify his human enemies outright with Antichrist.

---

[177] *Reg.* 4.18, to the canons of le Puy, 23 Mar. 1077, p. 324/21–7.

[178] *Reg.* 7.27, to Robert Curthose, 8 May 1080, p. 508/33–6; 8.3, to King Alphonso of León–Castile, (27 June 1080), p. 519/16–21.

[179] *Reg.* 8.21, pp. 555/13–16, 556/5–7.

[180] *Reg.* 2.27, to the faithful of St Peter, 16 Dec. 1074, p. 173/7–12; 2.49, to Abbot Hugh of Cluny, 22 Jan. 1075, p. 189/14–19.

[181] *Reg.* 4.24, to the faithful in Germany, 31 May 1077, p. 337/27–32.

[182] *Epp. vag.* no. 47, to Count Robert of Flanders, (1082/3), pp. 114–15; *Reg.* 9.35, to the bishops and lay princes of Flanders, (1083), p. 624/4–6.

[183] *Reg.* 1.11, to Countesses Beatrice and Matilda of Tuscany, 24 June 1073, p. 18/13–18; 1.15, to the faithful in Lombardy, 1 July 1073, pp. 23/32–24/1; cf. the description of those present at the synod of Brixen in 1080 as 'disciples of Satan': 8.5, to the bishops of South Italy, 21 July 1080, pp. 521/32–532/2, 23–9.

[184] *Reg.* 8.5, p. 522/23–33, 8.12–13, to the bishops of Tuscan March, Fermo, and the exarchate, and to the clergy and laity of Ravenna, 15 Oct. 1080, pp. 531–4, esp. 533/12–14; 8.14, to the clerical and lay authorities of the exarchate, the Pentapolis, Fermo, and Spoleto, 11 Dec. 1080, pp. 534–5.

[185] *Epp. vag.* no. 54, to all the faithful, (1084), pp. 132–5.

As a consequence, Gregory always kept open the possibility that his opponents might be converted. He held to the conviction that God's mercies are infinite and that there is always hope for the penitent, however great the sin and however delayed the penitence. This held good even for the excommunicate, for Gregory would have regarded Christ's promise that whatever he bound in earth would be bound in heaven (Matt. 16: 19) as not only establishing a judicial sentence but also providing a medicine which might avail to the salvation of one who duly reacted with penitence and amendment. Gregory made his position clear in his second apologia to Bishop Hermann of Metz:

Just as the elect are indissolubly united to the head, so, too, the reprobate are resolutely in league with him who is the head of wickedness, particularly against the good. In opposition to such men, we assuredly should not engage in controversy but rather should plead for them with tearful lamentation that Almighty God should deliver them from the snare of Satan in which they are held captive, and that, after whatever dangers, he should bring them to the knowledge of the truth.[186]

In the record of his last testament at Salerno, Gregory is said to have acted consistently with this statement. He did, indeed, except Henry IV of Germany, Archbishop Guibert of Ravenna, and their principal supporters, from the general absolution which he promised to all the excommunicated who acknowledged his power to pronounce it; but he also provided that the exception would not apply if, in his hearers' judgement, the king and the anti-pope made due and canonical satisfaction.[187]

Especially during his final years, Gregory's call to repent was not only addressed to his opponents but also to his own partisans. He believed that the church in his day was subject to the judgement of a just God upon its own members ('peccatis nostris exigentibus') and that its consequent afflictions were to be borne with patience. Patience should be accompanied by hope in the mercy of a God who, if he was strong to put down the proud, was also strong to exalt the humble. Thus, he called for the repentance of catholics no less than of their enemies:

If only we bring the medication of penitence to the sickness of our sins, and if by strictly correcting our transgressions and negligence we order the course of our lives according to the pattern of righteousness, with the aid of power from heaven the madness of our enemies will swiftly perish and holy church will receive the peace and safety that it has long desired.[188]

Gregory looked for repentance on the part of his supporters no less than of his opponents. Such repentance was the condition of the coming of better times. Gregory's calls upon men to repent in no way diminished his belief in the direct action in the world of God and of the devil; rather, they followed from his conviction that every man must choose to which service and to which solidarity he would belong.

---

[186] *Reg.* 8.21, 15 Mar. 1081, pp. 557/23–558/3.
[187] *H* no. 35, p. 75/18–25; see, too, the final words of his sentence against Henry IV in 1080: *Reg.* 7.14*a*, p. 487/16–19.
[188] *Reg.* 8.9, to the faithful in Germany, 22 Sept. 1080, pp. 527/35–538/1.

TABLE. *A list of the passages at the end of Gregory's letters which begin with the* Omnipotens Deus *(or similar) formula*

	Reference		Pages	Date	Addressees
1.	*Reg.*	1.15	24–5	1 July 1073	All the faithful, esp. in Lombardy
2.		1.38	61	17 Dec. 1073	Duke Wratislav II of Bohemia
3.		1.40	63	3 Jan. 1074	Countess Matilda of Tuscany
4.		1.50	77	4 Mar. 1074	Countesses Beatrice and Matilda of Tuscany
5.		1.62	91	19 Mar. 1074	Abbot Hugh of Cluny
6.		1.77	111	15 Apr. 1074	Countesses Beatrice and Matilda of Tuscany
7.		1.83	119	9 May 1074	King Alphonso VI of León–Castile
8.		2.7	136	22 Sept. 1074	Duke Wratislav II of Bohemia
9.		2.8	138	22 Sept. 1074	Bishop John of Olmütz
10.		2.31	168	7 Dec. 1074	King Henry IV of Germany
11.		2.37	173	16 Dec. 1074	All the faithful of St Peter
12.	*Epp. vag.*	15	12	(1074, after 16 Dec.)	Countess Matilda of Tuscany
13.	*Reg.*	2.44	182	10 Jan. 1075	Queen Judith of Hungary
14.		2.70	230	17 Apr. 1075	Duke Gésa of Hungary and his subjects
15.		2.71	232	17 Apr. 1075	Duke Wratislav II of Bohemia
16.		2.73	235	20 Apr. 1075	Duke Boleslav II of Poland
17.		2.74	237	17 Apr. 1075	Prince Demetrius of Russia and his wife
18.		3.7	259	1075, early Sept.	King Henry IV of Germany
19.		3.15	277	1076 (Apr.)	The Milanese knight Wifred
20.		4.1	292	15 July 1076	All the faithful in Germany
21.		4.2	297	25 Aug. 1076	Bishop Hermann of Metz and all the faithful in Germany
22.		4.17	323	31 Mar. 1077	King William I of England, Queen Matilda, and their children

(*cont.*)

	Reference		Pages	Date	Addressees
23.	*Reg.*	5.10	363	6 Nov. 1077	King Harold Hein of Denmark
24.		5.21	385	7 May 1078	Abbot Hugh of Cluny and all his monks
25.		6.1	391	1 July 1078	All in Germany who who were not excommunicated
26.		6.3	396	22 Aug. 1078	Bishop Hugh of Die and Abbot Hugh of Cluny
27.		6.13	417–18	15 Dec. 1078	King Olav III of Norway and his subjects
28.		6.14	419	30 Dec. 1078	Duke Welf IV of Bavaria and his followers
29.		6.15	420	3 Jan. 1079	The monks of Saint-Victor at Marseilles
30.		6.29	422	21 Mar. 1079	King Ladislaus I of Hungary
31.		6.35	452	20 Apr. 1079	The archbishops of Rouen, Tours, and Sens
32.	*Epp. vag.*	31	84	(1079, July/Oct.)	Cardinal-bishop Peter of Albano and Bishop Ulrich of Padua
33.	*Reg.*	7.23	502–3	24 Apr. 1080	King William I of England
34.		8.1	513–14	24 Apr. 1080	Archbishop Gregory of Tsamandos
35.		8.22	565	(1081)	Queen Adelaide of Hungary
36.		9.2	572	(1081)	King Alphonso VI of León–Castile and his subjects
37.	*Epp. vag.*	47	114	(1082/3)	Count Robert I of Flanders
38.		54	134	(1084, July/Nov.)	All the faithful

8.5 The Liberty of the Church

In the last encyclical that Gregory dispatched from Salerno in 1084, he declared his greatest concern as pope to have been 'that holy church, the bride of Christ, our lady and mother, should return to her true glory and stand free, chaste, and catholic' ('libera, casta, et catholica'). It was by reason of this concern that the devil, as the ancient enemy of mankind, had armed his human members against Gregory.[189] Gregory's concept of Christian liberty, and of the liberty of the church, was derived from his conviction that two services, that of Christ and that of the devil, radically divided mankind. As the distinguishing quality of the service of Christ, liberty was no abstract concept, but the mark of those who were his members, not those of Satan.

It was a quality of corporate and individual living to which all Christians should aspire.[190] It had two aspects: first and negatively, it was freedom from any lordship, subjection, or services which contradicted or limited the service of Christ and of St Peter to whom Christ had committed authority over his church upon earth; second and positively, it was a complete and exclusive commitment in time and in eternity to Christ whose service is perfect freedom, through St Peter as Christ had commissioned him to be the prince of the apostles in the New Testament. Viewed retrospectively, liberty was the birthright of the Christian religion in which Christ founded it and in which it must always be renewed; prospectively, as embodied in whoever followed Christ in humility, it had the power to raise men from a condition that was servile and transient to one of emancipation and eternal duration.[191] It was the distinguishing quality of both the Christian and the church.

Gregory's commitment to vindicating the liberty of the church was apparent from the beginning of his pontificate, especially in his dealings over the church of Milan and through them with King Henry IV of Germany. In 1074, using language which anticipated that of his last encyclical, he praised Henry's mother the Empress Agnes because, in company with Countesses Beatrice and Matilda of Tuscany, she had striven that the church should rise again to its pristine liberty; as though instructed by angels, she had urged other princes to help a struggling church.[192] In the contest for the archbishopric of Milan, the issue for Gregory was whether that church would be joined to Christ as his bride or whether it would be shamefully subject to the devil. A church which had once shone forth for its religion, liberty, and special glory had now been bought by its new archbishop, Godfrey, as if it were a slave-girl; having been the free bride of Christ, the church of Milan had been prostituted by him in servitude to the devil. Gregory trusted that, in such circumstances, Bishop William of Pavia would signify his willingness to fight with Gregory for the liberty of holy church against those who assailed it. When he summoned the bishops of the province of Aquileia to his Lent synod of 1074, he reminded them that the rulers of the world were using the bride of Christ as a vile slave-girl; he summoned them to the defence of the church's proper liberty and religion.[193]

---

[189] *Epp. vag.* no. 54, to all the faithful, (1084), pp. 132–3.

[190] The most useful studies of Gregory's idea of liberty are Tellenbach, *Church, State, and Christian Society*, and Szabó-Bechstein, *Libertas ecclesiae*, esp. pp. 138–92.

[191] *Reg.* 2.42, to Archbishop Guibert of Ravenna, 4 Jan. 1075, p. 179/21–5; 8.21, to Bishop Hermann of Metz, 15 Mar. 1081, p. 562/20–5.

[192] *Reg.* 1.85, 15 June 1074, p. 122/17–23.

[193] *Reg.* 1.12, to Bishop William of Pavia, 29 June 1073, p. 20/9–17; 1.15, to the faithful in Lombardy, 1 July 1073, p. 24/1–19; 1.42, to Archbishop Sigehard of Aquileia and his suffragans, 24 Jan. 1074, pp. 64–5; cf. 2.42, to Archbishop Guibert of Ravenna, 4 Jan. 1075, p. 179/13–25.

The liberty that came from free and unhampered subjection to Christ himself was the prerogative of the church universal as the bride of Christ.[194] It was, therefore, the noblest objective for which a Christian might strive in the conflicts the beset western Christendom. As Gregory wrote in 1081 of his supporters in Germany:

We know that our brothers are wearied by their long struggle and manifold vexations. But by general consent it is more noble to contend for a long time for the liberty of holy church than to be wretchedly subject in servitude to the devil. For these wretches—I mean the members of the devil—strive only so that they may be subject to his wretched slavery; by contrast, the members of Christ strive so that such wretches as these may be restored to Christian liberty.[195]

The upholding of Christian liberty was, accordingly, a prime duty of kings,[196] the more so because the pristine liberty of the church was at risk from latter-day custom, such as (in Gregory's eventual evaluation of it) lay investiture, as well as simony and like infringements.[197]

It was in individual churches, and especially metropolitan sees, that the liberty of the church as it was supremely exemplifed in the church of Rome was most critically at stake; the liberty of the church universal was represented in microcosm in each and every church, and it was everywhere at stake in their vicissitudes. Apart from Milan, Gregory considered this to be especially so in his dealings with the church of Ravenna, especially after Henry IV of Germany's choice in 1080 of Archbishop Guibert to be his anti-pope. Thus, Gregory wrote to the clergy and laity of Ravenna:

Do not any longer allow your church to be treated like a slave-girl and oppressed by godless hands, but like good sons exert yourselves to free ('vendicare') it in the liberty of its mother, that is, of the Roman church. By so doing, you will both show that you love the honour of God when you hold dear the liberty of holy church which is his spouse, and as free sons you can and should deservedly hope for the inheritance of eternal blessedness.[198]

In similar vein, when Gregory eventually charged the clergy and people of Rheims, under the guidance of his legate Bishop Hugh of Die, to elect a new archbishop in place of the *pseudopastor* Manasses I, the purpose was to renew the ancient liberty of their church.[199] When he instructed the clergy and people of Chartres to replace the deposed Bishop Robert, he reminded them that the source of their liberty which they must vindicate was Christ himself:

---

[194] *Reg.* 3.10, to Henry IV of Germany, (8 Dec.) 1075, p. 267/10–14; 9.3, to Bishop Altmann of Passau and Abbot William of Hirsau, (Mar. 1081), p. 574/29–30.

[195] *Reg.* 9.3, p. 575/6–13. Gregory could also refer ironically to the 'wretched liberty' of those who shook off the yoke of St Peter: 8.21, to Bishop Hermann of Metz, 15 Mar. 1081, p. 548/18–25.

[196] *Reg.* 1.75, to King Philip of France, 13 Apr. 1074, pp. 106/34–107/4; 3.10, to Henry IV of Germany, (8 Dec.), 1075, p. 267/7–14; 4.28, to the kings and lay magnates of Spain, 28 June 1077, p. 344/23–7.

[197] *Reg.* 4.3, to the faithful in Germany, 3 Sept. 1076, pp. 298/36–299/2; 5.7, to Archbishop Udo of Trier and his suffragans, 30 Sept. 1077, p. 358/6–12; 7.14a(2), record of the Lent synod of 1080, 7 Mar. 1080, pp. 480/26–481/3.

[198] *Reg.* 8.13, 15 Oct. 1080, p. 534/1–8; cf. 8.12, to the bishops, clergy, and laity of the marches of Tuscany and Fermo and of the exarchate, 15 Oct. 1080, p. 532/11–19.

[199] *Reg.* 8.17, 17 Dec. 1080, p. 539/15–20.

Remember that no one suffered for you, no one died for you, but Christ. As beloved sons of God, cling to and defend his liberty. Do not allow the yoke of iniquity, or any lordship, to be in any way imposed upon you to the destruction of your souls, knowing that, in this cause, papal authority and defence will never let you down.[200]

The liberty of the church universal, and of every church as part of it, consisted in unfettered and unqualified subjection to the lordship of Christ the Redeemer. It was formed and sustained in the continuing struggle of Christ against the devil to which all men were committed on one side or the other.

It was, therefore, to be generally transmitted through the church and through Christian society. In Gregory's eyes, whatever vicissitudes his legates might experience, they represented the Roman church which was the fountain-head of liberty; they must be the upholders and champions of its truth and liberty.[201] Archbishops and bishops, too, were invested with a liberty that belonged to their office ('libertas vestri sacerdotalis officii') in which they should stand fast to the death against the tyranny of kings and against the disorders of church and society.[202] As Gregory told Abbot Hugh of Cluny, there was a liberty of rightful conduct and government ('libertas rectitudinis') to which the leaders of human affairs, especially, should adhere, although few of them in fact did so.[203] The defining and the prosecution of liberty in and through whatever strife might be involved was a prime duty of all faithful churchmen.

8.6 Free Elections

The liberty that Gregory sought for the church became an issue whenever there was an election to a bishopric or abbey, and the demand for freedom of election was a watchword of his pontificate.[204] So far as bishoprics are concerned, it must be borne in mind that, in Gregory's day, the emergence of organized cathedral chapters composed exclusively of clergy was far from complete in any part of western Christendom.[205] Although the opposition to their bishops of cathedral establishments such as that of Bamberg was well known to Gregory, he never in his letters addressed a cathedral corporation as such; his usual addressees were, in traditional terms from which he had no thought of departing, the 'clerus et populus' of the church.[206] This was always the case with regard to episcopal elections. He did not seek to eliminate the laity from all part in elections by enforcing election by cathedral

---

[200] *Reg.* 4.14, 4 Mar. 1077, p. 318/24–9.

[201] *Reg.* 2.12, to Bishop Burchard of Halberstadt, 26 Oct. 1074, pp. 143/30–144/1.

[202] *Reg.* 2.5, to the bishops of France, 10 Sept. 1074, p. 132/10–16; cf. 4.20, to Bishop Josfred of Paris, 25 Mar. 1077, p. 329/9–15; *Epp. vag.* no. 14, to all the faithful in Germany, (summer 1076), pp. 34–5.

[203] *Reg.* 8.2, 27 June 1080, pp. 517/32–518/2; cf. 8.23, to Cardinal-bishop Peter of Albano and Prince Gisulf of Salerno, (1084), p. 567/4–7.

[204] The best study of canonical elections remains Schmid, *Der Begriff der kanonischen Wahl.*

[205] On the emergence of chapters in Germany, see R. Schieffer, *Die Entstehung von Domkapiteln* and 'Die ältesten Papsturkunden'.

[206] *Reg.* 3.1–3, to the clergy and people of Bamberg, to Archbishop Siegfried of Mainz, and to King Henry IV of Germany, 20 July 1075, pp. 242–7.

chapters. Rather, his concern was to ensure that, according to the established canonical principle 'docendus non sequendus populus', the clergy of a church should take a lead which the laity should obediently follow. Nor was he concerned to exclude external authorities from the procedure of elections. Among the clergy, metropolitans and comprovincial bishops had a rightful part to play in ensuring a free and canonical election; as the final step in an electoral process, a king, too, if in good standing might signify his consent to what had been done and perform appropriate consequential acts in introducing a bishop to his see.[207] Such was the authentic order, hallowed from the earliest days of the church, which Gregory deemed from 1075 to be given definitive expression in canon twenty-two of the fourth council of Constantinople, and which seems to have guided the development of his thought about the three interrelated issues of free elections, simony, and lay investiture.[208]

Italy, France, and Germany provide the most telling illustrations. Too much should not be made of the situation at Milan in the early years of Gregory's pontificate. The elections of the rival archbishops Godfrey and Atto did, indeed, set out in the sharpest terms the rival claims of the German king and of the Roman pope, and the Milanese clergy and people were profoundly concerned about their respective rights. But all parties concerned pressed their claims too hard for Milan to be other than an exceptional case. The clergy of the city were too consciously particularist in their outlook, and too much involved in practices that were simoniacal. The self-awareness and activity of the Milanese people, especially during the ascendancy of the lay Patarene leader Erlembald, were too powerful for it to respect the principle 'docendus non sequendus populus'. Too much was at stake for both king and pope for an archiepiscopal election at Milan to be left to its own clergy and people.[209] Gregory's requirements for elections are, therefore, most clearly apparent elsewhere.

The kingdom of France provides the most telling evidence, for Gregory's relations with King Philip I were, for the most part, restrained and without confrontation. From his dealings over the see of Mâcon in 1074 to those over that of Rheims six years later, Gregory's requirements were remarkably consistent. The paradigm is provided by the arrangements which he proposed for Rheims, with election by clergy and people with due advice from a papal legate, protection of the security of the election by well-disposed local lay magnates, the concurrence of the suffragan bishops of the province, and finally but integrally the assent of the Capetian king to what had been done.[210]

The vicissitudes of Gregory's dealings with Germany resulted in there being greater development in Gregory's requirements about free election in lands that were subject to Henry IV. Until Gregory's break with Henry in January 1076, his requirements were similar to those which he expressed as regards France. This

---

[207] See e.g. the discussion of Cardinal Deusdedit's *Coll. can.* in Cowdrey, *The Age of Abbot Desiderius*, pp. 188–90.
[208] See above, 3.2.4.
[209] See esp. Arnulf of Milan, 3.20–5.5, pp. 196–224, and the discussion above, 4.3.
[210] See above, 5.2.1.

emerges with regard to the see of Bamberg after the deposition in 1075 of Bishop Hermann. The provision of a successor was a matter for God and for St Peter as patron saint of the see.[211] Gregory entrusted the oversight of a new election to Archbishop Siegfried of Mainz in his capacity as metropolitan. He insisted that the appointment of a new bishop should take place 'secundum sanctorum instituta patrum', by which he clearly meant a canonical election by clergy and people from which all simony was excluded. King Henry IV, too, was to ensure that an election took place duly ('secundum Deum') and with the counsel of religious men.[212]

After Gregory restored Henry to communion at Canossa and after the election of Rudolf of Swabia as anti-king by the German princes at Forchheim, Gregory enlarged upon his understanding of free election. The first occasion was in September 1077, after the clergy and people of Aquileia had elected their archdeacon to be patriarch.[213] Gregory prefaced a letter to them by what he considered to be the essential guideline for such elections: the words of Christ himself in the Gospel, that 'he who enters by the door is the shepherd of the sheep; he who does not enter the door but climbs in by another way is a thief and robber' (John 10: 1–2). Gregory commented that, through human sins, this requirement had for long been neglected and corrupted by evil customs; he was determined to revive and restore it. In order to rule the people of God in every church according to the needs of the time, such a bishop should be elected, and his election should be so performed, that he might indeed not be a thief and robber, but might be worthy of the name and office of a shepherd. Gregory's concern was no less with the person of the bishop than with the manner of his election, and he dedicated himself to the task of implementing his concern.

With an eye to Henry IV whose interests were at stake in Aquileia, Gregory balanced his requirement for the freedom of the electoral process itself by a recognition of the king's rightful claims when the election was complete.

However, we by no means deny or hinder what pertains to the service and due allegiance ('fidelitas') of the king. And, thus, we are seeking to introduce nothing new and nothing of our own devising, but we seek only what the well-being ('salus') of all and necessity alike demand, that in the appointment of bishops the authority of the Gospel and of the church's law should before all else be secured, according to the common understanding and approval of the holy fathers of the church.

Gregory was, in effect, leaving a way open for the king to confer what would increasingly be called the *regalia*—the complex of service, rights, lands, and renders which were owed to the king because of royal endowments and of the temporal position of the bishops. As would also be the case at Rheims in 1080, Gregory utilized legates to

---

[211] *Reg.* 2.76, to the clergy and people of Bamberg, 20 Apr. 1075, p. 240/4–6.

[212] *Reg.* 3.2–3, to Archbishop Siegfried of Mainz, and to King Henry IV of Germany, 20 July 1075, pp. 244–7, esp. pp. 245/12–17, 247/22–30. In Dec. 1074, Gregory had been willing for an election to be made to the see of Fermo 'regis consilio': 2.38, to the count, clergy, and people of Fermo, 22 Dec. 1074, p. 174/20–4.

[213] For the circumstances, see above, 4.4.

oversee the election at Aquileia, and he called upon the suffragan bishops of the see to ensure the integrity of the election.[214]

In the following spring, the election of Bishop Wigold of Augsburg provides further evidence of Gregory's current aspirations for the freedom of the church as expressed in an episcopal election. The Swabian annalist Berthold, who is the principal source for what happened, wrote of Wigold's consecration at Goslar where the anti-king Rudolf of Swabia kept Easter. Wigold had already been canonically elected by clergy and people as well as by others who were rightfully involved ('a meliori et maiori parte aecclesiasticae militiae'). At Goslar, Gregory's legate, the cardinal-deacon Bernard, confirmed the election, and Wigold was consecrated by Archbishop Siegfried of Mainz and nine other bishops. Only after all that legally belonged to his election had been completed with his receiving from the archbishop his ring, staff, and episcopal throne did the anti-king Rudolf confer upon him what appertained to the temporal aspect of his office ('rex . . . ex sua parte quicquid regii iuris fuit in procurandis bonis aecclesiasticis diligenter commendavit'). 'For,' as Berthold explained, 'because the king was abundantly obedient in all things, he safeguarded what had lately (*nuper*) been laid down in the Roman synod, . . . that no layman should confer churches and ecclesiastical offices and tithes upon any person as though they were his own property (*quasi proprium suum*), nor should any laymen venture to claim them for himself against the canons.'[215] As in Gregory's own reflections upon the election at Aquileia, so in the account of Wigold's at Augsburg, every suggestion that a layman, even the king, might confer spiritual offices or rights as though they were his property was to be excluded. At Goslar, indeed, investiture with ring and staff was expressly reserved for the spiritual hands of the metropolitan. But in both cases, the king was allowed after the election was in every respect complete to confer the *regalia*.

The two elections to the sees of Aquileia and Augsburg made clear Gregory's insistence that, for there to be a free election, no layman might transmit the episcopate, or any spiritual appurtenance of it, as though it were his own property ('quasi proprium suum'). Gregory required, first, the election of a duly accredited clerk who was personally worthy of his office, and secondly, an electoral process in which the clergy took the lead while the laity obediently followed, while no kind of spiritual gift was transmitted by lay hands. Such was the way in which a true shepherd entered by the door.

At his Lent synod of 1080, Gregory published decrees which brought to a head this quest to provide for free elections which would promote the liberty of the church. If any bishop, abbot, or lesser minister were to receive his office at lay hands, his office was to be accounted vacant and he himself was to be deemed excommunicate; for he had fallen into the sins of ambition and disobedience which were as the sin of idolatry (cf. 1 Sam. 15: 23). On the lay side, a similar penalty of excommunication

---

[214] *Reg.* 5.5–6, to the clergy and people of Aquileia, and to the suffragans of the see of Aquileia, 17 Sept. 1077, pp. 352–5, esp. p. 353/5–27.
[215] Berthold, *a.* 1078, pp. 309/35–310/13.

was visited upon any authority from emperors down to local lords who carried out investitures with bishoprics or lesser churches; the layman responsible would be excommunicate until he repented and restored to its proper liberty the church concerned.[216] Gregory sought further to safeguard the freedom of episcopal elections by a 'law of devolution' which placed them exclusively under ecclesiastical authority. In the event of a vacancy, a new shepherd—the word 'pastor' evoked John 10: 1–2—was to be supplied at the instance of the episcopal visitor or overseer;[217] the clergy and people of the see were to put aside all secular ambition, fear, or favour and to elect a successor subject to the consent of the papacy (if the see were among those directly subject to it) or of the metropolitan see concerned (in other cases). If the proper procedure were not followed, the election would be null; it would pass to the discretion of the papacy or of the metropolitan see, whichever might be appropriate.[218]

Gregory's breach in 1080 with King Henry IV of Germany and the consequent turmoils were not favourable to further developments, and Gregory's mature position about elections must take due account of his proposed procedure at Rheims in 1080.[219] But there can be no mistaking his cumulative determination, probably intensified by his reading of canon twenty-two of the fourth council of Constantinople, to eliminate lay influence from the processes whereby bishops and other clergy came to their offices in the church and to limit lay influence thereafter to such forms as ecclesiastical authority might define and concede. Only so could the liberty of the church be secured and the unfettered service of Christ be made possible.

8.7 Simony

Gregory's citation of the Johannine text about the shepherd who enters by the door by contrast with the thief and robber who climbs in by another way (John 10: 1–2) in connection with freedom of episcopal elections is an indication of the extent to which he regarded his opposition to simony as part of his purpose of securing the liberty of the church; for the text was also a main warrant for his requirement that simony should be eliminated from all ecclesiastical ordinations and promotions.

In the second half of the eleventh century, simony was a term of increasingly comprehensive and complex meaning which described abuses in the church that reformers of all kinds wished to eradicate. It was derived from Simon Magus, the mercenary figure who saw St Peter at Samaria conferring the gift of the Holy Spirit, and who offered Peter silver in order that he might receive a like gift; Peter refused with the rebuke, 'Your silver perish with you, because you thought you could obtain the gift of God with money!' (Acts 8: 9–24). An eleventh-century example of simony in its basic sense is the tariff of payments that, in 1059, Peter Damiani informed

---

[216] *Reg.* 7.14*a*(1)(2), 7 Mar. 1080, pp. 480–1.

[217] For the term *visitator*, see Niermeyer, *Mediae Latinitatis Lexicon Minus*, s.v. *visitator*, 2, 3.

[218] *Reg.* 7.14*a*(6), p. 482; for the election at Arles which prepared the way for this decree, see above, 5.4.3.

[219] See above, 5.2.1.

Hildebrand that he found in force at Milan whenever holy orders were conferred.[220] As Gregory VII's letters illustrate, the writings about simony of Pope Gregory the Great provided material for a more wide-ranging conception of simony as being of three kinds—simony by the hand ('a manu') when monetary payments passed, simony by service ('ab obsequio') when the discharge of some duty was the *quid pro quo* for promotion, and simony by the tongue ('a lingua'), when there was an offer of favours, advocacy, or promises. Pope Gregory the Great also gave currency to the proscription of simony as the 'simoniac heresy'.[221]

Such was the view of simony that predominated in Gregory VII's letters. Alongside the tradition about Simon Magus as the would-be trafficker in sacred things, there had been another, legendary presentation of him as the magician and wonder-worker who was the life-long adversary of St Peter who, after engaging him in debate before the Emperor Nero, brought about the martyrdom at Rome of St Peter and St Paul.[222] This tradition was familiar in reforming circles at eleventh-century Rome, for example to Peter Damiani.[223] Moreover, the most elaborate version of Gregory's lifetime was in a poetic work composed at Montecassino by the monk Amatus and dedicated to Gregory himself.[224] It is testimony to Gregory's own sober attitude to legend, however powerful it might be as propaganda for his cause, that he referred to Simon Magus's contest with St Peter but seldom. He did so only in two letters addressed after Archbishop Guibert of Ravenna was chosen to be anti-pope at the synod of Brixen and dispatched from South Italy, where Amatus's poem suggests that legends about the contest were especially current.[225]

Gregory was, nevertheless, convinced that Simon Magus was still personally active in the church, and he could present the struggle against him in personal and heroic terms. Thus, he told Bishop-elect Albert of Acqui that no churchman could make himself more the debtor of St Peter and of himself as Peter's vicar than if, armed with the shield of faith and the helmet of salvation (cf. Eph. 6: 16–17), he fought with them against Simon Magus, who had wretchedly infected the church of St Ambrose at Milan with the poison of his venality, and if he helped the Patarene leader Erlembald, a most strenuous knight of Christ, in deeds which belonged to the worship of God and the religion of holy church.[226] However, as Gregory presented it, the struggle against Simon Magus was not a matter of past legend but of the present spiritual and moral state of the Christian religion. The simonists now disparaged the church as the bride of Christ; the church belonged wholly to Christ, yet the

---

[220] *Briefe*, no. 65, 2.228–47, esp. pp. 240/11–241/2.

[221] *Reg.* 6.34, to Archbishop Gebuin of Lyons, 20 Apr. 1079, p. 448/9–17; cf. Gregory I, *Hom. XL in Evang.* 1.4.4, col. 1092.

[222] For the legends, see Cowdrey, 'Simon Magus in South Italy', esp. pp. 78–83.

[223] *Briefe*, no. 89, 2.572.

[224] Lentini, *Il poema*. For the dedication to Gregory, see 1.60/10–15. Unfortunately the dedicatory letter to Gregory is largely lost through damage to the sole MS: 1.57.

[225] *Reg.* 8.2, to Abbot Hugh of Cluny, 27 June 1080, p. 517/24–9, and more overtly, 8.5, to the bishop of South Italy, 21 July 1080, p. 523/5–12; see Cowdrey, 'Simon Magus in South Italy', pp. 85–6.

[226] *Reg.* 1.27, 13 Oct. 1073, pp. 44/29–45/3.

simonists presumed to buy it like a common woman. Archbishop Godfrey of Milan had dared to buy the church of Milan like a vile slave-girl, to prostitute the church of Christ to the devil, to separate it from the Christian faith, and to taint it with the crime of the simoniac heresy.[227] Gregory made much of the polluting effect of simony upon the churches concerned as well as those individuals who practised it. Thus, guilty German bishops were 'symoniaca labe fedati'; again, when Gregory suspended the simoniacal Bishop Stephen of le Puy and committed the oversight of the see to another bishop, he spoke of the expulsion from the see of every contagion of the simoniac heresy and of the presence henceforth of a lawful bishop, so that the clergy and people might offer pure services to Christ and to his Mother, the patron of their see.[228]

Despite the intensity of his language about pollution and contagion, with its over-tones of the religious and social taboos attaching to leprosy, Gregory almost certainly had in mind primarily the moral rather than the cultic and ceremonial purity of the church. This is indicated, first, by his manifest restraint, by contrast with his ex-tremer confrères at Rome and allies in the church at large, in never treating the sacra-ments and ministrations of simoniacs as absolutely null and void.[229] Second, Gregory's preoccupation with the moral qualities of the clergy, rather than with ritual disqualification, is clear in his reply to an Italian clerk, that mercy should be shown to those who had been ordained by a simoniacal bishop without knowledge of his simony and payment on their part, before Pope Nicholas II's strict ruling in 1059; they were to be confirmed in their orders by the laying on of hands, provided only that their own lives were beyond reproach.[230] Third, for Gregory, freedom from simony was itself a mark of a bishop's zeal for Christian righteousness and of his exhibiting the key virtue of Christian obedience. When exhorting Count Robert of Flanders to resist simoniacal bishops, he characteristically drew upon a multiplicity of biblical passages to place simony in a wider moral, rather than ceremonial, context:

He who said, 'Let everyone who hears say: Come' (Rev. 22: 17), excluded no one of any order. And whosoever would receive a penny from the master of the household, let him dedicate him-self to working in the vineyard of the Lord (cf. Matt. 20: 1–16). The universal mother [the church] commands those who are called bishops to proclaim these things, as is rightful. But what kind of men they are, you can know by their fruits (cf. Matt. 7: 16), because those who do not enter the sheepfold by the door but climb in elsewhere are thieves and robbers (cf. John 10:

---

[227] *Reg.* 1.15, to the faithful of St Peter in Lombardy, 1 July 1073, p. 24/1–9.

[228] *Reg.* 1.77, to Countesses Beatrice and Matilda, 15 Apr. 1074, p. 109/26; cf. 3.4, to Archbishop Siegfried of Mainz, 3 Sept. 1075, p. 249/16–18; 1.80, to the clergy and people of le Puy, 13 Apr. 1074, p. 111/24–30.

[229] For the problem of reordinations, see esp. Saltet, *Les Réordinations*, pp. 173–217. For extremer manifestations, see e.g. the Patarenes' disparagement of their opponents' sacraments as 'dog's dung': Arnulf of Milan, 3.9, cf. 4.5–6, pp. 177, 209–10; also Bishop Amatus of Oloron's ruling at the council of Gerona (1078): canon 11, Mansi, 19.519–20; and his subsequent description of chrism consecrated by the simoniacal Bishop Frotard of Albi as 'not consecrated but execrated, and more fit for anointing asses than Christians': *Not. de eccles. s. Eugenii*, p. 50CD.

[230] *Reg.* 6.39, to Bishop Raynald of Como, 21 June 1079, p. 457/1–8. For Nicholas II's canon, see *MGH Const.* 1.547, no. 384, canon 6.

1). Whoever is made bishop according to the holy canons enters by the door, that is, by Christ. For the saying of holy scripture, that 'Evil priests are a people's ruin' (cf. 1 Sam. 2: 2–17), is borne out in our own time more clearly than daylight. Many of those who are called bishops not only do not uphold righteousness but also strive by any devices to obscure it lest it should shine forth. You should regard such men not as bishops but as enemies of Christ. As they have no concern to obey the apostolic see, by the same token you should pay them no obedience.[231]

For Gregory, simony was at root a moral disorder which detracted from the moral purity of the church as the bride of Christ and contradicted the demand of righteousness. The extirpation of it was a prime means by which, throughout his pontificate, he promoted his concern 'that holy church, the bride of Christ, our lady and mother, should return to her true glory and stand free, chaste, and catholic'.[232]

8.8 Lay Investiture

The question of Gregory's attitude to lay investiture has already been discussed in relation to German and French history during his pontificate.[233] Between his Lent synods of 1075 and 1080, his attitude hardened until, in the latter year, his synodal decrees confirmed his already formulated requirement that no bishop, abbot, or lesser member of the clergy should receive his office from the hands of a lay person on pain of exclusion from the membership and from the duties of his ecclesiastical order; those guilty were deprived of the grace of St Peter and from entry into a church until they repented and abandoned the office that they had entered through the crime of ambition and disobedience, which was as the sin of idolatry (cf. 1 Sam. 15: 23). Gregory's tendency to dwell on the moral aspect of issues is here apparent. He now added a sentence of excommunication upon any laymen, from emperors and kings down to petty lords, who presumed to confer investiture with a bishopric or any other ecclesiastical office; unless such transgressors repented and restored its proper liberty to the church concerned, they must expect divine punishment in this world and in the next.[234]

These synodal decrees constitute the fullest statement that survives of Gregory's final position about lay investiture. The development in hostility to it of Gregory himself, and probably of the Roman church as well, since the early months of Gregory's pontificate had been very great. Before he became pope the polemic against it of Cardinal Humbert in his *Adversus simoniacos* (1057/8) seems to have made little impression at Rome, and particularly not upon the mind of Hildebrand.[235] The current practice of kings in investing bishops and abbots with the ring and staff before they received consecration was not subject to question, unless there were unusual circumstances. At about the time that Humbert wrote his polemic, Hildebrand

---

[231] *Reg.* 4.11, 10 Nov. 1076, pp. 310/23–311/7.
[232] *Epp. vag.* no. 54, to all Christians, (1084), pp. 132–3.
[233] See above, 3.2.4, 5.4.2.   [234] *Reg.* 7.14a(1), (2), pp. 480–1.
[235] For Humbert's attacks on lay investiture, see *Libri III adversus simoniacos*, 3.6, 11–12, pp. 205–6, 211–13. For comment on the limited manuscript tradition and influence of Humbert's treatise, see Schieffer, *Die Entstehung des päpstlichen Investiturverbots*, pp. 41–7.

was in Germany as a papal legate and made no difficulty about being present at the episcopal consecration of Bishop Gundechar of Eichstätt, who had already received his pastoral staff from the Empress Agnes.[236] In 1073, Gregory showed similar openness of attitude when he confirmed to Anselm, the bishop-elect of Lucca, his earlier direction to refrain from receiving investiture with his bishopric at the hands of King Henry IV until the king had made satisfaction for his association with his excommunicated counsellors; Gregory envisaged Anselm's investiture if and when the king made proper satisfaction.[237]

Anselm of Lucca may have played a critical part in initiating a change in Gregory's mind. The chronicler Hugh of Flavigny states that, after Hugh was elected in October 1073 to the Burgundian see of Die, he went to Rome for ordination. Probably while awaiting Gregory's return from the south in December, he formed a close friendship there with Anselm, who had come for a similar purpose. Before Hugh's consecration, a messenger came from Henry IV with a request to Gregory not to act contrary to the custom of his predecessors by ordaining bishop two clerks who had been elected but not yet invested by the king. Gregory consulted the cardinals about what should be his answer to the king, and also his procedure at Rome. Upon their advice, Gregory agreed to defer Anselm's ordination, but he proceeded, on 16 March 1074, to perform Hugh's.[238] After being invested by Henry, no doubt after the king's restoration to communion at Eastertide 1074, the *Life* of Anselm says that, as a result of studying various written authorities ('perscrutatis diversarum auctoritatum libris'), he developed grave scruples; he fled to Gregory at Rome and abandoned into Gregory's hands whatever he had received from the king.[239] There is no evidence as to which authorities Anselm had read, but it is a reasonable conjecture that they may have included canon twenty-two of the fourth council of Constantinople, which may also have been at the heart of Gregory's synodal legislation of Lent 1075, and to which Gregory certainly appealed when instructing Hugh of Die in 1077 about his resistance to lay investiture in France.[240]

Whether or not Anselm of Lucca brought it to Gregory's attention, if canon twenty-two at this juncture became critical for Gregory's understanding of the place of the laity in the making of bishops and abbots, its rulings go far to illuminate his progressive hardening of attitude against lay investiture. The canon above all insisted that, from first to last, the process of making a bishop should be a matter for ecclesiastical persons and bodies alone. There is evidence in Gregory's letters that the Lent synod of 1075 saw the beginning of his regarding lay investiture as in itself an intrinsically unwarrantable intrusion of laymen in the process of an ecclesiastical appointment. His later comments on the elections of Bishop Gerard of Cambrai and Huzmann of Speyer make it clear that, in 1075, he had made a prohibition of lay investiture which, whatever its terms, he considered that they should have obeyed.

---

[236] Gundechar, *Lib. pontif. Eichst.* pp. 245–6. [237] *Reg.* 1.21, 1 Sept. 1073, pp. 34–5.
[238] 2, pp. 411/35–412/4. [239] *Vita Anselmi ep. Lucensis*, cap. 4, p. 14.
[240] See above, 3.2.4.

In the case of Gerard of Cambrai (1076–92) who acknowledged that he had received the gift of the episcopate ('donum episcopatus') from King Henry IV but who pleaded lack of information about Gregory's decree ('decretum') prohibiting such an acceptance, Gregory pointed out how serious a matter it was to transgress even in ignorance a synodal decree ('synodale decretum') of the apostolic see. To Huzmann of Speyer (1075–90), Gregory expressed a fear that he had received his pastoral staff from the king knowingly and rashly against a decree of the apostolic see ('contra decretum apostolicae sedis'); because Huzmann claimed to have had no certain knowledge of the decree before his investiture, Gregory now permitted him to perform the episcopal duties from which he had hitherto been inhibited, but when opportunity arose he must make satisfaction for his transgression before Gregory or his legates.[241]

Other evidence shows that, despite the excuses made by these two bishops, the prohibition gained publicity even in a distant region. In March 1077, Gregory said that the princes of Brittany had not only responded favourably to it but had understood it in a wider context of rightful episcopal appointments; they had done so with respect to the see of Dol:

When we heard that the princes of this land, in derogation of an ancient and evil custom and out of reverence for Almighty God and the apostolic see, wished no longer when bishops were appointed to exercise the lordship of investiture or to seek pecuniary advantage, so that in this see [Dol] a lawful bishop might be appointed according to the statutes of the holy fathers, we rejoiced greatly in their devotion and gladly acceded to their petition.[242]

Gregory took further steps in his synodal legislation of 1078 and 1080. Lay investiture as an abuse in itself now played prominent role in his purpose of securing the freedom of the churches concerned. In November 1078, he passed a decree against it from the side of the involvement of the clergy; in March 1080, he condemned it stringently from the lay side, as well.[243] It had come to epitomize in itself the uncanonical interference of laymen against which, in his view, the church had always in its authentic legislation striven.

Canon twenty-two also envisaged that, so long as the exclusive right of ecclesiastical persons in the making of a bishop was safeguarded, they might at their discretion invite laymen to assist and collaborate in appropriate ways. Compatibly with this provision, if not guided by it, Gregory counterbalanced his own progress towards a full synodical prohibition of lay investiture in several ways.

First, in Lent 1075, his decree concerning it seems to have had conditions and delays attached to it in order to facilitate a willing acceptance of it by Henry IV, for whom Gregory's legislation was as much a new departure as it was for the pope himself. He accorded Henry an opportunity to propose responsibly formulated

---

[241] *Reg.* 4.22, to Bishop Hugh of Die, 12 May 1077, pp. 330/27–331/11; 5.18, to Bishop Huzmann of Speyer, 19 Mar. 1078, p. 381/13–20; see also, with reference to Archbishop Henry of Aquileia, Berthold, *a.* 1079, p. 317/43–7.

[242] *Reg.* 4.13, to Archbishop Ralph of Tours, 1 Mar. 1077, p. 316/26–34.

[243] *Reg.* 6.5*b*(3), p. 403; 7.14*a*(1),(2), pp. 480–1.

modifications which might be made, subject to preserving the integrity of its principal intention.[244] Moreover, during the rest of 1075, Gregory did not press upon Henry his prohibition of lay investiture in relation to episcopal elections that took place. In the light of Gregory's later dealings with Bishops Gerard of Cambrai and Huzmann of Speyer, it seems that, in February 1075, Gregory postponed the operation of the sanctions imposed by his decree for so long as Henry showed obedience to Gregory; only when it had become clear that he had been disobedient, especially by not dismissing his excommunicate counsellors, did Gregory deem the sanctions to have been operative from the first: since Henry's disobedience was open and notorious in Germany, his subjects should have recognized that the sanctions had been triggered.[245] Gregory's attempt to invite Henry's collaboration had failed from the start through the king's disobedience.

Second, although in 1080 Gregory's synodal legislation at Rome had found its culmination in an outright prohibition of lay investiture as such, his provisions in practice for the appointment of bishops concentrated upon the comprehensive exclusion of lay participation that canon twenty-two required, rather than upon the ceremony of lay investiture. This is especially clear in his directions at the end of 1080 for the election of an archbishop of Rheims, which read like a model presentation of how such an appointment free from improper lay involvement should in practice be made.[246] Even in his letter to King Philip I of France, Gregory made no allusion to lay investiture. It is unlikely that, given Hugh of Die's campaign in France and his own synodal legislation in the previous March, Gregory was unmindful of it. Probably, after the appointment had been completed in accordance with his directions, Gregory intended to raise the matter with an obedient King Philip as he had hoped to raise it in 1075 with an obedient King Henry IV.

Third, the recognition in canon twenty-two that ecclesiastical authorities might, at their discretion, make arrangements for appropriate lay involvement may have contributed, in the late 1070s, to the first steps in Gregorian circles towards the practice whereby the king might properly confer the *regalia*, that is, the secular rights and possessions of a bishop as distinct from his spiritual functions. Such a recognition of the king's role, discharged after the process of an episcopal appointment was complete, is described in the annalist Berthold's account of the succession in April 1078 of Bishop Wigold of Augsburg. At Eastertide, Wigold, who was a canon of Augsburg and so a prime candidate, was first canonically elected by clergy and people; next, he was approved by the papal legate Cardinal Bernard and by his own metropolitan, Archbishop Siegfried of Mainz, and nine other bishops. Then he was canonically consecrated and enthroned; the archbishop of Mainz conferred upon him his ring, staff, and episcopal throne. He was thus completely set in office by clerical hands. Only thereafter, the anti-king Rudolf of Swabia, for his part, conferred upon the new bishop 'whatever belonged to royal right in administering ecclesiastical goods (*quicquid regii iuris fuerit in procurandis bonis aecclesiasticis*); for, most obedient as he

---

[244] *Reg.* 3.10, pp. 266/24–367/4.
[245] As nn. 241, 244; also *Epp. vag.* no. 14, pp. 36–7.   [246] See above, 5.4.3.

[Rudolf] was in all things, he safeguarded what had lately been canonically decreed in a Roman synod.'[247] That Gregory's own mind had been proceeding on similar lines is suggested by his declaration to the clergy and people of Aquileia in September 1077 about their own archiepiscopal election that he had no wish in any way to deny or hinder whatever belonged to the king's service and rightful fealty ('ad servitium et debitam fidelitatem regis'); he sought only to uphold the authority of the gospel and of the canons in the ordination of bishops.[248] These two cases provide circumstantial evidence that the lines set by canon twenty-two facilitated the beginnings of the distinction between the *spiritualia* and the *regalia* of a bishop upon which the resolution of the Investiture Contest eventually took place, and that Gregory had a part in drawing the distinction.

Despite his rigorous prohibition of lay investiture at his Lent synod of 1080, Gregory never raised it as an issue outside the kingdoms of Germany, Italy, Burgundy, and France. He never, for example, challenged its practice by William I, the masterful ruler of the Anglo-Norman kingdom. Gregory had no wish to alienate powerful rulers of the peripheral lands of Latin Christendom, especially when, like William, he regarded their attitudes and actions as conducing to the well-being of the churches of their realms. Gregory's restraint in his demands despite his stringent synodal prohibition repeated on a larger scale the prudent modification of his requirement for laymen to surrender tithes that he instructed his legates in France to adopt in the case of knights who co-operated in resisting clerical fornication and simony.[249] Even in so critical a matter as lay investiture, Gregory set the fostering of concord and co-operation with well-disposed laymen above the rigorous and universal enforcement for the time being of enacted ecclesiastical decrees.

8.9 Clerical Chastity

In common with almost everyone who, in the second half of the eleventh century, was concerned with the condition of the church, Gregory strongly and continually sought to secure the observance in the Latin church of a strict rule of chastity by all who were in major ecclesiastical orders, that is, who were priests (including bishops), deacons, or subdeacons. He was, therefore, determined to extirpate fornication, in the sense of any kind of sexual commerce, whether marriage, concubinage, or casual, amongst all who were ordained to these orders. His measures against simony and clerical fornication were closely associated. This was particularly the case in his letters to the German and Italian churches before and after the Lent synod of 1075; Gregory used such phrases as 'these plagues which are to be detested—the simoniac heresy and the fornication of ministers of the sacred altar'.[250]

---

[247] *a.* 1078, pp. 309/48–310/8.
[248] *Reg.* 5.5, p. 353/20–7; see above, 4.4.   [249] See above, 8.2.
[250] *Reg* 2.55, to the church of Lodi, 3 Mar. 1075, p. 200/19–22; cf. 2.61, to Bishop Dietwin of Liège, 23 Mar. 1075, pp. 215/27–216/13; 2.62, to Archbishop Sigehard of Aquileia, 23 Mar. 1075, p. 217; 2.67, to Archbishop Anno of Cologne, 29 Mar. 1075, pp. 223–5; also Gregory's letters of 1075 to German recipients: *Epp. vag.* nos. 6–11, pp. 14–27.

As in his opposition to simony Gregory largely disregarded the legends about Simon Magus as the magician who waged a lifelong struggle with St Peter, so in his campaign against clerical fornication he paid little heed to the more extravagant legends that were current, not least among such figures at Rome during his archidiaconate as Cardinals Humbert and Peter Damiani. Breaches of chastity on the part of the clergy were widely subsumed under the name 'nicolaitism'. Their origin was alleged to be bound up with the obscure biblical references to the sect of the Nicolaitans, whose offences included fornication (Rev. 2: 6, 14–15) and whose name came to be associated, however groundlessly, with that of Nicholas, one of the first seven deacons of the Christian church (Acts 6: 1–6), so that he acquired the reputation of being the first fornicator among the Christian clergy.[251] Thus, in 1059, Peter Damiani wrote to Archdeacon Hildebrand himself that 'clerks who are coupled with women against the rule of ecclesiastical chastity are called Nicolaites'.[252] Yet in the letters in his Register, Gregory made no use of this term, and he did so only once in his *extravagantes,* when he referred to Bishop Juhel of Dol as someone who 'as though he accounted it little or nothing to be a simoniac, . . . hastened also to be a nicolaite' ('nicolaita').[253] It seems clear that Gregory set little store by such legendary propaganda. Instead, his letters suggest that he took his stand upon three lines of defence for a rule of clerical chastity: first, what was intrinsically fitting in the light of the structure of Christian society and of Christian tradition; second, the cultic demands and proprieties of Christian worship; and third, the precepts of Christian morality.

The argument from the structure of Christian society was in itself decisive. Writing in 1075 to Bishop Otto of Constance, Gregory argued that the Christian church was divided into three orders, to one or another of which every Christian must belong: the virgin, the continent, and the married. For many centuries, clergy in major orders had been excluded from the order of the married by papal legislation which went back to Leo I (440–61) and was confirmed by subsequent popes, especially Gregory the Great (590–604); it absolutely prohibited their marriage. Gregory, therefore, based his argument from church order and legislation upon the *a fortiori* consideration that, if even a married layman who associated with a mistress was debarred from the sacraments, how much more impossible was it that a clerk should dispense the sacraments from which, by reason of his fornication, he could not be even a partaker?[254] Gregory accordingly normally withheld the name of wife from a woman married to a clerk, as when he referred to Bishop Pibo of Toul as allegedly

---

[251] For legends about nicolaitism, see Cowdrey, 'Simon Magus in South Italy', esp. pp. 88–90.

[252] *Briefe*, no. 65, 2.230–1.

[253] *Epp. vag.* no. 16, to King William I of England, (1076, after 27 Sept.), pp. 44–7. This letter also gives evidence of Gregory's opposition to clerical marriage on the grounds of its leading to the dispersal and alienation of church lands and revenues.

[254] *Epp. vag.* no. 9, to Bishop Otto of Constance, (late 1075), pp. 20–1. Gregory no doubt relied on passages like Leo I, *Epp.* 14.4, 167.3, *PL* 54.672–3, 1204; Gregory I, *Epp.* 1.42, 4.34, vol. 1.54–5, 254. For the review of the older legislation since the time of Pope Leo IX, see *Reg.* 2.45, to the South German dukes, 11 Jan. 1075, pp. 183/18–184/9.

'lying in fornication with a certain woman by whom he has begotten a son, although rumour has it that he has bound himself to her after the manner of the laity by vows and espousal'.[255] Whether they were thus formally married, or whether they kept women on a long-term basis, or whether they engaged in occasional irregularities, clergy who entered upon a sexual relationship were 'fornicatores clerici' and, therefore, guilty of the crime of fornication ('iaceant in crimine fornicationis'); all those who connived in their misconduct by accepting their ministrations were guilty of the grave offence of disobedience to the apostolic see.[256]

Second, Gregory based his demand for clerical chastity upon the cultic demands and proprieties of Christian worship as he envisaged them. In 1075, he urged Archbishop Anno of Cologne to promote the chastity of the clergy in his province, 'so that the acceptable service of a pure and spotless household may be presented to the bride of Christ which knows neither spot nor wrinkle (cf. Eph. 5: 27)'.[257] Yet Gregory seldom argued in terms of a merely ritual purity. Only once did he expressly argue, as was done with increasing force and frequency by reformers after his death, that for a priest to touch the body of a woman rendered him unfit to touch the body of Christ while saying mass. In 1076, he wrote to Count Robert of Flanders,

It has reached the apostolic see that, in the land under your rule, some who are called priests but who lie in fornication are not ashamed to sing mass and to touch the body and blood of Christ. They pay no heed to what madness and to how great an offence it is at one and the same time to handle the body of a harlot and the body of Christ.[258]

Furthermore, it should be observed that Gregory had no special vocabulary with which to condemn the sexual improprieties of the clergy; he used similarly emotive words in dealing with simony as with fornication. A simoniacal promotion was 'symonica sorde . . . foedata', while offending clergy were 'symoniaca labe fedati';[259] yet Gregory's objection to simony was, at root, a moral one. In a similar way, the purity that should clothe the servants of Christ was at heart moral rather cultic. Gregory continued his letter of 1075 to Archbishop Anno of Cologne by urging him to remind his clergy that the chastity which was necessary for those in sacred orders and befitting for those who were chamberlains ('cubicularii') of a virgin bridegroom (Christ) and a virgin bride (the church) was a great virtue ('virtus').[260]

Thus, thirdly, in Gregory's eyes, the demand that only those who served God in chastity ('caste') should minister at the altar had its deepest justification in the

---

[255] *Reg.* 2.10, to Archbishop Udo of Trier, 16 Oct. 1074, pp. 140/34–141/4, cf. *Epp. vag.* no. 16, pp. 44–5.

[256] *Reg.* 2.62, to Archbishop Sigehard of Aquileia, 23 Mar. 1075, p. 217/28–9; 9.5 to Bishops Hugh of Die and Amatus of Oloron, (1081), p. 580/21. *Epp. vag.* no. 32, to the faithful of Germany and Italy, (1079), pp. 84–7.

[257] *Reg.* 2.67, 29 Mar. 1075, p. 223/26–31.

[258] *Reg.* 4.11, 10 Nov. 1076, p. 310/14–19. In general terms, the assertion that Gregory VII, 'novus morum corrector', insisted upon clerical chastity for cultic reasons was strongly made by Sigebert of Gembloux in his *Apologia*: cap. 5, p. 440.

[259] *Reg.* 1.32, to Bishop Arald of Chartres, 27 Nov. 1073, p. 53/17; 1.77, to Countesses Beatrice and Matilda of Tuscany, 15 Apr. 1074, p. 109/26.

[260] *Reg.* 2.67, p. 224/11–16.

requirements of a Christian morality which was one and indivisible. In this connection as in others, Gregory was concerned to emphasize the moral aspect of current issues. In part, he did so with respect to the individual lives of the clergy concerned. Chastity was more than a matter of ritual suitability to handle the sacrament of Christ's body and blood; it was one of moral conformity to Christ and his bride the church in the completeness of their union. In an earlier letter to Anno of Cologne, Gregory accordingly made clear the moral value that he set upon clerical chastity: Anno was to confirm his clergy in it, 'since, as you well know, in God's eyes other virtues avail nothing without chastity, just as chastity avails nothing without other virtues'.[261] Gregory set clerical chastity still more insistently within a moral context in the directions that he gave, not to the generality of the clergy in respect of their individual lives, but to all in authority, whether clerical or lay, whom he wished to impose discipline and right order upon the church by whatever means. He made the enforcement of clerical chastity a matter of due obedience on the part of those in authority to the directions of the apostolic see. Such obedience was not primarily a matter of outward conformity but of inner commitment. He grounded his requirement of obedience in the Bible and in the comment of his predecessor, Pope Gregory the Great. Five times in letters about the enforcement of clerical chastity, he urged his correspondents to obedience by citing the prophet Samuel's rebuke of the disobedient King Saul: 'To obey is better than sacrifices and to hearken than the fat of rams. For rebellion is as the sin of witchcraft, and stubbornness is as iniquity and idolatry' (1 Sam. 14: 22–3). Pope Gregory I's comment upon this text was that obedience constitutes true sacrifice, and that it carries the reward of faith.[262] By thus setting his campaign against clerical unchastity in a context of obedience to the church and its authorities and lay agents, Gregory directed it away from cultic considerations towards moral ones and towards the gaining of human salvation. As he wrote in 1079 with regard to clerical chastity, 'I beseech you, obey our apostolic precepts that you may attain to your inheritance in the kingdom of heaven'.[263]

The cultic element in Gregory's campaign for clerical chastity, although important, should not be isolated or exaggerated. His campaign had more to do with chastity as an innate requirement of Christian order and tradition as God had constituted Christian society. But, above all, chastity was a moral virtue arising from his vision of a free and uncompromised church, ruled by proper and inner obedience, which was dedicated to the following of Christ who himself lived a life of virginity.[264]

---

[261] *Reg.* 2.25, 18 Nov. 1074, p. 157/14–19.

[262] Gregory I, *Moralia in Iob*, 35.14, vol. 3.1792–3. For Gregory VII's citations, see *Reg.* 2.45, to the South German dukes, 11 Jan. 1075, p. 184/5–9; 2.66, to Bishop Burchard of Halberstadt, 29 Mar. 1075, p. 222/1–9; 4.11, to Count Robert of Flanders, 10 Nov. 1076, pp. 310/31–311/10; *Epp. vag.* nos. 10, to the clergy and laity of the diocese of Constance, (1075, late), pp. 24–7; 32, to the faithful of Italy and Germany, (1079), pp. 86–7.

[263] *Epp. vag.* no. 32, pp. 86–7.

[264] For fuller discussion, see Cowdrey, 'Pope Gregory VII and the Chastity of the Clergy'.

8.10 Gregory VII's Demands upon Christians

Gregory's resistance to simony and clerical fornication illustrates how deeply his aims and actions were motivated by the demands of morality as he envisaged them. He set great store by respect for divine order as scripture and tradition revealed it, and by the virtue of chastity. Six further human dispositions invite special comment on account of their prominence among Gregory's demands upon Christians, whether upon himself, upon the clergy, or upon the laity, alike in their individual lives and in their social relations. Gregory related them closely to each other. Their propagation both individually and together was at the heart of his conception of the papal office.

8.10.1 Charity

As his citations and comments make clear, Gregory set store by St Paul's praise of charity in 1 Corinthians 13. In accordance with it, Gregory declared that true charity is to be preferred by all Christians to all other virtues; indeed, it is the mother of them. If it were lacking, whatever good anyone might do lacked all fruitfulness for his salvation. Charity had compelled God himself to come down from heaven to earth and to share the wretchedness of the human condition. It provided men and women, and not least lay rulers, with a compelling motive to persist in their duties in the world. 'Charity does not seek its own' (1 Cor. 13: 5); the cries of widows and orphans and the pleas of priests and monks should hold them, even against their own inclination, in the performance of their temporal functions. Charity was a gift from God which must be accepted and cultivated as he willed.[265] If it should provide an overriding motive to a secular ruler, so, too, those who were by true vocation monks should aspire to 'the perfection of the highest charity' as the culmination of the monastic life.[266]

As for those in the world, Gregory had learnt from Pope Gregory the Great that God had appointed for each Christian his own share of adversity and of prosperity.[267] It behoved all Christians to share in charity the human burden of adversity. Thus, during King Henry IV's attacks on Rome in the 1080s, Gregory explained to his supporters that, since when one member of the body suffers, all other members suffer with it (1 Cor. 12: 26), the charity of God which was poured into their hearts could be recognized in a singleness of will that all the ungodly should repent and return to their Creator, in a singleness of desire that the church which was now everywhere shaken, divided, and confused should recover its original poise and stability, and in a singleness of religious goal that God might be glorified in Gregory and his followers

---

[265] *Reg.* 1.47, to Countess Matilda of Tuscany, 16 Feb. 1074, pp. 71/25–72/1; 1.50, to Countesses Beatrice and Matilda, 4 Mar. 1074, pp. 76–7; 1.61, to Duke Wratislav II of Bohemia, 18 Mar. 1074, p. 89/21–5; 6.17, to Duke Hugh I of Burgundy, 2 Jan. 1079, pp. 423/34–424/7; 8.21, to Bishop Hermann of Metz, 15 Mar. 1081, p. 562/15–20.

[266] *Reg.* 6.17, p. 424/23–6.

[267] *Reg.* 1.11, to Countesses Beatrice and Matilda of Tuscany, 24 June 1073; cf. Gregory I, *Moralia in Iob.* 12.2.2, vol. 2. 628–9.

and that they might attain to eternal life with their brothers—even with those who were persecuting them.[268]

Since charity should thus embrace and direct the whole of Christian life, Gregory envisaged the papal office itself as one whose duties must be discharged in a spirit of paternal charity which was also the charity of Christ: it was safer for a pope to suffer death than to desert Christ's law, or to show respect to the ungodly who were powerful ('potentes') rather than to follow the poor ('pauperes') who loved Christ's commandments.[269] The pope's duty of charity required that he hold no Christian in hatred. To all without exception, from emperors and kings to the least of Christians, he had a duty of always maintaining the charity which, like the wedding garment in Christ's parable (Matt. 22: 11–12), was necessary for acceptance by God.[270] Following Christ's example, for the pope and for all Christians, the ultimate test of charity was a willingness to lay down one's life for one's friends. He expressed this with especial commitment in his plans of 1074 for an expedition which he would himself lead to relieve Constantinople from the attacks of the Seljuks.[271] But it was no less incumbent upon all Christians, since their religion bound them to the imitation of Christ.[272] If charity required that they be prepared to die for their brothers, so, too, it was their principal motive for fortitude in the tribulations which were the lot of all Christians; in it, they should persevere to the end and be saved.[273]

8.10.2 Obedience

If charity was, for Gregory, the mother of all virtues, obedience was the virtue to which he made most frequent reference.[274] Early in his pontificate, he wrote to the Saxon magnates that his own life had always been directed by the will of God. He had deemed himself unequal to bearing the weight of the papal office and had sought to avoid it.

But, since the way of a man is not in his own hand (cf. Jer. 10: 23) but is at the disposition of him by whom the steps of men are directed (cf. Prov. 20: 24), it was impossible for me to defend against the divine will the purposes that I had formed ('concepta vota defendere').[275]

This letter shows that, like Gregory's understanding of charity, his sense of obedience as required both of himself and of all Christians had biblical roots and was nourished by direct reading of the biblical text. But two ancient Latin sources seem to have been especially effective in forming his understanding of the biblical virtue of

---

[268] *Reg.* 9.21, to all the faithful, (1082), pp. 601/26–607/11.

[269] *Reg.* 2.12, to Bishop Burchard II of Halberstadt, 26 Oct. 1074, p. 144/4–11.

[270] *Reg.* 1.19, to the clergy and people of Carthage, 15 Sept. 1073, p. 37/20; 2.31, to King Henry IV, 7 Dec. 1074, pp. 165/30–166/3.

[271] *Reg.* 1.49, to all the faithful, 1 Mar. 1074, p. 75/22–6; 2.37, to all the faithful of St Peter, 16 Dec. 1074, p. 172/26–9.

[272] *Reg.* 3.20, to the clergy and people of Bougie, (May 1076), p. 287/2–15.

[273] *Reg.* 7.3, to all the faithful in Germany, 1 Oct. 1079, p. 463/10–14.

[274] See Caspar's Index, s.v. *obedientia*: *Reg.* pp. 696–7.

[275] *Reg.* 1.39, 20 Dec. 1073, p. 61/32–8, cf. 2.73, to Duke Boleslav II of Poland, 20 Apr. 1075, p. 234/7–14.

obedience. One was the Rule of St Benedict, to his early training in which he seems to have owed his commitment to obedience.[276] He never cited the Rule at length, although his letters sometimes echoed it verbally. But the opening words of St Benedict's Prologue, which itself drew upon the Bible, admirably summarize Gregory's own reasons for requiring obedience:

Hear, my son, the precepts of the master and incline the ear of your heart. Receive gladly and perform effectually the admonitions of your father in God, so that you may return by the toil of obedience to him from whom you departed by the sloth of disobedience. Therefore my present word is addressed to whoever you may be who, by abandoning his own acts of will in order that he may serve the Lord Christ as the true king, is taking up the most powerful and glorious weapons of obedience.[277]

Gregory once urged a newly elected abbot 'to bind himself in the marrow of his being to the holy Rule' ('sanctae regulae medullitus te astringas').[278] His own utterances about obedience suggest an inner acceptance of the obedience that the Rule inculcates. Thus, for example, in 1075 he commented to the clergy and people of Constance upon whether their bishop, if himself disobedient to the apostolic see, could expect obedience from his own subjects. He dwelt upon the unfittingness that one who refused to be under a master should seek himself to stand as master over his own disciples. The overtones are those of obedience as taught by the Rule.[279]

The other Latin source was Pope Gregory the Great's reflections on obedience near the end of his *Moralia*, where he commented upon King Saul's disobedience to the prophet Samuel: after Saul's victory over the Amalekites, he disobeyed Samuel's instructions that he should utterly destroy the Amalekites and their possessions by sparing their king, Agag, and the choicest of their flocks and herds. Gregory I cited Samuel's rebuke to Saul:

> Does the Lord wish for burnt offerings and sacrifices,
>   And not, rather, that men should obey the voice of the Lord?
> Obedience is better than victims,
>   And to hearken is better than to offer the fat of rams.
> For to rebel is like the sin of divination,
>   And to concur is like the crime of idolatry.
> Therefore, because you have rejected the word of the Lord,
>   He has rejected you from being king.

(1 Sam. 15: 22–3)

---

[276] On the monastic background of Gregory's idea of obedience, see esp. Benz, 'Die Regula Benedicti' and 'Kirche and Gehorsam'.

[277] *Reg. Ben. Prol.* 1–3. Some examples of possible echoes of its language and thought in Gregory's letters are: *Reg.* 1.17 to Duke Wratislav II of Bohemia, 8 July 1073, p. 28/12–15; 2.3, to Count William of Poitou, 10 Sept. 1074, p. 127/4–7; 2.56, to Archbishop Manasses I of Rheims, 4 Mar. 1075, pp. 209/36–210/2.

[278] *Reg.* 7.7, to Cardinal Richard of Marseilles, 2 Nov. 1079, p. 468/20–6.

[279] *Epp. vag.* no. 10, (late 1075), pp. 24–5; cf. Gregory's counsels about monastic obedience in *Reg.* 2.65, to the monks of Saint-Denis, 25 Mar. 1075, p. 220/22–9.

Gregory I added his own comment, which Gregory VII copied at length in his letter about obedience to the clergy and people of Constance.[280] It placed stress upon the ethical aspects of obedience, setting aside cultic considerations in order to commend moral ones: Samuel placed obedience before sacrifice because, whereas sacrifice involves putting to death flesh other than one's own, by obedience men put to death their own wills; obedience, therefore, sets a curb upon human pride of will. As for Samuel's comparison of disobedience with witchcraft, Gregory I explained that Samuel's purpose was to emphasize how great a virtue was obedience and to bring home how highly it was to be prized.[281]

In his letters, Gregory VII cited or drew upon Samuel's rebuke some twenty-two times, making a number of allusions to Gregory I's commentary.[282] There can be no doubt that its moralizing interpretation had entered deeply into his mind. He frequently cited Samuel's words to point the duty of kings to obey the directions of churchmen, as of subjects to refuse obedience to kings if they were recalcitrant. It was also a sanction for universal obedience to papal decrees against simony and clerical fornication. Gregory brought it to bear upon prelates like Guibert of Ravenna who were guilty of major disobedience to the apostolic see, and as a warning to Lanfranc of Canterbury who was remiss in visiting Rome. He used it against the cathedral canons of Lucca when they failed to obey a direction that they adopt a full canonical life. Whatever political use Gregory made of Samuel's words, they ensured that the positive commands of the pope or of the apostolic see were not merely an exercise of arbitrary power; as Gregory intended them, they carried the deeper moral authority with which Pope Gregory the Great invested the concept of obedience.

In Gregory VII's estimation, it followed that whether or not men preferred God to their own will and whether they obeyed his commands rather than those of men was the touchstone of whether they were members of Christ or of Antichrist.[283] Obedience was owed first and foremost to the Roman church as the mother of all churches, to St Peter as prince of the apostles, and to the pope as Peter's vicar.[284] But it was also due from their subjects to archbishops and bishops who were themselves in good standing.[285] Gregory exhibited it not only as a duty but also as a source of blessing, as when the meticulous obedience of Joshua in the Old Testament made possible even the suspension of the ordinary operation of the elements, so that the Israelites could cross the River Jordan dry-footed, could arrest the course of the sun,

---

[280] *Epp. vag.* no. 10, pp. 24–7.

[281] *Moralia in Iob*, 35.14.18, vol. 3.1792–3. Gregory also wrote of obedience that 'Sola namque virtus est quae virtutes ceteras menti inserit, insertasque custodit.'

[282] Most of the citations are noted in the indexes of *Reg.* p. 650 and *Epp. vag.* p. 169.

[283] *Reg.* 4.2, to Bishop Hermann of Metz, 25 Aug. 1076, p. 295/14–17, where the biblical echoes of Acts 5: 29 and 1 Cor. 6: 15, 12: 27, are to be noted; cf. 4.27, to Doge Dominicus Silvius of Venice, 9 June 1077, p. 342/11–22.

[284] e.g. *Reg.* 2.1, to the bishops and abbots of Brittany, 28 Aug. 1074, p. 124/18–25; 3.9, to the bishops of the province of Milan, 8 Dec. 1075, p. 262/16–20; 4.16, to the clergy of Romans, 21 Mar. 1077, p. 321/19–24; 8.10, to Judge Orzoccor of Cagliari, 5 Oct. 1080, p. 529/9–15.

[285] This was a repeated requirement by Gregory, e.g. *Reg.* 7.15, to the bishops of Brittany and to the clergy and people of Tours, 8 Mar. 1080, p. 489/15–25.

and could bring down the walls of Jericho by the sound of trumpets.[286] Because of their connection with the giving or withholding of God's blessing, obedience and disobedience were prominent among the touchstones by which kings rose and fell.[287]

8.10.3 Humility

As Gregory required it of Christians, humility was closely related to obedience and, indeed, was often virtually synonymous with it; it was also an expression of the charity that sprang from the imitation of Christ: in humility and love, the whole law of God was to be found.[288] Humility had, therefore, none of the connotations of the modern word humiliation; rather, it ennobled and raised those who exhibited it to their full stature as men. At its heart was obedience to the law and to the righteousness of God and to the admonitions of those upon earth who were his accredited spokesmen—especially to the Roman church and to the pope. Its contrary was the pride ('superbia') that raised men up against them. Christ supported the few and the humble against the many and the proud;[289] Gregory several times alluded to the biblical warning that 'God resists the proud (*superbis*), but he gives grace to the humble (*humilibus*)' (James 4: 6).

In Gregory's eyes, humility was, above all, the distinguishing virtue of a good king. If King Saul was his exemplar of disobedience to the word of God as authoritatively communicated through Samuel as his spokesmen upon earth and of the reprobation that followed from disobedience, his successor King David showed how humility won the favour of God.[290] Another exemplar of humility was the Emperor Constantine who, at the council of Nicaea, took the last place after the bishops, because he was mindful that God resists the proud, but gives grace to the humble.[291] Amongst the kings of his own day, Gregory commended the humility that he saw in King Alphonso VI of León–Castile, particularly on account of his obedience to papal and other ecclesiastical mentors in replacing the Hispanic by the Roman liturgical order.[292] He urged humility upon other kings as upon Alphonso. He admonished William I of England that 'the more the powerful of this world are blinded by their pride (*superbia*) and by their godly deeds, the more it becomes you, who in preference to them have been found most dear to God, to be raised up by dutiful humility (*pie humiliando*) and exalted by obedience'. When urging King Sweyn Estrithson of Denmark to seek the guidance of the apostolic see, Gregory reflected that the more humble before St Peter a people was, the greater was its strength.[293]

---

[286] *Reg.* 2.68, to Archbishop Werner of Magdeburg, 29 Mar. 1075, p. 225/19–29.
[287] e.g. *Reg.* 7.14*a*, record of the Lent synod 1080, 7 Mar. 1080, pp. 486/27–487/3.
[288] *Reg.* 1.71, to Queen Matilda of England, 4 Apr. 1074, p. 103/1–6; 7.2, to the clergy and people of Lucca, 1 Oct. 1079, pp. 460/29–461/10; 8.21, to Bishop Hermann of Metz, 15 Mar. 1081, p. 562/20–5.
[289] *Reg.* 1.15, to the faithful in Lombardy, 1 July 1073, p. 24/26–33.
[290] *Reg.* 3.10, to King Henry IV of Germany, (8 Dec.) 1075, p. 267/17–24.
[291] *Reg.* 4.2, to Bishop Hermann of Metz, 25 Aug. 1076, p. 296/4–7.
[292] *Reg.* 7.6, 15 Oct. 1079, pp. 466/7–467/11, 9.2, (1081), p. 570/27–41.
[293] *Reg.* 2.75, to the king of Denmark, 17 Apr. 1075, p. 238/8–18; 7.23, to King William I, 24 Apr. 1080, p. 501/13–22.

Gregory's most insistent promptings to exhibit humility were directed to those in Germany who claimed the royal authority. Henry IV's early protestations of obedience to Gregory had seemed to proclaim his humility, and, in 1075, the Saxons' defeat at his hands on the Unstrut seemed to be a divine punishment for their pride ('superbia') in unjustly resisting him. At Canossa, Gregory regarded Henry as 'humiliatus ad paenitentiam'; as Gregory saw matters, a responsible return to Christian obedience and humility thus prepared the way for his absolution.[294] In 1080, a major consideration in determining Gregory's rejection of Henry and acceptance of Rudolf of Swabia as German king was that, whereas Henry had exhibited pride ('superbia') by resisting papal admonitions, Rudolf had been humble ('humilis') in heeding them.[295] After Rudolf had been killed, the king who should succeed him must be obedient and humbly ('humiliter') devoted and useful to holy church, as a Christian king should be and as Gregory had hoped that Rudolf was.[296] Gregory showed that he looked for a comparable disposition of humility in churchmen, as well.[297]

8.10.4 Righteousness

One of Gregory's most stringent demands upon those with whom he dealt was that they should observe the requirements of righteousness ('iustitia'). It was bound up with his emphasis upon the virtues of obedience and humility. Nevertheless, he referred to it less as an inner human quality or virtue than as an objective norm standing outside men to which they should conform, albeit in a spirit of love and of duty. Like religion itself, it was established by God and it depended directly upon him and his providence.[298] But Gregory came near to giving it a personification of its own, with its own sovereignty and power of discernment, as when he made the test of which side righteousness favoured ('cui amplius iustitia faveret') the criterion in the disputed succession between 1077 and 1080 to the German crown.[299] Throughout his letters, to have ('habere') or to do righteousness ('facere iustitia') was often simply a matter of distributive justice in a legal forum. At root, however, righteousness was religious: it was the intrinsic quality of the law of God which had as its end the attainment of eternal blessedness and which should inform and guide all human law. It was a quality for which men should strive and if necessary suffer throughout their earthly lives.[300] Not only to uphold but also to live by it was an especial duty of kings

---

[294] *Reg.* 3.7, (early Sept. 1075), p. 258/5–8, 3.10, (8 Dec.) 1075, p. 264/10–17; 4.12, to the German princes, (late Jan. 1077), p. 312/11–16.

[295] *Reg.* 7.14a, record of the Lent synod 1080, 7 Mar. 1080, pp. 486/27–487/3; cf. 4.24, to the faithful in Germany, 31 May 1077, pp. 337/27–338/8 for Gregory's ideas at this time.

[296] *Reg.* 9.3, to Bishop Altmann of Passau and Abbot William of Hirsau, (Mar. 1081), p. 575/19–33.

[297] e.g. *Reg.* 1.77, to Countesses Beatrice and Matilda of Tuscany, 15 Apr. 1074, p. 109/21–9; 7.2, to the clergy and people of Lucca, 1 Oct. 1079, pp. 460/31–461/10.

[298] *Reg.* 1.9, to Duke Godfrey of Lorraine, 6 May 1073, p. 14/20–6.

[299] e.g. *Reg.* 7.14a, record of the Lent synod 1080, 7 Mar. 1080, pp. 485/6–486/4.

[300] *Reg.* 1.11, to Countesses Beatrice and Matilda of Tuscany, 24 June 1073, p. 18/1–7; 2.9, to the same, 22 Sept. 1074, p. 140/2–6.

and lay rulers, who should so govern that they offered the sacrifice of righteousness (cf. Ps. 4: 6). As a requirement of God, righteousness should rule the hearts of kings as well as their actions. To this end, their keeping to the path of righteousness depended upon following papal instructions and counsels and in ruling according to divine and human laws.[301] Righteousness became a human virtue in so far as it was a matter of acquiescence from the heart in the laws and guidance of God and of his representative upon earth. It resulted from accepting and never deviating from such guidance as would enable men to follow the straight path of righteousness, safeguarding the just right of other men with commitment of heart ('concorditer') and with prompt obedience. Righteousness was thus associated, not only with outward obedience to the law of God and of the church, but also with moral integrity ('morum honestate').[302] Yet it remained a divine imperative standing over man to which the virtues of obedience and humility were the due human response; Gregory was, therefore, reticent about it in itself as a quality of the individual Christian, whether powerful or humble. It was known by its fruits.

8.10.5 Mercy

As the motto which most often appears in the rota at the foot of his charters, Gregory adapted a verse from the Psalms: 'Your compassions (*miserationes*), Lord, are over all your works' (cf. Ps. 144: 9).[303] Gregory's references to mercy ('misericordia') in his letters make it clear that this was no mere rhetorical decoration; the verse expressed Gregory's deepest convictions about the nature of God and about the consequent obligations of those who were his earthly representatives. His zeal to declare and to implement the righteousness of God was balanced and informed by his concern to recognize and to exhibit the mercy of God.

This mercy was apparent in every aspect of God's providence for his creation; indeed, it was virtually a synonym for that providence. Its power was strong to raise up the lowliness of the faithful and to cast down the pride that set itself against this lowliness. It was ever active to recall the fallen to the way of truth and to bring the righteous to salvation.[304] It was tantamount to a divine providence which protected them in all dangers and could be relied upon to deliver them in present

---

[301] *Reg.* 1.9, p. 15/4–12, 1.75, to King Philip I of France, 13 Apr. 1074, pp. 106/34–107/8; 2.51, to King Sweyn II Estrithson of Denmark, 25 Jan. 1075, p. 193/12–18; 4.28, to the kings and magnates of Spain, 28 June 1077, p. 345/26–9.

[302] *Reg.* 3.8, to the 'clerk' Tedald of Milan, 8 Dec. 1075, p. 259/23–6; 3.14, to Patriarch Dominicus IV of Grado, (Apr.) 1076, p. 276/1–11; 4.28, to the kings and princes of Spain, 28 June 1077, p. 344/12–27; 6.29, to King Ladislaus I of Hungary, 21 Mar. 1079, p. 442/12–17, 30–5; 8.21, to Bishop Hermann of Metz, 15 Mar. 1081, p. 562/1–5; 9.23, to a Count C., (1082), p. 604/3–8.

[303] See *QF* plates, *passim*. The text is that of the Roman Psalter.

[304] For passages which illustrate Gregory's understanding of the divine mercy, see *Reg.* 1.49, to all Christians, 1 Mar. 1074, p. 75/26–9; 4.23, to Gregory's legates in Germany, 31 May 1077, p. 335/1–5; 4.28, to the kings and princes of Spain, 28 June 1077, p. 346/16–21; 6.13, to King Olaf III of Norway, 15 Dec. 1078, pp. 416/10–20, 417/37–40; 8.9, to the faithful in Germany, pp. 527/30–4, 528/16–18; 9.14, to the kings of Sweden, (1081), p. 593/12–15.

tribulations.[305] The righteous might count upon it when they came to judgement at the end of their lives.[306] Thus considered, mercy was no mere religious cliché; it was a foundation stone of the Christian life, both as a grace which was received from God and as a quality to be shown to one's fellow men.

Gregory himself trusted in the mercy of God as brought to him through the merits of St Peter.[307] His letters repeatedly referred to his own duty of clemency ('mansuetudo', 'clementia'), to which the adjective 'apostolica' was habitually prefixed, partly, no doubt, to associate it with the papal office, but partly to evoke the repeated references to it in the Pauline scriptures (1 Cor. 4: 21, 2 Cor. 10: 11, Gal. 5: 23, Eph. 4: 2, 1 Tim. 6: 11, Titus 3: 1).[308] The frequency of the reference suggests a commonplace of chancery drafting, yet Gregory's own concern in practice to temper justice with mercy is often evident, as when he instructed the sometimes overzealous legate Archbishop Hugh of Lyons to reconsider the case of an unnamed French abbot with whom he had dealt severely:

We wish that, for love of St Peter from whom no one should come away without mercy ('a quo sine misericordia nemo regredi debet'), in so far as you can with justice do so, you should treat this man mercifully, and that through your clemency he should not feel that he had undertaken in vain so great an effort in coming to the apostolic see.[309]

Gregory expressed a preference for first applying merciful measures; only if they failed should recourse be made to severity.[310] Where possible, he sought to temper justice with mercy and to take a middle course.[311] It was an approach he urged upon kings as well as preferring it for himself.[312]

The severity in tone and content of Gregory's sentences upon Henry IV of Germany in 1076 and in 1080 must be recognized;[313] but they should not obscure the extent to which, in his overall dealings with Henry, Gregory sought to temper justice with mercy.[314] It remains true that Gregory acquired in Germany a reputation for

[305] e.g. *Reg.* 1.11, to Countesses Beatrice and Matilda of Tuscany, 24 June 1073, p. 18/24–7; 4.6, to Bishop Henry of Liège, 28 Oct. 1076, p. 304/22–9; 4.7, to the faithful at Milan, 31 Oct. 1076, p. 305/30–1, *Epp. vag.* no. 51, to all the faithful, (summer 1083), pp. 122–5.

[306] e.g. *Reg.* 1.58, to Duke Gésa of Hungary, 17 Mar. 1074, p. 85/23–9; 7.10, to the inhabitants of Brittany, 25 Nov. 1079, p. 472/22–6.

[307] *Reg.* 2.31, to King Henry IV of Germany, 7 Dec. 1074, p. 165/26–30.

[308] For a list of occurrences, see the index in Caspar, *Reg.* pp. 677–8.

[309] *Reg.* 9.19, (1082–3), p. 599/29–36.

[310] *Reg.* 1.22, to the clergy and people of Carthage, 15 Sept. 1073, pp. 38/30–39/4.

[311] e.g. *Reg.* 1.34, to Bishop Remigius of Lincoln, 2 Dec. 1073, p. 55/14–24; 1.77, to Countesses Beatrice and Matilda of Tuscany, 14 Apr. 1074, pp. 109/21–110/8, 34–9; 4.25, to Archbishop Nehemiah of Gran, 9 June 1077, pp. 339/25–340/10.

[312] e.g. *Reg.* 5.10, to King Harold Hein of Denmark, 6 Nov. 1077, p. 362/32–5; 7.21, to the same, 19 Apr. 1080, p. 498/8–12.

[313] *Reg.* 3.10a, record of the Lent synod 1076, pp. 270–1; 7.14a, record of that of 1080, pp. 483–7; though the final prayer of the latter, that the apostles' judgement against Henry should bring about his fall and confusion, also sought his penitence, that his spirit might be saved in the day of the Lord (cf. 1 Cor. 5: 5).

[314] e.g. *Epp. vag.* 14, to the faithful in Germany, (summer 1076), pp. 36–7, *Reg.* 4.3, to the faithful in Germany, 3 Sept. 1076, p. 298/20–30; 4.12, to the German bishops and lay princes, (late Jan. 1077), pp. 313/26–314/4.

severity and for giving play to personal resentment which he was at pains to dispel in a letter to the faithful in Germany which perforce presented his principal motive as zeal for righteousness.[315]

The severe image that Gregory acquired in Germany through his dealings with Henry IV should not disguise the extent to which, in his dealings with other parts of Christendom, the merciful side of his personality was apparent and sometimes uppermost. This was especially so in his dealings with France and Burgundy. To the clergy and laity of these regions, recourse to Gregory at Rome was a road to mercy in face of the rigour of local prelates and of Gregory's legates, who were liable to act with a severity that Gregory did not intend. Gregory was well aware that a reputation for mercy was of importance in encouraging recourse to the papacy; two letters well illustrate Gregory's concern to exhibit the apostolic see in this light. First, in 1077, he wrote to Bishop Josfred of Paris with instructions to investigate on his behalf the cases of several persons who had appealed to the apostolic see from the excessive severity of Archbishop Manasses of Rheims. Walter, castellan of Douai, had besought Gregory, 'by the mercy of our apostolic kindness', to intervene with Manasses; Canon Azzo of Saint-Aimé at Douai had sought 'the clemency of apostolic mercy' in securing his readmission to his community; two monks of Saint-Remi at Rheims sought mitigation of their archbishop's severity against their community; the cruelty of the people of Cambrai in burning a man—Ramihrd—who had opposed clerical simony and fornication should be investigated with a view to the punishment of the perpetrators.[316] Second, in 1078, Gregory reversed the severe sentences imposed by his legate Hugh of Die upon a number of French and Burgundian bishops who appealed to him in Rome. He prefaced his decisions by the observation that, in setting aside Hugh's sentences of suspension or inhibition, he had been mindful of the custom of the holy Roman church in tolerating or even overlooking some offences and that he had himself applied a restraint proceeding from his own discretion rather than the severity of the law.[317] In his long-term dealings with both King Philip I of France and Archbishop Manasses I of Rheims, Gregory showed comparable restraint and moderation.[318] In thus showing moderation, Gregory appealed to the traditions of the Roman church, and his attitude to petitioners from France suggests that he well appreciated the value for papal authority in France of identifying it with mercy rather than with rigour. Gregory's image as one who showed mercy was evidently a powerful factor in drawing French clergy and laity to Rome for the consideration of their business and thus in opening France to Gregory's counsels and aspirations for the church. Gregory's way of proceeding had the effect of distancing him from his most committed legates, Hugh of Die/Lyons and Amatus of Oloron, and of tending to identify him with the measure and restraint of a figure like Abbot Hugh of Cluny. Such an image of moderation and mercy favoured Gregory's own

---

[315] *Epp. vag.* no. 14, pp. 32–41; cf. no. 13, to Bishop Henry of Trent, (Mar.–July 1076), pp. 30–3.
[316] *Reg.* 4.20, 25 Mar. 1077, pp. 326–8; cf. 4.22, to Bishop Hugh of Die, 12 May 1077, pp. 330–2.
[317] *Reg.* 5.17, 9 Mar. 1078, pp. 378–80; see above, 5.3.2.1.
[318] See above, 5.2.1.

purposes in France. But Gregory's own reflections upon the quality of divine mercy establish that it was more than a matter of expediency; it sprang from his religious sense of the virtues that were appropriate in a Christian, especially if he were in high authority.

8.10.6 Loyalty

Gregory also looked to Christians for a loyalty which was best expressed in the term 'fidelitas' which currently expressed the bond of service and protection between men and their seniors in both ecclesiastical and lay relationships.[319] As Gregory propounded it, it rested upon the obligation to perform services, and it was closely associated with the duty of obedience in the pursuit of righteousness. It had a strong moral value which arose from a man's faithful continuance in the service and loyalty that a duly accredited superior required.

Against this background, Gregory could himself point to his own life-long *fidelitas* to St Peter, for which he incurred the hatred of evil men.[320] But *fidelitas* was above all a bond of laymen which had its guarantee in the oath of fealty. Gregory characteristically used the term *fidelitas* to express the personal obedience and service for which he looked from kings and lay princes, claiming it for the princes of the apostles, St Peter and St Paul, and for the Roman church.[321] Its conditions varied from person to person. Especially where well established arrangements existed, *fidelitas* to the papacy might be based upon strictly formal conditions, with a sworn obligation to the discharge of specific services arising from papal enfeoffment with a principality and its lands.[322] From the Normans in South Italy, in particular, Gregory demanded a *fidelitas* of binding strength which carried both legal and moral obligations.[323] Nevertheless, a sworn nexus between a ruler and the apostolic see was not the only, or even the main, bond which was possible. In 1080, when King William I of England politely but firmly declined such a nexus, Gregory was content with an obligation to obedience and service which rested upon gratitude and devotion on the part of the king.[324] To the people of Bohemia, Gregory wrote of a loyalty in devoted service ('devotissimi servitii fidelitas') which had its ground in the necessity of securing St Peter's patronage at the last judgement.[325]

---

[319] For Gregory's use of the terms *fidelitas, fidelis,* and *fides,* see Caspar's Index: *Reg.* pp. 688–9.

[320] *Reg.* 3.10a, record of the Lent synod 1076, p. 270/2–5.

[321] e.g. *Reg.* 1.63, to King Sancho II of Aragon, 20 Mar. 1074, pp. 91/32–92/1; 1.72, to Duke Godfrey of Lorraine, 7 Apr. 1074, p. 103/27–9.

[322] e.g. *Reg.* 1.21a, *iusiurandum fidelitatis* of Prince Richard of Capua, 14 Sept. 1973, pp. 35–6, 8.1a–c, investiture of Robert Guiscard, 29 June 1080, pp. 514–17.

[323] e.g. *Reg.* 2.9, to Countesses Beatrice and Matilda of Tuscany, 16 Oct. 1074, p. 139/13–16; 3.15, to the Milanese knight Wifred, (Apr.) 1076, p. 277/2–4; 9.4, to Abbot Desiderius of Montecassino, (Feb. 1081), p. 578/17–26.

[324] Lanfranc, *Letters,* no. 39, (summer 1080), pp. 130–3; *Reg.* 7.23, to King William I, 24 Apr. 1080, pp. 499–502, in which Gregory seems already to have envisaged the possibility that William might refuse a formal doing of fealty.

[325] *Reg.* 2.72, 17 Apr. 1075, p. 233/10–18.

The noun *fidelitas* has no background in the Latin Bible. Added range and depth were added to Gregory's expectation of loyalty by his use of the biblical words 'fides' (faith) and 'fidelis' (faithful). It brought into play a broad spectrum of meaning from religious commitment and zeal, through right belief, to service of and obedience to St Peter and the Roman church, as when he wrote of the church of Cologne as bound to that of Rome in especial closeness 'by faith, love, and services (*fide et dilectione atque obsequiis*)'.[326] In Gregory's vocabulary, the words *caritas*, *devotio*, and *dilectio* were regularly paired with *fidelitas* as expressing the duty of kings, bishops, and other great men to the apostolic see. Gregory similarly employed the word *fideles* with a broad range of meanings from Christians in general to committed servants of Christ, St Peter, or the Roman church; in the more intensive sense, he also used the word of the retainers or agents of kings, bishops, or other great men.[327] The greater the benefits which were received from the Roman church, the more a recipient was canonically committed to be faithful ('fidelis'), to exhibit love ('dilectio'), and to obey the apostolic see from the heart.[328] Such words overlapped in meaning with the less often used but expressive designations *militia* (or *miles*) *Christi* (or *sancti Petri*),[329] which shared the ambiguity of the verb *militare* as having the sense both of 'to fight' with weapons and also 'to serve' in a wider capacity. Gregory's use of this group of words calls for care in not exaggerating the degree to which he used them of armed warfare in a temporal sense; other forms of service, both temporal and spiritual, might be intended. Thus, the *fideles sancti Petri* were understood by Gregory as serving St Peter in all the vicissitudes of papal needs.[330] Gregory's demands for loyalty, service, and obedience were all-pervading; but their content and urgency were primarily derived from the spiritual and biblical background of the words that he used. Their temporal, and especially their feudal, connotations, although often important, were secondary and negotiable.

8.11 Gregory VII's Principal Concerns as Pope

Writing in 1078 to Bishop Hermann of Metz, Gregory referred to his concerns as pope in the following terms:

We both wish to and must extend to all the duty of our concern, since we have received the care ('cura') of all; and we desire and long for the salvation of all, because, although we are unworthy by our own merits, we have undertaken to direct the government ('regimen') of the universal church.[331]

The vocabulary is reminiscent of that of Pope Gregory I and especially of his treatise on the pastoral office which he wrote soon after becoming pope. The word 'cura'

---

[326] *Reg.* 2.27, to Archbishop Anno of Cologne, 29 Mar. 1075, p. 223/16–20.
[327] e.g. *Reg.* 1.25, to Erlembald of Milan, 27 Sept. 1073, p. 42/20 (of Henry IV of Germany); 2.47, to inhabitants of the county of Chiusi, 13 Jan. 1075, p. 187/14 (of a bishop of Chiusi).
[328] *Reg.* 2.28, to Archbishop Liemar of Bremen, 12 Dec. 1074, p. 160/15–21.
[329] For illustrations of Gregory's usage, see Caspar's Index, *Reg.* pp. 695–6.
[330] e.g. *Reg.* 2.49, to Abbot Hugh of Cluny, 22 Jan. 1075, p. 290/12–24.
[331] *Reg.* 1.53, 14 Mar. 1074, p. 80/16–19.

begins Gregory the Great's letter to a Bishop John who had reproved him for a reluctance, such as Gregory VII himself felt and exhibited, to undertake the 'pastoralis curae pondera'.[332] Gregory the Great used the word 'regimen', particularly in the first book of his treatise when he was discussing accession to the pastoral office, to signify more than the administrative and political government of the church; above all, it signified the direction of men collectively and individually in the way of salvation: 'With what rashness is pastoral instruction undertaken by the unskilled! For the government of souls is the art of arts' ('Ab imperitis ergo pastorale magisterium qua temeritate suscipitur, quando ars est artium regimen animarum').[333] To the mentors among his predecessors as pope, especially Gregory the Great, whom Gregory VII was committed to imitating, the papal office was, accordingly, before all else a pastoral office. The pope himself was committed to fulfilling it, and he must encourage all others in authority to share and to exercise it over the subjects who were committed to them. It included the interrelated functions of 'rector' or ruler of men and administrator of church property, 'pastor' or director of souls, 'sacerdos' or president of a church's round of liturgical worship, 'doctor' or teacher of the faith, 'praedicator' or herald who brought home the truths and demands of the faith to each and all of his subjects, and 'praepositus' or leader of the faithful through the shoals of the world to the harbour of eternal salvation.[334]

For Gregory I, the office of preaching ('praedicatio'), in the sense of announcing the depth and range of Christian faith and conduct by word and by example to all who would hear, was at the heart of the pastoral office. This may be illustrated by his comment upon a scriptural verse that also made a deep impression upon Gregory VII:

The key that opens is the word of rebuke, for by reproof it reveals a fault of which even he who commits it is often unaware. . . . Hence, the Lord warns by Isaiah, saying, 'Cry out, do not cease, raise up your voice like a trumpet' (Isa. 58: 1). And, in truth, whoever is raised to the priesthood undertakes the office of a herald, so that he goes ahead, crying aloud, before the advent of the Judge who follows and strikes dread. Thus, if a priest is reluctant to preach, whatever message of crying aloud will he deliver, this dumb herald?[335]

Such instructions as this, which Gregory VII found in the writings of the earlier popes whom he aspired to follow and especially Gregory I, provide the key to his understanding of the pastoral care of all Christians and of the government of the universal church to which he was committed.

8.11.1 The Proclamation of the Gospel

In the light of Gregory I's presentation of the pastoral office, Gregory VII appropriately expanded his statement to Bishop Hermann of Metz of his concerns as pope by

[332] Gregory I, *Reg. past.*, dedicatory epistle, vol. 1.124/3–5.
[333] Gregory I, *Reg. past.* 1.1, vol. 1.128/3–5.
[334] See Judic, introduction to Gregory I, *Reg. past.*, 1.68–88.
[335] Gregory I, *Reg. past.* 2.4, vol. 1.188/31–190/43.

invoking St Paul's words: 'We have received a ministry of preaching the gospel; woe to us, if we do not preach the gospel' (cf. 1 Cor. 9: 16).[336] As Gregory understood such a ministry, it was not directed towards the conversion of the heathen outside the bounds of Christendom; it was exceptional when, by sponsoring the preaching of the sometime Cluniac monk Anastasius, he promoted the conversion to Christianity of Saracens in Spain, which in any case he regarded as part of Christendom. In North Africa, where Christians were a minority in provinces lost centuries ago to Islam, Gregory was concerned, not with the conversion of Muslims, but with the faithful witness of a Christian minority which would win their respect for Christianity.[337] So far as can be seen from his letters, in Gregory's eyes the frontiers of active Christian endeavour were set by those of regions where Christianity had already been established and was currently represented. Adapting for his purpose a claim of St Paul, he asserted that the voice of the gospel had already reached the ends of the earth, having exceeded the limits even of the Roman empire.[338]

Christendom ('Christianitas') was, therefore, in effect defined by the regions of the organized Christian kingdoms, principalities, and churches to which Gregory sent letters and messengers. In what may broadly be described as the Latin world, his purpose was to build up Christian states with episcopal structures; elsewhere as in the Christian east, he sought concord with rulers and churches so that they might be drawn towards an acceptance of his claims for the apostolic see of Rome and for the faith and practice of which it was the custodian. He showed no sign that he began to comprehend the scale or population of the Muslim world, let alone of the peoples and religions that lay beyond it. Instead, his perspective was set by his understanding of St Paul's assertions, as he understood them, that although he had a duty of preaching to all men, his first concern was with those who were of the household of faith (Rom. 1: 14–15, Eph. 6: 10, 1 Tim. 5: 8). He made this clear to the lay rulers of Spain:

The holy and apostolic see is the prince and the universal mother of all the churches and peoples which God's mercy has foreordained to come by way of the teachings of the gospels and of the apostles to the confession of his name in the faith of our Lord and Saviour Jesus Christ. The apostolic see should show them this care and perpetual solicitude, that it should provide instructions and salutary warnings with a view alike to maintaining the truth of the catholic faith and to investigating and upholding righteousness ('iustitia'). . . . We know that we were debtors to those who are near and to those who are afar (cf. Eph. 2: 17), nor shall we be able to find any ground for excuse before the supernal Judge, if by our keeping silence their salvation is neglected or their guilt encouraged. Of this fact, in the prophetic books as in the gospels many warnings and examples carrying fearful threats have been set forth; with respect to them, the illustrious preacher and apostle himself says, 'A necessity is laid upon me to preach the gospel; for woe is me if I do not preach the gospel' (1 Cor. 9: 16).[339]

---

[336] *Reg.* 1.53, p. 80/19–20.   [337] See above, 7.3.
[338] *Reg.* 2.75, to King Sweyn Estrithson of Denmark, 17 Apr. 1075, pp. 237/30–238/1; cf. Rom. 10: 18, citing Ps. 18: 5.
[339] *Reg.* 4.28, 28 June 1077, pp. 343/25–344/8.

Gregory's imperative was the more pressing because of his fear that, everywhere in Christendom, princes and rulers of the world despised the law of God; hardened in the disobedience that, as seen in Saul, the prophet Samuel likened to disobedience, they were deaf to papal representations.[340]

Gregory's preaching was first and foremost addressed to the world at large in so far as its peoples, and especially its spiritual and temporal rulers, would listen. From the beginning of his pontificate, he understood and proclaimed his message on the model of the prophetic office in the Old Testament, especially as fulfilled by the greater prophets, Isaiah, Jeremiah, and Ezekiel. In July 1073, he declared that he was set in a place from which he must announce truth and righteousness ('veritatem et iustitiam') to all peoples but especially to Christians; as warrant, he made three citations from the greater prophets which, often in combination, recurred prominently in his letters.[341] All had been used of the pastoral office by Pope Gregory the Great, and Gregory VII seems to have brought them together on the basis of his reading as an epitome of the duties that had been placed upon him.

First, he drew on the book of Isaiah: 'Cry out, do not cease, raise up your voice like a trumpet and announce to my people their transgressions' (Isa. 58: 1).[342] Gregory's citations of this verse established his duty to speak out, and to continue to speak out, in face of all hostility against the transgressions of the people of God and the sins of the church.[343] He twice prefaced it by the Lord's command to Isaiah, 'Ascend into a high mountain, you who preach in Sion; lift up your voice with strength, you who preach in Jerusalem' (Isa. 10: 9; cf. Exod.19: 3).[344] He thus underlined the publicity of his preaching to Christians in face of the evil customs of the times. Second, he turned to God's words to Ezekiel: 'If you do not announce to the wicked man his iniquity, I shall require his soul at your hands' (cf. Ezek. 3: 18).[345] He thus recalled his own duty of seeking the amendment of sinners and of speaking with boldness on pain of his own having to answer to God at the last judgement. Third, he added the warning of Jeremiah: 'Cursed is the man who withholds his sword from blood' (Jer. 48: 10).[346] As often when citing a text, Gregory added an explanation, in this case, 'that is, who withholds the word of preaching from the chastisement of the carnal' ('a carnalium increpatione'). In interpreting Gregory's use of the imagery of the sword, it must be remembered that he evidently had in mind two paragraphs from Gregory the Great's book on the pastoral rule which, though starkly formulated, were allegorical in their sense:

---

[340] *Reg.* 2.75, p. 238/1–8; cf. 2.29, to Abbot Hugh of Cluny, 22 Jan. 1075, p. 189/20–7; 4.1, to the faithful in Germany, 25 July 1076, pp. 289/30–290/3.

[341] *Reg.* 1.15, to the faithful of St Peter especially in Lombardy, 1 July 1073, p. 23/23–32.

[342] Cited by Gregory I in *Reg. past.* 2.4, vol. 1.190/38–9; *Epp.* 1.24, 33, vol. 1.16/137, 39/5–6.

[343] Gregory referred to it five times in the Register and once in his *Epistolae vagantes*.

[344] See Gregory I, *Reg. past.* 2.3, vol. 1.180/10–182/2, *Reg.* 1.24, vol. 1.23/63–4.

[345] See Gregory I, *Ep.* 1.33, vol. 1.39/9–40/15; also the passages from Gregory I that Gregory VII associated with it in *Reg.* 9.35, to the bishops of Flanders, (1083), p. 624/28–36; Gregory VII made five citations in the Register of Ezek. 3: 18.

[346] Gregory VII referred to this text ten times in the Register.

And so it is well said through the prophet, 'Cursed is he who withholds his sword from blood'. Now, to withhold the sword from blood is to hold back the word of preaching from the putting to death of a carnal life.

Therefore, it is also rightly added, 'Let each man kill his brother and friend and neighbour' (cf. Exod. 32: 27). For a man kills his brother and friend and neighbour when, finding in them things deserving punishment, he does not spare from the sword of chastisement ('ab increpationis gladio') even those whom he loves through kinship. If, then, one who is incited by the love of God to strike at faults is called a man of God, then certainly he who refuses, so far as he can, to chastise the life of those who are carnal ('increpare vitam carnalium') denies that he is a man of God.[347]

In the light of these passages, Gregory VII's prime intention was to insist that, when crying aloud and when announcing to the wicked their sins, he himself, and any bishop true to his calling, must persist to the end in announcing truth and righteousness. When saying that the sword must not be withheld from blood, Gregory VII, like his mentor, spoke metaphorically; he did not set out to justify the employment by the church of the material sword. Moreover, the object of the preacher's sword was the sin and not the sinner, with whom as a person Gregory VII tempered justice with mercy.

Nevertheless, under pressure from the events of the early years of his pontificate, Gregory VII was led to gloss Jeremiah's verse in terms which were more suggestive of physical coercion than those which his mentor had used. In his letter of 1074, Gregory went on from citing his three prophetic texts to urge his followers at Milan to carry their resistance to Archbishop Godfrey to the point at which, as sons of God, they would respond 'by all means', by which Gregory implied physical resistance and armed coercion, thereby to provide an all-out defence of the Christian faith by which they were being saved.[348] Thus far Gregory carried his preaching, and it is significant that, over the years he gradually hardened the gloss that he put upon Jeremiah's injunction: he progressed from Gregory I's terms, 'that is, who withholds the word of preaching from the chastisement of the carnal', to a less clearly metaphorical wording: 'that is, who withholds the word of preaching from the killing of the life of the carnal.'[349] While his later formulation remained patient of interpretation in Gregory I's allegorical sense, there was little safeguard against its being understood literally by Gregory VII's more fervent partisans. However, despite

---

[347] *Reg. past.* 3.35, vol. 2.430/33–6, 434/90–6.   [348] *Reg.* 1.15, p. 24/24–6.

[349] The development of the gloss in Gregory VII's letters was as follows: (i) 'id est verbum predicationis a carnalium increpatione': 1.15, p. 23/21–2; 2.66, to Bishop Burchard of Halberstadt, 29 Mar. 1075, pp. 221/32–222/1. (ii) 'hoc est, sicut ipsi bene intelligitis, qui verbum predicationis a carnalium hominum retinet increpatione': 2.5, to the archbishops and bishops of France, 10 Sept. 1074, p. 131/20–1; 'id est verbum correctionis (or praedicationis) a prave viventium increpatione': 4.1, to all the faithful in the Roman empire, 15 July 1076, pp. 291/31–292/1, 27. (iii) 'id est verbum predicationis a carnalis vitae interfectione [retinere]': 3.4, to Archbishop Siegfried of Mainz, 3 Sept. 1075, p. 249/10–11; 4.2, to Bishop Hermann of Metz, 25 Aug. 1076, p. 296/21; 8.21, to the same, 15 Mar. 1081, longer version, p. 563/25. (iv) 'id est qui doctrinam subtrahit ab occisione carnalis vitae': 7.23, to King William I of England, 24 Apr. 1080, p. 500/25–6.

Gregory VII's characteristic sharpening of Gregory I's words, his use of Jeremiah 48: 10 affords no evidence that he expressly moved from an allegorical to a literal meaning which directly encouraged the physical use of the sword to shed blood. The text remained a signal statement of his understanding of the duty of the pope to preach truth and righteousness without weakening or compromise, and to deal rigorously with those who sinned and remained incorrigible.[350]

Gregory's preaching, as he understood it, was by no means addressed only to the church at large or to groups of people; his preaching 'from a high mountain' was complemented by preaching through letters to individuals, and especially to kings and princes with their consorts. Since, in the ordering of the church and in pursuit of its freedom, Gregory was committed to securing lay rulers who followed and did not lead in matters of religion and whose sacrality he was concerned to reduce, and since he upon occasion expressed despair of the conduct of his contemporary kings and rulers, it is at first sight surprising that he should have directed his publication of the Christian message so largely to and through them. But he did so necessarily, since in most of Christendom public authority rested in their hands, while especially around its periphery church structures were rudimentary or at best underdeveloped. Gregory, therefore, recognized that his own publication of Christianity required the co-operation of kings and that it was necessary for him to seek to instruct them. As he expressed this need to King Philip I of France.

Thus, while it is neither safe for or open to us to hide away or anywhere to silence the word of preaching, yet the higher the rank and the more exalted the person, the more urgent the care and address that we should have in directing him in the right way; for the Lord warns us by the prophet, 'Cry out, do not cease, raise up your voice like a trumpet.' This is especially so because the power of Christian princes should be at one with ourselves in the oversight of Christian service in the camp of the heavenly King ('precipue cum virtus christianorum principum in eiusdem Regis castris ad custodiam christianae militiae nobiscum convenire debeat').[351]

Hence Gregory's concern to correct the youthful misconduct of Philip as of Henry IV of Germany.[352] Hence, too, the pastoral expositions of Christian faith and dispositions that he often addressed to rulers of the peripheral states of Christendom;[353] those who, for reason of distance, he could not exhort by word of mouth he must of necessity instruct by letter.

---

[350] *Reg.* 1.17, to Duke Wratislav II of Bohemia, 8 July 1073, p. 28/26–7.

[351] *Reg.* 1.75, 13 Apr. 1074, p. 107/10–17.

[352] Philip I: *Reg.* 1.75; 8.20, 27 Dec. 1080, p. 542/20–33; Henry IV: *Epp. vag.* no. 14, to all the faithful in Germany, (summer 1076), pp. 34–9.

[353] The principal examples are: Spain *Reg.* 4.28, to the kings and lay magnates, 28 June 1077, pp. 343–7; 9.2, to King Alphonso VI of León–Castile, (1081), pp. 569–72. England: 7.23, 25–7, to King William I and his family, 24 Apr. and 8 May 1080, pp. 499–502, 505–8. Ireland: *Epp. vag.* no. 57, to the king and people, (1074/84), pp. 138–41. Poland: *Reg.* 2.73, to Duke Boleslav II, 30 Apr. 1075, pp. 233–5. Hungary: 8.22, to Queen Adelaide, (1081), pp. 564–5. Denmark: 5.10, to King Harold, 6 Nov. 1077, pp. 361–3. Norway: 6.13, to King Olaf III, 15 Dec. 1078, pp. 415–18. See also Flanders: 9.35, to the bishops serving under Count Robert, (1083), pp. 622–7.

There should be no mistaking the pastoral earnestness of this aspect of Gregory's preaching. He wrote to kings and princes above all for their own salvation ('de salute vestra'),[354] though also because upon them depended the spiritual welfare of their peoples. Gregory therefore offered full and balanced expositions of the Christian faith with copious reference to the text of the Bible.[355] He made much of the last judgement, when priests must answer for kings; with the judgement in mind, Gregory repeatedly pressed home the message that, according to the thought of the collect for the third Sunday after Pentecost which seems especially to have appealed to him, kings should so pass through things temporal that finally they did not lose things eternal.[356] If kings should, accordingly, be obedient to Gregory's precepts, he also made much of the excellence of kingship as an office held from God; royal resources of arms, wealth, and power might be honourably employed if directed, not to worldly show, but to the honour and service of the eternal King.[357] For this reason, Gregory saw in the fostering of Christian kingship a principal dimension of his preaching of the gospel.

8.11.2 The Implementation of Righteousness

Gregory's overmastering concern to uphold righteousness ('iustitia') was an aspect of his zeal, in his terms, to preach the gospel. He himself wrote of his concern to promote truth and righteousness, and the two concepts were closely related to his mind. But the truth of the catholic faith was essentially a settled body of belief, based upon revelation, which was to be conserved and proclaimed, as it had come down; righteousness, although also rooted in the dispensation of God, must often be sought out afresh by diligent human inquiry.[358]

As Gregory used the word, *iustitia* is not satisfactorily translated by the English word 'justice', with its largely forensic connotation. It has strong biblical overtones arising from the nature and activity of God which are better expressed by the word 'righteousness'. From the Old Testament, it derived a sense of the power and purpose of a God who intervened in human affairs to save his people; from the New Testament and especially from the Pauline writings, it followed from the new and restored relation of man to God which was established by the redemption. From one aspect, it proclaimed God's sovereignty over men; from another, it enforced their duty to conform to his revealed will. Righteousness was whatever ought to be, and whatever men should embrace and love, according to God's purpose for the world. If *iustitia* thus took its meaning from biblical righteousness, it also included human justice, conveying the demands of the law and requiring conformity with it. Its

---

354 *Reg.* 4.28, p. 344/10.   355 See, e.g. *Reg.* 4.28, 7.23.

356 e.g. *Reg.* 4.28, pp. 344/38–345/13, 8.22, p. 564/13–15. This was an especial theme of the concluding prayers with which Gregory ended many of his letters to lay rulers, e.g. 5.10, p. 363/17–21, 6.13, pp. 417/17–418/3; for further comment, see above, 8.4, and Cowdrey, 'The Spirituality', esp. pp. 4–5.

357 *Reg.* 4.28, p. 345/24–6.

358 *Reg.* 4.28, to the kings and magnates of Spain, 28 June 1077, p. 343/32–3: the apostolic see should so exercise care and oversight of all churches and peoples, 'ut sicut ad conservandam catholicae fidei veritatem, ita quoque ad cognoscendam et tenendam iustitiam documenta et salutifera amministret monita.'

demands were the more stringent because Gregory came near to personifying it as the voice of God, both as guide and as judge, in all the contingencies of human life, whether collective or individual.

Gregory may be regarded as having sought to promote righteousness in three principal ways. First, he sought to secure recognition of it as a commitment that all Christians, clerical and lay, should accept. Those who wished to share in the adoption of the children of God (Rom. 8: 23) must establish their lives, not on a prudent calculation of advantage and disadvantage, but upon limitless tenacity in seeking and performing the righteousness of God, which will never lack blessedness as its end.[359] Increasingly during his latter years, Gregory proclaimed the especial blessedness of those who suffer for righteousness' sake (Matt. 5: 10).[360] Righteousness was not only a cause to be served; it was also a pattern of life. Based upon conformity with the law of God, it was more than an essential quality of good men in their lives as individuals; it was also the key to resolving the ills of a Christian society that was fraught with disorder:

If only we will bring the medicine of penitence to the diseases of our sins and if we will shape our way of life according to the pattern of righteousness, then assuredly, with God's help, the madness of our enemies will quickly perish and holy church will receive long-desired peace and security.[361]

Second, having established the claim of righteousness, Gregory was concerned to make known its demands. These were sometimes clearly stated in existing law which must be insistently publicized, and within due limits of prudence enforced, by the appropriate authorities, ecclesiastical and lay, but especially by the apostolic see. Sometimes, however, the pope must actively devise new means for the implementation of old laws, especially in such imperative matters as the eradication of simony and clerical marriage; as he put it, 'It seems to us much better to rebuild the righteousness of God even by new measures, than to destroy the souls of men along with laws that are being neglected.'[362] When it came to applying the law rather than to simply stating it, greater uncertainties arose about the requirements of righteousness. As Gregory understood his duty, his task became one of discerning and declaring by thorough inquiry which of the parties to a dispute righteousness, as an actively discriminating revelation of God's will, most favoured. That he regularly resolved judicial business in such a way is suggested by a case that was heard at Rome in 1078. Certain clerks of the church of Orleans raised objections against their bishop-elect Sanzo. According to Gregory's account, he therefore caused inquiry to be made

---

359 *Reg.* 1.11, to Countesses Beatrice and Matilda of Tuscany, 24 June 1073, pp. 17/34–18/7.

360 e.g. *Epp. vag.* no. 26, to Rudolf of Swabia and his followers, (late Feb. 1079), pp. 66–9; *Reg.* 7.20, to Archbishop Manasses of Rheims, 17 Apr. 1080, p. 496/23–5; 9.2, to King Alphonso VI of León–Castile, p. 570/19–25; 9.21, to all the faithful, (1082), p. 602/31–6; 9.24, to the people of Tours and Anjou, (1082/3), p. 606/11–16; 9.35, to the bishops and magnates of Flanders, (1083), pp. 623/3–7, 624/4–10.

361 8.9, to the faithful in Germany, 22 Sept. 1080, pp. 527/35–528/1.

362 *Reg.* 2.45, to the South German dukes, 11 Jan. 1075, p. 184/14–16 (for the transitive use of *deperire*, cf. 2 Sam. 13: 2).

before the Roman bishops so that, the arguments of both sides having been heard, he might be in a position to determine the case. Sanzo destroyed his adversaries' arguments so comprehensively as to prove to Gregory which party righteousness more favoured ('Sanzo ipse confutans sibi magis favere iustitiam nobis dignis assertionibus demonstravit').[363]

Between 1077 and 1080, Gregory adapted this mode of inquiry to seek out the sentence of righteousness as between the rivals for the German crown, Henry IV and Rudolf of Swabia. The issue was equally simple with that in the case of Sanzo: whether righteousness favoured Henry or Rudolf for the government of the kingdom. But proceedings were longer and less well-established. Gregory was frustrated in his purpose of convening a German assembly at which, with the counsel of the God-fearing clergy and laity of the kingdom, he or his legates might hear the case of the two kings, both of whom had appealed to the apostolic see, and at which it might be ascertained by careful inquiry which of them righteousness favoured. Gregory had, therefore, himself to settle the matter at Rome. He did so at his Lent synod of 1080, mainly using the criterion that whichever king had disobediently sought to impede the German assembly had thereby condemned himself at the tribunal of righteousness; he also applied the test of the moral qualities that he claimed were apparent in both kings—in Henry, pride, disobedience, and falsehood, but in Rudolf, humility, obedience, and truth.[364] The sentence of righteousness thus became clear.

Third, when the demands of righteousness had been both proclaimed and, by whatever means, discovered, the pope had a universal concern to see to their implementation. This might be by his direct order, or it might be through legates or through archbishops and bishops who acted locally at his command. Kings and princes, too, if worthy, were the agents of righteousness as Gregory conceived it and as he established its demands and rulings. In his exhortation of kings, Gregory insisted that righteousness must rule in their minds; in the succession of their dynasties they should adhere to it from generation to generation, and their daily doings should reflect the inherent righteousness of the Christian order ('iustitia christianae legis').[365]

8.11.3 The Power of the Keys

The full force of Gregory's concern, in his terms, to preach the gospel and to implement righteousness throughout Christendom and to do so especially amongst its

---

[363] *Reg.* 5.14, to the clergy and people of Orleans, 29 Jan. 1078, pp. 367–8.

[364] See esp. *Reg.* 4.23–4, to Gregory's legates in Germany, and to all the faithful in Germany, 31 May 1077, pp. 334–8; 5.14a (6), record of the Lent synod of 1078, pp. 370–1; 5.15, to the faithful in Germany, 9 Mar. 1078, p. 375/13–26; 5.16, to Archbishop Udo of Trier, 9 Mar. 1078, pp. 377/39–378/3, 6.4, to Bishop Henry of Liège, 9 Oct. 1078, p. 397/26–31; 6.17a(2–3), record of the Lent synod of 1079, pp. 427–8; *Epp. vag.* no. 27, to Rudolf of Swabia and his supporters, (Mar.–Apr. 1079), pp. 70–1; *Reg.* 7.14a(7), record of the Lent synod of 1080, pp. 485/6–487/3.

[365] *Reg.* 1.75, to King Philip I of France, 13 Apr. 1074, p. 107/18–24; 2.9, to Countesses Beatrice and Matilda of Tuscany, 16 Oct. 1074, p. 140/2–6.

rulers is to be appreciated only when it is set against the authority which he believed that he received on the day of his ordination as bishop at the tomb of St Peter whose vicar he then became: 'Whatsoever you bless shall be blessed, and whatsoever you loose upon earth shall be loosed also in heaven.'[366] He gave his most considered summary of what this commission involved in 1083 to the clergy and lay magnates of Flanders; it imposed upon him at once a pastoral office expressed in Christ's commission to feed his sheep, and also a judicial office which perpetuated in the pope for the time being St Peter's power to bind and loose upon earth by a sentence that was also binding in heaven.[367]

Historians have understandably concentrated upon the more dramatic exercises by Gregory of his Petrine authority and upon his eloquent justification of them in his dealings with King Henry IV of Germany. But before such great matters are discussed, it is appropriate to recall how great a part the exercise of the power of the keys played in both the regular business at Rome of the pope and the Roman church, and the pope's more ordinary dealings with the leaders and peoples of Christendom. Pope Alexander III (1159–81) indicated the priorities of the great popes of the central Middle Ages in his alleged answer when someone acclaimed him as a good pope: 'If I judge well, if I preach well, and if I award penance, I shall be a good pope.'[368] As pope, Gregory's letters suggest that he had as a prime concern of his office the awarding of penance and the granting of the apostolic absolution and blessing.

Thus, as bishop of Rome, Gregory was pastor of souls with regard to the clergy and people of his own diocese and of the Central Italian dioceses which were directly subject to the Roman church. He can occasionally be seen in the exercise of his pastoral concern for them. An attractive vignette of his sure touch in bringing a sinner to penitence and absolution is provided by the Hildebrandine anecdote of how, when travelling south of Rome with Abbot Hugh of Cluny, Gregory became aware that a monk at Rome who was his valued supporter had committed fornication; he discreetly used Abbot Hugh to bring him gently but speedily to repentance and confession.[369] Moreover, by Gregory's time, penitential pilgrimages to Rome were an established institution which had been regulated by church councils in order both to safeguard the position of diocesan bishops and to regulate the means of approach to papal authority.[370] Gregory's personal dealings with a pilgrim who came to Rome for purposes of devotion are well illustrated by the experiences there of Count Simon of Crépy, upon whose first visit Gregory himself determined the conditions upon which the count should be granted penance.[371] The penitential journey to Rome of Adelelme, later abbot of la Chaise-Dieu (1078) provides a graphic account of the

---

[366] *Epp. vag.* no. 18, to all the faithful in Germany, (Dec. 1076), pp. 48–9.

[367] Cited above, 8.3.

[368] Peter Cantor, *Verbum abbreviatum*, cap. 65, *PL* 205.199C.

[369] Alexander, *De mirac.* cap. 30, in Southern and Schmitt, *Memorials*, pp. 218–19.

[370] See the council of Seligenstadt (1023), canons 16, 18, *MGH Const.* 1.638, no. 437; council of Limoges (1031), Mansi, 19.546–8 (in this source, the hand of Adhemar of Chabannes must be allowed for).

[371] *Vita beati Simonis*, cap. 3, cols. 1213C–1214A.

austerities of a penitential journey in quest of absolution at the see of St Peter.[372] Again, those who had sinned grievously at home came to Rome for papal penance. An example is Peter Raymundi, son of Count Raymond Berengar I of Barcelona, who in 1071 murdered his stepmother; in 1073, he came to Rome where Gregory referred to the Roman cardinals the task of assigning him a penance.[373] Because such exercise of the power of the keys was a regular papal concern, it only occasionally finds specific record in surviving sources. But for a pope like Gregory, it is likely to have been a main activity of his official routine. Penitents and pilgrims returning from Rome are likely to have fostered a general awareness of the powers of St Peter as they were daily exercised.

By an extension of the power which he thus possessed at Rome, Gregory was concerned to bring Petrine blessing and discipline to bear upon all in Christendom with whom the pope had dealings. For the power of the keys had wider applications than the functions of judgement, penance, and absolution. By reason of its efficacy, papal expressions of both blessing and warning were not merely words and wishes; like the blessings and the cursings of the Old Testament they drew upon a reserve of supernatural energy which made them effective and self-fulfilling. Gregory could bring or withhold, and he had a duty to bring or withhold, prosperity both spiritual and material, according to whether men obeyed, ignored, or disobeyed his words. Thus, the concluding prayers which Gregory sometimes addressed to those whom he favoured were not mere wishes; they were intended to convey the blessing that they expressed. They were an effective assurance of heavenly aid to the obedient of which the Petrine sources of papal authority were the guarantee.[374] Gregory was concerned to distribute blessings, such as absolution from their sins, which would both win loyalty from those who received them and promote the moral quality and the prosperity of their lives. For example, when Bishop Remigius of Lincoln sent to Gregory for judgement about his clerical status a clerk who had committed homicide, Gregory added to his decision a blessing for Remigius himself:

As you have asked, we have also, by the authority of the princes of the apostles Peter and Paul on whose behalf we act, thought proper to send you the absolution of your sins, provided that, by cleaving to good works and by weeping for the sins that you have committed, you maintain the habitation of your body as a temple which is clean as from God (cf. 1 Cor. 3: 16, 6: 19).[375]

Conversely, in 1082, Gregory warned Archbishop Lanfranc of Canterbury that disobedience to his summons to come to Rome would entail the loss of St Peter's favour as well as the incurring of sanctions imposed by his authority.[376] Gregory similarly sought by promoting obedience to bring princes and their peoples to enjoy blessings and prosperity here and hereafter of which St Peter was the source.[377]

---

[372] Ralph, *Vita s. Adelelmi*, cap. 3, pp. 844–7.

[373] Kehr, 'Das Papsttum und der katalanische Prinzipat', pp. 80–1, no. 7.

[374] See esp. *Reg.* 1.15, to the faithful of St Peter in Lombardy, 1 July 1073, pp. 24/34–25/2; 2.27, to Duke Gésa of Hungary, 17 Apr. 1075, p. 230/26–8.

[375] *Reg.* 1.34, 2 Dec. 1073, p. 55/24–9.   [376] *Reg.* 9.20, (May/June 1082), pp. 600–1.

[377] *Reg.* 2.71–2, to Duke Wratislav II, and to the people of Bohemia, 17 Apr. 1075, pp. 231–3.

Much of Gregory's concern with the power of the keys was thus bound up with the daily discharge at Rome of the papal duty of judging well and awarding penance, and with the capacity granted to the prince of the apostles and entrusted to the pope as his vicar of directing blessing and warning, as might be appropriate, to all those in Christendom with whom it might fall to the pope to deal. Nevertheless, it is such exceptional use of the power of the keys as was involved in Gregory's dealings in 1076–7 and 1080 with Henry IV of Germany that most signally illustrate the force of his concern to bring St Peter's authority to bear in the affairs of Christendom.

His sanctions against Henry were foreshadowed in a sentence of March 1075 upon Bishop Dionysius of Piacenza, when at his Lent synod he deposed the bishop from his see without hope of reconciliation and absolved all who had sworn him fealty from the bond of their oaths.[378] Dionysius's case is likely to have been in Gregory's mind when he formulated the last clause of the *Dictatus papae*: 'That the pope can absolve subjects from their fealty to wicked men',[379] which he implemented against Henry IV in 1076 and 1080. His sentence of deposition and excommunication against Henry at his Lent synods of those years took the form of impassioned addresses respectively to St Peter and to St Peter and St Paul, and were based upon the authority to bind and loose in heaven and upon earth which was committed to him.[380] In 1076, Gregory expressly derived from it his inhibition of Henry from governing the German kingdom and his absolution of his subjects from all their oaths to him, so that none might serve him as king. In 1080, his sentence was still more comprehensively expressed:

And again, on behalf of Almighty God and of yourselves, in debarring him from the kingdom of the Germans and of Italy I take away from him all royal power and dignity. I forbid that any Christian should obey him as king, and I absolve from the promise of their oath all who have sworn to him, or shall swear, regarding his rulership of the kingdom.

Oaths were the bond of contemporary society. It is not surprising that Gregory's exercise of the power of the keys to annul them should have become the central issue in polemic about Gregory's claims.

Accordingly, at an interval after each sentence, Gregory set out his authority and the duty to exercise it in letters to Bishop Hermann of Metz.[381] In these connections, Gregory was above all concerned to assert that kings were in no way excepted from Christ's commission to Peter to feed his sheep, and from the power of the keys that was committed to Peter. If spiritual rulers were subject to the judgement of the prince of the apostles, how much more so were emperors and kings, who depended upon priests for their salvation. Gregory was thus concerned to bring kings firmly

---

[378] *Reg.* 2.54, to the faithful at Piacenza, 3 Mar. 1075, pp. 198–9; cf. *Epp. vag.* no. 46, to the clergy and people of Thérouanne, (1082), pp. 110–13.

[379] *Reg.* 2.55a, p. 208. The measures that Gregory contemplated in 1074 against King Philip I of France should be borne in mind: *Reg.* 2.5, to the archbishops and bishops of France, 10 Sept. 1074, p. 132/29–41.

[380] *Reg.* 3.10a, pp. 270–1; 7.14a, pp. 483–7.

[381] *Reg.* 4.2, 25 Aug. 1076, pp. 293–7; 8.21, 15 Mar. 1081, pp. 544–63.

under St Peter's authority to bind and loose. Who, indeed, could think himself exempt, Gregory asked, except perhaps a wretched man who, being unwilling to bear the yoke of the Lord (Matt. 11: 30), placed himself under the burden of the devil? Such miserable liberty profited nothing, and was merely the expression of a pride which would lead to eternal damnation.[382]

Accordingly, in his sentences against Henry IV, Gregory had three purposes in mind with regard to the power of the keys. First, he sought to vindicate the authority of the princes of the apostles and to secure the obedience of kings to their exercise of their authority in and through the church: 'now let kings and all princes of the world learn how great you are,' Gregory asked, 'and what you can do; and let them fear to disregard the command of your church.'[383] Second, he sought so to bring to bear the sanctions of excommunication and anathema as to demonstrate that a ruler who incurred them lost all blessing and prosperity in this world, even to the point of becoming incapable of military victory.[384] But, third, the power of the keys and the purpose of its being committed to the church were such that, swift and sure though its sentence might be, the ultimate goal of any exercise of it must be the repentance of a sinner, at least in the day of judgement. Thus, Gregory concluded his second sentence against Henry with the plea to the apostles Peter and Paul:

And execute your judgement upon Henry so swiftly, that everyone may know that he falls and is put to confusion not by chance but by your power—would that it may be to repentance, that the spirit may be saved in the day of the Lord (1 Cor. 5: 5).[385]

Such was Gregory's view of the power of the keys at the limit of its exercise.

8.11.4 The Promotion of Peace and Concord

The force and directness of Gregory's preaching, his zeal to implement righteousness as he envisaged it, and his tone of overmastering authority when twice applying the power of the keys to pass sentence upon Henry IV of Germany, should not conceal the fact that much of his public concern bears a somewhat different stamp. Broadly speaking, his masterfulness was to the fore when he was denouncing grave sins—simony and fornication on the part of the clergy, disobedience on that of kings. But human affairs are complex and do not always reduce themselves to simple issues that are appropriate for the prophet's voice. Nor do matters always come to a head in points of crisis at which the fully panoply of apostolic power may be appropriate. Thus, Gregory's concern to announce righteousness and to bring to judgement was

---

[382] See esp. *Reg.* 4.2, p. 295; 7.14*a*, p. 487; 8.21, pp. 548, 552–3.

[383] *Reg.* 7.14*a*, p. 487/14–16; cf. the advice to kings in 5.10, to King Harold Hein of Denmark, 6 Nov. 1077, p. 362/12–30; 7.6, to King Alphonso VI of León–Castile, 15 Oct. 1079, p. 465/34–8.

[384] For Gregory's repeated insistence upon the loss of earthly power and blessing by reprobate kings and princes, see esp. *Epp. vag.* no. 13, to Bishop Henry of Trent, (Mar./July 1076), pp. 30–1; *Reg.* 5.14*a*, record of the Lent synod of 1078, pp. 370/31–371/5, to all in Germany, 9 Mar. 1078, p. 376/4–10; 6.1, to all in Germany, 1 July 1078, p. 390/17–21; 6.16, to Bishop Berengar of Gerona, 2 Jan. 1079, p. 422/8–23; 7.14*a*, record of the Lent synod of 1080, p. 486/20–7.

[385] *Reg.* 7.14*a*, p. 487/14–19.

complemented by a concern to promote peace ('pax') and concord ('concordia'). Separately and together, they are key words in his vocabulary.[386]

Whereas Gregory set his own stamp upon the term 'righteousness', his use of 'peace' and 'concord' followed the tradition of a millennium during which these words expressed two of the profoundest aspirations that men cherished for human society. At Rome, Gregory will have been familiar with the temples of Peace and Concord which recalled the values of pagan days—peace, as realized in the *pax Augusta* with its promise of quiet at home and abroad guaranteed by strong and popular government, and concord, as the harmony and agreement of the state and of bodies within it. From St Paul to St Augustine, Christian writers cherished the two words, which retained much of their classical meaning. Thus, in 1079, Gregory cited to the archbishops of Rouen, Sens, and Tours a passage from Gregory I's letters about the requirements of a well-ordered society in which each member performed his appointed function under a duly constituted head: a single concord ('concordia') should arise from diversity, while peace ('pax') and charity should embrace each other, and a firm foundation should be established of concord ('concordia') in men's love for each other and for God.[387] In its legislation and in its political theory, the Carolingian age, too, proclaimed peace and concord as objectives for good government. Throughout the Christian centuries and not least during the eleventh century, there was no more evocative social model than that of the early Jerusalem church in the Acts of the Apostles, when concord prevailed among the number of believers: 'multitudinis autem credentium erat cor et anima una' (Acts 4: 32, cf. 2: 44–7).[388]

The social objectives of peace and concord were not only handed down by long and active tradition; they were also to the fore in Gregory's day because of legal conventions that were widely current in lay as in ecclesiastical circles. When attempts were made peaceably to resolve disputes, the primary object was not to apply legal rules and to ascertain facts so that the rules might be rigorously satisfied to the letter; it was to mend fractured human relationships and loyalties and so to restore peace among those in conflict. Matters affecting rights and property that might be at stake were to be dealt with by way of compromise. Peace among men was to be renewed by a concord which represented, not an ideal solution, but the best bargain that could be contrived in order that hitherto unreconciled adversaries might henceforth live in peace and harmony. It was unlikely that such a bargain would satisfy entirely the claims of any party.[389] Eleventh-century sources provide no better example of an attempt by a superior authority to achieve peace and concord by such means than Gregory's dealings with Bohemia which centred upon the *lis et discordia* between the sees of Prague and Olmütz. Gregory's overriding intention was to restore relations

---

[386] For Gregory's use of these words, see Caspar's Index, *Reg.* pp. 682, 699–700.

[387] *Reg.* 6.35, 20 Apr. 1079, pp. 450/22–451/9, citing Gregory I, *Reg.* 5, 59, vol. 1.357/1–358/17; cf. p. 452/3–7.

[388] See Cowdrey, 'From the Peace of God to the First Crusade'.

[389] For a discusson of general principles and of a relevant 11th-cent. case, see Dier, 'The Proper Relationship'.

between the bishops concerned and between them and the ducal house. While the claims of righteousness were to be paramount, rights and property were to be disposed of by compromise in the interest of restoring a proper pattern of human relationships and loyalties. Gregory hoped by this means to foster peace in the whole of Bohemia and to settle the relations of the duchy with the papacy and with the German king.[390] The failure of his intentions in no way detracts from them as an example of his purpose, according to the usages of his time, to proceed by way of negotiation and compromise under the aegis of papal authority as well as by the direct exercise of papal prerogatives.

Gregory's concern to promote peace and concord was active in his dealings both ecclesiastical and political, and it tempered the masterfulness which was also characteristic of him. In the church, he declared it at the beginning of his pontificate to the leading clergy and laity to whom he gave notice of his election. Thus, writing to Archbishop Guibert of Ravenna, he sought to establish the relations between the churches of Rome and Ravenna upon a basis of peace, concord, and charity:

You should not doubt that we desire to join the Roman church and that over which by God's authority you preside by such concord ('concordia') and, so far as we shall be able saving their common honour by such charity, that in our own hearts lasting peace and entire love may always be conjoined.[391]

The reality, but also the limits of Gregory's concern to restore human relationships by negotiation and pacification when tensions were in need of relaxation became apparent in the exarchate during June 1073. The citizens of Imola complained to Gregory that Archbishop Guibert was wrongfully seeking to exact from them an oath of fealty. Gregory acted in the spirit of his letter to Guibert by urging Count Guy of Imola to restore the situation by mediation:

Whatever discord there may be between them or whatever source of vexation, we earnestly ask you to try to quieten it and, if you can saving the honour of St Peter, to settle it by a firm peace.

If he could not, the count should seek to contain the situation until papal legates might arrive:

For we ardently desire to have peace, if it be possible, with all men (cf. Rom. 12: 18), but with God's help we do not shrink from resisting as well by power as by righteousness ('tam virtute quam iustitia') the designs of those who seek to aggrandize themselves to the detriment of St Peter whose servant we are.[392]

Gregory was concerned to establish throughout the church a concord which had as its foundation the faith, unity, and discipline of the Roman church: he made this clear in *Dictatus papae* 26: 'That he is not to be held catholic who does not conform to the Roman church.'[393] Accordingly, the Roman see might never deviate from Christian

---

[390] See above, 6.5.
[391] *Reg.* 1.3, 26 Apr. 1073, p. 6/19–23, cf. 1.4, p. 7. Gregory seems to have had in mind Gregory I's words as referred to above: as n. 387
[392] *Reg.* 1.10, to Count Guy of Imola, 1 June 1073, pp. 16–17.
[393] *Reg.* 2.55a, p. 207, cf. 7.24, to Abbot William of Hirsau, 8 May 1080, pp. 504/21–505/7.

concord as enshrined in the canonical tradition ('a concordia canonicae traditionis'): yet for good reason it might show a measure of tolerance in practice.[394] Its duty of promoting concord in current contingencies left considerable room for dialogue and tolerance no less than for command, and for a genuine search for mutual knowledge and comprehension.

This is especially apparent in Gregory's dealings with the eastern churches. At the beginning of his pontificate, he expressed a purpose to renew the ancient concord between the Roman church and its daughter of Constantinople as well as the eastern empire, and he hoped so far as in him lay to have peace with all men. In 1074, he believed that the Byzantine, Armenian, and most other eastern churches were ready for a papal initiative in bringing them towards concord in the faith of St Peter. This was a major motive for his 'Crusading' plan of that year.[395] The conciliatory approach that he was prepared to adopt is illustrated by his letter of 1080 to the Armenian catholicos Gregory of Tsamandos, which made a sustained attempt to seek common ground. It expressed surprising tolerance of the use of leavened bread in the eucharist by the Greeks, and it ended with a tactfully worded prayer for the catholicos's progress in the way of peace towards convergence with the Roman church:

May Almighty God, from whom comes whatever we rightly know or feel or believe, himself the more abundantly illuminate your mind ('mentem tuae fraternitatis') and direct it in the way of sound understanding. May he preserve you in the concordant unity of the faithful ('in concordi fidelium unitate') and may he so direct and keep you that you may be able effectively to instruct the peoples subject to you in the knowledge of divine truth, and also enter with them into eternal glory and with them win through to receive eternal rewards.[396]

Gregory's concern for peace and concord in the bond of charity led him to seek to bring eastern Christians to the unity of faith by defending them against the violence of the Seljuks and by dialogue, rather than by ecclesiastical sanctions and by command.

A comparable concern to proceed where possible by agreement is apparent in Gregory's dealings in the Latin west. Gregory's studied moderation in French and Burgundian church affairs was animated by a purpose of restoring loyalties, due services, and collaboration amongst the human agents involved; his intervention in 1079 to relieve tension about rights and property between the abbot of Cluny and the bishop of Mâcon provides an excellent example of his overriding concern to restore concord between them.[397] In Germany, Gregory's attempted mediation in 1075 between Bishop Otto of Constance and Abbot Ekkehard of Reichenau shows a similar concentration upon restoring peace between them. Both had appealed to Gregory; he ruled that, first of all, impartial local mediators should be sought who might settle

---

394 *Reg.* 2.20, to King Sancho I of Aragon, 24 Jan. 1075, p. 191/24–6.

395 *Reg.* 1.18, to Emperor Michael VII Ducas, 9 July 1073, pp. 29/30–30/4; 2.31, to King Henry IV of Germany, 7 Dec. 1074, pp. 166/32, 167/15.

396 *Reg.* 8.1, 6 June 1080, pp. 510–14.

397 See above, 5.3.2.4, with Cowdrey, *The Cluniacs*, and id., 'Cardinal Peter of Albano's Legatine Journey'.

their dispute equitably and by general consent. If this failed, they should come to Rome where Gregory himself would bring their prolonged discord to a just conclusion. In the meantime, both should observe firm peace and abstain from mutual provocation as though they were subject to the sanction of St Peter who would be the guarantor of the restored relationship which it was Gregory's aim to establish:

For you should regard it as no light matter when such a mediator was interposed to break the terms of peace, for whoever does not show respect and trust towards apostolic authority as expressed in this decree will turn credibility and judgement against himself and his cause by the very impiety of his boldness.398

Thus a pattern of obligation and loyalties was established within which the resolution of disputes might take place. Gregory also sought to forestall disputes that might threaten human relationships. Thus, in South Italy, he asked Count Roger of Sicily duly to consider the metropolitan rights of the church of Reggio/Calabria when setting up the new see of Mileto; for, if Reggio's rights proved to be well founded, the count should proceed equitably in the things of God, taking care to avoid breaking the bond of brotherly charity and concord.399 By such means, Gregory sought to promote the settlement of ecclesiastical disputes and uncertainties by way of mediation and concord.400

The pursuit of peace and concord was no less Gregory's declared objective in his political aspirations and dealings. The pope's duty to foster them in Christian society was especially strongly in his mind in relation to Germany, both before and after his first breach with Henry IV in 1076. Comparably to the way in which he aspired to restore the ancient concord between the apostolic see and the Byzantine empire,401 in the early months of his pontificate he hoped to establish it between Rome and the western empire. As present king and future emperor, Henry IV was to be instructed, without the hindrance of evil counsellors, in a ruler's proper attributes of loving religion, of listening to good advisers whom he unfeignedly loved, and of increasing and defending the property of churches. In 1074, Gregory praised Henry's mother, the Empress Agnes, for her labours on behalf of the peace and concord of the universal church and for seeking the unity in charity of the papacy and the empire.402 Until quite a late date in 1075, Gregory was prepared to believe that Henry himself might be amenable; but he then became anxious lest the king were lapsing into a desire that peace should not be arranged ('pacem componi') and lest he were listening to counsellors who preferred discord to the concord between king and pope that it was Gregory's purpose to establish.403

---

398 *Reg.* 2.60, to Bishop Otto of Constance, 13 Mar. 1075, pp. 214–15.

399 *Reg.* 9.25, 1081, before 4 Feb., pp. 607–8.

400 Gregory's frequent use of the verbs *componere* and *facere* in connection with peace is significant: see Caspar's Index, s.v. *pax*, *Reg.* p. 700.

401 *Reg.* 1.18, p. 30/1–4.   402 *Reg.* 1.85, 15 June 1074, p. 121/20–4.

403 *Reg.* 1.20, to Bishop Raynald of Como, 1 Sept. 1073, pp. 33/28–24/14; 3.7, to King Henry IV, (early Sept. 1075), p. 257. 8–11; 3.5, to Countesses Beatrice and Matilda of Tuscany, 11 Sept. 1075, p. 252/3–9; cf. the language which Henry IV adopted when writing to Gregory: *Epp. HIV* nos. 5,7, pp. 54/24–30, 58/16–20.

Between Canossa and his second excommunication of Henry IV in 1080, a main theme of Gregory's dealings with the German kingdom was a search for peace and concord there. Immediately after Canossa, Gregory informed the faithful in Germany of his intention of himself coming to Germany at the first opportunity, 'in order that, as we have long desired, we may with God's help more fully repair all things (*omnia plenius coaptare*), to the peace of the church and the concord of the kingdom'; later, he declared his purpose as being 'to arrange (*componere*) peace and concord between King Henry and the princes of the land.'[404] At Canossa, Henry was, accordingly, required to swear that, with regard to the grievances that the ecclesiastical and lay princes had against him, he would, by a set date, 'implement either righteousness according to Gregory's sentence or concord according to his counsel'.[405] The alternative 'aut iustitiam aut concordiam' was a well established convention of eleventh-century judicial procedure. It offered the parties to a dispute the alternative either of accepting the definitive sentence of an accredited judge or of themselves coming by way of compromise to a mutual agreement; in either case, the ultimate aim was to secure the reconciliation of the parties concerned.[406] The use of the formula demonstrates Gregory's willingness, in order to achieve the pope's ultimate concern to promote peace, to be flexible as between proceeding by his own act of judgement or by the promotion of concord between king and princes.

The election of Rudolf of Swabia as anti-king added a double complication from Gregory's viewpoint. First, it became necessary to decide between the rival kings, and secondly, besides dealing with the kingship, it was necessary to take increasing thought for the kingdom by seeking general peace in the renewed civil wars. Germany was afflicted by a 'motus et perturbatio' which brought slaughter, arson, and other perils of war to its people. Gregory deemed it his duty to bring peace to the whole land; the 'lis et perturbatio regni' became a major item in the agenda of his Roman synods.[407] He continued to hold out in Germany the alternative solutions of concord or judgement.[408] Thus in 1078, he told the German people that his legates' task was to restore the concord of their kingdom; in the projected assembly, the legates would either (by agreement) arrange peace between the two German parties, or else determine (by judgement) which of the two parties righteousness favoured.

---

[404] *Reg.* 4.12, to the German princes, (late Jan. 1077), p. 413/19–22; 4.25, to Archbishop Nehemiah of Gran, 9 June 1077, p. 339/17–20; see also 4.23, to Gregory's legates in Germany, 31 May 1077, p. 335/1–5; 7.14a, record of the Lent synod 1080, p. 484/16–20.

[405] *Reg.* 4.12a, Henry IV's *iusiurandum*, 28 Jan. 1077, pp. 314/22–315/6.

[406] See esp. *The Letters and Poems of Fulbert of Chartres*, ed. Behrens, pp. 152–5, no. 86; also the remaining citations in Niermeyer, *Mediae Latinitatis Lexicon Minus*, s.v. *concordia*.

[407] *Reg.* 5.7, to Archbishop Udo of Trier, 30 Sept. 1077, pp. 356–8. For the synods, see for Lent 1078: 5.14a(6), pp. 370–1, with 5.15–16, to all the faithful in Germany, and to Archbishop Udo of Trier, 9 Mar. 1078, pp. 374–8; 6.1, to all the faithful in Germany, 1 July 1078, pp. 389–91. For Nov. 1078, 6.5b, pp. 400–1, with 6.14, to Duke Welf IV of Bavaria, 30 Dec. 1078; pp. 418–19; *Epp. vag.* no. 25, to the supporters of both parties in Germany, (late Nov. 1078), pp. 64–7; no. 26, to the anti-king Rudolf and his followers, (late Feb. 1079), pp. 66–9. For Lent 1079; *Reg.* 6.17a(2–3), pp. 427–8.

[408] *Reg.* 7.14a, p. 485/15–18.

He also told them that his legates were to decide between the two kings as individual rulers according to the test of righteousness.[409]

Underlying Gregory's sustained purpose of bringing peace to Germany was a conviction that, when public authority broke down, the pope had a function and a duty to restore peace and security in the interests of those who were most vulnerable —churches and clergy, widows, children, and travellers. Gregory was thereby claiming a role in making and sanctioning peace that had been claimed and contended for by rulers both clerical and lay since the attempts to establish the Peace and the Truce of God which had marked the early decades of the eleventh century.[410] In 1074, Gregory had adumbrated his claim during his period of sharp conflict with Philip I of France; he had expressed the fear that the anarchy into which he believed France to be falling might overflow, if unchecked, to the limits of Christendom.[411] Between 1077 and 1080, Gregory more strongly and continually asserted his purpose to restore public peace, if possible by his coming to Germany and holding a national assembly, but if not by the instrumentality of his legates. From Henrician bishops, Gregory stimulated the reply that, far from being a source of peace for their land, he was the cause of the prevailing warfare and bloodshed.[412]

After his second excommunication of Henry IV in 1080, Gregory was no longer concerned with the problem of deciding between rival kings. In the years of his bitter propaganda and military contest with Henry IV, he was left with a concern to establish a peace which was general, rather than merely national, in its scope. Henry's manifestos to the Roman citizens goaded Gregory to express and to seek to implement a concern to make peace and concord wherever in Christendom they were needful. Probably in 1083, he addressed Christians everywhere, saying that in some safe place, and therefore not at Rome, he planned a general synod to which clergy and laity, both friendly and hostile, would come from all regions. He blamed Henry outright for the prevalent homicides, perjuries, sacrileges, acts of simony, and treacheries. All whom such calamities moved, or whom fear of God moved to seek peace and concord, should strive for the convening of a synod that would relieve and strengthen the church in head and body. Soon afterwards, an encylical letter to the French and German prelates summoned them to a November synod that would take counsel about establishing the peace of God and healing the schism.[413]

It was Gregory's final, and in the event ineffectual, attempt to claim for himself as pope the function of making peace and concord in Christendom, wherever it might be needed. It was also a landmark on the way to the momentous assembly that Pope Urban II would hold at Clermont in November 1095.[414]

---

[409] *Reg.* 5.15, 6.1.

[410] See Cowdrey, 'From the Peace of God to the First Crusade'.

[411] *Reg.* 5.7, p. 358/6–12; cf. 2.5, to the archbishops and bishops of France, 10 Sept. 1074, 131/12–15, and the discussion above, 5.2.1.

[412] See above, 3.5.1.

[413] *Reg.* 9.29, to all clergy and laity not under excommunication, (summer 1083), pp. 612–13; *Epp. vag.* no. 51, to the loyal archbishops, bishops, and abbots in France and Germany, summer 1083, pp. 122–5.

[414] See Cowdrey, 'From The Peace of God to the First Crusade'.

8.12 Conclusion

It should not be concluded that Gregory was by intention a political pope or that he was predominantly motivated by a drive for power in a this-worldly sense. In the last encyclical which, in 1084, he dispatched from Salerno, he insisted that, as pope, his greatest concern had been that the church which was the bride of Christ 'should return to her former glory and stand free, chaste, and catholic'.[415] The foregoing discussion suggests that, by 'free', he meant that the church as bride should be in unfettered and unqualified subjection to the lordship of Christ as bridegroom and to the authority that Christ had vested in St Peter and, through him, in the apostolic see of Rome; the lay order should be separate from the clerical and obedient to it. By 'chaste', he meant that monks and clergy should eschew all sexual relationships and that laity should shun fornication; but he also required that all orders in the church, whether clerical or lay, should cultivate all the virtues that were appropriate to them. By 'catholic', he sought the universal concord of all Christians in the faith which Peter confessed and of which the apostolic see must be the custodian and guarantor to the end of time.

Gregory's concerns were, as he himself declared, at root religious and moral. He was a true disciple of his mentor, Pope Gregory the Great. For both popes, a prime concern of their office was *praedicatio*, in the sense of proclaiming the demands of Christianity to all peoples and especially to their kings and rulers. Gregory VII's discharge of his office as *praedicator* is to be seen in many of his letters; its results are embodied in the proceedings and decrees of his Lateran synods, in so far as they were directed to the moral and spiritual regeneration of the church, of Christian society, and of individual Christians. The sanctions which, through St Peter, he commanded flowed from his understanding of the power of the keys. But his purpose to act effectively was by no means restricted to the wielding of the spiritual sword, and still less to the directing of the material sword. Righteousness and justice must be tempered with mercy and directed towards reconciliation. Throughout Christian society, and in all regions of the world which were accessible to his action, the pope had a duty of promoting peace and concord. Especially where societies were divided and where rulers were ineffective and useless, the pope had a duty to be himself the promoter of justice and order, and to protect the weak and unprotected against their oppressors. Such was Gregory's vision of the papal office.

[415] *Epp. vag.* no. 54, pp. 132–3.

The Ordering of the Church

The purpose of this chapter is to offer some general observations on how Gregory's government of the church operated in practice, both at Rome and in his relations with the church at large and especially its higher clergy.

9.1 The Roman Church

The still underdeveloped structure of the Roman church by comparison with its constitution in the twelfth and thirteenth centuries, and also the differing and often contrasting currents within the eleventh-century Roman church, have already been discussed. The evidence of Gregory's letters suggests that, at least until he experienced the full pressures of Henry IV's attacks upon Rome in the 1080s, Gregory behaved with prudence and restraint in accepting things as they were and in refraining from pressing matters to a crisis.[1] In practice, Gregory seems to have maintained a balance between acting upon his personal authority as pope apart from the other constituent members of the Roman church, and acting with them as counsellors and coadjutors. Gregory was himself aware that his discharge of his office was differently viewed by different observers:

Neither does it escape us how diverse is the opinion and the judgement of us that some men have, since with respect to the same matters and actions some call us inhuman and others excessively mild. To all such persons, we consider no reply to be truer and more apposite than the Apostle's: 'To me it is of very little account that I am judged by you or by any human tribunal' (1 Cor. 4: 3).[2]

The implication is that Gregory felt himself to be pursuing a middle course, but that for his judgements he was responsible to God alone and that they were for him individually to make.

Apart from the assertion of the prerogatives of the pope himself as well as of the Roman church that characterizes the *Dictatus papae*,[3] there is powerful evidence for Gregory's acting in practice upon a basis of his own right and apart from the corporateness of the Roman church in both judicial and political matters. Judicially, for example, his sentences against Henry IV of Germany at his Lent synods of 1076 and 1080 took the form of addresses of the pope himself to St Peter or to St Peter and St Paul. His sentences were expressed in the first person singular, and they were delivered by him as vicar of the apostles rather than as spokesman of the synod. In 1080,

---

[1] See esp. above, 4.7.
[2] *Reg.* 1.77, to Countesses Beatrice and Matilda of Tuscany, 15 Apr. 1074, p. 110/34–9.
[3] Esp. clauses 5, 7, 12–14, 16–19, 24–5, 27, *Reg.* 2.55a, pp. 203–8.

Gregory spoke expressly of his hearers as acquiescing in his sentence and not as contributing to it:

Because you [St Peter and St Paul] are disciples and lovers of the truth, give me your aid that I may declare the truth to you with all falsehood such as you altogether abhor being altogether banished, so that my brothers may the better agree with me, and may know and understand that by confidence in you, after God and his mother Mary ever-virgin, I resist the perverse and wicked but bring help to those who are faithful to you.[4]

Politically, Gregory's journey to Germany at the end of 1076 was his own decision made against the advice of almost all his Roman entourage; in 1082, his use of church property to finance his resistance to Archbishop Guibert of Ravenna lacked the sanction of the Roman church and was resisted by an assembly of its leading members, many of whom were supporters of his cause.[5]

Such examples of Gregory's acting at his own discretion must, however, be balanced against a considerable body of evidence which suggests that, especially in matters of regular business, he habitually acted in consultation with the Roman bishops and with the Roman priests and deacons of the cardinalate. Thus, in the awarding of penance, when in 1073 Peter Raymundi, son of Count Raymond Berengar I of Barcelona, came to Rome seeking penance for the murder of his stepmother Almodis, Gregory referred him for the settlement of its terms to the cardinals of the Roman church.[6] Gregory made similar consultations with regard to judicial matters. In 1073, when his legate Cardinal Gerald of Ostia referred to him the difficult case of Archbishop William of Auch, Gregory came to a decision after consulting 'our brothers and fellow-bishops and the cardinals'. In 1074, Gregory's *confratres* at Rome were instrumental in securing from Gregory a merciful decision in the case of Bishop Werner of Strassburg. In 1075, before Gregory answered an inquiry from King Sancho of Aragon concerning canonical problems arising from the succession of the bishops of Huesca, he not only took long thought on his own part but also discussed them with his clergy ('cum filiis sanctae Romanae ecclesiae'). When, in 1078, some clerks of Orleans petitioned Gregory against their bishop-elect Sanzo, he caused both parties to be diligently examined by the Roman bishops ('coram episcoporum nostrorum presentia') in order that he himself might know which party to reject and which to approve. In 1081, Gregory's brothers ('fratres') at Rome advised him when the bishops of Paris and Orleans appealed against a sentence of Gregory's legate, Bishop Hugh of Die.[7]

---

4 *Reg.* 3.10a, record of the Lent synod of 1076, pp. 270–1; 7.14a, record of the Lent synod of 1080, pp. 483–7, citation from p. 483/4–10.

5 See above, 3.5.7.

6 Kehr, 'Das Papsttum und der katalanische Prinzipat', p. 80, no. 7.

7 *Reg.* 1.16, to Cardinal Gerald of Ostia, 1 July 1073, p. 26/7–23; 1.77, to Countesses Beatrice and Matilda of Tuscany, 15 Apr. 1074, pp. 109/29–110/8; 2.50, to King Sancho I of Aragon, 24 Jan. 1075, p. 191/6–10; 5.14, to the clergy and people of Orleans, 29 Jan. 1078, pp. 367–8; 9.15, to Bishop Hugh of Die, 4 Dec. (1081), p. 595/17–23; see also the evidence for consultation in Hugh of Flavigny, *Chron.* 2, p. 411/53–5; *Chron. s. Andreae castris Camerac.* cap. 1, p. 540/2–5; Berthold, *Ann. a.* 1079, p. 322/44–8; *Vita s. Brunonis ep. Signien.* p. 497E; *Vita s. Altmanni*, cap. 14, p. 233/35–7.

It would be anachronistic to conclude that Gregory was already deliberating about matters of business with a consistory in the developed, twelfth-century sense of a regular assembly, normally meeting formally in the Lateran, whether of cardinals alone or of cardinals afforced by other appropriate persons. Yet it is often overlooked that meetings of broadly such a character had a long history in the Roman church, and that they were evidently taking place during Gregory's time as archdeacon.[8] The incidental references to consultations in his letters suggest that he habitually consulted the Roman bishops and cardinals, that they had regular and recognized functions in the local and general government of the church, and that Gregory paid considerable attention to their deliberations and decisions. Such consultation was not a later hiving off of business from the Roman synods in spring and autumn as they developed in Gregory's time; it already took place regularly alongside the synods in order to deal with matters of business when they arose and, no doubt, to reduce the burden of the synods themselves. It provides an undertone of concerted action between the pope and the *ecclesia Romana*, and it casts doubt upon the justice of the later allegation of the schismatic Cardinal Beno that, from the beginning of his pontificate, 'he removed the cardinals of the holy see from his counsels'.[9]

9.2 Roman Synods

Whatever consultation Gregory may have maintained with the Roman bishops and with the cardinals was complemented by the work of the Roman synods which were a regular feature of his pontificate. The testimony of his Register and other letters, as well as of chronicles and other sources, points to their having been a principal means whereby he demonstrated his apostolic authority and sought to order the spiritual, moral, and political life of Christendom. Gregory's Roman synods were established upon ancient foundations. They were the linear continuation of the synods that popes since late antiquity had held as bishops of the Roman church who also had direct authority over many bishoprics in Central Italy. Such episcopal synods were attended by the suburbicarian bishops and by a greater or smaller number of other bishops, as well as by lesser clergy and laity.[10] But their weight and the range of attendance and business were greatly augmented by the traditions of the imperial councils held by the Ottonian and Salian rulers of Germany over which the emperor had presided either by himself or jointly with the pope. Such councils were widely attended by bishops and by others, and they dealt with ecclesiastical business throughout the emperor's realms.[11] The pontificate of Leo IX (1049–54) was a critical time for the development of papal councils and synods. The year 1049 saw Leo both sitting at Mainz with the Emperor Henry III at an imperial council of the familiar kind and also holding outside the empire, at Rheims, a papal synod of bishops from

---

[8] See above, 2.2.5. [9] Beno, 1, 2, p. 370.

[10] The membership and business of an early 11th-cent. Roman synod are well illustrated by Pope John XIX's bulls of Dec. 1026 concerning the rights and possessions of the see of Silva Candida: Zimmermann, *Papsturkunden*, nos. 568–9, 2.1075–83.

[11] See e.g. *MGH Const.* 1, pp. 70–8, no. 34 (Pavia, 1022), pp. 82–4, no. 38 (Rome, 1027).

many lands which issued reforming canons for the whole church.[12] Under the popes up to 1073, Roman synods were frequently held after Easter for the discharge of ecclesiastical business and for the reform of the church in many lands.[13]

Alexander's II's last synod in 1073 had been held in Lent rather than after Easter; Gregory VII followed suit by holding a Lent synod in the Lateran basilica during each year of his pontificate save 1077, when he was travelling in North Italy after his encounter with Henry IV at Canossa, and 1082-5, when military and political circumstances made the holding of Lent synods at Rome impracticable.[14] In 1074 and 1078, he held an additional synod in November; he also held a synod in November 1083, although attendance at it was small.[15] About a year later, a further synod took place at Salerno.[16]

Gregory's synods were normally attended by a wide cross-section of Christian society, a feature which has an obvious parallel in the crown-wearings of contemporary kings.[17] Bishops and abbots provided the majority of those present: bishops were expected to enforce the decrees of Roman synods in their own provinces or dioceses and through their own synods; the abbots whose attendance was a feature of Roman synods from the time of Pope Leo IX were expected to play an important part in their localities by implementing the moral and penitential rulings of the synods amongst the considerable clerical and lay public who looked to them.[18] But lower clergy and laity also had their place; as, for Gregory, a local church was constituted by its clergy and people, so a Roman synod which was convened to represent the whole church comprised both. In terms of numbers, it is probable that the constant attendance at Gregory's synods was made up of the suburbicarian bishops and the bishops of the 'Roman church province' of Central Italy who were directly subject to Roman jurisdiction. It is probably significant that, in 1079, the record of the Lent synod referred to the attendance, in this order, of neighbouring archbishops, bishops, and religious persons, and then of those of different provinces, and that, in Lent 1080, the decree about the right of devolution in episcopal elections provided first for sees directly subject to Rome and thereafter for those subject to other metropolitans.[19] In

---

[12] *MGH Const.* 1, pp. 97–100, no. 51; Anselme de Saint-Remy, *Histoire*, esp. caps. 20–34, pp. 234–53.

[13] The synods are noted in JL; see also Tangl, *Die Teilnehmer*, pp. 129–52. For their annual meeting, see *Reg.* 1.43, to the suffragans of Milan, 25 Jan. 1074, p. 66/8–11.

[14] For the synods, see JL, and G. Tangl, *Die Teilnehmer*, pp. 152–69; Gregory himself referred to a synod in Nov. 1074: *Reg.* 2.33, to Bishop Cunibert of Turin, 12 Dec. 1074, p. 169/20–2. Gregory's reason for preferring to hold his regular synods before rather than after Easter does not emerge; he may have had in mind canon 5 of the council of Nicaea (325): *COD* p. 8; or perhaps he wished to enable those summoned to leave Rome before the months of heat and pestilence and so to preclude an excuse for non–attendance.

[15] *Reg.* 9.35*a*, record of the Nov. synod 1093, p. 628/4–5.

[16] Bernold, *Chron. a.* 1084, p. 441/34–5.

[17] For attendance at Gregory's synods, see Tangl, *Die Teilnehmer*, pp. 152–69.

[18] See e.g. the role assigned to 'eos, qui religione et scripturarum doctrina instructi viam veritatis et salutis . . . ostendere valeant' in *Reg.* 7.14*a*(6), p. 482/12–18. For an illustration of the place of monasteries in raising pastoral standards outside their walls through hagiography and canon law, see Cowdrey, *The Age of Abbot Desiderius*, pp. 43–4.

[19] *Reg.* 6.17*a*, p. 425/19–23, 7.14*a*, p. 482.

November 1083, when access to Rome was largely barred to those travelling from the north, the archbishops, bishops, and abbots 'of Campania, the principates, and Apulia' remained as the solid core of the assembly.[20]

Nevertheless, both the status of the synods in the Lateran as general councils of the church[21] and the universal applicability of much of their business served to ensure that the synods had an authority that was commensurate with Gregory's universal jurisdiction. It also ensured that, partly upon Gregory's summons and partly by local and individual initiative, many of all grades of the clergy would attend from widespread regions of the church. Gregory himself on several occasions summoned *en bloc* the upper clergy of regions about which he was particularly concerned. Thus, in 1074, he summoned the archbishop of Aquileia and his suffragans, and the bishops and abbots of Lombardy; in 1075, the bishops and abbots at Brittany, and the archbishop of Mainz and his many suffragans; and in 1078, the archbishop of Ravenna and his suffragans together with a wide circle of bishops and abbots.[22] Gregory also summoned individual bishops whose presence at a Roman synod he deemed necessary, whether for the internal business of their own churches or for the wider affairs of their regions.[23] Many persons also came to Rome at the time of Gregory's synods in order to secure their own interests. They did so in response to the general right of medieval subjects, however humble and remote, to petition their rulers for grace or for justice.[24] One should envisage that, at most of Gregory's synods, there was a concourse of attenders that was sufficient to fill the Lateran basilica and to provide an impressive theatre for the exercise of papal authority; in Lent 1078, the bishops who were present numbered almost a hundred, apart from abbots, lesser clergy, and laity.[25]

Gregory was wont to set these assemblies against the background of his sombre view of the predicament of a church which was being shaken like a ship in a storm and which was in peril of shipwreck. By way of the deliberation of the Roman synods, it needed protection alike from the lay rulers of this world who sought only what was their own while treading the church, the bride of Christ, underfoot like a common slave-girl, and from a worldly clergy who sought nothing but their own worldly glory and advancement. In face of such derogations of duty, a Christian people deprived of proper guidance and care needed to have restored to it a lively faith and the practice of true religion. Accordingly, Gregory could declare his purpose in summoning

---

[20] *Reg.* 9.35*a*, p. 627/20–2.

[21] *Reg.* 1.43, to the suffragans of Milan, 25 Jan. 1074, p. 66/8–11.

[22] *Reg.* 1.42, to Archbishop Sigehard of Aquileia, 24 Jan. 1074, pp. 65–5, see esp. 65/21–9; 1.43, 2.1, to the bishops and abbots of Brittany, 28 Aug. 1074, pp. 124–5; 2.29, to Archbishop Siegfried of Mainz, 4 Dec. 1074, pp. 161–2; cf. 2.30, to King Henry IV of Germany, 7 Dec. 1074, pp. 164/27–165/7; 5.13, to Archbishop Guibert of Ravenna, his suffragans, and other bishops and abbots, 28 Jan. 1078, pp. 366–7.

[23] e.g. *Reg.* 2.42, to Archbishop Guibert of Ravenna, 4 Jan. 1075, p. 179; 4.9, to Archbishop Richer of Sens, 2 Nov. 1076, pp. 307–8.

[24] e.g. *Reg.* 1.54, to the canons of Saint-Hilaire at Poitiers, 16 Mar. 1074, pp. 81–2; 7.17, to the monks of Déols, 24 Mar. 1080, pp. 491–2.

[25] *Reg.* 5.14*a*, p. 368/34–41, cf. Deusdedit, *Coll. can.* 4.185, p. 491, 'episcoporum XCV'; Berthold gave the number as 'fere LXX'; *a.* 1078, p. 306/37–8.

bishops to his synod to be that, through their prudence and their spiritual fortitude and wisdom, the wicked might be restrained from their designs and that the Christian religion might be confirmed in the liberty and peace of its original foundation.[26] The records of Gregory's synods could describe their purpose as being 'for the renewal (*restauratio*) of holy church' (Lent 1078) and 'for the honour of God and the building up (*hedeficatio*) of holy church, and also for the salvation of both bodies and souls' (Lent 1079).[27]

Such was Gregory's approach to his Lent and November synods. Since they had the character of general synods, his personal authority over them was marked by the decisiveness that was expressed in *Dictatus papae* 16 and 17—that no synod might be called general without his precept, and that no legal chapter ('capitulum') could be deemed canonical without his authority.[28] Consistently with these claims, the chapters ('capitula') which were read out when the synods were solemnly terminated took the form of papal pronouncements which were expressed in the first person plural of majesty.[29] During the synods, the authority of the pope himself was apparent in judicial decisions such as those involving the deposition or restoration of bishops.[30] Still more, it was exhibited in such exceptional matters as the sentences of 1076 and 1080 upon Henry IV of Germany; thus, in 1080, Gregory's sentence had the form of a personal address to the apostles Peter and Paul in which Gregory's brothers in the synod would concur.[31] Such a procedure later elicited the bitter complaint of the schismatic cardinals that, in 1076, Gregory precipitately excommunicated Henry against the cardinals' will and advice and in derogation of proper canonical procedure, so that none of the cardinals subscribed to Henry's excommunication.[32]

The official phraseology that recurs in the records of Gregory's synods confirms that they were deemed to be held in order to facilitate the exercise of the pope's own authority:

The lord pope himself celebrated a synod . . . in which, in corroboration of apostolic rulings, he corrected many things that needed correction and confirmed many things that needed confirmation. Therefore, amongst other things, at the conclusion of the dismissal of the synod he appended these items and commanded that they should be written down as a permanent record for future generations. He spoke thus: [the *decreta* of the synod follow].[33]

---

[26] *Reg.* 1.42, pp. 64–5; 2.1, pp. 124–5; 2.42, p. 179.

[27] *Reg.* 6.5*b*, p. 400/29; 6.17*a*, p. 425/19–23.   [28] *Reg.* 2.55*a*, p. 205/6–9.

[29] For emphasis upon the pope's authority, see esp. *Reg.* 5.14*a*, record of the Lent synod 1078, pp. 368/36–373/11; 7.14*a*, record of the Lent synod 1080, pp. 480/6–482/18. The less emphatically papal formulation of most of the record of the Nov. synod 1078 should also be noticed: 6.5*b*, pp. 400–6.

[30] Cf. Leo IX, *Epp.* 83–4, *PL* 143.728CD, 730AB.

[31] *Reg.* 7.14*a*, pp. 483–7, esp. p. 483/4–10: 'Quia veritatis estis discipuli et amatores, adiuvate, ut veritatem vobis dicam omni remota falsitate, . . . ut fratres mei melius michi adquiescant et sciant et intellegant, quia ex vestra fiducia post Deum et matrem eius semper virginem Mariam pravis et iniquis resisto, vestris autem fidelibus auxilium presto.'

[32] Beno, 1.3, p. 370.

[33] *Reg.* 5.14*a*, record of the Lent synod 1078, pp. 368/36–369/3; 7.14*a*, record of the Lent synod 1080, p. 480/6–13.

According to Gregory himself, synods were convened by the pope to assist him in his apostolic office; whatever they achieved was the work of the Holy Spirit who worked by the agency of the pope:

Consider [he wrote in 1078 to Duke Welf IV of Bavaria] what the Holy Spirit deigned to decree through us, unworthy though we are, in the holy synod which was held at Rome in the Lent of this year, and you will recognize how august are the authority and power of St Peter and how much they can avail.[34]

Yet there is a further dimension to Gregory's synods. Decisions taken at them did not arise from the will and authority of the pope alone. In another connection, Gregory professed his belief in the especial value of corporate decisions, for he firmly recalled Christ's words that where two or three are gathered together in his name, they are enlightened by his presence (cf. Matt. 18: 20).[35] Furthermore, like lay rulers of his age his authority was the greater when it was supported by the counsel and consent of his associates. Accordingly, he could declare that his decrees at the Lent synod of 1074 were issued 'with the counsel of our brothers [the bishops] and with the consent of the whole assembly'.[36]

It is evident that the references to synodal counsel and consent were more than formalities; in many items of business, there was open discussion and active participation by the synod in decisions that were reached. A striking example is the debate in Lent 1079 about the eucharistic teaching of Berengar of Tours. This was a matter about which Gregory himself had for decades been hesitant and uncertain. At the synod, arguments on both sides were put fully and forcibly, and Berengar made his eventual submission before the whole assembly ('coram concilio frequenti').[37] According to the Reichenau annalist Berthold in his account of the Lent synod of 1078, the problems of the German kingdom were likewise a matter for open and careful debate.[38] Gregory's letters yield further examples of general discussions and of participation by the synod in the decisions that were made. Thus, in 1075, the intractable dispute between the sees of Prague and Olmütz was ventilated at length with the two bishops presenting their case; Gregory's eventual ruling was made 'cum consilio patrum nostrorum'. At the same synod, the deposition of Bishop Dionysius of Piacenza was effected 'by the immutable sentence of the holy synod and the irrevocable counsel of all the brothers who were seated there'. In 1080, there was a prolonged synodal consideration of the dispute between the archbishop of Tours and the bishop of Dol about the latter's claim to receive a *pallium*; and a provisional adjudication was made between the bishop of Limoges and the monks of Déols about the possession of two monasteries which Gregory described as having been reached 'according to the consent and counsel of our brothers'.[39] After his synods, Gregory's

34 *Reg.* 2.1, p. 124/15–23, 6.14, to Duke Welf IV of Bavaria, 30 Dec. 1078, p. 418/22–7.
35 *Reg.* 4.24, to the faithful in Germany, 31 May 1077, pp. 337/34–338/4.
36 *Reg.* 2.62, to Archbishop Sigehard of Aquileia, 23 Mar. 1075, p. 217/14–18.
37 *Reg.* 6.17a, pp. 425–6; see above, 8.1.1.   38 *a.* 1078, p. 307/35–49.
39 *Reg.* 2.53, sentence of the Lent synod 1075, 2 Mar. 1075, pp. 197–8; 2.54, to the church of Piacenza, 3 Mar. 1075, pp. 198–9; 7.15, to the bishops of Brittany and the clergy and people of the province of Tours, 8 Mar. 1080, pp. 488–9, 7.17, pp. 491–2.

hand was strengthened when implementing their *decreta* because he could represent them as decisions made with collective support.[40] Gregory's synods were by no means only theatres for the demonstration of his personal authority; they also served to complement and to reinforce it.

The collective aspect of the synods was reinforced by their procedure. They normally occupied some three to five days, during the inside of the week. They had the character of religious, as well as of administrative and judicial, occasions. Given Gregory's temperament, the level of emotion could run high, as during his excommunications of Henry IV of Germany, or at his November synod of 1083. In 1083, according to the brief official record,

On the third day, the lord pope, with the tongue not of a man but of an angel, publicly gave an exposition of the elements of the faith and the demands of the Christian religion, and also of the strength and constancy of spirit that were called for in the current straits. He moved almost the whole assembly to sighs and tears. Then the council, gladdened by the apostolic blessing, departed in peace.[41]

Since the Lent synod of 1078 of which the Swabian annalist Berthold gave a long and evidently informed account,[42] the synodal agenda was dominated by the problems of Germany—the royal succession and the establishment of peace and concord within the kingdom. Berthold brings out Gregory's caution and his purpose of proceeding with due counsel. But there was always an extensive agenda concerned with matters of church order and discipline; compared with the papal synods of the next century, a great deal of judicial business, especially with regard to the disciplining of errant bishops, was also transacted. Such agenda seem to have been set out in such lists of *capitula* as appear in the record of the November synod of 1078.[43] There was often open discussion. Where Gregory himself had strong views, he might express them in such an address from the papal throne as is preserved in his allocution of Lent 1080 in favour of the abbey of Cluny, the record of which also preserves the answering cries of 'Placeat, laudamus' from the assembled synod.[44] At the same synod, the deliberations about penance appear to have included a papal homily about true repentance and the need for Christians to take proper spiritual advice, traces of which survive in the synodal record.[45] At the end of the synod when the pope pronounced its final dismissal, the decisions that had been agreed were solemnly read out with a view to their being recorded in writing as the *decreta* of the synod.

---

[40] *Reg.* 1.54, pp. 81–2; 2.53, pp. 197–8; 2.62, p. 217; 2.67, to Archbishop Anno of Cologne, 29 Mar. 1075, pp. 223–5; 6.19, to the *ministeriales* of the church of Bamberg, 17 Feb. 1079, pp. 430–1.

[41] *Reg.* 9.35*a*, p. 628/16–21.

[42] *a*.1078, pp. 306/37–309/34. Berthold's account is also important for showing that Gregory's *suffraganei*, by whom seem to be meant the Roman suburbicarian bishops, had a special place during synods as his advisers and associates.

[43] *Reg.* 6.5*b*, pp. 401/2.   [44] *Epp. vag.* no. 39, pp. 96–9.

[45] *Reg.* 7.14*a*(5), pp. 481–2. The homiletic element is implied by the verbs 'ammonemus' and 'vos hortamus et monemus'; it is significant that some of the more directly homiletic phrases were not included in the handbook summary of the Volterra *Liber capitularis: De sancti Hugonis actis liturgicis*, cap. 58, p. 79.

Such synodal procedure enabled a pope of Gregory's eloquence, force, and conviction to set the impress of his religion and demands upon the wide range of persons who attended, whether regularly or occasionally. He was at pains to disseminate the decrees of his synods. The evidence of the *Liber capitularis* of Volterra suggests that, amongst Italian sees directly subject to Rome, due note was taken of Gregory's decrees, which were recorded along with the rulings of other popes.[46] Further afield, letters in and outside Gregory's Register show that, immediately after his synods, he was at pains to communicate their business to those whom he particularly wished to be informed. Examples are his letters to Germany about his rulings in 1075 and 1079 against simony and clerical fornication, and his letters to French destinations in 1080 about particular decisions regarding that region.[47] Before and after Gregory's synods, the pace of registration quickened. But secretarial resources at Rome were still limited and ill-organized. Gregory therefore looked to his legates and to metropolitans and other bishops to propagate and apply his rulings at their synods and by whatever other means they could.[48] He was well aware that publicity depended all too much upon the chance of the movements of his own legates and messengers, and also upon the goodwill and the good offices of those who had happened to be present at Roman synods. That being so, there was all too large a risk of Gregory's decisions not getting through to the localities of Christendom, and also of a deaf ear being turned to them by those who did not wish to hear.[49]

9.3 Papal Legates

The problems of effective communication and of securing the implementation of papal decisions and decrees caused Gregory to depend heavily upon papal legates whose activities in one form or another were a constant feature of his pontificate. The employment of legates had become common under the reform popes since Leo IX; before he became pope, Gregory himself had extensive experience of legatine service in Italy, France, and Germany. It has already been noticed that, in connection with his employment of legates in France and Spain, he himself regarded their dispatch as a custom of the Roman church from its earliest days; he understood their functions not only in administrative and judicial terms but also as reflecting the popes' duty to proclaim salvation, to promote virtue, and to instruct the world in sound doctrine.[50]

---

[46] For material relating to Gregory VII, see caps. 58, 64, 114, 134, 136, 138, 262, pp. 79, 84, 129–30, 149, 51–3, 221. The phrase 'Gregorius papa septimus in generali sinodo residens dixit' on pp. 129, 149, and 153 should be noticed, as well as the prominence of Gregory's synodal rulings on liturgical matters.

[47] *Epp. vag.* nos. 6–11, 32, pp. 14–27, 84–7; cf. *Reg.* 2.66, to Bishop Burchard II of Halberstadt, 29 Mar. 1075, p. 221/13–19; 7.15, to the bishops of Brittany and the clergy and people of Tours, 8 Mar. 1080, pp. 488–9; 7.16, to Bishop Hubert of Thérouanne, 26 Mar. 1080, pp. 489–91; 7.17, to the monks of Déols, 24 Mar. 1080, pp. 491–2.

[48] e.g. *Reg.* 2.28, to Archbishop Liemar of Bremen, 12 Dec. 1074, p. 161/6–11; 2.67, to Archbishop Anno of Cologne, 29 Mar. 1075, pp. 223–5; 4.20 to Bishop Josfred of Paris, 25 Mar. 1077, pp. 328/35–329/15; 4.22, to Bishop Hugh of Die, 12 May 1077, pp. 331–4.

[49] e.g. *Reg.* 4.22, pp. 330/27–331/29; 6.4, to Bishop Henry I of Liège, 9 Oct. 1078, pp. 396–7.

[50] See above, 5.3.2. Gregory's fullest statement of his conception of the function of legates was made,

It was his opinion that the apostolic see had latterly been remiss by failing duly to send its envoys to the more distant regions of Christendom; by extending the employment of legates, he was introducing no novelty but was implementing what should always have been a papal concern.[51] Legates were to be regarded as a regular and necessary part of the church's functioning. It should also be remembered that, in respect to the pope's authority over bishops everywhere, there was an active memory in the late eleventh-century Lateran of Constantine's law of the fourth day according to the *Actus Silvestri*, that in the Roman world, the bishops had the pope as their head and prince just as all the secular judges had the emperor as theirs; accordingly, the cardinal-priests of the Roman church, in particular, had the power to pass judgement on the bishops of the whole Roman empire in all councils and synods to which they were summoned or at which they were present.[52]

In Gregory's letters, however, the word *legatus* is used to describe a wide spectrum of agents from great and long-standing figures like Hugh, bishop of Die and archbishop of Lyons, to humble messengers who, it should be remembered, not only carried letters but were also entrusted with oral communications that might be no less important than the letters themselves. *Legati* in the sense of occasional messengers were not distinguishable in function from the *legati* of prominent men who might come to Gregory. In the circumstances of the late eleventh century, it would be premature to attempt a rigid classification of different kinds of papal legate; Gregory was more concerned with persons performing services in differing contingencies than with office and rank. Nevertheless, he himself once drew a distinction between 'those of any nationality upon whom the Roman pontiff may impose some particular embassy' ('quibus Romanus pontifex aliquam legationem iniungat') and those whom, 'what is more weighty, he may empower to act in his place' ('quod maius est, vicem suam indulgeat') or, as he later expressed it with reference to Hugh of Die, those to whom, in some region of the church, the pope especially committed the representation of his pastoral care in all matters ('cum nos in partibus illis Diensi episcopo precipue sollicitudinis nostrae vicem de omnibus commiserimus'). Gregory went on to assign to Hugh the function that he was himself said to discharge universally in his Roman synods: in an appropriate matter of business, Hugh was 'to correct what may need correction and to confirm what may need confirmation'.[53]

Hugh of Die and Lyons is the archetypal example of the select group of men who acted *vice* the pope, or as his *vicarius* or *legatus*, on a long-term basis and in an extensive and more or less defined region. The role that he came to perform in France especially as from 1077 was broadly performed as from that year in southern France

apropos Amatus of Oloron, in *Epp. vag.* no. 21, (*c*.28 June 1077), pp. 56–7; cf. *Reg.* 5.2, to the clergy and people of Corsica, 1 Sept. 1077, p. 349/22–32.

[51] *Reg.* 1.17, to Duke Wratislav II of Bohemia, 8 July 1073, p. 27/15–30.

[52] *Desc. eccles. Lateran.* pp. 544, 546; for the law of the fourth day, see Linder, 'Constantine's "Ten Laws"', p. 494.

[53] *Reg.* 4.26, to Patriarch Dominicus of Grado, 9 June 1077, p. 341/10–19; 6.2, to Archbishop Manasses I of Rheims, 22 Aug. 1078, p. 392/10–13; 7.1, to the Roman subdeacon Hubert, 23 Sept. 1079, p. 460/1–6.

and northern Spain by Bishop Amatus of Oloron, and from *c.* 1081 in Lombardy by Bishop Anselm II of Lucca and in southern Germany by Bishop Altmann of Passau. Their services to Gregory have already been discussed in connection with the regions in which they were active.[54] It is sufficient now to notice that none was, or ever became, a clerk of the Roman church itself; none, for example, was or became a cardinal, whether local or 'external'. All were natives of the regions in which they served. At the time when their characteristic activities began, all were bishops, and in Hugh's case upon appointment a youthful bishop, of sees that were of minor, or at least of not more than medium, size and importance. Before 1073, and even before 1077, their position and role were unexampled in the western church. They emerged gradually in response partly to the mounting pressure of business upon Gregory and the still rudimentary resources of the Roman church, but much more to changing circumstances in Gregory's dealings with the two major western kingdoms of France and Germany. As their role as papal vicar developed, they represent Gregory's most distinctive individual contribution to the government of the church. Nevertheless, in the longer development of the institutions of papal government, their role was transient; in the twelfth century, the expansion of the papal administration made it largely otiose.

Provided that the line is not sharply drawn, Gregory's distinction between those legates, notably the four who have just been discussed, whom the pope empowered to act in his place and those upon whom he imposed some particular embassy is a useful one. In the second of these categories, Gregory employed a wide variety of persons, whom he selected according to his estimate of their loyalty and capability and according to the demands of each embassy. In circumstances of weight or urgency, he tended to use cardinal-bishops. Both the cardinal-bishops of Ostia, the senior men of that rank, served as legates—Gerald was already in France at the beginning of Gregory's pontificate, and in 1074 Gregory sent him to Germany with Cardinal-bishop Hubert of Palestrina; his successor Odo was sent alone to Germany in 1084–5. Peter of Albano was in Germany in 1079, he was then sent to resolve the crisis of 1079–80 between Cluny and its neighbouring bishops, and he was back in France in 1084–5. The beginning of Gregory's pontificate saw the cardinal-priest Hugh Candidus being again dispatched in Spain, although in general Gregory made little use of the Roman priests in a legatine capacity, perhaps because of their liturgical duties at Rome. He more often employed Roman clerks of the lesser ranks of deacon and subdeacon in which he had himself done legatine service. Such clerks had the recommendations that they could be expected to know Gregory's mind and that they could readily be held accountable. They were of St Peter's household and family.[55] He made considerable use of abbots, sometimes of Roman monasteries but especially those whose monastic empires gave them widespread prestige and

54 For Hugh, see esp. above, 5.3.2.1; for Amatus, 5.3.2.2; for Anselm, 4.5; and for Altmann, 3.6.2.

55 *Reg.* 4.26, p. 341/22–3. So, too, Gregory's legates from Salerno in 1084 were 'most faithful servants of St Peter and, each of them in his order, . . . amongst the leading men of his household': *Epp. vag.* no. 54, pp. 130–1.

connections. Thus, Abbot Hugh of Cluny was a trusted legate, as were Abbots Bernard and Richard of Saint-Victor at Marseilles. Bishops, too, were occasionally involved, as when, in 1079, Bishop Ulrich of Padua went to Germany in company with Cardinal Peter of Albano. Particular tasks of a legatine nature were performed by Bishop Landulf of Pisa, of whom in 1077 Gregory wrote as a papal vicar in Corsica, and by Bishop Leodegar of Gap who in 1079 was given a legatine role in relation to settling the archiepiscopal succession at Arles.[56] Gregory very seldom used lesser clergy of churches other than the Roman.[57] His only lay legate was Gisulf, formerly prince of Salerno, whom he dispatched to France in 1084 with Cardinal Peter of Albano; since Robert Guiscard expelled him from his principality he had found refuge at Rome in Gregory's service. Gregory's legates did not usually act alone. Even a papal vicar like Hugh of Die often acted in concert with his counterpart Amatus of Oloron; at other times, Gregory might balance his zeal by associating with him Abbot Hugh of Cluny as a representative of apostolic mercy and discretion.

Although a legate might be described as being 'of the Roman church' or 'of the apostolic see', he was more commonly said to be 'legatus noster'—the envoy of the pope himself.[58] He might come on behalf of St Peter, or of St Peter and the pope,[59] but he was always a bearer of papal authority. In *Dictatus papae* 4, Gregory ruled that the pope's legate, even if of inferior rank in holy orders, took precedence in a council over all bishops, and that he could pass sentence of deposition against bishops.[60] It was his frequent claim that, when a legate spoke, it was as though the pope himself were speaking. A legate came, as it were, from the pope's own bosom, as one in whom the pope's pastoral care and divinely entrusted authority were represented and exercised ('utpote per quem nostra apud vos sollicitudo et a domino Deo nobis concessae potestatis auctoritas vicaria dispensatione representatur et geritur').[61]

Such being the relationship between the pope and his legates, problems of control and accountability were inevitably pressing. At the beginning of his pontificate, Gregory wrote to the legates Gerald of Ostia and the Roman subdeacon Rainbald who were already in France that they should urgently return to Rome so that Gregory might be informed about what they had done and might review their instructions.[62] In 1079, he reminded Cardinal Peter of Albano and Bishop Ulrich of Padua of the evidently very precise instructions that he had given them and from which some informants had sought to persuade Gregory that they had deviated.[63]

---

[56] *Reg.* 5.2, to the people of Corsica, 1 Sept. 1077, pp. 349–50; 6.21, to the clergy and people of Arles, 1 Mar. 1079, pp. 432–4.

[57] But see the role of Wighard, a clerk of Besançon: *Epp. vag.* no. 23, to Archbishop Ralph of Tours, (summer 1078), pp. 60–1.

[58] For Gregory's usage, see Caspar's Index: *Reg.* pp. 694–5.

[59] *Reg.* 2.32, to Archbishop Manasses I of Rheims, 8 Dec. 1074, p. 169/1–6; 2.74, to Prince Demetrius of Russia, 17 Apr. 1075, p. 237/8–9.

[60] *Reg.* 2.55a, p. 203/1–3, cf. clause 2, p. 202/9–10, and *Desc. eccles. Lateran.* p. 546.

[61] *Reg.* 4.26, p. 341/19–27, 6.21, p. 434/2–5; cf. 1.7, to French princes minded to go to Spain, 30 Apr. 1073, p. 12/19–23; 2.40, accreditation of his legates to the Pentapolis, 2 Jan. 1075, p. 177.

[62] *Reg.* 1.6, 30 Apr. 1073, p. 10/22–7; 1.16, 1 July 1073, pp. 25–6.

[63] *Epp. vag.* no. 31, pp. 80–3.

But the range of matters with which legates might be expected to have to deal could not always be foreseen; Gregory was sometimes compelled to give his occasional legates, let alone his long-term papal vicars, a wide liberty to act on his behalf according to the guidelines of canon law and church discipline.[64] Some safeguards could be made against the exceeding of instructions by legates. Thus, legates should return regularly to Gregory at Rome, and should do so especially after they had held a council, so that Gregory might be informed of and able to review their decisions as taken in his name; legates who delayed in so returning were subject to severe censure.[65] Even the sentences of so experienced a legate as Bishop Hugh of Die were subject to scrutiny and confirmation by Gregory's Roman synods.[66]

But, despite all the controls that Gregory sought to maintain, the problem of legates who exceeded their instructions was always a pressing one. It was not least acute and intractable in the cases of Gregory's vicars in France, Hugh of Die/Lyons and Amatus of Oloron, whose persistent fault as legates was excessive zeal and rigour in promoting reform; Gregory had several times to temper the severity of Hugh, in particular, by reversing his sentences.[67] Again, legates could exceed Gregory's intentions in matters of high politics, as when, in 1077 at Forchheim, the Roman cardinal-deacon Bernard and Abbot Bernard of Saint-Victor at Marseilles gave a concurrence to the election of Rudolf of Rheinfelden as anti-king which was not in line with Gregory's wishes; at his Lent synod of 1080, he declared Rudolf's election to have taken place without his counsel.[68] If the dispatch of legates was an essential part of Gregory's administration of the church and exercise of his pastoral duty, it also gave rise to considerable problems.

9.4 Primates and Metropolitans

Gregory's extensive and intensive use of legates to give effect to his pastoral and judicial authority in the localities of the church raised profound questions of doctrine and of practice about his attitude to the episcopal hierarchy which was the solid framework of the government of the church. They were especially acute in relation to the primates and metropolitans who, often in a succession that went back for many centuries, stood at the head of the bishops of regions which often coincided with temporal kingdoms and principalities. Gregory was confronted with the problem of securing their obedience and active participation in what he believed to be a shared pastoral office, and at the same time of respecting and supporting their own rightful

---

[64] e.g. his legates to Venice: *Reg.* 4.16, to Patriarch Dominicus of Grado and the bishops of his region, 9 June 1077, p. 341/10–19.

[65] Gerald of Ostia: *Reg.* 1.16, pp. 25–6; the Roman subdeacon Hubert, 7.1, 23 Sept. 1079, pp. 458/29–459/7.

[66] *Reg.* 7.20, to Archbishop Manasses I of Rheims, 17 Apr. 1080, p. 496/4–7; 8.17, to the clergy and people of Rheims, 27 Dec. 1080, p. 538/24–31.

[67] See above, 5.3.2.1; also Gregory's sharp rebuke to Abbot Richard of Marseilles, *Epp. vag.* no. 50, (?1082), pp. 120–1.

[68] See above, 3.4.1; for the Lent synod of 1080, *Reg.* 7.14a, p. 484/21–4.

headship of their provinces. Due weight must be given to both aspects of Gregory's problem.[69]

Gregory's key requirement of a metropolitan was that, as he expressed it to Archbishop Siegfried of Mainz in 1075, that he should be the pope's agent in respects in which the pope called for his collaboration, so that the Roman church might rejoice in him as a most dear brother and zealous fellow-worker.[70] The participation of a metropolitan in the pastoral office that the pope exercised in its fullness was symbolized by the ancient liturgical ornament, the *pallium*, a narrow scarf of lamb's wool which was placed on the altar of St Peter's basilica before being conferred upon a new pope and upon a metropolitan, as well as upon a small number of bishops. The pastoral character of the obligation that it was deemed to impose is well expressed in the ancient formulas of the *Liber diurnus* of the Roman church which enlarged upon its use.[71] Since Gregory made much of the *pallium* as a bond between pope and archbishops, it is well duly to notice his understanding of it.

It was an established rule upon which he strongly insisted that those seeking the *pallium* should receive it in person at Rome.[72] He made exceptions when travel there was inexpedient or impossible; thus in 1079 in view of warfare in the lands of Henry IV of Germany, he sent it to Archbishops Gebuin of Lyons and Hartwig of Magdeburg.[73] But these were rare exceptions. To Archbishop William of Rouen, Gregory cited a canonical rule that those who postponed coming to Rome for more than three consecutive months after their consecration would be subject to censure; he accordingly inhibited the archbishop from performing ordinations of bishops and priests and from consecrating churches until he had duly sought at Rome the *pallium* which Gregory described as the complement of his office ('honoris tui supplementum').[74] Besides receiving the *pallium*, archbishops were expected to take an oath of fidelity and canonical obedience to the Roman church.[75]

The *pallium* was normally conferred upon conditions governing its liturgical use that were traditional for each see and enshrined in earlier papal privileges.[76] But Gregory was insistent that its conferment was not a right; it depended upon the pope's being satisfied in every case that the metropolitan had come to his see by due canonical process and that his character was such as beseemed his office.[77] It was thus a means by which the pope might control the succession of metropolitans. He was no less insistent that it not only conferred an entitlement to liturgical rights but that it

---

[69] In this section, I owe a particular debt to Robinson, "'*Periculosus homo*'".

[70] *Epp. vag.* no. 6, (Feb. 1075), pp. 14–17.

[71] cap. 45, cf. caps. 46–7, ed. Foerster, pp. 101–6.

[72] *Epist. pont. Rom. ined.*, ed. Loewenfeld, nos. 76, 81, pp. 41, 43.

[73] Gebuin: *RHGF* 14.668, no. 2, see above, 5.3.3.2; Hartwig: *Gest. archiep. Magd.* cap. 22, pp. 403–4.

[74] *Reg.* 1.24, to Bishop Bruno of Verona, 24 Sept. 1073, p. 41/9–18; 9.1, to Archbishop William of Rouen, (1081), p. 569/9–16.

[75] *Reg.* 2.28, to Archbishop Liemar of Bremen, 12 Dec. 1074, p. 160/15–21; 6.17a, record of the Lent synod 1079, pp. 428–9 (oath of Archbishop Henry of Aquileia).

[76] e.g. *QF* no. 212, privilege for Archbishop Alcherius of Palermo, 16 Apr. 1083, pp. 253–4.

[77] *Reg.* 4.5, to the bishops of Brittany, 27 Sept. 1076, p. 302/11–17.

also committed its recipient to an outstanding quality of moral and spiritual life. Gregory gave expression to this in 1083 to Archbishop Alcherius of Palermo, when, in characteristic terms, he insisted upon the need for inner conversion of life, for the exercise of all the virtues but especially of charity, and for the bearer of the *pallium* duly to maintain justice both by his fervent zeal for righteousness and by his vigilance never to exceed the bounds of moderation.[78]

Since the *pallium* was a mark of papal favour to an approved petitioner and not a matter of right, the pope could and must withhold it from the wicked and disobedient; but he could also reward virtuous archbishops *ad hominem* by adding to the liturgical privileges that they enjoyed.[79] Since Gregory deemed the *pallium* to symbolize the pastoral and moral share that a metropolitan had in the universal office of the pope, Gregory expected metropolitans to pay regular *ad limina* visits to Rome. He could remind a metropolitan of his duty with tact and restraint; but he particularly censured Archbishop Lanfranc of Canterbury for his neglect of this duty, and he complained bitterly against King William I of England for his unwillingness to allow the archbishops of England and Normandy duly to travel to Rome.[80]

In effect, by the urgency of his demand, Gregory was making active and positive a relationship, symbolized by the *pallium*, between the pope and metropolitan which hitherto had been latent and formal. Even if they were of a reforming frame of mind, metropolitans everywhere were, in 1073, habituated to the older ways of a papacy that left them pretty much to themselves and confined the exercise of papal authority largely to responses to the occasional initiatives of metropolitans. Gregory's insistence that they should regularly and obediently regard themselves as the pope's zealous fellow-workers impinged on them as an innovation and as the exercise of invasive, if not of aggressive, power so far as their own rights were concerned.

In face of Gregory's determination to activate the obedient collaboration in the light of his own interpretation of the pastoral office that he expected of metropolitans, some, like Lanfranc of Canterbury, were non-co-operative and pursued their own task as they envisaged it. But, especially in the earlier stages of Gregory's pontificate, many others were openly resentful and hostile. Such metropolitans have already been studied; it is sufficient now to refer back to some conspicious examples. Thus, Gregory was concerned to contradict the claim of the Ambrosian church at Milan to virtual independence of Roman authority, and to secure the succession of an archbishop who would be obedient to Rome, especially in the struggle against simony and clerical fornication. In Germany, Gregory challenged the contention of Archbishop Siegfried of Mainz with regard to the sees of Prague and Olmütz, that all major ecclesiastical business should first be treated locally, and referred to Rome only in

---

[78] *QF* no. 212, p. 254.

[79] *Reg.* 6.38, to Archbishop Henry of Aquileia, 16 June 1079, pp. 454–5; the address 'karissimo in Christo fratri et coepiscopo Aquilegiensi' should be noted.

[80] *Reg.* 2.32, to Archbishop Manasses I of Rheims, 8 Dec. 1074, p. 168/17–21; 6.30, to Archbishop Lanfranc, 25 Mar. 1079, pp. 443–4; 9.20, to the same, (May–June 1082), pp. 600–1, 7.1, to the Roman subdeacon Hubert, 23 Sept. 1079, p. 459/8–25.

exceptional circumstances and at the discretion of the metropolitan. In 1074 and 1075, Gregory's campaign against simony and clerical fornication, and the consequent dispatch of Cardinal-bishops Gerald of Ostia and Hubert of Palestrina, represented a challenge to the German metropolitans, even if themselves of a reforming disposition, to which Archbishops Siegfried of Mainz, Liemar of Bremen, and Udo of Trier all reacted in terms of resentment and complaint. In Italy and France, Gregory's dealings respectively with Archbishops Guibert of Ravenna and Manasses I of Rheims further illustrate the problems which were created when Gregory's claims impinged upon metropolitans who were rooted in an older order of things.[81]

These claims may be summarized under four headings. First, Gregory interpreted the traditional theme of pastoral collaboration of pope and metropolitans in terms of a duty of active obedience which committed metropolitans to total concurrence with papal commands and which was enforced by rigorous sanctions if it were not immediately forthcoming. Second, the duty of obedience to the pope as supreme was to take precedence over the solidarity and fraternity of the episcopal order as enshrined in the collaboration and consultation of a metropolitan with his episcopal suffragans. Third, a metropolitan should deem himself personally the *fidelis* of the Roman church, bound to it by oath as well as by the demands of his office; disobedience thus carried with it the stigma of *infidelitas* of a kind that was comparable with the failure of duty to a secular lord.[82] Fourth, Gregory was so urgently concerned to implement his demands of reform, especially in respect of simony and clerical fornication, that if metropolitans did not promptly take the steps that he called for, he claimed the duty of himself invoking lay sanctions against the clergy which, although familiar to the south of the Alps, were especially resented by German metropolitans as a novelty in their lands.

The active and obedient collaboration that Gregory expected in practice from metropolitans is a recurrent theme of his letters. In the first two years of his pontificate, in particular, every one of the German metropolitans was called upon to show such collaboration; not one of them was at ease with Gregory's call. The principal matter involved was the moral reform of the church, especially by eliminating simony and clerical fornication. The first to be challenged was Gebhard of Salzburg, whom, in November 1073, Gregory rebuked for his disobedience in not implementing Pope Alexander II's synodal prohibition in 1063 of clerical fornication; Gregory admonished him by papal authority with all rigour to constrain his errant clerks. During 1074 and in early 1075, the other metropolitans were involved. Besides Siegfried of Mainz, Anno of Cologne received a reminder of the charity which bound the sees of Rome and Cologne and was urged himself to hold a synod that would enforce Roman rulings. Gregory sharply reminded Werner of Magdeburg of his duty of zeal and obedience in implementing his directions. Liemar of Bremen was

---

[81] For the principal discussions, see above, 4.3 (Milan), 3.2.5 (Prague–Olmütz and the German episcopate, 1074–5), 4.6 (Ravenna), 5.3.3.1 (Rheims).

[82] See esp. *Reg.* 2.28, pp. 160/15–161/6.

suspended for his resistance to the reforming endeavours of Gregory's legates in Germany and Udo of Trier was urged to intervene decisively in the dispute between Bishop Pibo of Toul and his canons who had accused him of simony and concubinage.[83] In Italy, Gregory similarly, if in somewhat milder terms, called upon Archbishop Sigehard of Aquileia to implement his reforms.[84] During the same years, Gregory also sought to command the active support of French metropolitans. Manasses I of Rheims was expected to be Gregory's obedient agent in his proceedings against King Philip I.[85] Manasses and other French archbishops were to implement Gregory's directives against bishops whom he sought to discipline.[86]

Gregory's demands upon metropolitans and his subordination of their authority to that of the apostolic see should not, however, obscure the extent to which he recognized both in theory and in practice the rights and the necessity of their office, and their just place in the structure of the church. When confirming the primacy of Lyons, he expressed his wish to follow the tradition of his predecessors by defending the rights and dignities which had been granted to all the churches.[87] With regard to Poland, he declared that it was his own primary concern for its bishops to be made duly subject to the *magisterium* of a metropolitan. In North Africa, he was anxious for Archbishop Cyriacus of Carthage to have sufficient bishops under him for him to be able himself to perform ordinations. In South Italy, he insisted that the bishop of Conza should be canonically subject to Archbishop Alfanus of Salerno; neighbouring bishops, abbots, clergy, and people must likewise obey Alfanus, showing him due reverence as their special father and archbishop, if they desired the goodwill of St Peter and of the pope.[88] In anticipation of the choice of an archbishop in the Spanish church, Gregory told King Alphonso VI of León–Castile that a man should be chosen who was well educated, characterized by good personal qualities rather than noble birth, and whose religion and teaching would bring honour and salvation to the land.[89] In an extreme case, Gregory told the clergy and people of Carthage, whose archbishop, Cyriacus, was suffering Saracen persecution, that he was not only their archbishop and master, but also in truth their anointed one ('vero vestri christum').[90]

For all the power that Gregory vested in his legates, he showed concern that, when it was possible to do so, they should rather reinforce than cut across the authority of metropolitans. Three letters of 1074 illustrate this point. In one, Gregory noted that

---

[83] Gebhard of Salzburg: *Reg.* 1.30, 15 Nov. 1073, pp. 50–1. Siegfried of Mainz: *Epp. vag.* no. 6, (Feb. 1075), pp. 14–17; *Reg.* 2.29, 4 Dec. 1074, pp. 161–2. Anno of Cologne: 1.79, 18 Apr. 1074, pp. 112–113. Werner of Magdeburg: *Epp. vag.* no. 7, (Feb. 1075), pp. 16–17; *Reg.* 2.68, 29 Mar. 1075, pp. 225–6. Liemar of Bremen: 2.28, 12 Dec. 1074, pp. 160–1. Udo of Trier: 2.10, 16 Oct. 1074, pp. 140–2.

[84] *Reg.* 2.62, 23 Mar. 1075, p. 217.   [85] *Reg.* 2.32, 8 Dec. 1074, pp. 168–9.

[86] e.g. *Reg.* 2.56, to Archbishop Manasses I of Rheims, 4 Mar. 1075, pp. 209–10; 2.58, to the same, 5 Mar. 1075, pp. 211–12; 1.36, to Archbishop Humbert of Lyons, 4 Dec. 1073, pp. 57–8; 2.4, to Archbishop Gozelin of Bordeaux, 10 Sept. 1074, pp. 128–9.

[87] *Reg.* 6.34, 19/20 Apr. 1080, pp. 447/25–448/4; cf. 1.24, to Bishop Bruno of Verona, 24 Sept. 1073, p. 41/16–18.

[88] *Reg.* 2.73, to Duke Wratislav II of Poland, 20 Apr. 1075, p. 234/15–25, 3.19, to Archbishop Cyriacus of Carthage, June 1076, p. 285; *QF* no. 27, pp. 12–13.

[89] *Reg.* 9.2, (1081), p. 571/5–23.   [90] *Reg.* 1.22, 15 Sept. 1073, p. 38/16–21.

his legate Gerald of Ostia had urged the suffragans of Archbishop William of Auch to pay their metropolitan due respect. William complained to Gregory that they still did not do so; Gregory therefore wrote to them enjoining them to pay him proper respect and obedience. A similar scenario of Gregory seeking to uphold the joint authority of a legate and a metropolitan, in this case Amatus of Oloron and Gozelin of Bordeaux, arose in respect of their dealings with the delinquent Bishop Isembert II of Poitiers. In Germany, Gregory commissioned Archbishop Anno of Cologne to take over and to settle canonically the conflict over tithes between Bishop Benno of Osnabrück and the abbey of Corvey which had been left unsettled by the legates Hubert of Palestrina and Gerald of Ostia.[91]

In the general run of business, Gregory showed himself prepared firmly to uphold the position of metropolitans, especially in relation to their suffragans. Even when a bishop's subjects laid a complaint against him at Rome, as did the monks of Saint-Hilaire at Poitiers in 1074, Gregory ruled that their complaint should first come before the metropolitan, Archbishop Gozelin of Bordeaux, at his provincial council; only should Gozelin fail to resolve the case must the matter come to Rome.[92] In return for his respect for their rights, Gregory expected metropolitans so to act that appropriate business was referred to them.[93] Thus, his letters illustrate his purpose of working with metropolitans in respect of their suffragans and, in the interests of efficiency, of having matters so far as possible settled by them, subject to their duly reporting their decisions to him. Such, for example was the pattern of events in 1074, after Bishop Thierry of Verdun brought to Gregory complaints against the monks of Saint-Michel at Verdun, whom he had placed under interdict. Thierry had ignored earlier papal directives; Gregory referred the matter for resolution to the metropolitan, Archbishop Udo of Trier, acting with two of his suffragans, so that the matter might find a solution either by episcopal or by papal authority as might prove necessary. 'For', Gregory commented, 'we were not set in authority to deal arbitrarily rather than justly with those committed to our oversight.'[94] In a similar way, he referred a complaint made at Rome by Abbot Hubert of Pothières, an abbey under immediate papal jurisdiction, against the church of Langres to Archbishop Humbert of Lyons and his suffragans for investigation, for the practical reason that it was hard for Gregory at Rome to understand the abbot's detailed complaints about local matters.[95] Gregory's concern was to balance papal and metropolitan authority in such a way as to find just and effectual solutions to difficult problems. Metropolitans were to act, as Gregory said to Archbishop Humbert, 'nostra vice et apostolica auctoritate'; yet justice and convenience required him to work through them and not against them. As Gregory's dealings with France in 1074 illustrate, metropolitans,

[91] *Reg.* 1.55, 16 Mar. 1074, pp. 82–3; 2.2, to Bishop Isembert II of Poitiers, 10 Sept. 1074, pp. 125–6; 2.25, to Archbishop Anno of Cologne, 18 Nov. 1074, pp. 156–7.

[92] *Reg.* 1.73, to Bishop Isembert II of Poitiers, 12 Apr. 1074, pp. 104–5.

[93] *Reg.* 2.56, to Archbishop Manasses I of Rheims, 4 Mar. 1074, p. 209/17–23.

[94] 'Neque ad hoc prelati sumus, ut nostrae commissos providentiae potenter magis quam iuste tractemus': *Reg.* 1.81, to Archbishop Udo of Trier, 6 May 1074, pp. 115–16.

[95] *Reg.* 2.15, 11 Nov. 1074, pp. 147–8; cf. 4.16, to the clerks of Romans, 21 Mar. 1077, pp. 320–1.

from their side, found working with Gregory to be useful. There was a common interest in the working together of pope, legates, and metropolitans.[96] The collaboration that was often apparent especially in French affairs must be set against the tension that was apparent in German affairs.

Gregory's cautious attitude towards the episcopal hierarchy is further evident in his dealings with regard to those claiming the titles of patriarch or primate, and therefore a status and function superior to those of all metropolitans. The eleventh century saw many archbishops and their sees drawing upon the resources of local tradition and legend in order to heighten their prestige and to advance their claims to autonomy and authority. Conspicuous examples were the North Italian sees of Milan and Ravenna; in such cases, Gregory was concerned to resist them resolutely and to reduce their claims to what he deemed proper.[97] Yet he manifestly had no general intention of resisting all claims to patriarchal and primatial status and authority, provided that they were authentic within his criteria and that they were exercised in harmony with the universal authority of the apostolic see of Rome. The lines of Gregory's dealings were close to those set out in the Pseudo-Isidorian letters attributed to the first-century popes Clement and Anacletus, which purported to establish the arrangements of the very earliest days of the church. The letters both assigned to patriarchs and primates their established places within the church and affirmed that the Roman church was the hinge and head of all the churches.[98]

With such testimony to the right order of the church in mind, in 1073 Gregory made no difficulty about referring to Dominicus IV Cerbano of Grado as his own *confrater* and as 'patriarch of Venice'; he described him as being most faithful ('fidelissimus') to the Roman church and to the emperor of Constantinople. Writing a year later to the doge of Venice, Gregory described the establishment of the patriarchate of Grado as a work of divine providence by which the see was given an eminence that it shared only with the four others of Antioch, Alexandria, Constantinople, and Jerusalem. The doge and people of Venice should ensure that the impoverished patriarch was provided for according to his proper dignity.[99]

As regards primacies, whatever reservations Gregory may have had before becoming pope about the primatial claims of Lanfranc of Canterbury, having become pope he was prepared to seek Lanfranc's goodwill by at least tacitly recognizing his jurisdiction over the Irish, whose marriage customs he was urged to remedy.[100] Lanfranc's unpreparedness to journey to Rome, rather than any refusal on Gregory's part, prevented any further steps towards the consideration of the primacy by the papacy during their lifetime. For Gregory was far from being inimical to the notion of primacies. His view of them was expressly developed in one major instance when,

---

[96] This is made particularly clear in the series of letters that Gregory dispatched to French addresses on 15 and 16 Nov. 1074: *Reg.* 2.19–24, pp. 151–6.

[97] See above, 4.3,6; also Cowdrey, 'The Papacy, the Patarenes and the Church of Milan'.

[98] Hinschius, pp. 39, 66–87, esp. pp. 79–80, 82–4.

[99] *Reg.* 1.18, to the Emperor Michael VII Ducas, 9 July 1073, pp. 29–30; 2.39, to Doge Dominicus Silvius and the people of Venice, 31 Dec. 1074, pp. 175–6.

[100] *Epp. vag.* no. 1, pp. 4–5; see above, 6.9.

in April 1079, he confirmed the primacy of Lyons over the provinces of Lyons, Rouen, Tours, and Sens, that is, over the ancient Roman imperial province of Gallia Lugdunensis.[101] It is most unlikely that Gregory rehabilitated the primacy of Lyons with a view to undermining the see of Rheims and its troublesome archbishop, Manasses I.[102] Indeed, as lately as the previous August, Gregory had reassured Manasses that he did not intend unreasonably to break or diminish the privileges of the church of Rheims, although he hoped for a face-to-face talk with Manasses before long at their common leisure. This reads like a hint that Gregory wished to work out more precisely and clearly with Manasses what the privileges of Rheims actually were.[103] As regards Lyons, Gregory took a decisive step. He confirmed its primacy, not in a novel way, but as he believed that its ancient dignity had been recognized by apostolic authority, giving Archbishop Gebuin and his worthily elected successors a primacy over the four provinces.

His covering letter to the archbishops of Rouen, Tours, and Sens is of the utmost importance for his explanation why he was forthwith confirming what he deemed to be the pristine and traditional arrangement. His explanation consisted entirely of two passages directly cited from the Pseudo-Isidorian Decrees. The first was from a letter attributed to Pope Boniface II (530–604).[104] It set out in principle the need for an ordered and graded hierarchy on earth as in heaven, and for an earthly order of peace, charity, concord, and sincerity which was best secured when there was a single person in charge ('prepositus') to whom all might have recourse. Such a *prepositus*, it is to be inferred, was the pope or, if he were not conveniently accessible, a local representative of his authority. The second passage was from the letters of Pseudo-Anacletus. It set forth how, in the very earliest years of the church, apostolic authority had established an order which gave practical expression to this principle. According to it, the apostles transferred to the church a structure of jurisdiction that was already to hand in the pagan empire. In the capital cities of the imperial provinces, there had long been established judges of the highest rank and chief judicial authority ('primates legis erant seculi et prima iudiciaria potestas'). Therefore, all who could not for any reason go to the imperial or royal court for redress of oppressions and injustice might find it nearer home. In the empire, other metropolitan cities had judges who, however exalted their titles, were of minor standing and who must obey the *primates legis seculi*. Similarly in the church, there were, from virtually the beginning of its history, patriarchs or primates (in this passage of Pseudo-Isidore, the terms were synonymous) with authority in divine and ecclesiastical law; to them, the bishops were subject. There were also metropolitans and archbishops who ruled over their own provinces but owed obedience to primates. In the light of this wholly

---

[101] *Reg.* 6.34, to Archbishop Gebuin of Lyons, 20 Apr. 1074, pp. 447–9 = *QF* no. 171, pp. 196–8 (dated 19 Apr.); 6.35, to the archbishops of Rouen, Tours, and Sens, 20 Apr. 1079, pp. 450–2; 6.36, to the canons of Lyons, 20 Apr. 1079, pp. 452–3.

[102] See above, 5.3.3.2.

[103] *Reg.* 6.2, to Archbishop Manasses I of Rheims, 22 Aug. 1078, p. 393/22–4.

[104] *Reg.* 6.35, pp. 450/22–451/9; cf. Hinschius, p. 703/17–30 and *Reg. Greg. I*, 5.59, vol. 1.357/3–358/19.

unhistorical account of their origin, Pseudo-Anacletus defined the powers of primates precisely:

They are those to whom, after the apostolic see, the highest matters of business appertain, so that they may relieve those in need and bring about just redress. Those unjustly oppressed should be by them justly restored and sustained; by them, pleas of bishops and the highest matters of business should, subject to papal authority, be most justly settled.[105]

Thus ran Gregory's citations from Pseudo-Isidore. It was highly unusual for him to send letters which in this way consisted largely of undigested citations; the sole comparable example is his advice about frequent communion to Countess Matilda of Tuscany, to whom he sent a catena of passages from the ancient fathers upon the subject of eucharistic theology about which he was for long uncertain.[106] It is probable that, in 1079, he had no settled view of ecclesiastical primacies, but was feeling his way towards a resolution of the problems of the relations with one another of pope, primates, and metropolitans, and of the relations of papal vicars like Bishop Hugh of Die with them all. If so, he took in 1079 a step in the process which he advanced further towards resolution in 1082/3 when he brought about Hugh of Die's succession to the see of Lyons. In the meanwhile, he was concerned to explore and to implement what he believed to be the order of things that was established in the earliest days of the church. Perhaps the most remarkable feature of Gregory's thinking is the fullness and peculiarity of the power that, on the authority of Pseudo-Isidore, should be ascribed to primates. Far from breaking down their power, he was impelled by canonical tradition to augment it.

Except that Gregory in 1079 was seeking to move from ancient documents towards principles whereas in 1075 he was seeking to move in the reverse direction, there is a parallel with the *Dictatus papae*. The documents of 1079, like that of 1075, probably do not represent a considered and settled position on Gregory's part; rather, they were an attempt to investigate how the structure of ecclesiastical authority should be renewed in the light of what in nature of things ought to be and of ancient precedent so far as documentary sources provided it. Like the *Dictatus papae*, the attempt was straining both principle and practicality too far, and it was implemented only to a limited extent. Within Gallia Lugdunensis, it was never likely that much notice would be taken by the province of Rouen,[107] and after 1079 Gregory did not actively attempt to extend the experiment of that year to other parts of even the French church. While the renewal of the primacy of Lyons is a reminder of how far Gregory was from being radically hostile in principle to the claims of major sees, it is a unique event which, while it shows how surprisingly far Gregory might be drawn when he explored the supposed precedents of the church in its earliest days, cannot be made the basis of generalization about his settled views of the structure of the church.

[105] *Reg.* 6.35, pp. 451/10–452/2; cf. Hinschius, pp. 79/21–80/6.
[106] *Reg.* 1.47, 16 Feb. 1074, pp. 72/2–73/22; for Gregory's uncertainties about eucharistic theology, see above, 8.1.1.
[107] For the attitude of Archbishop Ralph of Tours, see above, 5.3.3.3.

9.5 Bishops

So far bishops in general were concerned, Gregory required that they like their metropolitans should be diligent, active, and obedient collaborators with the pope in the discharge of his pastoral office; at the same time, if they were duly obedient, he was committed to upholding them in the discharge of their own office. It must be recognized that, by and large, he took an unfavourable view of the spiritual and moral qualities of the bishops of his day; therefore he laid corresponding emphasis upon papal prerogatives in relation to them. Thus, in 1074, he wrote to Count Albert of Calw in Germany that bishops who were called to win souls and to teach their subjects by word and example were led astray by the devil so that they not only deserted but also overthrew the law of God.[108] Soon afterwards, he wrote to Abbot Hugh of Cluny that, in whatever direction he looked, he found scarcely any bishops who ruled the Christian people through love of Christ and not through secular ambition.[109] Gregory was led to place great weight upon papal prerogatives and papal action to discipline bishops. As a temporal lord required the support of his *fideles* in major matters, so did St Peter, to whose purview belonged the business of the whole church.[110] He reminded Bishop Henry of Liège, who had roundly condemned Gregory's absolution of someone from his diocese at the Roman synod of Lent 1078, that the apostolic see had authority to bind and to loose whomever it saw fit and wherever it saw fit.[111] It is not surprising that a prime feature of Gregory's *Dictatus papae* of 1075 was an exploration of the means of papal control over bishops. The pope alone and without a synodal assembly might depose and reconcile them. His legate, although their inferior in holy orders, took precedence over them in councils and might pronounce their deposition. The pope might translate bishops from see to see, and he might himself ordain a clerk of any church. Whereas no one might review his own judicial sentence, he might review those of everyone. No one was to condemn an appellant to the apostolic see, and the major cases of all churches should be referred to it. Upon the pope's command and licence, subjects might accuse their superiors.[112] In so far as these propositions were adopted and enforced, they imposed a thoroughgoing papal control of bishops everywhere.

Yet, provided that bishops showed what Gregory deemed to be proper obedience and co-operated with his purposes, he was at the same time concerned to vindicate the dignity and rights of the episcopal office as such. It was an institution of divine mercy ('pietas') and was intrinsically always directed towards the heavenly life.[113] The laity should obey their bishops as their spiritual fathers and pastors, bringing them all possible support in upholding the rights and duties of their office.[114]

---

[108] *Reg.* 2.11, 26 Oct. 1074, pp. 142/24–143/6.
[109] *Reg.* 2.29, 22 Jan. 1075, p. 189/20–3.
[110] *Reg.* 8.18, to Count Ebolus of Roucy, 27 Dec. 1080, p. 540/22–6.
[111] *Reg.* 6.4, 3 Oct. 1078, p. 396/21–7.
[112] Clauses 3, 4, 13, 14, 28, 20–1, 25, *Reg.* 2.55a, pp. 202–7.
[113] *Reg.* 4.2, to Bishop Hermann of Metz, 25 Aug. 1076, p. 295/20–4.
[114] *Reg.* 1.69, to Count William of Die and the subjects of the church of Die, 23 Mar. 1074, p. 99/25–30; 1.74, to the clergy and people of Beauvais, 13 Apr. 1074, p. 106/4–10; 1.80, to the clergy and

Rebellion against a bishop, as when the people of Ragusa arbitrarily imprisoned and replaced their bishop, or accusing a bishop before pagan authorities as some of the people of Carthage accused Archbishop Cyriacus, elicited Gregory's strong support for the bishop concerned.[115]

Such examples serve as a reminder of the presumptions, by the late eleventh century somewhat old-fashioned, which underlay Gregory's conception of the universal church. Important though its organization into provinces was, it was made up of dioceses in which, if matters were in good order, the clergy were followed by the people in canonically electing a bishop who became their head and representative in maintaining the liturgical, pastoral, and administrative life of a city and its surrounding region. Whatever the claims and the implementation of papal authority, Gregory sought the well-being of the diocesan organization of the church according to a pattern that had come down from Christian antiquity, at first to meet the needs of the urbanized Mediterranean world and then by somewhat uneasy modification to those of the less or non-urbanized lands that lay beyond. Dioceses were the essential building-bricks of the church. To a large degree, the church remained both in fact and in Gregory's mind a federation of dioceses; he was feeling towards, but did not in his day articulate or establish, the unitary papal monarchy of the central Middle Ages.

9.6 Rome and the Church Universal

As regards Gregory's ordering of the church, it should finally be emphasized that his attempts to explore and to implement the privileges of the Roman church upon his own initiative were balanced by his need to settle specific matters that were brought to his notice from the localities of the church. As was the case with all rulers in antiquity and in the Middle Ages, a large part of papal business was not initiated by the pope but came to him at the instance of petitioners who came with petitions for justice or grace in matters of local importance. The revival of such business at Rome under the reform popes, and especially under Gregory VII, is signalled by the reappearance after several centuries of letters with such incipits as 'Pervenit ad nos', or 'Pervenit ad aures nostras'.[116] Such letters illustrate a need on the part of the pope, not so much to extend the jurisdiction and the direct authority of the papacy, as to make the existing ecclesiastical structure function more effectively in its own terms and to restrain the excesses of legates and others who were acting as papal agents. Thus, *c.* 1082, Gregory rebuked Abbot Richard of Saint-Victor at Marseilles for unjustly excommunicating Cluniac monks who had already duly withdrawn from Saint-Sernin at Toulouse, on the grounds that 'to exercise authority intemperately

---

people of le Puy, 13 Apr. 1074, p. 114/24–30, 6.20, to Count Centullus of Béarn, 25 Feb. 1079, p. 432/15–19; 9.16, to the clergy and people of Chartres, (late 1081), pp. 596/22– 597/4.

[115] *Reg.* 1.65, to the people of Ragusa, 20 Mar. 1074, pp. 94–5; 1.22, to the clergy and people of Carthage, 15 Sept. 1073, pp. 36–9.

[116] See the indexes of incipits in *Reg.* p. 641 and *Epp. vag.* p. 166; cf. JL 2.803, where such incipits are extremely scarce between the mid-8th and the mid-11th cents.

or rashly against men of good report must assuredly detract from its force'.[117] Similarly, in 1078, Gregory acted through a legate, Bishop Hugh of Die, to restrain another legate, the Roman subdeacon Hubert, and Bishop Hugh of Langres, who had exceed their authority by excommunicating Count Robert of Flanders.[118] When, in 1074, it came to Gregory's ears that Bishop Vitalis of Ragusa had been imprisoned and replaced by his subjects, he instructed Archbishop Gerald of Siponto as his legate to do justice and to restore order in the see.[119] Complaints by bishops themselves might be attended to; thus, in 1078, when 'Archbishop' Evenus of Dol came to Gregory with a complaint about a challenge to his succession to his see, Gregory made detailed proposals about how his legates might compose the dispute.[120] If Gregory sometimes used his legates to establish the rights of bishops and others according to the proper order of local churches, he also remitted cases for settlement on his behalf by bishops themselves. In 1079, he referred to Bishop Isembert II of Poitiers a local dispute that had been brought to him at Rome about a property.[121] Later in the same year, he commissioned three North Italian bishops to settle, subject to his own confirmation, a marriage case that had come to his notice and which concerned the Aledramid Marquis Boniface of Vasto.[122] Soon afterwards, Bishop Thierry of Verdun was instructed to do synodal justice upon Count Arnulf of Chiny who had robbed Bishop Henry of Liège while he was on his way to Rome.[123] Such cases are a reminder that Gregory's dealings with the church at large were a two-way process. On the one hand, he was concerned to assert the prerogatives of the Roman church as the mother of all the churches which could in cases of need intervene directly in their affairs, even to the extent of himself ordaining bishops and claiming a right of devolution if ordinary electoral procedures failed. Yet, on the other hand, in response to the increasing attraction to Rome of ecclesiastical business sometimes of a local and even trivial kind, he was also concerned to prompt bishops to act positively and appropriately in their own spheres and to restrain excessive or heavy-handed behaviour by Roman legates. Relations under Gregory between Rome and other churches must be recognized to have developed, not only upon the initiative of the pope in asserting the prerogatives of the apostolic see, but also upon that of local and often humble churches and people in seeking out papal assistance.

---

[117] *Epp. vag.* no. 50, pp. 120–1.

[118] *Epp. vag.* no. 14, to Bishop Hugh of Langres, (*c.*25 Nov. 1078), pp. 62–3; cf. *Reg.* 6.7, to Bishop Hugh of Die, 25 Nov. 1078, pp. 407–8.

[119] *Reg.* 1.65, to the people of Ragusa, 20 Mar. 1074, pp. 94–5.

[120] *Reg.* 5.22–3, to the subdeacon Hubert and the monk Teuzo, and to the counts of Brittany, 22 May 1078, pp. 385–8.

[121] *Reg.* 6.32, 13 Apr. 1079, pp. 445–6.

[122] *Reg.* 7.9, to the bishops of Asti and Turin and the bishop-elect of Acqui, 3 Nov. 1079, pp. 470–1.

[123] *Reg.* 7.13, 30 Jan. 1080, pp. 477–8.

Sacerdotium *and* Regnum

10.1 Gregory VII's View of the Relationship between *Sacerdotium* and *Imperium/Regnum*

With regard to the question of relations between the priestly element in Christian society, the *sacerdotium*, and the royal element, the *imperium* or *regnum*, Gregory was in no way an original thinker.[1] His thought remained within the broad lines that had been established in late antiquity by Pope Gelasius I in his letter of 494 to the Eastern Emperor Anastasius:

There are two things, venerable emperor, by which this world is supremely ('principaliter') ruled: the hallowed authority of pontiffs and the royal power ('auctoritas sacrata pontificum et regalis potestas'). As between them, the burden of priests is greater inasmuch as, at the divine judgement, they will render account even for the souls of kings themselves. And indeed, most gracious son, you are aware that, although by your office you govern the human race, you nevertheless devoutly bow the neck to those who have charge of things divine. You seek from them the means of your salvation, and you acknowledge that hence, in receiving and administering as is fitting the heavenly mysteries, you should submit yourself in the order of religion rather than command. In such matters, you should rely upon their judgement and not wish that they should be subject to your will.[2]

Gregory's thought was not closely tied to that of Gelasius, for he came to refer to it only after 1080, and he always selected and accentuated those aspects of it that told in favour of papal authority. Moreover, at successive stages of his pontificate he responded differently to changing contingencies. These contingencies arose mainly, but by no means only, from his dealings with the German kingdom. They may be studied in three phases: up to his first breach with Henry IV early in 1076; the immediate consequences of this breach; and the further consequences of his second sentence against Henry at his Lent synod of 1080.

Gregory's first recorded statement which bears upon the relations of *sacerdotium* and *imperium* was addressed in July 1073 to the Byzantine emperor, when he replied to a letter in which, in face of the Seljuk threat to his empire, Michael VII Ducas had shown himself well disposed towards the Roman church. Gregory's reply avoided any express pronouncement on the relation of *sacerdotium* and *imperium*, although his selection as his envoy to Constantinople of Patriarch Dominicus of Grado echoed Gelasian views of their harmony since he regarded Dominicus as 'most faithful to the Roman church and to your imperial majesty' ('Romane ecclesiae et imperio vestro

---

[1] For a fuller discussion to which this chapter is greatly indebted, see Robinson, 'Church and Papacy', in *CHMPT*, pp. 252–305.

[2] *Ep.* 12, 2–3, E. Schwartz, 'Publizistische Sammlungen', p. 20.

fidelissimum'). Gregory's emphasis was upon the moral quest for concord and peace, rooted in charity, that he declared to be the ancient quality of the good relations that he sought to renew. He said that he desired not only to renew concord between the Roman church and the church and empire of Constantinople but also, so far as in him lay, to have peace with all men.[3]

During the months that followed, his dealings in the west with regard to Henry IV of Germany struck a similar note in relations between *sacerdotium* and *imperium*. For Gregory, it was a time of hope: under the constraint of the Saxon revolt, Henry had sent to Gregory his two penitent letters; in April 1074, Henry was freed from the excommunication that he was deemed to have incurred by infection from his counsellors; Gregory was increasingly able to envisage his coming to Rome and being granted imperial coronation; there was the prospect of harmonious collaboration between the two predominant powers in human society.

In September 1073, Gregory already sought to set the stage for such collaboration by seeking to initiate conversations at Rome which would involve the Empress-mother Agnes, Duke Rudolf of Swabia, Countess Beatrice of Tuscany and her daughter Matilda, Bishop Raynald of Como, and other God-fearing persons.[4] Writing to Rudolf, Gregory said that the empire would be more illustriously ruled and the strength of the church would be consolidated by the joining together of *sacerdotium* and *imperium* in the unity of concord. Gregory compared them to the two eyes of the human body: as this body was guided by temporal light, so the body of the church was directed and enlightened by spiritual light when the two dignities were concordant in true religion. A comparison with the Gelasian formulation, to which Gregory at this time made no express allusion, is instructive. On the one hand, Gregory laid no stress upon the subordination of royal power to the hallowed authority of pontiffs upon which Gelasius insisted; his simile of the two eyes told in the direction of equality and comparability. On the other hand, whereas Gelasius had associated the two powers in the government of the world and had separated spiritual from temporal functions, Gregory placed the two eyes together within the body of the church. Gelasius's dual society was replaced by a unitary one of which both papacy and empire were aspects. Nevertheless, Gregory's studied restraint should be observed: not only was he silent about Gelasius's subordination of the royal power;[5] he also declared himself prepared to consider on their merits any additions to or subtractions from his own view of *sacerdotium* and *imperium* that his German and Italian advisers might propose. Such a dialogue was, for Gregory, the path to establishing the concord that he sought.

---

3 *Reg.* 1.18, 9 July 1073, pp. 29–30. The reference to Rom. 12: 18 may be compared with that in 1.10, to Count Guy of Imola, 23 June 1073, p. 17/7–9, as an illustration of Gregory's aspiration for peace at this stage of his pontificate.

4 *Reg.* 1.19–21, to Duke Rudolf of Swabia, Bishop Raynald of Como, and Bishop-elect Anselm of Lucca, 1 Sept. 1073, pp. 31–5.

5 Writing in 1075 to King Sweyn Estrithson of Denmark, probably with Gelasius's letter to Anastasius in mind, he argued that both popes and kings would similarly render account for their subjects at the last judgement: *Reg.* 2.51, 25 Jan. 1075, p. 193/20–5.

In this context, too much should not be read into Gregory's description to Bishop Raynald of Como of King Henry IV as head of the laity ('laicorum caput').[6] Gregory was not referring to any desacralization of monarchy or restriction of the king to lay status. His emphasis was upon the word 'caput', not 'laicorum': if any lay individual or lay noble ('princeps') brought profit to the church by his virtue and religion, how much more might Henry do so, since he was king and prospective emperor. Gregory was writing of personal moral and religious suitability, not of objective sacral quality; he was anticipating by an *a fortiori* argument the point that he later made positively in letters to Henry, that Henry was placed by God in the highest office of all ('in summo culmine rerum').[7]

Accordingly, in the circumstances which prevailed until the end of 1073, Gregory's emphasis lay upon the partnership and concord of *sacerdotium* and *imperium* and upon the need to resist those who sought to sow discord.[8] Papacy and empire were to be held together by the bond of charity.[9] His expectation of collaboration found eloquent expression in his 'Crusading' plans of 1074. Although Henry had not been crowned emperor, Gregory spoke of his own charity towards Henry that was elicited by (in this order) the imperial majesty and the mild power of the apostolic see ('imperatoria maiestas et apostolicae sedis mansueta potestas'). Gregory could contemplate leaving Henry to protect the Roman church 'as a holy mother' while he himself led the expedition to the east.[10]

Such moderate and conciliatory language as addressed to Henry about the relations of *sacerdotium* and *imperium* did not prevent Gregory from also exploring more privately the intrinsic superiority of the *sacerdotium*. *Dictatus papae* 8 and 9 proposed that the pope alone could use imperial insignia and that all *principes* or rulers should kiss the feet of the pope alone. Gregory was here exploring the pre-eminent rather than the exclusive prerogatives of the pope.[11] More challenging and specific were *Dictatus papae* 12, that the pope might depose emperors, and clause 27, that the pope might release subjects from fealty to evil men.[12] The theses of the *Dictatus papae* received no collective publicity, and it is hard to know how integrally they became rooted in Gregory's working conception of papal authority. But at the end of 1075, when his relations with Henry IV underwent rapid deterioration, Gregory began to place more weight upon the prerogatives of the *sacerdotium*. To the clerk Tedald whom Henry intruded into the see of Milan, Gregory insisted that no objective trust could be placed in the aid of the king, or in the power of his own noble birth, or in the

---

[6] *Reg.* p. 33/33–4.

[7] *Reg.* 2.31, 7 Dec. 1074, p. 165/32; 3.7, (early Sept. 1075), p. 257/4–5. The representation of the emperor as head of the lay order was, in any case, no innovation of Gregory's: see e.g. Burchard of Worms, *Decretum*, 15, Argumentum, col. 895B.

[8] *Reg.* 2.31, p. 166/3–7.   [9] *Reg.* 1.85, to the Empress Agnes, 15 June 1074, p. 121/20–8.

[10] *Reg.* 2.31, esp. pp. 165/26–30, 167/15–20; see also the reference to the exaltation of Henry's rule ('dominationis tuae altitudinem') in 2.30, to King Henry IV, 7 Dec. 1074, p. 164/21–3.

[11] The interpretation of the word 'solus' in *Dictatus papae* 7–10 is made difficult by *Dictatus papae* 10, in which it is not easy to envisage that Gregory intended the liturgical recitation of no name but the pope's.

[12] *Reg.* 2.55a, pp. 203–4.

resources of the Milanese citizens, for against papal prerogatives ('apostolica iura') and God's omnipotence the strength ('virtus') of kings and emperors, like all merely human endeavour, was mere ash and chaff.[13] In his final letter to Henry before their breach, Gregory stressed a king's duty to reverence and obey St Peter as master of the church and to hear the pope's commands as Peter's own.[14] In Gregory's estimation, it may be concluded that more turned upon the moral and religious disposition of the ruler than upon the niceties of political theory: if a ruler were obedient, the bond of charity drew *sacerdotium* and *imperium* into something approaching an equality of esteem within the body of the church; but if he were recalcitrant, the prerogative of St Peter to bind and to loose, and the capacity of the pope as vicar of St Peter, brought princes to their knees before the *sacerdotium* and placed in jeopardy even the rule of emperors.

With the sentence of deprivation of the power to rule and of excommunication that Gregory passed upon Henry IV at his Lent synod of 1076, his express comments on the relations of *sacerdotium* and *imperium* ceased; he concentrated upon the single issue of the applicability even to kings of the powers that Christ in the New Testament conferred upon St Peter and that Peter passed on to his vicars who succeeded him. The grounds of his sentence upon Henry were that, by St Peter's grace, the Christian people, that is, all Christians at all times, was committed by Christ specifically ('specialiter') to Peter; it must specifically ('specialiter') obey Gregory because of Peter's vicariate that was entrusted to him. By Peter's grace, power from God was committed to Gregory to bind in heaven and on earth, and this sufficed to warrant the pope's sentence upon the king. Hence Gregory's twofold sentence upon Henry: first, because Henry by unheard-of pride had risen up against Peter's church, Gregory inhibited him from the government of the German and Italian kingdom, and released all Christians from oaths taken to him, 'for it was appropriate that one who sought to diminish the dignity (*honor*) of Peter's church should himself forfeit the dignity (*honor*) that he seemed to have'; second, because of Henry's contemptuous disobedience in continuing his association with his excommunicated counsellors, of his spurning of Gregory's salutary admonitions, and of his separating himself from Peter's church which he had endeavoured to rend apart, Gregory bound Henry with the chains of anathema.[15]

Because Gregory set his sentence upon the single basis of his Petrine authority, he did not in 1076 directly address the broader arguments of Henry's propagandists, who drew upon a modified Gelasian view of the duality of *sacerdotium* and *regnum* and of Christ's pronouncement about the two swords (Luke 22: 38).[16] After the Lent

---

[13] *Reg.* 3.8, (8 Dec. 1075), p. 261/6–16.

[14] *Reg.* 3.10, (8 Dec.) 1075, pp. 264/27–265/26.

[15] *Reg.* 3.10a, pp. 270–1; cf. *Epp. vag.* no. 14, to the faithful in Germany, (summer 1076), pp. 38–41.

[16] *Epp. HIV* nos. 10–13, pp. 60–72, esp. p. 70/7–15; it should be observed that the two swords, priestly and royal, were wielded within the church. Gregory himself never, in his letters, cited Luke 22: 38, although he spoke separately of the spiritual sword as committed to the clergy and of the material sword in a literal sense as the weapon of laity: see *Reg.* pp. 676, s.v. *anathema*, 687, s.v. *excommunicatio*, 689, s.v. *gladius*.

synod, he concentrated his argument upon the objection that came from Germany about the validity of his sentence: whether the pope could rightly excommunicate a king and release his subjects from their oaths. Thus, in his hastily dictated letter of 25 August to Bishop Hermann of Metz, he argued upon an extremely narrow front.[17] The German objection was so foolish as barely to deserve an answer. Gregory therefore merely referred cursorily to ancient texts and examples which said little about the excommunication of kings in particular and he commented only weakly upon their forfeiture of their power to rule. For the rest, Gregory avoided addressing the actual arguments of his German critics about the relations of *regnum* and *sacerdotium* but, instead, set up hypothetical positions of his own formulation which kept the argument upon his own ground. Perhaps his critics thought that, when committing his sheep to St Peter, God excepted kings? Gregory merely replied by *a fortiori* assertions: those who would not be bound could not be loosed, and so separated themselves from Christ; if the apostolic see was divinely empowered to judge in spiritual matters, it was so empowered in secular ones; all men, including kings and princes, were members either of Christ or of Antichrist, and if spiritual men who were members of Christ were subject to papal judgement, how much more so were worldly men in respect of their wickedness. Or perhaps his critics held that the royal dignity was superior to the episcopal ('episcopalem precellat')? As a statement of the Henrician case, this was doubly a travesty: his propagandists did not claim the superiority of the royal power,[18] and they did not broaden the spiritual power by referring to it, as Gregory implied, as episcopal. Without explanation, Gregory dismissed the royal dignity as an invention of human pride which strove only for vain glory, while the episcopal was a gift of divine mercy which strove after the heavenly life.[19] A brief reference to ancient authorities included St Ambrose's comparison of the episcopal and royal dignities to gold and lead.

All in all, the letter of 1076 to Hermann of Metz is the most weakly argued of Gregory's major letters. It suggests that, at the time of his breach with Henry, he had no considered and well grounded theory of *sacerdotium* and *imperium* which could survive the breakdown of his earlier hope for their concord; that he did not, in this area, engage with the view of his German critics; and that he rested his position on the one argument of which he was assured—that of the power of St Peter to bind and loose as established in the Gospels, which was conveyed by Peter to his vicar upon earth.

When Gregory again passed sentence upon Henry IV at his Lent synod of 1080, his much longer allocution, this time addressed to both the apostles St Peter and St Paul, again turned upon the universal power of the pope, as vicar of the apostles, to

[17] *Reg.* 4.2, pp. 293–7, esp. 294/4–296/7; 4.3, to the faithful in Germany, 3 Sept. 1076, p. 298/9–15; cf. *Epp. vag.* no. 14, pp. 32–3.

[18] Although the two powers were pointedly listed in the order *regnum–sacerdotium*.

[19] Gregory seems to have been comparing Old Testament kingship as pejoratively presented in 1 Sam. 8: 4–18 with Christ's words to Peter in the Gospels; he seems also to have been influenced by St Augustine's discussion of the origins of government in *De doct. Christ* 1. 23, pp. 18–19. See Carlyle and Carlyle, *A History of Medieval Political Theory*, 2. 144–5, 3. 93–8.

bind and to loose.[20] On this occasion, Gregory passed sentence of excommunication before, not after, he passed that of deposition. This was evidently done for the practical reason that, in 1080, he deemed Henry to have already incurred excommunication by his disobedience in impeding the planned German assembly; but the religious terms in which he introduced his sentence suggest that, upon maturer consideration than time allowed him in 1076, he now thought it appropriate to place the spiritual sentence of excommunciation and anathema before the temporal sentence of deprivation of earthly power.

In two respects, Gregory intensified his sentence by comparison with that of 1076 in a manner that implied the superiority of the priestly to the secular power: when again inhibiting ('interdicens') Henry's rule over the German and Italian kingdom, he in addition took away his royal dignity ('dignitatem illi regiam tollo'); in releasing his subjects from their oaths, he expressly referred to the oaths as being taken in respect of Henry's lordship over the kingdom ('de regni dominatione'). Thus, whereas in his sentence of 1076 Gregory envisaged Henry in his royal person, in 1080 he also referred to him in his royal office. Consonantly with so doing, in 1080 he developed considerably the *a fortiori* arguments about the superiority of the spiritual power over the royal which he had adumbrated in the aftermath of his sentence in 1076: if the princes of the apostles could bind and loose in heaven, how much more could they in accordance with a ruler's merits take away and grant all grades of earthly dominion from empires and kingdoms down to the least of human possessions; if they could transfer from wicked men to good the whole range of ecclesiastical patriarchates, primacies, archbishoprics, and bishoprics, thus judging spiritual things, how much more could they judge secular things; if they would, according to St Paul (cf. 1 Cor. 6: 3), judge the angels who stand behind proud princes, how much more could they judge the human agents of those angels? All kings and all princes of the world should learn the nature and the power of Peter and Paul, and fear to treat lightly the command of their church. Their power was now extended from persons to embrace all spiritual and secular offices. Gregory's step forward shows that, by 1080, he had come to a more sophisticated and positive understanding of the superiority of *sacerdotium* to *regnum* than he had expressed up to 1076.

From 1080, this was apparent in his letters. It was so mainly in those concerning Germany, but also in his correspondence with other kings, especially the Anglo-Norman ruler William I. His letters bore the mark of further reflection and research by himself or on his behalf, particularly into the Pseudo-Isidorian Decrees and the writings of Pope Gregory I. The prime example is the longest and the most widely noticed of all Gregory's letters—that which he sent on 15 March 1081 to Bishop Hermann of Metz in order to justify his second excommunication and deposition of Henry IV in the previous year.[21] Gregory greatly developed and augmented arguments that he had deployed to Hermann in his letter of 1076; as then, the letter took its start from questions that arose in Germany: did the apostolic see have authority to

---

[20] *Reg.* 7.14a(7), pp. 483–7.   [21] *Reg.* 8.21, pp. 544–61.

excommunicate a king and to release his subjects from their oaths? Once again, though more fully, Gregory began by referring to the gospel record of Christ's commission to St Peter and by insisting that kings were not excluded from the sheep that the Son of God entrusted to the pope. Now, however, he also enlarged upon the position of the Roman church as universal mother, whose judgements and teachings were binding everywhere. The Roman church had a universal *principatus*, defined by the Petrine texts, which warranted the claim which was the core of his presentation of the superiority of the *sacerdotium* to the *regnum*: that where there was divinely conferred power to judge heavenly things, there was *a fortiori* the power to judge earthly things, even to the extent of depriving disobedient kings of their capacity to rule.

Gregory had already adverted to the relative standing of the spiritual and secular dignities ('dignitates') in a letter of almost exactly a year earlier to King William I of England.[22] He drew upon Pope Gelasius I's letter to the Emperor Anastasius, to which, however, he referred as though it were a text from holy scripture.[23] When writing to a king of whom he, on balance, approved, Gregory expressed himself in favourable terms about the royal dignity: he declared that the papal and royal dignities ('dignitates') were more exalted than all others that God had set in this world for its governance ('huic mundo ad eius regimine').[24] Nevertheless, if the two dignities were complementary, they were now displayed as far from equal: just as God had appointed sun and moon to be superior to all other luminaries in enlightening his creation at their proper times, so creation was to be ruled by the papal and royal dignities through different agencies ('officia'). The Christian religion enforced such a difference of greater and lesser that, after God, the royal dignity was governed by papal care and guidance. Thus—here Gregory cited Pope Gelasius—the pope would represent kings as all other men before God at the last judgement and render account to him of their transgressions.

Gregory's qualified but genuine appreciation, as here expressed, of the excellence of the royal, as well as the papal, dignity was possible because he deemed William to be, on balance, a good Christian ruler. In the light of Gregory's later exposition of kingship to Hermann of Metz, he was to be numbered with those who were the body of Christ the true king, not with those who were the body of the devil.[25] In a world where division between the two bodies was stark and divisive, obedience to Christ within the order of grace redeemed the kingly dignity. Writing to Hermann of Metz, Gregory envisaged a kingship of Henry IV which was not so redeemed. He referred, not to the excellence of kingship when truly exercised in the body of Christ, but to its origins in the pride of men which was the sinful consequence of the fall. Following a Stoic and patristic tradition that had been epitomized by St Augustine in his *De doctrina Christiana*, Gregory posited a creation in which all men were originally equal.[26]

---

[22] *Reg.* 7.25, 8 May 1080, pp. 505–6.   [23] *Reg.* p. 506/8.

[24] Cf. Gelasius I's formula, 'duo . . . sunt quibus principaliter mundus hic regitur': as n. 2.

[25] *Reg.* 8.21, p.557/11–19.

[26] Augustine, *De doct. Christ.* 1.23, pp. 18–19, cited in *Reg.* 8.21, p. 556/2–5, the sole citation of Augustine in Gregory's letters; cf. Augustine, *De civ. Dei*, 5.19, 19.25, vol. 1.154–6, 2.696.

Kingship was imposed upon fallen men by other fallen men who, as gentile kings, had no knowledge of God ('dignitas a secularibus etiam Deum ignorantibus inventa'). The credentials of unredeemed kingship, whether gentile, Jewish, or supposedly Christian, were everywhere false and its operation harmful and even diabolical:

> Who may not know that kings and dukes took their origin ('principium') from those who, not knowing God and incited by the prince of the world, namely the devil, through pride, acts of rapine, perfidy, murders, in short by almost every kind of crime, presumed from blind greed and intolerable presumption to lord it over their equals—that is, men. When such as these strive to bow the priests of the Lord before their feet, to whom may they more rightly be compared than to him who is head over all the sons of pride (cf. Job 41: 25)? . . . Who may doubt that the priests of Christ should be reckoned the fathers and masters of kings and princes, and of all the faithful?[27]

Only by acknowledging this could kingship become truly a dignity in the sense in which Gregory had written of it to William the Conqueror.

Gregory's understanding of the origin of royal power led him to be concerned, not for the desacralization of kingship to which he never alluded, but for its moralization. How might an institution which was the invention of human pride be brought to cherish and to exhibit humility? How might an institution which was characterized by greed and by presumption in lording it over equals be brought to obedience to its proper fathers and masters, the priests of Christ? How might kings in Christendom whose persistence in pride and unjust dominion left them members of the devil be so converted or replaced that they become members of Christ? How might even kings who were members of Christ be restrained from a deterioration similar to that in the Israel of old, by which, from being good and humble men, Saul and David as kings worsened in character?[28] Gregory's remaining thoughts about *sacerdotium* and *regnum* in his letter to Hermann of Metz turned primarily, not upon theoretical considerations although these were important, but upon such practical issues as how a royal dignity with its origins in pride might be so moralized as to make kings indeed the members of Christ.

Gregory, therefore, argued that the priestly dignity had a fourfold superiority over the kingly. First, it had a superiority in giving judgement which was based upon the Petrine power to bind and loose in heaven and upon earth. 'Is it not to be recognized as pitiable madness for a son to subject to himself a father, or a disciple a master, and to try by wrongful bonds to make subject to his own power one by whom he believes that he can be bound and loosed not only in earth but also in heaven?' Gregory cited approvingly the Emperor Constantine's alleged refusal, though he was lord of almost all the world, to sit in judgement on bishops at the council of Nicaea. He also cited the Gelasian text about the two powers; he adapted it for his purpose by omitting Gelasius's reference to the division of authority between the two powers, thus enabling him to claim Gelasius's warrant for the view that emperors altogether depended upon the judgement of priests whom they might not venture to reduce to

---

[27] *Reg.* 8.21, pp. 552/5–553/2.   [28] *Reg.* 8.21, p. 561/1–6.

their own will.[29] Gregory also cited St Ambrose's opinion, which he would again cite when rebuking King William I of England for imprisoning his episcopal half-brother Odo of Bayeux, that the priestly dignity was superior to kingly power as gold was superior to lead; because of its superiority by divine ordinance, the priestly dignity should be inviolable.[30]

Second, Gregory argued for the superiority of the priestly dignity to the royal on account of the powers with which it was endowed. The humblest members of the spiritual order commanded the demons to whom emperors and kings were subject. To appreciate Gregory's argument, one must bear in mind his rigorous division of mankind between members of Christ and members of the devil, and his view of kingship as by origin rooted in the pride of fallen men, although it was capable of being guided towards excellence if made obedient to the spiritual power. Gregory began his comments on the respective powers of priests and emperors by alluding to the text of the ordination rite for exorcists, who ranked among those in minor orders: exorcists were ordained 'in order that they might be spiritual emperors to cast out demons from the bodies of the possessed, with all their manifold wickedness'.[31] But kings and princes who did not live religiously and in the fear of God were subject to demons. If exorcists have command ('imperium') over demons, how much more did they command those men who were subject to and members of demons? And if exorcists thus ranked above kings, how much more did priests rank above them?[32] The everyday course of priestly ministrations confirmed the superiority of the powers of those in major orders. Since priestly power looked to things eternal, kings were beholden to priests for help in the hour of death. No emperor or king could, by virtue of his office, confer baptism, by the word of his mouth make the Lord's body and blood, or bind and loose in heaven and on earth. Only bishops could ordain other bishops, and only with the pope's authority could they depose them. In all these powers, priests were superior to kings; if kings were judged by priests in respect of their sins, from whom, Gregory asked with papal jurisdiction over bishops tacitly in view, could kings be more rightly judged than by the Roman pontiff?[33]

Gregory's claim to the superiority of the priestly dignity on grounds of the powers that it exercised led, thirdly, to an assertion of its superiority on account of the spiritual and transcendental solidarities to which priests and kings characteristically belonged. He began with a pejorative estimate of kingship, observing that any good Christians could more properly be called kings than could evil princes. For the former were the body of Christ the true king, while the latter were members of the devil. Good Christians commanded themselves ('sibi imperant'), to the end that they might rule eternally with Christ the true emperor ('imperator'); the powers of evil

---

[29] *Reg.* 8.21, p. 553/3–22.
[30] *Reg.* 8.21, pp. 554/11–555/9; 9.37, to King William I, (late 1083), pp. 630/33–631/18.
[31] *PRG* 15.18, vol. 1.17.
[32] *Reg.* 8.21, pp. 555/10–556/9.
[33] *Reg.* 8.21, pp. 556/10–557/10. The limits set on the status and power of kings in the formulas of the *RGP* should be borne in mind: see above, 3.1.1.

princes so operated that they would perish eternally with the prince of darkness, who was king over all the sons of pride (cf. Job 41: 25).[34]

When untutored by Christian obedience, the royal office was as far below the priestly as the body of the devil was below the body of Christ; tutored by the priestly office, the royal was capable of excellence, but only after the manner of a son in relation to a father or a disciple to a master.[35] Thus, fourthly, and in a manner particularly characteristic of his thought during his last years as pope, Gregory regarded the priestly dignity as having a superiority of sanctity over the royal. He therefore turned his attention from kings and emperors who, puffed up by worldly glory, reigned not for God but for themselves, to consider their Christian counterparts. He bade them remember the spiritual and moral dangers of their office. Whereas Gregory claimed, with some exaggeration, that in one see alone, that of St Peter, almost a hundred popes had been numbered among the saints,[36] only a very few emperors and kings were saved, while not more than a handful bore the mark of sanctity through the quality of their religion and the testimony of miracles.[37] Even exemplary emperors —Gregory named only Constantine,[38] Theodosius I, Honorius, Charlemagne, and Louis the Pious—whom the church rightly venerated had no such record of miracles as had the apostles, martyrs, and holy abbots. Given this contrast, only culpable pride would lead kings and princes to arrogate themselves above those whose sanctity was so abundantly proven. The moral contrast between secular rulers and religious popes, made holy by the merits of St Peter, was clear: 'being too much devoted to worldly activity, the former set little store by things spiritual; earnestly meditating upon things heavenly, the latter despise whatever is of this world.'[39] The climax to which Gregory drew his second letter to Hermann of Metz leaves little doubt that, for him, this moral criterion provided the decisive proof of the almost incalculable superiority of the *sacerdotium* over the *imperium* or *regnum*, at least as he came to estimate it by the early 1080s.

34 *Reg.* 8.21, p. 557/11–19; for the reference to Job, cf. p. 552/18–20.

35 This goes far to explain Gregory's use of the Bible in relation to the temporal power. He never cited such words of Christ as 'Render to Caesar the things that are Caesar's' (Matt. 22: 21) or his reply to Pontius Pilate, 'You would have no power against me unless it were given you from above' (John 19: 11). When citing—but only once—Paul's text, 'Let every soul be subject to the governing authorities' (Rom. 13: 1; cf. *Reg.* 1.22, to the clergy and people of Carthage, 15 Sept. 1073, p. 38/9–14), Gregory omitted the sequel: 'there is no authority except from God, and those that exist have been instituted by God'; he made the characteristic, *a fortiori* point that if subjection is owed to temporal authorities, how much more is it owed to spiritual ones: see Arquillière, *Saint Grégoire VII*, pp. 241–2.

36 For the number of saintly popes as understood in Gregory's day, see Jounel, *Le Culte des saints*, esp. pp. 169–81.

37 *Reg.* 8.21, p. 558/21–5. In the Register, no number of saintly kings is given, but the number seven is added in the recipients' versions. The number is unexplained; Jounel, *Le Culte des saints*, provides no evidence for the cult of saintly kings in the 11th-cent. Lateran and Vatican basilicas. Gregory elsewhere referred to the examples set by *christianissimi principes*: *Reg.* 4.28, to the kings and magnates of Spain, 28 June 1077, pp. 346/16–21, 347/5–8.

38 For western estimates of Constantine, see Cowdrey, 'Eleventh-Century Reformers' Views of Constantine'.

39 *Reg.* 8.21, pp. 558/4–560/13.

10.2 The Government of Kings and Princes

It is helpful to consider Gregory's view of the power of kings together with that of dukes and counts who were rulers of major principalities, since he brought to bear similar considerations in all cases. In concert with his thought about the relations of *sacerdotium* and *regnum*, his attitudes to kings and princes underwent development, particularly after 1080. In either case, his concern was less with theoretical formulations than with propagating in lay rulers through his role as preacher after the manner of Pope Gregory the Great what he deemed to be appropriate religious and moral qualities and dispositions.

His letters suggest that he began his pontificate with an approach to kingship that was less radical and distinctive than it later became. He shared in a conventional way many of the expectations about lay rulers that were general amongst his contemporaries, when family stock and lineage were at a premium; although the fact of changes of ruling houses, as in France in 987, Germany in 1024, or England in 1066, had to be accommodated. Ordered descent and succession were part of the bed-rock of human societies. The considerable number of letters of his own dictation that he dispatched to emperors, kings, dukes, and counts in order to convey spiritual, moral, and personal guidance testify to his desire for established rulers themselves to rule effectively in his terms, and to hand on their effective rule to children who shared their blood and governed in their likeness. Chance remarks attest his sense of the inherent worth of royal and aristocratic stock, in accordance with the ancient concept of the *stirps regia*. It was particularly apparent with regard to the Salian house in Germany, although Gregory centred his admiration for it not upon the first Salian emperor, Conrad II, but upon the imperial pair who succeeded him, Henry III and Agnes of Poitou. In 1075, he wrote a pastoral letter to their daughter Judith, who was married to King Solomon of Hungary, extolling the benefits that she had brought to Hungary by reason of her family stock: 'Among a savage and unknown people, you have done honour to the fame of your family (*generis tui gloriam*), because, as one born at the summit of empire, you have so far shown in your deeds and deportment nothing but imperial decorum'; and again, 'So behave, that in all that the royal dignity confers, you will show yourself the more pre-eminent as you remember that such things, which belong to your nature and the imperial seed (*germen*) that is in you, can be changed by no vicissitudes of success or adversity.'[40] A year earlier, Gregory had reminded Judith's brother, Count William VI of Poitou who was also duke of Aquitaine, of the damage to his family stock that would ensue from his remarriage within the prohibited degrees. To renounce such a union safeguarded not only William's salvation but also the excellence of stock ('generositas') that had always marked his line. For the nobility of a family ('nobilitas generis') was debased when offspring were begotten otherwise than in fully lawful marriage. Gregory assured the count that 'the Roman church has always loved you and your house and lineage (*prosapia*) with such singular and outstanding charity that it could not suffer your

---

[40] *Reg.* 2.44, 10 Jan. 1075, pp. 181/8–11, 32/182/3.

remaining in such great danger.'[41] When, in 1079, Gregory wrote to Ladislas I upon his gaining the Hungarian crown, he wrote of his following the best kings by exemplifying both a pattern of righteousness in his way of life and the lineage of nobility in his blood ('lineam nobilitatis in sanguine').[42] In 1080, on the other hand, he urged King Alphonso VI of León–Castile to withdraw from a marriage to a kinswoman of his former queen 'lest you place a stain upon your glory, and lest you render the posterity of your body useless and reprobate' ('ne in gloria tua maculam ponas, ne posteritatem carnis tuae inutilem et reprobam facias').[43]

Gregory was not concerned with ancient lineage as such; he looked primarily to exemplary figures imbued with the aspirations of the reform papacy from whom ruling families might stem. In Germany, he looked to the Emperor Henry III and his empress, Agnes of Poitou, as pre-eminently such figures.[44] In Sweden, the praiseworthy reputation of King Stenkil (1060–6) was to be a pattern for the sons who succeeded him.[45] In Catalonia, he viewed Count Raymond Berengar of Barcelona in a similar light.[46] In England and Denmark, Gregory was at pains to build up Kings William I and Sweyn II Estrithson respectively as models of suitability and as heads of royal families. Gregory eulogized William as a most powerful ruler whose prosperity was in itself a mark of divine favour; Gregory was at pains so to admonish him that he set a standard of righteousness and a pattern of obedience for all kings upon earth.[47] In Denmark, he built up Sweyn Estrithson after his death still more sedulously. As an immaculate model of kingly virtue based upon obedience to the apostolic see, his merits exceeded even those of Henry III of Germany.[48] As for the Capetian line that had ruled France since 987, Gregory singled out no individual king; but he reminded King Philip I, at the low point of his dealings with him, of his illustrious predecessors ('antecessores') whose royal majesty had been vigilant to defend the church and to uphold righteousness; such forebears he should emulate.[49]

Gregory's predilection for royal and family stock and his preparedness to recognize exemplars of Christian rulership in recent or contemporary kings and princes made him anxious to promote the passing on of a kingdom or principality from father to son. Gregory seems to have envisaged the succession of the eldest son, but above all he sought to ensure that whichever son might succeed would rule after the

[41] *Reg.* 2.3, 10 Sept. 1074, p. 127/14–24.

[42] *Reg.* 6.29, 21 Mar. 1079, p. 441/26–31.

[43] *Reg.* 8.3, (27 June 1080), p. 520/4–9.

[44] *Reg.* 2.44, to Queen Judith of Hungary, 10 Jan. 1075, pp. 180/28–181/7; 4.3 to all the faithful in Germany, 3 Sept. 1076, p. 298/22–5; 7.21, to King Harold Hein of Denmark, 19 Apr. 1080, p. 497/26–30.

[45] *Reg.* 9.14, to Kings Inge and Alsten of Sweden, (1081), pp. 593/31–594/2.

[46] *Reg.* 6.16, to Bishop Berengar of Gerona, 2 Jan. 1079, p. 421/28–34.

[47] Especially in the following letters to William: *Reg.* 1.70, 4 Apr. 1074, p. 101/7–29; 4.17, 21 Mar. 1077, p. 323/6–19; 7.23, 24 Apr. 1080, pp. 500/26–501/22; 7.25, 8 May 1080, pp. 505/18–507/5; 9.37, (late 1083), pp. 630–1.

[48] *Reg.* 5.10, to King Harold Hein of Denmark, 6 Nov. 1077, pp. 361/20–362/30; 7.21, to the same, 19 Apr. 1080, pp. 497/21/498/12.

[49] *Reg.* 1.75, to King Philip I, 13 Apr. 1074, pp. 106/34–107/8, 18–24; cf. 2.18, to Count William VI of Poitou, 13 Nov. 1074, p. 151/4–6.

example of a worthy father. Gregory's endeavours to this end were apparent in the peripheral kingdoms of Latin Christendom, and they continued throughout his pontificate. Thus, in England, Gregory in 1080 spoke of King William's prosperous kingship as being granted to himself and to his heirs; he urged William's eldest son Robert Curthose, who had been in prolonged rebellion against his father, henceforth to maintain proper filial obedience. Gregory reminded Robert that his father had valiantly established his kingdom with the intention of leaving it to an heir of his own; Robert should fulfil the biblical command to honour his father and mother so that his days might be long upon earth.[50] In Denmark, Gregory rejoiced that a son of the, in his eyes, exemplary king Sweyn Estrithson, Harold Hein, had succeeded as heir to his kingdom.[51] In 1080, he wrote to Harold with regard to his father that

we desire, urge, and again counsel that you set him before you as an example, so that you may copy and show forth the ornaments of the virtues that you evidently derive from your most noble lineage of blood.[52]

When he had earlier heard that Harold's brothers were seeking to compel Harold to divide the kingdom with them, Gregory wrote to King Olaf III of Norway to prevent any such division: Olaf was to urge Harold to receive his brothers back into Denmark, making adequate provision for them as subordinate members of his family lest the order or honour of the kingdom be infringed. Gregory pointed the need for a similar national kingship in Norway itself.[53] In Sweden, the inheritance of King Stenkil was already divided between his two sons Inge and Halstan; Gregory there sought to promote unity by urging them to maintain mutual concord by following their father's example.[54] In Kievan Russia, Gregory conferred the kingly office upon Jaropulk, son of the reigning prince Isjavlav, with his father's knowledge so that the son might reign in due course.[55] In the county of Barcelona, Gregory sought to reconcile the sons of Count Raymond Berengar who were feuding for the inheritance into such a concord as he recognized in Sweden, or else to secure a juridical decision by Bishop Berengar of Gerona as to which of the two showed appropriate dispositions, so that the son who was worthy might receive undivided his father's inheritance and rulership.[56]

At the outset of his pontificate, Gregory's approach to the kingdoms of Germany and France was similar. In Germany, his genuine goodwill towards the young king Henry IV was prompted, not only by admiration for his parents, the imperial pair Henry III and Agnes of Poitou, but also by a sense of his own personal closeness to the Salian family: in early letters as pope, he said that he loved the Empress Agnes as a mother and her daughter Queen Judith of Hungary as though she were his own

---

[50] *Reg.* 7.23, to King William I, 19 Apr. 1080, p. 501/4–6; 7.27, to Robert Curthose, 8 May 1080, p. 508/19–29.

[51] *Reg.* 5.10, p. 362/6–11.   [52] *Reg.* 7.21, 19 Apr. 1080, p. 497/30–4.

[53] *Reg.* 7.13, 15 Dec. 1078, p. 417/3–21.

[54] *Reg.* 9.14 (1081), pp. 593/16–594/2.

[55] *Reg.* 2.74, to Prince Isjavlav of Russia, 17 Apr. 1075, pp. 236–7.

[56] *Reg.* 6.16, to Bishop Berengar of Gerona, 2 Jan. 1079, pp. 421/27–422/23.

sister; his close association with the Salian court under Henry III began a process of events through which he felt a special reponsibility of tutelage over Henry IV as he grew from childhood towards manhood and a dedication to Christian kingship which, especially in 1075, Gregory believed that he might be brought to manifest.[57] In France, the Capetian king Philip I was much of an age with Henry. In a retrospect made at the end of 1080, Gregory wrote to him in terms of his having spared the king for his youthful faults and of his having sought to bring about his amendment; his language was similar to that which he used of his dealings with Henry IV up to 1075.[58] In the case of both young men, Gregory wished to bring a rightful successor to the throne through the turbulence of youth to the practice of Christian kingship as he himself understood it.

To this extent, Gregory embarked upon his pontificate, and in large degree continued throughout it, with an appraisal of rulership which was based upon family stock, upon models provided by exemplary ancestors, and upon succession passing from father to eldest son. Such an appraisal was widely shared by the kings and princes with whom he dealt; the areas of common, or at least of comparable, ground made Gregory's goodwill and backing of appreciable value to many of them. But, also from the beginning of his pontificate, but to an increasing extent as it developed, Gregory expected kings and princes to satisfy two further criteria which had little to do with dynasty and of which the pope claimed to be himself the judge. They were, first, that a ruler should be serviceable ('utilis'), and second that he should prove himself suitable ('idoneus') in the role to which he was called.[59] These criteria overlapped but were distinguishable. Serviceableness was a matter of practical effectiveness and was to be judged primarily in terms of past performance; suitability turned upon personal and moral qualities, and was to be judged mainly in terms of future expectations. The criteria overlapped because a ruler could be *utilis*, profitable to his subjects by providing strong and effective rule, only on condition that he possessed the blessing of God and St Peter. Such blessing would be forthcoming only if he satisfied the test of suitability by exhibiting personal and moral qualities that were pleasing to God. Suitability was thus the precondition and basis of serviceableness.

Gregory's understanding of the need for a king to be serviceable ('utilis') is apparent from his presentation in his letter of 1081 to Bishop Hermann of Metz of what he regarded as Pope Zacharias's deposition of the last of the Merovingian kings: the

---

57 *Reg.* 2.3, to Count William of Poitou, 10 Sept. 1074, p. 127/24–7; 2.44, to Queen Judith of Hungary, 10 Jan. 1075, p. 181/12–13; 1.19, to Duke Rudolf of Swabia, 1 Sept. 1073, pp. 31/35–32/8; 3.3, to King Henry IV, 20 July 1075, p. 246/15–25; 3.7, to the same, (early Sept. 1075), pp. 254/8–259/6; 3.10, to the same, (8 Dec.) 1075, p. 264/10–29; 4.1, to the faithful in Germany, 25 July 1076, p. 290/12–20; *Epp. vag.* no. 14, to the same, (summer 1076), pp. 34–9.

58 *Reg.* 8.20, 27 Dec. 1080, pp. 542/20–33, 543/15–22; cf. *Epp. vag.* no. 14, as in n. 18.

59 For Gregory's use of the word 'utilis', see Caspar's Index, *Reg.* p. 707. Gregory used the word 'idoneus' less often. He used it of a king in *Reg.* 9.3, to Bishop Altmann of Passau and Abbot William of Hirsau, (Mar. 1081), pp. 574/29–575/6, as the opposite of a king who was 'indignus' in respect of 'mores et cetera, quae regi oportet inesse'. *Idoneus* was normally used of practical competence in bishops, legates, and messengers, e.g. *Reg.* pp. 191/33, 299/5, 337/12, 340/15, 370/14, 18, 375/20, 463/4, 530/24.

pope deposed the *rex Francorum* not so much for his iniquities as because he was not
practically effective in such a public office ('non tam pro suis iniquitatibus quam pro
eo, quod tantae potestati non erat utilis').[60] Conversely, in 1077, Gregory admonished the Danish king, Harold Hein, that he must oversee the kingdom divinely
entrusted to him with proper competence: 'with all zeal, skill, and expertise' ('omni
industria sollertia peritiaque').[61] A year later, Gregory sought to ward off a division
of the Danish kingdom on the grounds that a divided kingdom was ineffective in protecting churches, warding off pagan assaults from without, and upholding order and
well-being within.[62]

What Gregory expected of kings by way of serviceableness, at least during the
1070s, may be summarized quite simply on the basis of his reiterated admonitions to
kings and rulers. First, they must love religion; second, they must assist according to
their station in seeing that bishops were duly elected and thereafter competent in the
discharge of their pastoral duties; third, they must increase and defend the goods of
the church; fourth, they must have good counsellors; fifth, they should provide good
peace and justice for all their subjects; and sixth, they should have an especial care for
the unprotected, especially the clergy, widows and orphans, and the poor.[63] Gregory
especially insisted upon the discharge of the last two of these functions; he looked to
rulers to reinforce their lands and governments by a bond of inviolable peace
('fortissimae pacis foedere').[64] The insistence of Gregory's demand for strong and
effective rulership in terms of his own criteria should not be underestimated.

Such a demand played a leading part in adverse judgements that he passed upon
rulers in France and Germany. In 1074, his wrath against King Philip I of France was
in part directed against scandals and outrages which he had individually perpetrated
—Gregory was incensed by his greed in despoiling merchants from Italy. But it was
much more strongly occasioned by Gregory's conviction that Philip was ruling, by
his criteria, *inutiliter*. Law and justice had collapsed in France, which, owing partly to
the king's own acts of violence and partly to those that his subjects perpetrated by
way of imitation, had lapsed into a devastating warfare of all against all. There was no
protection for the vulnerable, and the violence threatened to overflow beyond the
country's borders. To the ecclesiastical and to trusted lay princes in France, Gregory

---

[60] *Reg.* 8.21, p. 554/3–5.   [61] *Reg.* 5.10, 6 Nov. 1077, p. 362/31–2.

[62] *Reg.* 6.13 to King Olaf III of Norway, 15 Dec. 1078, p. 417/3–21.

[63] Gregory's advice as regards kings and rulers which bears mainly upon their serviceableness occurs
in *Reg.* 1.20, to Bishop Raynald of Como, 1 Sept. 1073, pp. 33/35–34/4; 1.37, to Countess Adelaide of
Turin, 7 Dec. 1073, p. 59/8–11; 1.50, to Countesses Beatrice and Matilda of Tuscany, 4 Mar. 1074, pp.
76/29–77/11; 1.70, to King William I of England, 4 Apr. 1074, p. 101/19–21; 2.18, to Count William VI
of Poitou, 13 Nov. 1074, p. 151/1–8; 2.30, to King Henry IV of Germany, 1 Dec. 1074, p. 164/17–26; 5.10,
to King Harold Hein of Denmark, 6 Nov. 1077, p. 362/31–8; 5.19, to King William I of England, 4 Apr.
1078, pp. 382–3; 6.20, to Count Centullus of Béarn, 25 Nov. 1079, p. 432/1–4; 7.21, to King Harold Hein
of Denmark, 19 Apr. 1080, p. 498/8–38; 7.26, to Queen Matilda of England, 8 May 1080, p. 507/24–7;
8.11, to King Inge of Sweden, 4 Oct. 1080, p. 530/28–31; 8.20, to King Philip I of France, 27 Dec. 1080,
p. 542/27–33; 8.22, to Queen Adelaide of Hungary, (1081), p. 565/12–20; 9.14, to Kings Inge and Halsten
of Sweden, (1081), p. 593/22–7.

[64] *Reg.* 2.71, to Duke Wratislav II of Bohemia, 17 Apr. 1074, pp. 231/30–232/2.

outlined a sequence of sanctions which, if they did not succeed in recalling the king to his ruling functions, would culminate in the pope's exercise of his duty to wrest the kingdom from Philip's possession by all means ('modis omnibus regnum Franciae de eius occupatione adiuvante Deo temptemus eripere'). Again, he would excommunicate Philip in a Roman synod, and would inhibit ('sequestrabimus') both the king and all who showed him honour or obedience.[65] Almost certainly having in mind his interpretation of the papal deposition of Childeric in 751, Gregory already went far towards anticipating the papal power over a king who had ceased to be *utilis* which he claimed over Henry IV of Germany in 1081:

Another Roman pope [Zacharias] deposed a king of the Franks less for his iniquities than because he was not useful ('utilis') in such a public office. He substituted Pippin, father of the Emperor Charlemagne, in his place and released all the race of the Franks from the oath of fealty which they had made to him.[66]

In the sequel to his Lent synod of 1078, Gregory began to add a similar allegation of unserviceableness to his charges against Henry IV of Germany. In 1076, he had deposed and excommunicated him, whatever other reasons may have been in the background, exclusively for the moral reason of his unheard-of pride.[67] In his sentence of 1080, he made only an initial reference to Henry's pride. He grounded what was now his principal accusation, that of disobedience which is as the sin of idolatry, in a train of events since 1078 for which Henry was responsible and which gave rise to such national bloodshed and anarchy as he had represented in 1074 as evidence for Philip I's unserviceability.[68] At first sight, Gregory's accusation of unserviceability against Henry is paradoxical; for, at Canossa, Gregory had expressly restored Henry to communion but not to his royal authority and power to govern;[69] how could a king without power to govern be deemed to govern unprofitably? But, as Gregory saw matters, since his Lent synod of 1078 the duty of relieving the *lis et pertubatio* of Germany had devolved upon himself as pope. A main purpose of the national assembly that he planned was to put an end by his own authority to strife and to create peace and concord.[70] In 1080, Gregory contended that, by hindering a national assembly, Henry, not fearing the sin of disobedience, had both already brought renewed excommunication upon himself and had incurred responsibility for the horrors of warfare in Germany—for the death of a great multitude of Christians, for the destruction of churches, and for almost the whole German kingdom being consigned to desolation.[71] No less than Philip I in 1074, Henry by 1080 had forfeited his claim to utility

---

[65] *Reg.* 2.5, to the archbishops and bishops of France, 10 Sept. 1074, pp. 129–33; 2.18, to Count William VI of Poitou, 13 Nov. 1074, pp. 150–1; cf. 1.75, to King Philip I, 13 Apr. 1074, pp. 106–7; 8.20, to the same, 27 Dec. 1080, pp. 542–3.

[66] *Reg.* 8.21, to Bishop Hermann of Metz, 15 Mar. 1081, p. 554/3–8.

[67] *Reg.* 3.10a, record of the Lent synod 1076, p. 270/15–21.

[68] *Reg.* 7.14a, record of the Lent synod 1080, p. 486/4–10.

[69] *Reg.* 7.14a, p. 484/10–15.

[70] *Reg.* 5.15a, record of the Lent synod 1078, pp. 370–1; cf. 5.15–16, to all the faithful in Germany, and to Archbishop Udo of Trier, 9 Mar. 1078, pp. 374–8.

[71] *Reg.* 7.14a, p. 486/4–10.

as Gregory understood it. In Gregory's subsequent comments upon him, this reason for his repudiation as king was emphasized:

If Henry, the so-called king, and his party had preserved the obedience that he had promised to us or rather to St Peter, I confidently declare that, with God's help, so many evils—homicides, perjuries, sacrileges, pestilences of the simoniac heresy, betrayals—would not have happened.[72]

Princes who were morally virtuous and otherwise praiseworthy were also open to Gregory's censure on grounds of failure to be properly serviceable to their subjects in terms of Gregory's criteria of usefulness. This might occur in connection with a wish to enter the monastic life. Gregory was insistent that they had an overriding duty, rooted in charity, to provide peace and protection for their subjects. In 1074, he restrained Countess Matilda of Tuscany and her mother from the thought of entering a nunnery, arguing that true charity placed helping the wretched and oppressed before all prayers, fasts, and vigils. Only if there were another person to whom her responsibilities might safely be entrusted could Gregory advise Matilda to leave the world and its cares.[73] Similarly, in 1079, when Gregory learned that Abbot Hugh of Cluny had admitted to the cloister Duke Hugh I of Burgundy leaving no provision for its future order, he depicted the duchy as suffering from a ruler who had defaulted in his obligation of serviceability to his subjects: a hundred thousand Christians lacked a protector.[74] The abbot and the duke shared responsibility for a high-minded lapse of princely utility which had consequences that were potentially as damaging within the duchy of Burgundy as the most sinful lapses of the kings of France and Germany were within their kingdoms.

With the demand that rulers be practically serviceable, Gregory combined the further demand that they be morally suitable. In 1077, he set forth to the kings and princes of Spain his reasons for being concerned as pope with rulers' inner dispositions. The apostolic see was 'the prince and the universal mother of all churches and peoples'; it must, therefore, issue salutary admonitions not only to defend the truth of the catholic faith but also to secure the knowledge and implementation of righteousness ('iustitia'). The instruction of lay rulers was thus at the heart of a pope's sense of mission, in accordance with St Paul's declaration that 'a necessity of preaching the gospel is laid upon me; woe is me if I do not preach the gospel' (1 Cor. 9: 16). Again, he declared in 1081 that

Because it belongs to our office to issue admonitions to everyone according to the order and dignity in which he seems to stand, we are concerned on God's behalf to provide for emperors and kings as well as other princes the weapons of humility so that they can suppress the swelling of the sea and the billows of pride. For we know that worldly glory and secular concerns are accustomed most readily to draw those who rule into the swelling up ('ad elationem')

---

[72] *Reg.* 8.21, pp. 547/20–1, 550/19–571/8; 9.29, to all the faithful, summer 1083, pp. 612/27–36, 613/15–19.

[73] *Reg.* 1.50, to Countesses Beatrice and Matilda of Tuscany, 4 Mar. 1074, pp. 76/27–77/11.

[74] *Reg.* 7.17, to Abbot Hugh of Cluny, 2 Jan. 1079, pp. 423/23–424/20.

through which they always neglect humility and seek their own glory, and as a consequence try to stand superior to their brothers.[75]

The sense of such a duty to admonish accounts for Gregory's early concern for the youthful rulers Henry IV of Germany and Philip I of France, whom he sought to guide through the waywardness of youth to his conception of mature Christian kingship and, in Henry's case, to the imperial dignity.[76] Still more, it underlay his set-piece instructions to rulers all round Europe in the qualities which, rooted in the doctrines of the Christian religion, were the proper basis upon which they should stand.[77] Two virtues above all were held out to kings as essential for right ruling—humility and obedience. The example of King Saul in the Old Testament, as expounded by Pope Gregory the Great, pointed up the close relation between the sins of pride and disobedience, and between the virtues of humility and obedience.[78] It was in respect of these vices and virtues that Henry IV primarily stood condemned in 1076 and 1080, for, as Gregory proclaimed on the second occasion, it was according to their moral deserts ('pro meritis') that all earthly rulers, from emperors and kings to the pettiest of local lords, must expect the princes of the apostles to withhold or confer their dominion upon earth just as they were empowered to bind and loose in heaven.[79] The primacy of Gregory's moral concern when admonishing rulers was further confirmed by his underlying spiritual message to them, that they should so pass through this world that they did not finally lose things eternal.

After Gregory's excommunication and deposition of Henry in 1080, his thought about the moral suitability of kings underwent a marked development in relation to the kingly office in Germany. There though not elsewhere he placed an exclusive emphasis upon it which led to a virtual elimination of concern for family stock and for an inheritance descending from father to son. Instead, he concentrated upon the necessity for an elective kingship based chiefly upon considerations of personal

[75] *Reg.* 4.28, to the kings and princes of Spain, 28 June 1077, pp. 343/25–344/12; 8.21, to Bishop Hermann of Metz, 15 Mar. 1081, p. 558/5–10.

[76] Henry IV: *Reg.* 1.9, to Duke Godfrey of Lorraine, 6 May 1073, pp. 14/34–15/7; 1.11, to Countesses Beatrice and Matilda of Tuscany, 24 June 1073, p. 19/5–10; *Epp. vag.* no. 14, to all the faithful in Germany, (summer 1076), pp. 34–5. Philip I: *Reg.* 1.75, to the king, 13 Apr. 1074, pp. 106–7; 8.20, to the same, 27 Dec. 1080, p. 542/14–33.

[77] For Gregory's most intensive campaign of instruction, see his letters of 17–20 Apr. 1075 addressed to rulers and people of Hungary, Bohemia, Poland, Russia, and Denmark: *Reg.* 2.70–5, pp. 229–38; see above, 6.1. Amongst Gregory's other letters, the following are particularly noteworthy. Spain *Reg.* 4.28, to the kings and princes of Spain, 28 July 1077, pp. 343–7; 7.6, to King Alphonso VI of León–Castile, 15 Oct. 1079, pp. 465–7; *Epp. vag.* no. 65, to King Sancho Ramírez of Aragon, (1076–85), pp. 146–9. Scandinavia: *Reg.* 2.51, to King Sweyn Estrithson, 25 Jan. 1075, pp. 192–4; 6.13, to King Olaf III of Norway, 15 Dec. 1078, pp. 415–18; 7.5, to King Harold Hein of Denmark, 15 Oct. 1079, pp. 464–5; 7.21, to the same, 19 Apr. 1080, pp. 497–8. Bohemia: 7.11, to Duke Wratislav II, 2 Jan. 1080, pp. 473–5. England: 7.23, to King William I, 24 Apr. 1080, pp. 499–502; 7.25, to the same, 8 May 1080, pp. 505–7. Ireland: *Epp. vag.* no. 57, to Toirdhealbhach Ó Briain, king of Munster, (1074/84), pp. 138–41.

[78] *Reg.* 3.10, to King Henry IV of Germany, (8 Dec.) 1075, p. 267/17–24; 8.21, to Bishop Hermann of Metz, 15 Mar. 1081, p. 561/1–25.

[79] *Reg.* 3.10a, record of the Lent synod of 1076, p. 270/19–20, 25/271/3; 7.14a, record of the Lent synod of 1080, pp. 484/7–8, 486/4–6, 27/487/13.

suitability, but reinforced by those of functional usefulness, since the second flowed from the first. The change of view was adumbrated in 1080 in relation to Spain, during the transient but acute crisis in which he momentarily contemplated severe measures against King Alphonso VI of León–Castile. He warned the king that he should obey papal demands with regard to a canonically objectionable marriage, lest both he and his posterity should forfeit their royal authority and innate power to rule ('ne te ipsum despicias, ne in gloria tua maculam ponas, ne posteritatem carnis tuae inutilem et reprobam facias').[80] Nevertheless, for the rest of his pontificate Gregory showed no change of ideas in relation to monarchies other than the German: in Spain, he quickly renewed his approval of Alphonso VI's rule in recognition of his *humilitas* in obeying papal wishes about the Roman rite and sought an accommodation in respect of the king's marriage; the effectiveness of King William I's rule in England led Gregory to be tolerant of his recalcitrance in some major matters; and he wrote to the kings of Sweden in his usual way about the duties and the family solidarity appropriate for kingship.[81]

His sponsoring of elective kingship in Germany was gradually forced upon him by events: he later insisted that the election of Rudolf of Swabia in 1077 had taken place neither by his advice nor at his command.[82] The test of righteousness had seemed to vindicate Rudolf in 1080, but it had been quickly followed by the trauma of his death in battle. Gregory was presented with the necessity of declaring upon what basis a new king should succeed. In the spring of 1081, he wrote to his leading supporters in Germany, Bishop Altmann of Passau and Abbot William of Hirsau, about what must be done if pressure to recognize Henry IV was to be resisted. The succession should be by way of election and upon the basis of moral suitability: whatever time might be necessary should be devoted to finding a candidate who was not 'indignus' but 'ad honorem sanctae ecclesiae rex . . . idoneus'. The choice should be of a king who would be to the church as a defender and protector ('defensorem et rectorem'); it should reject anyone who did not satisfy the demands of suitability, together with those of usefulness—who was not 'ita oboediens et sanctae ecclesiae humilis et utilis, quemadmodum christianum regem oportet et sicut de R[odulfo] speravimus'). Gregory sent from Rome a pattern oath for the new king to take to St Peter and the reigning pope, which laid emphasis upon these qualities.[83]

In the most widely influential of his writings, his letter of 1081 to Bishop Hermann of Metz, Gregory circulated in Germany and elsewhere his justification not only for his renewed sentence against Henry IV but also for his novel requirement that German kingship should be elective. In effect, he transferred to the royal office in Germany the view of succession that he appears always to have held in respect of the

---

[80] *Reg.* 8.3, 27 June 1080, p. 520/4–9; see above 6.11.
[81] Spain *Reg.* 9.2, to King Alphonso, (1081), pp. 570/26–571/4. England: 9.5, to his legates Bishops Hugh of Die and Amatus of Oloron, (1081), pp. 579/27–580/19; 9.37, to King William I, (late 1083), pp. 630–1. Sweden: 9.14, to Kings Inge and Halstan, (1081), pp. 592–4.
[82] *Reg.* 7.14a, p. 484/21–4, 9.29, to all the faithful, (summer 1083), p. 613/6–13.
[83] *Reg.* 9.3, pp. 574/29–576/19.

imperial dignity.[84] Henceforth, just as the pope was the judge of the suitability of a future emperor and of his readiness to enter upon his high office, so it was to be with the German king: it was holy church that called a person alike to rulership, that is, kingship, and to the imperial office; it did so of its own will and mature counsel, and the corollary was a king's duty of humble obedience ('. . . quos sancta ecclesia sua sponte ad regimen vel imperium deliberato consilio advocat non pro transitoria gloria, sed pro multorum salute, humiliter obaediant . . .').[85]

Gregory's argument about kingship in the latter part of his letter proposed a moralization of it which is startling in its implications and in its novelty.[86] Its background is Gregory's concern with the problems of penitence that is manifest between his Roman synods of 1078 and 1080.[87] In those years, Gregory had considered the penance of warriors, merchants, and lay officials whose avocations could not be pursued without sin—hatred, deceit, falsehood, envy, or deception. In 1081, he turned similarly to consider kings, who seldom ruled without falling foul of worldly glory, secular advantage, and elation of soul. Up to 1080, he had called upon lesser men to make full restitution of goods wrongly seized and, in 1080, to turn wholly to God and do penance for all their sins. In 1081, he called upon kings to show similarly thoroughgoing repentance accompanied by restitution:

If the judgement of holy church strongly binds a sinner who slays just one man, how shall it be with those who, for the honour of this world, deliver to death many thousands? And although such men sometimes say with their lips 'Mea culpa' for the killing of many, in their heart they nevertheless rejoice for the increase of their supposed honour, and they do not wish they had not done what they have done; nor do they grieve that they have driven their brothers to hell. When they do not repent with their whole heart and when they are not willing to abandon what they have acquired or defended at the cost of human blood, in God's eyes their penance remains devoid of the fruit of due repentance.[88]

Gregory was demanding specifically of kings and princes the deep and complete repentance of which he had spoken more generally in 1080. As he had then advised those who aspired to true penitence to have recourse to religious men—clergy and monks who were true guides to salvation, so in 1081 princes 'were not to walk in the counsel of the ungodly (cf. Ps. 1: 1), but they should cleave to religious men with ever-obedient heart'. They should strive to honour holy church as was fitting by especially recognizing its eyes, that is the priests of the Lord, as their masters and fathers.[89]

---

[84] For Gregory's view of the imperial office, see below, 10.4.

[85] *Reg.* 8.21, p. 561/14–17. The word *regimen* takes up the citation from Pope Gregory I's *Reg. past.*: p. 560/19.

[86] The relevant section of the letter is pp. 558/5–562/11.

[87] *Reg.* 7.14*a*(5), record of the Lent synod 1080, pp. 481–2; cf. 6.5*b*(6), record of the Nov. synod 1078, p. 404; 7.10, to the bishops and magnates of Brittany, 25 Nov. 1079, p. 472/1–15.

[88] *Reg.* 8.21, p. 559/19–28. If this argument were pressed, the Normans of South Italy and England, for example, should have been willing to abandon their conquests; but Gregory used very different language when writing about their affairs: see esp. *Reg.* 7.23, to King William I, 24 Apr. 1080, pp. 499–502; 7.27, to Robert Curthose, 8 May 1080, p. 508; 9.4, to Abbot Desiderius of Montecassino, (Feb. 1081), p. 578/11–26.

[89] *Reg.* 8.21, p. 562/1–7.

Gregory drew towards the conclusion of his letter to the bishop of Metz by turning to the *Regula pastoralis* of his mentor Pope Gregory the Great.[90] He pointed the need for all Christians who would reign with Christ to rise superior to all ambition for secular power: whoever came to a ruler's office ('ad regimen') should do so only under compulsion and fortified with virtues ('virtutibus pollens'); a man devoid of virtues should not succeed, even under compulsion.[91] Like Christ himself, no man should seek his own transitory glory (John 8: 50, Mark 10: 44), but, following the call of the church, he should rule with humble obedience.[92] He concluded by challenging the practice of the Salian house in Germany, whereby a father designated his newborn eldest son for the kingship during his own lifetime; Henry III had done this, not without the complicity of the young Hildebrand, in the case of Henry IV,[93] while Henry IV had followed suit at Christmastide 1075 with his own infant son Conrad.[94] Now, despite all that he had written in the past, Gregory castigated the practice as inappropriate and irreligious; only by facilitating the free election of whoever was most virtuous and therefore most serviceable could rulers hope to fulfil their Christian duty and therefore aspire themselves in the end to rise from the low estate of an earthly kingdom to the eternal kingdom in heaven:

Let them not be allured by love of their own flesh to contrive the setting of a son of their own over the flock for which Christ shed his blood, if they can find someone better and more serviceable than him ('si meliorem illo et utiliorem possunt invenire'); lest by loving their own son more than God they inflict enormous damage on holy church. For he is manifestly convicted of not loving God and his neighbour as a Christian should, who fails to provide to the best of his ability for so great an interest and for something so essential for holy mother church ('qui tantae utilitati tamque necessariae sanctae matri ecclesiae, prout melius potest, negligit providere'). For if this virtue, I mean charity, is neglected, whatever good a man does will be devoid of all the fruits of salvation. Therefore, by humbly doing the things that they should do and by upholding the love of God and their neighbour as it behoves, they may trust in the mercy of him who said, 'Learn of me, for I am meek and humble in heart' (Matt. 11: 29). If they have humbly imitated him, they will pass from a servile and transient kingdom to a kingdom of true liberty and of eternity.[95]

To such lengths the vicissitudes of the German kingdom after 1078 brought Gregory when they impelled him in its case to explore the moralization of earthly avocation and office in the light of his concern for the prevailing system of penance. Between his Roman synods of November 1078 and Lent 1080, he had mainly in view warriors, merchants, and officials; now, his attention was drawn to the German king. Like his mentor Pope Gregory the Great, the heart of his thought concerned not theology, or law, or political thought, but morality—not as a matter of theory, but as applied to the

---

90 See Brown, *The Rise of Western Christendom*, pp. 137–44, 161.
91 *Reg.* 8.21, pp., 560/14–561/1, citing Gregory I, *Reg. past.* 1.9, vol. 1.160/37–9.
92 *Reg.* 8.21, pp. 561/14–562/1.
93 Hermann of Reichenau, *Chron. aa.* 1051, 1053, pp. 692/22–4, 704/23–5; *Ann. Wirziburg. a.* 1056, p. 31; *Reg.* 1.19, to Duke Rudolf of Swabia, 1 Sept. 1073, pp. 31/35–32/10.
94 Lampert of Hersfeld, *Ann. a.* 1076, pp. 340–3; Bernold, *Chron. a.* 1076, p. 431/13–14.
95 *Reg.* 8.21, p. 562/11–25.

lives of his fellow-men. There were no limits to where it might lead him in his demands for what was suitable and useful.

10.3 The *Regna* of Europe

Thus far, attention has been concentrated upon Gregory's attitude to the persons of kings and princes. But he was also in some measure responsible for changes in how his contemporaries thought and felt about the nature and identity of the kingdoms of Europe when viewed as human associations which interacted corporately with the papacy and with each other.

Most signally, these changes are apparent in Germany, where the phrase *regnum Teutonicum* (or *Teutonicorum*) became widely current from the middle decades of the eleventh century.[96] It was by no means universally adopted. Paradoxical as this may seem at first glance, the concept of a *regnum Teutonicum* became established in circles that were at a distance from the German king, Henry IV. In his own forty-two surviving letters, there is no mention of it before 1105; in his diplomas, of which there are nearly 500, it does not occur at all.[97] His master propagandist, Gotteschalk of Aachen, made no use of it, and Henrician writers in general used it sparingly. Henrician circles kept within the familiar concepts of Ottonian and early Salian rulership. A supranational idea of empire checked the development of 'nationalist' approaches. Of especial significance were, first, the persistence of a personal and functional idea of the ruler, which embraced his whole authority over the many lands that he ruled; second, the lack, until the twelfth century, of a clear distinction between the concepts of *regnum* and *imperium*, as respectively national and supranational; and, third, the legacy of the notion of the king as *vicarius Christi*, which defined his authority in relation to God rather than to a human entity such as his *gens*. Thus, for example, Henry IV's letters usually referred to the *rex* and his *regnum*, without the addition of any adjective or noun in the genitive case. In his day, Salian kingship provided little basis for a *regnum Teutonicum*, however defined—whether personally, institutionally, territorially, or ethnically.

Until *c*.1075, it was not to the north of the Alps that the phrase *regnum Teutonicum* began to be significantly current. This first took place in parts of the Italian peninsula—the south and Venice—that were adjacent to the Byzantine world. Thence it spread, from *c*.1056, to Imperial Italy. In Italian usage, it marked Italy off from the other world beyond the Alps. There, it first began to appear at all regularly in the annals of the Bavarian abbey of Niederaltaich, which were written down *c*.1075. In them, it was used quite commonly in connection with events after 1028. The king himself was usually either *rex* or *imperator* without addition, but he and the princes together constituted a *regnum* or *Reich*. The *regnum Teutonicum* was essentially

[96] The indispensable monograph is Müller-Mertens, *Regnum Teutonicum*, to which this and the next sections are deeply indebted, even though I differ from Müller-Mertens's conclusions with regard to the imperial title and idea.
[97] *Epp. HIV* no. 34, p. 108/22 ('in Teutonico regno'); *MGH DDHIV*.

a political and administrative entity; the phrase had little territorial significance.[98] In so far as it caught on in Germany, it did so in anti-Henrician circles. The outstanding witness is the *Annales* of the monk Lampert of Hersfeld, completed *c*.1077/8. He had a deep and eloquent pride in the 'auctoritas et arma Teutonici regni'. His concept of the *regnum* was rich and complex. If it could stand for the king's personal authority, it was more often an impersonal, institutional reality, superior to the king, which he and the princes should together uphold. Lampert was indebted to the classical idea of a *res publica*; for him, the young Henry IV's ways of using his royal power through a selfish aggregation of lands, castles, and *ministeriales* were a derogation of it as a sum of public rights and interests, and an affront to the princes. His conception of a *regnum Teutonicum* also implied a circumscribed locality; it stood over against such territorial regions as Italy, Poland, Hungary, or Bohemia. As the bitter enemy of the king and as the advocate of the princes who opposed him, Lampert was the exponent of a German and national concept of a *regnum Teutonicum*, as well as of a highly centralized national consciousness.

Simultaneously with the formation in Germany of the notion of a *regnum Teutonicum*, Gregory VII, too, as the opponent of Henry IV, did much to propagate this concept. He had grown up in an Italy where the term had been slowly disseminated before it became widely current north of the Alps. As pope, he came to use *regnum Teutonicum/Teutonicorum* as his standard form of address to a German public; for example, a widely circulated letter of summer 1076 began: 'Gregory, bishop, servant of the servants of God, to all bishops, dukes, counts, and other faithful men *in regno Theutonicorum* who are defending the Christian religion, greeting and apostolic blessing.'[99]

Between his accession to the papacy and his first breach with Henry IV three years later, Gregory's views had already begun to undergo a transformation. Through his dealings with the Salian royal family, he began by falling in with the imperial and hegemonial character of German rulership according to the Ottonian and Salian tradition. But during 1074, in circumstances in which he deemed it necessary to vindicate the claims of the apostolic see, he began to refer to Henry as *rex Teutonicorum*, when, in a letter to King Solomon of Hungary, he rebuked the latter for having received his kingdom as a fief ('in beneficium') from the German king. Gregory claimed that the *regnum Ungariae* had been commended by its first king, Stephen, to the Roman church; as kings, Henry and Solomon were equal in their possession of the royal title and of the independence that went with it.[100] The series of letters that Gregory wrote in April 1075 to the most important lands to Germany's east and north showed a similar concern for the consolidation of rulers' power over their *regna* or *terrae*.[101] No less significant was Gregory's treatment of the German church. His dispatch in 1074 of the legates Gerald of Ostia and Hubert of Palestrina in pursuit of

---

98 *Ann. Altah. maior.*   99 *Epp. vag.* no. 14, pp. 32–3.
100 *Reg.* 2.13, to King Solomon of Hungary, 28 Oct. 1074, p. 145/2–14; cf. 2.70, to Duke Gésa of Hungary, 17 Apr. 1075, p. 230/5–17.
101 *Reg.* 2.70–5, to Hungary, Bohemia, Poland, Kievan Russia, and Denmark.

his plan for a national synod of the German church showed his intention of treating Germany as a single entity and as having a specifically German church under Roman oversight. It was eloquent of this intention that, in March 1075, he referred to Cologne's special place in papal favour 'inter caeteras regni Teutonici ecclesias'.[102] Even before his first breach with Henry IV, Gregory was already defining the *regnum Teutonicum/Teutonicorum* negatively over against other *regna* like Hungary, and positively by correlation with the overall German ecclesiastical structure.

After 1076, Gregory treated the German ruler, whether a restored Henry or whether a rival like Rudolf of Swabia or Hermann of Salm, simply as ruler of a *regnum Teutonicum*. He no longer made references to the prospect of imperial coronation at Rome. Nor did he refer to the kingdoms of Italy and Burgundy, while he regarded Hungary, Poland, and Bohemia as separate entities. In his energetic propaganda Gregory naturalized the concept of a *regnum Teutonicum* among his German followers. The chroniclers indicate his importance in doing so. In Berthold of Reichenau, the phrases 'regnum Teutonicorum', 'Teutonicae partes', and 'partes nostrae' were frequently used when the annalist was recording the impact of Gregory upon the German church and kingdom. Bernold of St Blasien used such concepts sparingly in his earlier annals, but from *c*.1083, when Gregorian propaganda had had time to make its mark, he used them more often. An important part of Gregory's impact upon Germany was thus to assist with the formation and dissemination of the notion of a *regnum Teutonicum*.[103]

To the west, Gregory followed a similar line of thinking with regard to France, both in its relation to Germany and as a kingdom in its own right. Almost certainly with deliberate intent, Gregory in his letters never used the term *Germania* to designate lands to the east of the River Rhine over against those to its west which constituted *Gallia*.[104] He used his phrase *regnum Teutonicorum* of Salian dominions on both banks of the Rhine, including the whole of Lorraine; he reserved the word *Gallia* and its derivatives for lands under the suzerainty of the Capetian king. Thus, France was the *regnum Franciae*, or the *regnum Francorum*; Philip I, *rex Francorum*,

---

[102] *Reg.* 2.67, to Archbishop Anno of Cologne, 29 Mar. 1075, p. 223/16–20.

[103] Müller-Mertens's overall conclusion is that 'In the struggles between the kingdom and empire and the papacy, and between royal centralization and princely regionalism, the church and princes of the *Reich* entered upon a new relationship with the papacy, while the *Reich* itself received a new order and the state a new form. The origins of these developments are to be found in the revolutionary events of 1073–7, which marked the beginning of the Investiture Context and the revolt of the princes, and which called into fundamental question the hitherto prevailing order of church and state. It was these events which led to the emergence in German historical writing of the concept of a *regnum Teutonicum*. This did not arise from within the existing order. The concept of a German *Reich* was introduced from Rome through the reform papacy of Gregory VII and disseminated in the Gregorian and anti-Henrician camp. Simultaneously it also emerged in Germany in reaction against Henry IV's new policies of the rehabilitation of royal power': *Regnum Teutonicum*, p. 327; for an analysis of vocabulary in the sources, see pp. 145–302. It is an irony of the history of the period that the sole surviving manuscript of Tacitus's *Germania* lay unread in Lampert's abbey of Hersfeld, and so did not colour contemporary terminology.

[104] When writing to an Italian layman, Gregory once referred to Henry IV as 'rex Alamanniae': *Reg.* 3.15, to the Milanese knight Wifred, (Apr.) 1076, p. 277/5.

was the oppressor of French churches ('Gallicanae ecclesiae').[105] Just as in Germany the bishops and lay magnates were to attend to the welfare of the *regnum Teutonicorum*, so in France, in September 1074, Gregory charged the bishops of *Francia* to apply pressure to the king by holding a national council (his plans for the German church in 1074 should be borne in mind); the ultimate sanction against King Philip was that Gregory would seek by all means to wrest the *regnum Franciae* from his possession.[106] Two months later, Count William of Poitou was to associate himself with the *nobiliores Franciae*.[107] Medieval France and medieval Germany were to develop among different lines, and Gregory made no such decisive contribution to French collective self-awareness as his concept of a *regnum Teutonicorum* made to German. But in his letters, the *regnum Teutonicorum* and the *regnum Franciae* were political entities of comparable standing. They were juxtaposed with a new sharpness of distinction, and their boundaries were those of the suzerainty of their kings.

Gregory undoubtedly invested the concept of a kingdom ('regnum') with fresh significance when, especially in the years 1074 and 1075, he thus designated Germany a *regnum Teutonicorum* which stood alongside the established *regnum Franciae* to the west and over against the emerging *regna* or *terrae* to the east and north. Gregory in this way made a critical contribution to the process whereby the kingdoms and peoples of Europe found and established their identities. It is thus necessary to guard against too negative an interpretation of Gregory's concept of the *regnum*, in terms of a doctrinal *Augustinisme politique* that accorded it significance only when viewed in straight dependence upon the *sacerdotium*. According to such a view, Gregory's evaluation of the *regnum* tended towards the high-medieval interpretation of the two swords of Luke 22: 38, that 'kingship is of its essence ecclesiastical and spiritual. In its origin and end, if not in its means, it belongs virtually to the pope as recipient of the plenitude of spiritual power.'[108] While there is some truth in this view, it is doubtful whether it depicts the avenue by which Gregory's concept of the *regnum* is best approached. In the critical case of the *regnum Teutonicorum*, Gregory set out, not from politico-theological propositions, but from current Italian usage whereby the kingdom to the north of the Alps was *de facto* so described. From October 1074, he deliberately projected this designation upon Germany. He did so without intrinsic theological overtones, to designate a German *regnum* which was upheld by the bishops, dukes, counts, and other faithful men, but, if he were obedient, by the king above all. In this sense, the *regnum* was confirmed as an entity in its own right. Moreover, it was not exclusively a lay and secular entity; ecclesiastical and lay magnates were integrated in a single society in which bishops owed a rightful loyalty to a worthy king as well as to the pope. There was room for bishops to depend upon the king for their *regalia*, and there was a potential that was larger than Gregory

---

[105] *Reg.* 1.35, to Bishop Roclin of Chalon-sur-Saône, 4 Dec. 1073, p. 56/17–23, cf. p. 57/9–13, where Gregory threatened the *Franci* with a general anathema if they failed to dissociate themselves from the king's simony.

[106] *Reg.* 2.5, to all the bishops of France, 10 Sept. 1074, pp. 130/2–9, 132/25–41.

[107] *Reg.* 2.18, 13 Nov. 1074, pp. 150–1.   [108] See esp. Arquillière, *Saint Grégoire VII*, pp. 285–8.

perhaps appreciated for ecclesiastical and lay princes to become associated as a single princely class in the structure of the kingdom.

But in guarding against a too negative interpretation of Gregory's view of the *regnum*, it is necessary to avoid the opposite extreme of asserting too much. Gregory's ways of thinking remained within the older view of what German historians have called a *Personenverbandstaat*—a hierarchical structure of interlocking personal rather than institutional loyalties in which bonds of homage and fealty, rather than land and judicial arrangements, were critical in holding society together. Only indirectly did he prepare the way for the centralized, administrative states of the twelfth century,[109] or even for the position reached by the end of the Investiture Contest, whereby, in the Concordat of Worms (1122) a sharp distinction between *imperium* and *regnum* made possible the idea of a single empire with the three constituent kingdoms of Germany, Italy, and Burgundy.[110] The *regnum* as Gregory conceived it was not a closed institutional entity, but a structure of persons in which the pope not only made rightful demands upon the king for obedience and humility, but might also directly seek the fidelity and service to St Peter of all grades of laymen as well as of bishops and clergy. The interventions of Gregory in the kingdoms and lands of Europe prepared the way for the developments of the twelfth century, but they did not determine them or make them inevitable, let alone substantially anticipate them.

10.4 Emperors

Gregory was concerned with the disposition of the imperial no less than with the royal office in human society. During his lifetime, the title emperor was associated with three figures in Christendom. First, from the mid-1070s, it was claimed, in the simple form *imperator* and soon in the title *imperator totius Hispaniae*, by King Alphonso VI of León–Castile, by reason of the paramount authority that he wielded over the Christian regions of the Iberian peninsula. There was a possibility of conflict with Gregory's assertion that the 'regnum Hyspaniae' belonged to St Peter 'in ius et proprietatem'. But Alphonso seems to have intended no challenge to papal prerogatives, which Gregory did not press upon him. Nor, if he knew of Alphonso's use of the imperial title, did Gregory make any recorded comment. Thus, the use of the imperial title in Spain contributes nothing to an understanding of Gregory's position in its regard.[111]

Second, Gregory was concerned with the Byzantine empire, where there was a continuous succession of emperors from Constantine in the early fourth century. For Gregory as for all his contemporaries, Constantine was a model emperor; for the reform papacy, he was a ruler of true religion who deferred as was his duty to papal and

---

[109] As was the view esp. of Brackmann, 'Die Ursachen'.

[110] For the text of the concordat, *MGH Const.* 1.159–61, nos. 107–8; see esp. the comments of Müller-Mertens, *Regnum Teutonicum*, pp. 375–83, and Classen, 'Das Wormser Konkordat', esp. p. 458.

[111] For the title in Spain, see Cowdrey, *The Cluniacs*, pp. 225–6.

episcopal authority and jurisdiction.[112] The long-term result of the confrontation between churchmen of the Latin and the Greek obediences at Constantinople in 1054 was to confirm this picture of him and to remind Roman churchmen that Rome and Constantinople were related as mother and daugher. For Gregory, Seljuk attacks on Byzantium constituted a strong reason for bringing help to the Byzantine empire, and he entertained sanguine expectations that, through such help, both church and emperor in Byzantium might be drawn towards due obedience to Rome.

The ruling emperor at the time of Gregory's accession, Michael VII Ducas (1071–8), needed all the aid that he could get after the disaster that overcame his predecessor, Romanus IV Diogenes, in the battle of Manzikert (1071). He lost no time in making a well calculated démarche to Gregory which won him the pope's enduring favour. In July 1073, he sent a letter which Gregory read as being eloquent of his goodwill and of his no small devotion to the holy Roman church. Gregory, therefore, was encouraged to look for such a concord between Rome and Constantinople as he also hoped to foster with the western empire under an amenable Henry IV.[113] Even after the pantomime events that followed Michael's dethronement in 1078 by Nicephorus III Botanaites (1078–81), Gregory clung to the view that Michael was the most glorious Constantinopolitan emperor, who had been rejected from the height of imperial pre-eminence improperly and maliciously, not justly and reasonably; he therefore deserved St Peter's help to secure his restoration to the empire.[114] At his Lent synod of 1078, Gregory excommunicated Nicephorus, although there was no mention of a sentence of deposition.[115] It is far from clear how far, in his *Dictatus papae* of 1075, Gregory had been directly concerned with papal prerogatives in relation to Byzantium. Since, just before their inclusion in his Register, Gregory had entertained hopes of ecclesiastical concord between Rome and Constantinople but had quickly expressed disillusion,[116] he may have had some regard to the east. Yet, even though he claimed a papal right to depose emperors,[117] in 1078 he only excommunicated Nicephorus, and in 1080 he sought his removal not through a papal sentence but by giving religious and moral support to a proposed expedition against him under Norman leadership which would aid and defend the deposed Michael as supposedly the rightful emperor.[118] Likewise, Gregory seems to have done no more than excommunicate the next emperor, Alexius I Comnenus (1081–1118), in spite of his support for Henry IV of Germany.[119] There were no signs of Gregory's invoking such extremer claims as were canvassed in the *Dictatus papae*.

[112] See Cowdrey, 'Eleventh-Century Reformers' Views'.
[113] *Reg.* 1.18, to the Emperor Michael VII, 9 July 1073, pp. 29–30; for Gregory's comparable expectation of Henry IV, see e.g. 2.31, to King Henry IV, 7 Dec. 1074, pp. 165/26–166/2.
[114] *Reg.* 8.6, to the bishops of Apulia and Calabria, 25 July 1080, pp. 523–4.
[115] *Reg.* 6.5*b*, record of the Nov. synod 1078, pp. 400/28–9, 401/28.
[116] *Reg.* 2.31, pp. 166/32–167/15; 2.49, to Abbot Hugh of Cluny, 22 Jan. 1075, p. 189/14–19.
[117] *Dictatus papae*, clause 12, *Reg.* 2.55*a*, p. 204/5.
[118] *Reg.* 8.6.
[119] Gregory congratulated Robert Guiscard on his victory over Alexius at Durazzo on 18 Oct. 1081: *Reg.* 9.17, (late 1081), pp. 597–8.

His letters suggest that, as was inevitable, he accepted the fact and the order of the empire of Constantinople as he found them. He showed no awareness of a problem in the existence in Christendom of two emperors, of the east and of the west. He aspired to establish in practice a concord between the papacy and the eastern empire which was similar to that which he sought to establish in the west. He praised an eastern emperor in so far as he seemed to incline towards the obedience as between mother and daughter that would foster the requisite concord. He was prepared to use against an eastern emperor the spiritual sanction of excommunication, but he made no reference to any power of deposition, save in so far as the removal of a supposed intruder might be effected by military means. Effectively, Gregory's view of the pope's relation to the eastern emperor in the circumstances of his time was limited to encouraging concord and obedience in an emperor whose power could be regarded as legitimate, and to combining the spiritual sanction of excommunication with the sponsoring of military resistance when an emperor was deemed to have usurped or misused his position.

Third, as regards the empire in the west, the pope claimed greater powers, and he had greater room for their exercise. In the east, the imperial succession, by means fair or foul, had been continuously maintained over the centuries. In the west, the succession was far from continuous. Since 962, the Ottonian and Salian rulers of Germany had, indeed, an expectation of imperial coronation which was enhanced when, from the 1040s, the German kings adopted the title *rex Romanorum*.[120] But for imperial coronation, they must go to Rome, and they depended on the pope's willingness to perform the ceremony. Thus, there were regularly periods when there was no crowned emperor: Henry II of Germany, king from 1002, was crowned emperor only in 1014; in the case of Conrad II, there was a gap from 1024 to 1027; Henry III succeeded him as king in 1039, but was crowned emperor only in 1046. When Gregory became pope in 1073, Henry IV had been king since 1056; the lapse of time was getting rather long, and his imperial coronation had already been considered. It was inevitably high on the papal agenda; but circumstances must be right and, above all, Gregory must be satisfied that the young Henry was personally suitable in his conduct, religion, and political disposition to come to Rome and receive the crown.

Between 1073 and the autumn of 1075, and so both before and after Henry's restoration to communion in 1074 by Gregory's legates in Germany, a major concern of Gregory's was the need and, indeed, the duty, of promoting his advancement from the royal office which was his already by succession to his father, to the imperial office which it was the pope's prerogative to withhold or to confer. Although Gregory did not respond in any way to Henry's use in his penitent letter of 1073 of the title 'Romanorum Dei gratia rex',[121] he expressed his awareness, both before and after he became pope, of a commitment to Henry. The commitment arose both from the imperial dignity to which Henry was the presumptive successor, and from respect for

---

[120] For the title 'rex Romanorum', see Ullmann, '*Dies ortus imperii*', pp. 685–6.

[121] *Epp. HIV* no. 5 (late Aug. 1073), p. 54/22 = *Reg.* 1.29a, p. 48/3–4. The implication of the words *Dei gratia* that Henry had a divinely-given claim to the empire should be observed.

his father and mother, the imperial pair Henry III and Agnes, in whose progeny imperial qualities were to be anticipated.[122] In the order of things, the imperial dignity, which Gregory could describe to Henry as the 'imperatoria maiestas', was the counterpart to the papal; it was necessary that they should act in a partnership of peace and concord.[123] In such persons as Beatrice and Matilda of Tuscany, the Roman empire already had princes whose personal qualities matched up to its demands;[124] Gregory's task was to admonish and instruct Henry himself in the virtues that belonged to the imperial dignity, and then, when he was satisfied that Henry had adopted them, he must at Rome make him, by God's permission and gift, emperor. In this sense, imperial coronation was not the right of the prospective recipient but a divine gift bestowed at the pope's discretion when he was satisfied that the candidate was morally suitable and therefore practically useful to the church in the highest office of the lay order.[125] In September 1075, Gregory intimated to Henry that he was so satisfied.[126]

The events that culminated in February 1076 with Gregory's inhibition of Henry from the exercise of his kingly office and with his excommunication put what proved to be a final end to the possibility that Gregory might proceed to Henry's imperial coronation at Rome. It is possible to read Gregory's letters during the ensuing years as establishing that, save in occasional and formal ways, he paid no regard to the concept of a western empire and to the claim of a German king to succeed to it. Henceforth, his concern and that of his followers in Germany was increasingly centred upon a *regnum Teutonicorum* that disregarded the position of the German king as king also of Italy and of Burgundy, and that in effect represented him as being one king among many. Such a view was especially apparent in his dealings with the German anti-kings Rudolf of Swabia and Hermann of Salm, of whom he never spoke save as kings of Germany with no reference to the possibility of their eventual advancement to the imperial title, which Gregory perhaps intended to discard. Thus, for example, in 1080, when recognizing Rudolf as king, Gregory declared him to have been elected by the Germans ('Teutonici') to rule and defend the German kingdom ('regnum Teutonicorum').[127]

It is, however, likely that, in so expressing himself, Gregory was reacting to a current situation rather than envisaging a radical change in the pattern of public authority. He never lost sight of such model emperors as Constantine and Henry III. Even in his sentence of 1080 against Henry IV he referred to the latter as 'Heinrici imperatoris filius'; empires stood at the head of the list of kingdoms, principalities,

---

[122] *Epp. vag.* no. 14, to the faithful in Germany, (summer, 1076), pp. 34–5, cf. *Reg.* 2.44, to Queen Judith of Hungary, 10 Jan. 1075, p. 181/10–11, 39.
[123] *Reg.* 1.19, to Duke Rudolf of Swabia, 1 Sept. 1073, p. 31/28–32/15; 1.85, to the Empress-mother Agnes, 15 June 1074, p. 121/20–4; 2.31, to King Henry IV, 7 Dec. 1074, pp. 165/26–166/2; 3.7, to the same, (early Sept. 1075), p. 257/8–11.
[124] *Reg.* 1.50, to Countesses Beatrice and Matilda, 4 Mar. 1074, p. 76/23–7.
[125] *Reg.* 1.11, to Countesses Beatrice and Matilda, 24 June 1073, p. 19/5–10; 1.20, to Bishop Raynald of Como, 1 Sept. 1073, pp. 33/24–34/4; *Epp. vag.* no. 14, pp. 34–5.
[126] *Reg.* 3.7, p. 257/8–21.   [127] *Reg.* 7.14a, record of the Lent synod 1080, p. 486/22–5.

duchies, marches, counties, and other lordships that the princes of the apostles could give or withhold according to the merits or offences of the individuals who were concerned.[128] In both his sentences against Henry IV, Gregory used a carefully formulated phrase which took account of his kingship in respect of both Germany and Italy: he forbade him the *regnum Teutonicorum et Italiae*, thereby acknowledging the *de facto* extent of his power.[129] In a similar way, between 1076 and 1080 Gregory referred to the *imperium Romanum* as an object of his own continuing concern. The decision about who should be recognized as the German king should be guided, among other things, by the needs of the Christian religion and the welfare of the whole empire; for by the pride and disobedience of an evil ruler, the Roman empire was brought to desolation and destruction. This was true of past, of present, and of future. Gregory acknowledged his own problem as being that, in his later years as pope, no persons could be found who were equal to governing the empire as Henry III and Agnes had governed it. It was far from Gregory's mind that the imperial title and office should permanently lapse; his problem was that they must remain in suspense until a suitable and useful candidate should be available. No such candidate was in sight.[130]

Such remained the theme of his letters after 1080. He continued to refer to the paradigm emperors of the past who had measured up to the church's moral demands upon rulers, especially Constantine, Charlemagne, and Henry III.[131] Throughout his exposition of Christian rulership to Bishop Hermann of Metz in 1081, he associated the royal and the imperial dignities; both were now to be exercised only by those who satisfied the moral demands that Gregory made upon rulers and who were called by the church to rule. By his misdeeds, Henry IV had made himself the destroyer ('destructor') of the empire.[132] To repair human society, Gregory sought the succession of rulers who met what was required in both kings and emperors. He insisted that, by contrast with those constituting the *sacerdotium*, both alike had but humble and limited functions to discharge; both must, therefore, shun the worldly glory that made them seek to rule for themselves and not for God. At considerable length, Gregory enlarged upon the proper moral dispositions of kings and emperors

---

[128] *Reg.* 7.14a, pp. 484/3–4, 487/4–8.

[129] *Reg.* 3.10a, record of the Lent synod 1076, p. 270/20–1, 7.14a, p. 486/15–20, cf. *Epp. vag.* no. 32, to the faithful 'per totum Italicum regnum et Teutonicorum' (1079), p. 84. Gregory's long-standing disregard of Henry's position as king of Burgundy was probably occasioned by his lack of power there rather than by constitutional considerations.

[130] For Gregory's use of the words 'imperator' and 'imperium' between 1076 and 1080, see *Epp. vag.* no. 14, to all the faithful, (summer 1076), p. 34; *Reg.* 3.15, to the Milanese knight Wifred, (Apr.) 1076, p. 276/31–2; 4.1, to all the faithful 'in Romanum imperium', 25 July 1076, p. 289/23–4; 4.3, to all the faithful in Germany, 3 Sept. 1076, pp. 298/22–9, 299/15–16; 4.23, to his legates in Germany, 31 May 1077, p. 335/30; 4.24, to all the faithful in Germany, 31 May 1077, p. 337/18–19.

[131] Constantine: *Reg.* 9.3, to Bishop Altmann of Passau and Abbot William of Hirsau, (Mar. 1081), p. 576/6 (part of the form of oath for a future German king); 9.37, to King William I of England, (late 1083), p. 631/7 ('piae memoriae Constantinus precipuus . . . imperator'). Charlemagne: 8.23, to Cardinal Peter of Albano and Prince Gisulf of Salerno, (1084), pp. 565–7. Henry III: 7.21, to King Harold Hein of Denmark, 19 Apr. 1080, p. 497/28. See also 8.21, to Bishop Hermann of Metz, 15 Mar. 1081, p. 559/5–8.

[132] *Reg.* 8.21, p. 547/19–22.

alike.[133] When advising about the choice of a new ruler, he expressly declared that the church must seek someone morally apt either for the kingship or for the imperial office ('ad regimen vel imperium').[134]

Nothing was further from Gregory's mind than the setting aside of the imperial office in the west. His concern was that, given its weighty responsibilities in concert with the *sacerdotium*, it should in due time be worthily filled. This could occur only when a candidate had proved himself in the exercise of the kingship; hence Gregory's preoccupation in the early 1080s with the election of a German king. But his repeated linking of kings and emperors in his letter to Hermann of Metz places it beyond question that, God being willing, the empire that Henry IV had destroyed by his conduct would be renewed in someone who had proved himself to be worthy of it.

10.5 The Bonds of Loyalty and Service

Throughout his pontificate, Gregory sought to establish and to consolidate bonds of loyalty and service between the Roman church and the kingdoms and principalities, and therefore the rulers and the more powerful laity, of Latin Christendom. The nature and extent of these bonds has been much discussed, often in terms of whether Gregory had a policy, sometimes designated a 'feudal' policy, of binding some if not all Christian peoples in a comprehensive system of 'feudal' suzerainty.[135]

Probably, however, the most helpful approach to Gregory's conception of service to the Roman church is along avenues that are more religious than political. For him, St Peter, by virtue of the position that Christ assigned to him according to the Gospels, possessed a lordship of a comprehensive kind over all the peoples of the world. Peter was the father of all Christians and, after Christ, their first shepherd. The church whose government Christ had committed to Peter was set over all the kingdoms of the world; all principalities and powers were subject to it. To Peter and his vicar at Rome, the whole world owed obedience and service.[136] Accordingly, the princes of the apostles, St Peter and St Paul, could both withhold and grant the kingdoms and principalities of this world according to the personal merits of their rulers.[137] Since Peter possessed this universal lordship, all kingdoms and rulers should seek his patronage ('patrocinium') in order to procure their welfare in this world and the next.

The forms and the consequences of this patronage differed from lordship to lordship and person to person. The pope's role was, above all, to bring lay rulers to a recognition of their debt to St Peter in a way that included the politics of this world

---

[133] *Reg.* 8.21, pp. 555/10–16, 558/3–559/12; cf. 8.22, to Queen Adelaide of Hungary, (1081), p. 565/10–12.

[134] *Reg.* 8.21, p. 561/14–17.

[135] For a general survey, see Robinson, *The Papacy*, pp. 302–9. On Gregory's 'feudal' policy, see esp. Jordan, 'Das Eindringen' and 'Das Reformpapsttum'; for a minimizing view, see Reynolds, *Fiefs and Vassals*, pp. 211–14.

[136] *Reg.* 1.69, to King Sancho II of Aragon, 20 Mar. 1074, p. 72/11–13; *Epp. vag.* no. 54, to all the faithful, (July–Nov. 1084), pp. 134–5; no. 57, to Toirdhealbhach Ó Briain, king of Ireland (1074/84), pp. 138–9.

[137] *Reg.* 7.14*a*, report of the Lent synod 1080, p. 487/4–8.

but also transcended it. They were to acknowledge the patronage ('patrocinium') which St Peter either actively conferred or could be brought to confer in proportion to a ruler's recognition of his duty of loyalty and serviceability. But a ruler's recognition of St Peter's patronage might take a wide variety of forms, by no means all of which can usefully be described as feudal. They arose from a ruler's perception of what from time to time was feasible and appropriate for him as well as from papal demands, and they might be variously worked out by the negotiation of the pope with the ruler.

The nature of the response that, in Gregory's view, a lay ruler might show towards St Peter's patronage is well illustrated by his dealings after 1080 with Robert Guiscard, duke of Apulia and Calabria, upon whom he especially counted for armed aid against Henry IV of Germany. Gregory wrote to Robert in the wake of the latter's victory over the army of Alexius Comnenus at Durazzo in October 1081, with a view to directing Robert's arms against Henry. Only in a secondary way did he appeal to Robert's contractual obligation to help the apostolic see as it had been renewed by the oaths of Ceprano. Gregory dwelt most urgently upon the patronage ('patrocinium') of St Peter, the powerful results of which were manifest in Robert's mighty deeds. Robert should now repay the benefits that Peter had conferred and should further make Peter his debtor of whom he could expect to receive still more bounty to requite the services that he would in future perform—Gregory clearly understood by resisting Henry. Next, he should remember the trust that his mother, the holy Roman church, placed in him. Only thereafter did he rank Robert's sworn promises at Ceprano; even so, he added the comment that, had they not been made, Robert would still have been obliged to the service of the Roman church by the general law of Christendom ('ex iure christianitatis').[138] So subordinately did Robert's sworn promises rank in Gregory's estimation; he put before them the obligations that arose from St Peter's *patrocinium* and the obedience that arose from the general law.

The nature of St Peter's patronage as Gregory envisaged it had a further consequence which added to the obligations to which it gave rise: for rulers and peoples alike, its benefits were to be looked for not only in earthly matters but, above all, when men appeared at the final judgement before the just Judge. In this life they should, therefore, both so flee carnal desires and pursue virtues, and also make St Peter their debtor by their faithfulness in his service ('devotissimi servitii fidelitate'), that on the last day they would have his patronage ('patrocinium') and not his condemnation. In these terms Gregory exhorted the people of Bohemia in 1075; in 1079, he sent King Alphonso VI of León–Castile a relic of St Peter's chains so that, by Peter's patronage here and now ('per eius presentia patrocinia') he might enjoy richer blessings ('beneficia') than even before, and so that by his intercessions he might hereafter enter eternal joy.[139] The patronage of St Peter that men should seek by doing him due service transcended earthly bounds.

---

[138] *Reg.* 9.17, (after 18 Oct. 1081), pp. 597–8.
[139] *Reg.* 2.72, to the people of Bohemia, 17 Apr. 1075, p. 233/10–18; 7.6, to King Alphonso VI of León–Castile, 15 Oct. 1079, p. 467/12–20.

The language in which Gregory expressed the bonds of loyalty and service was similarly broad in its spectrum of meaning. The *fidelitas* of which Gregory frequently spoke ranged from personal loyalty and obligation of a temporal sort, through specific promises of legal fealty, to religious commitment of the deepest kind. The noun *fides* and the adjective *fidelis* had similar complexities of meaning, from the bond of a man to his lord according to the norms of secular law and society, through loyalty to St Peter in accordance with papal purposes, to the quality of the good Christian according to the catholic faith as rooted in the New Testament.[140] Similarly, the term *beneficium* comprehended both lands granted by ecclesiastical or lay lords to be held in return for appropriate earthly services and spiritual blessings in time and eternity as well as good deeds in general.[141] Again, the verb *militare* and the nouns *militia* and *miles* could refer to earthly warfare waged with material weapons of war. But they could also refer to services of a wider, including those of a religious, kind. *Militia*, in fact, could be synonymous with *servitium* in all its range of meanings.[142] The breadth of significance, religious and secular, temporal and eternal, which marked the language of loyalty, service, and dependence in Gregory's letters must be constantly borne in mind.

Because the patronage of St Peter had so many facets and applications and because the language of loyalty and service had such a broad spectrum of meaning, the ways in which Gregory sought to bind Christians whether as organized in kingdoms and principalities or as individuals to the purposes of St Peter and the Roman church cannot be reduced to simple formulas. This is particularly true of states; Gregory's claims upon and dealings with them showed flexibility and differences from state to state and from time to time.

Over some regions, notably South Italy, Spain, and the islands of the western Mediterranean, he claimed for the pope a direct lordship which appears to have been grounded in the passages of the *Constitutum Constantini* by which Constantine had allegedly conferred upon the pope 'all the provinces, places, and cities of Italy and of the western regions', and put at his disposal resources in 'Judaea, Greece, Asia, Thrace, Africa, and Italy, and in various islands'.[143] Gregory's claims were at their most intensive and sustained in the Norman provinces of South Italy. From a formal and legal point of view, they were embodied in oaths taken by rulers and in acts of investiture by the pope which followed formulas essentially settled in the days of Popes Nicholas II and Alexander II.[144] Such formulas reflected the needs both of the

[140] For Gregory's vocabulary and its range of meanings, see Erdmann, *Die Entstehung*, pp. 185–211, Eng. trans. pp. 201–28. For *fidelitas* and related terms in Gregory's letters, see Caspar's Index, *Reg.* pp. 688–9, and, for discussion, Zerbi, 'Il termine "fidelitas"'.

[141] Caspar, Index, *Reg.* p. 679.

[142] Ibid. pp. 695–6. Gregory's use of the verb 'militare' of service in a general sense with no reference to earthly warfare is illustrated by *Dictatus papae*, clause 15, *Reg.* 2.55a, p. 205.

[143] *Das Constitutum Constantini*, ed. Fuhrmann, lines 203–8, 261–70, pp. 85–6, 93–4. It should, however, be remembered that Gregory made no direct reference to this document: see Cowdrey, 'Eleventh-Century Reformers' Views'. For its significance, and also for that of grants to the papacy by Carolingian and later rulers, see Deér, *Papsttum und Normannen*, pp. 76–92.

[144] Oath of fidelity of Robert Guiscard to Pope Nicholas II and promise of annual *pensio*, 1059: *Lib.*

Norman invaders of South Italy to secure title to lands that they had invaded and seized, and of the papacy to promote the security of its own lands from Norman incursions and, in the long run, from hostile German intervention in Central and South Italy. Upon the succession of a new pope or of a new temporal ruler, the commitments involved were to be renewed. Formulas involving the princes of Capua and the dukes of Apulia established both the personal obligations of the rulers concerned to the Roman church, the apostolic see, and the pope himself, and also the conditions of dependent tenure upon which they held their lands.[145] Thus, the rulers swore to be personally loyal ('fidelis') and to implement their loyalty by appropriate obligations of counsel ('consilium') and aid ('tibique adiutor ero', 'adiuvabo te'), especially by defending the lands of St Peter ('terra sancti Petri') in the restricted sense of lands under direct papal lordship (the 'patrimonium Petri').[146] The rulers also acknowledged the status of dependent tenure that attached to their principalities. They constituted a *terra sancti Petri* in a broader sense of lands outside the patrimony which belonged to the Roman church by some such title as the *Constitutum Constantini* or grants by Carolingian or later emperors. The pope invested the Norman rulers with such lands. In recognition of such Roman lordship, an annual payment ('pensio') was due to the Roman church. Moreover, to confirm the transfer of his lands and in token of the fealty that was due ('ad confirmationem traditionis et ad recognitionem fidelitatis') Robert Guiscard also paid an annual rent ('census') for all his lands that were held in demesne and not granted to his Norman followers.

In their essentials, such formulas were settled before Gregory became pope, and their language was widely current in the later eleventh century.[147] In his day, they were copied by Cardinal Deusdedit into his canonical collection.[148] But Gregory's dealings with the Normans of South Italy showed a marked tendency on his part to augment such legal expressions of loyalty to the Roman church and to the pope by appeals to St Peter, whose name was not prominently used in current formularies such as Deusdedit copied. Gregory's emphasis upon religious appeals based upon the patronage of St Peter as a basis for loyalty and service was most signally expressed in his last letter to Robert Guiscard after the latter's victory at Durazzo when he needed Norman help against Henry IV of Germany.[149] But, if the chronicler Amatus is to be believed, Robert Guiscard had already understood Gregory's religious motive when, in 1076, he diplomatically parried Henry IV's bid to have him receive

cens. caps. 162–3, vol. 1.421–2; oath of fidelity of Richard of Capua to Pope Alexander II, 2 Oct. 1061: Albinus, 10.42, vol. 2.93–4; Deusdedit, *Coll. can.* 3.288 (159), pp. 395–6.

[145] See esp. for Capua: *Reg.* 1.21*a*, oath of fidelity of Prince Richard, 14 Sept. 1073, pp. 35–6; Deusdedit, *Coll. can.* 3.289(159), oath of fidelity of Prince Jordan, 10 June 1080, p. 396. For Apulia: *Reg.* 8.1*a–c*, oath of fidelity of Robert Guiscard, investiture by Gregory VII, and promise by Robert of an annual *pensio*, 29 June 1080, pp. 514–17. See also the version of the act of fidelity preserved in a Bible belonging to St Paul's-without-the-Walls, Deér, *Das Papsttum und die süditalienischen Normannenstaaten*, no. 9.18*b*, p. 32.

[146] For the ambiguity of the phrase 'terra sancti Petri', see Deér, *Papsttum und Normannen*, pp. 67–96.

[147] See Deér, *Papsttum und Normannen*, pp. 63–4.

[148] *Coll. can.* 3.283 (155)–289, pp. 392–6.

[149] *Reg.* 9.17, pp. 597–8.

his lands by royal gift. Robert Guiscard is said to have insisted upon the supreme value of the patronage of the apostles; he would not set an earthly power above God's and the apostles'; in order that his lords St Peter and St Paul, to whom all the kingdoms of the world were subject, might pray to God for his safety in so many military dangers, he wished to be subject to their vicar, the pope, with all his conquests.[150] As for Gregory himself, when restraining the Normans from depredations of the lands of St Peter, he appealed, not to their fealty or to the obligations of tenure, but to what morally befitted Christian men and to the danger of exchanging St Peter's blessing for his wrath.[151] In warfare against Henry IV and Archbishop Guibert of Ravenna, Gregory looked to the Normans for service in terms of the renewed oaths taken at Ceprano. But Robert Guiscard was also to urge his nephew Robert of Loritello to desist from depredations so that he might not forfeit St Peter's patronage; by restraining himself for the future, he might make Peter favourable to him: for in Peter's anger he would find ruin, but in his favour life and felicity.[152] Gregory addressed similar counsels about winning and losing Peter's favour with respect to Prince Jordan of Capua.[153] While Gregory always insisted upon the obligations that were imposed by the legal commitments of the Norman rulers to the papacy, he strongly reinforced them by advancing reasons for loyalty and service that arose from the deeper and essentially religious need for Peter's patronage to secure well-being in this world and the next.

With respect to Spain, a similar pattern of thought may be observed. During the first four years of his pontificate, Gregory advanced strong claims to papal proprietorship of the whole peninsula. In 1073, he told Frenchmen who might campaign there that the *regnum Hyspaniae* of old belonged to the immediate jurisdiction of St Peter ('proprii iuris sancti PETRI fuisse'); despite pagan occupation, it rightly belonged to no mortal man but exclusively to the apostolic see; recovered lands should, therefore, be held of St Peter alone.[154] In 1077, Gregory addressed to the kings and magnates of Spain a general reminder that, upon the evidence of ancient ordinances, the *regnum Hyspaniae* had been granted to St Peter and the holy Roman church *in ius et proprietatem*.[155] The commendation of the kingdom of Aragon to the apostolic see in 1068 implied a recognition of this claim, yet, even in his dealings with Aragon, Gregory made little of it. In an early letter to King Sancho Ramírez, he preferred to emphasize the patronage of St Peter whom Christ had set over all the kingdoms of the world, together with the duty of a *fidelitas* which was a matter more of religious faith than of legal fealty. Gregory desired to have the same friendship ('amicitia') with Sancho that the kings of Spain had enjoyed of old with the Roman pontiffs.[156]

---

[150] Amatus, 7.27, pp. 320–1.   [151] *Reg.* 7.14a, record of the Lent synod 1080, p. 481/20–5.

[152] *Reg.* 8.7, to the faithful of St Peter, (summer 1080), p. 525/10–15; 9.4, to Abbot Desiderius of Montecassino, (early Feb. 1081), p. 578/27–36.

[153] *Reg.* 6.37, 21 Apr. 1079, pp. 453–4; 9.27, to Archbishop John of Naples, (after 24 June 1082), p. 610/21–6.

[154] *Reg.* 1.7, 30 Apr. 1073, pp. 11–12.   [155] *Reg.* 4.28, 28 June 1077, pp. 345/35–346/21.

[156] *Reg.* 1.63, 20 Mar. 1074, pp. 91–2; cf. the absence of temporal claims in *Epp. vag.* no. 65, to King Sancho Ramírez, (1076–85), pp. 146–9.

It is highly significant that, in the last months of his pontificate, Gregory granted Bishop García of Jaca a privilege in which he recalled how his father, King Ramiro, had made himself and his kingdom tributary to St Peter, the bearer of the keys. The notion of proprietary right expressed in a *census* was evidently still present in Gregory's mind. Yet Gregory declared Ramiro's motive as having been the religious one of securing St Peter's patronage ('quo post discessionem terreni regni in celo cum sanctis gloriosius regnaret'). His good works as king were likewise religious: having first made his kingdom tributary, he replaced the superstition of the Toledan (Hispanic) rite by Roman law and customs, so that the faith and the number of Christians increased through the zeal of surrounding kings and princes while papal authority was upheld in all things.[157]

With regard to the strongest of the Spanish kings, Alphonso VI of León–Castile, Gregory never referred expressly in letters directed individually to him to the proprietary rights of the Roman church. His emphasis was upon the benefits of St Peter's patronage both now and in the world to come. Gregory expressed himself especially warmly when he sent the king a relic of St Peter's chains, 'so that through his present patronage you may feel his more abundant blessings toward you'. After the resolution of the crisis of 1080, Gregory rejoiced that Alphonso had chosen St Peter as his patron, thus showing a ruler's proper concern for the welfare of his subjects.[158]

It may be concluded that, in Spain, Gregory never forgot the claim of the apostolic see to a temporal right and proprietorship based upon ancient ordinances and confirmed by tribute. But this claim was increasingly overlaid by exhortations to the Spanish kings to be mindful of the present and future benefits that they, like all kings, might expect to accrue from fidelity in a religious sense to St Peter as their heavenly patron. Gregory supposed, and probably rightly, that claims for the legal loyalty of kings and princes that were based upon temporal ordinances of long ago were less compelling than the blessings that would surely follow both now and in eternity from placing themselves under the ever-vigilant patronage of the prince of the apostles.

Probably, though never explicitly, on the basis of the *Constitutum Constantini*, Gregory claimed papal proprietorship of the islands of Sardinia and Corsica. Their position and resources made them important for the struggle in North Italy between the supporters and the opponents of the reform papacy; Gregory was, therefore, anxious to revive and confirm papal rights over them. Nevertheless, his caution and pragmatism are evident in his dealings with them. Sardinia was the first of them to receive his attention. In October 1073, he wrote to the judges, or governors, of five of its towns from concern, as he said, both for the welfare of their souls and for the safety of their country. His declared motive in writing was to maintain the proper vigilance of the Roman church as the universal mother of all Christians, but he also referred cryptically to a special and even private care that Rome had for Sardinia. Constantine, the archbishop of Torres, whom Gregory had recently consecrated at Rome, and a legate whom he planned soon to send, would communicate further about Gregory's

---

[157] *QF* no. 215 (1084–5), pp. 258–9.
[158] *Reg.* 7.6, 15 Oct. 1079, p. 467/12–20; 9.2, (1081), p. 570/26–41.

plans for the Sardinians' welfare and benefit. In January 1074, a further letter to the
judge of Cagliari referred to Gregory's intention no longer to leave St Peter's right
and honour in Sardinia unpursued.[159] It was a clear hint that papal rights to jurisdiction
and proprietorship would be revived.

Nothing more is known of Gregory's purpose until October 1080, when he again
wrote to the judge of Cagliari. This time, he made a threefold reference to Sardinia's
relation to apostolic lordship. First, he began and ended his letter by promising the
blessings that, through the pope, would accrue from St Peter's patronage: 'If you
continue in faithfulness to him (*in ipsius familiaritate*), we promise you beyond doubt
the aid of St Peter, which will not fail you here and in the future.' Second, to this new
line of approach, he added a reference to his earlier hint of Petrine proprietorship:
the Roman church was the mother of all the churches, but specially ('specialiter') so
to that of Sardinia. Third, he disclosed to the judge that many peoples—Normans,
Tuscans, Lombards, and even ultramontanes (he probably meant Duke Godfrey of
Lorraine)—had sought his permission to invade Sardinia. If successful, they had
promised great services to the papacy, and that they would leave half the land for the
benefit of the Roman church while promising fidelity to the pope for the other half
('maxima servitia . . . fuisse promissa, ita ut medietatem totius terrae nostro usui vel-
lent relinquere partemque alteram ad fidelitatem nostram sibi habere'). There had
evidently been proposed some such papal-princely condominium as had existed in
South Italy, with the implication that the papacy was recognized as having comparable proprietorship in the two regions.[160]

About Corsica, Gregory advanced expressly the claim that about Sardinia he advanced only tentatively. He first did so in 1077, when he believed that the Corsicans
themselves wished, as was proper, to return to apostolic obedience ('ad honorem et
iustitiam apostolici principatus'). Corsica had been under Frankish and then Pisan
domination. Save that it had not been under Saracen rule, Gregory regarded it as he
regarded Spain. It rightly belonged to no one save the holy Roman church ('nulli
mortalium nullique potestati nisi sanctae Romanae ecclesiae ex debito vel iuris proprietate pertinere'). Those who had seized it violently and without yielding service,
fidelity ('fidelitas'), and obedience to St Peter were guilty of sacrilege. Gregory,
therefore, dispatched Bishop Landulf of Pisa to Corsica where he would not only act
on Gregory's behalf in spiritual matters but also recover the island temporally on
behalf of St Peter ('ut terram ex parte beati Petri et nostra vice suscipiat et eam cum
omni studio et diligentia regat et de omnibus rebus ac causis beato PETRO et nobis
per illum pertinentibus se intromittat'). The Corsicans should promise fidelity
('fidelitas') to Landulf, but overridingly to St Peter and to Gregory and his successors.[161] In his privilege of 1078 for the see of Pisa, Gregory commented that
Corsica had been wrongly alienated from the dominion of the Roman church ('a iure

---

[159] *Reg.* 1.29, to the judges of Sardinia, 14 Oct. 1073, pp. 46–7; cf. 1.85*a*, summary of the year 1073–4,
(28 June 1074), p. 123/16–18; 1.41, to Orzoccor, judge of Cagliari, 16 Jan. 1074, pp. 63–4.
[160] *Reg.* 8.10, to Orzoccor, judge of Cagliari, 5 Oct. 1080, pp. 528–30.
[161] *Reg.* 5.4, to the Corsicans, 16 Sept. 1077, pp. 351–2, cf. 5.2; to the same, 1 Sept. 1077, pp. 349–50.

et dominio sanctae Romanae ecclesiae') but was now being restored to that dominion; he set out in detail the judicial, financial, and military requirements of the Roman church.[162] In 1082, Gregory charged Hermann, cardinal-priest of SS. Quatro Coronati, with the oversight of an episcopal election on the island; he insisted that, as in the papal patrimony, a bishop-elect must be known to Gregory before he laid hands upon him.[163]

A privilege for the abbey of Sainte-Croix at Quimperlé carries a strong implication that Gregory also regarded the apostolic see as having a special superiority over Brittany. Its *arenga* claimed that, on the testimony of the Bretons themselves, not only emperors but also its own inhabitants had committed it to the protection and defence of the holy Roman church ('tutelae et defensioni sanctae Romanae ecclesiae'). His own predecessors had carelessly allowed this provision to lapse, but in issuing his privilege he recognized that the Bretons had from devotion subjected themselves to the patronage ('patrocinium') of St Peter.[164] There can be little doubt that the papal claim was tacitly founded upon the section of the *Constitutum Constantini* in which Constantine delivered to the papacy 'omnes . . . occidentalium regionum provincias.'[165] The claim no doubt helps to explain Gregory's exceptional pastoral solicitude for the totality of Breton society, both clerical and lay, although in his letters he explained his concern in terms of the universal care of the Roman church and the general benefit of St Peter's patronage.[166]

A claim for the temporal superiority of the apostolic see might also arise from recent title. This was the case with Hungary.[167] As Gregory interpreted matters, the kingdom of Hungary was the property of the holy Roman church which, in 1000, King Stephen had conferred upon St Peter with full right and power. Gregory based his claim upon no written document, for there was none, but upon the living memory of the elders of the Hungarian kingdom. He drew the conclusion that the Hungarian crown was a gift ('beneficium') not of the German king but of the Roman pope.[168]

As his dealings with successive rulers developed, he placed increasing weight upon the sanction of the giving or withholding of St Peter's favour, rather than upon the proprietary rights of the Roman church.[169] Gregory's approach to Bohemia further illustrates the flexibility of his approach.[170] He confirmed to the duke the right

---

[162] *Reg.* 6.12, 30 Nov. 1078, pp. 414/27–415/23.

[163] *Reg.* 9.28, pp. 611–612. For Hermann, see Hüls, *Kardinäle*, p. 202. Landulf of Pisa had died in 1079: G. Schwartz, *Die Besetzung*, p. 217.

[164] *QF* no. 153, 25 Mar. 1078, pp. 174–5; for discussion of Gregory's claim, see Pocquet du Haut-Jussé, 'La Bretagne'.

[165] *Das Constitutum Constantini*, ed. Fuhrmann, lines 263–6, p. 93.

[166] Esp. *Reg.* 2.1, to all the bishops and abbots of Brittany, 28 Aug. 1074, pp. 124–5; 5.23, to the counts of Brittany, 22 May 1078; pp. 387–8, 7.10, to the Breton clergy and laity, 25 Nov. 1079, pp. 471–2.

[167] See above, 6.4.

[168] *Reg.* 2.13, to King Solomon of Hungary, 28 Oct. 1074, p. 145/2–5, 17–22; cf. 2.63, to Duke Gésa of Hungary, 23 Mar. 1075, p. 218/24–31; 6.29, to King Ladislas of Hungary, 21 Mar. 1079, pp. 441/22–6, 442/8–12.

[169] *Reg.* 2.63, pp. 218/31–219/4; 2.70, to Duke Gésa, 17 Apr. 1075, p. 230/11–28; 6.29, p. 442/30–5.

[170] See above, 6.5.

to wear a mitre in return for an annual *census* to the Roman church of his own weight in silver. However, he advanced no express claim to Roman proprietorship or jurisdiction in any special sense; he spoke, instead, of the duke's devotion and obedience to the apostolic see, and of the blessings with which St Peter would requite the duke's love and humility. He also wrote of the duke's faithfulness ('fidelitas').[171] When defining the duty that the regions of Christendom owed to the apostolic see, Gregory chose his ideas and his language to suit what he took to be the needs and circumstances of each case.

He also showed flexibility and accommodation in theory and practice with regard to two kingdoms, England and Denmark, which had an acknowledged obligation to pay Peter's Pence to Rome. In the summer of 1080, and therefore in the aftermath of his second breach with Henry IV of Germany, he sought to draw the Norman king of England, William, into a closer temporal relationship with the Roman church, at a time when he was also reviewing the obligations of the Norman princes of South Italy.[172] From the papal side, no record survives of the terms of Gregory's definitive request to William; it was, in any case, communicated verbally by the legate Hubert, and it is not clear that it was also presented to the king in written form. Gregory's approach was gradual. In a letter dispatched in April, he already approached him for help 'as his most beloved son and as a faithful servant ('fidelis') of St Peter and of ourself'; he held out before William the tribulations of his mother the Roman church and the irresistible necessity of bringing help to the pope ('inevitabilis nos succurrendi necessitas'). He solicited a response that befitted the king's majesty and devotion.[173] Within days, he again wrote to the English king and queen as well as to their son, Robert Curthose, as the sequel to a reconciliation between father and son; it had been facilitated by Count Simon of Crépy, currently a hermit at Rome, and Gregory may have considered that the manner of the reconciliation increased William's indebtedness to the apostolic see. He also announced the coming to the royal presence of his legate Hubert.[174] It was probably soon after that Hubert, on Gregory's behalf, urged the king to perform an act of fidelity ('fidelitatem facere') to Gregory and his successors.[175] Hitherto the faithful servant ('fidelis') of the pope, William was invited to intensify and formalize his relationship by a bond which, in the king's eyes, must have seemed like the oath of fealty which he required of his own subjects. Its terms were probably comparable to at least some of those embodied in Robert Guiscard's oath at Ceprano on 29 June 1080, especially the obligation to help Gregory to hold the Roman papacy with security and honour, and the promise to maintain his fidelity ('hanc fidelitatem') to Gregory's properly promoted successors.[176]

It does not emerge on what grounds Gregory based his request to William; it can only be speculation that he had in mind the *Constitutum Constantini*, of which there

---

[171] *Reg.* 1.38, to Duke Wratislav, 17 Dec. 1073, pp. 60–1; 2.7, 22 Sept. 1074, pp. 135–6.
[172] See above, 6.9.   [173] *Reg.* 7.23, 24 Apr. 1080, p. 500/11–14, 26–31.
[174] *Reg.* 7.25–7, 8 May 1080, pp. 505–8.   [175] Lanfranc, *Letters*, nos. 38–9, pp. 128–33.
[176] *Reg.* 8.1a, pp. 514–1; cf. the oath prepared in 1081 for Count Bertrand of Provence: 9.12a, p. 590/11–16.

is no verbal echo in the surviving evidence. William, in any case, firmly but courteously declined to perform any act of fidelity; he claimed that he had made no such promise, and that he did not find that his Anglo-Saxon predecessors had done so to earlier popes. But he acceded to, and took steps to comply with, Gregory's other request, that for the future Peter's Pence be paid regularly to Rome.

Gregory did not press matters further. William had pointedly opened his reply to Gregory with the greeting 'salutem cum amicicia' and it is probably no coincidence that, in 1083, Gregory wrote to William of their common devotion to St Peter and to the *amicitia* that had for long joined them.[177] From classical times, friendship between rulers had overtones of co-operation which was not sanctioned by formal bonds of superiority and obligation. Gregory and his entourage were probably satisfied when a willing friendship emerged as the best available basis for securing William's loyalty and a hope for the services that the 'irresistable necessity' of a papacy under military threat might seem to call for.[178]

The papacy also claimed Peter's Pence from Denmark;[179] but as in the case of England, it had associated with their payment no claim to special lordship. Thus, in 1075, Gregory left it for King Sweyn Estrithson to propose ways in which he might commit his kingdom to the prince of the apostles in godly devotion and receive the support of his authority in return; Gregory also hoped for military services to the Roman church as part of the king's response. The overriding motive that Gregory proposed was one of making St Peter the king's debtor and of the king's winning Peter's signal patronage ('nobile patrocinium') for himself and his kingdom.[180] Gregory continued to extol to the Danish kings the benefits of St Peter's favour;[181] but they showed no disposition to intensify their formal and temporal relationship with the apostolic see, nor did Gregory press the matter. His written counsels to the kings remained at root moral rather than legal or political.

In other cases, for reasons that might be both political and religious, rulers were moved to seek the patronage of St Peter in this life and the next by placing themselves or their lands under his special authority. In the Dalmatian principalities of Croatia and Zeta, which were subject to pressures from Byzantium and from the Normans, rulers had strong political reasons for underpinning their own authority by holding their lands of the Roman church.[182] Likewise, in Kievan Russia, political circumstances led Prince Jaropolk to receive the land that he would inherit from Gregory's hands as a gift from St Peter, although the influence of his mother, the Polish-born Gertrude, contributed a background of Petrine devotion.[183]

---

[177] *Reg.* 9.37, p. 630/13–15, cf. Gregory's earlier allusion to his long-standing 'amicitia' with William: 7.1, to the subdeacon Hubert, 23 Sept. 1079, p. 459/20–5.

[178] *H* no. 1, pp. 15–17.   [179] See above, 6.8.

[180] *Reg.* 2.51, to King Sweyn Estrithson, 25 Jan. 1075, pp. 193/35–194/17, 2.75, to the same, 17 Apr. 1075, p. 238/8–26.

[181] *Reg.* 5.10, to King Harold Hein, 6 Nov. 1077, p. 362/12–30; 7.21, to the same, 19 Apr. 1080, p. 499/14–22.

[182] See above, 6.3.   [183] See above, 6.7.

In Spain and the south of France, several rulers seem to have been brought by a genuine desire for St Peter's patronage to commend themselves or their churches or lands to the Roman church. In 1077, Count Bernard of Besalú not only provided that seven monasteries in his county should pay annual *census* for the use of St Peter ('ad opus beati Petri') but he also similarly bound himself; in order that he might be St Peter's special knight or servant ('peculiarem militem'), he promised an annual *census* in recognition of his obligation to be of service ('mee milicie'). No mention was made of a commendation of the county as such, nor was reference made to Gregory's over-all claims to papal proprietorship of the Spanish kingdom. Bernard's expressed concern was to show gratitude to God and St Peter for the legatine work of Bishop Amatus of Oloron and to fulfil a personal desire to serve St Peter.[184]

In the south of France, two lords committed themselves and their inheritances to the papacy during the last years of Gregory's papacy—in 1080 Count Bertrand of Provence and in 1085 Count Peter of Substantion and Melgueil.[185] The latter grant, which was made through Gregory's legate Cardinal-bishop Peter of Albano, may have been, in part, a response to Gregory's last encyclical from Salerno which he ended by pleading the duty and the interest that his supporters had to help St Peter and the Roman church, in view of the blessing and peace that they would receive in this world and the next.[186] Desire on the part of rulers to maximize the patronage of St Peter may have been the leading motive behind these rulers' actions. It may also have prompted Countess Matilda of Tuscany to offer all her proprietary possessions to St Peter's at Rome,[187] since the gift was apparently made to the saint himself with-out mention of his vicar or of the apostolic see.

During most of his reign, Gregory made no attempt to claim direct temporal su-periority of any kind over the two largest kingdoms of Latin Christendom—France and Germany; his attentions were directed towards the periphery. But in 1081, with a view to the election of a new German anti-king to succeed Rudolf of Swabia, Gregory prepared the draft of an oath to the Roman church which the new king would take.[188] In some respects, its language followed that of oaths that Gregory took from rulers like Robert Guiscard over whose lands he claimed proprietorship: the new king was to be faithful ('fidelis') to St Peter and to his vicar the pope; whatever the pope commanded him under the sanction of true obedience ('per verum obaedi-entiam') he was to perform faithfully ('fideliter'); and at the first opportunity, he was faithfully to make himself a knight or servant of St Peter and of the pope by a cere-mony of placing his hands between the pope's ('Et eo die, quando illum primitus videro, fideliter per manus meas miles sancti Petri et illius efficiar'). It would be wrong to place upon this oath a narrowly military or secular interpretation.[189]

---

[184] *Lib. feud. maior,* no. 501, 2.16–17; see above, 6.11.
[185] See above, 5.2.2.   [186] *Epp. vag.* no. 54, pp. 134–5.
[187] *MGH Const.* 1.653–5, no. 444; Matilda's stated motive, in retrospect from 1102, was said to be 'pro remedio animae meae et parentum meorum'. See above, 4.5.
[188] *Reg.* 9.3, to Bishop Altmann of Passau and Abbot William of Hirsau, (Mar. 1081), pp. 575/14–576/19.
[189] See the comments of Flori, *L'Essor,* pp. 76–7.

Rather, it should be understood in the light of the moralization of kingship, and especially of German kingship, to which Gregory gave expression during his final years as pope.[190] The oath was couched entirely in terms of the king and not the kingdom. It concentrated upon the king's personal duty to be suitable in respect of his character and useful in respect of his government: he was to the defender and protector ('defensor et protector') of whom the church had need; he was to show due obedience and to be humbly devoted and useful to holy church as a Christian king should be. His promise to be faithful through true faith ('fidelis ero per rectam fidem') thus had a religious, rather than a secular, significance. As a *miles sancti Petri*, he was less a knight in a military or lay sense than a servant and supporter in all respects, including military service but not limited to it, that his religion demanded of a Christian king.

All in all, the evidence that has been surveyed does not bear out the contention that Gregory sought to secure the loyalty and service of the rulers of Latin Christendom according to consistent secular norms that might be described as feudal. He had no overall *Lehnspolitik*. His dealings with various regions proceeded piecemeal; he reacted to circumstances without seeking to make them conform to a preconceived pattern. When, as in South Italy, Spain, and the islands of the western Mediterranean, he believed that the Roman church had ancient proprietary and juridical rights, he sought to secure them; although his endeavours to do so were more active in the earlier than in the latter years of his pontificate. He increasingly turned from an emphasis upon the legal and temporal rights of the Roman church to a concentration upon the religious concept of the patronage of St Peter which offered to rulers prosperity and well-being in this world, and, after they had lived a good life in it, salvation and felicity in the next, to which St Peter controlled the keys of admission. As St Peter's vicar, the pope could assist in ensuring such benefits to rulers who humbly, obediently, and diligently served the prince of the apostles. Rulers could thus secure St Peter's favour not only by honouring legal and temporal undertakings according to the documents of the past but, far more, by maintaining due religious behaviour according to the spiritual and moral demands of the present and future.

As the examples of England and Denmark especially show, Gregory was prepared to concede to rulers who were in good standing with him a breadth of interpretation of what *fidelitas* to St Peter called for and to negotiate the benefits that they should bring to St Peter without imposing his own interpretation. For, from the side of kings and rulers, the sense of the value of St Peter's patronage should not be underestimated; they, too, were aware of a need for it and its benefits in this world and the next. Hence, Gregory was concerned, not to impose a single pattern of subjection and service, but to attract the *fidelitas* of kings and rulers upon a broad spectrum of interpretation ranging between religious commitment and secular fealty. Conditions were to be settled by negotiation and compromise, so long as appropriate dispositions of obedience and humility could be discerned in the several rulers.

---

[190] See above, 10.2.

10.6 Kings, Knights, and Warfare

Amongst the most striking features of Gregory's exercise of the papal office is the frequency and the forcefulness with which he sought to recruit the laity of western Christendom, from kings and princes to the broad knightly classes, for one form of another of military service by placing their arms at the disposal of the apostolic see.[191] Gregory set such service, in whatever form he claimed it, under the patronage of St Peter, to whom it was owed, through whom it might expect to be victorious, and from whom those who were engaged in it might expect an eternal reward. Thus, service in pursuit of papal ends was a *militia sancti Petri*, and the individual who provided it was a *miles sancti Petri*. The purpose of this section is to examine the contrast between the assurance with which, in practice, Gregory sought to involve the military classes in many forms of warfare for the purposes of the papacy, and the tentativeness and even inner contradiction of his thought and legislation about the bearing of arms by Christian laymen. For, in this matter, Gregory the man of action outran Gregory the man of ideas.

Gregory's practical engagement in warfare has already been abundantly illustrated in the foregoing parts of this study; it is necessary here only to bring together in summary its principal manifestations. Involvement in military organization and action was prominent in Gregory's local concerns in and around Rome itself. Gregory shared the obligation of every contemporary ecclesiastical ruler to safeguard the security and property of his church and its patron saint—in his case, the *terra sancti Petri* or papal patrimony in the narrower sense of the term. The patrimony had its own fortifications, garrisons, and obligations to service over which Gregory exercised direct and vigilant control. Over and above its own resources, he could, according to their willingness, seek military support from the Normans of South Italy who were sworn to the papal service; he once described knights so solicited as being dispatched 'for the household service of St Peter' ('in familiari militia beati Petri').[192] He also sought from the king of Denmark, who was not sworn to his service, the dispatch of his son to campaign further afield; he was invited to resist 'heretics', probably in Dalmatia, as a form of service to the papal palace ('apostolicae aulae militandum'); accompanied by a posse of knights, he would become the general, prince, and defender of Christendom ('ducem ac principem et defensorem christianitatis').[193] For such service on behalf of the papal household whether locally or further afield, Gregory also recruited, apparently piecemeal, from bishops, whether or not they were specially sworn to fidelity to the pope: thus, in 1079, the oath of Archbishop Henry of Aquileia included an undertaking faithfully to help the Roman church by secular service ('per secularem militiam') when called upon to do so;[194] informally, in 1076, Gregory called for knights from Bishop Henry of Trent to

---

[191] Erdmann, *Die Entstehung*, remains the indispensable starting-point for a consideration of this subject. For further discussion, see Cowdrey, 'Pope Gregory VII and the Bearing of Arms'.

[192] *Reg.* 9.4, to Abbot Desiderius of Montecassino, (Feb. 1081), p. 578/14–17.

[193] *Reg.* 2.51, to King Sweyn Estrithson, 25 Jan. 1075, p. 194/8–17.

[194] *Reg.* 6.17a(4), record of the Lent synod of 1079, pp. 428–9.

be sent according to his capacity for the service of St Peter; and, in 1078, he sought the dispatch of knights by Archbishop Manasses of Rheims.[195] Such an endeavour to secure the availability of knights was both less and more than a plan to have available a kind of papal equivalent of the Varangian guard at Constantinople. There was no such standing force, if only because it could not be financially afforded by the papacy. But, in its fullest extension, Gregory's aspiration to have at his disposal for papal service all the knights of western Christendom who duly acknowledged and understood St Peter's patronage found expression in his letter of January 1075 to Abbot Hugh of Cluny:

And because we ought to use either hand as a right hand (Judg. 3: 15) to subdue the violence of wicked men, it is needful, seeing that there is no prince who attends to such matters, for ourselves to protect the life of religious men. With brotherly charity we enjoin you to the best of your ability to extend your hand with watchful zeal by warning, beseeching, and urging those who love St Peter that, if they would truly be his sons and knights ('milites'), they should not hold secular princes more dear than him. For secular princes reluctantly grant wretched and transient things; but he, by loosing from all sins, promises things blessed and eternal, and by the power committed to him (Matt. 16: 19) he brings men to a heavenly home. I wish to know who are truly loyal ('fideles') to him, and who love their heavenly prince for heavenly glory no less than those to whom they are subject for an earthly and wretched hope.

Especially in his last years as pope, Gregory issued a clarion and general call to the service of St Peter to those knights who were willing to devote their arms to his immediate service.[196]

A further dimension to the active service for which Gregory looked in the military classes of society was his concern that laymen should apply coercion to clergy who were guilty of simony or unchastity. Especially eloquent of his preparedness to enlist the use of armed force was his sponsorship of the fierce Patarenes of Milan and their violent leader Erlembald, whom, in 1078, Gregory virtually canonized.[197] More widely, he called for the use of force by his supporters in Germany, as when, in 1075, he called upon the South German dukes and all men who were trustworthy in faith and devotion to debar offending clergy from taking part in divine service, 'even by force if it should be necessary' ('etiam vi si oportuerit'); some years later, a letter to his legates in France shows that, with his concurrence, knights there were similarly bringing coercive sanctions to bear upon offending clergy.[198]

As well as such general appeals to the military classes for coercive action to defend Christian righteousness and to resist its enemies, Gregory's pontificate was punctuated by plans for particular military enterprises which, although they came to little result, demonstrated Gregory's warlike intentions in pursuit of his objectives as

---

[195] *Epp. vag.* no. 13, pp. 32–3; *RHGF* 14.612C, no. 76.

[196] *Reg.* 2.49, to Abbot Hugh of Cluny, 22 Jan. 1075, p. 190; see also 9.21, to all the faithful, (1082), pp. 601–3; *Epp. vag.* no. 51, to the clergy of France and Germany, (summer 1083), pp. 122–5; no. 54, to all the faithful, (late 1084), pp. 130–5.

[197] See above, 4.3.

[198] *Reg.* 2.45, to the South German dukes, 11 Jan. 1075, pp. 184/17–185/4; 9.5, to Bishops Hugh of Die and Amatus of Oloron, (1081), p. 580/20–5.

pope. In 1074, he canvassed his 'crusading' plans to overawe the dissident Normans of South Italy and then to bring help to the Eastern Christians who were subject to the attacks and depredations of the Seljuk Turks; Gregory cast himself as the general and pontiff ('dux et pontifex') of his expedition in its ultimate form.[199] In the same year, the nadir of Gregory's relations with King Philip I of France led him to envisage the involvement of the armed force of French society in order to wrest the kingdom from a tyrannical and unprofitable ruler.[200] Between 1077 and 1080, Gregory sought increasingly to inject into the warfare of a German kingdom divided between the claims of Henry IV and of Rudolf of Swabia the notion of a holy war in which whoever was on the side of righteousness had the guarantee of earthly victory; those who fought for it were guaranteed, through the apostles Peter and Paul whose warfare they were waging, both prosperity in this life and remission of sins and blessings in the life to come.[201] The middle months of 1080 saw Gregory canvassing three military expeditions, the first and third of which he envisaged that he might lead in person: against the forces of Archbishop Guibert of Ravenna; to support the supposedly rightful Emperor Michael at Constantinople; and to bring to a right mind King Alphonso VI of León–Castile.[202] In 1081, he sought to organize the Normans to fight, if need be in Lent when they habitually refrained from warfare, in order to reduce South Italian rebels to submission.[203] Thereafter, Gregory sought to recruit and to direct military forces in the defence of Rome itself against Henry IV and Archbishop Guibert of Ravenna.[204] In view of all this military activity, there is warrant for Erdmann's comment that, judged in the light of what he intended to do, Gregory was the most warlike pope who had ever sat in St Peter's chair.[205]

As regards the spiritual and moral justification of warfare, Gregory's approach was far from showing the confidence and certainty that marked his actions.[206] This was partly owing to the lack of an adequate framework of ideas about war in the eleventh-century inheritance from the patristic past and in the current canon-law repertoire of guidance. In particular, St Augustine of Hippo's teachings about the just war, which might have provided such a framework, were unknown to Gregory and had no discernible influence upon his thought.[207] Instead, Gregory seems to have drawn upon a strong and established tradition about holy war that had characterized Ottonian Germany in the tenth century, and with which the papacy had been associated both in ninth- and early tenth-century military campaigns against the Saracens in Italy and in Pope Leo IX's campaign of 1053 against the Normans.[208] This tradition gave rise to an attempt, especially apparent in the liturgical tradition,

---

[199] See above, 7.1.   [200] See above, 5.2.1.   [201] See above, 3.4.5–8.

[202] See above, 3.5.3, 7.1, 6.10.

[203] *Reg.* 9.4, to Abbot Desiderius of Montecassino, (Feb. 1081), p. 578.

[204] See above, 3.5.6–9.

[205] 'Mißt man ihn an dem, was er gewollt hat, so war er wohl der kriegerischste Papst, der je auf Petri Stuhl gesessen hat': *Die Entstehung*, p. 161, Eng. trans. p. 177.

[206] See Cowdrey, 'Pope Gregory VII and the Bearing of Arms'.

[207] For Augustine's teachings, see Russell, *The Just War*, esp. pp. 15–26.

[208] See Erdmann, *Die Entstehung*, pp. 22–4, 86–97, 107–15, Eng. trans. pp. 26–8, 95–107, 118–27.

to direct the motives and outlook of those who fought towards a warfare which was fully acceptable on Christian terms. The attempt is well illustrated in the Romano-Germanic Pontifical, compiled at Mainz *c*.960, which, over the next hundred years, spread widely through western Christendom. It included a prayer for the army which asked both that, in fighting, warriors should have a right motive ('proeliandi recta voluntas'), and that in the hour of victory they should imitate Christ as the model victor who by the humility of his passion triumphed on the cross over death and the prince of death.[209]

The twin concepts of a right motive in warfare and of the imitation of Christ in battle and victory were active in the minds of Gregory and his Italian supporters. The first of them was developed by Bishop Anselm II of Lucca in the thirteenth book of his *Collectio canonum*, in which he was concerned to establish the freedom from sin of those who took part in warfare that was, in his view, just—that is, in warfare against Christian heretics and schismatics. Largely in the writings of St Augustine and of Pope Gregory the Great, he found authority for such *capitula* as 'that Moses did nothing cruel when, at the Lord's command, he slew certain men', 'concerning punishment (*vindicta*), that it should be performed not from hate but from love', and that 'those who fight can also be righteous (*iusti*), and that necessity not choice should be the reason for laying low an enemy'.[210] Such teaching can be seen in practice when, in 1084, a clerk from Anselm's circle instructed those about to take part in the battle of Sorbaria about 'on what grounds and with what intention they should fight' ('quo pacto quave intentione deberent pugnare').[211] Theirs was to be, indeed, a 'proeliandi recta voluntas'.

Gregory himself developed the other concept in the Romano-Germanic Pontifical —that of an imitation of Christ by the warrior which raised his warfare above the reproach of being sinful. This was an especial theme of Gregory's letters about his 'Crusading' plans, by which he sought to recruit and himself to lead military forces to relieve eastern Christians whom the pagan Seljuks were slaughtering like cattle. Gregory set before fighting men the supreme inner motive of self-sacrifice to the point of martyrdom which should inspire their warfare. The example of the Redeemer himself should be allied to the duty of brotherly love in order to recruit armed relief, 'for as he laid down his life for us, so ought we to lay down our life for our brothers' (1 John 3: 16).[212] Gregory's call to such self-sacrificial service under arms was the more compelling because he was willing himself to cross the sea and if need be to lay down his life for Christ which was the highest of human motives: 'for if, as some say, it is a noble thing to die for our country (Horace, *Carmina*, 3.2.13), it is a far nobler and truly praiseworthy thing to give our corruptible flesh for Christ,

---

[209] *RGP* no. 245, 2.380. For discussion of this and similar prayers, see Erdmann, *Die Entstehung*, pp. 334–5.

[210] For the relevant material, see Pásztor, 'Lotta per le investiture', pp. 375–421, esp. pp. 405–21.

[211] *Vita Anselmi ep. Lucensis*, cap. 23, p. 20.

[212] *Reg.* 1.49, to all wishing to defend the Christian faith, 1 Mar. 1074, p. 75/22–6; 2.31, to King Henry IV of Germany, 7 Dec. 1074, p. 166/20–6; 2.37, to all the faithful of St Peter, 16 Dec. 1074, p. 173/12–14.

who is life eternal.'²¹³ Papally-proclaimed warfare carried with it the possibility of a martyrdom which raised it to a wholly good and saving activity for those who made its declared motive their own. During his last years, Gregory challenged those upon whom he called to resist Archbishop Guibert of Ravenna and King Henry IV of Germany by citing St Paul's words about the Christian's sharing Christ's death and resurrection: 'If we suffer with him, we shall also reign with him' ('Si compatimur, et conregnabimus') (2 Tim. 12: 2). He also praised the few who, for love of Christ's law, were determined to stand fast to the death in face of the ungodly.²¹⁴ For the fighting man, being under arms was a following of Christ which required him to perfect his motive in fighting and which carried the promise of sharing Christ's death and resurrection. It was another route to a 'proeliandi recta voluntas'.

Therefore, when military endeavours whether general or particular were not under Gregory's immediate guidance as when he planned to be *dux et pontifex* of his final 'Crusading' plan in 1074, he preferred to set recruitment under the spiritual direction of abbots and bishops. In 1074, Abbot Hugh of Cluny was to urge knights who loved St Peter to rally duly to his service in the expectation of heavenly glory and reward.²¹⁵ More particularly, in 1076, on St Peter's behalf Gregory imposed upon Archbishop Arnald of Acerenza the pastoral charge of imposing penance upon and of absolving Count Roger of Calabria and Sicily together with the knights who were to campaign with him in Sicily; in order that they might deserve victory, the archbishop was to instruct them to refrain from capital crimes and to commend Christianity before the pagan Saracens.²¹⁶ In 1080, he instructed all the bishops of Apulia and Calabria with respect to the prospective expedition of Robert Guiscard to restore the supposed Emperor Michael VII to power in Constantinople that they should direct those who would fight in the faithful discharge of their task. They should be guided towards a right moral disposition and state of life in their fighting; the bishops were to urge them

most diligently, as your duty demands, to perform due penance and, as becomes Christians, to keep true faith with [Robert Guiscard and the Emperor Michael]. In all that they do they should keep the fear and love of God before their eyes, and they should persist in good works. Thus, supported by our own authority or rather by the power of St Peter, you should absolve them from their sins.²¹⁷

In 1081, Abbot Desiderius of Montecassino was to explore the circumstances in which Robert Guiscard and his followers might be employed to restrain depredations against the lands of St Peter.²¹⁸ In the last case, the claims of expediency came near to displacing those of morality. But, in general, Gregory was concerned that, through appropriate penance and absolution and through appropriate guidance by religious men, warfare should be raised above unworthy motives and states of mind, so that it might become holy in its intention as well as in its objectives.

---

²¹³ *Epp. vag.* no. 5, to Countess Matilda of Tuscany, (Dec. 1074), pp. 12–13.
²¹⁴ *Reg.* 9.21, to all the faithful, (1082), pp. 602/28–603/2; *Epp. vag.* no. 54, to all the faithful, (1084), pp. 132–3.   ²¹⁵ *Reg.* 2.49.   ²¹⁶ *Reg.* 3.11, 14 Mar. 1076, pp. 271/18–272/7.
²¹⁷ *Reg.* 8.6, 25 July 1080, pp. 523–4.   ²¹⁸ *Reg.* 9.4.

Gregory thus sought to proclaim a warfare which was morally acceptable, and even a matter of obligation, for those who would truly serve the cause of St Peter from motives of love for their neighbour and of imitating Christ in his death and resurrection. But this aspect of his thinking was difficult to reconcile with the long-standing understanding in the west that certain avocations, of which that of the knight was the most often discussed, could not by their very nature be pursued without falling into grave sin. Thus, for example, killings and woundings that knights inflicted even in warfare for a legitimate purpose under the command of a duly constituted ruler must be atoned for by substantial penance. Such a view was propagated by so influential a canon-law collection as that of Burchard of Worms; it was given effect in the penances that were imposed, under the supervision of a papal legate, upon those who fought in 1066 at the battle of Hastings; many in Gregory's own circle at Rome had been disturbed by his own sponsorship of such bloodshed as occurred in this battle.[219]

The problem of the necessarily sinful associations of the knight's activities came to the fore in the legislation about penance that took place between Gregory's November synod of 1078 and his Lent synod of 1080.[220] In 1078, a decree associated the knight with the merchant and the official, such as the steward of a lord, as those whose avocations could not by their nature be followed without sin, for it necessarily involved hatred in the heart and the violent and unjust detention of others' property. Therefore, a knight who sought penance for any major sin, like murder, adultery, or perjury, must lay aside his arms and have recourse to them only in order to defend his legitimate interests. In so doing, he should act on the advice of 'religious bishops', whose primary role was now not to perfect his motives but to instruct him in the terms upon which he might take up his arms.[221] When, in 1080, a further canon deepened the concept of penance to include the complete inner and external turning from all sins, it continued to exclude from true penance those who persisted in the knight's habitual and wrongful inner dispositions of hatred and self-enrichment. The canon intensified the call for penitents to seek the guidance of prudent and spiritual men about the terms of their penance. The new emphasis on inner motive no doubt mitigated the position of the knight, who was not explicitly named in the canon; but its terms perpetuated the stigma of inherent sinfulness that attached to the knight's way of life.[222]

[219] Burchard, *Decretum*, 6.23, cols. 770–1; penitential ordinance: *Councils and Synods*, no. 88, 2.581–4; *Reg.* 7.23, to King William I of England, 24 Apr. 1080, pp. 499/31–500/11. See also Cowdrey, 'Bishop Ermenfrid of Sion'.

[220] See above, 8.1.3.

[221] *Reg.* 6.5*b*(6), p. 404, together with 7.10, to the clergy and people of Brittany, 25 Nov. 1079, p. 472/5–15, where Gregory adopted a similar approach but enlarged the reasons for which a penitent knight might be allowed to bear arms to include protecting the interests of his lord, his friend, or the poor, and the defence of churches.

[222] *Reg.* 7.14*a*(5), pp. 481–2, where the comment concerning knights, merchants, and officials on p. 482/4–12, introduced by the words 'In quibus verbis manifeste datur intellegi', reads like an explanatory gloss on Gregory's initial and more radical statement; it does not appear in the version in the Volterra chapter-book: *De sancti Hugonis actis*, cap. 58, p. 79.

The persistence of a stigma upon the actual waging of warfare is graphically illustrated by Gregory's attempt to prescribe a fully moralized model for German kingship in his letter of March 1081 to Bishop Hermann of Metz. According to it, the rigour with which the church treated a sinner who had committed only a single homicide was compounded in the case of a ruler who consigned thousands to death from a motive of worldly glory which he was prone to conceal behind a façade of penitence while rejoicing at heart for what he had done. For a king's penitence to be sufficient, he should, in the terms of the canon of 1080, repent with his whole heart, and he must physically surrender all the gains which he had won or defended through the shedding of human blood.[223] Upon this teaching, kings should be prepared to surrender all their conquests, and there would be no scope for them to show the wrath ('ira') or the power to reward their followers that were essential for contemporary kingship as it actually operated.[224]

There was, no doubt, a theoretical possibility that Gregory's exemplary king might have committed himself to the service of St Peter and to the motives of warfare that Gregory attached to this service; if so, the inherent sinfulness of a military avocation might have been transcended. But, in actuality, Gregory never satisfactorily bridged the gap between the justification for warfare in the service of St Peter that he sought to establish and the current canonical understanding that the engagement of knights, and by extension of kings, in acts of violence inevitably involved grave sinfulness. The contradictions in Gregory's attitude to warfare were made the more apparent by the transmission of his canons on the subject. Surprisingly few of Gregory's letters or decrees passed into the canonical tradition of the western church.[225] The main exception is the decrees of the November synod of 1078. As a result of it, Gregory was for many decades remembered for his decree which asserted that the avocation of the knight could not, by its very nature, be followed without sin. Gregory's decree of 1080, which adumbrated a fresh approach to the problem of penance which would free the avocation of knight, merchant, and official from the stigma of being necessarily associated with sin, was seldom cited; although it is likely that, in the long term, it helped to open the way for Pope Urban II in 1095 to announce the Crusade as a way by which the knight, by conversion of life, turning from all sins, and released from all penance, might embark upon a warfare that was morally acceptable and religiously justifying. By his decree of 1078, Gregory was responsible for a prolongation of the view that the knight's way of life necessarily involved sin; by that of 1080, he opened the way for the view that it might be made a means of sanctification.

Was Gregory responsible for a wholesale transformation of the attitude of western Christians to the carrying of arms and the waging of war? It is important to avoid

---

[223] *Reg.* 8.21, p. 559/19–28.

[224] Gregory had himself threatened the 'iram nostrae malevolentiae' as a canonical sanction: *Reg.* 1.66, to the monks and others associated with SS. Quirico e Giulitta in Antrodoco, 20 Mar. 1074, p. 96/9–11; cf. 6.25, to Abbot Arnald of Saint-Sever, 8 Mar. 1079, p. 438/5–8; 6.31, to the people of Provence, 31 Mar. 1079, p. 445/4–10.

[225] See Gilchrist, 'The Reception of Gregory VII'.

such over-simplification as that of Gregory's severe critic Sigebert of Gembloux, who accused him of the innovation of presenting papally sanctioned warfare as in itself, without the accompaniment of confession and penance, a guarantee of salvation for those who took part.[226] Sigebert, who had lived through Gregory's pontificate, in 1103 reacted strongly against a letter from Pope Paschal II to Count Robert II of Flanders in which he applauded the count's warfare against imperialists in the bishopric of Cambrai and exhorted him to undertake a military campaign against 'excommunicated pseudo-clerks' at Liège. Sigebert commented upon the pope's letter phrase by phrase, and he was especially critical of its final sentence: 'We address this command to you and to your knights for the remission of sins and for the household service of the apostolic see, so that by these labours and victories you may, the Lord being your helper, attain to the heavenly Jerusalem.'[227] Sigebert condemned such an outright association of warfare with the remission of sins as a novel confusion of the functions of binding and loosing, which the papacy had hitherto kept separate by requiring confession and penance before men were released from their sins:

To such a custom of separating binding from loosing you have hitherto held fast, and you have commanded us to hold it fast, O holy mother Roman church. Whence, therefore, do you derive this novel authority by which, without confession and penance, the guilty are offered impunity for past sins and *carte blanche* for future ones? How wide a window for wickedness have you hereby opened up to men!

For such a flying in the face of the precepts of the scriptural and canonical tradition, Sigebert blamed 'Pope Hildebrand', when he commanded Countess Matilda of Tuscany to fight against the Emperor Henry IV for the remission of her sins.[228]

If Sigebert here fairly represented Gregory's command, he indeed made a new departure by straitly and simply attaching the remission of sins to participation in papally sanctioned warfare. But there are reasons for suspecting that Sigebert misleadingly over-simplified Gregory's position and exaggerated its novelty. Sigebert wrote some eighteen years after Gregory's death, by which time the preaching and popular understanding of the First Crusade may have coloured what he said. Even during Gregory's lifetime, Sigebert had probably exaggerated the extent to which Gregory opposed clerical unchastity for reasons of ritual, rather than moral purity;[229] he cannot be assumed more faithfully to have reported his theory of warfare. Neither Gregory's own letters nor other sources provide confirmation that Gregory counselled Countess Matilda in the sense that Sigebert stated. The date of any advice that he gave her must have been after 1080, for before that date it is impossible to identify a possible occasion. While evidence in Tuscan sources for the early 1080s, such as that concerning clerical preaching before the battle of Sorbaria,

---

[226] *Leodicensium epistola*. For its circumstances, see Erdmann, *Die Entstehung*, pp. 243–6, Eng. trans. pp. 262–3; J. Beumann, *Sigebert von Gembloux*, pp. 36–7; for Sigebert's career, ibid. pp. 7–38.

[227] 'Hoc tibi ac militibus tuis in peccatorum remissionem et apostolicae sedis familiaritatem precipimus, ut his laboribus et triumphis ad caelestem Ierusalem Domino prestante pervenias': *Leodicensium epistola*, cap. 1, pp. 451–2.

[228] *Leodicensium epistola*, cap. 13, pp. 463–4. [229] *Apologia*, cap. 5, p. 440.

sheds no direct light upon the practice of confession and penance, it is not excluded; indeed, those who had associated with excommunicates were required to seek absolution.[230] As for Gregory himself, he insisted that those who fought in campaigns that he sponsored should do so under the direction of religious clergy who were to provide for penance and absolution.[231] During the 1080s, the thrust of Gregory's own teaching was to insist upon, and not as Sigebert implied to diminish, the moralization of knighthood and kingship in respect of warfare and violence.

Especially when considered together with his provisions as regards penance, Gregory's ideas about the military service of the church were epoch-making in the developments that they began and for the moral intensity with which he took up a long tradition of holy war and enhanced it by the religious motivation that he brought to bear. But his thinking was too imperfectly elaborated and integrated, too fraught with inner contradictions, and, especially during the crisis years of the early 1080s, too unrealistic and pressed to extremes, for it in itself to have constituted a major and rounded reassessment of warfare, settled in its formulation and consolidated by effective application in practice. It was not by reason of his settled ideas that Gregory's pontificate marks a turning-point in the western Christian attitude to warfare and the profession of arms. Gregory's concerns as pope and the energy with which he proclaimed and pursued them ensured that his pontificate should mark a decisive stage in the association of the church with warfare and the bearing of arms. By the same token, it was a necessary, though perhaps not a sufficient, preparation for the emergence in the 1090s of the idea of Crusade. But it remained for future generations, assisted by the Crusade, to reconcile both in theory and in practice the contrasting appraisals of warfare that are discernible in Gregory's mind, words, and actions.

---

[230] *Vita Anselmi ep. Lucensis*, cap. 23, p. 20.   [231] See above, nn. 216–7.

Gregory VII and the Monastic Order

11.1 Gregory VII and the Protection of Monasteries

Gregory's background as a monk by early training and lasting loyalty ensured that, throughout his pontificate, he would maintain close relations with the monastic order to whose objectives he was committed. He would seek both to promote its well-being and to benefit from its services, spiritual and practical. Equally, many monastic houses would look to him for help and provide him with support. Especially with regard to Cluny and to Montecassino, these subjects have already been studied in work that was preparatory for the present book.[1] The purpose of this chapter is to summarize and complement earlier discussions by considering four matters which especially illustrate Gregory's distinctive concern with the monastic order.

A little-regarded passage from one of Gregory's privileges in favour of monasteries will serve to establish both the context of overall pastoral concern for the church in which his monastic dealings were set and also the sense of a close bond between the apostolic see and the monastic order that characterized his own pontificate:

Bearing in mind the mercy of Heaven, we have so assumed the oversight of the universal church and we so discharge the responsibility of apostolic government, that we meet with zealous bounty the rightful wishes of those who make supplications to us and that we may also fulfil the duty, according to the power that God gives us, of assisting by means of the scales of equity all those who find themselves in need. However, we believe that, so far as by God's aid the possibility is given us, we should especially devote thought and effort to the security of venerable places [that is, of monasteries] ('de venerabilium locorum stabilitate') and thus promote the rightful honour of the supreme and apostolic see of which such places are members.

These formal and rhetorical sentences form the *arenga* of the privilege that Gregory issued on 1 February 1075 for the Apulian monastery of S. Maria at Banzi (dioc. Venosa).[2] Despite the insignificance of this monastery, there are good reasons for citing them as the starting-point of a consideration of Gregory's dealings with, and appraisal of, the monastic order of the church. The privilege for Banzi was inserted into the beginning of Gregory's Register to serve as a paradigm for privileges which gave papal protection to monasteries which, like Banzi, were constitutionally subject to the exclusive jurisdiction of the Roman and apostolic see.[3] The *arenga* itself was expressed in traditional terms, in that it was adapted from formulas 85–6 of the *Liber*

---

[1] See Cowdrey, *The Cluniacs* and *The Age of Abbot Desiderius*; also 'Pope Gregory VII and la Chaise-Dieu', 'Cluny and Rome', and 'The Gregorian Papacy and Eremitical Monasticism'.

[2] *QF* no. 95, pp. 76–9. The proximity in date to the registration of the *Dictatus papae* and to the Lent synod of 1075 should be noticed.

[3] Registrum Vaticanum 2, fos. b–c; see *Reg.* pp. 632–5.

diurnus of the popes.[4] These formulas had been seldom used, the most recent authentic example being in a privilege of Pope Silvester II dated 1002.[5] But under Gregory VII, the *arenga* of the privilege for Banzi was substantially reproduced in no fewer than thirty-one genuine documents that survive, the latest of them being dated at Salerno on 9 May 1085.[6] Thereafter, there is no further example of its use, even under Pope Urban II. It may, therefore, be regarded as distinctively representative of the practice of papal officials between 1075 and 1085 as guided by Gregory himself, and as embodying his own estimate of monasticism.

The privilege for Banzi was the model for the treatment of monasteries which their founders or patrons had placed under the special care of St Peter; over recent centuries, they had done so at first by making them the property of the papacy, but in the later eleventh century it became usual, as with Banzi, for them to be made subject to the exclusive jurisdiction of the apostolic see.[7] The *arenga* of the privilege for Banzi registered two points of especial importance about such monasteries. First, the pope acknowledged their welfare, both spiritual and material, to be a particularly urgent part of his duty of oversight of the universal church. Second, monasteries that were committed to the proprietorship or to the exclusive jurisdiction of the apostolic see became members of it; they were not merely distant objects of its concern but were intrinsically connected to it as the limbs of the body are connected to its head.

The dispositive clauses of the privilege for Banzi made it clear that the oversight exercised by the papacy was threefold: first, it was concerned to secure the inviolability of monasteries and of their property wherever situated from every kind of inroad by lay or ecclesiastical outsiders; second, the internal life of the monastery was to be protected, especially in respect of the free election of the abbot; third, detailed provisions were made for the external relations of monasteries in order to secure their freedom from exactions by lay or ecclesiastical powers. The provisions of privileges based upon that for Banzi varied in detail according to the histories, circumstances, and needs of each monastery; but their basic structure and purpose remained constant.

Gregory was vigilantly active in helping monasteries under papal protection whose privileges were challenged or infringed. He acted strongly upon the complaints ('clamores') of their monks; as he reminded Archbishop Lanfranc of Canterbury in face of Bishop Herfast of Elmham's challenge to Bury St Edmunds:

The holy Roman church, by a God-given right, defends for itself the consecrations of churches, priests, and bishops, which it can and will perform without leave of anyone. It has provided, and by God's consent will continue to provide, the most strenuous defence for its

---

4 *Liber diurnus*, ed. Foerster, pp. 408–12.

5 Zimmermann, *Papsturkunden*, no. 403, 2.765–7 (formula 85), no. 71, 1.118–20 (formula 86).

6 Listed in *QF* pp. 473–4; no other *incipit* occurs more than four times in the index of *QF*. Similar formulas also occur e.g. in *QF* nos. 70, 74, 76, pp. 46, 54, 57.

7 For discussion of papal privileges for monasteries, see esp. Robinson, *The Papacy*, pp. 209–42, to which this section is much indebted.

own people in the present case as well, for they have come to Rome and have besought the counsel and aid of the apostolic see.[8]

Accordingly, for example, Gregory also heard the *clamor* of the abbot of Aurillac against a *vicomte* who unjustly held his abbey's lands, and he insisted upon the due return to Aurillac of two monasteries and their dependent lands and churches of which it had been wrongfully deprived.[9] Because monasteries which were directly subject to the apostolic see had the status of its members, inroads upon their property were tantamount to inroads upon the lands of St Peter themselves. Thus, those responsible incurred the sin of sacrilege, and Gregory could use language implying that their behaviour was treasonable against the apostolic see.[10]

Gregory was, therefore, active to further the well-being of such monasteries both by his own intervention and by calling upon whomever might best be able to secure their material and spiritual welfare. An appeal to him might be answered by a brief but urgent reply which was similar in tone to the royal writs of the Anglo–Norman kingdom. Thus, in 1074, when the monks, laymen, and feudatories of the monastery of SS. Quirico e Giulitta in Antrodoco, which belonged to St Peter's at Rome, failed duly to obey Bishop Rainer of Rieti to whose oversight Gregory had committed their monastery, Gregory called for their obedience 'according as you wish to have St Peter's favour and our own; otherwise you will not escape the wrath of our ill-will (*iram nostrae malivolentiae*) or the fetter of excommunciation.'[11] In examples already discussed, he called upon a metropolitan, Archbishop Lanfranc of Canterbury, to safeguard the rights of Bury St Edmunds; the people of three whole ecclesiastical provinces were to help the monks of Aurillac.[12] Similarly, he called upon legates to take necessary action, as Abbot Richard of Saint-Victor at Marseilles was to protect the newly restored canonical order at Saint-Sernin at Toulouse against those who, at the devil's prompting, were endeavouring to subvert it.[13] In a number of cases, the necessary renewal of the religious life in houses that were directly subject to St Peter was an urgent concern for Gregory. For example, in 1075/6, he charged Abbot Hugh of Cluny with the monastic reform of Montierneuf at Poitou, Saint-Pierre at Gigny, and Saint-Gilles; in 1081, he entrusted the southern French houses of Saint-Pierre at Montmajour and Sainte-Marie at Grasse to the similar attention of Abbot Richard of Saint-Victor.[14]

Although the pope's official concern was especially vigilant in respect to monasteries which, like Banzi, were directly subject to St Peter and were therefore regarded as members of the apostolic see, it was by no means confined to them; it was an especially intensive part of the papacy's universal care for houses of monks and regular

---

[8] *Reg.* 1.31, 20 Nov. 1073, pp. 51–2.

[9] *Reg.* 7.19, to all in the provinces of Bourges, Narbonne, and Bordeaux, 12 Apr. 1080, pp. 494–5.

[10] Sacrilege: *Reg.* 6.31, to all in Provence concerning the monastery of Montmajour, 31 Mar. 1079, p. 444/30–4; 7.18, to Archbishop William of Auch, 12 Apr. 1080, p. 493/27–9; 7.19, p. 495/2–5. Treason: 1.68, to Bishop Froterius of Nîmes, 22 Mar. 1074, p. 98/7–8.

[11] *Reg.* 1.66, 20 Mar. 1074, pp. 95–6.   [12] *Reg.* 1.31, 7.12.

[13] *Reg.* 9.30 (1082–3), p. 615.

[14] *QF* nos. 108–10, pp. 100–5; *Reg.* 9.6, 18 Apr. 1081, pp. 581–3.

canons. Two examples may serve to illustrate this general care as Gregory sought to discharge it. The first is his solicitude for the abbey of Saint-Remi at Rheims in face of its oppression by Archbishop Manasses I.[15] No less than monasteries specially commended to St Peter, Saint-Remi was regarded as a 'venerabilis locus' in the language of the *Liber diurnus*. Gregory received the complaints ('clamores') of its monks, and he repeatedly reminded Archbishop Manasses of his duty to oversee the appointment of an abbot who would attend to the material and spiritual well-being of the community. Manasses should himself respect both its goods and the persons of its individual members. Failure on his part would show a lack of respect for St Peter as well as for the pope himself; recalcitrance would call forth from Gregory apostolic severity and wrath ('apostolicam severitatem et iracundiam') against Manasses. It was not only to the archbishop that Gregory looked for the security of the monastic life of Saint-Remi. In 1074, he enlisted the aid of Abbot Hugh of Cluny to supervise Manasses's behaviour and to report upon it to Rome. In 1077, renewed complaints from the monks led Gregory to give Bishop Josfred of Paris a similar responsibility; if necessary, it might be extended to Bishop Hugh of Die and other legates, while, if all else failed, the grievances of the monks should be referred to Rome for Gregory's own direct action.

A different approach which might be adopted is illustrated by Gregory's action in 1073 on behalf of the Lombard monasteries of S. Benigno at Fruttuaria and S. Michele della Chiusa. Both were subject to severe vexation by outside assailants. Gregory therefore sought the assistance of a devout lay ruler, Countess Adelaide of Turin, whose zeal in support of monasteries he praised. He charged her by his command and by St Peter's authority to redouble her support. He appealed to his own understanding of the proper responsibility and interest of lay rulers; they should so provide for the material needs of holy places and their religious inhabitants that they might themselves share in the spiritual benefits, that is the intercessions, that the monastic order secured by its devout observances. Gregory commended the monastery and monks of Fruttuaria to Adelaide's care by way of her providing counsel and strong defence against the assaults of their adversaries; he likewise commended the abbot and monastery of S. Michele to her vigilant care and protection.[16]

By such means as he adopted at Rheims and in the case of the Lombard monasteries, Gregory sought to implement the prime duty of the apostolic see to ensure the inviolability of monasteries in the performance of spiritual duties which were at the centre of the proper life and witness of the church.

11.2 Gregory VII's Expectations of Monasticism

Gregory's personal expectations of the monastic order of the church must be understood in the light of this official practice of the Roman church of his day in respect of

---

[15] For details, see above, 5.3.3.1; the letters concerned are *Reg.* 1.13–14, 52–3, 4.20.
[16] *Reg.* 1.37, 7 Dec. 1073, pp. 58–9.

the protection of monasteries and other religious houses. His expectations also reflected the widespread view, which he shared, of the universal church as consisting of three orders—the virgins, the chaste, and the married.[17] Those who consecrated themselves to a life of virginity which they lived in common with others according to such a Rule as that of St Benedict had a recognized place in the church as followers of a more excellent way. Gregory was himself a monk who continued to wear the monastic habit as a token of his abiding commitment to it.[18] So hostile a witness as Bishop Guy of Ferrara recorded in generous terms the monastic life-style which Gregory maintained both as archdeacon and as pope:

He was also a defender of widows and minors, a supporter of orphans, a helper of the poor; all that he could come by he gave to the needy and the weak, the wretched and the poor. Constant in fasting, zealous in prayer, given to sacred study, he made his body the temple of Christ. For however weary, he curtailed his sleep. He gladly suffered hunger, although he abounded with the most exquisite food. He bore thirst and other bodily discomforts, although all things were at his beck and call. . . . When others were busy with secular business and were striving for the desires and pursuits of the world, he rose above all such things by the virtue of his soul, for he reckoned this life to be an exile, not a home ('peregrinationem, non patriam'). And more: who can adequately tell how courteous, amenable, and available he was to everyone? He gave the law to servants and masters, princes and subjects, parents and children, wives and husbands, and he guided the lives of all in every respect by his godly advice. . . . No one ever went empty away who approached him for a hearing. As we ourselves have observed at first hand, he received abundantly from the Lord the grace of tears, so that at his daily mass—for no day passed without his offering the Lord's body and blood—he poured out his own self at the time of sacrifice in lamentation and tears, and thus made a double sacrifice to the Lord. He ate only once in each day, and he prolonged his fast into the evening. His table was graced with the most precious dishes and covered with the choicest food. It abounded with stags and roe-deer, hares, boars, birds, and fattened poultry of every kind, as the papal dignity required. Amongst so many delicate dishes, while others feasted he nevertheless fed only on wild herbs and vegetables served with chick-peas.[19]

Allowance must be made for Guy of Ferrara's rhetorical purpose of setting Gregory in a favourable light before he presented an adverse case which he deemed to outweigh it. But it is hard to escape the conclusion that those who, like Guy, observed Gregory at first hand must have been impressed by his monastic style of living.

There can be little doubt that Gregory's adoption of this style was part of his response to the example and the teachings of the first pope who had been a monk, Gregory the Great. For Gregory I, monasticism, especially as taught by St Benedict himself, was and always remained a decisive influence. He had given up the office of city prefect at Rome in order to establish a monastic community on the slopes of the Caelian hill in what had been his family home. It was a centre of austerity, devotion, and study; to it, his mother brought a diet of cooked vegetables such as St Benedict had prescribed and such as Gregory VII was to follow. After Gregory I was

---

[17] *Epp. vag.* no. 9, to Bishop Otto of Constance, (late 1075), pp. 20–1.   [18] See above, 2.1.

[19] *De scis. Hild.* 1.2, pp. 534–6, cf. Wenric of Trier, *Epistola*, cap. 1, pp. 285–6; also, for Gregory's vegetarian diet, Benzo of Alba, *Ad Heinricum*, 6.6, p. 666/1–13.

unwillingly called from his monastery to the active service of the Roman church and to the papal office, he looked back to his monastic years as the happiest period of his life, when he could shun the idle pursuits of the world and give his mind to prayer. When called to the pastoral office, he could not sustain the recollection that had before been possible; with a mind that was divided and rent, he became immersed in the care of churches, monasteries, and individuals. He accepted this as his calling, but longed for his days of monastic quiet. He expressed himself in the imagery that Gregory VII would borrow in his own letters as pope, of being shaken by the waves of the sea and battered by tempest, while longing for the repose of the shore that he had left behind. Gregory I's own letters illustrate his continuing concern as pope to secure both the interior discipline and the external security of monasteries in which the prayerful, disciplined, and cultivated life was being maintained for the benefit not only of the monks but of all Christian people.[20]

Gregory VII, too, was always insistent upon the intrinsic excellence of the monastic life. He made his own the phrase that the draftsmen of his privileges for monasteries derived from the *Liber diurnus* in order to describe them: considered as houses of prayer, they were 'venerabiles loci'.[21] They were to be fostered as places of rest ('quies'), not in the sense of idle repose but of havens of peace and tranquillity in the midst of the tumults of the world; in them, the worship of God might be single-mindedly performed.[22] As for monks themselves, they were 'spiritual men', the simplicity and purity of whose lives established them as an élite among Christians in respect of all that was authentic in the Christian life. The life of the monk who was true to his profession was one of progress from virtue to virtue, and its goal was the perfection of charity according to its truest expression.[23] Communities of monks provided a beacon light to guide and inspire their neighbours outside the cloister upon whom their witness made a compelling impact.[24] Their prayers and works were, therefore, especially pleasing to God, so that they were able to intercede with him on behalf of others, like Gregory himself, who were immersed in the business of the world.[25]

Especially in the earliest days of his pontificate, Gregory was urgently concerned to secure the intercessory support of monastic communities, wherever it could be

---

[20] For Gregory I's years as a monk, see John the Deacon, *S. Greg. magni vita*, 1.4–25, cols. 64–72. For his appraisal of the monastic life, see esp. *Dialogues*, Prol. 1–6, vol. 1.10–15, *Hom. in Hiezech.* 1.11.6, pp. 171–2, *Moralia*, *Epistola*, 1, vol. 1.10–15. Gregory devoted the second book of his *Dialogues* to St Benedict: 2.126–249. But for sharp criticism of those who might be useful to others by their preaching (*praedicatio*) but who refrain in order to seek their own tranquillity (*quies*), see *Regula pastoralis*, 1.5, vol. 1.144–9. For examples of Gregory's letters which bear on monastic affairs, see *Reg.* 1.38–41, 3.3, 5.4, 5.55, 14.16, vols. 1.44–9, 148–9, 269–70, 350, 2.1089–90.

[21] *Reg.* 1.8, to the legates Hubert and Albert, 30 Apr. 1073, p. 13/19–24.

[22] *Reg.* 1.14, to Abbot Hugh of Cluny, 30 June 1073, p. 23/3–6; 2.69, to Bishop Cunibert of Turin, 9 Apr. 1075, p. 227/12–17, 25–30.

[23] *Reg.* 6.17, to Abbot Hugh of Cluny, 2 Jan. 1079, p. 424/23–6; cf. 6.15, to the monks of Saint-Victor at Marseilles, 2 Jan. 1079, p. 420/29–37.

[24] *Epp. vag.* no. 2, to the community of Vallombrosa, (after 12 July 1073), pp. 4–7.

[25] *Reg.* 1.9, to Duke Godfrey of Lorraine, 6 May 1073, p. 14/17–20; 2.49, to Abbot Hugh of Cluny, 22 Jan. 1075, p. 190/7–12.

recruited. On the day after his election, he asked Abbot Desiderius of Montecassino to urge his monks to pray for him, 'so that the prayer which should have ensured my freedom [from the burden of the papal office] may at least defend me from running into danger now that I am set in the midst of it'. He asked Prince Gisulf of Salerno to transmit a similar request to Abbot Leo of La Cava and to other monastic figures in South Italy.[26] A week later, two of his legates in France were to seek prayers for him in whatever monasteries their travels might bring them to, 'so that Almighty God, who knows that my desire has not been set upon this office, may mercifully grant to my infirmity all powers that are necessary for bearing so heavy a burden which, once it was imposed upon me, I could not refuse for fear of him'.[27] Gregory continued earnestly to desire such prayers from monastic communities both for himself and for the renewal and safety of the Roman church.[28]

He also sought to secure monastic prayers for others who stood in especial need of them, and to ensure that prayers were set in the context of proper advice to those for whom they were offered. Monks were especially to assist with Gregory's bid to ensure the proper administration of penance. At his Lent synod of 1080, he accordingly encouraged those who knew themselves to be guilty of grave sin to open their soul to 'prudent and religious men'.[29] What Gregory expected of monks in this connection is well illustrated by a letter that he soon afterwards wrote to Abbot Peter of Fucecchio and Prior Rudolf of Camaldoli. Gregory declined their request that he should absolve Ughiccio, count of Fucecchio, a member of the powerful Cadolingi family, who had invaded the property of the church of Lucca and who had compounded his offence by helping to expel from that see Gregory's ardent supporter, Bishop Anselm II. Gregory insisted that the count must show true repentance by acknowledging his fault and seeking pardon with his whole heart. Gregory explained the offences that the count must fully acknowledge, and called upon the two religious superiors to be diligent in their intercessory support:

Therefore we urge and beseech you to remember especially to pour out your prayers daily for him to the Lord, imploring God's mercy to visit, soften, and turn to penitence his heart and mind, so that repenting, bewailing, and asking pardon for his sins he may in the future by his performance of good works prove worthy to be reckoned amongst the members of holy church.[30]

In April 1079, Gregory's intervention at Montecassino further illustrates his concern to achieve a right relationship between a monastery and a powerful lay

---

[26] *Reg.* 1.1, 2, 23 Apr. 1073, p. 4/2–6, 26–30; on 28 Apr., Gregory wrote in similar terms to the abbots of Cluny and of Saint-Victor at Marseilles: 1.4, p. 7; cf. 1.62, to Abbot Hugh of Cluny, 19 Mar. 1074, p. 91/10–15.

[27] *Reg.* 1.8, p. 13/19–24, cf. 1.9, p. 14/16–20.

[28] *Reg.* 1.62, p. 91/6–15, 2.27, to the monks of S. Savino at Piacenza, 27 Nov. 1074, p. 159/33–6; 2.65, to the monks of Saint-Denis, 25 Mar. 1075, p. 220/34–5; 5.21, to Abbot Hugh of Cluny, 7 May 1078, p. 384/30–3; 6.17, to the same, 2 Jan. 1079, p. 424/23–6; *Epp. vag.* no. 29, to the monks of Montecassino, (Apr. 1079), pp. 76–7.

[29] *Reg.* 7.14*a*(5), p. 481/30–4; see above, 8.1.3.   [30] *Epp. vag.* no. 43, (? 1081), pp. 104–7.

neighbour and to direct its intercessions towards his temporal and eternal well-being. Gregory had a number of grievances against Prince Jordan of Capua, one of which was the violent seizure by his knights from the abbey church at Montecassino of valuables that had been deposited there. Gregory took the drastic step of laying Montecassino itself under interdict, partly because he judged Abbot Desiderius to have been remiss in himself punishing the outrage, and partly in order to punish Jordan's pride and violence by depriving him and his men of the monks' intercessory support. In the event, Gregory quickly raised the interdict in order that the monks might observe the feast of the Ascension. He did so with a plea that they would re-double their intercessory support of both friends and enemies, and especially of Prince Jordan of Capua:

Also you should offer your prayers for him who has invaded so holy and world-famous a place, that God may give him a contrite heart and so turn him to himself that he may deserve to have God's grace in this life and in the next.[31]

Gregory's dealings with Fucecchio, Camaldoli, and Montecassino as recorded in these letters illustrate his concern to ensure the internal and external integrity of monasteries in all matters relating to their spiritual observance and material posses-sions. An important reason for it was their contribution to the church at large and to their own immediate neighbourhood by the power of their intercessions and the value of their counsel, especially with regard to the penitence of laymen for grave public and private offences. Gregory's concern was matched by his vigilance to secure the observance of the Rule of St Benedict in both the spirit and the letter. Thus, in 1079, when his legate to Spain, Cardinal Richard of Saint-Victor at Marseilles, was elected abbot by the monks in succession to his brother Bernard, Gregory was prompt to urge him, in respect of his new office, to bind himself strictly to the holy Rule in the depth of his being ('medullitus'), lest by reason of his youth his monastery should suffer any harm in its religious observance.[32] Gregory was especially anxious to ensure the election of abbots according to the provisions of the Rule of St Benedict, so that monasteries might be rightly and regularly governed and so that the monastic life might be sustained in religious integrity and brotherly con-cord.[33] There was more than a formal reference to Gregory's priorities as pope in the *arenga* of one of his late privileges for a monastery, when it asserted that, although his apostolic office required him to provide to the limit of his ability for all the churches, his vigilance and care were especially called for in respect of monasteries and for those in them who served God devotedly.[34]

---

[31] For the events concerned, see *Chron. Cas.* 3.46, p. 424; *Reg.* 6.37, to Prince Jordan of Capua, 21 Apr. 1079, pp. 453–4. For Gregory's response, *Epp. vag.* nos. 28–9, (Apr. 1079), pp. 72–7.

[32] *Reg.* 7.7, 2 Nov. 1079, p. 468/20–6.

[33] *Reg.* 1.52, to Archbishop Manasses of Rheims, 14 Mar. 1074, pp. 79/15–80/1; 2.27, to the monks of S. Savino at Piacenza, 27 Nov. 1074, p. 159/30–6; 9.6, to Abbot Richard of Saint-Victor at Marseilles, 18 Apr. 1081, pp. 582/19–583/5.

[34] *QF* no. 217, to Abbot Madelmus of S. Sophia at Benevento, 11 Dec. 1084, p. 262.

11.3 Montecassino and Cluny

Amongst the monasteries of Latin Christendom, those which Gregory most highly esteemed and from which he most earnestly sought both spiritual and temporal support were the South Italian abbey of Montecassino and the Burgundian abbey of Cluny. Their significance for him was the greater because each of them was ruled throughout his pontificate by an abbot of outstanding capability and experience who was personally well known to him—Montecassino by Abbot Desiderius (1058–87) and Cluny by Abbot Hugh of Semur (1049–1109).[35] In important respects, the two abbeys stood in contrast to each other. Montecassino was by many centuries the older, for its community traced its history to the settlement there in the sixth century of St Benedict himself, whereas Cluny had less than two centuries of history behind it; it had been founded in 909/10 by Duke William the Pious of Aquitaine. Partly on account of their difference of age, the two abbeys stood in different relationships to the apostolic see. Cluny was one of the monasteries which, in line with the formula of the privilege for Banzi, had so close a relationship with the apostolic see that they were in its especial care; Cluny was joined to Rome by a special right ('speciali iure').[36] Montecassino was not numbered among such monasteries; Gregory dealt with its legal affairs and institutional interests as it were from a distance, as an impartial arbiter.[37] Yet, if Montecassino was constitutionally at a greater distance from the apostolic see than was Cluny, in terms of personalities and of services rendered, Montecassino had a close standing relationship which was not paralleled by Cluny. Unlike Abbot Hugh, Abbot Desiderius for as long as he was abbot was also an 'external' cardinal-priest of the Roman church, with the important title of S. Cecilia in Trastevere.[38] Cluny had no dependent house in Rome, but, from the days of Pope Alexander II, Montecassino occupied the monastery of S. Maria in Pallara on the Palatine, where a small community of monks served both the abbey and the papacy.[39] Against this institutional presence of Cassinese monks must be set the outstanding loyalty and service to Gregory of two former monks and grand priors of Cluny who ceased to be monks of that house when they were promoted to the senior cardinal-bishopric, that of Ostia—Gerald (1072/3–77) and his successor Odo (c.1080–8), the future Pope Urban II.[40] The dominant note of the Gregorian papacy's relations with Cluny was trust and cordiality, whereas that with Montecassino was respect and convenience. Moreover, it is likely that, on balance, Gregory stood in greater need of help from Montecassino than Montecassino stood in need of help from him; whereas with Cluny, the position was reversed: in view of the hostility of its neighbouring

---

[35] For fuller discussions of the relations between Gregorian papacy and the two abbeys, see Cowdrey, *The Cluniacs* and *The Age of Abbot Desiderius*. The purpose of the present section is mainly to take account of some points of similarity and difference.

[36] See the use of the Banzi formula in Gregory's privilege for Cluny of 1075/6: *QF* no. 107, p. 95; the Cluny privilege, like a number of others, adopts the variant 'apostolicae sedis, cui speciali iure adhaerent' instead of the Banzi reading 'apostolicae sedis, cuius membra sunt'.

[37] *QF* no. 162, pp. 189–91; Gregory issued no privilege for Montecassino itself.

[38] Ganzer, *Die Entwicklung*, pp. 17–23.   [39] Cowdrey, *The Age of Abbot Desiderius*, pp. 60–8.

[40] Hüls, *Kardinäle*, pp. 100–3.

bishops, Cluny needed papal support more than the pope needed that of Cluny, at least in temporal matters.

As the monastery of St Benedict and as a holy and world-famous place, Gregory expressed his high regard for Montecassino.[41] He was concerned to defend both the lands and the monastery of St Benedict against Norman attacks and depredations; in 1079, he imposed the sanction of his own interdict upon the abbey in order to remedy what he construed as Abbot Desiderius's infirmity of purpose in punishing an outrage against it by Prince Jordan of Capua.[42] At the beginning and in the final years of his pontificate, Gregory recognized his pressing need for Desiderius's counsel and assistance. It is eloquent of Gregory's sense of dependence upon Cassinese aid that, along with the Lombard prince Gisulf of Salerno, Desiderius was the first major figure whom Gregory notified of his succession to the papacy; he urged both men to come to him as soon as possible, for, as he told each of them, 'you know how greatly the Roman church needs you and what confidence it has in your prudence'.[43] In 1081, Gregory again addressed Desiderius in such terms. Addressing him as a beloved brother ('amande frater'), he urged him to do what was fitting by so adhering to Gregory that the well-being ('honor') of his holy mother the church, which trusted greatly in him, might now and always gain strength; once again, Gregory asked Desiderius to come to him.[44] In 1080, Desiderius had been instrumental in bringing about the renewal of the oaths of the Norman princes Robert Guiscard and Jordan of Capua to the papacy.[45] From this time, Gregory looked to him for co-operation in ecclesiastical matters in South Italy, as in dealing with the Armenian impostor Macharus and in composing the mutual hostility of the bishop and church of Valva.[46] He also looked to Desiderius to exert a beneficial influence on his difficult ally Robert Guiscard, both to negotiate about the provisions of knights to impose peace and order in South Italy and also, more sensitively, to report upon and if necessary to counteract Guiscard's supposed negotiations in 1081 with King Henry IV of Germany.[47]

Set upon a rocky eminence and at the centre of a 'terra sancti Benedicti' which Desiderius extended and developed, Montecassino was strategically placed just to the south of the papal patrimony near the ancient Via Latina which led from Rome to the south of Italy and which was coming under ever more effective Norman control.

---

[41] *Epp. vag.* nos. 28–9, to the monks of Montecassino, (Apr. 1079), pp. 74–7.

[42] Gregory legislated to defend the lands and goods of St Benedict at his Roman synods: *Reg.* 6.5*b*, record of the Nov. synod 1078, pp. 401/14–15, 403/6–10; 7.14*a*(4), record of the Lent synod 1080, p. 481; for the incident of 1079, see above, n. 31.

[43] *Reg.* 1.1–2, 23 Apr. 1073, pp. 3–4; Gregory wrote to Abbot Hugh of Cluny five days later: 1.4, p. 7. Gregory's note of urgency in his letters of Desiderius and Gisulf was probably in part the result of the false report of the death of Robert Guiscard: Amatus, 7.7, pp. 297–8; it is an illustration of the cruciality of Norman affairs.

[44] *Reg.* 9.11, (May 1081), pp. 588–9.   [45] See above, 6.2.

[46] *Reg.* 7.28, to Archbishop Roffred of Benevento, (1080), pp. 509–10; 8.15, to the people of Valva, 12 Dec. 1080, pp. 353–6.

[47] *Reg.* 9.4, (Feb. 1081), pp. 577–9, 9.11.

In 1059, the reform papacy had committed itself to alliance with the Normans; at the same juncture, Desiderius had decided that they were neighbours whose presence must be accepted and therefore built upon for the advantage of Montecassino. During the decades that followed, both the papacy and the abbey had relationships with the Normans that were necessary to them but never easy. Since the Normans of Capua and Apulia were near at hand, Montecassino was impelled to give priority to its relations with them over the immediate interests of the papacy. Gregory VII's repeated excommunication of Robert Guiscard was an especial source of strain. Nevertheless, in the longer term, the papacy could never forget its dependence upon Montecassino as an intermediary with its troublesome Norman allies, upon whom it had to rely for military and political backing in face of the problems set by Henry IV as king and, from 1084, as emperor. Thus, Abbot Desiderius was always a major figure in papal concerns and calculations. As his *Dialogues*, written between 1076 and 1079, illustrate,[48] Desiderius's commitment to papal aspirations for the reform of the church should not be underestimated. But political considerations, and especially the interests of Montecassino, always played a major part in determining relations between Desiderius and the papacy. Roman dependence upon the great and ancient abbey in the south was set in the context of the abbey's need to secure its own position. Abbot Desiderius could be expected to give the papacy his full and unqualified support only when his own position with respect to the Normans was settled and clear, and when the Norman leaders were acting in substantial agreement with each other and with the abbey. Such conditions of harmony were seldom prevalent.

Gregory VII's relations with the Burgundian abbey of Cluny were orientated differently to his relations with Montecassino. Unlike the ancient abbey of St Benedict, Cluny was numbered among the monasteries that were in a special sense commended to St Peter and to the apostolic see. Its status was already established in its foundation charter, and throughout the tenth and eleventh centuries the popes had frequently renewed and intensified its close bond with the papacy.[49] This bond was strong, partly because of the value that the popes set upon Cluny's liberty, with its direct and exclusive subjection to the lordship of St Peter, and partly because of Cluny's own pressing need for the papal protection of its immunity and exemption against the sometimes forcefully advanced counter-claims of the local episcopate. Papal defence of Cluny's liberty was signally provided and shown to be effective in the legatine missions of Cardinal Peter Damiani in 1063 and Cardinal Peter of Albano in 1080.[50]

In Gregory's eyes, Cluny as a monastic institution possessed in the most intensive form that was possible the bond with the apostolic see that was expressed in the *arenga* of the privilege for Banzi; as pope, he had a corresponding duty to protect and to propagate it. He gave memorable expression to his evaluation of Cluny in his

---

[48] For the *Dialogues*, see Cowdrey *The Age of Abbot Desiderius*, pp. 21–2, 79–83.
[49] Cowdrey, *The Cluniacs*, pp. 3–63.
[50] Cowdrey, *The Cluniacs*, pp. 47–51, 52–7, and id., 'Cardinal Peter of Albano's Legatine Journey'.

allocution in its praise which, synchronously with Peter of Albano's legatine mission, he delivered to his Lent synod in 1080.[51] In it, he praised the liberty ('libertatis immunitatem') with which the popes had endowed Cluny. From its foundation 170 years before, it had been an exemplar of the freedom from external authorities and of the exclusive subjection to St Peter which represented the Gregorian ideal of liberty: 'its abbots and monks have never in any way dishonoured their sonship of this [the Roman] church nor bowed the knee to Baal and the Baalim' (cf. 1 Kgs 19: 18). Cluny, therefore, had a unique place amongst monasteries north of the Alps. It belonged to the Roman church by a special right ('speciali iure') as a peculiar possession. Gregory dwelt upon the qualities of its abbots: 'under its religious and holy abbots . . . it surpasses all other monasteries . . . in the service of God and in spiritual fervour. . . . For there has never been an abbot there who was not *sanctus*—holy.' Gregory's language recalls that which he applied to the succession of popes themselves in *Dictatus papae* 23 and towards the close of his letter of March 1081 to Bishop Hermann of Metz: 'the Roman pontiff, if he has been canonically instituted, is indubitably made *sanctus* by the merits of St Peter.'[52] The abbots and monks of Cluny had a comparable endowment of official and personal holiness: 'They have always copied the liberty and dignity of this holy Roman see which they have enjoyed from the beginning, and from generation to generation they have nobly preserved for themselves its authority. For they never bent their necks before any outsider or earthly power, but they have remained under the exclusive obedience and protection of St Peter and this [the Roman] church.' As St Peter's merits devolved upon a canonically elected pope and made him *sanctus*, similar merits devolved upon the abbots of Cluny 'per successionis seriem'.

Such being Gregory's appraisal of Cluny's institutional standing in relation to the apostolic see, it is not surprising that, at about the time of his synodal allocution, he was using it as a model for the liberty of other monastic houses. Such houses were not constitutionally subject to Cluny; indeed, they did not necessarily have any relationship with it. There was no relationship between Cluny and Saint-Victor at Marseilles, which, early in 1079, Gregory wished to reward for the long absence upon papal service of its abbot, Bernard. Because of the claim upon St Peter and St Paul which this absence established, Gregory established a monastic union between Saint-Victor and the Roman monastery of St Paul's-without-the-Walls. Thus, upon the model of Cluny's relationship with the apostolic see, Saint-Victor might be especially joined to the apostolic see and might enjoy its aid and blessing.[53] In 1080, Gregory committed to Abbot William of Hirsau the oversight of the monastery of All Saints' at Schaffhausen, which was already subject to the apostolic see

---

[51] *Epp. vag.* no. 39, pp. 96–9.

[52] *Reg.* 2.55*a*, p. 207/3–4, 8.21, pp. 559/28–561/6.

[53] *Reg.* 6.15, to the monks of Saint-Victor, 2 Jan. 1079, p. 420/15–23; according to Berthold, Gregory incorporated Bernard into the Roman church as *primicerius* of St Paul's: *a.* 1079, pp. 323/48–324/4; 14 Apr. 1074. Gregory referred to him as 'Sancti Pauli abbatem': *Reg.* 6.33, to Abbot Hugh of Cluny, p. 447/4–5.

('iuris apostolicae sedis'). In derogation of the arrangements of his predecessor Alexander II, he provided for its absolute freedom from all secular powers and for its reposing in the liberty of the Roman see as did the monasteries of Cluny and Marseilles.[54] Gregory again used the model of Cluny's liberty in 1083 when he issued a privilege to Bernard, the Cluniac abbot of the Leónese monastery of Sahagún. Sahagún was to be specially joined to the apostolic see on the model of Cluny, which shone forth through almost the whole world for the renown of its religion and good report. As Cluny in France, so Sahagún in Spain was to stand out for its prerogative of liberty and protection by the apostolic see, to which it would be joined as a member of the body is joined to its head.[55] Both in itself and on account of its replicability within the conventions established by Gregory's privilege for Banzi, Cluny's liberty gave it a prestige in Gregory's eyes which marked it off from a monastery like Montecassino that primarily relied for its well-being upon its independent standing and its own regional impact upon spiritual and temporal affairs.

To move from Cluny's institutional status as expressed in its liberty and in its ideal closeness to the apostolic see into the actuality of the relations between the Cluny of Abbot Hugh and the papacy calls for a considerable adjustment of perspective.[56] Like Abbot Desiderius of Montecassino, Abbot Hugh of Cluny loomed large in Gregory's considerations; but both men had minds of their own and were committed to the spiritual and temporal welfare of their abbeys and their monastic families. It was remembered at Cluny that, while he was pope, Gregory used to call Hugh 'the persuasive tyrant (*blandus tirannus*), for he knew him to be a lion towards the untamed and a lamb towards the meek, and to be not unpractised in sparing the submissive and chastening the proud'.[57] Gregory's characterization of Hugh blended approval and admiration with a recognition that Hugh was his own master, and someone who might be persuaded but not compelled.

Gregory's letters show him to have been critical of Hugh for tardiness in coming to Rome and for being preoccupied with the internal and external affairs of his own monastery.[58] The two men met but seldom during Gregory's pontificate. In January 1077, Hugh was present at Gregory's encounter at Canossa with Hugh's godson Henry IV of Germany; according to the German annalist Berthold, during his contacts with Henry Hugh incurred excommunication from which Gregory had to release him.[59] Hugh did not come to Rome until, at earliest, the second quarter of 1079, when it is probable that a personal meeting led to the resolution of a complex of problems that threatened their understanding and renewed in Gregory the approval of

---

[54] *Reg.* 7.24, to Abbot William of Hirsau, 8 May 1080, pp. 503/19–504/10. For Hirsau itself and Cluniac monasticism, see above, 3.6.3.

[55] *QF* no. 209, pp. 244–5. The use of phrases from the *arenga* of the privilege for Banzi should be noticed.

[56] For fuller discussions, see Cowdrey, 'St Hugh and Gregory VII', and id., 'Cluny and Rome'.

[57] Gilo, *Vita sancti Hugonis*, 1.7, p. 57, echoing Virgil, *Aeneid*, 6.853.

[58] *Reg.* 1.62, 19 Mar. 1074, p. 91–2; 6.17, 2 Jan. 1079, p. 423/16–23.

[59] See above, 3.3.5.

Cluny to which he gave expression in his synodal allocution of 1080.[60] Hugh certainly came to Rome in 1083.[61]

Gregory nevertheless regarded Hugh with an approval and warmth such as he expressed to few others of his contemporaries. In letters written at times of frustration and self-questioning, he opened his heart to Hugh in terms of confidence and candour.[62] In public matters, Hugh represented that side of Gregory which valued the quality of mercy and strove for concord. He enlisted his aid as a legate to balance the more rigorous Bishop Hugh of Die.[63] Having regard to their envisaged collaboration, Gregory urged them jointly 'to act manfully and wisely, and let all your deeds be in charity, so that the oppressed may find you their wise defenders and so that the oppressors may find you to be lovers of righteousness'.[64] When, in 1080, Gregory was incensed by reports from Spain about the Cluniac monk Robert he carefully dissociated Abbot Hugh from what the monk was believed to have done wrong. Instead, he praised Hugh for his habitual concord with the Roman church: 'you have given us long-standing proof (*antiquum experimentum*) of being of one mind with us concerning the honour of the Roman church, and of having kept your freedom of action for the performance of a righteousness (*iustitia*) which, since love has grown cold, has now all but departed from the earth.' In a parallel letter addressed to King Alphonso VI of León–Castile, he reiterated his concord with Abbot Hugh: 'the abbot of Cluny will imitate us in what we do, for we walk by the same way, by the same mind, and by the same spirit' ('eadem enim via eodem sensu eodem spiritu ambulamus').[65] This may be taken as a fair statement of Gregory's estimate of Abbot Hugh of Cluny. It is consistent with it that Gregory was understood to have sought from Abbot Hugh monks whom he might ordain to the episcopate, the most noteworthy of whom was

---

[60] The case for suspecting a visit to Rome in 1079 rests on the following considerations: (i) Gregory undoubtedly expected a visit for which he had agenda relating to Archbishop Ralph of Tours: *Epp. vag.* no. 37, (1078/9), pp. 92–3. (ii) At Cluny, Hugh was in dispute with Bishop Landeric of Mâcon about certain properties; Landeric had gained Gregory's ear by himself going to Rome, where Gregory stipulated that, if necessary, there should be an adjudication by his legates Bishop Hugh of Die and Abbot Bernard of Marseilles: *Reg.* 6.33, to Abbot Hugh, 14 Apr. 1079, pp. 446–7. Hugh may well have thought fit to hasten to Rome in person and to head off such an adjudication by legates whose goodwill towards Cluny could not be counted upon. Gregory's concession in his synodal allocution that no legate should ever intervene at Cluny seems to reflect further negotiation between Gregory and Hugh which may have been face-to-face; *Epp. vag.* no. 39, pp. 98–9. (iii) Besides the matter of Cluny's relations with local bishops and papal legates, Gregory had incurred Gregory's censure for admitting to the cloister Duke Hugh of Burgundy: *Reg.* 6.17. It would be difficult to account for Gregory's favour for Cluny during the winter of 1079–80 by sending Cardinal Peter of Albano to vindicate it against the bishops and by his synodal allocution unless the air had been cleared by a personal visit. The departure from Cluny in 1080 of the grand prior, Odo, to be cardinal-bishop of Ostia may have been Hugh's *quid pro quo* for having admitted the duke of Burgundy to the cloister. (iv) Gregory's letter of 27 June 1080 to Abbot Hugh in protest against the supposed misdoings of the Cluniac monk Robert in León–Castile: *Reg.* 8.2, pp. 517–18, can be read as presupposing a recent meeting. Despite the renewed crisis involving a Cluniac monk, there should be no recriminations in advance of another such meeting as had recently taken place to resolve sensitive matters. For fuller discussion, see Cowdrey, 'Cluny and Rome', p. 263.

[61] See above, 3.5.8.   [62] *Reg.* 2.49, 22 Jan. 1075, pp. 188–90; 5.21, 7 May 1078, pp. 384–5.
[63] For Hugh as legate, see above, 5.3.2.3.   [64] *Reg.* 6.3, 22 Aug. 1078, pp. 395/32–396/2.
[65] *Reg.* 8.2–3, 27 June 1080, pp. 517/29–518/3, 520/19–20.

the grand prior of Cluny, Odo, who *c*.1080 became cardinal-bishop of Ostia and, in 1088, Pope Urban II.[66]

11.4 Gregory VII and Conversion to the Monastic Life

Although, throughout the eleventh century, many monks, like Abbots Hugh of Cluny and Desiderius of Montecassino themselves, entered the cloister in childhood or early youth, numerous men and women also converted to the religious life in mature years and in old age. Not infrequently, lay rulers—princes and even kings— were minded to lay aside their secular dignities and possessions in order to seek re- mission of their sins by becoming monks. Gregory himself was concerned with several rulers who made or contemplated such conversions. His responses to them were somewhat different and have often been misunderstood; taken together, they shed considerable light upon his view of the religious life both as it affected individ- uals and as it formed part of the total life of Christian church and society.

His earliest dealings as pope were with Countess Matilda of Tuscany who, in 1074, was the sole surviving child and prospective successor of Countess Beatrice. The two women were exercising what came near to being joint rule. Matilda was some 28 years old. Her marriage to Duke Godfrey the Hunchback of Lower Lorraine had failed, and she had no surviving child. Two letters survive in which Gregory ex- plained his reasons for dissuading her from taking the veil as a nun. The first was addressed to her alone. Gregory explained his reason for so advising her as having been the demand of charity that she should not desert the subjects who needed her care in order that she might seek the benefit only of her own soul. He therefore coun- selled her about the devotional life of a good lay person who was active in the world, with emphasis upon the daily receiving of holy communion and upon devotion to the Blessed Virgin.[67] Soon after, Gregory wrote jointly to Countesses Beatrice and Matilda. The occasion was a request for them to settle a dispute between Bishop Dodo of Roselle and Count Ugolino of the Aldobrandeschi family. Gregory wrote of his unique confidence in the countesses amongst all the princes of the Roman em- pire. He extrapolated from their role in settling a minor and local dispute that threat- ened public peace to generalize about the duty of rulers such as the countesses. It was overridingly to persist in such works of righteousness as that to which he directed them at Roselle. He affirmed that, in whatever they did, he was seeking to direct them to the honour of God and to their own salvation. He was insistent that rulers such as they should not enter the religious life at the expense of the provision of justice and peace for their subjects:

And so I say with the Prophet, 'Sacrifice the sacrifice of righteousness and hope in the Lord' (Ps. 4: 6), and again, 'Vindicate the fatherless and defend widows, and come and reason with

---

[66] *Historiae Tornacenses*, 4.11, pp. 340–1; Orderic Vitalis, 2, vol. 2.298–300. For Cluniacs as bishops, see Mehne, 'Cluniacenserbischöfe', pp. 254–63; Gregory did not so strongly look to Montecassino for potential bishops: Cowdrey, *The Age of Abbot Desiderius*, pp. 67–8.

[67] *Reg.* 1.47, 16 Feb. 1074, pp. 71–3.

me, says the Lord' (Isa. 1: 17–18). Indeed, I place before prayers, fasting, vigils, and all other good works whatsoever [that is, the concerns of the monastic life] the bringing of help to the needy and aid to the oppressed [that is, the works of the Christian lay ruler] when they proceed from the love of one's neighbour which springs from love of God. For, with the Apostle, I do not hesitate to set true charity above all other virtues (cf. 1 Cor. 13: 13).[68]

In 1073, Gregory had adduced similar arguments in his own case. He himself, however unwillingly, had accepted the divine summons to exchange the monastic life for a course that brought him to the papacy. The near-shipwreck of the universal church as it was battered by the storms of the world compelled him to accept this burden:

Since the life of a man is not in his own hand but is at the disposal of him by whom man's footsteps are guided (cf. Prov. 16: 9, Jer. 10: 23), it was not possible for me to maintain the intentions that I had formed ('concepta vota defendere').

Gregory went on to refer to his concern to bring to an end the discord and homicidal enmities that were ravaging the German kingdom and to promote its peace and concord.[69] For the Christian ruler, the overriding demands of charity thus required that, so long as he was needed in the world to uphold justice, to defend the weak, and to foster the peace of Christian society, he must lay aside all thought of seeking the welfare of his own soul in the cloister, whatever the merits of the religious life might be.

Exactly such considerations lay behind Gregory's severe rebuke of Abbot Hugh of Cluny in January 1079 after Hugh had admitted to the cloister Duke Hugh I of Burgundy (1075–8).[70] Gregory condemned the duke's selfish concern for his own salvation: 'Lo! those who seem to fear or love God flee from the warfare of Christ, put second the safety of their fellow men (*salutem fratrum*), and seek peace (*quietem*) as though loving only themselves.' Because Abbot Hugh had received the duke into the cloister, 100,000 Christians lacked a protector. If the abbot was deaf to the admonitions of the apostolic see, at least he should be moved by the lot of the Christians who now lacked the defence of a Christian prince—the groans of the poor, the tears of widows, the devastation of churches, the cries of orphans, the complaints of priests and monks; and he should act upon the Apostle's saying, 'Charity does not seek its own' (1 Cor. 13: 5). Gregory accepted the *fait accompli* so far as the duke was concerned: 'If no one worse than he succeeds to his rulership, we can find consolation.' But Abbot Hugh should be more careful in the future, setting love of God and of his neighbour before all other virtues. To do this would confirm Hugh and his monks in the vocation that was truly their own:

Let this love also compel you to stretch out hands of prayer for us, and also to seek to move all monks entrusted to you so that you and they may avail to progress from virtue to virtue and to attain to the perfection of the highest charity.

Monks were to blend the pursuit of their own vocation within the monastery with the exercise of due charity towards those outside its walls, so that the legitimate needs

---

[68] *Reg.* 1.50, 4 Mar. 1074, pp. 76–7.
[69] *Reg.* 1.39, to the Saxon bishops and princes, 20 Dec. 1073, pp. 61–2.
[70] *Reg.* 6.17, 2 Jan. 1079, pp. 423–4.

and purposes both of the monks and of human society might be met and harmonized.

Abbot Hugh seems to have taken the point, which he may have discussed further with Gregory if, as is likely, they met at Rome in 1079 to resolve their various differences. He was later said to have refused the request of King Alphonso VI of León–Castile to be admitted to the cloister.[71] On Gregory's side, it should be noticed that on the very day of his sending his rebuke to Abbot Hugh, he also expressed to the monks of Saint-Victor at Marseilles his recognition of the close bond between Cluny and the apostolic see, and the help and blessing that Cluny deserved from the papacy.[72] Gregory experienced no fundamental disenchantment with Cluny or with the monastic order.

Gregory, in fact always maintained a high regard for monasticism. It would be wrong to conclude from the examples of Countess Matilda of Tuscany and Duke Hugh of Burgundy that he was necessarily opposed to the departure of lay princes for the monastic life. On the contrary, when circumstances permitted and when a prince had made what Gregory deemed to be proper provision for the peace, security, and well-being of his subjects, such a conversion might have his warm approval. Such was the case with Count Simon of Crépy, whose monastic conversion calls for comparison with that of Duke Hugh of Burgundy.[73] The comparison is the more necessary because it was Simon's conversion, which took place in the spring of 1077, that prompted Hugh of Burgundy and other French laymen, including Count Guy of Mâcon, themselves to enter the cloister.[74] Simon had also been advised by Abbot Hugh of Cluny, especially about the liturgical commemoration of his father and perhaps about his own monastic vocation. When he entered the austere monastery of Saint-Oyend in the Jura, he did so without immediately consulting Gregory.[75] Yet, after Simon had moved on to the life of a hermit, Gregory himself summoned him to Rome and installed him and his companions in a hermitage near the church of S. Thecla on the Ostian Way.[76] Until his death in 1081/2, he enjoyed Gregory's favour. He was buried amongst the popes in St Peter's basilica with an epitaph, allegedly composed by Pope Urban II, which warmly applauded his progress from prince to hermit.[77]

Why did Gregory rebuke the monastic conversion of Hugh of Burgundy but welcome that of Simon of Crépy? The reason seems to be that, as Gregory regarded the obligations and services of a prince, Simon had duly prepared the way for his conversion while Hugh had not. Hugh's conversion was sudden and made no provision for the peace of his subjects: as Gregory put it, 100,000 Christians were left without a guardian. But Simon had done all that he could have done to establish, under the

---

[71] Bernold, *Chron. a.* 1093, p. 457/23–9; see also Hugh's later comments to Archbishop Anselm of Canterbury about the roles of Mary and Martha in Hugh's *Ep.* 6, Cowdrey, 'Two Studies', pp. 151–6.

[72] *Reg.* 6.15, 2 Jan. 1079, p. 420/19–22.

[73] For a fuller discussion of Count Simon, see Cowdrey, 'Count Simon of Crépy's Monastic Conversion'.

[74] *Vita beati Simonis*, cap. 6, col. 1216D.   [75] *Vita beati Simonis*, cap. 6, col. 1216C.

[76] Ibid. cap. 12, col. 1220B–D.   [77] Ibid. cap. 15, cols. 1223B–1224A.

guidance of Gregory himself and of other spiritual men like Abbot Hugh of Cluny, the peace and concord for his subjects which were Gregory's requirements for a settled society. Considerations such as that of the political balance of power between the royal demesne and the adjacent principalities which might seem critical to modern historians were not present in Gregory's mind. Simon had duly pacified his neighbours by bringing back his father's body from burial in a place that he had unjustly seized and had buried it, with that of his first and rightful wife, at the heart of his rightful dominions.[78] On a penitential pilgrimage to Rome in 1076, he had obeyed Gregory's direction that he should atone for the sins of his earlier warfare with King Philip I and should resume the governance of his principality under the guidance of Bishop Hugh of Die and Abbot Hugh of Cluny 'until he had renewed peace with the king'. He prosecuted his feud with the king until he was victorious, and until an assembly of magnates from both sides promoted concord by adjudicating about what properly belonged to Simon's inheritance. Thus, 'peace was restored and all things were set in order that had been in disorder during the long period of warfare'.[79] Once peace and concord were thus established and the well-being of his subjects was, in Gregory's eyes, secured, Gregory was willing for him to enter a monastery. Gregory was the more willing because, as a monk, Simon continued in his role of a peacemaker both in France and neighbouring regions, where, for example, he was instrumental in reconciling King William I of England and his son Robert Curthose,[80] and in South Italy, where he played a part in the negotiations which brought about the renewal in 1080 of the oaths of the Norman princes to the papacy.[81] After his monastic conversion as before it, Simon of Crépy was a willing and successful agent of the peace and concord that Gregory placed at the centre of his social objectives.

Matilda of Tuscany was, for Gregory, the model of a ruler who sacrificed a desire to enter the peace of the cloister in order to fulfil the demands of charity towards those who needed a ruler's care and protection and to serve the papacy by dedicating her political and military resources to its service; Simon of Crépy was the model of a ruler who, no less properly, fulfilled a religious vocation that he entered upon under advice, with due regard for the peace of his subjects, and with a blending of strict religious observance with a care for wider concerns which, according to the demands of charity, promoted peace and concord as Gregory envisaged them. If the case of Hugh of Burgundy shows how easily the precipitate admission of a prince to the cloister might contravene Gregory's requirements, the rapid restoration of understanding between Gregory and Cluny suggests that, in Gregory's eyes, the monastic order of his time was, on balance, successful in providing both the spiritual and the social services for which Gregory looked in the ways in which he sought them.

---

[78] *Recueil des actes de Philippe Ier*, no. 88, pp. 229–30; *Vita beati Simonis*, cap. 2, cols. 1212C–1213A.
[79] *Vita beati Simonis*, cap. 3, cols. 1213C–1214A.   [80] Ibid. cap. 11, col. 1219BC.
[81] Ibid. cap. 13, cols. 1220D–1221B. During his excursion to Robert Guiscard, Simon was said to have been responsible for the monastic conversion of almost sixty knights.

Death in Exile

12.1 The Last Months at Salerno

Gregory VII died at Salerno on 25 May 1085.[1] He seems to have fallen seriously ill at about the beginning of the year. The record of his final testament, followed by the Montecassino Chronicle, suggests that he was for a considerable period in the grip of major illness. According to Paul of Bernried, his sufferings at an early stage of it were such that he was consoled by a heavenly message: 'these cleansings will benefit him and will suffice for him in eternity, nor need he fear any chastisement after death.' A remission of his illness may have followed; again according to Paul of Bernried, at about the beginning of January he foreknew that he would die at about the beginning of June. He continued to attend to business. His last surviving privilege which is dated was issued on 9 May in favour of the abbey of S. Salvatore at Fucecchio; it was requested in person by the abbot, Peter, and the cordial address to him as 'Petre, fili karissime' indicates that Gregory may have spoken directly with him.[2]

Some days before he died, Gregory appears to have suffered a relapse. He was attended by an entourage of bishops and cardinals who seem to have been essentially those who had left Rome with him. Also present were a number of chaplains. If he died 'poor and in exile' ('pauperem et in exilio'),[3] his poverty was a matter of the moral indifference to possessions which was proper for a Christian, not of enforced material need or human isolation. The only named witness throughout his last illness

---

[1] The principal sources for Gregory's sickness and death are: Paul of Bernried, caps. 108–10, 124, pp. 538–40, 545–6; *Chron. Cas.* 3.65, p. 447; *Vita Anselmi ep. Lucensis*, cap. 38, p. 24; Notice of Gregory's final testament, *H* no. 35, pp. 75–6. Of other sources, the most interesting is an account attributed to Bishop Agano of Autun who, returning from a two-year pilgrimage to Jerusalem, was in Salerno at the time of Gregory's burial. According to it, Gregory foretold a week in advance ('ante octo dies') the day and hour of his death. On his last day, he made a public profession in church before the clergy and people of Salerno, first of his belief as regards the body and blood of Christ in the eucharist, and then of a vindication of his life's work ('de intentione totius suae operis'). He absolved all whom he had excommunicated; then, proceeding on hands and knees to the altar, he received the viaticum. He returned to his lodging where he died at the hour which he had foretold. He committed to Bishop Agano the duties of officiating at his burial and of disposing of his few earthly possessions: ed. Waitz, *MGH SS* 5.563 n. 58; see also *Archiv*, 7 (1839), 220–1. Orderic Vitalis believed Gregory to have died at Benevento and to have been buried there in the crypt of the church of S. Bartolomeo; his is the only account that speaks of many miracles as having occurred at the place of his death: 8.7, vol. 4.164–6. An altogether incredible Henrician manifesto claimed that, *in extremis*, Gregory disowned all his acts as pope and released Henry IV and his followers from the sentences that he had imposed upon them: Cowdrey, *The Age of Abbot Desiderius*, p. 250; for further references, see Meyer von Knonau, 4.60 n. 105.

[2] *QF* no. 218, pp. 265–7.

[3] *Vita Anselmi ep. Lucensis*, cap. 38, p. 24. The author drew a comparison between Gregory and Anselm II of Lucca, who like his master died poor and in exile.

was Abbot Desiderius of Montecassino, who, however, according to Paul of Bernried, fulfilled Gregory's prophecy by being absent at the hour of his death in order to bring relief to one of his abbey's castles to which some Normans were laying siege. Desiderius returned for Gregory's burial, which took place *honorabiliter* in the cathedral of St Matthew which he lately consecrated. According to Paul of Bernried, he was buried in the crypt. As commonly happened during the Middle Ages after the death of popes and great men, robbers sought to break into his tomb in order to plunder the pontifical vestments in which he had been buried. However, by a miracle the lamps in the crypt were extinguished and the would-be robbers were struck by temporary madness.[4]

12.2 The Final Testament

Probably quite soon after Gregory's death, a brief record was made of his utterances during his terminal illness; it became widely known among his followers.[5] When, where, and by whom it was compiled are not certain. The phraseology of the opening sentence ('apud Salernum . . . episcopi et cardinales Romani qui ibidem aderant') may imply that it was written elsewhere than at Salerno. Because the Roman bishops and cardinals are referred to in the third person, it is unlikely to have originated with someone of their number. One of Gregory's chaplains of whom the *Vita Anselmi episcopi Lucensis* speaks as having been at his bedside may have been responsible for it, perhaps after reporting to the circle of Countess Matilda of Tuscany. However this may be, the record makes it clear that Gregory's pronouncements, which were set down in *oratio recta*, were spoken over a considerable period of time, and that they represent but a small selection from many precepts which Gregory uttered to his entourage.

The first pronouncement was Gregory's reply to a request from the Roman bishops and cardinals that he should disclose to them whom he wished to be elected as his successor in the papal office. His answer, after reflection, was that they should

---

4 For such happenings, see Elze, '*Sic transit gloria mundi*'. There is no further evidence for Gregory's being buried in the crypt of the cathedral of Salerno. The scanty evidence suggests that, during most of the middle ages, his body may have been placed in the nave of the cathedral and then in its south-eastern apse. Interest in his remains revived when his tomb was opened in 1578 and again in 1605. After the first opening, his tomb was said to be almost invisible and his memory at Salerno almost extinct ('fere exoletam'). He was, therefore, placed in a marble tomb. In 1583, Pope Gregory XIII caused his name to be included in the Roman Martyrology. In 1609, Paul V authorized his commemoration at Salerno by a special office and in 1728 Benedict XIII extended his feast to the whole church. For a brief account of these developments, see Miccoli, 'Gregorio VII', cols. 367–9; Carucci, *Il sepolcro*.

5 The principal source for the final testament is the early 16th-cent. transcript in the section of Hildesheim letters in the Hanover letter-collection: *H* no. 35, pp. 75–6. A copy of its first two dispositions, introduced by the words 'Dixit Urbanus papa in quadam epistola sua', is inserted into the autograph MS of Hugh of Flavigny's *Chronicon*: 2, p. 466; no such letter of Pope Urban II is otherwise known. Another abbreviated version appears in the *Codex Udalrici*: no. 71, pp. 143–4. The final testament appears to have been known to the authors of *Chron. Cas.* 3.65, p. 447, the *Vita Anselmi ep. Lucensis*, cap. 38, p. 24, and to Paul of Bernried, caps. 108–10, pp. 538–40. For further discussion of its authenticity and content, see Cowdrey, 'Death-Bed Testaments', esp. pp. 707–12, 722–4.

choose as pope whichever of the following they could procure—Bishop Anselm II of Lucca, Cardinal-bishop Odo of Ostia, or Archbishop Hugh of Lyons. The likelihood that, of these, Anselm of Lucca was Gregory's prime choice is suggested, not only by his being placed first in order, but also by stories of Gregory's dispatching to him a mitre which he himself had worn.[6] But Anselm died on 28 March 1086, before an election proved to be possible. Thereafter it was quickly noised abroad that Gregory had named as his successor Abbot Desiderius of Montecassino.[7] An interpretation of events in 1085 and 1086 must turn largely upon how the confused and repetitive evidence of the Montecassino Chronicle is to be unravelled.[8] From what seems to be the earliest information that it embodies,[9] it appears that, upon Gregory's death, prompt steps were taken to secure an election. At Pentecost (8 June), Desiderius somewhere met two of Gregory's partisans who were travelling south from Rome, Bishop Hubald of Sabina and a certain Gratian. They were joined by the Normans, Prince Jordan of Capua and Count Rainald of Caiazzo, whom Desiderius found to be willing to serve the Roman church. He therefore urged the cardinals urgently to set in train the election of a new pope. They should send a letter to Countess Matilda of Tuscany asking her to encourage Gregory's three episcopal nominees (there was no hint of a non-episcopal nominee such as Desiderius himself) and others whom she might deem fit for the papal office to hasten to Rome. In these negotiations, Desiderius was the executor of Gregory's dying directions, not a possible beneficiary. Not until 1086 did he emerge as such; records of Gregory's having nominated him should be regarded as *ex post facto* justification of this development. So far as the naming of possible successors is concerned, the record of Gregory's final testament in the Hanover letter-collection is in all probability authentic.

According to this record, Gregory was similarly asked about those who were under sentence of excommunication. He responded with the charity and forgiveness that were appropriate upon a death-bed. He excepted Henry 'the so-called king' and his own supplanter as pope, the archbishop of Ravenna, together with all leading persons who by counsel or aid had favoured their iniquity and impiety, unless they should come forward to the Roman bishops and cardinals and perform due and canonical satisfaction. Otherwise, Gregory absolved and blessed all who unhesitatingly believed that he had the spiritual power to do this on behalf of the apostle Peter.

Gregory, the record continued, admonished the Roman bishops and cardinals about many further matters, of which one was selected for verbatim citation. Reverting to the papal succession, Gregory solemnly charged them on behalf of God and by the authority of St Peter and St Paul to have no one as Roman pope who was not canonically elected and instituted by the authority of the holy fathers ('nisi

---

[6] *Vita Anselmi ep. Lucensis*, cap. 32, pp. 32–3; Rangerius, *Vita Anselmi*, 5.6348–50, p. 1288, Paul of Bernried, cap. 111, p. 540.

[7] Guy of Ferrara, 1.20, p. 549/32–7, written in 1086. For later references, see *Chron. Cas.* 3.65, p. 447/1–12; Paul of Bernried, cap. 109, p. 539.

[8] For an analysis, see Cowdrey, *The Age of Abbot Desiderius*, pp. 185–206, 251–6. Reference may also be made to these discussions for a fuller account of the sequel to Gregory's death.

[9] 3.65, pp. 447/27–448/1.

canonice electum et sanctorum patrum auctoritate ordinatum'). Especially in view of
Henry IV's recent promotion of Archbishop Guibert of Ravenna to be the anti-pope
Clement III, it is apparent that Gregory wished to exclude all improper lay involvement and to entrust the election to those who were appropriate among the Roman
clergy. It does not, however, clearly emerge what positive criteria he had in mind. In
view of the fierce hostility to the Election Decree of 1059 which was expressed by so
strong a supporter of Gregory among the cardinal-priests as Deusdedit of S. Pietro
in Vincoli,[10] it is scarcely conceivable that the dying pope sought to commend it. He
more likely referred to such older guidance as was provided by canon twenty-two of
the fourth council of Constantinople (869–70), with its emphatic exclusion of lay
participation in an election save in so far as it might be specially and rightly conceded.[11]

Finally, the record preserved Gregory's alleged last words: 'I have loved righteousness and hated iniquity, therefore I die in exile' ('Dilexi iustitiam et odivi iniquitatem, propterea morior in exilio').[12] They also appear in this form in the Life of
Bishop Anselm of Lucca, where they are cited on the authority of Gregory's own
faithful chaplains ('ab ipsius capellanis . . . religiosis').[13] In form, they open with an
adaptation of Psalm 44: 8 which figures in the triumphant catena from the Psalms in
Hebrews 1: 5–13: 'You have loved righteousness and hated iniquity, therefore God,
your God, has anointed you with the oil of gladness above your fellows' ('Dilexisti
iustitiam et odisti iniquitatem, propterea unxit te Deus, Deus tuus, oleo laetitiae prae
consortibus tuis'); but Gregory replaced the latter half of the verse by referring to the
circumstance of his dying at Salerno in exile from Rome. The interpretation of
Gregory's words manifestly caused perplexity from an early date. In recording them,
Paul of Bernried added that, upon hearing them, 'a certain venerable bishop' whom
he did not name was said to have replied, 'My lord, you cannot die in exile, for on
behalf of Christ and his apostles you have received from God the peoples for your
inheritance and the ends of the earth for your possession' (cf. Ps. 2: 8).[14] But, when
drawing a parallel between the deaths of Gregory and of Bishop Anselm of Lucca,
the latter's biographer rightly confirmed Gregory's meaning of an earthly exile
which was a matter of deep moral significance.[15]

Much modern comment upon that significance has interpreted it in terms of
Gregory's expressing bitterness and disillusion; yet it is more than unlikely that it
conveys any such meaning.[16] Such an interpretation is confirmed by no other words
or actions on his part; indeed, it conflicts with the tone of all his other utterances at
Salerno, particularly his confident and defiant final encyclical.[17] More credible is an
alternative interpretation, that Gregory saw in his exile at Salerno a token of the

---

[10] *Coll. can.*, Dedicatory Epistle, pp. 4–5; *Libellus contra invasores*, caps. 11–13, pp. 309–13.

[11] See above, 3.2.4.

[12] Erdmann's punctuation, with a dash between the words *propterea* and *morior*, has no manuscript
authority.

[13] *Vita Anselmi ep. Lucensis*, cap. 38, p. 24.   [14] cap. 110, p. 540.   [15] As n. 13.

[16] As was decisively established by Hübinger, *Die letzten Worte*.

[17] *Epp. vag.* no. 54, pp. 128–35.

blessedness that Christ promised to those who suffer persecution for righteousness'
sake: 'Beati qui persecutionem patiuntur propter iustitiam, quoniam ipsorum est
regnum caelorum' (Matt. 5: 10).

As thus understood, the conviction expressed in his alleged last words runs deeply
through his letters and is a credible epitome of them. In his last encyclical from
Salerno, he was concerned that his followers everywhere should ponder deeply
about why he was undergoing distresses and afflictions at the hands of the enemies of
the Christian religion; he affirmed that it was because of his steadfast concern that
'holy church, our lady and mother, should return to her true glory and stand free,
chaste, and catholic.'[18] As long ago as 1076, he had reminded his Milanese followers
of St Paul's words that all who wish to live godly lives in Christ Jesus must suffer
persecution (cf. 2 Tim. 3: 12); this pronouncement had come down to Gregory himself, along with his occupancy of the apostolic see, as if by hereditary right.[19] If need
be, it was, therefore, better that he should suffer bodily death at the hands of tyrants
than that he should be party to the destruction of the Christian religion through
silence, fear, or seeking an easy way.[20] Such thoughts were repeated with heightened
force in letters of his final years. In 1081, he affirmed that to suffer for righteousness
was the crown of a bishop's vocation:

From the brevity of this life and from the nature of temporal advantages we have assuredly
concluded that no man can ever better be a bishop than when he is suffering persecution for
righteousness' sake; we have determined rather to incur the enmity of wicked men by obeying
divine commandments than by wrongfully placating them to incur the wrath of God.[21]

A year or so later, he urged his followers:

If we wish with God's help quickly and bravely to rout the ancient enemy and to reckon his devices as nothing, let us strive not only not to avoid the persecution that he inflicts and death for
righteousness, but from love of God and for the defence of the Christian religion even to desire them.[22]

Fortified by such thoughts, Gregory averred that nothing would divert him from the
path of righteousness; it would be better to suffer death at his enemies' hands than to
accede to their ungodliness or to depart from a righteousness that he must uphold
until the end.[23]

As well as envisaging death as the price of defending righteousness, Gregory wrote
of the contingency of exile. He described the clerks of the church of Rheims who had
for long resisted Archbishop Manasses as having undergone exile for righteousness
('pro iustitia exilium passi sunt').[24] In 1083, Count Robert of Flanders was to restore

---

[18] *Epp. vag.* no. 54, pp. 132–4.
[19] *Reg.* 4.7, 31 Oct. 1076, p. 305/13–16; cf. *Epp. vag.* no. 26, to the anti-king Rudolf and his supporters
in Saxony, late Feb. 1079, pp. 66–9.
[20] *Reg.* 4.1, to the faithful in the Roman empire, 25 July 1076, p. 292/4–12.
[21] *Reg.* 9.2, to King Alphonso VI of León–Castile, p. 570/19–25.
[22] *Reg.* 9.21, pp. 602/21–603/7.
[23] *Reg.* 9.11, to Abbot Desiderius of Montecassino, (May 1081), p. 588/23–33; 9.35, to the bishops and
princes of Flanders, (1083), p. 623/3–7.
[24] *Reg.* 7.20, to Archbishop Manasses I of Rheims, 17 Apr. 1080, p. 496/23–5.

to clerks of the church of Thérouanne who had been exiled for righteousnessness ('clericis pro iustitia exulatis') whatever had been seized from them.[25] At about the same time, he wrote of his brother-bishop, Archbishop Ralph of Tours, as having suffered extrusion from his see and persecution on account of righteousness ('propter iustitiam pulsas et persecutionem perpessus est').[26] Upon his own deathbed at Salerno, it would have been a short and natural step for Gregory to transfer to himself the theme of exile for righteousness, and to do so not in bitterness or disillusion but in confidence that his own sufferings carried the guarantee offered in the New Testament that they were a pledge of the kingdom of heaven.

There can be no assurance of either the authenticity or the true interpretation of Gregory's supposed last words. But thus understood, they are consistent with convictions that he had expressed over many years, and they have the ring of truth as an affirmation by him of his invincible hope and confidence to the very end.

[25] *Reg.* 9.35, p. 624/4–8.
[26] *Reg.* 9.24, to the clergy and people of Tours and Angers, (1082/3), p. 606/11–16.

13

Conclusion

As early in his pontificate as 1074, Gregory commented to Countesses Beatrice and Matilda of Tuscany both upon the contrasting views that were current of him and his work and also upon his own indifference to all human judgements:

Neither does it escape us how diverse is the opinion and the judgement of us that men have, since with respect to the same matters and actions some call us inhuman and others excessively mild. To all such persons, we consider no reply to be truer and more apposite than the Apostle's: 'To me it is of very little account that I am judged by you or by any human tribunal' (1 Cor. 4: 3).[1]

In similar vein, one who had observed Gregory at first hand, Bishop Guy of Ferrara, a year or so after his death observed that:

The Christian people was divided into two, some saying that he was a good man but others calling him an impostor and one who lived at odds with what befits a monk and a Christian.[2]

According to their standpoint, Gregory's contemporaries came to the most divergent conclusions about him. He could either attract or repel these who came into close contact with him, as he attracted Abbot William of Hirsau during his stay in Rome during the winter of 1075–6, but as he repelled Cardinal Hugh Candidus; from being a sponsor of his election to the papacy, Hugh quickly and lastingly became his virulent and implacable foe. Bishops and archbishops like Anselm II of Lucca, Hugh of Die and Lyons, Odo of Ostia, and Peter of Albano, were his profoundly committed collaborators; conservatively reforming figures like Liemar of Bremen and Guibert of Ravenna were impelled to exasperation and enmity; a more ambivalent figure, so far as reform was concerned, like Benzo of Alba, was unremitting and unmeasured in his vituperation; others, like Lanfranc of Canterbury, kept their distance and, while not resisting Gregory, went their own way; others again, like Siegfried of Mainz and Udo of Trier, broadly approved what Gregory was doing but wished that he would not behave in a way that disturbed their own ecclesiastical and political world. Few figures in history have elicited so wide a range of reactions among their contemporaries. Few have been as indifferent as Gregory was to human judgement as he pursued the course that he deemed to be providentially marked out for him to follow.

After his death, and especially in the twelfth century, Gregory for the most part receded from memory with remarkable speed and completeness. Leaders of Christian thought and spirituality like Bernard of Clairvaux seldom mentioned him or

---

[1] *Reg.* 1.77, 15 Apr. 1074, p. 110/34–9. [2] 1.2, p. 535/43–5.

showed awareness of him. He left little mark upon the developing tradition of canon law; the all-important *Decretum* of Gratian cited his predecessor Alexander II and his next successor who reigned for any length of time, Urban II, more often and more significantly than it cited Gregory. By and large, twelfth-century chroniclers paid only brief attention to the pope who, according to some modern perspectives, gave his name to a 'Gregorian reform'; thus, Otto of Freising, while recognizing that Gregory was 'of outstanding zeal and authority among all priests and Roman popes', drew the sixth book of his *Chronicle* to an end with Gregory's death in exile and pessimistically noted it as a historical juncture which saw a lapse from well-being to decline ('tanquam a perfectione ad defectum vergente tempore').[3] But since interest in Gregory revived with the Reformation of the sixteenth century, Gregory has again been judged in a variety of ways ranging from eulogy to harsh criticism, according to the ecclesiastical, national, and political standpoints of the observers. There is little possibility of forming a generally acceptable conclusion about him. However much the historian may set out to present him *sine ira et studio*, Gregory strikes chords that echo too deeply in men's being to permit of detachment or objectivity.

Other factors besides the standpoint of the observer make it difficult to draw generally acceptable conclusions about Gregory. His character, and therefore the motives and actions that flowed from it, were of infinite complexity. Different and contrasting facets of his personality and ideas were for ever being manifested; it is seldom indeed that any conclusion can be drawn about him which does not call out to be balanced and modified by a contrasting judgement. As springs of papal action, he claimed to value both justice and mercy. The rigour and insistence of his demands upon the German episcopate, especially in 1074–5, stand in the sharpest contrast with his prolonged forbearance with regard to Archbishop Manasses I of Rheims; if, in Germany, Archbishop Siegfried of Mainz pleaded with Gregory to temper justice with apostolic mercy, in France, Gregory's legate Bishop Hugh of Die had reason to wonder at Gregory's preferring of apostolic mercy to the zealous disciplining of the bishops according to the demands of righteousness that Hugh undertook in Gregory's name. Gregory's eventual advocacy of elective kingship in Germany stands in contrast with the value that he usually set upon royal families and upon strong though obedient hereditary kingship. If Gregory's resolute pursuit of the prerogatives of the apostolic see prepared the way for the papal monarchy of the central Middle Ages, his own values and aspirations placed him in many respects nearer to Pope Gregory the Great five centuries ago than to successors in the next two centuries like Alexander III and Innocent III. In Gregory, the ascetic ideals of the monk and the priest were always alive if not paramount; yet Gregory was convinced that his vocation to act upon and in the world must always, in the end, rule out any desire on his part to withdraw from the world. Gregory thus presents himself as a complex of opposites, a man of whom it is difficult to take a view that is comprehensive, balanced, and just.

---

3 *Chronica*, 6.36, pp. 492–3.

A further characteristic of Gregory that makes an overall assessment difficult is his titanic energy—an energy that is the more remarkable since he was probably in his late fifties when he became pope, and since his energy continued unabated until the end. As pope, his horizons extended from Iceland and Ireland in the west to Kievan Russia, Armenia, and Jerusalem in the east, and from Norway and Sweden in the north to North Africa in the south. His letters and privileges suggest a detailed and retentive memory of the persons and places with which he dealt. No single individual in the Latin west of his lifetime is likely to have achieved a comparable knowledge of the world, both religious and temporal, and of how it was peopled and ruled. Besides building up this extensive knowledge, Gregory's mental and personal energies led him to outbursts of reproof and threatening which concentrated and directed the spiritual and physical powers of which he believed himself to dispose. Examples are his sentences against Henry IV of Germany in 1076 and in 1080, or his explosion of wrath about what he believed to be the falling away of the kingdom of León–Castile from the Roman liturgical observance in 1080. Yet Gregory could also show patience, compassion, and pastoral concern, as well as restraint and willingness to compromise towards rulers such as William of England who went some, but not all, of the way towards behaving as Gregory thought that a Christian ruler should behave. Another consequence of Gregory's indomitable energy was that, far from ruling as pope with a fixed and established set of principles, he was always learning and modifying his ideas and springs of action in response to changing circumstances and to changed perceptions of past precedents and present needs. His reactions were often unpredictable and unexpected. Like his attitude to Berengar of Tours in 1078–9, his mind could undergo sudden and radical changes of direction in response to promptings that were known to himself alone.

It was of critical importance for Gregory that his early years provided him and his world with the shared legacy of two models, of an emperor and of a pope, which were well remembered by him throughout his lifetime. In most people's eyes, the Emperor Henry III, who was responsible for the renewal of the papacy in 1046, was a model king and emperor. He was seen as having been devout, the bringer of peace and order, and as solicitous for the needs of the church in his dominions and elsewhere. His good deeds had included the advancement to the papacy in 1049 of his kinsman, Leo IX. Everyone admired Leo as the opponent of simony and clerical unchastity, as the unwearied holder of papal councils, not only at Rome, but also in Italy, France, and Germany; above all, he was revered as a saint. Leo died under the shadow of the military defeat of his army by the Normans at the battle of Civitate in 1053. But it was soon accepted that his men who had fallen in the battle were shown by Heaven to have been martyrs in a holy war, and the aura of sanctity embraced Leo himself. It was a landmark for the papacy. Most popes of the early Christian centuries were venerated as martyrs and confessors, but none who had reigned since the mid-ninth century was so regarded. On the contrary: during most of the tenth and early eleventh centuries, the papacy was at one of the lowest ebbs in its history, and many popes were more noteworthy for scandal than for sanctity. In Leo IX, the papacy again had a saint, without whose reputation Gregory could scarcely have made his claim that the Roman pontiff, if canonically elected, was indubitably made holy by the merits of St Peter. Like most of his contemporaries, Gregory acknowledged and valued the models of Christian rulership that Henry III and Leo IX provided. They were the firstfruits of a new age for Christian society and for the papacy. Gregory and many of his contemporaries shared common ground because they had such perceptions of exemplary rulership.

Yet the complexity of Gregory's personality, his inexhaustible energy, and his capacity to learn and to change under the onward progress of events, ensured that his pontificate could not be contained within the limits of such models. In many respects, he broke their mould, or at least was ambivalent in respect of them. The ways in which he differed from Leo IX and from the other reforming popes from 1046 to 1073 have been much discussed,[4] but they deserve fresh consideration; taken together, they underline Gregory's uniqueness among the popes of all time.

First, from what the sources call his 'adolescentia'—from while he was still a young man, Gregory was a monk, whereas, for most of their lifetimes at least, his pre-decessors since 1046 were not. If, as seems likely, he was a monk of the tenth-century Benedictine foundation of St Mary's-on-the-Aventine at Rome, he had belonged to a house which had associations with the great abbots of Cluny Odo and Odilo, with Abbot Aligernus who restored Montecassino, and with Archbishop Adalbert of Prague, the martyr-bishop who died in 997 while preaching to the heathen in Pomerania. Gregory always wore the monastic habit in token of his renunciation, like such men, of all ties with the world. A critical observer, Bishop Guy of Ferrara, who observed him at first hand, testified to the monastic austerity of his personal life-style while pope. His way of presenting the Christian duty of obedience had more in com-mon with the ancient traditions of Benedictine monasticism about the personal obedience of a monk to his abbot than with the still largely unformed canon law and institutions of the papal monarchy which, in the twelfth century and after, would propagate obedience to enacted law and ruler sovereignty.

Second, the seven reform popes between 1046 and 1073 were all of aristocratic, even royal, connections: Leo IX was a kinsman of the German emperor, Stephen IX was a brother of the duke of Lorraine, and so forth. Gregory was the son of modest parents: 'vir de plebe', Abbot Walo of Metz hailed him upon his accession to the papacy, in terms reminiscent of David, the shepherd-boy who became king; while Bishop Benzo of Alba mocked him as one whose father was a goatherd and whose mother was from a suburb. Gregory's skeletal remains indicate that he was strong and well nourished, so that there may be exaggeration in such phrases. But he was evidently born to parents who counted for nothing in the great world. His modest birth seems to have had ambivalent consequences upon his outlook. On the one hand, he owed his advancement to be archdeacon and pope to his personal qualities and to his burning zeal; he was beholden to no human kinsman or benefactor. He

---

4 See esp. Caspar, 'Gregor VII. in seinen Briefen'.

manifested a personal devotion to 'pauper Jesus'—Jesus the poor man. On the other hand, like many who have made their own way in life, he was far from despising family and rank; he showed a tendency to value kingly dynasty and aristocratic stock and to associate himself with them. In particular, with the exemplary emperor Henry III in mind, he identified himself with the Salian family. Early in his pontificate, he wrote of the young Henry IV as someone towards whom he regarded himself a debtor, because he had himself elected him king (Gregory probably alluded to his presence at one of the acts of princely homage to the infant king in the 1050s); because the young king's father, the illustrious Henry III, and Agnes his wife had honoured him, as the young Hildebrand, at the German court above all other Italians, and had received him there 'caritative'—with love; and because on his deathbed Henry III had commended his son to the Roman church.[5] Gregory told Henry IV's sister, Queen Judith of Hungary, that he 'loved her as his own sister' ('in loco germane sororis te diligimus').[6] He claimed to love the Empress Agnes like a mother.[7] So close was the bond thus established between Gregory and the Salian royal family that the drama of his eventual dealings with Henry IV must be appreciated in the light, not only of Gregory's humble origins and Roman identity, but also of his personal self-identification with the Salian family. As so often, Gregory presents a paradox: he made his own way in the world and was beholden to no one; yet he drew close in spirit and feeling to the greatest in the world, and especially the Salian dynasty.

Third, Gregory's Roman identity set him apart from the popes who preceded him after 1046. Besides being high-born, they had, for most if not all of their lives, lived and worked away from Rome—in dioceses of the German church, or in North Italian cities like Florence and Lucca. Their non-Roman connections were the more significant because, while they were pope, they also retained their previous sees or abbeys.[8] Hildebrand was probably not born in Rome but at Sovana in South Tuscany. But, on his mother's side, he had relations in Rome, and he lived in Rome from childhood. He was, therefore, Roman through and through, and he never held ecclesiastical office of any kind save in the Roman church. He had no loyalty other than to the city of the popes and to the church within which their authority primarily resided.

Above all, along with this sense of Roman identity, Gregory differed from the earlier reform popes by his overmastering sense that, from boyhood, he belonged to the household of St Peter himself and that he was, therefore, uniquely indebted to the prince of the apostles. He gave this debt to St Peter striking expression at the crisis-points of his pontificate, for example, in the address to St Peter which included his sentence of deposition and excommunication upon Henry IV in 1076.[9] Gregory

---

[5] *Reg.* 1.20, to Duke Rudolf of Swabia, 1 Sept. 1073, pp. 31/34– 32/6.

[6] *Reg.* 2.44, to Queen Judith, 10 Jan. 1075, p. 181/12–13.

[7] *Reg.* 2.3, to Duke William of Aquitaine, 10 Sept. 1074, p. 127/26.

[8] See Goez, '*Papa qui et episcopus*'.

[9] *Reg.* 3.10a, pp. 270–1, see above, 3.3.2; cf. his similar address to St Peter and St Paul when renewing his sentence in 1080; *Reg.* 7.14a, pp. 483–7.

never thought or spoke of himself as the vicar of Christ but always as the vicar of St Peter. For him, because of his life-long bond of service with Peter, the prince of the apostles was no distant and nominal patron; he consciously and deliberately acted in and through his earthly vicar. As Gregory warned Henry IV in December 1075:

So long as we, such as we are, a sinner and unworthy, by God's providence act as the vicar of St Peter's power in his seat and apostolic stewardship, whatever you may send us in writing or by word of mouth, he himself receives. When we read the letter or hear the messenger's words, he perceives by sure insight from what state of mind your message comes.[10]

Gregory's total identity with St Peter according to his commission in the New Testament was the mainspring of his life. No pope before or since has so exalted his own personal and official role: he was in St Peter and St Peter was in him.

Gregory's singleness of mind and purpose as the vicar of St Peter was a source of great strength to him and to his cause. It provided the assurance and conviction that sustained him through the vicissitudes of his pontificate and that found expression in the last encyclical that he wrote during his final exile at Salerno.[11] Yet it was also a source of weakness. At no time in the long history of the papacy has it been wise for a pope to forget that the office that he holds is greater and more enduring than himself, or that he has a duty to maintain the office intact and to hand it on to his successor as a working entity. The very intensity of Gregory's self-identification with St Peter led him, no doubt unwittingly, sometimes to speak and to behave as though the person of the pope transcended the office. Gregory may be absolved from the most serious accusations that have been brought against him of ruling autocratically and without counsel, or of disregarding the agencies, such as the Roman bishops and cardinals, by which he was surrounded.[12] Yet the half-century between the accession in 1049 of Pope Leo IX and the death in 1099 of Pope Urban II was one of the most critical periods in history for the development of the institutions of papal government, such as the college of cardinals; Gregory contributed little to this development. If he was successful in holding together the disparate elements among his followings at Rome and elsewhere until the crisis of his last months, he did so by the force and charisma of his personality, rather than by laying firm foundations for future developments such as took place in the entourages of the anti-pope Clement III and then of Urban II. The way in which the Gregorian party fell apart after his death in 1085, the internal enmities of the next three years, and the situation from which Urban II had to rescue the papacy, illustrate the weaknesses inherent in Gregory VII's too-personal style of rule as vicar of St Peter.[13]

Still more pronouncedly than giving rise to points of strength and weakness in Gregory's exercise of papal authority, his unique position amongst the eleventh-century popes gave rise to ambiguity. He genuinely kept before his own and others' eyes as models to follow the Olympian figures of his youth—the Emperor Henry III

---

[10] *Reg.* 3.10, 8 Dec. 1075, p. 265/4–10
[11] *Epp. vag.* no. 54, pp. 128–35; see above, 3.5.11.   [12] See above, 9.1.
[13] For a fuller examination, see Cowdrey, *The Age of Abbot Desiderius*, pp. 177–217.

and Pope Leo IX. Yet these men were establishment figures of the existing world-order. Gregory was himself not of the social and political establishment: for a superior, he looked solely to St Peter whose vicar he was; for agents, he tended to bypass the mighty of this world and to seek his friends in wider circles of new and upwards-thrusting men over whom his control was less than he intended or required in order to fulfil his purposes. This was most apparent in his dealings with the Milanese Patarenes, both while he was Archdeacon Hildebrand and after he became pope in 1073. The Patarenes were in fanatical and militant protest against the clerical and aristocratic establishment of Milan and its region, and they were zealots against simony and the unchastity of the clergy. Hildebrand forged an alliance with their lay leader, the knight Erlembald who was a man of the sword. Only after Erlembald perished in 1075 during bloody street-fighting could Gregory's true objectives be set in the way of attainment at Milan.[14] No less ambivalent was Gregory's alliance with the lately-arrived Normans of South Italy, who had undermined the Byzantine and Lombard establishments there. For Gregory as pope, they became necessary allies in face of the German ruler with whom he became at loggerheads. But Robert Guiscard, the Norman duke of Apulia, was the least dependable of friends: three times Gregory excommunicated him; he tended to be not available or to be un-amenable when Gregory most needed his aid; when he belatedly came to Gregory's rescue, the result in 1084 was one of the worst sackings in Rome's history; Gregory thereafter died in exile as his unwilling guest at Salerno. There was a profound ambiguity about a Gregory who both revered the 'establishment' models of Henry III and Leo IX and also sought partners and allies in the upstart Patarenes and Normans.

The mixture of strength, weakness, and ambiguity in Gregory's presentation of himself as vicar of St Peter is symptomatic of his being, despite the apparent confidence of his pronouncements, far from sure in his own mind about what his prerogatives as pope really were. Both in principle and in practice, he was always searching for them, and to a large degree his conclusions, even in his letter of 1081 to Bishop Hermann of Metz,[15] remained tentative and open to change.

A revealing incident in his search for light about papal prerogatives occurred in his early days as archdeacon. In 1059, Cardinal Peter Damiani pointed out to him how his dealings with the Patarenes at Milan had aroused in him an awareness of, and a need further to explore, the 'privilegium Romanae aecclesiae', by which he meant the prerogatives of the Roman church. 'What great powers these prerogatives have', Peter wrote, 'to uphold the rules of canonical equity and righteousness, he alone knows who is used to labouring in ecclesiastical business.' He said that by dint of his experiences at Milan, he now understood why Hildebrand had often urged him to work through the decrees and precedents of the Roman popes and to search out whatever seemed especially relevant to the authority of the apostolic see, writing them in a small book.[16] Neither Peter nor anyone else took up the challenge of thoroughly investigating these prerogatives until Gregory's pontificate was well

---

[14] See Cowdrey, 'The Papacy, the Patarenes, and the Church of Milan'.
[15] *Reg.* 8.21, pp. 544–63.   [16] *Briefe*, no. 65, 2.228–47, esp. 229–30.

advanced. When Cardinal Deusdedit did so at Rome, his emphasis differed from Gregory's own by laying the emphasis upon the Roman church rather than on the pope himself.[17]

As this difference illustrates, both before and during his pontificate, views at Rome of the nature and application of papal authority were anything but monolithic, uniform, and settled, even with respect to the most pressing issues of the day. With all the force of his energy and commitment, Gregory stood alone and developed his own ideas and reactions to events. Before 1073, he was the disciple neither of Cardinal Humbert nor of Cardinal Peter Damiani, but he formed his own outlook in detachment from them both. There is no basis whatsoever for deeming him to have been a follower of the extremist Cardinal Humbert; he differed from him in his long suspension of judgement about the eucharistic teaching of Berengar of Tours, and he cannot be shown to have owed any debt whatsoever to Humbert's polemic against lay investiture, since his own hostility to it grew only gradually and long after Humbert was dead, in the course of his own pontificate.[18] His lack of interest in polemic against clerical unchastity in terms of the 'nicolaitism' against which the two cardinal-bishops wrote, and in the legends of Simon Magus in his contest with St Peter which Peter Damiani canvassed, is symptomatic of his very different cast of mind. To Peter Damiani, Hildebrand was 'my holy Satan', the gadfly who challenged and tested him, not the receptive listener who learned from him. As pope, Gregory testified to his practice of taking decisions that were his own and that he sometimes arrived at against the advice of his counsellors at Rome, for example his decisions at the end of 1076 to make a journey across the Alps to Germany.[19]

Neither before nor after 1073 did Gregory have any party of supporters from amongst the variety of outlooks and emphases that, throughout his active lifetime, characterized the church of Rome. It was, perhaps, this very independence that enabled him for most of his pontificate to retain the loyalty and co-operation of most of the Roman bishops, cardinals, and clergy even when, like Cardinal Deusdedit, their views were markedly different from his own. Gregory had an exceptional capacity to inspire personal loyalty and devotion even in those who, in important respects, differed from him; it persisted in many of his entourage even to the last events of his deathbed. In the church at large, too, he won and retained the loyalty and commitment of many of the outstanding figures of an age of great churchmen. Among bishops, he did so especially in the cases of those who became his papal vicars—Hugh of Die and Lyons, Amatus of Oloron, Anselm II of Lucca, and Altmann of Passau, and among monks, of figures so different from himself as Hugh of Cluny and Desiderius of Montecassino, as well as of men more similar to him, like William of Hirsau or Bernard and Richard of Marseilles. Like no other pope in the recent past,

---

[17] See above, 8.3.

[18] For Humbert on lay investiture, see *Adv. simoniacos* 3.6, 11, 15, pp. 205–6, 211–12, 216–17; for the limited influence of this treatise in general, see Schieffer, *Die Entstehung des päpstlichen Investiturverbots*, pp. 41–7.

[19] See *Epp. vag.* nos. 17–18, pp. 46–51.

Gregory's charisma and energetic action forced men everywhere who were concerned with the renewal of the church to adopt a considered stance towards him. If some rejected him and what he stood for, many others, of a wide variety of temperaments and backgrounds, were drawn to co-operate with him.

They did so the more readily because Gregory exhibited a remarkable blend of ideas and action. The power of his thought should not be underestimated. It has often, and rightly, been remarked that he was not of a speculative turn of mind, nor was he greatly concerned with fundamental issues of dogmatic theology. He exhibited no such encyclopaedic learning as that of Peter Damiani; his thought was always austerely directed to spiritual guidance and practical action. He was slow to appreciate the dogmatic dangers that many of his contemporaries, from Cardinal Humbert onwards, claimed to see in the eucharistic teachings of Berengar of Tours, upon which he for long suspended judgement in the belief that they were insufficient rather than erroneous. While convinced, like all his close associates, of the indefectibility of the Roman church in which the truth would always be found and by which it would always be safeguarded, the concept of a personal attribute of infallibility with which the pope was endowed and which he was bound to exercise formed no part of his world of thought. When it came to passing judgement on such a matter as Berengar's teachings at his Lent synod of 1079, Gregory seems to have depended, not upon dialectical argument or ancient authorities, but upon the manifestation of a sign from heaven.[20] Gregory seems to have depended considerably upon such signs. His admiring biographer Paul of Bernried presented him as one who was often granted them and who expected to be guided by them.[21] His enemies made much of his dependence upon the dreams and divinations of himself and of others.[22] The extent to which Gregory depended for direction upon supernatural manifestations of one kind or another should not be underestimated. In this, he was a man of his time.

He was no less a man of his time in that his mind was a deeply cultivated one through knowledge of and reflection upon the books of the Old and the New Testaments. Frequency of scriptural citation and allusion is rightly regarded as a mark of letters that were of his own dictation; it is significant that a high proportion of his scriptural references have the form of allusions rather than of direct citations, and that his scriptural passages were well digested into his arguments and exhortations.[23] His knowledge of other ancient Christian authors was uneven. He cited Augustine of Hippo only once,[24] and he displayed little clear evidence of having read his works. But he referred to Pope Gregory the Great much more often, especially in relation to matters like Christian obedience. In this connection, he also seems to have

---

[20] See above, 8.1.1.

[21] Paul of Bernried, caps. 11, 13, 17–20, 23–6, 30–6, pp. 478–90.

[22] See e.g. the decree of the synod of Brixen (1080), Anhang C, *Quellen HIV* pp. 478/1–5, 480/21–5; Beno, 1.4, 6–7, 9, pp. 370–3; Peter Crassus, *Defensio*, cap. 7, pp. 451–2.

[23] See the indexes of biblical references in *Reg.* pp. 644–8 and *Epp. vag.* p. 169.

[24] Augustine, *De doctrina Christiana*, 1.23, at *Reg.* 8.21, p. 556/2–5.

reflected much upon the Rule of St Benedict, to which he once urged an abbot to bind himself in the depth of his being ('Volumus etiam et monemus, ut . . . sanctae regulae medullitus te astringas').[25] The profoundest influences on Gregory's mind seem to have been writers like Gregory I and Benedict whose teachings had a strongly moral purpose. Gregory's profound and systematic reflection upon scripture and upon authors concerned with moral formation is apparent in the expositions of the Christian faith and its moral consequences that he addressed to Christian kings and princes in the hope that they would both themselves assimilate them and pass them on to the kingdoms and peoples over whom they ruled.[26] In this sense, the preaching of the Gospel to which Gregory felt himself to be constrained was directed by much more than by practical maxims of action; he intended it to express a wholeness of Christian teaching which was formed through deep reflection, after the manner of Pope Gregory I.

In certain respects, Gregory's sense of moral purpose led to his showing a moderation and balance with which he has not usually been credited. Towards eastern Christians, and not least to the Greeks, his approach was conspicuously moderate and restrained, and he genuinely sought to promote concord amongst the churches. Even Muslims, if they were in his eyes peaceable and politically stable, formed a religious group amongst whom a Christian minority should strive to live well and commend its faith; he did not see them as aliens and enemies fitted only for extirpation. Within Christendom, even such antagonists as Gregory came to recognize in Henry IV of Germany and Archbishop Guibert of Ravenna were not usually described outright as Antichrist; rather, for so long as they persisted in their enmity, they were his members. Gregory was accordingly able to leave room even to the end for their repentance and at least for their spiritual reconciliation. From being members of Antichrist, they could always return to being members of Christ.

In other respects, however, Gregory pressed matters to extremes, and did so impetuously and with daemonic intensity. He was thus impelled to situations of confrontation and conflict that consorted ill with his genuine wish to promote peace and concord both in the church and in lay society. His sharp distinction between the followers of Christ and those of Antichrist, and his insistence that every human being followed the one or the other, had the effect of polarizing men absolutely, at least when Gregory found himself in circumstances of mental and physical conflict. If they lived on the periphery of the Latin world, rulers like William I of England who were reputable and well disposed might be tolerated and humoured even though they did not measure up to Gregory's standard of obedience. But nearer to the centre of things, in Italy, Germany, or France, in times of crisis all was black and white; there was no light and shade. Those who were not for Gregory were against him. The record of the Lent synods of 1076 and 1080 embody the force of the judgement to which he was, therefore, impelled.

[25] *Reg.* 7.7, to Cardinal Richard of Marseilles, 2 Nov. 1079, p. 468/20–4.
[26] e.g. *Reg.* 4.28, to the kings and princes of Spain, 28 June 1077, pp. 343–6; 6.13, to King Olaf III of Norway, 15 Dec. 1078, pp. 415–18.

Within his scheme of thought and values, Gregory maintained a high degree of personal integrity, and he can be cleared of most of the moral charges that have been levelled against him both by his contemporaries and by more recent historians; even if the paradoxes and ambiguities of Gregory's personality and actions leave scope for differing judgements upon him. He could, indeed, occasionally when under intense pressure act without due scrupulousness, as when, in 1081, he wished the Normans to depart from their good custom of not fighting in Lent so that they might defend the interest of the Roman church, and when in 1082, he was prepared to mortgage church property in order to finance his resistance to Archbishop Guibert of Ravenna during Henry IV's expedition to Rome; he thereby called forth the combined opposition of a cross-section of the Roman clergy in a public *conventus* that firmly restrained him.[27] But, in general, accusations that, both before and after he became pope, Gregory was excessively preoccupied with matters of finance and warfare are misplaced. Papal finances in the mid-eleventh century were rudimentary, and Gregory was justified in the steps that he normally took to maximize them. He had a responsibility for the order and security of Rome and of the papal lands which he seems to have discharged with effect, in view of their usual quietness during his pontificate. With regard to Christendom at large, too little weight has been given to Gregory's genuine concern to promote peace and concord in human situations both great and small. Similarly, allegations that Gregory was personally harsh and even cruel must be tempered by regard to the pastoral concern that was a leading quality of his treatment of others, and to his recognition of the duty of tempering justice with mercy. Not for nothing did he choose as the motto in the rota of many of his charters the Psalmist's words that the mercies of the Lord are over all his works (Ps. 144: 9).

Gregory's awareness of the divine mercy was at the heart of his religious outlook. It was associated in his mind with a sense of personal isolation and even of insecurity that he felt amongst his associates at Rome, in spite of his own lifelong association with the city and his membership of the household of St Peter and of his consequent protection by the prince of the apostles whose vicar he was. His sense of isolation and consequent dependence upon the divine mercy emerges in his letters of self-disclosure to Abbot Hugh of Cluny, to whom alone he seems to have opened his soul as a kind of surrogate abbot of his own. Thus, in January 1075, he wrote to Abbot Hugh that 'those among whom I live, the Romans that is, the Lombards, and the Normans, as I often tell them, I accuse of being worse than the Jews and the heathen'. His sense of isolation threw him back upon the divine mercy: 'When I return to myself, I find myself so burdened by the weight of my own actions that no hope of safety is left, save solely in the mercy of Christ.'[28] In May 1078, Gregory wrote to Hugh again in similar vein but still more poignantly of his sense of isolation under the burden of the papal office: 'We are oppressed by such constraints and wearied by such great labours, that those who are with us are not only unable to sustain them but they cannot even conceive them.' As St Paul had complained, his life was

---

[27] See above, 3.5.7, 6.2.
[28] *Reg.* 2.49, p. 189/25–30; cf. Gregory I, *Reg. past.* 4, title, vol. 2.534.

burdensome to him, and he desired to be dead (cf. Phil. 1: 23). Once again, Gregory's recourse was to turn directly to Jesus, envisaged as a poor man ('pauper Jesus') and as a merciful comforter ('pius consolator'). Gregory's encounter with Jesus was immediate: when Jesus, true God and true man, extended his hand, he made Gregory glad, not sorrowful and afflicted; when Jesus turned him away ('memet dimittit'), Gregory was greatly dismayed. 'For', he explained, 'in myself I am always dying, but in him I sometimes live.' When Gregory's strength altogether failed, he turned to Jesus and pleaded about the burden that he bore, placing his papal office in the hands of Jesus and of 'his Peter'. He indicated to Abbot Hugh the habitual lines of his prayer by referring to three biblical themes: the Lord's mercy upon the weak—'Have mercy upon me, Lord, for I am weak' (Ps. 6: 3); the Lord's strength to save—'I have become a monster to many, but you are my strong helper' (Ps. 70: 7); and God's almighty power—'For God is able from these stones to raise up children to Abraham' (cf. Matt. 3: 9).[29]

Such letters reveal in Gregory an inner spirituality that has been insufficiently appreciated.[30] It underlay all his dealings with leading persons of his time, whether monastic, clerical, or lay. It found expression in the concluding prayers, beginning with the phrase 'Omnipotens Deus' or similar words, which occur in thirty-eight of his letters.[31] As an example, that which ended a letter of January 1079 to the monks of Saint-Victor at Marseilles runs as follows:

May Almighty God, from whom all good things come, by the merits and intercession of the Virgin Mother of God and through the authority of Blessed Peter and Paul, the princes of the apostles, look with favour upon you, may he continually renew and keep you, may he reveal to you what is the 'new song' (Rev. 14: 3), and may he inflame you in holy jubilation; so that you may fully know how to weep for human frailty and how to experience the unspeakable goodness of God; and so that, by growing continually in his love, you may, with the Mother of Heaven as guide, deserve to come to the true knowledge of him and to his marvellous joy.[32]

Gregory's own grace of tears while saying mass was noticed by his contemporaries.[33] Moreover, there may be observed in this prayer undertones of the liturgical collect for the third Sunday after Pentecost: 'that we may so pass through things temporal that we do not finally lose things eternal.' Gregory incorporated these words almost verbatim in the concluding prayer of a letter of April 1075 to Duke Wratislav II of Bohemia:

May Almighty God illuminate your mind, and so may he make you pass through temporal good things that you may deserve to attain to things eternal.[34]

Not only does this theme occur in many of Gregory's concluding prayers, but it informs a remarkable number of Gregory's letters as addressed to the great men and

---

[29] *Reg.* 5.21, pp. 384–5.   [30] See Cowdrey, 'The Spirituality of Pope Gregory VII'.
[31] See Table at the end of 8.4, above. Caspar's figure of thirty examples in the Register is incorrect: *Reg.* p. 25 n. 1 and *passim*.
[32] *Reg.* 6.15, p. 420/29–37.
[33] *Vita Iohannis Gualberti*, cap. 85, p. 1102; Guy of Ferrara, 1.2, p. 535/12–16.
[34] *Reg.* 2.71, p. 232/3–4.

women of his time. Gregory especially addressed it to kings and lay rulers as the ground theme of his exhortations to Christian rulership.[35] So widely circulated a letter as that of March 1081 to Bishop Hermann of Metz had as its climax an impassioned plea to look to things eternal:

For if this virtue, I mean charity, be neglected, no matter what degree of good a man shall perform, he will be lacking in any fruit of salvation. Therefore, by humbly doing the things that I have said and by duly maintaining love of God and their neighbour, men may count upon the mercy of him who said, 'Learn of me, for I am meek and humble of heart' (Matt. 11: 29). If they will humbly copy him, they will pass from a kingdom that is mean and transient to one that is truly free and eternal.[36]

The deepest springs of Gregory's thought and action are not to be found in any politician's urge to wield power and to humble his adversaries, nor in any abuse of priestly power by seeking domination over the souls of others and, above all, of kings and of the lay orders of society. Before all else, his motives were religious. They arose from an informed and reflective familiarity with the books of the Bible, in its overall presentation of man's destiny through his creation, his fallen state, his redemption by Christ and consequent choice between obedience and disobedience, and the ever-present expectation of the final judgement. He interpreted the biblical message above all through the writings of Pope Gregory the Great whose papal name he took, and through the Rule of St Benedict by whose monastic Rule his early life had been formed. His values were those which arose from such a background. Charity, obedience, humility, righteousness, mercy, and the pursuit of peace and concord were pre-eminent among them. It cannot be too strongly insisted that, in respect to such values and to his appraisal of them, he stood far closer to the tradition of Gregory and Benedict in the sixth century than to the lawyer-popes like Alexander III and Innocent III who were soon to follow him, and to the age of canon law as ushered in by the *Decretum* of Gratian. However much Gregory's exploration of the prerogatives of the apostolic see opened the way for the papal monarchy of the central Middle Ages, he was its forerunner, not its founder. His values were too deeply rooted in an older time.

Gregory's essentially religious motivation, on lines that were familiar to his many contemporaries who were steeped in the Bible, in the works of Pope Gregory the Great, and in the Rule of St Benedict, was a source both of strength and of weakness. It was a source of strength, because it was in line with the aspirations of many of the outstanding persons of his time. His appeal was the stronger, not only because of the force of his own personality and conviction, but also because, for all his rootedness in the past, he also foreshadowed and prepared the way for some of the most vital developments of the twelfth century—not least in his radical attempt to overhaul the ways of penance by insisting upon the total and inner conversion of the individual

---

35 Some examples are his letters to the kings and princes of Spain, *Reg.* 4.28, 28 June 1077, pp. 343–7; to King William I of England, 24 Apr. 1080, pp. 499–502; and to King Inge of Sweden, 8.11, 4 Oct. 1080, p. 530.
36 *Reg.* 8.21, p. 562/18–25.

Christian. This insistence was accompanied by a resolute quest for the moralization of church and society which owed much of its inspiration to Gregory the Great's conception of the pastoral office, but which also prepared the way for new orders such as the Carthusians and the Cistercians, and for the greater ethical sophistication of early scholastic thought.[37]

But within the perspectives that governed his mind, Gregory's religious motivation was also a source of weakness. In the west, Pope Gregory the Great had not had to contend with such structures of ecclesiastical and temporal authority as were being vigorously founded in the later eleventh century. Gregory's mental formation led him to regard archbishops and bishops, and no less kings and princes, as owing to St Peter and his vicar an obedience which was like that of the monastery. His demands were not adapted to the various sorts and conditions of men who made up the world at large. His attempted moralization of kingship, in particular, was incapable of being realized in the hard reality of a rough and brutal world. All too often, in the demands that he made of human beings both individually and collectively, Gregory worked across the grain of human nature, rather than with it. Few judgements on Gregory are more to the point than that of Erdmann: 'Gregory did not reckon with men as they actually are.'[38] By the same token, Gregory did not grasp the complexities of political life. In Germany, for example, he was never able to comprehend the realities of a three-cornered struggle of pope, king, and princes, in which many of his own apparent allies were primarily motivated by hostility to the king. Again, Gregory's determination, which was especially manifest in relation to Germany during the years after Canossa, that the pope should be the source of peace and order in divided societies, had an intrinsic nobility and high motivation. But it ran counter to the constructive development whereby, during the eleventh and twelfth centuries, the Peace of God as fostered by churchmen gave place to the peace of temporal rulers. In the long run, it was they who developed the legal power and the instruments of government to provide for civil security and order.[39] In his pastoral dealings, Gregory often showed depths of human sympathy and understanding; in ecclesiastical and political connections, his aspirations and endeavours were too often flawed by over-simple and impulsive thinking.

But a final judgement on Gregory should not be a matter of striking a balance; his qualities were too strong and positive for this to be sufficient. He was a man of the eleventh century, when the force and impact of personality had not yet given way as the foundation of effective rulership to ordered administration and skilfully formulated and enforced laws. Gregory's greatness as a pope lay in the larger-than-life personal qualities that enabled him to encompass within his mind and to make an impact upon the churchmen, lay rulers, and peoples of both the central and the peripheral regions of Latin Christendom. With a comprehensiveness and an intensity not

[37] See, for one line of development, Cowdrey, 'The Carthusians and their Contemporary World'.

[38] 'Gregor VII. rechnete nicht, mit den Menschen, wie sie waren', *Die Entstehung*, p. 210, Eng. trans. p. 227.

[39] See Cowdrey, 'The Peace and Truce of God', and id., 'From the Peace of God to the First Crusade'.

achieved by his recent predecessors, even Leo IX, he brought Christendom as a whole into the effective purview of papal authority, and he defined its peoples and regions with a clarity that ensured the persistence of his vision. His overriding purpose was, on the model of Pope Gregory the Great, to announce universally by way of preaching as he understood it the order of society and the manner of individual life that God had prepared by means of the redemption. The vision of the church that he cherished as the bride of Christ who should, as the result of his stewardship, return to her true glory and stand free, chaste, and catholic, would soon by overlaid by the papal monarchy of the central Middle Ages. But that monarchy could scarcely have been constructed unless Gregory had expanded men's minds, and especially those of the popes, by the fullness of his vision. This fullness was both spatial, in that it comprehended the whole of Christendom as an ordered family of peoples and kingdoms, and transcendent, in that he sought to bring universally to bear upon it the mercies of God which were over all his works. His concern was to renew a timeless Christian order which was founded upon the New Testament, which was consolidated by the fathers and councils of the church, and which was warranted by the Petrine authority of the popes who were its custodians; although latter-day negligence had caused it to be obscured.

By seeking to renew this order, Gregory prepared the way for the centralized and organized church of his twelfth-century papal successors, and especially of Pope Innocent III. But he saw himself above all as a pope who, in whatever he said and did, was a 'praedicator' after the model of Pope Gregory the Great. Thus, he belonged to an earlier age than that of the lawyer-popes, the canonists, and the schoolmen who followed him; they understandably showed little sense of measurable indebtedness to him. The comprehensiveness of his vision marked him off from the past, while its formation upon ancient models marked him off from the future. In such terms, he was, indeed, the great innovator in the history of the papacy, who nevertheless stands alone.[40] He was the towering forerunner and prophet of the papal monarchy of the central Middle Ages, but not its architect or builder.

---

[40] See esp. Caspar's judgement that 'Er ist eben doch, trotz aller Vorläufer, der große Anfänger, der auf sich selbst allein steht': 'Gregor VII. in seinen Briefen', p. 30.

BIBLIOGRAPHY

1. SOURCES

Acta Lanfranci, in *Two of the Saxon Chronicles Parallel*, pp. 287–92.

Acta Murensia, ed. M. Kiem, *QSG* 3 (1883), 16–100.

Actus Silvestri, in B. Mombritius, *Sanctuarium seu Vitae sanctorum*, 2 vols. (Paris, 1910), 2. 508–31.

ADAM OF BREMEN, *Historia Hammaburgensis ecclesiae pontificum*, ed. B. Schmeidler and W. Trillmich, in *Quellen der 9. und 11. Jahrhunderts*, pp. 137–503.

ALBINUS: *Eglogarum digesta pauperis scholaris Albini*, in *Lib. cens.* 2. 2–4, 87–137.

Altercatio inter Urbanum et Clementem, ed. E. Sackur, *MGH L. de L.* 2. 169–71.

AMATUS: *Storia dei Normanni di Amato di Montecassino*, ed. V. de Bartholomeis, *Fonti*, 76 (Rome, 1935).

ANDREW OF STRUMI, *Vita sancti Arialdi*, ed. F. Baethgen, *MGH SS* 30/2 (1929), 1049–75.

—— *Vita sancti Iohannis Gualberti*, ed. F. Baethgen, *MGH SS* 30/2 (1929), 1076–104.

ANNA COMNENA: *Anne Comnène, Alexiade*, ed. B. Leib, 4 vols. (Paris, 1937–76).

Annales Altahenses maiores, with *Annalium Ratisbonensium maiorum fragmentum*, 2nd edn., ed. W. von Giesbrecht and E. L. B. von Oefele, *MGH SRG* (1891).

Annales Augustani, ed. G. H. Pertz, *MGH SS* 3 (1839), 124–36.

Annales Beneventani, ed. G. H. Pertz, *MGH SS* 3 (1839), 173–85.

Annales Casinenses, ed. G. Smidt, *MGH SS* 30/2 (1926–34), 1408–29.

Annales Cavenses, ed. G. H. Pertz, *MGH SS* 3 (1839), 186–97.

Annales Corbeienses, ed. G. H. Pertz, *MGH SS* 3 (1839), 1–18.

Annales Magdeburgenses, ed. G. H. Pertz, *MGH SS* 16 (1859), 107–96.

Annales Palidenses, ed. G. H. Pertz, *MGH SS* 16 (1859), 48–96.

Annales Patherbrunnenses, in P. Schieffer-Boichorst, *Eine verlorene Quellenschrift des xii. Jahrhunderts, aus Brüchstuchen wiederhergestellt* (Innsbruck, 1870), 92–170.

Annales Pegavienses, ed. G. H. Pertz, *MGH SS* 16 (1859), 234–70.

Ann. Rom.: *Annales Romani*, in *LP* 2. 331–50.

Annales sancti Vitoni Virdunensis, ed. G. Waitz, *MGH SS* 10 (1852), 525–30.

Annalista Saxo, ed. G. Waitz, *MGH SS* 6 (1844), 550–777.

Annalium Ratisbonensium maiorum fragmentum: see *Annales Altahenses maiores*.

Anonymi Vita Hludowici, in *Quellen zur karolingischen Reichsgeschichte*, ed. R. Rau, *Aus. Quellen* 5, 3 vols. (Darmstadt, 1968), 1. 257–381.

ANSELM, Archbishop of Canterbury, *Opera omnia*, ed. F. S. Schmitt, 6 vols. (Edinburgh, 1946–61).

ANSELM OF LIÈGE, *Gesta episcoporum Leodiensium*, ed. G. Waitz, *MGH SS* 7 (1846), 189–234.

ANSELM OF LUCCA, *Collectio canonum*, ed. F. Thaner, 1 (Innsbruck, 1906–11).

—— *Liber contra Wibertum*, ed. E. Bernheim, *MGH L. de L.* 1. 517–28.

Anselme de Saint-Remy: *Histoire de la dédicace de Saint-Remi*, ed. J. Hourlier, in *La Champagne Bénédictine*, Travaux de l'Académie nationale de Reims, 160 (Reims, 1981).

ARNULF OF MILAN, *Liber gestorum recentium*, ed. C. Zey, *MGH SRG* 67 (Hanover, 1994).

AUGUSTINE OF HIPPO, St, *De civitate Dei*, ed. B. Dombart and A. Kalb, 2 vols., *CCL* 47–8 (1955).

AUGUSTINE OF HIPPO *De doctrina Christiana*, ed. J. Martin, *CCL* 32 (1962).

AUTENRIETH, J., 'Der bisher unbekannte Schluss des Briefs Gregors VII. am Mathilde von Tuscien vom 16. Februar 1074 (*Reg.* 1.47)', *DA* 13 (1957), 534–8.

BEN. CAN.: Benedictus Canonicus, *Liber politicus*, in *Lib. cens.* 2.2–4, 144–77; also in Valentini–Zucchetti, pp. 197–222.

BENO: *Benonis et aliorum cardinalium schismaticorum contra Gregorium VII. et Urbanum II. scripta*, ed. K. Francke, *MGH L. de L.* 2. 366–422.

BENZO OF ALBA, *Ad Heinricum IV imperatorem libri VII*, ed. K. Pertz, *MGH SS* 11 (1854), 597–681.

BERENGERIUS TURONENSIS, *Rescriptum contra Lanfrannum*, 1: *Text*, ed. R. B. C. Huygens, 2: *Facsimile*, with introd. by W. Milde, *CCM* 84, 84A (Turnhout, 1988).

BERNOLD OF ST BLASIEN, *Chronicon*, ed. G. Waitz, *MGH SS* 5 (1844), 385–467.

—— *Libelli*, ed. F. Thaner, *MGH L. de L.* 2. 1–168: 1. *De incontinentia sacerdotum*, pp. 7–26; 2. *De damnatione scismaticorum*, pp. 26–58; 3. *Apologeticus*, pp. 58–88; 4. *De sacramentis excommunicatorum*, pp. 89–94; 5. *Apologeticae rationes contra scismaticorum obiectiones*, pp. 94–101; 6. *De lege excommunicationis*, pp. 101–3; 7. *De eadem re*, pp. 103–6; 8. *De emptione ecclesiarum*, pp. 106–8; 9. *Pro Gebhardo episcopo Constantiensi epistola apologetica*; 10. *De excommunicatis vitandis*, pp. 112–41; 11. *De presbyteris*, pp. 142–6; 12. *De solutione iuramentorum*, pp. 146–9; 13. *Fragmentum libelli deperditi*, p. 149; 14. *De reordinatione vitanda*, pp. 150–6; 15. *De statutis ecclesiasticis*, pp. 156–60; 16. *De libro mittendo*, p. 160; Appendix. *Libellus de sententia excommunicationis*, pp. 160–8.

—— *Micrologus*, *PL* 151. 977–1022.

BERTHOLD OF REICHENAU, *Chronicon*, ed. G. H. Pertz, *MGH SS* 5 (1844), 264–326.

BONIZO OF SUTRI, *Liber ad amicum*, ed. E. Dümmler, *MGH L. de L.* 1. 568–620.

—— *Liber de vita christiana*, ed. E. Perels (Berlin, 1930).

Briefe Berengars von Tours, in *Briefsammlungen der Zeit Heinrichs IV.*, pp. 132–87.

Briefsammlungen der Zeit Heinrichs IV., ed. C. Erdmann and N. Fickermann, *MGH Briefe*, 5 (Weimar, 1950).

BRUNO, *Saxonicum bellum*, ed. E. Lohmann, in *Quellen HIV* pp. 28–84, 191–405.

BRUNO OF SEGNI, *Expositio in Leviticum*, *PL* 164. 377–464.

—— *Libellus de symoniacis*, ed. E. Sackur, *MGH L. de L.* 2. 543–62.

BURCHARD, Bishop of Worms, *Decretorum libri viginti*, *PL* 140. 537–1058.

Calendar of the Manuscripts of the Dean and Chapter of Wells, 2 vols. (Historical Manuscripts Commission, London, 1907–14).

Cameracensium et Noviomensium clericorum epistolae, ed. H. Boehmer, *MGH L. de L.* 3. 573–8.

Canterbury Professions, ed. M. Richter, *The Canterbury and York Society*, 140 (1972–3).

Carmen de bello Saxonico, ed. O. Holder-Egger, in *Quellen HIV* pp. 20–7, 143–89.

Cartulaire de l'abbaye cardinale de la Trinité de Vendôme, ed. C. Métais, 5 vols. (Paris, 1893–1904).

Cartulaire de l'abbaye de Saint-André-le-Bas de Vienne, ed. C. U. J. Chevalier (Vienne and Lyons, 1869).

Cartulaire de l'abbaye de Saint-Victor de Marseille, ed. M. Guérard, 2 vols. (Paris, 1857).

Cartulaire manceau de Marmoutier, ed. E. Laurain, 2 vols. (Laval, 1911–45).

Cartulario de San Juan de la Peña, ed. A. Ubieto Arteta, 2 vols. (Valencia, 1962–3).

CASSIODORUS, *Historia ecclesiastica tripartita*, ed. W. Jacob and R. Hanslik, *CSEL* 71 (Vienna, 1952).

Casuum Sancti Galli continuatio secunda, ed. I. von Arx, *MGH SS* 2 (1829), 148–63.

Chron. Cas.: *Chronica monasterii Casinensis*, ed. H. Hoffmann, *MGH SS* 34 (1980).

Chronica sancti Benedicti, *MGH SS* 3 (1839), 197–213.

Chronicon Burgense, *ES* 23 (1767), 305–10.

Chronicon Ebersheimense, ed. L. Weiland, *MGH SS* 23 (1874), 427–53.

Chronicon Malleacense (*Chronicon sancti Maxentii*), in *Chroniques des églises d'Anjou*, ed. Marchegay and Mabille, pp. 351–433.

Chronicon monasterii Watinensis, ed. O. Holder-Egger, *MGH SS* 14 (1883), 163–75.

Chronicon sancti Andreae castri Cameracensii, ed. L. C. Bethmann, *MGH SS* 7 (1846), 526–50.

Chronicon sancti Benigni Divionensis, ed. G. Waitz, *MGH SS* 7 (1846), 235–8.

Chronicon sancti Huberti Andaginensis, ed. L. C. Bethmann and W. Wattenbach, *MGH SS* 8 (1848), 565–630.

Chronicon Sublacense, ed. R. Morghen, *RIS²* 24/6 (Rome, 1927).

Chronicon Vulturnense, ed. V. Federici, 3 vols., *Fonti*, 58–60 (1925–40).

Chronicon Wirziburgense, ed. G. Waitz, *MGH SS* 6 (1844), 17–32.

Chroniques des églises d'Anjou, ed. P. Marchegay and E. Mabille (Paris, 1869).

COD: *Conciliorum oecumenicorum decreta*, ed. J. Alberigo *et al.* (3rd edn., Bologna, 1973).

Codex diplomaticus regni Croatiae, Dalmatiae et Slavoniae, 1: *743–1100*, ed. M. Kostrenčić (Zagreb, 1967).

Cod. dipl. Trem.: *Codice diplomatico de monastero benedettino di S. Maria di Tremiti (1005–1237)*, ed. A. Petrucci, 3 vols., *Fonti*, 98/1–3 (1960).

Consuetudines Hirsaugienses, *PL* 150. 927–1146.

Cosmas of Prague, *Chronica Bohemorum*, ed. B. Bretholz, *MGH SRG* NS 2 (1923).

Councils and Synods with Other Documents relating to the English Church, 1: *AD 871–1204*, ed. D. Whitelock, M. Brett, and C. N. L. Brooke, 2 vols. (Oxford, 1981).

Crónica Najerense: Cirot, G., 'Une chronique léonaise inédite', *BH* 11 (1909), 259–82, 13 (1922), 133–56, 381–439.

CU: *Udalrici Babenbergensis Codex*, in *Monumenta Bambergensia*, Jaffé, *Bibl.* 5 (1869), 17–469.

Cuozzo, E., 'Il "Breve chronicon Northmannicum"', *BISI* 83 (1971), 131–232.

Das Constitutum Constantini (Konstantinische Schenkung): Text, ed. H. Fuhrmann, *MGH Font. iur. Ger. ant.* (Hanover, 1968).

Das Verbrüderungsbuch der Abtei Reichenau, ed. J. Autenrieth, D. Geuenich, and K. Schmid, *MGH Lib. mem.* NS 1 (Hanover, 1979).

De episcopis Eichstetensibus, ed. L. Bethmann, *MGH SS* 7 (1846), 254–67.

Deér, J., *Das Papsttum und die süditalienischen Normannenstaaten, 1053–1212* (Göttingen, 1969).

De iniusta vexatione Willelmi episcopi primi, in *English Lawsuits*, no. 134, pp. 90–106.

De ordinando pontifice, in H. H. Anton, *Der sogenannte Traktat 'De ordinando pontifice'* (Bonn, 1982), pp. 75–83.

De sancti Hugonis actis liturgicis, ed. M. Bocci (Florence, 1984).

De sancto Petro episcopo Anagniae in Italia, *AA. SS. Boll.* Aug. 1. 233–41.

Descriptio ecclesiae Lateranensis, in Georgi, *De liturgia*, 3. 542–55; later version in Valentini–Zuccetti, pp. 319–73.

Desiderius of Montecassino, *Dialogi de miraculis sancti Benedicti*, ed. G. Schwartz and A. Hofmeister, *MGH SS* 30/2 (1926–34), 1111–51.

Deusdedit, *Coll. can.*: *Die Kanonessammlung des Kardinals Deusdedit*, ed. V. Wulf von Glanvell, 1 (Paderborn, 1905).

DEUSDEDIT *Liber contra invasores et symoniacos et reliquos scismaticos*, ed. E. Sackur, *MGH L. de L.*, 2. 300–65.

Dicta cuiusdam de discordia papae et regis, ed. K. Francke, *MGH L. de L.* 1. 454–60.

Die Briefe des Abtes Walo von St Arnulf vor Metz, ed. B. Schütte, *MGH S. und T.* 10 (Hanover, 1995).

Die Chronik des Klosters Petershausen, ed. O. Feder (Lindau and Constance, 1956).

Die falschen Investiturprivilegien, ed. C. Märtl, *MGH Font. iur. Ger. ant.* 13 (Hanover, 1986).

DIEHL, E., *Inscriptiones Latinae Christianae veteres*, 3 vols. (Berlin, 1925–31).

Dipl. Danic.: *Diplomatarium Danicum*, 1 Raekke, pt. 2: *1053–1169*, ed. N. Skyum-Nielsen and L. Weibull (Copenhagen, 1963).

Diversorum patrum sententie, siue Collectio in LXXIV titulos digesta, ed. J. Gilchrist (Vatican City, 1973).

DONIZO, *Vita Matildis*, ed. L. Bethmann, *MGH SS* 12 (1856), 348–409.

EADMER, *Historia novorum in Anglia*, ed. M. Rule, *RS* 81 (London, 1884).

EBO, *Vita Ottonis episcopi Bambergensis*, ed. R. Köpke, *MGH SS* 12 (1856), 822–83.

EKKEHARD OF AURA, *Chronicon*, in *Frutolfs und Ekkehards Chroniken*, pp. 124–209.

English Lawsuits from William I to Richard I, 1: *William I to Stephen*, ed. R. C. van Caenegem, Selden Society 106 (London, 1990).

Ennodius, *Libellus adversus eos qui contra synodum scribere praesumpserunt*, ed. F. Vogel, *MGH AA* 7 (1885), 48–67.

Epistolae pontificum Romanorum ineditae, ed. S. Loewenfeld (Leipzig, 1885).

Epitaphium sancti Kanuti, *VSD* 76.

Epp. HIV: *Epistolae Heinrici IV.*, in *Quellen HIV* pp. 5–20, 51–141, 470–83.

Epp. vag.: *The Epistolae vagantes of Pope Gregory VII*, ed. and trans. H. E. J. Cowdrey (Oxford 1972).

EWALD, P., 'Die Papstbriefe der Brittischen Sammlung', *NA* 5/2 (1880), 277–596.

Frutolfi Chronica, in *Frutolfs und Ekkehards Chroniken*, pp. 47–121.

Frutolfs und Ekkehards Chroniken und die anonyme Kaiserchronik, ed. F.-J. Schmale and I. Schmale-Ott, *Aus. Quell.* 15 (Darmstadt, 1977).

FLODOARD, *Historia Remensis ecclesiae*, ed. J. Heller and G. Waitz, *MGH SS* 13 (1881), 409–599.

GALTERIUS, *Vita sancti Anastasii*, *PL* 149. 423–32.

GEBHARD OF SALZBURG, *Epistola ad Herimannum Mettensem episcopum data*, ed. K. Francke, *MGH L. de L.* 1. 260–79.

GEOFFREY MALATERRA: Gaufredus Malaterra, *De rebus gestis Rogerii Calabriae et Siciliae comitis et Roberti Guiscardi ducis fratris eius*, ed. R. Pontieri, *RIS²* (1925–8), 5/1.

GEORGI, D., *De liturgia Romani pontificis*, 3 vols. (Rome, 1731–44).

GERHOH OF REICHERSBERG, *Commentarius in Psalmum LXIV*, ed. E. Sackur, *MGH L. de L.* 3. 439–92.

—— *De investigatione Antichristi*, ed. E. Sackur, *MGH L. de L.* 3. 304–95.

Gesta archiepiscoporum Magdeburgensium, ed. W. Schum, *MGH SS* 14 (1883), 374–484.

Gesta episcoporum Cameracensium, ed. L. C. Bethmann, *MGH SS* 7 (1846), 402–510.

Gesta Treverorum, ed. G. Waitz, *MGH SS* 8 (1848), 111–260.

GILO, *Vita sancti Hugonis abbatis*, in Cowdrey, 'Two Studies', pp. 43–117.

Graphia aureae urbis, in Valentini–Zucchetti, pp. 67–110.

GREGORY I, *Dialogues*, ed. A. de Vogüé and P. Antin, 3 vols., *SC* 251, 260, 265 (Paris, 1978–80).

—— *Homiliae in Hiezechielem prophetam*, ed. M. Adriaen, *CCL* 142 (Turnhout, 1971).

—— *Homiliae XL in Evangelia*, *PL* 76. 1075–312.

—— *Moralia in Iob*, ed. M. Adriaen, 3 vols., *CCL* 143, 143A, 143B, (Turnhout, 1979–85).

—— *Registrum epistularum*, ed. D. Norberg, 2 vols., *CCM* 140, 140A (Turnhout, 1982).

—— *Reg. past.*: Grégoire le Grand, *Règle pastorale*, ed. B. Judic, F. Rommel, and C. Morel, 2 vols., *SC* 381–2 (Paris, 1992).

GREGORY VII: see *Reg., Epp. vag., QF*.

GUIBERT DE NOGENT, *Autobiographie*, ed. E.-R. Labande (Paris, 1981).

GUIGO PRIOR CARTHUSIENSIS, *Vita sancti Hugonis episcopi Gratianopolitani*, *PL* 153. 759–84.

GUNDECHAR, *Liber pontificalis Eichstetensis*, ed. L. C. Bethmann, *MGH SS* 7 (1846), 239–53.

GUY OF FERRARA, *De scismate Hildebrandi*, ed. R. Wilmans and E. Dümmler, *MGH L. de L.* 1. 529–67.

HALLER, J., *Die Quellen zur Geschichte der Entstehung des Kirchenstaates* (Leipzig and Berlin, 1907).

HELGASON, J., *Byskupa Sogur*, 2 vols. (Copenhagen, 1938–78).

HERBORD, *Dialogus de vita Ottonis episcopi Bambergensis*, ed. G. H. Pertz, *MGH SRG* 33 (1868).

HERMANN OF REICHENAU, *Chronicon*, ed. G. Pertz and H. Buchner, in *Quellen des 9. und 11. Jahrhunderts*, pp. 615–707.

HILDEBERT OF LE MANS, *Carmina minora*, ed. A. B. Scott (Leipzig, 1967).

HINSCHIUS: *Decretales Pseudo-Isidorianae et Capitula Angilramni*, ed. P. Hinschius (Leipzig, 1863).

Historiae Tornacenses, ed. G. Waitz, *MGH SS* 14 (1883), 327–52.

Historia Hirsaugiensis monasterii, ed. G. Waitz, *MGH SS* 14 (1883), 254–65.

HOLDER-EGGER, O., 'Fragment eines Manifestes aus der Zeit Heinrichs IV.', *NA* 31 (1906), 183–93.

HUGH OF FLAVIGNY, *Chronicon*, ed. G. Pertz, *MGH SS* 8 (1848), 288–502.

HUGH THE CHANTER, *The History of the Church of York*, *1066–1127*, ed. and trans. C. Johnson (2nd edn., Oxford, 1990).

HUMBERT, *Libri III adversus simoniacos*, ed. G. Thaner, *MGH L. de L.* 1. 95–253.

IOHANNES LONGUS, *Chronicon monasterii sancti Bertini*, ed. O. Holder-Egger, *MGH SS* 25 (1880), 747–866.

I Placiti del 'Regnum Italiae', ed. C. Manaresi, *Fonti*, 92, 96–7, 3 vols. (Rome, 1958–60).

ISIDORE OF SEVILLE, *Etymologiarum sive originum libri XX*, ed. W. M. Lindsay, 2 vols. (Oxford, 1911).

IVO OF CHARTRES: *Yves de Chartres, Correspondance*, 1: *1090–1098*, ed. J. Leclercq (Paris, 1949).

JOHN OF LODI, *Vita sancti Petri Damiani*, *PL* 144. 113–46.

JOHN OF MANTUA: *Iohannis Mantuani In Cantica canticorum et De sancta Maria tractatus ad Comitissam Matildam*, ed. B. Bischoff and B. Taeger (Freiburg, 1973).

JOHN THE DEACON, *S. Gregorii magni vita*, *PL* 75. 59–242.

KEHR, P. F., 'Papsturkunden in Rom: Erster Bericht', *Nach. Gött.* 1900, 111–97.

—— 'Papsturkunden in Spanien', 1–2, *Abh. Gött.* NF, 18, 22 (1926, 1928).

LAMPERT OF HERSFELD, *Annales*, ed. O. Holder-Egger and W. D. Fritz, *Aus. Quell.* 13 (Berlin, n.d.).

—— *Libellus de institutione Herveldensis ecclesiae*, in *Opera*, 342–54.

—— *Opera*, ed. O. Holder-Egger, *MGH SRG* 38 (Hanover and Leipzig, 1894).

LANDULF SENIOR, *Historia Mediolanensis*, ed. L. C. Bethman and W. Wattenbach, *MGH SS* 8 (1848), 32–100.

LANFRANC, *Letters*: *The Letters of Lanfranc, Archbishop of Canterbury*, ed. H. Clover and M. Gibson (Oxford, 1979).

LAURENTIUS MONACHUS CASINENSIS ARCHIEPISCOPUS AMALFITANUS, *Opera*, ed. F. Newton, *MGH Quell. Geistesgesch.* 7 (1973).

LENTINI, A., *Il poema di Amato su S. Pietro apostolo*, 2 vols., *Misc. cassin.* 30–1 (Montecassino, 1958–9).

—— and AVAGLIANO, F., *I carmi di Alfano I, arcivescovo di Salerno*, *Misc. cassin.* 38 (Montecassino, 1974).

Lettres des premiers chartreux, 1: *S. Bruno - Guigues - S. Anthelme*, ed. a Carthusian, *SC* 88 (2nd edn., Paris, 1988).

Lib. cens.: *Le Liber censuum de l'église romaine*, edd. P. Fabre and L. Duchesne, 3 vols., *Reg. pap. XIIIes.* (1889–1952).

Liber de unitate ecclesiae conservanda, ed. W. Schwenkenbecker, *MGH L. de L.* 2. 173–284.

Liber diurnus Romanorum pontificum, ed. H. Foerster (Berne, 1958).

Liber feudorum maior, ed. F. M. Rosell, 2 vols. (Barcelona, 1945–7).

Liber monasterii de Hyda, ed. E. Edwards, *RS* 45 (London, 1866).

LIEBERMANN, F., 'Lanfranc and the Antipope', *EHR* 16 (1901), 328–32.

LOKRANTZ, M., *L'opera poetica di S. Pier Damiani* (Stockholm, 1964).

LORENZO VALLA, *De falso credita et ementita Constantini donatione*, ed. W. Setz, *MGH Quell. Geistesgesch.* (1976).

LP: *Le Liber pontificalis*, ed. L. Duchesne, 3 vols., *Reg. pap. XIIes.* (1886–1957).

LUPUS PROTOSPATARIUS, *Chronicon*, ed. G. H. Pertz, *MGH SS* 5 (1844), 51–63.

Mainzer Urkundenbuch, 1: *bis 1137*, ed. M. Stimming (Darmstadt, 1932).

MANEGOLD OF LAUTENBACH, *Contra Wolfelmum Coloniensem* (excerpts), ed. K. Francke, *MGH L. de L.* 1. 303–8.

—— *Ad Gebehardum liber*, ed. K. Francke, *MGH L. de L.* 1. 300–430.

MANSI: *Sacrorum conciliorum nova et amplissima collectio*, ed. J. D. Mansi, 31 vols. (Florence and Venice, 1759–98).

MANSILLA, D., *La documentación pontificia hasta Inocencio III (965–1216)* (Rome, 1955).

MARIANUS SCOTTUS, *Chronicon*, ed. G. Waitz, *MGH SS* 5 (1844), 481–568.

MARTÈNE, E., and DURAND, U., *Thesaurus novus anecdotorum*, 5 vols. (Paris, 1717).

—— *Veterum scriptorum et monumentorum, historicorum, dogmaticorum, moralium, amplissima collectio*, 9 vols. (Paris, 1724–33).

MATRONOLA, M., *Un testo inedito di Berengario di Tours e il concilio Romano del 1079* (Milan, 1936).

MÉNAGER, L.-R., *Recueil des actes des ducs normands d'Italie (1046–1127)*, 1: *Les premiers ducs (1046–1087)* (Bari, 1981).

MEYER, W., 'Ein Gedicht und ein Brief aus Freising von den Jahren 1084 und 1085 und ein Labyrinth mit Versen', *SB München*, 1982, pp. 253–300.

MEYSZTOWICZ, V., 'Manuscriptum Gertrudae filiae Mesconis II regis Poloniae', *Antemurale*, 2 (1955), 103–57.

MITTARELLI, G. B., and COSTADONI, A., *Annales Camaldulenses ordinis sancti Benedicti*, 9 vols. (Venice, 1755–73).

MOMMSEN, T. E., and MORRISON, K. F., *Imperial Lives and Letters of the Eleventh Century* (Columbia, 1962).

MORICE, H., *Mémoires pour servir des preuves à l'histoire ecclésiastique et civile de Bretagne*, 3 vols. (Paris, 1742–6).

MORIN, G., 'Règlements inédits du pape St Grégoire VII pour les chanoines réguliers', *RB* 18 (1901), 177–83.

—— 'Bérenger contre Bérenger. Un document inédit des luttes théologiques du xiᵉ siècle', *RTAM* 4 (1932), 109–33.

MURATORI, *Antiq.*: *Antiquitates italicae medii aevi*, ed. L. A. Muratori, 17 vols. (Arezzo, 1777–80).

MUSSET, L., 'Les actes de Guillaume le Conquérant et de la reine Matilde pour les abbayes Caennaises', *Mémoires de la Société des Antiquaires de Normandie*, 37 (Caen, 1967).

Notitia de ecclesia sancti Eugenii de Viancio, *RHGF* 14. 49–52.

ORDERIC VITALIS: *The Ecclesiastical History of Orderic Vitalis*, ed. M. Chibnall, 6 vols. (Oxford, 1969–80).

OTTO OF FREISING, *Chronica sive Historia de duabus civitatibus*, ed. A. Hofmeister and W. Lammers, *Aus. Quell.* 16 (Darmstadt, 1961).

—— and RAHEWIN, *Gesta Frederici*, ed. G. Waitz and B. Simson, revised by F.-J. Schmale, *Aus. Quell.* 17 (Darmstadt, 1965).

Passio sancti Kanuti regis er martyris, *VSD* pp. 62–71.

PAUL OF BERNRIED, *Vita Gregorii VII*, Watterich, 1. 474–545.

PETER CRASSUS, *Defensio Heinrici IV regis*, ed. L. de Heinemann, *MGH L. de L.* 1. 432–53.

PETER DAMIANI, *Briefe*: *Die Briefe des Petrus Damiani*, ed. K. Reindel, 4 vols., *MGH Briefe*, 4 (1983–93).

—— *Vita sancti Rudolphi episcopi Eugubii et sancti Dominici Loricati*, *PL* 144. 1007–24.

PET. MALL.: *Petri Mallii Descriptio basilicae Vaticanae aucta atque emendata a Romano presbitero*, Valentini–Zucchetti, pp. 375–442.

PETER THE DEACON, *De viris illustribus Casinensium opusculum*, *PL* 173. 1003–50.

—— *Ortus et vita iustorum cenobii Casinensis*, ed. R. H. Rodgers (Berkeley, Los Angeles, and London, 1972).

PFLUGK-HARTTUNG, J. VON, *Acta pontificum Romanorum inedita*, 3 vols. (Tübingen, 1881–6).

—— *Iter Italicum* (Stuttgart, 1883).

PONCELET, A., 'Vie et miracles de S. Léon IX', *AB* 25 (1906), 258–97.

PSEUDO-AUGUSTINE, *De vera et falsa penitentia*, *PL* 40. 1113–30.

PSEUDO-UDALRICUS, *Epistola de continentia clericorum*, ed. L. de Heinemann, *MGH L. de L.* 1. 254–60.

QF: *Quellen und Forschungen zum Urkunden- und Kanzleiwesen Papst Gregors VII.*, 1: *Quellen*: *Urkunden. Regesten. Facsimilia*, ed. L. Santifaller, *ST* 190 (Vatican City, 1957).

Quellen des 9. und 11. Jahrhunderts zur Geschichte des Hamburgischen Kirche und des Reiches, ed. W. Trillmich and R. Buchner, *Aus. Quell.* 11 (Darmstadt, 1961).

Quellen HIV: *Quellen zur Geschichte Kaiser Heinrichs IV.*, ed. F.-J. Schmale and I. Schmale-Ott, *Aus. Quell.* 12 (Darmstadt, 1963).

Quellen zum Investiturstreit, ed. F.-J. Schmale and I. Schmale-Ott, 2 vols., *Aus. Quell.* 12 (Darmstadt, 1978–84).

RALPH, *Vita sancti Adelelmi*, *ES* 27 (1772), 841–66.

RALPH GLABER, *Rodulfus Glaber Opera*, ed. J. France, N. Bulst, and P. Reynolds (Oxford, 1989).

RANGERIUS OF LUCCA, *Vita metrica s. Anselmi Lucensis episcopi*, ed. E. Sackur *et al.*, *MGH SS* 30/2 (1926–34), 1152–1307.

Recueil des actes de Philippe Ier, roi de France (1059–1108), ed. M. Prou (Paris, 1908).

Recueil des chartes de l'abbaye de Cluny, edd. A. Bernard and A. Bruel, 6 vols. (Paris, 1876–1903).

Reg.: Das Register Gregors VII., ed. E. Caspar, *MGH Epp. sel.* 2 (1920–3).

Reg. Farf.: Il Regesto di Farfa compilato da Gregorio di Catino, ed. I. Georgi and U. Balzani, 5 vols (Rome, 1883–1914).

Reg. Greg. I: S. Gregorii Magni Registrum epistularum, ed. D. Norberg, 2 vols., *CCM* 140, 140A (Turnhout, 1982).

Reg. Inn. III: Die Register Innocenz' III., 1: *Pontifikatsjahr 1198/1199*, ed. O. Hageneder and A. Haidacher (Graz, Cologne, and Vienna, 1964); 2: *Pontifikatsjahr 1199–1200*, ed. O. Hageneder, W. Maleczek, and A. A. Strnad (Rome and Vienna, 1979).

Regula Sancti Benedicti: La Règle de saint Benoît, ed. A. de Vogüé and others, 6 vols., *SC* 181–6 (Paris, 1971–2).

REYNALD OF VÉZELAY, *Vita s. Hugonis abbatis Cluniacensis*, *PL* 149. 893–910.

RGP: Le Pontifical Romano-Germanique du dixième siècle, ed. C. Vogel and R. Elze, 3 vols., *ST* 226–7, 269 (Vatican City, 1963–72).

ROMUALD OF SALERNO, *Chronicon*, ed. C. A. Garufi, *RIS*², 7/1 (1909–35).

SAXO GRAMMATICUS, *Danorum regum heroumque historia*, Books *X–XVI*, trans. E. Christiansen, 3 vols. (Oxford, 1980–1).

SCHMEIDLER, B., 'Ein Brief Bischof Imads von Paderborn an Papst Gregor VII.', *NA* 37 (1912), 804–9.

SIGEBERT OF GEMBLOUX, *Catalogus de viris illustribus*, ed. R. Witte, Lateinische Sprache und Literatur des Mittelalters, 1 (Frankfurt and Berne, 1974).

—— *Apologia contra eos qui calumniantur missas coniugatorum sacerdotum*, ed. E. Sackur, *MGH L. de L.* 2. 436–88.

—— *Chronicon*, ed. L. C. Bethmann, *MGH SS* 6 (1844), 300–74.

—— *Leodicensium epistola adversus Paschalem papam*, ed. E. Sackur, *MGH L. de L.* 2. 449–64.

SOUTHERN, R. W., and SCHMITT, F. S., *Memorials of St Anselm* (Oxford, 1969).

Stories of the Bishops of Iceland, [ed. M. Leith] (London, 1895).

Tabula Othiniensis, *VSD* pp. 60–2.

The Anglo-Saxon Chronicle, ed. D. Whitelock with D. C. Douglas and S. I. Tucker (London, 1961).

The Domesday Monachorum of Christ Church, Canterbury, ed. D. C. Douglas (London, 1944).

The Letters and Poems of Fulbert of Chartres, ed. and trans. F. Behrens (Oxford, 1976).

THIETMAR OF MERSEBURG, *Chronicon*, ed. R. Holtzmann and W. Trillmich, *Aus. Quell.* 9 (Darmstadt, 1962).

Triumphus s. Remacli de Malmundariensi coenobio, ed. W. Wattenbach, *MGH SS* 11 (1854), 433–61.

Two of the Saxon Chronicles Parallel, ed. C. Plummer (2 vols, Oxford, 1892–9).

Ughelli–Coleti: Ughelli, F., Italia sacra, new edn. by N. Coleti, 10 vols. (Venice, 1717–22).

ULRICH, *Antiquiores consuetudines Cluniacensis monasterii*, *PL* 149. 635–778.

VALENTINI–ZUCCHETTI: *Codice topografico della città di Roma*, edd. R. Valentini and G. Zucchetti, 4 vols., *Fonti*, 81, 88, 90–1 (Rome, 1940–53).

Vetera analecta, ed. J. Mabillon (2nd edn., Paris, 1723).

VILLARD, F., *Recueil des documents relatifs à l'histoire de Montierneuf de Poitiers (1076–1319)*, Archives historiques de Poitou, 59 (Poitiers, 1973).

Vita Altmanni episcopi Pataviensis, ed. W. Wattenbach, *MGH SS* 12 (1856), 226–43.

Vita Annonis archiepiscopi Coloniensis, ed. R. Köpke, *MGH SS* 11 (1854), 465–514.

Vita Anselmi episcopi Lucensis, ed. R. Wilmans, *MGH SS* 12 (1856), 1–35.

Vita beati Simonis comitis Crespeiensis auctore synchrono, *PL* 156. 1211–24.

Vita Bennonis II episcopi Osnabrugensis auctore Norberto abbate, ed. H. Bresslau, in *Lebensbeschreibungen einiges Bischöfe des 10.–12. Jahrhunderts*, ed. H. Kallfelz, *Aus. Quell.* 22 (Darmstadt, 1973), pp. 363–441.

Vita HIV: Vita Heinrici IV imperatoris, ed. W. Wattenbach and W. Eberhard, in *Quellen HIV* pp. 35–46, 407–467.

Vita Iohannis Gualberti auctore anonymo, ed. F. Baethgen, *MGH SS* 34/2 (1926–34), 1084–104.

Vita sancti Bernardi Menthoniensis, *AA. SS. Boll.* Jul. 2. 1083–5.

Vita sancti Brunonis episcopi Signieniensis, *AA. SS. Boll.* Jul. 4. 478–84.

Vita Theodorici abbatis Andaginensis, ed. W. Wattenbach, *MGH SS* 12 (1856), 36–57.

Vita Willihelmi abbatis Hirsaugiensis auctore Haimone, ed. W. Wattenbach, *MGH SS* 12 (1856), 209–25.

WATTERICH: *Pontificum Romanorum qui fuerunt inde ab exeunte saeculo IX usque ad finem saeculi XIII vitae ab aequalibus conscriptae*, ed. J. B. M. Watterich, 2 vols. (Leipzig, 1862).

WEISWEILER, H., 'Die vollständige Kampfschrift Bernolds von St. Blasien: *De veritate corporis et sanguinis Domini*', *Scholastik*, 12 (1937), 58–93.

WENRIC OF TRIER, *Epistola sub Theoderici episcopi Virdunensis nomine composita*, ed. K. Francke, *MGH L. de L.* 1. 280–99.

WIBERT, *Vita Leonis IX*, in Watterich, 1. 127–70.

WILL, C., *Acta et scripta quae de controversiis ecclesiae Graecae et Latinae saeculo undecimo composita extant* (Leipzig and Marburg, 1861).

WILLIAM OF APULIA: Guillaume de Pouille, *La Geste de Robert Guiscard*, ed. M. Mathieu (Palermo, 1961).

WILLIAM OF CHIUSA, *Vita sancti Benedicti abbatis Clusensis*, ed. L. Bethmann, *MGH SS* 12 (1856), 196–208.

WILLIAM OF HIRSAU, *Consuetudines Hirsaugienses*, *PL* 150. 923–1146.

WILLIAM OF MALMESBURY, *De gestis pontificum Anglorum libri quinque*, ed. N. E. S. A. Hamilton, *RS* 52 (London, 1870).

—— *De gestis regum Anglorum libri quinque*, ed. W. Stubbs, 2 vols., *RS* 90 (London, 1887–9).

WILLIAM OF POITIERS: Guillaume de Poitiers, *Histoire de Guillaume le Conquérant*, ed. and trans. R. Foreville (Paris, 1952).

WIPO, *Opera*, ed. H. Bresslau, 3rd edn., *MGH SRG* (Hanover and Leipzig, 1915).

ZIMMERMANN, *Papsturkunden: Papsturkunden 896–1046*, ed. H. Zimmermann, 3 vols. (2nd edn., Vienna, 1988–9).

2. MODERN AUTHORITIES

ACCROCCA, F., ' "Pastorem secundum Deum eligite": la partecipiazione del popolo all'elezione dei vescovi nell'epistolario di Gregorio VII', *AHP* 28 (1980), 343–55.

Actes du xie Congrès international d'archéologie chrétienne. Lyon, Vienne, Grenoble, Genève et Aosta (21–28 septembre 1986), 3 vols. (Rome, 1989).

ADHÉMAR, J., *Influences antiques dans l'art du moyen âge français* (London, 1939).

ALBERIGO, G., *Cardinalato e collegialità. Studi sull'ecclesiologia tra l'xi e il xiv secolo* (Florence, 1969).

ALTHOFF, G., 'Demonstration und Inszenierung. Spielregeln der Kommunikation in mittelalterliche Öffentlichkeit', *FS* 27 (1993), 27–50.

ALZATI, C., 'Tradizione e disciplina ecclesiastica nel debattito tra Ambrosiani e Patarini a Milano nell'età di Gregorio VII', *SG* 14 (1991), 175–94.

AMANN, É., and DUMAS, A., *L'Église au pouvoir des laïques (888–1057)*, Histoire de l'Église, ed. A. Fliche and V. Martin, 7 (Paris, 1948).

ANCIAUX, P., *La Théologie du sacrement de pénitence au xiie siècle* (Louvain, 1949).

ANTON, H. H., 'Beobachtungen zur henrizianischen Publizistik: Die *Defensio Heinrici IV. regis*', in Berg and Goetz (eds.), *Historiographia Mediaevalis*, pp. 149–67.

ARDUINI, M. L., ' "Interventu precii": Gregorio VII e il problema della simonia come eresia', *SG* 14 (1991), 103–19.

ARQUILLIÈRE, H.-X., *Saint Grégoire VII: essai sur sa conception du pouvoir pontifical* (Paris, 1934).

—— 'La Signification théologique du pontificat de Grégoire VII', *Revue de l'Université d'Ottawa*, 20 (1950), 140–61; Germ. trans. in Kämpf (ed.), *Canossa als Wende*, pp. 337–62.

—— 'Le Sens juridique de l'absolution de Canossa (1077)', in *Actes du congrès de droit canonique* (Paris, 1950), pp. 157–64; Germ. trans. in Kampf (ed.), *Canossa als Wende*, pp. 299–310.

—— 'Grégoire VII, à Canossa, a-t-il rédintegré Henri IV dans sa fonction royale?', *SG* 4 (1952), 1–25; Germ. trans. in Kämpf (ed.), *Canossa als Wende*, pp. 265–98.

—— *L'Augustinisme politique: essai sur la formation des théories politiques du moyen âge* (2nd edn., Paris, 1955).

AUTENRIETH, J., *Die Domschule von Konstanz zur Zeit des Investiturstreits* (Stuttgart, 1956).

—— 'Bernold von Konstanz und die erweitete 74-Titelsammlung', *DA* 14 (1958), 375–94.

BAETHGEN, F., 'Zur Tribur-Frage', *DA* 4 (1941), 394–411, repr. *Mediaevalia*, 1. 71–84.

—— *Mediaevalia. Aufsätze, Nachrufe, Besprechungen, MGH Schriften*, 17, 2 vols. (Stuttgart, 1960).

BALDACCHINI, L., 'Cencio', *DBI* 23 (1979), 520–5.

BARDY, G., 'Saint Grégoire VII et la réforme canoniale au xie siècle', *SG* 1 (1947), 47–64.

BASKEN, G., and SCHMIDT, R. (eds.), *Königtum, Burgen und Königsfreie. Königsumritt und Huldigung in ottonisch-salischer Zeit*, Vorträge und Forschungen, 6 (Sigmaringen, 1961).

BECKER, A., *Studien zum Investiturproblem in Frankreich* (Saarbrücken, 1955).

—— *Papst Urban II., MGH Schriften*, 19/1– , 3 vols. (Stuttgart, 1964–).

BENZ, K. J., 'Escatologisches Gedankengut bei Gregor VII.', *ZKG* 97 (1986), 1–35.

—— 'Die Regula Benedicti in den Briefen Gregors VII.', in *Itinera Domini. Gesammelte Aufsätze aus Liturgie und Mönchstum. Emmanuel von Severus OSB zur Vollendung des 70. Lebensjahres am 24. August 1988 dargeboten* (Münster, 1988), pp. 263–79.

—— 'Kirche und Gehorsam bei Papst Gregor VII. Neue Überlegungen zu einem alten Thema', in *Papsttum und Kirchenreform*, pp. 97–150.

—— 'Eschatologie und Politik bei Gregor VII.', *SG* 14 (1991), 1–20.

—— 'Noch einmal Joh. 10.1–14 in der theologischen Argumentation Gregors VII. gegen Simonie und Laieninvestitur', *DA* 49 (1993), 191–206.

BERG, D., and GOETZ, H.-W. (eds.), *Historiographia mediaevalis. Studien zur Geschichtsschreibung und Quellenkunde des Mittelalters. Festschrift für F.-J. Schmale* (Darmstadt, 1988).

BERGES, W., 'Gregor VII. und das deutsche Designationsrecht', *SG* 2 (1947), 199–209.

—— 'Zur Geschichte des Werla-Goslarer Reichsbezirks von neunten bis zur elften Jahrhundert', *Deutsche Königspfalzen*, 1 (1963), 113–57.

BERNHEIM, E., *Mittelalterliche Zeitanschauungen in ihrem Einfluss auf Politik und Geschichtsschriebung*, 1 (Tübingen, 1918).

BERSCHIN, W., *Bonizo von Sutri. Leben und Werk* (Berlin, 1972).

—— 'Die publizistische Reaktion auf den Tod Gregors VII.', *SG* 14 (1991), 121–35.

BERTOLINI, M. G., 'Beatrice di Lorena', *DBI* 7 (1965), 352–63.

BEULERTZ, S., *Das Verbot der Laieninvestitur im Investiturstreit, MGH S. und T. 2* (Hanover, 1991).

BEUMANN, H., 'Tribur, Rom und Canossa', in Fleckenstein (ed.), *Investiturstreit und Reichsverfassung*, pp. 33–60.

—— 'Regnum Teutonicorum et rex Teutonicorum in ottonischer und salischer Zeit. Bemerkungen zu einem Buch von Eckhard Müller-Mertens', *AK* 55 (1973), 215–23.

—— (ed.), *Historische Forschungen für Walter Schlesinger* (Cologne, 1974).

BEUMANN, J., *Sigebert von Gembloux und der Traktat De invesititura episcoporum* (Sigmaringen, 1976).

BIENVENU, J.-M., 'Les Charactères originaux de la réforme grégorienne dans le diocèse d'Angers', *BPH* 2 (1968/71), 545–60.

BISHKO, C. J., 'Fernando I and the Origins of the Leonese-Castilian Alliance with Cluny', in *Studies in Medieval Spanish Frontier History* (London, 1980), no. 2.

BLAUL, O., 'Studien zum Register Gregors VII.', *AU* 4 (1912), 113–228.

BLET, P., *Histoire de la représentation diplomatique du saint siège des origines à l'aube du xixe siècle* (Vatican City, 1982).

BLOCH, H., *Monte Cassino in the Middle Ages*, 3 vols. (Rome, 1986).

BLUM, O. J., 'Alberic of Monte Cassino and a Letter of St Peter Damian to Hildebrand', *SG* 5 (1956), 291–8.

BLUMENTHAL, U.-R., 'Canossa and Royal Ideology in 1077: Two Unknown Manuscripts of *De penitentia regis Salomonis*', *Manuscripta*, 22 (1978), 92–6.

—— *Der Investiturstreit* (Stuttgart, 1982); Eng. trans. *The Investiture Controversy: Church and Monarchy from the Ninth to the Twelfth Century* (Philadelphia, 1988).

—— 'Fälschungen bei kanonisten der Kirchenreform des 11. Jahrhunderts', in *Fälschungen*, 2.241–62.

—— 'Papal and Local Councils: the Evidence of the *pax* and *treuga Dei*', *SG* 14 (1991), 137–44.

—— 'Rom in der Kanonistik', in *Rom im hohen Mittelalter*, pp. 29–39.

BORINO, G. B., 'Per la storia della riforma della chiesa nel sec. xi', *ASP* 38 (1915), 453–513.

—— 'L'elezione e la depozitione de Gregorio VI', *ASP* 39 (1916), 141–252, 295–410.

—— 'Un ipotesi sul "Dictatus papae" di Gregorio VII', *ASP* 67 (1944), 237–52.

—— 'Quando e dove si fece monaco Ildebrando?' in *Miscellanea Giovanni Mercati*, 5, *ST* 125 (Vatican City, 1946), 218–62.

—— 'Invitus ultra montes cum domno papa Gregorio abii', *SG* 1 (1947), 3–46.

—— 'Una sottoscrizione di Ildebrando arcidiacono, 24 maggio 1061', *SG* 2 (1947), 525–8.

—— 'L'arcidiaconato di Ildebrando', *SG* 3 (1948), 463–516.

—— 'Cencio del prefetto Stefano, l'attentore di Gregorio VII', *SG* 4 (1952), 373–440.

—— 'Ildebrando non si fece monaco a Roma', *SG* 4 (1952), 441–56.

—— 'Perché Gregorio VII non annunziò la sua elezione ad Enrico IV e non ne richiese il consenso', *SG* 5 (1956), 313–43.

—— 'L'investitura laica dal decreto di Nicolò II al decreto di Gregorio VII', *SG* 5 (1956), 345–59.

BORINO, G. B., 'Le monacato e l'investitura di Anselmo vescovo di Lucca', *SG* 5 (1956), 361–74.

—— 'Può il Reg. Vat. 2 (Registro di Gregorio VII) essere il registro della cancelleria?' *SG* 5 (1956), 391–402.

—— 'La lettera di Walone abate di S. Arnolfo di Metz e di S. Remigio di Reims a Gregorio VII (1073)' *La bibliofila*, 60 (1958), 28–33.

—— 'Le lettere di Gregorio VII e di Sigifrido arcivescovo di Magonza che si scambiarono fino al principio del 1075', *SG* 6 (1959–61), 265–75.

—— 'I decreti di Gregorio VII contro i simoniaci e i nicolaitismo sono del sinodo quaresimale del 1074', *SG* 6 (1959–61), 277–95.

—— 'La lettera di Enrico IV alla madre Agnese imperatrice (1074)', *SG* 6 (1959–61), 297–310.

—— 'Il decreto di Gregorio VII contro le investiture fu "promulgato" nel 1075', *SG* 6 (1959–61), 329–48.

—— 'Le persone che consigliarono Gregorio VII di andare in Germania (1076)', *SG* 6 (1959–61), 349–54.

—— 'Ildebrando predicò, nella chiesa cattedrale di Arezzo, alla presenza di Niccolo II (1059)', *SG* 6 (1959–61), 357–9.

BORNSCHEUER, T., *Miseriae regum. Untersuchungen zum Krisen- und Todesgedankens in den herrschaftstheologischen Vorstellungen der ottonisch-salischen Zeit* (Berlin, 1968).

BOSHOF, E., *Heinrich IV., Herrscher an einer Zeitenwende* (Göttingen, 1979).

—— *Die Salier* (Stuttgart, 1987).

BOSL, K., *Die Reichsministerialität der Salier und Staufer, MGH Schriften*, 10, 2 vols. (Stuttgart, 1950–1).

—— (ed.), *Handbuch der Geschichte der Böhmischen Länder*, 4 vols. (Stuttgart, 1967–70).

BRACKMANN, A., 'Die Anfänge von Hirsau', in *Papsttum und Kaisertum*, pp. 215–32; repr. in *Zur politischen Bedeutung*, pp. 47–75, and in *Gesammelte Aufsätze*, pp. 272–89.

—— 'Heinrich IV. als Politiker beim Ausbruch des Investiturstreites', *SB Berlin*, 32 (1927), 393–411; repr. in Kämpf (ed.), *Canossa als Wende*, pp. 61–88.

—— 'Die politische Wirkung der kluniazensischen Bewegung', *HZ* 139 (1929), 24–47; repr. in *Zur politischen Bedeutung*, pp. 7–25, and *Gesammelte Aufsätze*, pp. 290–302.

—— 'Die Ursachen der geistigen und politischen Wandlung Europas im 11. und 12. Jahrhundert', *HZ* 149 (1934), 229–39; repr. *Zur politischen Bedeutung*, pp. 29–46, *Gesammelte Aufsätze*, pp. 356–66.

—— 'Tribur', *Abh. Berlin*, 1939, pp. 3–37; repr. in Kämpf (ed.), *Canossa als Wende*, pp. 182–228, *Gesammelte Aufsätze*, pp. 303–38.

—— 'Canossa und das Reich', in *Stufen und Wandlung der deutschen Einheit* (Stuttgart, 1943), pp. 9–32; repr. in Kämpf (ed.), *Canossa als Wende*, pp. 311–36.

—— 'Gregor VII. und die kirchliche Reformbewegung in Deutschland', *SG* 2 (1947), 7–30; repr. *Gesammelte Aufsätze*, pp. 529–52.

—— *Zur politischen Bedeutung der kluniazensischen Bewegung* (Darmstadt, 1955).

—— *Gesammelte Aufsätze* (2nd edn., Darmstadt, 1967).

BRAKEL, C. H., 'Die vom Reformpapsttum geförderten Heiligenkulte', *SG* 9 (1972), 241–311.

BREENGAARD, C., *Muren om Israels hus: regnum og sacerdotium i Danmark, 1050–1170* (Copenhagen, 1982).

BRESSLAU, H., *Handbuch der Urkundenlehre für Deutschland und Italien*, 2 vols. (Leipzig, 1913–31).

Brezzi, P., *Roma e l'impero medioevale (774–1252)*, Storia di Roma (Bologna, 1947).

Brieger, P. H., 'Bible Illustration and Gregorian Reform', *SCH* 2 (1965), 154–64.

Brooke, C. N. L., *The Twelfth Century Renaissance* (London, 1969).

—— *Medieval Church and Society* (London, 1971).

Brooke, Z. N., *The English Church and the Papacy from the Conquest to the Reign of John* (Cambridge, 1931).

—— 'Lay Investiture and its Relation to the Conflict of Empire and Papacy', *PBA* 25 (1939), 217–47; repr. in L. S. Sutherland (ed.), *Studies in History. British Academy Lectures*, (London, 1966), pp. 50–77.

Brown, P., *The Rise of Western Christendom* (Cambridge, Mass., and Oxford, 1996).

Bruns, H., *Das Gegenkönigtum Rudolfs von Rheinfelden und seine zeitpolitischen Voraussetzungen* (Berlin, 1939).

Bulst-Thiele, M. L., *Die Kaiserin Agnes* (Leipzig and Berlin, 1933).

Busch, J. W., '*Landulfi senioris Historia Mediolanensis* – Überlieferung, Datierung und Intention', *DA* 45 (1989), 1–30.

Büttner, H., 'Die Bischofsstädte von Basel bis Mainz in der Zeit des Investiturstreites', in Fleckenstein (ed.), *Investiturstreit und Reichsverfassung*, pp. 351–61.

Cantelli, S., 'Il commento al Cantico dei Cantici di Giovanni da Mantova', *SM* 3rd ser., 26 (1985), 101–84.

Capitani, O., 'La lettera di Goffredo II Martello conte d'Angiò a Ildebrando', *SG* 5 (1956), 19–31.

—— 'La riforma gregoriana e la lotta per le investiture nella recente storiografia', *Cultura e scuola*, 6 (1962/3), 108–15.

—— 'La figura del vescovo in alcune collezioni canoniche della seconda metà del secolo xi', in *Vescovi e diocesi in Italia nel medioevo (sec. ix–xiii)*, Italia sacra 5 (Rome, 1964), pp. 161–91.

—— 'Esiste un "età gregoriana"? Considerazioni sulle tendenze di una storiografia medievistica', *Rivista di storia e letteratura religiosa*, 1 (1965), 454–81; repr. *Tradizione ed interpretazione*, pp. 11–48.

—— *Immunità vescovile ed ecclesiologia in età 'pregregoriana' e 'gregoriana'* (Spoleto, 1966).

—— 'Ancora della lettera di Odilone ad Enrico imperatore', in *Miscellanea Gilles Gerard Meersseman*, 1, Studi e documenti di storia ecclesiastica, 15 (Padua, 1970), 89–106.

—— 'Episcopato ed ecclesiologia nell'età gregoriana', in *Le istituzioni ecclesiastiche*, pp. 316–73; repr. *Tradizione ed interpretazione*, pp. 85–150.

—— 'Al di là di una commemorazione', *SG* 9 (1972), 17–35.

—— 'Canossa: una lezione da meditare', *DSP Modena*, NS 44 repr. *RSCI* 32 (1978), 359–81.

—— ' "Ecclesia romana" e riforma: "utilitas" in Gregorio VII', in *Chiesa, diritto e ordinamento*, pp. 26–69; repr. *Tradizione ed interpretazione*, pp. 185–232.

—— 'Il papato di Gregorio VII nella pubblicistica del suo tempo: notazioni sul "Liber ad Gebehardum" ', *SG* 13 (1989), 373–97; repr. *Tradizione ed interpretazione*, pp. 233–60.

—— *Tradizione ed interpretazione: dialettiche ecclesiologiche del sec. XI* (Rome, 1990).

Cappelletti, G., *Le chiese d'Italia*, 21 vols. (Venice, 1844–70).

Carlyle, R. W., and Carlyle, A. J., *A History of Mediaeval Political Thought in the West*, 6 vols. (2nd edn., Edinburgh and London, 1927–36).

Carucci, A., *Il sepolcro di S. Gregorio VII in Salerno* (Salerno, n.d.)

Caspar, E., 'Gregor VII. in seinen Briefen', *HZ* 130 (1924), 1–30.

Cauchie, A., *La Querelle des investitures dans les diocèses de Liège et de Cambrai*, 2 vols. (Louvain and Paris, 1890–1).

CECCHELLI, C., 'Castel S. Angelo al tempo di Gregorio VII', *SG* 2 (1947), 103–23.

CESSI, R., 'Venezia e Gregorio VII', *SG* 1 (1947), 491–500.

—— 'La crisi Veneziana al tempo di Gregorio VII', *SG* 5 (1956), 109–13.

CHALANDON, F., *Histoire de la domination normande en Italie et en Sicile*, 2 vols. (Paris, 1907).

Chiesa, diritto e ordinamento della 'societas christiana' dei sec. XI–XII (Milan, 1986).

CHOUX, J., *L'Épiscopat de Pibon (1069–1107): recherches sur la diocèse de Toul au temps de la réforme grégorienne* (Nancy, 1952).

CHRISTENSEN, C. A., NIELSEN, H., WEIBULL, L., and SKYUM-NIELSEN N., (eds.), *Diplomatarium Danicum*, 1 Raekke: 3/2 (Copenhagen, 1963–75).

CILENTO, N., 'La riforma gregoriana, Bizanzio e l'Italia meridionale', *SG* 13 (1989), 353–72.

CLASSEN, P., *Gerhoch von Reichersberg* (Wiesbaden, 1960).

—— 'Gerhoch von Reichersberg und die Regularkanoniker in Bayern und Oesterreich', *La vita comune del clero*, 1. 304–48.

—— 'Heinrichs IV. Briefe im Codex Udalrici', *DA* 20 (1964), 115–29.

—— 'Das Wormser Konkordat in der deutschen Verfassungsgeschichte', in Fleckenstein (ed.), *Investiturstreit und Reichsverfassung*, pp. 411–60.

CLAUDE, D., *Geschichte des Erzbistums Madgeburg bis in das 12. Jahrhundert*, 2 vols. (Cologne and Vienna, 1972–5).

CONGAR, Y. M.-J., 'Der Platz des Papsttums in der Kirchenfrömmigkeit der Reformer des 11. Jahrhundert', in *Sentire ecclesiam: Festschrift Hugo Rahner* (Freiburg, 1961), 196–217.

—— *L'Ecclésiologie du haut moyen-âge* (Paris, 1968).

CONSTABLE, G., *Monastic Tithes* (Cambridge, 1964).

COURTOIS, C., 'Grégoire VII et l'Afrique du Nord. Remarques sur les communautés d'Afrique au XIe siècle', *RH* 195 (1945), 97–122, 193–226.

COWDREY, H. E. J., 'The Papacy, the Patarenes and the Church of Milan', *TRHS*, 5th ser., 18 (1968), 25–48; repr. *Popes, Monks and Crusaders*, no. V.

—— 'The Succession of the Archbishops of Milan in the Time of Pope Urban II', *EHR* 83 (1968), 285–94; repr. *Popes, Monks and Crusaders*, no. VI.

—— 'Bishop Ermenfrid of Sion and the Penitential Ordinance Following the Battle of Hastings', *JEH* 20 (1969), 225–42.

—— *The Cluniacs and the Gregorian Reform* (Oxford, 1970).

—— 'The Peace and Truce of God in the Eleventh Century', *Past and Present*, no. 46 (1970), 42–67; repr. *Popes, Monks and Crusaders*, no. VII.

—— 'Pope Gregory VII and the Anglo-Norman Church and Kingdom', *SG* 9 (1972), 79–114, repr. *Popes, Monks and Crusaders*, no. IX.

—— 'Cardinal Peter of Albano's Legatine Journey to Cluny (1080)', *JTS*, NS 24 (1973), 481–91; repr. *Popes, Monks and Crusaders*, no. XI.

—— 'Two Studies in Cluniac History', *SG* 11 (1978), 1–298.

—— 'Pope Gregory VII's "Crusading" Plans of 1074', in Kedar, Mayer, and Smail (eds.), *Outremer*, pp. 27–40; repr. *Popes, Monks and Crusaders*, no. X.

—— *The Age of Abbot Desiderius: Montecassino, the Papacy and the Normans in the Late Eleventh Century* (Oxford, 1983).

—— *Popes, Monks and Crusaders* (London, 1984).

—— 'The Gregorian Papacy, Byzantium, and the First Crusade', in *Byzantium and the West*, *c*.850–*c*.1200, ed. J. Howard-Johnston (Amsterdam, 1988), pp. 145–69.

—— 'Death-Bed Testaments', in *Fälschungen*, 4. 703–24.

—— 'Hugh of Avalon, Carthusian and Bishop', in Sargent (ed.), *De cella in seculum*, pp. 41–57.

—— 'The Gregorian Reform in the Anglo-Norman Lands and in Scandinavia', *SG* 13 (1989), 321–52.

—— 'St Hugh and Gregory VII', in *Le Gouvernement d'Hugues de Semur à Cluny* (Cluny, 1990), pp. 173–90.

—— 'The Papacy and the Berengarian Controversy', in Ganz, Huygens, and Niewöhner (eds.), *Auctoritas und Ratio*, pp. 109–38.

—— 'Pope Gregory VII', *MH* 1 (1991), 23–38.

—— 'Pope Gregory VII and la Chaise-Dieu', in *Maisons de Dieu*, pp. 25–35.

—— 'The Carthusians and their Contemporary World: the Evidence of Twelfth-century Bishops' *Vitae*', in *Die Karthäuser*, 1. 26–43.

—— 'Count Simon of Crépy's Monastic Conversion', in *Papauté, monachisme*, 1. 253–66.

—— 'Pope Gregory VII and the Bishoprics of Central Italy', *SM* 3rd ser., 34 (1993), 51–64.

—— 'Simon Magus in South Italy', *ANS* 15 1993), 77–90.

—— 'Lanfranc, the Papacy, and the See of Canterbury', in *Lanfranco di Pavia*, pp. 439–500.

—— 'Cluny and Rome', *RM* NS 5 (1994), 258–65.

—— 'The Enigma of Archbishop Lanfranc', *HSJ* 6 (1994), 129–52.

—— 'The Spirituality of Pope Gregory VII', in Hogg (ed.), *The Mystical Tradition*, 1. 1–22.

—— 'The Gregorian Papacy and Eremitical Monasticism', in *San Bruno e la Certosa di Calabria: Atti del Convegno internazionale di studi per il IX centenario della certosa di Sierra S. Bruno (1991)*, ed. P. De Leo (Soveria Mannelli, 1995), pp. 31–54.

—— 'Pope Urban II and the Idea of Crusade', *SM* 3rd ser., 36 (1995), 721–42.

—— 'Eleventh-century Reformers' Views of Constantine', forthcoming, in L. Garland, (ed.), *Conformity and Non-Conformity in Byzantium*, Byzantinische Forschungen, 24 (1997), 63–91.

—— 'Pope Gregory VII and the Bearing of Arms', in B. Z. Kedar, R. Hiestand, and J. Riley-Smith (eds.) *Montjoie: Studies in Crusade History in Honour of Hans Eberhard Mayer* (Aldershot, 1997), pp. 21–35.

—— 'The Reform Papacy and the Origin of the Crusades', in *Le Concile de Clermont de 1095 et l'Appel à la Croisade* (Rome, 1997), pp. 65–83.

—— 'From the Peace of God to the First Crusade', forthcoming, in L. García-Guijarro Ramos (ed.), *La primera cruzada, novecientos años después: el concilio de Clermont y los orígenes del movimento cruzado* (Castellón, 1997).

—— 'Pope Gregory VII and the Chastity of the Clergy', forthcoming in M. Frassetto (ed.) *Medieval Purity and Piety: Essays on Clerical Celibacy and Religious Reform* (New York, 1997)

—— 'The Structure of the Church, 1024–1073', forthcoming, in D. Luscombe and J. Riley-Smith (eds.), *The New Cambridge Medieval History*, 4/1: *c.1024–1198*.

CUSHING, K. G., 'Anselm of Lucca, Reform and the Canon Law, *c.*1046–1086: the Beginnings of Systematization' (Univ. of Oxford D. Phil. thesis, 1991).

—— 'Anselm of Lucca and the Doctrine of Coercion: the Legal Impact of the Schism of 1080?' *CHR* 71 (1995), 353–71.

DAHLHAUS, J., 'Aufkommen und Bedeutung der Rota in den Urkunden des Papstes Leo IX', *AHP* 27 (1989), 7–84.

—— and KOHNLE, A. (eds.), *Papstgeschichte und Landesgeschichte. Festschrift für Hermann Jakobs zum 65. Geburtstag* (Cologne, Weimar, and Vienna, 1995).

DAVID, C. W., *Robert Curthose, Duke of Normandy* (Cambridge, Mass., 1920).

DAVID, P., *Études historiques sur la Galice et le Portugal du vi^e au xiie siècle* (Lisbon, 1947).

DAVIDSOHN, R., *Geschichte von Florenz*, 4 vols. (Berlin, 1896–1925).

DEÉR, J., *Papsttum and Normannen*, Studien und Quellen zur Welt Kaiser Friedrichs II., 1 (Cologne and Vienna, 1972).

DENZLER, G., *Das Papsttum und der Amtszölibat*, Päpste und Papsttum, 5, 2 vols. (Stuttgart, 1973–6).

DEREINE, C., 'Le Problème de la vie commune chez les canonistes d'Anselme de Lucques à Gratien', *SG* 3 (1948), 278–98.

—— 'La Prétendue Règle de Grégoire VII pour chanoines réguliers', *RB* 71 (1961), 108–18.

Deutsche Königspfalzen: Beiträge zu ihrer historischen und archäologischen Erforschung, 3 vols. (Göttingen, 1963–79).

Die Kartäuser und ihre Welt—Kontakte und gegenseitige Einflüsse, *AC* 62, 2 vols. (Salzburg, 1993).

DIENER, H., 'Das Verhältnis Clunys zu den Bischöfen vor allem in der Zeit Abtes Hugo (1049–1109)', in Tellenbach (ed.), *Neue Forschungen*, pp. 219–352.

DIER, C. L., 'The Proper Relationship between Lord and Vassal: Toward a Rationale for Anglo-Norman Litigation', *HSJ* 6 (1994), 1–12.

D'ONOFRIO, C., *Castel S. Angelo* (Rome, 1971).

D'ONOFRIO, G. (ed.), *Lanfranco di Pavia e l'Europa del secolo XI nel IX centenario della morte* (Rome, 1993).

DRESSLER, F., *Petrus Damiani: Leben und Werk*, *SA* 39 (Rome, 1954).

DVORNIK, F., *The Photian Schism: History and Legend* (Cambridge, 1948).

—— *The Making of Central and Eastern Europe* (London, 1949).

EHRLE, F., 'Die Frangipani und der Untergang des Archivs und der Bibliothek der Päpste am Anfang des 13. Jahrhundert', in *Mélanges . . . Chatelain*, pp. 448–85.

EICHMANN, E., *Die Weihe und Krönung der Papsten im Mittelalter* (Munich, 1951).

ELZE, R., 'Das sacrum palatium Lateranense im 10. und 11. Jahrhundert', *SG* 4 (1952), 27–54; repr. *Päpste—Kaiser—Könige*, no. 1.

—— '*Sic transit gloria mundi*. Zum Tode des Papstes in Mittelalter', *DA* 34 (1978), 1–18; repr. *Päpste—Kaiser—Könige*, no. 4.

—— 'Über die Leistungsfähigkeit vom Gesandtschaften und Boten im 11. Jahrhundert. Aus der Vorgeschichte von Canossa, 1075–1077', in W. Paravicini and K. F. Werner (eds.), *Histoire comparée de l'administration (iv*e*–xviii*e* siècle)*, (Munich, 1980); repr. *Päpste— Kaiser—Könige*, no. 14.

—— *Päpste—Kaiser—Könige und die mittelalterliche Herrschaftssymbolik* (London, 1982).

—— 'Gregor VII. und die römische Liturgie', *SG* 13 (1989), 179–88.

ERDMANN, C., 'Gregor VII. und Berengar von Tours', *QFIAB* 28 (1927), 48–74.

—— *Die Entstehung des Kreuzzugsgedankens* (Stuttgart, 1935); Eng. trans. by M. W. Baldwin and W. Goffart, *The Origin of the Idea of Crusade* (Princeton, 1977).

—— 'Die Anfänge des staatlichen Propaganda im Investiturstreit', *HZ* 154 (1936), 491–512; repr. in Kerner (ed.), *Ideologie und Herrschaft*, pp. 1–23.

—— 'Die Bamberger Domschule im Investiturstreit', *ZBLG* 9 (1936), 1–46.

—— 'Tribur und Rom. Zur Vorgeschichte der Canossafahrt', *DA* 1 (1937), 361–88; repr. in Kämpf (ed.), *Canossa als Wende*, pp. 89–117.

—— *Studien zum Briefliteratur Deutschlands im elften Jahrhundert*, *MGH Schriften*, 1 (Stuttgart, 1938).

—— 'Untersuchungen zu den Briefen Heinrichs IV.', *AU* 16 (1939), 184–253.

Bibliography

—— 'Zum Fürstentag von Tribur', *DA* 4 (1941), 486–95; repr. in Kämpf (ed.), *Canossa als Wende*, pp. 240–9.

—— and VON GLADISS, D., 'Gotteschalk von Aachen im Dienste Heinrichs IV.', *DA* 3 (1939), 115–74.

ERKENS, F.-R., *Die Trierer Kirchenprovinz im Investiturstreit* (Cologne and Vienna, 1987).

FABRE, P., *Étude sur le Liber censuum de l'église romaine* (Rome, 1892).

Fälschungen im Mittelalter. Internationaler Kongress der MGH, München, 16.–19. September 1986. MGH Schriften, 33, 6 vols. (Hanover, 1988–9).

FEDELE, P., 'Le famiglie di Anacleto II e di Gelasio II', *ASP* 27 (1904), 399–449.

FEINE, H. E., *Kirchliche Rechtsgeschichte*, 1: *Die katholische Kirche* (3rd edn., Weimar, 1955).

FENSKE, L., *Adelsopposition und kirchliche Reformbewegung im östlichen Sachsen* (Göttingen, 1977).

—— RÖSMER, W., and ZOTZ, T. (eds.), *Institutionen, Kultur und Gesellschaft im Mittelalter. Festschrift für Josef Fleckenstein zu seinem 65. Geburtstag* (Sigmaringen, 1984).

FERNANDEZ CONDE, J. (ed.), *Historia de la Iglesia en España: 2/1, La Iglesia en la España de los siglos VIII al XIV* (Madrid, 1982).

FERRUA, A., 'La donazione della contessa Matilde', *Storia e civiltà*, 4 (1988), 3–13.

FICHTENAU, H., 'Neues zum Problem der italienischen Riesenbibeln', *MIÖG* 58 (1950), 50–67.

—— 'Cluny und der Mönch Hildebrand (Gregor VII.)' in *Beiträge zur Mediävistik*, 3 vols. (Stuttgart, 1975–86), 3. 122–46.

FICKER, J., *Forschungen zur Reichs- und Rechtsgeschichte Italiens*, 4 vols. (Innsbruck, 1848–74).

FITA, F., 'El monasterio toledano de San Servando en la segunda mitad del siglo xi', *BRAH* 49 (1906), 280–331.

—— 'El concilio nacional de Burgos en 1080', *BRAH* 49 (1906), 337–84.

FLECKENSTEIN, J., *Die Hofkapelle der deutschen Könige, MGH Schriften*, 16, 2 vols. (Stuttgart, 1959–66).

—— 'Heinrich IV. und der deutsche Episkopat in den Anfängen des investiturstreites. Eine Beitrag zur Problematik von Worms, Tribur und Canossa', in Fleckenstein and Schmid (eds.), *Adel und Kirche*, pp. 221–36.

—— 'Zum Begriff der ottonisch-salischen Reichskirche', in *Ordnungen und formende Kräfte*, pp. 211–21.

—— 'Hofkapelle und Reichespiskopat unter Heinrich IV.', in *Investiturstreit und Reichsverfassung*, pp. 117–40; repr. *Ordnungen und formende Kräfte*, pp. 243–68.

—— (ed.), *Investiturstreit und Reichsverfassung* (Sigmaringen, 1973).

—— *Ordnungen und formende Kräfte des Mittelalters* (Göttingen, 1989).

—— and SCHMID, K. (eds.), *Adel und Kirche. Gerd Tellenbach zum 65. Geburtstag dargebracht von Freunden und Schülern* (Freiburg, Basle, and Vienna, 1968).

FLICHE, A., *Le Règne de Philippe I, roi de France* (Paris, 1912).

—— 'L'Élection de Grégoire VII', *Le Moyen Age*, 2nd ser., 26 (1924), 71–90.

—— *La Réforme grégorienne*, 3 vols. (Louvain and Paris, 1926–37).

—— *La Réforme grégorienne et la reconquête chrétienne*, in A. Fliche and V. Martin (eds.), *Histoire de l'Église*, 6 (Paris, 1946).

—— 'Grégoire VII, à Canossa, a-t-il rédintégré Henri IV dans sa fonction royale?' *SG* 1 (1947), 373–86; Germ. trans. Kämpf (ed.), *Canossa als Wende*, pp. 250–64.

FLORI, J., *L'Essor de la chevalerie, xie–xiie siècles* (Geneva, 1986).

FONSECA, C. D., 'Gregorio VII e il movimento canonicale: un caso di sensibilità gregoriana', *Ben.* 33 (1968), 11–23 .

—— 'La memoria "gregoriana" di Anselmo da Lucca', in Golinelli (ed.), *Sant'Anselmo, Mantova e la lotta'*, pp. 15–25.

FORNACIARI, G., and MALLEGNI, F., 'La ricognizione dei resti scheletrici di S. Gregorio VII: risultati antropologici, paleopatologici e paleonutrizionali', *SG* 13 (1989), 399–425.

FORNACIARI, G., MALLEGNI, F., and VULTAGGIO, C., 'Il regime di vita e il quadro fisio-clinico di Gregorio VII', *Rassegna Storica Salernitana*, NS 2 (1985), 31–90.

FORNASARI, G., 'La reconciliazione di Canossa nel storiografia. A proposito di un libro recente di Harald Zimmermann', *RSCI* 30 (1976), 515–39.

—— 'Del nuovo su Gregorio VII? Riflessioni su un problema storiografico "non esaurito" ', *SM* 3rd ser., 24 (1983), 314–53.

—— 'Coscienza ecclesiale e storia della spiritualità. Per un ridefinizione della Riforma di Gregorio VII', *Ben.* 33 (1986), 25–50.

—— 'Verità, tradimento della verità e falsità nell'epistolario di Gregorio VII: un abbozzo di recerca', in *Fälschungen*, 2. 217–40.

—— 'La riforma gregoriana nel "Regnum Italiae" ', *SG* (1989), 281–320.

FOURNIER, P., and LE BRAS, G., *Histoire des collections canoniques en occident depuis les Fausses Décrétales jusqu'au Décret de Gratien*, 2 vols. (Paris, 1931–2).

FRANSEN, G., 'Papes, conciles généraux et oecumeniques', in *Le instituzione ecclesiastiche*, pp. 203–28.

—— 'Anselme de Lucques canoniste?' in Violante (ed.), *Sant'Anselmo, vescovo di Lucca*, pp. 143–55.

FRIED, J., 'Der Regalienbegriff im 11. und 12. Jahrhundert', *DA* 29 (1973), 450–528.

—— (ed.), *Die abendländische Freiheit vom 10. zum 14. Jahrhundert* (Sigmaringen, 1991).

—— 'Der päpstliche Schutz für Laienfürsten: Die politische Geschichte des päpstlichen Schutzprivilegs für Laien', *Abh. Heidelberg*, 1980–1.

FUHRMANN, H., 'Studien zur Geschichte mittelalterlicher Patriarchate', 1–3, *ZRG kan. Abt.* 39 (1953), 112–76, 40 (1954), 1–84, 41 (1955), 95–183.

—— 'Zur Benutzung des Registers Gregors VII. durch Pauls von Bernried', *SG* 5 (1956), 299–312.

—— 'Die Wahl des Papstes—Ein historischer Überblick', *Geschichte in Wissenschaft und Unterricht*, 9 (1958), 782–80.

—— *Einfluss und Verbreitung der pseudoisidorischen Fälschungen*, *MGH Schriften*, 24, 3 vols. (Stuttgart, 1972–4).

—— 'Das Reformpapsttum und Rechtswissenschaft', in Fleckenstein (ed.), *Investiturstreit und Reichsverfassung*, pp. 175–203.

—— '"Volkssouveränität" und "Herrschaftsvertrag" bei Manegold von Lautenbach', in Gagner, Schlosser, and Wiegand (eds.), *Festschrift für Hermann Krause*, pp. 21–42.

—— *'Quod catholicus non habeatur, qui non concordat Romanae ecclesiae*. Randnotizen zum *Dictatus papae*', in Jäschke and Wenskus (eds.), *Festschrift für Helmut Beumann*, pp. 263–87.

—— 'Pseudoisidor, Otto von Ostia (Urban II.) und der Zitatenkampf von Gerstungen (1085)', *ZRG kan. Abt.* 68 (1982), 52–69.

—— 'Gregor VII., "Gregorianische Reform", und Investiturstreit', in M. Greschat (ed.), *Gestalten der Kirchengeschichte*, 11/1 Stuttgart, 1985), pp. 155–75.

—— 'Papst Gregor VII. und das Kirchenrecht. Zum problem des *Dictatus papae*', *SG* 13

(1989), 123–49.

FÜRST, C. G., *Cardinalis. Prolegomena zu einer Rechtsgeschichte des römischen Kardinalskollegiums* (Munich, 1967).

—— 'Gregorio VII, cardinali e amministrazione pontifica', *SG* 13 (1989), 17–31.

GAGNER, S., SCHLOSSER, H., and WIEGAND, W. (eds.) *Festschrift für Hermann Krause* (Cologne and Vienna, 1975).

GANZ, P., HUYGENS, R. B. C., and NIEWÖHNER, F. (eds.), *Auctoritas und ratio. Studien zu Berengar von Tours* (Wiesbaden, 1990).

GANZER, K., *Die Entwicklung des auswärtigen Kardinalats im hohen Mittelalter* (Tübingen, 1963).

—— 'Das roemischer Kardinalkollegium', in *Le instuzioni ecclesiastiche*, pp. 153–84.

GARCÍA Y GARCÍA, A., 'Reforma gregoriana e idea de la *militia sancti Petri* en los reinos ibéricos', *SG* 13 (1989), 241–62.

GATTULA [GATTOLA], E., *Historia abbatiae Cassinensis* (Venice, 1733).

—— *Ad historiam abbatiae Cassinensis accessiones* (Venice, 1734).

GAUDEMET, J., 'Grégoire VII et la France', *SG* 13 (1989), 213–40.

GAUSS, J., 'Die Dictatus-Thesen Gregors VII. als Unionsforderungen. Ein historischer Erklärungsversuch', *ZRG kan. Abt.*, 60 (1940), 1–115.

—— *Ost und West in den Kirchen- und Papstgeschichte des 11. Jahrhunderts* (Zürich, 1967).

GAWLICK, A., 'Analekten zu den Urkunden Heinrichs IV.', *DA* 31 (1975), 370–419.

GERNHUBER, J., *Die Landfriedensbewegung in Deutschland bis zum Mainzer Reichslandfrieden von 1235* (Bonn, 1952).

GHIRARDINI, L. L., *L'imperatore a Canossa* (2nd edn., Parma, 1965).

—— *L'enigma di Canossa* (Bologna, 1968).

—— *Chi ha vinto a Canossa?* (Bologna, 1970).

GIESE, W., *Der Stamm der Sachsen und das Reich in ottonischer und salischer Zeit* (Wiesbaden, 1979).

GIESEBRECHT, W., *Geschichte der deutschen Kaiserzeit*, 6 vols. (Brunswick and Leipzig, 1863–95).

GILCHRIST, J., 'Gregory VII and the Juristic Sources of his Ideology', *Stud. Grat.* 12 (1967), 1–37.

—— 'Eleventh and Early Twelfth Century Canonical Collections and the Economic Policy of Gregory VII', *SG* 9 (1972), 375–417.

—— 'The Reception of Pope Gregory VII into the Canon Law (1073–1141)', *ZRG kan. Abt.* 90 (1973), 35–82, 110 (1980), 192–229.

GIRY, A., 'Grégoire VII et les évêques de Térouanne', *RH* 1 (1876), 387–409.

GIUSTI, M., 'Le canoniche della città e diocesi di Lucca al tempo della Riforma Gregoriana', *SG* 3 (1948), 321–67.

GNILKA, C., 'Ultima verba', *Jahrbuch für Antike und Christentum*, 22 (1979), 5–21.

GOETTING, H., 'Die Gandersheimer Originalsupplik an Papst Paschalis II. als Quelle für eine unbekannte Legation Hildebrands nach Sachsen', *NJL* 21 (1949), 93–122.

—— *Die Bistümer der Kirchenprovinz Mainz: Der Bistum Hildesheim*, 3: *Die Hildesheimer Bischöfe von 815 bis 1221 (1227)*, *GP* 20 (Berlin and New York, 1984).

GOETZ, H.-W., 'Tradition und Geschichte im Denken Gregors VII.', in Berg and Goetz (eds.), *Historiographia mediaevalis*, pp. 138–48.

GOEZ, E., *Beatrix von Canossa und Tuszien. Eine Untersuchung zur Geschichte des 11. Jahrhunderts* (Sigmaringen, 1995).

GOEZ, W., 'Zur Erhebung und ersten Absetzung Papst Gregors VII.', *RQ* 63 (1968), 117–44.

—— '*Papa qui et episcopus*. Zum Selbstverstandnis des Reformpapsttums im Mittelalter', *AHP* 8 (1970), 7–59.

—— 'Reformpapsttum, Adel und monastische Erneuerung in der Toscana', in Fleckenstein (ed.), *Investiturstreit und Reichsverfassung*, pp. 205–39.

—— 'Rainald von Como, ein Bischof des elften Jahrhunderts zwischen Kurie und Kron', in Beumann (ed.), *Historische Forschungen für Walther Schlesinger*, pp. 462–94.

—— 'Zur Persönlichkeit Gregors VII.', *RQ* 73 (1978), 193–216.

—— 'Riforma ecclesiastica—Riforma Gregoriana', *SG* 13 (1989), 167–78.

GOLINELLI, P., 'Dall'agiografia alla storia: le "Vitae" di Sant'Anselmo di Lucca', in *Sant'Anselmo, Mantova e la lotta*, pp. 27–61.

—— (ed.), *Sant'Anselmo, Mantova e la lotta per le investiture* (Bologna, 1987).

—— 'Sulla successione a Gregorio VII: Matilde di Canossa e la sconfitta del reformismo intransigente', in Matteis (ed.), *A Ovidio Capitani*, pp. 67–86.

—— 'Prima di Canossa. Considerazioni e notazioni sui rapporti di Gregorio VII con Beatrice e Matilde', *SG* 14 (1991), 195–206.

GOTTLOB, A., *Kreuzablass und Almosenablass* (Stuttgart, 1906).

GRÉGOIRE, R., *La vocazione sacerdotale. I canonici regolari nel medioevo* (Rome, 1982).

GREGOROVIUS, F., *Geschichte der Stadt Rom im Mittelalter von V. bis XVI. Jahrhundert*, 3 vols. (new edn. by W. Kampf, Darmstadt, 1963).

GRISAR, H., *Das Missale im Lichte römische Stadtgeschichte. Stationen/Perikopen/Gebräuche* (Freiburg-im-Breisgau, 1925).

GUERRINI, P., 'Un cardinale gregoriano a Brescia: il vescovo Arimanno', *SG* 2 (1947), 361–85.

GUILLOTEL, H., 'La Pratique du cens épiscopal dans l'éveché de Nantes', *Le Moyen Age*, 80 (1974), 5–49.

GYUG, R., 'The Milanese Church and the Gregorian Reform', *Scintilla*, 2–3 (1985–6), 29–65.

HÄGERMANN, D., 'Untersuchungen zum Papstwahldekret von 1059', *ZRG kan. Abt.* 56 (1970), 157–93.

HAIDER, S., *Passau—St Florian—St Pölten. Beiträge zur Geschichte des Diözese Passau im 11. Jahrhundert* (Vienna, Cologne, and Graz, 1971).

—— 'Zu den Anfängen der päpstlichen Kapelle', *MIÖG* 87 (1979), 38–70.

HALFTER, P., *Das Papsttum und die Armenier im frühen und hohen Mittelalter. Von den ersten Kontakten bis zur fixierung der Kirchenunion im Jahre 1198* (Cologne, Weimar, and Vienna, 1996).

HALLER, J., 'Der Weg nach Canossa', *HZ* 160 (1939), 229–85; repr. in Kämpf (ed.), *Canossa als Wende*, pp. 118–81.

—— 'Pseudoisidors erstes Auftreten im Investiturstreit', *SG* 2 (1947), 91–101.

—— *Das Papsttum. Idee und Wirklichkeit*, 5 vols. (2nd edn., Darmstadt, 1962).

HALLINGER, K., *Gorze-Kluny. Studien zu den monastischen Lebensformen und Gegensätzen im Hochmittelalter*, *SA* 22–5, 2 vols. (Rome, 1950–1).

HALPHEN, L., *Le Comté d'Anjou au xie siècle* (Paris, 1906).

—— *Études sur l'administration de Rome au moyen âge (751–1252)*, Bibliothèque de l'École des hautes études, 166 (Paris, 1907).

HAMILTON, B., *Monastic Reform, Catharism and the Crusades (900–1300)* (London, 1979).

HAMPE, K., *Deutsche Kaisergeschichte im Zeitalter der Salier und Staufer* (10th edn. by F. Baethgen, Heidelberg, 1949); Eng. trans. by R. Bennett, *Germany under the Salian and Hohenstaufen Emperors* (Oxford, 1973).

—— *Herrschergestalten des deutschen Mittelalters* (7th edn., Darmstadt, 1967).

HASSINGER, E. (ed.), *Geschichte, Wirtschaft, Gesellschaft. Festschrift für Clemens Bauer zum 75. Geburtstag* (Berlin, 1974).

HAUCK, A., *Kirchengeschichte Deutschlands*, 5 vols. (3rd and 4th edn., Leipzig, 1914–20).

HEIDRICH, U., *Ravenna unter Erzbischof Wibert (1073–1100). Untersuchungen zur Stellung des Erzbischofs und Gegenpapstes Clemens III. in seiner Metropole* (Sigmaringen, 1984).

HENSEL, W., *La Naissance de la Pologne* (Wrocław, Warsaw, and Krakow, 1966).

HERBERHOLD, F., 'Die Angriff des Cadalus von Parma (Gegenpapst Hororius II.) auf Rom in den Jahren 1062 und 1063', *SG* (1947), 477–503.

HERBERT, K., KORTÜM, H.-H., and SERVATIUS, C. (eds.), *Ex ipsis rerum documentis: Beiträge zur Mediävistik. Festschrift für Harald Zimmermann* (Sigmaringen, 1991).

HERDE, P., 'Das Papsttum und die greichische Kirche in Süditalien vom 11. bis zum 13. Jahrhundert', *DA* 26 (1970), 1–46.

HERGEMÖLLER, B.-U., 'Die Namen der Reformpäpste (1046–1145)', *AHP* 24 (1986), 7–47.

HERRMANN, K.-J., *Das Tuskulanerpapsttum (1012–1046)*, Päpste und Papsttum, 4 (Stuttgart, 1973).

HETTINGER, A., *Die Beziehungen des Papsttums zu Afrika von der Mitte des 11. bis zum Ende des 12. Jahrhunderts* (Cologne, Weimar, and Vienna, 1993).

HILL, L., and HILL, J., *Raymond IV de St-Gilles, comte de Toulouse* (Toulouse, 1959).

HILPERT, H.-E., 'Zu den Rubriken im Register Gregors VII.', *DA* 40 (1984), 606–11.

—— 'Zum ersten Investiturverbot nach Arnulf von Mailand', *DA* 43 (1987), 185–93.

HILS, K., *Die Grafen von Nellenburg im 11. Jahrhundert. Ihre Stellung zum Adel, zum Reich und zur Kirche* (Freiburg-im-Breisgau, 1967).

HIRSCH, H., 'Reichskanzlei und Reichspolitik im Zeitalter der salischen Kaiser', *MIÖG* 42 (1927), 1–22.

—— *Die Klosterimmunität seit dem Investiturstreit* (2nd edn., with postscript by H. Büttner, Darmstadt, 1967).

HLAWITSCHKA, E. (ed.), *Königswahl und Thronfolge in ottonisch-frühdeutschen Zeit*, WF 178 (Darmstadt, 1971).

—— 'Zwischen Tribur und Canossa', *HJ* 94 (1974), 25–45.

HOFFMAN, E., 'Knut der Heilige und die Wende der dänischen Geschichte im 11. Jahrhundert', *HZ* 218 (1974), 529–70.

HOFFMAN, G., 'Papst Gregor VII. und der christliche Osten', *SG* 1 (1947), 169–81.

—— 'La Vie de prière dans les lettres de Grégoire VII', *RAM* 25 (1949), 225–33.

HOFFMANN, H., 'Ivo von Chartres und die Lösung des Investiturproblems', *DA* 15 (1959), 393–440.

—— 'Von Cluny zum Investiturstreit', *AK* 45 (1963), 165–203; repr. in Richter (ed.), *Cluny*, pp. 319–203.

—— *Gottesfriede und Treuga Dei*, MGH Schriften, 20 (Stuttgart, 1964).

—— 'Petrus Diaconus, die Herren von Tusculum und der Sturz Oderisius' II. von Montecassino', *DA* 27 (1971), 1–109.

—— 'Zum Register und zu den Briefen Papst Gregors VII.', *DA* 32 (1976), 86–130.

HOFFMANN, K., *Der Dictatus papae Gregors VII. Eine rechtsgeschichtliche Erklärung* (Paderborn, 1933).

—— 'Der "Dictatus papae" Gregors VII. als Index einer Kanonessammlung?' *SG* 1 (1947), 531–7.

HOGG, J., (ed.), *The Mystical Tradition and the Carthusians*, 14 vols., AC 130 (1995–7).

HOLDER-EGGER, O., 'Berichtigung zur Bonizo- und Beno-Ausgabe', *NA* 19 (1894), 680–2.

HOLTZMANN, W., 'Laurentius von Amalfi, ein Lehrer Hildebrands', *SG* 1 (1947), 207–36; repr. *Beiträge*, pp. 9–33.

—— *Beiträge zur Reichs- und Papstgeschichte des hohen Mittelalters* (Bonn, 1957).

—— 'Ein Gegner Wiberts von Ravenna', *RQ* 57 (1962), 189–91.

HÓMAN, B., *Geschichte des ungarischen Mittelalters*, 1: *Von den ältesten Zeiten bis zum Ende des XII. Jahrhunderts* (Berlin, 1940).

HÜBINGER, P. E., *Die letzten Worte Papst Gregors VII.* (Opladen, 1973).

HÜLS, K., *Kardinäle, Klerus und Kirchen Roms, 1049–1130* (Tübingen, 1977).

HUSSEY, J. M., *The Orthodox Church in the Byzantine Empire* (Oxford, 1986).

HUYGENS, R. B. C., 'Bérenger de Tours, Lanfranc et Bernold de Constance', *SE* 16 (1965), 355–403.

HUYGHEBAERT, N., 'Un Légat de Grégoire VII en Flandre, Warmond de Vienne', *RHE* 40 (1944–5), 187–200.

I laici nella 'societas christiana' dei secoli XI e XII, La Mendola, 5 (Milan, 1968).

Il monachesimo e la riforma ecclesiastica (1049–1122), La Mendola, 6 (Milan, 1971).

ISERLOH, E. and REPGEN, K. (eds.), *Reformata reformanda. Festgabe für Hubert Jedin zum 17. Juni 1965*, 2 vols. (Münster, 1965).

JAKOBS, H., *Die Hirsauer. Ihre Ausbreitung und Rechtsstellung im Zeitalter der Investiturstreit* (Cologne and Graz, 1961).

—— *Der Adel in der Klosterreform von St. Blasien* (Cologne and Graz, 1968).

—— 'Die Cluniazenser und das Papsttum im 10. und 11. Jahrhundert. Bemerkungen zum Cluny-Bild eines neuen Buches', *Francia*, 2 (1974), 643–63.

—— 'Rudolf von Rheinfelden und die Kirchenreform', in *Investiturstreit und Reichsverfassung*, pp. 87–115.

—— 'Das Hirsauer Formular und seine Papsturkunde', *FBAM* 10/2 (1991), 85–100.

—— 'Eine Urkunde und ein Jahrhundert. Zur Bedeutung des Hirsauer Formulars', *ZGO* 140 (1991), 39–59.

JÄSCHKE, K.-U., 'Studien zu Quellen und Geschichte des Osnabrücker Zehntstreits unter Heinrich IV.', *AD* 11/12 (1965/6), 280–401.

JÄCHSKE K.-U., and WENSKUS, R. (eds.), *Festschrift für Helmut Beumann zum 65. Geburtstag* (Sigmaringen, 1977).

JASPER, D., *Das Papstwahldekret von 1059. Überlieferung und Textgestalt* (Sigmaringen, 1986).

JENAL, G., *Erzbischof Anno II. von Köln (1056–75) und sein politisches Wirken*, 2 vols. (Stuttgart, 1974–5).

JORDAN, K., 'Das Eindringen des Lehnswesens in das Rechtslebens der römischen Kurie', *AU* 12 (1931), 13–110; repr. with appendix (Darmstadt, 1971).

—— 'Zur päpstlichen Finanzgeschichte im 11. und 12. Jahrhundert', *QFIAB* 25 (1933–4), 61–104; repr. *Ausgewählte Aufsätze*, pp. 85–128.

—— 'Ravennater Fälschungen aus den Anfängen des Investiturstreites', *AU* 15 (1938), 426–48; repr. *Ausgewählte Aufsätze*, pp. 75–84.

—— 'Der Kaisergedanke in Ravenna zur Zeit Heinrichs IV. Ein Beitrag zur Vorgeschichte der staufischen Reichsidee', *DA* 2 (1938), 85–128; repr. *Ausgewählte Aufsätze*, pp. 21–51.

—— 'Die Entstehung der römischen Kurie', *ZRG kan. Abt.* 28 (1939), 97–152; repr. with Appendix (Darmstadt, 1962).

—— 'Die päpstliche Verwaltung im Zeitalter Gregors VII.', *SG* 1 (1947), 111–35; repr. *Ausgewählte Aufsätze*, pp. 129–53.

—— 'Ravenna und Rom im Zeitalter Gregors VII.', *Spoleto* 1952 (Spoleto, 1953), pp. 193–8.

—— 'Die Stellung Wiberts von Ravenna in der Publizistik des Investiturstreits', *MIÖG* 62 (1954), 155–64; repr. *Ausgewählte Aufsätze*, pp. 75–84.

—— 'Das Reformpapsttum und die abendländische Staatenwelt', *WG* 18 (1958), 122–37; repr. *Ausgewählte Aufsätze*, pp. 154–69.

—— 'Das Zeitalter des Investiturstreites als politische und geistige Wende des abendländischen Mittelalters', *Geschichte in Wissenschaft und Unterricht*, 23 (1972), 513–22; repr. *Ausgewählte Aufsätze*, pp. 11–20.

—— *Ausgewählte Aufsätze zur Geschichte des Mittelalters* (Stuttgart, 1980).

JOUNEL, P., *Le Culte des saints dans les basiliques du Latran et du Vatican au douzième siècle* (Rome, 1977).

KAMP, N., and WOLLASCH, J. (eds.), *Tradition als historische Kraft* (Berlin and New York, 1982).

KÄMPF, H. (ed.), *Canossa als Wende, WF* 12 (Darmstadt, 1969).

KAPOIAN-KOUYMJIAN, A., 'Le Catholicos Grégoire II le Martyrophile (Vkayaser) et ses pérégrinations', *Bazmavep. Revue des études arméniennes*, 132 (1974), 306–25.

KEDAR, B. Z., MAYER, H. E., and SMAIL, R. C. (eds.), *Outremer: Studies in the History of the Crusading Kingdom of Jerusalem* (Jerusalem, 1982)

KEHR, P. F., 'Zur Geschichte Wiberts von Ravenna (Clemens III.)', *SB Berlin*, 1921, 355–68, 973–88.

—— 'Das Papsttum und der katalanische Prinzipat bis sur Vereinigung mit Aragon', *Abh. Berlin*, 1926, no. 1.

—— 'Wie und wann wurde das Reich Aragon ein Lehen der römischen Kirche?', *SB Berlin*, 1928, 196–223.

—— 'Das Papsttum und die Königreiche Navarra und Aragon bis zur Mitte des 12. Jahrhunderts', *Abh. Berlin*, 1928, no. 5.

—— 'Die Belehnung der süditalienischen Normannenfürsten durch die Päpste, 1059–1192', *Abh. Berlin*, 1934, no. 1.

KELLER, H., ' "Adelsheiliger" und Pauper Christi in Ekkeberts Vita sancti Haimeradi', in Fleckenstein and Schmid (eds.), *Adel und Kirche*, pp. 307–24.

—— 'Pataria und Stadtverfassung, Stadtgemeinde und Reform. Mailand im "Investiturstreit" ', in Fleckenstein (ed.), *Investiturstreit und Reichsverfassung*, pp. 321–50.

—— *Adelsherrschaft und städtische Gesellschaft in Oberitalien (9. bis 12. Jahrhundert)* (Tübingen, 1979).

—— *Zwischen regionaler Begrenzung und universaler Horizont. Deutschland im Imperium der Salier und Staufer 1024 bis 1250* (Berlin, 1986).

—— 'Die Investitur. Ein Beitrag zum Problem der "Staatssymbolik" in Hochmittelalter', *FS* 27 (1993), 51–86.

KEMPF, F., 'Pier Damiani und das Papstwahldekret von 1059', *AHP* 2 (1964), 73–89.

—— 'Ein zweiter *Dictatus papae* Gregors VII.? Ein Beitrag zum Depositionsanspruch Gregors VII.', *AHP* 13 (1975), 119–39.

—— 'Die Eingliederung der überdiozesanen Hierarchie in die Papalsystem des kanonischen Rechts bis zu Innocenz III.', *AHP* 18 (1980), 57–96.

KEMPF, F., review of: Schieffer, *Die Entstehung des päpstlichen Investiturverbots*, in *AHP* 20 (1982), 409–16.

KEMPF, F., BECK, H.-G., EWIG, E., and JUNGMANN, J. A., *Die mittelalterliche Kirche*, 1: *Vom kirchlichen Frühmittelalter zur gregorianischen Reform*, Handbuch der Kirchengeschichte, ed. H. Jedin, 3/1 (Freiburg, Basle, and Vienna, 1966).

KERN, F., *Gottesgnadentum und Widerstandsrecht im früheren Mittelalter. Zur Entwicklungsgeschichte der Monarchie* (6th edn. by R. Buchner, Darmstadt, 1973); Eng. trans. by S. B. Chrimes, *Kingship and Law in the Middle Ages* (Oxford, 1948).

KERNER, M. (ed.), *Ideologie und Herrschaft im Mittelalter*, WF 530 (Darmstadt, 1982).

KÉRY, L., *Die Einrichtung des Bistums Arras (1093/1094)* (Sigmaringen, 1994).

KING, P., 'English Influence on the Church at Odense in the Middle Ages', *JEH* 13 (1962), 144–55.

KIRSCH, J. P., *Die Stationskirchen des Missale Romanum* (Freiburg-im-Breisgau, 1926).

KITTEL, E., 'Der Kampf um die Reform des Domkapitels in Lucca im 11. Jahrhundert', in Santifaller (ed.), *Festschrift Albert Brackmann*, pp. 207–47.

KLAUSER, T., 'Die liturgischen Austauschbeziehungen zwischen der römischen und der fränkisch-deutschen Kirche vom achten bis zum elften jahrhundert', *HJ* 53 (1933), 169–89.

KLEWITZ, H.-W., 'Die Entstehung des Kardinalkollegiums', *ZRG kan. Abt.* 25 (1936), 115–21; repr. *Reformpapsttum*, pp. 9–134.

—— *Reformpapsttum und Kardinalkolleg* (Darmstadt, 1957).

KNOX, R., 'Finding the Law: Developments in Canon Law during the Gregorian Reform', *SG* 9 (1972), 419–66.

KOEBNER, R., 'Der Dictatus papae', in *Kritische Beiträge zur Geschichte des Mittelalters. Festschrift für Robert Holtzmann zum sechzigsten Geburtstag* (Berlin, 1933), pp. 64–92.

KÖHNKE, O., *Wibert von Ravenna (Papst Clemens III.)* (Berlin, 1888).

KOHNLE, A., *Abt Hugo von Cluny (1049–1109)* (Sigmaringen, 1993).

KÖLMEL, W., 'Imago Mundi. Das Weltverständnis im Schrifttum des Investiturstreites', *SG* 9 (1972), 166–98.

KOŠĆAK, V., 'Gregorio VII e la Croazia. Presopposti politico-sociali', *SG* 14 (1991), 253–64.

KOST, O.-H., *Das östliche Niedersachsen im Investiturstreit. Studien zum Brunos Buch vom Sachsenkrieg* (Göttingen, 1962).

KOTTJE, R., 'Zur Bedeutung des Bischofsstädte für Heinrich IV.', *HJ* 97–8 (1978), 131–57.

KRAUSE, H.-G., 'Das Papstwahldekret von 1059 und seine Rolle im Investiturstreit', *SG* 7 (1960).

KRAUSE, H., 'Königtum und Rechtsordnung in der Zeit der sächsischen und salischen Herrscher', *ZRG germ. Abt.* 92 (1965), 1–98.

KRAUTHEIMER, R., *Rome. Profile of a City* (Princeton, 1980).

KUTTNER, S., 'Cardinalis: the History of a Canonical Concept', *Traditio*, 3 (1945), 129–214; repr. *The History of Ideas*, no. IX and *Retractationes*, pp. 14–18.

—— 'Liber canonicus: a Note on the *Dictatus papae, c. 17*', *SG* 2 (1947), 387–401; repr. *The History of Ideas*, no. II and Retractationes, pp. 2–3.

—— 'St Jón of Hólar: Canon Law and Hagiography in Medieval Iceland', *Analecta Cracoviensia*, 7 (1976), 367–75; repr. in *The History of Ideas*, no. VIII.

—— *The History of Ideas and Doctrines of Canon Law in the Middle Ages* (London, 1980).

LADNER, G. B., 'Two Gregorian Letters on the Sources and Nature of Gregory VII's Reform Ideology', *SG* 5 (1956), 221–42.

—— *Theologie und Politik vor dem Investiturstreit* (2nd edn., Darmstadt, 1968).

—— 'Gregory the Great and Gregory VII', *Viator*, 4 (1973), 1–26.

LAEHR, G., *Die Konstantinische Schenkung in der abendländischen Literatur des Mittelalters bis zur Mitte des 14. Jahrhunderts* (Berlin, 1926).

LANGE, K.-H., 'Die Stellung der Grafen von Nordheim in der Reichsgeschichte des 11. und frühen 12. Jahrhunderts', *NJL* 33 (1961), 1–108.

LAUDAGE, J., *Priesterbild und Reformpapsttum im 11. Jahrhundert* (Cologne, 1984).

—— 'Gregor VII. und die *electio canonica*', *SG* 14 (1991), 83–101.

—— *Gregorianische Reform und Investiturstreit* (Darmstadt, 1993).

La vita comune del clero nei secoli xi e xii', La Mendola, 3 (1959), 2 vols. (Milan, 1962).

LECCISOTTI, T., 'Il racconto della dedicazione della basilica desideriana nel Codice Cassinese 47', *Misc. cassin.* 36 (1973).

LECLERCQ, J., 'Un Témoignage sur l'influence de Grégoire VII dans la réforme canoniale', *SG* 6 (1959), 173–227.

—— *Saint Pierre Damien, ermite et homme d'église* (Rome, 1960).

—— 'Die Bibel in der gregorianischen Reform', *Concilium*, 2 (1966), 507–14.

—— *The Love of Learning and the Desire for God*, trans. C. Misrahi (London, 1978).

LEHMGRÜBNER, H., *Benzo von Alba, ein Verfechter der kaiserlichen Staatsidee unter Heinrich IV. Sein Leben und der sogenannte 'Panegyrikus'* (Berlin, 1887).

Le istituzioni ecclesiastiche della 'Societas christiana' dei secoli XI–XII. Papato, cardinalato ed episcopato, La Mendola, 5 (Milan, 1974).

LEMARIGNIER, J.-F., *Le Gouvernement royal aux premiers temps capétiens (987–1108)* (Paris, 1965).

LENTINI, A., *Scritti vari*, ed. F. Avagliano, *Misc. cassin.* 57 (Montecassino, 1988).

LERNER, F., *Kardinal Hugo Candidus* (Munich and Berlin, 1931).

LEVILLAIN, P. (ed.), *Dictionnaire historique de la papauté*, (Paris, 1994).

LEWALD, U., 'Köln im Investiturstreit', in Fleckenstein (ed.), *Investiturstreit und Reichsverfassung*, pp. 373–93.

LEYSER, K., 'The Polemics of the Papal Revolution', in Smalley (ed.), *Trends*, pp. 42–74; repr. *Medieval Germany*, pp. 139–60.

—— *Rule and Conflict in Early Medieval Saxony: Ottonian Saxony* (London, 1979).

—— *Medieval Germany and its Neighbours 900–1250* (London, 1982).

—— 'Early Medieval Canon Law and the Beginnings of Knighthood', in Fenske, Rösmer, and Zotz (eds.), *Institutionen, Kultur und Gesellschaft*, pp. 549–66; repr. *Communications and Power*, 1. 51–71.

—— 'The Crisis of Medieval Germany', *PBA* 69 (1983), 409–43; repr. *Communications and Power*, 2. 21–49.

—— 'Gregory VII and the Saxons', *SG* 14 (1992), 231–8; repr. *Communications and Power*, 2. 69–75.

—— 'Von sächsischen Freiheiten zum Freiheit Sachsens. Die Krise des 11. Jahrhunderts', in *Die abendländische Freiheit*, pp. 67–84; Eng. trans. 'From Saxon Freedoms to the Freedom of Saxony', in *Communications and Power*, 2. 41–67.

—— *Communications and Power in Medieval Europe*, 1: *The Carolingian and Ottonian Centuries*. 2: *The Gregorian Revolution and Beyond*, 2 vols. (London, 1994).

LINDER, A., 'Constantine's "Ten Laws" Series', in *Fälschungen*, 2. 491–507.

LINEHAN, P., *History and the Historians of Medieval Spain* (Oxford, 1993).

LLORCA, B., 'Derechos de la Santa Sede sobre España. El pensamiento de Gregorio VII', in *Sacerdozio e regno*, pp. 79–105.

LOPEZ, R. S., 'A propos d'une virgule: le facteur économique dans la politique africaine des papes', *RH* 198 (1947), 178–88.

LÜCK, D., 'Erzbischof Anno II. von Köln. Standesverhältnisse, verwandschaftliche Beziehungen und Werdegang bis zur Bishofsweihe', *Annalen des Historischen Vereins für den Niederrhein*, 172 (1970), 7–112.

LÜHE, W., *Hugo von Die und Lyon, Legat Gallien* (Breslau, 1898).

MACCARRONE, M., *Vicarius Christi: storia del titolo papale* (Rome, 1952).

—— 'I fondamenti "petrini" del primato romano di Gregorio VII', *SG* 13 (1989), 55–122; repr. *Romana ecclesia*, 2. 671–756.

—— *Romana ecclesia cathedra Petri*, ed. P. Zerbi, R. Volpini, and A. Galuzzi, 2 vols. (Rome, 1991).

MAGNOU, E., *L'Introduction de la réforme grégorienne à Toulouse (fin xie–début xiie siècle)* (Toulouse, 1958).

MAGNOU-NORTIER, E., *La Société laïque et l'église dans la province ecclésiastique de Narbonne* (Toulouse, 1974).

Maisons de Dieu et hommes d'église: florilège en l'honneur de Pierre-Roger Gaussin (Saint-Étienne, 1992).

MARCHETTI-LONGHI, G., 'Richerche sulla famiglia di Gregorio VII', *SG* 2 (1947), 287–333.

MANDIĆ, D., 'Gregorio VII e l'occupazione veneta del Dalmazia nell'anno 1076', in Pertusi (ed.), *Venezia e il Levante*, pp. 453–91.

MARTIN, G., 'Der salische Herrscher als *Patricius Romanorum*', *FS* 28 (1994), 257–95.

MÄRTL, C., 'Ein angebliche Text zum Bussgang von Canossa: *De paenitentia regum*', *DA* 38 (1982), 555–63.

—— 'Zur Überlieferung des *Liber contra Wibertum* Anselms von Lucca', *DA* 41 (1985), 192–202.

—— 'Regensburg in den geistigen Auseinandersetzungen des Investiturstreites', *DA* 42 (1986), 145–91.

MATTEIS, M. C. De (ed.), *A Ovidio Capitani: scritti degli allievi bolognesi* (Bologna, 1990).

MAURER, H., 'Die Konstanzer Bürgerschaft im Investiturstreit', in Fleckenstein (ed.), *Investiturstreit und Reichsverfassung*, pp. 363–71.

MAY, O. H., *Regesten der Erzbischöfe von Bremen*, 1: *787–1306* (Hanover, 1928–31).

MAYER, T., *Fürsten und Staat. Studien zur Verfassungsgeschichte des deutschen Mittelalters* (Weimar, 1950).

MAYER-PFANNHOLZ, A., 'Die Wende von Canossa. Eine Studie zum Sacrum Imperium', *Hochland*, 30 (1932–3), 385–404; repr. in Kämpf (ed.), *Canossa als Wende*, pp. 1–26.

—— 'Heinrich IV. und Gregor VII. im Lichte der Geistesgeschichte', *ZDG* 2 (1936), 153–65; repr. in Kämpf (ed.), *Canossa als Wende*, pp. 27–50.

MEHNE, J., 'Cluniacenserbischöfe', *FS* 11 (1977), 241–87.

Mélanges offerts à M. Émile Chatelain (Paris, 1910).

MERCATI, A., 'Gregorio VII a Nonantola', *SG* 1 (1947), 413–16.

MEULENBERG, L. F. J., *Der Primat der römischen Kirche im Denken und Handeln Gregors VII.* (The Hague, 1965).

MEYER, O., 'Reims und Rom unter Gregor VII.', *ZRG kan. Abt.* 59 (1939), 418–52.

MEYER VON KNONAU, G., *Jahrbücher des deutschen Reiches unter Heinrich IV. und Heinrich V.*, 7 vols. (Leipzig, 1890–1909).

MEYSZTOWICZ, V., 'L'Union de Kiev avec Rome sous Grégoire VII', *SG* 5 (1956), 83–108.

MEYVAERT, P., 'A Spurious Signature of Pope Gregory VII', *RB* 65 (1955), 259–62.

—— 'Bérenger de Tours contre Albéric du Mont-Cassin', *RB* 70 (1960), 324–32.

MICCOLI, G., 'Gregorio VII, papa, santo', *BS* 7. 294–379.

—— 'Il valore dell'assoluzione de Canossa', *Annali della Scuola Normale Superiore di Pisa*, 2nd ser., 27 (1958), 149–68; repr. *Chiesa gregoriana*, pp. 203–23.

—— 'Il problema delle ordinazioni simoniache e le sinodi lateranensi del 1060 e 1061', *SG* 5 (1956), 33–81.

—— *Pietro Igneo. Studi sull'età gregoriana* (Rome, 1960).

—— 'Le ordinizione simoniache nel pensiero di Gregorio VII. Un capitolo della dottrina del primato?' *SM* 3rd ser., 4 (1963), 104–35; repr. *Chiesa gregoriana*, pp. 169–201.

—— *Chiesa gregoriana* (Florence, 1966).

MICHEL, A., 'Die folgenschweren Ideen des Kardinals Humbert und ihr Einfluß auf Gregor VII.', *SG* 1 (1947), 65–92.

—— 'Pseudo-Isidor, die Sentenzen Humberts und Burkhard von Worms im Investiturstreit', *SG* 3 (1948), 149–61.

—— 'Humbert und Hildebrand bei Nikolaus II. (1059/61)', *HJ* 72 (1953), 133–61.

MIKOLETZKY, H. L., 'Der "fromme" Kaiser Heinrich IV', *MIÖG* 68 (1960), 250–65.

MIRBT, C., *Die Wahl Gregors VII.* (Marburg, 1891).

—— *Die Publizistik im Zeitalter Gregors VII.* (Leipzig, 1894).

MISCOLL-RECKERT, I. J., *Kloster Petershausen als bischöflich-konstanzischer Eigenkloster. Studien über das Verhältnis zu Bischof, Adel und Reform von 10. bis 12. Jahrhundert* (Freiburg and Munich, 1973).

MOIS, J., *Das Stift Rottenbuch in der Kirchenreform des XI.–XII. Jahrhunderts* (Munich and Freising, 1953).

MOLLAT, G., 'La Restitution des églises privées au patrimoine ecclésiastique en France du ixe au xie siècle', *RDFE* 67 (1949), 399–423.

MONTCLOS, J. de, *Lanfranc et Bérenger: la controverse eucharistique du xie siècle* (Louvain, 1971).

MORDEK, H., '*Proprie auctoritates apostolice sedis*: ein zweiter *Dictatus papae* Gregors VII.?' *DA* 27 (1972), 105–32.

—— (ed.), *Überlieferung und Geltung normativer Texte des frühen und hohen Mittelalters* (Sigmaringen, 1986).

MORGHEN, R., 'Questioni gregoriane', *ASP* 65 (1942), 14–62.

—— 'Gregoriana', *ASP* 66 (1943), 213–23.

—— *L'origine e la formazione del programma della riforma gregoriana* (Rome, 1959).

MORRIS, C., *The Papal Monarchy: The Western Church from 1050 to 1250* (Oxford, 1989).

MORRISON, K. F., 'Canossa: a Revision', *Traditio*, 18 (1962), 121–48.

MORTON, C., 'Pope Alexander II and the Norman Conquest', *Latomus*, 34 (1975), 362–82.

MÜLLER, K., 'Der Umschwung in der Lehre von der Busse während des 12. Jahrhunderts', in *Theologische Abhandlungen Carl von Weizsäcker zu seinem siebsigsten Geburtstage* (Freiburg, 1892), pp. 287–320.

MÜLLER-MERTENS, E., *Regnum Teutonicum. Aufkommen und Verbreitung der deutschen Reichs- und Königsauffassung im früheren Mittelalter* (Vienna and Cologne, 1970).

MURJANOFF, M. F., 'Über eine Darstellung der Kiever Malerei des 11. Jahrhunderts', *SG* 9 (1972), 367–73.

MURRAY, A., 'Pope Gregory VII and his Letters', *Traditio*, 22 (1966), 149–201.

Müssigbrod, A., 'Zur Necrologüberlieferung aus cluniacensischen Klöstern', *RB* 98 (1988), 62–113.
—— 'Das Necrolog von Saint-Pons de Thomières', in Neiske, Poeck, and Sandmann (eds.), *Vinculum societatis*, pp. 83–117.
Müsy, J., 'Mouvements populaires et hérésies au xie siècle en France', *RH* 253 (1975), 33–76.
Neiske, F., Poeck, D., and Sandmann, M. (eds.), *Vinculum societatis. Joachim Wollasch zum 60. Geburtstag* (Sigmaringendorf, 1991).
Neuss, W., and Oediger, F. W. (eds.), *Geschichte des Erzbistums Köln, 1: Das Bistum Köln von den Anfängen bis zum Ende des 12. Jahrhundert* (Cologne, 1964).
Niermeyer, J. F., *Mediae Latinitatis Lexicon Minus* (Leiden, 1976).
Nitschke, A., 'Die Wirksamkeit Gottes in der Welt Gregors VII.', *SG* 5 (1956), 115–219.
—— 'Das Verständnis für Gregors Reformen im 11. Jahrhundert', *SG* 9 (1972), 141–66.
Norden, W., *Das Papsttum und Byzanz* (Berlin, 1903).
O'Callaghan, J. F., 'The Integration of Christian Spain into Europe: the Role of Alfonso VI of León–Castile', in Reilly (ed.), *Santiago, Saint-Denis, and Saint Peter*, pp. 101–20.
Oliver, A., ' "Regnum Hispaniae" en el programa de reforma de Gregorio VII', *SG* 14 (1991), 75–82 .
Oppermann, C. J. A., *The English Missionaries in Sweden and Finland* (London, 1937).
Overmann, A., *Gräfin Mathilde von Tuszien. Ihre Besitzung, ihres Gutes von 1115–1230 und ihre Regesten* (Innsbruck, 1895).
Pantoni, A., *Le vicende della basilica di Montecassino attraverso la documentazione archaeologica, Misc. Cassin.* 32 (1973).
Papauté, monachisme et théories politiques, 1: Le pouvoir et l'institution ecclésiale; 2: Les églises locales (Lyons, 1994).
Papsttum und Kaisertum. Festschrift P. Kehr (Munich, 1926).
Partner, P., *The Lands of St Peter* (London, 1972).
Pásztor, E., 'Sacerdozio e regno nella *Vita Anselmi episcopi Lucensis*', *AHP* 2 (1964), 91–115.
—— 'Motivi dell'ecclesiologia di Anselmo di Lucca. In margini a un sermone inedito', *BISI* 77 (1965), 45–104.
—— 'Lotta per le investiture e "ius belli": la posizione di Anselmo di Lucca', in Golinelli (ed.), *Sant'Anselmo, Mantova e la lotta*, pp. 375–421.
—— 'La "Vita" anonima di Anselmo di Lucca. Una rilettura', in Violante (ed.), *Sant'Anselmo vescovo di Lucca*, pp. 207–22.
Pauler, R., *Das Regnum Italiae in ottonischen Zeit* (Tübingen, 1982).
Peitz, W. M., 'Das Originalregister Gregors VII. im Vatikanischen Archiv (Reg. Vat. 2) nebst Beiträgen zur Kenntnis der Originalregister Innocenz' III. und Honorius III. (Reg. Vat. 4–11)', *SB Wien*, 1911.
Pertusi, A. (ed.), *Venezia e il Levante fino al secolo xv,* 1/1 (Florence, 1973).
Pflugk-Harttung, J. Von, *Iter italicum* (Stuttgart, 1883).
Picasso, G., ' "Studi Gregoriani" e storigrafia gregoriana', *Ben.* 33 (1986), 51–60.
—— 'Gregorio VII e la disciplina canonica: clero e vita monastica', *SG* 13 (1989), 151–66.
Picotti, G. B., 'Della supposta parentela ebraica di Gregorio VI e Gregorio VII', *ASI* 10 (1942), 3–44.
—— 'Sul luogo, data di nascita e genitori di Gregorio VII', *Annali della R. scuola normale superiore di Pisa*, 2nd ser., 11 (1942), 201–13.
Piccotti, G. B., and Morghen, R., 'Ancora una parola su certe questioni gregoriani', *ASP* 69 (1946), 117–30.

POCQUET DU HAUT-JUSSÉ, B.-A., 'La Bretagne a-t-elle été vassale du saint-siège?', *SG* 1 (1947), 189–96.

POLY, J.-P., *La Provence et la société féodale (879–1166)* (Paris, 1976).

PONTAL, O., *Les Conciles de la France capétienne jusqu'en 1215* (Paris, 1995).

POOLE, R. L., *Studies in Chronology and History* (Oxford, 1934).

—— 'Benedict IX and Gregory VI', in *Studies*, pp. 185–222.

RÁBANOS, J. M. S., 'Introducción del rito romano en los reinos de España. Argumentos del papa Gregorio VII', *SG* 14 (1991), 161–74.

RAMACKERS, J., 'Analekten zur Geschichte des Papsttums im 11. Jahrhundert. Zum Itinerar Gregors VII. im Frühjahr 1077', *QFIAB* 25 (1933–4), 56–60.

REEKMANS, L., 'L'Implantation monumentale chrétienne dans le paysage urbain de Rome de 300 à 850', *Actes du XIᵉ congrès international d'archéologie chrétienne*, 2. 861–915.

REILLY, B. F. (ed.), *Santiago, Saint-Denis, and Saint Peter: The Reception of the Roman Liturgy in León–Castile in 1080* (New York, 1985).

—— *The Kingdom of León-Castilla under King Alphonso VI, 1065–1109* (Princeton NJ, 1988).

RENTSCHLER, M. *Liutprand von Cremona. Eine Studie zum ost-westlichen Kulturgefälle im Mittelalter* (Frankfurt-am-Main, 1981).

REUTER, T., 'The "Imperial Church System" of the Ottonian and Salian Rulers: a Reconsideration', *JEH* 23 (1982), 347–74.

—— 'Unruhestiftung, Fehde, Rebellion, Widerstand: Gewalt und Frieden in der Politik der Salierzeit', in Weinfurter (ed.), *Die Salier und das Reich*, 3. 297–325.

REYNOLDS, S., *Fiefs and Vassals: the Medieval Evidence Reinterpreted* (Oxford, 1994).

RICHARD, J., *Les Ducs de Bourgogne et la formation du duché du xiᵉ au xivᵉ siècle* (Paris, 1954).

RICHTER, H. (ed.), *Cluny*, *WF* 241 (Darmstadt, 1975)

RIVERA RECIO, J. F., *La iglesia de Toledo en el siglo XI (1086–1208)*, 2 vols. (Rome, 1966; Toledo, 1976).

ROBINSON, I. S., 'Gregory VII and the Soldiers of Christ', *History*, 58 (1973), 161–92.

—— 'The Metrical Commentary on Genesis of Donizo of Canossa', *RTAM* 41 (1974), 5–37.

—— 'The "colores rhetorici" in the Investiture Contest', *Traditio*, 32 (1976), 209–38.

—— '*Periculosus homo*: Pope Gregory VII and Episcopal Authority', *Viator*, 9 (1978), 103–31.

—— 'The Friendship Network of Gregory VII', *History*, 63 (1978), 1–22.

—— 'Zur Arbeitsweise Bernolds von Konstanz und seiner Kreises. Untersuchungen zum Schlettstäter Codex 13', *DA* 34 (1978), 51–122.

—— *Authority and Resistance in the Investiture Contest: The Polemical Literature of the Late Eleventh Century* (Manchester, 1978).

—— 'Pope Gregory VII, the Princes and the *Pactum*, 1077–1080', *EHR* 104 (1979), 721–56.

—— 'The Dissemination of the Letters of Pope Gregory VII during the Investiture Contest', *JEH* 34 (1983), 175–93.

—— ' "Political Allegory" in the Biblical Exegesis of Bruno of Segni', *RTAM* 50 (1983), 69–98.

—— 'Pope Gregory VII (1073–1085)', *JEH* 36 (1985), 439–83.

—— 'Church and Papacy', in *CHMPT* pp. 252–305.

—— 'Bernold von Konstanz und der gregorianischen Reformkreis um Bischof Gebhard III.', *FDA* 3rd ser., 109 (1989), 155–88.

—— *The Papacy, 1073–1198: Continuity and Innovation* (Cambridge, 1990).

Rome et les églises nationales, viiᵉ–xiiiᵉ siècles (Colloque de Malmédy, 2–3 juin 1988) (Aix-en-Provence, 1991).

RUBEUS, H., *Historiarum Ravennatum libri decem* (Venice, 1589).

RUGGIERI, C., 'Alcuni usi dell'Antico Testamento nella controversia gregoriana', *Cristianesimo nella storia*, 8 (1987), 51–91.

RUSSELL, F. H., *The Just War in the Middle Ages* (Cambridge, 1975).

RYAN, J. J., *Saint Peter Damiani and his Canonical Sources* (Toronto, 1956).

SÄBEKOW, G., *Die päpstlichen Legaten nach Spanien und Portugal bis zum Ausgang des XII. Jahrhunderts* (Berlin, 1931).

Sacerdozio e regno da Gregorio VII a Bonifacio VIII, *MHP* 18 (1953).

SACKUR, E., 'Zur *Iotsaldi vita Odilonis* und Verse auf Odilo', *NA* 15 (1889), 117–26.

—— *Die Cluniacenser in ihrer kirchlichen und allgemeingeschichtlichen Wirksamkeit bis zur Mitte des elften Jahrhunderts*, 2 vols. (Halle-an-der-Saale, 1892–4).

—— 'Der Dictatus papae und die Canonsammlung des Deusdedit', *NA* 18 (1893), 135–53.

SALMON, P., 'Un *Libellus officialis* du xie siècle', *RB* 87 (1977), 257–88.

—— 'Un Témoin de la vie chrétienne dans une église de Rome au xie siècle', *RSCI* 33 (1979), 65–73.

—— 'La Composition d'une *Libellus precum* à l'époque de la réforme grégorienne', *Ben.* 26 (1979), 285–322.

SALTET, L., *Les Réordinations: étude sur le sacrement de l'ordre* (Paris, 1907).

SANDER, P., *Der Kampf Heinrichs IV. und Gregors VII.* (Berlin, 1893).

ŠANJEK, F., 'La Réforme grégorienne en Croatie sous le règne de Démétrius Zwonimir (1075–1089)', *SG* 14 (1991), 245–51.

San Pier Damiano nel IX centenario della morte (1072–1972), 4 vols. (Cesena, 1972–9).

SANTIFALLER, L. (ed.), *Festschrift Albert Brackmann* (Weimar, 1931).

—— 'Saggio di uno elenco dei funzionari, impiegati e scrittori della cancellaria pontificia dall'inizio all'anno 1099', *BISI* 56 (1940).

—— 'Beiträge zur Geschichte der Beschreibstoffe im Mittelalter. Mit besonderer Berucksichtigung der päpstlichen Kanzlei', *MIÖG* Erg. Bd. 16/1, 1953.

—— 'Zur Geschichte des ottonisch-salischen Reichskirchensystems', *SB Wien*, 229/1 (2nd edn., Vienna, 1964).

SARGENT, M. G. (ed.), *De cella in seculum: Religious and Secular Life and Devotion in Late Medieval England* (Cambridge, 1989).

SAUERLÄNDER, W., 'Cluny und Speyer', in Fleckenstein (ed.), *Investiturstreit und Reichsverfassung*, pp. 9–32.

SAXER, V., 'L'Utilisation par la liturgie de l'espace urbain et suburbain: l'exemple de Rome dans l'antiquité et le haut moyen âge', *Acta du xie congrès international d'archéologie chrétienne*, 2. 917–1033.

SCHARNAGL, A., *Der Begriff der Investitur in den Quellen und der Literatur des Investiturstreites* (Stuttgart, 1908).

SCHEBLER, A., *Die Reordinationen in der 'altkatholischen' Kirche* (Bonn, 1936).

SCHIEFFER, R., 'Die Romreise deutsche Bischöfe im Frühjahr 1070. Anno von Köln, Siegfried von Mainz und Hermann von Bamberg bei Alexander II.', *Rheinische Vierteljahrsblätter*, 35 (1971), 152–74.

—— 'Tomus Gregorii papae. Bemerkungen zur Diskussion um das Register Gregors VII.', *AD* 17 (1971), 169–84.

—— '*Spirituales latrones*. Zu den Hintergründen der Simonieprozesse in Deutschland zwischen 1069 und 1075', *HJ* 92 (1972), 19–60.

—— 'Von Mailand nach Canossa. Ein Beitrag zur Geschichte der christlichen Herrscherbusse von Theodosius der Grosse bis zu Heinrich IV.', *DA* 28 (1972), 333–70.

—— *Die Entstehung von Domkapiteln in Deutschland* (Bonn, 1976).

—— 'Gregor VII. Ein Versuch über die historische Grosse', *HJ* 97/98 (1978), 87–107.

—— *Die Entstehung des päpstlichen Investiturverbots für den deutschen König, MGH Schriften* 28 (Stuttgart, 1981).

—— 'Rechtstexte des Reformpapsttums und ihre zeitgenössische Resonanz', in Mordek (ed.), *Überlieferung und Geltung*, pp. 51–69.

—— 'Gregor VII. und die Könige Europas', *SG* 13 (1989), 189–211.

—— 'Freiheit und Kirche von 9. zum 11. Jahrhundert', in Fried (ed.), *Die abendländische Freiheit*, pp. 49–66.

—— 'Die ältesten Papsturkunden für deutsche Domkapitel', in Dalhaus and Kohnle (eds.), *Papstgeschichte und Landesgeschichte*, pp. 135–55.

SCHIEFFER, T., *Die päpstlichen Legaten in Frankreich vom Vertrage von Meersen (870) bis zum Schisma von 1130* (Berlin, 1935).

SCHIMMELPFENNIG, B., *Die Zeremoniebücher der römischen Kurie im Mittelalter* (Tübingen, 1973).

—— 'Die Bedeutung Roms in päpstlichen Zeremoniell', in Schimmelpfennig and Schmugge (eds.), *Rom im hohen Mittelalter*, pp. 47–61.

SCHIMMELPFENNIG, B., and SCHMUGGE, L. (eds.), *Rom im hohen Mittelalter. Studien zu den Romvorstellungen und zur Rompolitik vom 10. bis zum 12. Jahrhundert* (Sigmaringen, 1992).

SCHLESINGER, W., *Kirchengeschichte Sachsens in Mittelalter*, 2 vols. (Cologne and Graz, 1962).

—— 'Die Wahl Rudolfs von Scwaben zum Gegenkönig 1077 in Forchheim', in Fleckenstein (ed.), *Investiturstreit und Reichsverfassung*, pp. 61–85.

SCHUCK, M., *Die Vita Heinrich IV. imperatoris* (Sigmaringen, 1979).

SCHMALE, F.-J., 'Papsttum und Kurie zwischen Gregor VII. und Innocenz III.', *HZ* 193 (1961), 265–85.

—— 'Die "Absetzung" Gregors VI. in Sutri und die synodale Tradition', *AHC* 11 (1979), 55–103.

SCHMEIDLER, B., *Kaiser Heinrich IV. und seine Helfer im Investiturstreit* (Leipzig, 1927).

SCHMID, K., 'Heinrich III. und Gregor VI. in Gebetsgedächtnis von Piacenza des Jahres 1046. Bericht über ein Quellenfund', in H. Fromm, W. Harms, and U. Ruberg (eds.), *Beiträge zur mediävistischen Bedeutungsforschung. Studien zu Semantik und Sinntradition im Mittelalter* (Munich, 1975), pp. 79–97.

—— 'Adel und Reform in Schwaben', in Fleckenstein (ed.), *Investiturstreit und Reichsverfassung*, pp. 295–319.

—— 'Der Stifter und sein Gedenken', in Kamp and Wollasch (eds.), *Tradition als historische Kraft*, pp. 297–322.

—— 'Frutolfs Bericht zum Jahr 1077 oder Der Rückzug Rudolfs von Schwaben', in Berg and Goetz (eds.), *Historiographia mediaevalis*, pp. 181–98.

—— (ed.), *Reich und Kirche vor dem Investiturstreit. Vorträge beim wissenschaftlichen Kolloquium aus Anlass des 80. Geburtstag von G. Tellenbach* (Sigmaringen, 1985).

SCHMID, P., *Der Begriff der kanonischen Wahl in den Anfängen des Investiturstreits* (Stuttgart, 1926).

SCHMIDINGER, H., *Patriarch und Landesherr. Die weltliche Herrschaft des Patriarchen von Aquileja bis zum Ende der Staufer* (Graz and Cologne, 1954).

SCHMIDT, T., 'Die Kanonikerreform in Rom und Papst Alexander II.' *SG* 9 (1972), 199–221.

—— 'Zur Hildebrands Eid vor Kaiser Heinrich III.', *AHP* 11 (1973), 374–86.

—— 'Hildebrand, Kaiserin Agnes und Gandersheim', *NJL* 46–7 (1974/5), 299–309.

—— *Alexander II. (1061–1073) und die römische Reformgruppe seiner Zeit* (Stuttgart, 1977).

SCHMIDT, U., 'Die Wahl Hermanns von Salm zum Gegenkönig 1081', in Herbert, Kortüm, and Servatius (eds.), *Ex ipsis rerum documentis*, pp. 477–91.

SCHMITT, F. S., 'Neue und alte Hildebrand-Anekdoten aus den *Dicta Anselmi*', *SG* 5 (1956), 1–18.

SCHNEIDER, C., *Prophetisches Sacerdotium und heilsgeschichtliches Regnum in Dialog, 1073–1077. Zur Geschichte Gregors VII. und Heinrichs IV.* (Munich, 1972).

SCHRAMM, P. E., *Kaiser, Rom und Renovatio*, 2 vols. (Leipzig, 1929; 2nd edn. of vol. 1 with additional notes, Darmstadt, 1957).

—— 'Das Zeitalter Gregors VII.', *GGA* 207 (1953), 62–140.

—— 'Sacerdotium und Regnum im Austauch ihrer Vorrechte', *SG* 1 (1947), 403–57.

SCHREIBER, G., *Gemeinschaften des Mittelalters* (Regensberg and Münster, 1948).

SCHUBERT, O., *Die päpstlichen Legaten in Deutschland zur Zeit Henrichs IV. und Heinrichs V. (1056–1125)* (Marburg, 1912).

SCHWAIGER, G. (ed.), *Konzil und Papst. Historische Beiträge zur Frage der höchsten Gewalt in der Kirche. Festschrift für H. Tüchle* (Munich and Paderborn, 1975).

SCHWARTZ, E., 'Publizistische Sammlungen zum Acacianischen Schisma', *Abh. Bay.* NF 10 (1934).

SCHWARTZ, G., *Die Besetzung der Bistümer Reichsitaliens unter den sächsischen und salischen Kaisern mit den Listen der Bischöfe, 951–1122* (repr. with introd. by O. Capitani, Spoleto, 1993).

SCHWARZ, U., *Amalfi im frühen Mittelalter (9.–11. Jahrhundert)* (Tübingen, 1978).

SCHWARZ, W., 'Der Investiturstreit in Frankreich', *ZKG* 42 (1923), 255–328; 43 (1924), 92–150.

SCHWARZMEIER, H., 'Das Kloster S. Benedetto di Polirone in seiner cluniacensischen Umwelt', in Fleckenstein and Schmid (eds.), *Adel und Kirche*, pp. 280–94.

—— *Lucca und das Reich bis zum Ende des 11. Jahrhunderts* (Tübingen, 1972).

SCHWIENKÖPFER, B., *Königtum und Städte bis zum Ende des Investiturstreits. Die Politik der Ottonen und Salier gegenüber den werdenden Städten im östlichen Sachsen und Nordthüringen* (Sigmaringen, 1977).

SCIURIE, H., 'Die Merseburger Grabplatte König Rudolfs von Schwaben und die Bewertung des Herrschers im 11. Jahrhundert', *JGF* 6 (1982), 173–83.

SEEGRÜN, W., *Das Papsttum und Skandinavien bis zur Vollendung der nordischen Kirchenorganisation (1164)* (Neumünster, 1967).

—— *Das Erzbistum Hamburg in seinen älteren Papsturkunden* (Cologne and Vienna, 1976).

SEMMLER, J., *Die Klosterreform von Siegburg. Ihre Ausbreitung und ihr Reformprogramm im 11. und 12. Jahrhundert* (Bonn, 1959).

—— 'Klosterreform und Gregorianische Reform. Die Chorherrstifter Marbach und Hördt im Investiturstreit', *SG* 6 (1959/61), 165–72.

—— 'Ein Herrschaftsmaxime im Wandel. Pax et concordia im karolingischen Frankenreich', in *Frieden in Geschichte und Gegenwart* (Düsseldorf, n.d.), pp. 24–34.

SERRANO, L., *El obispado de Burgos y Castilla primitiva desde el siglo V al XIII*, 3 vols. (Madrid, 1935).

SERVATIUS, C., *Paschalis II. (1099–1118). Studien zu seiner Person und seiner Politik* (Stuttgart, 1979).

SIEGWART, J., *Die Chorherren- und Chorfrauengemeinschaften in der deutschsprachigen Schweiz vom 6. Jahrhundert bis 1160* (Freiburg, 1962).

SHEPARD, J., and FRANKLIN, S. (eds.), *Byzantine Diplomacy* (Aldershot, 1992).

SIMEONI, L., 'Il contributo della contessa Matilda al papato nella lotta per le investiture', *SG* 1 (1947), 353–72.

ŠIŠIĆ, F. VON, *Geschichte der Kroaten*, 1 (Zagreb, 1917).

SMALLEY, B. (ed.), *Trends in Medieval Political Thought* (Oxford, 1963).

SOMERVILLE, R., 'The Case against Berengar of Tours—a New Text', *SG* 9 (1972), 53–75.

—— 'Anselm of Lucca and Wibert of Ravenna', *BMCL NS* 10 (1980), 1–13.

SOMERVILLE, R., with KUTTNER, S., *Pope Urban II, the Collectio Britannica and the Council of Melfi (1089)* (Oxford, 1996).

SOT, M., 'Le Mythe des origines romaines de Reims au Xᵉ siècle', in *Rome et les églises nationales*, pp. 55–74.

SPINELLI, G., 'Ildebrando *archidiaconus et sancti Pauli rector*', *Ben.* 33 (1996), 61–78.

Spiritualità cluniacense, Convegni Todi, 1960.

SPÖRL, J., 'Gregor VII. und das Problem der Autorität. Eine Besinnung', *Reformata reformanda*, 1. 59–73.

SPREMIĆ, M., 'Gregorio VII e gli Slavi del sud', *SG* 14 (1991), 239–43.

STAAB, F., 'Zur "romanitas" bei Gregor VII.', in E.-D. Hehl, H. Siebert, and F. Staab (eds.), *Deus qui mutat tempora. Menschen und Institutionen im Wandel des Mittelalters. Festschrift für A. Becker* (Sigmaringen, 1987), pp. 101–13.

—— 'Die Mainzer Kirche. Konzeption und Verwirklichung in der Bonifatius- und Theonesttradition', in *Die Salier und das Reich*, 2. 31–77.

STEINDORFF, E., *Jahrbücher des deutschen Reichs unter Heinrich III.*, 2 vols. (Leipzig, 1874–81).

STENGEL, E. E., 'Die Entwicklung des Kaiserprivilegs für die Römische Kurie 817–962. Ein Beitrag zur ältesten Geschichte des Kirchenstaates', *HZ* 134 (1926), 216–41; repr. *Abhandlungen und Untersuchungen*, pp. 218–48.

—— 'Lampert von Hersfeld der erste Abt von Hasungen', *Aus Verfassungs- und Landesgeschichte. Festschrift für Th. Mayer* (Lindau, 1955), 2. 245–58; repr. *Abhandlungen und Untersuchungen*, pp. 342–59.

—— *Abhandlungen und Untersuchungen zur mittelalterlichen Geschichte* (Cologne and Graz, 1960).

STICKLER, A. M., 'Il potere coattivo materiale della chiesa nella Riforma Gregoriana secondo Anselmo di Lucca', *SG* 2 (1947), 235–85.

—— 'I presupposti storico-giuridici della riforma gregoriana e della azione personale di Gregorio VII', *SG* 13 (1989), 1–15.

STÖRMER, W., *Früher Adel. Studien zur politischen Führungsschicht im frankish-deutschen Reich vom 8. bis 11. Jahrhundert* (Stuttgart, 1973).

STRUVE, T., 'Lampert von Hersfeld. Persönlichkeit und Weltbild eines Geschichtsschreibers am Beginn des Investiturstreits', *Hessisches Jahrbuch für Landesgeschichte*, 19 (1969), 1–123, 20 (1970), 32–142.

—— 'Zwei Briefe der Kaiserin Agnes', *HJ* 104 (1984), 411–24.

—— 'Johann Haller—ein Romancier? Kritische Bemerkungen zur Schilderung des päpstlich-königlichen Versöhnungsmahl auf Canossa (1077)', *HJ* 109 (1989), 206–10.

—— 'Das Problem der Eideslösung in den Streitschriften des Investiturstreites', *ZRG kan. Abt.* 75 (1989), 107–32.

—— 'Der Bild des Gegenkönigs Rudolf von Schwaben in der zeitgenössischen

Historiographie', in Herbert, Kortüm, and Servatius (eds.), *Ex ipsis rerum documentis*, pp. 459–75.

—— 'Gregor VII. und Heinrich IV. Stationen einer Auseinandersetzung', *SG* 14 (1991), 29–67.

Studi sul medioevo cristiano offerti a Raffaello Morghen, 2 vols. (Rome, 1974).

STÜRNER, W., 'Das Königswahlparagraph im Papstwahldekret von 1059', *SG* 9 (1972), 39–52.

—— 'Das Papstwahldekret von 1059 und seine Verfälschungen', in *Fälschungen*, 2. 157–90.

—— *Peccatum und Potestas. Der Sündenfall und die Entstehung der herrschaftlichen Gewalt im mittelalterlichen Staatsdenken* (Sigmaringen, 1987).

SWEENEY, J. R., 'Gregory VII, the Reform Program, and the Hungarian Church at the End of the Eleventh Century', *SG* 14 (1991), 265–75.

SYDOW, J., 'Cluny und die Anfänge der Apostolischen Kammer. Studien zur Geschichte der päpstlichen Finanzverwaltung im 11. und 12. Jahrhundert', *SMGBO* 73 (1951), 45–66; repr. *Cum omni mensura*, pp. 31–52.

—— 'Untersuchungen zur kurialen Verwaltungsgeschichte im Zeitalter des Reformpapsttums', *DA* 11 (1954–5), 18–73.

—— *Cum omni mensura et ratione. Ausgewählte Aufsätze*, ed. H. Maurer (Sigmaringen, 1991).

—— 'Der Jahr 1078 und Tübingen. Der November-Feldzug Heinrichs IV. in den zeitgenössischen Geschichtsquellen', in *Cum omni mensura*, pp. 329–36.

SZABÓ-BECHSTEIN, B., *Libertas ecclesiae. Ein Schlüsselbegriff des Investiturstreits und seine Vorgeschichte*, *SG* 12 (Rome, 1985).

—— '*Libertas ecclesiae* vom 12. bis zur Mitte des 13. Jahrhunderts. Verbreitung und Wandel des Begriffs seit seiner Prägung durch Gregory VII.', in Fried (ed.), *Die abendländische Freiheit*, pp. 147–75.

SZÉKELY, G., 'Ideologische Fragen des europäischen Hochfeudalismus in den Ländern Ost- und Mitteleuropas während des 11. Jahrhundert', *JGF* 6 (1982), 87–101.

TANGL, G., *Die Teilnehmer an den allgemeinen Konzilien des Mittelalters* (Weimar, 1932).

TANGL, M., 'Gregors VII. jüdischer Herkunft?' *NA* 31 (1905), 159–79.

TAVIANI-CAROZZI, H., *La Principauté lombarde de Salerne, ixe–xie siècle*, 2 vols. (Rome, 1991).

—— 'Aspects de la réforme de l'église à Salerne jusqu'au pontificat de Grégoire VII', *SG* 14 (1991), 207–29.

—— *La Terreur du monde: Robert Guiscard et la conquête normande en Italie* (Paris, 1996).

TELLENBACH, G., *Libertas. Kirche und Weltordnung im Zeitalter des Investiturstreites* (Leipzig, 1935); Eng. trans. by R. F. Bennett, *Church, State and Christian Society at the Time of the Investiture Controversy* (Oxford, 1940).

—— 'Zwischen Worms und Canossa (1076/7)', *HZ* 162 (1940), 316–25; repr. in Kämpf (ed.), *Canossa als Wende*, pp. 229–39.

—— 'Il monachesimo riformato ed i laici nei secoli XI e XII', in *I laici*, pp. 118–51; Germ. trans. in Richter (ed.), *Cluny*, pp. 371–400.

—— (ed.), *Neue Forschungen über Cluny und die Cluniacenser* (Freiburg, 1959).

—— *Die westliche Kirche vom 10. bis zum frühen 12. Jahrhundert* (Göttingen, 1988); Eng. trans. by T. Reuter, *The Church in Western Europe from the Tenth to the Early Twelfth Century* (Cambridge, 1993).

THOMAS, H., 'Erzbischof Siegfried I. von Mainz und die Tradition seiner Kirche', *DA* 26 (1970), 368–99.

THUMSER, M., 'Die Frangipane. Abriss der Geschichte einer Adelsfamilie im hochmittelalterlichen Rom', *QFIAB* 71 (1991), 106–63.

TIRELLI, V., 'Osservazioni sui rapporti tra sede apostolica, Capua e Napoli durante i pontificati di Gregorio VII e di Urbano II', in *Studi . . . Morghen*, 1. 961–1010.

TONDELLI, L., 'Il valore dell'assoluzione di Enrico IV a Canossa', *La Scuola Cattolica*, 77 (1949), 109–20.

—— 'Scavi archeologici a Canossa. Le tre mura di cintra', *SG* 4 (1952), 365–71; Germ. trans. in Kämpf (ed.), *Canossa als Wende*, pp. 51–60

TÖPFER, B., 'Tendenzen zur Entsacralisierung der Herrscherwürde in der Zeit des Investiturstreits', *JGF* 6 (1982), 163–71.

—— et al. (eds.), *Deutsche Geschichte*, 2: *Die entfaltete Feudalgesellschaft von der Mitte des 11. bis zu den siebzigen Jahren des 15. Jahrhundert* (Berlin, 1983).

TOUBERT, H., *Un Art dirigé. Réforme grégorienne et iconographie* (Paris, 1990).

TOUBERT, P., *Les Structures du Latium méridional et la Sabine du ixe à la fin du xiie siècle*, 2 vols. (Rome, 1973).

—— 'Église et état au xie siècle: la signification du moment grégorien pour la genèse de l'état moderne', in *État et église dans la genèse de l'état moderne* (Madrid, 1986), 9–22.

TRAUBE, L., '*O Roma nobilis*', *Abh. Bay.* 19 (1891), 299–392.

TRITZ, H., 'Die hagiographischen Quellen zur Geschichte Papst Leos IX.', *SG* 4 (1952), 191–353.

ULLMANN, W., 'Cardinal Humbert and the Ecclesia Romana', *SG* 4 (1952), 111–27; repr. in *The Papacy and Political Ideas*, no. I.

—— '*Romanus pontifex indubitanter efficitur sanctus*: Dictatus papae 23 in Retrospect and Prospect', *SG* 6 (1959–61), 229–64.

—— '*Dies ortus imperii*: a Note on the Glossa Ordinaria on C.III.12.7(5)', in *Atti del Convegno internazionali di studi Accursiani* (Milan, 1968), pp. 663–94, repr. *The Papacy and Political Ideas*, no. VI.

—— *The Growth of Papal Government in the Middle Ages* (3rd edn., London, 1970).

—— 'A Note on Inalienability in Gregory VII', *SG* (1972), 115–40.

—— *The Papacy and Political Ideas in the Middle Ages* (London, 1976).

VAN DIJK, S. J. P., and HAZELDEN WALKER, J., *The Origins of the Modern Roman Liturgy* (London, 1960).

VANDVIK, E., *Latinske Dokument til Norsk Historie* (Oslo, 1959).

VAN LAARHOVEN, J., ' "Christianitas" et réforme grégorienne', *SG* 6 (1959–61), 1–98.

VEDOVATO, G. (ed.), *Camaldoli e la sua congregazione dalle origini al 1184: storia e documentazione* (Cesena, 1994).

VEHSE, O., 'Benevent als Territorium des Kirchenstaates bis zum Beginn der avignonesischen Epoche', *QFIAB* 22 (1930–1), 87–160.

VILLARD, F., 'Primatie des Gaules et réforme grégorienne', *BÉC* 149 (1991), 421–34.

VIC, C. DE, and VAISSETTE, J. (eds.), *Histoire générale de Languedoc*, 16 vols. (new edn., Toulouse, 1872–1907).

VIOLANTE, C., *La Pataria Milanese e la riforma ecclesiastica*, 1: *Le premese* (Rome, 1955).

—— 'Anselmo da Baggio', *DBI* 3. 399–407.

—— 'Il monachesimo cluniacense di fronte al mondo politico ed ecclesiastico (secoli x e xi)', *Spiritualità cluniacense*, pp. 153–242; repr. *Studi sulla cristianità medioevale*, pp. 3–37.

—— 'Venezia fra papato e impero nel secolo xi', in *La Venezia del mille* (Florence, 1965), 45–84; repr. *Studi sulla christianità medioevale*, pp. 291–322.

—— *Studi sulla cristianità medioevale* (Milan, 1972).

—— 'Discorso di chiusura', *SG* 13 (1989), 417–31.

VIOLANTE, C. (ed.), *Sant'Anselmo, vescovo di Lucca (1073–1086), nel quadro della trasformazioni sociali e della riforma ecclesiastica* (Rome, 1992).

VLASTO, A. P., *The Entry of Slavs into Christendom: An Introduction to the Medieval History of the Slavs* (Cambridge, 1972).

VOGEL, C., 'La *Descriptio ecclesiae Lateranensis* du diacre Jean: histoire du texte manuscrit', in *Mélanges en l'honneur de Monseigneur Michel Andrieu* (Strasbourg, 1956), pp. 457–76.

—— *Le Pécheur et la pénitence au moyen âge* (Paris, 1969).

VOGEL, J., 'Gregors VII. Abzug aus Rom und sein letztes Pontifikatsjahr in Salerno', in Kamp and Wollasch (eds.), *Tradition als historische Kraft*, pp. 341–9.

—— 'Zur Kirchenpolitik Henrichs IV. nach seiner Kaiserkrönung und zur Wirksamkeit der Legaten Gregors VII. und Clemens' (III.) im deutschen Reich, 1084/5', *FS* 16 (1982), 161–92.

—— *Gregor VII. und Heinrich IV. nach Canossa. Zeugnisse ihres Selbstverstandnisses* (Berlin and New York, 1983).

—— 'Rudolf von Rheinfelden, die Fürstenopposition gegen Heinrich IV. im Jahr 1072 und die Reform des Klosters St Blasien', *ZGO* 232 (1984), 1–30.

—— Gottschalk von Aachen (Adalbero C) und Heinrichs IV. Briefe an die Römer (1081, 1082), *Zeitschrift des Aachener Geschichtsvereins*, 90/91 (1983/4), 55–68.

VOLLRATH, H., 'Kaisertum und Patriziat in den Anfängen des Investiturstreits', *ZKG* 85 (1974), 11–44.

VON DEN BRINCKEN, A.-D., *Studien zur lateinischen Weltchronistik bis in das Zeitalter Ottos von Freising* (Düsseldorf, 1957).

VON DEN STEINEN, W., *Canossa. Heinrich IV. und die Kirche* (2nd edn., Darmstadt, 1969).

VON FALKENHAUSEN, V., *Untersuchungen über die byzantinische Herrschaft in Süditalien von 9. bis ins 11. Jahrhundert* (Wiesbaden, 1967).

—— 'Olympias, eine normannische Prinzessin in Konstantinopel', in *Bizanzio e l'Italia, Raccolta di studi in memoria di Agostino Pertusi* (Milan, 1982), pp. 56–72.

VON GUTTENBERG, E., (ed.), *Die Regesten der Bischöfe und des Domkapitels von Bamberg* (Würzburg, 1932–63).

VOOSEN, E., *Papauté et pouvoir civile à l'époque de Grégoire VII* (Gembloux, 1927)

WADLE, E., 'Heinrich IV. und die deutsche Friedensbewegung', in Fleckenstein (ed.), *Investiturstreit und Reichsverfassung*, pp. 141–73.

—— 'Frühe deutsche Landfrieden', in Mordek (ed.), *Überlieferung und Geltung*, pp. 71–92.

WALDMÜLLER, L., *Die Synoden in Dalmatien, Kroatien und Ungarn von der Völkerwanderung bis zum Ende der Arpaden (1311)* (Paderborn, 1987).

WALEY, D., *The Papal State in the Thirteenth Century* (London, 1961).

WEINFURTER, S., 'Neuere Forschung zu den Regularkanonikern im deutschen Reich des 11. und 12. Jahrhunderts', *HZ* 224 (1977), 379–97.

—— 'Reformkanoniker und Reichsepiskopat im Hochmittelalter', *HJ* 97–8 (1978), 158–93.

—— 'Herrschaftslegitimation und Königsautorität im Wandel. Die Salier und ihr Dom zu Speyer', in *Die Salier und das Reich*, 1. 55–96.

—— (ed.),*Die Salier und das Reich*, 3 vols. (Sigmaringen, 1991).

WEISWEILER, H., 'Die päpstliche Gewalt in den Schriften Bernolds von St Blasien aus dem Investiturstreit', *SG* 4 (1952), 129–47.

WEITLAUF, M., and HEUSBERGER K. (eds.), *Papsttum und Kirchenreform: Historische Beiträge. Festschrift für Georg Schwaiger zum 65. Geburtstag* (St Ottolien, 1990).

WENDEHORST, A., 'Bischof Adalbero von Würzburg (1045–90) zwischen Papst und Kaiser', *SG* 6 (1969–61), 147–64.

WERMINGHOFF, A., 'Die Beschlüsse des Aachener Concils im Jahre 816', *NA* 27 (1902), 605–75.

WERNER, E., *Die gesellschaftliche Grundlagen der Klosterreform im 11. Jahrhundert* (Berlin, 1953).

—— *Pauperes Christi. Studien zu social-religiösen Bewegungen im Zeitalter des Reformpapsttums* (Leipzig, 1956).

—— *Zwischen Canossa und Worms. Staat und Kirche 1077–1122* (2nd edn., Berlin, 1975).

—— 'Konstantinopel und Canossa. Lateinisches Selbstverständnis im 11. Jahrhundert', *SB Ak. DDR*, 1977, no. 41A, pp. 3–35.

—— 'Ideologie und Gesellschaft im europäischen Mittelalter', *JGF* 6 (1982), 11–52.

WHITTON, D., 'The *Annales Romani* and Codex Vaticanus latinus 1984', *BISI* 84 (1972–3), 125–44.

—— 'Papal Policy in Rome, 1012–1124' (Univ. of Oxford D. Phil. thesis 1979).

WILKE, S., 'Das Goslarer Reichsgebiet und seine Beziehungen zu den territorialen Nachbargewalten', *Veröffentlichungen der Max-Planck-Instituts für Geschichte*, 32 (1970).

WILLIAMS, J. R., 'Archbishop Manasses of Reims and Pope Gregory VII', *AHR* 54 (1949), 804–24.

WILMART, A., 'Une Lettre de S. Pierre Damien à l'impératrice Agnès', *RB* 49 (1932), 125–46.

—— 'Cinque Textes de prières composés par Anselme de Lucques pour la comtesse Mathilde', *RAM* 19 (1938), 23–72.

WINTER, E., *Russland und das Papsttum*. 1: *Quellen und Studien zur Geschichte Osteuropas*, vol. 6/1 (Berlin, 1960).

WISCHERMANN, E. M., *Marcigny-sur-Loire. Gründungs- und Frühgeschichte des ersten Cluniacenserinnenpriorates (1055–1150)* (Munich, 1986).

WOJTOWYTSCH, M., 'Proprie auctoritates apostolice sedis. Bemerkungen zu einer bisher unbeachteten Überlieferung', *DA* 40 (1984), 612–21.

WOLF, A., 'Königskandidatur und Königsverwandtschaft. Hermann von Schwaben als Prüfstein für das "Prinzip der freien Wahl" ', *DA* 47 (1991), 45–117.

WOLLASCH, J., 'Die Wahl des Papstes Nikolaus II.', in Fleckenstein and Schmid (eds.), *Adel und Kirche*, pp. 205–20; also in *Il monachesimo*, pp. 54–78.

—— 'Reform und Adel in Burgund', in Fleckenstein, (ed.), *Investiturstreit und Reichsverfassung*, pp. 277–93.

WOODY, K. M., '*Sagena piscatoris*: Peter Damiani and the Papal Election Decree of 1959', *Viator*, 1 (1970), 33–54.

WÜHR, W., *Studien zu Gregor VII. Kirchenreform und Weltpolitik* (Munich, 1936).

ZACCARIA, F. A., *Anecdotorum medii aevi maximam partem ex archivis Pistoriensibus collectio* (Turin, 1755).

—— *Dell'antichissima badia di Leno libri tre* (Venice, 1767).

ZAFARANA, Z., 'Sul "conventus" del clero romano nel maggio 1082', *SM* 3rd ser., 7 (1966), 399–403.

—— 'Richerche sul "Liber de unitate ecclesiae conservanda" ', *SM* 3rd ser., 7 (1966), 617–700.

ZEMA, D. B., 'Economic Reorganization of the Roman See during the Gregorian Reform', *SG* 1 (1947), 137–68.

—— 'The Houses of Tuscany and of Pierleone in the Crisis of Rome in the Eleventh Century', *Traditio*, 2 (1974), 155–75.

ZERBI, P., 'Il termine "fidelitas" nelle lettere di Gregorio VII', *SG* 3 (1948), 129–48.

ZIEGLER, A. W., 'Gregor VII. und der Kijewer Grossfürst Isjaslav', *SG* 1 (1947), 387–411.

ZIESE, J., *Historische Beweisführungen in Streitschriften des Investiturstreits* (Munich, 1972).

—— 'Bischofsamt und Königtum', *HJ* 97–8 (1978), 108–30.

—— *Wibert von Ravenna: Der Gegenpapst Clemens III. (1084–1100)* (Stuttgart, 1982).

ZIMMERMANN, H., *Papstabsetzungen des Mittelalters* (Vienna, Cologne, and Graz, 1968).

—— 'Wurde Gregor VII. 1076 in Worms abgesetzt?' *MIÖG* 78 (1970), 121–31.

—— *Der Canossagang von 1077. Wirkungen und Wirklichkeit* (Mainz, 1975).

—— 'Die "gregorianische Reform" in deutschen Landen', *SG* 13 (1989), 263–79.

—— 'Anselm II. zwischen Gregor VII., Mathilde von Canossa und Heinrich IV.' in Violante (ed.), *Sant'Anselmo vescovo di Lucca*, pp. 129–42.

INDEX